INFORMATION FOR CPA EXAMINATION CANDIDATES

by the AICPA Board of Examiners

INTRODUCTION

This document has been prepared by the Board of Examiners of the American Institute of Certified Public Accountants (AICPA) and is intended for those preparing to take the Uniform Certified Public Accountant Examination. Individuals who want information on how to apply to become a CPA should contact the board of accountancy in the jurisdiction from which they seek the CPA designation.

Certified Public Accountant

Certified Public Account (CPA) is a designation conferred by a state or similar governmental jurisdiction that authorizes the holder to practice as a certified public accountant in that jurisdiction. Licensing of CPAs helps to protect the public from substandard work performed by incompetent individuals.

Boards of Accountancy

Specific requirements for becoming a CPA and the rights and obligations of a licensed CPA are set forth in the laws and regulations of fifty-four United States jurisdictions. These jurisdictions appear on the map on page ii.

The laws of each jurisdiction establish a board of accountancy as an administrative branch of the jurisdiction's government. The board is responsible for safeguarding the public interest by ensuring the competence and integrity of those who hold themselves out to the public as CPAs. The board evaluates the qualifications of candidates, administers examinations, issues certificates and licenses to practice, promulgates rules of professional conduct, investigates complaints, holds hearings, and takes disciplinary actions.

Each jurisdiction has specific requirements for a candidate to become licensed as a certified public accountant. The requirements, which vary among the jurisdictions, may include precertification education, passing the Uniform CPA Examination, and experience. Those who practice as CPAs must understand and abide by the specific laws and regulations of the jurisdiction in which they practice.

National Association of State Boards of Accountancy

The National Association of State Boards of Accountancy (NASBA) is a voluntary organization that coordinates the activities of the fifty-four boards of accountancy. NASBA provides numerous programs and services to assist state boards in discharging their responsibilities.

- The CPA Examination Review Board, appointed by NASBA, annually reviews the preparation, grading, security, and administration of the Examination.
- The Computerized Grade Reporting and Statistical Information Program assists the boards of accountancy in processing examination grades and in compiling jurisdictional and national statistical information on examination performance.

Additional information about NASBA may be obtained by writing to NASBA, 150 Fourth Avenue North, Nashville, TN 37219-2417.

THE UNIFORM CPA EXAMINATION

Background

Examinations were first used to test the qualifications of public accountants in New York State in 1896. As the country and profession grew, more states enacted accountancy laws that required individuals to pass an examination to qualify as certified public accountants. The Uniform CPA Examination was first administered in 1917. By the 1960's, all jurisdictions in the United States required new CPAs to have passed the Uniform CPA Examination prepared by the AICPA and graded by its Advisory Grading Service. Acceptance of the Uniform CPA Examination by all jurisdictions has greatly improved the ability of the CPAs to obtain reciprocal recognition by other jurisdictions.

Nondisclosure of Examination Questions and Answers

Effective with the May 1996 Examination, the Uniform CPA Examination became nondisclosed. Nondisclosure means that candidates are not allowed to retain or receive their question booklets after the examination. However, the AICPA updates and publishes *Selected Questions & Unofficial Answers Indexed to Content Specification Outlines* which contains pre-1996 examination questions and nondisclosed examination questions that will not be used on future examinations.

There are three major benefits to not disclosing items on the Uniform CPA Examination:
1. Examination quality can be improved through the use of pretested items.
2. By using statistical equating methods, examinations given at different times can be compared to each other and adjusted for variations in difficulty.
3. Computer administration of future Uniform CPA Examinations will be facilitated.

© American Institute of Certified Public Accountants, Inc.

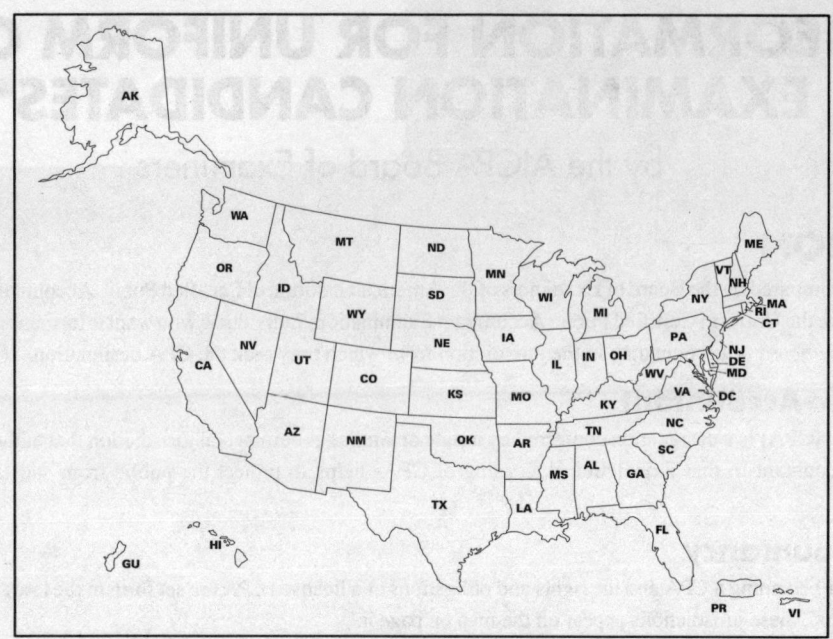

The first two benefits further help to ensure that the examination is fair to all candidates by keeping the examination and the standards required for passing consistent over time. The third benefit may reduce the time it takes most candidates to complete the examination and may make it possible for boards of accountancy to offer the examination more frequently than twice a year.

To realize these benefits, Uniform CPA Examination questions and answers must remain nondisclosed. Since questions may be reused on examinations to achieve the benefits described, it is necessary to require that candidates and others not divulge the questions after the examination has been administered. Candidates are required to read the following policy statement on each Uniform CPA Examination Booklet and to sign and date the front of the Booklet, signifying that they agree to comply with the policy before they are allowed to open the Booklet.

> I hereby attest that I will not divulge the nature or content of any question or answer to any individual or entity, and I will report to the board of accountancy any solicitations or disclosures of which I become aware. I will not remove, or attempt to remove, any Uniform CPA Examination materials, notes, or other unauthorized materials from the examination room. I understand that failure to comply with this attestation may result in the invalidation of my grades, disqualification from future examinations, and possible civil and criminal penalties.

Statutes and rules of the jurisdictions in which the Uniform CPA Examination is administered stipulate various penalties associated with disclosure of examination material. These may differ across jurisdictions but could include withholding examination scores and a variety of administrative and legal penalties.

The Board of Examiners and the Examinations Team

The Board of Examiners (the Board) is an executive committee of the AICPA with overall responsibility for preparing and grading the examination. This responsibility is carried out by five subcommittees that report to the Board of Examiners: Auditing, Financial Accounting & Reporting; Accounting & Reporting—Taxation, Managerial, and Governmental and Not-for-Profit Organizations; Business Law & Professional Responsibilities; and Standard Setting. Each of the subcommittees, other than Standard Setting, is responsible for the preparation of its section of the examination. This responsibility includes reviewing questions and unofficial answers for technical accuracy, relevance to practice as a CPA, compliance with content specification outlines, and appropriate range and level of skills and knowledge needed to practice as a CPA. The Standard Setting Subcommittee is responsible for establishing the grading bases for each examination section.

Member of the Board and its subcommittees are practitioners or educators selected for their knowledge of the subject matter relevant to the practice of public accountancy. The members of the Board include the chair of each preparation subcommittee and members of the Board's other subcommittees. The Standard Setting Subcommittee is made up of the chairs of the preparation subcommittees and other individuals with relevant skills.

The AICPA Examinations Team, which carries out the Board's policies, consists of CPAs and attorneys who specialize in the technical content of the Uniform CPA Examination; testing specialists; desktop publishing professionals; systems management personnel; and administrative personnel. The staff is responsible for developing, producing, shipping, and grading the Uniform CPA Examination.

Additional information about the AICPA and the Examinations Team is available on the AICPA's Website (*AICPA Online:* http://www.aicpa.org; *Examinations Team:* http//www.aicpa.org/exams). Visitors to the Website can access profession-related information and discover the latest developments in accountancy.

Examination Dates, Structure, and Times

The examination is given twice each year, in May and November, as follows:

1999 — May 5, 6
  November 3, 4
2000 — May 3, 4
  November 1, 2
2001 — May 2, 3
  November 7, 8
2002 — May 8, 9
  November 6, 7

The examination is administered only within the boundaries of the fifty-four United States jurisdictions that use the examination. The examination consists of four separate sections. These sections are administered over a two-day period with the following time allocations.

Section	Hours	Day	Time
Business Law & Professional Responsibilities	3.0	Wednesday	9:00 A.M. - 12:00 NOON
Auditing	4.5	Wednesday	1:30 P.M. - 6:00 P.M.
Accounting & Reporting — Taxation & Managerial, and Governmental and Not-for-Profit Organizations	3.5	Thursday	8:30 A.M. - 12:00 NOON
Financial Accounting & Reporting	4.5	Thursday	1:30 P.M. - 6:00 P.M.
Total	15.5		

The examination questions and answers are given and graded only in English.

Candidates' knowledge and skills are assessed by requiring responses to questions in three different formats:

- Four-option multiple-choice format
- Other objective answer format
- Essay question or problem format

These formats are assigned the following percentages for each examination sections:

Section	Format		
	Four Option Multiple-Choice	Other Objective Answer Formats	Essay Questions or Problems
Business Law & Professional Responsibilities	50-60%	20-30%	20-30%
Auditing	50-60%	20-30%	20-30%
Accounting & Reporting— Taxation, Managerial, and Governmental and Not-for Profit Organizations	50-60%	40-50%	None
Financial Accounting & Reporting	50-60%	20-30%	20-30%

Pretesting

About 10 percent of the multiple choice questions on each section of the Uniform CPA Examination are included for pretesting only and are not included in a candidate's final grade. The ability to pretest questions increases the quality of future examinations by eliminating questions that candidates find ambiguous and contributes to a more consistent level of examination difficulty.

Cheating

Boards of accountancy and the Board of Examiners take cheating on the Uniform CPA Examination very seriously. If a board of accountancy determines that a candidate has cheated, the candidate will be subject to a variety of penalties including, but not limited to, invalidation of grades and disqualification from subsequent examination administrations. In cases where cheating is discovered after a candidate has obtained a CPA certificate, a board may rescind the certificate.

Some actions, among others, that may be considered cheating are:
- Falsifying credentials
- Copying answers from another candidate during the examination
- Helping another candidate during the examination
- Unauthorized communication with another individual, in or out of the examination room, during the examination
- Using unauthorized materials during the examination
- Taking written materials, notes, etc. from the examination room
- Divulging examination information in violation of the nondisclosed examination policies

Boards of accountancy use a variety of procedures of prevent candidates from cheating on the examination. Proctors are trained to watch for unusual behavior and incidents during the examination and to document the occurrence of any unusual activity.

During the grading process, the AICPA Advisory Grading Service instructs graders to report all cases of unusually similar responses. After grading is complete, the Advisory Grading System sends to each board of accountancy a report that identifies candidates whose patterns of answers are unusually similar. Boards of accountancy may use this report to support an existing investigation into possible cheating or to initiate such an investigation.

EXAMINATION FOCUS AND CONTENT
Focus of the Examination

The focus of the examination is on the broad range of knowledge and skills CPAs need to plan and implement a public accounting engagement. Thus, the examination tests a broad range of skills, at various cognitive levels, that are necessary to practice as a CPA. The cornerstone to answering examination questions is knowledge and the comprehension of that knowledge. In addition to knowledge, many answers require application and analytical skills related to business information. Still other answers, especially essays and problem solutions, require evaluation, judgment, presentation, and decision-making ability related to accounting and auditing information in business situations.

All sections of the examination test a candidate's analytical skills. Examples of these skills are:
- Analyzing information and identifying data relevant to the situation.
- Assessing materiality and identifying risk.
- Identifying and explaining auditing procedures, accounting and reporting situations, and potential legal issues.
- Understanding and evaluating information technology.
- Evaluating situations, formulating conclusions, and making recommendations.
- Preparing auditing and accounting findings, conclusions, and recommendations in written report format.

General Content of the Examination

The content of the examination is based primarily on the results of two national studies of public accounting practice and the evaluations of CPA practitioners and educators. The content of each examination section is described in outline form. These outlines provide a framework, or "blueprint," for the knowledge and skills tested on the Uniform CPA Examination. Each major content area in the outlines is preceded by a roman numeral and is followed by a percentage that represents the approximate weight given to that content area. Examination items are selected from the content represented by the capital letters and numerals listed under each roman numeral.

In addition to testing technical knowledge and skills, selected essays on the auditing, financial accounting & reporting, and business law & professional responsibilities sections are graded for writing skills. Evaluation of candidates' writing skills in each of these three sections accounts for 5 percent of the respective section's grade.

Study Aids

The Examinations Team continues to publish *Selected Questions and Unofficial Answers Indexed to Content Specification Outlines,* which includes questions from nondisclosed examinations that will not appear on future examinations. This publication also includes a chart listing the total number of multiple-choice, other objective answer format, and essay questions and problems by each section's content specification outline, beginning with the May 1996 Uniform CPA Examination. This book, and other Examination Team publications, may be ordered from the AICPA by contacting the AICPA Order Department.

Sample examination questions are also available on the AICPA's Website (*AICPA Online:* http://www.aicpa.org/exams).

CONTENT BY SECTION

The Content Specification Outlines, which were effective for the May 1998 Examination, have been revised to reflect new pronouncements and changes in the profession, such as the integration of information technology.

Auditing

The auditing sections covers knowledge of generally accepted auditing standards and procedures and the skills needed to apply them in auditing and other attestation engagements. This section tests the knowledge and skills, as appropriate, in the context of the four broad engagement tasks that follow.

Auditing content specification outline

I. Plan the engagement, evaluate the prospective client and engagement, decide whether to accept or continue the client and the engagement, and enter into an agreement with the client (40%)
   A. Determine nature and scope of engagement
      1. Generally accepted auditing standards
      2. Standards for accounting and review services
      3. Standards for attestation engagements
      4. Compliance auditing applicable to governmental entities and other recipients of governmental financial assistance
      5. Other assurance services
      6. Appropriateness of engagement to meet client's needs
   B. Assess engagement risk and the CPA firm's ability to perform the engagement
      1. Engagement responsibilities
      2. Staffing and supervision requirements
      3. Quality control considerations
      4. Management integrity
      5. Researching information sources for planning and performing the engagement
   C. Communicate with the predecessor accountant/auditor
   D. Decide whether to accept or continue the client and engagement
   E. Enter into an agreement with the client as to the terms of the engagement
   F. Obtain an understanding of the client's operations, business, and industry
   G. Perform analytical procedures
   H. Determine preliminary engagement materiality
   I. Assess inherent risk and risk of misstatements
      1. Errors
      2. Fraud
      3. Illegal acts by clients
   J. Consider internal control
      1. Obtain and document an understanding of internal control—automated and manual
      2. Assess risk control
      3. Consider limitations of internal control
      4. Consider the effects of information technology on internal control
      5. Consider the effects of service organizations on internal control
   K. Consider other planning matters
      1. Using the work of other independent auditors
      2. Using the work of a specialist
      3. Internal audit function
      4. Related parties and related party transactions
      5. Electronic evidence
   L. Identify financial statement assertions and formulate audit objectives
      1. Accounting estimates
      2. Routine financial statement balances, classes of transactions, and disclosures
      3. Unusual financial statement balances, classes of transactions, and disclosures
   M. Determine and prepare the work program defining the nature, timing, and extent of the auditor's procedures

II. Obtain and document information to form a basis for conclusions (35%)
   A. Perform planned procedures including planned applications of audit sampling
      1. Tests of controls
      2. Analytical procedures
      3. Confirmation of balances and/or transactions with third parties
      4. Physical examination of inventories and other assets
      5. Other tests of details
      6. Computer assisted audit techniques
      7. Substantive tests prior to the balance sheet date
      8. Tests of unusual year-end transactions
   B. Evaluate contingencies
   C. Obtain and evaluate lawyers' letters
   D. Review subsequent events

E. Obtain representations from management
F. Identify reportable conditions and other control deficiencies
G. Identify matters for communication with audit committees

III. Review the engagement to provide reasonable assurance that objectives are achieved and evaluate information obtained to reach and to document engagement conclusions (5%)
   A. Perform analytical procedures
   B. Evaluate the sufficiency and competence of audit evidence and document engagement conclusions
      1. Consider substantial doubt about an entity's ability to continue as a going concern
      2. Evaluate whether financial statements are free of material misstatements
      3. Consider other information in documents containing audited financial statements
   C. Review the work performed to provide reasonable assurance that objectives are achieved

IV. Prepare communications to satisfy engagement objectives (20%)
   A. Prepare reports
      1. Reports on audited financial statements
      2. Reports on reviewed and compiled financial statements
      3. Reports required by Government Auditing Standards
      4. Reports on compliance with laws and regulations
      5. Reports on internal control
      6. Reports on prospective financial information
      7. Reports on agreed-upon procedures
      8. Reports on other assurance services
      9. Reports on the processing of transactions by service organizations
      10. Reports on supplementary financial information
      11. Other special reports
      12. Reissuance of reports
   B. Prepare letters and other required communications
      1. Errors and fraud
      2. Illegal acts
      3. Special reports
      4. Communication with audit committees
      5. Other reporting considerations covered by statements on auditing standards and statements on standards for attestation engagements
   C. Other matters
      1. Subsequent discovery of facts existing at the date of the auditor's report
      2. Consideration of omitted procedures after the report date

Suggested publications to study—auditing
- AICPA Statements on Auditing Standards
- AICPA Statements on Standards for Accounting and Review Services
- AICPA Statements on Quality Control Standards
- AICPA Statements on Standards for Attestation Engagements
- U.S. General Accounting Office Government Auditing Standards
- AICPA Audit and Accounting Guides:
  — Audit Sampling
  — Consideration of Internal Control in a Financial Statement Audit
- Textbooks and articles on auditing and other assurance services
- AICPA Auditing Procedures Studies
- AICPA Top 10 Technologies and Their Impact on CPAs
- AICPA Top 10 Technology Opportunities: Tips and Tools
- The CPA's Guide to Web Commerce
- The CPA's Guide to Information Security
- AICPA Risk Alerts
- SECPS Practice Alerts
- Single Audit Act, as amended
- Information on auditing and other assurance services on the AICPA Website

Sample questions for auditing are included on the AICPA's Website at http://www.aicpa.org/exams.

Financial accounting & reporting

The financial accounting & reporting section tests candidates' knowledge of generally accepted accounting principles for business enterprises and the skills needed to apply them in a public accounting engagement. Content covered in this section includes financial accounting concepts and standards as well as their application in a public accounting engagement. Candidates will

- Obtain and document entity information for use in financial statement presentations
- Evaluate, analyze, and process entity information for reporting in financial statements
- Communicate entity information and conclusions
- Analyze information and identify data relevant to financial accounting and reporting
- Identify financial accounting and reporting methods and select those that are suitable
- Perform calculations and formulate conclusions
- Present results in writing in a financial statement format or other appropriate format

Financial accounting & reporting content specification outline

I. Concepts and standards for financial statements (20%)
   A. Financial accounting concepts
   B. Financial accounting standards for presentation and disclosures in general purpose financial statements
      1. Consolidated and combined financial statements
      2. Balance sheet
      3. Statement(s) of income, comprehensive changes in equity accounts
      4. Statement of cash flows
      5. Accounting policies and other notes to financial statements
   C. Other presentations of financial data
      1. Financial statements prepared in conformity with comprehensive bases of accounting other than generally accepted accounting principles
      2. Personal financial statements
      3. Prospective financial information
   D. Financial statement analysis

II. Recognition, measurement, valuation, and presentation of typical items in financial statements in conformity with generally accepted accounting principles (40%)
   A. Cash, cash equivalents, and marketable securities
   B. Receivables
   C. Inventories
   D. Property, plant, and equipment
   E. Investments
   F. Intangible and other assets
   G. Payables and accruals
   H. Deferred revenues
   I. Notes and bonds payable
   J. Other liabilities
   K. Equity accounts
   L. Revenue, cost, and expense

III. Recognition, measurement, valuation, and presentation of specific types of transactions and events in financial statements in conformity with generally accepted accounting principles (40%)
   A. Accounting changes and corrections of errors
   B. Business combinations
   C. Cash flow components — financing, investing, and operating
   D. Contingent liabilities and commitments
   E. Discontinued operations
   F. Earnings per share
   G. Employee benefits
   H. Extraordinary items
   I. Financial instruments
   J. Foreign currency transactions and translation
   K. Income taxes
   L. Interest costs
   M. Interim financial reporting

N. Leases
O. Nonmonetary transactions
P. Quasi-reorganizations, reorganizations, and changes in entity
Q. Related parties
R. Research and development costs
S. Segment reporting

Suggested publications to study—financial accounting & reporting
- Financial Accounting Standards Board (FASB) Statements of Financial Accounting Standards and Interpretations, Accounting Principles Board Opinions, and AICPA Accounting Research Bulletins
- FASB Technical Bulletins
- AICPA Statement on Auditing Standards No. 69, "The Meaning of *Present Fairly in Conformity With Generally Accepted Accounting Principles* in the Independent Auditor's Report," and Statement on Auditing Standards No. 62, "Special Reports"
- AICPA Personal Financial Statements Guide
- FASB Statements of Financial Accounting Concepts
- AICPA Statements of Position
- Books and articles on accounting

Sample questions for financial accounting & reporting are included on the AICPA's Website at http://www.aicpa.org/exams.

Accounting & reporting—taxation, managerial, and governmental and not-for-profit organizations

The accounting & reporting—taxation, managerial, and governmental and not-for-profit organizations section tests candidates' knowledge of principles and procedures for federal taxation, managerial accounting, and accounting for governmental and not-for-profit organizations, and the skills needed to apply them in a public accounting engagement.

Federal taxation

This portion covers knowledge applicable to federal taxation and its application in practice. Candidates will
- Analyze information and identity data relevant for tax purposes
- Identify issues, elections, and alternative tax treatments
- Perform required calculations
- Formulate conclusions

Federal taxation content specification outline
I. Federal taxation—individuals (20%)
   A. Inclusions in gross income
   B. Exclusions and adjustments to arrive at adjusted gross income
   C. Deductions from adjusted gross income
   D. Filing status and exemptions
   E. Tax accounting methods
   F. Tax computations, credits, and penalties
   G. Alternative minimum tax
   H. Tax procedures
II. Federal taxation—corporations (20%)
   A. Determination of taxable income or loss
   B. Tax accounting methods
   C. S corporations
   D. Personal holding companies
   E. Consolidated returns
   F. Tax computations, credits and penalties
   G. Alternative minimum tax
   H. Other
      1. Distributions
      2. Incorporation, reorganization, liquidation, and dissolution
      3. Tax procedures
III. Federal taxation—partnerships (10%)
   A. Basis of partner's interest and bases of assets contributed to the partnership
   B. Determination of partner's share of income, credits, and deductions
   C. Partnership and partner elections
   D. Partner dealing with own partnership

E. Treatment of partnership liabilities
F. Distribution of partnership assets
G. Termination of partnership
IV. Federal taxation—estates and trusts, exempt organizations, and preparers' responsibilities (10%)
    A. Estates and trusts
        1. Income taxation
        2. Determination of beneficiary's share of taxable income
        3. Estate and gift taxation
    B. Exempt organizations
        1. Types of organizations
        2. Requirements for exemption
        3. Unrelated business income tax
    C. Preparers' responsibilities

Suggested publications to study—federal taxation
- Internal Revenue Code and Income Tax Regulations
- Internal Revenue Service Circular 230
- AICPA Statements on Responsibilities in Tax Practice
- Income tax textbooks

Governmental and not-for-profit organizations

This portion covers knowledge applicable to accounting for governmental and not-for-profit organizations and its application in practice. Candidates will

- Analyze and identify information relevant to governmental and not-for-profit accounting and reporting
- Identify alternative accounting and reporting policies and select those appropriate in specific situations
- Distinguish the relative weight of authority of differing sources of generally accepted accounting principles
- Perform procedures, formulate conclusions, and present results

Governmental and not-for-profit organizations content specification outline

V. Accounting for governmental and not-for-profit organizations (30%)
    A. Governmental entities
        1. Measurement focus and basis of accounting
        2. Objectives of financial reporting
        3. Uses of fund accounting
        4. Budgetary process
        5. Financial reporting entity
        6. Elements of financial statements
        7. Conceptual reporting issues
        8. Accounting and financial reporting for state and local governments
            a. Governmental-type funds and account groups
            b. Proprietary-type funds
            c. Fiduciary-type funds
        9. Accounting and financial reporting for governmental not-for-profit organizations (including hospitals, colleges and universities, voluntary health and welfare organizations, and other governmental not-for-profit organizations)
    B. Nongovernmental—not-For-Profit Organizations
        1. Objectives of financial reporting
        2. Elements of financial statements
        3. Formats of financial statements
        4. Accounting and financial reporting for nongovernmental not-for-profit organizations
            a. Revenues and contributions
            b. Restrictions on resources
            c. Expenses, including depreciation

Suggested publications to study—governmental and not-for-profit organizations
- Governmental Accounting Standards (GASB) Statements, Interpretations, and Technical Bulletins
- Financial Accounting Standards Board (FASB) Statements of Financial Accounting Standards and Interpretations, Accounting Principles Board Opinions, AICPA Accounting Research Bulletins, and FASB Technical Bulletins
- FASB Statement of Financial Accounting Concepts No. 4, "Objectives of Financial Reporting by Nonbusiness Organizations," and FASB Statement of Financial Concept, No. 6, "Elements of Financial Statements"

- AICPA Statement on Auditing Standards No. 69, "The Meaning of *Present Fairly in Conformity With Generally Accepted Accounting Principles* in the Independent Auditior's Report"
- AICPA Audit and Accounting Guides and Statements of Position relating to governmental and not-for-profit organizations
- Governmental and not-for-profit accounting textbooks and other accounting textbooks containing pertinent chapters

Managerial accounting

This portion covers knowledge applicable to managerial accounting and its application in accounting practice. Candidates will
- Analyze and interpret information as a basis for decision making
- Determine product and service costs
- Prepare and interpret information for planning and control

Managerial accounting content specification outline

VI. Managerial accounting (10%)
- A. Cost estimation, cost determination, and cost drivers
- B. Job costing, process costing, and activity based costing
- C. Standard costing and flexible budgeting
- D. Inventory planning, inventory control, and just-in-time purchasing
- E. Budgeting and responsibility accounting
- F. Variable and absorption costing
- G. Cost-volume-profit analysis
- H. Cost allocation and transfer pricing
- I. Joint and by-product costing
- J. Capital budgeting
- K. Special analyses for decision making
- L. Product and service pricing

Suggested publications to study—managerial accounting

- Managerial accounting textbooks and other accounting textbooks containing pertinent chapters
- Accounting periodicals

Sample questions for accounting & reporting are included on the AICPA's Website at http://www.aicpa.org/exams.

Business law & professional responsibilities

The business law & professional responsibilities section tests candidates' knowledge of CPA's professional responsibilities and of the legal implications of business transactions, particularly as they relate to accounting and auditing. Content covered in this section includes a CPA's professional responsibilities, business organizations, contracts, debtor-creditor relationships, government regulation of business, the Uniform Commercial Code, and property. Candidates will be required to
- Recognize relevant legal issues
- Recognize the legal implications of certain business situations
- Apply the underlying principles of law to accounting and auditing situations

This section deals with federal and widely adopted uniform laws. If there is no federal or uniform law on a topic, the questions are intended to test knowledge of the law of the majority of jurisdictions. Professional ethics questions are based on the AICPA *Code of Professional Conduct* because it is national in its application, whereas codes of other organizations and jurisdictions may be limited in their application.

Business law & professional responsibilities content specification outline

I. Professional code and legal responsibilities (15%)
- A. Code of professional conduct
- B. Proficiency, independence, and due care
- C. Responsibilities in other professional services
- D. Disciplinary systems imposed by the profession and state regulatory bodies
- E. Common law liability to clients and third parties
- F. Federal statutory liability
- G. Privileged communications and confidentiality
- H. Responsibilities of CPAs in business and industry, and in the public sector

II. Business organizations (20%)
- A. Agency
  1. Formation and termination
  2. Duties of agents and principals
  3. Liabilities and authority of agents and principals

    B. Partnership, and other unincorporated associations
        1. Formation, operation, and termination
        2. Liabilities and authority of partners and owners
    C. Corporations
        1. Formation and operation
        2. Stockholders, directors, and officers
        3. Financial structure, capital, and distributions
        4. Reorganization and dissolution
    D. Estates and trusts
        1. Formation, operation, and termination
        2. Allocation between principal and income
        3. Fiduciary responsibilities
        4. Distributions
III. Contracts (10%)
    A. Formation
    B. Performance
    C. Third party assignments
    D. Discharge, breach, and remedies
IV. Debtor-creditor relationships (10%)
    A. Rights, duties, and liabilities of debtors and creditors
    B. Rights, duties, and liabilities of guarantors
    C. Bankruptcy
V. Government regulations of business (15%)
    A. Federal securities acts
    B. Employment regulation
    C. Environmental regulation
VI. Uniform commercial code (20%)
    A. Negotiable instruments
    B. Sales
    C. Secured transactions
    D. Documents of title
VII. Property (10%)
    A. Real property including insurance
    B. Personal property including bailments and computer technology rights

Suggested publications to study—business law & professional responsibilities

- AICPA *Code of Professional Conduct*
- AICPA Statements on Auditing Standards dealing explicitly with proficiency, independence, and due care
- AICPA Statement on Standards for Consulting Services
- AICPA Statements on Responsibilities in Personal Finance Planning Practice
- Books covering business law, auditing, accounting

Sample questions for business law & professional responsibilities are included on the AICPA's website at http://www.aicpa.org/exams.

EFFECTIVE DATES OF PRONOUNCEMENTS

Candidates are responsible for knowing accounting and auditing pronouncements, including knowing the governmental and not-for-profit organization areas, six months after a pronouncement's *effective* date, unless early application is permitted. When early application is permitted, candidates are responsible for knowing the new pronouncement six months after the *issuance* date. In this case, candidates are responsible for knowing both the old and the new pronouncements until the old pronouncement is superseded. For the federal taxation area, candidates are responsible for knowing the Internal Revenue Code and federal tax regulations in effect six months before the examination date. For the business law & professional responsibilities section, candidates are responsible for knowing federal laws six months after their *effective* date and knowing uniform acts one year after their adoption by a simple majority of the jurisdictions.

EVALUATION OF WRITING SKILLS
Writing Skills

Selected essay answers in the business law & professional responsibilities, auditing, and financial accounting & reporting sections are used to assess candidates' writing skills. Five percent of the total points available on each of these sections will be allocated to writing skills. Effective writing can be characterized by the following six elements:

1. *Coherent organization.* The writer arranges ideas in a smooth, logical flow, enabling the reader to easily follow the train of thought. The writer develops each main idea in a separate paragraph and places the idea in the first sentence of the paragraph. Sentences that follow describe, define, clarify, illustrate, or explain the principal idea. Connectives and transition words link sentences to paragraphs.
2. *Conciseness.* The writer conveys points in as few as possible without scrimping on important detail or substance. Short sentences and simple wording contribute to concise writing.
3. *Clarity.* A clearly written response expresses the writer's meaning or reasoning to the intended reader. Well-constructed sentences and carefully chosen words, including proper technical terms, contribute to clarity.
4. *Use of standard English.* Effective responses use standard English, which is defined in the *Business Writer's Handbook* as follows:
   > There are two broad varieties of written English: standard and nonstandard. These varieties are determined through **usage** of those who write in the English language. Standard English...is used to carry on the daily business of the nation. It is the language of business, industry, government, education, and the professions. Standard English is characterized by exacting standards of **punctuation** and capitalization, by accurate **spelling,** by exact **diction,** by an expressive vocabulary, and by knowledgeable usage choices[1].
5. *Responsiveness to the requirements of the question.* The writer should address the requirements of the question and demonstrate awareness of the purpose of the writing task. Answers should not be broad expositions on the general subject but should focus on the specific elements presented in the question. However, answers should not be so narrowly focused that they omit key elements of the requirements.
6. *Appropriateness for the reader.* Writing that is appropriate for the reader takes into account the reader's background, knowledge of the subject, interests, and concerns. Some essay questions may require candidates to prepare a written document for a specific reader, such as a memorandum to a CPA's client. In such cases, technical terms may have to be defined for the specific reader. When the requirements do not identify a specific reader, the candidate should assume the intended reader is a knowledgeable CPA.

Writing Skills Samples

Writing skills are assessed at levels ranging from weak to very good. The following example includes a question followed by two sample answers illustrating weak writing skills and very good writing skills, respectively. Each answer is followed by an assessment of the writing skills demonstrated.

Question:
How has technology changed work in the business environment? Explain your answer with specific examples.

Weak:
People have to get used to new things. Like computers and Faxes and all. And they have to learn how to use things like voice mail. Which can get confusing for some people. Technology eliminates a lot of jobs because it can do things faster and better and cheaper than a lot of people. Though computers can't think. Can a computer handle a complaint from a customer? Teleconferencing helps a group of people have a group meeting over the phone. They don't have to all spend a lot of money for planes and hotels and stuff to go to a meeting. They can all stay in their own office and meet over the phone.

Assessment:
The passage is weak in coherence. It does not introduce any principal idea and lumps various types of examples and comments together into one paragraph. Some of what is in the paragraph is irrelevant to the topic of the essay. Further, the writing jumps from one thought to another without any connecting link. There are a number of grammatical errors, such as sentence fragments and faulty agreement. The passage addresses the question, however, and answers with specific examples.

Very Good:
As technology evolved over the last 15 years, it radically changed office equipment and the way Americans work. The word processor has replaced the typewriter and the computer has become the nerve center of the office. With the personal computer, vast amounts of information from various sources are available to office workers in an instant. Using such equipment as the modem and laptop computer, people can work almost anywhere—on planes, at home, at an off-site location. Even the telephone has seen significant change. For example, some telephones have become facsimile machine, enabling workers to transmit paper documents over telephone lines, with a paper reproduction arriving at the other end.

---

[1] Charles T. Brusaw, Gerald J. Alred, and Walter E. Oliu, *The Business Writer's Handbook,* 4th ed. (New York: St. Martin's Press, 1993), page 223.

These kinds of technological innovations have enabled many companies to reduce expenses while improving services. For instance, with improved technology, office payroll usually can be trimmed. Expenses can be further decreased by changing from a paper-based filling system to a computer-based system. At the same time, customer service improves, as workers can respond to customer needs more quicker using faxes or voice mail. Workers can research numerous topics more quicker and thoroughly, using a variety of electronic data sources. Further, changes and updates to customer documents can be done with little delay by using a word processor.

Assessment:

This essay is coherent. It introduces the principal ideas in the first sentence of each paragraph and uses the remaining sentences to explain those ideas. There is no irrelevant information in either paragraph. The passage makes its points concisely and clearly. There are no ambiguous or misused words, and some of the vocabulary is quite expressive: "radically," "nerve center" and "payroll can be trimmed." The passage gets high marks for its use of standard English, as it is relatively free of errors in punctuation, spelling and grammar. The errors "filling" and "more quicker" can be overlooked in such a well-written essay. The essay speaks to the question, answering it with specifics. The content and language are appropriate for the reader. Note the explanation of how the facsimile machine works, given just in case the reader may not know the device.

GRADING THE EXAMINATION

The objective of the Advisory Grading Service is to grade candidates' examination papers fairly and uniformly. This objective is attained by developing grading bases and consistently applying grading guides to candidates' objective, essay, and problem answers, with as many as two subsequent reviews of each paper.

Grading Bases

Grading guides are created as the examination is developed and are approved by the subcommittees and the Board of Examiners. The grading guides the machine-gradable objective-answer-type questions are the answer key and the point value assigned to each answer. For the essay questions and problems, the grading guides consist of the model answers, each concept being elicited, and each concept's assigned point value. If a question requires a candidate to prepare an income statement, an example of a grading concept might be "proper heading".

Writing skills are graded using the holistic grading method. As the term implies, "holistic grading" treats the writing sample as a whole. Graders assign a single writing skills rating based on the six characteristics listed in the section "Evaluation of Writing Skills".

To establish the grading bases, the grading guides are applied to a sample of papers. As a result of the sample grading, modifications to the grading guides may be made. For essay question and problems, additional acceptable concepts may be gleaned from candidates' answers. Also, alternative approaches to the questions and alternative interpretations of data and statements presented in the essay questions and problems are evaluated. If the alternative approaches to the questions and alternative interpretations are deemed acceptable by the Standard Setting Subcommittee of the Board of Examiners, the grading guide is adjusted.

Objective questions are also analyzed during the sample grading. If a substantial number of candidates select an answer different from the correct answer indicated by the grading guide, the question is reviewed by experts in the field of knowledge tested. If the candidates' answer is found to be valid, the grading guide is appropriately revised. After the sample grading is completed, the Standard Setting Subcommittee approves the final grading guides.

Candidate Concerns About Examination Questions

Candidates who identify possible defective questions while taking the Uniform CPA Examination have the opportunity to request that such questions be reviewed by the Advisory Grading Service. This procedure, described below, is designed to assure candidates that all technically accurate answers will be considered in the grading and to speed technical review immediately after the examination is administered.

Candidates who believe one or more questions contain errors and want their concerns evaluated must fax to the AICPA their comments, including the precise nature of any defect; their rationale; and if possible, references. The fax must be received by the AICPA within four days of the completion of the examination administration. Comments should be faxed to (201)938-3443. This will ensure that all comments are reviewed before the grading bases for the Uniform CPA Examination are confirmed.

GRADING PROCESS

Candidate anonymity is preserved throughout the grading process. The only information available to the grading staff is the candidate identification number, which appears on the examination papers. The graders have no access to information about a candidate's name, education, experience, age, number of sittings or other personal characteristics. A candidate's performance on the examination is measured solely on the basis of the answers submitted.

Initial production grading. Objective questions are graded using an optical scanner. Samples of answer sheets are continually verified manually to ensure that the scanner has not malfunctioned.

Answers to essay questions and problems are graded by a professional staff of CPAs and attorneys specifically engaged for this purpose. In general, a candidate must correctly identify all gradable concepts to earn the maximum number of points. Some questions, however, may allow full credit for a less-than-perfect solution. For example, in a ten-point essay question that has fifteen gradable concepts (where each concept is worth one point), a candidate may receive full credit for providing any ten of the fifteen gradable concepts.

Graders are assigned to individual essay questions or problems and then trained intensively to apply the grading guide consistently. As a result, graders are proficient both in the subject matter and in the evaluation of candidates' answers. This promotes grading that is both objective and uniform.

First review. When the initial grading is complete, first review is performed by highly experienced graders who review essays or problem solutions for candidates with adjusted scores in the 65-74 range. This review serves as confirmation of the initial grade and as a quality control mechanism over the consistency of the grading process because reviewers are able to compare the work of different graders. In this manner, there is continual verification that all graders are properly applying the essay and problem solution grading guides. Based on this review, candidate scores are corrected for any scoring errors.

Second review. Papers with adjusted scores in the range between 72 and 74 are reviewed a second time as follows:

1. Manual verification of the accuracy of the objective answer grade.
2. Independent verification of the accuracy of the essay and problem grading by a reviewer who did not perform the first review.

Based on this review, candidate grades are corrected for any scoring errors.

A second review is also performed for failing papers of those candidates whose grades are just below the minimum grade requirement to receive conditional credit for other sections, according to jurisdictional statue.

Passing Grade for Each Section

Each section of the Uniform CPA Examination is graded separately. All grades are reported to boards of accountancy on a scale ranging from 0 to 100, with a passing grade of 75 for each section.

Setting the Passing Standard

The passing standard for each section of the Uniform CPA Examination is based on the Angoff passing standard studies held during 1996. For these studies, more than 100 CPAs rated the questions given on the May 1996 Examination to estimate the percentage of newly licensed CPAs that would answer the question correctly. The estimates were used to determine a minimum passing score, which was then converted to a grade of 75.

The minimum passing score for subsequent examinations is statistically determined through a process known as *equating*. Equating adjusts for differences in the difficulty level of the examinations and differences in the ability level of the groups of candidates taking the examinations. Using this process the score on a subsequent examination that corresponds to the same ability level as the minimum passing score is then converted to a grade of 75. All scores above that score are assigned passing advisory grades of 75 through 100 and scores below that score are assigned failing advisory grades of 0 through 74.

Grade Reporting

All boards of accountancy mail candidates' grades approximately 90 days after the examination is administered. This day is referred to as the Uniform Mailing Date.

Conditional status may be granted to those candidates who receive a passing grade on some but not all sections. Many boards require a minimum grade in the sections failed for a candidate to receive conditional credit for the sections passed. Candidates receiving conditional status are generally allowed limited number of additional opportunities to pass the remaining sections. If the conditional credit lapses, candidates must be reexamined on all sections. Candidates are encouraged to familiarize themselves with the rules and regulations governing the granting of conditional status in their jurisdiction.

Candidate Diagnostic Report

Boards of accountancy may report information to candidates about how they performed on each content area of the Examination by including a Candidate Diagnostic Report with the candidates' grades. The report provides information that may be useful to candidates who must retake one or more sections of the Examination.

The report indicates the percent coverage of each content area for each Examination section. It provides the grade for each section taken and indicates the approximate percentage of points the candidate has earned in each content area. Candidates should use caution in interpreting percentages of area earned, especially those that are based on relatively small numbers of questions.

Review Service

The AICPA accepts requests for review of candidate papers from boards of accountancy through September 20th for the preceding May Examination and through March 20th for the preceding November Examination.

The AICPA Advisory Grading Service reviews a candidate's paper by manually verifying the accuracy of the objective answers scores; independently verifying the original scoring of essays or problem solutions by a technical manager who did not participate in the original grading; and recomputing the total score.

In reporting the results to the board of accountancy, a "no change" is issued unless a failing grade is increased to a passing grade or to a minimum grade required on a failed section to retain credit for sections passed on the current or previous examinations.

The grading of all candidate papers is subject to very high quality controls. At least two experienced graders, other than the original grader, review all failing papers near either the passing grade or the minimum grade. Thus, the Advisory Grading Service review process rarely results in a grade change.

WRITING THE EXAMINATION

Application Forms

Application forms to sit for the examination may be obtained from the board of accountancy from which the candidate is seeking a CPA certificate. Most boards must receive the application at least sixty days before the examination date.

Candidates requiring special accommodations under the American with Disabilities Act should contact their board of accountancy for specific guidelines and procedures.

Rules for Examination Day

The examination is a closed-book examination and no reference materials are permitted to be taken to an examination site. Candidates are not permitted to bring calculators, computers, other electronic data storage devices, or communication devices into the examination room.

At the examination site, candidates are provided with Examination Question and Answer Booklets for each section they are taking. In addition, for the accounting & reporting—taxation, managerial, and governmental and not-for-profit organizations and financial accounting & reporting sections, candidates are given calculators identified for the specific examination. Candidates should bring an adequate supply of Number 2 pencils and erasers.

The general candidate instructions are as follows:

1. Prior to the start of the examination, you will be required to sign a *Statement of Confidentiality,* which states:

   I hereby attest that I will not divulge the nature or content of any question or answer to any individual or entity, and I will report to the board of accountancy any solicitations and disclosures of which I become aware. I will not remove, or attempt to remove, any Uniform CPA Examination materials, notes, or other unauthorized materials from the examination room. I understand that failure to comply with this attestation may result in invalidation of my grades, disqualification from future examinations, and possible civil and criminal penalties.

2. The only aids you are allowed to take to the examination tables are pens, pencils and erasers.

3. You will receive a Prenumbered Identification Card (or Admission Notice) with your 7-digit candidate number on it. The Prenumbered Identification Card must be available for inspection by the proctors throughout the examination.

4. Any reference during the examination to books or other materials or the exchange of information with other persons shall be considered misconduct sufficient to bar you from further participation in the examination. Penalties will be imposed on any candidate who is caught cheating before, during, or after the examination. These penalties may include expulsion from the examination and denial of applications for future examinations.

5. You must observe the fixed time for each session. It is your responsibility to be ready at the start of the session and to stop writing when told to do so.

6. The following is an example of point values for each question as they might appear in the *Examination Questions* portion of the *Examination Question and Answer Booklet (Booklet).*

	Point Value
No. 1	60
No. 2	10
No. 3	10
No. 4	10
No. 5	10
Total	100

   When answering each question, you should allocate the total examination time in proportion to the question's point value.

7. The *Booklet* will be distributed shortly before each session begins. Do not break the seal around the *Examinations Questions* portion of the *Booklet* until you are told to do so.

   Prior to the start of the examination, you are permitted to complete page 1 of the *Booklet* by recording your 7-digit candidate number in the boxes provided in the upper right-hand corner of the page and by filling out and signing the *Attendance Record.* You are also permitted to turn the *Booklet* over and record your 7-digit candidate number and State on the *Objective Answer Sheet* portion of the *Booklet.*

   You must also check the booklet numbers on the *Attendance Record, Examination Questions, Objective Answer Sheet* and *Essay Paper.* Notify the proctor if any of these numbers are not identical.

   You must also review the *Examination Questions* (after you are told to break the seal), *Objective Answer Sheet,* and *Essay Paper* for any possible defects, such as missing pages, blurred printing, or stray marks (*Objective Answer Sheet* only). If any defects are found, request an entirely new *Examination Question and Answer Booklet* from a proctor before you answer any questions.

8. For the Business Law & Professional Responsibilities (LPR), Auditing (AUDIT), and Financial Accounting & Reporting (FARE) sections, your answers to the essay questions or problems must be written on the paper provided in the *Essay Paper* portion of the *Booklet.* After the start of the examination, you should record your 7-digit candidate number, State, and question number on the first page of the *Essay Paper* portion of the *Booklet* and on the other pages where indicated.

9. For the Accounting & Reporting—Taxation, Managerial, and Not-For-Profit Organizations (ARE) and FARE examination sections, you will be given a calculator. You should test the calculator in accordance with the instructions on the cover page of the *Booklet*. Inform your proctor if your calculator is defective. Calculators will not be provided for the LPR and AUDIT examination sections because the number of questions requiring calculations is minimal and the calculations are simple.
10. All amounts given in questions are to be considered material unless otherwise stated.
11. Answer all objective items on the *Objective Answer Sheet* provided. Use a No.2 pencil only. You should attempt to answer all objective items, as there is no penalty for incorrect responses. Since the objective items are scanned optically, all your comments and calculations associated with them are not considered. You should blacken the ovals as darkly as possible and erase clearly any marks you wish to change. You should make no stray marks.
12. The *Objective Answer Sheet* may vary for each section of the examination. It is important to pay strict attention to the manner in which your *Objective Answer Sheet* is structured. As you proceed with the examination, be certain that you blacken the oval that corresponds exactly with the item number in the *Examination Questions* portion of your *Booklet,* be certain that you transfer them to the *Objective Answer Sheet* before the session ends. Your examination paper will not be graded if you fail to record your answers on the *Objective Answer Sheet.* You will not be given additional time to record your answers.
13. If an objective item requires you to record a numerical answer, blacken the ovals on the *Objective Answer Sheet.* If zeros precede your numerical answer, blacken the zeros in the ovals preceding your answer. You cannot receive credit for your answers if you fail to blacken an oval in each column. You may write the numbers in the boxes provided to facilitate blackening ovals; however, the numbers written in the boxes will not be graded.
14. Answer all essay questions and problems on the *Essay Paper* provided. Always begin your answer to a question on the top of a new page, which may be the reverse side of a sheet of paper. Cross out anything that you do not want graded.
15. Selected essay responses will be graded for writing skills.
16. Include all computations to the problem in the FARE section. This may assist the graders in understanding your answers.
17. You may not leave the examination room with any examination materials, nor may you take notes about the examination with you from the examination room. You are required to turn in by the end of each session:
    a. *Attendance Record* and *Statement of Confidentiality*
    b. *Examination Questions*
    c. *Essay Paper* (for LPR, AUDIT, and FARE). Do not remove unused pages.
    d. *Objective Answer Sheet.*
    e. Calculator (for ARE and FARE)
    f. All unused examination materials.
    g. Prenumbered Identification Card (or Admission Notice) at the last examination section for which you sit (if required by your examining jurisdiction).
    Your examination will not be graded unless you hand in the above-listed items before you leave the examination room.
18. If you believe one or more questions contain errors and want your concerns evaluated, you must fax to the AICPA your comments, including the precise nature of any defect; your rationale; and if possible, references. The fax should include your 7-digit candidate number and must be received by the AICPA within 4 days of the completion of the examination administration. Comments should be faxed to (201)938-3443. This will ensure that all comments are reviewed before the grading bases for the Uniform CPA Examination are confirmed. Although the AICPA cannot respond directly to each fax, it will investigate all comments received within the 4-day period.
19. Contact your board of accountancy for information regarding any other applicable rules.

Calculators

Each candidate receives a calculator at the examination site to use on the accounting & reporting—taxation, managerial, and governmental and not-for-profit organizations and financial accounting & reporting sections. The purpose of providing calculators is to save the time candidates spend on performing and rechecking manual calculations; it is not intended t allow for more difficult and complex calculations and problems. In other words, the calculations required to answer multiple-choice and problem-type questions will be at the same level of complexity as they were before calculators were provided.

Occasionally, candidates are required to perform calculations to answer questions on the business law & professional responsibilities and auditing sections. However, since the number of questions requiring calculations is minimal and the calculations are simple, calculators will not be provided for either of these sections.

The candidate should only need to use the calculator's four primary functions—add, subtract, multiply, and divide. However, the calculator also has function keys for square root, percentage and memory. The candidate is given an opportunity to test the calculator to ensure that the calculator is functioning properly by using the test calculations printed in the examination booklets. It is the candidate's responsibility to notify one of the proctors immediately in the event of a malfunction. Replacement calculators are available.

THE AICPA'S UNIFORM CPA EXAM

Edited by the Staff of the AICPA Examinations Team:

James D. Blum, CPA, Ph.D.
Director

Ahava Z. Goldman, CPA
Senior Technical Manager

Mary E. Moore
Copy editor

Technical Managers:
Edward R. Gehl, CPA, J.D.
Joel Koppelman, J.D.
Charles H. Offerman, CPA

Kevin P. Sweeney, Ph.D.
Assistant Director, Psychometrics

Bruce H. Biskin, Ph.D.
Senior Psychometrician

Andrew Wiley, M.A.
Psychometrican

Previously published as: *Uniform CPA Examination Selected Questions and Unofficial Answers*

Macmillan USA

Macmillan General Reference
A Simon & Schuster Macmillan Company
1633 Broadway
New York, NY 10019-6785

Copyright © 1999, 1998, 1997, 1996, 1995, 1994, 1993, 1992, 1991
by the American Institute of Certified Public Accountants, Inc.
All rights reserved. No part of this book may be reproduced or transmitted in any form or by any means, electronic or mechanical, including photocopying, recording, or by any information storage and retrieval system, without permission in writing from the Publisher.

An Arco Book

MACMILLAN is a registered trademark of Macmillan, Inc.

ISBN 0-02-862688-5

Manufactured in the United States of America

10 9 8 7 6 5 4 3 2 1

FOREWORD

The Uniform CPA Examination is prepared by the Board of Examiners of the American Institute of Certified Public Accountants, and is used by the examining boards of all fifty states, the District of Columbia, Puerto Rico, Guam, and the Virgin Islands as a prerequisite for issuance of CPA certificates.

This book contains selected questions and unofficial answers from past Uniform Certified Public Accountant Examinations. To assist candidates in studying for the Examination, the selected questions and unofficial answers have been indexed in accordance with the Content Specification Outlines.

All disclosed questions—those that appeared on Examinations *before* May 1996—are identified by a boldface code indicating the month (May [**M**] or November [**N**]); the year (**89** through **95**); and the question number in the original examination. All nondisclosed questions—those that appeared on Examinations *beginning with and after* May 1996—are identified by a boldface code that begins with **R** and the year (**96**). The nondisclosed questions have been renumbered sequentially, beginning with **1**. Within the content specification areas and groups, all questions and answers have been arranged in reverse chronological order.

Each individual multiple-choice question is indexed according to the area and group and in some cases the topic it tests. In some cases, a common fact pattern is used for two or more multiple-choice questions. In such cases, where different areas and groups are being tested by questions referring to a common fact pattern, the fact pattern is repeated to accompany the questions indexed in each applicable area or group.

Each other objective answer format question is indexed according to the area it tests and in certain cases to the group or group and topic it tests. Where an other objective answer format question and its answer involve more than one area, they have been separated and indexed according to areas tested. Thus, all parts of a question and its answer may not appear in their original examination sequence.

Each essay question or problem is indexed according to the area it tests and in certain cases to the group or group and topic it tests. Where an essay question or problem and its answer involve more than one part—for example, part a. and part b.—they have been separated and indexed according to areas and groups tested. Thus, all parts of a question and its answer may not appear in their original examination sequence.

Although the questions and unofficial answers may be used for many purposes, the principal reason for their publication is to help candidates to prepare for and write the Uniform CPA Examination. Candidates are also encouraged to read the 14th Edition of *Information for Uniform CPA Examination Candidates*, which describes the content, grading, and other administrative aspects of the Uniform CPA Examination.

The questions were selected by the staff of the Examinations Team on the basis of current value and pertinence. The unofficial answers were prepared by the staff of the Examinations Team and reviewed by the Board of Examiners but are not purported to be official positions of the American Institute of Certified Public Accountants.

Arleen R. Thomas, *Vice President—Professional Standards and Services*
American Institute of Certified Public Accountants

October 1998

BOARD OF EXAMINERS

Stephen M. Walker, CPA, JD, *Chair*
Rogoff, Erickson, Diamond & Walker, LLP
Albuquerque, NM

Quinton Booker, CPA, DBA
Jackson State University
Jackson, MS

Robert R. Hill, CPA
Crowe Chizek & Company LLP
Louisville, KY

Robert M. Keith, CPA, PhD
University of South Florida
Tampa, FL

Charles Wayne Alderman, CPA, DBA
Auburn University
Auburn, AL

Vincent C. Brenner, CPA, PhD
Louisiana State University
Baton Rouge, LA

Jesse W. Hughes, CPA, PhD
Old Dominion University
Norfolk, VA

David B. Pearson, CPA, DBA
Ernst & Young, LLP
Cleveland, OH

Michael A. Bolas, CPA, JD
Miken Companies, Inc.
Buffalo, NY

Robert E. Fleming, CPA
Urbach Kahn & Werlin, P.C.
Albany, NY

Richard D. Isserman, CPA
KPMG Peat Marwick LLP (Retired)
New York, NY

PREPARATION SUBCOMMITTEES

Business Law & Professional Responsibilities

Michael A. Bolas, CPA, JD, *Chair*
Miken Companies, Inc.
Buffalo, NY

Brent B. Nicholson, CPA
Bowling Green State University
Bowling Green, OH

Richard D. Isserman, CPA
KPMG Peat Marwick LLP (Retired)
New York, NY

Edward J. Roche, CPA, JD
University of Denver
Denver, CO

Richard L. Jungck, CPA
Baird, Kurtz & Dobson
Kansas City, MO

Richard J. Vierk, CPA
Deloitte & Touche LLP
Lincoln, NE

Auditing

David B. Pearson, CPA, DBA, *Chair*
Ernst & Young, LLP
Cleveland, OH

Robert E. Fleming, CPA
Urbach Kahn & Werlin, P.C.
Albany, NY

Charles Wayne Alderman, CPA, DBA
Auburn University
Auburn, AL

Charles James McElroy, CPA
Larson, Allen, Weishair & Co. LLP
Minneapolis, MN

Lyndee J. Black, CPA
Thomas, Watts, and Hershberger, P.C.
Lincoln, NE

Thomas R. Weirich, CPA, PhD
Central Michigan University
Mt. Pleasant, MI

Tax, Managerial, and Governmental Accounting & Reporting

Robert R. Hill, CPA, *Chair*
Crowe Chizek & Company LLP
Louisville, KY

Stuart H. Harden, CPA
Silva Harden & Adolph
Fresno, CA

L. Gayle Rayburn, CPA, PhD
SE Missouri State University
Cape Girardeau, MO

Steven C. Darr, CPA
Thomas Havey LLP
Washington, D.C.

Jesse W. Hughes, CPA, PhD
Old Dominion University
Norfolk, VA

John D. Rossi, III, CPA
Rossi & Co.
Allentown, PA

Anna C. Fowler, CPA, PhD
University of Texas
Austin, TX

Robert M. Pielech, CPA
Pielech & Pielech, CPAs, P.C.
New Bedford, MA

Dennis F. Togo, CPA
University of New Mexico
Albuquerque, NM

Financial Accounting & Reporting

Quinton Booker, CPA, DBA
Jackson State University
Jackson, MS

Robert M. Keith, CPA, PhD
University of South Florida
Tampa, FL

Vincent C. Brenner, CPA, PhD
Louisiana State University
Baton Rouge, LA

Linda M. Nichols, CPA
Texas Tech University
Lubbock, TX

Jacob J. Cohen, CPA
Walpert, Smullian & Blumenthal, P.A.
Baltimore, MD

EXAMINATIONS TEAM STAFF

Arleen R. Thomas, CPA
Vice President—Professional Standards and Services

Yolanda deJesus
Senior Manager

Tamara Bond
Grading Manager

Xiaohui Guo
Research Assistant

Edward Lake, Jr.
Production Manager

Kathleen Phillips
Grading Project Manager

James D. Blum, CPA, PhD
Director

Ahava Z. Goldman, CPA
Senior Technical Manager

Joan Clements, MS
Systems & Operations Manager

Carola Jacobs
Research Assistant

Mary E. Moore
Copy Editor

Steven Walme
Materials Control Supervisor

Anat Kendal, CPA
Director, Reformation and Computerization of the Examination

Bruce Biskin, PhD
Senior Psychometrician

Edward R. Gehl, CPA, JD
Technical Manager

Joel Koppelman, JD
Technical Manager

Charles H. Offerman, CPA
Technical Manager

Andrew Wiley, MA
Psychometrician

CONTRIBUTORS TO THE UNIFORM CPA EXAMINATION

Henry R. Anderson, *Orlando, FL*
Andrew H. Barnett, *San Diego State University*
James E. Brown, *Baird, Kurtz & Dobson, Joplin, MO*
James L. Brown, *Crowe Chizek & Company LLP, South Bend, IN*
Donald Deis, *Louisiana State University, Baton Rouge*
Joseph E. Gibson, *Charlottesville, VA*
Gregory W. Geisert, *Phibbs, Burkholder, Geisert, & Huffman, Harrisonburg, VA*
G. William Glezan, *University of Arkansas, Fayetteville*
Michael Granof, *University of Texas, Austin*
John K. Harris, *Tulsa, OK*
Earl Keller, *San Luis Obispo, CA*
Larry N. Killough, *Virginia Polytechnic Institute & State University, Blacksburg*
Kevin Leifer, *Ernst & Young, New York, NY*
W. Douglas Logan, *Athens, AL*
Mary L. Montoya, *Klanerud, Montoya, Wuebben & Freehan, PC, Sioux Falls, SD*
Steven Rubin, *Weissbarth, Altman & Michaelson, LLP, CPAs, New York, NY*
Florence Sharp, *Ohio University, Athens*
Nancy Stara, *Lincoln, NE*
Susan M. Vance, *Granger, IN*
Carl Warren, *University of Georgia, Athens*
Nancy C. Youngblood, *Roberts, Cherry & Co., Shreveport, LA*

FUTURE UNIFORM CPA EXAMINATION DATES

1999 — May 5, 6
November 3, 4
2000 — May 3, 4
November 1, 2

2001 — May 2, 3
November 7, 8

2002 — May 8, 9
November 6, 7

CONTENTS

Uniform CPA Examination Selected Questions & Unofficial Answers, *1999 Edition*

Business Law & Professional Responsibilities   **B**

Auditing   **A**

Accounting & Reporting–Taxation, Managerial, and
Governmental and Not-for-Profit Organizations   **AR**

Financial Accounting & Reporting   **FA**

Content Specification Outlines   **CSO**

**Summary of Coverage – May 1996
through May 1998 Uniform CPA Examinations**   **S**

Uniform CPA Examination

Business Law & Professional Responsibilities

Selected Questions And Unofficial Answers Indexed To Content Specification Outline

TABLE OF CONTENTS

Selected Questions	Multiple Choice Items	Other Objective Answer Formats	Essays
I. Professional and Legal Responsibilities	B-1	B-93	B-129
A. Code of Professional Conduct	B-1	*	B-129
B. Proficiency, Independence, and Due Care	B-2	*	*
C. Responsibilities in Other Professional Services	B-4	*	*
D. Disciplinary Systems Imposed by the Profession and State Regulatory Bodies	B-5	*	*
E. Common Law Liability to Clients and Third Parties	B-5	*	B-129
F. Federal Statutory Liability	B-8	B-93	B-132
G. Privileged Communications and Confidentiality	B-10	*	*
H. Responsibilities of CPAs in Business and Industry, and in the Public Sector	*	*	*
II. Business Organizations	B-12	B-94	B-133
A. Agency	B-12	B-94	B-133
B. Partnership, Joint Ventures, and Other Unincorporated Associations	B-15	B-94	B-134
C. Corporations	B-20	B-96	B-136
D. Estates and Trusts	B-23	B-97	B-137
III. Contracts	B-27	B-98	B-139
A. Formation	B-27	†	†
B. Performance	B-31	†	†
C. Third Party Assignments	B-32	†	†
D. Discharge, Breach, and Remedies	B-33	†	†
IV. Debtor-Creditor Relationships	B-40	B-100	B-144
A. Rights, Duties, and Liabilities of Debtors and Creditors	B-40	*	*
B. Rights, Duties, and Liabilities of Guarantors	B-41	*	*
C. Bankruptcy	B-43	B-100	B-144
V. Government Regulation of Business	B-49	B-102	B-146
A. Federal Securities Acts	B-49	B-102	B-146
B. Employment Regulation	B-56	*	*
C. Environmental Regulation	B-60	*	*
VI. Uniform Commercial Code	B-60	B-106	B-146
A. Negotiable Instruments	B-60	B-106	B-146
B. Sales	B-66	B-111	B-150
C. Secured Transactions	B-73	B-112	B-153
D. Documents of Title	B-77	*	*
VII. Property	B-78	B-113	B-155
A. Real Property Including Insurance	B-78	B-113	B-155
B. Personal Property Including Bailments and Computer Technology Rights	B-85	*	*

* No questions were indexed for this group.
† Questions in this area are not classified according to group.

	Pages
Selected Multiple Choice Items — Unofficial Answers	B-87
Other Objective Answer Formats — Selected Questions	B-93
Selected Other Objective Answer Formats — Unofficial Answers	B-119
Essays — Selected Questions	B-129
Selected Essays — Unofficial Answers	B-159
Suggested References	B-180
Content Specification Outline	CSO-2
Summary of Coverage — May 1996 through May 1998 Uniform CPA Examinations	S-1

MULTIPLE CHOICE ITEMS — SELECTED QUESTIONS

I. Professional and Legal Responsibilities

A. Code of Professional Conduct

N95#1. According to the ethical standards of the profession, which of the following acts is generally prohibited?
a. Purchasing a product from a third party and reselling it to a client.
b. Writing a financial management newsletter promoted and sold by a publishing company.
c. Accepting a commission for recommending a product to an audit client.
d. Accepting engagements obtained through the efforts of third parties.

N95#2. According to the ethical standards of the profession, which of the following acts is generally prohibited?
a. Issuing a modified report explaining a failure to follow a governmental regulatory agency's standards when conducting an attest service for a client.
b. Revealing confidential client information during a quality review of a professional practice by a team from the state CPA society.
c. Accepting a contingent fee for representing a client in an examination of the client's federal tax return by an IRS agent.
d. Retaining client records after an engagement is terminated prior to completion and the client has demanded their return.

M95#2. Which of the following best describes what is meant by the term generally accepted auditing standards?
a. Rules acknowledged by the accounting profession because of their universal application.
b. Pronouncements issued by the Auditing Standards Board.
c. Measures of the quality of the auditor's performance.
d. Procedures to be used to gather evidence to support financial statements.

N94#1. The profession's ethical standards most likely would be considered to have been violated when a CPA represents that specific consulting services will be performed for a stated fee and it is apparent at the time of the representation that the
a. Actual fee would be substantially higher.
b. Actual fee would be substantially lower than the fees charged by other CPAs for comparable services.
c. CPA would **not** be independent.
d. Fee was a competitive bid.

N94#2. According to the profession's ethical standards, which of the following events may justify a departure from a Statement of Financial Accounting Standards?

	New legislation	Evolution of a new form of business transaction
a.	No	Yes
b.	Yes	No
c.	Yes	Yes
d.	No	No

M94#1. Which of the following actions by a CPA most likely violates the profession's ethical standards?
a. Arranging with a financial institution to collect notes issued by a client in payment of fees due.
b. Compiling the financial statements of a client that employed the CPA's spouse as a bookkeeper.
c. Retaining client records after the client has demanded their return.
d. Purchasing a segment of an insurance company's business that performs actuarial services for employee benefit plans.

M94#2. Which of the following statements best explains why the CPA profession has found it essential to promulgate ethical standards and to establish means for ensuring their observance?
a. A distinguishing mark of a profession is its acceptance of responsibility to the public.
b. A requirement for a profession is to establish ethical standards that stress primary responsibility to clients and colleagues.
c. Ethical standards that emphasize excellence in performance over material rewards establish a reputation for competence and character.
d. Vigorous enforcement of an established code of ethics is the best way to prevent unscrupulous acts.

M93#1. A violation of the profession's ethical standards most likely would have occurred when a CPA
a. Issued an unqualified opinion on the 1992 financial statements when fees for the 1991 audit were unpaid.
b. Recommended a controller's position description with candidate specifications to an audit client.

c. Purchased a CPA firm's practice of monthly write-ups for a percentage of fees to be received over a three-year period.
d. Made arrangements with a financial institution to collect notes issued by a client in payment of fees due for the current year's audit.

N91#2. A violation of the profession's ethical standards **least** likely would have occurred when a CPA
a. Purchased another CPA's accounting practice and based the price on a percentage of the fees accruing from clients over a three-year period.
b. Received a percentage of the amounts invested by the CPA's audit clients in a tax shelter with the clients' knowledge and approval.
c. Had a public accounting practice and also was president and sole stockholder of a corporation that engaged in data processing services for the public.
d. Formed an association — **not** a partnership — with two other sole practitioners and called the association "Adams, Betts and Associates."

M91#57. A violation of the profession's ethical standards most likely would have occurred when a CPA
a. Compiled the financial statements of a client that employed the CPA's spouse as a bookkeeper.
b. Received a fee for referring audit clients to a company that sells limited partnership interests.
c. Purchased the portion of an insurance company that performs actuarial services for employee benefit plans.
d. Arranged with a financial institution to collect notes issued by a client in payment of fees due.

N89#56. The profession's ethical standards would most likely be considered to have been violated when a CPA
a. Continued an audit engagement after the commencement of litigation against the CPA alleging excessive fees filed in a stockholders' derivative action.
b. Represented to a potential client that the CPA's fees were substantially lower than the fees charged by other CPAs for comparable services.
c. Issued a report on a financial forecast that omitted a caution regarding achievability.
d. Accepted an MAS consultation engagement concerning data processing services for which the CPA lacked independence.

B. Proficiency, Independence, and Due Care

N95#3. According to the standards of the profession, which of the following activities may be required in exercising due care?

	Consulting with experts	Obtaining specialty accreditation
a.	Yes	Yes
b.	Yes	No
c.	No	Yes
d.	No	No

N95#4. According to the standards of the profession, which of the following activities would most likely **not** impair a CPA's independence?
a. Providing extensive advisory services for a client.
b. Contracting with a client to supervise the client's office personnel.
c. Signing a client's checks in emergency situations.
d. Accepting a luxurious gift from a client.

M95#1. According to the standards of the profession, which of the following circumstances will prevent a CPA performing audit engagements from being independent?
a. Obtaining a collateralized automobile loan from a financial institution client.
b. Litigation with a client relating to billing for consulting services for which the amount is immaterial.
c. Employment of the CPA's spouse as a client's internal auditor.
d. Acting as an honorary trustee for a not-for-profit organization client.

N94#3. To exercise due professional care an auditor should
a. Critically review the judgment exercised by those assisting in the audit.
b. Examine all available corroborating evidence supporting management's assertions.
c. Design the audit to detect all instances of illegal acts.
d. Attain the proper balance of professional experience and formal education.

N94#4. Must a CPA in public practice be independent in fact and appearance when providing the following services?

	Compilation of personal financial statements	Preparation of a tax return	Compilation of a financial forecast
a.	Yes	No	No
b.	No	Yes	No
c.	No	No	Yes
d.	No	No	No

M94#3. Which of the following reports may be issued only by an accountant who is independent of a client?
a. Standard report on an examination of a financial forecast.
b. Report on consulting services.
c. Compilation report on historical financial statements.
d. Compilation report on a financial projection.

M94#4. According to the profession's ethical standards, an auditor would be considered independent in which of the following instances?

a. The auditor is the officially appointed stock transfer agent of a client.
b. The auditor's checking account that is fully insured by a federal agency is held at a client financial institution.
c. The client owes the auditor fees for more than two years prior to the issuance of the audit report.
d. The client is the only tenant in a commercial building owned by the auditor.

N93#1. According to the profession's ethical standards, a CPA would be considered independent in which of the following instances?
a. A client leases part of an office building from the CPA, resulting in a material indirect financial interest to the CPA.
b. The CPA has a material direct financial interest in a client, but transfers the interest into a blind trust.
c. The CPA owns an office building and the mortgage on the building is guaranteed by a client.
d. The CPA belongs to a country club client in which membership requires the acquisition of a pro rata share of equity.

N93#2. Which of the following best describes what is meant by the term generally accepted auditing standards?
a. Pronouncements issued by the Auditing Standards Board.
b. Rules acknowledged by the accounting profession because of their universal application.
c. Procedures to be used to gather evidence to support financial statements.
d. Measures of the quality of the auditor's performance.

M93#4. A CPA's duty of due care to a client most likely will be breached when a CPA
a. Gives a client an oral instead of written report.
b. Gives a client incorrect advice based on an honest error of judgment.
c. Fails to give tax advice that saves the client money.
d. Fails to follow generally accepted auditing standards.

N92#1. To exercise due professional care an auditor should
a. Attain the proper balance of professional experience and formal education.
b. Design the audit to detect all instances of illegal acts.
c. Critically review the judgment exercised by those assisting in the audit.
d. Examine all available corroborating evidence supporting management's assertions.

N92#2. In which of the following situations would a CPA's independence be considered to be impaired?

I. The CPA maintains a checking account that is fully insured by a government deposit insurance agency at an audit-client financial institution.
II. The CPA has a direct financial interest in an audit client, but the interest is maintained in a blind trust.
III. The CPA owns a commercial building and leases it to an audit client. The rental income is material to the CPA.

a. I and II.
b. II and III.
c. I and III.
d. I, II, and III.

M92#56. Must a CPA in public practice be independent in fact and appearance when providing the following services?

	Compilation of personal financial statements	Preparation of a tax return	Compilation of a financial forecast
a.	No	No	No
b.	No	No	Yes
c.	Yes	No	No
d.	No	Yes	No

N90#2. A CPA owes a duty to
a. Provide for a successor CPA in the event death or disability prevents completion of an audit.
b. Advise a client of errors contained in a previously filed tax return.
c. Disclose client fraud to third parties.
d. Perform an audit according to GAAP so that fraud will be uncovered.

N90#37. An accountant who is **not** independent of a client is precluded from issuing a
a. Report on management advisory services.
b. Compilation report on historical financial statements.
c. Compilation report on prospective financial statements.
d. Special report on compliance with contractual agreements.

N90#39. Which of the following standards requires a critical review of the work done and the judgment exercised by those assisting in an audit at every level of supervision?
a. Proficiency.
b. Audit risk.
c. Inspection.
d. Due care.

M90#46. The first general standard requires that an audit of financial statements is to be performed by a person or persons having
a. Seasoned judgment in varying degrees of supervision and review.
b. Adequate technical training and proficiency.

c. Knowledge of the standards of field work and reporting.
d. Independence with respect to the financial statements and supplementary disclosures.

M90#47. The exercise of due professional care requires that an auditor
a. Examine all available corroborating evidence.
b. Critically review the judgment exercised at every level of supervision.
c. Reduce control risk below the maximum.
d. Attain the proper balance of professional experience and formal education.

M89#3. According to the profession's ethical standards, an auditor would be considered independent in which of the following instances?
a. The auditor's checking account, which is fully insured by a federal agency, is held at a client financial institution.
b. The auditor is also an attorney who advises the client as its general counsel.
c. An employee of the auditor donates service as treasurer of a charitable organization that is a client.
d. The client owes the auditor fees for two consecutive annual audits.

C. Responsibilities in Other Professional Services

R98#1. According to the standards of the profession, which of the following would be considered a part of a consulting services engagement?

I. Expressing a conclusion about the reliability of a client's financial statements.
II. Reviewing and commenting on a client-prepared business plan.

a. I only.
b. II only.
c. Both I and II.
d. Neither I nor II.

R96#1. Which of the following services may a CPA perform in carrying out a consulting service engagement for a client?

I. Review of the client-prepared business plan.
II. Preparation of information for obtaining financing.

a. I only.
b. II only.
c. Both I and II.
d. Neither I nor II.

N95#5. Under the Statements on Standards for Consulting Services, which of the following statements best reflects a CPA's responsibility when undertaking a consulting services engagement? The CPA must
a. Not seek to modify any agreement made with the client.
b. Not perform any attest services for the client.
c. Inform the client of significant reservations concerning the benefits of the engagement.
d. Obtain a written understanding with the client concerning the time for completion of the engagement.

N95#6. According to the standards of the profession, which of the following sources of information should a CPA consider before signing a client's tax return?

I. Information actually known to the CPA from the tax return of another client.
II. Information provided by the client that appears to be correct based on the client's returns from prior years.

a. I only.
b. II only.
c. Both I and II.
d. Neither I nor II.

N95#7. According to the standards of the profession, which of the following statements is(are) correct regarding the action to be taken by a CPA who discovers an error in a client's previously filed tax return?

I. Advise the client of the error and recommend the measures to be taken.
II. Withdraw from the professional relationship regardless of whether or not the client corrects the error.

a. I only.
b. II only.
c. Both I and II.
d. Neither I nor II.

M95#3. According to the standards of the profession, which of the following events would require a CPA performing a consulting services engagement for a nonaudit client to withdraw from the engagement?

I. The CPA has a conflict of interest that is disclosed to the client and the client consents to the CPA continuing the engagement.
II. The CPA fails to obtain a written understanding from the client concerning the scope of the engagement.

a. I only.
b. II only.
c. Both I and II.
d. Neither I nor II.

N94#5. According to the profession's standards, which of the following is **not** required of a CPA performing a consulting engagement?
a. Complying with Statements on Standards for Consulting Services.
b. Obtaining an understanding of the nature, scope, and limitations of the engagement.

c. Supervising staff who are assigned to the engagement.
d. Maintaining independence from the client.

N94#6. According to the profession's standards, which of the following would be considered consulting services?

	Advisory services	Implementation services	Product services
a.	Yes	Yes	Yes
b.	Yes	Yes	No
c.	Yes	No	Yes
d.	No	Yes	Yes

M94#5. Which of the following services may a CPA perform in carrying out a consulting service for a client?

I. Analysis of the client's accounting system.
II. Review of the client's prepared business plan.
III. Preparation of information for obtaining financing.

a. I and II only.
b. I and III only.
c. II and III only.
d. I, II, and III.

M94#6. Nile, CPA, on completing an audit, was asked by the client to provide technical assistance in implementing a new EDP system. The set of pronouncements designed to guide Nile in this engagement is the Statement(s) on
a. Quality Control Standards.
b. Auditing Standards.
c. Standards for Accountants' EDP Services.
d. Standards for Consulting Services.

N93#14. Which of the following statements applies to consulting services engagements?
a. A practitioner should obtain an understanding of the internal control structure to assess control risk.
b. A practitioner is **not** permitted to compile a financial forecast.
c. A practitioner should obtain sufficient relevant data to complete the engagement.
d. A practitioner is to maintain an appearance of independence.

M93#5. A pervasive characteristic of a CPA's role in a consulting services engagement is that of being a(an)
a. Objective advisor.
b. Independent practitioner.
c. Computer specialist.
d. Confidential reviewer.

N91#14. Which of the following general standards apply to consulting services engagements and consultations?

	Due professional care	Independence in mental attitude	Planning and supervision
a.	No	Yes	No
b.	No	Yes	Yes
c.	Yes	No	Yes
d.	Yes	No	No

N89#57. If requested to perform a review engagement for a nonpublic entity in which an accountant has an immaterial direct financial interest, the accountant is
a. Independent because the financial interest is immaterial and, therefore, may issue a review report.
b. Not independent and, therefore, may **not** be associated with the financial statements.
c. Not independent and, therefore, may **not** issue a review report.
d. Not independent and, therefore, may issue a review report, but may **not** issue an auditor's opinion.

D. Disciplinary Systems Imposed by the Profession and State Regulatory Bodies

R96#2. Which of the following bodies ordinarily would have the authority to suspend or revoke a CPA's license to practice public accounting?
a. The SEC.
b. The AICPA.
c. A state CPA society.
d. A state board of accountancy.

E. Common Law Liability to Clients and Third Parties

R97#1. Which of the following statements is generally correct regarding the liability of a CPA who negligently gives an opinion on an audit of a client's financial statements?
a. The CPA is only liable to those third parties who are in privity of contract with the CPA.
b. The CPA is only liable to the client.
c. The CPA is liable to anyone in a class of third parties who the CPA knows will rely on the opinion.
d. The CPA is liable to all possible foreseeable users of the CPA's opinion.

N95#8. Under the "Ultramares" rule, to which of the following parties will an accountant be liable for negligence?

	Parties in privity	Foreseen parties
a.	Yes	Yes
b.	Yes	No
c.	No	Yes
d.	No	No

N95#9. When performing an audit, a CPA will most likely be considered negligent when the CPA fails to

a. Detect all of a client's fraudulent activities.
b. Include a negligence disclaimer in the client engagement letter.
c. Warn a client of known internal control weaknesses.
d. Warn a client's customers of embezzlement by the client's employees.

N95#10. Which of the following is the best defense a CPA firm can assert in a suit for common law fraud based on its unqualified opinion on materially false financial statements?
a. Contributory negligence on the part of the client.
b. A disclaimer contained in the engagement letter.
c. Lack of privity.
d. Lack of scienter.

N94#9. In a common law action against an accountant, lack of privity is a viable defense if the plaintiff
a. Is the client's creditor who sues the accountant for negligence.
b. Can prove the presence of gross negligence that amounts to a reckless disregard for the truth.
c. Is the accountant's client.
d. Bases the action upon fraud.

N94#10. Under common law, which of the following statements most accurately reflects the liability of a CPA who fraudulently gives an opinion on an audit of a client's financial statements?
a. The CPA is liable only to third parties in privity of contract with the CPA.
b. The CPA is liable only to known users of the financial statements.
c. The CPA probably is liable to any person who suffered a loss as a result of the fraud.
d. The CPA probably is liable to the client even if the client was aware of the fraud and did **not** rely on the opinion.

M94#9. If a CPA recklessly departs from the standards of due care when conducting an audit, the CPA will be liable to third parties who are unknown to the CPA based on
a. Negligence.
b. Gross negligence.
c. Strict liability.
d. Criminal deceit.

N93#1. Beckler & Associates, CPAs, audited and gave an unqualified opinion on the financial statements of Queen Co. The financial statements contained misstatements that resulted in a material overstatement of Queen's net worth. Queen provided the audited financial statements to Mac Bank in connection with a loan made by Mac to Queen. Beckler knew that the financial statements would be provided to Mac. Queen defaulted on the loan. Mac sued Beckler to recover for its losses associated with Queen's default. Which of the following must Mac prove in order to recover?

I. Beckler was negligent in conducting the audit.
II. Mac relied on the financial statements.

a. I only.
b. II only.
c. Both I and II.
d. Neither I nor II.

N93#2. Which of the following statements best describes whether a CPA has met the required standard of care in conducting an audit of a client's financial statements?
a. The client's expectations with regard to the accuracy of audited financial statements.
b. The accuracy of the financial statements and whether the statements conform to generally accepted accounting principles.
c. Whether the CPA conducted the audit with the same skill and care expected of an ordinarily prudent CPA under the circumstances.
d. Whether the audit was conducted to investigate and discover all acts of fraud.

M93#1. Sun Corp. approved a merger plan with Cord Corp. One of the determining factors in approving the merger was the financial statements of Cord that were audited by Frank & Co., CPAs. Sun had engaged Frank to audit Cord's financial statements. While performing the audit, Frank failed to discover certain irregularities that later caused Sun to suffer substantial losses. For Frank to be liable under common law negligence, Sun at a minimum must prove that Frank
a. Knew of the irregularities.
b. Failed to exercise due care.
c. Was grossly negligent.
d. Acted with scienter.

M93#2. A CPA will most likely be negligent when the CPA fails to
a. Correct errors discovered in the CPA's previously issued audit reports.
b. Detect all of a client's fraudulent activities.
c. Include a negligence disclaimer in the CPA's engagement letter.
d. Warn a client's customers of embezzlement by the client's employees.

M93#3. Which of the following elements, if present, would support a finding of constructive fraud on the part of a CPA?
a. Gross negligence in applying generally accepted auditing standards.
b. Ordinary negligence in applying generally accepted accounting principles.
c. Identified third party users.
d. Scienter.

N91#1. Cable Corp. orally engaged Drake & Co., CPAs, to audit its financial statements. Cable's management informed Drake that it suspected the accounts receivable were materially overstated. Though the financial statements Drake audited included a materially overstated accounts receivable balance, Drake issued an unqualified opinion. Cable used the financial statements to obtain a loan to expand its operations. Cable defaulted on the loan and incurred a substantial loss.

If Cable sues Drake for negligence in failing to discover the overstatement, Drake's best defense would be that Drake did **not**
  a. Have privity of contract with Cable.
  b. Sign an engagement letter.
  c. Perform the audit recklessly or with an intent to deceive.
  d. Violate generally accepted auditing standards in performing the audit.

N91#3. Ford & Co., CPAs, issued an unqualified opinion on Owens Corp.'s financial statements. Relying on these financial statements, Century Bank lent Owens $750,000. Ford was unaware that Century would receive a copy of the financial statements or that Owens would use them to obtain a loan. Owens defaulted on the loan.

To succeed in a common law fraud action against Ford, Century must prove, in addition to other elements, that Century was
  a. Free from contributory negligence.
  b. In privity of contract with Ford.
  c. Justified in relying on the financial statements.
  d. In privity of contract with Owens.

N91#4. Hark, CPA, failed to follow generally accepted auditing standards in auditing Long Corp.'s financial statements. Long's management had told Hark that the audited statements would be submitted to several banks to obtain financing. Relying on the statements, Third Bank gave Long a loan. Long defaulted on the loan. In a jurisdiction applying the *Ultramares* decision, if Third sues Hark, Hark will
  a. Win because there was **no** privity of contract between Hark and Third.
  b. Lose because Hark knew that banks would be relying on the financial statements.
  c. Win because Third was contributorily negligent in granting the loan.
  d. Lose because Hark was negligent in performing the audit.

N91#5. A CPA who fraudulently performs an audit of a corporation's financial statements will
  a. Probably be liable to any person who suffered a loss as a result of the fraud.
  b. Be liable only to the corporation and to third parties who are members of a class of intended users of the financial statements.
  c. Probably be liable to the corporation even though its management was aware of the fraud and did **not** rely on the financial statements.
  d. Be liable only to third parties in privity of contract with the CPA.

N90#1. A CPA firm issues an unqualified opinion on financial statements not prepared in accordance with GAAP. The CPA firm will have acted with scienter in all the following circumstances **except** where the firm

  a. Intentionally disregards the truth.
  b. Has actual knowledge of fraud.
  c. Negligently performs auditing procedures.
  d. Intends to gain monetarily by concealing fraud.

N90#4. In a common law action against an accountant, lack of privity is a viable defense if the plaintiff
  a. Can prove the presence of gross negligence which amounts to a reckless disregard for the truth.
  b. Bases the action upon fraud.
  c. Is the client's creditor who sues the accountant for negligence.
  d. Is the accountant's client.

N90#5. Mix and Associates, CPAs, issued an unqualified opinion on the financial statements of Glass Corp. for the year ended December 31, 1989. It was determined later that Glass' treasurer had embezzled $300,000 from Glass during 1989. Glass sued Mix because of Mix's failure to discover the embezzlement. Mix was unaware of the embezzlement. Which of the following is Mix's best defense?
  a. The audit was performed in accordance with GAAS.
  b. The treasurer was Glass' agent and, therefore, Glass was responsible for preventing the embezzlement.
  c. The financial statements were presented in conformity with GAAP.
  d. Mix had **no** actual knowledge of the embezzlement.

M89#1. Krim, President and CEO of United Co., engaged Smith, CPA, to audit United's financial statements so that United could secure a loan from First Bank. Smith issued an unqualified opinion on May 20, 1988, but the loan was delayed. On August 5, 1988, on inquiry to Smith by First Bank, Smith, relying on Krim's representation, made assurances that there was no material change in United's financial status. Krim's representation was untrue because of a material change which took place after May 20, 1988. First relied on Smith's assurances of no change. Shortly thereafter, United became insolvent. If First sues Smith for negligent misrepresentation, Smith will be found
  a. Not liable, because Krim misled Smith, and a CPA is **not** responsible for a client's untrue representations.
  b. Liable, because Smith should have undertaken sufficient auditing procedures to verify the status of United.
  c. Not liable, because Smith's opinion only covers the period up to May 20.
  d. Liable, because Smith should have contacted the chief financial officer rather than the chief executive officer.

M89#2. If a stockholder sues a CPA for common law fraud based on false statements contained in the financial statements audited by the CPA, which of the following, if present, would be the CPA's best defense?

a. The stockholder lacks privity to sue.
b. The false statements were immaterial.
c. The CPA did **not** financially benefit from the alleged fraud.
d. The contributory negligence of the client.

M89#6. When CPAs fail in their duty to carry out their contracts for services, liability to clients may be based on

	Breach of contract	Strict liability
a.	Yes	Yes
b.	Yes	No
c.	No	No
d.	No	Yes

M89#7. Which one of the following, if present, would support a finding of constructive fraud on the part of a CPA?
a. Privity of contract.
b. Intent to deceive.
c. Reckless disregard.
d. Ordinary negligence.

F. Federal Statutory Liability

N95#11. Under the anti-fraud provisions of Section 10(b) of the Securities Exchange Act of 1934, a CPA may be liable if the CPA acted
a. Negligently.
b. With independence.
c. Without due diligence.
d. Without good faith.

N95#13. Ocean and Associates, CPAs, audited the financial statements of Drain Corporation. As a result of Ocean's negligence in conducting the audit, the financial statements included material misstatements. Ocean was unaware of this fact. The financial statements and Ocean's unqualified opinion were included in a registration statement and prospectus for an original public offering of stock by Drain. Sharp purchased shares in the offering. Sharp received a copy of the prospectus prior to the purchase but did not read it. The shares declined in value as a result of the misstatements in Drain's financial statements becoming known. Under which of the following Acts is Sharp most likely to prevail in a lawsuit against Ocean?

	Securities Exchange Act of 1934, Section 10(b), Rule 10b-5	Securities Act of 1933, Section 11
a.	Yes	Yes
b.	Yes	No
c.	No	Yes
d.	No	No

N94#11. Under the provisions of Section 10(b) and Rule 10b-5 of the Securities Exchange Act of 1934, which of the following activities must be proven by a stock purchaser in a suit against a CPA?

I. Intentional conduct by the CPA designed to deceive investors.
II. Negligence by the CPA.

a. I only.
b. II only.
c. Both I and II.
d. Neither I nor II.

N94
Items 12 and 13 are based on the following:

Under the liability provisions of Section 11 of the Securities Act of 1933, a CPA may be liable to any purchaser of a security for certifying materially misstated financial statements that are included in the security's registration statement.

12. Under Section 11, a CPA usually will **not** be liable to the purchaser
    a. If the purchaser is contributorily negligent.
    b. If the CPA can prove due diligence.
    c. Unless the purchaser can prove privity with the CPA.
    d. Unless the purchaser can prove scienter on the part of the CPA.

13. Under Section 11, which of the following must be proven by a purchaser of the security?

	Reliance on the financial statements	Fraud by the CPA
a.	Yes	Yes
b.	Yes	No
c.	No	Yes
d.	No	No

N93
Items 3 through 5 are based on the following:

While conducting an audit, Larson Associates, CPAs, failed to detect material misstatements included in its client's financial statements. Larson's unqualified opinion was included with the financial statements in a registration statement and prospectus for a public offering of securities made by the client. Larson knew that its opinion and the financial statements would be used for this purpose.

3. Which of the following statements is correct with regard to a suit against Larson and the client by a purchaser of the securities under Section 11 of the Securities Act of 1933?
    a. The purchaser must prove that Larson was negligent in conducting the audit.
    b. The purchaser must prove that Larson knew of the material misstatements.

c. Larson will **not** be liable if it had reasonable grounds to believe the financial statements were accurate.
d. Larson will be liable unless the purchaser did **not** rely on the financial statements.

4. In a suit by a purchaser against Larson for common law negligence, Larson's best defense would be that the
   a. Audit was conducted in accordance with generally accepted auditing standards.
   b. Client was aware of the misstatements.
   c. Purchaser was **not** in privity of contract with Larson.
   d. Identity of the purchaser was **not** known to Larson at the time of the audit.

5. In a suit by a purchaser against Larson for common law fraud, Larson's best defense would be that
   a. Larson did **not** have actual or constructive knowledge of the misstatements.
   b. Larson's client knew or should have known of the misstatements.
   c. Larson did **not** have actual knowledge that the purchaser was an intended beneficiary of the audit.
   d. Larson was **not** in privity of contract with its client.

N93#6. Jay and Co., CPAs, audited the financial statements of Maco Corp. Jay intentionally gave an unqualified opinion on the financial statements even though material misstatements were discovered. The financial statements and Jay's unqualified opinion were included in a registration statement and prospectus for an original public offering of Maco stock. Which of the following statements is correct regarding Jay's liability to a purchaser of the offering under Section 10(b) and Rule 10b-5 of the Securities Exchange Act of 1934?
   a. Jay will be liable if the purchaser relied on Jay's unqualified opinion on the financial statements.
   b. Jay will be liable if Jay was negligent in conducting the audit.
   c. Jay will **not** be liable if the purchaser's loss was under $500.
   d. Jay will **not** be liable if the misstatement resulted from an omission of a material fact by Jay.

M93#5. To be successful in a civil action under Section 11 of the Securities Act of 1933 concerning liability for a misleading registration statement, the plaintiff must prove the

	Defendant's intent to deceive	Plaintiff's reliance on the registration statement
a.	No	Yes
b.	No	No
c.	Yes	No
d.	Yes	Yes

M93#10. An accountant will be liable for damages under Section 10(b) and Rule 10b-5 of the Securities Exchange Act of 1934 only if the plaintiff proves that
   a. The accountant was negligent.
   b. There was a material omission.
   c. The security involved was registered.
   d. The security was part of an original issuance.

M92
Items 2 through 5 are based on the following:

Dart Corp. engaged Jay Associates, CPAs, to assist in a public stock offering. Jay audited Dart's financial statements and gave an unqualified opinion, despite knowing that the financial statements contained misstatements. Jay's opinion was included in Dart's registration statement. Larson purchased shares in the offering and suffered a loss when the stock declined in value after the misstatements became known.

2. In a suit against Jay and Dart under the Section 11 liability provisions of the Securities Act of 1933, Larson must prove that
   a. Jay knew of the misstatements.
   b. Jay was negligent.
   c. The misstatements contained in Dart's financial statements were material.
   d. The unqualified opinion contained in the registration statement was relied on by Larson.

3. If Larson succeeds in the Section 11 suit against Dart, Larson would be entitled to
   a. Damages of three times the original public offering price.
   b. Rescind the transaction.
   c. Monetary damages only.
   d. Damages, but only if the shares were resold before the suit was started.

4. In a suit against Jay under the anti-fraud provisions of Section 10(b) and Rule 10b-5 of the Securities Exchange Act of 1934, Larson must prove all of the following **except**
   a. Larson was an intended user of the false registration statement.
   b. Larson relied on the false registration statement.
   c. The transaction involved some form of interstate commerce.
   d. Jay acted with intentional disregard of the truth.

5. If Larson succeeds in the Section 10(b) and Rule 10b-5 suit, Larson would be entitled to
   a. Only recover the original public offering price.
   b. Only rescind the transaction.
   c. The amount of any loss caused by the fraud.
   d. Punitive damages.

N91#6. Quincy bought Teal Corp. common stock in an offering registered under the Securities Act of 1933. Worth & Co., CPAs, gave an unqualified opinion on Teal's financial statements that were included in the registration statement filed with the SEC. Quincy sued Worth

under the provisions of the 1933 Act that deal with omission of facts required to be in the registration statement. Quincy must prove that
   a. There was fraudulent activity by Worth.
   b. There was a material misstatement in the financial statements.
   c. Quincy relied on Worth's opinion.
   d. Quincy was in privity with Worth.

N91#7. For a CPA to be liable for damages under the antifraud provisions of Section 10(b) and Rule 10b-5 of the Securities Exchange Act of 1934, a plaintiff must prove all of the following **except** that
   a. The plaintiff relied on the financial statements audited by the CPA.
   b. The CPA violated generally accepted auditing standards.
   c. There was a material misrepresentation of fact in the financial statements audited by the CPA.
   d. The CPA acted with scienter.

N91#8. Jay, CPA, gave an unqualified opinion on Nast Power Co.'s financial statements. Larkin bought Nast bonds in a public offering subject to the Securities Act of 1933. The registration statement filed with the SEC included Nast's financial statements. Larkin sued Jay for misstatements contained in the financial statements under the provisions of Section 11 of the Securities Act of 1933. To prevail, Larkin must prove

	Scienter	Reliance
a.	Yes	No
b.	Yes	Yes
c.	No	No
d.	No	Yes

N90#6. Holly Corp. engaged Yost & Co., CPAs, to audit the financial statements to be included in a registration statement Holly was required to file under the provisions of the Securities Act of 1933. Yost failed to exercise due diligence and did not discover the omission of a fact material to the statements. A purchaser of Holly's securities may recover from Yost under Section 11 of the Securities Act of 1933 only if the purchaser
   a. Brings a civil action within one year of the discovery of the omission and within three years of the offering date.
   b. Proves that the registration statement was relied on to make the purchase.
   c. Proves that Yost was negligent.
   d. Establishes privity of contract with Yost.

N90
Items 7 and 8 are based on the following:

Petty Corp. made a public offering subject to the Securities Act of 1933. In connection with the offering, Ward & Co., CPAs, rendered an unqualified opinion on Petty's financial statements included in the SEC registration statement. Huff purchased 500 of the offered shares. Huff has brought an action against Ward under Section 11 of the Securities Act of 1933 for losses resulting from misstatements of facts in the financial statements included in the registration statement.

7. To succeed, Huff must prove that
   a. Ward performed the audit negligently.
   b. The misstatements were material.
   c. Ward rendered its opinion with knowledge of material misstatements.
   d. Huff relied on the financial statements included in the registration statement.

8. Ward's weakest defense would be that
   a. Huff knew of the misstatements when Huff purchased the stock.
   b. Huff's losses were **not** caused by the misstatements.
   c. Ward was **not** in privity of contract with Huff.
   d. Ward conducted the audit in accordance with GAAS.

M89#8. Burt, CPA, issued an unqualified opinion on the financial statements of Midwest Corp. These financial statements were included in Midwest's annual report and Form 10-K filed with the SEC. As a result of Burt's reckless disregard for GAAS, material misstatements in the financial statements were not detected. Subsequently, Davis purchased stock in Midwest in the secondary market without ever seeing Midwest's annual report or Form 10-K. Shortly thereafter, Midwest became insolvent and the price of the stock declined drastically. Davis sued Burt for damages based on Section 10(b) and Rule 10b-5 of the Securities Exchange Act of 1934. Burt's best defense is that
   a. There has been **no** subsequent sale for which a loss can be computed.
   b. Davis did **not** purchase the stock as part of an initial offering.
   c. Davis did **not** rely on the financial statements or Form 10-K.
   d. Davis was **not** in privity with Burt.

G. Privileged Communications and Confidentiality

N95#14. Which of the following statements is correct regarding a CPA's working papers? The working papers must be
   a. Transferred to another accountant purchasing the CPA's practice even if the client hasn't given permission.
   b. Transferred permanently to the client if demanded.
   c. Turned over to any government agency that requests them.
   d. Turned over pursuant to a valid federal court subpoena.

N95#15. Thorp, CPA, was engaged to audit Ivor Co.'s financial statements. During the audit, Thorp discovered that Ivor's inventory contained stolen goods. Ivor was

indicted and Thorp was subpoenaed to testify at the criminal trial. Ivor claimed accountant-client privilege to prevent Thorp from testifying. Which of the following statements is correct regarding Ivor's claim?
    a. Ivor can claim an accountant-client privilege only in states that have enacted a statute creating such a privilege.
    b. Ivor can claim an accountant-client privilege only in federal courts.
    c. The accountant-client privilege can be claimed only in civil suits.
    d. The accountant-client privilege can be claimed only to limit testimony to audit subject matter.

M95#5. A CPA is permitted to disclose confidential client information without the consent of the client to

I. Another CPA firm if the information concerns suspected tax return irregularities.
II. A state CPA society voluntary quality control review board.

    a. I only.
    b. II only.
    c. Both I and II.
    d. Neither I nor II.

N94#14. Which of the following statements concerning an accountant's disclosure of confidential client data is generally correct?
    a. Disclosure may be made to any state agency without subpoena.
    b. Disclosure may be made to any party on consent of the client.
    c. Disclosure may be made to comply with an IRS audit request.
    d. Disclosure may be made to comply with Generally Accepted Accounting Principles.

N94#15. To which of the following parties may a CPA partnership provide its working papers, without being lawfully subpoenaed or without the client's consent?
    a. The IRS.
    b. The FASB.
    c. Any surviving partner(s) on the death of a partner.
    d. A CPA before purchasing a partnership interest in the firm.

M94#10. Which of the following statements is correct with respect to ownership, possession, or access to a CPA firm's audit working papers?
    a. Working papers may **never** be obtained by third parties unless the client consents.
    b. Working papers are **not** transferable to a purchaser of a CPA practice unless the client consents.
    c. Working papers are subject to the privileged communication rule which, in most jurisdictions, prevents any third-party access to the working papers.
    d. Working papers are the client's exclusive property.

N93#10. A CPA's working papers
    a. Need **not** be disclosed under a federal court subpoena.
    b. Must be disclosed under an IRS administrative subpoena.
    c. Must be disclosed to another accountant purchasing the CPA's practice even if the client hasn't given permission.
    d. Need **not** be disclosed to a state CPA society quality review team.

M93#6. A CPA is permitted to disclose confidential client information without the consent of the client to

I. Another CPA who has purchased the CPA's tax practice.
II. Another CPA firm if the information concerns suspected tax return irregularities.
III. A state CPA society voluntary quality control review board.

    a. I and III only.
    b. II and III only.
    c. II only.
    d. III only.

M93#9. Pym, CPA, was engaged to audit Silo Co.'s financial statements. During the audit Pym discovered that Silo's inventory contained stolen goods. Silo was indicted and Pym was subpoenaed to testify at the criminal trial. Silo claimed accountant-client privilege to prevent Pym from testifying. Silo will be able to prevent Pym from testifying
    a. If the action is brought in a federal court.
    b. About the nature of the work performed in the audit.
    c. Due to the common law in the majority of the states.
    d. Where a state statute has been enacted creating such a privilege.

M92#1. In a jurisdiction having an accountant-client privilege statute, to whom may a CPA turn over workpapers without a client's permission?
    a. Purchaser of the CPA's practice.
    b. State tax authorities.
    c. State court.
    d. State CPA society quality control panel.

N90#3. Mell Corp. engaged Davis & Co., CPAs, to audit Mell's financial statements. Mell's management informed Davis it suspected that the accounts receivable were materially overstated. Although the financial statements did include a materially overstated accounts receivable balance, Davis issued an unqualified opinion. Mell relied on the financial statements in deciding to obtain a loan from County Bank to expand its operations. County relied on the financial statements in making the loan to Mell. As a result of the overstated accounts receivable balance, Mell has defaulted on the loan and has incurred a substantial loss.

If County sues Davis for fraud, must Davis furnish County with the audit working papers?
   a. Yes, if the working papers are lawfully subpoenaed into court.
   b. Yes, provided that Mell does **not** object.
   c. No, because of the privileged communication rule, which is recognized in a majority of jurisdictions.
   d. No, because County was **not** in privity of contract with Davis.

N90#9. Locke, CPA, was engaged to perform an audit for Vorst Co. During the audit, Locke discovered that Vorst's inventory contained stolen goods. Vorst was indicted and Locke was validly subpoenaed to testify at the criminal trial. Vorst has claimed accountant-client privilege to prevent Locke from testifying. Locke may be compelled to testify
   a. Only with Vorst's consent.
   b. In any federal court located in the 50 states.
   c. In any state court.
   d. Only about the nature of the work performed in the audit.

N90#10. A CPA partnership may, without being lawfully subpoenaed or without the client's consent, make client workpapers available to
   a. An individual purchasing the entire partnership.
   b. The IRS.
   c. The SEC.
   d. Any surviving partner(s) on the death of a partner.

II. Business Organizations

A. Agency

R96#3. Which of the following statements represent(s) a principal's duty to an agent who works on a commission basis?

I. The principal is required to maintain pertinent records, account to the agent, and pay the agent according to the terms of their agreement.
II. The principal is required to reimburse the agent for all authorized expenses incurred unless the agreement calls for the agent to pay expenses out of the commission.

   a. I only.
   b. II only.
   c. Both I and II.
   d. Neither I nor II.

M95#6. Trent was retained, in writing, to act as Post's agent for the sale of Post's memorabilia collection. Which of the following statements is correct?

I. To be an agent, Trent must be at least 21 years of age.
II. Post would be liable to Trent if the collection was destroyed before Trent found a purchaser.

   a. I only.
   b. II only.
   c. Both I and II.
   d. Neither I nor II.

M95#7. Thorp was a purchasing agent for Ogden, a sole proprietor, and had the express authority to place purchase orders with Ogden's suppliers. Thorp placed an order with Datz, Inc. on Ogden's behalf after Ogden was declared incompetent in a judicial proceeding. Thorp was aware of Ogden's incapacity. Which of the following statements is correct concerning Ogden's liability to Datz?

   a. Ogden will be liable because Datz was **not** informed of Ogden's incapacity.
   b. Ogden will be liable because Thorp acted with express authority.
   c. Ogden will **not** be liable because Thorp's agency ended when Ogden was declared incompetent.
   d. Ogden will **not** be liable because Ogden was a nondisclosed principal.

M95#8. When a valid contract is entered into by an agent on the principal's behalf, in a nondisclosed principal situation, which of the following statements concerning the principal's liability is correct?

	The principal may be held liable once disclosed	The principal must ratify the contract to be held liable
a.	Yes	Yes
b.	Yes	No
c.	No	Yes
d.	No	No

M95#9. Young Corp. hired Wilson as a sales representative for six months at a salary of $5,000 per month plus 6% of sales. Which of the following statements is correct?
   a. Young does **not** have the power to dismiss Wilson during the six-month period without cause.
   b. Wilson is obligated to act solely in Young's interest in matters concerning Young's business.
   c. The agreement between Young and Wilson is **not** enforceable unless it is in writing and signed by Wilson.
   d. The agreement between Young and Wilson formed an agency coupled with an interest.

N94#16. Which of the following actions requires an agent for a corporation to have a written agency agreement?
  a. Purchasing office supplies for the principal's business.
  b. Purchasing an interest in undeveloped land for the principal.
  c. Hiring an independent general contractor to renovate the principal's office building.
  d. Retaining an attorney to collect a business debt owed the principal.

N94#17. Bolt Corp. dismissed Ace as its general sales agent and notified all of Ace's known customers by letter. Young Corp., a retail outlet located outside of Ace's previously assigned sales territory, had never dealt with Ace. Young knew of Ace as a result of various business contacts. After his dismissal, Ace sold Young goods, to be delivered by Bolt, and received from Young a cash deposit for 20% of the purchase price. It was not unusual for an agent in Ace's previous position to receive cash deposits. In an action by Young against Bolt on the sales contract, Young will
  a. Lose, because Ace lacked any implied authority to make the contract.
  b. Lose, because Ace lacked any express authority to make the contract.
  c. Win, because Bolt's notice was inadequate to terminate Ace's apparent authority.
  d. Win, because a principal is an insurer of an agent's acts.

N94#18. Easy Corp. is a real estate developer and regularly engages real estate brokers to act on its behalf in acquiring parcels of land. The brokers are authorized to enter into such contracts, but are instructed to do so in their own names without disclosing Easy's identity or relationship to the transaction. If a broker enters into a contract with a seller on Easy's behalf,
  a. The broker will have the same actual authority as if Easy's identity had been disclosed.
  b. Easy will be bound by the contract because of the broker's apparent authority.
  c. Easy will **not** be liable for any negligent acts committed by the broker while acting on Easy's behalf.
  d. The broker will **not** be personally bound by the contract because the broker has express authority to act.

N94#19. An agent will usually be liable under a contract made with a third party when the agent is acting on behalf of a(an)

	Disclosed principal	Undisclosed principal
a.	Yes	Yes
b.	Yes	No
c.	No	Yes
d.	No	No

N93#11. Noll gives Carr a written power of attorney. Which of the following statements is correct regarding this power of attorney?
  a. It must be signed by both Noll and Carr.
  b. It must be for a definite period of time.
  c. It may continue in existence after Noll's death.
  d. It may limit Carr's authority to specific transactions.

N93#13. Generally, a disclosed principal will be liable to third parties for its agent's unauthorized misrepresentations if the agent is an

	Employee	Independent Contractor
a.	Yes	Yes
b.	Yes	No
c.	No	Yes
d.	No	No

N93#14. Which of the following rights will a third party be entitled to after validly contracting with an agent representing an undisclosed principal?
  a. Disclosure of the principal by the agent.
  b. Ratification of the contract by the principal.
  c. Performance of the contract by the agent.
  d. Election to void the contract after disclosure of the principal.

N93#15. North, Inc. hired Sutter as a purchasing agent. North gave Sutter written authorization to purchase, without limit, electronic appliances. Later, Sutter was told not to purchase more than 300 of each appliance. Sutter contracted with Orr Corp. to purchase 500 tape recorders. Orr had been shown Sutter's written authorization. Which of the following statements is correct?
  a. Sutter will be liable to Orr because Sutter's actual authority was exceeded.
  b. Sutter will **not** be liable to reimburse North if North is liable to Orr.
  c. North will be liable to Orr because of Sutter's actual and apparent authority.
  d. North will **not** be liable to Orr because Sutter's actual authority was exceeded.

M92#6. A principal and agent relationship requires a
  a. Written agreement.
  b. Power of attorney.
  c. Meeting of the minds and consent to act.
  d. Specified consideration.

M92#7. Young was a purchasing agent for Wilson, a sole proprietor. Young had the express authority to place purchase orders with Wilson's suppliers. Young conducted business through the mail and had little contact with Wilson. Young placed an order with Vanguard, Inc. on Wilson's behalf after Wilson was declared incompetent in a judicial proceeding. Young was aware of Wilson's incapacity. With regard to the contract with Vanguard, Wilson (or Wilson's legal representative) will
  a. Not be liable because Vanguard dealt only with Young.

b. Not be liable because Young did **not** have authority to enter into the contract.
c. Be liable because Vanguard was unaware of Wilson's incapacity.
d. Be liable because Young acted with express authority.

M92#8. Long Corp. is a real estate developer and regularly engages real estate brokers to act on its behalf in acquiring parcels of land. The brokers are authorized to enter into such contracts, but are instructed to do so in their own names without disclosing Long's identity or Long's relationship to the transaction. If a broker enters into a contract with a seller on Long's behalf,
  a. Long will **not** be liable for any negligent acts committed by the broker while acting on Long's behalf.
  b. The broker will have the same actual authority as if Long's identity had been disclosed.
  c. The broker will **not** be personally bound by the contract because the broker has express authority to act.
  d. Long will be bound by the contract because of the broker's apparent authority.

M92#9. Ogden Corp. hired Thorp as a sales representative for nine months at a salary of $3,000 per month plus 4% of sales. Which of the following statements is correct?
  a. Thorp is obligated to act solely in Ogden's interest in matters concerning Ogden's business.
  b. The agreement between Ogden and Thorp formed an agency coupled with an interest.
  c. Ogden does **not** have the power to dismiss Thorp during the nine-month period without cause.
  d. The agreement between Ogden and Thorp is **not** enforceable unless it is in writing and signed by Thorp.

N91#11. Forming an agency relationship requires that
  a. The agreement between the principal and agent be supported by consideration.
  b. The principal and agent **not** be minors.
  c. Both the principal and agent consent to the agency.
  d. The agent's authority be limited to the express grant of authority in the agency agreement.

N91#12. When an agent acts for an undisclosed principal, the principal will **not** be liable to third parties if the
  a. Principal ratifies a contract entered into by the agent.
  b. Agent acts within an implied grant of authority.
  c. Agent acts outside the grant of actual authority.
  d. Principal seeks to conceal the agency relationship.

M91#1. Simpson, Ogden Corp.'s agent, needs a written agency agreement to
  a. Enter into a series of sales contracts on Ogden's behalf.
  b. Hire an attorney to collect a business debt owed Ogden.
  c. Purchase an interest in undeveloped land for Ogden.
  d. Retain an independent general contractor to renovate Ogden's office building.

M91#2. Kent, without authority, contracted to buy computer equipment from Fox Corp. for Ace Corp. Kent told Fox that Kent was acting on Ace's behalf. For Ace to ratify the contract with Fox,
  a. Kent must be a general agent of Ace.
  b. Ace must know all material facts relating to the contract at the time it is ratified.
  c. Ace must notify Fox that Ace intends to ratify the contract.
  d. Kent must have acted reasonably and in Ace's best interest.

M91#3. Frost's accountant and business manager has the authority to
  a. Mortgage Frost's business property.
  b. Obtain bank loans for Frost.
  c. Insure Frost's property against fire loss.
  d. Sell Frost's business.

M90#1. Generally, an agency relationship is terminated by operation of law in all of the following situations **except** the
  a. Principal's death.
  b. Principal's incapacity.
  c. Agent's renunciation of the agency.
  d. Agent's failure to acquire a necessary business license.

M90#2. Pine, an employee of Global Messenger Co., was hired to deliver highly secret corporate documents for Global's clients throughout the world. Unknown to Global, Pine carried a concealed pistol. While Pine was making a delivery, he suspected an attempt was being made to steal the package, drew his gun and shot Kent, an innocent passerby. Kent will **not** recover damages from Global if
  a. Global discovered that Pine carried a weapon and did nothing about it.
  b. Global instructed its messengers **not** to carry weapons.
  c. Pine was correct and an attempt was being made to steal the package.
  d. Pine's weapon was unlicensed and illegal.

M90#4. Able, as agent for Baker, an undisclosed principal, contracted with Safe to purchase an antique car. In payment, Able issued his personal check to Safe. Able could not cover the check but expected Baker to give him cash to deposit before the check was presented for payment. Baker did not do so and the check was dishonored. Baker's identity became known to Safe. Safe may **not** recover from
  a. Baker individually on the contract.
  b. Able individually on the contract.

c. Baker individually on the check.
d. Able individually on the check.

M90#5. Ace engages Butler to manage Ace's retail business. Butler has the implied authority to do all of the following, **except**
 a. Purchase inventory for Ace's business.
 b. Sell Ace's business fixtures.
 c. Pay Ace's business debts.
 d. Hire or discharge Ace's business employees.

N09#2. A principal will not be liable to a third party for a tort committed by an agent
 a. Unless the principal instructed the agent to commit the tort.
 b. Unless the tort was committed within the scope of the agency relationship.
 c. If the agency agreement limits the principal's liability for the agent's tort.
 d. If the tort is also regarded as a criminal act.

N89#3. Parc contracted with Furn Brothers Corp. to buy hotel furniture and fixtures on behalf of Global Motor House, a motel chain. Global instructed Parc to use Parc's own name and not to disclose to Furn that Parc was acting on Global's behalf. Who is liable to Furn on this contract?

	Parc	Global
a.	Yes	No
b.	No	Yes
c.	Yes	Yes
d.	No	No

M89#11. Pell is the principal and Astor is the agent in an agency coupled with an interest. In the absence of a contractual provision relating to the duration of the agency, who has the right to terminate the agency before the interest has expired?

	Pell	Astor
a.	Yes	Yes
b.	No	Yes
c.	No	No
d.	Yes	No

M89#12. Neal, an employee of Jordan, was delivering merchandise to a customer. On the way, Neal's negligence caused a traffic accident that resulted in damages to a third party's automobile. Who is liable to the third party?

	Neal	Jordan
a.	No	No
b.	Yes	Yes
c.	Yes	No
d.	No	Yes

M89#13. Simmons, an agent for Jensen, has the express authority to sell Jensen's goods. Simmons also has the express authority to grant discounts of up to 5% of list price. Simmons sold Hemple goods with a list price of $1,000 and granted Hemple a 10% discount. Hemple had not previously dealt with either Simmons or Jensen. Which of the following courses of action may Jensen properly take?
 a. Seek to void the sale to Hemple.
 b. Seek recovery of $50 from Hemple only.
 c. Seek recovery of $50 from Simmons only.
 d. Seek recovery of $50 from either Hemple or Simmons.

D. Partnership, Joint Ventures, and Other Unincorporated Associations

R98#2. On February 1, Addison, Bradley, and Carter, physicians, formed ABC Medical Partnership. Dr. Bradley was placed in charge of the partnership's financial books and records. On April 1, Dr. Addison joined the City Hospital Medical Partnership, retaining the partnership interest in ABC. On May 1, ABC received a writ of attachment from the court attaching Dr. Carter's interest in ABC. The writ resulted from Dr. Carter's failure to pay a credit card bill. On June 1, Dr. Addison was adjudicated bankrupt. On July 1, Dr. Bradley was sued by the other partners of ABC for an accounting of ABC's revenues and expenses. Under the Uniform Partnership Act, which of the preceding events resulted in the dissolution of the ABC Medical Partnership?
 a. Dr. Addison joining the City Hospital Medical Partnership.
 b. Dr. Carter's interest in the partnership being attached by the court.
 c. Dr. Addison being adjudicated bankrupt.
 d. Dr. Bradley being sued for an accounting by the other partners of ABC.

R97#2. Which of the following statements is correct regarding the apparent authority of a partner to bind the partnership in dealings with third parties? The apparent authority
 a. Must be derived from the express powers and purposes contained in the partnership agreement.
 b. Will be effectively limited by a formal resolution of the partners of which third parties are unaware.
 c. May allow a partner to bind the partnership to representations made in connection with the sale of goods.
 d. Would permit a partner to submit a claim against the partnership to arbitration.

R96#11. Under the Uniform Partnership Act, which of the following statements concerning the powers and duties of partners in a general partnership is(are) correct?

I. Each partner is an agent of every other partner and acts as both a principal and an agent in any business transaction within the scope of the partnership agreement.
II. Each partner is subject to joint liability on partnership debts and contracts.

a. I only.
b. II only.
c. Both I and II.
d. Neither I nor II.

N95#16. Generally, under the Uniform Partnership Act, a partnership has which of the following characteristics?

	Unlimited duration	Obligation for payment of federal income tax
a.	Yes	Yes
b.	Yes	No
c.	No	Yes
d.	No	No

N95#17. Which of the following statements is(are) usually correct regarding general partners' liability?

I. All general partners are jointly and severally liable for partnership torts.
II. All general partners are liable only for those partnership obligations they actually authorized.

a. I only.
b. II only.
c. Both I and II.
d. Neither I nor II.

N95#18. Which of the following statements is correct regarding the division of profits in a general partnership when the written partnership agreement only provides that losses be divided equally among the partners? Profits are to be divided
a. Based on the partners' ratio of contribution to the partnership.
b. Based on the partners' participation in day to day management.
c. Equally among the partners.
d. Proportionately among the partners.

N95#19. Which of the following statements best describes the effect of the assignment of an interest in a general partnership?
a. The assignee becomes a partner.
b. The assignee is responsible for a proportionate share of past and future partnership debts.
c. The assignment automatically dissolves the partnership.
d. The assignment transfers the assignor's interest in partnership profits and surplus.

N95#20. Park and Graham entered into a written partnership agreement to operate a retail store. Their agreement was silent as to the duration of the partnership. Park wishes to dissolve the partnership. Which of the following statements is correct?
a. Park may dissolve the partnership at any time.
b. Unless Graham consents to a dissolution, Park must apply to a court and obtain a decree ordering the dissolution.
c. Park may **not** dissolve the partnership unless Graham consents.
d. Park may dissolve the partnership only after notice of the proposed dissolution is given to all partnership creditors.

N94#20. Unless otherwise provided in a general partnership agreement, which of the following statements is correct when a partner dies?

	The deceased partner's executor would automatically become a partner	The deceased partner's estate would be free from any partnership liabilities	The partnership would be dissolved automatically
a.	Yes	Yes	Yes
b.	Yes	No	No
c.	No	Yes	No
d.	No	No	Yes

N94#21. Which of the following statements is correct concerning liability when a partner in a general partnership commits a tort while engaged in partnership business?
a. The partner committing the tort is the only party liable.
b. The partnership is the only party liable.
c. Each partner is jointly and severally liable.
d. Each partner is liable to pay an equal share of any judgment.

N94#22. The partnership agreement for Owen Associates, a general partnership, provided that profits be paid to the partners in the ratio of their financial contribution to the partnership. Moore contributed $10,000, Noon contributed $30,000, and Kale contributed $50,000. For the year ended December 31, 1993, Owen had losses of $180,000. What amount of the losses should be allocated to Kale?
a. $ 40,000
b. $ 60,000
c. $ 90,000
d. $100,000

N94#23. Lark, a partner in DSJ, a general partnership, wishes to withdraw from the partnership and sell Lark's interest to Ward. All of the other partners in DSJ have agreed to admit Ward as a partner and to hold Lark harmless for the past, present, and future liabilities of DSJ. As a result of Lark's withdrawal and Ward's admission to the partnership, Ward
a. Acquired only the right to receive Ward's share of DSJ profits.
b. Has the right to participate in DSJ's management.
c. Is personally liable for partnership liabilities arising before and after being admitted as a partner.
d. Must contribute cash or property to DSJ to be admitted with the same rights as the other partners.

N94#24. The partners of College Assoc., a general partnership, decided to dissolve the partnership and agreed that none of the partners would continue to use the partnership name. Under the Uniform Partnership Act, which of the following events will occur on dissolution of the partnership?

	Each partner's existing liability would be discharged	Each partner's apparent authority would continue
a.	Yes	Yes
b.	Yes	No
c.	No	Yes
d.	No	No

N93#12. The apparent authority of a partner to bind the partnership in dealing with third parties
  a. Will be effectively limited by a formal resolution of the partners of which third parties are aware.
  b. Will be effectively limited by a formal resolution of the partners of which third parties are unaware.
  c. Would permit a partner to submit a claim against the partnership to arbitration.
  d. Must be derived from the express powers and purposes contained in the partnership agreement.

N93#16. Which of the following requirements must be met to have a valid partnership exist?

I. Co-ownership of all property used in a business.
II. Co-ownership of a business for profit.

  a. I only.
  b. II only.
  c. Both I and II.
  d. Neither I nor II.

N93#18. Unless the partnership agreement prohibits it, a partner in a general partnership may validly assign rights to

	Partnership property	Partnership distributions
a.	Yes	Yes
b.	Yes	No
c.	No	Yes
d.	No	No

M93
Items 11 through 13 are based on the following:

Downs, Frey, and Vick formed the DFV general partnership to act as manufacturers' representatives. The partners agreed Downs would receive 40% of any partnership profits and Frey and Vick would each receive 30% of such profits. It was also agreed that the partnership would not terminate for five years. After the fourth year, the partners agreed to terminate the partnership. At that time, the partners' capital accounts were as follows: Downs, $20,000; Frey, $15,000; and Vick, $10,000. There also were undistributed losses of $30,000.

11. Which of the following statements about the form of the DFV partnership agreement is correct?
  a. It must be in writing because the partnership was to last for longer than one year.
  b. It must be in writing because partnership profits would **not** be equally divided.
  c. It could be oral because the partners had explicitly agreed to do business together.
  d. It could be oral because the partnership did **not** deal in real estate.

12. Vick's share of the undistributed losses will be
  a. $0
  b. $ 1,000
  c. $ 9,000
  d. $10,000

13. If Frey died before the partnership terminated
  a. Downs and Vick, as a majority of the partners, would have been able to continue the partnership.
  b. The partnership would have continued until the five-year term expired.
  c. The partnership would automatically dissolve.
  d. Downs and Vick would have Frey's interest in the partnership.

M93#14. Locke and Vorst were general partners in a kitchen equipment business. On behalf of the partnership, Locke contracted to purchase 15 stoves from Gage. Unknown to Gage, Locke was not authorized by the partnership agreement to make such contracts. Vorst refused to allow the partnership to accept delivery of the stoves and Gage sought to enforce the contract. Gage will
  a. Lose, because Locke's action was **not** authorized by the partnership agreement.
  b. Lose, because Locke was **not** an agent of the partnership.
  c. Win, because Locke had express authority to bind the partnership.
  d. Win, because Locke had apparent authority to bind the partnership.

M93#15. Cobb, Inc., a partner in TLC Partnership, assigns its partnership interest to Bean, who is not made a partner. After the assignment, Bean asserts the rights to

I. Participate in the management of TLC.
II. Cobb's share of TLC's partnership profits.

Bean is correct as to which of these rights?
  a. I only.
  b. II only.
  c. I and II.
  d. Neither I **nor** II.

M92#10. A partnership agreement must be in writing if
a. Any partner contributes more than $500 in capital.
b. The partners reside in different states.
c. The partnership intends to own real estate.
d. The partnership's purpose **cannot** be completed within one year of formation.

M92#11. Which of the following statements is correct with respect to a limited partnership?
a. A limited partner may **not** be an unsecured creditor of the limited partnership.
b. A general partner may **not** also be a limited partner at the same time.
c. A general partner may be a secured creditor of the limited partnership.
d. A limited partnership can be formed with limited liability for all partners.

M92
Items 12 and 13 are based on the following:

Dowd, Elgar, Frost, and Grant formed a general partnership. Their written partnership agreement provided that the profits would be divided so that Dowd would receive 40%; Elgar, 30%; Frost, 20%; and Grant, 10%. There was no provision for allocating losses. At the end of its first year, the partnership had losses of $200,000. Before allocating losses, the partners' capital account balances were: Dowd, $120,000; Elgar, $100,000; Frost, $75,000; and Grant, $11,000. Grant refuses to make any further contributions to the partnership. Ignore the effects of federal partnership tax law.

12. What would be Grant's share of the partnership losses?
   a. $ 9,000
   b. $20,000
   c. $39,000
   d. $50,000

13. After losses were allocated to the partners' capital accounts and all liabilities were paid, the partnership's sole asset was $106,000 in cash. How much would Elgar receive on dissolution of the partnership?
   a. $37,000
   b. $40,000
   c. $47,500
   d. $50,000

M92#14. Blake, a partner in QVM, a general partnership, wishes to withdraw from the partnership and sell her interest to Nolan. All of the other partners in QVM have agreed to admit Nolan as a partner and to hold Blake harmless for the past, present, and future liabilities of QVM. As a result of Blake's withdrawal and Nolan's admission to the partnership, Nolan
a. Must contribute cash or property to QVM to be admitted with the same rights as the other partners.
b. Is personally liable for partnership liabilities arising before and after being admitted as a partner.
c. Has the right to participate in QVM's management.
d. Acquired only the right to receive Nolan's share of QVM's profits.

N91#14. A general partnership must
a. Pay federal income tax.
b. Have two or more partners.
c. Have written articles of partnership.
d. Provide for apportionment of liability for partnership debts.

N91#15. In a general partnership, the authorization of all partners is required for an individual partner to bind the partnership in a business transaction to
a. Purchase inventory.
b. Hire employees.
c. Sell goodwill.
d. Sign advertising contracts.

N91#16. In a general partnership, a partner's interest in specific partnership property is
a. Transferable to a partner's individual creditors.
b. Subject to a partner's liability for alimony.
c. Transferable to a partner's estate upon death.
d. Subject to a surviving partner's right of survivorship.

N91#17. On dissolution of a general partnership, distributions will be made on account of:

I. Partners' capital accounts
II. Amounts owed partners with respect to profits
III. Amounts owed partners for loans to the partnership

in the following order
   a. III, I, II.
   b. I, II, III.
   c. II, III, I.
   d. III, II, I.

N90#11. Which of the following is **not** necessary to create an express partnership?
a. Execution of a written partnership agreement.
b. Agreement to share ownership of the partnership.
c. Intention to conduct a business for profit.
d. Intention to create a relationship recognized as a partnership.

N90#12. Eller, Fort, and Owens do business as Venture Associates, a general partnership. Trent Corp. brought a breach of contract suit against Venture and Eller individually. Trent won the suit and filed a judgment against both Venture and Eller. Trent will generally be able to collect the judgment from
a. Partnership assets only.
b. The personal assets of Eller, Fort, and Owens only.

B-18

c. Eller's personal assets only after partnership assets are exhausted.
d. Eller's personal assets only.

N90#13. Acorn and Bean were general partners in a farm machinery business. Acorn contracted, on behalf of the partnership, to purchase 10 tractors from Cobb Corp. Unknown to Cobb, Acorn was not authorized by the partnership agreement to make such contracts. Bean refused to allow the partnership to accept delivery of the tractors and Cobb sought to enforce the contract. Cobb will
  a. Lose because Acorn's action was beyond the scope of Acorn's implied authority.
  b. Prevail because Acorn had implied authority to bind the partnership.
  c. Prevail because Acorn had apparent authority to bind the partnership.
  d. Lose because Acorn's express authority was restricted, in writing, by the partnership agreement.

N90#14. Lewis, Clark, and Beal entered into a written agreement to form a partnership. The agreement required that the partners make the following capital contributions: Lewis, $40,000; Clark, $30,000; and Beal, $10,000. It was also agreed that in the event the partnership experienced losses in excess of available capital, Beal would contribute additional capital to the extent of the losses. The partnership agreement was otherwise silent about division of profits and losses. Which of the following statements is correct?
  a. Profits are to be divided among the partners in proportion to their relative capital contributions.
  b. Profits are to be divided equally among the partners.
  c. Losses will be allocated in a manner different from the allocation of profits because the partners contributed different amounts of capital.
  d. Beal's obligation to contribute additional capital would have an effect on the allocation of profit or loss to Beal.

N89#4. A joint venture is a(an)
  a. Association limited to no more than two persons in business for profit.
  b. Enterprise of numerous co-owners in a non-profit undertaking.
  c. Corporate enterprise for a single undertaking of limited duration.
  d. Association of persons engaged as co-owners in a single undertaking for profit.

N89#5. Which of the following statements regarding a limited partner is(are) generally correct?

	The limited partner is subject to personal liability for partnership debts	The limited partner has the right to take part in the control of the partnership
a.	Yes	Yes
b.	Yes	No
c.	No	Yes
d.	No	No

N89#6. Gillie, Taft, and Dall are partners in an architectural firm. The partnership agreement is silent about the payment of salaries and the division of profits and losses. Gillie works full-time in the firm, and Taft and Dall each work half-time. Taft invested $120,000 in the firm, and Gillie and Dall invested $60,000 each. Dall is responsible for bringing in 50% of the business, and Gillie and Taft 25% each. How should profits of $120,000 for the year be divided?
  a. Gillie $60,000, Taft $30,000, Dall $30,000.
  b. Gillie $40,000, Taft $40,000, Dall $40,000.
  c. Gillie $30,000, Taft $60,000, Dall $30,000.
  d. Gillie $30,000, Taft $30,000, Dall $60,000.

N89#7. A partner's interest in specific partnership property is

	Assignable to the partner's individual creditors	Subject to attachment by the partner's individual creditors
a.	Yes	Yes
b.	Yes	No
c.	No	Yes
d.	No	No

M89#14. Rivers and Lee want to form a partnership. For the partnership agreement to be enforceable, it must be in writing if
  a. Rivers and Lee reside in different states.
  b. The agreement cannot be completed within one year from the date on which it will be entered into.
  c. Either Rivers or Lee is to contribute more than $500 in capital.
  d. The partnership intends to buy and sell real estate.

M89#15. Cass is a general partner in Omega Company general partnership. Which of the following unauthorized acts by Cass will bind Omega?
  a. Submitting a claim against Omega to arbitration.
  b. Confessing a judgment against Omega.
  c. Selling Omega's goodwill.
  d. Leasing office space for Omega.

M89#16. Kroll, Inc., a partner in JKL Partnership, assigns its interest in the partnership to Trell, who is not made a partner. After the assignment, Trell asserts the rights to

I. Receive Kroll's share of JKL's profits and
II. Inspect JKL's books and records.

Trell is correct as to which of the rights?
  a. I only.
  b. II only.
  c. I and II.
  d. Neither I nor II.

C. Corporations

R98#3. Under the Revised Model Business Corporation Act, which of the following statements regarding a corporation's bylaws is(are) correct?

I. A corporation's initial bylaws shall be adopted by either the incorporators or the board of directors.
II. A corporation's bylaws are contained in the articles of incorporation.

    a. I only.
    b. II only.
    c. Both I and II.
    d. Neither I nor II.

R98#4. For what purpose will a stockholder of a publicly held corporation be permitted to file a stockholders' derivative suit in the name of the corporation?
    a. To compel payment of a properly declared dividend.
    b. To enforce a right to inspect corporate records.
    c. To compel dissolution of the corporation.
    d. To recover damages from corporate management for an *ultra vires* management act.

R97#3. Which of the following actions may be taken by a corporation's board of directors without stockholder approval?
    a. Purchasing substantially all of the assets of another corporation.
    b. Selling substantially all of the corporation's assets.
    c. Dissolving the corporation.
    d. Amending the articles of incorporation.

R96#12. Under the Revised Model Business Corporation Act, a corporate director is authorized to
    a. Rely on information provided by the appropriate corporate officer.
    b. Serve on the board of directors of a competing business.
    c. Sell control of the corporation.
    d. Profit from insider information.

N95#21. Which of the following facts is(are) generally included in a corporation's articles of incorporation?

	Name of registered agent	Number of authorized shares
a.	Yes	Yes
b.	Yes	No
c.	No	Yes
d.	No	No

N95#22. Which of the following statements best describes an advantage of the corporate form of doing business?
    a. Day to day management is strictly the responsibility of the directors.
    b. Ownership is contractually restricted and is **not** transferable.
    c. The operation of the business may continue indefinitely.
    d. The business is free from state regulation.

N95#23. To which of the following rights is a stockholder of a public corporation entitled?
    a. The right to have annual dividends declared and paid.
    b. The right to vote for the election of officers.
    c. The right to a reasonable inspection of corporate records.
    d. The right to have the corporation issue a new class of stock.

N95#24. Carr Corp. declared a 7% stock dividend on its common stock. The dividend
    a. Must be registered with the SEC pursuant to the Securities Act of 1933.
    b. Is includable in the gross income of the recipient taxpayers in the year of receipt.
    c. Has **no** effect on Carr's earnings and profits for federal income tax purposes.
    d. Requires a vote of Carr's stockholders.

N95#25. Which of the following statements is a general requirement for the merger of two corporations?
    a. The merger plan must be approved unanimously by the stockholders of both corporations.
    b. The merger plan must be approved unanimously by the boards of both corporations.
    c. The absorbed corporation must amend its articles of incorporation.
    d. The stockholders of both corporations must be given due notice of a special meeting, including a copy or summary of the merger plan.

N94#25. A parent corporation owned more than 90% of each class of the outstanding stock issued by a subsidiary corporation and decided to merge that subsidiary into itself. Under the Revised Model Business Corporation Act, which of the following actions must be taken?
    a. The subsidiary corporation's board of directors must pass a merger resolution.
    b. The subsidiary corporation's dissenting stockholders must be given an appraisal remedy.
    c. The parent corporation's stockholders must approve the merger.
    d. The parent corporation's dissenting stockholders must be given an appraisal remedy.

M94#11. Under the Revised Model Business Corporation Act, which of the following must be contained in a corporation's articles of incorporation?
    a. Quorum voting requirements.
    b. Names of stockholders.
    c. Provisions for issuance of par and non-par shares.
    d. The number of shares the corporation is authorized to issue.

M94#12. Under the Revised Model Business Corporation Act, which of the following statements is correct regarding corporate officers of a public corporation?
  a. An officer may not simultaneously serve as a director.
  b. A corporation may be authorized to indemnify its officers for liability incurred in a suit by stockholders.
  c. Stockholders always have the right to elect a corporation's officers.
  d. An officer of a corporation is required to own at least one share of the corporation's stock.

M94#13. Which of the following rights is a holder of a public corporation's cumulative preferred stock always entitled to?
  a. Conversion of the preferred stock into common stock.
  b. Voting rights.
  c. Dividend carryovers from years in which dividends were **not** paid, to future years.
  d. Guaranteed dividends.

M94#14. Under the Revised Model Business Corporation Act, a merger of two public corporations usually requires all of the following **except**
  a. A formal plan of merger.
  b. An affirmative vote by the holders of a majority of each corporation's voting shares.
  c. Receipt of voting stock by all stockholders of the original corporations.
  d. Approval by the board of directors of each corporation.

N93#17. Which of the following securities are corporate debt securities?

	Convertible bonds	Debenture bonds	Warrants
a.	Yes	Yes	Yes
b.	Yes	No	Yes
c.	Yes	Yes	No
d.	No	Yes	Yes

N93#19. Which of the following provisions must a for-profit-corporation include in its Articles of Incorporation to obtain a corporate charter?

I. Provision for the issuance of voting stock.
II. Name of the corporation.

  a. I only.
  b. II only.
  c. Both I and II.
  d. Neither I nor II.

N93#20. The corporate veil is most likely to be pierced and the shareholders held personally liable if
  a. The corporation has elected S corporation status under the Internal Revenue Code.
  b. The shareholders have commingled their personal funds with those of the corporation.
  c. An ultra vires act has been committed.
  d. A partnership incorporates its business solely to limit the liability of its partners.

N92#1. Which of the following statements is correct concerning the similarities between a limited partnership and a corporation?
  a. Each is created under a statute and must file a copy of its certificate with the proper state authorities.
  b. All corporate stockholders and all partners in a limited partnership have limited liability.
  c. Both are recognized for federal income tax purposes as taxable entities.
  d. Both are allowed statutorily to have perpetual existence.

N92#2. A stockholder's right to inspect books and records of a corporation will be properly denied if the stockholder
  a. Wants to use corporate stockholder records for a personal business.
  b. Employs an agent to inspect the books and records.
  c. Intends to commence a stockholder's derivative suit.
  d. Is investigating management misconduct.

N92#3. Which of the following must take place for a corporation to be voluntarily dissolved?
  a. Passage by the board of directors of a resolution to dissolve.
  b. Approval by the officers of a resolution to dissolve.
  c. Amendment of the certificate of incorporation.
  d. Unanimous vote of the stockholders.

N92#4. Generally, a merger of two corporations requires
  a. That a special meeting notice and a copy of the merger plan be given to all stockholders of both corporations.
  b. Unanimous approval of the merger plan by the stockholders of both corporations.
  c. Unanimous approval of the merger plan by the boards of both corporations.
  d. That all liabilities owed by the absorbed corporation be paid before the merger.

M92#15. Assuming all other requirements are met, a corporation may elect to be treated as an S corporation under the Internal Revenue Code if it has
  a. Both common and preferred stockholders.
  b. A partnership as a stockholder.
  c. Thirty-five or fewer stockholders.
  d. The consent of a majority of the stockholders.

M92#16. Generally, a corporation's articles of incorporation must include all of the following **except** the
  a. Name of the corporation's registered agent.
  b. Name of each incorporator.
  c. Number of authorized shares.
  d. Quorum requirements.

M92#17. Unless prohibited by the organization documents, a stockholder in a publicly held corporation and the owner of a limited partnership interest both have the right to
 a. Ownership of the business' assets.
 b. Control management of the business.
 c. Assign their interest in the business.
 d. An investment that has perpetual life.

M92#18. A corporate stockholder is entitled to which of the following rights?
 a. Elect officers.
 b. Receive annual dividends.
 c. Approve dissolution.
 d. Prevent corporate borrowing.

M92#19. Price owns 2,000 shares of Universal Corp.'s $10 cumulative preferred stock. During its first year of operations, cash dividends of $5 per share were declared on the preferred stock but were never paid. In the second year, dividends on the preferred stock were neither declared nor paid. If Universal is dissolved, which of the following statements is correct?
 a. Universal will be liable to Price as an unsecured creditor for $10,000.
 b. Universal will be liable to Price as a secured creditor for $20,000.
 c. Price will have priority over the claims of Universal's bond owners.
 d. Price will have priority over the claims of Universal's unsecured judgment creditors.

M92#20. Which of the following actions may a corporation take without its stockholders' consent?
 a. Consolidate with one or more corporations.
 b. Merge with one or more corporations.
 c. Dissolve voluntarily.
 d. Purchase 55% of another corporation's stock.

M91#4. Which of the following statements is correct with respect to the differences and similarities between a corporation and a limited partnership?
 a. Stockholders may be entitled to vote on corporate matters but limited partners are prohibited from voting on any partnership matters.
 b. Stock of a corporation may be subject to the registration requirements of the federal securities laws but limited partnership interests are automatically exempt from those requirements.
 c. Directors owe fiduciary duties to the corporation and limited partners owe such duties to the partnership.
 d. A corporation and a limited partnership may be created only under a state statute and each must file a copy of its organizational document with the proper governmental body.

M91#5. Davis, a director of Active Corp., is entitled to
 a. Serve on the board of a competing business.
 b. Take sole advantage of a business opportunity that would benefit Active.
 c. Rely on information provided by a corporate officer.
 d. Unilaterally grant a corporate loan to one of Active's shareholders.

M91#6. The limited liability of a stockholder in a closely held corporation may be challenged successfully if the stockholder
 a. Undercapitalized the corporation when it was formed.
 b. Formed the corporation solely to have limited personal liability.
 c. Sold property to the corporation.
 d. Was a corporate officer, director, or employee.

M91#7. A consolidation of two corporations usually requires all of the following **except**
 a. Approval by the board of directors of each corporation.
 b. Receipt of voting stock by all stockholders of the original corporations.
 c. Provision for an appraisal buyout of dissenting stockholders.
 d. An affirmative vote by the holders of a majority of each corporation's voting shares.

N90#15. Knox, president of Quick Corp., contracted with Tine Office Supplies, Inc. to supply Quick's stationery on customary terms and at a cost less than that charged by any other supplier. Knox later informed Quick's board of directors that Knox was a majority stockholder in Tine. Quick's contract with Tine is
 a. Void because of Knox's self-dealing.
 b. Void because the disclosure was made after execution of the contract.
 c. Valid because of Knox's full disclosure.
 d. Valid because the contract is fair to Quick.

N90#16. A stockholder's right to inspect books and records of a corporation will be properly denied if the purpose of the inspection is to
 a. Commence a stockholder's derivative suit.
 b. Obtain stockholder names for a retail mailing list.
 c. Solicit stockholders to vote for a change in the board of directors.
 d. Investigate possible management misconduct.

N90#17. All of the following distributions to stockholders are considered asset or capital distributions, **except**
 a. Liquidating dividends.
 b. Stock splits.
 c. Property distributions.
 d. Cash dividends.

M90#6. In general, which of the following must be contained in articles of incorporation?
 a. Names of the initial officers and their terms of office.
 b. Classes of stock authorized for issuance.

c. Names of states in which the corporation will be doing business.
d. Name of the state in which the corporation will maintain its principal place of business.

M90#7. Absent a specific provision in its articles of incorporation, a corporation's board of directors has the power to do all of the following, **except**
a. Repeal the bylaws.
b. Declare dividends.
c. Fix compensation of directors.
d. Amend the articles of incorporation.

M90#8. An owner of common stock will **not** have any liability beyond actual investment if the owner
a. Paid less than par value for stock purchased in connection with an original issue of shares.
b. Agreed to perform future services for the corporation in exchange for original issue par value shares.
c. Purchased treasury shares for less than par value.
d. Failed to pay the full amount owed on a subscription contract for no-par shares.

M90#9. Johns owns 400 shares of Abco Corp. cumulative preferred stock. In the absence of any specific contrary provisions in Abco's articles of incorporation, which of the following statements is correct?
a. Johns is entitled to convert the 400 shares of preferred stock to a like number of shares of common stock.
b. If Abco declares a cash dividend on its preferred stock, Johns becomes an unsecured creditor of Abco.
c. If Abco declares a dividend on its common stock, Johns will be entitled to participate with the common stock shareholders in any dividend distribution made after preferred dividends are paid.
d. Johns will be entitled to vote if dividend payments are in arrears.

D. Estates and Trusts

R97#6. Which of the following parties is necessary to create an express trust?

	A remainderman	A successor trustee
a.	Yes	Yes
b.	Yes	No
c.	No	Yes
d.	No	No

R97#7. When a trust instrument is silent regarding a trustee's powers, which of the following implied powers does a trustee generally have?

	The power to make distributions of principal to income beneficiaries	The power to lease trust property to third parties
a.	Yes	Yes
b.	Yes	No
c.	No	Yes
d.	No	No

R97#8. Which of the following assets generally will be distributed outside of the probate estate and regardless of intestacy laws, provided the estate is not the named beneficiary?

	Proceeds from insurance policies	Totten trusts
a.	Yes	Yes
b.	Yes	No
c.	No	Yes
d.	No	No

R97#9. Generally, which of the following parties would have the first priority to receive the estate of a person who dies without a will?
a. The state.
b. A child of the deceased.
c. A parent of the deceased.
d. A sibling of the deceased.

R96#4. Which of the following investments generally will be a violation of a trustee's fiduciary duty to the trust?
a. Secured first mortgages on land.
b. High interest unsecured loans.
c. Tax-exempt municipal bonds.
d. Guaranteed savings certificates.

M95#10. On the death of the grantor, which of the following testamentary trusts would fail?
a. A trust created to promote the public welfare.
b. A trust created to provide for a spouse's health care.
c. A trust created to benefit a charity.
d. A trust created to benefit a childless person's grandchildren.

M95#11. An irrevocable trust that contains **no** provision for change or termination can be changed or terminated only by the
a. Courts.
b. Income beneficiaries.
c. Remaindermen.
d. Grantor.

M95#12. Frost's will created a testamentary trust naming Hill as life income beneficiary, with the principal to Brown when Hill dies. The trust was silent on allocation of principal and income. The trust's sole asset was a commercial office building originally valued at $100,000 and having a current market value of $200,000. If the building was sold, which of the following statements

would be correct concerning the allocation of the proceeds?
a. The entire proceeds would be allocated to principal and retained.
b. The entire proceeds would be allocated to income and distributed to Hill.
c. One half of the proceeds would be allocated to principal and one half to income.
d. One half of the proceeds would be allocated to principal and one half distributed to Brown.

M95#13. Which of the following fiduciary duties may be violated by the trustee if the trustee, without express direction in the trust instrument, invests trust assets in unsecured loans to a co-trustee?

I. Duty to invest prudently.
II. Duty of loyalty to the trust.

a. I only.
b. II only.
c. Both I and II.
d. Neither I nor II.

M95#14. Absent specific directions, which of the following parties will ordinarily receive the assets of a terminated trust?
a. Income beneficiaries.
b. Remaindermen.
c. Grantor.
d. Trustee.

M95#15. Cord's will created a trust to take effect on Cord's death. The will named Cord's spouse as both the trustee and personal representative (executor) of the estate. The will provided that all of Cord's securities were to be transferred to the trust and named Cord's child as the beneficiary of the trust. Under the circumstances,
a. Cord has created an inter vivos trust.
b. Cord has created a testamentary trust.
c. The trust is invalid because it will **not** become effective until Cord's death.
d. Cord's spouse may **not** serve as both the trustee and personal representative because of the inherent conflict of interest.

M94#15. Which of the following is **not** necessary to create an express trust?
a. A successor trustee.
b. A trust corpus.
c. A beneficiary.
d. A valid trust purpose.

M94#16. Which of the following expenditures resulting from a trust's ownership of commercial real estate should be allocated to the trust's principal?
a. Building management fees.
b. Insurance premiums.
c. Sidewalk assessments.
d. Depreciation.

M94#17. In a written trust containing **no** specific powers, the trustee will have all of the following implied powers **except**
a. Sell trust property.
b. Pay management expenses.
c. Accumulate income.
d. Employ a CPA to prepare trust tax returns.

M94#18. Which of the following fiduciary duties will a trustee violate by borrowing money from the trust?
a. Duty of loyalty.
b. Duty to properly account.
c. Duty to safeguard the trust res.
d. Duty to properly manage the trust.

M94#19. An irrevocable testamentary trust was created by Park, with Gordon named as trustee. The trust provided that the income will be paid to Hardy for life with the principal then reverting to Park's estate to be paid to King. The trust will automatically end on the death of
a. Park.
b. Gordon.
c. Hardy.
d. King.

M94#20. Which of the following events will terminate an irrevocable spendthrift trust established for a period of five years?
a. Grantor dies.
b. Income beneficiaries die.
c. Grantor decides to terminate the trust.
d. Income beneficiaries agree to the trust's termination.

M93
Items 16 through 18 are based on the following:

Arno plans to establish a spendthrift trust naming Ford and Sims life income beneficiaries, Trip residuary beneficiary, and Bing as trustee. Arno plans to fund the trust with an office building.

16. For the trust to be enforceable, Arno must
a. Execute a written trust instrument.
b. Provide for Bing's trustee fees.
c. Designate a successor trustee.
d. Deed the property to Bing as trustee.

For items 17 and 18, assume an enforceable trust was formed.

17. Sims has the following personal creditors:

I. Bank holding a home mortgage note deficiency judgment.
II. Judgment creditor as a result of an automobile accident.

To which of these creditors can Bing pay Sims' share of trust income?

a. I only.
b. II only.
c. Both I and II.
d. Neither I nor II.

18. Which of the following will be allocated to trust principal?

	Annual property tax	Monthly mortgage principal payment
a.	Yes	Yes
b.	Yes	No
c.	No	Yes
d.	No	No

M93#19. Colt's will created a testamentary trust for the benefit of Colt's spouse. Colt's sister and Colt's spouse were named as co-trustees of the trust. The trust provided for discretionary principal distributions to Colt's spouse. It also provided that, on the death of Colt's spouse, any remaining trust property was to be distributed to Colt's children. Part of the trust property consisted of a very valuable baseball card collection. After Colt's death, which of the following statements would be correct?
   a. The co-trustees must use the same degree of skill, judgment, and care in managing the trust assets as reasonably prudent persons would exercise in managing their own affairs.
   b. The co-trustees must employ an investment advisor to manage the trust assets.
   c. Colt's sister may delegate her duties as co-trustee to the spouse and thereby **not** be liable for the administration of the trust.
   d. Under **no** circumstances could the spouse purchase the baseball card collection from the trust without breaching fiduciary duties owed to the trust and Colt's children.

M93#20. An irrevocable trust that contains **no** provision for change or termination can be changed or terminated only by the
   a. Trustee.
   b. Grantor.
   c. Courts.
   d. Consent of the majority of the beneficiaries.

N92#5. Which of the following situations would cause a resulting trust to be created?

I. Failure of an express trust.
II. Application of the *cy pres* doctrine.
III. Fulfillment of the trust purpose.

   a. I and II.
   b. I and III.
   c. II and III.
   d. I, II, and III.

N92#6. Cox transferred assets into a trust under which Smart is entitled to receive the income for life. After Smart's death, the remaining assets are to be given to Mix. In 1991, the trust received rent of $1,000, stock dividends of $6,000, interest on certificates of deposit of $3,000, municipal bond interest of $4,000, and proceeds of $7,000 from the sale of bonds. Both Smart and Mix are still alive. What amount of the 1991 receipts should be allocated to trust principal?
   a. $ 7,000
   b. $ 8,000
   c. $13,000
   d. $15,000

N92#7. If **not** expressly granted, which of the following implied powers would a trustee have?

I. Power to sell trust property.
II. Power to borrow from the trust.
III. Power to pay trust expenses.

   a. I and II.
   b. I and III.
   c. II and III.
   d. I, II and III.

N92#8. To which of the following trusts would the rule against perpetuities **not** apply?
   a. Charitable.
   b. Spendthrift.
   c. Totten.
   d. Constructive.

N92#9. A decedent's will provided that the estate was to be divided among the decedent's issue, per capita and not per stirpes. If there are two surviving children and three grandchildren who are children of a predeceased child at the time the will is probated, how will the estate be divided?
   a. $1/2$ to each surviving child.
   b. $1/3$ to each surviving child and $1/9$ to each grandchild.
   c. $1/4$ to each surviving child and $1/6$ to each grandchild.
   d. $1/5$ to each surviving child and grandchild.

N92#10. Which of the following would ordinarily be distributed to a trust income beneficiary?

I. Royalties.
II. Stock received in a stock split.
III. Cash dividends.
IV. Settlements of claims for damages to trust property.

   a. I and II.
   b. I and III.
   c. II and III.
   d. II and IV.

N91#19. A trustee's fiduciary duty will probably be violated if the trustee
   a. Invests trust property in government bonds.
   b. Performs accounting services for the trust.
   c. Sells unproductive trust property.
   d. Borrows money from the trust.

N91#20. An irrevocable spendthrift trust established for a period of ten years will be terminated if the
   a. Income beneficiaries die.
   b. Trustee resigns.
   c. Income beneficiaries agree to the trust's termination.
   d. Grantor decides to terminate the trust.

M91#8. To properly create an inter vivos trust funded with cash, the grantor must
   a. Execute a written trust instrument.
   b. Transfer the cash to the trustee.
   c. Provide for payment of fees to the trustee.
   d. Designate an alternate trust beneficiary.

M91#9. Farrel's will created a testamentary trust naming Gordon as life income beneficiary, with the principal going to Hall on Gordon's death. The trust's sole asset was a commercial office building valued at $200,000. The trustee sold the building for $250,000. To what amount of the sale price is Gordon entitled?
   a. $0
   b. $ 50,000
   c. $200,000
   d. $250,000

M91#10. Mason's will created a testamentary trust for the benefit of Mason's spouse. Mason's sister and Mason's spouse were named as co-trustees of the trust. The trust provided for discretionary principal distributions to Mason's spouse. It also provided that, on the death of Mason's spouse, any remaining trust property was to be distributed to Mason's children. Part of the trust property consisted of a very valuable coin collection. After Mason's death, which of the following statements would be correct?
   a. Mason's spouse may **not** be a co-trustee because the spouse is also a beneficiary of the trust.
   b. Mason's sister may delegate her duties as co-trustee to the spouse and thereby **not** be liable for the administration of the trust.
   c. Under **no** circumstances could the spouse purchase the coin collection from the trust without breaching fiduciary duties owed to the trust and Mason's children.
   d. The co-trustees must use the same degree of skill, judgment, and care in managing the trust assets as reasonably prudent persons would exercise in managing their own affairs.

N90#19. Which of the following expenditures resulting from a trust's ownership of commercial real estate would be allocated to the trust's principal?
   a. Sidewalk assessments.
   b. Building management fees.
   c. Real estate taxes.
   d. Electrical repairs.

N90#20. A trust will be terminated if
   a. A beneficiary becomes incompetent.
   b. The trustee dies.
   c. The grantor dies.
   d. The trust term expires.

M90#10. Jay properly created an inter vivos trust naming Kroll as trustee. The trust's sole asset is a fully rented office building. Rental receipts exceed expenditures. The trust instrument is silent about the allocation of items between principal and income. Among the items to be allocated by Kroll during the year are insurance proceeds received as a result of fire damage to the building and the mortgage interest payments made during the year. Which of the following items is(are) properly allocable to principal?

	Insurance proceeds on building	Current mortgage interest payments
a.	No	No
b.	No	Yes
c.	Yes	No
d.	Yes	Yes

N89#8. Harper transferred assets into a trust under which Drake is entitled to receive the income for life. Upon Drake's death, the remaining assets are to be paid to Neal. In 1988, the trust received rent of $1,000, royalties of $3,000, cash dividends of $5,000, and proceeds of $7,000 from the sale of stock previously received by the trust as a stock dividend. Both Drake and Neal are still alive. How much of the receipts should be distributed to Drake?
   a. $ 4,000.
   b. $ 8,000.
   c. $ 9,000.
   d. $16,000.

M89#17. Generally, an estate is liable for which debts owed by the decedent at the time of death?
   a. All of the decedent's debts.
   b. Only debts secured by the decedent's property.
   c. Only debts covered by the statute of frauds.
   d. None of the decedent's debts.

M89#18. A trust agreement is silent on the allocation of the following trust receipts between principal and income:

- Cash dividends on investments in common stock $1,000
- Royalties from property subject to depletion $2,000

What is the total amount of the trust receipts that should be allocated to trust income?
   a. $0
   b. $1,000
   c. $2,000
   d. $3,000

M89#19. A personal representative of an estate would breach fiduciary duties if the personal representative
   a. Combined personal funds with funds of the estate so that both could purchase treasury bills.
   b. Represented the estate in a lawsuit brought against it by a disgruntled relative of the decedent.

c. Distributed property in satisfaction of the decedent's debts.
d. Engaged a non-CPA to prepare the records for the estate's final accounting.

M89#20. A trust was created in 1980 to provide funds for sending the settlor's child through medical school. The trust agreement specified that the trust was to terminate in 1987. The child entered medical school in 1983, took a leave of absence in 1984, and died in 1986. This trust terminated in
    a. 1983
    b. 1984
    c. 1986
    d. 1987

III. Contracts

A. Formation

M95#16. Which of the following facts must be proven for a plaintiff to prevail in a common law negligent misrepresentation action?
    a. The defendant made the misrepresentations with a reckless disregard for the truth.
    b. The plaintiff justifiably relied on the misrepresentations.
    c. The misrepresentations were in writing.
    d. The misrepresentations concerned opinion.

M95#17. A building subcontractor submitted a bid for construction of a portion of a high-rise office building. The bid contained material computational errors. The general contractor accepted the bid with knowledge of the errors. Which of the following statements best represents the subcontractor's liability?
    a. Not liable because the contractor knew of the errors.
    b. Not liable because the errors were a result of gross negligence.
    c. Liable because the errors were unilateral.
    d. Liable because the errors were material.

M95#18. Where the parties have entered into a written contract intended as the final expression of their agreement, which of the following agreements will be admitted into evidence because they are **not** prohibited by the parol evidence rule?

	Subsequent oral agreements	Prior written agreements
a.	Yes	Yes
b.	Yes	No
c.	No	Yes
d.	No	No

M93#21. All of the following are effective methods of ratifying a contract entered into by a minor **except**
    a. Expressly ratifying the contract after reaching the age of majority.
    b. Failing to disaffirm the contract within a reasonable time after reaching the age of majority.
    c. Ratifying the contract before reaching the age of majority.
    d. Impliedly ratifying the contract after reaching the age of majority.

M93#22. Which of the following statements correctly applies to a typical statute of limitations?
    a. The statute requires that a legal action for breach of contract be commenced within a certain period of time after the breach occurs.
    b. The statute provides that only the party against whom enforcement of a contract is sought must have signed the contract.
    c. The statute limits the right of a party to recover damages for misrepresentation unless the false statements were intentionally made.
    d. The statute prohibits the admission into evidence of proof of oral statements about the meaning of a written contract.

M93#23. Long purchased a life insurance policy with Tempo Life Insurance Co. The policy named Long's daughter as beneficiary. Six months after the policy was issued, Long died of a heart attack. Long had failed to disclose on the insurance application a known pre-existing heart condition that caused the heart attack. Tempo refused to pay the death benefit to Long's daughter. If Long's daughter sues, Tempo will
    a. Win, because Long's daughter is an incidental beneficiary.
    b. Win, because of Long's failure to disclose the pre-existing heart condition.
    c. Lose, because Long's death was from natural causes.
    d. Lose, because Long's daughter is a third-party donee beneficiary.

N92#11. On February 12, Harris sent Fresno a written offer to purchase Fresno's land. The offer included the following provision: "Acceptance of this offer must be by registered or certified mail, received by Harris no later than February 18 by 5:00 p.m. CST." On February 18, Fresno sent Harris a letter accepting the offer by private overnight delivery service. Harris received the letter on February 19. Which of the following statements is correct?
    a. A contract was formed on February 19.
    b. Fresno's letter constituted a counteroffer.
    c. Fresno's use of the overnight delivery service was an effective form of acceptance.
    d. A contract was formed on February 18 regardless of when Harris actually received Fresno's letter.

N92#12. In determining whether the consideration requirement to form a contract has been satisfied, the consideration exchanged by the parties to the contract must be
    a. Of approximately equal value.
    b. Legally sufficient.
    c. Exchanged simultaneously by the parties.
    d. Fair and reasonable under the circumstances.

N92#13. On June 15, Peters orally offered to sell a used lawn mower to Mason for $125. Peters specified that Mason had until June 20 to accept the offer. On June 16, Peters received an offer to purchase the lawn mower for $150 from Bronson, Mason's neighbor. Peters accepted Bronson's offer. On June 17, Mason saw Bronson using the lawn mower and was told the mower had been sold to Bronson. Mason immediately wrote to Peters to accept the June 15 offer. Which of the following statements is correct?
    a. Mason's acceptance would be effective when received by Peters.
    b. Mason's acceptance would be effective when mailed.
    c. Peters' offer had been revoked and Mason's acceptance was ineffective.
    d. Peters was obligated to keep the June 15 offer open until June 20.

N92#16. Which of the following statements is true with regard to the Statute of Frauds?
    a. All contracts involving consideration of more than $500 must be in writing.
    b. The written contract must be signed by all parties.
    c. The Statute of Frauds applies to contracts that can be fully performed within one year from the date they are made.
    d. The contract terms may be stated in more than one document.

N92#18. Maco, Inc. and Kent contracted for Kent to provide Maco certain consulting services at an hourly rate of $20. Kent's normal hourly rate was $90 per hour, the fair market value of the services. Kent agreed to the $20 rate because Kent was having serious financial problems. At the time the agreement was negotiated, Maco was aware of Kent's financial condition and refused to pay more than $20 per hour for Kent's services. Kent has now sued to rescind the contract with Maco, claiming duress by Maco during the negotiations. Under the circumstances, Kent will
    a. Win, because Maco refused to pay the fair market value of Kent's services.
    b. Win, because Maco was aware of Kent's serious financial problems.
    c. Lose, because Maco's actions did **not** constitute duress.
    d. Lose, because Maco **cannot** prove that Kent, at the time, had **no** other offers to provide consulting services.

M92#21. On September 10, Harris, Inc., a new car dealer, placed a newspaper advertisement stating that Harris would sell 10 cars at its showroom for a special discount only on September 12, 13, and 14. On September 12, King called Harris and expressed an interest in buying one of the advertised cars. King was told that five of the cars had been sold and to come to the showroom as soon as possible. On September 13, Harris made a televised announcement that the sale would end at 10:00 PM that night. King went to Harris' showroom on September 14 and demanded the right to buy a car at the special discount. Harris had sold the 10 cars and refused King's demand. King sued Harris for breach of contract. Harris' best defense to King's suit would be that Harris'
    a. Offer was unenforceable.
    b. Advertisement was **not** an offer.
    c. Television announcement revoked the offer.
    d. Offer had **not** been accepted.

M92#22. On April 1, Fine Corp. faxed Moss an offer to purchase Moss' warehouse for $500,000. The offer stated that it would remain open only until April 4 and that acceptance must be received to be effective. Moss sent an acceptance on April 4 by overnight mail and Fine received it on April 5. Which of the following statements is correct?
    a. No contract was formed because Moss sent the acceptance by an unauthorized method.
    b. No contract was formed because Fine received Moss' acceptance after April 4.
    c. A contract was formed when Moss sent the acceptance.
    d. A contract was formed when Fine received Moss' acceptance.

M92#23. Which of the following will be legally binding despite lack of consideration?
    a. An employer's promise to make a cash payment to a deceased employee's family in recognition of the employee's many years of service.
    b. A promise to donate money to a charity on which the charity relied in incurring large expenditures.
    c. A modification of a signed contract to purchase a parcel of land.
    d. A merchant's oral promise to keep an offer open for 60 days.

M92#24. In which of the following situations does the first promise serve as valid consideration for the second promise?
    a. A police officer's promise to catch a thief for a victim's promise to pay a reward.
    b. A builder's promise to complete a contract for a purchaser's promise to extend the time for completion.
    c. A debtor's promise to pay $500 for a creditor's promise to forgive the balance of a $600 liquidated debt.
    d. A debtor's promise to pay $500 for a creditor's promise to forgive the balance of a $600 disputed debt.

M91#11. Nix sent Castor a letter offering to employ Castor as controller of Nix's automobile dealership. Castor received the letter on February 19. The letter provided that Castor would have until February 23 to consider the offer and, in the meantime, Nix would not withdraw it. On February 20, Nix, after reconsidering the offer to Castor, decided to offer the job to Vick, who accepted immediately. That same day, Nix called Castor and revoked the offer. Castor told Nix that an acceptance of Nix's offer was mailed on February 19. Under the circumstances,
  a. Nix's offer was irrevocable until February 23.
  b. No contract was formed between Nix and Castor because Nix revoked the offer before Nix received Castor's acceptance.
  c. Castor's acceptance was effective when mailed.
  d. Any revocation of the offer would have to be in writing because Nix's offer was in writing.

M91#12. Carson Corp., a retail chain, asked Alto Construction to fix a broken window at one of Carson's stores. Alto offered to make the repairs within three days at a price to be agreed on after the work was completed. A contract based on Alto's offer would fail because of indefiniteness as to the
  a. Price involved.
  b. Nature of the subject matter.
  c. Parties to the contract.
  d. Time for performance.

M91#16. Kay, an art collector, promised Hammer, an art student, that if Hammer could obtain certain rare artifacts within two weeks, Kay would pay for Hammer's postgraduate education. At considerable effort and expense, Hammer obtained the specified artifacts within the two-week period. When Hammer requested payment, Kay refused. Kay claimed that there was no consideration for the promise. Hammer would prevail against Kay based on
  a. Unilateral contract.
  b. Unjust enrichment.
  c. Public policy.
  d. Quasi contract.

N90#21. Which of the following requires consideration to be binding on the parties?
  a. Material modification of a contract involving the sale of real estate.
  b. Ratification of a contract by a person after reaching the age of majority.
  c. A written promise signed by a merchant to keep an offer to sell goods open for 10 days.
  d. Material modification of a sale of goods contract under the UCC.

M90#11. To satisfy the consideration requirement for a valid contract, the consideration exchanged by the parties must be
  a. Legally sufficient.
  b. Payable in legal tender.
  c. Simultaneously paid and received.
  d. Of the same economic value.

M90#12. On September 27, Summers sent Fox a letter offering to sell Fox a vacation home for $150,000. On October 2, Fox replied by mail agreeing to buy the home for $145,000. Summers did not reply to Fox. Do Fox and Summers have a binding contract?
  a. No, because Fox failed to sign and return Summers' letter.
  b. No, because Fox's letter was a counteroffer.
  c. Yes, because Summers' offer was validly accepted.
  d. Yes, because Summers' silence is an implied acceptance of Fox's letter.

M90#13. On November 1, Yost sent a telegram to Zen offering to sell a rare vase. The offer required that Zen's acceptance telegram be sent on or before 5:00 P.M. on November 2. On November 2, at 3:00 P.M., Zen sent an acceptance by overnight mail. It did not reach Yost until November 5. Yost refused to complete the sale to Zen. Is there an enforceable contract?
  a. Yes, because the acceptance was made within the time specified.
  b. Yes, because the acceptance was effective when sent.
  c. No, because Zen did **not** accept by telegram.
  d. No, because the offer required receipt of the acceptance within the time specified.

M90#14. Opal offered, in writing, to sell Larkin a parcel of land for $300,000. If Opal dies, the offer will
  a. Terminate prior to Larkin's acceptance only if Larkin received notice of Opal's death.
  b. Remain open for a reasonable period of time after Opal's death.
  c. Automatically terminate despite Larkin's prior acceptance.
  d. Automatically terminate prior to Larkin's acceptance.

M90#15. King sent Foster, a real estate developer, a signed offer to sell a specified parcel of land to Foster for $200,000. King, an engineer, had inherited the land. On the same day that King's letter was received, Foster telephoned King and accepted the offer. Which of the following statements is correct under the Statute of Frauds?
  a. No contract was formed because Foster did **not** sign the offer.
  b. No contract was formed because King is **not** a merchant and, therefore, King's letter is **not** binding on Foster.
  c. A contract was formed, although it would be enforceable only against King.
  d. A contract was formed and would be enforceable against both King and Foster because Foster is a merchant.

M90#16. Which of the following will be legally binding on all parties despite lack of consideration?
  a. An irrevocable oral promise by a merchant to keep an offer open for 60 days.

b. A promise to donate money to a charity which the charity relied upon in incurring large expenditures.
c. A promise to pay for the college education of the child of a person who saved the promisor's life.
d. A signed modification to a contract to purchase a parcel of land.

M90#17. Payne entered into a written agreement to sell a parcel of land to Stevens. At the time the agreement was executed, Payne had consumed alcoholic beverages. Payne's ability to understand the nature and terms of the contract was not impaired. Stevens did not believe that Payne was intoxicated. The contract is
a. Void as a matter of law.
b. Legally binding on both parties.
c. Voidable at Payne's option.
d. Voidable at Stevens' option.

M90#20. With regard to an agreement for the sale of real estate, the Statute of Frauds
a. Does **not** require that the agreement be signed by all parties.
b. Does **not** apply if the value of the real estate is less than $500.
c. Requires that the entire agreement be in a single writing.
d. Requires that the purchase price be fair and adequate in relation to the value of the real estate.

N89#9. The mailbox rule generally makes acceptance of an offer effective at the time the acceptance is dispatched. The mailbox rule does **not** apply if
a. Both the offeror and offeree are merchants.
b. The offer proposes a sale of real estate.
c. The offer provides that an acceptance shall **not** be effective until actually received.
d. The duration of the offer is **not** in excess of three months.

N89#10. For there to be consideration for a contract, there must be
a. A bargained-for detriment to the promisor(ee) or a benefit to the promisee(or).
b. A manifestation of mutual assent.
c. Genuineness of assent.
d. Substantially equal economic benefits to both parties.

N89#12. The Statute of Frauds
a. Prevents the use of oral evidence to contradict the terms of a written contract.
b. Applies to all contracts having consideration valued at $500 or more.
c. Requires the independent promise to pay the debt of another to be in writing.
d. Applies to all real estate leases.

M89#21. Martin wrote Dall and offered to sell Dall a building for $200,000. The offer stated it would expire 30 days from April 1. Martin changed his mind and does not wish to be bound by his offer. If a legal dispute arises between the parties regarding whether there has been a valid acceptance of the offer, which one of the following is correct?
a. The offer cannot be legally withdrawn for the stated period of time.
b. The offer will **not** expire before the 30 days even if Martin sells the property to a third person and notifies Dall.
c. If Dall categorically rejects the offer on April 10, Dall cannot validly accept within the remaining stated period of time.
d. If Dall phoned Martin on May 3, and unequivocally accepted the offer, a contract would be created, provided that Dall had **no** notice of withdrawal of the offer.

M89#22. Which of the following statements concerning the effectiveness of an offeree's rejection and an offeror's revocation of an offer is generally correct?

	An offeree's rejection is effective when	An offeror's revocation is effective when
a.	Received by offeror	Sent by offeror
b.	Sent by offeree	Received by offeree
c.	Sent by offeree	Sent by offeror
d.	Received by offeror	Received by offeree

M89#23. An offer is **not** terminated by operation of law solely because the
a. Offeror dies.
b. Offeree is adjudicated insane.
c. Subject matter is destroyed.
d. Subject matter is sold to a third party.

M89#24. Dye sent Hill a written offer to sell a tract of land located in Newtown for $60,000. The parties were engaged in a separate dispute. The offer stated that it would be irrevocable for 60 days if Hill would promise to refrain from suing Dye during this time. Hill promptly delivered a promise not to sue during the term of the offer and to forego suit if Hill accepted the offer. Dye subsequently decided that the possible suit by Hill was groundless and therefore phoned Hill and revoked the offer 15 days after making it. Hill mailed an acceptance on the 20th day. Dye did not reply. Under the circumstances,
a. Dye's offer was supported by consideration and was **not** revocable when accepted.
b. Dye's written offer would be irrevocable even without consideration.
c. Dye's silence was an acceptance of Hill's promise.
d. Dye's revocation, **not** being in writing, was invalid.

M89#25. To announce the grand opening of a new retail business, Hudson placed an advertisement in a local newspaper quoting sales prices on certain items in stock. The grand opening was so successful that Hudson was unable

to totally satisfy customer demands. Which of the following statements is correct?
   a. Hudson made an invitation seeking offers.
   b. Hudson made an offer to the people who read the advertisement.
   c. Anyone who tendered money for the items advertised was entitled to buy them.
   d. The offer by Hudson was partially revocable as to an item once it was sold out.

B. Performance

M95#19. Which of the following types of conditions affecting performance may validly be present in contracts?

	Conditions precedent	Conditions subsequent	Concurrent conditions
a.	Yes	Yes	Yes
b.	Yes	Yes	No
c.	Yes	No	Yes
d.	No	Yes	Yes

M95#20. Grove is seeking to avoid performing a promise to pay Brook $1,500. Grove is relying on lack of consideration on Brook's part. Grove will prevail if he can establish that
   a. Prior to Grove's promise, Brook had already performed the requested act.
   b. Brook's only claim of consideration was the relinquishment of a legal right.
   c. Brook's asserted consideration is only worth $400.
   d. The consideration to be performed by Brook will be performed by a third party.

N93#21. Egan, a minor, contracted with Baker to purchase Baker's used computer for $400. The computer was purchased for Egan's personal use. The agreement provided that Egan would pay $200 down on delivery and $200 thirty days later. Egan took delivery and paid the $200 down payment. Twenty days later, the computer was damaged seriously as a result of Egan's negligence. Five days after the damage occurred and one day after Egan reached the age of majority, Egan attempted to disaffirm the contract with Baker. Egan will
   a. Be able to disaffirm despite the fact that Egan was **not** a minor at the time of disaffirmance.
   b. Be able to disaffirm only if Egan does so in writing.
   c. Not be able to disaffirm because Egan had failed to pay the balance of the purchase price.
   d. Not be able to disaffirm because the computer was damaged as a result of Egan's negligence.

N92#14. Castle borrowed $5,000 from Nelson and executed and delivered to Nelson a promissory note for $5,000 due on April 30. On April 1 Castle offered, and Nelson accepted, $4,000 in full satisfaction of the note. On May 15, Nelson demanded that Castle pay the $1,000 balance on the note. Castle refused. If Nelson sued for the $1,000 balance Castle would
   a. Win, because the acceptance by Nelson of the $4,000 constituted an accord and satisfaction.
   b. Win, because the debt was unliquidated.
   c. Lose, because the amount of the note was not in dispute.
   d. Lose, because no consideration was given to Nelson in exchange for accepting only $4,000.

M91#13. On reaching majority, a minor may ratify a contract in any of the following ways **except** by
   a. Failing to disaffirm within a reasonable time after reaching majority.
   b. Orally ratifying the entire contract.
   c. Acting in a manner that amounts to ratification.
   d. Affirming, in writing, some of the terms of the contract.

M91#14. Nolan agreed orally with Train to sell Train a house for $100,000. Train sent Nolan a signed agreement and a down payment of $10,000. Nolan did not sign the agreement, but allowed Train to move into the house. Before closing, Nolan refused to go through with the sale. Train sued Nolan to compel specific performance. Under the provisions of the Statute of Frauds,
   a. Train will win because Train signed the agreement and Nolan did **not** object.
   b. Train will win because Train made a down payment and took possession.
   c. Nolan will win because Nolan did **not** sign the agreement.
   d. Nolan will win because the house was worth more than $500.

N90#22. Which of the following would be unenforceable because the subject matter is illegal?
   a. A contingent fee charged by an attorney to represent a plaintiff in a negligence action.
   b. An arbitration clause in a supply contract.
   c. A restrictive covenant in an employment contract prohibiting a former employee from using the employer's trade secrets.
   d. An employer's promise **not** to press embezzlement charges against an employee who agrees to make restitution.

M89#27. Able hired Carr to restore Able's antique car for $800. The terms of their oral agreement provided that Carr was to complete the work within 18 months. Actually, the work could be completed within one year. The agreement is
   a. Unenforceable because it covers services with a value in excess of $500.
   b. Unenforceable because it covers a time period in excess of one year.
   c. Enforceable because personal service contracts are exempt from the Statute of Frauds.
   d. Enforceable because the work could be completed within one year.

C. Third Party Assignments

R97#10. Which of the following statements is(are) correct regarding a valid assignment?

I. An assignment of an interest in a sum of money must be in writing and must be supported by legally sufficient consideration.
II. An assignment of an insurance policy must be made to another party having an insurable interest in the property.

  a. I only.
  b. II only.
  c. Both I and II.
  d. Neither I nor II.

M95#21. Generally, which of the following contract rights are assignable?

	Option contract rights	Malpractice insurance policy rights
a.	Yes	Yes
b.	Yes	No
c.	No	Yes
d.	No	No

M95#22. One of the criteria for a valid assignment of a sales contract to a third party is that the assignment must
  a. Be supported by adequate consideration from the assignee.
  b. Be in writing and signed by the assignor.
  c. Not materially increase the other party's risk or duty.
  d. Not be revocable by the assignor.

M93#24. On February 1, Burns contracted in writing with Nagel to sell Nagel a used car. The contract provided that Burns was to deliver the car on February 15 and Nagel was to pay the $800 purchase price not later than March 15. On February 21, Burns assigned the contract to Ross for $600. Nagel was not notified of the assignment. Which of the following statements is correct?
  a. By making the assignment, Burns impliedly warranted Nagel would pay the full purchase price.
  b. The assignment to Ross is invalid because Nagel was **not** notified.
  c. Ross will **not** be subject to any contract defenses Nagel could have raised against Burns.
  d. By making the assignment, Burns impliedly warranted a lack of knowledge of any fact impairing the value of the assignment.

N92#24. Wilcox Co. contracted with Ace Painters, Inc. for Ace to paint Wilcox's warehouse. Ace, without advising Wilcox, assigned the contract to Pure Painting Corp. Pure failed to paint Wilcox's warehouse in accordance with the contract specifications. The contract between Ace and Wilcox was silent with regard to a party's right to assign it. Which of the following statements is correct?
  a. Ace remained liable to Wilcox despite the fact that Ace assigned the contract to Pure.
  b. Ace would **not** be liable to Wilcox if Ace had notified Wilcox of the assignment.
  c. Ace's duty to paint Wilcox's warehouse was nondelegable.
  d. Ace's delegation of the duty to paint Wilcox's warehouse was a breach of the contract.

M92#31. Baxter Inc. and Globe entered into a contract. After receiving valuable consideration from Clay, Baxter assigned its rights under the contract to Clay. In which of the following circumstances would Baxter **not** be liable to Clay?
  a. Clay released Globe.
  b. Globe paid Baxter.
  c. Baxter released Globe.
  d. Baxter breached the contract.

M92#34. Egan contracted with Barton to buy Barton's business. The contract provided that Egan would pay the business debts Barton owed Ness and that the balance of the purchase price would be paid to Barton over a 10 year period. The contract also required Egan to take out a decreasing term life insurance policy naming Barton and Ness as beneficiaries to ensure that the amounts owed Barton and Ness would be paid if Egan died.

Barton's contract rights were assigned to Vim, and Egan was notified of the assignment. Despite the assignment, Egan continued making payments to Barton. Egan died before completing payment and Vim sued Barton for the insurance proceeds and the other payments on the purchase price received by Barton after the assignment. To which of the following is Vim entitled?

	Payments on purchase price	Insurance proceeds
a.	No	Yes
b.	No	No
c.	Yes	Yes
d.	Yes	No

N91#24. Yost contracted with Egan for Yost to buy certain real property. If the contract is otherwise silent, Yost's rights under the contract are
  a. Assignable only with Egan's consent.
  b. Nonassignable because they are personal to Yost.
  c. Nonassignable as a matter of law.
  d. Generally assignable.

M91#28. One of the criteria for a valid assignment of a sales contract to a third party is that the assignment must
  a. Not materially increase the other party's risk or duty.
  b. Not be revocable by the assignor.
  c. Be supported by adequate consideration from the assignee.
  d. Be in writing and signed by the assignor.

M90#22. On August 1, Neptune Fisheries contracted in writing with West Markets to deliver to West 3,000 pounds of lobsters at $4.00 a pound. Delivery of the lobsters was due October 1 with payment due November 1. On August 4, Neptune entered into a contract with Deep Sea Lobster Farms which provided as follows: "Neptune Fisheries assigns all the rights under the contract with West Markets dated August 1 to Deep Sea Lobster Farms." The best interpretation of the August 4 contract would be that it was
   a. Only an assignment of rights by Neptune.
   b. Only a delegation of duties by Neptune.
   c. An assignment of rights and a delegation of duties by Neptune.
   d. An unenforceable third-party beneficiary contract.

N89#18. Moss entered into a contract to purchase certain real property from Shinn. Which of the following statements is **not** correct?
   a. If Shinn fails to perform the contract, Moss can obtain specific performance.
   b. The contract is nonassignable as a matter of law.
   c. The Statute of Frauds applies to the contract.
   d. Any amendment to the contract must be agreed to by both Moss and Shinn.

M89#33. Generally, which one of the following transfers will be valid without the consent of the other parties?
   a. The assignment by the lessee of a lease contract where rent is a percentage of sales.
   b. The assignment by a purchaser of goods of the right to buy on credit without giving security.
   c. The assignment by an architect of a contract to design a building.
   d. The assignment by a patent holder of the right to receive royalties.

D. Discharge, Breach, and Remedies

R97#11. Which of the following statements is correct regarding the effect of the expiration of the period of the statute of limitations on a contract?
   a. Once the period of the statute of limitations has expired, the contract is void.
   b. The expiration of the period of the statute of limitations extinguishes the contract's underlying obligation.
   c. A cause of action barred by the statute of limitations may **not** be revived.
   d. The running of the statute of limitations bars access to judicial remedies.

M95#23. Which of the following actions will result in the discharge of a party to a contract?

	Prevention of performance	Accord and satisfaction
a.	Yes	Yes
b.	Yes	No
c.	No	Yes
d.	No	No

M95#24. Under a personal services contract, which of the following circumstances will cause the discharge of a party's duties?
   a. Death of the party who is to receive the services.
   b. Cost of performing the services has doubled.
   c. Bankruptcy of the party who is to receive the services.
   d. Illegality of the services to be performed.

M95#25. Ordinarily, in an action for breach of a construction contract, the statute of limitations time period would be computed from the date the
   a. Contract is negotiated.
   b. Contract is breached.
   c. Construction is begun.
   d. Contract is signed.

N93#22. Teller brought a lawsuit against Kerr ten years after an oral contract was made and eight years after it was breached. Kerr raised the statute of limitations as a defense. Which of the following allegations would be most important to Kerr's defense?
   a. The contract was oral.
   b. The contract could **not** be performed within one year from the date made.
   c. The action was **not** timely brought because the contract was entered into ten years prior to the commencement of the lawsuit.
   d. The action was **not** timely brought because the contract was allegedly breached eight years prior to the commencement of the lawsuit.

N93#23. To prevail in a common law action for fraud in the inducement, a plaintiff must prove that the
   a. Defendant was an expert with regard to the misrepresentations.
   b. Defendant made the misrepresentations with knowledge of their falsity and with an intention to deceive.
   c. Misrepresentations were in writing.
   d. Plaintiff was in a fiduciary relationship with the defendant.

N93#24. Which of the following offers of proof are inadmissible under the parol evidence rule when a written contract is intended as the complete agreement of the parties?

I. Proof of the existence of a subsequent oral modification of the contract.
II. Proof of the existence of a prior oral agreement that contradicts the written contract.

   a. I only.
   b. II only.
   c. Both I and II.
   d. Neither I nor II.

N93#26. Ames Construction Co. contracted to build a warehouse for White Corp. The construction specifications required Ames to use Ace lighting fixtures. Inadvertently, Ames installed Perfection lighting fixtures which

are of slightly lesser quality than Ace fixtures, but in all other respects meet White's needs. Which of the following statements is correct?
   a. White's recovery will be limited to monetary damages because Ames' breach of the construction contract was **not** material.
   b. White will **not** be able to recover any damages from Ames because the breach was inadvertent.
   c. Ames did **not** breach the construction contract because the Perfection fixtures were substantially as good as the Ace fixtures.
   d. Ames must install Ace fixtures or White will **not** be obligated to accept the warehouse.

M93#25. Master Mfg., Inc. contracted with Accur Computer Repair Corp. to maintain Master's computer system. Master's manufacturing process depends on its computer system operating properly at all times. A liquidated damages clause in the contract provided that Accur pay $1,000 to Master for each day that Accur was late responding to a service request. On January 12, Accur was notified that Master's computer system failed. Accur did not respond to Master's service request until January 15. If Master sues Accur under the liquidated damage provision of the contract, Master will
   a. Win, unless the liquidated damage provision is determined to be a penalty.
   b. Win, because under all circumstances liquidated damage provisions are enforceable.
   c. Lose, because Accur's breach was **not** material.
   d. Lose, because liquidated damage provisions violate public policy.

N92#15. Rail, who was 16 years old, purchased an $800 computer from Elco Electronics. Rail and Elco are located in a state where the age of majority is 18. On several occasions Rail returned the computer to Elco for repairs. Rail was very unhappy with the computer. Two days after reaching the age of 18, Rail was still frustrated with the computer's reliability, and returned it to Elco, demanding an $800 refund. Elco refused, claiming that Rail no longer had a right to disaffirm the contract. Elco's refusal is
   a. Correct, because Rail's multiple requests for service acted as a ratification of the contract.
   b. Correct, because Rail could have transferred good title to a good faith purchaser for value.
   c. Incorrect, because Rail disaffirmed the contract within a reasonable period of time after reaching the age of 18.
   d. Incorrect, because Rail could disaffirm the contract at any time.

N92#17. On June 1, 1992, Decker orally guaranteed the payment of a $5,000 note Decker's cousin owed Baker. Decker's agreement with Baker provided that Decker's guaranty would terminate in 18 months. On June 3, 1992, Baker wrote Decker confirming Decker's guaranty. Decker did not object to the confirmation. On August 23, 1992, Decker's cousin defaulted on the note and Baker demanded that Decker honor the guaranty. Decker refused. Which of the following statements is correct?
   a. Decker is liable under the oral guaranty because Decker did **not** object to Baker's June 3 letter.
   b. Decker is **not** liable under the oral guaranty because it expired more than one year after June 1.
   c. Decker is liable under the oral guaranty because Baker demanded payment within one year of the date the guaranty was given.
   d. Decker is **not** liable under the oral guaranty because Decker's promise was **not** in writing.

N92#19. The statute of limitations for an alleged breach of contract
   a. Does **not** apply if the contract was oral.
   b. Requires that a lawsuit be commenced and a judgment rendered within a prescribed period of time.
   c. Is determined on a case by case basis.
   d. Generally commences on the date of the breach.

N92#20. Miller negotiated the sale of Miller's liquor store to Jackson. Jackson asked to see the prior year's financial statements. Using the store's checkbook, Miller prepared a balance sheet and profit and loss statement as well as he could. Miller told Jackson to have an accountant examine Miller's records because Miller was not an accountant. Jackson failed to do so and purchased the store in reliance on Miller's financial statements. Jackson later learned that the financial statements included several errors that resulted in a material overstatement of assets and net income. Miller was not aware that the errors existed. Jackson sued Miller, claiming Miller misrepresented the store's financial condition and that Jackson relied on the financial statements in making the decision to acquire the store. Which of the following statements is correct?
   a. Jackson will prevail if the errors in the financial statements were material.
   b. Jackson will **not** prevail because Jackson's reliance on the financial statements was **not** reasonable.
   c. Money damages is the only remedy available to Jackson if, in fact, Miller has committed a misrepresentation.
   d. Jackson would be entitled to rescind the purchase even if the errors in the financial statements were **not** material.

N92#22. In negotiations with Andrews for the lease of Kemp's warehouse, Kemp orally agreed to pay one-half of the cost of the utilities. The written lease, later prepared by Kemp's attorney, provided that Andrews pay all of the utilities. Andrews failed to carefully read the lease and signed it. When Kemp demanded that Andrews pay all of the utilities, Andrews refused, claiming that the lease did not accurately reflect the oral agreement. Andrews also learned that Kemp intentionally misrepresented the condition of the structure of the warehouse during the negotiations between the parties. Andrews sued to rescind the lease and intends to introduce evidence of the parties' oral agreement about sharing the utilities and the fraudulent statements made by Kemp. The parol evidence rule will prevent the admission of evidence concerning the

	Oral agreement regarding who pays the utilities	Fraudulent statements by Kemp
a.	Yes	Yes
b.	No	Yes
c.	Yes	No
d.	No	No

N92#23. Rogers and Lennon entered into a written computer consulting agreement that required Lennon to provide certain weekly reports to Rogers. The agreement also stated that Lennon would provide the computer equipment necessary to perform the services, and that Rogers' computer would not be used. As the parties were executing the agreement, they orally agreed that Lennon could use Rogers' computer. After executing the agreement, Rogers and Lennon orally agreed that Lennon would report on a monthly, rather than weekly, basis. The parties now disagree on Lennon's right to use Rogers' computer and how often Lennon must report to Rogers. In the event of a lawsuit between the parties, the parol evidence rule will
- a. Not apply to any of the parties' agreements because the consulting agreement did **not** have to be in writing.
- b. Not prevent Lennon from proving the parties' oral agreement that Lennon could use Rogers' computer.
- c. Not prevent the admission into evidence of testimony regarding Lennon's right to report on a monthly basis.
- d. Not apply to the parties' agreement to allow Lennon to use Rogers' computer because it was contemporaneous with the written agreement.

N92#25. On June 15, 1990, Alpha, Inc. contracted with Delta Manufacturing, Inc. to buy a vacant parcel of land Delta owned. Alpha intended to build a distribution warehouse on the land because of its location near a major highway. The contract stated that: "Alpha's obligations hereunder are subject to the vacant parcel being rezoned to a commercial zoning classification by July 31, 1991." Which of the following statements is correct?
- a. If the parcel is **not** rezoned by July 31, and Alpha refuses to purchase it, Alpha would **not** be in breach of contract.
- b. If the parcel is rezoned by July 31, and Alpha refuses to purchase it, Delta would be able to successfully sue Alpha for specific performance.
- c. The contract is **not** binding on either party because Alpha's performance is conditional.
- d. If the parcel is rezoned by July 31, and Delta refuses to sell it, Delta's breach would **not** discharge Alpha's obligation to tender payment.

M92#25. West, an Indiana real estate broker, misrepresented to Zimmer that West was licensed in Kansas under the Kansas statute that regulates real estate brokers and requires all brokers to be licensed. Zimmer signed a contract agreeing to pay West a 5% commission for selling Zimmer's home in Kansas. West did not sign the contract. West sold Zimmer's home. If West sued Zimmer for nonpayment of commission, Zimmer would be
- a. Liable to West only for the value of services rendered.
- b. Liable to West for the full commission.
- c. Not liable to West for any amount because West did **not** sign the contract.
- d. Not liable to West for any amount because West violated the Kansas licensing requirements.

M92#26. Carson agreed orally to repair Ives' rare book for $450. Before the work was started, Ives asked Carson to perform additional repairs to the book and agreed to increase the contract price to $650. After Carson completed the work, Ives refused to pay and Carson sued. Ives' defense was based on the Statute of Frauds. What total amount will Carson recover?
- a. $0
- b. $200
- c. $450
- d. $650

M92#27. In an action for breach of contract, the statute of limitations time period would be computed from the date of the
- a. Breach of the contract.
- b. Signing of the contract.
- c. Negotiation of the contract.
- d. Commencement of the action.

M92#28. Which of the following, if intentionally misstated by a seller to a buyer, would be considered a fraudulent inducement to make a contract?
- a. Nonexpert opinion.
- b. Appraised value.
- c. Prediction.
- d. Immaterial fact.

M92#29. If a buyer accepts an offer containing an immaterial unilateral mistake, the resulting contract will be
- a. Void as a matter of law.
- b. Void at the election of the buyer.
- c. Valid as to both parties.
- d. Voidable at the election of the seller.

M92#30. Under the parol evidence rule, oral evidence will be excluded if it relates to
- a. A contemporaneous oral agreement relating to a term in the contract.
- b. Failure of a condition precedent.
- c. Lack of contractual capacity.
- d. A modification made several days after the contract was executed.

M92#32. To cancel a contract and to restore the parties to their original positions before the contract, the parties should execute a

a. Novation
b. Release
c. Rescission
d. Revocation

M92#33. Egan contracted with Barton to buy Barton's business. The contract provided that Egan would pay the business debts Barton owed Ness and that the balance of the purchase price would be paid to Barton over a 10 year period. The contract also required Egan to take out a decreasing term life insurance policy naming Barton and Ness as beneficiaries to ensure that the amounts owed Barton and Ness would be paid if Egan died.

Which of the following would describe Ness' status under the contract and insurance policy?

	Contract	Insurance policy
a.	Donee beneficiary	Donee beneficiary
b.	Donee beneficiary	Creditor beneficiary
c.	Creditor beneficiary	Donee beneficiary
d.	Creditor beneficiary	Creditor beneficiary

M92#35. Kaye contracted to sell Hodges a building for $310,000. The contract required Hodges to pay the entire amount at closing. Kaye refused to close the sale of the building. Hodges sued Kaye. To what relief is Hodges entitled?
a. Punitive damages and compensatory damages.
b. Specific performance and compensatory damages.
c. Consequential damages or punitive damages.
d. Compensatory damages or specific performance.

N91#21. The intent, or scienter, element necessary to establish a cause of action for fraud will be met if the plaintiff can show that the
a. Defendant made a misrepresentation with a reckless disregard for the truth.
b. Defendant made a false representation of fact.
c. Plaintiff actually relied on the defendant's misrepresentation.
d. Plaintiff justifiably relied on the defendant's misrepresentation.

N91#22. Under the UCC Sales Article, a plaintiff who proves fraud in the formation of a contract may
a. Elect to rescind the contract and need **not** return the consideration received from the other party.
b. Be entitled to rescind the contract and sue for damages resulting from the fraud.
c. Be entitled to punitive damages provided physical injuries resulted from the fraud.
d. Rescind the contract even if there was **no** reliance on the fraudulent statement.

N91#23. Two individuals signed a contract that was intended to be their entire agreement. The parol evidence rule will prevent the admission of evidence offered to
a. Explain the meaning of an ambiguity in the written contract.
b. Establish that fraud had been committed in the formation of the contract.
c. Prove the existence of a contemporaneous oral agreement modifying the contract.
d. Prove the existence of a subsequent oral agreement modifying the contract.

N91#25. On May 25, 1991, Smith contracted with Jackson to repair Smith's cabin cruiser. The work was to begin on May 31, 1991. On May 26, 1991, the boat, while docked at Smith's pier, was destroyed by arson. Which of the following statements is correct with regard to the contract?
a. Smith would **not** be liable to Jackson because of mutual mistake.
b. Smith would be liable to Jackson for the profit Jackson would have made under the contract.
c. Jackson would **not** be liable to Smith because performance by the parties would be impossible.
d. Jackson would be liable to repair another boat owned by Smith.

M91#15. In 1959, Dart bought an office building from Graco under a written contract signed only by Dart. In 1991, Dart discovered that Graco made certain false representations during their negotiations concerning the building's foundation. Dart could have reasonably discovered the foundation problems by 1965. Dart sued Graco claiming fraud in the formation of the contract. Which of the following statements is correct?
a. The parol evidence rule will prevent the admission into evidence of proof concerning Dart's allegations.
b. Dart will be able to rescind the contract because both parties did **not** sign it.
c. Dart must prove that the alleged misrepresentations were part of the written contract because the contract involved real estate.
d. The statute of limitations would likely prevent Dart from prevailing because of the length of time that has passed.

M91#17. Bond and Spear orally agreed that Bond would buy a car from Spear for $475. Bond paid Spear a $100 deposit. The next day, Spear received an offer of $575, the car's fair market value. Spear immediately notified Bond that Spear would not sell the car to Bond and returned Bond's $100. If Bond sues Spear and Spear defends on the basis of the statute of frauds, Bond will probably
a. Lose, because the agreement was for less than the fair market value of the car.
b. Win, because the agreement was for less than $500.
c. Lose, because the agreement was **not** in writing and signed by Spear.
d. Win, because Bond paid a deposit.

M91#18. Dunne and Cook signed a contract requiring Cook to rebind 500 of Dunne's books at 80¢ per book. Later, Dunne requested, in good faith, that the price be

reduced to 70¢ per book. Cook agreed orally to reduce the price to 70¢. Under the circumstances, the oral agreement is
   a. Enforceable, but proof of it is inadmissible into evidence.
   b. Enforceable, and proof of it is admissible into evidence.
   c. Unenforceable, because Dunne failed to give consideration, but proof of it is otherwise admissible into evidence.
   d. Unenforceable, due to the statute of frauds, and proof of it is inadmissible into evidence.

M91#19. Wilk bought an apartment building from Dix Corp. There was a mortgage on the building securing Dix's promissory note to Xeon Finance Co. Wilk took title subject to Xeon's mortgage. Wilk did not make the payments on the note due Xeon and the building was sold at a foreclosure sale. If the proceeds of the foreclosure sale are less than the balance due on the note, which of the following statements is correct regarding the deficiency?
   a. Xeon must attempt to collect the deficiency from Wilk before suing Dix.
   b. Dix will **not** be liable for any of the deficiency because Wilk assumed the note and mortgage.
   c. Xeon may collect the deficiency from either Dix or Wilk.
   d. Dix will be liable for the entire deficiency.

M91#20. Johns leased an apartment from Olsen. Shortly before the lease expired, Olsen threatened Johns with eviction and physical harm if Johns did not sign a new lease for twice the old rent. Johns, unable to afford the expense to fight eviction, and in fear of physical harm, signed the new lease. Three months later, Johns moved and sued to void the lease claiming duress. The lease will be held
   a. Void because of the unreasonable increase in rent.
   b. Voidable because of Olsen's threat to bring eviction proceedings.
   c. Void because of Johns' financial condition.
   d. Voidable because of Olsen's threat of physical harm.

M91#21. To prevail in a common law action for innocent misrepresentation, the plaintiff must prove
   a. The defendant made the false statements with a reckless disregard for the truth.
   b. The misrepresentations were in writing.
   c. The misrepresentations concerned material facts.
   d. Reliance on the misrepresentations was the only factor inducing the plaintiff to enter into the contract.

M91#22. Graham contracted with the city of Harris to train and employ high school dropouts residing in Harris. Graham breached the contract. Long, a resident of Harris and a high school dropout, sued Graham for damages. Under the circumstances, Long will
   a. Win, because Long is a third-party beneficiary entitled to enforce the contract.
   b. Win, because the intent of the contract was to confer a benefit on all high school dropouts residing in Harris.
   c. Lose, because Long is merely an incidental beneficiary of the contract.
   d. Lose, because Harris did **not** assign its contract rights to Long.

M91#23. Maco Corp. contracted to sell 1,500 bushels of potatoes to LBC Chips. The contract did not refer to any specific supply source for the potatoes. Maco intended to deliver potatoes grown on its farms. An insect infestation ruined Maco's crop but not the crops of other growers in the area. Maco failed to deliver the potatoes to LBC. LBC sued Maco for breach of contract. Under the circumstances, Maco will
   a. Lose, because it could have purchased potatoes from other growers to deliver to LBC.
   b. Lose, unless it can show that the purchase of substitute potatoes for delivery to LBC would make the contract unprofitable.
   c. Win, because the infestation was an act of nature that could **not** have been anticipated by Maco.
   d. Win, because both Maco and LBC are assumed to accept the risk of a crop failure.

M91#24. In general, a clause in a real estate contract entitling the seller to retain the purchaser's down payment as liquidated damages if the purchaser fails to close the transaction, is enforceable
   a. In all cases, when the parties have a signed contract.
   b. If the amount of the down payment bears a reasonable relationship to the probable loss.
   c. As a penalty, if the purchaser intentionally defaults.
   d. Only when the seller cannot compel specific performance.

N90#23. For a purchaser of land to avoid a contract with the seller based on duress, it must be shown that the seller's improper threats
   a. Constituted a crime or tort.
   b. Would have induced a reasonably prudent person to assent to the contract.
   c. Actually induced the purchaser to assent to the contract.
   d. Were made with the intent to influence the purchaser.

N90#25. Parc hired Glaze to remodel and furnish an office suite. Glaze submitted plans that Parc approved. After completing all the necessary construction and painting, Glaze purchased minor accessories that Parc rejected because they did not conform to the plans. Parc refused to allow Glaze to complete the project and refused to pay Glaze any part of the contract price. Glaze sued for the value of the work performed. Which of the following statements is correct?

a. Glaze will lose because Glaze breached the contract by **not** completing performance.
b. Glaze will win because Glaze substantially performed and Parc prevented complete performance.
c. Glaze will lose because Glaze materially breached the contract by buying the accessories.
d. Glaze will win because Parc committed anticipatory breach.

M90#19. Union Bank lent $200,000 to Wagner. Union required Wagner to obtain a life insurance policy naming Union as beneficiary. While the loan was outstanding, Wagner stopped paying the premiums on the policy. Union paid the premiums, adding the amounts paid to Wagner's loan. Wagner died and the insurance company refused to pay the policy proceeds to Union. Union may
a. Recover the policy proceeds because it is a creditor beneficiary.
b. Recover the policy proceeds because it is a donee beneficiary.
c. Not recover the policy proceeds because it is **not** in privity of contract with the insurance company.
d. Not recover the policy proceeds because it is only an incidental beneficiary.

M90#21. Steele, Inc. wanted to purchase Kalp's distribution business. On March 15, 1990, Kalp provided Steele with copies of audited financial statements for the period ended December 31, 1989. The financial statements reflected inventory in the amount of $1,200,000. On March 29, 1990, Kalp discovered that the December 31 inventory was overstated by at least $400,000. On April 3, 1990, Steele, relying on the financial statements, purchased all of Kalp's business. On April 29, 1990, Steele discovered the inventory overstatement. Steele sued Kalp for fraud. Which of the following statements is correct?
a. Steele will lose because it should **not** have relied on the inventory valuation in the financial statements.
b. Steele will lose because Kalp was unaware that the inventory valuation was incorrect at the time the financial statements were provided to Steele.
c. Steele will prevail because Kalp had a duty to disclose the fact that the inventory value was overstated.
d. Steele will prevail but will **not** be able to sue for damages.

M90#23. Paco Corp., a building contractor, offered to sell Preston several pieces of used construction equipment. Preston was engaged in the business of buying and selling equipment. Paco's written offer had been prepared by a secretary who typed the total price as $10,900, rather than $109,000, which was the approximate fair market value of the equipment. Preston, on receipt of the offer, immediately accepted it. Paco learned of the error in the offer and refused to deliver the equipment to Preston unless Preston agreed to pay $109,000. Preston has sued Paco for breach of contract. Which of the following statements is correct?
a. Paco will **not** be liable because there has been a mutual mistake of fact.
b. Paco will be able to rescind the contract because Preston should have known that the price was erroneous.
c. Preston will prevail because Paco is a merchant.
d. The contract between Paco and Preston is void because the price set forth in the offer is substantially less than the equipment's fair market value.

M90#24. Rice contracted with Locke to build an oil refinery for Locke. The contract provided that Rice was to use United pipe fittings. Rice did not do so. United learned of the contract and, anticipating the order, manufactured additional fittings. United sued Locke and Rice. United is
a. Entitled to recover from Rice only, because Rice breached the contract.
b. Entitled to recover from either Locke or Rice because it detrimentally relied on the contract.
c. Not entitled to recover because it is a donee beneficiary.
d. Not entitled to recover because it is an incidental beneficiary.

M90#25. Wren purchased a factory from First Federal Realty. Wren paid 20% at the closing and gave a note for the balance secured by a 20-year mortgage. Five years later, Wren found it increasingly difficult to make payments on the note and defaulted. First Federal threatened to accelerate the loan and foreclose if Wren continued in default. First Federal told Wren to make payment or obtain an acceptable third party to assume the obligation. Wren offered the land to Moss, Inc. for $10,000 less than the equity Wren had in the property. This was acceptable to First Federal and at the closing Moss paid the arrearage, assumed the mortgage and note, and had title transferred to its name. First Federal released Wren. The transaction in question is a(an)
a. Purchase of land subject to a mortgage.
b. Assignment and delegation.
c. Third party beneficiary contract.
d. Novation.

N89#11. Kent, a 16-year old, purchased a used car from Mint Motors, Inc. Ten months later, the car was stolen and never recovered. Which of the following statements is correct?
a. The car's theft is a *de facto* ratification of the purchase because it is impossible to return the car.
b. Kent may disaffirm the purchase because Kent is a minor.
c. Kent effectively ratified the purchase because Kent used the car for an unreasonable period of time.
d. Kent may disaffirm the purchase because Mint, a merchant, is subject to the UCC.

N89#14. Bradford sold a parcel of land to Jones who promptly recorded the deed. Bradford then resold the land to Wallace. In a suit against Bradford by Wallace, recovery will be based on the theory of
   a. Bilateral mistake.
   b. Ignorance of the facts.
   c. Unilateral mistake.
   d. Fraud.

N89#15. A party to a contract who seeks to rescind the contract because of that party's reliance on the unintentional but materially false statements of the other party will assert
   a. Reformation.
   b. Actual fraud.
   c. Misrepresentation.
   d. Constructive fraud.

N89#16. Ward is attempting to introduce oral evidence in an action relating to a written contract between Ward and Weaver. Weaver has pleaded the parol evidence rule. Ward will be prohibited from introducing parol evidence if it relates to
   a. A modification made several days after the contract was executed.
   b. A change in the meaning of an unambiguous provision in the contract.
   c. Fraud in the inducement.
   d. An obvious error in drafting.

N89#17. Jones owned an insurance policy on her life, on which she paid all the premiums. Smith was named the beneficiary. Jones died and the insurance company refused to pay the insurance proceeds to Smith. An action by Smith against the insurance company for the insurance proceeds will be
   a. Successful because Smith is a third party donee beneficiary.
   b. Successful because Smith is a proper assignee of Jones' rights under the insurance policy.
   c. Unsuccessful because Smith was **not** the owner of the policy.
   d. Unsuccessful because Smith did **not** pay any of the premiums.

N89#19. Nagel and Fields entered into a contract in which Nagel was obligated to deliver certain goods to Fields by September 10. On September 3, Nagel told Fields that Nagel had no intention of delivering the goods required by the contract. Prior to September 10, Fields may successfully sue Nagel under the doctrine of
   a. Promissory estoppel.
   b. Accord and satisfaction.
   c. Anticipatory repudiation.
   d. Substantial performance.

M89#26. Tell, an Ohio real estate broker, misrepresented to Allen that Tell was licensed in Michigan under Michigan's statute regulating real estate brokers. Allen signed a standard form listing contract agreeing to pay Tell a 6% commission for selling Allen's home in Michigan. Tell sold Allen's home. Under the circumstances, Allen is
   a. Not liable to Tell for any amount because Allen signed a standard form contract.
   b. Not liable to Tell for any amount because Tell violated the Michigan licensing requirements.
   c. Liable to Tell only for the value of services rendered under a quasi-contract theory.
   d. Liable to Tell for the full commission under a promissory estoppel theory.

M89#30. Which of the following remedies is available to a party who has entered into a contract in reliance upon the other contracting party's innocent misrepresentations as to material facts?

	Compensatory damages	Punitive damages	Rescission
a.	No	No	No
b.	Yes	No	Yes
c.	No	No	Yes
d.	Yes	Yes	No

M89#32. Ace contracted with Big City to train and employ handicapped, unemployed veterans residing in Big City. Ace breached the contract and Bell, a resident of Big City who is a handicapped, unemployed veteran, sues Ace for damages. Under the circumstances, Bell will
   a. Lose, because Bell is merely an incidental beneficiary of the contract.
   b. Win, because Bell is a third-party beneficiary entitled to enforce the contract.
   c. Lose, because Big City did **not** assign its contract rights to Bell.
   d. Win, because the intent of the contract was to confer a benefit on all handicapped, unemployed veterans residing in Big City.

M89#34. In September 1988, Cobb Company contracted with Thrifty Oil Company for the delivery of 100,000 gallons of heating oil at the price of 75¢ per gallon at regular specified intervals during the forthcoming winter. Due to an unseasonably warm winter, Cobb took delivery on only 70,000 gallons. In a suit against Cobb for breach of contract, Thrifty will
   a. Lose, because Cobb acted in good faith.
   b. Lose, because both parties are merchants and the UCC recognizes commercial impracticability.
   c. Win, because this is a requirements contract.
   d. Win, because the change of circumstances could have been contemplated by the parties.

M89#35. Jones, CPA, entered into a signed contract with Foster Corp. to perform accounting and review services. If Jones repudiates the contract prior to the date performance is due to begin, which of the following is **not** correct?

a. Foster could successfully maintain an action for breach of contract after the date performance was due to begin.
b. Foster can obtain a judgment ordering Jones to perform.
c. Foster could successfully maintain an action for breach of contract prior to the date performance is due to begin.
d. Foster can obtain a judgment for the monetary damages it incurred as a result of the repudiation.

IV. Debtor-Creditor Relationships

A. Rights, Duties, and Liabilities of Debtors and Creditors

R98#5. The federal Credit Card Fraud Act protects a credit card holder from loss by
a. Restricting the interest rate charged by the credit card company.
b. Limiting the card holder's liability for unauthorized use.
c. Requiring credit card companies to issue cards to qualified persons.
d. Allowing the card holder to defer payment of the balance due on the card.

R96#13. Which of the following will enable a creditor to collect money from a debtor's wages?
a. An order of receivership.
b. An order of garnishment.
c. A writ of execution.
d. A writ of attachment.

N95#26. Which of the following statements is(are) correct regarding debtors' rights?

I. State exemption statutes prevent all of a debtor's personal property from being sold to pay a federal tax lien.
II. Federal social security benefits received by a debtor are exempt from garnishment by creditors.

a. I only.
b. II only.
c. Both I and II.
d. Neither I nor II.

N95#27. Which of the following liens generally require(s) the lienholder to give notice of legal action before selling the debtor's property to satisfy the debt?

	Mechanic's lien	Artisan's lien
a.	Yes	Yes
b.	Yes	No
c.	No	Yes
d.	No	No

N94#26. Under the Federal Fair Debt Collection Practices Act, which of the following would a collection service using improper debt collection practices be subject to?
a. Abolishment of the debt.
b. Reduction of the debt.
c. Civil lawsuit for damages for violating the Act.
d. Criminal prosecution for violating the Act.

N94#27. Which of the following actions between a debtor and its creditors will generally cause the debtor's release from its debts?

	Composition of creditors	Assignment for the benefit of creditors
a.	Yes	Yes
b.	Yes	No
c.	No	Yes
d.	No	No

N94#28. Which of the following prejudgment remedies would be available to a creditor when a debtor owns **no** real property?

	Writ of attachment	Garnishment
a.	Yes	Yes
b.	Yes	No
c.	No	Yes
d.	No	No

M94#21. A debtor may attempt to conceal or transfer property to prevent a creditor from satisfying a judgment. Which of the following actions will be considered an indication of fraudulent conveyance?

	Debtor remaining in possession after conveyance	Secret conveyance	Debtor retains an equitable benefit in the property conveyed
a.	Yes	Yes	Yes
b.	No	Yes	Yes
c.	Yes	Yes	No
d.	Yes	No	Yes

M94#22. A homestead exemption ordinarily could exempt a debtor's equity in certain property from post-judgment collection by a creditor. To which of the following creditors will this exemption apply?

	Valid home mortgage lien	Valid IRS Tax lien
a.	Yes	Yes
b.	Yes	No
c.	No	Yes
d.	No	No

M94#23. Which of the following methods will allow a creditor to collect money from a debtor's wages?
   a. Arrest.
   b. Mechanic's lien.
   c. Order of receivership.
   d. Writ of garnishment.

B. Rights, Duties, and Liabilities of Guarantors

N95#28. Which of the following rights does one cosurety generally have against another cosurety?
   a. Exoneration.
   b. Subrogation.
   c. Reimbursement.
   d. Contribution.

N95#29. Which of the following acts always will result in the total release of a compensated surety?
   a. The creditor changes the manner of the principal debtor's payment.
   b. The creditor extends the principal debtor's time to pay.
   c. The principal debtor's obligation is partially released.
   d. The principal debtor's performance is tendered.

N95#30. When a principal debtor defaults and a surety pays the creditor the entire obligation, which of the following remedies gives the surety the best method of collecting from the debtor?
   a. Exoneration.
   b. Contribution.
   c. Subrogation.
   d. Attachment.

M95#26. Green was unable to repay a loan from State Bank when due. State refused to renew the loan unless Green provided an acceptable surety. Green asked Royal, a friend, to act as surety on the loan. To induce Royal to agree to become a surety, Green fraudulently represented Green's financial condition and promised Royal discounts on merchandise sold at Green's store. Royal agreed to act as surety and the loan was renewed. Later, Green's obligation to State was discharged in Green's bankruptcy. State wants to hold Royal liable. Royal may avoid liability
   a. If Royal can show that State was aware of the fraudulent representations.
   b. If Royal was an uncompensated surety.
   c. Because the discharge in bankruptcy will prevent Royal from having a right of reimbursement.
   d. Because the arrangement was void at the inception.

M95#27. Wright cosigned King's loan from Ace Bank. Which of the following events would release Wright from the obligation to pay the loan?
   a. Ace seeking payment of the loan only from Wright.
   b. King is granted a discharge in bankruptcy.
   c. Ace is paid in full by King's spouse.
   d. King is adjudicated mentally incompetent.

N94#29. Which of the following defenses would a surety be able to assert successfully to limit the surety's liability to a creditor?
   a. A discharge in bankruptcy of the principal debtor.
   b. A personal defense the principal debtor has against the creditor.
   c. The incapacity of the surety.
   d. The incapacity of the principal debtor.

N94#30. Which of the following rights does a surety have?

	Right to compel the creditor to collect from the principal debtor	Right to compel the creditor to proceed against the principal debtor's collateral
a.	Yes	Yes
b.	Yes	No
c.	No	Yes
d.	No	No

N94#31. Ingot Corp. lent Flange $50,000. At Ingot's request, Flange entered into an agreement with Quill and West for them to act as compensated co-sureties on the loan in the amount of $100,000 each. Ingot released West without Quill's or Flange's consent, and Flange later defaulted on the loan. Which of the following statements is correct?
   a. Quill will be liable for 50% of the loan balance.
   b. Quill will be liable for the entire loan balance.
   c. Ingot's release of West will have no effect on Flange's and Quill's liability to Ingot.
   d. Flange will be released for 50% of the loan balance.

M94#24. A party contracts to guaranty the collection of the debts of another. As a result of the guaranty, which of the following statements is correct?
   a. The creditor may proceed against the guarantor without attempting to collect from the debtor.
   b. The guaranty must be in writing.
   c. The guarantor may use any defenses available to the debtor.
   d. The creditor must be notified of the debtor's default by the guarantor.

M94#25. Which of the following events will release a noncompensated surety from liability?
   a. Release of the principal debtor's obligation by the creditor but with the reservation of the creditor's rights against the surety.
   b. Modification by the principal debtor and creditor of their contract that materially increases the surety's risk of loss.
   c. Filing of an involuntary petition in bankruptcy against the principal debtor.
   d. Insanity of the principal debtor at the time the contract was entered into with the creditor.

N93#25. Nash, Owen, and Polk are co-sureties with maximum liabilities of $40,000, $60,000 and $80,000, respectively. The amount of the loan on which they have agreed to act as co-sureties is $180,000. The debtor defaulted at a time when the loan balance was $180,000. Nash paid the lender $36,000 in full settlement of all claims against Nash, Owen, and Polk. The total amount that Nash may recover from Owen and Polk is
 a. $0
 b. $ 24,000
 c. $ 28,000
 d. $140,000

N92#26. Ivor borrowed $420,000 from Lear Bank. At Lear's request, Ivor entered into an agreement with Ash, Kane, and Queen for them to act as co-sureties on the loan. The agreement between Ivor and the co-sureties provided that the maximum liability of each co-surety was: Ash, $84,000; Kane, $126,000; and Queen, $210,000. After making several payments, Ivor defaulted on the loan. The balance was $280,000. If Queen pays $210,000 and Ivor subsequently pays $70,000, what amounts may Queen recover from Ash and Kane?
 a. $0 from Ash and $0 from Kane.
 b. $42,000 from Ash and $63,000 from Kane.
 c. $70,000 from Ash and $70,000 from Kane.
 d. $56,000 from Ash and $84,000 from Kane.

N92#27. Which of the following acts will always result in the total release of a compensated surety?
 a. The creditor extends the principal debtor's time to pay.
 b. The principal debtor's performance is tendered.
 c. The place of payment is changed.
 d. The principal debtor's obligation is partially released.

N92#28. A distinction between a surety and a co-surety is that only a co-surety is entitled to
 a. Reimbursement (Indemnification).
 b. Subrogation.
 c. Contribution.
 d. Exoneration.

N91#26. Mane Bank lent Eller $120,000 and received securities valued at $30,000 as collateral. At Mane's request, Salem and Rey agreed to act as uncompensated co-sureties on the loan. The agreement provided that Salem's and Rey's maximum liability would be $120,000 each.
 Mane released Rey without Salem's consent. Eller later defaulted when the collateral held by Mane was worthless and the loan balance was $90,000. Salem's maximum liability is
 a. $30,000
 b. $45,000
 c. $60,000
 d. $90,000

N91#38. Brown was unable to repay a loan from Safe Bank when due. Safe refused to renew the loan unless Brown provided an acceptable surety. Brown asked King, a friend, to act as surety on the loan. To induce King to agree to become a surety, Brown fraudulently represented Brown's financial condition and promised King discounts on merchandise sold at Brown's store. King agreed to act as surety and the loan was renewed. Later, Brown's obligation to Safe was discharged in Brown's bankruptcy. Safe wants to hold King liable. King may avoid liability
 a. Because the discharge in bankruptcy will prevent King from having a right of reimbursement.
 b. Because the arrangement was void at the inception.
 c. If King was an uncompensated surety.
 d. If King can show that Safe was aware of the fraudulent representations.

M91#26. Edwards Corp. lent Lark $200,000. At Edwards' request, Lark entered into an agreement with Owen and Ward for them to act as compensated co-sureties on the loan in the amount of $200,000 each. If Edwards releases Ward without Owen's or Lark's consent, and Lark later defaults, which of the following statements is correct?
 a. Lark will be released for 50% of the loan balance.
 b. Owen will be liable for the entire loan balance.
 c. Owen will be liable for 50% of the loan balance.
 d. Edwards' release of Ward will have **no** effect on Lark's and Owen's liability to Edwards.

M91#27. Lane promised to lend Turner $240,000 if Turner obtained sureties to secure the loan. Turner agreed with Rivers, Clark, and Zane for them to act as cosureties on the loan from Lane. The agreement between Turner and the cosureties provided that compensation be paid to each of the cosureties. It further indicated that the maximum liability of each cosurety would be as follows: Rivers $240,000, Clark $80,000, and Zane $160,000. Lane accepted the commitments of the sureties and made the loan to Turner. After paying ten installments totaling $100,000, Turner defaulted. Clark's debts, including the surety obligation to Lane on the Turner loan, were discharged in bankruptcy. Later, Rivers properly paid the entire outstanding debt of $140,000. What amount may Rivers recover from Zane?
 a. $0
 b. $56,000
 c. $70,000
 d. $84,000

N90#26. Sorus and Ace have agreed, in writing, to act as guarantors of collection on a debt owed by Pepper to Towns, Inc. The debt is evidenced by a promissory note. If Pepper defaults, Towns will be entitled to recover from Sorus and Ace unless
 a. Sorus and Ace are in the process of exercising their rights against Pepper.
 b. Sorus and Ace prove that Pepper was insolvent at the time the note was signed.
 c. Pepper dies before the note is due.
 d. Towns has **not** attempted to enforce the promissory note against Pepper.

N89#20. Burns borrowed $240,000 from Dollar Bank as additional working capital for his business. Dollar required that the loan be collateralized to the extent of 20%, and that an acceptable surety for the entire amount be obtained. Surety Co. agreed to act as surety on the loan and Burns pledged $48,000 of negotiable bearer bonds. Burns defaulted. Which of the following statements is correct?
    a. Dollar must first liquidate the collateral before it can proceed against Surety.
    b. Surety is liable in full immediately upon default by Burns, but will be entitled to the collateral upon satisfaction of the debt.
    c. Dollar must first proceed against Burns and obtain a judgment before it can proceed against the collateral.
    d. Surety may proceed against Burns for the full amount of the loan even if Surety settles with Dollar for a lower amount.

N89#21. If a debtor defaults and the debtor's surety satisfies the obligation, the surety acquires the right of
    a. Subrogation.
    b. Primary lien.
    c. Indemnification.
    d. Satisfaction.

C. Bankruptcy

R97#12. Under the liquidation provisions of Chapter 7 of the federal Bankruptcy Code, a debtor will be denied a discharge in bankruptcy if the debtor
    a. Fails to list a creditor.
    b. Owes alimony and support payments.
    c. Cannot pay administration expenses.
    d. Refuses to satisfactorily explain a loss of assets.

M95
Items 28 through 33 are based on the following:

Dart Inc., a closely held corporation, was petitioned involuntarily into bankruptcy under the liquidation provisions of Chapter 7 of the Federal Bankruptcy Code. Dart contested the petition.

Dart has not been paying its business debts as they became due, has defaulted on its mortgage loan payments, and owes back taxes to the IRS. The total cash value of Dart's bankruptcy estate after the sale of all assets and payment of administration expenses is $100,000.

Dart has the following creditors:

- Fracon Bank is owed $75,000 principal and accrued interest on a mortgage loan secured by Dart's real property. The property was valued at and sold, in bankruptcy, for $70,000.

- The IRS has a $12,000 recorded judgment for unpaid corporate income tax.

- JOG Office Supplies has an unsecured claim of $3,000 that was timely filed.

- Nanstar Electric Co. has an unsecured claim of $1,200 that was not timely filed.

- Decoy Publications has a claim of $14,000, of which $2,000 is secured by Dart's inventory that was valued and sold, in bankruptcy, for $2,000. The claim was timely filed.

28. Which of the following creditors must join in the filing of the involuntary petition?

    I. JOG Office Supplies
    II. Nanstar Electric Co.
    III. Decoy Publications

    a. I, II, & III.
    b. II & III.
    c. I & II.
    d. III only.

29. Which of the following statements would correctly describe the result of Dart's opposing the petition?
    a. Dart will win because the petition should have been filed under Chapter 11.
    b. Dart will win because there are **not** more than 12 creditors.
    c. Dart will lose because it is **not** paying its debts as they become due.
    d. Dart will lose because of its debt to the IRS.

30. Which of the following events will follow the filing of the Chapter 7 involuntary petition?

	A trustee will be appointed	A stay against creditor collection proceedings will go into effect
a.	Yes	Yes
b.	Yes	No
c.	No	Yes
d.	No	No

For **Items 31 through 33** assume that the bankruptcy estate was distributed.

31. What dollar amount would Nanstar Electric Co. receive?
    a. $0
    b. $ 800
    c. $1,000
    d. $1,200

32. What total dollar amount would Fracon Bank receive on its secured and unsecured claims?
    a. $70,000
    b. $72,000
    c. $74,000
    d. $75,000

33. What dollar amount would the IRS receive?
    a. $0
    b. $ 8,000
    c. $10,000
    d. $12,000

M95
Items 34 and 35 are based on the following:

Strong Corp. filed a voluntary petition in bankruptcy under the reorganization provisions of Chapter 11 of the Federal Bankruptcy Code. A reorganization plan was filed and agreed to by all necessary parties. The court confirmed the plan and a final decree was entered.

34. Which of the following parties ordinarily must confirm the plan?

	½ of the secured creditors	⅔ of the shareholders
a.	Yes	Yes
b.	Yes	No
c.	No	Yes
d.	No	No

35. Which of the following statements best describes the effect of the entry of the court's final decree?
    a. Strong Corp. will be discharged from all its debts and liabilities.
    b. Strong Corp. will be discharged only from the debts owed creditors who agreed to the reorganization plan.
    c. Strong Corp. will be discharged from all its debts and liabilities that arose before the date of confirmation of the plan.
    d. Strong Corp. will be discharged from all its debts and liabilities that arose before the confirmation of the plan, except as otherwise provided in the plan, the order of confirmation, or the Bankruptcy Code.

N94#33. Which of the following claims will **not** be discharged in bankruptcy?
    a. A claim that arises from alimony or maintenance.
    b. A claim that arises out of the debtor's breach of a contract.
    c. A claim brought by a secured creditor that remains unsatisfied after the sale of the collateral.
    d. A claim brought by a judgment creditor whose judgment resulted from the debtor's negligent operation of a motor vehicle.

N94#34. Under the liquidation provisions of Chapter 7 of the Federal Bankruptcy Code, which of the following statements applies to a person who has voluntarily filed for and received a discharge in bankruptcy?
    a. The person will be discharged from all debts.
    b. The person can obtain another voluntary discharge in bankruptcy under Chapter 7 after three years have elapsed from the date of the prior filing.
    c. The person must surrender for distribution to the creditors amounts received as an inheritance, if the receipt occurs within 180 days after filing the bankruptcy petition.
    d. The person is precluded from owning or operating a similar business for two years.

N94#37. Under the reorganization provisions of Chapter 11 of the Federal Bankruptcy Code, after a reorganization plan is confirmed, and a final decree closing the proceedings entered, which of the following events usually occurs?
    a. A reorganized corporate debtor will be liquidated.
    b. A reorganized corporate debtor will be discharged from all debts except as otherwise provided in the plan and applicable law.
    c. A trustee will continue to operate the debtor's business.
    d. A reorganized individual debtor will **not** be allowed to continue in the same business.

N93#27. The filing of an involuntary bankruptcy petition under the Federal Bankruptcy Code
    a. Terminates liens on exempt property.
    b. Terminates all security interests in property in the bankruptcy estate.
    c. Stops the debtor from incurring new debts.
    d. Stops the enforcement of judgment liens against property in the bankruptcy estate.

N93#29. Which of the following conditions, if any, must a debtor meet to file a voluntary bankruptcy petition under Chapter 7 of the Federal Bankruptcy Code?

	Insolvency	Three or more creditors
a.	Yes	Yes
b.	Yes	No
c.	No	Yes
d.	No	No

N93#30. Which of the following transfers by a debtor, within ninety days of filing for bankruptcy, could be set aside as a preferential payment?
    a. Making a gift to charity.
    b. Paying a business utility bill.
    c. Borrowing money from a bank secured by giving a mortgage on business property.
    d. Prepaying an installment loan on inventory.

N93#31. Which of the following acts by a debtor could result in a bankruptcy court revoking the debtor's discharge?

I. Failure to list one creditor.
II. Failure to answer correctly material questions on the bankruptcy petition.

    a. I only.
    b. II only.
    c. Both I and II.
    d. Neither I nor II.

N93#32. Robin Corp. incurred substantial operating losses for the past three years. Unable to meet its current obligations, Robin filed a petition for reorganization under Chapter 11 of the Federal Bankruptcy Code. Which of the following statements is correct?
 a. The creditors' committee must select a trustee to manage Robin's affairs.
 b. The reorganization plan may only be filed by Robin.
 c. A creditors' committee, if appointed, will consist of unsecured creditors.
 d. Robin may continue in business only with the approval of a trustee.

N93#33. A reorganization under Chapter 11 of the Federal Bankruptcy Code requires all of the following **except** the
 a. Liquidation of the debtor.
 b. The filing of a reorganization plan.
 c. Confirmation of the reorganization plan by the court.
 d. Opportunity for each class of claims to accept the reorganization plan.

N93#34. Which of the following statements is correct with respect to the reorganization provisions of Chapter 11 of the Federal Bankruptcy Code?
 a. A trustee must always be appointed.
 b. The debtor must be insolvent if the bankruptcy petition was filed voluntarily.
 c. A reorganization plan may be filed by a creditor anytime after the petition date.
 d. The commencement of a bankruptcy case may be voluntary or involuntary.

N93#39. Which of the following types of claims would be paid first in the distribution of a bankruptcy estate under the liquidation provisions of Chapter 7 of the Federal Bankruptcy Code if the petition was filed July 15, 1993?
 a. A secured debt properly perfected on March 20, 1993.
 b. Inventory purchased and delivered August 1, 1993.
 c. Employee wages due April 30, 1993.
 d. Federal tax lien filed June 30, 1993.

N92#30. A party involuntarily petitioned into bankruptcy under Chapter 7 of the Federal Bankruptcy Code who succeeds in having the petition dismissed could recover

	Court costs and attorney's fees	Compensatory damages	Punitive damages
a.	Yes	Yes	Yes
b.	Yes	Yes	No
c.	No	Yes	Yes
d.	Yes	No	No

N92#31. Under Chapter 11 of the Federal Bankruptcy Code, which of the following actions is necessary before the court may confirm a reorganization plan?
 a. Provision for full payment of administration expenses.
 b. Acceptance of the plan by all classes of claimants.
 c. Preparation of a contingent plan of liquidation.
 d. Appointment of a trustee.

N92#32. Under Chapter 11 of the Federal Bankruptcy Code, which of the following would **not** be eligible for reorganization?
 a. Retail sole proprietorship.
 b. Advertising partnership.
 c. CPA professional corporation.
 d. Savings and loan corporation.

N92
Items 37 through 39 are based on the following:

On August 1, 1992, Hall filed a voluntary petition under Chapter 7 of the Federal Bankruptcy Code.
Hall's assets are sufficient to pay general creditors 40% of their claims.
The following transactions occurred before the filing:

- On May 15, 1992, Hall gave a mortgage on Hall's home to National Bank to secure payment of a loan National had given Hall two years earlier. When the loan was made, Hall's twin was a National employee.

- On June 1, 1992, Hall purchased a boat from Olsen for $10,000 cash.

- On July 1, 1992, Hall paid off an outstanding credit card balance of $500. The original debt had been $2,500.

37. The National mortgage was
 a. Preferential, because National would be considered an insider.
 b. Preferential, because the mortgage was given to secure an antecedent debt.
 c. Not preferential, because Hall is presumed insolvent when the mortgage was given.
 d. Not preferential, because the mortgage was a security interest.

38. The payment to Olsen was
 a. Preferential, because the payment was made within 90 days of the filing of the petition.
 b. Preferential, because the payment enabled Olsen to receive more than the other general creditors.
 c. Not preferential, because Hall is presumed insolvent when the payment was made.
 d. Not preferential, because the payment was a contemporaneous exchange for new value.

39. The credit card payment was
 a. Preferential, because the payment was made within 90 days of the filing of the petition.

b. Preferential, because the payment was on account of an antecedent debt.
c. Not preferential, because the payment was for a consumer debt of less than $600.
d. Not preferential, because the payment was less than 40% of the original debt.

N91#29. To file for bankruptcy under Chapter 7 of the Federal Bankruptcy Code, an individual must
a. Have debts of any amount.
b. Be insolvent.
c. Be indebted to more than three creditors.
d. Have debts in excess of $5,000.

N91#31. By signing a reaffirmation agreement on April 15, 1991, a debtor agreed to pay certain debts that would be discharged in bankruptcy. On June 20, 1991, the debtor's attorney filed the reaffirmation agreement and an affidavit with the court indicating that the debtor understood the consequences of the reaffirmation agreement. The debtor obtained a discharge on August 25, 1991. The reaffirmation agreement would be enforceable only if it was
a. Made after discharge.
b. Approved by the bankruptcy court.
c. Not for a household purpose debt.
d. Not rescinded before discharge.

N91
Items 42 through 45 are based on the following:

On February 28, 1991, Master, Inc. had total assets with a fair market value of $1,200,000 and total liabilities of $990,000. On January 15, 1991, Master made a monthly installment note payment to Acme Distributors Corp., a creditor holding a properly perfected security interest in equipment having a fair market value greater than the balance due on the note. On March 15, 1991, Master voluntarily filed a petition in bankruptcy under the liquidation provisions of Chapter 7 of the Federal Bankruptcy Code. One year later, the equipment was sold for less than the balance due on the note to Acme.

42. If a creditor challenged Master's right to file, the petition would be dismissed
a. If Master had less than 12 creditors at the time of filing.
b. Unless Master can show that a reorganization under Chapter 11 of the Federal Bankruptcy Code would have been unsuccessful.
c. Unless Master can show that it is unable to pay its debts in the ordinary course of business or as they come due.
d. If Master is an insurance company.

43. If Master's voluntary petition is filed properly,
a. Master will be entitled to conduct its business as a debtor-in-possession unless the court appoints a trustee.
b. A trustee must be appointed by the creditors.
c. Lawsuits by Master's creditors will be stayed by the Federal Bankruptcy Code.
d. The unsecured creditors must elect a creditors' committee of three to eleven members to consult with the trustee.

44. Master's payment to Acme could
a. Be set aside as a preferential transfer because the fair market value of the collateral was greater than the installment note balance.
b. Be set aside as a preferential transfer unless Acme showed that Master was solvent on January 15, 1991.
c. Not be set aside as a preferential transfer because Acme was oversecured.
d. Not be set aside as a preferential transfer if Acme showed that Master was solvent on March 15, 1991.

45. Which of the following statements correctly describes Acme's distribution from Master's bankruptcy estate?
a. Acme will receive the total amount it is owed, even if the proceeds from the sale of the collateral were less than the balance owed by Master.
b. Acme will have the same priority as unsecured general creditors to the extent that the proceeds from the sale of its collateral are insufficient to satisfy the amount owed by Master.
c. The total proceeds from the sale of the collateral will be paid to Acme even if they are less than the balance owed by Master, provided there is sufficient cash to pay all administrative costs associated with the bankruptcy.
d. Acme will receive only the proceeds from the sale of the collateral in full satisfaction of the debt owed by Master.

M91#30. A voluntary petition filed under the liquidation provisions of Chapter 7 of the Federal Bankruptcy Code
a. Is **not** available to a corporation unless it has previously filed a petition under the reorganization provisions of Chapter 11 of the Federal Bankruptcy Code.
b. Automatically stays collection actions against the debtor **except** by secured creditors.
c. Will be dismissed unless the debtor has 12 or more unsecured creditors whose claims total at least $5,000.
d. Does **not** require the debtor to show that the debtor's liabilities exceed the fair market value of assets.

M91#31. In general, which of the following debts will be discharged under the voluntary liquidation provisions of Chapter 7 of the Federal Bankruptcy Code?
a. A debt due to the negligence of the debtor arising before filing the bankruptcy petition.
b. Alimony payments owed the debtor's spouse under a separation agreement entered into two years before the filing of the bankruptcy petition.

c. A debt incurred more than 90 days before the filing of the bankruptcy petition and **not** disclosed in the petition.
d. Income taxes due within two years before the filing of the bankruptcy petition.

M91#32. Peters Co. repairs computers. On February 9, 1991, Stark Electronics Corp. sold Peters a circuit tester on credit. Peters executed an installment note for the purchase price, a security agreement covering the tester, and a financing statement that Stark filed on February 11, 1991. On April 13, 1991, creditors other than Stark filed an involuntary petition in bankruptcy against Peters. What is Stark's status in Peters' bankruptcy?
  a. Stark will be treated as an unsecured creditor because Stark did **not** join in the filing against Peters.
  b. Stark's security interest constitutes a voidable preference because the financing statement was **not** filed until February 11.
  c. Stark's security interest constitutes a voidable preference because the financing statement was filed within 90 days before the bankruptcy proceeding was filed.
  d. Stark is a secured creditor and can assert a claim to the circuit tester that will be superior to the claims of Peters' other creditors.

M91
Items 33 and 34 are based on the following:

On May 1, 1991, two months after becoming insolvent, Quick Corp., an appliance wholesaler, filed a voluntary petition for bankruptcy under the provisions of Chapter 7 of the Federal Bankruptcy Code. On October 15, 1990, Quick's board of directors had authorized and paid Erly $50,000 to repay Erly's April 1, 1990, loan to the corporation. Erly is a sibling of Quick's president. On March 15, 1991, Quick paid Kray $100,000 for inventory delivered that day.

33. Which of the following is **not** relevant in determining whether the repayment of Erly's loan is a voidable preferential transfer?
  a. Erly is an insider.
  b. Quick's payment to Erly was made on account of an antecedent debt.
  c. Quick's solvency when the loan was made by Erly.
  d. Quick's payment to Erly was made within one year of the filing of the bankruptcy petition.

34. Quick's payment to Kray would
  a. Not be voidable, because it was a contemporaneous exchange.
  b. Not be voidable, unless Kray knew about Quick's insolvency.
  c. Be voidable, because it was made within 90 days of the bankruptcy filing.
  d. Be voidable, because it enabled Kray to receive more than it otherwise would receive from the bankruptcy estate.

M91#35. Decal Corp. incurred substantial operating losses for the past three years. Unable to meet its current obligations, Decal filed a petition for reorganization under Chapter 11 of the Federal Bankruptcy Code. Which of the following statements is correct?
  a. A creditors' committee, if appointed, will consist of unsecured creditors.
  b. The court must appoint a trustee to manage Decal's affairs.
  c. Decal may continue in business only with the approval of a trustee.
  d. The creditors' committee must select a trustee to manage Decal's affairs.

N90#27. On June 5, 1989, Gold rented equipment under a four-year lease. On March 8, 1990, Gold was petitioned involuntarily into bankruptcy under the Federal Bankruptcy Code's liquidation provisions. A trustee was appointed. The fair market value of the equipment exceeds the balance of the lease payments due. The trustee
  a. May **not** reject the equipment lease because the fair market value of the equipment exceeds the balance of the lease payments due.
  b. May elect **not** to assume the equipment lease.
  c. Must assume the equipment lease because its term exceeds one year.
  d. Must assume and subsequently assign the equipment lease.

N90#28. Flax, a sole proprietor, has been petitioned involuntarily into bankruptcy under the Federal Bankruptcy Code's liquidation provisions. Simon & Co., CPAs, has been appointed trustee of the bankruptcy estate. If Simon also wishes to act as the tax return preparer for the estate, which of the following statements is correct?
  a. Simon is prohibited from serving as both trustee and preparer under any circumstances because serving in that dual capacity would be a conflict of interest.
  b. Although Simon may serve as both trustee and preparer, it is entitled to receive a fee only for the services rendered as a preparer.
  c. Simon may employ itself to prepare tax returns if authorized by the court and may receive a separate fee for services rendered in each capacity.
  d. Although Simon may serve as both trustee and preparer, its fee for services rendered in each capacity will be determined solely by the size of the estate.

N90#29. A contested involuntary petition in bankruptcy will be dismissed if the debtor
  a. Owes unsecured obligations exceeding $5,000 to less than three creditors.
  b. Had all its property taken to enforce a lien within 120 days of filing.
  c. Is failing to pay undisputed debts as they become due.
  d. Is an individual engaged in the business of farming.

N90#30. Larson, an unemployed carpenter, filed for voluntary bankruptcy on August 14, 1990. Larson's liabilities are listed below.

Credit card charges due May 2, 1989	$3,000
Bank loan incurred June 1990	5,000
Medical expenses incurred June 1983	7,000
Alimony due during 1988	1,000

Under the provisions of Chapter 7 of the Federal Bankruptcy Code, Larson's discharge will **not** apply to the unpaid
- a. Credit card charges.
- b. Bank loan.
- c. Medical expenses.
- d. Alimony.

N90#32. Chapter 7 of the Federal Bankruptcy Code will deny a debtor a discharge when the debtor
- a. Made a preferential transfer to a creditor.
- b. Accidentally destroyed information relevant to the bankruptcy proceeding.
- c. Obtained a Chapter 7 discharge 10 years previously.
- d. Is a corporation or a partnership.

N90#33. A claim will **not** be discharged in a bankruptcy proceeding if it
- a. Is brought by a secured creditor and remains unsatisfied after receipt of the proceeds from the disposition of the collateral.
- b. Is for unintentional torts that resulted in bodily injury to the claimant.
- c. Arises from an extension of credit based upon false representations.
- d. Arises out of the breach of a contract by the debtor.

N90#34. On May 24, Knurl, an appliance dealer, filed for bankruptcy under the provisions of Chapter 7 of the Federal Bankruptcy Code. A trustee was appointed and an order for relief was entered. Knurl's nonexempt property was converted to cash, which is available to satisfy the following claims and expenses:

Claim by Card Corp. (one of Knurl's suppliers) for toasters ordered on May 11, and delivered on credit to Knurl on May 15.	$50,000
Fee earned by the bankruptcy trustee.	$12,000
Claim by Hill Co. for the delivery of televisions to Knurl on credit. The televisions were delivered on April 9, and a financing statement was properly filed on April 10. These televisions were sold by the trustee with Hill's consent for $7,000, their fair market value.	$ 7,000
Fees earned by the attorneys for the bankruptcy estate.	$ 8,000

The cash available for distribution includes the proceeds from the sale of the televisions. What amount will be distributed to Card if the cash available for distribution is $50,000?
- a. $23,000
- b. $30,000
- c. $31,000
- d. $43,000

N90#35. A bankrupt who filed voluntarily and received a discharge in bankruptcy under the provisions of Chapter 7 of the Federal Bankruptcy Code
- a. May obtain another voluntary discharge in bankruptcy under Chapter 7 after five years have elapsed from the date of the prior filing.
- b. Will receive a discharge of any and all debts owed.
- c. Is precluded from owning or operating a similar business for two years.
- d. Must surrender for distribution to the creditors any amount received as an inheritance if received within 180 days after filing the petition.

N89#22. Rolf, an individual, filed a voluntary petition in bankruptcy. A general discharge in bankruptcy will be denied if Rolf
- a. Negligently made preferential transfers to certain creditors within 90 days of filing the petition.
- b. Unjustifiably failed to preserve Rolf's books and records.
- c. Filed a fraudulent federal income tax return two years prior to filing the petition.
- d. Obtained a loan by using financial statements that Rolf knew were false.

N89#25. Filing a valid petition in bankruptcy acts as an automatic stay of actions to

	Garnish the debtor's wages	Collect alimony from the debtor
a.	Yes	Yes
b.	Yes	No
c.	No	Yes
d.	No	No

N89#26. Eagle Corp. is a general creditor of Dodd. Dodd filed a petition in bankruptcy under the liquidation provisions of the Bankruptcy Code. Eagle wishes to have the bankruptcy court either deny Dodd a general discharge or not have its debt discharged. The discharge will be granted and it will include Eagle's debt even if
- a. Dodd filed for and received a previous discharge in bankruptcy under the liquidation provisions within five years of the filing of the present petition.
- b. Eagle's debt is unscheduled.
- c. Eagle was a secured creditor **not** fully satisfied from the proceeds obtained on disposition of the collateral.

d. Dodd unjustifiably failed to preserve the records from which Dodd's financial condition might be ascertained.

N89#27. Which of the following assets would be included in a debtor's bankruptcy estate in a liquidation proceeding?
    a. Proceeds from a life insurance policy received 90 days after the petition was filed.
    b. An inheritance received 270 days after the petition was filed.
    c. Property from a divorce settlement received 365 days after the petition was filed.
    d. Wages earned by the debtor after the petition was filed.

N89#28. Which of the following unsecured debts of $500 each would have the highest relative priority in the distribution of a bankruptcy estate in a liquidation proceeding?
    a. Tax claims of state and municipal governmental units.
    b. Liabilities to employee benefit plans arising from services rendered during the month preceding the filing of the petition.
    c. Claims owed to customers who gave deposits for the purchase of undelivered consumer goods.
    d. Wages earned by employees during the month preceding the filing of the petition.

N89#29. As an alternative to bankruptcy liquidation, a business may reorganize under Chapter 11 of the Bankruptcy Code. Such a reorganization
    a. Requires the appointment of a trustee to administer the debtor organization.
    b. May be commenced by filing either a voluntary or involuntary petition.
    c. Never requires the appointment of a creditors' committee.
    d. May **not** be confirmed unless all creditors accept the plan.

V. Government Regulation of Business

A. Federal Securities Acts

R96#5. Under the Securities Exchange Act of 1934, the SEC is responsible for all of the following activities **except**
    a. Requiring disclosure of facts concerning offerings of securities listed on national securities exchanges.
    b. Prosecuting criminal violations of federal securities laws.
    c. Regulating the activities of securities brokers.
    d. Investigating securities fraud.

R96#6. Under the registration requirements of the Securities Act of 1933, which of the following items is (are) considered securities?

	Investment contracts	Collateral-trust certificates
a.	Yes	Yes
b.	Yes	No
c.	No	Yes
d.	No	No

N94#41. Under the Securities Act of 1933, which of the following statements most accurately reflects how securities registration affects an investor?
    a. The investor is provided with information on the stockholders of the offering corporation.
    b. The investor is provided with information on the principal purposes for which the offering's proceeds will be used.
    c. The investor is guaranteed by the SEC that the facts contained in the registration statement are accurate.
    d. The investor is assured by the SEC against loss resulting from purchasing the security.

N94#42. Which of the following securities would be regulated by the provisions of the Securities Act of 1933?
    a. Securities issued by not-for-profit, charitable organizations.
    b. Securities guaranteed by domestic governmental organizations.
    c. Securities issued by savings and loan associations.
    d. Securities issued by insurance companies.

N94#43. Which of the following requirements must be met by an issuer of securities who wants to make an offering by using shelf registration?

	Original registration statement must be kept updated	The offeror must be a first-time issuer of securities
a.	Yes	Yes
b.	Yes	No
c.	No	Yes
d.	No	No

N94#44. Under the Securities Act of 1933, which of the following statements concerning an offering of securities sold under a transaction exemption is correct?
    a. The offering is exempt from the anti-fraud provisions of the 1933 Act.
    b. The offering is subject to the registration requirements of the 1933 Act.
    c. Resales of the offering are exempt from the provisions of the 1933 Act.
    d. Resales of the offering must be made under a registration or a different exemption provision of the 1933 Act.

N94

Items 45 through 47 are based on the following:

Link Corp. is subject to the reporting provisions of the Securities Exchange Act of 1934.

45. Which of the following situations would require Link to be subject to the reporting provisions of the 1934 Act?

	Shares listed on a national securities exchange	More than one class of stock
a.	Yes	Yes
b.	Yes	No
c.	No	Yes
d.	No	No

46. Which of the following documents must Link file with the SEC?

	Quarterly reports (Form 10-Q)	Proxy statements
a.	Yes	Yes
b.	Yes	No
c.	No	Yes
d.	No	No

47. Which of the following reports must also be submitted to the SEC?

	Report by any party making a tender offer to purchase Link's stock	Report of proxy solicitations by Link stockholders
a.	Yes	Yes
b.	Yes	No
c.	No	Yes
d.	No	No

N94#48. Which of the following facts will result in an offering of securities being exempt from registration under the Securities Act of 1933?
   a. The securities are nonvoting preferred stock.
   b. The issuing corporation was closely held prior to the offering.
   c. The sale or offer to sell the securities is made by a person other than an issuer, underwriter, or dealer.
   d. The securities are AAA-rated debentures that are collateralized by first mortgages on property that has a market value of 200% of the offering price.

N94#52. Which of the following statements concerning an initial intrastate securities offering made by an issuer residing in and doing business in that state is correct?
   a. The offering would be exempt from the registration requirements of the Securities Act of 1933.
   b. The offering would be subject to the registration requirements of the Securities Exchange Act of 1934.
   c. The offering would be regulated by the SEC.
   d. The shares of the offering could **not** be resold to investors outside the state for at least one year.

M94#31. Which of the following statements concerning the prospectus required by the Securities Act of 1933 is correct?
   a. The prospectus is a part of the registration statement.
   b. The prospectus should enable the SEC to pass on the merits of the securities.
   c. The prospectus must be filed after an offer to sell.
   d. The prospectus is prohibited from being distributed to the public until the SEC approves the accuracy of the facts embodied therein.

M94#32. A preliminary prospectus, permitted under SEC Regulations, is known as the
   a. Unaudited prospectus.
   b. Qualified prospectus.
   c. "Blue-sky" prospectus.
   d. "Red-herring" prospectus.

M94#33. A tombstone advertisement
   a. May be substituted for the prospectus under certain circumstances.
   b. May contain an offer to sell securities.
   c. Notifies prospective investors that a previously-offered security has been withdrawn from the market and is therefore effectively "dead."
   d. Makes known the availability of a prospectus.

M94#34. Which of the following factors, by itself, requires a corporation to comply with the reporting requirements of the Securities Exchange Act of 1934?
   a. Six hundred employees.
   b. Shares listed on a national securities exchange.
   c. Total assets of $2 million.
   d. Four hundred holders of equity securities.

M94#35. Which of the following events must be reported to the SEC under the reporting provisions of the Securities Exchange Act of 1934?

	Tender offers	Insider trading	Soliciting proxies
a.	Yes	Yes	Yes
b.	Yes	Yes	No
c.	Yes	No	Yes
d.	No	Yes	Yes

M94#37. Which of the following transactions will be exempt from the full registration requirements of the Securities Act of 1933?
   a. All intrastate offerings.
   b. All offerings made under Regulation A.

c. Any resale of a security purchased under a Regulation D offering.
d. Any stockbroker transaction.

M94#38. Under the Securities Exchange Act of 1934, which of the following types of instruments is excluded from the definition of "securities"?
a. Investment contracts.
b. Convertible debentures.
c. Nonconvertible debentures.
d. Certificates of deposit.

M94#39. If securities are exempt from the registration provisions of the Securities Act of 1933, any fraud committed in the course of selling such securities can be challenged by

	SEC	Person defrauded
a.	Yes	Yes
b.	Yes	No
c.	No	Yes
d.	No	No

M94#40. Under Regulation D of the Securities Act of 1933, which of the following conditions apply to private placement offerings? The securities
a. Cannot be sold for longer than a six month period.
b. Cannot be the subject of an immediate unregistered reoffering to the public.
c. Must be sold to accredited institutional investors.
d. Must be sold to fewer than 20 non-accredited investors.

N93#37. One of the elements necessary to recover damages if there has been a material misstatement in a registration statement filed under the Securities Act of 1933 is that the
a. Issuer and plaintiff were in privity of contract with each other.
b. Issuer failed to exercise due care in connection with the sale of the securities.
c. Plaintiff gave value for the security.
d. Plaintiff suffered a loss.

N93#38. Lux Limited Partnership intends to offer $300,000 of its limited partnership interests under Rule 504 of Regulation D of the Securities Act of 1933. Which of the following statements is correct?
a. The resale of the limited partnership interests by a purchaser generally will be restricted.
b. The limited partnership interests may be sold only to accredited investors.
c. The exemption under Rule 504 is **not** available to an issuer of limited partnership interests.
d. The limited partnership interests may **not** be sold to more than 35 investors.

N93#40. An offering made under the provisions of Regulation A of the Securities Act of 1933 requires that the issuer
a. File an offering circular with the SEC.
b. Sell only to accredited investors.
c. Provide investors with the prior four years' audited financial statements.
d. Provide investors with a proxy registration statement.

N93#41. Adler, Inc. is a reporting company under the Securities Exchange Act of 1934. The only security it has issued is voting common stock. Which of the following statements is correct?
a. Because Adler is a reporting company, it is **not** required to file a registration statement under the Securities Act of 1933 for any future offerings of its common stock.
b. Adler need **not** file its proxy statements with the SEC because it has only one class of stock outstanding.
c. Any person who owns more than 10% of Adler's common stock must file a report with the SEC.
d. It is unnecessary for the required annual report (Form 10K) to include audited financial statements.

N93#42. Which of the following persons is **not** an insider of a corporation subject to the Securities Exchange Act of 1934 registration and reporting requirements?
a. An attorney for the corporation.
b. An owner of 5% of the corporation's outstanding debentures.
c. A member of the board of directors.
d. A stockholder who owns 10% of the outstanding common stock.

N93
Items 43 and 44 are based on the following:

Pix, Corp. is making a $6,000,000 stock offering. Pix wants the offering exempt from registration under the Securities Act of 1933.

43. Which of the following provisions of the Act would Pix have to comply with for the offering to be exempt?
a. Regulation A.
b. Regulation D, Rule 504.
c. Regulation D, Rule 505.
d. Regulation D, Rule 506.

44. Which of the following requirements would Pix have to comply with when selling the securities?
a. No more than 35 investors.
b. No more than 35 nonaccredited investors.
c. Accredited investors only.
d. Nonaccredited investors only.

N93#45. Frey, Inc. intends to make a $2,000,000 common stock offering under Rule 505 of Regulation D of the Securities Act of 1933. Frey
a. May sell the stock to an unlimited number of investors.

b. May make the offering through a general advertising.
c. Must notify the SEC within 15 days after the first sale of the offering.
d. Must provide all investors with a prospectus.

M93#29. Which of the following disclosures must be contained in a securities registration statement filed under the Securities Act of 1933?
a. A list of all existing stockholders.
b. The principal purposes for which the offering proceeds will be used.
c. A copy of the corporation's latest proxy solicitation statement.
d. The names of all prospective accredited investors.

M93#30. Which of the following is **least** likely to be considered a security under the Securities Act of 1933?
a. Stock options.
b. Warrants.
c. General partnership interests.
d. Limited partnership interests.

M93#31. Corporations that are exempt from registration under the Securities Exchange Act of 1934 are subject to the Act's
a. Antifraud provisions.
b. Proxy solicitation provisions.
c. Provisions dealing with the filing of annual reports.
d. Provisions imposing periodic audits.

M93#32. Under the Securities Exchange Act of 1934, a corporation with common stock listed on a national stock exchange
a. Is prohibited from making private placement offerings.
b. Is subject to having the registration of its securities suspended or revoked.
c. Must submit Form 10-K to the SEC except in those years in which the corporation has made a public offering.
d. Must distribute copies of Form 10-K to its stockholders.

M93#33. The Securities Act of 1933 provides an exemption from registration for

	Bonds issued by a municipality for governmental purposes	Securities issued by a not-for-profit charitable organization
a.	Yes	Yes
b.	Yes	No
c.	No	Yes
d.	No	No

M93#34. Which of the following securities is exempt from registration under the Securities Act of 1933?
a. Shares of nonvoting common stock, provided their par value is less than $1.00.
b. A class of stock given in exchange for another class by the issuer to its existing stockholders without the issuer paying a commission.
c. Limited partnership interests sold for the purpose of acquiring funds to invest in bonds issued by the United States.
d. Corporate debentures that were previously subject to an effective registration statement, provided they are convertible into shares of common stock.

M93#35. Regulation D of the Securities Act of 1933
a. Restricts the number of purchasers of an offering to 35.
b. Permits an exempt offering to be sold to both accredited and nonaccredited investors.
c. Is limited to offers and sales of common stock that do **not** exceed $1.5 million.
d. Is exclusively available to small business corporations as defined by Regulation D.

M92
Items 39 and 40 are based on the following:

World Corp. wanted to make a public offering of its common stock. On May 10, World prepared and filed a registration statement with the SEC. On May 20, World placed a "tombstone ad" announcing that it was making a public offering. On May 25, World issued a preliminary prospectus and the registration statement became effective on May 30.

39. On what date may World first make oral offers to sell the shares?
a. May 10.
b. May 20.
c. May 25.
d. May 30.

40. On what date may World first sell the shares?
a. May 10.
b. May 20.
c. May 25.
d. May 30.

M92
Items 41 and 42 are based on the following:

Integral Corp. has assets in excess of $4 million, has 350 stockholders, and has issued common and preferred stock. Integral is subject to the reporting provisions of the Securities Exchange Act of 1934. For its 1991 fiscal year, Integral filed the following with the SEC: quarterly reports, an annual report, and a periodic report listing newly appointed officers of the corporation. Integral did not notify the SEC of stockholder "short swing" profits; did not report that a competitor made a tender offer to Integral's stockholders; and did not report changes in the price of its stock as sold on the New York Stock Exchange.

41. Under SEC reporting requirements, which of the following was Integral required to do?
    a. Report the tender offer to the SEC.
    b. Notify the SEC of stockholder "short swing" profits.
    c. File the periodic report listing newly appointed officers.
    d. Report the changes in the market price of its stock.

42. Under the Securities Exchange Act of 1934, Integral must be registered with the SEC because
    a. It issues both common and preferred stock.
    b. Its shares are listed on a national stock exchange.
    c. It has more than 300 stockholders.
    d. Its shares are traded in interstate commerce.

M92#43. Under the Securities Act of 1933, which of the following securities must be registered?
    a. Bonds of a railroad corporation.
    b. Common stock of an insurance corporation.
    c. Preferred stock of a domestic bank corporation.
    d. Long-term notes of a charitable corporation.

M92#44. Data, Inc. intends to make a $375,000 common stock offering under Rule 504 of Regulation D of the Securities Act of 1933. Data
    a. May sell the stock to an unlimited number of investors.
    b. May make the offering through a general advertising.
    c. Must offer the stock for a period of more than 12 months.
    d. Must provide all investors with a prospectus.

M92#45. For an offering to be exempt under Regulation D of the Securities Act of 1933, Rules 504, 505, and 506 each require that
    a. There be a maximum of 35 unaccredited investors.
    b. All purchasers receive the issuer's financial information.
    c. The SEC be notified within 10 days of the first sale.
    d. The offering be made without general advertising.

N91#35. Exemption from registration under the Securities Act of 1933 would be available for
    a. Promissory notes maturing in 12 months.
    b. Securities of a bank.
    c. Limited partnership interests.
    d. Corporate bonds.

N91#36. When a common stock offering requires registration under the Securities Act of 1933,
    a. The registration statement is automatically effective when filed with the SEC.
    b. The issuer would act unlawfully if it were to sell the common stock without providing the investor with a prospectus.
    c. The SEC will determine the investment value of the common stock before approving the offering.
    d. The issuer may make sales 10 days after filing the registration statement.

N91#37. Under the Securities Act of 1933, an initial offering of securities must be registered with the SEC, unless
    a. The offering is made through a broker-dealer licensed in the states in which the securities are to be sold.
    b. The offering prospectus makes a fair and full disclosure of all risks associated with purchasing the securities.
    c. The issuer's financial condition meets certain standards established by the SEC.
    d. The type of security or the offering involved is exempt from registration.

N91#39. The reporting and registration provisions of the Securities Exchange Act of 1934
    a. Do **not** require registration by a corporation if its stock was originally issued under an offering exempt from registration under the Securities Act of 1933.
    b. Do **not** require registration by a corporation unless its stock is listed on a national securities exchange.
    c. Require a corporation reporting under the Act to register any offering of its securities under the Securities Act of 1933.
    d. Require a corporation reporting under the Act to file its proxy statements with the SEC even if it has only one class of stock outstanding.

N91#40. Kamp is offering $10 million of its securities. Under Rule 506 of Regulation D of the Securities Act of 1933,
    a. The securities may be debentures.
    b. Kamp must be a corporation.
    c. There must be more than 35 purchasers.
    d. Kamp may make a general solicitation in connection with the offering.

M91#39. Bird Corp. made a $500,000 exempt common stock offering under Rule 504 of Regulation D of the Securities Act of 1933. This made the shares restricted securities. As the issuer of restricted securities, Bird must
    a. Make a reasonable effort to determine that purchasers are buying for themselves and **not** for others.
    b. Publicly advertise that the shares are **not** registered.
    c. Provide information to all purchasers as to how they can register their shares so that resale will be permitted.
    d. Apply to the SEC for contingent exemptions so that purchasers may resell their shares as exempt.

M91#40. Universal Corp. intends to sell its common stock to the public in an interstate offering that will be registered under the Securities Act of 1933. Under the Act,
   a. Universal can make offers to sell its stock before filing a registration statement, provided that it does **not** actually issue stock certificates until after the registration is effective.
   b. Universal's registration statement becomes effective at the time it is filed, assuming the SEC does **not** object within 20 days thereafter.
   c. A prospectus must be delivered to each purchaser of Universal's common stock unless the purchaser qualifies as an accredited investor.
   d. Universal's filing of a registration statement with the SEC does **not** automatically result in compliance with the "blue-sky" laws of the states in which the offering will be made.

M91#41. The registration of a security under the Securities Act of 1933 provides an investor with
   a. A guarantee by the SEC that the facts contained in the registration statement are accurate.
   b. An assurance against loss resulting from purchasing the security.
   c. Information on the principal purposes for which the offering's proceeds will be used.
   d. Information on the issuing corporation's trade secrets.

M91#42. Which of the following statements is correct regarding the proxy solicitation requirements of Section 14(a) of the Securities Exchange Act of 1934?
   a. A corporation does **not** have to file proxy revocation solicitations with the SEC if it is a reporting company under the Securities Exchange Act of 1934.
   b. Current unaudited financial statements must be sent to each stockholder with every proxy solicitation.
   c. A corporation must file its proxy statements with the SEC if it is a reporting company under the Securities Exchange Act of 1934.
   d. In a proxy solicitation by management relating to election of officers, all stockholder proposals must be included in the proxy statement.

M91#44. The antifraud provisions of Rule 10b-5 of the Securities Exchange Act of 1934
   a. Apply only if the securities involved were registered under either the Securities Act of 1933 or the Securities Exchange Act of 1934.
   b. Require that the plaintiff show negligence on the part of the defendant in misstating facts.
   c. Require that the wrongful act must be accomplished through the mail, any other use of interstate commerce, or through a national securities exchange.
   d. Apply only if the defendant acted with intent to defraud.

M91#45. Which of the following securities is exempt from the registration requirements of the Securities Act of 1933?
   a. Common stock with **no** par value.
   b. Warrants to purchase preferred stock.
   c. Bonds issued by a charitable foundation.
   d. Convertible debentures issued by a corporation.

M91#46. Winslow, Inc. intends to make a $450,000 common stock offering under Rule 504 of Regulation D of the Securities Act of 1933. Winslow
   a. May make the offering through a general advertising.
   b. Must provide all investors with a prospectus.
   c. May sell the stock to an unlimited number of investors.
   d. Must offer the stock for a period of 24 months.

N90#39. The registration requirements of the Securities Act of 1933 are intended to provide information to the SEC to enable it to
   a. Evaluate the financial merits of the securities being offered.
   b. Ensure that investors are provided with adequate information on which to base investment decisions.
   c. Prevent public offerings of securities when management fraud or unethical conduct is suspected.
   d. Assure investors of the accuracy of the facts presented in the financial statements.

N90#40. The registration provisions of the Securities Exchange Act of 1934 require disclosure of all of the following information **except** the
   a. Names of owners of at least five (5) percent of any class of nonexempt equity security.
   b. Bonus and profit-sharing arrangements.
   c. Financial structure and nature of the business.
   d. Names of officers and directors.

N90#43. Imperial Corp. is offering $450,000 of its securities under Rule 504 of Regulation D of the Securities Act of 1933. Under Rule 504, Imperial is required to
   a. Provide full financial information to all nonaccredited purchasers.
   b. Make the offering through general solicitation.
   c. Register the offering under the provisions of the Securities Exchange Act of 1934.
   d. Notify the SEC within 15 days after the first sale of the securities.

N90#44. Hamilton Corp. is making a $4,500,000 securities offering under Rule 505 of Regulation D of the Securities Act of 1933. Under this regulation, Hamilton is
   a. Required to provide full financial information to accredited investors only.
   b. Allowed to make the offering through a general solicitation.

c. Limited to selling to **no** more than 35 nonaccredited investors.
d. Allowed to sell to an unlimited number of investors both accredited and nonaccredited.

N90#45. A $10,000,000 offering of corporate stock intended to be made pursuant to the provisions of Rule 506 of Regulation D of the Securities Act of 1933 would **not** be exempt under Rule 506 if
a. The offering was made through a general solicitation or advertising.
b. Some of the investors are nonaccredited.
c. There are more than 35 accredited investors.
d. The SEC was notified 14 days after the first sale of the securities.

M90#29. Under the Securities Act of 1933, the registration of an interstate securities offering is
a. Required only in transactions involving more than $500,000.
b. Mandatory, unless the cost to the issuer is prohibitive.
c. Required, unless there is an applicable exemption.
d. Intended to prevent the marketing of securities which pose serious financial risks.

M90#30. Dice, Inc. is a reporting company under the Securities Exchange Act of 1934. The only security Dice issued is voting common stock. With regard to Dice's proxy solicitation requirements, which of the following statements is correct?
a. Dice must file its proxy statements with the SEC even though it has only one class of stock outstanding.
b. Dice's current unaudited financial statements must be sent to each shareholder with every proxy solicitation.
c. Shareholder proposals need **not** be included in the proxy statements unless consented to by a majority of Dice's board of directors.
d. Dice need **not** provide any particular information to its shareholders unless Dice is soliciting proxies from them.

M90#31. Under the Securities Exchange Act of 1934, which of the following individuals would **not** be subject to the insider reporting provisions?
a. An owner of ten percent of a corporation's stock.
b. An owner of five percent of a corporation's voting stock.
c. The vice-president of marketing.
d. A member of the board of directors.

M90#32. Which of the following are exempt from the registration requirements of the Securities Act of 1933?
a. Bankers' acceptances with maturities at the time of issue ranging from one to two years.
b. Participation interests in money market funds that consist wholly of short-term commercial paper.
c. Corporate stock offered and sold only to residents of the state in which the issuer was incorporated and is doing all of its business.
d. All industrial development bonds issued by municipalities.

M90#33. Pate Corp. is offering $3 million of its securities solely to accredited investors. Under Regulation D of the Securities Act of 1933, Pate is
a. Not required to provide any specified information to the accredited investors.
b. Permitted to make a general solicitation.
c. Not allowed to sell to investors using purchaser representatives.
d. Required to provide accredited investors with audited financial statements for the three most recent fiscal years.

M90#37. Zack Limited Partnership intends to sell $6,000,000 of its limited partnership interests. Zack conducts all of its business activities in the state in which it was organized. Zack intends to use the offering proceeds to acquire municipal bonds. Which of the following statements is correct concerning the offering and the registration exemptions that might be available to Zack under the Securities Act of 1933?
a. The offering is exempt from registration because of the intended use of the offering proceeds.
b. Under Rule 147 (regarding intrastate offerings), Zack may make up to five offers to non-residents without jeopardizing the Rule 147 exemption.
c. If Zack complies with the requirements of Regulation D, any subsequent resale of a limited partnership interest by a purchaser is automatically exempt from registration.
d. If Zack complies with the requirements of Regulation D, Zack may make an unlimited number of offers to sell the limited partnership interests.

N89#33. One of the elements necessary to recover damages if there has been a material misstatement in a registration statement filed pursuant to the Securities Act of 1933 is that the
a. Plaintiff suffered a loss.
b. Plaintiff gave value for the security.
c. Issuer and plaintiff were in privity of contract with each other.
d. Issuer failed to exercise due care in connection with the sale of the securities.

N89#34. To be successful in a civil action under Section 11 of the Securities Act of 1933 concerning liability for a misleading registration statement, the plaintiff must prove

	Defendant's intent to deceive	Plaintiff's reliance on the registration statement
a.	Yes	Yes
b.	Yes	No
c.	No	Yes
d.	No	No

N89#35. An issuer making an offering under the provisions of Regulation A of the Securities Act of 1933 must file a(an)
a. Prospectus.
b. Offering statement.
c. Shelf registration.
d. Proxy.

N89#37. Rule 504 of Regulation D of the Securities Act of 1933 provides issuers with an exemption from registration for certain small issues. Which of the following statements is correct?
a. The rule allows sales to an unlimited number of investors.
b. The rule requires certain financial information to be furnished to the investors.
c. The issuer must offer the securities through general public advertising.
d. The issuer is **not** required to file anything with the SEC.

N89#38. Securities available under a private placement made pursuant to Regulation D of the Securities Act of 1933
a. Cannot be subject to the payment of commissions.
b. Must be sold to accredited institutional investors.
c. Must be sold to fewer than 20 non-accredited investors.
d. Cannot be the subject of an immediate unregistered reoffering to the public.

N89#39. Which of the following types of securities are generally exempt from registration under the Securities Act of 1933?

	Securities of nonprofit charitable organizations	Securities of savings and loan associations
a.	Yes	Yes
b.	Yes	No
c.	No	Yes
d.	No	No

M89#40. Acme Corp. intends to make a public offering in several states of 250,000 shares of its common stock. Under the Securities Act of 1933,
a. Acme must sell the common stock through licensed securities dealers.
b. Acme must, in all events, file a registration statement with the SEC because the offering will be made in several states.
c. Acme's use of any prospectus delivered to an unsophisticated investor must be accompanied by a simplified explanation of the offering.
d. Acme may make an oral offer to sell the common stock to a prospective investor after a registration statement has been filed but before it becomes effective.

M89#41. Pace Corp. previously issued 300,000 shares of its common stock. The shares are now actively traded on a national securities exchange. The original offering was exempt from registration under the Securities Act of 1933. Pace has $2,500,000 in assets and 425 shareholders. With regard to the Securities Exchange Act of 1934, Pace is
a. Required to file a registration statement because its assets exceed $2,000,000 in value.
b. Required to file a registration statement even though it has fewer than 500 shareholders.
c. Not required to file a registration statement because the original offering of its stock was exempt from registration.
d. Not required to file a registration statement unless insiders own at least 5% of its outstanding shares of stock.

M89#42. Rice, Inc. is a reporting company under the Securities Exchange Act of 1934. The only security it has issued is its voting common stock. Which one of the following statements is correct?
a. Any person who owns more than 5% of Rice's common stock must file a report with the SEC.
b. Rice need **not** file its proxy statements with the SEC because it has only one class of stock outstanding.
c. It is unnecessary for the required annual report (Form 10-K) to include audited financial statements.
d. Because Rice is a reporting company, it is **not** required to file a registration statement under the Securities Act of 1933 for any future offerings of its common stock.

M89
Item 45 is based on the following:

Maco Limited Partnership intends to sell $6,000,000 of its limited partnership interests. The state in which Maco was organized is also the state in which it carries on all of its business activities.

45. If Maco intends to offer the limited partnership interests in reliance on Rule 506 of Regulation D under the Securities Act of 1933 to prospective investors residing in several states, which of the following statements is correct?
a. The offering will be exempt from the anti-fraud provisions of the Securities Exchange Act of 1934.
b. Any subsequent resale of a limited partnership interest by a purchaser will be exempt from registration.
c. Maco may make an unlimited number of offers to sell the limited partnership interests.
d. No more than 35 purchasers may acquire the limited partnership interests.

B. Employment Regulation

R97#4. Which of the following statements is(are) correct regarding the authority of the Occupational Safety and Health Administration (OSHA)?

Selected Questions

I. OSHA is authorized to establish standards that protect employees from exposure to substances that may be harmful to their health.
II. OSHA is authorized to develop safety equipment and require employers to instruct employees in its use.

   a. I only.
   b. II only.
   c. Both I and II.
   d. Neither I nor II.

R96#14. Under the federal Age Discrimination in Employment Act, which of the following practices is prohibited?
   a. Termination of employees between the ages of 65 and 70 for cause.
   b. Mandatory retirement of any employee.
   c. Unintentional age discrimination.
   d. Termination of employees as part of a rational business decision.

N95#31. Under the Federal Insurance Contributions Act (FICA), which of the following acts will cause an employer to be liable for penalties?

	Failure to supply taxpayer identification numbers	Failure to make timely FICA deposits
a.	Yes	Yes
b.	Yes	No
c.	No	Yes
d.	No	No

N95#33. Which of the following claims is(are) generally covered under workers' compensation statutes?

	Occupational disease	Employment aggravated pre-existing disease
a.	Yes	Yes
b.	Yes	No
c.	No	Yes
d.	No	No

N95#34. Generally, which of the following statements concerning workers' compensation laws is correct?
   a. The amount of damages recoverable is based on comparative negligence.
   b. Employers are strictly liable without regard to whether or **not** they are at fault.
   c. Workers' compensation benefits are **not** available if the employee is negligent.
   d. Workers' compensation awards are payable for life.

N95#35. Under the Age Discrimination in Employment Act, which of the following remedies is(are) available to a covered employee?

	Early retirement	Back pay
a.	Yes	Yes
b.	Yes	No
c.	No	Yes
d.	No	No

N95#36. Which of the following Acts prohibit(s) an employer from discriminating among employees based on sex?

	Equal Pay Act	Title VII of the Civil Rights Act
a.	Yes	Yes
b.	Yes	No
c.	No	Yes
d.	No	No

N95#37. Under the Fair Labor Standards Act, which of the following pay bases may be used to pay covered, nonexempt exployees who earn, on average, the minimum hourly wage?

	Hourly	Weekly	Monthly
a.	Yes	Yes	Yes
b.	Yes	Yes	No
c.	Yes	No	Yes
d.	No	Yes	Yes

N95#38. Under the Fair Labor Standards Act, if a covered, nonexempt employee works consecutive weeks of 45, 42, 38, and 33 hours, how many hours of overtime must be paid to the employee?
   a. 0
   b. 7
   c. 18
   d. 20

N95#39. Under the Employee Retirement Income Security Act of 1974 (ERISA), which of the following areas of private employer pension plans is(are) regulated?

	Employee vesting	Plan funding
a.	Yes	Yes
b.	Yes	No
c.	No	Yes
d.	No	No

N95#40. Which of the following employee benefits is(are) exempt from the provisions of the National Labor Relations Act?

	Sick pay	Vacation pay
a.	Yes	Yes
b.	Yes	No
c.	No	Yes
d.	No	No

M95#37. Under which of the following conditions is an on-site inspection of a workplace by an investigator from

the Occupational Safety and Health Administration (OSHA) permissible?
a. Only if OSHA obtains a search warrant after showing probable cause.
b. Only if the inspection is conducted after working hours.
c. At the request of employees.
d. After OSHA provides the employer with at least 24 hours notice of the prospective inspection.

M95#38. Under the provisions of the Americans With Disabilities Act of 1990, in which of the following areas is a disabled person protected from discrimination?

	Public transportation	Privately operated public accommodations
a.	Yes	Yes
b.	Yes	No
c.	No	Yes
d.	No	No

M95#39. When verifying a client's compliance with statutes governing employees' wages and hours, an auditor should check the client's personnel records against relevant provisions of which of the following statutes?
a. National Labor Relations Act.
b. Fair Labor Standards Act.
c. Taft-Hartley Act.
d. Americans With Disabilities Act.

M95#40. Under the provisions of the Employee Retirement Income Security Act of 1974 (ERISA), which of the following statements is correct?
a. Employees are entitled to have an employer established pension plan.
b. Employers are prevented from unduly delaying an employee's participation in a pension plan.
c. Employers are prevented from managing retirement plans.
d. Employees are entitled to make investment decisions.

N94#36. Which of the following provisions is basic to all workers' compensation systems?
a. The injured employee must prove the employer's negligence.
b. The employer may invoke the traditional defense of contributory negligence.
c. The employer's liability may be ameliorated by a co-employee's negligence under the fellow-servant rule.
d. The injured employee is allowed to recover on strict liability theory.

N94#38. Under the Federal Age Discrimination in Employment Act, which of the following practices would be prohibited?

	Compulsory retirement of employees below the age of 65	Termination of employees between the ages of 65 and 70 for cause
a.	Yes	Yes
b.	Yes	No
c.	No	Yes
d.	No	No

N94#39. Under the Federal Fair Labor Standards Act, which of the following would be regulated?

	Minimum wage	Overtime	Number of hours in the workweek
a.	Yes	Yes	Yes
b.	Yes	No	Yes
c.	Yes	Yes	No
d.	No	Yes	Yes

N94#40. Which of the following statements correctly describes the funding of noncontributory pension plans?
a. All of the funds are provided by the employees.
b. All of the funds are provided by the employer.
c. The employer and employee each provide 50% of the funds.
d. The employer provides 90% of the funds, and each employee contributes 10%.

M94#27. Which of the following statements is correct regarding the scope and provisions of the Occupational Safety and Health Act (OSHA)?
a. OSHA requires employers to provide employees a workplace free from risk.
b. OSHA prohibits an employer from discharging an employee for revealing OSHA violations.
c. OSHA may inspect a workplace at any time regardless of employer objection.
d. OSHA preempts state regulation of workplace safety.

M94#28. Under Title VII of the 1964 Civil Rights Act, which of the following forms of discrimination is **not** prohibited?
a. Sex.
b. Age.
c. Race.
d. Religion.

M94#29. Which of the following statements is correct under the Federal Fair Labor Standards Act?
a. Some workers may be included within the minimum wage provisions but exempt from the overtime provisions.
b. Some workers may be included within the overtime provisions but exempt from the minimum wage provisions.
c. All workers are required to be included within both the minimum wage provisions and the overtime provisions.

d. Possible exemptions from the minimum wage provisions and the overtime provisions must be determined by the union contract in effect at the time.

M94#30. Under the Federal Consolidated Budget Reconciliation Act of 1985 (COBRA), when an employee voluntarily resigns from a job, the former employee's group health insurance coverage that was in effect during the period of employment with the company
 a. Automatically ceases for the former employee and spouse, if the resignation occurred before normal retirement age.
 b. Automatically ceases for the former employee's spouse, but continues for the former employee for an 18-month period at the former employer's expense.
 c. May be retained by the former employee at the former employee's expense for at least 18 months after leaving the company, but must be terminated for the former employee's spouse.
 d. May be retained for the former employee and spouse at the former employee's expense for at least 18 months after leaving the company.

N93#36. Which one of the following statements concerning workers' compensation laws is generally correct?
 a. Employers are strictly liable without regard to whether or **not** they are at fault.
 b. Workers' compensation benefits are **not** available if the employee is negligent.
 c. Workers' compensation awards are **not** reviewable by the courts.
 d. The amount of damages recoverable is based on comparative negligence.

M93#28. Kroll, an employee of Acorn, Inc., was injured in the course of employment while operating a forklift manufactured and sold to Acorn by Trell Corp. The forklift was defectively designed by Trell. Under the state's mandatory workers' compensation statute, Kroll will be successful in

	Obtaining workers' compensation benefits	A negligence action against Acorn
a.	Yes	Yes
b.	Yes	No
c.	No	Yes
d.	No	No

M92#38. Workers' Compensation Acts require an employer to
 a. Provide coverage for all eligible employees.
 b. Withhold employee contributions from the wages of eligible employees.
 c. Pay an employee the difference between disability payments and full salary.
 d. Contribute to a federal insurance fund.

N91#33. An unemployed CPA generally would receive unemployment compensation benefits if the CPA

 a. Was fired as a result of the employer's business reversals.
 b. Refused to accept a job as an accountant while receiving extended benefits.
 c. Was fired for embezzling from a client.
 d. Left work voluntarily without good cause.

N91#34. Workers' Compensation laws provide for all of the following benefits **except**
 a. Burial expenses.
 b. Full pay during disability.
 c. The cost of prosthetic devices.
 d. Monthly payments to surviving dependent children.

M91#36. Social security benefits may include all of the following **except**
 a. Payments to divorced spouses.
 b. Payments to disabled children.
 c. Medicare payments.
 d. Medicaid payments.

M91#38. The primary purpose for enacting Workers' Compensation statutes was to
 a. Eliminate all employer-employee negligence lawsuits.
 b. Enable employees to recover for injuries regardless of negligence.
 c. Prevent employee negligence suits against third parties.
 d. Allow employees to recover additional compensation for employer negligence.

N90#38. If an employee is injured, full workers' compensation benefits are **not** payable if the employee
 a. Was injured because of failing to abide by written safety procedures.
 b. Was injured because of the acts of fellow employees.
 c. Intentionally caused self-inflicted injury.
 d. Brought a civil suit against a third party who caused the injury.

M90#26. Tower drives a truck for Musgrove Produce, Inc. The truck is owned by Musgrove. Tower is paid on the basis of a formula that takes into consideration the length of the trip, cargo, and fuel consumed. Tower is responsible for repairing or replacing all flat tires. Musgrove is responsible for all other truck maintenance. Tower drives only for Musgrove. If Tower is a common law employee and **not** an independent contractor, which of the following statements is correct?
 a. All social security retirement benefits are fully includible in the determination of Tower's federal taxable income if certain gross income limitations are exceeded.
 b. Musgrove remains primarily liable for Tower's share of FICA taxes if it fails to withhold and pay the taxes on Tower's wages.
 c. Musgrove would **not** have to withhold FICA taxes if Tower elected to make FICA contributions as a self-employed person.

B-59

d. Bonuses or vacation pay that are paid to Tower by Musgrove are **not** subject to FICA taxes because they are **not** regarded as regular compensation.

N89#31. Which of the following statements is **not** correct concerning federal unemployment insurance?
    a. Federal law provides general guidelines, standards, and requirements for the program.
    b. The states administer the benefit payments under the program.
    c. The program is funded by taxes imposed on employers and employees.
    d. The federal unemployment tax is calculated as a fixed percentage of each covered employee's salary up to a stated maximum.

N89#32. An employee will generally be precluded from collecting full workers' compensation benefits when the injury is caused by

	Noncompliance with the employer's rules	An intentional, self-inflicted action
a.	No	No
b.	Yes	Yes
c.	No	Yes
d.	Yes	No

M89#37. Under the Federal Insurance Contributions Act (FICA) and the Social Security Act (SSA),
    a. Persons who are self-employed are **not** required to make FICA contributions.
    b. Employees who participate in private retirement plans are **not** required to make FICA contributions.
    c. Death benefits are payable to an employee's survivors only if the employee dies before reaching the age of retirement.
    d. The receipt of earned income by a person who is also receiving social security retirement benefits may result in a reduction of such benefits.

M89#38. Which one of the following statements concerning workers' compensation laws is generally correct?
    a. Workers' compensation laws are very narrowly construed against employees.
    b. The amount of damages recoverable is based on comparative negligence.
    c. Employers are strictly liable without regard to whether or not they are at fault.
    d. Workers' compensation benefits are **not** available if the employee is grossly negligent.

C. Environmental Regulation

R96#7. Under the federal Clean Air Act, which of the following statements is correct?
    a. Power plants are required to eliminate all air polluting emissions.
    b. Factories that emit toxic air pollutants are required to reduce emissions by installing the best available emission control technology.
    c. Automobile manufacturers are required to have emission control equipment installed on previously manufactured vehicles.
    d. Homeowners are required to remove all pollutants from their residences.

N95#57. Which of the following activities is(are) regulated under the Federal Water Pollution Control Act (Clean Water Act)?

	Discharge of heated water by nuclear power plants	Dredging of wetlands
a.	Yes	Yes
b.	Yes	No
c.	No	Yes
d.	No	No

M95#56. Under the Comprehensive Environmental Response, Compensation, and Liability Act (CERCLA), commonly known as Superfund, which of the following parties would be liable to the Environmental Protection Agency (EPA) for the expense of cleaning up a hazardous waste disposal site?

I. The current owner or operator of the site.
II. The person who transported the wastes to the site.
III. The person who owned or operated the site at the time of the disposal.

    a. I and II.
    b. I and III.
    c. II and III.
    d. I, II, and III.

VI. Uniform Commercial Code

A. Negotiable Instruments

R96#8. Under the Negotiable Instruments Article of the UCC, when an instrument is indorsed "Pay to John Doe" and signed "Faye Smith," which of the following statements is(are) correct?

	Payment of the instrument is guaranteed	The instrument can be further negotiated
a.	Yes	Yes
b.	Yes	No
c.	No	Yes
d.	No	No

M95#41. Under the Negotiable Instruments Article of the UCC, which of the following documents would be considered an order to pay?

I. Draft
II. Certificate of deposit

  a. I only.
  b. II only.
  c. Both I and II.
  d. Neither I nor II.

M95#42.

```
To: Middlesex National Bank
    Nassau, N.Y.
                                  September 15, 1994

Pay to the order of   Robert Silver    $4,000.00

Four Thousand and xx/100      Dollars

on October 1, 1994

                                    Lynn Dexter
                                    Lynn Dexter
```

The above instrument is a
  a. Draft.
  b. Postdated check.
  c. Trade acceptance.
  d. Promissory note.

M95#43. Under the Negotiable Instruments Article of the UCC, for an instrument to be negotiable it must
  a. Be payable to order or to bearer.
  b. Be signed by the payee.
  c. Contain references to all agreements between the parties.
  d. Contain necessary conditions of payment.

M95#44. Under the Negotiable Instruments Article of the UCC, which of the following circumstances would prevent a promissory note from being negotiable?
  a. An extension clause that allows the maker to elect to extend the time for payment to a date specified in the note.
  b. An acceleration clause that allows the holder to move up the maturity date of the note in the event of default.
  c. A person having a power of attorney signs the note on behalf of the maker.
  d. A clause that allows the maker to satisfy the note by the performance of services or the payment of money.

M95#45. Under the Negotiable Instruments Article of the UCC, which of the following requirements must be met for a transferee of order paper to become a holder?

I. Possession
II. Endorsement of transferor

  a. I only.
  b. II only.
  c. Both I and II.
  d. Neither I nor II.

M95#46. Under the Negotiable Instruments Article of the UCC, which of the following requirements must be met for a person to be a holder in due course of a promissory note?
  a. The note must be payable to bearer.
  b. The note must be negotiable.
  c. All prior holders must have been holders in due course.
  d. The holder must be the payee of the note.

M95#47. Under the Negotiable Instruments Article of the UCC, which of the following circumstances would prevent a person from becoming a holder in due course of an instrument?
  a. The person was notified that payment was refused.
  b. The person was notified that one of the prior endorsers was discharged.
  c. The note was collateral for a loan.
  d. The note was purchased at a discount.

M95#48. Under the Negotiable Instruments Article of the UCC, which of the following statements best describes the effect of a person endorsing a check "without recourse"?
  a. The person has **no** liability to prior endorsers.
  b. The person makes **no** promise or guarantee of payment on dishonor.
  c. The person gives **no** warranty protection to later transferees.
  d. The person converts the check into order paper.

M95#49. Under the Negotiable Instruments Article of the UCC, in a nonconsumer transaction, which of the following are real defenses available against a holder in due course?

	Material alteration	Discharge in bankruptcy	Breach of contract
a.	No	Yes	Yes
b.	Yes	Yes	No
c.	No	No	Yes
d.	Yes	No	No

M95#50.

```
         Pay to Ann Tyler
           Paul Tyler

           Ann Tyler



          Mary Thomas

          ~~Betty Ash~~


        Pay George Green Only
           Susan Town
```

Susan Town, on receiving the above instrument, struck Betty Ash's endorsement. Under the Negotiable Instruments Article of the UCC, which of the endorsers of the above instrument will be completely discharged from secondary liability to later endorsers of the instrument?
    a. Ann Tyler
    b. Mary Thomas
    c. Betty Ash
    d. Susan Town

M93
Items 36 through 39 are based on the following:

On February 15, 1993, P.D. Stone obtained the following instrument from Astor Co. for $1,000. Stone was aware that Helco, Inc. disputed liability under the instrument because of an alleged breach by Astor of the referenced computer purchase agreement. On March 1, 1993, Willard Bank obtained the instrument from Stone for $3,900. Willard had no knowledge that Helco disputed liability under the instrument.

                           February 12, 1993

Helco, Inc. promises to pay to Astor Co. or bearer the sum of $4,900 (four thousand four hundred and 00/100 dollars) on March 12, 1993 (maker may elect to extend due date to March 31, 1993) with interest thereon at the rate of 12% per annum.

                HELCO, INC.

        By: _A.J. Help_____
             A.J. Help, President

Reference: Computer purchase agreement dated February 12, 1993

The reverse side of the instrument is endorsed as follows:

Pay to the order of Willard Bank, without recourse

                _P.D. Stone_____
                P.D. Stone
---

36. The instrument is a
    a. Promissory note.
    b. Sight draft.
    c. Check.
    d. Trade acceptance.

37. The instrument is
    a. Nonnegotiable, because of the reference to the computer purchase agreement.
    b. Nonnegotiable, because the numerical amount differs from the written amount.
    c. Negotiable, even though the maker has the right to extend the time for payment.
    d. Negotiable, when held by Astor, but nonnegotiable when held by Willard Bank.

38. Which of the following statements is correct?
    a. Willard Bank **cannot** be a holder in due course because Stone's endorsement was without recourse.
    b. Willard Bank must endorse the instrument to negotiate it.
    c. Neither Willard Bank **nor** Stone are holders in due course.
    d. Stone's endorsement was required for Willard Bank to be a holder in due course.

39. If Willard Bank demands payment from Helco and Helco refuses to pay the instrument because of Astor's breach of the computer purchase agreement, which of the following statements would be correct?
    a. Willard Bank is **not** a holder in due course because Stone was **not** a holder in due course.
    b. Helco will **not** be liable to Willard Bank because of Astor's breach.
    c. Stone will be the only party liable to Willard Bank because he was aware of the dispute between Helco and Astor.
    d. Helco will be liable to Willard Bank because Willard Bank is a holder in due course.

M93#40. An instrument reads as follows:

$10,000   Ludlow, Vermont   February 1, 1993

I promise to pay to the order of Custer Corp. $10,000 within 10 days after the sale of my two-carat diamond ring. I pledge the sale proceeds to secure my obligation hereunder.

                              _R. Harris_____
                              R. Harris

Which of the following statements correctly describes the above instrument?
- a. The instrument is nonnegotiable because it is **not** payable at a definite time.
- b. The instrument is nonnegotiable because it is secured by the proceeds of the sale of the ring.
- c. The instrument is a negotiable promissory note.
- d. The instrument is a negotiable sight draft payable on demand.

M93#41. The following endorsements appear on the back of a negotiable promissory note payable to Lake Corp.

Pay to John Smith only
Frank Parker, President of Lake Corp.

John Smith

Pay to the order of Sharp, Inc., without recourse, but only if Sharp delivers computers purchased by Mary Harris by March 15, 1993
Mary Harris

Sarah Sharp, President of Sharp, Inc.

Which of the following statements is correct?
- a. The note became nonnegotiable as a result of Parker's endorsement.
- b. Harris' endorsement was a conditional promise to pay and caused the note to be nonnegotiable.
- c. Smith's endorsement effectively prevented further negotiation of the note.
- d. Harris' signature was **not** required to effectively negotiate the note to Sharp.

M93#42. Robb, a minor, executed a promissory note payable to bearer and delivered it to Dodsen in payment for a stereo system. Dodsen negotiated the note for value to Mellon by delivery alone and without endorsement. Mellon endorsed the note in blank and negotiated it to Bloom for value. Bloom's demand for payment was refused by Robb because the note was executed when Robb was a minor. Bloom gave prompt notice of Robb's default to Dodsen and Mellon. None of the holders of the note were aware of Robb's minority. Which of the following parties will be liable to Bloom?

	Dodsen	Mellon
a.	Yes	Yes
b.	Yes	No
c.	No	No
d.	No	Yes

M93#43. Vex Corp. executed a negotiable promissory note payable to Tamp, Inc. The note was collateralized by some of Vex's business assets. Tamp negotiated the note to Miller for value. Miller endorsed the note in blank and negotiated it to Bilco for value. Before the note became due, Bilco agreed to release Vex's collateral. Vex refused to pay Bilco when the note became due. Bilco promptly notified Miller and Tamp of Vex's default. Which of the following statements is correct?
- a. Bilco will be unable to collect from Miller because Miller's endorsement was in blank.
- b. Bilco will be able to collect from either Tamp or Miller because Bilco was a holder in due course.
- c. Bilco will be unable to collect from either Tamp or Miller because of Bilco's release of the collateral.
- d. Bilco will be able to collect from Tamp because Tamp was the original payee.

N92#33. Which of the following negotiable instruments is subject to the UCC Negotiable Instruments Article?
- a. Corporate bearer bond with a maturity date of January 1, 2001.
- b. Installment note payable on the first day of each month.
- c. Warehouse receipt.
- d. Bill of lading payable to order.

N92#34. Which of the following conditions, if present on an otherwise negotiable instrument, would affect the instrument's negotiability?
- a. The instrument is payable six months after the death of the maker.
- b. The instrument is payable at a definite time subject to an accelerated clause in the event of a default.
- c. The instrument is postdated.
- d. The instrument contains a promise to provide additional collateral if there is a decrease in value of the existing collateral.

N92#40. A maker of a note will have a real defense against a holder in due course as a result of any of the following conditions **except**
- a. Discharge in bankruptcy.
- b. Forgery.
- c. Fraud in the execution.
- d. Lack of consideration.

M92#46. The following endorsements appear on the back of a negotiable promissory note made payable "to bearer." Clark has possession of the note.

Pay to Sam North
Alice Fox

Sam North

(without recourse)

Which of the following statements is correct?
- a. Clark's unqualified endorsement is required to further negotiate the note.
- b. To negotiate the note, Clark must have given value for it.

B-63

c. Clark is **not** a holder because North's qualified endorsement makes the note nonnegotiable.
d. Clark can negotiate the note by delivery alone.

M92#47. To the extent that a holder of a negotiable promissory note is a holder in due course, the holder takes the note free of which of the following defenses?
a. Minority of the maker where it is a defense to enforcement of a contract.
b. Forgery of the maker's signature.
c. Discharge of the maker in bankruptcy.
d. Nonperformance of a condition precedent.

M92#48. Which of the following actions does **not** discharge a prior party to a commercial instrument?
a. Good faith payment or satisfaction of the instrument.
b. Cancellation of that prior party's endorsement.
c. The holder's oral renunciation of that prior party's liability.
d. The holder's intentional destruction of the instrument.

N91
Items 46 and 47 relate to the following instrument:

```
                                    May 19, 1991

I promise to pay to the order of A.B. Shark $1,000
(One thousand and one hundred dollars) with inter-
est thereon at the rate of 12% per annum.

                    T. T. Tile
                    ─────────
                    T. T. Tile

                    Guaranty

I personally guaranty payment by T. T. Tile.

                    N. A. Abner
                    ─────────
                    N. A. Abner
```

46. The instrument is a
    a. Promissory demand note.
    b. Sight draft.
    c. Check.
    d. Trade acceptance.

47. The instrument is
    a. Nonnegotiable even though it is payable on demand.
    b. Nonnegotiable because the numeric amount differs from the written amount.
    c. Negotiable even though a payment date is **not** specified.
    d. Negotiable because of Abner's guaranty.

N91#48. For a person to be a holder in due course of a promissory note

a. The note must be payable in U.S. currency to the holder.
b. The holder must be the payee of the note.
c. The note must be negotiable.
d. All prior holders must have been holders in due course.

N91#50. A subsequent holder of a negotiable instrument may cause the discharge of a prior holder of the instrument by any of the following actions **except**
a. Unexcused delay in presentment of a time draft.
b. Procuring certification of a check.
c. Giving notice of dishonor the day after dishonor.
d. Material alteration of a note.

N90#46. Union Co. possesses the following instrument:

```
Holt, MT            $4,000         April 15, 1990

Fifty days after date, or sooner, the undersigned
promises to pay to the order of

                    Union Co.
                    ─────────
                    Four Thousand            Dollars
at                  Salem Bank, Holt, MT

            Ten percent interest per annum.

This instrument is secured by the maker's business
inventory.

                                EASY, INC.

                    BY: ─────Thomas Foy─────
                            Thomas Foy, President
```

Assuming all other requirements of negotiability are satisfied, this instrument is
a. Not negotiable because of a lack of a definite time for payment.
b. Not negotiable because the amount due is unspecified.
c. Negotiable because it is secured by the maker's inventory.
d. Negotiable because it is payable in a sum certain in money.

N90#47. A $5,000 promissory note payable to the order of Neptune is discounted to Bane by blank endorsement for $4,000. King steals the note from Bane and sells it to Ott who promises to pay King $4,500. After paying King $3,000, Ott learns that King stole the note. Ott makes no further payment to King. Ott is
a. A holder in due course to the extent of $5,000.
b. An ordinary holder to the extent of $4,500.
c. A holder in due course to the extent of $3,000.
d. An ordinary holder to the extent of $0.

N90#48. A maker of a note will have a valid defense against a holder in due course as a result of any of the following conditions **except**
    a. Lack of consideration.
    b. Infancy.
    c. Forgery.
    d. Fraud in the execution.

N90#49. The following note was executed by Elizabeth Quinton on April 17, 1990 and delivered to Ian Wolf:

(Face)

April 17, 1990

On demand, the undersigned promises to pay to the order of Ian Wolf

Seven Thousand and 00/100 ---------------DOLLARS

Elizabeth Quinton
Elizabeth Quinton

(Back)

Ian Wolf
Ian Wolf

Pay: George Vernon
Samuel Thorn
Samuel Thorn

Pay: Alan Yule
George Vernon
George Vernon

Alan Yule
Alan Yule

In sequence, beginning with Wolf's receipt of the note, this note is properly characterized as what type of commercial paper?
    a. Bearer, bearer, order, order, order.
    b. Order, bearer, order, order, bearer.
    c. Order, order, bearer, order, bearer.
    d. Bearer, order, order, order, bearer.

M90#36. Below is a copy of a note Prestige Properties obtained from Tim Hart in connection with Hart's purchase of land located in Hunter, MT. The note was given for the balance due on the purchase and was secured by a first mortgage on the land.

$200,000.00   Hunter, MT
November 30, 1989

    For value received, six years after date, I promise to pay to the order of Prestige Properties TWO HUNDRED THOUSAND and 00/100 DOLLARS with interest at 11% compounded annually until fully paid. This instrument arises out of the sale of land located in MT and the law of MT is to be applied to any question which may arise. It is secured by a first mortgage on the land conveyed. It is further agreed that:
1. Maker will pay the costs of collection including attorney's fees upon default.
2. Maker may repay the amount outstanding on any anniversary date of this note.

Tim Hart
Tim Hart

This note is a
    a. Nonnegotiable promissory note because it is secured by a first mortgage.
    b. Negotiable promissory note.
    c. Nonnegotiable promissory note because it permits prepayment and requires the maker's payment of the costs of collection and attorney's fees.
    d. Negotiable investment security under the UCC.

M90#38. Bond fraudulently induced Teal to make a note payable to Wilk, to whom Bond was indebted. Bond delivered the note to Wilk. Wilk negotiated the instrument to Monk, who purchased it with knowledge of the fraud and after it was overdue. If Wilk qualifies as a holder in due course, which of the following statements is correct?
    a. Monk has the standing of a holder in due course through Wilk.
    b. Teal can successfully assert the defense of fraud in the inducement against Monk.
    c. Monk personally qualifies as a holder in due course.
    d. Teal can successfully assert the defense of fraud in the inducement against Wilk.

M90#39. A holder in due course will take free of which of the following defenses?
    a. Infancy, to the extent that it is a defense to a simple contract.
    b. Discharge of the maker in bankruptcy.
    c. A wrongful filling-in of the amount payable that was omitted from the instrument.
    d. Duress of a nature that renders the obligation of the party a nullity.

N89#42. Which of the following is required to make an instrument negotiable?
    a. Stated date of issue.
    b. An indorsement by the payee.

c. Stated location for payment.
d. Payment only in legal tender.

M89#46. On April 2, 1989, Harris agreed to sell a computer to Cross for $390. At the time of delivery, Cross gave Harris $90 and a written instrument, signed by Cross, in which Cross promised to pay Harris the balance on April 20, 1989. The instrument also made a reference to the sale of the computer. Under the UCC Negotiable Instruments Article, the instrument is a
   a. Promissory note.
   b. Non-negotiable draft.
   c. Trade acceptance.
   d. Negotiable time draft.

M89#48. The following instrument is in the possession of Bill North:

On May 30, 1989, I promise to pay Bill North, the bearer of this document, $1,800.

Joseph Peppers
Joseph Peppers

Re: Auto Purchase Contract

This instrument is
   a. Non-negotiable because it is undated.
   b. Non-negotiable because it is **not** payable to order or bearer.
   c. Negotiable even though it makes reference to the contract out of which it arose.
   d. Negotiable because it is payable at a definite time.

M89#49. Which one of the following aspects of an otherwise negotiable promissory note will render it non-negotiable?
   a. The maker is obligated to pay a sum certain to the payee but may instead deliver to the payee goods of equal value.
   b. The maker has the right to prepay the note, subject to a prepayment penalty of 10% of the amount prepaid.
   c. The maker is obligated to pay the payee's costs of collection upon default by the maker.
   d. The maker intentionally using a rubber stamp to sign the note.

M89#52. Jim Bass is in possession of a negotiable promissory note made payable "to bearer." Bass acquired the note from Mary Frank for value. The maker of the note was Fred Jackson. The following indorsements appear on the back of the note:

Sam Peters
Pay to Jim Bass

Mary Frank
Jim Bass
(without recourse)

Bass presented the note to Jackson, who refused to pay it because he was financially unable to do so. Which of the following statements is correct?
   a. Peters is **not** secondarily liable on the note because his indorsement was unnecessary for negotiation.
   b. Peters is **not** secondarily liable to Bass.
   c. Frank will probably **not** be liable to Bass unless Bass gives notice to Frank of Jackson's refusal to pay within a reasonable time.
   d. Bass would have had secondary liability to Peters and Frank if he had **not** qualified his indorsement.

B. Sales

R97#13. Under the Sales Article of the UCC, most goods sold by merchants are covered by certain warranties. An example of an express warranty would be a warranty of
   a. Usage of trade.
   b. Fitness for a particular purpose.
   c. Merchantability.
   d. Conformity of goods to sample.

R97#14. Under the Sales Article of the UCC, unless a contract provides otherwise, before title to goods can pass from a seller to a buyer, the goods must be
   a. Tendered to the buyer.
   b. Identified to the contract.
   c. Accepted by the buyer.
   d. Paid for.

N95#41. Under the Sales Article of the UCC, a firm offer will be created only if the
   a. Offer states the time period during which it will remain open.
   b. Offer is made by a merchant in a signed writing.
   c. Offeree gives some form of consideration.
   d. Offeree is a merchant.

N95#42. Under the Sales Article of the UCC, when a written offer has been made without specifying a means of acceptance but providing that the offer will only remain open for ten days, which of the following statements represent(s) a valid acceptance of the offer?

I. An acceptance sent by regular mail the day before the ten-day period expires that reaches the offeror on the eleventh day.
II. An acceptance faxed the day before the ten-day period expires that reaches the offeror on the eleventh day, due to a malfunction of the offeror's printer.

a. I only.
b. II only.
c. Both I and II.
d. Neither I nor II.

N95#43. Under the Sales Article of the UCC, the warranty of title
a. Provides that the seller cannot disclaim the warranty if the sale is made to a bona fide purchaser for value.
b. Provides that the seller deliver the goods free from any lien of which the buyer lacked knowledge when the contract was made.
c. Applies only if it is in writing and signed by the seller.
d. Applies only if the seller is a merchant.

N95#44. To establish a cause of action based on strict liability in tort for personal injuries that result from the use of a defective product, one of the elements the injured party must prove is that the seller
a. Was aware of the defect in the product.
b. Sold the product to the injured party.
c. Failed to exercise due care.
d. Sold the product in a defective condition.

N95#45. Under the Sales Article of the UCC, which of the following factors is most important in determining who bears the risk of loss in a sale of goods contract?
a. The method of shipping the goods.
b. The contract's shipping terms.
c. Title to the goods.
d. How the goods were lost.

N95#46. Under the Sales Article of the UCC, in an F.O.B. place of shipment contract, the risk of loss passes to the buyer when the goods
a. Are identified to the contract.
b. Are placed on the seller's loading dock.
c. Are delivered to the carrier.
d. Reach the buyer's loading dock.

N95#47. Under the Sales Article of the UCC, which of the following rights is(are) available to the buyer when a seller commits an anticipatory breach of contract?

	Demand assurance of performance	Cancel the contract	Collect punitive damages
a.	Yes	Yes	Yes
b.	Yes	Yes	No
c.	Yes	No	Yes
d.	No	Yes	Yes

N95#48. Under the Sales Article of the UCC, and unless otherwise agreed to, the seller's obligation to the buyer is to
a. Deliver the goods to the buyer's place of business.
b. Hold conforming goods and give the buyer whatever notification is reasonably necessary to enable the buyer to take delivery.
c. Deliver all goods called for in the contract to a common carrier.
d. Set aside conforming goods for inspection by the buyer before delivery.

N95#49. Under the Sales Article of the UCC, which of the following statements regarding liquidated damages is(are) correct?

I. The injured party may collect any amount of liquidated damages provided for in the contract.
II. The seller may retain a deposit of up to $500 when a buyer defaults even if there is no liquidated damages provision in the contract.

a. I only.
b. II only.
c. Both I and II.
d. Neither I nor II.

N95#50. Under the Sales Article of the UCC, which of the following rights is available to a seller when a buyer materially breaches a sales contract?

	Right to cancel the contract	Right to recover damages
a.	Yes	Yes
b.	Yes	No
c.	No	Yes
d.	No	No

N94#50. Under the Sales Article of the UCC, which of the following statements is correct?
a. The obligations of the parties to the contract must be performed in good faith.
b. Merchants and nonmerchants are treated alike.
c. The contract must involve the sale of goods for a price of more than $500.
d. None of the provisions of the UCC may be disclaimed by agreement.

N94#51. Under the Sales Article of the UCC, which of the following statements is correct regarding the warranty of merchantability arising when there has been a sale of goods by a merchant seller?
a. The warranty must be in writing.
b. The warranty arises when the buyer relies on the seller's skill in selecting the goods purchased.
c. The warranty cannot be disclaimed.
d. The warranty arises as a matter of law when the seller ordinarily sells the goods purchased.

N94#53. High sues the manufacturer, wholesaler, and retailer for bodily injuries caused by a power saw High purchased. Which of the following statements is correct under strict liability theory?
a. Contributory negligence on High's part will always be a bar to recovery.
b. The manufacturer will avoid liability if it can show it followed the custom of the industry.

c. Privity will be a bar to recovery insofar as the wholesaler is concerned if the wholesaler did **not** have a reasonable opportunity to inspect.
d. High may recover even if he **cannot** show any negligence was involved.

N94#54. Under the Sales Article of the UCC, which of the following events will result in the risk of loss passing from a merchant seller to a buyer?

	Tender of the goods at the seller's place of business	Use of the seller's truck to deliver the goods
a.	Yes	Yes
b.	Yes	No
c.	No	Yes
d.	No	No

N94#55. Under the Sales Article of the UCC, which of the following events will release the buyer from all its obligations under a sales contract?
a. Destruction of the goods after risk of loss passed to the buyer.
b. Impracticability of delivery under the terms of the contract.
c. Anticipatory repudiation by the buyer that is retracted before the seller cancels the contract.
d. Refusal of the seller to give written assurance of performance when reasonably demanded by the buyer.

N94#56. Rowe Corp. purchased goods from Stair Co. that were shipped C.O.D. Under the Sales Article of the UCC, which of the following rights does Rowe have?
a. The right to inspect the goods before paying.
b. The right to possession of the goods before paying.
c. The right to reject nonconforming goods.
d. The right to delay payment for a reasonable period of time.

M94#42. Under the UCC Sales Article, which of the following statements is correct concerning a contract involving a merchant seller and a non-merchant buyer?
a. Whether the UCC Sales Article is applicable does **not** depend on the price of the goods involved.
b. Only the seller is obligated to perform the contract in good faith.
c. The contract will be either a sale or return or sale on approval contract.
d. The contract may **not** involve the sale of personal property with a price of more than $500.

M94#43. Vick bought a used boat from Ocean Marina that disclaimed "any and all warranties" in connection with the sale. Ocean was unaware the boat had been stolen from Kidd. Vick surrendered it to Kidd when confronted with proof of the theft. Vick sued Ocean. Who is likely to prevail and why?

a. Vick, because the implied warranty of title has been breached.
b. Vick, because a merchant **cannot** disclaim implied warranties.
c. Ocean, because of the disclaimer of warranties.
d. Ocean, because Vick surrendered the boat to Kidd.

M94#44. Larch Corp. manufactured and sold Oak a stove. The sale documents included a disclaimer of warranty for personal injury. The stove was defective. It exploded causing serious injuries to Oak's spouse. Larch was notified one week after the explosion. Under the UCC Sales Article, which of the following statements concerning Larch's liability for personal injury to Oak's spouse would be correct?
a. Larch **cannot** be liable because of a lack of privity with Oak's spouse.
b. Larch will **not** be liable because of a failure to give proper notice.
c. Larch will be liable because the disclaimer was **not** a disclaimer of all liability.
d. Larch will be liable because liability for personal injury **cannot** be disclaimed.

M94#45. Quick Corp. agreed to purchase 200 typewriters from Union Suppliers, Inc. Union is a wholesaler of appliances and Quick is an appliance retailer. The contract required Union to ship the typewriters to Quick by common carrier, "F.O.B. Union Suppliers, Inc. Loading Dock." Which of the parties bears the risk of loss during shipment?
a. Union, because the risk of loss passes only when Quick receives the typewriters.
b. Union, because both parties are merchants.
c. Quick, because title to the typewriters passed to Quick at the time of shipment.
d. Quick, because the risk of loss passes when the typewriters are delivered to the carrier.

M94#46. Webstar Corp. orally agreed to sell Northco, Inc. a computer for $20,000. Northco sent a signed purchase order to Webstar confirming the agreement. Webstar received the purchase order and did not respond. Webstar refused to deliver the computer to Northco, claiming that the purchase order did not satisfy the UCC Statute of Frauds because it was not signed by Webstar. Northco sells computers to the general public and Webstar is a computer wholesaler. Under the UCC Sales Article, Webstar's position is
a. Incorrect because it failed to object to Northco's purchaser order.
b. Incorrect because only the buyer in a sale-of-goods transaction must sign the contract.
c. Correct because it was the party against whom enforcement of the contract is being sought.
d. Correct because the purchase price of the computer exceeded $500.

M94#47. Under the UCC Sales Article, which of the following legal remedies would a buyer **not** have when

a seller fails to transfer and deliver goods identified to the contract?
- a. Suit for specific performance.
- b. Suit for punitive damages.
- c. Purchase substitute goods (cover).
- d. Recover the identified goods (capture).

N93#49. Which of the following statements applies to a sale on approval under the UCC Sales Article?
- a. Both the buyer and seller must be merchants.
- b. The buyer must be purchasing the goods for resale.
- c. Risk of loss for the goods passes to the buyer when the goods are accepted after the trial period.
- d. Title to the goods passes to the buyer on delivery of the goods to the buyer.

N93#50. Which of the following statements would **not** apply to a written contract governed by the provisions of the UCC Sales Article?
- a. The contract may involve the sale of personal property.
- b. The obligations of a nonmerchant may be different from those of a merchant.
- c. The obligations of the parties must be performed in good faith.
- d. The contract must involve the sale of goods for a price of $500 or more.

N93
Item 52 is based on the following:

On May 2, Handy Hardware sent Ram Industries a signed purchase order that stated, in part, as follows:

> "Ship for May 8 delivery 300 Model A-X socket sets at current dealer price. Terms 2/10/net 30."

Ram received Handy's purchase order on May 4. On May 5, Ram discovered that it had only 200 Model A-X socket sets and 100 Model W-Z socket sets in stock. Ram shipped the Model A-X and Model W-Z sets to Handy without any explanation concerning the shipment. The socket sets were received by Handy on May 8.

52. Assuming a contract exists between Handy and Ram, which of the following implied warranties would result?

- I. Implied warranty of merchantability.
- II. Implied warranty of fitness for a particular purpose.
- III. Implied warranty of title.

  - a. I only.
  - b. III only.
  - c. I and III only.
  - d. I, II and III.

N93#54. To establish a cause of action based on strict liability in tort for personal injuries resulting from using a defective product, one of the elements the plaintiff must prove is that the seller (defendant)
- a. Failed to exercise due care.
- b. Was in privity of contract with the plaintiff.
- c. Defectively designed the product.
- d. Was engaged in the business of selling the product.

N93#55. Bond purchased a painting from Wool, who is not in the business of selling art. Wool tendered delivery of the painting after receiving payment in full from Bond. Bond informed Wool that Bond would be unable to take possession of the painting until later that day. Thieves stole the painting before Bond returned. The risk of loss
- a. Passed to Bond at Wool's tender of delivery.
- b. Passed to Bond at the time the contract was formed and payment was made.
- c. Remained with Wool, because the parties agreed on a later time of delivery.
- d. Remained with Wool, because Bond had **not** yet received the painting.

N93#56. Smith contracted in writing to sell Peters a used personal computer for $600. The contract did not specifically address the time for payment, place of delivery, or Peters' right to inspect the computer. Which of the following statements is correct?
- a. Smith is obligated to deliver the computer to Peters' home.
- b. Peters is entitled to inspect the computer before paying for it.
- c. Peters may **not** pay for the computer using a personal check unless Smith agrees.
- d. Smith is **not** entitled to payment until 30 days after Peters receives the computer.

N93#57. Cara Fabricating Co. and Taso Corp. agreed orally that Taso would custom manufacture a compressor for Cara at a price of $120,000. After Taso completed the work at a cost of $90,000, Cara notified Taso that the compressor was no longer needed. Taso is holding the compressor and has requested payment from Cara. Taso has been unable to resell the compressor for any price. Taso incurred storage fees of $2,000. If Cara refuses to pay Taso and Taso sues Cara, the most Taso will be entitled to recover is
- a. $ 92,000
- b. $105,000
- c. $120,000
- d. $122,000

M92
Items 51 through 53 are based on the following:

On May 2, Lace Corp., an appliance wholesaler, offered to sell appliances worth $3,000 to Parco, Inc., a household appliances retailer. The offer was signed by Lace's president, and provided that it would not be withdrawn before June 1. It also included the shipping terms: "FOB — Parco's warehouse." On May 29, Parco mailed an acceptance of Lace's offer. Lace received the acceptance June 2.

51. Which of the following statements is correct if Lace sent Parco a telegram revoking its offer, and Parco received the telegram on May 25?
    a. A contract was formed on May 2.
    b. Lace's revocation effectively terminated its offer on May 25.
    c. Lace's revocation was ineffective because the offer could **not** be revoked before June 1.
    d. No contract was formed because Lace received Parco's acceptance after June 1.

52. Risk of loss for the appliances will pass to Parco when they are
    a. Identified to the contract.
    b. Shipped by Lace.
    c. Tendered at Parco's warehouse.
    d. Accepted by Parco.

53. If Lace inadvertently ships the wrong appliances to Parco and Parco rejects them two days after receipt, title to the goods will
    a. Pass to Parco when they are identified to the contract.
    b. Pass to Parco when they are shipped.
    c. Remain with Parco until the goods are returned to Lace.
    d. Revert to Lace when they are rejected by Parco.

M92#54. On May 2, Mason orally contracted with Acme Appliances to buy for $480 a washer and dryer for household use. Mason and the Acme salesperson agreed that delivery would be made on July 2. On May 5, Mason telephoned Acme and requested that the delivery date be moved to June 2. The Acme salesperson agreed with this request. On June 2, Acme failed to deliver the washer and dryer to Mason because of an inventory shortage. Acme advised Mason that it would deliver the appliances on July 2 as originally agreed. Mason believes that Acme has breached its agreement with Mason. Acme contends that its agreement to deliver on June 2 was not binding. Acme's contention is
    a. Correct, because Mason is **not** a merchant and was buying the appliances for household use.
    b. Correct, because the agreement to change the delivery date was **not** in writing.
    c. Incorrect, because the agreement to change the delivery date was binding.
    d. Incorrect, because Acme's agreement to change the delivery date is a firm offer that **cannot** be withdrawn by Acme.

M92#55. Which of the following conditions must be met for an implied warranty of fitness for a particular purpose to arise in connection with a sale of goods?

I. The warranty must be in writing.
II. The seller must know that the buyer was relying on the seller in selecting the goods.

   a. I only.
   b. II only.
   c. Both I and II.
   d. Neither I nor II.

M92#56. On February 15, Mazur Corp. contracted to sell 1,000 bushels of wheat to Good Bread, Inc. at $6.00 per bushel with delivery to be made on June 23. On June 1, Good advised Mazur that it would not accept or pay for the wheat. On June 2, Mazur sold the wheat to another customer at the market price of $5.00 per bushel. Mazur had advised Good that it intended to resell the wheat. Which of the following statements is correct?
    a. Mazur can successfully sue Good for the difference between the resale price and the contract price.
    b. Mazur can resell the wheat only after June 23.
    c. Good can retract its anticipatory breach at any time before June 23.
    d. Good can successfully sue Mazur for specific performance.

M92#57. Under the UCC Sales Article, an action for breach of the implied warranty of merchantability by a party who sustains personal injuries may be successful against the seller of the product only when
    a. The seller is a merchant of the product involved.
    b. An action based on negligence can also be successfully maintained.
    c. The injured party is in privity of contract with the seller.
    d. An action based on strict liability in tort can also be successfully maintained.

M92#58. Morgan is suing the manufacturer, wholesaler, and retailer for bodily injuries caused by a power saw Morgan purchased. Which of the following statements is correct under the theory of strict liability?
    a. The manufacturer will avoid liability if it can show it followed the custom of the industry.
    b. Morgan may recover even if he **cannot** show any negligence was involved.
    c. Contributory negligence on Morgan's part will always be a bar to recovery.
    d. Privity will be a bar to recovery insofar as the wholesaler is concerned if the wholesaler did **not** have a reasonable opportunity to inspect.

M92#59. Under the UCC Sales Article, a seller will be entitled to recover the full contract price from the buyer when the
    a. Goods are destroyed after title passed to the buyer.
    b. Goods are destroyed while risk of loss is with the buyer.
    c. Buyer revokes its acceptance of the goods.
    d. Buyer rejects some of the goods.

M92#60. Which of the following factors result(s) in an express warranty with respect to a sale of goods?

I. The seller's description of the goods as part of the basis of the bargain.
II. The seller selects goods knowing the buyer's intended use.

a. I only.
b. II only.
c. Both I and II.
d. Neither I nor II.

M91#49. Under a contract governed by the UCC Sales Article, which of the following statements is correct?
    a. Unless both the seller and the buyer are merchants, neither party is obligated to perform the contract in good faith.
    b. The contract will **not** be enforceable if it fails to expressly specify a time and a place for delivery of the goods.
    c. The seller may be excused from performance if the goods are accidentally destroyed before the risk of loss passes to the buyer.
    d. If the price of the goods is less than $500, the goods need **not** be identified to the contract for title to pass to the buyer.

M91#50. Under the UCC Sales Article, the implied warranty of merchantability
    a. May be disclaimed by a seller's oral statement that mentions merchantability.
    b. Arises only in contracts involving a merchant seller and a merchant buyer.
    c. Is breached if the goods are **not** fit for all purposes for which the buyer intends to use the goods.
    d. Must be part of the basis of the bargain to be binding on the seller.

M91#51. Yost Corp., a computer manufacturer, contracted to sell 15 computers to Ivor Corp., a computer retailer. The contract specified that delivery was to be made by truck to Ivor's warehouse. Instead, Yost shipped the computers by rail. When Ivor claimed that Yost did not comply with the contract, Yost told Ivor that there had been a trucker's strike when the goods were shipped. Ivor refused to pay for the computers. Under these circumstances, Ivor
    a. Is obligated to pay for the computers because Yost made a valid substituted performance.
    b. Is obligated to pay for the computers because title to them passed to Ivor when Ivor received them.
    c. May return the computers and avoid paying for them because of the way Yost delivered them.
    d. May return the computers and avoid paying for them because the contract was void under the theory of commercial impracticability.

M91#54. West purchased a painting from Noll, who is not in the business of selling art. Noll tendered delivery of the painting after receiving payment in full from West. West informed Noll that West would be unable to take possession of the painting until later that day. Thieves stole the painting before West returned. The risk of loss
    a. Remained with Noll, because West had **not** yet received the painting.
    b. Remained with Noll, because the parties agreed on a later time of delivery.
    c. Passed to West at the time the contract was formed and payment was made.
    d. Passed to West on Noll's tender of delivery.

M91
Items 55 and 56 are based on the following:

Lazur Corp. agreed to purchase 100 radios from Wizard Suppliers, Inc. Wizard is a wholesaler of small home appliances and Lazur is an appliance retailer. The contract required Wizard to ship the radios to Lazur by common carrier, "F.O.B. Wizard Suppliers, Inc. Loading Dock."

55. Risk of loss for the radios during shipment to Lazur would be on
    a. Lazur, because the risk of loss passes when the radios are delivered to the carrier.
    b. Wizard, because the risk of loss passes only when Lazur receives the radios.
    c. Wizard, because it is a shipment contract.
    d. Lazur, because title to the radios passes to Lazur at the time of shipment.

56. Under the UCC Sales Article
    a. Title to the radios passes to Lazur at the time they are delivered to the carrier, even if the goods are nonconforming.
    b. Lazur must inspect the radios at the time of delivery or waive any defects and the right to sue for breach of contract.
    c. Wizard must pay the freight expense associated with the shipment of the radios to Lazur.
    d. Lazur would have the right to reject any shipment if Wizard fails to notify Lazur that the goods have been shipped.

M90#40. To satisfy the UCC Statute of Frauds regarding the sale of goods, which of the following must generally be in writing?
    a. Designation of the parties as buyer and seller.
    b. Delivery terms.
    c. Quantity of the goods.
    d. Warranties to be made.

M90#42. Under the UCC Sales Article, the warranty of title may be excluded by
    a. Merchants or non-merchants provided the exclusion is in writing.
    b. Non-merchant sellers only.
    c. The seller's statement that it is selling only such right or title that it has.
    d. Use of an "as is" disclaimer.

M90#43. An important factor in determining if an express warranty has been created is whether the
    a. Statements made by the seller became part of the basis of the bargain.
    b. Sale was made by a merchant in the regular course of business.
    c. Statements made by the seller were in writing.
    d. Seller intended to create a warranty.

M90#44. Cey Corp. entered into a contract to sell parts to Deck, Ltd. The contract provided that the goods would be shipped "F.O.B. Cey's warehouse." Cey shipped parts different from those specified in the contract. Deck rejected the parts. A few hours after Deck informed Cey that the parts were rejected, they were destroyed by fire in Deck's warehouse. Cey believed that the parts were conforming to the contract. Which of the following statements is correct?
   a. Regardless of whether the parts were conforming, Deck will bear the loss because the contract was a shipment contract.
   b. If the parts were nonconforming, Deck had the right to reject them, but the risk of loss remains with Deck until Cey takes possession of the parts.
   c. If the parts were conforming, risk of loss does **not** pass to Deck until a reasonable period of time after they are delivered to Deck.
   d. If the parts were nonconforming, Cey will bear the risk of loss, even though the contract was a shipment contract.

M90#45. Pulse Corp. maintained a warehouse where it stored its manufactured goods. Pulse received an order from Star. Shortly after Pulse identified the goods to be shipped to Star, but before moving them to the loading dock, a fire destroyed the warehouse and its contents. With respect to the goods, which of the following statements is correct?
   a. Pulse has title but **no** insurable interest.
   b. Star has title and an insurable interest.
   c. Pulse has title and an insurable interest.
   d. Star has title but **no** insurable interest.

M90#46. Jefferson Hardware ordered three hundred Ram hammers from Ajax Hardware. Ajax accepted the order in writing. On the final date allowed for delivery, Ajax discovered it did not have enough Ram hammers to fill the order. Instead, Ajax sent three hundred Strong hammers. Ajax stated on the invoice that the shipment was sent only as an accommodation. Which of the following statements is correct?
   a. Ajax's note of accommodation cancels the contract between Jefferson and Ajax.
   b. Jefferson's order can only be accepted by Ajax's shipment of the goods ordered.
   c. Ajax's shipment of Strong hammers is a breach of contract.
   d. Ajax's shipment of Strong hammers is a counteroffer and **no** contract exists between Jefferson and Ajax.

M90#47. On September 10, Bell Corp. entered into a contract to purchase 50 lamps from Glow Manufacturing. Bell prepaid 40% of the purchase price. Glow became insolvent on September 19 before segregating, in its inventory, the lamps to be delivered to Bell. Bell will **not** be able to recover the lamps because
   a. Bell is regarded as a merchant.
   b. The lamps were **not** identified to the contract.
   c. Glow became insolvent fewer than 10 days after receipt of Bell's prepayment.
   d. Bell did **not** pay the full price at the time of purchase.

N89#45. Which of the following factors is least important in determining whether a manufacturer is strictly liable in tort for a defective product?
   a. The negligence of the manufacturer.
   b. The contributory negligence of the plaintiff.
   c. Modifications to the product by the wholesaler.
   d. Whether the product caused injuries.

N89#46. Cookie Co. offered to sell Distrib Markets 20,000 pounds of cookies at $1.00 per pound, subject to certain specified terms for delivery. Distrib replied in writing as follows:

> "We accept your offer for 20,000 pounds of cookies at $1.00 per pound, weighing scale to have valid city certificate."

Under the UCC
   a. A contract was formed between the parties.
   b. A contract will be formed only if Cookie agrees to the weighing scale requirement.
   c. No contract was formed because Distrib included the weighing scale requirement in its reply.
   d. No contract was formed because Distrib's reply was a counteroffer.

N89#47. DaGama bought a used boat from Magellan Marina, which disclaimed "any and all warranties" in connection with the sale. Magellan was unaware that the boat had been stolen from Colon. DaGama surrendered it to Colon when confronted with proof of the theft. DaGama sued Magellan. Who is likely to prevail and why?
   a. Magellan, because of the general disclaimer.
   b. Magellan, because it was unaware of the theft.
   c. DaGama, because the warranty of title has been breached.
   d. DaGama, because Magellan is a merchant.

N89#48. Which of the following factors is most important in deciding who bears the risk of loss between merchants when goods are destroyed during shipment?
   a. The agreement of the parties.
   b. Whether the goods are perishable.
   c. Who has title at the time of the loss.
   d. The terms of applicable insurance policies.

N89#49. On Monday, Wolfe paid Aston Co., a furniture retailer, $500 for a table. On Thursday, Aston notified Wolfe that the table was ready to be picked up. On Saturday, while Aston was still in possession of the table, it was destroyed in a fire. Who bears the loss of the table?
   a. Wolfe, because Wolfe had title to the table at the time of loss.
   b. Aston, unless Wolfe is a merchant.

c. Wolfe, unless Aston breached the contract.
d. Aston, because Wolfe had **not** yet taken possession of the table.

N89#52. Under the UCC Sales Article, if a buyer wrongfully rejects goods, the aggrieved seller may

	Resell the goods and sue for damages	Cancel the agreement
a.	Yes	Yes
b.	Yes	No
c.	No	Yes
d.	No	No

M89#54. With regard to a contract governed by the UCC Sales Article, which one of the following statements is correct?
  a. Merchants and non-merchants are treated alike.
  b. The contract may involve the sale of any type of personal property.
  c. The obligations of the parties to the contract must be performed in good faith.
  d. The contract must involve the sale of goods for a price of more than $500.

M89
Items 55 through 58 are based on the following:

Lazur Corp. entered into a contract with Baker Suppliers, Inc. to purchase a used word processor from Baker. Lazur is engaged in the business of selling new and used word processors to the general public. The contract required Baker to ship the goods to Lazur by common carrier pursuant to the following provision in the contract: "F.O.B. — Baker Suppliers, Inc. loading dock." Baker also represented in the contract that the word processor had been used for only 10 hours by its previous owner. The contract included the provision that the word processor was being sold "as is" and this provision was in a larger and different type style than the remainder of the contract.

55. With regard to the contract between Lazur and Baker,
  a. An implied warranty of merchantability does **not** arise unless both Lazur and Baker are merchants.
  b. The "as is" provision effectively disclaims the implied warranty of title.
  c. No express warranties are created by the contract.
  d. The "as is" provision would **not** prevent Baker from being liable for a breach of any express warranties created by the contract.

56. *For this item only,* assume that during shipment to Lazur the word processor was seriously damaged when the carrier's truck was involved in an accident. When the carrier attempted to deliver the word processor, Lazur rejected it and has refused to pay Baker the purchase price. Under the UCC Sales Article,
  a. Lazur rightfully rejected the damaged computer.
  b. The risk of loss for the computer was on Lazur during shipment.
  c. At the time of the accident, risk of loss for the computer was on Baker because title to the computer had **not** yet passed to Lazur.
  d. Lazur will **not** be liable to Baker for the purchase price of the computer because of the F.O.B. provision in the contract.

57. *For this item only,* assume that the contract between Lazur and Baker is otherwise silent. Under the UCC Sales Article,
  a. Lazur must pay Baker the purchase price before Baker is required to ship the word processor to Lazur.
  b. Baker does **not** warrant that it owns the word processor.
  c. Lazur will be entitled to inspect the word processor before it accepts or pays for it.
  d. Title to the word processor passes to Lazur when it takes physical possession.

58. *For this item only,* assume that Lazur refused to accept the word processor even though it was in all respects conforming to the contract and that the contract is otherwise silent. Under the UCC Sales Article,
  a. Baker can successfully sue for specific performance and make Lazur accept and pay for the word processor.
  b. Baker may resell the word processor to another buyer.
  c. Baker must sue for the difference between the market value of the word processor and the contract price plus its incidental damages.
  d. Baker cannot successfully sue for consequential damages unless it attempts to resell the word processor.

C. Secured Transactions

N94#57. Under the Secured Transactions Article of the UCC, which of the following requirements is necessary to have a security interest attach?

	Debtor has rights in the collateral	Proper filing of a security agreement	Value given by the creditor
a.	Yes	Yes	Yes
b.	Yes	Yes	No
c.	Yes	No	Yes
d.	No	Yes	Yes

N94#58. Under the Secured Transactions Article of the UCC, which of the following purchasers will own consumer goods free of a perfected security interest in the goods?
  a. A merchant who purchases the goods for resale.
  b. A merchant who purchases the goods for use in its business.

c. A consumer who purchases the goods from a consumer purchaser who gave the security interest.
d. A consumer who purchases the goods in the ordinary course of business.

N94#59. Under the Secured Transactions Article of the UCC, what would be the order of priority for the following security interests in consumer goods?

I. Financing agreement filed on April 1.
II. Possession of the collateral by a creditor on April 10.
III. Financing agreement perfected on April 15.

a. I, II, III.
b. II, I, III.
c. II, III, I.
d. III, II, I.

N94#60. Under the Secured Transactions Article of the UCC, which of the following remedies is available to a secured creditor when a debtor fails to make a payment when due?

	Proceed against the collateral	Obtain a general judgment against the debtor
a.	Yes	Yes
b.	Yes	No
c.	No	Yes
d.	No	No

M94#48. Under the UCC Secured Transactions Article, which of the following events will always prevent a security interest from attaching?
a. Failure to have a written security agreement.
b. Failure of the creditor to have possession of the collateral.
c. Failure of the debtor to have rights in the collateral.
d. Failure of the creditor to give present consideration for the security interest.

M94#49. Under the UCC Secured Transactions Article, which of the following after-acquired property may be attached to a security agreement given to a secured lender?

	Inventory	Equipment
a.	Yes	Yes
b.	Yes	No
c.	No	Yes
d.	No	No

M94#50. Under the UCC Secured Transactions Article, which of the following actions will best perfect a security interest in a negotiable instrument against any other party?
a. Filing a security agreement.
b. Taking possession of the instrument.
c. Perfecting by attachment.
d. Obtaining a duly executed financing statement.

M94#51. Under the UCC Secured Transactions Article, perfection of a security interest by a creditor provides added protection against other parties in the event the debtor does not pay its debts. Which of the following parties is **not** affected by perfection of a security interest?
a. Other prospective creditors of the debtor.
b. The trustee in a bankruptcy case.
c. A buyer in the ordinary course of business.
d. A subsequent personal injury judgment creditor.

M94#52. Under the UCC Secured Transactions Article, what is the order of priority for the following security interests in store equipment?

I. Security interest perfected by filing on April 15, 1994.
II. Security interest attached on April 1, 1994.
III. Purchase money security interest attached April 11, 1994 and perfected by filing on April 20, 1994.

a. I, III, II.
b. II, I, III.
c. III, I, II.
d. III, II, I.

M94#53. Larkin is a wholesaler of computers. Larkin sold 40 computers to Elk Appliance for $80,000. Elk paid $20,000 down and signed a promissory note for the balance. Elk also executed a security agreement giving Larkin a security interest in Elk's inventory, including the computers. Larkin perfected its security interest by properly filing a financing statement in the state of Whiteacre. Six months later, Elk moved its business to the state of Blackacre, taking the computers. On arriving in Blackacre, Elk secured a loan from Quarry Bank and signed a security agreement putting up all inventory (including the computers) as collateral. Quarry perfected its security interest by properly filing a financing statement in the state of Blackacre. Two months after arriving in Blackacre, Elk went into default on both debts. Which of the following statements is correct?
a. Quarry's security interest is superior because Larkin's time to file a financing statement in Blackacre had expired prior to Quarry's filing.
b. Quarry's security interest is superior because Quarry had **no** actual notice of Larkin's security interest.
c. Larkin's security interest is superior even though at the time of Elk's default Larkin had **not** perfected its security interest in the state of Blackacre.
d. Larkin's security interest is superior provided it repossesses the computers before Quarry does.

M94
Items 54 and 55 are based on the following:

Drew bought a computer for personal use from Hale Corp. for $3,000. Drew paid $2,000 in cash and signed a security agreement for the balance. Hale properly filed the security agreement. Drew defaulted in paying the balance of the purchase price. Hale asked Drew to pay the balance. When Drew refused, Hale peacefully repossessed the computer.

54. Under the UCC Secured Transactions Article, which of the following remedies will Hale have?
   a. Obtain a deficiency judgment against Drew for the amount owed.
   b. Sell the computer and retain any surplus over the amount owed.
   c. Retain the computer over Drew's objection.
   d. Sell the computer without notifying Drew.

55. Under the UCC Secured Transactions Article, which of the following rights will Drew have?
   a. Redeem the computer after Hale sells it.
   b. Recover the sale price from Hale after Hale sells the computer.
   c. Force Hale to sell the computer.
   d. Prevent Hale from selling the computer.

N93#58. Winslow Co., which is in the business of selling furniture, borrowed $60,000 from Pine Bank. Winslow executed a promissory note for that amount and used all of its accounts receivable as collateral for the loan. Winslow executed a security agreement that described the collateral. Winslow did not file a financing statement. Which of the following statements best describes this transaction?
   a. Perfection of the security interest occurred even though Winslow did **not** file a financing statement.
   b. Perfection of the security interest occurred by Pine having an interest in accounts receivable.
   c. Attachment of the security interest did **not** occur because Winslow failed to file a financing statement.
   d. Attachment of the security interest occurred when the loan was made and Winslow executed the security agreement.

N93#59. Grey Corp. sells computers to the public. Grey sold and delivered a computer to West on credit. West executed and delivered to Grey a promissory note for the purchase price and a security agreement covering the computer. West purchased the computer for personal use. Grey did not file a financing statement. Is Grey's security interest perfected?
   a. Yes, because Grey retained ownership of the computer.
   b. Yes, because it was perfected at the time of attachment.
   c. No, because the computer was a consumer good.
   d. No, because Grey failed to file a financing statement.

N93#60. Noninventory goods were purchased and delivered on June 15, 1993. Several security interests exist in these goods. Which of the following security interests has priority over the others?
   a. Security interest in future goods attached June 10, 1993.
   b. Security interest attached June 15, 1993.
   c. Security interest perfected June 20, 1993.
   d. Purchase money security interest perfected June 24, 1993.

M93#46. On March 1, Green went to Easy Car Sales to buy a car. Green spoke to a salesperson and agreed to buy a car that Easy had in its showroom. On March 5, Green made a $500 downpayment and signed a security agreement to secure the payment of the balance of the purchase price. On March 10, Green picked up the car. On March 15, Easy filed the security agreement. On what date did Easy's security interest attach?
   a. March 1.
   b. March 5.
   c. March 10.
   d. March 15.

M93#47. Mars, Inc. manufactures and sells VCRs on credit directly to wholesalers, retailers, and consumers. Mars can perfect its security interest in the VCRs it sells without having to file a financing statement or take possession of the VCRs if the sale is made to
   a. Retailers.
   b. Wholesalers that sell to distributors for resale.
   c. Consumers.
   d. Wholesalers that sell to buyers in the ordinary course of business.

M93#48. Which of the following transactions would illustrate a secured party perfecting its security interest by taking possession of the collateral?
   a. A bank receiving a mortgage on real property.
   b. A wholesaler borrowing to purchase inventory.
   c. A consumer borrowing to buy a car.
   d. A pawnbroker lending money.

M93#49. A party who filed a security interest in inventory on April 1, 1993, would have a superior interest to which of the following parties?
   a. A holder of a mechanic's lien whose lien was filed on March 15, 1993.
   b. A holder of a purchase money security interest in after acquired property filed on March 20, 1993.
   c. A purchaser in the ordinary course of business who purchased on April 10, 1993.
   d. A judgment lien creditor who filed its judgment on April 15, 1993.

M93#50. Under the UCC Secured Transactions Article, which of the following statements is correct concerning the disposition of collateral by a secured creditor after a debtor's default?
   a. A good faith purchaser for value and without knowledge of any defects in the sale takes free of any subordinate liens or security interests.

b. The debtor may **not** redeem the collateral after the default.
c. Secured creditors with subordinate claims retain the right to redeem the collateral after the collateral is sold to a third party.
d. The collateral may only be disposed of at a public sale.

N92#45. Under the UCC Secured Transactions Article, which of the following conditions must be satisfied for a security interest to attach?
a. The debtor must have title to the collateral.
b. The debtor must agree to the creation of the security interest.
c. The creditor must be in possession of part of the collateral.
d. The creditor must properly file a financing statement.

N92#46. Under the UCC Secured Transactions Article, when collateral is in a secured party's possession, which of the following conditions must also be satisfied to have attachment?
a. There must be a written security agreement.
b. The public must be notified.
c. The secured party must receive consideration.
d. The debtor must have rights to the collateral.

N92#47. Under the UCC Secured Transactions Article, what is the effect of perfecting a security interest by filing a financing statement?
a. The secured party can enforce its security interest against the debtor.
b. The secured party has permanent priority in the collateral even if the collateral is removed to another state.
c. The debtor is protected against all other parties who acquire an interest in the collateral after the filing.
d. The secured party has priority in the collateral over most creditors who acquire a security interest in the same collateral after the filing.

N92#48. A secured creditor wants to file a financing statement to perfect its security interest. Under the UCC Secured Transactions Article, which of the following must be included in the financing statement?
a. A listing or description of the collateral.
b. An after-acquired property provision.
c. The creditor's signature.
d. The collateral's location.

N92#49. On July 8, Ace, a refrigerator wholesaler, purchased 50 refrigerators. This comprised Ace's entire inventory and was financed under an agreement with Rome Bank that gave Rome a security interest in all refrigerators on Ace's premises, all future acquired refrigerators, and the proceeds of sales. On July 12, Rome filed a financing statement that adequately identified the collateral. On August 15, Ace sold one refrigerator to Cray for personal use and four refrigerators to Zone Co. for its business. Which of the following statements is correct?
a. The refrigerators sold to Zone will be subject to Rome's security interest.
b. The refrigerator sold to Cray will **not** be subject to Rome's security interest.
c. The security interest does **not** include the proceeds from the sale of the refrigerators to Zone.
d. The security interest may **not** cover after-acquired property even if the parties agree.

N92#50. Under the UCC Secured Transactions Article, if a debtor is in default under a payment obligation secured by goods, the secured party has the right to

	Peacefully repossess the goods without judicial process	Reduce the claim to a judgment	Sell the goods and apply the proceeds toward the debt
a.	Yes	Yes	Yes
b.	No	Yes	Yes
c.	Yes	Yes	No
d.	Yes	No	Yes

M91#59. On June 15, Harper purchased equipment for $100,000 from Imperial Corp. for use in its manufacturing process. Harper paid for the equipment with funds borrowed from Eastern Bank. Harper gave Eastern a security agreement and financing statement covering Harper's existing and after-acquired equipment. On June 21, Harper was petitioned involuntarily into bankruptcy under Chapter 7 of the Federal Bankruptcy Code. A bankruptcy trustee was appointed. On June 23, Eastern filed the financing statement. Which of the parties will have a superior security interest in the equipment?
a. The trustee in bankruptcy, because the filing of the financing statement after the commencement of the bankruptcy case would be deemed a preferential transfer.
b. The trustee in bankruptcy, because the trustee became a lien creditor before Eastern perfected its security interest.
c. Eastern, because it had a perfected purchase money security interest without having to file a financing statement.
d. Eastern, because it perfected its security interest within the permissible time limits.

M91#60. Wine purchased a computer using the proceeds of a loan from MJC Finance Company. Wine gave MJC a security interest in the computer. Wine executed a security agreement and financing statement, which was filed by MJC. Wine used the computer to monitor Wine's personal investments. Later, Wine sold the computer to Jacobs, for Jacobs' family use. Jacobs was unaware of MJC's security interest. Wine now is in default under the MJC loan. May MJC repossess the computer from Jacobs?
a. No, because Jacobs was unaware of the MJC security interest.
b. No, because Jacobs intended to use the computer for family or household purposes.

c. Yes, because MJC's security interest was perfected before Jacobs' purchase.
d. Yes, because Jacobs' purchase of the computer made Jacobs personally liable to MJC.

N89#50. Under the UCC Secured Transactions Article, for a security interest to attach, the
a. Debtor must agree to the creation of the security interest.
b. Creditor must properly file a financing statement.
c. Debtor must be denied all rights in the collateral.
d. Creditor must take and hold the collateral.

N89#53. Perfection of a security interest permits the secured party to protect its interest by
a. Avoiding the need to file a financing statement.
b. Preventing another creditor from obtaining a security interest in the same collateral.
c. Establishing priority over the claims of most subsequent secured creditors.
d. Denying the debtor the right to possess the collateral.

N89#54. Roth and Dixon both claim a security interest in the same collateral. Roth's security interest attached on January 1, 1989, and was perfected by filing on March 1, 1989. Dixon's security interest attached on February 1, 1989, and was perfected on April 1, 1989, by taking possession of the collateral. Which of the following statements is correct?
a. Roth's security interest has priority because Roth perfected before Dixon perfected.
b. Dixon's security interest has priority because Dixon's interest attached before Roth's interest was perfected.
c. Roth's security interest has priority because Roth's security interest attached before Dixon's security interest attached.
d. Dixon's security interest has priority because Dixon is in possession of the collateral.

N89#55. Under the UCC Secured Transactions Article, if a debtor is in default under a payment obligation secured by goods, the secured party has the right to

	Reduce the claim to a judgment	Sell the goods and apply the proceeds toward the debt	Take possession of the goods without judicial process
a.	Yes	Yes	No
b.	Yes	No	Yes
c.	No	Yes	Yes
d.	Yes	Yes	Yes

M89#47. Acorn Marina, Inc. sells and services boat motors. On April 1, 1989, Acorn financed the purchase of its entire inventory with GAC Finance Company. GAC required Acorn to execute a security agreement and financing statement covering the inventory and proceeds of sale. On April 14, 1989, GAC properly filed the financing statement pursuant to the UCC Secured Transactions Article. On April 27, 1989, Acorn sold one of the motors to Wilks for use in his charter business. Wilks, who had once worked for Acorn, knew that Acorn regularly financed its inventory with GAC. Acorn has defaulted on its obligations to GAC. The motor purchased by Wilks is
a. Subject to the GAC security interest because Wilks should have known that GAC financed the inventory purchase by Acorn.
b. Subject to the GAC security interest because Wilks purchased the motor for a commercial use.
c. Not subject to the GAC security interest because Wilks is regarded as a buyer in the ordinary course of Acorn's business.
d. Not subject to the GAC security interest because GAC failed to file the financing statement until more than 10 days after April 1, 1989.

M89#60. Burn Manufacturing borrowed $500,000 from Howard Finance Co., secured by Burn's present and future inventory, accounts receivable, and the proceeds thereof. The parties signed a financing statement that described the collateral and it was filed in the appropriate state office. Burn subsequently defaulted in the repayment of the loan and Howard attempted to enforce its security interest. Burn contended that Howard's security interest was unenforceable. In addition, Green, who subsequently gave credit to Burn without knowledge of Howard's security interest, is also attempting to defeat Howard's alleged security interest. The security interest in question is valid with respect to
a. Both Burn and Green.
b. Neither Burn nor Green.
c. Burn but **not** Green.
d. Green but **not** Burn.

D. Documents of Title

R97#5. Under the Documents of Title Article of the UCC, which of the following terms must be contained in a warehouse receipt?

I. A statement indicating whether the goods received will be delivered to the bearer, to a specified person, or to a specified person or his/her order.
II. The location of the warehouse where the goods are stored.

a. I only.
b. II only.
c. Both I and II.
d. Neither I nor II.

R97#15. Under the Documents of Title Article of the UCC, a negotiable document of title is "duly negotiated" when it is negotiated to
a. Any holder by indorsement.
b. Any holder by delivery.

c. A holder who takes the document in payment of a money obligation.
d. A holder who takes the document for value, in good faith, and without notice of any defense or claim to it.

R96#15. Under the Documents of Title Article of the UCC, which of the following statements is(are) correct regarding a common carrier's duty to deliver goods subject to a negotiable, bearer bill of lading?

I. The carrier may deliver the goods to any party designated by the holder of the bill of lading.
II. A carrier who, without court order, delivers goods to a party claiming the goods under a missing negotiable bill of lading is liable to any person injured by the misdelivery.

a. I only.
b. II only.
c. Both I and II.
d. Neither I nor II.

VII. Property

A. Real Property Including Insurance

R96#10. Which of the following losses, resulting from a fire, generally may be recovered under a standard fire insurance policy?

	Water damage resulting from extinguishing the fire	Loss of income due to business interruption
a.	Yes	Yes
b.	Yes	No
c.	No	Yes
d.	No	No

N95#51. Long, Fall, and Pear own a building as joint tenants with the right of survivorship. Long gave Long's interest in the building to Green by executing and delivering a deed to Green. Neither Fall nor Pear consented to this transfer. Fall and Pear subsequently died. After their deaths, Green's interest in the building would consist of

a. A $1/3$ interest as a joint tenant.
b. A $1/3$ interest as a tenant in common.
c. No interest because Fall and Pear did **not** consent to the transfer.
d. Total ownership due to the deaths of Fall and Pear.

N95#52. A method of transferring ownership of real property that most likely would be considered an arm's-length transaction is transfer by

a. Inheritance.
b. Eminent domain.
c. Adverse possession.
d. Sale.

N95#53. Which of the following provisions must be included to have an enforceable written residential lease?

	A description of the leased premises	A due date for the payment of rent
a.	Yes	Yes
b.	Yes	No
c.	No	Yes
d.	No	No

N95#54. Which of the following elements must be contained in a valid deed?

	Purchase price	Description of the land
a.	Yes	Yes
b.	Yes	No
c.	No	Yes
d.	No	No

N95#55. Rich purchased property from Sklar for $200,000. Rich obtained a $150,000 loan from Marsh Bank to finance the purchase, executing a promissory note and a mortgage. By recording the mortgage, Marsh protects its

a. Rights against Rich under the promissory note.
b. Rights against the claims of subsequent bona fide purchasers for value.
c. Priority against a previously filed real estate tax lien on the property.
d. Priority against all parties having earlier claims to the property.

N95#60. Which of the following statements correctly describes the requirement of insurable interest relating to property insurance? An insurable interest

a. Must exist when any loss occurs.
b. Must exist when the policy is issued and when any loss occurs.
c. Is created only when the property is owned in fee simple.
d. Is created only when the property is owned by an individual.

M95#51. On August 15, 1994, Tower, Nolan, and Oak were deeded a piece of land as tenants in common. The deed provided that Tower owned $1/2$ the property and Nolan and Oak owned $1/4$ each. If Oak dies, the property will be owned as follows:

a. Tower $1/2$, Nolan $1/4$, Oak's heirs $1/4$.
b. Tower $1/3$, Nolan $1/3$, Oak's heirs $1/3$.
c. Tower $5/8$, Nolan $3/8$.
d. Tower $1/2$, Nolan $1/2$.

M95#52. Which of the following provisions must be included in a residential lease agreement?

a. A description of the leased premises.
b. The due date for payment of rent.
c. A requirement that the tenant have public liability insurance.
d. A requirement that the landlord will perform all structural repairs to the property.

M95#53. For a deed to be effective between a purchaser and seller of real estate, one of the conditions is that the deed must
a. Be recorded within the permissible statutory time limits.
b. Be delivered by the seller with an intent to transfer title.
c. Contain the actual sales price.
d. Contain the signatures of the seller and purchaser.

M95#54. Generally, which of the following federal acts regulate mortgage lenders?

	Real Estate Settlement Procedures Act (RESPA)	Federal Trade Commission Act
a.	Yes	Yes
b.	Yes	No
c.	No	Yes
d.	No	No

M95#59. Clark Corp. owns a warehouse purchased for $150,000 in 1990. The current market value is $200,000. Clark has the warehouse insured for fire loss with Fair Insurance Corp. and Zone Insurance Co. Fair's policy is for $150,000 and Zone's policy is for $75,000. Both policies contain the standard 80% coinsurance clause. If a fire totally destroyed the warehouse, what total dollar amount would Clark receive from Fair and Zone?
a. $225,000
b. $200,000
c. $160,000
d. $150,000

M95#60. Which of the following parties has an insurable interest?

I. A corporate retailer in its inventory.
II. A partner in the partnership property.

a. I only.
b. II only.
c. Both I and II.
d. Neither I nor II.

M94#56. Court, Fell, and Miles own a parcel of land as joint tenants with right of survivorship. Court's interest was sold to Plank. As a result of the sale from Court to Plank,
a. Fell, Miles, and Plank each own one-third of the land as joint tenants.
b. Fell and Miles each own one-third of the land as tenants in common.
c. Plank owns one-third of the land as a tenant in common.
d. Plank owns one-third of the land as a joint tenant.

M94#57. Which of the following is a defect in marketable title to real property?
a. Recorded zoning restrictions.
b. Recorded easements referred to in the contract of sale.
c. Unrecorded lawsuit for negligence against the seller.
d. Unrecorded easement.

M94#58. Which of the following conditions must be met to have an enforceable mortgage?
a. An accurate description of the property must be included in the mortgage.
b. A negotiable promissory note must accompany the mortgage.
c. Present consideration must be given in exchange for the mortgage.
d. The amount of the debt and the interest rate must be stated in the mortgage.

M94#59. Which of the following remedies is available against a real property owner to enforce the provisions of federal acts regulating air and water pollution?

	Citizen suits against the Environmental Protection Agency to enforce compliance with the laws	State suits against violators	Citizen suits against violators
a.	Yes	Yes	Yes
b.	Yes	Yes	No
c.	No	Yes	Yes
d.	Yes	No	Yes

M93#51. On July 1, 1992, Quick, Onyx, and Nash were deeded a piece of land as tenants in common. The deed provided that Quick owned $1/2$ the property and Onyx and Nash owned $1/4$ each. If Nash dies, the property will be owned as follows:
a. Quick $1/2$, Onyx $1/2$.
b. Quick $5/8$, Onyx $3/8$.
c. Quick $1/3$, Onyx $1/3$, Nash's heirs $1/3$.
d. Quick $1/2$, Onyx $1/4$, Nash's heirs $1/4$.

M93#52. Which of the following unities (elements) are required to establish a joint tenancy?

	Time	Title	Interest	Possession
a.	Yes	Yes	Yes	Yes
b.	Yes	Yes	No	No
c.	No	No	Yes	Yes
d.	Yes	No	Yes	No

M93#53. Which of the following warranties is(are) contained in a general warranty deed?

I. The grantor has the right to convey the property.
II. The grantee will **not** be disturbed in possession of the property by the grantor or some third party's lawful claim of ownership.

a. I only.
b. II only.
c. I and II.
d. Neither I **nor** II.

M93#54. A standard title insurance policy will generally insure that
a. There are **no** other deeds to the property.
b. The purchaser has good record title as of the policy's date.
c. All taxes and assessments are paid.
d. The insurance protection will be transferable to a subsequent purchaser.

M93#55. In general, which of the following statements is correct with respect to a real estate mortgage?
a. The mortgage may **not** be given to secure an antecedent debt.
b. The mortgage must contain the actual amount of the underlying debt.
c. The mortgage must be signed by both the mortgagor (borrower) and mortgagee (lender).
d. The mortgagee may assign the mortgage to a third party without the mortgagor's consent.

M93#57. On May 1, 1991, Chance bought a piece of property by taking subject to an existing unrecorded mortgage held by Hay Bank. On April 1, 1992, Chance borrowed money from Link Finance and gave Link a mortgage on the property. Link did not know about the Hay mortgage and did not record its mortgage until July 1, 1992. On June 1, 1992, Chance borrowed money from Zone Bank and gave Zone a mortgage on the same property. Zone knew about the Link mortgage but did not know about the Hay mortgage. Zone recorded its mortgage on June 15, 1992. Which mortgage would have priority if these transactions took place in a notice-race jurisdiction?
a. The Hay mortgage because it was first in time.
b. The Link mortgage because Zone had notice of the Link mortgage.
c. The Zone mortgage because it was the first recorded mortgage.
d. The Zone and Link mortgages share priority because neither had notice of the Hay mortgage.

M93#58. A mortgagor's right of redemption will be terminated by a judicial foreclosure sale unless
a. The proceeds from the sale are **not** sufficient to fully satisfy the mortgage debt.
b. The mortgage instrument does **not** provide for a default sale.
c. The mortgagee purchases the property for market value.
d. The jurisdiction has enacted a statutory right of redemption.

M93
Items 59 and 60 are based on the following:

In 1988, Pod bought a building for $220,000. At that time, Pod purchased a $150,000 fire insurance policy with Owners Insurance Co. and a $50,000 fire insurance policy with Group Insurance Corp. Each policy contained a standard 80% co-insurance clause. In 1992, when the building had a fair market value of $250,000, it was damaged in a fire.

59. How much would Pod recover from Owners if the fire caused $180,000 in damage?
a. $ 90,000
b. $120,000
c. $135,000
d. $150,000

60. How much would Pod recover from Owners and Group if the fire totally destroyed the building?
a. $160,000
b. $200,000
c. $220,000
d. $250,000

N92#51. Which of the following would change if an asset is treated as personal property rather than as real property?

	Requirements for transfer	Creditor's rights
a.	Yes	No
b.	No	Yes
c.	Yes	Yes
d.	No	No

N92#53. Which of the following forms of tenancy will be created if a tenant stays in possession of the leased premises without the landlord's consent, after the tenant's one-year written lease expires?
a. Tenancy at will.
b. Tenancy for years.
c. Tenancy from period to period.
d. Tenancy at sufferance.

N92#54. For a deed to be effective between the purchaser and seller of real estate, one of the conditions is that the deed must
a. Contain the signatures of the seller and purchaser.
b. Contain the actual sales price.
c. Be delivered by the seller with an intent to transfer title.
d. Be recorded within the permissible statutory time limits.

N92#55. Generally, in addition to being in writing, a real estate mortgage must
a. Be signed by both the mortgagor and mortgagee.
b. Be recorded to validate the mortgagee's rights against the mortgagor.
c. Contain a description of the real estate covered by the mortgage.
d. Contain the actual amount of the underlying debt and the interest rate.

N92#56. Hart owned a building with a fair market value of $400,000. The building was covered by a $300,000 fire insurance policy containing an 80% co-insurance clause. What amount would Hart recover if a fire totally destroyed the building?
a. $0
b. $240,000
c. $256,000
d. $300,000

N92#57. Daly tried to collect on a property insurance policy covering a house that was damaged by fire. The insurer denied recovery, alleging that Daly had no insurable interest in the house. In which of the following situations will the insurer prevail?
a. The house belongs to a corporation of which Daly is a 50% stockholder.
b. Daly is **not** the owner of the house but a long-term lessee.
c. The house is held in trust for Daly's mother and, on her death, will pass to Daly.
d. Daly gave an unsecured loan to the owner of the house to improve the house.

N92
Items 58 through 60 are based on the following:

On February 1, Frost bought a building from Elgin, Inc. for $250,000. To complete the purchase, Frost borrowed $200,000 from Independent Bank and gave Independent a mortgage for that amount; gave Elgin a second mortgage for $25,000; and paid $25,000 in cash. Independent recorded its mortgage on February 2 and Elgin recorded its mortgage on March 12.

The following transaction also took place:

- On March 1, Frost gave Scott a $20,000 mortgage on the building to secure a personal loan Scott had previously made to Frost.

- On March 10, Scott recorded this mortgage.

- On March 15, Scott learned about both prior mortgages.

- On June 1, Frost stopped making payments on all the mortgages.

- On August 1, the mortgages were foreclosed. Frost, on that date, owed Independent, $195,000; Elgin, $24,000; and Scott, $19,000.

A judicial sale of the building resulted in proceeds of $220,000 after expenses were deducted. The above transactions took place in a notice-race jurisdiction.

58. What amount of the proceeds will Scott receive?
a. $0
b. $ 1,000
c. $12,500
d. $19,000

59. Why would Scott receive this amount?
a. Scott knew of the Elgin mortgage.
b. Scott's mortgage was recorded before Elgin's and before Scott knew of Elgin's mortgage.
c. Elgin's mortgage was first in time.
d. After Independent is fully paid, Elgin and Scott share the remaining proceeds equally.

60. Frost may redeem the property before the judicial sale only if
a. There is a statutory right of redemption.
b. It is probable that the sale price will result in a deficiency.
c. All mortgages are paid in full.
d. All mortgagees are paid a penalty fee.

N91#51. A tenant's personal property will become a fixture and belong to the landlord if its removal would
a. Increase the value of the personal property.
b. Cause a material change to the personal property.
c. Result in substantial harm to the landlord's property.
d. Change the use of the landlord's property back to its prior use.

N91#53. To be enforceable, a residential real estate lease must
a. Require the tenant to obtain liability insurance.
b. Entitle the tenant to exclusive possession of the leased property.
c. Specify a due date for rent.
d. Be in writing.

N91#54. A purchaser who obtains real estate title insurance will
a. Have coverage for the title exceptions listed in the policy.
b. Be insured against all defects of record other than those excepted in the policy.
c. Have coverage for title defects that result from events that happen after the effective date of the policy.
d. Be entitled to transfer the policy to subsequent owners.

N91#55. A mortgage on real property must
a. Be acknowledged by the mortgagee.
b. State the exact amount of the debt.
c. State the consideration given for the mortgage.
d. Be delivered to the mortgagee.

N91#56. If a mortgagee fails to record its mortgage in a jurisdiction with a notice-race recording statute,
   a. A subsequent recording mortgagee who has **no** knowledge of the prior mortgage will have a superior security interest.
   b. A subsequent recording mortgagee who has knowledge of the prior mortgage will have a superior security interest.
   c. A subsequent purchaser for value who has **no** knowledge of the mortgage will take the property subject to the mortgage.
   d. A subsequent purchaser for value who has knowledge of the mortgage will take the property free of the prior security interest.

N91#57. Which of the following is correct regarding foreclosure of a purchase money mortgage by judicial sale of the property?
   a. The mortgagor has the right to any remaining sale proceeds after the mortgagee is paid.
   b. The purchaser at the sale is liable for any deficiency owed the mortgagee.
   c. The court must confirm any price received at the sale.
   d. The mortgagor can never be liable for a deficiency owed the mortgagee.

N91#58. Wyn bought real estate from Duke and gave Duke a purchase money mortgage. Duke forgot to record the mortgage. Two months later, Wyn gave a mortgage on the same property to Goode to secure a property improvement loan. Goode recorded this mortgage nine days later. Goode knew about the Duke mortgage. If these events took place in a notice-race statute jurisdiction, which mortgage would have priority?
   a. Duke's, because it was the first mortgage given.
   b. Duke's, because Goode knew of the Duke mortgage.
   c. Goode's, because it was the first mortgage recorded.
   d. Goode's, because it was recorded within ten days.

N91#59. In 1985, Ring purchased a building for $90,000 and insured it with a $90,000 fire insurance policy having a standard 80% coinsurance clause. Ring never increased the amount of the policy. In 1990, the building, worth $120,000, was destroyed by fire. What amount could Ring collect from the insurance company?
   a. $0
   b. $ 72,000
   c. $ 90,000
   d. $120,000

N91#60. Mason Co. maintained two standard fire insurance policies on one of its warehouses. Both policies included an 80% coinsurance clause and a typical "other insurance" clause. One policy was with Ace Fire Insurance, Inc., for $24,000, and the other was with Thrifty Casualty Insurance Co., for $16,000. At a time when the warehouse was worth $100,000, a fire in the warehouse caused a $40,000 loss. What amounts can Mason recover from Ace and Thrifty, respectively?
   a. $0 and $0.
   b. $10,000 and $10,000.
   c. $12,000 and $8,000.
   d. $24,000 and $16,000.

N90#51. Jones and Newton each own a one-half interest in certain real property as tenants in common. Jones' interest
   a. Will pass by operation of law to Newton on Jones' death.
   b. Will pass on Jones' death to Jones' heirs.
   c. May **not** be transferred during Jones' lifetime.
   d. Is considered a life estate.

N90#52. Bronson is a residential tenant with a 10-year written lease. In the absence of specific provisions in the lease to the contrary, which of the following statements is correct?
   a. The premises may **not** be sublet for less than the full remaining lease term.
   b. Bronson may **not** assign the lease.
   c. The landlord's death will automatically terminate the lease.
   d. Bronson's purchase of the property will terminate the lease.

N90#53. Unless an exception to title is noted in the title insurance policy, a title insurance company will be liable to a land purchaser for
   a. Closing costs.
   b. Recorded easements.
   c. Unrecorded assessments.
   d. Zoning violations.

N90#54. Sklar Corp. owns a factory that has a fair market value of $90,000. Dall Bank holds an $80,000 first mortgage and Rice Finance holds a $20,000 second mortgage on the factory. Sklar has discontinued payments to Dall and Rice, who have foreclosed on their mortgages. If the factory is properly sold to Bond at a judicial sale for $90,000, after expenses,
   a. Rice will receive $10,000 out of the proceeds.
   b. Dall will receive $77,500 out of the proceeds.
   c. Bond will take the factory subject to the unsatisfied portion of any mortgage.
   d. Rice has a right of redemption after the judicial sale.

N90#55. To be enforceable against the mortgagor, a mortgage must meet all the following requirements **except**
   a. Be delivered to the mortgagee.
   b. Be in writing and signed by the mortgagor.
   c. Be recorded by the mortgagee.
   d. Include a description of the debt and land involved.

N90#56. Which of the following deeds will give a real property purchaser the greatest protection?

a. Quitclaim.
b. Bargain and sale.
c. Special warranty.
d. General warranty.

N90#57. One of the primary purposes of including a coinsurance clause in a property insurance policy is to
  a. Encourage the policyholder to insure the property for an amount close to its full value.
  b. Make the policyholder responsible for the entire loss caused by some covered perils.
  c. Cause the policyholder to maintain a minimum amount of liability insurance that will increase with inflation.
  d. Require the policyholder to insure the property with only one insurance company.

N90#58. Ritz owned a building on which there was a duly recorded first mortgage held by Lyn and a recorded second mortgage held by Jay. Ritz sold the building to Nunn. Nunn assumed the Jay mortgage and had no actual knowledge of the Lyn mortgage. Nunn defaulted on the payments to Jay. If both Lyn and Jay foreclosed, and the proceeds of the sale were insufficient to pay both Lyn and Jay,
  a. Jay would be paid after Lyn was fully paid.
  b. Jay and Lyn would be paid proportionately.
  c. Nunn would be personally liable to Lyn but **not** to Jay.
  d. Nunn would be personally liable to Lyn and Jay.

N90#59. Gilmore borrowed $60,000 from Dix Bank. The loan was used to remodel a building owned by Gilmore as investment property and was secured by a second mortgage that Dix did not record. FCA Loan Company has a recorded first mortgage on the building. If Gilmore defaults on both mortgages, Dix
  a. Will **not** be entitled to any mortgage foreclosure sale proceeds, even if such proceeds are in excess of the amount owed to FCA.
  b. Will be unable to successfully claim any security interest in the building.
  c. Will be entitled to share in any foreclosure sale proceeds *pro rata* with FCA.
  d. Will be able to successfully claim a security interest that is subordinate to FCA's security interest.

N90#60. On February 1, Papco Corp. entered into a contract to purchase an office building from Merit Company for $500,000 with closing scheduled for March 20. On February 2, Papco obtained a $400,000 standard fire insurance policy from Abex Insurance Company. On March 15, the office building sustained a $90,000 fire loss. On March 15, which of the following is correct?

I. Papco has an insurable interest in the building.
II. Merit has an insurable interest in the building.

a. I only.
b. II only.
c. Both I and II.
d. Neither I nor II.

M90#50. A person may own property as a joint tenant with the right of survivorship with any of the following **except** a(an)
  a. Divorced spouse.
  b. Related minor child.
  c. Unaffiliated corporation.
  d. Unrelated adult.

M90#53. A tenant renting an apartment under a three-year written lease that does **not** contain any specific restrictions may be evicted for
  a. Counterfeiting money in the apartment.
  b. Keeping a dog in the apartment.
  c. Failing to maintain a liability insurance policy on the apartment.
  d. Making structural repairs to the apartment.

M90#54. Delta Corp. leased 60,000 square feet in an office building from Tanner under a written 25-year lease. Which of the following statements is correct?
  a. Tanner's death will terminate the lease and Delta will be able to recover any resulting damages from Tanner's estate.
  b. Tanner's sale of the office building will terminate the lease unless both Delta and the buyer consented to the assumption of the lease by the buyer.
  c. In the absence of a provision in the lease to the contrary, Delta does **not** need Tanner's consent to assign the lease to another party.
  d. In the absence of a provision in the lease to the contrary, Delta would need Tanner's consent to enter into a sublease with another party.

M90#55. On February 2, Mazo deeded a warehouse to Parko for $450,000. Parko did not record the deed. On February 12, Mazo deeded the same warehouse to Nexis for $430,000. Nexis was aware of the prior conveyance to Parko. Nexis recorded its deed before Parko recorded. Who would prevail under the following recording statutes?

	Notice statute	Race statute	Race-Notice statute
a.	Nexis	Parko	Parko
b.	Parko	Nexis	Parko
c.	Parko	Nexis	Nexis
d.	Parko	Parko	Nexis

M90#56. On April 6, Ford purchased a warehouse from Atwood for $150,000. Atwood had executed two mortgages on the property: a purchase money mortgage given to Lang on March 2, which was not recorded; and a mortgage given to Young on March 9, which was recorded the same day. Ford was unaware of the mortgage to Lang. Under the circumstances,

a. Ford will take title to the warehouse subject only to Lang's mortgage.
b. Ford will take title to the warehouse free of Lang's mortgage.
c. Lang's mortgage is superior to Young's mortgage because Lang's mortgage is a purchase money mortgage.
d. Lang's mortgage is superior to Young's mortgage because Lang's mortgage was given first in time.

M90#57. Sussex, Inc. had given a first mortgage when it purchased its plant and warehouse. Sussex needed additional working capital. It decided to obtain financing by giving a second mortgage on the plant and warehouse. Which of the following statements is true with respect to the mortgages?
a. Default on payment of the second mortgage will constitute default on the first mortgage.
b. The second mortgage may **not** be prepaid without the consent of the first mortgagee.
c. The second mortgagee may **not** pay off the first mortgage to protect its security.
d. If both mortgages are foreclosed, the first mortgage must be fully paid before paying the second mortgage.

M90#58. If a mortgagor defaults in the payment of a purchase money mortgage, and the mortgagee forecloses, the mortgagor may do any of the following **except**
a. Obtain any excess monies resulting from a judicial sale after payment of the mortgagee.
b. Remain in possession of the property after a foreclosure sale if the equity in the property exceeds the balance due on the mortgage.
c. Refinance the mortgage with another lender and repay the original mortgage.
d. Assert the equitable right of redemption by paying the mortgagee.

M90#59. Lawfo Corp. maintains a $200,000 standard fire insurance policy on one of its warehouses. The policy includes an 80% coinsurance clause. At the time the warehouse was originally insured, its value was $250,000. The warehouse now has a value of $300,000. If the warehouse sustains $30,000 of fire damage, Lawfo's insurance recovery will be a maximum of
a. $20,000
b. $24,000
c. $25,000
d. $30,000

M90#60. Orr is an employee of Vick Corp. Vick relies heavily on Orr's ability to market Vick's products and, for that reason, has acquired a $50,000 insurance policy on Orr's life. Half of the face value of the policy is payable to Vick and the other half is payable to Orr's spouse. Orr dies shortly after the policy is taken out but after leaving Vick's employ. Which of the following statements is correct?
a. Orr's spouse does **not** have an insurable interest because the policy is owned by Vick.
b. Orr's spouse will be entitled to all of the proceeds of the policy.
c. Vick will **not** be entitled to any of the proceeds of the policy because Vick is **not** a creditor or relative of Orr.
d. Vick will be entitled to its share of the proceeds of the policy regardless of whether Orr is employed by Vick at the time of death.

N89#56. A buyer of real estate who receives a title insurance policy will
a. Take title free of all defects.
b. Be able to transfer the policy to a subsequent buyer of the real estate.
c. Not have coverage for title exceptions listed in the insurance policy.
d. Not have coverage greater than the amount of any first mortgage.

N89#57. If a borrower is in default under a purchase money mortgage loan, the
a. Lender can file suit to have the borrower declared insolvent.
b. Person who sold the real estate to the borrower can be forced to assume the mortgage debt.
c. Lender may file suit for foreclosure.
d. Lender may unilaterally obtain title without a foreclosure suit.

N89#58. Ram Corp. owns a warehouse that has a fair market value of $280,000. Area Bank holds a first mortgage and Public Finance holds a second mortgage on the warehouse. Ram has discontinued payments to Area and Public. As a result, Area, which has an outstanding mortgage of $240,000, and Public, which has an outstanding mortgage of $60,000, have foreclosed on their respective mortgages. If the warehouse is properly sold to Quincy at a judicial sale for $280,000, after expenses,
a. Public will receive $40,000 out of the proceeds.
b. Area will receive $224,000 out of the proceeds.
c. Public has a right of redemption after the judicial sale.
d. Quincy will take the warehouse subject to the unsatisfied portion of any mortgage.

N89#59. McArthur purchased a house for $60,000. The house is insured for $64,000 and the insurance policy has an 80% coinsurance provision. Storms caused $12,000 worth of damage when the house had a fair market value of $120,000. What maximum amount will McArthur recover from the insurance company?
a. $ 8,000.
b. $ 9,000.
c. $ 9,600.
d. $12,000.

N89#60. To recover under a property insurance policy, an insurable interest must exist

	When the policy is purchased	At the time of loss
a.	Yes	Yes
b.	Yes	No
c.	No	Yes
d.	No	No

B. Personal Property Including Bailments and Computer Technology Rights

R96#9. Which of the following rights is(are) considered intangible personal property?

	An easement	A contract right
a.	Yes	Yes
b.	Yes	No
c.	No	Yes
d.	No	No

N95#56. Which of the following factors help determine whether an item of personal property is a fixture?

I. Degree of the item's attachment to the property.
II. Intent of the person who had the item installed.

a. I only.
b. II only.
c. Both I and II.
d. Neither I nor II.

N95#58. Which of the following methods of obtaining personal property will give the recipient ownership of the property?

	Lease	Finding abandoned property
a.	Yes	Yes
b.	Yes	No
c.	No	Yes
d.	No	No

N95#59. A common carrier bailee generally would avoid liability for loss of goods entrusted to its care if the goods are

a. Stolen by an unknown person.
b. Negligently destroyed by an employee.
c. Destroyed by the derailment of the train carrying them due to railroad employee negligence.
d. Improperly packed by the party shipping them.

M95#55. Which of the following factors help determine whether an item of personal property has become a fixture?

	Manner of affixation	Value of the item	Intent of the annexor
a.	Yes	Yes	Yes
b.	Yes	Yes	No
c.	Yes	No	Yes
d.	No	Yes	Yes

M95#57. Which of the following items is tangible personal property?
a. Share of stock.
b. Trademark.
c. Promissory note.
d. Oil painting.

M95#58. Which of the following standards of liability best characterizes the obligation of a common carrier in a bailment relationship?
a. Reasonable care.
b. Gross negligence.
c. Shared liability.
d. Strict liability.

M94#60. Which of the following requirements must be met to create a bailment?

I. Delivery of personal property to the intended bailee.
II. Possession by the intended bailee.
III. An absolute duty on the intended bailee to return or dispose of the property according to the bailor's directions.

a. I and II only.
b. I and III only.
c. II and III only.
d. I, II, and III.

SELECTED MULTIPLE CHOICE ITEMS — UNOFFICIAL ANSWERS

I. Professional and Legal Responsibilities

A. Code of Professional Conduct

N95# 1 c
N95# 2 d
M95# 2 c
N94# 1 a
N94# 2 c
M94# 1 c
M94# 2 a
*AM93# 1 a
*AN91# 2 a
*AM91#57 b
*AN89# 56 c

B. Proficiency, Independence, and Due Care

N95# 3 b
N95# 4 a
M95# 1 c
N94# 3 a
N94# 4 d
M94# 3 a
M94# 4 b
*AN93# 1 d
*AN93# 2 d
M93# 4 d
*AN92# 1 c
*AN92# 2 b
*AM92#56 a
N90# 2 b
*AN90# 37 d

*AN90# 39 d
*AM90#46 b
*AM90#47 b
*AM89# 3 a

C. Responsibilities in Other Professional Services

R98# 1 b
R96# 1 c
N95# 5 c
N95# 6 c
N95# 7 a
M95# 3 d
N94# 5 d
N94# 6 a
M94# 5 d
M94# 6 d
*AN93# 14 c
*AM93# 5 a
*AN91# 14 c
*AN89# 57 c

D. Disciplinary Systems Imposed by the Profession and State Regulatory Bodies

R96# 2 d

E. Common Law Liability to Clients and Third Parties

R97# 1 c

N95# 8 b
N95# 9 c
N95# 10 d
N94# 9 a
N94# 10 c
M94# 9 b
N93# 1 c
N93# 2 c
M93# 1 b
M93# 2 a
M93# 3 a
N91# 1 d
N91# 3 c
N91# 4 a
N91# 5 a
N90# 1 c
N90# 4 c
N90# 5 a
M89# 1 b
M89# 2 b
M89# 6 b
M89# 7 c

F. Federal Statutory Liability

N95# 11 d
N95# 13 c
N94# 11 a
N94# 12 b
N94# 13 d
N93# 3 c
N93# 4 a
N93# 5 a

N93# 6 a
M93# 5 b
M93# 10 b
M92# 2 c
M92# 3 c
M92# 4 a
M92# 5 c
N91# 6 b
N91# 7 b
N91# 8 c
N90# 6 a
N90# 7 b
N90# 8 c
M89# 8 c

G. Privileged Communications and Confidentiality

N95# 14 d
N95# 15 a
M95# 5 b
N94# 14 b
N94# 15 c
M94# 10 b
N93# 10 b
M93# 6 d
M93# 9 d
M92# 1 d
N90# 3 a
N90# 9 b
N90# 10 d

II. Business Organizations

A. Agency

R96# 3 c
M95# 6 d
M95# 7 c
M95# 8 b

M95# 9 b
N94# 16 b
N94# 17 c
N94# 18 a
N94# 19 c
N93# 11 d

N93# 13 b
N93# 14 c
N93# 15 c
M92# 6 c
M92# 7 b
M92# 8 b

M92# 9 a
N91# 11 c
N91# 12 c
M91# 1 c
M91# 2 b
M91# 3 c

*A—These questions are from Auditing Exams.

M90# 1 c	M93#15 b	M94#14 c	M95#12 a
M90# 2 d	M92#10 d	N93# 17 c	M95#13 c
M90# 4 c	M92#11 c	N93# 19 c	M95#14 b
M90# 5 b	M92#12 b	N93# 20 b	M95#15 b
N89# 2 b	M92#13 a	N92# 1 a	M94#15 a
N89# 3	M92#14 c	N92# 2 a	M94#16 c
M89#11 b	N91# 14 b	N92# 3 a	M94#17 c
M89#12 b	N91# 15 c	N92# 4 a	M94#18 a
M89#13 c	N91# 16 d	M92#15 c	M94#19 c
	N91# 17 a	M92#16 d	M94#20 b

B. Partnership, Joint Ventures, and Other Unincorporated Associations

	N90# 11 a	M92#17 c	M93#16 d
	N90# 12 c	M92#18 c	M93#17 d
	N90# 13 c	M92#19 a	M93#18 c
	N90# 14 b	M92#20 d	M93#19 a
	N89# 4 d	M91# 4 d	M93#20 c
R98# 2 c	N89# 5 d	M91# 5 c	N92# 5 b
R97# 2 c	N89# 6 b	M91# 6 a	N92# 6 c
R96# 11 c	N89# 7 d	M91# 7 b	N92# 7 b
N95# 16 d	M89#14 b	N90# 15 d	N92# 8 a
N95# 17 a	M89#15 d	N90# 16 b	N92# 9 d
N95# 18 c	M89#16 a	N90# 17 b	N92# 10 b
N95# 19 d		M90# 6 b	N91# 19 d
N95# 20 a	**C. Corporations**	M90# 7 d	N91# 20 a
N94# 20 d		M90# 8 c	M91# 8 b
N94# 21 c	R98# 3 a	M90# 9 b	M91# 9 a
N94# 22 d	R98# 4 d		M91#10 d
N94# 23 b	R97# 3 a	**D. Estates and Trusts**	N90# 19 a
N94# 24 c	R96# 12 a		N90# 20 b
N93# 12 a	N95# 21 a	R97# 6 d	M90#10 c
N93# 16 b	N95# 22 c	R97# 7 c	N89# 8 c
N93# 18 c	N95# 23 c	R97# 8 a	M89#17 a
M93#11 a	N95# 24 c	R97# 9 b	M89#18 d
M93#12 c	N95# 25 d	R96# 4 b	M89#19 d
M93#13 c	N94# 25 b	M95#10 d	M89#20 c
M93#14 d	M94#11 d	M95#11 a	
	M94#12 b		
	M94#13 c		

III. Contracts

A. Formation

	M90#11 a	N93# 21 a	M89#33 d
	M90#12 b	N92# 14 a	
M95#16 b	M90#13 c	M91#13 d	**D. Discharge, Breach, and Remedies**
M95#17 a	M90#14 d	M91#14 b	
M95#18 b	M90#15 c	N90# 22 d	
M93#21 c	M90#16 b	M89#27 d	
M93#22 a	M90#17 b		R97# 11 d
M93#23 b	M90#20 a	**C. Third Party Assignments**	M95#23 a
N92# 11 b	N89# 9 c		M95#24 d
N92# 12 b	N89# 10 a		M95#25 b
N92# 13 c	N89# 12 c	R97# 10 d	N93# 22 d
N92# 16 d	M89#21 c	M95#21 b	N93# 23 b
N92# 18 c	M89#22 d	M95#22 c	N93# 24 b
M92#21 b	M89#23 d	M93#24 d	N93# 26 a
M92#22 b	M89#24 a	N92# 24 a	M93#25 a
M92#23 b	M89#25 a	M92#31 a	N92# 15 c
M92#24 d		M92#34 c	N92# 17 d
M91#11 c	**B. Performance**	N91# 24 d	N92# 19 d
M91#12 a		M91#28 a	N92# 20 b
M91#16 a	M95#19 a	M90#22 c	N92# 22 c
N90# 21 a	M95#20 a	N89# 18 b	N92# 23 c
			N92# 25 a

B-88

Unofficial Answers

M92#25 d	N91# 22 b	M91#23 a	N89# 14 d
M92#26 d	N91# 23 c	M91#24 b	N89# 15 c
M92#27 a	N91# 25 c	N90# 23 c	N89# 16 b
M92#28 b	M91#15 d	N90# 25 b	N89# 17 a
M92#29 c	M91#17 b	M90#19 a	N89# 19 c
M92#30 a	M91#18 c	M90#21 c	M89#26 b
M92#32 c	M91#19 d	M90#23 b	M89#30 c
M92#33 d	M91#20 d	M90#24 d	M89#32 a
M92#35 d	M91#21 c	M90#25 d	M89#34 d
N91# 21 a	M91#22 c	N89# 11 b	M89#35 b

IV. Debtor-Creditor Relationships

A. **Rights, Duties, and Liabilities of Debtors and Creditors**

	N94# 29 c	M95#32 c	N91# 43 c
	N94# 30 d	M95#33 d	N91# 44 c
	N94# 31 a	M95#34 d	N91# 45 b
	M94#24 b	M95#35 d	M91#30 d
R98# 5 b	M94#25 b	N94# 33 a	M91#31 a
R96# 13 b	N93# 25 c	N94# 34 c	M91#32 d
N95# 26 b	N92# 26 b	N94# 37 b	M91#33 c
N95# 27 a	N92# 27 b	N93# 27 d	M91#34 a
N94# 26 c	N92# 28 c	N93# 29 d	M91#35 a
N94# 27 b	N91# 26 b	N93# 30 d	N90# 27 b
N94# 28 a	N91# 38 d	N93# 31 b	N90# 28 c
M94#21 a	M91#26 c	N93# 32 c	N90# 29 d
M94#22 d	M91#27 b	N93# 33 a	N90# 30 d
M94#23 d	N90# 26 d	N93# 34 d	N90# 32 d
	N89# 20 b	N93# 39 a	N90# 33 c
B. **Rights, Duties, and Liabilities of Guarantors**	N89# 21 a	N92# 30 a	N90# 34 a
		N92# 31 a	N90# 35 d
	C. **Bankruptcy**	N92# 32 d	N89# 22 b
		N92# 37 b	N89# 25 b
N95# 28 d	R97# 12 d	N92# 38 d	N89# 26 c
N95# 29 d	M95#28 d	N92# 39 c	N89# 27 a
N95# 30 c	M95#29 c	N91# 29 a	N89# 28 d
M95#26 a	M95#30 a	N91# 31 d	N89# 29 b
M95#27 c	M95#31 a	N91# 42 d	

V. Government Regulation of Business

A. **Federal Securities Acts**

	M94#35 a	M93#34 b	M91#44 c
	M94#37 b	M93#35 b	M91#45 c
	M94#38 d	M92#39 a	M91#46 c
R96# 5 b	M94#39 a	M92#40 d	N90# 39 b
R96# 6 a	M94#40 b	M92#41 c	N90# 40 a
N94# 41 b	N93# 37 d	M92#42 b	N90# 43 d
N94# 42 d	N93# 38 a	M92#43 b	N90# 44 c
N94# 43 b	N93# 40 a	M92#44 a	N90# 45 a
N94# 44 d	N93# 41 c	M92#45 d	M90#29 c
N94# 45 b	N93# 42 b	N91# 35 b	M90#30 a
N94# 46 a	N93# 43 d	N91# 36 b	M90#31 b
N94# 47 a	N93# 44 b	N91# 37 d	M90#32 c
N94# 48 c	N93# 45 c	N91# 39 d	M90#33 a
N94# 52 a	M93#29 b	N91# 40 a	M90#37 d
M94#31 a	M93#30 c	M91#39 a	N89# 33 a
M94#32 d	M93#31 a	M91#40 d	N89# 34 d
M94#33 d	M93#32 b	M91#41 c	N89# 35 b
M94#34 b	M93#33 a	M91#42 c	N89# 37 a

Business Law and Professional Responsibilities

N89# 38 d
N89# 39 a
M89#40 d
M89#41 b
M89#42 a
M89#45 c

B. Employment Regulation

R97# 4 a
R96# 14 c
N95# 31 a

N95# 33 a
N95# 34 b
N95# 35 c
N95# 36 a
N95# 37 a
N95# 38 b
N95# 39 a
N95# 40 d
M95#37 c
M95#38 a
M95#39 b
M95#40 b
N94# 36 d
N94# 38 b

N94# 39 a
N94# 40 b
M94#27 b
M94#28 b
M94#29 a
M94#30 d
N93# 36 a
M93#28 b
M92#38 a
N91# 33 a
N91# 34 b
M91#36 d
M91#38 b
N90# 38 c

M90#26 b
N89# 31 c
N89# 32 c
M89#37 d
M89#38 c

C. Environmental Regulation

R96# 7 b
N95# 57 a
M95#56 d

VI. Uniform Commercial Code

A. Negotiable Instruments

R96# 8 a
M95#41 a
M95#42 a
M95#43 a
M95#44 d
M95#45 c
M95#46 b
M95#47 a
M95#48 b
M95#49 b
M95#50 c
M93#36 a
M93#37 c
M93#38 b
M93#39 d
M93#40 a
M93#41 d
M93#42 d
M93#43 c
N92# 33 b
N92# 34 a
N92# 40 d
M92#46 d
M92#47 d
M92#48 c
N91# 46 a
N91# 47 c
N91# 48 c
N91# 50 c
N90# 46 d
N90# 47 c
N90# 48 a
N90# 49 b
M90#36 b
M90#38 a

M90#39 c
N89# 42 d
M89#46 a
M89#48 b
M89#49 a
M89#52 c

B. Sales

R97# 13 d
R97# 14 b
N95# 41 b
N95# 42 c
N95# 43 b
N95# 44 d
N95# 45 b
N95# 46 c
N95# 47 b
N95# 48 b
N95# 49 b
N95# 50 a
N94# 50 a
N94# 51 d
N94# 53 d
N94# 54 d
N94# 55 d
N94# 56 c
M94#42 a
M94#43 a
M94#44 d
M94#45 d
M94#46 a
M94#47 b
N93# 49 c
N93# 50 d
N93# 52 c
N93# 54 d
N93# 55 a
N93# 56 b
N93# 57 d

M92#51 c
M92#52 c
M92#53 d
M92#54 c
M92#55 b
M92#56 a
M92#57 a
M92#58 b
M92#59 b
M92#60 a
M91#49 c
M91#50 a
M91#51 a
M91#54 d
M91#55 a
M91#56 a
M90#40 c
M90#42 c
M90#43 a
M90#44 d
M90#45 c
M90#46 c
M90#47 b
N89# 45 a
N89# 46 a
N89# 47 c
N89# 48 a
N89# 49 d
N89# 52 a
M89#54 c
M89#55 d
M89#56 b
M89#57 c
M89#58 b

C. Secured Transactions

N94# 57 c
N94# 58 d

N94# 59 a
N94# 60 a
M94#48 c
M94#49 a
M94#50 b
M94#51 c
M94#52 c
M94#53 c
M94#54 a
M94#55 c
N93# 58 d
N93# 59 b
N93# 60 d
M93#46 c
M93#47 c
M93#48 d
M93#49 d
M93#50 a
N92# 45 b
N92# 46 d
N92# 47 d
N92# 48 a
N92# 49 b
N92# 50 a
M91#59 d
M91#60 c
N89# 50 a
N89# 53 c
N89# 54 a
N89# 55 d
M89#47 c
M89#60 a

D. Documents of Title

R97# 5 c
R97# 15 d
R96# 15 c

Unofficial Answers

VII. Property

A. Real Property Including Insurance

R96# 10 b
N95# 51 b
N95# 52 d
N95# 53 b
N95# 54 c
N95# 55 b
N95# 60 a
M95# 51 a
M95# 52 a
M95# 53 b
M95# 54 b
M95# 59 b
M95# 60 c
M94# 56 c
M94# 57 d
M94# 58 a
M94# 59 a
M93# 51 d

M93# 52 a
M93# 53 c
M93# 54 b
M93# 55 d
M93# 57 b
M93# 58 d
M93# 59 c
M93# 60 b
N92# 51 c
N92# 53 d
N92# 54 a
N92# 55 c
N92# 56 d
N92# 57 d
N92# 58 d
N92# 59 b
N92# 60 c
N91# 51 c
N91# 53 b
N91# 54 b
N91# 55 d
N91# 56 a
N91# 57 a

N91# 58 b
N91# 59 c
N91# 60 c
N90# 51 b
N90# 52 d
N90# 53 b
N90# 54 a
N90# 55 c
N90# 56 d
N90# 57 a
N90# 58 a
N90# 59 d
N90# 60 c
M90# 50 c
M90# 53 a
M90# 54 c
M90# 55 b
M90# 56 b
M90# 57 d
M90# 58 b
M90# 59 c

M90# 60 d
N89# 56 c
N89# 57 c
N89# 58 a
N89# 59 a
N89# 60 c

B. Personal Property Including Bailments and Computer Technology Rights

R96# 9 c
N95# 56 c
N95# 58 c
N95# 59 d
M95# 55 c
M95# 57 d
M95# 58 d
M94# 60 d

OTHER OBJECTIVE ANSWER FORMATS — SELECTED QUESTIONS

I. Professional and Legal Responsibilities

F. Federal Statutory Liability

M94
Number 2 (Estimated time —— 10 to 15 minutes)

Question Number 2 consists of 2 parts. Each part consists of 6 items. Select the **best** answer for each item. Use a No. 2 pencil to blacken the appropriate ovals on the Objective Answer Sheet to indicate your answers. **Answer all items.** Your grade will be based on the total number of correct answers.

A. Items 61 through 66 are based on the following:

Under Section 11 of the Securities Act of 1933 and Section 10(b), Rule 10b-5 of the Securities Exchange Act of 1934, a CPA may be sued by a purchaser of registered securities.

Required:
Items 61 through 66 relate to what a plaintiff who purchased securities must prove in a civil liability suit against a CPA. For each item determine whether the statement must be proven under Section 11 of the Securities Act of 1933, under Section 10(b), Rule 10b-5, of the Securities Exchange Act of 1934, both Acts, or neither Act, and blacken the corresponding oval on the Objective Answer Sheet.

- If the item must be proven **only** under Section 11 of the Securities Act of 1933, blacken Ⓐ on the Objective Answer Sheet.
- If the item must be proven **only** under Section 10(b), Rule 10b-5, of the Securities Exchange Act of 1934, blacken Ⓑ on the Objective Answer Sheet.
- If the item must be proven under **both** Acts, blacken Ⓒ on the Objective Answer Sheet.
- If the item must be proven under **neither** of the Acts, blacken Ⓓ on the Objective Answer Sheet.

Only Section 11	Only Section 10(b)	Both	Neither
Ⓐ	Ⓑ	Ⓒ	Ⓓ

The plaintiff security purchaser must allege or prove:

61. Material misstatements were included in a filed document.
62. A monetary loss occurred.
63. Lack of due diligence by the CPA.
64. Privity with the CPA.
65. Reliance on the document.
66. The CPA had scienter.

II. Business Organizations

A. Agency

N95
Number 2(a) (Estimated time — — 10 to 15 minutes)

Question Number 2 consists of two parts. Each part consists of five items. Select the **best** answer for each item. Use a No. 2 pencil to blacken the appropriate ovals on the *Objective Answer Sheet* to indicate your answers. **Answer all items.** Your grade will be based on the total number of correct answers.

a. Items 61 through 65 are based on the following:

Lace Computer Sales Corp. orally contracted with Banks, an independent consultant, for Banks to work part-time as Lace's agent to perform Lace's customers' service calls. Banks, a computer programmer and software designer, was authorized to customize Lace's software to the customers' needs, on a commission basis, but was specifically told not to sell Lace's computers.

On September 15, Banks made a service call on Clear Co. to repair Clear's computer. Banks had previously called on Clear, customized Lace's software for Clear, and collected cash payments for the work performed. During the call, Banks convinced Clear to buy an upgraded Lace computer for a price much lower than Lace would normally charge. Clear had previously purchased computers from other Lace agents and had made substantial cash down payments to the agents. Clear had no knowledge that the price was lower than normal. Banks received a $1,000 cash down payment and promised to deliver the computer the next week. Banks never turned in the down payment and left town. When Clear called the following week to have the computer delivered, Lace refused to honor Clear's order.

Required:
Items 61 through 65 relate to the relationships between the parties. For each item, select from List I whether only statement I is correct, whether only statement II is correct, whether both statements I and II are correct, or whether neither statement I nor II is correct. Blacken the corresponding oval on the *Objective Answer Sheet*.

List I
Ⓐ I only.
Ⓑ II only.
Ⓒ Both I and II.
Ⓓ Neither I nor II.

61. I. Lace's agreement with Banks had to be in writing for it to be a valid agency agreement.
    II. Lace's agreement with Banks empowered Banks to act as Lace's agent.

62. I. Clear was entitled to rely on Banks' implied authority to customize Lace's software.
    II. Clear was entitled to rely on Banks' express authority when buying the computer.

63. I. Lace's agreement with Banks was automatically terminated by Banks' sale of the computer.
    II. Lace must notify Clear before Banks' apparent authority to bind Lace will cease.

64. I. Lace is **not** bound by the agreement made by Banks with Clear.
    II. Lace may unilaterally amend the agreement made by Banks to prevent a loss on the sale of the computer to Clear.

65. I. Lace, as a disclosed principal, is solely contractually liable to Clear.
    II. Both Lace and Banks are contractually liable to Clear.

B. Partnership, Joint Ventures, and Other Unincorporated Associations

R97
Number 1

Question Number 1 consists of 5 items. Select the **best** answer for each item. Use a No. 2 pencil to blacken the appropriate ovals on the *Objective Answer Sheet* to indicate your answers. **Answer all items.** Your grade will be based on the total number of correct answers.

Items 1 through 5 are based on the following:

On March 1, 1995, Grove, Plane, and Range formed Techno Associates, a general partnership. They made capital contributions to the partnership as follows: Grove contributed $125,000; Plane contributed $250,000; and Range contributed $500,000. They prepared and executed a written partnership agreement that provided that profits would be shared equally, that the partnership would last for five years, and that the partnership use a calendar year for accounting purposes. There was no provision as to how losses would be allocated nor was there any provision regarding the continued use of the partnership name in the event of dissolution.

- On April 1, 1996, Range assigned Range's partnership interest to Blank. Blank notified Grove and Plane that Blank wanted to participate in the partnership business and vote on partnership issues.

- On June 10, 1996, a judgment was entered against Techno in a suit for breach of contract.
- On December 31, 1996, Grove resigned from the partnership.
- During the year-end closing, it was established that Techno had incurred an operating loss in 1996 as a result of the judgment. It was also established that Techno, being unable to pay its debts as they became due, was insolvent.
- On May 1, 1997, Techno filed for bankruptcy.

The Uniform Partnership Act applies.

Required:

For **Items 1 through 3,** select the correct answer from List I and blacken the corresponding oval on the *Objective Answer Sheet*. An answer may be selected once, more than once, or not at all.

1. What would be Range's liability for Techno's 1996 operating loss?
2. What would be Blank's liability for Techno's 1996 operating loss?
3. What would be Grove's liability for Techno's 1996 operating loss?

List I
Ⓐ No personal liability.
Ⓑ Liability limited to the amount contributed to the partnership.
Ⓒ Liability limited to the amount in the capital account.
Ⓓ Full personal liability for up to one-third of the total amount of the partnership debt.
Ⓔ Full personal liability for up to the total amount of the partnership debt.

For **Item 4,** select the correct answer from List II and blacken the corresponding oval on the *Objective Answer Sheet*.

4. As of January 1, 1997, who were the partners in Techno?

List II
Ⓐ Blank and Plane.
Ⓑ Plane and Range.
Ⓒ Blank, Plane, and Grove.
Ⓓ Grove, Plane, and Range.
Ⓔ Blank, Grove, Plane, and Range.

For **Item 5,** select the correct answer from List III and blacken the corresponding oval on the *Objective Answer Sheet*.

5. On May 1, 1997, what was the status of Techno?

List III
Ⓐ Dissolved.
Ⓑ Liquidated.
Ⓒ Terminated.

M95
Number 2(a) (Estimated time — — 10 to 15 minutes)

Question Number 2 consists of two parts. Each part consists of 6 items. Select the **best** answer for each item. Use a No. 2 pencil to blacken the appropriate ovals on the *Objective Answer Sheet* to indicate your answers. **Answer all items.** Your grade will be based on the total number of correct answers.

a. In 1992, Anchor, Chain, and Hook created ACH Associates, a general partnership. The partners orally agreed that they would work full time for the partnership and would distribute profits based on their capital contributions. Anchor contributed $5,000; Chain $10,000; and Hook $15,000.

For the year ended December 31, 1993, ACH Associates had profits of $60,000 that were distributed to the partners. During 1994, ACH Associates was operating at a loss. In September 1994, the partnership dissolved.

In October 1994, Hook contracted in writing with Ace Automobile Co. to purchase a car for the partnership. Hook had previously purchased cars from Ace Automobile Co. for use by ACH Associates partners. ACH Associates did not honor the contract with Ace Automobile Co. and Ace Automobile Co. sued the partnership and the individual partners.

Required:
Items 61 through 66 refer to the above facts. For each item, determine whether Ⓐ or Ⓑ is correct. On the *Objective Answer Sheet,* blacken the oval that corresponds to the correct statement.

61. A. The ACH Associates oral partnership agreement was valid.
    B. The ACH Associates oral partnership agreement was invalid because the partnership lasted for more than one year.

62. A. Anchor, Chain, and Hook jointly owning and conducting a business for profit establishes a partnership relationship.
    B. Anchor, Chain, and Hook jointly owning income producing property establishes a partnership relationship.

63. A. Anchor's share of ACH Associates' 1993 profits was $20,000.
    B. Hook's share of ACH Associates' 1993 profits was $30,000.

64. A. Anchor's capital account would be reduced by 1/3 of any 1994 losses.
    B. Hook's capital account would be reduced by 1/2 of any 1994 losses.

65. A. Ace Automobile Co. would lose a suit brought against ACH Associates because Hook, as a general partner, has no authority to bind the partnership.
    B. Ace Automobile Co. would win a suit brought against ACH Associates because Hook's authority continues during dissolution.

66. A. ACH Associates and Hook would be the only parties liable to pay any judgment recovered by Ace Automobile Co.
    B. Anchor, Chain, and Hook would be jointly and severally liable to pay any judgment recovered by Ace Automobile Co.

C. Corporations

R97
Number 2

Question Number 2 consists of 5 items. Select the **best** answer for each item. Use a No. 2 pencil to blacken the appropriate ovals on the *Objective Answer Sheet* to indicate your answers. **Answer all items.** Your grade will be based on the total number of correct answers.

Items 1 through 5 are based on the following:

Mill, Web, and Trent own all the outstanding and issued voting common stock of Sack Corp. Mill owns 40%, Web owns 30%, and Trent owns 30%. They also executed a written stockholders agreement in which Mill, Web, and Trent agreed to vote for each other as directors of Sack.

At the initial meeting of the incorporators, Mill, Web, and Trent were elected to the board of directors together with three non-stockholders. At the initial board of directors meeting, Mill, Web, and Trent were appointed as officers of the corporation and given three-year employment contracts.

During its first year of operations, Sack began experiencing financial difficulties, which caused disagreements among Mill, Web, and Trent as to how the business should be operated.

At the next annual stockholders' meeting, Mill was not elected to the board of directors. The new board fired Mill in a management reorganization despite there being two years left on the employment contract. The board, reasonably relying on assurances from Web and Trent regarding financial statements Web and Trent knew to be materially misstated, declared and paid a dividend that caused Sack to become insolvent.

Required:
For **Items 1 through 5,** select the correct answer from List IV and blacken the corresponding oval on the *Objective Answer Sheet*. An answer may be selected once, more than once, or not at all.

1. According to the stockholders' agreement, what party(ies) must be elected as director(s) of Sack?
2. According to the stockholders' agreement, what party(ies) must be appointed as officer(s) of the corporation?
3. What party(ies) is(are) liable to Mill for Mill's firing?
4. What party(ies) must return the dividend to the corporation?
5. What party(ies) would be liable for declaring the illegal dividend?

List IV
(A) Mill only.
(B) Web only.
(C) Trent only.
(D) Mill and Web only.
(E) Mill and Trent only.
(F) Web and Trent only.
(G) Mill, Web, and Trent.
(H) Neither Mill, Web, nor Trent.
(I) All directors.
(J) Sack Corp.

R96
Number 1 (Estimated time —— 10 to 15 minutes)

Question Number 1 consists of 6 items. Select the **best** answer for each item. Use a No. 2 pencil to blacken the appropriate ovals on the *Objective Answer Sheet* to indicate your answers. **Answer all items.** Your grade will be based on the total number of correct answers.

Drain Corp. has two classes of stock: 100,000 shares of authorized, issued, and outstanding voting common stock; and 10,000 shares of authorized, issued, and outstanding nonvoting 5% cumulative, nonparticipating preferred stock with a face value of $100 per share. In 1994, Drain's officers and directors intentionally allowed pollutants to be discharged by Drain's processing plant. These actions resulted in Drain having to pay penalties. Solely as a result of the penalties, no dividends were declared for the years ended December 31, 1994 and December 31, 1995. The total amount Drain paid in penalties was $1,000,000. In 1995, Drain was able to recover the full amount of the penalties from an insurance company that had issued Drain a business liability policy. Drain's directors refused to use this money to declare a dividend and decided to hold the $1,000,000 in a special fund to pay future bonuses to officers and directors.

Required:
Items 1 through 6 refer to the above fact pattern. For each item, select the correct answer that completes the statement and blacken the corresponding oval on the *Objective Answer Sheet*. An answer may be selected once, more than once, or not at all.

1. The actions by Drain's officers and directors in allowing pollutants to be discharged generally would be considered a violation of the
2. A stockholder's derivative suit, if successful, probably would result in the officers and directors being
3. A stockholder's derivative suit, if successful, probably would result in the $1,000,000 being considered
4. If the $1,000,000 was distributed to the shareholders in 1995, the distribution would be characterized as a
5. If the $1,000,000 was distributed in 1995, each share of 5% cumulative preferred stock would receive
6. If the $1,000,000 was distributed in 1995, each share of voting common stock would receive

Ⓐ	Available for distribution as a dividend.
Ⓑ	Fiduciary duty to prevent losses.
Ⓒ	Cash dividend.
Ⓓ	Fiduciary duty of care.
Ⓔ	Fiduciary duty of loyalty.
Ⓕ	Illegal dividend.
Ⓖ	Immune from liability.
Ⓗ	Liable for abuse of discretion.
Ⓘ	Liable to the corporation for $1,000,000.
Ⓙ	Property dividend.
Ⓚ	Stock dividend.
Ⓛ	Surplus or earnings held for expansion.
Ⓜ	$ 5.00.
Ⓝ	$ 9.00.
Ⓞ	$10.00.
Ⓟ	$18.00.

M95
Number 2(b) (Estimated time — — 10 to 15 minutes)

b. In 1990, Amber Corp., a closely-held corporation, was formed by Adams, Frank, and Berg as incorporators and stockholders. Adams, Frank, and Berg executed a written voting agreement which provided that they would vote for each other as directors and officers. In 1994, stock in the corporation was offered to the public. This resulted in an additional 300 stockholders. After the offering, Adams holds 25%, Frank holds 15%, and Berg holds 15% of all issued and outstanding stock. Adams, Frank, and Berg have been directors and officers of the corporation since the corporation was formed. Regular meetings of the board of directors and annual stockholders meetings have been held.

Required:
Items 67 through 72 refer to the formation of Amber Corp. and the rights and duties of its stockholders, directors, and officers. For each item, determine whether Ⓐ, Ⓑ, or Ⓒ is correct. On the *Objective Answer Sheet*, blacken the oval that corresponds to the correct statement.

67. A. Amber Corp. must be formed under a state's general corporation statute.
    B. Amber Corp.'s Articles of Incorporation must include the names of all stockholders.
    C. Amber Corp. must include its corporate bylaws in the incorporation documents filed with the state.

68. Amber Corp.'s initial bylaws ordinarily would be adopted by its
    A. Stockholders.
    B. Officers.
    C. Directors.

69. Amber Corp.'s directors are elected by its
    A. Officers.
    B. Outgoing directors.
    C. Stockholders.

70. Amber Corp.'s officers ordinarily would be elected by its
    A. Stockholders.
    B. Directors.
    C. Outgoing officers.

71. Amber Corp.'s day-to-day business ordinarily would be operated by its
    A. Directors.
    B. Stockholders.
    C. Officers.

72. A. Adams, Frank, and Berg must be elected as directors because they own 55% of the issued and outstanding stock.
    B. Adams, Frank, and Berg must always be elected as officers because they own 55% of the issued and outstanding stock.
    C. Adams, Frank, and Berg must always vote for each other as directors because they have a voting agreement.

D. Estates and Trusts

N95
Number 2(b) (Estimated time — — 10 to 15 minutes)

b. **Items 66 through 70** are based on the following:

Under the provisions of Glenn's testamentary trust, after payment of all administrative expenses and taxes, the entire residuary estate was to be paid to Strong and Lake as trustees. The trustees were authorized to invest the trust assets, and directed to distribute income annually to Glenn's children for their lives, then distribute the principal to Glenn's grandchildren, per capita. The trustees were also authorized to make such principal payments to the income beneficiaries that the trustees determined to be reasonable for the beneficiaries' welfare. Glenn died in 1992. On Glenn's death there were two surviving children, aged 21 and 30, and one two-year-old grandchild.

On June 15, 1995, the trustees made the following distributions from the trust:

- Paid the 1992, 1993, and 1994 trust income to Glenn's children. This amount included the proceeds from the sale of stock received by the trust as a stock dividend.

- Made a $10,000 principal payment for medical school tuition to one of Glenn's children.

- Made a $5,000 principal payment to Glenn's grandchild.

Required:
Items 66 through 70 relate to the above fact pattern. For each item, select from List II whether only statement I is correct, whether only statement II is correct, whether both statements I and II are correct, or whether neither statement I nor II is correct. Blacken the corresponding oval on the *Objective Answer Sheet*.

List II
Ⓐ I only.
Ⓑ II only.
Ⓒ Both I and II.
Ⓓ Neither I nor II.

66. I. Glenn's trust was valid because it did **not** violate the rule against perpetuities.
    II. Glenn's trust was valid even though it permitted the trustees to make principal payments to income beneficiaries.

67. I. Glenn's trust would be terminated if both of Glenn's children were to die.
    II. Glenn's trust would be terminated because of the acts of the trustees.

68. I. Strong and Lake violated their fiduciary duties by making any distributions of principal.
    II. Strong and Lake violated their fiduciary duties by failing to distribute the trust income annually.

69. I. Generally, stock dividends are considered income and should be distributed.
    II. Generally, stock dividends should be allocated to principal and remain as part of the trust.

70. I. The $10,000 principal payment was an abuse of the trustees' authority.
    II. The $5,000 principal payment was valid because of its payment to a non-income beneficiary.

III. Contracts

R98
Number 1

Question Number 1 consists of 10 items. Select the **best** answer for each item. Use a No. 2 pencil to blacken the appropriate ovals on the *Objective Answer Sheet* to indicate your answers. **Answer all items.** Your grade will be based on the total number of correct answers.

On January 15, East Corp. orally offered to hire Bean, CPA, to perform management consulting services for East and its subsidiaries. The offer provided for a three-year contract at $10,000 per month. On January 20, East sent Bean a signed memorandum stating the terms of the offer. The memorandum also included a payment clause that hadn't been discussed and the provision that Bean's acceptance of the offer would not be effective unless it was received by East on or before January 25. Bean received the memorandum on January 21, signed it, and mailed it back to East the same day. East received it on January 24. On January 23, East wrote to Bean revoking the offer. Bean received the revocation on January 25.

On March 1, East Corp. orally engaged Snow Consultants to install a corporate local area network system (LAN) for East's financial operations. The engagement was to last until the following February 15 and East would pay Snow $5,000 twice a month. On March 15, East offered Snow $1,000 per month to assist in the design of East's Internet homepage. Snow accepted East's offer. On April 1, citing excess work, Snow advised East that Snow would not assist with the design of the homepage. On April 5, East accepted Snow's withdrawal from the Internet homepage design project. On April 15, Snow notified East that Snow had assigned the fees due Snow on the LAN installation engagement to Band Computer Consultants. On April 30, East notified Snow that the LAN installation agreement was canceled.

Required:
Items 1 through 5 are based on the transaction between East Corp. and Bean. For each item, select the

best answer from List I and blacken the corresponding oval on the *Objective Answer Sheet*. An answer may be selected once, more than once, or not at all.

1. What was the effect of the event(s) that took place on January 20?
2. What was the effect of the event(s) that took place on January 21?
3. What was the effect of the event(s) that took place on January 23?
4. What was the effect of the event(s) that took place on January 24?
5. What was the effect of the event(s) that took place on January 25?

List I
Ⓐ Acceptance of a counteroffer.
Ⓑ Acceptance of an offer governed by the mailbox rule.
Ⓒ Attempted acceptance of an offer.
Ⓓ Attempted revocation of an offer.
Ⓔ Formation of an enforceable contract.
Ⓕ Formation of a contract enforceable only against East.
Ⓖ Invalid revocation because of prior acceptance of an offer.
Ⓗ Offer revoked by sending a revocation letter.
Ⓘ Submission of a counteroffer.
Ⓙ Submission of a written offer.

Items 6 through 10 are based on the transaction between East Corp. and Snow Consultants. For each item, select the best answer from List II and blacken the corresponding oval on the *Objective Answer Sheet*. An answer may be selected once, more than once, or not at all.

6. What was the effect of the event(s) that took place on March 1?
7. What was the effect of the event(s) that took place on March 15?
8. What was the effect of the event(s) that took place on April 5?
9. What was the effect of the event(s) that took place on April 15?
10. What was the effect of the event(s) that took place on April 30?

List II
Ⓐ Breach of contract.
Ⓑ Discharge from performance.
Ⓒ Enforceable oral contract modification.
Ⓓ Formation of a voidable contract.
Ⓔ Formation of an enforceable contract.
Ⓕ Formation of a contract unenforceable under the statute of frauds.
Ⓖ Invalid assignment.
Ⓗ Mutual rescission.
Ⓘ Novation.
Ⓙ Unilateral offer.
Ⓚ Valid assignment of rights.
Ⓛ Valid assignment of duties.
Ⓜ Valid assignment of rights and duties.

IV. Debtor-Creditor Relationships

C. Bankruptcy

N95
Number 3(a) (Estimated time — — 10 to 15 minutes)

Question Number 3 consists of two parts. Each part consists of five items. Select the **best** answer for each item. Use a No. 2 pencil to blacken the appropriate ovals on the *Objective Answer Sheet* to indicate your answers. **Answer all items.** Your grade will be based on the total number of correct answers.

a. Items 71 through 75 are based on the following:

On June 1, 1995, Rusk Corp. was petitioned involuntarily into bankruptcy. At the time of the filing, Rusk had the following creditors:

- Safe Bank, for the balance due on the secured note and mortgage on Rusk's warehouse.

- Employee salary claims.

- 1994 federal income taxes due.

- Accountant's fees outstanding.

- Utility bills outstanding.

Prior to the bankruptcy filing, but while insolvent, Rusk engaged in the following transactions:

- On February 1, 1995, Rusk repaid all corporate directors' loans made to the corporation.

- On May 1, 1995, Rusk purchased raw materials for use in its manufacturing business and paid cash to the supplier.

Required:
Items 71 through 75 relate to Rusk's creditors and the February 1 and May 1 transactions. For each item, select from List I whether only statement I is correct, whether only statement II is correct, whether both statements I and II are correct, or whether neither statement I nor II is correct. Blacken the corresponding oval on the *Objective Answer Sheet*.

List I
Ⓐ   I only.
Ⓑ   II only.
Ⓒ   Both I and II.
Ⓓ   Neither I nor II.

71.   I.   Safe Bank's claim will be the first paid of the listed claims because Safe is a secured creditor.
     II.   Safe Bank will receive the entire amount of the balance of the mortgage due as a secured creditor regardless of the amount received from the sale of the warehouse.

72.   I.   The employee salary claims will be paid in full after the payment of any secured party.
     II.   The employee salary claims up to $4,000 per claimant will be paid before payment of any general creditors' claims.

73.   I.   The claim for 1994 federal income taxes due will be paid as a secured creditor claim.
     II.   The claim for 1994 federal income taxes due will be paid prior to the general creditor claims.

74.   I.   The February 1 repayments of the directors' loans were preferential transfers even though the payments were made more than 90 days before the filing of the petition.
     II.   The February 1 repayments of the directors' loans were preferential transfers because the payments were made to insiders.

75.   I.   The May 1 purchase and payment was **not** a preferential transfer because it was a transaction in the ordinary course of business.
     II.   The May 1 purchase and payment was a preferential transfer because it occurred within 90 days of the filing of the petition.

M93
Number 2 (Estimated time — — 15 to 25 minutes)

Instructions

Question Number 2 consists of 15 items. Select the **best** answer for each item. Use a No. 2 pencil to blacken the appropriate ovals on the Objective Answer Sheet to indicate your answers. **Answer all items.** Your grade will be based on the total number of correct answers.

On April 15, 1992, Wren Corp., an appliance wholesaler, was petitioned involuntarily into bankruptcy under the liquidation provisions of Chapter 7 of the Federal Bankruptcy Code.

When the petition was filed, Wren's creditors included:

Secured creditors	Amount owed
Fifth Bank — 1st mortgage on warehouse owned by Wren	$50,000
Hart Manufacturing Corp. — perfected purchase money security interest in inventory	30,000
TVN Computers, Inc. — perfected security interest in office computers	15,000

Unsecured creditors	Amount owed
IRS — 1990 federal income taxes	$20,000
Acme Office Cleaners — services for January, February, and March 1992	750
Ted Smith (employee) — February and March 1992 wages	2,400
Joan Sims (employee) — March 1992 commissions	1,500
Power Electric Co. — electricity charges for January, February, and March 1992	600
Soft Office Supplies — supplies purchased in 1991	2,000

The following transactions occurred before the bankruptcy petition was filed:

- On December 31, 1991, Wren paid off a $5,000 loan from Mary Lake, the sister of one of Wren's directors.
- On January 30, 1992, Wren donated $2,000 to Universal Charities.
- On February 1, 1992, Wren gave Young Finance Co. a security agreement covering Wren's office fixtures to secure a loan previously made by Young.
- On March 1, 1992, Wren made the final $1,000 monthly payment to Integral Appliance Corp. on a two-year note.
- On April 1, 1992, Wren purchased from Safety Co., a new burglar alarm system for its factory, for $5,000 cash.

All of Wren's assets were liquidated. The warehouse was sold for $75,000, the computers were sold for $12,000, and the inventory was sold for $25,000. After paying the bankruptcy administration expenses of $8,000, secured creditors, and priority general creditors, there was enough cash to pay each nonpriority general creditor 50 cents on the dollar.

Required:

a. Items 61 through 65 represent the transactions that occurred before the filing of the bankruptcy petition. For each transaction, determine if the transaction would be set aside as a preferential transfer by the bankruptcy court. On the Objective Answer Sheet, blacken Ⓨ if the transaction would be set aside or Ⓝ if the transaction would **not** be set aside.

61. Payment to Mary Lake
62. Donation to Universal Charities
63. Security agreement to Young Finance Co.
64. Payment to Integral Appliance Corp.
65. Purchase from Safety Co.

b. Items 66 through 70 represent creditor claims against the bankruptcy estate. Select from List I each creditor's order of payment in relation to the other creditors named in items 66 through 70 and blacken the corresponding oval on the Objective Answer Sheet.

		List I
66.	Bankruptcy administration expense	A. First
67.	Acme Office Cleaners	B. Second
68.	Fifth Bank	C. Third
69.	IRS	D. Fourth
70.	Joan Sims	E. Fifth

V. Government Regulation of Business

A. Federal Securities Acts

N95
Number 3(b) (Estimated time —— 10 to 15 minutes)

b. **Items 76 through 80** are based on the following:

Coffee Corp., a publicly-held corporation, wants to make an $8,000,000 exempt offering of its shares as a private placement offering under Regulation D, Rule 506, of the Securities Act of 1933. Coffee has more than 500 shareholders and assets in excess of $1 billion, and has its shares listed on a national securities exchange.

Required:
Items 76 through 80 relate to the application of the provisions of the Securities Act of 1933 and the Securities Exchange Act of 1934 to Coffee Corp. and the offering. For each item, select from List II whether only statement I is correct, whether only statement II is correct, whether both statements I and II are correct, or whether neither statement I nor II is correct. Blacken the corresponding oval on the *Objective Answer Sheet*.

List II
Ⓐ I only.
Ⓑ II only.
Ⓒ Both I and II.
Ⓓ Neither I nor II.

76. I. Coffee Corp. may make the Regulation D, Rule 506, exempt offering.
    II. Coffee Corp., because it is required to report under the Securities Exchange Act of 1934, may **not** make an exempt offering.

77. I. Shares sold under a Regulation D, Rule 506, exempt offering may only be purchased by accredited investors.
    II. Shares sold under a Regulation D, Rule 506, exempt offering may be purchased by any number of investors provided there are **no** more than 35 non-accredited investors.

78. I. An exempt offering under Regulation D, Rule 506, must **not** be for more than $10,000,000.
    II. An exempt offering under Regulation D, Rule 506, has **no** dollar limit.

79. I. Regulation D, Rule 506, requires that all investors in the exempt offering be notified that for nine months after the last sale **no** resale may be made to a nonresident.
    II. Regulation D, Rule 506, requires that the issuer exercise reasonable care to assure that purchasers of the exempt offering are buying for investment and are **not** underwriters.

80. I. The SEC must be notified by Coffee Corp. within 5 days of the first sale of the exempt offering securities.
    II. Coffee Corp. must include an SEC notification of the first sale of the exempt offering securities in Coffee's next filed Quarterly Report (Form 10-Q).

The next question begins on page B-104.

Business Law and Professional Responsibilities

N92
Number 2 (Estimated time — — 15 to 25 minutes)

Question Number 2 is based on the following information. Question Number 2 consists of Items 61 through 75.

Butler Manufacturing Corp. planned to raise capital for a plant expansion by borrowing from banks and making several stock offerings. Butler engaged Weaver, CPA, to audit its December 31, 1989, financial statements. Butler told Weaver that the financial statements would be given to certain named banks and included in the prospectuses for the stock offerings.

In performing the audit, Weaver did not confirm accounts receivable and, as a result, failed to discover a material overstatement of accounts receivable. Also, Weaver was aware of a pending class action product liability lawsuit that was not disclosed in Butler's financial statements. Despite being advised by Butler's legal counsel that Butler's potential liability under the lawsuit would result in material losses, Weaver issued an unqualified opinion on Butler's financial statements.

In May 1990, Union Bank, one of the named banks, relied on the financial statements and Weaver's opinion in giving Butler a $500,000 loan.

Butler raised an additional $16,450,000 through the following stock offerings, which were sold completely:

- June 1990 — Butler made a $450,000 unregistered offering of Class B nonvoting common stock under Rule 504 of Regulation D of the Securities Act of 1933. This offering was sold over two years to 30 nonaccredited investors and 20 accredited investors by general solicitation. The SEC was notified eight days after the first sale of this offering.

- September 1990 — Butler made a $10,000,000 unregistered offering of Class A voting common stock under Rule 506 of Regulation D of the Securities Act of 1933. This offering was sold over two years to 200 accredited investors and 30 nonaccredited investors through a private placement. The SEC was notified 14 days after the first sale of this offering.

- November 1990 — Butler made a $6,000,000 unregistered offering of preferred stock under Rule 505 of Regulation D of the Securities Act of 1933. This offering was sold during a one-year period to 40 nonaccredited investors by private placement. The SEC was notified 18 days after the first sale of this offering.

Shortly after obtaining the Union loan, Butler began experiencing financial problems but was able to stay in business because of the money raised by the offerings. Butler was found liable in the product liability suit. This resulted in a judgment Butler could not pay. Butler also defaulted on the Union loan and was involuntarily petitioned into bankruptcy. This caused Union to sustain a loss and Butler's stockholders to lose their investments.

As a result:

- The SEC claimed that all three of Butler's offerings were made improperly and were not exempt from registration.

- Union sued Weaver for
  - Negligence
  - Common Law Fraud

- The stockholders who purchased Butler's stock through the offerings sued Weaver, alleging fraud under Section 10(b) and Rule 10b-5 of the Securities Exchange Act of 1934.

These transactions took place in a jurisdiction providing for accountant's liability for negligence to known and intended users of financial statements.

Selected Questions

Instructions

Question Number 2 consists of 15 items. Select the **best** answer for each item. Use a No. 2 pencil to blacken the appropriate ovals on the Objective Answer Sheet to indicate your answers. **Answer all items.** Your grade will be based on the total number of correct answers.

Example:
The following is an example of the manner in which your answer sheet should be marked.

Item

99. Does the SEC regulate the securities industry?

Answer Sheet

Item	Yes	No
99	●	Ⓝ

Required:

a. Items 61 through 65 are questions related to the June 1990 offering made under Rule 504 of Regulation D of the Securities Act of 1933. For each item, indicate your answer by blackening either yes Ⓨ or no Ⓝ on the Objective Answer Sheet.

61. Did the offering comply with the dollar limitation of Rule 504?
62. Did the offering comply with the method of sale restrictions?
63. Was the offering sold during the applicable time limit?
64. Was the SEC notified timely of the first sale of the securities?
65. Was the SEC correct in claiming that this offering was not exempt from registration?

b. Items 66 through 70 are questions related to the September 1990 offering made under Rule 506 of Regulation D of the Securities Act of 1933. For each item, indicate your answer by blackening either yes Ⓨ or no Ⓝ on the Objective Answer Sheet.

66. Did the offering comply with the dollar limitation of Rule 506?
67. Did the offering comply with the method of sale restrictions?
68. Was the offering sold to the correct number of investors?
69. Was the SEC notified timely of the first sale of the securities?
70. Was the SEC correct in claiming that this offering was not exempt from registration?

c. Items 71 through 75 are questions related to the November 1990 offering made under Rule 505 of Regulation D of the Securities Act of 1933. For each item, indicate your answer by blackening either yes Ⓨ or no Ⓝ on the Objective Answer Sheet.

71. Did the offering comply with the dollar limitation of Rule 505?
72. Was the offering sold during the applicable time limit?
73. Was the offering sold to the correct number of investors?
74. Was the SEC notified timely of the first sale of the securities?
75. Was the SEC correct in claiming that this offering was not exempt from registration?

VI. Uniform Commercial Code

A. Negotiable Instruments

R96
Number 2(a) (Estimated time —— 10 to 15 minutes)

Question Number 2 consists of two parts. Each part consists of 5 items. Select the **best** answer for each item. Use a No. 2 pencil to blacken the appropriate ovals on the *Objective Answer Sheet* to indicate your answers. **Answer all items.** Your grade will be based on the total number of correct answers.

    a. Under the Negotiable Instruments Article of the UCC, a note must conform to certain requirements to be negotiable. Similarly, a note's negotiability may be restricted or prevented.

Required:
    Items 1 through 5 are examples of terms, conditions, and indorsements that may appear on a note. For each item, select the effect each term, condition, or indorsement would have on the note's negotiability from List I and blacken the corresponding oval on the *Objective Answer Sheet*. An answer may be selected once, more than once, or not at all.

1. The note is postdated.

2. No place of payment is indicated on the note.

3. The note is payable to the order of a named individual.

4. The note is indorsed "For Collection."

5. The note is payable in either money or goods.

List I—Effect on Negotiability
Ⓐ Has no effect on negotiability.
Ⓑ Restricts negotiability.
Ⓒ Must be negotiated by delivery.
Ⓓ Must be indorsed to be negotiated.
Ⓔ Results in nonnegotiability.

The next question begins on page B-108.

Business Law and Professional Responsibilities

N94
Number 3 (Estimated time — — 10 to 15 minutes)

Question Number 3 consists of 2 parts. Part A consists of 5 items and Part B consists of 8 items. Select the **best** answer for each item. Use a No. 2 pencil to blacken the appropriate ovals on the Objective Answer Sheet to indicate your answers. **Answer all items.** Your grade will be based on the total number of correct answers.

During an audit of Trent Realty Corp.'s financial statements, Clark, CPA, reviewed the following instruments:

A. Instrument 1.

> $300,000   Belle, MD
>   September 15, 1993
>
> For value received, ten years after date, I promise to pay to the order of Dart Finance Co. Three Hundred Thousand and 00/100 dollars with interest at 9% per annum compounded annually until fully paid.
>
> This instrument arises out of the sale of land located in MD.
>
> It is further agreed that:
>
> 1. Maker will pay all costs of collection including reasonable attorney fees.
> 2. Maker may prepay the amount outstanding on any anniversary date of this instrument.
>
>   G. Evans
>   ─────────
>   G. Evans

The following transactions relate to Instrument 1.

- On March 15, 1994, Dart endorsed the instrument in blank and sold it to Morton for $275,000.
- On July 10, 1994, Evans informed Morton that Dart had fraudulently induced Evans into signing the instrument.
- On August 15, 1994, Trent, which knew of Evans' claim against Dart, purchased the instrument from Morton for $50,000.

Required:
    Items 76 through 80 relate to Instrument 1. For each item, select from List I the correct answer and blacken the corresponding oval on the Objective Answer Sheet. An answer may be selected once, more than once, or not at all.

List I

76. Instrument 1 is a (type of instrument)

77. Instrument 1 is (negotiability)

78. Morton is considered a (type of ownership)

79. Trent is considered a (type of ownership)

80. Trent could recover on the instrument from (liable party (s))

A. Draft
B. Promissory Note
C. Security Agreement
D. Holder
E. Holder in due course
F. Holder with rights of a holder in due course under the Shelter Provision
G. Negotiable
H. Nonnegotiable
I. Evans, Morton, and Dart
J. Morton and Dart
K. Only Dart

B. Instrument 2.

Front:
```
To: Pure Bank
    Upton, VT

                              April 5, 1994

Pay to the order of M. West  $1,500.00
One Thousand Five Hundred and 00/100
Dollars on May 1, 1994

                    W. Fields
                    ─────────
                    W. Fields
```

Back:
```
M. West

Pay to C. Larr
T. Keetin

C. Larr
without recourse
```

Required:
   Items 81 through 88 relate to Instrument 2. For each item, select from List II the correct answer and blacken the corresponding oval on the Objective Answer Sheet. An answer may be selected once, more than once, or not at all.

List II

A. Bearer paper
B. Blank
C. Check
D. Draft
E. Negotiable
F. Nonnegotiable
G. Note
H. Order paper
I. Qualified
J. Special

81. Instrument 2 is a (type of instrument)

82. Instrument 2 is (negotiability)

83. West's endorsement makes the instrument (type of instrument)

84. Keetin's endorsement makes the instrument (type of instrument)

85. Larr's endorsement makes the instrument (type of instrument)

86. West's endorsement would be considered (type of endorsement)

87. Keetin's endorsement would be considered (type of endorsement)

88. Larr's endorsement would be considered (type of endorsement)

Business Law and Professional Responsibilities

M94
Number 3 (Estimated time — 10 to 15 minutes)

Question Number 3 consists of 2 parts. Each part consists of 6 items. Select the **best** answer for each item. Use a No. 2 pencil to blacken the appropriate oval on the Objective Answer Sheet to indicate your answers. **Answer all items.** Your grade will be based on the total number of correct answers.

A. **Items 73 through 78** are based on the following documents:

Document I (face)

April 1, 1994

On demand, the undersigned promises to pay to the order of

MARK EDEN

Three Thousand Two Hundred and $^{NO}/_{100}$ ($3,300.00) .... dollars

Alice Long
Alice Long

Document I (back)

Mark Eden

Pay Joyce Noon
Harold Storm

Document II (face)

April 15, 1994

On May 1, 1994, or sooner, pay to the order of

EDWARD THARP

Two Thousand and $^{NO}/_{100}$ ($2,000.00) .... dollars

To: Henry Gage
100 East Way
Capital City, ND

Patricia Rite
Patricia Rite

Document II (back)

Edward Tharp

Nancy Ferry
without recourse

Ann Archer

Required:
Items 73 through 78 relate to the nature and negotiability of the above documents and the nature of several of the endorsements. For each item select from List A the response that best completes that statement and blacken the corresponding oval on the Objective Answer Sheet. A response may be selected more than once.

		List A
73. Document I is a (type of instrument)	A.	Blank
74. Document II is a (type of instrument)	B.	Check
75. Document I is (negotiability)	C.	Draft
76. Document II is (negotiability)	D.	Negotiable
77. The endorsement by Mark Eden is (type of endorsement)	E.	Nonnegotiable
78. The endorsement by Nancy Ferry is (type of endorsement)	F.	Promissory Note
	G.	Qualified
	H.	Special

B. Sales

M95
Number 3(a) (Estimated time — — 10 to 15 minutes)

Question Number 3 consists of two parts. Each part consists of 6 items. Select the **best** answer for each item. Use a No. 2 pencil to blacken the appropriate ovals on the *Objective Answer Sheet* to indicate your answers. **Answer all items.** Your grade will be based on the total number of correct answers.

a. On February 1, 1995, Grand Corp., a manufacturer of custom cabinets, contracted in writing with Axle Co., a kitchen contractor, to sell Axle 100 unique, custom-designed, kitchen cabinets for $250,000. Axle had contracted to install the cabinets in a luxury condominium complex. The contract provided that the cabinets were to be ready for delivery by April 15 and were to be shipped F.O.B. sellers loading dock. On April 15, Grand had 85 cabinets complete and delivered them, together with 15 standard cabinets, to the trucking company for delivery to Axle. Grand faxed Axle a copy of the shipping invoice, listing the 15 standard cabinets. On May 1, before reaching Axle, the truck was involved in a collision and all the cabinets were damaged beyond repair.

Required:
Items 73 through 78 refer to the above fact pattern. For each item, determine whether Ⓐ, Ⓑ, or Ⓒ is correct. On the *Objective Answer Sheet*, blacken the oval that corresponds to the correct statement.

73. A. The contract between Grand and Axle was a shipment contract.
    B. The contract between Grand and Axle was a destination contract.
    C. The contract between Grand and Axle was a consignment contract.

74. A. The risk of loss for the 85 custom cabinets passed to Axle on April 15.
    B. The risk of loss for the 100 cabinets passed to Axle on April 15.
    C. The risk of loss for the 100 cabinets remained with Grand.

75. A. The contract between Grand and Axle was invalid because **no** delivery date was stated.
    B. The contract between Grand and Axle was voidable because Grand shipped only 85 custom cabinets.
    C. The contract between Grand and Axle was void because the goods were destroyed.

76. A. Grand's shipment of the standard cabinets was a breach of the contract with Axle.
    B. Grand would **not** be considered to have breached the contract until Axle rejected the standard cabinets.
    C. Grand made a counteroffer by shipping the standard cabinets.

77. A. Had the cabinets been delivered, title would **not** transfer to Axle until Axle inspected them.
    B. Had the cabinets been delivered, title would have transferred on delivery to the carrier.
    C. Had the cabinets been delivered, title would **not** have transferred because the cabinets were nonconforming goods.

78. A. Axle is entitled to specific performance from Grand because of the unique nature of the goods.
    B. Axle is required to purchase substitute goods (cover) and is entitled to the difference in cost from Grand.
    C. Axle is entitled to punitive damages because of Grand's intentional shipment of nonconforming goods.

C. Secured Transactions

R96
Number 2(b) (Estimated time — 10 to 15 minutes)

b. Under the Secured Transactions Article of the UCC, any transaction intended to establish a security interest in personal property is governed by requirements for the creation and satisfaction of that interest.

Required:
Items 6 through 10 relate to situations involved in the creation and/or satisfaction of a security interest. For each item, select the effect that will result from each situation from List II and blacken the corresponding oval on the *Objective Answer Sheet.* An answer may be selected once, more than once, or not at all.

6. The security interest obtained by a creditor who lends money to a debtor to purchase goods used in the debtor's business will be

7. A seller of consumer goods who obtains an oral security agreement from a purchaser in the ordinary course of business will have

8. A creditor who is transferred collateral to hold as security by a debtor, pursuant to agreement, will have

9. A creditor who files a financing statement would, at the most, have

10. A creditor who files a financing statement on October 15 will have priority over another creditor who has a signed but unfiled security agreement dated October 1 because of

List II—Effect
Ⓐ An attached security interest.
Ⓑ A priority due to attachment.
Ⓒ A priority due to perfection.
Ⓓ A priority due to chronological order.
Ⓔ A purchase money security interest.
Ⓕ A security interest in receivables.
Ⓖ A security interest perfected by filing.
Ⓗ A security interest perfected without filing.
Ⓘ No security interest.

M95
Number 3(b) (Estimated time — 10 to 15 minutes)

b. On January 2, 1994, Gray Interiors Corp., a retailer of sofas, contracted with Shore Furniture Co. to purchase 150 sofas for its inventory. The purchase price was $250,000. Gray paid $50,000 cash and gave Shore a note and security agreement for the balance. On March 1, 1994, the sofas were delivered. On March 10, 1994, Shore filed a financing statement.

On February 1, 1994, Gray negotiated a $1,000,000 line of credit with Float Bank, pledged its present and future inventory as security, and gave Float a security agreement. On February 20, 1994, Gray borrowed $100,000 from the line of credit. On March 5, 1994, Float filed a financing statement.

On April 1, 1994, Dove, a consumer purchaser in the ordinary course of business, purchased a sofa from Gray. Dove was aware of both security interests.

Required:
Items 79 through 84 refer to the above fact pattern. For each item, determine whether Ⓐ, Ⓑ, or Ⓒ is correct.

On the *Objective Answer Sheet,* blacken the oval that corresponds to the correct statement.

79. Shore's security interest in the sofas attached on
   A. January 2, 1994.
   B. March 1, 1994.
   C. March 10, 1994.

80. Shore's security interest in the sofas was perfected on
   A. January 2, 1994.
   B. March 1, 1994.
   C. March 10, 1994.

81. Float's security interest in Gray's inventory attached on
   A. February 1, 1994.
   B. March 1, 1994.
   C. March 5, 1994.

82. Float's security interest in Gray's inventory was perfected on
   A. February 1, 1994.
   B. February 20, 1994.
   C. March 5, 1994.

83. A. Shore's security interest has priority because it was a purchase money security interest.
    B. Float's security interest has priority because Float's financing statement was filed before Shore's.
    C. Float's security interest has priority because Float's interest attached before Shore's.

84. A. Dove purchased the sofa subject to Shore's security interest.
    B. Dove purchased the sofa subject to both the Shore and Float security interests.
    C. Dove purchased the sofa free of either the Shore or Float security interests.

VII. Property

A. Real Property Including Insurance

R97
Number 3

Question Number 3 consists of 5 items. Select the **best** answer for each item. Use a No. 2 pencil to blacken the appropriate ovals on the *Objective Answer Sheet* to indicate your answers. **Answer all items.** Your grade will be based on the total number of correct answers.

Items 1 through 5 are based on the following:

Wolf purchased a factory building for $800,000. At the time of the purchase, Wolf obtained a fire insurance policy with a face value of $400,000 from Acme Fire Insurance Co. At the same time, Wolf obtained another fire insurance policy with a face value of $200,000 from Prevent Fire Insurance Corp. Each policy contained a standard 80% coinsurance clause and a pro rata clause. Two years later, when the building had a fair market value of $1,000,000, a fire caused $600,000 damage.

Required:

For **Items 1 through 5,** select the correct answer from List I and blacken the corresponding oval on the *Objective Answer Sheet.* An answer may be selected once, more than once, or not at all.

1. What dollar amount of fire insurance coverage should Wolf have obtained when purchasing the building to avoid being considered a coinsurer?
2. What dollar amount of fire insurance coverage should Wolf have at the time of the fire to avoid being considered a coinsurer?
3. What dollar amount should Wolf recover from Acme and Prevent under the fire insurance policies?
4. What dollar amount should Wolf recover under the Acme fire insurance policy?
5. What dollar amount should Wolf recover under the Prevent fire insurance policy?

List I			
Ⓐ	$0	Ⓗ	$450,000
Ⓑ	$150,000	Ⓘ	$480,000
Ⓒ	$160,000	Ⓙ	$600,000
Ⓓ	$200,000	Ⓚ	$640,000
Ⓔ	$300,000	Ⓛ	$750,000
Ⓕ	$360,000	Ⓜ	$800,000
Ⓖ	$400,000		

N93
Number 2 (Estimated time —— 15 to 25 minutes)

Question Number 2 consists of 12 items. Select the best answer for each item. Use a No. 2 pencil to blacken the appropriate ovals on the Objective Answer Sheet to indicate your answers. **Answer all items.** Your grade will be based on the total number of correct answers.

On June 1, 1990, Anderson bought a one family house from Beach for $240,000. At the time of the purchase, the house had a market value of $200,000 and the land was valued at $40,000. Anderson assumed the recorded $150,000 mortgage Beach owed Long Bank, gave a $70,000 mortgage to Rogers Loan Co., and paid $20,000 cash. Rogers did not record its mortgage. Rogers did not know about the Long Mortgage.

Beach gave Anderson a quitclaim deed that failed to mention a recorded easement on the property held by Dalton, the owner of the adjacent piece of property. Anderson purchased a title insurance policy from Edge Title Insurance Co. Edge's policy neither disclosed nor excepted Dalton's easement.

On August 1, 1992, Anderson borrowed $30,000 from Forrest Finance to have a swimming pool dug. Anderson gave Forrest a $30,000 mortgage on the property. Forrest, knowing about the Long mortgage but not the Rogers mortgage, recorded its mortgage on August 10, 1992. After the digging began, Dalton sued to stop the work claiming violation of the easement. The court decided in Dalton's favor.

At the time of the purchase, Anderson had taken out two fire insurance policies; a $120,000 face value policy with Harvest Fire Insurance Co., and a $60,000 face value policy with Grant Fire Insurance Corp. Both policies contained a standard 80% coinsurance clause.

On December 1, 1992, a fire caused $180,000 damage to the house. At that time, the house had a market value of $250,000. Harvest and Grant refused to honor the policies claiming that the house was under insured.

Anderson made no mortgage payments after the fire and on June 1, 1993, after the house had been rebuilt, the mortgages were foreclosed. The balances due for principal and accrued interest were as follows: Long, $140,000; Rogers, $65,000; and Forrest, $28,000. At a foreclosure sale, the house and land were sold. After payment of all expenses, $200,000 of the proceeds remained for distribution. As a result of the above events, the following actions took place:

- Anderson sued Harvest and Grant for the face values of the fire insurance policies.

- Anderson sued Beach for failing to mention Dalton's easement in the quitclaim deed.

- Anderson sued Edge for failing to disclose Dalton's easement.

- Long, Rogers, and Forrest all demanded full payment of their mortgages from the proceeds of the foreclosure sale.

The preceding took place in a "Notice-Race" jurisdiction.

Selected Questions

Required:

a. Items 61 through 63 relate to Anderson's suit against Harvest and Grant. For each item, select from *List I* the dollar amount Anderson will receive and blacken the corresponding oval on the Objective Answer Sheet.

		List I
61.	What will be the dollar amount of Anderson's total fire insurance recovery?	A. $ 0
62.	What dollar amount will be payable by Harvest?	B. $ 20,000
63.	What dollar amount will be payable by Grant?	C. $ 48,000
		D. $ 54,000
		E. $ 60,000
		F. $ 80,000
		G. $ 96,000
		H. $108,000
		I. $120,000
		J. $144,000
		K. $162,000
		L. $180,000

b. Items 64 through 66 have not been selected.

c. Items 67 through 69 have not been selected.

d. Items 70 through 72 relate to the demands Long, Rogers, and Forrest have made to have their mortgages satisfied out of the foreclosure proceeds. For each item, select from *List II* the dollar amount to be paid and blacken the corresponding oval on the Objective Answer Sheet.

		List II
70.	What dollar amount of the foreclosure proceeds will Long receive?	A. $ 0
		B. $ 28,000
71.	What dollar amount of the foreclosure proceeds will Rogers receive?	C. $ 32,000
		D. $ 65,000
72.	What dollar amount of the foreclosure proceeds will Forrest receive?	E. $107,000
		F. $135,000
		G. $140,000

Business Law and Professional Responsibilities

M92
Number 2 (Estimated time — — 15 to 20 minutes)

Instructions

Question Number 2 consists of 18 items. Select the **best** answer for each item. Use a No. 2 pencil to blacken the appropriate ovals on the Objective Answer Sheet to indicate your answers. **Answer all items.** Your grade will be based on the total number of correct answers.

Example:
The following is an example of the manner in which the answer sheet should be marked.

Item

Select from List A the order in which one goes through school in the United States.

99. First school attended.

Answer Sheet

Item	List A (select one)
99	Ⓐ Ⓑ ●

List A
a. High School
b. College
c. Elementary School

On June 10, 1990, Bond sold real property to Edwards for $100,000. Edwards assumed the $80,000 recorded mortgage Bond had previously given to Fair Bank and gave a $20,000 purchase money mortgage to Heath Finance. Heath did not record this mortgage. On December 15, 1991, Edwards sold the property to Ivor for $115,000. Ivor bought the property subject to the Fair mortgage but did not know about the Heath mortgage. Ivor borrowed $50,000 from Knox Bank and gave Knox a mortgage on the property. Knox knew of the unrecorded Heath mortgage when its mortgage was recorded. Ivor, Edwards, and Bond defaulted on the mortgages. Fair, Heath, and Knox foreclosed and the property was sold at a judicial foreclosure sale for $60,000. At the time of the sale, the outstanding balance of principal and accrued interest on the Fair mortgage was $75,000. The Heath mortgage balance was $18,000 and the Knox mortgage was $47,500.

Fair, Heath, and Knox all claim that their mortgages have priority and should be satisfied first from the sale proceeds. Bond, Edwards, and Ivor all claim that they are not liable for any deficiency resulting from the sale.

The above transactions took place in a jurisdiction that has a notice-race recording statute and allows foreclosure deficiency judgments.

Required:
a. Items 61 through 63. For each mortgage, select from List A the priority of that mortgage and blacken the corresponding oval on the Objective Answer Sheet. Blacken Ⓐ if the mortgage has first priority, blacken Ⓑ if the mortgage has second priority, and blacken Ⓒ if the mortgage has third priority. A priority should be selected only once.

List A

61. Knox Bank.   a. First Priority.
62. Heath Finance.   b. Second Priority.
63. Fair Bank.   c. Third Priority.

Selected Questions

b. Items 64 through 66. For each mortgage, select from List B the reason for its priority and blacken the corresponding oval on the Objective Answer Sheet. A reason may be selected once, more than once, or not at all.

List B

64. Knox Bank.
65. Heath Finance.
66. Fair Bank.

a. An unrecorded mortgage has priority over any subsequently recorded mortgage.
b. A recorded mortgage has priority over any unrecorded mortgage.
c. The first recorded mortgage has priority over all subsequent mortgages.
d. An unrecorded mortgage has priority over a subsequently recorded mortgage if the subsequent mortgagee knew of the unrecorded mortgage.
e. A purchase money mortgage has priority over a previously recorded mortgage.

---

c. Items 67 through 69. For each mortgage, select from List C the amount of the sale proceeds that each mortgagee would be entitled to receive and blacken the corresponding oval on the Objective Answer Sheet. An amount may be selected once, more than once, or not at all.

List C

67. Knox Bank.
68. Heath Finance.
69. Fair Bank.

a. $0.
b. $12,500.
c. $18,000.
d. $20,000.
e. $42,000.
f. $47,500.
g. $60,000.

---

d. Items 70 through 72. Determine whether each party would be liable to pay a mortgage foreclosure deficiency judgment on the Fair Bank mortgage. If the party would be held liable, select from List D the reason for the party's liability and blacken the corresponding oval on the Objective Answer Sheet. If you determine there is **no** liability, blacken Ⓓ on the Objective Answer Sheet. A reason may be selected once, more than once, or not at all.

List D

70. Edwards.
71. Bond.
72. Ivor.

a. Original mortgagor.
b. Assumed the mortgage.
c. Took subject to the mortgage.
d. Not liable.

---

e. For items 73 through 75, determine whether each party would be liable to pay a mortgage foreclosure deficiency judgment on the Heath Finance mortgage. If the party would be held liable, select from List E the reason for that party's liability and blacken the corresponding oval on the Objective Answer Sheet. If you determine there is **no** liability, blacken Ⓓ on the Objective Answer Sheet. A reason may be selected once, more than once, or not at all.

List E

73. Edwards.
74. Bond.
75. Ivor.

a. Original mortgagor.
b. Assumed the mortgage.
c. Took subject to the mortgage.
d. Not liable.

---

f. For items 76 through 78, determine whether each party would be liable to pay a mortgage foreclosure deficiency judgment on the Knox Bank mortgage. If the party would be held liable, select from List F the reason for that party's liability and blacken the corresponding oval on the Objective Answer Sheet. If you determine there is **no** liability, blacken Ⓓ on the Objective Answer Sheet. A reason may be selected once, more than once, or not at all.

List F

76. Edwards.
77. Bond.
78. Ivor.

a. Original mortgagor.
b. Assumed the mortgage.
c. Took subject to the mortgage.
d. Not liable.

SELECTED OTHER OBJECTIVE ANSWER FORMATS — UNOFFICIAL ANSWERS

I. Professional and Legal Responsibilities

F. Federal Statutory Liability

M94
Answer 2A

Item	A (Select one)			
61	Ⓐ	Ⓑ	●	Ⓓ
62	Ⓐ	Ⓑ	●	Ⓓ
63	Ⓐ	Ⓑ	Ⓒ	●
64	Ⓐ	Ⓑ	Ⓒ	●
65	Ⓐ	●	Ⓒ	Ⓓ
66	Ⓐ	●	Ⓒ	Ⓓ

II. Business Organizations

A. Agency

N95
Answer 2(a)

a. Item	Select one			
61	Ⓐ	●	Ⓒ	Ⓓ
62	●	Ⓑ	Ⓒ	Ⓓ
63	Ⓐ	●	Ⓒ	Ⓓ
64	Ⓐ	Ⓑ	Ⓒ	●
65	●	Ⓑ	Ⓒ	Ⓓ

Business Law and Professional Responsibilities

B. Partnership, Joint Ventures, and Other Unincorporated Associations

R97
Answer 1

ANSWER 1

	List I (Select one)		List II (Select one)		List III (Select one)
1	Ⓐ Ⓑ Ⓒ Ⓓ ●	4	Ⓐ ● Ⓒ Ⓓ Ⓔ	5	● Ⓑ Ⓒ
2	● Ⓑ Ⓒ Ⓓ Ⓔ				
3	Ⓐ Ⓑ Ⓒ Ⓓ ●				

M95
Answer 2(a)

ANSWER 2

a. Item	Select one	
61	●	Ⓑ
62	●	Ⓑ
63	Ⓐ	●
64	Ⓐ	●
65	Ⓐ	●
66	Ⓐ	●

C. Corporations

R97
Answer 2

ANSWER 2

	List IV (Select one)
1	Ⓐ Ⓑ Ⓒ Ⓓ Ⓔ Ⓕ ● Ⓗ Ⓘ Ⓙ
2	Ⓐ Ⓑ Ⓒ Ⓓ Ⓔ Ⓕ Ⓖ ● Ⓘ Ⓙ
3	Ⓐ Ⓑ Ⓒ Ⓓ Ⓔ Ⓕ Ⓖ Ⓗ Ⓘ ●
4	Ⓐ Ⓑ Ⓒ Ⓓ Ⓔ Ⓕ ● Ⓗ Ⓘ Ⓙ
5	Ⓐ Ⓑ Ⓒ Ⓓ Ⓔ ● Ⓖ Ⓗ Ⓘ Ⓙ

R96
Answer 1

Item	Select one
1	Ⓐ Ⓑ Ⓒ Ⓓ ● Ⓕ Ⓖ Ⓗ Ⓘ Ⓙ Ⓚ Ⓛ Ⓜ Ⓝ Ⓞ Ⓟ
2	Ⓐ Ⓑ Ⓒ Ⓓ Ⓔ Ⓕ Ⓖ ● Ⓘ Ⓙ Ⓚ Ⓛ Ⓜ Ⓝ Ⓞ Ⓟ
3	● Ⓑ Ⓒ Ⓓ Ⓔ Ⓕ Ⓖ Ⓗ Ⓘ Ⓙ Ⓚ Ⓛ Ⓜ Ⓝ Ⓞ Ⓟ
4	Ⓐ Ⓑ ● Ⓓ Ⓔ Ⓕ Ⓖ Ⓗ Ⓘ Ⓙ Ⓚ Ⓛ Ⓜ Ⓝ Ⓞ Ⓟ
5	Ⓐ Ⓑ Ⓒ Ⓓ Ⓔ Ⓕ Ⓖ Ⓗ Ⓘ Ⓙ Ⓚ Ⓛ Ⓜ Ⓝ ● Ⓟ
6	Ⓐ Ⓑ Ⓒ Ⓓ Ⓔ Ⓕ Ⓖ Ⓗ Ⓘ Ⓙ Ⓚ Ⓛ Ⓜ ● Ⓞ Ⓟ

M95
Answer 2(b)

b. Item	Select one
67	● Ⓑ Ⓒ
68	Ⓐ Ⓑ ●
69	Ⓐ Ⓑ ●
70	Ⓐ ● Ⓒ
71	Ⓐ Ⓑ ●
72	Ⓐ Ⓑ ●

D. Estates and Trusts

N95
Answer 2(b)

b. Item	Select one
66	Ⓐ Ⓑ ● Ⓓ
67	● Ⓑ Ⓒ Ⓓ
68	Ⓐ ● Ⓒ Ⓓ
69	Ⓐ ● Ⓒ Ⓓ
70	Ⓐ Ⓑ Ⓒ ●

Business Law and Professional Responsibilities

III. Contracts

R98
Answer 1 (10 points)

ANSWER 1

List I (Select one)

1. (A) (B) (C) (D) (E) (F) (G) (H) (I) ●
2. (A) (B) ● (D) (E) (F) (G) (H) (I) (J)
3. (A) (B) (C) ● (E) (F) (G) (H) (I) (J)
4. (A) (B) (C) (D) ● (F) (G) (H) (I) (J)
5. (A) (B) (C) (D) (E) (F) ● (H) (I) (J)

List II (Select one)

6. (A) (B) (C) (D) ● (F) (G) (H) (I) (J) (K) (L) (M)
7. (A) (B) (C) (D) ● (F) (G) (H) (I) (J) (K) (L) (M)
8. (A) (B) (C) (D) (E) (F) ● (H) (I) (J) (K) (L) (M)
9. (A) (B) (C) (D) (E) (F) (G) (H) (I) (J) ● (L) (M)
10. ● (B) (C) (D) (E) (F) (G) (H) (I) (J) (K) (L) (M)

IV. Debtor-Creditor Relationships

C. Bankruptcy

N95
Answer 3(a)

a. Item	Select one			
71	●	(B)	(C)	(D)
72	(A)	●	(C)	(D)
73	(A)	●	(C)	(D)
74	(A)	(B)	●	(D)
75	●	(B)	(C)	(D)

B-122

M93
Answer 2

ANSWER 2

a.
Item	Select One	
61	●	N
62	Y	●
63	●	N
64	Y	●
65	Y	●

b.
Item	Select One				
66	A	●	C	D	E
67	A	B	C	D	●
68	●	B	C	D	E
69	A	B	C	●	E
70	A	B	●	D	E

V. Government Regulation of Business

A. Federal Securities Acts

N95
Answer 3(b)

ANSWER 3

b. Item	Select one			
76	●	B	C	D
77	A	●	C	D
78	A	●	C	D
79	A	●	C	D
80	A	B	C	●

N92
Answer 2

ANSWER 2

Item	Yes	No
61	●	N
62	Y	●
63	Y	●
64	●	N
65	●	N

Item	Yes	No
66	●	N
67	●	N
68	●	N
69	●	N
70	Y	●

Item	Yes	No
71	Y	●
72	●	N
73	Y	●
74	Y	●
75	●	N

Business Law and Professional Responsibilities

VI. Uniform Commercial Code

A. Negotiable Instruments

R96
Answer 2(a)

ANSWER 2

a.

Item	List I (Select one)
1	● B C D E
2	● B C D E
3	A B C ● E
4	A ● C D E
5	A B C D ●

N94
Answer 3

ANSWER 3

A. Item — List I (Select one)

Item	A	B	C	D	E	F	G	H	I	J	K
76	A	●	C	D	E	F	G	H	I	J	K
77	A	B	C	D	E	F	●	H	I	J	K
78	A	B	C	D	●	F	G	H	I	J	K
79	A	B	C	D	E	●	G	H	I	J	K
80	A	B	C	D	E	F	G	H	●	J	K

B. Item — List II (Select one)

Item	A	B	C	D	E	F	G	H	I	J
81	A	B	C	●	E	F	G	H	I	J
82	A	B	C	D	●	F	G	H	I	J
83	●	B	C	D	E	F	G	H	I	J
84	A	B	C	D	E	F	●	H	I	J
85	●	B	C	D	E	F	G	H	I	J
86	A	●	C	D	E	F	G	H	I	J
87	A	B	C	D	E	F	G	H	I	●
88	A	B	C	D	E	F	G	H	●	J

M94
Answer 3A

	Item	A (Select one)							
ANSWER 3	73	A	B	C	D	E	●	G	H
	74	A	B	●	D	E	F	G	H
	75	A	B	C	●	E	F	G	H
	76	A	B	C	●	E	F	G	H
	77	●	B	C	D	E	F	G	H
	78	A	B	C	D	E	F	●	H

B. Sales

M95
Answer 3(a)

	a. Item	Select one		
ANSWER 3	73	●	B	C
	74	A	B	●
	75	A	●	C
	76	●	B	C
	77	A	B	●
	78	●	B	C

C. Secured Transactions

R96
Answer 2(b)

	b. Item	List II (Select one)								
ANSWER 2	6	A	B	C	D	●	F	G	H	I
	7	A	B	C	D	E	F	G	H	●
	8	A	B	C	D	E	F	G	●	I
	9	A	B	C	D	E	F	●	H	I
	10	A	B	●	D	E	F	G	H	I

M95
Answer 3(b)

b. Item	Select one		
79	Ⓐ	●	Ⓒ
80	Ⓐ	Ⓑ	●
81	●	Ⓑ	Ⓒ
82	Ⓐ	Ⓑ	●
83	Ⓐ	●	Ⓒ
84	Ⓐ	Ⓑ	●

VII. Property

A. Real Property Including Insurance

R97
Answer 3

List I (Select one)

ANSWER 3	A	B	C	D	E	F	G	H	I	J	K	L	M
1	Ⓐ	Ⓑ	Ⓒ	Ⓓ	Ⓔ	Ⓕ	Ⓖ	Ⓗ	Ⓘ	Ⓙ	●	Ⓛ	Ⓜ
2	Ⓐ	Ⓑ	Ⓒ	Ⓓ	Ⓔ	Ⓕ	Ⓖ	Ⓗ	Ⓘ	Ⓙ	Ⓚ	Ⓛ	●
3	Ⓐ	Ⓑ	Ⓒ	Ⓓ	Ⓔ	Ⓕ	Ⓖ	●	Ⓘ	Ⓙ	Ⓚ	Ⓛ	Ⓜ
4	Ⓐ	Ⓑ	Ⓒ	Ⓓ	●	Ⓕ	Ⓖ	Ⓗ	Ⓘ	Ⓙ	Ⓚ	Ⓛ	Ⓜ
5	Ⓐ	●	Ⓒ	Ⓓ	Ⓔ	Ⓕ	Ⓖ	Ⓗ	Ⓘ	Ⓙ	Ⓚ	Ⓛ	Ⓜ

N93
Answer 2 (10 points)

a.

Item	List I (select one)
61	Ⓐ Ⓑ Ⓒ Ⓓ Ⓔ Ⓕ Ⓖ Ⓗ Ⓘ Ⓙ ● Ⓛ
62	Ⓐ Ⓑ Ⓒ Ⓓ Ⓔ Ⓕ Ⓖ ● Ⓘ Ⓙ Ⓚ Ⓛ
63	Ⓐ Ⓑ Ⓒ ● Ⓔ Ⓕ Ⓖ Ⓗ Ⓘ Ⓙ Ⓚ Ⓛ

d.

Item	List II (select one)
70	Ⓐ Ⓑ Ⓒ Ⓓ Ⓔ Ⓕ ●
71	Ⓐ Ⓑ ● Ⓓ Ⓔ Ⓕ Ⓖ
72	Ⓐ ● Ⓒ Ⓓ Ⓔ Ⓕ Ⓖ

M92
Answer 2 (10 points)

Item	List A (select one)	Item	List D (select one)
61	Ⓐ Ⓑ ●	70	Ⓐ ● Ⓒ Ⓓ
62	Ⓐ ● Ⓒ	71	● Ⓑ Ⓒ Ⓓ
63	● Ⓑ Ⓒ	72	Ⓐ Ⓑ Ⓒ ●

Item	List B (select one)	Item	List E (select one)
64	Ⓐ Ⓑ Ⓒ ● Ⓔ	73	● Ⓑ Ⓒ Ⓓ
65	Ⓐ Ⓑ Ⓒ ● Ⓔ	74	Ⓐ Ⓑ Ⓒ ●
66	Ⓐ Ⓑ ● Ⓓ Ⓔ	75	Ⓐ Ⓑ Ⓒ ●

Item	List C (select one)	Item	List F (select one)
67	● Ⓑ Ⓒ Ⓓ Ⓔ Ⓕ Ⓖ	76	Ⓐ Ⓑ Ⓒ ●
68	● Ⓑ Ⓒ Ⓓ Ⓔ Ⓕ Ⓖ	77	Ⓐ Ⓑ Ⓒ ●
69	Ⓐ Ⓑ Ⓒ Ⓓ Ⓔ Ⓕ ●	78	● Ⓑ Ⓒ Ⓓ

ESSAYS — SELECTED QUESTIONS

I. Professional and Legal Responsibilities

A. Code of Professional Conduct

R96
Number 2(a) (Estimated time — — 15 to 25 minutes)

Dredge Corp. engaged Crew, a CPA licensed by a state board of accountancy, to perform an audit of Dredge's financial statements so that Dredge could obtain a large capital improvement loan. During the audit, Bold, Dredge's CFO, asked Crew to accept a consulting engagement to assist Dredge with the installation of a new computerized accounting system. Crew accepted the consulting engagement and performed it simultaneously with the audit.

While performing the audit, Crew discovered material misstatements in Dredge's financial statements resulting from management fraud committed by Bold. Crew notified Bold of the discovery and was told to disregard it or Crew would lose the consulting engagement. Believing that the consulting engagement would be lost, Crew intentionally did not notify Dredge's audit committee of the fraud, and rendered an unqualified opinion on Dredge's financial statements.

Dredge submitted to Ocean Bank the materially misstated financial statements together with Crew's auditor's report. Ocean relied on the opinion in agreeing to finance Dredge's capital improvement.

While performing the consulting engagement, Crew failed to discover that Dredge's new computerized accounting system had insufficient control procedures because Crew omitted steps in order to complete the engagement on time. The insufficient control procedures had allowed and were allowing employees to steal from the corporation.

As a result of Bold's fraud, Dredge defaulted on the Ocean loan and was petitioned into bankruptcy under Chapter 11 of the Federal Bankruptcy Code.

The following events resulted from the above situation:

- Dredge Corp. reported Crew's actions to the state board of accountancy that licensed Crew.

- Dredge Corp. sued Crew for negligence in performing the consulting engagement.

- Ocean Bank sued Crew for common law fraud for giving an unqualified opinion on Dredge's financial statements.

Required:
a. 1. Determine whether or not Crew violated the profession's standards in the areas of independence (when accepting the engagements), due care, and acts discreditable to the profession, and give the reasons for your conclusions.
2. State the actions the state board of accountancy may take against Crew.

E. Common Law Liability to Clients and Third Parties

R96
Number 2(b) (Estimated time — — 15 to 25 minutes)

Dredge Corp. engaged Crew, a CPA licensed by a state board of accountancy, to perform an audit of Dredge's financial statements so that Dredge could obtain a large capital improvement loan. During the audit, Bold, Dredge's CFO, asked Crew to accept a consulting engagement to assist Dredge with the installation of a new computerized accounting system. Crew accepted the consulting engagement and performed it simultaneously with the audit.

While performing the audit, Crew discovered material misstatements in Dredge's financial statements resulting from management fraud committed by Bold. Crew notified Bold of the discovery and was told to disregard it or Crew would lose the consulting engagement. Believing that the consulting engagement would be lost, Crew intentionally did not notify Dredge's audit committee of the fraud, and rendered an unqualified opinion on Dredge's financial statements.

Dredge submitted to Ocean Bank the materially misstated financial statements together with Crew's auditor's report. Ocean relied on the opinion in agreeing to finance Dredge's capital improvement.

While performing the consulting engagement, Crew failed to discover that Dredge's new computerized accounting system had insufficient control procedures because Crew omitted steps in order to complete the engagement on time. The insufficient control procedures had allowed and were allowing employees to steal from the corporation.

As a result of Bold's fraud, Dredge defaulted on the Ocean loan and was petitioned into bankruptcy under Chapter 11 of the Federal Bankruptcy Code.

The following events resulted from the above situation:

- Dredge Corp. reported Crew's actions to the state board of accountancy that licensed Crew.

- Dredge Corp. sued Crew for negligence in performing the consulting engagement.

- Ocean Bank sued Crew for common law fraud for giving an unqualified opinion on Dredge's financial statements.

Required:
   b. 1. State the outcome of Dredge Corp.'s suit against Crew for negligence in performing the consulting engagement, and give the reasons for your conclusion.
       2. State the outcome of Ocean Bank's suit against Crew for common law fraud for giving an unqualified opinion on Dredge's financial statements, and give the reasons for your conclusion.

M95
Number 4 (Estimated time — — 15 to 25 minutes)

Verge Associates, CPAs, were retained to perform a consulting service engagement by Stone Corp. Verge contracted to advise Stone on the proper computers to purchase. Verge was also to design computer software that would allow for more efficient collection of Stone's accounts receivable. Verge prepared the software programs in a manner that allowed some of Stone's accounts receivable to be erroneously deleted from Stone's records. As a result, Stone's expense to collect these accounts was increased greatly.

During the course of the engagement, a Verge partner learned from a computer salesperson that the computers Verge was recommending to Stone would be obsolete within a year. The salesperson suggested that Verge recommend a newer, less expensive model that was more efficient. Verge intentionally recommended, and Stone purchased, the more expensive model. Verge received a commission from the computer company for inducing Stone to purchase that computer.

Stone sued Verge for negligence and common law fraud.

Required:
   a. State whether Stone will be successful in its negligence suit against Verge and describe the elements of negligence shown in the above situation that Stone should argue.

   b. State whether Stone will be successful in its fraud suit against Verge and describe the elements of fraud shown in the above situation that Stone should argue.

M92
Number 3 (Estimated time — — 15 to 20 minutes)

Goodwin, a CPA, and Jensen, a banker, were the trustees of the Moore Family Trust. The trust was created as a spendthrift trust and provided for distribution of income annually to the four Moore adult children for life, with the principal to be distributed to their issue after the death of the last income beneficiary. The trust was funded with commercial and residential real estate and a stock portfolio.

Goodwin, in addition to being a trustee, was lawfully employed as the trust's accountant. Goodwin, as the trust's accountant, prepared and signed all trust tax returns, kept the trust's accounting records, and supervised distributions to the income beneficiaries.

In 1990, Goodwin and Jensen, as trustees, sold a building owned by the trust for $400,000, its fair market value. The building had been valued at $250,000 when acquired by the trust. The $150,000 gain was allocated to income. In addition, the trust had rental, interest, and dividend income of $1,500,000 in 1990. Expenses for taxes, replacement of plumbing fixtures, roof repairs, utilities, salaries, and fees and commissions totaled $1,050,000.

On December 31, 1990, Goodwin and Jensen prepared and signed four $150,000 trust account checks and sent three of them to three of the income beneficiaries and the fourth one to a creditor of the fourth beneficiary. This beneficiary had acknowledged that the creditor was owed $200,000.

In February 1991, Goodwin discovered that Jensen had embezzled $200,000 by secretly selling part of the trust's stock portfolio. Goodwin agreed not to reveal Jensen's embezzlement if Jensen would pay Goodwin $25,000.

In April 1991, Goodwin prepared the 1990 trust income tax return. The return was signed by Goodwin as preparer and by Jensen and Goodwin as trustees and was filed with the IRS. Goodwin also prepared the 1990 income tax returns for the income beneficiaries. In an attempt to hide the embezzlement, Goodwin, in preparing the trust tax return, claimed nonexistent losses and improper credits. The beneficiaries' returns reflected the same nonexistent losses and improper credits. Consequently, the beneficiaries' taxes were underpaid. As a result of an IRS audit, the embezzlement was uncovered, the nonexistent losses and improper credits were disallowed, and the beneficiaries were assessed additional taxes, penalties, and interest.

Jensen cannot be located.

As a result of the above, the income beneficiaries sued Goodwin for negligence, fraud, and breach of fiduciary duty.

Required:
Answer the following questions and give the reasons for your conclusions.

Will the income beneficiaries win their suits against Goodwin for:

a. accountant's negligence?

b. actual fraud?

c. breach of fiduciary duty as a trustee?

M90
Number 3 (Estimated time —— 15 to 20 minutes)

Astor Electronics, Inc. is engaged in the business of marketing a wide variety of computer-related products throughout the United States. Astor's officers decided to raise $1,000,000 by selling shares of Astor's common stock in an exempt offering under Regulation D of the Securities Act of 1933. In connection with the offering, Astor engaged Apple & Co., CPAs, to audit Astor's 1989 financial statements. The audited financial statements, including Apple's unqualified opinion, were included in the offering memorandum given to prospective purchasers of Astor's stock. Apple was aware that Astor intended to include the statements in the offering materials.

On Astor's financial statements, certain inventory items were reported at a cost of $930,000 when, in fact, they had a fair market value of less than $100,000 because of technological obsolescence. Apple accepted the assurances of Astor's controller that cost was the appropriate valuation, despite the fact that Apple was aware of ongoing sales of the products at prices substantially less than cost. All of this was thoroughly documented in Apple's working papers.

Musk purchased 10,000 shares of Astor's common stock in the Regulation D offering at a total price of $300,000. In deciding to make the purchase, Musk had reviewed the audited financial statements of Astor that accompanied the other offering materials and Musk was impressed by Astor's apparent financial strength.

Shortly after the stock offering was completed, Astor's management discovered that the audited financial statements reflected the materially overstated valuation of the company's inventory. Astor advised its shareholders of the problem.

Musk, upon receiving notice from Astor of the overstated inventory amount, became very upset because the stock value was now substantially less than what it would have been had the financial statements been accurate. In fact, the stock is worth only about $200,000.

Musk has commenced an action against Apple alleging that Apple is liable to Musk based on the following causes of action:

- Common law fraud.
- Negligence.
- A violation of Section 10(b) and Rule 10b-5 of the Securities Exchange Act of 1934.

During the course of the litigation, Apple has refused to give to Musk its working papers pertaining to the Astor audit, claiming that these constituted privileged communications. The state in which the actions have been commenced has no accountants' privileged communication statute.

The state law applicable to this action follows the *Ultramares* decision with respect to accountants' liability to third parties for negligence or fraud.

Apple has also asserted that the actions should be dismissed because of the absence of any contractual relationship between Apple and Musk, i.e., a lack of privity.

Required:
Answer the following, setting forth reasons for any conclusions stated.

a. Will Apple be required to give Musk its working papers?

b. What elements must be established by Musk to support his cause of action based on negligence?

c. What elements must be established by Musk to support his cause of action based on a Rule 10b-5 violation?

d. Is Apple's assertion regarding lack of privity correct with regard to Musk's causes of action for negligence and fraud?

N89
Number 3 (Estimated time —— 15 to 20 minutes)

Astor Inc. purchased the assets of Bell Corp. A condition of the purchase agreement required Bell to retain a CPA to audit Bell's financial statements. The purpose of the audit was to determine whether the unaudited financial statements furnished to Astor fairly presented Bell's financial position. Bell retained Salam & Co., CPAs, to perform the audit.

While performing the audit, Salam discovered that Bell's bookkeeper had embezzled $500. Salam had some evidence of other embezzlements by the bookkeeper. However, Salam decided that the $500 was immaterial and that the other suspected embezzlements did not require further investigation. Salam did not discuss the matter with Bell's management. Unknown to Salam, the bookkeeper had, in fact, embezzled large sums of cash from Bell. In addition, the accounts receivable were significantly overstated. Salam did not detect the overstatement because of Salam's inadvertent failure to follow its audit program.

Despite the foregoing, Salam issued an unqualified opinion on Bell's financial statements and furnished a copy of the audited financial statements to Astor. Unknown to Salam, Astor required financing to purchase Bell's assets and furnished a copy of Bell's audited financial statements to City Bank to obtain approval of the loan. Based on Bell's audited financial statements, City loaned Astor $600,000.

Astor paid Bell $750,000 to purchase Bell's assets. Within six months, Astor began experiencing financial difficulties resulting from the undiscovered embezzlements and overstated accounts receivable. Astor later defaulted on the City loan.

City has commenced a lawsuit against Salam based on the following causes of action:

- Constructive fraud
- Negligence

Required: In separate paragraphs, discuss whether City is likely to prevail on the causes of action it has raised, setting forth reasons for each conclusion.

F. Federal Statutory Liability

N92
Number 3 (Estimated time — — 15 to 25 minutes)

Butler Manufacturing Corp. planned to raise capital for a plant expansion by borrowing from banks and making several stock offerings. Butler engaged Weaver, CPA, to audit its December 31, 1989, financial statements. Butler told Weaver that the financial statements would be given to certain named banks and included in the prospectuses for the stock offerings.

In performing the audit, Weaver did not confirm accounts receivable and, as a result, failed to discover a material overstatement of accounts receivable. Also, Weaver was aware of a pending class action product liability lawsuit that was not disclosed in Butler's financial statements. Despite being advised by Butler's legal counsel that Butler's potential liability under the lawsuit would result in material losses, Weaver issued an unqualified opinion on Butler's financial statements.

In May 1990, Union Bank, one of the named banks, relied on the financial statements and Weaver's opinion in giving Butler a $500,000 loan.

Butler raised an additional $16,450,000 through the following stock offerings, which were sold completely:

- June 1990 — Butler made a $450,000 unregistered offering of Class B nonvoting common stock under Rule 504 of Regulation D of the Securities Act of 1933. This offering was sold over two years to 30 nonaccredited investors and 20 accredited investors by general solicitation. The SEC was notified eight days after the first sale of this offering.

- September 1990 — Butler made a $10,000,000 unregistered offering of Class A voting common stock under Rule 506 of Regulation D of the Securities Act of 1933. This offering was sold over two years to 200 accredited investors and 30 nonaccredited investors through a private placement. The SEC was notified 14 days after the first sale of this offering.

- November 1990 — Butler made a $6,000,000 unregistered offering of preferred stock under Rule 505 of Regulation D of the Securities Act of 1933. This offering was sold during a one-year period to 40 nonaccredited investors by private placement. The SEC was notified 18 days after the first sale of this offering.

Shortly after obtaining the Union loan, Butler began experiencing financial problems but was able to stay in business because of the money raised by the offerings. Butler was found liable in the product liability suit. This resulted in a judgment Butler could not pay. Butler also defaulted on the Union loan and was involuntarily petitioned into bankruptcy. This caused Union to sustain a loss and Butler's stockholders to lose their investments.

As a result:

- The SEC claimed that all three of Butler's offerings were made improperly and were not exempt from registration.

- Union sued Weaver for
  - Negligence
  - Common Law Fraud

- The stockholders who purchased Butler's stock through the offerings sued Weaver, alleging fraud under Section 10(b) and Rule 10b-5 of the Securities Exchange Act of 1934.

These transactions took place in a jurisdiction providing for accountant's liability for negligence to known and intended users of financial statements.

Required:
Answer the following questions and give the reasons for your conclusions:

a. Will Union be successful in its suit against Weaver for:
1. Negligence?
2. Common law fraud?

b. Will the stockholders who purchased Butler's stock through the 1990 offerings succeed against Weaver under the anti-fraud provisions of Section 10(b) and Rule 10b-5 of the Securities Exchange Act of 1934?

M91
Number 5 (Estimated time — — 15 to 20 minutes)

Sleek Corp. is a public corporation whose stock is traded on a national securities exchange. Sleek hired Garson Associates, CPAs, to audit Sleek's financial statements. Sleek needed the audit to obtain bank loans and to make a public stock offering so that Sleek could undertake a business expansion program.

Before the engagement, Fred Hedge, Sleek's president, told Garson's managing partner that the audited financial statements would be submitted to Sleek's banks to obtain the necessary loans.

During the course of the audit, Garson's managing partner found that Hedge and other Sleek officers had embezzled substantial amounts of money from the corporation. These embezzlements threatened Sleek's financial stability. When these findings were brought to Hedge's attention, Hedge promised that the money would be repaid and begged that the audit not disclose the embezzlements.

Hedge also told Garson's managing partner that several friends and relatives of Sleek's officers had been advised about the projected business expansion and proposed stock offering, and had purchased significant amounts of Sleek's stock based on this information.

Garson submitted an unqualified opinion on Sleek's financial statements, which did not include adjustments for or disclosures about the embezzlements and insider stock transactions. The financial statements and audit report were submitted to Sleek's regular banks including Knox Bank. Knox, relying on the financial statements and Garson's report, gave Sleek a $2,000,000 loan.

Sleek's audited financial statements were also incorporated in a registration statement prepared under the provisions of the Securities Act of 1933. The registration statement was filed with the SEC in conjunction with Sleek's public offering of 100,000 shares of its common stock at $100 per share.

An SEC investigation of Sleek disclosed the embezzlements and the insider trading. Trading in Sleek's stock was suspended and Sleek defaulted on the Knox loan.

As a result, the following legal actions were taken:

- Knox sued Garson.

- The general public purchasers of Sleek's stock offerings sued Garson.

Required:
Answer the following questions and give the reasons for your conclusions.

    a. Would Knox recover from Garson for fraud?

    b. Would the general public purchasers of Sleek's stock offerings recover from Garson
        1. Under the liability provisions of Section 11 of the Securities Act of 1933?
        2. Under the anti-fraud provisions of Rule 10b-5 of the Securities Exchange Act of 1934?

II. Business Organizations

A. Agency

N92
Number 4 (Estimated time — — 15 to 25 minutes)

Exotic Pets, Inc. hired Peterson to be the manager of one of its stores. Exotic sells a wide variety of animals. Peterson was given considerable authority by Exotic to operate the store, including the right to buy inventory. Peterson was told that any inventory purchase exceeding $2,000 required the approval of Exotic's general manager.

On June 1, 1992, Peterson contracted with Creatures Corp. to buy snakes for $3,100. Peterson had regularly done business with Creatures on Exotic's behalf in the past, and on several occasions had bought $1,000 to $1,750 worth of snakes from Creatures. Creatures was unaware of the limitation on Peterson's authority to buy inventory.

Peterson occasionally would buy, for Exotic, a certain breed of dog from Premier Breeders, Inc., which was owned by Peterson's friend. Whenever Exotic bought dogs from Premier, Premier paid Peterson 5% of the purchase price as an incentive to do more business with Premier. Exotic's management was unaware of these payments to Peterson.

On June 20, 1992, Mathews went to the Exotic store managed by Peterson to buy a ferret. Peterson allowed Mathews to handle one of the ferrets. Peterson knew that this particular ferret had previously bitten one of the store's clerks. Mathews was bitten by the ferret and seriously injured.

On July 23, 1992, Peterson bought paint and brushes for $30 from Handy Hardware. Peterson charged the purchase to Exotic's account at Handy. Peterson intended to use the paint and brushes to repaint the pet showroom. Exotic's management had never specifically discussed with Peterson whether Peterson had the authority to charge purchases at Handy. Although Exotic paid the Handy bill, Exotic's president believes Peterson is obligated to reimburse Exotic for the charges.

On August 1, 1992, Exotic's president learned of the Creatures contract and advised Creatures that Exotic would neither accept delivery of the snakes, nor pay for them, because Peterson did not have the authority to enter into the contract.

Exotic's president has also learned about the incentive payments Premier made to Peterson.

Exotic has taken the following positions:

- It is not liable to Creatures because Peterson entered into the contract without Exotic's consent.

- Peterson is obligated to reimburse Exotic for the charges incurred by Peterson at Handy Hardware.

- Peterson is liable to Exotic for the incentive payments received from Premier.

Mathews has sued both Peterson and Exotic for the injuries sustained from the ferret bite.

Required:
    a. State whether Exotic's positions are correct and give the reasons for your conclusions.

    b. State whether Mathews will prevail in the lawsuit against Exotic and Peterson and give the reasons for your conclusions.

N90
Number 3 (Estimated time — — 15 to 20 minutes)

Prime Cars, Inc. buys and sells used automobiles. Occasionally Prime has its salespeople purchase used cars from third parties without disclosing that the salesperson is in fact buying for Prime's used car inventory. Prime's management believes better prices can be negotiated using this procedure. One of Prime's salespeople, Peterson, entered into a contract with Hallow in accordance with instructions from Prime's sales manager. The car was to be delivered one week later. After entering into the contract with Hallow, and while driving back to Prime's place of business, Peterson was involved in an automobile accident with another vehicle. Peterson's negligence, and the resulting collision, injured Mathews, the driver of the other car involved in the accident.

Prime terminated Peterson's employment because of the accident. Following Prime's general business practices, Prime published an advertisement in several trade journals that gave notice that Peterson was no longer employed by Prime. Shortly thereafter, Peterson approached one of Prime's competitors, Bagley Autos, Inc., and contracted to sell Bagley several used cars in Prime's inventory. Bagley's sales manager, who frequently purchased cars out of Prime's inventory from Peterson, paid 25% of the total price to Peterson, with the balance to be paid ten days later when the cars were to be delivered. Bagley's sales manager was unaware of Peterson's termination. Prime refused to deliver the cars to Bagley or to repay Bagley's down payment, which Prime never received from Peterson.

Prime also refused to go through with the contract entered into by Peterson with Hallow. Mathews sued both Peterson and Prime for the injuries sustained in the automobile accident. Bagley sued Prime for failing to deliver the cars or return the down payment paid to Peterson.

Required:
Answer each of the following questions, setting forth the reasons for your conclusions.

a. What rights does Hallow have against Prime or Peterson?

b. Will Mathews prevail in the lawsuit against Prime and Peterson?

c. Will Bagley prevail in its lawsuit against Prime?

B. Partnership, Joint Ventures, and Other Unincorporated Associations

M94
Number 4 (Estimated time — — 15 to 25 minutes)

Best Aviation Associates is a general partnership engaged in the business of buying, selling and servicing used airplanes. Best's original partners were Martin and Kent. They formed the partnership on January 1, 1992, under an oral partnership agreement which provided that the partners would share profits equally. There was no agreement as to how the partners would share losses. At the time the partnership was formed, Martin contributed $320,000 and Kent contributed $80,000.

On December 1, 1993, Best hired Baker to be a salesperson and to assist in purchasing used aircraft for Best's inventory. On December 15, 1993, Martin instructed Baker to negotiate the purchase of a used airplane from Jackson without disclosing that Baker was acting on Best's behalf. Martin thought that a better price could be negotiated by Baker if Jackson was not aware that the aircraft was being acquired for Best. Baker contracted with Jackson without disclosing that the airplane was being purchased for Best. The agreement provided that Jackson would deliver the airplane to Baker on January 2, 1994, at which time the purchase price was to be paid. On January 2, 1994, Jackson attempted to deliver the used airplane purchased for Best by Baker. Baker, acting on Martin's instructions, refused to accept delivery or pay the purchase price.

On December 20, 1993, Kent assigned Kent's partnership interest in Best to Green. On December 31, 1993, Kent advised Martin of the assignment to Green. On January 11, 1994, Green contacted Martin and demanded to inspect the partnership books and to participate in the management of partnership affairs, including voting on partnership decisions.

On January 13, 1994, it was determined that Best had incurred an operating loss of $160,000 in 1993. Martin demanded that Kent contribute $80,000 to the partnership to account for Kent's share of the loss. Kent refused to contribute.

On January 28, 1994,** Laco Supplies, Inc., a creditor of Best, sued Best and Martin for unpaid bills totalling $92,000. Best had not paid the bills because of a cash shortfall caused by the 1993 operating loss.

Jackson has taken the following position:

- Baker is responsible for any damages incurred by Jackson as a result of Best's refusal to accept delivery or pay the purchase price.

Martin has taken the following positions:

- Green is not entitled to inspect the partnership books or participate in the management of the partnership.

- Only the partnership is liable for the amounts owed to Laco, or, in the alternative, Martin's personal liability is limited to 50% of the total of the unpaid bills.

Kent has taken the following positions:

- Only Martin is liable for the 1993 operating loss because of the assignment to Green of Kent's partnership interest.

- Any personal liability of the partners for the 1993 operating loss should be allocated between them on the basis of their original capital contributions.

Required:
a. Determine whether Jackson's position is correct and state the reasons for your conclusions.

b. Determine whether Martin's positions are correct and state the reasons for your conclusions.

c. Determine whether Kent's positions are correct and state the reasons for your conclusions.

*Originally misprinted as contracted.
**Originally misprinted as 1993.

M91
Number 2 (Estimated time — — 15 to 20 minutes)

Prime Cars Partnership is a general partnership engaged in the business of buying, selling, and servicing used cars. Prime's original partners were Baker and Mathews, who formed the partnership three years ago under a written partnership agreement, which provided that:

- Profits and losses would be allocated 60% to Baker and 40% to Mathews.
- Baker would be responsible for supervising Prime's salespeople and for purchasing used cars for inventory. Baker could not, without Mathews' consent, enter into a contract to purchase more than $15,000 worth of used cars at any one time.
- Mathews would be responsible for supervising Prime's service department.

On May 1, 1990, Baker entered into a contract on Prime's behalf with Jaco Auto Wholesalers, Inc. to purchase 11 used cars from Jaco for a total purchase price of $40,000. Baker's agreement with Jaco provided that the cars would be delivered to Prime on September 1. Baker did not advise Mathews of the terms and conditions of the contract with Jaco. Baker had regularly done business with Jaco on behalf of Prime in the past, and on several occasions had purchased $12,000 to $15,000 of used cars from Jaco. Jaco was unaware of the limitation on Baker's authority.

Baker also frequently purchased used cars for Prime from Top Auto Auctions, Ltd., a corporation owned by Baker's friend. Whenever Prime purchased cars from Top, Baker would personally receive up to 5% of the total purchase price from Top as an incentive to do more business with Top. Baker did not tell Mathews about these payments.

On August 1, 1990, Baker and Mathews agreed to admit KYA Auto Restorers, Inc. as a partner in Prime to start up and supervise a body shop facility. KYA made a $25,000 capital contribution and Prime's partnership agreement was amended to provide that Prime's profits and losses would be shared equally by the partners.

On September 1, 1990, Mathews learned of the Jaco contract and refused to accept delivery of the cars. Mathews advised Jaco that Baker had entered into the contract without Mathews' consent as required by their agreement. Jaco has demanded a payment of $10,000 from Prime for Jaco's lost profits under the contract.

Mathews has also learned about the incentive payments made to Baker by Top.

Mathews has taken the following positions:

- Prime is not liable to Jaco because Baker entered into the contract without Mathews' consent.
- In any event, Mathews is not liable to Jaco for more than 40% of Jaco's lost profits because of the original partnership provisions concerning the sharing of profits and losses.
- Baker is liable to Mathews for any liability incurred by Mathews under the Jaco contract.
- Baker is liable to Prime for accepting the incentive payments from Top.

KYA contends that none of its $25,000 capital contribution should be applied to the Jaco liability and that, in any event, KYA does not have any responsibility for the obligation.

Required:

a. State whether Mathews' positions are correct and give the reasons for your conclusions.

b. State whether KYA's contentions are correct and give the reasons for your conclusions.

M90
Number 4 (Estimated time — — 15 to 20 minutes)

Smith, Edwards, and Weil formed Sterling Properties Limited Partnership to engage in the business of buying, selling and managing real estate. Smith and Edwards were general partners. Weil was a limited partner entitled to 50% of all profits.

Within a few months of Sterling's formation, it became apparent to Weil that Smith's and Edwards' inexperience was likely to result in financial disaster for the partnership. Therefore, Weil became more involved in day-to-day management decisions. Weil met with prospective buyers and sellers of properties; assisted in negotiating partnership loans with its various lenders; and took an active role in dealing with personnel problems. Things continued to deteriorate for Sterling, and the partners began blaming each other for the partnership's problems.

Finally, Smith could no longer deal with the situation, and withdrew from the partnership. Edwards reminded Smith that the Sterling partnership agreement specifically prohibited withdrawal by a general partner without the consent of all the other partners. Smith advised Edwards and Weil that she would take no part in any further partnership undertaking and would not be responsible for partnership debts incurred after this withdrawal.

With Sterling on the verge of collapse, the following situations have occurred:

- Weil demanded the right to inspect and copy the partnership's books and records and Edwards refused to allow Weil to do so, claiming that Weil's status as a limited partner precludes that right.
- Anchor Bank, which made a loan to the partnership prior to Smith's withdrawal, is suing Sterling and each partner individually, including Smith, because the loan is in default. Weil denied any liability based on his limited partner status. Smith denies liability based on her withdrawal.

- Edwards sued Smith for withdrawing from the partnership and is uncertain about the effect of her withdrawal on the partnership.
- Weil wants to assign his partnership interest to Fred Alberts, who wants to become a substitute limited partner. Weil is uncertain about his right to assign this interest to Alberts and, further, the right of Alberts to become a substitute limited partner. Edwards contends that Edwards' consent is necessary for the assignment or the substitution of Alberts as a limited partner and that without this consent any such assignment would cause a dissolution of the partnership. The Sterling partnership agreement and certificate are silent in this regard.

Required:
Answer the following questions, setting forth reasons for the conclusions stated.

a. Is Weil entitled to inspect and copy the books and records of the partnership?

b. Are Weil and/or Smith liable to Anchor Bank?

c. Will Edwards prevail in the lawsuit against Smith for withdrawing from the partnership?

d. What is the legal implication to the partnership of Smith's withdrawal?

e. Can Weil assign his partnership interest to Alberts?

f. Can Edwards prevent the assignment to Alberts or the substitution of Alberts as a limited partner?

g. What rights does Alberts have as assignee of Weil's partnership interest?

h. What effect does an assignment have on the partnership?

C. Corporations

M93
Number 3 (Estimated time — — 15 to 25 minutes)

Edwards, a director and a 10% stockholder in National Corp., is dissatisfied with the way National's officers, particularly Olsen, the president, have been operating the corporation. Edwards has made many suggestions that have been rejected by the board of directors, and has made several unsuccessful attempts to have Olsen removed as president.

National and Grand Corp. had been negotiating a merger that Edwards has adamantly opposed. Edwards has blamed Olsen for initiating the negotiation and has urged the board to fire Olsen. National's board refused to fire Olsen. In an attempt to defeat the merger, Edwards approached Jenkins, the president of Queen Corp., and contracted for Queen to purchase several of National's assets. Jenkins knew Edwards was a National director, but had never done business with National. When National learned of the contract, it notified Queen that the contract was invalid.

Edwards filed an objection to the merger before the stockholders' meeting called to consider the merger proposal was held. At the meeting, Edwards voted against the merger proposal.

Despite Edwards' efforts, the merger was approved by both corporations. Edwards then orally demanded that National purchase Edwards' stock, citing the dissenters' rights provision of the corporation's by-laws, which reflects the Model Business Corporation Act.

National's board has claimed National does not have to purchase Edwards' stock.

As a result of the above:

- Edwards initiated a minority stockholder's action to have Olsen removed as president and to force National to purchase Edwards' stock.

- Queen sued National to enforce the contract and/or collect damages.

- Queen sued Edwards to collect damages.

Required:
Answer the following questions and give the reasons for your answers.

a. Will Edwards be successful in a lawsuit to have Olsen removed as president?

b. Will Edwards be successful in a lawsuit to have National purchase the stock?

c. 1. Will Queen be successful in a lawsuit against National?
   2. Will Queen be successful in a lawsuit against Edwards?

N91
Number 2 (Estimated time — — 15 to 20 minutes)

Frost, Glen, and Bradley own 50%, 40%, and 10%, respectively, of the authorized and issued voting common stock of Xeon Corp. They had a written stockholders' agreement that provided they would vote for each other as directors of the corporation.

At the initial stockholders' meeting, Frost, Glen, Bradley, and three others were elected to a six-person board of directors. The board elected Frost as president of the corporation, Glen as secretary, and Bradley as vice president. Frost and Glen were given two-year contracts with annual salaries of $50,000. Bradley was given a two-year contract for $10,000 per year.

At the end of its first year of operation, Xeon was in financial difficulty. Bradley disagreed with the way Frost and Glen were running the business.

At the annual stockholders' meeting, a new board of directors was elected. Bradley was excluded because

Frost and Glen did not vote for Bradley. Without cause, the new board fired Bradley as vice president even though 12 months remained on Bradley's contract.

Despite the corporation's financial difficulties, the new board, relying on the assurances of Frost and Glen and based on fraudulent documentation provided by Frost and Glen, declared and paid a $200,000 dividend. Payment of the dividend caused the corporation to become insolvent.

- Bradley sued Frost and Glen to compel them to follow the written stockholders' agreement and reelect Bradley to the board.

- Bradley sued the corporation to be reinstated as an officer of the corporation, and for breach of the employment contract.

- Bradley sued each member of the board for declaring and paying an unlawful dividend, and demanded its repayment to the corporation.

Required:
State whether Bradley would be successful in each of the above suits and give the reasons for your conclusions.

N89
Number 5 (Estimated time — — 15 to 20 minutes)

On May 12, 1987, West purchased 6% of Ace Corp.'s outstanding $3 cumulative preferred stock and 7% of Ace's outstanding common stock. These are the only two classes of stock authorized by Ace's charter. Both classes of stock are traded on a national stock exchange. Ace uses the calendar year for financial reporting purposes.

During 1987 and 1988, Ace neither declared dividends nor recorded dividends in arrears as a liability on its books. West was disturbed about this and, on February 8, 1989, sent a written demand to examine Ace's books and records to determine Ace's financial condition. Ace has refused to permit West to examine its books and records.

On May 8, 1989, West lost the stock certificate representing the shares of preferred stock. On May 9, 1989, West notified Ace of the lost stock certificate and requested that Ace issue a new stock certificate. West offered to file an indemnity bond with Ace and to fulfill any reasonable requests made by Ace. Although Ace has no knowledge that any other party has acquired the lost stock certificate, Ace refused to issue a new stock certificate or accept the indemnity bond.

As a result of the foregoing, West has made the following assertions:

- Ace should have recorded the dividends in arrears for 1987 and 1988 as a liability that, in effect, would treat West as a general creditor to the extent of the dividends in arrears.
- West is entitled to examine Ace's books and records.
- West is entitled to receive a new stock certificate to replace the lost stock certificate.

Required: In separate paragraphs, discuss West's assertions. Indicate whether such assertions are correct and the reasons therefor. Do **not** consider securities laws.

M89
Number 4 (Estimated time — — 15 to 20 minutes)

On May 1, 1987, Cray's board of directors unanimously voted to have Cray reacquire 100,000 shares of its common stock. On May 25, 1987, Cray did so, paying current market price. In determining whether to reacquire the shares, the board of directors relied on reports and financial statements that were negligently prepared by Cray's internal accounting department under the supervision of the treasurer and reviewed by its independent accountants. The reports and financial statements indicated that, as of April 30, 1987, Cray was solvent and there were sufficient funds to reacquire the shares. Subsequently, it was discovered that Cray had become insolvent in March 1987 and continued to be insolvent after the reacquisition of the shares. As a result of the foregoing, Cray experienced liquidity problems and losses during 1987 and 1988.

The board of directors immediately fired the treasurer because of the treasurer's negligence in supervising the preparation of the reports and financial statements. The treasurer had three years remaining on a binding five-year employment agreement which, among other things, prohibited the termination of the treasurer's employment for mere negligence.

Required: Discuss the following assertions, indicating whether such assertions are correct and the reasons therefor.

- It was improper for the board of directors to authorize the reacquisition of Cray's common stock while Cray was insolvent.
- The members of the board of directors are personally liable because they voted to reacquire shares while Cray was insolvent.
- Cray will be liable to the treasurer as a result of his termination by the board of directors.

D. Estates and Trusts

N94
Number 4 (Estimated time — — 15 to 25 minutes)

On January 1, 1993, Stone prepared an *inter vivos* spendthrift trust. Stone wanted to provide financial security for several close relatives during their lives, with the remainder payable to several charities. Stone funded the trust by transferring stocks, bonds, and a commercial building to the trust. Queen Bank was named as Trustee. The trust was to use the calendar year as its accounting period. The trust instrument contained no provision for the allocation of receipts and disbursements to principal and income.

The following transactions involving trust property occurred in 1993:

- The trust sold stock it owned for $50,000. The cost basis of the stock was $10,000. $40,000 was allocated to income and $10,000 to principal.

- The trust received a stock dividend of 500 shares of $10 par value common stock selling, at the time, for $50 per share. $20,000 was allocated to income and $5,000 to principal.

- The trust received bond interest of $18,000, which was allocated to income. The interest was paid and received semiannually on May 1 and November 1.

- The trust made mortgage amortization payments of $40,000 on the mortgage on the commercial building. The entire amount was allocated to principal.

On December 31, 1993, all the income beneficiaries and the charities joined in a petition to have the court allow the trust to be terminated and all trust funds distributed.

Required:

a. State the requirements to establish a valid *inter vivos* spendthrift trust and determine whether the Stone trust meets those requirements.

b. State whether the allocations made in the four transactions were correct and, if not, state the proper allocation to be made under the majority rule. Disregard any tax effect of each transaction.

c. State whether the trust will be terminated by the court and give the reasons for your conclusion.

N93
Number 3 (Estimated time —— 15 to 25 minutes)

In 1990, Park, after consulting a CPA and an attorney, decided to have an *inter vivos* trust and will prepared. Park wanted to provide for the welfare of three close relatives: Archer, Book, and Cable, during Park's lifetime and after Park's death.

The trust was funded by cash and real estate transfers. The trust contained spendthrift provisions directing the trustees to pay the income to only the trust beneficiaries, Archer, Book, and Cable. Park also provided for $10,000 "sprinkling" provisions allowing for the annual distribution of up to $10,000 of principal to each beneficiary at the trustees' discretion.

Park's will provided for a "pour-over" transfer of any residuary estate to the trust.

Young, a CPA, and Zack, a stockbroker, were named trustees of the trust and executors of the will. Young and Zack were directed to perform their duties as "prudent business people" in investing and protecting the assets of the trust and estate.

During 1991, Young and Zack properly allocated income and principal and paid the trust income to Park's relatives as directed. They also made $5,000 principal payments to two of the beneficiaries for a medical emergency and to pay college tuition.

During 1992, Zack, with Young's consent, borrowed $10,000 from the trust. Zack agreed to repay the loan at a higher interest rate than the trust normally received on its investments. Archer, one of the trust beneficiaries, asked for and received a $15,000 principal payment. The money was used to enable Archer to invest in a joint venture with Zack.

In January 1993, Park died and the will was probated. After payment of all taxes, debts, and bequests, the residuary estate was transferred to the trust. Archer, Book, and Cable sued:

- To have the court allow distribution of the residuary estate instead of the residuary being transferred to the trust.

- To have the spendthrift trust terminated.

- To remove Young and Zack as trustees for making the $5,000 principal payments.

- To remove Young and Zack as trustees for allowing Zack to borrow money from the trust.

- To remove Young and Zack as trustees for making the $15,000 principal payment to Archer.

Required:
Determine whether Archer, Book, and Cable will be successful in the lawsuits and give the reasons for your conclusions.

M92
Number 3 (Estimated time —— 15 to 20 minutes)

Goodwin, a CPA, and Jensen, a banker, were the trustees of the Moore Family Trust. The trust was created as a spendthrift trust and provided for distribution of income annually to the four Moore adult children for life, with the principal to be distributed to their issue after the death of the last income beneficiary. The trust was funded with commercial and residential real estate and a stock portfolio.

Goodwin, in addition to being a trustee, was lawfully employed as the trust's accountant. Goodwin, as the trust's accountant, prepared and signed all trust tax returns, kept the trust's accounting records, and supervised distributions to the income beneficiaries.

In 1990, Goodwin and Jensen, as trustees, sold a building owned by the trust for $400,000, its fair market value. The building had been valued at $250,000 when acquired by the trust. The $150,000 gain was allocated to income. In addition, the trust had rental, interest, and dividend income of $1,500,000 in 1990. Expenses for taxes, replacement of plumbing fixtures, roof repairs, utilities, salaries, and fees and commissions totaled $1,050,000.

On December 31, 1990, Goodwin and Jensen prepared and signed four $150,000 trust account checks and sent three of them to three of the income beneficiaries and the fourth one to a creditor of the fourth beneficiary. This beneficiary had acknowledged that the creditor was owed $200,000.

In February 1991, Goodwin discovered that Jensen had embezzled $200,000 by secretly selling part of the trust's stock portfolio. Goodwin agreed not to reveal Jensen's embezzlement if Jensen would pay Goodwin $25,000.

In April 1991, Goodwin prepared the 1990 trust income tax return. The return was signed by Goodwin as preparer and by Jensen and Goodwin as trustees and was filed with the IRS. Goodwin also prepared the 1990 income tax returns for the income beneficiaries. In an attempt to hide the embezzlement, Goodwin, in preparing the trust tax return, claimed nonexistent losses and improper credits. The beneficiaries' returns reflected the same nonexistent losses and improper credits. Consequently, the beneficiaries' taxes were underpaid. As a result of an IRS audit, the embezzlement was uncovered, the nonexistent losses and improper credits were disallowed, and the beneficiaries were assessed additional taxes, penalties, and interest.

Jensen cannot be located.

As a result of the above, the income beneficiaries sued Goodwin for negligence, fraud, and breach of fiduciary duty.

Required:
Answer the following questions and give the reasons for your conclusions.

Will the income beneficiaries win their suits against Goodwin for:

- **a.** accountant's negligence?
- **b.** actual fraud?
- **c.** breach of fiduciary duty as a trustee?

N89
Number 2 (Estimated time — — 15 to 20 minutes)

On May 1, 1988, Mary Stein sold a commercial building to Sam Bean and Bean's son, Bob, as equal tenants in common. At the time of the sale, there was a recorded existing mortgage on the building in favor of Fale Bank. The mortgage and the note it secured were silent as to whether the entire amount outstanding on the loan would become due upon the sale of the building. Sam and Bob did not assume the mortgage and it was not paid off when they purchased the building.

On June 15, 1989, Sam died leaving a will naming his wife, Rita Bean, as the beneficiary of his entire estate, except for certain stocks which were to be transferred to a spendthrift trust created for the benefit of Bob. The will named Rita as the trustee and Bob as the sole beneficiary of the trust. The provision in the will creating the spendthrift trust stated in part that:

> Payments and distributions to the beneficiary shall be made only to the beneficiary in person or upon his personal receipt, and no interest of the beneficiary in the income or principal of the trust estate shall be assignable in anticipation of payment, either by the voluntary or involuntary act of the beneficiary or by operation of law, or be liable in any way for the debts of the beneficiary.

Required:
- **a.** Discuss the personal liability of Sam Bean and Bob Bean, and the personal liability of Mary Stein, if there is a default on the mortgage to Fale and a foreclosure sale results in a deficiency.

- **b.** Discuss the effect Sam Bean's death will have on the ownership of the building.

- **c.** Discuss the major purposes/benefits of a spendthrift trust such as the one created by Sam Bean.

- **d.** Discuss whether
    1. A trust may generally be terminated by its beneficiaries; and
    2. The spendthrift trust created by Sam Bean could be terminated by Bob Bean.

III. Contracts

R97
Number 1(a)

On April 1, Thorn and Birch negotiated the sale of Thorn's shopping center to Birch for $2.1 million ($2 million for the buildings and $100,000 for the land). The parties orally agreed on the following terms:

- Birch would make a cash down payment of $600,000.

- Birch would give Thorn a $1.5 million first mortgage on the property to secure the balance of the purchase price.

- The contract would contain an anti-assignment clause prohibiting assignment of the contract of sale or the mortgage.

- The contract would contain a "time of the essence" clause requiring that the closing take place on June 1.

No discussion took place regarding any existing mortgages or liens on the property. On April 14, the parties signed a written contract containing the above provisions.

On April 20, Birch took out a $1.5 million fire insurance policy with Acme Fire Insurance Co. on the buildings. The policy contained a standard 80% coinsurance clause.

On April 25, a title insurance report ordered by Birch revealed that there was an existing $500,000 mortgage on the property that had been recorded the previous February. The title report failed to disclose another mortgage for $50,000 that had been given years earlier by a prior owner of the land and had not been recorded. Thorn was aware of the $500,000 mortgage but not the earlier mortgage. The title report also disclosed that there were unpaid property taxes outstanding.

On May 1, Thorn agreed to assign to a third party the prospective mortgage payments Thorn would receive from Birch.

When Birch received the title report and found out about Thorn's assignment of the mortgage payments, Birch accused Thorn of breach of contract for failing to disclose the prior mortgages and for violating the anti-assignment clause in the contract. Birch also insisted on postponing the contract closing date.

Thorn and Birch were able to resolve their differences.

- Birch reduced the mortgage being given to Thorn and assumed the previously recorded mortgage.

- The closing took place on July 1.

- Thorn recorded Birch's mortgage on July 5.

- The previously unrecorded mortgage was recorded on July 10.

On August 1, a fire caused $160,000 damage to the buildings. On that date, the fair market value of the buildings was $2 million. Acme contested payment of the claim, contending that Birch had no insurable interest in the buildings when the policy was taken out. Acme also contended that, even if Birch had an insurable interest, Birch would not be entitled to recover the entire amount of the loss because Birch is a coinsurer.

After the insurance issues were resolved and the buildings repaired, Birch stopped making payments on the mortgages and they were foreclosed. After payment of all foreclosure expenses, there was $1 million available to pay the outstanding mortgages. Thorn's mortgage had a principal and accrued interest balance of $950,000. The mortgage recorded in February had a principal and accrued interest balance of $475,000. The mortgage recorded on July 10 had a principal and accrued interest balance of $60,000.

The above transactions took place in a notice-race jurisdiction.

Required:
a. 1. State whether there was an enforceable contract for the sale of real property and list the requirements necessary to form such a contract.
2. State whether Thorn breached the contract by assigning the mortgage payments and give the reasons supporting your decision.
3. State and explain the remedies available to Birch if a court determined that Thorn, in any way, breached the contract.

N95
Number 4 (Estimated time — — 15 to 25 minutes)

On July 5, 1995, Korn sent Wilson a written offer to clear Wilson's parking lot whenever it snowed through December 31, 1995. Korn's offer stated that Wilson had until October 1 to accept.

On September 28, 1995, Wilson mailed Korn an acceptance with a request that the agreement continue through March, 1996. Wilson's acceptance was delayed and didn't reach Korn until October 3.

On September 29, 1995, Korn saw weather reports indicating the snowfall for the season would be much heavier than normal. This would substantially increase Korn's costs to perform under the offer.

On September 30, 1995, Korn phoned Wilson to insist that the terms of the agreement be changed. When Wilson refused, Korn orally withdrew the offer and stated that Korn would not perform.

Required:
a. State and explain the points of law that Korn would argue to show that there was **no** valid contract.

b. State and explain the points of law that Wilson would argue to show that there was a valid contract.

c. Assuming that a valid contract existed:

1. Determine whether Korn breached the contract and the nature of the breach and
2. State the common law remedies available to Wilson.

M94
Number 5 (Estimated time — — 15 to 25 minutes)

Suburban Properties, Inc. owns and manages several shopping centers.

On May 4, 1993, Suburban received from Bridge Hardware, Inc., one of its tenants, a signed letter proposing that the existing lease between Suburban and Bridge be modified to provide that certain utility costs be equally shared by Bridge and Suburban, effective June 1, 1993. Under the terms of the original lease, Bridge was obligated to pay all utility costs. On May 5, 1993, Suburban sent Bridge a signed letter agreeing to share the utility costs as proposed. Suburban later changed its opinion and refused to share in the utility costs.

On June 4, 1993, Suburban received from Dart Associates, Inc. a signed offer to purchase one of the shopping centers owned by Suburban. The offer provided as follows: a price of $9,250,000; it would not be withdrawn before July 1, 1993; and an acceptance must be received by Dart to be effective. On June 9, 1993, Suburban mailed Dart a signed acceptance. On June 10, before Dart had received Suburban's acceptance, Dart telephoned Suburban and withdrew its offer. Suburban's acceptance was received by Dart on June 12, 1993.

On June 22, 1993, one of Suburban's shopping centers was damaged by a fire, which started when the center was struck by lightning. As a result of the fire, one of the tenants in the shopping center, World Popcorn Corp., was forced to close its business and will be unable to reopen until the damage is repaired. World sued Suburban claiming that Suburban is liable for World's losses resulting from the fire. The lease between Suburban and World is silent in this regard.

Suburban has taken the following positions:

- Suburban's May 5, 1993,* agreement to share equally the utility costs with Bridge is not binding on Suburban.

- Dart could not properly revoke its June 4 offer and must purchase the shopping center.

- Suburban is not liable to World for World's losses resulting from the fire.

Required:
In separate paragraphs, determine whether Suburban's positions are correct and state the reasons for your conclusions.

*Originally misprinted as 1994.

N93
Number 4 (Estimated time —— 15 to 25 minutes)

Victor Corp. engaged Bell & Co., CPAs, to audit Victor's financial statements for the year ended December 31, 1992. Victor is in the business of buying, selling, and servicing new and used construction equipment. While reviewing Victor's 1992 records, Bell became aware of the following disputed transactions:

- On September 8, Victor sent Ambel Contractors, Inc. a signed purchase order for several pieces of used construction equipment. Victor's purchase order described twelve different pieces of equipment and indicated the price Victor was willing to pay for each item. As a result of a mathematical error in adding up the total of the various prices, the purchase price offered by Victor was $191,000 rather than the correct amount of $119,000. Ambel, on receipt of the purchase order, was surprised by Victor's high price and immediately sent Victor a written acceptance. Ambel was aware that the fair market value of the equipment was approximately $105,000 to $125,000. Victor discovered the mistake in the purchase order and refused to purchase the equipment from Ambel. Ambel claims that Victor is obligated to purchase the equipment at a price of $191,000, as set forth in the purchase order.

- On October 8, a Victor salesperson orally contracted to service a piece of equipment owned by Clark Masons, Inc. The contract provided that for a period of 36 months, commencing November 1992, Victor would provide routine service for the equipment at a fixed price of $15,000, payable in three annual installments of $5,000 each. On October 29, Clark's president contacted Victor and stated that Clark did not intend to honor the service agreement because there was no written contract between Victor and Clark.

- On November 3, Victor received by mail a signed offer from GYX Erectors, Inc. The offer provided that Victor would service certain specified equipment owned by GYX for a two-year period for a total price of $81,000. The offer also provided as follows:

  > "We need to know soon whether you can agree to the terms of this proposal. You must accept by November 15, or we will assume you can't meet our terms."

  On November 12, Victor mailed GYX a signed acceptance of GYX's offer. The acceptance was not received by GYX until November 17, and by then GYX had contracted with another party to provide service for its equipment. Victor has taken the position that GYX is obligated to honor its November 3 offer. GYX claims that no contract was formed because Victor's November 12 acceptance was not received timely by GYX.

- On December 19, Victor contracted in writing with Wells Landscaping Corp. The contract required Victor to deliver certain specified new equipment to Wells by December 31. On December 23, Victor determined that it would not be able to deliver the equipment to Wells by December 31 because of an inventory shortage. Therefore, Victor made a written assignment of the contract to Master Equipment, Inc. When Master attempted to deliver the equipment on December 31, Wells refused to accept it, claiming that Victor could not properly delegate its duties under the December 19 contract to another party without the consent of Wells. The contract is silent with regard to this issue.

Required:
State whether the claims of Ambel, Clark, GYX, and Wells are correct and give the reasons for your conclusions.

M93
Number 4 (Estimated time — — 15 to 25 minutes)

West Corp. is involved in the following disputes:

- On September 16, West's president orally offered to hire Dodd Consultants, Inc. to do computer consulting for West. The offer provided for a three-year contract at $5,000 per month. West agreed that Dodd could have until September 30 to decide whether to accept the offer. If Dodd chose to accept the offer, its acceptance would have to be received by September 30.

  On September 27, Dodd sent West a letter accepting the offer. West received the letter on October 2. On September 28, West's president decided that West's accounting staff could handle West's computer problems and notified Dodd by telephone that the offer was withdrawn. Dodd argued that West had no right to revoke its offer, and that Dodd had already accepted the offer by mail.

  Dodd claims that it has a binding contract with West because:

  - West's offer could not be revoked before September 30.

  - Dodd's acceptance was effective on September 27, when the letter accepting the offer was mailed.

  West's president claims that if an agreement exists that agreement would not be enforceable against West because of the Statute of Frauds requirement that the contract be in writing.

- On March 1, West signed a lease with Abco Real Estate, Inc. for warehouse space. The lease required that West repair and maintain the warehouse. On April 14, West orally asked Abco to paint the warehouse. Despite the lease provision requiring West to repair and maintain the warehouse, Abco agreed to do so by April 30. On April 29, Abco advised West that Abco had decided not to paint the warehouse. West demanded that Abco paint the warehouse under the April 14 agreement. Abco refused and has taken the following positions:

  - Abco's April 14 agreement to paint the warehouse is not binding on Abco because it was a modification of an existing contract.

  - Because the April 14 agreement was oral and the March 1 lease was in writing, West would not be allowed to introduce evidence in any litigation relating to the April 14 oral agreement.

Required:
   a. State whether Dodd's claims are correct and give the reasons for your conclusions.

   b. State whether West's president's claim is correct and give the reasons for your conclusion.

   c. State whether Abco's positions are correct and give the reasons for your conclusions.

N91
Number 3 (Estimated time — — 15 to 20 minutes)

In a signed letter dated March 2, 1991, Stake offered to sell Packer a specific vacant parcel of land for $100,000. Stake had inherited the land, along with several apartment buildings in the immediate vicinity. Packer received the offer on March 4. The offer required acceptance by March 10 and required Packer to have the property surveyed by a licensed surveyor so the exact legal description of the property could be determined.

On March 6, Packer sent Stake a counteroffer of $75,000. All other terms and conditions of the offer were unchanged. Stake received Packer's counteroffer on March 8, and, on that day, telephoned Packer and accepted it. On learning that a survey of the vacant parcel would cost about $1,000, Packer telephoned Stake on March 11 requesting that they share the survey cost equally. During this conversation, Stake agreed to Packer's proposal.

During the course of the negotiations leading up to the March communications between Stake and Packer, Stake expressed concern to Packer that a buyer of the land might build apartment units that would compete with those owned by Stake in the immediate vicinity. Packer assured Stake that Packer intended to use the land for a small shopping center. Because of these assurances, Stake was willing to sell the land to Packer. Contrary to what Packer told Stake, Packer had already contracted conditionally with Rolf for Rolf to build a 48-unit apartment development on the vacant land to be purchased from Stake.

During the last week of March, Stake learned that the land to be sold to Packer had a fair market value of $200,000. Also, Stake learned that Packer intended to build apartments on the land. Because of this information, Stake sued Packer to rescind the real estate contract, alleging that:

- Packer committed fraud in the formation of the contract thereby entitling Stake to rescind the contract.

- Stake's innocent mistake as to the fair market value of the land entitles Stake to rescind the contract.

- The contract was not enforceable against Stake because Stake did not sign Packer's March 6 counteroffer.

Required:
State whether Stake's allegations are correct and give the reasons for your conclusions.

Selected Questions

N90
Number 2 (Estimated time —— 15 to 20 minutes)

The following letters were mailed among Jacobs, a real estate developer, Snow, the owner of an undeveloped parcel of land, and Eljay Distributors, Inc., a clothing wholesaler interested in acquiring Snow's parcel to build a warehouse:

a. *January 21, 1990* — Snow to Jacobs: "My vacant parcel (Lot 2, Birds Addition to Cedar Grove) is available for $125,000 cash, closing within 60 days. You must accept by January 31 if you are interested."

This was received by Jacobs on January 31.

b. *January 29, 1990* — Snow to Jacobs: "Ignore my January 21 letter to you; I have decided not to sell my lot at this time."

This was received by Jacobs on February 3.

c. *January 31, 1990* — Jacobs to Snow: "Per your January 21 letter, you have got a deal."

Jacobs inadvertently forgot to sign the January 31 letter, which was received by Snow on February 4.

d. *February 2, 1990* — Jacobs to Eljay: "In consideration of your promise to pay me $10,000, I hereby assign to you my right to purchase Snow's vacant lot (Lot 2, Birds Addition to Cedar Grove)."

This was received by Eljay on February 5.

All of the letters were signed, except as noted above, and properly stamped and addressed.

Snow has refused to sell the land to Jacobs or Eljay, asserting that no contract exists because:

- Jacobs' acceptance was not received on a timely basis.
- Snow had revoked the January 21 offer.
- Jacobs' acceptance was not signed.
- Jacobs had no right to assign the contract to Eljay.

Required:
For each of Snow's assertions, indicate whether the assertion is correct, setting forth reasons for your conclusion.

N89
Number 4 (Estimated time —— 15 to 20 minutes)

Anker Corp., a furniture retailer, engaged Best & Co., CPAs, to audit Anker's financial statements for the year ended December 31, 1988. While reviewing certain transactions entered into by Anker during 1988, Best became concerned with the proper reporting of the following transactions:

- On September 8, 1988, Crisp Corp., a furniture manufacturer, signed and mailed a letter offering to sell Anker 50 pieces of furniture for $9,500. The offer stated it would remain open until December 20, 1988. On December 5, 1988, Crisp mailed a letter revoking this offer. Anker received Crisp's revocation the following day. On December 12, 1988, Anker mailed its acceptance to Crisp, and Crisp received it on December 13, 1988.
- On December 6, 1988, Dix Corp. signed and mailed a letter offering to sell Anker a building for $75,000. The offer stated that acceptance could only be made by certified mail, return receipt requested. On December 10, 1988, Anker telephoned Dix requesting that Dix keep the offer open until December 20, 1988 because it was reviewing Dix's offer. On December 12, 1988, Dix signed and mailed a letter to Anker indicating that it would hold the offer open until December 20, 1988. On December 19, 1988, Anker sent its acceptance to Dix by a private express mail courier. Anker's acceptance was received by Dix on December 20, 1988.

After reviewing the documents concerning the foregoing transactions, Best spoke with Anker's president who made the following assertions:

- The September 8, 1988 offer by Crisp was irrevocable until December 20, 1988, and therefore a contract was formed by Anker's acceptance on December 12, 1988.
- Dix's letter dated December 12, 1988 formed an option contract with Anker.
- Anker's acceptance on December 19, 1988 formed a contract with Dix.

Required:
In separate paragraphs, discuss the assertions made by Anker's president. Indicate whether the assertions are correct and the reasons therefor.

IV. Debtor-Creditor Relationships

C. Bankruptcy

R96
Number 1 (Estimated time — — 15 to 25 minutes)

In 1995, Fender was petitioned involuntarily into bankruptcy under the liquidation provisions of Chapter 7 of the Federal Bankruptcy Code.

At the time of the filing, Fender listed the following unsecured claims:

Judgment creditor	$4,000
Alimony and maintenance due under divorce decree	1,200
IRS assessment for 1993 taxes	500
1994 state income tax due	750
Unsecured personal loan from Ranch Bank	7,000
Rent on residence	2,000
Electricity charges on residence	200
Ace Finance Co.	1,000

The Ace Finance Company claim is listed because, in 1993, Fender agreed to guarantee payment of a $1,000 loan by Ace Finance Co. to Fender's cousin. The cousin defaulted on the loan and Ace is attempting to collect from Fender.

Fender had not been paying bills and obligations as they became due.

Required:
    a. State and name the fewest number of creditors which would have had to join in filing the petition against Fender and give the reasons for your decision.
    b. State which two creditor claims would be satisfied first from the bankruptcy estate and give the reasons for your decision.
    c. State which claim(s) would not be discharged if unpaid and give the reasons for your decision.
    d. State whether Fender's guarantee of payment would be discharged and give the reasons for your decision.

M92
Number 4 (Estimated time — — 15 to 20 minutes)

Techno, Inc. is a computer equipment dealer. On February 3, 1992, Techno was four months behind in its payments to Allied Building Maintenance, Cleen Janitorial Services, Inc., and Jones and Associates, CPAs, all of whom provide monthly services to Techno. In an attempt to settle with these three creditors, Techno offered each of them a reduced lump-sum payment for the past due obligations and full payment for future services. These creditors rejected Techno's offer and on April 9, 1992, Allied, Cleen and Jones filed an involuntary petition in bankruptcy against Techno under the provisions of Chapter 7 of the Federal Bankruptcy Code. At the time of the filing, Techno's liability to the three creditors was $10,500,* all of which was unsecured.

Techno, at the time of the filing, had liabilities of $229,000 (owed to 23 creditors) and assets with a fair market value of $191,000. During the entire year before the bankruptcy filing, Techno's liabilities exceeded the fair market value of its assets.

Included in Techno's liabilities was an installment loan payable to Dollar Finance Co., properly secured by cash registers and other equipment.

The bankruptcy court approved the involuntary petition.

On April 21, 1992, Dollar filed a motion for relief from automatic stay in bankruptcy court claiming it was entitled to take possession of the cash registers and other equipment securing its loan. Dollar plans to sell these assets immediately and apply the proceeds to the loan balance. The fair market value of the collateral is less than the loan balance and Dollar claims to lack adequate protection. Also, Dollar claims it is entitled to receive a priority distribution, before distribution to unsecured creditors, for the amount Techno owes Dollar less the proceeds from the sale of the collateral.

During the course of the bankruptcy proceeding, the following transactions were disclosed:

- On October 6, 1991, Techno paid its president $9,900 as repayment of an unsecured loan made to the corporation on September 18, 1989.

- On February 19, 1992, Techno paid $1,150 to Alexis Computers, Inc. for eight color computer monitors. These monitors were delivered to Techno on February 9, 1992, and placed in inventory.

- On January 12, 1992, Techno bought a new delivery truck from Maple Motors for $7,900 cash. On the date of the bankruptcy filing, the truck was worth $7,000.

Required:
Answer the following questions and give the reasons for your conclusions.

    a. What circumstances had to exist to allow Allied, Cleen, and Jones to file an involuntary bankruptcy petition against Techno?

    b. 1. Will Dollar's motion for relief be granted?
        2. Will Dollar's claim for priority be approved by the bankruptcy court?

    c. Are the payments to Techno's president, Alexis, and Maple preferential transfers?

---
*This question has been revised to reflect changes in the Federal Bankruptcy Code.

Selected Questions

M90
Number 2 (Estimated time — — 15 to 20 minutes)

On February 1, 1990, Drake, a sole proprietor operating a retail clothing store, filed a bankruptcy petition under the liquidation provisions of the Bankruptcy Code. For at least six months prior to the filing of the petition, Drake had been unable to pay current business and personal obligations as they came due. Total liabilities substantially exceeded the total assets. A trustee was appointed who has converted all of Drake's nonexempt property to cash in the amount of $96,000. Drake's bankruptcy petition reflects a total of $310,000 of debts, including the following:

- A judgment against Drake in the amount of $19,500 as a result of an automobile accident caused by Drake's negligence.
- Unpaid federal income taxes in the amount of $4,300 for the year 1983. (Drake filed an accurate tax return for 1983.)
- A $3,200 obligation payable on June 1, 1990, described as being owed to Martin Office Equipment, when, in fact, the debt is owed to Bartin Computer Supplies (Bartin has no knowledge of Drake's bankruptcy and the time for filing claims has expired).
- Unpaid child support in the amount of $780 arising from a support order incorporated in Drake's 1982 divorce judgment.

Prior to the filing of the petition, Drake entered into the following transactions:

- January 13, 1990 — paid Safe Bank $7,500, the full amount due on an unsecured loan given by Safe on November 13, 1989 (Drake had used the loan proceeds to purchase a family automobile).
- October 21, 1989 — conveyed to his brother, in repayment of a $2,000 debt, a painting that cost Drake $125 and which had a fair market value of $2,000.
- November 15, 1989 — borrowed $23,000 from Home Savings and Loan Association, giving Home a first mortgage on Drake's residence, which has a fair market value of $100,000.
- November 9, 1989 — paid $4,300 to Max Clothing Distributors for clothing delivered to Drake 60 days earlier (Drake had for several years purchased inventory from Max and his other suppliers on 60-day credit terms).

Required:
Answer the following questions, setting forth reasons for any conclusions stated.

a. Will the four debts described above be discharged in Drake's bankruptcy?

b. What factors must the bankruptcy trustee show to set aside a transaction as a preferential transfer?

c. State whether each transaction entered into by Drake is a preferential or non-preferential transfer.

M89
Number 2 (Estimated time — — 15 to 20 minutes)

On March 23, 1989, Tine, a sole proprietor, was involuntarily petitioned into bankruptcy under the liquidation provisions of the Bankruptcy Code. The petition was filed by Lux, Squire, and Rusk, who were creditors of Tine with unsecured claims of $5,000,* $4,000, and $2,000, respectively. Tine also has 10 other unsecured creditors, three partially secured creditors, and two fully secured creditors, none of whom joined in the filing of the bankruptcy petition. For the six-month period before the filing of the bankruptcy petition, Tine had been unable to pay current obligations as they became due. At the time the petition was filed, Tine had a negative net worth.

Before March 23, 1989, Tine entered into the following transactions:

- On December 29, 1988, Tine borrowed $250,000 from Safe Finance. On January 31, 1989, after learning of Tine's financial problems, Safe requested that Tine execute a mortgage on Tine's residence naming Safe as mortgagee. On January 31, 1989, Tine executed the mortgage and delivered it to Safe and it was recorded that same day. The residence had a fair market value of $300,000 at all times.
- On May 5, 1988, Rich Bank loaned Tine $50,000 based on Tine's personal financial statements. Tine knew the financial statements submitted to Rich substantially overstated Tine's net worth because of misrepresentations that were difficult to detect.

Required: Answer the following, setting forth reasons for any conclusions stated.

a. Discuss whether the requirements necessary for the commencement of an involuntary bankruptcy proceeding were met.

b. Assuming that the requirements necessary for the commencement of an involuntary bankruptcy were met, discuss the following:
  1. What action may the court take regarding the transactions between Tine and Safe?
  2. What action may the court take regarding the transaction between Tine and Rich if Rich challenges the discharge of its debt?

---
*This question has been revised to reflect changes in the Federal Bankruptcy Code.

V. Government Regulation of Business

A. Federal Securities Acts

M95
Number 5 (Estimated time — — 15 to 25 minutes)

Perry, a staff accountant with Orlean Associates, CPAs, reviewed the following transactions engaged in by Orlean's two clients: World Corp. and Unity Corp.

WORLD CORP.

During 1994, World Corp. made a $4,000,000 offering of its stock. The offering was sold to 50 nonaccredited investors and 150 accredited investors. There was a general advertising of the offering. All purchasers were provided with material information concerning World Corp. The offering was completely sold by the end of 1994. The SEC was notified 30 days after the first sale of the offering.

World did not register the offering and contends that the offering and any subsequent resale of the securities are completely exempt from registration under Regulation D, Rule 505, of the Securities Act of 1933.

UNITY CORP.

Unity Corp. has 750 equity stockholders and assets in excess of $100,000,000. Unity's stock is traded on a national stock exchange. Unity contends that it is not a covered corporation and is not required to comply with the reporting provisions of the Securities Exchange Act of 1934.

Required:

a. 1. State whether World is correct in its contention that the offering is exempt from registration under Regulation D, Rule 505, of the Securities Act of 1933. Give the reason(s) for your conclusion.
   2. State whether World is correct in its contention that on subsequent resale the securities are completely exempt from registration. Give the reason(s) for your conclusion.

b. 1. State whether Unity is correct in its contention that it is not a covered corporation and is not required to comply with the reporting requirements of the Securities Exchange Act of 1934 and give the reason(s) for your conclusion.
   2. Identify and describe two principal reports a covered corporation must file with the SEC.

VI. Uniform Commercial Code

A. Negotiable Instruments

N95
Number 5 (Estimated time — — 15 to 25 minutes)

On October 30, 1995, Dover, CPA, was engaged to audit the financial records of Crane Corp., a tractor manufacturer. During the review of notes receivable, Dover reviewed a promissory note given to Crane by Jones Corp., one of its customers, in payment for a tractor. The note appears below.

(Face)

```
                                              July 18, 1995

Sixty (60) days from date, the undersigned promises
to

Pay to the order of _____Jones Corp._____
Twenty Thousand and 00/100 ($20,000)........dollars
at West Bank

                    OVAL CORP.

                    G.J. Small
                By: G.J. Small, Pres.
```

(Back)

```
            Jones Corp.
          Without Recourse
             R. Mall
          By: R. Mall, Pres.

            Crane Corp.
           For Collection

          Payment Refused
```

On the note's due date, Crane deposited the note for collection and was advised by the bank that Oval had refused payment. After payment was refused, Crane contacted Oval. Oval told Crane that Jones fraudulently induced Oval into executing the note and that Jones knew about Oval's claim before Jones indorsed the note to Crane.

Dover also reviewed a security agreement signed by Harper, a customer, given to Crane to finance Harper's purchase of a tractor for use in Harper's farming business. On October 1, 1995, Harper made a down payment and gave Crane a purchase money security interest for the balance of the price of the tractor. Harper executed a financing statement that was filed on October 10, 1995. The tractor had been delivered to Harper on October 5, 1995. On October 8, 1995, Harper gave Acorn Trust a security agreement covering all of Harper's business equipment, including the tractor. Harper executed a financing statement that Acorn filed on October 9, 1995.

Required:
As the auditor on this engagement, write a memo to the partner-in-charge identifying, explaining, and stating your conclusions about the legal issues pertaining to the note and the security interest.

The memo should address the following:

- Whether Crane is a holder in due course
- Whether Oval will be required to pay the note
- Whether Jones is liable to pay the note
- When Crane's security interest was perfected and whether it had priority over Acorn's security interest

---

N93
Number 5 (Estimated time — — 15 to 25 minutes)

Williams Co. provides financial consulting services to the business community. On occasion, Williams will purchase promissory notes from its clients. The following transactions involving promissory notes purchased by Williams have resulted in disputes:

- Williams purchased the following promissory note from Jason Computers, Inc.:

> January 3, 1992
>
> For value received, Helco Distributors Corp. promises to pay $3,000 to the order of Jason Computers, Inc. with such payment to be made out of the proceeds of the resale of the computer components purchased this day from Jason Computers, Inc. and to be used as part of the customized computer systems sold to our customers. Payment shall be made two weeks after such proceeds become available.
>
> *J. Helco*
> J. Helco, President

Helco executed and delivered the note to Jason in payment for the computer components referred to in the note. Jason represented to Helco that all the components were new when, in fact, a large number of them were used and had been reconditioned. Williams was unaware of this fact at the time it acquired the note from Jason for $2,000. Jason endorsed and delivered the note to Williams in exchange for the $2,000 payment. Williams presented the promissory note to Helco for payment. Helco refused to pay, alleging that Jason misrepresented the condition of the components. Helco also advised Williams that the components had been returned to Jason within a few days after Helco had taken delivery.

Williams commenced an action against Helco, claiming that:

- the note is negotiable;
- Williams is a holder in due course; and
- Helco cannot raise Jason's misrepresentation as a defense to payment of the note.

- Williams Co. purchased a negotiable promissory note from Oliver International, Inc. that Oliver had received from Abco Products Corp., as partial payment on the sale of goods by Oliver to Abco. The maker of the note was Grover Corp., which had executed and delivered the note to Abco as payment for services rendered by Abco. When Oliver received the note from Abco, Oliver was unaware of the fact that Grover disputed its obligation under the note because Grover was dissatisfied with the quality of the services Abco rendered. Williams was aware of Grover's claims at the time Williams purchased the note from Oliver. The reverse side of the note was endorsed as follows:

> Pay to the order of Oliver
>
> *F. Smith*
> F. Smith, President of Abco Products Corp.
>
> Pay to the order of Williams Co. without recourse
>
> *N. Oliver*
> N. Oliver, President of Oliver International, Inc.

When the promissory note became due Williams demanded that Grover pay the note. Grover refused, claiming that Abco breached its contractual obligations to Grover and that Williams was aware of this fact at the time Williams acquired the note. Williams immediately advised both Abco and Oliver of Grover's refusal to pay and demanded payment from Oliver in the event Grover fails to pay the note.

Required:
Answer the following questions and give the reasons for your conclusions.

a. Are Williams' claims correct regarding the Helco promissory note?

b. Is Grover correct in refusing to pay its note?

c. What are the rights of Williams against Oliver in the event Grover is not required to pay its note?

M92
Number 5 (Estimated time — — 15 to 20 minutes)

Rustic Equipment, Inc. manufactures lathes and other woodworking equipment. It sells these products to hardware stores, often on credit. Rustic usually requires its credit customers to place large signs in their stores indicating that Rustic products are made available through financing provided by Rustic.

On February 1, 1992, Rustic sold and delivered five lathes to Friendly Hardware Corp. for $25,000. Friendly sells woodworking tools and equipment, among other things, to the general public. Friendly made a 10% downpayment and delivered a promissory note for the balance, along with a security agreement and a financing statement covering the lathes. Rustic properly filed the financing statement on February 9, 1992. Rustic required Friendly to display a sign in its store indicating that Rustic provided financing for the lathes.

On February 6, 1992, Friendly borrowed $100,000 from National Bank, and gave National a promissory note, a security agreement, and a financing statement covering Friendly's inventory, fixtures, and equipment. Friendly intended to use the loan proceeds to remodel its store. National properly filed the financing statement on February 7, 1992. National was not aware of Rustic's security interest in the lathes included in Friendly's inventory.

On March 8, 1992, Friendly sold one of the Rustic lathes to Karry, whose hobby was woodworking. Karry paid 20% of the purchase price, and gave Friendly a promissory note for the balance and a security agreement covering the lathe. Karry, at the time of the purchase, saw the sign publicizing the financing arrangement between Rustic and Friendly. Friendly did not file a financing statement.

The following is the promissory note Karry gave to Friendly:

March 8 , 199 2

I promise to pay Friendly Hardware Corp. or bearer $ 900.00 , with interest thereon at 12 % per annum.

S.J. Karry
Maker

Reference: Sale of Lathe
Invoice #6734

On March 10, 1992, Friendly delivered Karry's promissory note, without endorsement, to Queen Bank in exchange for $750. Queen, a holder in due course, was unaware that Karry had advised Friendly that the lathe was not operating properly and that Karry had no intention of paying the note. Queen then delivered the note to Abcor Factors, Inc. in exchange for $800. At the time Abcor acquired the note from Queen, it knew that Karry disputed any obligation under the note because the lathe was not working properly.

Friendly has experienced serious financial difficulties and defaulted on its obligations to Rustic and National. Abcor has demanded that Karry pay the note given to Friendly, but Karry has refused to do so.

Rustic and Karry have taken the following positions:

- Rustic claims that its security interest in the lathes, including the one sold to Karry, is superior to that of National and that Karry purchased the lathe subject to Rustic's security interest.

- Karry refuses to honor the note held by Abcor claiming that:

   It is nonnegotiable because it is not payable at a definite time and it references the sales invoice.

   Abcor has no rights under the note because it was not endorsed by Friendly.

   Abcor was aware of Karry's claim that the lathe was not working properly and, therefore, took the note subject to that claim.

Required:
State whether the claims of Rustic and Karry are correct and give the reasons for your conclusions.

M91
Number 3 (Estimated time — — 15 to 20 minutes)

River Oaks is a wholesale distributor of automobile parts. River Oaks received the promissory note shown below from First Auto, Inc., as security for payment of a $4,400 auto parts shipment. When River Oaks accepted the note as collateral for the First Auto obligation, River Oaks was aware that the maker of the note, Hillcraft, Inc., was claiming that the note was unenforceable because Alexco Co. had breached the license agreement under which Hillcraft had given the note. First Auto had acquired the note from Smith in exchange for repairing several cars owned by Smith. At the time First Auto received the note, First Auto was unaware of the dispute between Hillcraft and Alexco. Also, Smith, who paid Alexco $3,500 for the note, was unaware of Hillcraft's allegations that Alexco had breached the license agreement.

```
                    PROMISSORY NOTE

                                     Date: 1/14/90

         Hillcraft, Inc.       promises to pay to

      Alexco Co. or bearer     the sum of $4,400

      Four Thousand and 00/100           Dollars

on or before    May 15, 1991 (maker may elect

to extend due date by 30 days)      with interest

thereon at the rate of    9 1/2%    per annum.

                            Hillcraft, Inc.
                            By: P.J. Hill
                            P.J. Hill, President

Reference: Alexco Licensing Agreement
```

The reverse side of the note was endorsed as follows:

```
Pay to the order of First Auto without recourse

   E. Smith
   E. Smith

Pay to the order of River Oaks Co.

   First Auto
   By: G. First
   G. First, President
```

First Auto is now insolvent and unable to satisfy its obligation to River Oaks. Therefore, River Oaks has demanded that Hillcraft pay $4,400, but Hillcraft has refused, asserting:

- The note is nonnegotiable because it references the license agreement and is not payable at a definite time or on demand.
- River Oaks is not a holder in due course of the note because it received the note as security for amounts owed by First Auto.
- River Oaks is not a holder in due course because it was aware of the dispute between Hillcraft and Alexco.
- Hillcraft can raise the alleged breach by Alexco as a defense to payment.
- River Oaks has no right to the note because it was not endorsed by Alexco.
- The maximum amount that Hillcraft would owe under the note is $4,000, plus accrued interest.

Required:
State whether each of Hillcraft's assertions are correct and give the reasons for your conclusions.

M90
Number 5 (Estimated time — — 15 to 20 minutes)

On February 12, 1990, Mayfair & Associates, CPAs, was engaged to audit the financial statements of University Book Distributors, Inc. University operates as a retail and wholesale distributor of books, newspapers, magazines, and other periodicals. In conjunction with the audit of University's cash, notes, and accounts receivable, University's controller gave Mayfair's staff accountant certain instruments that University had received from its customers during 1989 in the ordinary course of its business. The instruments are:

- A signed promissory note dated June 30, 1989, in the amount of $3,100 payable "to Harris on December 31, 1989." The maker of the note was Peters and it was indorsed in blank by Harris, who delivered it to University as payment for a shipment of magazines. University demanded that Peters pay the note but Peters refused, claiming that he gave the note as a result of misrepresentations by Harris related to a real estate transaction between the two of them. University advised Harris immediately of Peters' refusal to pay.
- A signed promissory note dated July 31, 1989, in the amount of $1,800 payable "to the order of Able on January 15, 1990." The maker of the note was Cole and it further provided that it was given "pursuant to that certain construction contract dated June 1, 1989." The note had been given to University as payment for books by one of its customers, Baker, who did not indorse it. The note bears Able's blank indorsement. University demanded payment from Cole. Cole refused to honor the note claiming that:

  - The note's reference to the construction contract renders it nonnegotiable; and
  - University has no rights to the note because it was not indorsed by Baker.

University immediately advised Baker of Cole's refusal to pay.

University is uncertain of its rights under the two notes.

Required:
Answer the following questions, setting forth reasons for your conclusions.

a. With regard to the note executed by Peters, is University a holder in due course?

b. Can Peters raise Harris' alleged misrepresentations as a defense to University's demand for payment?

c. Are Cole's claims valid?

B. Sales

R98
Number 1

On June 1, Classic Corp., a manufacturer of desk chairs, orally agreed to sell 100 leather desk chairs to Rand Stores, a chain of retail furniture stores, for $50,000. The parties agreed that delivery would be completed by September 1, and the shipping terms were "F.O.B. seller's loading dock." On June 5, Classic sent Rand a signed memorandum of agreement containing the terms orally agreed to. Rand received the memorandum on June 7 and made no response.

On July 31, Classic identified the chairs to be shipped to Rand and placed them on its loading dock to be picked up by the common carrier the next day. That night, a fire on the loading dock destroyed 50 of the chairs. On August 1, the remaining 50 chairs were delivered to the common carrier together with 50 vinyl chairs. The truck carrying the chairs was involved in an accident, resulting in extensive damage to 10 of the leather chairs and 25 of the vinyl chairs.

On August 10, the chairs were delivered to Rand. On August 12, Rand notified Classic that Rand was accepting 40 of the leather chairs and 10 of the vinyl chairs, but the rest of the shipment was being rejected. Rand also informed Classic that, due to Classic's failure to perform under the terms of the contract, Rand would seek all remedies available under the Sales Article of the UCC.

Classic contended that it has no liability to Rand and that the shipment was strictly an accommodation to Rand because Rand failed to sign the memorandum of agreement, thus preventing a contract from being formed.

The above parties and transactions are governed by the provisions of the Sales Article of the UCC.

Required:
    a. Determine whether Classic's contention is correct and give the reasons for your conclusion.

    b. Assuming that a valid contract exists between Classic and Rand, answer the following questions and give the reasons for your conclusions. Do not consider any possible liability owed by the common carrier.
        1. Who bears the risk of loss for the 50 destroyed leather chairs?
        2. Who bears the risk of loss for the 25 damaged vinyl chairs?
        3. What is the earliest date that title to any of the chairs would pass to Rand?

    c. With what UCC requirements must Rand comply to be entitled to recover damages from Classic?

    d. Assuming that a valid contract exists between Classic and Rand, state the applicable remedies to which Rand would be entitled. Do not consider any possible liability owed by the common carrier.

M93
Number 5 (Estimated time — — 15 to 25 minutes)

Angler Corp., a food distributor, is involved in the following disputes:

- On September 8, Angler shipped the wrong grade of tuna to Mason Restaurants, Inc. under a contract that stated as follows: "F.O.B. — Angler's loading dock." During shipment, the tuna was destroyed in an accident involving the common carrier's truck. Mason has refused to pay for the tuna, claiming the risk of loss belonged to Angler at the time of the accident.

- On October 3, Angler shipped 100 bushels of peaches to Classic Foods, Inc., a retail grocer. Because of a delay in shipping, the peaches rotted. Classic elected to reject the peaches and notified Angler of this decision. Angler asked Classic to return the peaches at Angler's expense. Classic refused the request, claiming it had no obligation to do so.

- On October 23, Angler orally contracted to sell Regal Fast-Food 1,000 pounds of hamburger meat for $900. Delivery was to be made on October 31. On October 29, after Angler had shipped the hamburger meat to Regal, Regal sent Angler the following signed correspondence:

    "We are not going to need the 1,000 pounds of meat we ordered on October 23. Don't ship."

Regal rejected the shipment and claimed it is not obligated to purchase the hamburger meat because there is no written contract between Angler and Regal.

Required:
    a. State whether Mason's claim is correct and give the reasons for your conclusion.

    b. State whether Classic's claim is correct and give the reasons for your conclusion.

    c. State whether Regal's claim is correct and give the reasons for your conclusion.

N92
Number 5 (Estimated time — — 15 to 25 minutes)

    Debco Electronics, Inc. sells various brands of computer equipment to retail and business customers. An audit of Debco's 1991 financial statements has revealed the following transactions:

- On September 1, 1991, a Debco salesperson orally agreed to sell Rapid Computers, Inc. eight TMI computers for $11,000, to be delivered on October 15, 1991. Rapid sells computers to the general public. The Debco salesperson sent Rapid a signed confirmation of the sales agreement. Rapid received the confirmation on September 3, but did not respond to it. On October

15, 1991, Debco tendered delivery of the computers to Rapid. Rapid refused to accept delivery, claiming it had no obligation to buy the computers because it had not signed a contract with Debco.

- On October 12, 1991, Debco mailed TMI Computers, Inc. a signed purchase order for certain specified computers for delivery by November 30, 1991. The purchase order also stated the following:

  > This purchase order will not be withdrawn on or before October 31, 1991. You must accept by that date or we will assume you cannot meet our terms. Ship F.O.B. — our loading dock.

  TMI received the purchase order on October 15, 1991.

- On October 25, Debco mailed the following signed correspondence to TMI, which TMI received on October 29:

  > Cancel our October 12, 1991, purchase order. We have found a better price on the computers.

- On October 31, 1991, TMI mailed the following signed correspondence to Debco, which Debco received on November 3:

  > We have set aside the computers you ordered and turned down other offers for them. Therefore, we will ship the computers to you for delivery by November 30, 1991, F.O.B. — your loading dock with payment terms 2/10; net 30.

There were no further communications between TMI and Debco.

TMI shipped the computers on November 15, and Debco received them on November 29. Debco refused to accept delivery. In justifying its refusal to accept delivery, Debco claimed the following:

- Its October 25 correspondence prevented the formation of a contract between Debco and TMI;

- TMI's October 31 correspondence was not an effective acceptance because it was not received by Debco until November 3;

- TMI's October 31 correspondence was not an effective acceptance because it added payment terms to Debco's purchase order.

Debco, Rapid, and TMI are located in a jurisdiction that has adopted the UCC.

Required:
  a. State whether Rapid's claim is correct and give the reasons for your conclusions.

  b. State whether Debco's claims are correct with regard to the transaction involving TMI and give the reasons for your conclusions.

N91
Number 4 (Estimated time — — 15 to 20 minutes)

On October 10, Vesta Electronics contracted with Zap Audio to sell Zap 200 18" stereo speakers. The contract provided that the speakers would be shipped F.O.B. seller's loading dock. The contract was silent as to when risk of loss for the speakers would pass to Zap. Delivery was to be completed by November 10.

On October 18, Vesta identified the speakers to be shipped to Zap and moved them to the loading dock. Before the carrier picked up the goods, a fire on Vesta's loading dock destroyed 50 of the speakers. On October 20, Vesta shipped, by common carrier, the remaining 150 18" speakers and 50 16" speakers. The truck carrying the speakers was involved in an accident resulting in damage to 25 of the 16" speakers. Zap received the 200 speakers on October 25, and on October 27 notified Vesta that 100 of the 18" speakers were being accepted but the rest of the shipment was being rejected. Zap also informed Vesta that, due to Vesta's failure to comply with the terms of the contract, Zap would contest paying the contract price and would sue for damages.

The above parties and transactions are subject to the Uniform Commercial Code (UCC).

Required:
Answer the following questions, and give the reasons for your conclusions.

  a. 1. Who bears the risk of loss for the 50 destroyed 18" speakers?
  2. Who bears the risk of loss for the 25 damaged 16" speakers?

  b. 1. Was Zap's rejection of the 16" speakers valid?
  2. Was Zap's acceptance of some of the 18" speakers valid?

  c. Under the UCC, what duties are required of Zap after rejecting all or part of the shipment?

N90
Number 4 (Estimated time — — 15 to 20 minutes)

Pharo Aviation, Inc. sells and services used airplanes. Sanders, Pharo's service department manager, negotiated with Secure Equipment Co. for the purchase of a used tug for moving airplanes in and out of Pharo's hangar. Secure sells and services tugs and related equipment. Sanders was unfamiliar with the various models, specifications, and capacities of the tugs sold by Secure; however, Sanders knew that the tug purchased needed to have the capacity to move airplanes weighing up to 10,000 pounds. Sanders and the sales representative discussed this specific need because Sanders was uncertain as to which tug would meet Pharo's requirements. The sales representative then recommended a particular make and model of tug. Sanders agreed to rely on the sales representative's advice and signed a purchase contract with Secure.

About a week after Sanders took delivery, the following occurred:

- Sanders determined that the tug did not have the capacity to move airplanes weighing over 5,000 pounds.
- Sanders was advised correctly by Maco Equipment Distributors, Inc. that Maco was the rightful owner of the tug, which it had left with Secure for repairs.

Pharo has commenced a lawsuit against Secure claiming that implied warranties were created by the contract with Secure and that these have been breached. Maco has claimed that it is entitled to the tug and has demanded its return from Pharo.

Required:
Answer each of the following questions, and set forth the reasons for your conclusions.

a. Were any implied warranties created by the contract between Pharo and Secure and, if so, were any of those warranties breached?

b. Is Maco entitled to the return of the tug?

N89
Number 4 (Estimated time — — 15 to 20 minutes)

Anker Corp., a furniture retailer, engaged Best & Co., CPAs, to audit Anker's financial statements for the year ended December 31, 1988. While reviewing certain transactions entered into by Anker during 1988, Best became concerned with the proper reporting of the following transactions:

- On September 8, 1988, Crisp Corp., a furniture manufacturer, signed and mailed a letter offering to sell Anker 50 pieces of furniture for $9,500. The offer stated it would remain open until December 20, 1988. On December 5, 1988, Crisp mailed a letter revoking this offer. Anker received Crisp's revocation the following day. On December 12, 1988, Anker mailed its acceptance to Crisp, and Crisp received it on December 13, 1988.
- On December 6, 1988, Dix Corp. signed and mailed a letter offering to sell Anker a building for $75,000. The offer stated that acceptance could only be made by certified mail, return receipt requested. On December 10, 1988, Anker telephoned Dix requesting that Dix keep the offer open until December 20, 1988 because it was reviewing Dix's offer. On December 12, 1988, Dix signed and mailed a letter to Anker indicating that it would hold the offer open until December 20, 1988. On December 19, 1988, Anker sent its acceptance to Dix by a private express mail courier. Anker's acceptance was received by Dix on December 20, 1988.

After reviewing the documents concerning the foregoing transactions, Best spoke with Anker's president who made the following assertions:

- The September 8, 1988 offer by Crisp was irrevocable until December 20, 1988, and therefore a contract was formed by Anker's acceptance on December 12, 1988.
- Dix's letter dated December 12, 1988 formed an option contract with Anker.
- Anker's acceptance on December 19, 1988 formed a contract with Dix.

Required: In separate paragraphs, discuss the assertions made by Anker's president. Indicate whether the assertions are correct and the reasons therefor.

M89
Number 5 (Estimated time — — 15 to 20 minutes)

On February 20, 1989, Pine, Inc. ordered a specially manufactured computer system consisting of a disk drive and a central processing unit (CPU) from Xeon Corp., a seller of computers and other office equipment. A contract was signed and the total purchase price was paid to Xeon by Pine on the same date. The contract required Pine to pick up the computer system at Xeon's warehouse on March 9, 1989, but was silent as to when risk of loss passed to Pine. The computer system was completed on March 1, 1989, and set aside for Pine's contemplated pickup on March 9, 1989. On March 3, 1989, the disk drive was stolen from Xeon's warehouse. On March 9, 1989, Pine picked up the CPU. On March 15, 1989, Pine returned the CPU to Xeon for warranty repairs. On March 18, 1989, Xeon mistakenly sold the CPU to Meed, a buyer in the ordinary course of business.

On April 12, 1989, Pine purchased and received delivery of five word processors from Jensen Electronics Corp. for use in its business. The purchase price of the word processors was $15,000. Pine paid $5,000 down and executed an installment purchase note and a security agreement for the balance. The security agreement contained a description of the word processors. Jensen never filed a financing statement. On April 1, 1989, Pine had given its bank a security interest in all of its assets. The bank had immediately perfected its security interest by filing. Pine has defaulted on the installment purchase note.

Required: Discuss the following assertions, indicating whether such assertions are correct and the reasons therefor.

- As of March 3, 1989, the risk of loss on the disk drive remained with Xeon.
- Meed acquired no rights in the CPU as a result of the March 18, 1989, transaction.
- Jensen's security interest in the word processors never attached and therefore Jensen's security interest is not enforceable against Pine.
- Jensen has a superior security interest to Pine's bank.

Selected Questions

C. Secured Transactions

N95
Number 5 (Estimated time — — 15 to 25 minutes)

On October 30, 1995, Dover, CPA, was engaged to audit the financial records of Crane Corp., a tractor manufacturer. During the review of notes receivable, Dover reviewed a promissory note given to Crane by Jones Corp., one of its customers, in payment for a tractor. The note appears below.

(Face)

```
                                    July 18, 1995

Sixty (60) days from date, the undersigned promises
to

Pay to the order of _____Jones Corp._____
Twenty Thousand and 00/100 ($20,000) ........dollars
at West Bank

                        OVAL CORP.

                        G.J. Small
                        By: G.J. Small, Pres.
```

(Back)

```
                        Jones Corp.
                      Without Recourse
                          R. Mall
                      By: R. Mall, Pres.

                        Crane Corp.
                       For Collection


                      Payment Refused
```

On the note's due date, Crane deposited the note for collection and was advised by the bank that Oval had refused payment. After payment was refused, Crane contacted Oval. Oval told Crane that Jones fraudulently induced Oval into executing the note and that Jones knew about Oval's claim before Jones indorsed the note to Crane.

Dover also reviewed a security agreement signed by Harper, a customer, given to Crane to finance Harper's purchase of a tractor for use in Harper's farming business. On October 1, 1995, Harper made a down payment and gave Crane a purchase money security interest for the balance of the price of the tractor. Harper executed a financing statement that was filed on October 10, 1995. The tractor had been delivered to Harper on October 5, 1995. On October 8, 1995, Harper gave Acorn Trust a security agreement covering all of Harper's business equipment, including the tractor. Harper executed a financing statement that Acorn filed on October 9, 1995.

Required:
As the auditor on this engagement, write a memo to the partner-in-charge identifying, explaining, and stating your conclusions about the legal issues pertaining to the note and the security interest.

The memo should address the following:

- Whether Crane is a holder in due course
- Whether Oval will be required to pay the note
- Whether Jones is liable to pay the note
- When Crane's security interest was perfected and whether it had priority over Acorn's security interest

---

M92
Number 5 (Estimated time — — 15 to 20 minutes)

Rustic Equipment, Inc. manufactures lathes and other woodworking equipment. It sells these products to hardware stores, often on credit. Rustic usually requires its credit customers to place large signs in their stores indicating that Rustic products are made available through financing provided by Rustic.

On February 1, 1992, Rustic sold and delivered five lathes to Friendly Hardware Corp. for $25,000. Friendly sells woodworking tools and equipment, among other things, to the general public. Friendly made a 10% down-payment and delivered a promissory note for the balance, along with a security agreement and a financing statement covering the lathes. Rustic properly filed the financing statement on February 9, 1992. Rustic required Friendly to display a sign in its store indicating that Rustic provided financing for the lathes.

On February 6, 1992, Friendly borrowed $100,000 from National Bank, and gave National a promissory note, a security agreement, and a financing statement covering Friendly's inventory, fixtures, and equipment. Friendly intended to use the loan proceeds to remodel its store. National properly filed the financing statement on February 7, 1992. National was not aware of Rustic's security interest in the lathes included in Friendly's inventory.

On March 8, 1992, Friendly sold one of the Rustic lathes to Karry, whose hobby was woodworking. Karry paid 20% of the purchase price, and gave Friendly a promissory note for the balance and a security agreement covering the lathe. Karry, at the time of the purchase, saw the sign publicizing the financing arrangement between Rustic and Friendly. Friendly did not file a financing statement.

The following is the promissory note Karry gave to Friendly:

March 8, 1992

I promise to pay Friendly Hardware Corp. or bearer $900.00, with interest thereon at 12% per annum.

S.J. Karry
Maker

Reference: Sale of Lathe
Invoice #6734

On March 10, 1992, Friendly delivered Karry's promissory note, without endorsement, to Queen Bank in exchange for $750. Queen, a holder in due course, was unaware that Karry had advised Friendly that the lathe was not operating properly and that Karry had no intention of paying the note. Queen then delivered the note to Abcor Factors, Inc. in exchange for $800. At the time Abcor acquired the note from Queen, it knew that Karry disputed any obligation under the note because the lathe was not working properly.

Friendly has experienced serious financial difficulties and defaulted on its obligations to Rustic and National. Abcor has demanded that Karry pay the note given to Friendly, but Karry has refused to do so.

Rustic and Karry have taken the following positions:

- Rustic claims that its security interest in the lathes, including the one sold to Karry, is superior to that of National and that Karry purchased the lathe subject to Rustic's security interest.

- Karry refuses to honor the note held by Abcor claiming that:

    It is nonnegotiable because it is not payable at a definite time and it references the sales invoice.

    Abcor has no rights under the note because it was not endorsed by Friendly.

    Abcor was aware of Karry's claim that the lathe was not working properly and, therefore, took the note subject to that claim.

Required:
State whether the claims of Rustic and Karry are correct and give the reasons for your conclusions.

N91
Number 5 (Estimated time — — 15 to 20 minutes)

Mead, a junior member of a CPA firm's audit staff, was assigned to assist in auditing Abco Electronics, Inc.'s financial statements. Abco sells various brands of computer equipment to the general public, and to distributors who sell the equipment to retail customers for personal and business use. One of Mead's assignments was to evaluate the following transactions:

- On September 1, Abco sold a CDM computer out of its inventory to Rice, who intended to use it for business purposes. Rice paid 25% of the purchase price and executed and delivered to Abco a promissory note for the balance. A security agreement was signed only by the Abco sales representative. Abco failed to file a financing statement. Rice is in default under the promissory note. Rice claimed that Abco does not have an effective security interest in the computer because Rice did not sign the security agreement, and because Abco did not file a financing statement.

- On August 18, Abco sold a computer to Baker, who intended to use it for business inventory and accounts payable control, and payroll processing. Baker paid 20% of the purchase price and executed and delivered to Abco a promissory note for the balance and a security agreement covering the computer. Abco filed a financing statement on August 27. On August 25, Baker borrowed $5,000 from Condor Finance Co., giving Condor a promissory note for the loan amount and a security agreement covering the computer. Condor filed a financing statement on August 26. Baker defaulted on the promissory note given to Abco and its obligation to Condor. Condor has asserted that its security interest in the computer is superior to Abco's.

Required:
State whether the claims of Rice and Condor are correct and give the reasons for your conclusions.

N90
Number 5 (Estimated time — — 15 to 20 minutes)

Wizard Computer Co. sells computers to the general public. On April 30, Wizard financed the purchase of its computer inventory with National Bank. Wizard executed and delivered a promissory note and a security agreement covering the inventory. National filed a financing statement on the same day.

On May 1, Wizard sold a computer out of its inventory to Kast, who intended to use it to do some household budgeting. Kast made a 10% down payment toward the purchase price. Kast executed and delivered to Wizard a promissory note for the balance and a security agreement covering the computer. Kast was aware that Wizard financed its inventory with National. Wizard did not file a financing statement.

On May 6, Kast, who was dissatisfied with the computer, sold it on credit to Marc, who intended to use it to assist in family budgeting. Marc, who was unaware that Kast had purchased the computer on credit, paid 25% of the purchase price and executed and delivered to Kast a promissory note for the balance and a security agreement covering the computer. Kast did not file a financing statement.

On May 12, Marc borrowed $6,000 from Alcor Finance. Marc gave Alcor a promissory note for the loan amount and a security agreement covering the computer and other household appliances owned by Marc. Alcor did not file a financing statement.

Marc failed to pay Alcor or Kast. In turn, Kast has been unable to pay Wizard. On June 2, Wizard defaulted on its obligation to National.

Kast and Marc take the following positions:
- Kast asserts that the computer was purchased from Wizard free of National's security interest.
- Marc asserts that the computer was purchased from Kast free of Wizard's security interest.
- Marc asserts that Alcor's security interest is unenforceable against Marc because Alcor failed to file a financing statement.

Required:
For each assertion, indicate whether it is correct, and set forth the reasons for your conclusion.

VII. Property

A. Real Property Including Insurance

R97
Number 1(b)

On April 1, Thorn and Birch negotiated the sale of Thorn's shopping center to Birch for $2.1 million ($2 million for the buildings and $100,000 for the land). The parties orally agreed on the following terms:

- Birch would make a cash down payment of $600,000.

- Birch would give Thorn a $1.5 million first mortgage on the property to secure the balance of the purchase price.

- The contract would contain an anti-assignment clause prohibiting assignment of the contract of sale or the mortgage.

- The contract would contain a "time of the essence" clause requiring that the closing take place on June 1.

No discussion took place regarding any existing mortgages or liens on the property. On April 14, the parties signed a written contract containing the above provisions.

On April 20, Birch took out a $1.5 million fire insurance policy with Acme Fire Insurance Co. on the buildings. The policy contained a standard 80% coinsurance clause.

On April 25, a title insurance report ordered by Birch revealed that there was an existing $500,000 mortgage on the property that had been recorded the previous February. The title report failed to disclose another mortgage for $50,000 that had been given years earlier by a prior owner of the land and had not been recorded. Thorn was aware of the $500,000 mortgage but not the earlier mortgage.

The title report also disclosed that there were unpaid property taxes outstanding.

On May 1, Thorn agreed to assign to a third party the prospective mortgage payments Thorn would receive from Birch.

When Birch received the title report and found out about Thorn's assignment of the mortgage payments, Birch accused Thorn of breach of contract for failing to disclose the prior mortgages and for violating the anti-assignment clause in the contract. Birch also insisted on postponing the contract closing date.

Thorn and Birch were able to resolve their differences.

- Birch reduced the mortgage being given to Thorn and assumed the previously recorded mortgage.

- The closing took place on July 1.

- Thorn recorded Birch's mortgage on July 5.

- The previously unrecorded mortgage was recorded on July 10.

On August 1, a fire caused $160,000 damage to the buildings. On that date, the fair market value of the buildings was $2 million. Acme contested payment of the claim, contending that Birch had no insurable interest in the buildings when the policy was taken out. Acme also contended that, even if Birch had an insurable interest, Birch would not be entitled to recover the entire amount of the loss because Birch is a coinsurer.

After the insurance issues were resolved and the buildings repaired, Birch stopped making payments on the mortgages and they were foreclosed. After payment of all foreclosure expenses, there was $1 million available to pay the outstanding mortgages. Thorn's mortgage had a principal and accrued interest balance of $950,000. The mortgage recorded in February had a principal and accrued interest balance of $475,000. The mortgage recorded on July 10 had a principal and accrued interest balance of $60,000.

The above transactions took place in a notice-race jurisdiction.

Required:
b. 1. Determine whether Acme's contentions are correct and give the reasons for your conclusions.
2. Compute the dollar amount to which Birch would be entitled if the policy was valid and show how this amount is arrived at.
3. Determine which mortgage(s) has(have) priority, give the reasons for your decision, and state how the foreclosure proceeds would be distributed.

N94
Number 5 (Estimated time — — 15 to 25 minutes)

On May 15, 1993, Strong bought a factory building from Front for $500,000. Strong assumed Front's $300,000 mortgage with Ace Bank, gave a $150,000 mortgage to Lane Finance Co., and paid $50,000 cash.

The Ace mortgage had never been recorded. Lane knew of the Ace mortgage and recorded its mortgage on May 20, 1993.

Strong bought the factory for investment purposes and, on June 1, 1993, entered into a written lease with Apex Mfg. for seven years. On December 1, 1993, Apex subleased the factory to Egan Corp. without Strong's permission. Strong's lease with Apex was silent concerning the right to sublease.

On May 15, 1993, Strong had obtained a fire insurance policy from Range Insurance Co. The policy had a face value of $400,000. Apex and Egan obtained fire insurance policies from Zone Insurance Co. Each policy contained a standard 80% coinsurance clause. On May 1, 1994, when the factory had a fair market value of $600,000, a fire caused $180,000 damage.

Strong made no mortgage payments after the fire and on September 1, 1994, after the factory had been repaired, the mortgages were foreclosed. The balances due for principal and accrued interest were: Ace, $275,000; and Lane, $140,000. At a foreclosure sale, the factory and land were sold. After payment of all expenses, $400,000 of the proceeds remained for distribution.

As a result of the above events, the following actions took place:

- Strong sued Apex for subleasing the factory to Egan without Strong's permission.

- Zone refused to honor the Apex and Egan fire insurance policies claiming neither Apex nor Egan had an insurable interest in the factory.

- Strong sued Range to have Range pay Strong's $180,000 loss. Range refused claiming Strong had insufficient coverage under the coinsurance clause.

- Ace and Lane both demanded full payment of their mortgages from the proceeds of the foreclosure sale.

The preceding took place in a "Notice-Race" jurisdiction.

Required:
Answer the following questions and give the reasons for your conclusions.

a. Would Strong succeed in the suit against Apex for subletting the factory to Egan without Strong's permission?

b. Is Zone correct in claiming that neither Apex nor Egan had an insurable interest in the factory at the time of the fire?

c. What amount will Strong be able to recover from Range?

d. What amount of the foreclosure proceeds will Lane recover?

M91
Number 4 (Estimated time — — 15 to 20 minutes)

On February 1, 1988, Tower and Perry, as tenants in common, purchased a two-unit apartment building for $250,000. They made a down payment of $100,000, and gave a $100,000 first mortgage to Midway Bank and a $50,000 second mortgage to New Bank.

New was aware of Midway's mortgage but, as a result of a clerical error, Midway did not record its mortgage until after New's mortgage was recorded.

At the time of purchase, a $200,000 fire insurance policy was issued by Acme Insurance Co. to Tower and Perry. The policy contained an 80% coinsurance clause and a standard mortgagee provision.

Tower and Perry rented an apartment to Young under a month-to-month oral lease. They rented the other apartment to Zimmer under a three-year written lease.

On December 8, 1989, Perry died leaving a will naming the Dodd Foundation as the sole beneficiary of Perry's estate. The estate was distributed on January 15, 1990. That same date, the ownership of the fire insurance policy was assigned to Tower and Dodd with Acme's consent. On January 21, 1990, a fire caused $180,000 in structural damage to the building. At that time, its market value was $300,000 and the Midway mortgage balance was $80,000 including accrued interest. The New mortgage balance was $40,000 including accrued interest.

The fire made Young's apartment uninhabitable and caused extensive damage to the kitchen, bathrooms, and one bedroom of Zimmer's apartment. On February 1, 1990, Young and Zimmer moved out. The resulting loss of income caused a default on both mortgages.

On April 1, 1990, Acme refused to pay the fire loss claiming that the required insurable interest did not exist at the time of the loss and that the amount of the insurance was insufficient to provide full coverage for the loss. Tower and Dodd are involved in a lawsuit contesting the ownership of the building and the claims they have both made for any fire insurance proceeds.

On June 1, 1990, Midway and New foreclosed their mortgages and are also claiming any fire insurance proceeds that may be paid by Acme.

On July 1, 1990, Tower sued Zimmer for breach of the lease and is seeking to collect the balance of the lease term rent.

The above events took place in a notice-race statute jurisdiction.

Required:

Answer the following questions and give the reasons for your conclusions.

a. Who had title to the building on January 21, 1990?

b. Did Tower and/or Dodd have an insurable interest in the building when the fire occurred? If so, when would such an interest have arisen?

c. Does Acme have to pay under the terms of the fire insurance policy? If so, how much?

d. Assuming the fire insurance proceeds will be paid, what would be the order of payment to the various parties and in what amounts?

e. Would Tower succeed in the suit against Zimmer?

N89
Number 2 (Estimated time — — 15 to 20 minutes)

On May 1, 1988, Mary Stein sold a commercial building to Sam Bean and Bean's son, Bob, as equal tenants in common. At the time of the sale, there was a recorded existing mortgage on the building in favor of Fale Bank. The mortgage and the note it secured were silent as to whether the entire amount outstanding on the loan would become due upon the sale of the building. Sam and Bob did not assume the mortgage and it was not paid off when they purchased the building.

On June 15, 1989, Sam died leaving a will naming his wife, Rita Bean, as the beneficiary of his entire estate, except for certain stocks which were to be transferred to a spendthrift trust created for the benefit of Bob. The will named Rita as the trustee and Bob as the sole beneficiary of the trust. The provision in the will creating the spendthrift trust stated in part that:

> Payments and distributions to the beneficiary shall be made only to the beneficiary in person or upon his personal receipt, and no interest of the beneficiary in the income or principal of the trust estate shall be assignable in anticipation of payment, either by the voluntary or involuntary act of the beneficiary or by operation of law, or be liable in any way for the debts of the beneficiary.

Required:

a. Discuss the personal liability of Sam Bean and Bob Bean, and the personal liability of Mary Stein, if there is a default on the mortgage to Fale and a foreclosure sale results in a deficiency.

b. Discuss the effect Sam Bean's death will have on the ownership of the building.

c. Discuss the major purposes/benefits of a spendthrift trust such as the one created by Sam Bean.

d. Discuss whether
 1. A trust may generally be terminated by its beneficiaries; and
 2. The spendthrift trust created by Sam Bean could be terminated by Bob Bean.

M89
Number 3 (Estimated time — — 15 to 20 minutes)

On March 2, 1988, Ash, Bale, and Rangel purchased an office building from Park Corp. as joint tenants with right of survivorship. There was an outstanding note and mortgage on the building, which they assumed. The note and mortgage named Park as the mortgagor (borrower) and Vista Bank as the mortgagee (lender). Vista has consented to the assumption.

Wein, Inc., a tenant in the office building, had entered into a 10-year lease dated May 8, 1985. The lease was silent regarding Wein's right to sublet. The lease provided for Wein to take occupancy on June 1, 1985, and that the monthly rent would be $5,000 for the entire 10-year term. On March 10, 1989, Wein informed Ash, Bale, and Rangel that it had agreed to sublet its office space to Nord Corp. On March 17, 1989, Ash, Bale, and Rangel notified Wein of their refusal to consent to the sublet. The following assertions have been made:

- The sublet from Wein to Nord is void because Ash, Bale, and Rangel did not consent.
- If the sublet is not void, Ash, Bale, and Rangel have the right to hold either Wein or Nord liable for payment of the rent.

On April 4, 1989, Ash transferred his interest in the building to his spouse.

Required: Answer the following, setting forth reasons for any conclusions stated.

a. *For this item only,* assume that Ash, Bale, and Rangel default on the mortgage note, that Vista forecloses, and a deficiency results. Discuss the personal liability of Ash, Bale, and Rangel to Vista and the personal liability of Park to Vista.

b. Discuss the assertions as to the sublet, indicating whether such assertions are correct and the reasons therefor.

c. *For this item only,* assume that Ash and Rangel died on April 20, 1989. Discuss the ownership interest(s) in the office building as of April 5, 1989, and April 21, 1989.

SELECTED ESSAYS — UNOFFICIAL ANSWERS

I. Professional and Legal Responsibilities

A. Code of Professional Responsibility

R96
Answer 2(a)

a. 1. Crew did not violate the profession's standards regarding independence when the engagements were accepted. A CPA may perform consulting services simultaneously with an audit engagement.

Crew violated the profession's standards in failing to perform the consulting engagement and the audit with due care. Crew acted without due care by failing to discover the insufficient control procedures because of omitting steps in the engagement and by issuing an unqualified opinion on the financial statements.

Crew committed acts discreditable to the profession by failing to notify Dredge's audit committee of the material misstatements contained in the financial statements, failing to disclose Bold's fraudulent activities, and profiting from withholding the information.

2. The state board of accountancy may permanently revoke Crew's license to practice or may suspend or restrict it for a period of time. If suspended or restricted, Crew may be required to take additional CPE courses as a condition of reinstatement.

E. Common Law Liability to Clients and Third Parties

R96
Answer 2(b)

b. 1. Dredge Corp. will be successful in its negligence suit against Crew. Crew owed a duty of care to Dredge to perform the consulting engagement according to the standards of the profession. Crew breached that duty by failing to discover that there were insufficient control procedures in Dredge's new computerized accounting system. Dredge was damaged by Crew's breach of duty because the insufficient control procedures had allowed and were continuing to allow employees to steal.

2. Ocean Bank will be successful in its common law fraud suit against Crew. Crew intentionally issued an unqualified opinion on Dredge's materially misstated financial statements. The financial statements and Crew's accountant's report were submitted to Ocean. Ocean justifiably relied on Crew's unqualified opinion in agreeing to finance Dredge's capital improvement. Ocean was damaged as a result of Dredge's default on the loan, which was caused by the fraud.

M95
Answer 4 (10 points)

a. Stone will be successful in its negligence suit against Verge. The elements of negligence are as follows:

- duty of care owed
- breach of the duty
- loss caused by the breach of duty

Verge Associates, CPAs owed a duty to its client, Stone Corp., to perform the consulting services engagement in a competent manner with the expertise necessary to perform the engagement. Verge breached this duty by incompetently preparing the computer software programs. As a result of the breach, Stone sustained damages through increased accounts receivable collection costs.

b. Stone will be successful in its fraud suit against Verge. The elements of fraud are as follows:

- false representation of a material fact
- done intentionally or with gross negligence
- justifiable reliance by the plaintiff
- resultant damages sustained by the plaintiff

Verge Associates falsely represented that it was recommending the best possible computer to Stone when, in fact, it was recommending an inferior product. The computer to be purchased was material to the entire engagement. Verge made its recommendation knowing that a better, less expensive computer was available. Stone, as Verge's client, justifiably relied on Verge's recommendation. Stone was damaged because it spent more money for an inferior computer.

M92
Answer 3 (10 points)

a. The income beneficiaries will win their suit for negligence against Goodwin. Goodwin was negligent in improperly allocating trust income and in paying a beneficiary's creditor. The beneficiaries sustained losses due to Goodwin's failure to exercise the due care required of a reasonable accountant.

b. The income beneficiaries will win their suit for fraud against Goodwin. Goodwin intentionally concealed the embezzlements and made material misstatements in the tax returns. These actions are considered fraud and will permit the beneficiaries, who relied on Goodwin to prepare the returns, to recover their losses.

c. The income beneficiaries will win their suit for breach of fiduciary duty against Goodwin. The following fiduciary duties were breached by Goodwin:

- The fiduciary duty of loyalty by personally benefitting from and concealing the embezzlements.

- The fiduciary duty of obedience by paying the beneficiary's creditor.

- The fiduciary duty of due care by misallocating trust principal and income, paying the creditor, and falsifying tax returns.

- The fiduciary duty to notify by failing to inform the beneficiaries of the embezzlements.

- The fiduciary duty to account by maintaining improper records and profiting from the embezzlements.

M90
Answer 3 (10 points)

a. Yes. Since there is no accountant-client privilege recognized at common law and there is no applicable state statute creating such a privilege, Apple will be required to produce its working papers. Furthermore, the right to assert the accountant-client privilege, when applicable, generally rests with the client and not with the accountant.

b. The elements necessary to establish negligence are:

- A legal duty to protect the plaintiff (Musk) from unreasonable risk.
- A failure by the defendant (Apple) to perform or report on an engagement with the due care or competence expected of members of its profession.
- A causal relationship, i.e., that the failure to exercise due care resulted in the plaintiff's loss.
- Actual damage or loss resulting from the failure to exercise due care.

c. The elements necessary to establish a violation of Rule 10b-5 include:

- A material misstatement or omission.
- The material misstatement or omission made by the defendant (Apple) with knowledge (scienter). Reckless disregard for the truth may constitute scienter.
- Justifiable reliance on the misstatement or omission.
- The reliance being in connection with the purchase or sale of a security.

d. Apple is not in privity of contract with Musk because there is no direct contractual relationship between them.

Therefore, in the absence of other factors, Apple would not be liable to Musk for Apple's alleged negligence based on the *Ultramares* decision. However, the privity defense would not protect Apple if Musk could prove that Apple had committed actual or constructive fraud (that is, Apple owes a duty to all persons, including third persons, to practice its profession in a non-fraudulent manner).

N89
Answer 3 (10 points)

City is likely to prevail against Salam based on constructive fraud. To establish a cause of action for constructive fraud, City must prove that:

- Salam made a materially false statement of fact.
- Salam lacked a reasonable ground for belief that the statement was true. Constructive fraud may be inferred from evidence of gross negligence or recklessness.
- Salam intended another to rely on the false statement.
- City justifiably relied on the false statement.
- Such reliance resulted in damages or injury.

Under the facts of this case, Salam is likely to be liable to City based on constructive fraud. Salam made a materially false statement of fact by rendering an unqualified opinion on Bell's financial statements. Salam lacked a reasonable ground for belief that the financial statements were fairly presented by recklessly departing from the standards of due care in that it failed to investigate other embezzlements, despite having knowledge of at least one embezzlement, and did not notify Bell's management of the matter. Salam intended that others rely on the audited financial statements. City justifiably relied on the audited financial statements in deciding to loan Astor $600,000 and damages resulted evidenced by Astor's default on the City loan.

City is not likely to prevail against Salam based on negligence. In order to establish a cause of action for negligence against Salam, City must prove that:

- Salam owed a legal duty to protect City.
- Salam breached that legal duty by failing to perform the audit with the due care or competence expected of members of the profession.
- City suffered actual losses or damages.
- Salam's failure to exercise due care proximately caused City to suffer damages.

The facts of this case establish that Salam was negligent by not detecting the overstatement of accounts receivable because of its inadvertent failure to follow its audit program. However, Salam will not be liable to City for negligence because Salam owed no duty to City. This is the case because Salam was not in privity of contract with City, and the financial statements were neither audited by Salam for the primary benefit of City, nor was City within a known and intended class of third party beneficiaries who were to receive the audited financial statements.

F. Federal Statutory Liability

N92
Answer 3 (10 points)

a. 1. Union Bank will be successful in its negligence suit against Weaver. To be successful in a lawsuit for accountant's negligence there must be:

- duty
- breach
- plaintiff must be a known intended user
- reliance
- loss

Weaver was negligent in performing the audit by failing to confirm accounts receivable, which resulted in failing to discover the overstatement of accounts receivable. Weaver's failure to confirm accounts receivable was a violation of Weaver's duty to comply with generally accepted auditing standards. Weaver knew that Union would receive the financial statements and was thereby an intended user. Union relied on Weaver's opinion in granting the loan and, as a result, suffered a loss.

2. Union will be successful in its common-law fraud suit against Weaver. To be successful in a lawsuit for common-law fraud there must be:

- an intentional material misstatement or omission
- reliance
- loss

Weaver was grossly negligent for failing to qualify its opinion after being advised of Butler's potential material losses from the product liability lawsuit by legal counsel. Weaver will be liable to anyone who relied on Weaver's opinion and suffered a loss as a result of this fraudulent omission.

b. Butler's stockholders who purchased stock under the 1990 offerings will also be successful in their suit against Weaver under Section 10(b) and Rule 10b-5 of the Securities Exchange Act of 1934. Under the Act stock purchased must show:

- intentional material misstatement or omission (scienter)
- reliance
- loss

Weaver's failure to qualify its opinion for Butler's potential legal liability was material and done intentionally (scienter). Weaver will be liable for losses sustained by the purchasers who relied on Weaver's opinion.

M91
Answer 5 (10 points)

a. Knox would recover from Garson for fraud. The elements of fraud are: the misrepresentation of a material fact (because Garson issued an unqualified opinion on misleading financial statements. Garson's opinion did not include adjustments for or disclosures about the embezzlements and insider stock transactions); with knowledge or scienter (because Garson was aware of the embezzlements and insider stock transactions); and a loss sustained by Knox (because of Sleek's default on the loan).

b. 1. The general public purchasers of Sleek's stock offerings would recover from Garson under the liability provisions of Section 11 of the Securities Act of 1933. Section 11 of the Act provides that anyone, such as an accountant, who submits or contributes to a registration statement or allows material misrepresentations or omissions to appear in a registration statement is liable to anyone purchasing the security who sustains a loss. Under the facts presented, Garson could not establish a "due diligence" defense to a Section 11 action because it knew that the registration statement failed to disclose material facts.

b. 2. The general public purchasers of Sleek's stock offerings would also recover from Garson under the antifraud provisions of Section 10(b) and Rule 10b-5 of the Securities Exchange Act of 1934. Under Rule 10b-5, Garson's knowledge that the registration statement failed to disclose a material fact, such as the insider trading and the embezzlements, is considered a fraudulent action. The omission was material. Garson's action was intentional or, at a minimum, a result of gross negligence or recklessness (scienter). These purchasers relied on Garson's opinion on the financial statements and incurred a loss.

II. Business Organizations

A. Agency

N92
Answer 4 (10 points)

a. Exotic's first position is incorrect. Although Peterson lacked actual authority to bind Exotic to the Creatures contract, from Creatures' perspective Peterson did have apparent authority to do so. Peterson was a store manager and had previously contracted with Creatures on Exotic's behalf. Creatures would not be bound by the limitation on Peterson's authority unless Creatures was aware of it.

Exotic's second position is incorrect. Although Peterson did not have express authority to charge purchases at Handy Hardware. Peterson had the implied authority as store manager to enter into contracts incidental to the express grant of authority to act as manager. Buying paint and brushes to improve Exotic's store would fall within Peterson's implied grant of authority.

Exotic's third position is correct. An agent owes a duty of loyalty to his or her principal. An agent may not benefit directly or indirectly from an agency relationship at the principal's expense. If an agent receives any profits from the principal/agent relationship without the consent of the principal, the agent must pay the profits to the principal. In this case, Peterson's incentive payments constituted a violation of Peterson's fiduciary duty to Exotic. Peterson must turn over all incentive payments to Exotic.

b. Peterson was negligent by allowing Mathews to handle a ferret that Peterson knew was dangerous. An employer is held liable for the torts of its employees if the tort occurs within the scope of employment and if the employee is subject to the employer's control. At the time of the accident, Peterson was acting within the scope of employment and subject to Exotic's control because this conduct occurred while on the job, during normal working hours, and with the intention of benefitting Exotic. Exotic, therefore, will be liable to Mathews because the accident occurred within the scope of Peterson's employment.

Peterson also will be liable to Mathews because all persons are liable for their own negligence.

N90
Answer 3 (10 points)

a. Peterson was acting for an undisclosed principal (Prime) with regard to the contract with Hallow. Peterson was acting with actual authority; therefore, Prime is liable to Hallow. Peterson is also liable to Hallow because agents acting on behalf of undisclosed principals are liable to the third parties on the contracts they enter into with such third parties on behalf of the principal. Hallow, however, cannot collect damages from both Peterson and Prime and must make an election between them.

b. At the time of the accident, Peterson was acting within the scope of employment because the conduct engaged in (that is, entering into a contract with Hallow) was authorized by Prime. Prime, therefore, will be liable to Mathews because the accident occurred within the scope of Peterson's employment.

Peterson will also be liable to Mathews because all persons are liable for their own negligence.

c. Peterson's actual authority to enter into contracts on Prime's behalf ceased on termination of employment by Prime. Peterson, however, continued to have apparent authority to bind Prime because:

- Peterson was acting ostensibly within the scope of authority as evidenced by past transactions with Bagley;
- Bagley was unaware of Peterson's termination.

The trade journal announcement was not effective notice to terminate Peterson's apparent authority in relation to Bagley because:

- Prime was obligated to give actual notice to Bagley that Peterson was no longer employed;
- Actual notice is required because of Bagley's past contact with Peterson while Peterson was employed by Prime.

B. Partnership, Joint Ventures, and Other Unincorporated Associations

M94
Answer 4 (10 points)

a. Jackson is correct. Baker, as an agent acting on behalf of an undisclosed principal (Best), is personally liable for any contracts entered into in that capacity.

b. Martin's first position that Green is not entitled to inspect the partnership books or participate in partnership management is correct. Green, as an assignee of Kent's partnership interest, is entitled to receive Kent's share of partnership profits only. Green is not entitled, as an assignee of Kent's partnership interest, to inspect the partnership records or to participate in the management of the partnership.

Martin's second position that only the partnership is responsible for the debt owed Laco is incorrect. Although the partnership is primarily liable for the unpaid bills, both Martin and Kent, as Best's partners, are personally liable for the unpaid amount of the debt. Laco will be entitled to seek recovery against Martin or Kent for the full amount owed.

c. Kent's first position that only Martin is liable for the 1993 operating loss because of the assignment of Kent's partnership interest to Green is incorrect. A partner's assignment of a partnership interest does not terminate that partner's liability for the partnership's losses and debts.

Kent's second position that any personal liability of the partners for the 1993 operating loss should be allocated on the basis of their original capital contributions is incorrect. The 1993 loss will be allocated in the same way that profits were to be allocated between the parties, that is, equally, because Martin and Kent had not agreed on the method for allocating losses between themselves.

M91
Answer 2 (10 points)

a. 1. Mathews' first position is incorrect. A partner is considered an agent of the partnership in carrying out its usual business. In this case, Baker lacked actual authority to bind Prime to the Jaco contract; however, Baker did have, from Jaco's perspective, apparent authority to do so because of the general character of Prime's business and, more important, because Baker had previously purchased cars from Jaco on Prime's behalf. Jaco was not

Unofficial Answers

bound by the limitation on Baker's authority unless Jaco was aware of it.

2. Mathews' second position is also incorrect. As a general rule, a partner is liable for the debts of the partnership, and a third party is not bound by the profit and loss sharing agreements between partners because the third party is not a party to the partnership agreement. Therefore, Jaco can look to Prime's assets and Mathews' personal assets to satisfy the obligation.

3. Mathews' third position is correct. A partner is liable to other partners for any liability associated with contracts entered into ostensibly on behalf of the partnership but outside the partner's actual authority. In this case, because Baker violated the agreement with Mathews concerning the $15,000 limitation on used car purchases, Baker will be liable to Mathews for any liability that Mathews may have to Jaco.

4. Mathews' fourth position is also correct. A partner owes a fiduciary duty (that is, a duty of loyalty) to the partnership and every other partner. A partner may not benefit directly or indirectly at the expense of the partnership. A partner must account to the partnership for any benefits derived from the partnership's business without the consent or knowledge of the other partners. In this case, Baker was not entitled to accept and retain the incentive payments made by Top. Doing so violated Baker's fiduciary duty to Prime and Mathews. Baker must account to Prime for all the incentive payments received.

b. KYA's contention that its $25,000 capital contribution cannot be used to satisfy Prime's obligation to Jaco is incorrect. A new partner is liable for partnership liabilities that arose prior to the new partner's admission, but the liability is limited to the partner's capital contribution and interest in partnership property. Therefore, KYA's liability is limited to its capital contribution and its interest as a partner in Prime's assets.

M90
Answer 4 (10 points)

a. Weil is entitled to inspect and copy Sterling's books and records. A limited partner such as Weil has the right to have the partnership books kept at the principal place of business of the partnership and to inspect and copy them at all times.

b. Generally, limited partners are not liable to partnership creditors except to the extent of their capital contribution. In Weil's case, however, he will probably be liable to Anchor Bank in the same manner as Sterling's general partners because he has taken part in the control of the business of the partnership and, therefore, has lost his limited liability. Smith, as a general partner, would also be personally liable to Anchor because liability was incurred prior to withdrawal.

c. Edwards will likely prevail in his lawsuit against Smith for withdrawing because the partnership agreement specifically prohibits a withdrawal by a general partner without the consent of the other partners. Therefore, Smith has breached the partnership agreement and will be liable to Edwards for any damages resulting from Smith's withdrawal.

d. The withdrawal (retirement) of a general partner dissolves the partnership unless the remaining general partners continue the business of the partnership under a right to do so provided in the limited partnership certificate, or unless all partners consent. Therefore, it is possible that Smith's withdrawal will result in Sterling's dissolution.

e. Weil is free to assign his limited partnership interests to Alberts in the absence of any prohibitions in the Sterling partnership agreement or certificate.

f. Alberts, however, cannot be a substitute limited partner without the consent of the remaining general partner, Edwards.

g. Therefore, Alberts, as an assignee of Weil's limited partnership interest, may not exercise any rights of a partner. Alberts is entitled only to any distributions from Sterling to which Weil would have been entitled.

h. Finally, the assignment by Weil of his partnership interest does not cause a dissolution of the partnership.

C. Corporations

M93
Answer 3 (10 points)

a. Edwards will not win the suit to have Olsen removed as president. The right to hire and fire officers is held by the board of directors. Individual stockholders, regardless of the size of their holding, have no vote in the selection of officers. Individual stockholders may exert influence in this area by voting for directors at the annual stockholders' meeting.

b. Edwards will lose the suit to have National purchase the stock. A stockholder who dissents from a merger may require the corporation to purchase his or her shares if the statutory requirements are met and would be entitled to the fair value of stock (appraisal remedy). To compel the purchase, Edwards would have had to file an objection to the merger before the stockholders' meeting at which the merger proposal was considered, vote against the merger proposal, and make a written demand that the corporation purchase the stock at an appraised price. Edwards will lose because the first two requirements were met but Edwards failed to make a written demand that the corporation purchase the stock.

c. 1. Queen will lose its suit against National to enforce the contract, even though Edwards was a National director. Jenkins may have assumed that Edwards was acting as National's agent, but Edwards had no authority to contract with Queen. A director has a fiduciary duty to the stockholders of a corporation but, unless expressly authorized by the board of directors or the officers of the corporation, has no authority to contract on behalf of the corporation. There is no implied agency authority merely by being a director.

2. Queen will win its suit against Edwards because Edwards had no authority to act for National. Edwards will be personally liable for Queen's damages.

N91
Answer 2 (10 points)

Bradley would be successful in the suit against Frost and Glen for failing to vote Bradley to the board of directors. The stockholders have the right to elect the directors of a corporation. The stockholders have the right to agree among themselves on how they will vote. Therefore, the voting provision of the stockholders' agreement between Bradley, Frost, and Glen is enforceable.

Bradley would be unsuccessful in attempting to be reinstated as vice president. A corporation's board oversees the operations of the business, which includes hiring officers and, at its discretion, dismissing officers with or without cause. Bradley would be successful in collecting some damages for the breach of the employment contract because there was no demonstrated cause for Bradley's dismissal.

Bradley would be successful in having Frost and Glen held personally liable to the corporation for declaring and paying the dividend because payment of a dividend that threatens a corporation's solvency is unlawful. Ordinarily, directors who approve such a dividend would be personally liable for its repayment to the corporation. However, the directors, other than Frost and Glen, in relying on the assurances and information supplied by Frost and Glen, as corporate officers, are protected by the business judgment rule. Therefore, only Frost and Glen would be held personally liable.

N89
Answer 5 (10 points)

West's assertion that Ace should have recorded the dividends in arrears for 1987 and 1988 as a liability is incorrect. A shareholder of cumulative preferred stock is entitled to receive all dividend arrearages plus any dividends for the current year before any dividends may be distributed to the shareholders of common stock. However, preferred stock represents a contribution of capital, not a debt of the corporation, and until a dividend is declared, a shareholder of cumulative preferred stock is not a creditor of the corporation. Thus, Ace was correct in not classifying the dividend arrearages as a liability because a dividend was not declared by Ace's board of directors. Ace should disclose the dividend arrearages in notes to its financial statements.

West's assertion that West is entitled to examine Ace's books and records is correct. A shareholder, upon written demand, is entitled to examine, at reasonable times, the books and records of the corporation, so long as the examination is for a proper purpose (in good faith). If the corporation refuses to permit the examination, the shareholder may obtain a court order compelling access to the books and records.

West's assertion that West is entitled to receive a new stock certificate to replace the lost stock certificate is correct. Because the subject matter in this case is a stock certificate of a corporation, the UCC Investment Securities Article applies. Under that article, the stock certificate of Ace is classified as a certificated security because it is one of a class of Ace's shares that is represented by an instrument in West's name and is traded on a national securities exchange. If the owner of a certificated security claims that the security has been lost, the issuer shall issue a new certificated security, or, at the option of the issuer, an equivalent uncertificated security in place of the original security if the owner makes a request before the issuer has notice that the security has been acquired by a bona fide purchaser; files a sufficient indemnity bond with the issuer; and satisfies any other reasonable requirements imposed by the issuer. Based on the facts of this case, West is entitled to receive a new stock certificate because West requested that a new stock certificate be issued before Ace had notice the lost certificate was acquired by any other party; offered to file an indemnity bond with Ace; and offered to cooperate with any reasonable requests made by Ace.

M89
Answer 4 (10 points)

The assertion that it was improper for the board of directors to authorize the reacquisition of Cray's common stock while Cray was insolvent is correct. A board of directors may authorize and the corporation may reacquire its shares of stock subject to any restriction in the articles of incorporation, except that no reacquisition may be made if, after giving effect thereto, either the corporation would be unable to pay its debts as they become due in the usual course of business or the corporation's total assets would be less than its total liabilities. Because Cray was insolvent before and after the reacquisition of Cray's common stock, it was improper for the board of directors to authorize the reacquisition.

The assertion that the members of Cray's board of directors are personally liable because Cray reacquired its own shares of Cray stock while Cray was insolvent is incorrect. In general, directors who vote or assent to a reacquisition by the corporation of its own shares while the corporation is insolvent will be jointly and severally liable to the corporation. However, the directors will not be liable if they acted in good faith, in a manner they reasonably believed to be in the best interests of the corporation, and with such care as an ordinarily prudent person in a like position would use under similar circumstances. In performing their duties, directors are entitled to rely on information, opinions, reports, or statements, including financial statements and other financial data prepared or presented by one or more officers or employees of the corporation whom the directors reasonably believe to be reliable and competent in the matters presented. The directors may rely on the same information prepared or presented by independent accountants that the directors reasonably believe to be within such person's professional competence. Based on the facts of this case, the directors' reliance on the reports and financial statements prepared by Cray's internal accounting department under the supervision of the treasurer and reviewed by its independent accountants was proper so long as the directors exercised due care, acted in good faith, and acted without knowledge that would cause such reliance to be unwarranted. In addition, the courts are precluded from substituting their business judgment for that of the board of directors if the directors have acted with due care and in good faith.

The assertion that Cray will be liable to the treasurer as a result of his termination by the board of directors is correct. An officer may be removed by the board of directors with or without cause whenever in its judgment the best interests of the corporation will be served by the removal. However, such removal is without prejudice to the contract rights of the person so removed. Thus, the board of directors had the power to remove the treasurer. The treasurer will prevail in a breach of contract action for damages against Cray because the firing violated the employment agreement.

D. Estates and Trusts

N94
Answer 4 (10 points)

a. The requirements to establish a valid *inter vivos* spendthrift trust are as follows:

- Grantor
- Trust Res
- Intent to create a trust
- Lawful purpose
- Trustee and separate beneficiaries

Stone created a valid spendthrift trust. As grantor, Stone transferred stocks, bonds, and real estate (res) to the trust with a present intent to create the trust for the express lawful purpose of providing income for life to close relatives with the remainder left to charity. Stone designated Queen Bank as trustee.

b.
- Incorrect. The entire proceeds from the sale of the stock should be allocated to principal.

- Incorrect. The entire amount of the stock dividend should be allocated to principal.

- Incorrect. One-third of the semiannual payment of bond interest received on May 1 had already accrued when the trust was created on January 1, 1993. Therefore, $3,000 should be allocated to principal and $15,000 to income.

- Correct/Incorrect. All mortgage payments representing a repayment of a mortgage debt should be allocated to principal. However, if any portion of the payment includes interest on the mortgage, that amount should be allocated to income.

c. The petition to have the trust terminated and distributed will fail. Even though all beneficiaries and remaindermen joined in the petition, termination of the trust, while any of the income beneficiaries is alive, would defeat the intent of the grantor in establishing a spendthrift trust.

N93
Answer 3 (10 points)

Archer, Book, and Cable will:

- Lose their lawsuit to have the residuary estate distributed. Park's inclusion of a "pour-over" provision in the will is a binding transfer of the residuary estate to the pre-existing spendthrift trust.

- Lose their lawsuit to have the trust terminated. Whereas a trust may ordinarily be terminated at the request of all beneficiaries, Park created the trust to protect the beneficiaries from their own possible financial mismanagement and to provide for their welfare during Park's lifetime and after Park's death. Terminating the trust at the request of the beneficiaries would defeat the purpose of the trust.

- Lose their lawsuit to have Young and Zack removed as trustees for making the $5,000 principal payments. Ordinarily trustees may not distribute trust principal to income beneficiaries. However, Park specifically authorized Young and Zack to make limited principal payments by providing "sprinkling" provisions in the trust instrument.

- Win their lawsuit to have Young and Zack removed as trustees for allowing Zack to borrow $10,000 from the trust. A trustee does not have the right to borrow money from a trust unless that right is specifically granted in the trust instrument. By allowing Zack to borrow the $10,000, Young and Zack violated their fiduciary duty of loyalty.

- Win their lawsuit to have Young and Zack removed as trustees for making the $15,000 principal payment to Archer. The payment exceeded the trustees' authority to make limited principal payments. By exceeding their authority, they violated their fiduciary duties to safeguard the trust, properly manage the trust, and have loyalty to the trust.

M92
Answer 3 (10 points)

a. The income beneficiaries will win their suit for negligence against Goodwin. Goodwin was negligent in improperly allocating trust income and in paying a beneficiary's creditor. The beneficiaries sustained losses due to

Goodwin's failure to exercise the due care required of a reasonable accountant.

b. The income beneficiaries will win their suit for fraud against Goodwin. Goodwin intentionally concealed the embezzlements and made material misstatements in the tax returns. These actions are considered fraud and will permit the beneficiaries, who relied on Goodwin to prepare the returns, to recover their losses.

c. The income beneficiaries will win their suit for breach of fiduciary duty against Goodwin. The following fiduciary duties were breached by Goodwin:

- The fiduciary duty of loyalty by personally benefitting from and concealing the embezzlements.

- The fiduciary duty of obedience by paying the beneficiary's creditor.

- The fiduciary duty of due care by misallocating trust principal and income, paying the creditor, and falsifying tax returns.

- The fiduciary duty to notify by failing to inform the beneficiaries of the embezzlements.

- The fiduciary duty to account by maintaining improper records and profiting from the embezzlements.

N89
Answer 2 (10 points)

a. Sam Bean and Bob Bean will not be personally liable to Fale for the deficiency resulting from the foreclosure sale because they did not assume the mortgage but instead purchased the building subject to the mortgage. In the absence of a state statute to the contrary, Stein will be personally liable for the deficiency because Stein was not released from liability on the note and mortgage.

b. There is no right of survivorship feature in a tenancy in common and, therefore, Rita Bean will acquire Sam Bean's one-half interest in the building under her husband's will. Thus, Rita Bean will own a one-half interest in the building as a tenant in common with Bob Bean.

c. In general, the purposes and benefits of creating a spendthrift trust are to provide a fund for the maintenance of another (the beneficiary); protect the fund from the beneficiary's financial mismanagement and improvidence; prohibit the beneficiary from transferring the right to future trust income or principal; and prohibit the beneficiary's interest from being subjected to the claims of the beneficiary's creditors.

d. 1. A trust may generally be terminated by the beneficiaries if all consent to the termination; all are legally competent to consent; and termination will not defeat a material purpose for which the trust was created.

2. The spendthrift trust created by Sam Bean cannot be terminated by Bob Bean because the major purpose of a spendthrift trust is to protect the beneficiary from mismanagement and improvidence. Thus, termination of the spendthrift trust would defeat the purpose for which it was created.

III. Contracts

R97
Answer 1(a) (10 points)

a. 1. There was an enforceable contract between Thorn and Birch. The requirements necessary to form an enforceable contract for the sale of real property are as follows:
   An offer.
   An acceptance.
   Legally sufficient consideration.
   Parties who have the legal capacity to enter into a contract.
   A legal purpose.
   A written contract document.
   2. Thorn did not breach the contract by assigning the mortgage payments to a third party. The right to receive a sum of money may be assigned even when a contract contains an anti-assignment clause.
   3. If a court determined that Thorn breached the contract, Birch would be entitled to sue for either compensatory damages or specific performance. Compensatory damages would reimburse Birch for all expenses as well as any additional amounts spent in obtaining substitute property as a result of Thorn's actions. Specific performance would require Thorn to complete the sale of the property to Birch because each parcel of real property is unique.

N95
Answer 4 (10 points)

a. Korn would argue two points of law to show there was no valid contract. Korn would argue that the July 5 offer was not accepted by Wilson before it was withdrawn on September 30. An offer can be withdrawn at any time before it is accepted even if it states that it will remain open for a definite period of time.

Korn would also argue that Wilson's response of September 28 was not a valid acceptance because Wilson included additional terms and Wilson's attempt to change the term of the contract was a rejection and a counteroffer.

b. Wilson would argue two points of law to show there was a valid contract. Wilson would argue that the mailing of the acceptance on September 28 was an effective acceptance under the mailbox rule. There is a valid contract because there was a valid acceptance before the offer was withdrawn.

Wilson would also argue that the attempt to extend the contract was not a condition of acceptance but a requested immaterial modification that did not negate the acceptance.

c. If a valid contract existed, Korn's September 30 telephone call resulted in Korn's anticipatory breach of the contract because Wilson could no longer rely on Korn performing.

Under common law, Wilson could either cancel the contract or sue to collect compensatory damages for the additional amount it would cost to obtain the services.

M94
Answer 5 (10 points)

Suburban is correct concerning the agreement to share utility costs with Bridge. A modification of a contract requires consideration to be binding on the parties. Suburban is not bound by the lease modification because Suburban did not receive any consideration in exchange for its agreement to share the cost of utilities with Bridge.

Suburban is not correct with regard to the Dart offer. An offer can be revoked at any time prior to acceptance. This is true despite the fact that the offer provides that it will not be withdrawn prior to a stated time. If no consideration is given in exchange for this promise not to withdraw the offer, the promise is not binding on the offeror. The offer provided that Suburban's acceptance would not be effective until received. Dart's June 10 revocation terminated Dart's offer. Thus, Suburban's June 9 acceptance was not effective.

Suburban is correct with regard to World's claim. The general rule is that destruction of, or damage to, the subject matter of a contract without the fault of either party terminates the contract. In this case, Suburban is not liable to World because Suburban is discharged from its contractual duties as a result of the fire, which made performance by it under the lease objectively impossible.

N93
Answer 4 (10 points)

Ambel is incorrect. The general rule is that when a party knows, or reasonably should know, that a mistake has been made in the making of an offer, the mistaken party will be granted relief from the offer. In this case, because Ambel was aware of the approximate fair market value of the equipment, it had reason to be aware of the mathematical error made by Victor and will not be allowed to take advantage of it.

Clark is correct. A contract that cannot by its terms be performed within one year from the date it is made must be evidenced by a writing that satisfies the requirements of the Statute of Frauds. The contract between Victor and Clark is not enforceable by Victor against Clark, because the contract was oral and provided for performance by the parties for longer than one year from the date the contract was entered into.

GYX is incorrect. An acceptance of an offer is effective when dispatched (in this case, when mailed), provided that the appropriate mode of communication is used. The general rule is that an offer shall be interpreted as inviting acceptance in any manner and by any medium reasonable in the circumstances. In this case, GYX made its offer by mail. An acceptance by mail, if properly addressed with adequate postage affixed, would be considered a reasonable manner and method of acceptance. Therefore, Victor's acceptance was effective (and a contract was formed) when the acceptance was mailed on November 12 and not when received by GYX on November 17.

Wells is incorrect. As a general rule, most contracts are assignable and delegable unless: prohibited in the contract, the duties are personal in nature, or the assignment or delegation is prohibited by statute or public policy. Victor was entitled to assign the contract to Master, because none of these exceptions apply to the contract.

M93
Answer 4 (10 points)

a. Dodd's claim, that West's offer could not be revoked before September 30, is incorrect. Offers can be revoked at any time before acceptance unless the offeror receives consideration to keep the offer open. West did not receive any consideration from Dodd in exchange for its promise to keep the offer open until September 30. Therefore, West effectively revoked its offer during the September 28 telephone conversation.

Dodd's claim, that the September 27 letter accepting West's offer was effective when mailed to West, is incorrect. The general rule is that an acceptance is effective when dispatched if the acceptance is made using a reasonable mode of communication. In this case, the offer required that the acceptance be received by West to be effective. Therefore, Dodd's acceptance could not have been effective until after the offer expired, because it was received after September 30.

b. West's claim, that any agreement that existed between West and Dodd would not be enforceable against West because of the Statute of Frauds, is correct. The term of the agreement was for three years. The Statute of Frauds requires that contracts that cannot be performed within one year from the date made must be in writing. Because this was an oral contract for a period of three years, it would not be enforceable under the Statute of Frauds. Dodd's attempted acceptance of the offer would not be such a writing because it was not signed by West and could not be enforceable against West.

c. Abco's first position, that the oral April 14 agreement regarding the painting of the warehouse is not binding, is correct. This agreement was intended to modify the existing lease between the parties. Under common law, agreements modifying existing contracts require consideration to be binding. Abco did not receive any consideration in exchange for its promise to paint the warehouse; therefore, the agreement is not enforceable against Abco.

Abco's second position, that evidence of the April 14 oral agreement could not be admitted into evidence, is incorrect. The parol evidence rule allows the admission of proof of a later oral agreement that modifies an existing written contract.

N91
Answer 3 (10 points)

Stake's first allegation, that Packer committed fraud in the formation of the contract, is correct and Stake may rescind the contract. Packer had assured Stake that the vacant parcel would be used for a shopping center when, in fact, Packer intended to use the land to construct apartment units that would be in direct competition with those owned by Stake. Stake would not have sold the land to Packer had Packer's real intentions been known. Therefore, the elements of fraud are present:

- A false representation;
- Of a fact;
- That is material;
- Made with knowledge of its falsity and intention to deceive;
- That is justifiably relied on.

Stake's second allegation, that the mistake as to the fair market value of the land entitles Stake to rescind the contract, is incorrect. Generally, mistakes as to adequacy of consideration or fairness of a bargain are insufficient grounds to entitle the aggrieved party to rescind a contract.

Stake's third allegation, that the contract was not enforceable against Stake because Stake did not sign the counteroffer, is correct. The contract between Stake and Packer involves real estate and, therefore, the Statute of Frauds requirements must be satisfied. The Statute of Frauds requires that a writing be signed by the party against whom enforcement is sought. The counteroffer is unenforceable against Stake, because Stake did not sign it. As a result, Stake is not obligated to sell the land to Packer under the terms of the counteroffer.

N90
Answer 2 (10 points)

Snow's assertion that Jacobs' acceptance was not received on a timely basis is incorrect. Jacobs' January 31 acceptance was effective when dispatched (mailed) under the complete-when-posted doctrine because:

- The letter was an authorized means of communication (because Snow's offer was by mail); and
- The letter was properly stamped and addressed.

Therefore, Jacobs' acceptance was effective on January 31, the last possible day under Snow's January 21 offer.

Snow's assertion that the January 21 offer was effectively revoked is incorrect because a revocation is not effective until received. In this case, the revocation was effective on February 3, and Jacobs' acceptance was effective on January 31.

Snow's assertion that Jacobs' failure to sign the January 31 acceptance prevents the formation of a contract is incorrect. The Statute of Frauds, which applies to contracts involving interests in real estate, requires only the signature of the party to be charged with enforcement of the contract. Therefore, because Snow had signed the January 21 offer, which was accepted by Jacobs, the contract is enforceable against Snow.

Snow's assertion that Jacobs had no right to assign the contract is incorrect. Contract rights, including the right to purchase real estate, are generally assignable unless the assignment:

- Would materially increase the risk or burden of the obligor;
- Purports to transfer highly personal contract rights;
- Is validly prohibited by the contract; or
- Is prohibited by law.

None of these limitations applies to the assignment by Jacobs to Eljay.

N89
Answer 4 (10 points)

The president's assertion that the September 8, 1988 offer by Crisp was irrevocable until December 20, 1988, and that, therefore, a contract was formed by Anker's acceptance on December 12, 1988, is incorrect. Because the offer made by Crisp involves a transaction in goods, i.e. furniture, the UCC Sales Article applies. The UCC Sales Article provides that an offer by a merchant to buy or sell goods in a signed writing which by its terms gives assurance that it will be held open is not revocable, for lack of consideration, during the time stated or, if no time is stated, for a reasonable time, but in no event may such period of irrevocability exceed three months. Under the facts of this case, Crisp's offer was a firm offer that could not be revoked because the offer was made by Crisp, a merchant, concerning the kind of goods being sold (furniture); was in writing and signed by Crisp; and stated that it would remain open until December 20, 1988. Despite the provision that the offer will remain open until December 20, 1988, a firm offer remains irrevocable for a three-month period. Therefore, Crisp's letter of revocation on December 5, 1988 did not terminate the firm offer because the three-month period had not yet expired. The revocation was effective on December 8, 1988, when the three-month period expired. Therefore, Anker's attempted acceptance on December 12, 1988 did not form a contract with Crisp. Instead, Anker's attempted acceptance is likely to be treated as an offer.

The president's assertion that Dix's December 12, 1988 letter formed an option contract is incorrect. To form an option contract, where the subject matter is real estate, all of the elements necessary to form a contract must be met. In this case, Anker did not furnish any consideration in return for Dix's promise to keep the offer open until December 20, 1988; therefore, an option contract was not formed.

The president's assertion that Anker's acceptance on December 19, 1988 formed a contract with Dix is incorrect. In general, acceptance of an offer is effective when it is dispatched. If, however, an offer specifically stipulates the method of communication to be utilized by the offeree, the acceptance to be effective must conform to that method. Thus, an acceptance by another method of communication is ineffective and no contract is formed. Under the facts of this case, Anker's acceptance on December 19, 1988 by a private express mail courier is ineffective, despite Dix's receipt of the acceptance on December 20, 1988, because Dix's offer specifically stipulated that acceptance could only be made by certified mail, return receipt requested. Instead, Anker's attempted acceptance is likely to be treated as a counteroffer.

IV. Debtor-Creditor Relationships

C. Bankruptcy

R96
Answer 1 (10 points)

a. Ranch Bank and the judgment creditor would have had to join in the involuntary bankruptcy petition. Fender had fewer than 12 unsecured creditors. Under the liquidation provisions of Chapter 7 of the Federal Bankruptcy Code, when there are fewer than 12 creditors one or more creditors having unsecured claims in the aggregate of $10,000 must join in the petition.

b. The $1,200 claim for alimony and maintenance due under a divorce decree would be the first creditor claim paid. The $500 IRS assessment for 1993 taxes and the $750 due for 1994 state income tax would be paid next.

Unsecured debts are paid according to the priority established by the Federal Bankruptcy Code. The claim with the highest applicable priority is the claim for alimony and maintenance. The next highest applicable priority is for taxes owed to governmental units for which a return is required within three years of the date of the filing of the petition. The IRS claim and the state claim would share *pro rata* if the assets of the bankruptcy estate were insufficient to pay both claims in full.

c. The alimony and maintenance claim and the tax claims would not be discharged if unpaid because these are two of the ten types of debts specifically excepted from discharge under the Federal Bankruptcy Code.

d. Fender's discharge in bankruptcy would discharge the guarantee of payment given to Ace. Bankruptcy of the guarantor is an absolute defense to payment, and any claim by Ace would be included in the bankruptcy proceeding and be discharged.

M92
Answer 4 (10 points)

a. An involuntary bankruptcy petition may be filed against a debtor having 12 or more creditors by at least three creditors having unsecured claims of at least $10,000,* provided the debtor is not paying its undisputed debts as they become due.

b. 1. Dollar's motion for relief will be granted. Dollar's claim that it is entitled to take possession of the collateral securing its loan is correct. Generally, a secured creditor is allowed to take possession of its collateral if there is no equity in it (that is, the debt balance exceeds the collateral's fair market value). Dollar would then be entitled to sell the collateral and apply the proceeds to the loan balance.

2. Dollar's claim that it is entitled to a priority distribution to the extent that the proceeds from the sale of its collateral are less than the loan balance will not be approved by the bankruptcy court. Dollar is entitled to the value of its collateral. As to any deficiency, Dollar will be treated as an unsecured creditor.

c. The payment to Techno's president would be regarded as a preferential transfer. Because the president is an "insider," any payments made on the unsecured loan during the year preceding the bankruptcy filing would be considered a preferential transfer.

The payment to Alexis was not a preferential transfer because it was made in the ordinary course of business and under ordinary business terms.

The $7,900 payment to Maple for the truck was not a preferential transfer because it was not made on account of an antecedent debt, but as a contemporaneous exchange for new value.

M90
Answer 2 (10 points)

a. The judgment against Drake arising from his negligence is dischargeable in his bankruptcy.

The unpaid federal income taxes are also dischargeable because they became due and owing more than three years prior to the filing of the bankruptcy petition.

---
*This question has been revised to reflect changes in the Federal Bankruptcy Code.

The obligation to Bartin will not be discharged because the debt was not included in Drake's bankruptcy petition schedules and the creditor did not have notice or actual knowledge of the bankruptcy in time to file a proof of claim.

The unpaid child support is not dischargeable in Drake's bankruptcy.

b. To establish a preferential transfer that can be set aside, the bankruptcy trustee must show

- A voluntary or involuntary transfer of nonexempt property to a creditor.
- The transfer was made during the ninety days immediately preceding the bankruptcy filing (or within one year in the case of an "insider").
- The transfer was on account of an antecedent debt.
- The transfer was made while the debtor was insolvent.
- The transfer allows the creditor to receive a greater percentage than would otherwise be received in the bankruptcy proceeding.

c. The payment to Safe will be regarded as a preference and may be set aside by the trustee.

The transfer by Drake to his brother can be set aside as a preference since his brother would be considered an insider and payment was made within one year of filing.

Giving the mortgage to Home is not a preference because it was not on account of an antecedent debt.

The payment to Max is not a preference because it was made in the ordinary course of the business of Max and Drake under ordinary business terms.

M89
Answer 2 (10 points)

a. The requirements necessary for the commencement of an involuntary bankruptcy proceeding were met because the petition was filed by Lux, Squire, and Rusk, who were creditors of Tine with unsecured claims aggregating more than $10,000.* To properly commence an involuntary bankruptcy proceeding in which the debtor

---
*This question has been revised to reflect changes in the Federal Bankruptcy Code.

has 12 or more creditors with unsecured claims, three or more creditors with unsecured claims aggregating at least $5,000 must sign the bankruptcy petition.

b. 1. The court may declare the January 31, 1989, mortgage delivered to Safe by Tine to be void as a preference. A preference occurs if there is a transfer of the interest in property:

- To or for the benefit of a creditor;
- For or on account of an antecedent debt owed by the debtor before such transfer was made;
- Made while the debtor was insolvent;
- Made within 90 days before the date of the filing of the bankruptcy petition (when the creditor is not an insider);
- That enables the creditor to receive more than the creditor would receive in a liquidation proceeding.

Under the facts of this case, the mortgage delivered by Tine to Safe was for Safe's benefit, on account of the $250,000 owed to Safe, given while Tine was unable to pay his current obligations (was insolvent), given on January 31, 1989 (which was within 90 days before the filing of the bankruptcy petition on March 23, 1989), and enabled Safe to receive more than it would have received in a liquidation proceeding ($250,000 as a secured creditor vs. a lesser amount as an unsecured creditor in liquidation).

2. The court can except Tine's debt to Rich Bank from Tine's discharge in bankruptcy. In general, the bankruptcy court will except a debt from discharge if the debtor obtains money by use of a statement in writing respecting the debtor's financial condition that is materially false; the creditor to whom the debtor is liable for such money reasonably relied on the statement, and the debtor caused the statement to be made or published with intent to deceive.

Based on the facts of this case, Tine obtained a $50,000 loan after furnishing Rich with personal financial statements, that he knew substantially overstated his net worth. Because it was difficult to detect the overstatement, Rich's reliance on the financial statements was reasonable. Therefore, the requirements necessary to except Rich's debt from Tine's discharge have been met.

V. Government Regulation of Business

A. Federal Securities Acts

M95
Answer 5 (10 points)

a. 1. World is incorrect in its first contention that the offering is exempt from registration under Regulation D, Rule 505, of the Securities Act of 1933. World did not comply with the requirements of Rule 505 for the following reasons: the offering was sold to more than 35 nonaccredited investors; there was a general advertising of the offering; and the SEC was notified more than 15 days after the first sale of the offering.

2. World is also incorrect in its second contention that the securities of the offering would be completely exempt from registration if the offering were exempt. Securities originally purchased under a Regulation D limited offering exemption are restricted securities. They must be registered prior to resale unless sold subject to another exemption.

b. 1. Unity is incorrect in its contention that it is not required to comply with the reporting requirements of the Securities Exchange Act of 1934. Unity must comply because it has more than 500 stockholders and total assets in excess of $5,000,000. Alternately, Unity must comply because its shares are traded on a national securities exchange.

2. A covered corporation must file the following reports with the SEC: Quarterly Reports (10-Q's); Annual Reports (10-K's); and Current Reports (8-K's). These reports are intended to provide a complete, current statement of all business operations and matters affecting the value of the corporation's securities.

VI. Uniform Commercial Code

A. Negotiable Instruments

N95
Answer 5 (10 points)

To:

From:

I have identified and explained the issues and offer my conclusions on the legal issues pertaining to the attached note and security interest:

- Is Crane a holder in due course?

Crane is a holder in due course because Crane took a negotiable note for value, in good faith, and without knowledge of any defenses by the maker. The later disclosure that Oval has a personal defense against Jones does not affect that status as a holder in due course.

- Will Crane be able to collect from Oval?

Crane should be able to collect from Oval because Oval's defense is personal and a holder in due course is not subject to personal defenses.

- Will Crane be able to collect from Jones?

Crane should be able to collect from Jones despite Jones' qualified indorsement (without recourse) of the note. Jones was aware of Oval's defense of fraud at the time Jones indorsed the note to Crane. This knowledge is a breach of the implied transfer warranty against defenses. Accordingly, Jones' qualified indorsement does not prevent Crane from collecting the note from Jones.

- Was Crane's security interest perfected and does it have priority over Acorn's security interest?

The perfection of the security interest relates back to the date Harper took possession of the tractor (collateral) (October 5, 1995) because the security interest was a non-inventory purchase money security interest, and the financing statement was filed on October 10, 1995 (within the statutory filing period). Accordingly, Crane's security interest has priority over Acorn's security interest despite Acorn's earlier filing on October 9, 1995.

N93
Answer 5 (10 points)

a. Williams' first claim that the promissory note is negotiable is incorrect. The note is nonnegotiable because:

- It is not payable at a definite time or on demand because payment is not required until two weeks after an event, the occurrence of which is uncertain.

- The note is only payable out of the proceeds of the resale of the computer components making the promise to pay the note conditional. This is referred to as the "particular fund doctrine."

Williams' second claim that it is a holder in due course is incorrect. Although Williams is a holder of the instrument, it cannot be a holder in due course because the instrument is nonnegotiable.

Williams' third claim that Helco cannot raise Jason's misrepresentation as a defense to payment of the note is incorrect. This defense is a personal defense and would not be valid against a holder in due course. Williams only has the rights of an assignee of the Helco note. It has no better rights than Jason. Thus, Helco can raise Jason's misrepresentation as a defense.

b. Grover is incorrect in refusing to pay its note. Williams took the note with notice of Grover's defense and, therefore, could not be a holder in due course in its own right. Williams took the note from Oliver, who was a holder in due course. Therefore, under the "shelter provision" of the UCC Commercial Paper Article, Williams has the rights of a holder in due course even though it does not qualify as one. As a result, Williams did not take the note subject to Grover's defense even though Williams was aware of it.

c. Williams will be unable to collect from Oliver in the event Grover is not required to pay the note. Oliver was unaware of the claims of Grover, its endorsement was without recourse and violated no transfer warranties. Therefore, Williams does not have any right to recover from Oliver.

M92
Answer 5 (10 points)

Rustic's first claim, that its security interest is superior to National's, is incorrect. Rustic's security interest was perfected at the time it filed its financing statement, February 9, 1992, because it was a purchase money security interest in inventory. National filed its financing statement on February 7, 1992, therefore, National's security interest was perfected before, and is superior to, Rustic's security interest.

Rustic's second claim, that Karry purchased the lathe subject to Rustic's security interest, is incorrect. Karry, as a buyer in the ordinary course of Friendly's business, purchased the lathe free of any security interest given by Friendly. The fact that Karry was aware of Rustic's security interest does not affect this conclusion.

Karry's first claim, that the note is nonnegotiable, is incorrect. For a promissory note to be negotiable, it must be payable on demand or at a definite time. An instrument is payable on demand when it states that it is so payable, or when it provides no specific time for payment. Therefore, the note would be considered payable on demand.

Also, Karry's promissory note is negotiable despite the reference to the sales invoice because the reference does not make the note subject to the sales contract; rather, the reference only notes the existence of the invoice.

Karry's second claim, that Abcor has no rights to Karry's note because Friendly did not endorse it, is incorrect. The note is a bearer instrument because it is made payable to Friendly or bearer. Bearer instruments may be negotiated by delivery of the instrument alone.

Karry's third claim, that Abcor took the note subject to Karry's dispute with Friendly, is incorrect. Karry's dispute with Friendly was a personal defense to Karry. Even though Abcor took the note knowing of Karry's dispute and, therefore, could not ordinarily be a holder in due course, Abcor did take the note from Queen, which was a holder in due course. Under the "shelter provision" of the UCC Commercial Paper Article, Abcor has the rights of a holder in due course even though it does not qualify as one. As a result, Abcor did not take the note subject to Karry's personal defense, despite knowing of Karry's claim.

M91
Answer 3 (10 points)

Hillcraft's first assertion, that the note is nonnegotiable because it references the license agreement and is not payable at a definite time or on demand, is incorrect. The note is negotiable despite the reference to the license agreement because it does not make the note subject to the terms of the agreement; rather, the reference is regarded only as a recital of its existence.

Also, Hillcraft's right to extend the time for payment does not make the note nonnegotiable because the extension period is for a definite period of time.

Hillcraft's second assertion, that River Oaks is not a holder in due course (HDC) because it received the note as security for an existing debt and, therefore, did not give value for it, is incorrect. Under the UCC Commercial Paper Article, a holder does give value for an instrument when it is taken in payment of, or as security for, an antecedent claim.

Hillcraft's third assertion, that River Oaks is not an HDC because River Oaks was aware of Alexco's alleged breach of the license agreement, is correct. If a holder of a note is aware of a dispute when it acquires the note, that holder cannot be an HDC because it took with notice.

Hillcraft's fourth assertion, that it can raise the alleged breach by Alexco as a defense to payment of the note, is incorrect. Even though River Oaks is not an HDC under the UCC "shelter provision," it is entitled to the protection of an HDC because it took the instrument from First Auto, which was an HDC. Therefore, River Oaks did not take the note subject to Hillcraft's defense based on the alleged breach by Alexco. Hillcraft's defense is considered a personal defense and can only be used by Hillcraft against Alexco.

Hillcraft's fifth assertion, that River Oaks has no right to the note because it was not endorsed by Alexco, is incorrect. River Oaks acquired rights to the Hillcraft note without Alexco's endorsement because the note was a bearer instrument as a result of it being payable to "Alexco Company or bearer." A bearer instrument can be negotiated by delivery alone.

Hillcraft's final assertion, that the maximum amount Hillcraft would owe under the note is $4,000, plus accrued interest, is correct. If there is a conflict between a number written in numerals and also described by words, the words take precedence. Therefore, Hillcraft's maximum potential principal liability is $4,000 under the note.

M90
Answer 5 (10 points)

a. University is not a holder in due course (HDC) with regard to Peters' note. To be an HDC, University must:

- Be a holder of a negotiable instrument.
- Take it for value.
- Take it in good faith.
- Take it without notice that it is overdue or has been dishonored.
- Take it without notice of any defense or claim to it.

All of the above requirements are met except the first. Peters' note is not negotiable because it is not made payable to bearer or to the order of a named payee.

b. University is an assignee of Harris' rights under Peters' note. Therefore, University "stands in the shoes" of Harris, and Peters can raise Harris' alleged misrepresentations as a defense against University.

c. 1. Cole's first claim is incorrect. The promissory note Cole executed is negotiable despite the reference to the construction contract, because it does not make the note subject to the other contract; rather, the reference is only a recital of that contract's existence.

2. Cole's second claim is incorrect. University acquired rights to the promissory note without Baker's

indorsement because the note had been converted to a bearer instrument as a result of Able's blank indorsement. Bearer paper can be negotiated by delivery alone.

B. Sales

R98
Answer 1

a. Classic's contention is incorrect. Under the provisions of the Sales Article of the UCC, a written memorandum stating an agreement between merchants does not have to be signed by both parties. The contract is enforceable against Classic because Classic signed the memorandum and against Rand because Rand did not object to the memorandum within 10 days of receiving it.

b. 1. Classic bears the risk of loss for the 50 leather chairs destroyed in the fire. Even though the goods were identified to the contract and placed on the loading dock, the risk of loss remains with Classic. The shipping terms "F.O.B. seller's loading dock" provide that risk of loss remains with the seller until the goods are delivered to the common carrier. The 50 leather chairs destroyed in the fire had not yet been delivered to the carrier.
2. Classic bears the risk of loss for the damaged vinyl chairs. Even though these goods were delivered to the common carrier, the risk of loss did not pass to Rand because the vinyl chairs were nonconforming goods.
3. August 1 was the earliest date that title to any of the chairs passed to Rand. Title passed when goods identified to the contract were delivered to the carrier.

c. Under the Sales Article of the UCC, for Rand to be entitled to damages from Classic, Rand must comply with the following requirements:

- Rand has to notify Classic of the rejection of the goods within a reasonable time.

- Rand must act in good faith with respect to the rejected goods by following any reasonable instructions from Classic.

- Rand must give Classic the opportunity to cure until the contract time of performance expires.

d. Rand would be entitled to the following remedies:

- The right to cancel the contract.

- The right of cover.

- The right to recover monetary damages for nondelivery.

M93
Answer 5 (10 points)

a. Mason's claim, that the risk of loss for the tuna belonged to Angler, is correct. Because Angler shipped the wrong grade of tuna, risk of loss remained with Angler until either it cured by shipping conforming goods to Mason or Mason elected to accept the tuna despite the fact that it was nonconforming.

b. Classic's claim, that it was not obligated to return the peaches to Angler, is incorrect. Classic is a merchant because it deals with the type of goods that is the subject of its contract with Angler. Therefore, Classic has an obligation, on rejecting goods, to follow any reasonable instructions from Angler. Angler's request that Classic ship the peaches back to Angler at Angler's expense is a reasonable instruction.

c. Regal's claim, that it is not obligated to purchase the hamburger meat, is incorrect. Because the price of the hamburger meat exceeds $500, the Uniform Commercial Code (UCC) Statute of Frauds applies and the contract between Angler and Regal must be evidenced by a writing and:

- Indicate that a contract for sale has been made;

- Be signed by the party against whom enforcement is sought; and

- Specify the quantity of goods sold.

Regal's correspondence to Angler, dated October 29, satisfies the UCC Statute of Frauds, so the contract will be enforceable against Regal.

N92
Answer 5 (10 points)

a. Rapid's claim is incorrect. Both Debco and Rapid are merchants under the UCC because they both deal in the type of goods involved in the transaction (computers).
The UCC provides that a confirmation satisfies the UCC Statute of Frauds, if an oral contract between merchants is:

- Confirmed in writing within a reasonable period of time, and

- The confirmation is signed by the party sending it and received by the other party

Both parties are bound even though the party receiving the confirmation fails to sign it. This is correct unless the party receiving the confirmation submits a written objection within 10 days of receipt. Rapid will be bound even though it did not sign the confirmation because no written objection was made.

b. Debco's first claim, that its October 25 correspondence prevented the formation of a contract, is incorrect. Debco's October 12 purchase order will be regarded as a firm offer under the UCC because:

- Debco is a merchant.
- The purchase order is in writing and signed.
- The purchase order states that it will not be withdrawn for the time specified.

Because Debco's October 12 purchase order is considered a firm offer, Debco cannot revoke it, and its October 25 attempt to do so is ineffective.

Debco's second claim, that TMI's October 31 correspondence is not an effective acceptance because it was not received until November 3, is incorrect. An acceptance of an offer is effective when dispatched (in this case, when mailed), provided that an appropriate mode of communication is used. The UCC provides that an offer shall be construed as inviting acceptance in any manner and by any medium reasonable in the circumstances. In this case, Debco made its offer by mail, which, if adequately addressed with proper postage affixed, would be considered a reasonable manner and medium for acceptance. As a result, TMI's acceptance was effective when mailed on October 31.

Debco's third claim, that TMI's acceptance is not effective because it added payment terms to Debco's offer, is also incorrect. The UCC provides that a definite and timely expression of acceptance of an offer will form a contract, even if the terms of the acceptance are different from those in the offer, unless acceptance is expressly made conditional on accepting the different terms. Therefore, TMI's October 31 correspondence, which expressly stated that TMI would ship the computers ordered by Debco, was an effective acceptance, and a contract was formed despite the fact that TMI added payment terms.

N91
Answer 4 (10 points)

a. 1. Vesta Electronics would bear the risk of loss for the 18" speakers destroyed by the fire on its loading dock. Even though Vesta identified and segregated the goods on its loading dock, the risk of loss remained with the seller because the contract's shipping terms "F.O.B. seller's loading dock" made it a shipping contract. Thus, risk of loss does not pass to Zap until the goods are delivered to the carrier.

2. The risk of loss for the 16" speakers also remained with Vesta. Even though the goods were delivered to the common carrier, risk of loss did not pass because Vesta shipped nonconforming goods.

b. 1. Zap may validly reject the 16" speakers because any buyer may reject nonconforming goods. To avoid potential liability, the rejection must be made within a reasonable time of receipt and must be communicated to the seller.

2. Zap may also validly accept some of the 18" speakers. A buyer may accept none, all, or any commercial unit of a shipment when nonconforming goods are shipped.

c. To be entitled to damages, Zap must comply with the UCC by notifying Vesta of the rejection of the goods within a reasonable time; acting in good faith with respect to the rejected goods by following any reasonable instructions of the seller; and giving Vesta the opportunity to cure until the contract time of performance expires.

N90
Answer 4 (10 points)

a. Under the UCC Sales Article, the contract between Pharo and Secure creates the following implied warranties:

- Implied warranty of merchantability;
- Implied warranty of fitness for a particular purpose;
- Implied warranty of title.

The implied warranty of merchantability requires the tug to be merchantable; that is, fit for the ordinary purpose intended. It is probable that the tug was fit for such ordinary purposes and, therefore, the implied warranty of merchantability was not breached.

The implied warranty of fitness for a particular purpose requires that the tug be fit for the particular purpose for which it was purchased. To show that the implied warranty of fitness for a particular purpose is present as a result of the contract, Pharo must show that:

- Secure knew of the particular needs of Pharo;
- Pharo relied on Secure to select a suitable tug;
- Secure knew that Pharo was relying on Secure to select a tug suitable for Pharo's needs.

The implied warranty of fitness for a particular purpose has been breached because the tug was not suitable for Pharo's particular needs (i.e., to move airplanes weighing up to 10,000 pounds).

The implied warranty of title requires that:

- Secure have good title;
- The transfer to Pharo would be rightful;
- The tug would be delivered free from any security interest or other lien.

The implied warranty of title has been breached because Maco was the rightful owner.

b. Maco will not be entitled to recover the tug from Pharo because:

- Maco had entrusted the tug to Secure, which deals in similar goods;
- That, as a result of such entrustment, Secure had the power to transfer Maco's rights to the tug to a buyer in the ordinary course of business;
- Pharo was a buyer in the ordinary course of business because Pharo purchased the tug in good faith and without knowledge of Maco's ownership interest.

N89
Answer 4 (10 points)

The president's assertion that the September 8, 1988 offer by Crisp was irrevocable until December 20, 1988, and that, therefore, a contract was formed by Anker's acceptance on December 12, 1988, is incorrect. Because the offer made by Crisp involves a transaction in goods, i.e. furniture, the UCC Sales Article applies. The UCC Sales Article provides that an offer by a merchant to buy or sell goods in a signed writing which by its terms gives assurance that it will be held open is not revocable, for lack of consideration, during the time stated or, if no time is stated, for a reasonable time, but in no event may such period of irrevocability exceed three months. Under the facts of this case, Crisp's offer was a firm offer that could not be revoked because the offer was made by Crisp, a merchant, concerning the kind of goods being sold (furniture); was in writing and signed by Crisp; and stated that it would remain open until December 20, 1988. Despite the provision that the offer will remain open until December 20, 1988, a firm offer remains irrevocable for a three-month period. Therefore, Crisp's letter of revocation on December 5, 1988 did not terminate the firm offer because the three-month period had not yet expired. The revocation was effective on December 8, 1988, when the three-month period expired. Therefore, Anker's attempted acceptance on December 12, 1988 did not form a contract with Crisp. Instead, Anker's attempted acceptance is likely to be treated as an offer.

The president's assertion that Dix's December 12, 1988 letter formed an option contract is incorrect. To form an option contract, where the subject matter is real estate, all of the elements necessary to form a contract must be met. In this case, Anker did not furnish any consideration in return for Dix's promise to keep the offer open until December 20, 1988; therefore, an option contract was not formed.

The president's assertion that Anker's acceptance on December 19, 1988 formed a contract with Dix is incorrect. In general, acceptance of an offer is effective when it is dispatched. If, however, an offer specifically stipulates the method of communication to be utilized by the offeree, the acceptance to be effective must conform to that method. Thus, an acceptance by another method of communication is ineffective and no contract is formed. Under the facts of this case, Anker's acceptance on December 19, 1988 by a private express mail courier is ineffective, despite Dix's receipt of the acceptance on December 20, 1988, because Dix's offer specifically stipulated that acceptance could only be made by certified mail, return receipt requested. Instead, Anker's attempted acceptance is likely to be treated as a counteroffer.

M89
Answer 5 (10 points)

The assertion that as of March 3, 1989 the risk of loss on the disk drive remained with Xeon is correct. Under the UCC Sales Article, if the agreement between the parties is otherwise silent, risk of loss passes to the buyer on the buyer's receipt of the goods if the seller is a merchant. Under the facts, Xeon is a merchant because it sells computer systems. Therefore, the risk of loss remained with Xeon because the disk drive was never received by Pine.

The assertion that Meed acquired no rights in the CPU as a result of the March 18, 1989 transaction is incorrect. Under the UCC Sales Article, any entrusting of possession of goods to a merchant who deals in goods of that kind gives the merchant power to transfer all rights of the entruster to the buyer in the ordinary course of business. Entrusting includes any delivery and any acquiescence in retention of possession regardless of any condition expressed between the parties to the delivery or acquiescence, and regardless of whether the possessor's disposition of the goods has been such as to be larcenous under the criminal law. For the merchant to acquire the power to transfer ownership and title, the entruster must be the rightful owner. Under the facts of this case, Pine had title at the time the CPU was returned to Xeon for repairs and this constituted an entrusting that gave Xeon the power to transfer all of Pine's rights in the CPU to Meed.

The assertion that Jensen's security interest in the word processors never attached and therefore Jensen's security interest is not enforceable against Pine with respect to the word processors is incorrect. A security interest in collateral will attach if: the collateral is in the possession of the secured party under an agreement, or the debtor has signed a security agreement that contains a description of the collateral; the secured party has given value; and the debtor has rights in the collateral. Based on the facts, Jensen's security interest attached on April 12, 1989, when Jensen sold and Pine received the word processors and Jensen received a security agreement executed by Pine that described the word processors. On attachment, Jensen's security interest became enforceable against Pine.

The assertion that Jensen has a superior security interest to Pine's bank is incorrect. Although Jensen has a purchase money security interest to the extent the security interest is taken by Jensen to secure the purchase price, Jensen's security interest will not be perfected by attachment alone. Jensen must file a financing statement to perfect its security interest because the collateral involved is goods used for business purposes and not consumer goods. Therefore, Jensen has an unperfected security interest in the word processors and the bank obtained a superior security interest by perfecting.

C. Secured Transactions

N95
Answer 5 (10 points)

To:

From:

I have identified and explained the issues and offer my conclusions on the legal issues pertaining to the attached note and security interest:

- Is Crane a holder in due course?

Crane is a holder in due course because Crane took a negotiable note for value, in good faith, and without knowledge of any defenses by the maker. The later disclosure that Oval has a personal defense against Jones does not affect that status as a holder in due course.

- Will Crane be able to collect from Oval?

Crane should be able to collect from Oval because Oval's defense is personal and a holder in due course is not subject to personal defenses.

- Will Crane be able to collect from Jones?

Crane should be able to collect from Jones despite Jones' qualified indorsement (without recourse) of the note. Jones was aware of Oval's defense of fraud at the time Jones indorsed the note to Crane. This knowledge is a breach of the implied transfer warranty against defenses. Accordingly, Jones' qualified indorsement does not prevent Crane from collecting the note from Jones.

- Was Crane's security interest perfected and does it have priority over Acorn's security interest?

The perfection of the security interest relates back to the date Harper took possession of the tractor (collateral) (October 5, 1995) because the security interest was a non-inventory purchase money security interest, and the financing statement was filed on October 10, 1995 (within the statutory filing period). Accordingly, Crane's security interest has priority over Acorn's security interest despite Acorn's earlier filing on October 9, 1995.

M92
Answer 5 (10 points)

Rustic's first claim, that its security interest is superior to National's, is incorrect. Rustic's security interest was perfected at the time it filed its financing statement, February 9, 1992, because it was a purchase money security interest in inventory. National filed its financing statement on February 7, 1992, therefore, National's security interest was perfected before, and is superior to, Rustic's security interest.

Rustic's second claim, that Karry purchased the lathe subject to Rustic's security interest, is incorrect. Karry, as a buyer in the ordinary course of Friendly's business, purchased the lathe free of any security interest given by Friendly. The fact that Karry was aware of Rustic's security interest does not affect this conclusion.

Karry's first claim, that the note is nonnegotiable, is incorrect. For a promissory note to be negotiable, it must be payable on demand or at a definite time. An instrument is payable on demand when it states that it is so payable, or when it provides no specific time for payment. Therefore, the note would be considered payable on demand.

Also, Karry's promissory note is negotiable despite the reference to the sales invoice because the reference does not make the note subject to the sales contract; rather, the reference only notes the existence of the invoice.

Karry's second claim, that Abcor has no rights to Karry's note because Friendly did not endorse it, is incorrect. The note is a bearer instrument because it is made payable to Friendly or bearer. Bearer instruments may be negotiated by delivery of the instrument alone.

Karry's third claim, that Abcor took the note subject to Karry's dispute with Friendly, is incorrect. Karry's dispute with Friendly was a personal defense to Karry. Even though Abcor took the note knowing of Karry's dispute and, therefore, could not ordinarily be a holder in due course, Abcor did take the note from Queen, which was a holder in due course. Under the "shelter provision" of the UCC Commercial Paper Article, Abcor has the rights of a holder in due course even though it does not qualify as one. As a result, Abcor did not take the note subject to Karry's personal defense, despite knowing of Karry's claim.

N91
Answer 5 (10 points)

Rice's assertion that Abco does not have an effective security interest in the CDM computer purchased by Rice is correct. For Abco to have an enforceable security interest in the collateral, the security interest claimed must have attached. Attachment requires that:

- The secured party (Abco) has given value;

- The debtor (Rice) has rights in the collateral; and

- The debtor (Rice) has executed and delivered to the creditor (Abco) a security agreement covering the collateral.

In this case, all but one of the requirements are met. The security agreement is ineffective because it was not signed by the debtor (Rice). Abco's failure to perfect its security interest by filing a financing statement would have no effect on the enforceability of the security interest against Rice.

Condor's assertion that its security interest in the computer is superior to Abco's is incorrect. Both Condor's and Abco's security interests are perfected. Condor's security interest was perfected when it filed its financing statement on August 26. Because Abco's security interest was a purchase money security interest in collateral other than inventory, its security interest was perfected at the time of the sale to Baker (August 18), provided it filed a financing statement at the time Baker took possession of the computer or within the UCC time period for perfection. Abco's security interest was perfected on August 18 before Condor's was perfected (on August 26), because Abco filed a financing statement within the applicable UCC time period. Therefore, Abco's security interest is superior to Condor's.

N90
Answer 5 (10 points)

Kast's assertion that the computer was purchased from Wizard free of National's security interest is correct. Kast, as a buyer in the ordinary course, purchased the computer free of any security interest given by Wizard. The fact that Kast was aware of the existence of National's security interest does not affect this conclusion.

Marc's assertion that the computer was purchased from Kast free of Wizard's security interest is correct. Marc purchased the computer from Kast free of Wizard's security interest because:

- Marc had no knowledge of the security interest;
- Marc was buying the computer for household use;
- Wizard's security interest had not been perfected by filing prior to Marc's purchase.

Marc's assertion that Alcor's security interest is unenforceable against Marc because Alcor failed to file a financing statement is incorrect. On attachment of Alcor's security interest, it became enforceable against Marc. Attachment has occurred because:

- The secured party (Alcor) gave value;
- The debtor (Marc) has rights in the collateral;
- The debtor (Marc) has executed and delivered a security agreement covering the collateral to the creditor (Alcor).

Alcor's failure to perfect its security interest has no effect on the enforceability of the security interest against Marc.

VII. Property

A. Real Property Including Insurance

R97
Answer 1(b) (10 points)

b. 1. Acme's first contention that Birch had no insurable interest in the property when the policy was issued is incorrect. Birch had an insurable interest in the property when the contract was signed, since a contract right is an insurable interest.

Acme's second contention that Birch is a coinsurer is correct. Birch's policy for $1.5 million is less than 80% of the value of the buildings.

2. Birch would recover $150,000 of the loss. This figure is computed by dividing the face value of the policy by 80% of the fair market value of the buildings and multiplying by the amount of the loss.

$$\frac{\text{Face value of policy}}{80\% \text{ of fair market value}} \times \text{amount of loss} = \text{recovery}$$

$$\frac{\$1,500,000}{.80 \times \$2,000,000} \times \$160,000 = \$150,000$$

3. The mortgage recorded in February would have first priority. In a notice-race jurisdiction, the first recorded mortgage has priority unless the holder of a later mortgage has knowledge of the earlier mortgage. Based on the facts presented, no one had notice of the earlier unrecorded mortgage and, consequently, it has no priority despite its being first in time. Accordingly, the February mortgage would be paid in full ($475,000) and the balance of the foreclosure proceeds ($525,000) would be paid to Thorn.

N94
Answer 5 (10 points)

a. Strong will lose its suit against Apex for subletting the factory to Egan without Strong's permission. Unless a lease provides otherwise, a tenant may sublet the premises without the landlord's consent.

b. Zone is incorrect in claiming that neither Apex nor Egan had an insurable interest in the factory. Apex has an insurable interest because it was the original lessee of the factory. Apex has a financial interest both in receiving rent from Egan and its liability to Strong under the original lease. Egan has an insurable interest and a financial interest as tenant in possession.

c. Strong will only recover $150,000 from Range. Strong's recovery is based on the coinsurance formula:

$$\frac{\text{Insurance carried (policy amount)}}{\text{Insurance required (coinsurance \% } \times \text{ fair market value of the property at the time of the loss)}} \times \text{The amount of loss} = \text{Recovery}$$

$$\frac{400,000}{.80 \times 600,000} \times 180,000 = \$150,000$$

Strong will be able to recover $150,000 from Range, despite having insufficient coverage.

d. Lane will recover $125,000 of the foreclosure proceeds. Lane's recovery is limited to the amount left after the satisfaction of the Ace mortgage. In a "Notice-Race" jurisdiction, Lane's recorded mortgage will not have priority over Ace's earlier unrecorded mortgage because Lane knew of the Ace mortgage.

M91
Answer 4 (10 points)

a. Tower and Perry owned the property as tenants in common. This form of ownership allows either party to dispose of his or her undivided interest by sale or on death. Any person purchasing or inheriting Perry's interest would become a tenant in common with Tower. Thus, on January 21, 1990, Tower and Dodd are tenants in common, each owning a one-half undivided interest in the house.

b. Both Tower and Dodd have an insurable interest in the house. Tower's interest arose when the property was purchased, continued when the insurance policy was purchased, and still existed at the time of the fire loss.

Dodd's interest arose when Dodd inherited Perry's interest in the house. Acme's consent to the assignment of the policy to Tower and Dodd entitles Dodd to a share of the proceeds of the policy.

c. Acme would have to honor the insurance contract and pay part of the loss. Despite Tower and Perry not maintaining insurance coverage of 80% of the property's market value, the coinsurance clause allows for a percentage of recovery. The formula is as follows:

$$\frac{\text{Amount of Coverage}}{\text{Actual Market Value} \times \text{Coinsurance \%}} \times \text{Amount of Loss}$$

This would allow a recovery as follows:

$$\frac{\$200,000}{\$300,000 \times .8} \times \$180,000 = \$150,000$$

d. The conflict between Midway and New would be resolved in favor of Midway. In a notice-race statute jurisdiction, New's knowledge of Midway's first mortgage would give Midway priority despite New's earlier filing. The insurance proceeds would be distributed as follows:

- $80,000 to Midway representing the balance due on the mortgage including accrued interest. This is due because Midway as a mortgagee is included as a contingent beneficiary in the policy.
- $40,000 to New for the same reasons as above but not paid unless and until Midway is fully paid.
- $30,000 to be divided equally between Tower and Dodd as tenants in common.

e. Tower would not be able to collect rent from Zimmer for the balance of the term of the lease because Zimmer moved as a result of the extensive fire damage to the apartment. The implied warranty of habitability would be considered breached by the landlord and a constructive eviction of Zimmer would be deemed to have taken place because the premises could no longer be used for their intended purpose. Constructive eviction releases both the landlord and the tenant from their obligations under the lease.

N89
Answer 2 (10 points)

a. Sam Bean and Bob Bean will not be personally liable to Fale for the deficiency resulting from the foreclosure sale because they did not assume the mortgage but instead purchased the building subject to the mortgage. In the absence of a state statute to the contrary, Stein will be personally liable for the deficiency because Stein was not released from liability on the note and mortgage.

b. There is no right of survivorship feature in a tenancy in common and, therefore, Rita Bean will acquire Sam Bean's one-half interest in the building under her husband's will. Thus, Rita Bean will own a one-half interest in the building as a tenant in common with Bob Bean.

c. In general, the purposes and benefits of creating a spendthrift trust are to provide a fund for the maintenance of another (the beneficiary); protect the fund from the beneficiary's financial mismanagement and improvidence; prohibit the beneficiary from transferring the right to future trust income or principal; and prohibit the beneficiary's interest from being subjected to the claims of the beneficiary's creditors.

d.1. A trust may generally be terminated by the beneficiaries if all consent to the termination; all are legally competent to consent; and termination will not defeat a material purpose for which the trust was created.

2. The spendthrift trust created by Sam Bean cannot be terminated by Bob Bean because the major purpose of a spendthrift trust is to protect the beneficiary from mismanagement and improvidence. Thus, termination of the spendthrift trust would defeat the purpose for which it was created.

M89
Answer 3 (10 points)

a. Ash, Bale, and Rangel will be personally liable to Vista for the deficiency resulting from the foreclosure sale because they became the principal debtors when they assumed the mortgage. Park will remain liable for the deficiency. Although Vista consented to the assumption of the mortgage by Ash, Bale, and Rangel, such assumption does not relieve Park from its obligation to Vista unless Park obtains a release from Vista or there is a novation.

b. The assertion that the sublet from Wein to Nord is void because Ash, Bale, and Rangel must consent to the sublet is incorrect. Unless the lease provides otherwise, a tenant may sublet the premises without the landlord's consent. Since the lease was silent regarding Wein's right to sublet, Wein may sublet to Nord without the consent of Ash, Bale, and Rangel.

The assertion that if the sublet was not void Ash, Bale, and Rangel have the right to hold either Wein or Nord liable for payment of rent is incorrect. In a sublease, the sublessee/subtenant (Nord) has no obligation to pay rent to the landlord (Ash, Bale, and Rangel).

The subtenant (Nord) is liable to the tenant (Wein), but the tenant (Wein) remains solely liable to the landlord (Ash, Bale, and Rangel) for the rent stipulated in the lease.

c. Ash's inter vivos transfer of his $1/3$ interest in the office building to his spouse on April 4, 1989 resulted in his spouse obtaining a $1/3$ interest in the office building as a tenant in common. Ash's wife did not become a joint tenant with Bale and Rangel because the transfer of a joint tenant's interest to an outside party destroys the joint tenancy nature of the particular interest transferred. Bale and Rangel will remain as joint tenants with each other.

As of April 21, 1989, the office building was owned by Ash's spouse who had a $1/3$ interest as tenant in common and Bale who had a $2/3$ interest as tenant in common.

Ash's death on April 20, 1989 will have no effect on the ownership of the office building because Ash had already transferred all of his interest to his wife on April 4, 1989.

Rangel's death on April 20, 1989 resulted in his interest being acquired by Bale because of the right of survivorship feature in a joint tenancy. Because there are no surviving joint tenants, Bale will become a tenant in common who owns $2/3$ of the office building. Ash's spouse will not acquire any additional interest due to Rangel's death because she was a tenant in common with Rangel.

SUGGESTED REFERENCES

Business Law & Professional Responsibilities

AICPA, Professional Standards; Code of Professional Conduct; U.S. Auditing Standards; Consulting Services; Personal Financial Planning.

Clarkson, Miller, Jentz, & Cross, *West's Business Law*, 7th ed. (West, 1998).

Federal Bankruptcy Code.

Mann & Roberts, *Smith & Roberson's Business Law*, 10th ed. (West, 1997).

Metzger, Mallor, Barnes, Bowers, & Phillips, *Business Law and the Regulatory Environment*, 8th ed. (Irwin, 1992).

Schantz & Jackson, *Business Law*, 2d ed. (West, 1987).

Uniform Commercial Code—Sales Article; Negotiable Instruments Article; Documents of Title Article; Secured Transactions Article.

Uniform CPA Examination

Auditing

Selected Questions And Unofficial Answers Indexed To Content Specification Outline

TABLE OF CONTENTS

	Multiple Choice Items	Other Objective Answer Formats	Essays
Selected Questions			
I. Plan, Evaluate, and Accept the Engagement	A-1	A-67	A-103
A. Determine Nature and Scope of Engagement	A-1	*	A-103
B. Assess Engagement Risk and the CPA Firm's Ability to Perform the Engagement	A-4	A-67	A-105
C. Communicate With the Predecessor Accountant/Auditor	A-5	*	*
D. Decide Whether to Accept or Continue the Client and Engagement	A-6	*	*
E. Enter Into an Agreement With the Client as to the Terms of the Engagement	A-6	*	*
F. Obtain an Understanding of the Client's Operations, Business, and Industry	A-6	*	*
G. Perform Analytical Procedures	A-7	A-68	A-106
H. Consider Preliminary Engagement Materiality	A-7	*	*
I. Assess Inherent Risk and Risk of Misstatements	A-8	*	A-106
J. Consider Internal Control	A-11	A-71	A-107
K. Consider Other Planning Matters	A-23	*	A-108
L. Identify Financial Statement Assertions and Formulate Audit Objectives	A-26	*	A-108
M. Determine and Prepare the Work Program	A-26	A-74	A-108
II. Obtain and Document Information to Form a Basis for Conclusions	A-28	A-76	A-109
A. Perform Planned Procedures Including Planned Applications of Audit Sampling	A-28	A-76	A-109
B. Evaluate Contingencies	*	*	*
C. Obtain and Evaluate Lawyers' Letters	A-40	*	A-114
D. Review Subsequent Events	A-40	*	*
E. Obtain Representations From Management	A-41	*	A-115
F. Identify Reportable Conditions and Other Control Deficiencies	A-42	*	*
G. Identify Matters for Communication With Audit Committees	A-42	*	A-115
III. Review the Engagement	A-43	*	A-116
A. Perform Analytical Procedures	A-43	*	*
B. Evaluate the Sufficiency and Competence of Audit Evidence and Document Engagement Conclusions	A-43	*	A-116
C. Review the Work Performed	A-44	*	A-117
IV. Prepare Communications to Satisfy Engagement Objectives	A-45	A-86	A-118
A. Prepare Reports	A-45	A-86	A-118
B. Prepare Letters and Other Required Communications	A-58	*	*
C. Other Matters	A-61	*	*

* No questions were indexed for this area or group.

	Pages
Selected Multiple Choice Items — Unofficial Answers	A-63
Other Objective Answer Formats — Selected Questions	A-67
Selected Other Objective Answer Formats — Unofficial Answers	A-93
Essays — Selected Questions	A-103
Selected Essays — Unofficial Answers	A-121
Suggested References	A-136
Content Specification Outline	CSO-3
Summary of Coverage — Uniform CPA Examinations, May 1996 through May 1998	S-3

MULTIPLE CHOICE ITEMS — SELECTED QUESTIONS

I. Plan, Evaluate, and Accept the Engagement

A. Determine Nature and Scope of Engagement

R98#1. Although the scope of audits of recipients of federal financial assistance in accordance with federal audit regulations varies, these audits generally have which of the following elements in common?
    a. The auditor is to determine whether the federal financial assistance has been administered in accordance with applicable laws and regulations.
    b. The materiality levels are lower and are determined by the government entities that provided the federal financial assistance to the recipient.
    c. The auditor should obtain written management representations that the recipient's internal auditors will report their findings objectively without fear of political repercussion.
    d. The auditor is required to express both positive and negative assurance that illegal acts that could have a material effect on the recipient's financial statements are disclosed to the inspector general.

R96#1. An accountant is required to comply with the provisions of Statements on Standards for Accounting and Review Services when

I. Reproducing client-prepared financial statements, without modification, as an accommodation to a client.
II. Preparing standard monthly journal entries for depreciation and expiration of prepaid expenses.

    a. I only.
    b. II only.
    c. Both I and II.
    d. Neither I nor II.

N95#36. Brown, CPA, has accepted an engagement to examine and report on Crow Company's written assertion about the effectiveness of Crow's internal control. In what form may Crow present its written assertion?

I. In a separate report that will accompany Brown's report.
II. In a representation letter to Brown.

    a. I only.
    b. II only.
    c. Either I or II.
    d. Neither I nor II.

N95#61. Harris, CPA, has been asked to audit and report on the balance sheet of Fox Co. but not on the statements of income, retained earnings, or cash flows. Harris will have access to all information underlying the basic financial statements. Under these circumstances, Harris may
    a. Not accept the engagement because it would constitute a violation of the profession's ethical standards.
    b. Not accept the engagement because it would be tantamount to rendering a piecemeal opinion.
    c. Accept the engagement because such engagements merely involve limited reporting objectives.
    d. Accept the engagement but should disclaim an opinion because of an inability to apply the procedures considered necessary.

M95#1. The element of the audit planning process most likely to be agreed upon with the client before implementation of the audit strategy is the determination of the
    a. Evidence to be gathered to provide a sufficient basis for the auditor's opinion.
    b. Procedures to be undertaken to discover litigation, claims, and assessments.
    c. Pending legal matters to be included in the inquiry of the client's attorney.
    d. Timing of inventory observation procedures to be performed.

M95#20. If requested to perform a review engagement for a nonpublic entity in which an accountant has an immaterial direct financial interest, the accountant is
    a. Not independent and, therefore, may **not** be associated with the financial statements.
    b. Not independent and, therefore, may **not** issue a review report.
    c. Not independent and, therefore, may issue a review report, but may **not** issue an auditor's opinion.
    d. Independent because the financial interest is immaterial and, therefore, may issue a review report.

M95#21. Kell engaged March, CPA, to submit to Kell a written personal financial plan containing unaudited personal financial statements. March anticipates omitting certain disclosures required by GAAP because the engagement's sole purpose is to assist Kell in developing a personal financial plan. For March to be exempt from

complying with the requirements of SSARS 1, *Compilation and Review of Financial Statements,* Kell is required to agree that the
- a. Financial statements will **not** be presented in comparative form with those of the prior period.
- b. Omitted disclosures required by GAAP are **not** material.
- c. Financial statements will **not** be disclosed to a non-CPA financial planner.
- d. Financial statements will **not** be used to obtain credit.

M95#22. An examination of a financial forecast is a professional service that involves
- a. Compiling or assembling a financial forecast that is based on management's assumptions.
- b. Limiting the distribution of the accountant's report to management and the board of directors.
- c. Assuming responsibility to update management on key events for one year after the report's date.
- d. Evaluating the preparation of a financial forecast and the support underlying management's assumptions.

N94#18. Which of the following conditions is necessary for a practitioner to accept an attest engagement to examine and report on an entity's internal control over financial reporting?
- a. The practitioner anticipates relying on the entity's internal control in a financial statement audit.
- b. Management presents its written assertion about the effectiveness of internal control.
- c. The practitioner is a continuing auditor who previously has audited the entity's financial statements.
- d. Management agrees **not** to present the practitioner's report in a general-use document to stockholders.

N94#19. Which of the following statements is correct concerning an auditor's responsibilities regarding financial statements?
- a. Making suggestions that are adopted about the form and content of an entity's financial statements impairs an auditor's independence.
- b. An auditor may draft an entity's financial statements based on information from management's accounting system.
- c. The fair presentation of audited financial statements in conformity with GAAP is an implicit part of the auditor's responsibilities.
- d. An auditor's responsibilities for audited financial statements are **not** confined to the expression of the auditor's opinion.

N94#20. An accountant has been engaged to review a nonpublic entity's financial statements that contain several departures from GAAP. If the financial statements are **not** revised and modification of the standard review report is **not** adequate to indicate the deficiencies, the accountant should
- a. Withdraw from the engagement and provide **no** further services concerning these financial statements.
- b. Inform management that the engagement can proceed only if distribution of the accountant's report is restricted to internal use.
- c. Determine the effects of the departures from GAAP and issue a special report on the financial statements.
- d. Issue a modified review report provided the entity agrees that the financial statements will **not** be used to obtain credit.

N94#22. Statements on Standards for Accounting and Review Services (SSARS) require an accountant to report when the accountant has
- a. Typed client-prepared financial statements, without modification, as an accommodation to the client.
- b. Provided a client with a financial statement format that does **not** include dollar amounts, to be used by the client in preparing financial statements.
- c. Proposed correcting journal entries to be recorded by the client that change client-prepared financial statements.
- d. Generated, through the use of computer software, financial statements prepared in accordance with a comprehensive basis of accounting other than GAAP.

N94#23. An accountant may accept an engagement to apply agreed-upon procedures to prospective financial statements provided that
- a. Distribution of the report is restricted to the specified users.
- b. The prospective financial statements are also examined.
- c. Responsibility for the adequacy of the procedures performed is taken by the accountant.
- d. Negative assurance is expressed on the prospective financial statements taken as a whole.

M94#9. North Co., a privately-held entity, asked its tax accountant, King, a CPA in public practice, to generate North's interim financial statements on King's microcomputer when King prepared North's quarterly tax return. King should **not** submit these financial statements to North unless, as a minimum, King complies with the provisions of
- a. Statements on Standards for Accounting and Review Services.
- b. Statements on Standards for Unaudited Financial Services.
- c. Statements on Standards for Consulting Services.
- d. Statements on Standards for Attestation Engagements.

M94#10. Which of the following is a conceptual difference between the attestation standards and generally accepted auditing standards?
    a. The attestation standards provide a framework for the attest function beyond historical financial statements.
    b. The requirement that the practitioner be independent in mental attitude is omitted from the attestation standards.
    c. The attestation standards do **not** permit an attest engagement to be part of a business acquisition study or a feasibility study.
    d. **None** of the standards of fieldwork in generally accepted auditing standards are included in the attestation standards.

M94#11. Because of the risk of material misstatement, an audit of financial statements in accordance with generally accepted auditing standards should be planned and performed with an attitude of
    a. Objective judgment.
    b. Independent integrity.
    c. Professional skepticism.
    d. Impartial conservatism.

M94#14. Accepting an engagement to examine an entity's financial projection most likely would be appropriate if the projection were to be distributed to
    a. All employees who work for the entity.
    b. Potential stockholders who request a prospectus or a registration statement.
    c. A bank with which the entity is negotiating for a loan.
    d. All stockholders of record as of the report date.

M94#37. Which of the following best describes a CPA's engagement to report on an entity's internal control over financial reporting?
    a. An attestation engagement to examine and report on management's written assertions about the effectiveness of its internal control.
    b. An audit engagement to render an opinion on the entity's internal control.
    c. A prospective engagement to project, for a period of time **not** to exceed one year, and report on the expected benefits of the entity's internal control.
    d. A consulting engagement to provide constructive advice to the entity on its internal control.

N93#2. Which of the following best describes what is meant by the term generally accepted auditing standards?
    a. Pronouncements issued by the Auditing Standards Board.
    b. Rules acknowledged by the accounting profession because of their universal application.
    c. Procedures to be used to gather evidence to support financial statements.
    d. Measures of the quality of the auditor's performance.

N93#9. In performing an attestation engagement, a CPA typically
    a. Supplies litigation support services.
    b. Assesses control risk at a low level.
    c. Expresses a conclusion about an assertion.
    d. Provides management consulting advice.

N93#12. A CPA is required to comply with the provisions of *Statements on Standards for Accounting and Review Services* when

	Processing financial data for clients of other CPA firms	Consulting on accounting matters
a.	Yes	Yes
b.	Yes	No
c.	No	Yes
d.	No	No

N93#56. A CPA is permitted to accept a separate engagement (**not** in conjunction with an audit of financial statements) to audit an entity's

	Schedule of accounts receivable	Schedule of royalties
a.	Yes	Yes
b.	Yes	No
c.	No	Yes
d.	No	No

M93#4. Which of the following is **not** an attestation standard?
    a. Sufficient evidence shall be obtained to provide a reasonable basis for the conclusion that is expressed in the report.
    b. The report shall identify the assertion being reported on and state the character of the engagement.
    c. The work shall be adequately planned and assistants, if any, shall be properly supervised.
    d. A sufficient understanding of internal control shall be obtained to plan the engagement.

N92#5. Which of the following accounting services may an accountant perform **without** being required to issue a compilation or review report under the Statements on Standards for Accounting and Review Services?

I. Preparing a working trial balance.
II. Preparing standard monthly journal entries.
    a. I only.
    b. II only.
    c. Both I and II.
    d. Neither I nor II.

M92#60. An attestation engagement is one in which a CPA is engaged to
    a. Issue a written communication expressing a conclusion about the reliability of a written assertion that is the responsibility of another party.

b. Provide tax advice or prepare a tax return based on financial information the CPA has **not** audited or reviewed.
c. Testify as an expert witness in accounting, auditing, or tax matters, given certain stipulated facts.
d. Assemble prospective financial statements based on the assumptions of the entity's management without expressing any assurance.

N91#13. Statements on Standards for Accounting and Review Services establish standards and procedures for which of the following engagements?
a. Assisting in adjusting the books of account for a partnership.
b. Reviewing interim financial data required to be filed with the SEC.
c. Processing financial data for clients of other accounting firms.
d. Compiling an individual's personal financial statement to be used to obtain a mortgage.

N91#59. Which of the following statements is correct concerning both an engagement to compile and an engagement to review a nonpublic entity's financial statements?
a. The accountant does **not** contemplate obtaining an understanding of internal control.
b. The accountant must be independent in fact and appearance.
c. The accountant expresses **no** assurance on the financial statements.
d. The accountant should obtain a written management representation letter.

M91#51. Which of the following professional services would be considered an attest engagement?
a. A management consulting engagement to provide EDP advice to a client.
b. An engagement to report on compliance with statutory requirements.
c. An income tax engagement to prepare federal and state tax returns.
d. The compilation of financial statements from a client's accounting records.

B. Assess Engagement Risk and the CPA Firm's Ability to Perform the Engagement

R98#2. During the initial planning phase of an audit, a CPA most likely would
a. Identify specific internal control activities that are likely to prevent fraud.
b. Evaluate the reasonableness of the client's accounting estimates.
c. Discuss the timing of the audit procedures with the client's management.
d. Inquire of the client's attorney as to whether any unrecorded claims are probable of assertion.

R97#1. Management's attitude toward aggressive financial reporting and its emphasis on meeting projected profit goals most likely would significantly influence an entity's control environment when
a. External policies established by parties outside the entity affect its accounting practices.
b. Management is dominated by one individual who is also a shareholder.
c. Internal auditors have direct access to the board of directors and the entity's management.
d. The audit committee is active in overseeing the entity's financial reporting policies.

N95#4. Which of the following auditor concerns most likely could be so serious that the auditor concludes that a financial statement audit **cannot** be conducted?
a. The entity has **no** formal written code of conduct.
b. The integrity of the entity's management is suspect.
c. Procedures requiring segregation of duties are subject to management override.
d. Management fails to modify prescribed controls for changes in conditions.

M95#5. The nature and extent of a CPA firm's quality control policies and procedures depend on

	The CPA firm's size	The nature of the CPA firm's practice	Cost-benefit considerations
a.	Yes	Yes	Yes
b.	Yes	Yes	No
c.	Yes	No	Yes
d.	No	Yes	Yes

M95#6. Would the following factors ordinarily be considered in planning an audit engagement's personnel requirements?

	Opportunities for on-the-job training	Continuity and periodic rotation of personnel
a.	Yes	Yes
b.	Yes	No
c.	No	Yes
d.	No	No

M95#7. The in-charge auditor most likely would have a supervisory responsibility to explain to the staff assistants
a. That immaterial irregularities are **not** to be reported to the client's audit committee.
b. How the results of various auditing procedures performed by the assistants should be evaluated.
c. What benefits may be attained by the assistants' adherence to established time budgets.
d. Why certain documents are being transferred from the current file to the permanent file.

M95#23. The third general standard states that due care is to be exercised in the performance of an audit. This standard is ordinarily interpreted to require

a. Thorough review of the existing safeguards over access to assets and records.
b. Limited review of the indications of employee fraud and illegal acts.
c. Objective review of the adequacy of the technical training and proficiency of firm personnel.
d. Critical review of the judgment exercised at every level of supervision.

N94#4. The senior auditor responsible for coordinating the field work usually schedules a pre-audit conference with the audit team primarily to
a. Give guidance to the staff regarding both technical and personnel aspects of the audit.
b. Discuss staff suggestions concerning the establishment and maintenance of time budgets.
c. Establish the need for using the work of specialists and internal auditors.
d. Provide an opportunity to document staff disagreements regarding technical issues.

N94#24. The primary purpose of establishing quality control policies and procedures for deciding whether to accept a new client is to
a. Enable the CPA firm to attest to the reliability of the client.
b. Satisfy the CPA firm's duty to the public concerning the acceptance of new clients.
c. Minimize the likelihood of association with clients whose management lacks integrity.
d. Anticipate before performing any field work whether an unqualified opinion can be expressed.

M94#3. The audit work performed by each assistant should be reviewed to determine whether it was adequately performed and to evaluate whether the
a. Auditor's system of quality control has been maintained at a high level.
b. Results are consistent with the conclusions to be presented in the auditor's report.
c. Audit procedures performed are approved in the professional standards.
d. Audit has been performed by persons having adequate technical training and proficiency as auditors.

N93#3. May a CPA hire for the CPA's public accounting firm a non-CPA systems analyst who specializes in developing computer systems?
a. Yes, provided the CPA is qualified to perform each of the specialist's tasks.
b. Yes, provided the CPA is able to supervise the specialist and evaluate the specialist's end product.
c. No, because non-CPA professionals are **not** permitted to be associated with CPA firms in public practice.
d. No, because developing computer systems is **not** recognized as a service performed by public accountants.

N93#4. The auditor with final responsibility for an engagement and one of the assistants have a difference of opinion about the results of an auditing procedure. If the assistant believes it is necessary to be disassociated from the matter's resolution, the CPA firm's procedures should enable the assistant to
a. Refer the disagreement to the AICPA's Quality Review Committee.
b. Document the details of the disagreement with the conclusion reached.
c. Discuss the disagreement with the entity's management or its audit committee.
d. Report the disagreement to an impartial peer review monitoring team.

N92#3. One of a CPA firm's basic objectives is to provide professional services that conform with professional standards. Reasonable assurance of achieving this basic objective is provided through
a. A system of quality control.
b. A system of peer review.
c. Continuing professional education.
d. Compliance with generally accepted reporting standards.

C. Communicate With the Predecessor Accountant/Auditor

R97#2. Before accepting an engagement to audit a new client, a CPA is required to obtain
a. An understanding of the prospective client's industry and business.
b. The prospective client's signature to the engagement letter.
c. A preliminary understanding of the prospective client's control environment.
d. The prospective client's consent to make inquiries of the predecessor auditor, if any.

R96#9. A successor auditor should request the new client to authorize the predecessor auditor to allow a review of the predecessor's

	Engagement letter	Working papers
a.	Yes	Yes
b.	Yes	No
c.	No	Yes
d.	No	No

M95#2. A successor auditor most likely would make specific inquiries of the predecessor auditor regarding
a. Specialized accounting principles of the client's industry.
b. The competency of the client's internal audit staff.
c. The uncertainty inherent in applying sampling procedures.
d. Disagreements with management as to auditing procedures.

M95#18. In auditing the financial statements of Star Corp., Land discovered information leading Land to

believe that Star's prior year's financial statements, which were audited by Tell, require substantial revisions. Under these circumstances, Land should
- a. Notify Star's audit committee and stockholders that the prior year's financial statements **cannot** be relied on.
- b. Request Star to reissue the prior year's financial statements with the appropriate revisions.
- c. Notify Tell about the information and make inquiries about the integrity of Star's management.
- d. Request Star to arrange a meeting among the three parties to resolve the matter.

N94#3. Hill, CPA, has been retained to audit the financial statements of Monday Co. Monday's predecessor auditor was Post, CPA, who has been notified by Monday that Post's services have been terminated. Under these circumstances, which party should initiate the communications between Hill and Post?
- a. Hill, the successor auditor.
- b. Post, the predecessor auditor.
- c. Monday's controller or CFO.
- d. The chairman of Monday's board of directors.

M94#1. Before accepting an audit engagement, a successor auditor should make specific inquiries of the predecessor auditor regarding the predecessor's
- a. Opinion of any subsequent events occurring since the predecessor's audit report was issued.
- b. Understanding as to the reasons for the change of auditors.
- c. Awareness of the consistency in the application of GAAP between periods.
- d. Evaluation of all matters of continuing accounting significance.

D. Decide Whether to Accept or Continue the Client and Engagement

R96#10. Which of the following factors most likely would cause a CPA **not** to accept a new audit engagement?
- a. The prospective client's unwillingness to permit inquiry of its legal counsel.
- b. The inability to review the predecessor auditor's working papers.
- c. The CPA's lack of understanding of the prospective client's operations and industry.
- d. The indications that management has **not** investigated employees in key positions before hiring them.

N94#2. Which of the following factors most likely would influence an auditor's determination of the auditability of an entity's financial statements?
- a. The complexity of the accounting system.
- b. The existence of related party transactions.
- c. The adequacy of the accounting records.
- d. The operating effectiveness of control activities.

M94#2. Which of the following factors most likely would cause an auditor **not** to accept a new audit engagement?
- a. An inadequate understanding of the entity's internal control.
- b. The close proximity to the end of the entity's fiscal year.
- c. Concluding that the entity's management probably lacks integrity.
- d. An inability to perform preliminary analytical procedures before assessing control risk.

E. Enter Into an Agreement With the Client as to the Terms of the Engagement

M95#3. Which of the following statements would **least** likely appear in an auditor's engagement letter?
- a. Fees for our services are based on our regular per diem rates, plus travel and other out-of-pocket expenses.
- b. During the course of our audit we may observe opportunities for economy in, or improved controls over, your operations.
- c. Our engagement is subject to the risk that material errors or irregularities, including fraud and defalcations, if they exist, will **not** be detected.
- d. After performing our preliminary analytical procedures we will discuss with you the other procedures we consider necessary to complete the engagement.

M94#12. Davis, CPA, accepted an engagement to audit the financial statements of Tech Resources, a nonpublic entity. Before the completion of the audit, Tech requested Davis to change the engagement to a compilation of financial statements. Before Davis agrees to change the engagement, Davis is required to consider the

	Additional audit effort necessary to complete the audit	Reason given for Tech's request
a.	No	No
b.	Yes	Yes
c.	Yes	No
d.	No	Yes

F. Obtain an Understanding of the Client's Operations, Business, and Industry

N94#6. To obtain an understanding of a continuing client's business in planning an audit, an auditor most likely would
- a. Perform tests of details of transactions and balances.
- b. Review prior-year working papers and the permanent file for the client.
- c. Read specialized industry journals.
- d. Reevaluate the client's internal control environment.

N94#7. In planning an audit of a new client, an auditor most likely would consider the methods used to process accounting information because such methods

a. Influence the design of internal control.
b. Affect the auditor's preliminary judgment about materiality levels.
c. Assist in evaluating the planned audit objectives.
d. Determine the auditor's acceptable level of audit risk.

M94#4. An auditor obtains knowledge about a new client's business and its industry to
a. Make constructive suggestions concerning improvements to the client's internal control.
b. Develop an attitude of professional skepticism concerning management's financial statement assertions.
c. Evaluate whether the aggregation of known misstatements causes the financial statements taken as a whole to be materially misstated.
d. Understand the events and transactions that may have an effect on the client's financial statements.

M94#46. May an accountant accept an engagement to compile or review the financial statements of a not-for-profit entity if the accountant is unfamiliar with the specialized industry accounting principles, but plans to obtain the required level of knowledge before compiling or reviewing the financial statements?

	Compilation	Review
a.	No	No
b.	Yes	No
c.	No	Yes
d.	Yes	Yes

N92#44. When compiling the financial statements of a nonpublic entity, an accountant should
a. Review agreements with financial institutions for restrictions on cash balances.
b. Understand the accounting principles and practices of the entity's industry.
c. Inquire of key personnel concerning related parties and subsequent events.
d. Perform ratio analyses of the financial data of comparable prior periods.

G. Perform Analytical Procedures

R97#3. Which of the following nonfinancial information would an auditor most likely consider in performing analytical procedures during the planning phase of an audit?
a. Turnover of personnel in the accounting department.
b. Objectivity of audit committee members.
c. Square footage of selling space.
d. Management's plans to repurchase stock.

M95#4. Which of the following procedures would an auditor most likely perform in planning a financial statement audit?

a. Inquiring of the client's legal counsel concerning pending litigation.
b. Comparing the financial statements to anticipated results.
c. Examining computer generated exception reports to verify the effectiveness of internal controls.
d. Searching for unauthorized transactions that may aid in detecting unrecorded liabilities.

M95#8. Analytical procedures used in planning an audit should focus on
a. Reducing the scope of tests of controls and substantive tests.
b. Providing assurance that potential material misstatements will be identified.
c. Enhancing the auditor's understanding of the client's business.
d. Assessing the adequacy of the available evidential matter.

M94#5. The objective of performing analytical procedures in planning an audit is to identify the existence of
a. Unusual transactions and events.
b. Illegal acts that went undetected because of internal control weaknesses.
c. Related party transactions.
d. Recorded transactions that were **not** properly authorized.

M93#30. Which of the following statements is correct concerning analytical procedures?
a. Analytical procedures usually involve comparisons of ratios developed from recorded amounts to assertions developed by management.
b. Analytical procedures used in planning an audit generally use data aggregated at a high level.
c. Analytical procedures can replace tests of controls in gathering evidence to support the assessed level of control risk.
d. Analytical procedures are more efficient, but **not** more effective, than tests of details and transactions.

N91#3. Which of the following procedures would an auditor most likely perform in planning a financial statement audit?
a. Reviewing investment transactions of the audit period to determine whether related parties were created.
b. Performing analytical procedures to identify areas that may represent specific risks.
c. Reading the minutes of stockholder and director meetings to discover whether any unusual transactions have occurred.
d. Obtaining a written representation letter from the client to emphasize management's responsibilities.

H. Consider Preliminary Engagement Materiality

R97#10. Which of the following would an auditor most likely use in determining the auditor's preliminary judgment about materiality?

a. The results of the initial assessment of control risk.
  b. The anticipated sample size for planned substantive tests.
  c. The entity's financial statements of the prior year.
  d. The assertions that are embodied in the financial statements.

R97#11. Holding other planning considerations equal, a decrease in the amount of misstatements in a class of transactions that an auditor could tolerate most likely would cause the auditor to
  a. Apply the planned substantive tests prior to the balance sheet date.
  b. Perform the planned auditing procedures closer to the balance sheet date.
  c. Increase the assessed level of control risk for relevant financial statement assertions.
  d. Decrease the extent of auditing procedures to be applied to the class of transactions.

M95#11. Which of the following would an auditor most likely use in determining the auditor's preliminary judgment about materiality?
  a. The anticipated sample size of the planned substantive tests.
  b. The entity's annualized interim financial statements.
  c. The results of the internal control questionnaire.
  d. The contents of the management representation letter.

N94#11. Which of the following statements is **not** correct about materiality?
  a. The concept of materiality recognizes that some matters are important for fair presentation of financial statements in conformity with GAAP, while other matters are **not** important.
  b. An auditor considers materiality for planning purposes in terms of the largest aggregate level of misstatements that could be material to any one of the financial statements.
  c. Materiality judgments are made in light of surrounding circumstances and necessarily involve both quantitative and qualitative judgments.
  d. An auditor's consideration of materiality is influenced by the auditor's perception of the needs of a reasonable person who will rely on the financial statements.

N93#6. In considering materiality for planning purposes, an auditor believes that misstatements aggregating $10,000 would have a material effect on an entity's income statement, but that misstatements would have to aggregate $20,000 to materially affect the balance sheet. Ordinarily, it would be appropriate to design auditing procedures that would be expected to detect misstatements that aggregate

  a. $10,000
  b. $15,000
  c. $20,000
  d. $30,000

N92#42. The concept of materiality for financial statements audited under the Single Audit Act of 1984 differs from materiality in an audit in accordance with generally accepted auditing standards. Under the Act, materiality is
  a. Determined by the federal agency requiring the audit.
  b. Ignored, because all account balances, regardless of size, are fully tested.
  c. Determined separately for each major federal financial assistance program.
  d. Calculated without consideration of the auditor's risk assessment.

M91#52. The concept of materiality would be **least** important to an auditor when considering the
  a. Adequacy of disclosure of a client's illegal act.
  b. Discovery of weaknesses in a client's internal control.
  c. Effects of a direct financial interest in the client on the CPA's independence.
  d. Decision whether to use positive or negative confirmations of accounts receivable.

I. Assess Inherent Risk and Risk of Misstatements

R97#12. Which of the following characteristics most likely would heighten an auditor's concern about the risk of material misstatements in an entity's financial statements?
  a. The entity's industry is experiencing declining customer demand.
  b. Employees who handle cash receipts are **not** bonded.
  c. Bank reconciliations usually include in-transit deposits.
  d. Equipment is often sold at a loss before being fully depreciated.

R97#13. Which of the following information discovered during an audit most likely would raise a question concerning possible illegal acts?
  a. Related party transactions, although properly disclosed, were pervasive during the year.
  b. The entity prepared several large checks payable to cash during the year.
  c. Material internal control weaknesses previously reported to management were **not** corrected.
  d. The entity was a campaign contributor to several local political candidates during the year.

N95#17. The diagram below depicts an auditor's estimated maximum deviation rate compared with the tolerable rate, and also depicts the true population deviation rate compared with the tolerable rate.

Selected Questions

Auditor's estimate based on sample results	True state of population	
	Deviation rate is less than tolerable rate	Deviation rate exceeds tolerable rate
Maximum deviation rate is less than tolerable rate	I.	III.
Maximum deviation rate exceeds tolerable rate	II.	IV.

As a result of tests of controls, the auditor assesses control risk too low and thereby decreases substantive testing. This is illustrated by situation
- a. I.
- b. II.
- c. III.
- d. IV.

M95#9. Which of the following relatively small misstatements most likely could have a material effect on an entity's financial statements?
- a. An illegal payment to a foreign official that was **not** recorded.
- b. A piece of obsolete office equipment that was **not** retired.
- c. A petty cash fund disbursement that was **not** properly authorized.
- d. An uncollectible account receivable that was **not** written off.

M95#10. Which of the following audit risk components may be assessed in nonquantitative terms?

	Control risk	Detection risk	Inherent risk
a.	Yes	Yes	No
b.	Yes	No	Yes
c.	Yes	Yes	Yes
d.	No	Yes	Yes

M95#12. As the acceptable level of detection risk decreases, an auditor may
- a. Reduce substantive testing by relying on the assessments of inherent risk and control risk.
- b. Postpone the planned timing of substantive tests from interim dates to the year-end.
- c. Eliminate the assessed level of inherent risk from consideration as a planning factor.
- d. Lower the assessed level of control risk from the maximum level to below the maximum.

M95#13. An auditor concludes that a client's illegal act, which has a material effect on the financial statements, has not been properly accounted for or disclosed. Depending on the materiality of the effect on the financial statements, the auditor should express either a(an)

- a. Adverse opinion or a disclaimer of opinion.
- b. Qualified opinion or an adverse opinion.
- c. Disclaimer of opinion or an unqualified opinion with a separate explanatory paragraph.
- d. Unqualified opinion with a separate explanatory paragraph or a qualified opinion.

M95#14. Which of the following characteristics most likely would heighten an auditor's concern about the risk of intentional manipulation of financial statements?
- a. Turnover of senior accounting personnel is low.
- b. Insiders recently purchased additional shares of the entity's stock.
- c. Management places substantial emphasis on meeting earnings projections.
- d. The rate of change in the entity's industry is slow.

N94#8. Inherent risk and control risk differ from detection risk in that they
- a. Arise from the misapplication of auditing procedures.
- b. May be assessed in either quantitative or nonquantitative terms.
- c. Exist independently of the financial statement audit.
- d. Can be changed at the auditor's discretion.

N94#9. The existence of audit risk is recognized by the statement in the auditor's standard report that the
- a. Auditor is responsible for expressing an opinion on the financial statements, which are the responsibility of management.
- b. Financial statements are presented fairly, in all material respects, in conformity with GAAP.
- c. Audit includes examining, on a test basis, evidence supporting the amounts and disclosures in the financial statements.
- d. Auditor obtains reasonable assurance about whether the financial statements are free of material misstatement.

N94#10. On the basis of audit evidence gathered and evaluated, an auditor decides to increase the assessed level of control risk from that originally planned. To achieve an overall audit risk level that is substantially the same as the planned audit risk level, the auditor would
- a. Decrease substantive testing.
- b. Decrease detection risk.
- c. Increase inherent risk.
- d. Increase materiality levels.

N94#12. During the annual audit of Ajax Corp., a publicly held company, Jones, CPA, a continuing auditor, determined that illegal political contributions had been made during each of the past seven years, including the year under audit. Jones notified the board of directors about the illegal contributions, but they refused to take any action because the amounts involved were immaterial to the financial statements.

Jones should reconsider the intended degree of reliance to be placed on the

a. Letter of audit inquiry to the client's attorney.
   b. Prior years' audit programs.
   c. Management representation letter.
   d. Preliminary judgment about materiality levels.

N94#13. Which of the following circumstances most likely would cause an auditor to consider whether material misstatements exist in an entity's financial statements?
   a. Management places little emphasis on meeting earnings projections.
   b. The board of directors makes all major financing decisions.
   c. Reportable conditions previously communicated to management are **not** corrected.
   d. Transactions selected for testing are **not** supported by proper documentation.

M94#6. Jones, CPA, is auditing the financial statements of XYZ Retailing, Inc. What assurance does Jones provide that direct effect illegal acts that are material to XYZ's financial statements, and illegal acts that have a material, but indirect effect on the financial statements will be detected?

	Direct effect illegal acts	Indirect effect illegal acts
a.	Reasonable	None
b.	Reasonable	Reasonable
c.	Limited	None
d.	Limited	Reasonable

M94#7. An auditor concludes that a client has committed an illegal act that has not been properly accounted for or disclosed. The auditor should withdraw from the engagement if the
   a. Auditor is precluded from obtaining sufficient competent evidence about the illegal act.
   b. Illegal act has an effect on the financial statements that is both material and direct.
   c. Auditor **cannot** reasonably estimate the effect of the illegal act on the financial statements.
   d. Client refuses to accept the auditor's report as modified for the illegal act.

N93#11. An auditor who discovers that client employees have committed an illegal act that has a material effect on the client's financial statements most likely would withdraw from the engagement if
   a. The illegal act is a violation of generally accepted accounting principles.
   b. The client does **not** take the remedial action that the auditor considers necessary.
   c. The illegal act was committed during a prior year that was **not** audited.
   d. The auditor has already assessed control risk at the maximum level.

N93#15. Which of the following circumstances most likely would cause an auditor to believe that material misstatements may exist in an entity's financial statements?
   a. Accounts receivable confirmation requests yield significantly fewer responses than expected.
   b. Audit trails of computer-generated transactions exist only for a short time.
   c. The chief financial officer does **not** sign the management representation letter until the last day of the auditor's field work.
   d. Management consults with other accountants about significant accounting matters.

N92#4. When an auditor becomes aware of a possible illegal act by a client, the auditor should obtain an understanding of the nature of the act to
   a. Evaluate the effect on the financial statements.
   b. Determine the reliability of management's representations.
   c. Consider whether other similar acts may have occurred.
   d. Recommend remedial actions to the audit committee.

N92#10. As the acceptable level of detection risk increases, an auditor may change the
   a. Assessed level of control risk from below the maximum to the maximum level.
   b. Assurance provided by tests of controls by using a larger sample size than planned.
   c. Timing of substantive tests from year end to an interim date.
   d. Nature of substantive tests from a less effective to a more effective procedure.

N92#56. Hill, CPA, is auditing the financial statements of Helping Hand, a not-for-profit organization that receives financial assistance from governmental agencies. To detect misstatements in Helping Hand's financial statements resulting from violations of laws and regulations, Hill should focus on violations that
   a. Could result in criminal prosecution against the organization.
   b. Involve reportable conditions to be communicated to the organization's trustees and the funding agencies.
   c. Have a direct and material effect on the amounts in the organization's financial statements.
   d. Demonstrate the existence of material weaknesses in the organization's internal control.

M92#57. Inherent risk and control risk differ from detection risk in that inherent risk and control risk are
   a. Elements of audit risk while detection risk is **not**.
   b. Changed at the auditor's discretion while detection risk is **not**.
   c. Considered at the individual account-balance level while detection risk is **not**.
   d. Functions of the client and its environment while detection risk is **not**.

N91#7. The risk that an auditor will conclude, based on substantive tests, that a material error does **not** exist

in an account balance when, in fact, such error does exist is referred to as
- a. Sampling risk.
- b. Detection risk.
- c. Nonsampling risk.
- d. Inherent risk.

N91#12. Which of the following circumstances most likely would cause an auditor to consider whether material misstatements exist in an entity's financial statements?
- a. Supporting records that should be readily available are frequently **not** produced when requested.
- b. Reportable conditions previously communicated have **not** been corrected.
- c. Clerical errors are listed on a monthly computer-generated exception report.
- d. Differences are discovered during the client's annual physical inventory count.

M91#26. The acceptable level of detection risk is inversely related to the
- a. Assurance provided by substantive tests.
- b. Risk of misapplying auditing procedures.
- c. Preliminary judgment about materiality levels.
- d. Risk of failing to discover material misstatements.

J. Consider Internal Control

R98#3. An entity has the following invoices in a batch:

Invoice #	Product	Quantity	Unit price
201	F10	150	$ 5.00
202	G15	200	$10.00
203	H20	250	$25.00
204	K35	300	$30.00

Which of the following numbers represents the record count?
- a. 1
- a. 4
- c. 810
- d. 900

R98#4. An entity has the following invoices in a batch:

Invoice #	Product	Quantity	Unit price
201	F10	150	$ 5.00
202	G15	200	$10.00
203	H20	250	$25.00
204	K35	300	$30.00

Which of the following most likely represents a hash total?
- a. FGHK80
- b. 4
- c. 204
- d. 810

R98#5. A customer intended to order 100 units of product Z96014, but incorrectly ordered nonexistent product Z96015. Which of the following controls most likely would detect this error?
- a. Check digit verification.
- b. Record count.
- c. Hash total.
- d. Redundant data check.

R98#6. A client is concerned that a power outage or disaster could impair the computer hardware's ability to function as designed. The client desires off-site backup hardware facilities that are fully configured and ready to operate within several hours. The client most likely should consider a
- a. Cold site.
- b. Cool site.
- c. Warm site.
- d. Hot site.

R98#7. Which of the following is considered a component of a local area network?
- a. Program flowchart.
- b. Loop verification.
- c. Transmission media.
- d. Input routine.

R98#8. Which of the following input controls is a numeric value computed to provide assurance that the original value has **not** been altered in construction or transmission?
- a. Hash total.
- b. Parity check.
- c. Encryption.
- d. Check digit.

R98#9. Which of the following represents an additional cost of transmitting business transactions by means of electronic data interchange (EDI) rather than in a traditional paper environment?
- a. Redundant data checks are needed to verify that individual EDI transactions are **not** recorded twice.
- b. Internal audit work is needed because the potential for random data entry errors is increased.
- c. Translation software is needed to convert transactions from the entity's internal format to a standard EDI format.
- d. More supervisory personnel are needed because the amount of data entry is greater in an EDI system.

R98#10. Many entities use the Internet as a network to transmit electronic data interchange (EDI) transactions. An advantage of using the Internet for electronic commerce rather than a traditional value-added network (VAN) is that the Internet
- a. Permits EDI transactions to be sent to trading partners as transactions occur.
- b. Automatically batches EDI transactions to multiple trading partners.

c. Possesses superior characteristics regarding disaster recovery.
d. Converts EDI transactions to a standard format without translation software.

R97#4. Which of the following procedures most likely would provide an auditor with evidence about whether an entity's internal control activities are suitably designed to prevent or detect material misstatements?
a. Reperforming the activities for a sample of transactions.
b. Performing analytical procedures using data aggregated at a high level.
c. Vouching a sample of transactions directly related to the activities.
d. Observing the entity's personnel applying the activities.

R97#14. Which of the following fraudulent activities most likely could be perpetrated due to the lack of effective internal controls in the revenue cycle?
a. Fictitious transactions may be recorded that cause an understatement of revenues and an overstatement of receivables.
b. Claims received from customers for goods returned may be intentionally recorded in other customers' accounts.
c. Authorization of credit memos by personnel who receive cash may permit the misappropriation of cash.
d. The failure to prepare shipping documents may cause an overstatement of inventory balances.

R96#2. Which of the following procedures concerning accounts receivable would an auditor most likely perform to obtain evidential matter in support of an assessed level of control risk below the maximum level?
a. Observing an entity's employee prepare the schedule of past due accounts receivable.
b. Sending confirmation requests to an entity's principal customers to verify the existence of accounts receivable.
c. Inspecting an entity's analysis of accounts receivable for unusual balances.
d. Comparing an entity's uncollectible accounts expense to actual uncollectible accounts receivable.

N95#2. In planning an audit, the auditor's knowledge about the design of relevant internal control activities should be used to
a. Identify the types of potential misstatements that could occur.
b. Assess the operational efficiency of internal control.
c. Determine whether controls have been circumvented by collusion.
d. Document the assessed level of control risk.

N95#3. Able Co. uses an online sales order processing system to process its sales transactions. Able's sales data are electronically sorted and subjected to edit checks. A direct output of the edit checks most likely would be a
a. Report of all missing sales invoices.
b. File of all rejected sales transactions.
c. Printout of all user code numbers and passwords.
d. List of all voided shipping documents.

N95#5. Management philosophy and operating style most likely would have a significant influence on an entity's control environment when
a. The internal auditor reports directly to management.
b. Management is dominated by one individual.
c. Accurate management job descriptions delineate specific duties.
d. The audit committee actively oversees the financial reporting process.

N95#6. Which of the following is a management control method that most likely could improve management's ability to supervise company activities effectively?
a. Monitoring compliance with internal control requirements imposed by regulatory bodies.
b. Limiting direct access to assets by physical segregation and protective devices.
c. Establishing budgets and forecasts to identify variances from expectations.
d. Supporting employees with the resources necessary to discharge their responsibilities.

N95
Items 7 and 8 are based on the following flowchart of a client's revenue cycle:

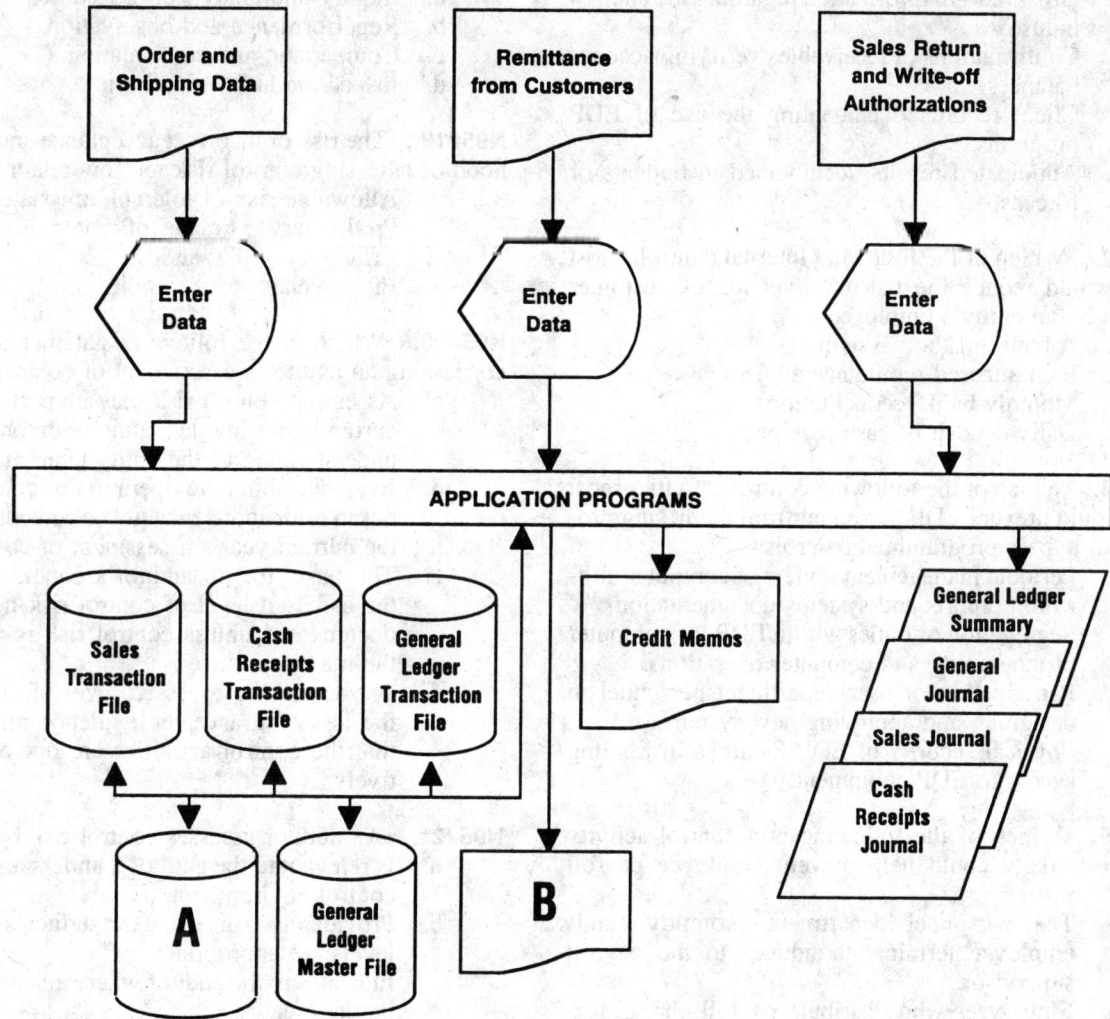

7. Symbol A most likely represents
   a. Remittance advice file.
   b. Receiving report file.
   c. Accounts receivable master file.
   d. Cash disbursements transaction file.

8. Symbol B most likely represents
   a. Customer orders.
   b. Receiving reports.
   c. Customer checks.
   d. Sales invoices.

N95#9. In an audit of financial statements in accordance with generally accepted auditing standards, an auditor is required to
   a. Document the auditor's understanding of the entity's internal control.
   b. Search for significant deficiencies in the operation of internal control.
   c. Perform tests of controls to evaluate the effectiveness of the entity's accounting system.
   d. Determine whether control activities are suitably designed to prevent or detect material misstatements.

N95#10. Which of the following is an example of a validity check?

   a. The computer ensures that a numerical amount in a record does **not** exceed some predetermined amount.
   b. As the computer corrects errors and data are successfully resubmitted to the system, the causes of the errors are printed out.
   c. The computer flags any transmission for which the control field value did **not** match that of an existing file record.
   d. After data for a transaction are entered, the computer sends certain data back to the terminal for comparison with data originally sent.

N95#11. Which of the following types of evidence would an auditor most likely examine to determine

whether internal control activities are operating as designed?
   a. Gross margin information regarding the client's industry.
   b. Confirmations of receivables verifying account balances.
   c. Client records documenting the use of EDP programs.
   d. Anticipated results documented in budgets or forecasts.

N95#12. Which of the following internal controls most likely would reduce the risk of diversion of customer receipts by an entity's employees?
   a. A bank lockbox system.
   b. Prenumbered remittance advices.
   c. Monthly bank reconciliations.
   d. Daily deposit of cash receipts.

N95#14. Which of the following control activities most likely could prevent EDP personnel from modifying programs to bypass programmed controls?
   a. Periodic management review of computer utilization reports and systems documentation.
   b. Segregation of duties within EDP for computer programming and computer operations.
   c. Participation of user department personnel in designing and approving new systems.
   d. Physical security of EDP facilities in limiting access to EDP equipment.

N95#15. Which of the following is a control activity that most likely could help prevent employee payroll fraud?
   a. The personnel department promptly sends employee termination notices to the payroll supervisor.
   b. Employees who distribute payroll checks forward unclaimed payroll checks to the absent employees' supervisors.
   c. Salary rates resulting from new hires are approved by the payroll supervisor.
   d. Total hours used for determination of gross pay are calculated by the payroll supervisor.

N95#16. Which of the following controls would a company most likely use to safeguard marketable securities when an independent trust agent is **not** employed?
   a. The investment committee of the board of directors periodically reviews the investment decisions delegated to the treasurer.
   b. Two company officials have joint control of marketable securities, which are kept in a bank safe-deposit box.
   c. The internal auditor and the controller independently trace all purchases and sales of marketable securities from the subsidiary ledgers to the general ledger.
   d. The chairman of the board verifies the marketable securities, which are kept in a bank safe-deposit box, each year on the balance sheet date.

N95#18. In assessing control risk, an auditor ordinarily selects from a variety of techniques, including
   a. Inquiry and analytical procedures.
   b. Reperformance and observation.
   c. Comparison and confirmation.
   d. Inspection and verification.

N95#19. The risk of incorrect acceptance and the likelihood of assessing control risk too low relate to the
   a. Allowable risk of tolerable misstatement.
   b. Preliminary estimates of materiality levels.
   c. Efficiency of the audit.
   d. Effectiveness of the audit.

N95#20. Which of the following statements is correct concerning an auditor's assessment of control risk?
   a. Assessing control risk may be performed concurrently during an audit with obtaining an understanding of the entity's internal control.
   b. Evidence about the operation of control activities in prior audits may **not** be considered during the current year's assessment of control risk.
   c. The basis for an auditor's conclusions about the assessed level of control risk need **not** be documented unless control risk is assessed at the maximum level.
   d. The lower the assessed level of control risk, the less assurance the evidence must provide that the control activities are operating effectively.

N95#21. An auditor assesses control risk because it
   a. Is relevant to the auditor's understanding of the control environment.
   b. Provides assurance that the auditor's materiality levels are appropriate.
   c. Indicates to the auditor where inherent risk may be the greatest.
   d. Affects the level of detection risk that the auditor may accept.

N95#22. Assessing control risk at below the maximum level most likely would involve
   a. Performing more extensive substantive tests with larger sample sizes than originally planned.
   b. Reducing inherent risk for most of the assertions relevant to significant account balances.
   c. Changing the timing of substantive tests by omitting interim-date testing and performing the tests at year end.
   d. Identifying specific internal control activities relevant to specific assertions.

N95#23. After assessing control risk at below the maximum level, an auditor desires to seek a further reduction in the assessed level of control risk. At this time, the auditor would consider whether
   a. It would be efficient to obtain an understanding of the entity's accounting system.
   b. The entity's internal control activities have been placed in operation.

c. The entity's internal control activities pertain to any financial statement assertions.
d. Additional evidential matter sufficient to support a further reduction is likely to be available.

N95#24. When assessing control risk below the maximum level, an auditor is required to document the auditor's

	Understanding of the entity's control environment	Basis for concluding that control risk is below the maximum level
a.	Yes	No
b.	No	Yes
c.	Yes	Yes
d.	No	No

N95#25. An auditor who uses statistical sampling for attributes in testing internal controls should reduce the planned reliance on a prescribed control when the
a. Sample rate of deviation plus the allowance for sampling risk equals the tolerable rate.
b. Sample rate of deviation is less than the expected rate of deviation used in planning the sample.
c. Tolerable rate less the allowance for sampling risk exceeds the sample rate of deviation.
d. Sample rate of deviation plus the allowance for sampling risk exceeds the tolerable rate.

N95#26. In addition to evaluating the frequency of deviations in tests of controls, an auditor should also consider certain qualitative aspects of the deviations. The auditor most likely would give broader consideration to the implications of a deviation if it was
a. The only deviation discovered in the sample.
b. Identical to a deviation discovered during the prior year's audit.
c. Caused by an employee's misunderstanding of instructions.
d. Initially concealed by a forged document.

N95#30. For effective internal control, the accounts payable department generally should
a. Stamp, perforate, or otherwise cancel supporting documentation after payment is mailed.
b. Ascertain that each requisition is approved as to price, quantity, and quality by an authorized employee.
c. Obliterate the quantity ordered on the receiving department copy of the purchase order.
d. Establish the agreement of the vendor's invoice with the receiving report and purchase order.

N95#32. In obtaining an understanding of a manufacturing entity's internal control concerning inventory balances, an auditor most likely would
a. Analyze the liquidity and turnover ratios of the inventory.
b. Perform analytical procedures designed to identify cost variances.
c. Review the entity's descriptions of inventory activities.
d. Perform test counts of inventory during the entity's physical count.

M95#24. The primary objective of procedures performed to obtain an understanding of internal control is to provide an auditor with
a. Knowledge necessary for audit planning.
b. Evidential matter to use in assessing inherent risk.
c. A basis for modifying tests of controls.
d. An evaluation of the consistency of application of management's policies.

M95#25. The overall attitude and awareness of an entity's board of directors concerning the importance of internal control usually is reflected in its
a. Computer-based controls.
b. System of segregation of duties.
c. Control environment.
d. Safeguards over access to assets.

M95#27. Control risk should be assessed in terms of
a. Specific control activities.
b. Types of potential fraud.
c. Financial statement assertions.
d. Control environment factors.

M95#28. As a result of tests of controls, an auditor assessed control risk too low and decreased substantive testing. This assessment occurred because the true deviation rate in the population was
a. Less than the risk of assessing control risk too low, based on the auditor's sample.
b. Less than the deviation rate in the auditor's sample.
c. More than the risk of assessing control risk too low, based on the auditor's sample.
d. More than the deviation rate in the auditor's sample.

M95#30. Sound internal control dictates that immediately upon receiving checks from customers by mail, a responsible employee should
a. Add the checks to the daily cash summary.
b. Verify that each check is supported by a prenumbered sales invoice.
c. Prepare a duplicate listing of checks received.
d. Record the checks in the cash receipts journal.

M95#33. After obtaining an understanding of internal control and assessing control risk, an auditor decided to perform tests of controls. The auditor most likely decided that
a. It would be efficient to perform tests of controls that would result in a reduction in planned substantive tests.
b. Additional evidence to support a further reduction in control risk is **not** available.

c. An increase in the assessed level of control risk is justified for certain financial statement assertions.
d. There were many internal control weaknesses that could allow errors to enter the accounting system.

N94#27. Which of the following statements is correct concerning statistical sampling in tests of controls?
a. As the population size increases, the sample size should increase proportionately.
b. Deviations from specific internal control activities at a given rate ordinarily result in misstatements at a lower rate.
c. There is an inverse relationship between the expected population deviation rate and the sample size.
d. In determining tolerable rate, an auditor considers detection risk and the sample size.

N94#28. In an audit of financial statements, an auditor's primary consideration regarding an internal control activity is whether the activity
a. Reflects management's philosophy and operating style.
b. Affects management's financial statement assertions.
c. Provides adequate safeguards over access to assets.
d. Enhances management's decision-making processes.

N94#30. The ultimate purpose of assessing control risk is to contribute to the auditor's evaluation of the risk that
a. Tests of controls may fail to identify activities relevant to assertions.
b. Material misstatements may exist in the financial statements.
c. Specified controls requiring segregation of duties may be circumvented by collusion.
d. Entity activities may be overridden by senior management.

N94#32. Which of the following is a step in an auditor's decision to assess control risk at below the maximum?
a. Apply analytical procedures to both financial data and nonfinancial information to detect conditions that may indicate weak controls.
b. Perform tests of details of transactions and account balances to identify potential errors and fraud.
c. Identify specific internal control activities that are likely to detect or prevent material misstatements.
d. Document that the additional audit effort to perform tests of controls exceeds the potential reduction in substantive testing.

N94#33. The likelihood of assessing control risk too high is the risk that the sample selected to test controls
a. Does **not** support the auditor's planned assessed level of control risk when the true operating effectiveness of internal control justifies such an assessment.
b. Contains misstatements that could be material to the financial statements when aggregated with misstatements in other account balances or transactions classes.
c. Contains proportionately fewer monetary errors or deviations from prescribed internal control activities than exist in the balance or class as a whole.
d. Does **not** support the tolerable error for some or all of management's assertions.

N94#34. Upon receipt of customers' checks in the mailroom, a responsible employee should prepare a remittance listing that is forwarded to the cashier. A copy of the listing should be sent to the
a. Internal auditor to investigate the listing for unusual transactions.
b. Treasurer to compare the listing with the monthly bank statement.
c. Accounts receivable bookkeeper to update the subsidiary accounts receivable records.
d. Entity's bank to compare the listing with the cashier's deposit slip.

N94#35. Proper authorization of write-offs of uncollectible accounts should be approved in which of the following departments?
a. Accounts receivable.
b. Credit.
c. Accounts payable.
d. Treasurer.

N94#37. Misstatements in a batch computer system caused by incorrect programs or data may **not** be detected immediately because
a. Errors in some transactions may cause rejection of other transactions in the batch.
b. The identification of errors in input data typically is **not** part of the program.
c. There are time delays in processing transactions in a batch system.
d. The processing of transactions in a batch system is **not** uniform.

N94#38. Which of the following controls is a processing control designed to ensure the reliability and accuracy of data processing?

	Limit test	Validity check test
a.	Yes	Yes
b.	No	No
c.	No	Yes
d.	Yes	No

N94#39. In assessing control risk for purchases, an auditor vouches a sample of entries in the voucher register to the supporting documents. Which assertion would this test of controls most likely support?

a. Completeness.
b. Existence or occurrence.
c. Valuation or allocation.
d. Rights and obligations.

N94#40. Which of the following internal control activities is **not** usually performed in the vouchers payable department?
a. Matching the vendor's invoice with the related receiving report.
b. Approving vouchers for payment by having an authorized employee sign the vouchers.
c. Indicating the asset and expense accounts to be debited.
d. Accounting for unused prenumbered purchase orders and receiving reports.

N94#41. Which of the following questions would an auditor **least** likely include on an internal control questionnaire concerning the initiation and execution of equipment transactions?
a. Are requests for major repairs approved at a higher level than the department initiating the request?
b. Are prenumbered purchase orders used for equipment and periodically accounted for?
c. Are requests for purchases of equipment reviewed for consideration of soliciting competitive bids?
d. Are activities in place to monitor and properly restrict access to equipment?

N94#42. The objective of tests of details of transactions performed as tests of controls is to
a. Monitor the design and use of entity documents such as prenumbered shipping forms.
b. Determine whether internal control activities have been placed in operation.
c. Detect material misstatements in the account balances of the financial statements.
d. Evaluate whether internal control activities operated effectively.

N94#43. Which of the following tests of controls most likely would help assure an auditor that goods shipped are properly billed?
a. Scan the sales journal for sequential and unusual entries.
b. Examine shipping documents for matching sales invoices.
c. Compare the accounts receivable ledger to daily sales summaries.
d. Inspect unused sales invoices for consecutive prenumbering.

N94#70. Which of the following computer-assisted auditing techniques allows fictitious and real transactions to be processed together without client operating personnel being aware of the testing process?
a. Integrated test facility.
b. Input controls matrix.
c. Parallel simulation.
d. Data entry monitor.

M94#16. Which of the following statements most likely represents a disadvantage for an entity that keeps microcomputer-prepared data files rather than manually prepared files?
a. Attention is focused on the accuracy of the programming process rather than errors in individual transactions.
b. It is usually easier for unauthorized persons to access and alter the files.
c. Random error associated with processing similar transactions in different ways is usually greater.
d. It is usually more difficult to compare recorded accountability with physical count of assets.

M94#18. An auditor's flowchart of a client's accounting system is a diagrammatic representation that depicts the auditor's
a. Assessment of control risk.
b. Identification of weaknesses in the system.
c. Assessment of the control environment's effectiveness.
d. Understanding of the system.

M94#22. Which of the following most likely would **not** be considered an inherent limitation of the potential effectiveness of an entity's internal control?
a. Incompatible duties.
b. Management override.
c. Mistakes in judgment.
d. Collusion among employees.

M94#23. When an auditor increases the assessed level of control risk because certain control activities were determined to be ineffective, the auditor would most likely increase the
a. Extent of tests of controls.
b. Level of detection risk.
c. Extent of tests of details.
d. Level of inherent risk.

M94#25. After obtaining an understanding of internal control and assessing control risk, an auditor decided not to perform additional tests of controls. The auditor most likely concluded that the
a. Additional evidence to support a further reduction in control risk was **not** cost-beneficial to obtain.
b. Assessed level of inherent risk exceeded the assessed level of control risk.
c. Internal control was properly designed and justifiably may be relied on.
d. Evidence obtainable through tests of controls would **not** support an increased level of control risk.

M94#27. Which of the following audit procedures would an auditor most likely perform to test controls

relating to management's assertion concerning the completeness of sales transactions?
  a. Verify that extensions and footings on the entity's sales invoices and monthly customer statements have been recomputed.
  b. Inspect the entity's reports of prenumbered shipping documents that have **not** been recorded in the sales journal.
  c. Compare the invoiced prices on prenumbered sales invoices to the entity's authorized price list.
  d. Inquire about the entity's credit granting policies and the consistent application of credit checks.

M94#28. Which of the following internal control activities most likely would assure that all billed sales are correctly posted to the accounts receivable ledger?
  a. Daily sales summaries are compared to daily postings to the accounts receivable ledger.
  b. Each sales invoice is supported by a prenumbered shipping document.
  c. The accounts receivable ledger is reconciled daily to the control account in the general ledger.
  d. Each shipment on credit is supported by a prenumbered sales invoice.

M94#29. An auditor most likely would assess control risk at the maximum if the payroll department supervisor is responsible for
  a. Examining authorization forms for new employees.
  b. Comparing payroll registers with original batch transmittal data.
  c. Authorizing payroll rate changes for all employees.
  d. Hiring all subordinate payroll department employees.

M94#31. An auditor most likely would introduce test data into a computerized payroll system to test internal controls related to the
  a. Existence of unclaimed payroll checks held by supervisors.
  b. Early cashing of payroll checks by employees.
  c. Discovery of invalid employee I.D. numbers.
  d. Proper approval of overtime by supervisors.

M94#32. Which of the following internal control activities most likely would prevent direct labor hours from being charged to manufacturing overhead?
  a. Periodic independent counts of work in process for comparison to recorded amounts.
  b. Comparison of daily journal entries with approved production orders.
  c. Use of time tickets to record actual labor worked on production orders.
  d. Reconciliation of work-in-process inventory with periodic cost budgets.

M94#33. Which of the following internal control activities most likely would be used to maintain accurate inventory records?
  a. Perpetual inventory records are periodically compared with the current cost of individual inventory items.
  b. A just-in-time inventory ordering system keeps inventory levels to a desired minimum.
  c. Requisitions, receiving reports, and purchase orders are independently matched before payment is approved.
  d. Periodic inventory counts are used to adjust the perpetual inventory records.

M94#34. When an entity uses a trust company as custodian of its marketable securities, the possibility of concealing fraud most likely would be reduced if the
  a. Trust company has **no** direct contact with the entity employees responsible for maintaining investment accounting records.
  b. Securities are registered in the name of the trust company, rather than the entity itself.
  c. Interest and dividend checks are mailed directly to an entity employee who is authorized to sell securities.
  d. Trust company places the securities in a bank safe-deposit vault under the custodian's exclusive control.

M94#35. An auditor tests an entity's policy of obtaining credit approval before shipping goods to customers in support of management's financial statement assertion of
  a. Valuation or allocation.
  b. Completeness.
  c. Existence or occurrence.
  d. Rights and obligations.

M94#44. The sample size of a test of controls varies inversely with

	Expected population deviation rate	Tolerable rate
a.	Yes	Yes
b.	No	No
c.	Yes	No
d.	No	Yes

N93#16. An advantage of using systems flowcharts to document information about internal control instead of using internal control questionnaires is that systems flowcharts
  a. Identify internal control weaknesses more prominently.
  b. Provide a visual depiction of clients' activities.
  c. Indicate whether control activities are operating effectively.
  d. Reduce the need to observe clients' employees performing routine tasks.

N93#18. Which of the following statements is **not** true of the test data approach to testing an accounting system?

a. Test data are processed by the client's computer programs under the auditor's control.
b. The test data need consist of only those valid and invalid conditions that interest the auditor.
c. Only one transaction of each type need be tested.
d. The test data must consist of all possible valid and invalid conditions.

N93#20. As a result of sampling procedures applied as tests of controls, an auditor incorrectly assesses control risk lower than appropriate. The most likely explanation for this situation is that
a. The deviation rates of both the auditor's sample and the population exceed the tolerable rate.
b. The deviation rates of both the auditor's sample and the population is less than the tolerable rate.
c. The deviation rate in the auditor's sample is less than the tolerable rate, but the deviation rate in the population exceeds the tolerable rate.
d. The deviation rate in the auditor's sample exceeds the tolerable rate, but the deviation rate in the population is less than the tolerable rate.

N93#21. An auditor may decide to assess control risk at the maximum level for certain assertions because the auditor believes
a. Control activities are unlikely to pertain to the assertions.
b. The entity's control environment, accounting system, and control activities are interrelated.
c. Sufficient evidential matter to support the assertions is likely to be available.
d. More emphasis on tests of controls than substantive tests is warranted.

N93#22. Which of the following statements concerning control risk is correct?
a. Assessing control risk and obtaining an understanding of an entity's internal control may be performed concurrently.
b. When control risk is at the maximum level, an auditor is required to document the basis for that assessment.
c. Control risk may be assessed sufficiently low to eliminate substantive testing for significant transaction classes.
d. When assessing control risk an auditor should **not** consider evidence obtained in prior audits about the operation of control activities.

N93#23. Regardless of the assessed level of control risk, an auditor would perform some
a. Tests of controls to determine the effectiveness of internal control activities.
b. Analytical procedures to verify the design of internal control activities.
c. Substantive tests to restrict detection risk for significant transaction classes.
d. Dual-purpose tests to evaluate both the risk of monetary misstatement and preliminary control risk.

N93#27. Which of the following internal control activities is **not** usually performed in the treasurer's department?
a. Verifying the accuracy of checks and vouchers.
b. Controlling the mailing of checks to vendors.
c. Approving vendors' invoices for payment.
d. Canceling payment vouchers when paid.

N93#28. The objectives of internal control for a production cycle are to provide assurance that transactions are properly executed and recorded, and that
a. Production orders are prenumbered and signed by a supervisor.
b. Custody of work in process and of finished goods is properly maintained.
c. Independent internal verification of activity reports is established.
d. Transfers to finished goods are documented by a completed production report and a quality control report.

N93#30. The purpose of segregating the duties of hiring personnel and distributing payroll checks is to separate the
a. Human resources function from the controllership function.
b. Administrative controls from the internal accounting controls.
c. Authorization of transactions from the custody of related assets.
d. Operational responsibility from the record keeping responsibility.

N93#32. Which of the following questions would an auditor most likely include on an internal control questionnaire for notes payable?
a. Are assets that collateralize notes payable critically needed for the entity's continued existence?
b. Are two or more authorized signatures required on checks that repay notes payable?
c. Are the proceeds from notes payable used for the purchase of noncurrent assets?
d. Are direct borrowings on notes payable authorized by the board of directors?

N93#33. Which of the following internal control activities would an entity most likely use to assist in satisfying the completeness assertion related to long-term investments?
a. Senior management verifies that securities in the bank safe deposit box are registered in the entity's name.
b. The internal auditor compares the securities in the bank safe deposit box with recorded investments.
c. The treasurer vouches the acquisition of securities by comparing brokers' advices with canceled checks.
d. The controller compares the current market prices of recorded investments with the brokers' advices on file.

N93#34. Equipment acquisitions that are misclassified as maintenance expense most likely would be detected by an internal control activity that provides for
 a. Segregation of duties of employees in the accounts payable department.
 b. Independent verification of invoices for disbursements recorded as equipment acquisitions.
 c. Investigation of variances within a formal budgeting system.
 d. Authorization by the board of directors of significant equipment acquisitions.

M93#7. The ultimate purpose of assessing control risk is to contribute to the auditor's evaluation of the
 a. Factors that raise doubts about the auditability of the financial statements.
 b. Operating effectiveness of internal control activities.
 c. Risk that material misstatements exist in the financial statements.
 d. Possibility that the nature and extent of substantive tests may be reduced.

M93#8. Which of the following controls most likely would assure that an entity can reconstruct its financial records?
 a. Hardware controls are built into the computer by the computer manufacturer.
 b. Backup diskettes or tapes of files are stored away from originals.
 c. Personnel who are independent of data input perform parallel simulations.
 d. System flowcharts provide accurate descriptions of input and output operations.

M93#14. Which of the following internal control activities most likely would deter lapping of collections from customers?
 a. Independent internal verification of dates of entry in the cash receipts journal with dates of daily cash summaries.
 b. Authorization of write-offs of uncollectible accounts by a supervisor independent of credit approval.
 c. Segregation of duties between receiving cash and posting the accounts receivable ledger.
 d. Supervisory comparison of the daily cash summary with the sum of the cash receipts journal entries.

M93#15. Which of the following most likely would be the result of ineffective internal control activities in the revenue cycle?
 a. Final authorization of credit memos by personnel in the sales department could permit an employee defalcation scheme.
 b. Fictitious transactions could be recorded, causing an understatement of revenues and an overstatement of receivables.
 c. Fraud in recording transactions in the subsidiary accounts could result in a delay in goods shipped.
 d. Omission of shipping documents could go undetected, causing an understatement of inventory.

M93#16. Mill Co. uses a batch processing method to process its sales transactions. Data on Mill's sales transaction tape are electronically sorted by customer number and are subjected to programmed edit checks in preparing its invoices, sales journals, and updated customer account balances. One of the direct outputs of the creation of this tape most likely would be a
 a. Report showing exceptions and control totals.
 b. Printout of the updated inventory records.
 c. Report showing overdue accounts receivable.
 d. Printout of the sales price master file.

M93#17. The authority to accept incoming goods in receiving should be based on a(an)
 a. Vendor's invoice.
 b. Materials requisition.
 c. Bill of lading.
 d. Approved purchase order.

M93#18. Mailing disbursement checks and remittance advices should be controlled by the employee who
 a. Matches the receiving reports, purchase orders, and vendors' invoices.
 b. Signs the checks last.
 c. Prepares the daily voucher summary.
 d. Agrees the check register to the daily check summary.

M93#20. Sound internal control activities dictate that defective merchandise returned by customers should be presented initially to the
 a. Accounts receivable supervisor.
 b. Receiving clerk.
 c. Shipping department supervisor.
 d. Sales clerk.

M93#21. Which of the following internal control activities most likely would justify a reduced assessed level of control risk concerning plant and equipment acquisitions?
 a. Periodic physical inspection of plant and equipment by the internal audit staff.
 b. Comparison of current-year plant and equipment account balances with prior-year actual balances.
 c. The review of prenumbered purchase orders to detect unrecorded trade-ins.
 d. Approval of periodic depreciation entries by a supervisor independent of the accounting department.

M93#22. Which of the following activities most likely would give the greatest assurance that securities held as investments are safeguarded?

a. There is **no** access to securities between the year end and the date of the auditor's security count.
b. Proceeds from the sale of investments are received by an employee who does **not** have access to securities.
c. Investment acquisitions are authorized by a member of the Board of Directors before execution.
d. Access to securities requires the signatures and presence of two designated officials.

M93#25. In performing tests of controls over authorization of cash disbursements, which of the following statistical sampling methods would be most appropriate?
a. Variables.
b. Stratified.
c. Ratio.
d. Attributes.

M93#41. To obtain evidence that online access controls are properly functioning, an auditor most likely would
a. Create checkpoints at periodic intervals after live data processing to test for unauthorized use of the system.
b. Examine the transaction log to discover whether any transactions were lost or entered twice due to a system malfunction.
c. Enter invalid identification numbers or passwords to ascertain whether the system rejects them.
d. Vouch a random sample of processed transactions to assure proper authorization.

N92#12. An online sales order processing system most likely would have an advantage over a batch sales order processing system by
a. Detecting errors in the data entry process more easily by the use of edit programs.
b. Enabling shipment of customer orders to be initiated as soon as the orders are received.
c. Recording more secure backup copies of the data base on magnetic tape files.
d. Maintaining more accurate records of customer accounts and finished goods inventories.

N92#13. Which of the following controls most likely would help ensure that all credit sales transactions of an entity are recorded?
a. The billing department supervisor sends copies of approved sales orders to the credit department for comparison to authorized credit limits and current customer account balances.
b. The accounting department supervisor independently reconciles the accounts receivable subsidiary ledger to the accounts receivable control account monthly.
c. The accounting department supervisor controls the mailing of monthly statements to customers and investigates any differences reported by customers.
d. The billing department supervisor matches prenumbered shipping documents with entries in the sales journal.

N92#16. When the shipping department returns non-conforming goods to a vendor, the purchasing department should send to the accounting department the
a. Unpaid voucher.
b. Debit memo.
c. Vendor invoice.
d. Credit memo.

N92#17. An entity's internal control requires for every check request that there be an approved voucher, supported by a prenumbered purchase order and a prenumbered receiving report. To determine whether checks are being issued for unauthorized expenditures, an auditor most likely would select items for testing from the population of all
a. Purchase orders.
b. Canceled checks.
c. Receiving reports.
d. Approved vouchers.

N92#19. In obtaining an understanding of a manufacturing entity's internal control concerning inventory balances, an auditor most likely would
a. Review the entity's descriptions of inventory activities.
b. Perform test counts of inventory during the entity's physical count.
c. Analyze inventory turnover statistics to identify slow-moving and obsolete items.
d. Analyze monthly production reports to identify variances and unusual transactions.

N92#20. If a control total were computed on each of the following data items, which would best be identified as a hash total for a payroll EDP application?
a. Total debits and total credits.
b. Net pay.
c. Department numbers.
d. Hours worked.

N92#21. Which of the following activities most likely would be considered a weakness in an entity's internal control over payroll?
a. A voucher for the amount of the payroll is prepared in the general accounting department based on the payroll department's payroll summary.
b. Payroll checks are prepared by the payroll department and signed by the treasurer.
c. The employee who distributes payroll checks returns unclaimed payroll checks to the payroll department.
d. The personnel department sends employees' termination notices to the payroll department.

N92#22. Which of the following controls would an entity most likely use in safeguarding against the loss of marketable securities?
  a. An independent trust company that has **no** direct contact with the employees who have record keeping responsibilities has possession of the securities.
  b. The internal auditor verifies the marketable securities in the entity's safe each year on the balance sheet date.
  c. The independent auditor traces all purchases and sales of marketable securities through the subsidiary ledgers to the general ledger.
  d. A designated member of the board of directors controls the securities in a bank safe-deposit box.

N92#25. In planning a statistical sample for a test of controls, an auditor increased the expected population deviation rate from the prior year's rate because of the results of the prior year's tests of controls and the overall control environment. The auditor most likely would then increase the planned
  a. Tolerable rate.
  b. Allowance for sampling risk.
  c. Risk of assessing control risk too low.
  d. Sample size.

N92#36. Processing data through the use of simulated files provides an auditor with information about the operating effectiveness of control activities. One of the techniques involved in this approach makes use of
  a. Controlled reprocessing.
  b. An integrated test facility.
  c. Input validation.
  d. Program code checking.

N92#37. An auditor most likely would test for the presence of unauthorized EDP program changes by running a
  a. Program with test data.
  b. Check digit verification program.
  c. Source code comparison program.
  d. Program that computes control totals.

M92#45. Which of the following controls most likely would be effective in offsetting the tendency of sales personnel to maximize sales volume at the expense of high bad debt write-offs?
  a. Employees responsible for authorizing sales and bad debt write-offs are denied access to cash.
  b. Shipping documents and sales invoices are matched by an employee who does **not** have authority to write off bad debts.
  c. Employees involved in the credit-granting function are separated from the sales function.
  d. Subsidiary accounts receivable records are reconciled to the control account by an employee independent of the authorization of credit.

M92#48. Which of the following internal control activities most likely would assist in reducing control risk related to the existence or occurrence of manufacturing transactions?
  a. Perpetual inventory records are independently compared with goods on hand.
  b. Forms used for direct material requisitions are prenumbered and accounted for.
  c. Finished goods are stored in locked limited-access warehouses.
  d. Subsidiary ledgers are periodically reconciled with inventory control accounts.

M92#53. Which of the following statements is correct concerning statistical sampling in tests of controls?
  a. Deviations from control activities at a given rate usually result in misstatements at a higher rate.
  b. As the population size doubles, the sample size should also double.
  c. The qualitative aspects of deviations are **not** considered by the auditor.
  d. There is an inverse relationship between the sample size and the tolerable rate.

M92#54. What is an auditor's evaluation of a statistical sample for attributes when a test of 50 documents results in 3 deviations if tolerable rate is 7%, the expected population deviation rate is 5%, and the allowance for sampling risk is 2%?
  a. Modify the planned assessed level of control risk because the tolerable rate plus the allowance for sampling risk exceeds the expected population deviation rate.
  b. Accept the sample results as support for the planned assessed level of control risk because the sample deviation rate plus the allowance for sampling risk exceeds the tolerable rate.
  c. Accept the sample results as support for the planned assessed level of control risk because the tolerable rate less the allowance for sampling risk equals the expected population deviation rate.
  d. Modify the planned assessed level of control risk because the sample deviation rate plus the allowance for sampling risk exceeds the tolerable rate.

M92#55. Decision tables differ from program flowcharts in that decision tables emphasize
  a. Ease of manageability for complex programs.
  b. Logical relationships among conditions and actions.
  c. Cost benefit factors justifying the program.
  d. The sequence in which operations are performed.

N91#32. Which of the following is a general internal control that would most likely assist an entity whose systems analyst left the entity in the middle of a major project?

a. Grandfather-father-son record retention.
b. Input and output validation routines.
c. Systems documentation.
d. Check digit verification.

N91#35. An auditor would most likely be concerned with internal control activities that provide reasonable assurance about the
a. Efficiency of management's decision-making process.
b. Appropriate prices the entity should charge for its products.
c. Methods of assigning production tasks to employees.
d. Entity's ability to process and summarize financial data.

N91#36. Which of the following most likely represents a significant deficiency in internal control?
a. The systems analyst reviews applications of data processing and maintains systems documentation.
b. The systems programmer designs systems for computerized applications and maintains output controls.
c. The control clerk establishes control over data received by the EDP department and reconciles control totals after processing.
d. The accounts payable clerk prepares data for computer processing and enters the data into the computer.

N91#55. To obtain evidence that user identification and password controls are functioning as designed, an auditor would most likely
a. Review the online transaction log to ascertain whether employees using passwords have access to data files and computer programs.
b. Examine a sample of assigned passwords and access authority to determine whether password holders have access authority incompatible with their other responsibilities.
c. Extract a random sample of processed transactions and ensure that transactions are appropriately authorized.
d. Observe the file librarian's activities to discover whether other systems personnel are permitted to operate computer equipment without restriction.

M91#16. An auditor would most likely be concerned with which of the following controls in a distributed data processing system?
a. Hardware controls.
b. Systems documentation controls.
c. Access controls.
d. Disaster recovery controls.

M91#28. An auditor would consider a cashier's job description to contain compatible duties if the cashier receives remittances from the mailroom and also prepares the

a. Prelist of individual checks.
b. Monthly bank reconciliation.
c. Daily deposit slip.
d. Remittance advices.

M91#31. In a computerized payroll system environment, an auditor would be **least** likely to use test data to test controls related to
a. Missing employee numbers.
b. Proper approval of overtime by supervisors.
c. Time tickets with invalid job numbers.
d. Agreement of hours per clock cards with hours on time tickets.

K. Consider Other Planning Matters

R97#5. Pell, CPA, decides to serve as principal auditor in the audit of the financial statements of Tech Consolidated, Inc. Smith, CPA, audits one of Tech's subsidiaries. In which situation(s) should Pell make reference to Smith's audit?

I. Pell reviews Smith's working papers and assumes responsibility for Smith's work, but expresses a qualified opinion on Tech's financial statements.
II. Pell is unable to review Smith's working papers; however, Pell's inquiries indicate that Smith has an excellent reputation for professional competence and integrity.

a. I only.
b. II only.
c. Both I and II.
d. Neither I nor II.

R96#3. For which of the following judgments may an independent auditor share responsibility with an entity's internal auditor who is assessed to be both competent and objective?

	Assessment of inherent risk	Assessment of control risk
a.	Yes	Yes
b.	Yes	No
c.	No	Yes
d.	No	No

N95#1. In assessing the objectivity of internal auditors, an independent auditor should
a. Evaluate the quality control program in effect for the internal auditors.
b. Examine documentary evidence of the work performed by the internal auditors.
c. Test a sample of the transactions and balances that the internal auditors examined.
d. Determine the organizational level to which the internal auditors report.

N95#53. The work of internal auditors may affect the independent auditor's

I. Procedures performed in obtaining an understanding of internal control.
II. Procedures performed in assessing the risk of material misstatement.
III. Substantive procedures performed in gathering direct evidence.

a. I and II only.
b. I and III only.
c. II and III only.
d. I, II, and III.

N95#54. Which of the following statements is correct concerning an auditor's use of the work of a specialist?
a. The auditor need **not** obtain an understanding of the methods and assumptions used by the specialist.
b. The auditor may **not** use the work of a specialist in matters material to the fair presentation of the financial statements.
c. The reasonableness of the specialist's assumptions and their applications are strictly the auditor's responsibility.
d. The work of a specialist who has a contractual relationship with the client may be acceptable under certain circumstances.

N95#58. Which of the following auditing procedures most likely would assist an auditor in identifying related party transactions?
a. Inspecting correspondence with lawyers for evidence of unreported contingent liabilities.
b. Vouching accounting records for recurring transactions recorded just after the balance sheet date.
c. Reviewing confirmations of loans receivable and payable for indications of guarantees.
d. Performing analytical procedures for indications of possible financial difficulties.

M95#59. An internal auditor's work would most likely affect the nature, timing, and extent of an independent CPA's auditing procedures when the internal auditor's work relates to assertions about the
a. Existence of contingencies.
b. Valuation of intangible assets.
c. Existence of fixed asset additions.
d. Valuation of related party transactions.

M95#60. During an audit an internal auditor may provide direct assistance to an independent CPA in

	Obtaining an understanding of internal control	Performing tests of controls	Performing substantive tests
a.	No	No	No
b.	Yes	No	No
c.	Yes	Yes	No
d.	Yes	Yes	Yes

M95#62. In using the work of a specialist, an auditor may refer to the specialist in the auditor's report if, as a result of the specialist's findings, the auditor

a. Becomes aware of conditions causing substantial doubt about the entity's ability to continue as a going concern.
b. Desires to disclose the specialist's findings, which imply that a more thorough audit was performed.
c. Is able to corroborate another specialist's earlier findings that were consistent with management's representations.
d. Discovers significant deficiencies in the design of the entity's internal control that management does **not** correct.

M95#68. When auditing related party transactions, an auditor places primary emphasis on
a. Ascertaining the rights and obligations of the related parties.
b. Confirming the existence of the related parties.
c. Verifying the valuation of the related party transactions.
d. Evaluating the disclosure of the related party transactions.

N94#1. Which of the following procedures would an auditor most likely include in the initial planning of a financial statement audit?
a. Obtaining a written representation letter from the client's management.
b. Examining documents to detect illegal acts having a material effect on the financial statements.
c. Considering whether the client's accounting estimates are reasonable in the circumstances.
d. Determining the extent of involvement of the client's internal auditors.

N94#25. When assessing the internal auditors' competence, the independent CPA should obtain information about the
a. Organizational level to which the internal auditors report.
b. Educational background and professional certification of the internal auditors.
c. Policies prohibiting the internal auditors from auditing areas where relatives are employed.
d. Internal auditors' access to records and information that is considered sensitive.

N94#65. Which of the following statements is correct about the auditor's use of the work of a specialist?
a. The specialist should **not** have an understanding of the auditor's corroborative use of the specialist's findings.
b. The auditor is required to perform substantive procedures to verify the specialist's assumptions and findings.
c. The client should **not** have an understanding of the nature of the work to be performed by the specialist.
d. The auditor should obtain an understanding of the methods and assumptions used by the specialist.

N94#68. In assessing the competence and objectivity of an entity's internal auditor, an independent auditor **least** likely would consider information obtained from
a. Discussions with management personnel.
b. External quality reviews of the internal auditor's activities.
c. Previous experience with the internal auditor.
d. The results of analytical procedures.

N94#69. After determining that a related party transaction has, in fact, occurred, an auditor should
a. Add a separate paragraph to the auditor's standard report to explain the transaction.
b. Perform analytical procedures to verify whether similar transactions occurred, but were **not** recorded.
c. Obtain an understanding of the business purpose of the transaction.
d. Substantiate that the transaction was consummated on terms equivalent to an arm's-length transaction.

M94#52. In using the work of a specialist, an auditor referred to the specialist's findings in the auditor's report. This would be an appropriate reporting practice if the
a. Client is **not** familiar with the professional certification, personal reputation, or particular competence of the specialist.
b. Auditor, as a result of the specialist's findings, adds an explanatory paragraph emphasizing a matter regarding the financial statements.
c. Client understands the auditor's corroborative use of the specialist's findings in relation to the representations in the financial statements.
d. Auditor, as a result of the specialist's findings, decides to indicate a division of responsibility with the specialist.

M94#57. Which of the following auditing procedures most likely would assist an auditor in identifying related party transactions?
a. Retesting ineffective internal control activities previously reported to the audit committee.
b. Sending second requests for unanswered positive confirmations of accounts receivable.
c. Reviewing accounting records for nonrecurring transactions recognized near the balance sheet date.
d. Inspecting communications with law firms for evidence of unreported contingent liabilities.

M93#6. When assessing an internal auditor's competence, a CPA ordinarily obtains information about all of the following **except**
a. Quality of working paper documentation.
b. Educational level and professional experience.
c. Audit programs and procedures.
d. Access to information about related parties.

N92#40. Which of the following most likely would indicate the existence of related parties?
a. Writing down obsolete inventory just before year end.
b. Failing to correct previously identified internal control deficiencies.
c. Depending on a single product for the success of the entity.
d. Borrowing money at an interest rate significantly below the market rate.

N92#51. Which of the following procedures ordinarily should be applied when an independent accountant conducts a review of interim financial information of a publicly held entity?
a. Verify changes in key account balances.
b. Read the minutes of the board of directors' meetings.
c. Inspect the open purchase order file.
d. Perform cut-off tests for cash receipts and disbursements.

M92#22. When using the work of a specialist, an auditor may refer to and identify the specialist in the auditor's report if the
a. Auditor expresses a qualified opinion as a result of the specialist's findings.
b. Specialist is **not** independent of the client.
c. Auditor wishes to indicate a division of responsibility.
d. Specialist's work provides the auditor greater assurance of reliability.

N91#30. In which of the following situations would a principal auditor **least** likely make reference to another auditor who audited a subsidiary of the entity?
a. The other auditor was retained by the principal auditor and the work was performed under the principal auditor's guidance and control.
b. The principal auditor finds it impracticable to review the other auditor's work or otherwise be satisfied as to the other auditor's work.
c. The financial statements audited by the other auditor are material to the consolidated financial statements covered by the principal auditor's opinion.
d. The principal auditor is unable to be satisfied as to the independence and professional reputation of the other auditor.

N91#56. After identifying related party transactions, an auditor most likely would
a. Substantiate that the transactions were consummated on terms equivalent to those prevailing in arms-length transactions.
b. Discuss the implications of the transactions with third parties, such as the entity's attorneys and bankers.
c. Determine whether the transactions were approved by the board of directors or other appropriate officials.
d. Ascertain whether the transactions would have occurred if the parties had **not** been related.

L. Identify Financial Statement Assertions and Formulate Audit Objectives

R97#6. In evaluating the reasonableness of an entity's accounting estimates, an auditor normally would be concerned about assumptions that are
 a. Susceptible to bias.
 b. Consistent with prior periods.
 c. Insensitive to variations.
 d. Similar to industry guidelines.

N95#38. An auditor may achieve audit objectives related to particular assertions by
 a. Performing analytical procedures.
 b. Adhering to a system of quality control.
 c. Preparing auditor working papers.
 d. Increasing the level of detection risk.

M95#16. An auditor should design the written audit program so that
 a. All material transactions will be selected for substantive testing.
 b. Substantive tests prior to the balance sheet date will be minimized.
 c. The audit procedures selected will achieve specific audit objectives.
 d. Each account balance will be tested under either tests of controls or tests of transactions.

M95#69. Which of the following procedures would an auditor ordinarily perform first in evaluating management's accounting estimates for reasonableness?
 a. Develop independent expectations of management's estimates.
 b. Consider the appropriateness of the key factors or assumptions used in preparing the estimates.
 c. Test the calculations used by management in developing the estimates.
 d. Obtain an understanding of how management developed its estimates.

N94#57. In evaluating the reasonableness of an accounting estimate, an auditor most likely would concentrate on key factors and assumptions that are
 a. Consistent with prior periods.
 b. Similar to industry guidelines.
 c. Objective and **not** susceptible to bias.
 d. Deviations from historical patterns.

M94#8. In designing written audit programs, an auditor should establish specific audit objectives that relate primarily to the
 a. Timing of audit procedures.
 b. Cost-benefit of gathering evidence.
 c. Selected audit techniques.
 d. Financial statement assertions.

M94#45. In evaluating an entity's accounting estimates, one of an auditor's objectives is to determine whether the estimates are
 a. Not subject to bias.
 b. Consistent with industry guidelines.
 c. Based on objective assumptions.
 d. Reasonable in the circumstances.

M. Determine and Prepare the Work Program

N95#52. A primary advantage of using generalized audit software packages to audit the financial statements of a client that uses an EDP system is that the auditor may
 a. Access information stored on computer files while having a limited understanding of the client's hardware and software features.
 b. Consider increasing the use of substantive tests of transactions in place of analytical procedures.
 c. Substantiate the accuracy of data through self-checking digits and hash totals.
 d. Reduce the level of required tests of controls to a relatively small amount.

M95#17. The audit program usually **cannot** be finalized until the
 a. Consideration of the entity's internal control has been completed.
 b. Engagement letter has been signed by the auditor and the client.
 c. Reportable conditions have been communicated to the audit committee of the board of directors.
 d. Search for unrecorded liabilities has been performed and documented.

M95#70. Which of the following pairs of accounts would an auditor most likely analyze on the same working paper?
 a. Notes receivable and interest income.
 b. Accrued interest receivable and accrued interest payable.
 c. Notes payable and notes receivable.
 d. Interest income and interest expense.

M95#71. An auditor's working papers serve mainly to
 a. Provide the principal support for the auditor's report.
 b. Satisfy the auditor's responsibilities concerning the Code of Professional Conduct.
 c. Monitor the effectiveness of the CPA firm's quality control procedures.
 d. Document the level of independence maintained by the auditor.

N94#16. Audit programs should be designed so that
 a. Most of the required procedures can be performed as interim work.
 b. Inherent risk is assessed at a sufficiently low level.
 c. The auditor can make constructive suggestions to management.
 d. The audit evidence gathered supports the auditor's conclusions.

N94#17. The permanent file of an auditor's working papers generally would **not** include
   a. Bond indenture agreements.
   b. Lease agreements.
   c. Working trial balance.
   d. Flowchart of the internal control structure.

N94#72. An auditor ordinarily uses a working trial balance resembling the financial statements without footnotes, but containing columns for
   a. Cash flow increases and decreases.
   b. Audit objectives and assertions.
   c. Reclassifications and adjustments.
   d. Reconciliations and tickmarks.

N94#73. Which of the following factors would **least** likely affect the quantity and content of an auditor's working papers?
   a. The condition of the client's records.
   b. The assessed level of control risk.
   c. The nature of the auditor's report.
   d. The content of the representation letter.

M94#51. Which of the following is required documentation in an audit in accordance with generally accepted auditing standards?
   a. A flowchart or narrative of the accounting system describing the recording and classification of transactions for financial reporting.
   b. An audit program setting forth in detail the procedures necessary to accomplish the engagement's objectives.
   c. A planning memorandum establishing the timing of the audit procedures and coordinating the assistance of entity personnel.
   d. An internal control questionnaire identifying activities that assure specific objectives will be achieved.

M94#58. Before applying principal substantive tests to the details of accounts at an interim date prior to the balance sheet date, an auditor should
   a. Assess control risk at below the maximum for the assertions embodied in the accounts selected for interim testing.
   b. Determine that the accounts selected for interim testing are **not** material to the financial statements taken as a whole.
   c. Consider whether the amounts of the year-end balances selected for interim testing are reasonably predictable.
   d. Obtain written representations from management that all financial records and related data will be made available.

M93#2. Which of the following procedures would an auditor **least** likely perform in planning a financial statement audit?
   a. Coordinating the assistance of entity personnel in data preparation.
   b. Discussing matters that may affect the audit with firm personnel responsible for non-audit services to the entity.
   c. Selecting a sample of vendors' invoices for comparison to receiving reports.
   d. Reading the current year's interim financial statements.

M93#39. Although the quantity and content of audit working papers vary with each particular engagement, an auditor's permanent files most likely include
   a. Schedules that support the current year's adjusting entries.
   b. Prior years' accounts receivable confirmations that were classified as exceptions.
   c. Documentation indicating that the audit work was adequately planned and supervised.
   d. Analyses of capital stock and other owners' equity accounts.

M93#40. An auditor would **least** likely use computer software to
   a. Construct parallel simulations.
   b. Access client data files.
   c. Prepare spreadsheets.
   d. Assess EDP control risk.

N92#35. Which of the following factors most likely would affect an auditor's judgment about the quantity, type, and content of the auditor's working papers?
   a. The assessed level of control risk.
   b. The likelihood of a review by a concurring (second) partner.
   c. The number of personnel assigned to the audit.
   d. The content of the management representation letter.

M92#24. Which of the following statements ordinarily is correct concerning the content of working papers?
   a. Whenever possible, the auditor's staff should prepare schedules and analyses rather than the entity's employees.
   b. It is preferable to have negative figures indicated in red figures instead of parentheses to emphasize amounts being subtracted.
   c. It is appropriate to use calculator tapes with names or explanations on the tapes rather than writing separate lists onto working papers.
   d. The analysis of asset accounts and their related expense or income accounts should **not** appear on the same working paper.

M92#47. Periodic or cycle counts of selected inventory items are made at various times during the year rather than a single inventory count at year end. Which of the following is necessary if the auditor plans to observe inventories at interim dates?
   a. Complete recounts by independent teams are performed.
   b. Perpetual inventory records are maintained.

c. Unit cost records are integrated with production accounting records.
d. Inventory balances are rarely at low levels.

M91#13. The current file of an auditor's working papers most likely would include a copy of the
a. Bank reconciliation.
b. Pension plan contract.
c. Articles of incorporation.
d. Flowchart of the internal control activities.

M91#15. An auditor using audit software probably would be **least** interested in which of the following fields in a computerized perpetual inventory file?
a. Economic order quantity.
b. Warehouse location.
c. Date of last purchase.
d. Quantity sold.

II. Obtain and Document Information to Form a Basis for Conclusions

A. Perform Planned Procedures Including Planned Applications of Audit Sampling

R98#11. In creating lead schedules for an audit engagement, a CPA often uses automated workpaper software. What client information is needed to begin this process?
a. Interim financial information such as third quarter sales, net income, and inventory and receivables balances.
b. Specialized journal information such as the invoice and purchase order numbers of the last few sales and purchases of the year.
c. General ledger information such as account numbers, prior-year account balances, and current-year unadjusted information.
d. Adjusting entry information such as deferrals and accruals, and reclassification journal entries.

R98#12. To reduce the risks associated with accepting e-mail responses to requests for confirmation of accounts receivable, an auditor most likely would
a. Request the senders to mail the original forms to the auditor.
b. Examine subsequent cash receipts for the accounts in question.
c. Consider the e-mail responses to the confirmations to be exceptions.
d. Mail second requests to the e-mail respondents.

R97#7. In testing plant and equipment balances, an auditor may inspect new additions listed on the analysis of plant and equipment. This procedure is designed to obtain evidence concerning management's assertions of

	Existence or occurrence	Presentation and disclosure
a.	Yes	Yes
b.	Yes	No
c.	No	Yes
d.	No	No

R97#15. Which of the following procedures would an auditor most likely perform to test controls relating to management's assertion about the completeness of cash receipts for cash sales at a retail outlet?
a. Observe the consistency of the employees' use of cash registers and tapes.
b. Inquire about employees' access to recorded but undeposited cash.
c. Trace the deposits in the cash receipts journal to the cash balance in the general ledger.
d. Compare the cash balance in the general ledger with the bank confirmation request.

R97#16. In determining the number of documents to select for a test to obtain assurance that all sales returns have been properly authorized, an auditor should consider the tolerable rate of deviation from the control activity. The auditor should also consider the

I. Likely rate of deviations.
II. Allowable risk of assessing control risk too high.

a. I only.
b. II only.
c. Both I and II.
d. Either I or II.

R97#17. Which of the following comparisons would an auditor most likely make in evaluating an entity's costs and expenses?
a. The current year's accounts receivable with the prior year's accounts receivable.
b. The current year's payroll expense with the prior year's payroll expense.
c. The budgeted current year's sales with the prior year's sales.
d. The budgeted current year's warranty expense with the current year's contingent liabilities.

R97#18. To reduce the risks associated with accepting fax responses to requests for confirmations of accounts receivable, an auditor most likely would
a. Examine the shipping documents that provide evidence for the existence assertion.
b. Verify the sources and contents of the faxes in telephone calls to the senders.
c. Consider the faxes to be nonresponses and evaluate them as unadjusted differences.
d. Inspect the faxes for forgeries or alterations and consider them to be acceptable if none are noted.

R97#19. In auditing accounts receivable, the negative form of confirmation request most likely would be used when
a. The total recorded amount of accounts receivable is immaterial to the financial statements taken as a whole.
b. Response rates in prior years to properly designed positive confirmation requests were inadequate.
c. Recipients are likely to return positive confirmation requests without verifying the accuracy of the information.
d. The combined assessed level of inherent risk and control risk relative to accounts receivable is low.

R96#4. For which of the following audit tests would an auditor most likely use attribute sampling?
a. Selecting accounts receivable for confirmation of account balances.
b. Inspecting employee time cards for proper approval by supervisors.
c. Making an independent estimate of the amount of a LIFO inventory.
d. Examining invoices in support of the valuation of fixed asset additions.

R96#5. An auditor observes the mailing of monthly statements to a client's customers and reviews evidence of follow-up on errors reported by the customers. This test of controls most likely is performed to support management's financial statement assertion(s) of

	Presentation and disclosure	Existence or occurrence
a.	Yes	Yes
b.	Yes	No
c.	No	Yes
d.	No	No

R96#11. An auditor usually tests the reasonableness of dividend income from investments in publicly-held companies by computing the amounts that should have been received by referring to
a. Dividend record books produced by investment advisory services.
b. Stock indentures published by corporate transfer agents.
c. Stock ledgers maintained by independent registrars.
d. Annual audited financial statements issued by the investee companies.

N95#27. When there are numerous property and equipment transactions during the year, an auditor who plans to assess control risk at a low level usually performs
a. Tests of controls and extensive tests of property and equipment balances at the end of the year.
b. Analytical procedures for current year property and equipment transactions.
c. Tests of controls and limited tests of current year property and equipment transactions.
d. Analytical procedures for property and equipment balances at the end of the year.

N95#28. An auditor suspects that a client's cashier is misappropriating cash receipts for personal use by lapping customer checks received in the mail. In attempting to uncover this embezzlement scheme, the auditor most likely would compare the
a. Dates checks are deposited per bank statements with the dates remittance credits are recorded.
b. Daily cash summaries with the sums of the cash receipts journal entries.
c. Individual bank deposit slips with the details of the monthly bank statements.
d. Dates uncollectible accounts are authorized to be written off with the dates the write-offs are actually recorded.

N95#29. In testing controls over cash disbursements, an auditor most likely would determine that the person who signs checks also
a. Reviews the monthly bank reconciliation.
b. Returns the checks to accounts payable.
c. Is denied access to the supporting documents.
d. Is responsible for mailing the checks.

N95#31. In determining the effectiveness of an entity's activities relating to the existence or occurrence assertion for payroll transactions, an auditor most likely would inquire about and
a. Observe the segregation of duties concerning personnel responsibilities and payroll disbursement.
b. Inspect evidence of accounting for prenumbered payroll checks.
c. Recompute the payroll deductions for employee fringe benefits.
d. Verify the preparation of the monthly payroll account bank reconciliation.

N95#33. Which of the following factors is(are) considered in determining the sample size for a test of controls?

	Expected deviation rate	Tolerable deviation rate
a.	Yes	Yes
b.	No	No
c.	No	Yes
d.	Yes	No

N95#39. The confirmation of customers' accounts receivable rarely provides reliable evidence about the completeness assertion because
a. Many customers merely sign and return the confirmation without verifying its details.
b. Recipients usually respond only if they disagree with the information on the request.

c. Customers may **not** be inclined to report understatement errors in their accounts.
d. Auditors typically select many accounts with low recorded balances to be confirmed.

N95#40. Which of the following sets of information does an auditor usually confirm on one form?
a. Accounts payable and purchase commitments.
b. Cash in bank and collateral for loans.
c. Inventory on consignment and contingent liabilities.
d. Accounts receivable and accrued interest receivable.

N95#41. An auditor's analytical procedures most likely would be facilitated if the entity
a. Segregates obsolete inventory before the physical inventory count.
b. Uses a standard cost system that produces variance reports.
c. Corrects material weaknesses in internal control before the beginning of the audit.
d. Develops its data from sources solely within the entity.

N95#42. To measure how effectively an entity employs its resources, an auditor calculates inventory turnover by dividing average inventory into
a. Net sales.
b. Cost of goods sold.
c. Operating income.
d. Gross sales.

N95#43. How would increases in tolerable misstatement and assessed level of control risk affect the sample size in a substantive test of details?

	Increase in tolerable misstatement	Increase in assessed level of control risk
a.	Increase sample size	Increase sample size
b.	Increase sample size	Decrease sample size
c.	Decrease sample size	Increase sample size
d.	Decrease sample size	Decrease sample size

N95#44. An advantage of statistical sampling over nonstatistical sampling is that statistical sampling helps an auditor to
a. Eliminate the risk of nonsampling errors.
b. Reduce the level of audit risk and materiality to a relatively low amount.
c. Measure the sufficiency of the evidential matter obtained.
d. Minimize the failure to detect errors and fraud.

N95#45. The usefulness of the standard bank confirmation request may be limited because the bank employee who completes the form may
a. Not believe that the bank is obligated to verify confidential information to a third party.
b. Sign and return the form without inspecting the accuracy of the client's bank reconciliation.
c. Not have access to the client's cutoff bank statement.
d. Be unaware of all the financial relationships that the bank has with the client.

N95#46. An auditor most likely would limit substantive audit tests of sales transactions when control risk is assessed as low for the existence or occurrence assertion concerning sales transactions and the auditor has already gathered evidence supporting
a. Opening and closing inventory balances.
b. Cash receipts and accounts receivable.
c. Shipping and receiving activities.
d. Cutoffs of sales and purchases.

N95#47. Which of the following procedures would an auditor most likely perform in searching for unrecorded liabilities?
a. Trace a sample of accounts payable entries recorded just before year end to the unmatched receiving report file.
b. Compare a sample of purchase orders issued just after year end with the year-end accounts payable trial balance.
c. Vouch a sample of cash disbursements recorded just after year end to receiving reports and vendor invoices.
d. Scan the cash disbursements entries recorded just before year end for indications of unusual transactions.

N95#48. An auditor traced a sample of purchase orders and the related receiving reports to the purchases journal and the cash disbursements journal. The purpose of this substantive audit procedure most likely was to
a. Identify unusually large purchases that should be investigated further.
b. Verify that cash disbursements were for goods actually received.
c. Determine that purchases were properly recorded.
d. Test whether payments were for goods actually ordered.

N95#49. Which of the following explanations most likely would satisfy an auditor who questions management about significant debits to the accumulated depreciation accounts?
a. The estimated remaining useful lives of plant assets were revised upward.
b. Plant assets were retired during the year.
c. The prior year's depreciation expense was erroneously understated.
d. Overhead allocations were revised at year end.

N95#50. Which of the following circumstances most likely would cause an auditor to suspect an employee payroll fraud scheme?
a. There are significant unexplained variances between standard and actual labor cost.
b. Payroll checks are disbursed by the same employee each payday.

c. Employee time cards are approved by individual departmental supervisors.
d. A separate payroll bank account is maintained on an imprest basis.

N95#51. The objective of tests of details of transactions performed as substantive tests is to
a. Comply with generally accepted auditing standards.
b. Attain assurance about the reliability of the accounting system.
c. Detect material misstatements in the financial statements.
d. Evaluate whether management's activities operated effectively.

M95#32. Tracing shipping documents to prenumbered sales invoices provides evidence that
a. No duplicate shipments or billings occurred.
b. Shipments to customers were properly invoiced.
c. All goods ordered by customers were shipped.
d. All prenumbered sales invoices were accounted for.

M95#34. To provide assurance that each voucher is submitted and paid only once, an auditor most likely would examine a sample of paid vouchers and determine whether each voucher is
a. Supported by a vendor's invoice.
b. Stamped "paid" by the check signer.
c. Prenumbered and accounted for.
d. Approved for authorized purchases.

M95#35. In determining the sample size for a test of controls, an auditor should consider the likely rate of deviations, the allowable risk of assessing control risk too low, and the
a. Tolerable deviation rate.
b. Risk of incorrect acceptance.
c. Nature and cause of deviations.
d. Population size.

M95#37. An auditor vouched data for a sample of employees in a payroll register to approved clock card data to provide assurance that
a. Payments to employees are computed at authorized rates.
b. Employees work the number of hours for which they are paid.
c. Segregation of duties exist between the preparation and distribution of the payroll.
d. Internal controls relating to unclaimed payroll checks are operating effectively.

M95#39. Which of the following types of audit evidence is the most persuasive?
a. Prenumbered client purchase order forms.
b. Client work sheets supporting cost allocations.
c. Bank statements obtained from the client.
d. Client representation letter.

M95#40. An auditor most likely would inspect loan agreements under which an entity's inventories are pledged to support management's financial statement assertion of
a. Presentation and disclosure.
b. Valuation or allocation.
c. Existence or occurrence.
d. Completeness.

M95#41. In auditing intangible assets, an auditor most likely would review or recompute amortization and determine whether the amortization period is reasonable in support of management's financial statement assertion of
a. Valuation or allocation.
b. Existence or occurrence.
c. Completeness.
d. Rights and obligations.

M95#42. Cutoff tests designed to detect purchases made before the end of the year that have been recorded in the subsequent year most likely would provide assurance about management's assertion of
a. Valuation or allocation.
b. Existence or occurrence.
c. Completeness.
d. Presentation and disclosure.

M95#43. An auditor most likely would make inquiries of production and sales personnel concerning possible obsolete or slow-moving inventory to support management's financial statement assertion of
a. Valuation or allocation.
b. Rights and obligations.
c. Existence or occurrence.
d. Presentation and disclosure.

M95#44. In confirming with an outside agent, such as a financial institution, that the agent is holding investment securities in the client's name, an auditor most likely gathers evidence in support of management's financial statement assertions of existence or occurrence and
a. Valuation or allocation.
b. Rights and obligations.
c. Completeness.
d. Presentation and disclosure.

M95#45. Which of the following statements is correct concerning the use of negative confirmation requests?
a. Unreturned negative confirmation requests rarely provide significant explicit evidence.
b. Negative confirmation requests are effective when detection risk is low.
c. Unreturned negative confirmation requests indicate that alternative procedures are necessary.
d. Negative confirmation requests are effective when understatements of account balances are suspected.

M95#46. When an auditor does **not** receive replies to positive requests for year-end accounts receivable confirmations, the auditor most likely would

a. Inspect the allowance account to verify whether the accounts were subsequently written off.
   b. Increase the assessed level of detection risk for the valuation and completeness assertions.
   c. Ask the client to contact the customers to request that the confirmations be returned.
   d. Increase the assessed level of inherent risk for the revenue cycle.

M95#48. Which of the following would **not** be considered an analytical procedure?
   a. Estimating payroll expense by multiplying the number of employees by the average hourly wage rate and the total hours worked.
   b. Projecting an error rate by comparing the results of a statistical sample with the actual population characteristics.
   c. Computing accounts receivable turnover by dividing credit sales by the average net receivables.
   d. Developing the expected current-year sales based on the sales trend of the prior five years.

M95#49. In confirming a client's accounts receivable in prior years, an auditor found that there were many differences between the recorded account balances and the confirmation replies. These differences, which were not misstatements, required substantial time to resolve. In defining the sampling unit for the current year's audit, the auditor most likely would choose
   a. Individual overdue balances.
   b. Individual invoices.
   c. Small account balances.
   d. Large account balances.

M95#50. In statistical sampling methods used in substantive testing, an auditor most likely would stratify a population into meaningful groups if
   a. Probability proportional to size (PPS) sampling is used.
   b. The population has highly variable recorded amounts.
   c. The auditor's estimated tolerable misstatement is extremely small.
   d. The standard deviation of recorded amounts is relatively small.

M95#51. The use of the ratio estimation sampling technique is most effective when
   a. The calculated audit amounts are approximately proportional to the client's book amounts.
   b. A relatively small number of differences exist in the population.
   c. Estimating populations whose records consist of quantities, but **not** book values.
   d. Large overstatement differences and large understatement differences exist in the population.

M95#52. While observing a client's annual physical inventory, an auditor recorded test counts for several items and noticed that certain test counts were higher than the recorded quantities in the client's perpetual records. This situation could be the result of the client's failure to record
   a. Purchase discounts.
   b. Purchase returns.
   c. Sales.
   d. Sales returns.

M95#53. To gain assurance that all inventory items in a client's inventory listing schedule are valid, an auditor most likely would trace
   a. Inventory tags noted during the auditor's observation to items listed in the inventory listing schedule.
   b. Inventory tags noted during the auditor's observation to items listed in receiving reports and vendors' invoices.
   c. Items listed in the inventory listing schedule to inventory tags and the auditor's recorded count sheets.
   d. Items listed in receiving reports and vendors' invoices to the inventory listing schedule.

M95#54. When control risk is assessed as low for assertions related to payroll, substantive tests of payroll balances most likely would be limited to applying analytical procedures and
   a. Observing the distribution of paychecks.
   b. Footing and crossfooting the payroll register.
   c. Inspecting payroll tax returns.
   d. Recalculating payroll accruals.

M95#55. In performing a search for unrecorded retirements of fixed assets, an auditor most likely would
   a. Inspect the property ledger and the insurance and tax records, and then tour the client's facilities.
   b. Tour the client's facilities, and then inspect the property ledger and the insurance and tax records.
   c. Analyze the repair and maintenance account, and then tour the client's facilities.
   d. Tour the client's facilities, and then analyze the repair and maintenance account.

M95#56. Which of the following procedures would an auditor most likely perform in auditing the statement of cash flows?
   a. Compare the amounts included in the statement of cash flows to similar amounts in the prior year's statement of cash flows.
   b. Reconcile the cutoff bank statements to verify the accuracy of the year-end bank balances.
   c. Vouch all bank transfers for the last week of the year and first week of the subsequent year.
   d. Reconcile the amounts included in the statement of cash flows to the other financial statements' balances and amounts.

M95#57. In determining whether transactions have been recorded, the direction of the audit testing should be from the

a. General ledger balances.
b. Adjusted trial balance.
c. Original source documents.
d. General journal entries.

M95#58. When providing limited assurance that the financial statements of a nonpublic entity require **no** material modifications to be in accordance with generally accepted accounting principles, the accountant should
    a. Assess the risk that a material misstatement could occur in a financial statement assertion.
    b. Confirm with the entity's lawyer that material loss contingencies are disclosed.
    c. Understand the accounting principles of the industry in which the entity operates.
    d. Develop audit programs to determine whether the entity's financial statements are fairly presented.

M95#72. When an auditor tests a computerized accounting system, which of the following is true of the test data approach?
    a. Several transactions of each type must be tested.
    b. Test data are processed by the client's computer programs under the auditor's control.
    c. Test data must consist of all possible valid and invalid conditions.
    d. The program tested is different from the program used throughout the year by the client.

M95#73. Which of the following procedures would an auditor **least** likely perform before the balance sheet date?
    a. Confirmation of accounts payable.
    b. Observation of merchandise inventory.
    c. Assessment of control risk.
    d. Identification of related parties.

M95#74. What type of analytical procedure would an auditor most likely use in developing relationships among balance sheet accounts when reviewing the financial statements of a nonpublic entity?
    a. Trend analysis.
    b. Regression analysis.
    c. Ratio analysis.
    d. Risk analysis.

M95#75. Which of the following procedures is ordinarily performed by an accountant in a compilation engagement of a nonpublic entity?
    a. Reading the financial statements to consider whether they are free of obvious mistakes in the application of accounting principles.
    b. Obtaining written representations from management indicating that the compiled financial statements will **not** be used to obtain credit.
    c. Making inquiries of management concerning actions taken at meetings of the stockholders and the board of directors.
    d. Applying analytical procedures designed to corroborate management's assertions that are embodied in the financial statement components.

N94#47. Which of the following presumptions is correct about the reliability of evidential matter?
    a. Information obtained indirectly from outside sources is the most reliable evidential matter.
    b. To be reliable, evidential matter should be convincing rather than persuasive.
    c. Reliability of evidential matter refers to the amount of corroborative evidence obtained.
    d. Effective internal control provides more assurance about the reliability of evidential matter.

N94#48. Which of the following auditing procedures most likely would provide assurance about a manufacturing entity's inventory valuation?
    a. Testing the entity's computation of standard overhead rates.
    b. Obtaining confirmation of inventories pledged under loan agreements.
    c. Reviewing shipping and receiving cutoff procedures for inventories.
    d. Tracing test counts to the entity's inventory listing.

N94#49. In establishing the existence and ownership of a long-term investment in the form of publicly-traded stock, an auditor should inspect the securities or
    a. Correspond with the investee company to verify the number of shares owned.
    b. Inspect the audited financial statements of the investee company.
    c. Confirm the number of shares owned that are held by an independent custodian.
    d. Determine that the investment is carried at the lower of cost or market.

N94#51. Determining that proper amounts of depreciation are expensed provides assurance about management's assertions of valuation or allocation and
    a. Presentation and disclosure.
    b. Completeness.
    c. Rights and obligations.
    d. Existence or occurrence.

N94#52. In auditing accounts receivable the negative form of confirmation request most likely would be used when
    a. Recipients are likely to return positive confirmation requests without verifying the accuracy of the information.
    b. The combined assessed level of inherent and control risk relative to accounts receivable is low.
    c. A small number of accounts receivable are involved but a relatively large number of errors are expected.
    d. The auditor performs a dual purpose test that assesses control risk and obtains substantive evidence.

N94#53. When using confirmations to provide evidence about the completeness assertion for accounts payable, the appropriate population most likely would be

a. Vendors with whom the entity has previously done business.
b. Amounts recorded in the accounts payable subsidiary ledger.
c. Payees of checks drawn in the month after the year end.
d. Invoices filed in the entity's open invoice file.

N94#54. Which of the following sampling methods would be used to estimate a numerical measurement of a population, such as a dollar value?
a. Attributes sampling.
b. Stop-or-go sampling.
c. Variables sampling.
d. Random-number sampling.

N94#55. Which of the following courses of action would an auditor most likely follow in planning a sample of cash disbursements if the auditor is aware of several unusually large cash disbursements?
a. Set the tolerable rate of deviation at a lower level than originally planned.
b. Stratify the cash disbursements population so that the unusually large disbursements are selected.
c. Increase the sample size to reduce the effect of the unusually large disbursements.
d. Continue to draw new samples until all the unusually large disbursements appear in the sample.

N94#56. Which of the following sample planning factors would influence the sample size for a substantive test of details for a specific account?

	Expected amount of misstatements	Measure of tolerable misstatement
a.	No	No
b.	Yes	Yes
c.	No	Yes
d.	Yes	No

N94#58. A client maintains perpetual inventory records in both quantities and dollars. If the assessed level of control risk is high, an auditor would probably
a. Increase the extent of tests of controls of the inventory cycle.
b. Request the client to schedule the physical inventory count at the end of the year.
c. Insist that the client perform physical counts of inventory items several times during the year.
d. Apply gross profit tests to ascertain the reasonableness of the physical counts.

N94#59. In auditing payroll, an auditor most likely would
a. Verify that checks representing unclaimed wages are mailed.
b. Trace individual employee deductions to entity journal entries.
c. Observe entity employees during a payroll distribution.
d. Compare payroll costs with entity standards or budgets.

N94#60. In auditing long-term bonds payable, an auditor most likely would
a. Perform analytical procedures on the bond premium and discount accounts.
b. Examine documentation of assets purchased with bond proceeds for liens.
c. Compare interest expense with the bond payable amount for reasonableness.
d. Confirm the existence of individual bondholders at year end.

N94#61. In performing tests concerning the granting of stock options, an auditor should
a. Confirm the transaction with the Secretary of State in the state of incorporation.
b. Verify the existence of option holders in the entity's payroll records or stock ledgers.
c. Determine that sufficient treasury stock is available to cover any new stock issued.
d. Trace the authorization for the transaction to a vote of the board of directors.

N94#62. An auditor analyzes repairs and maintenance accounts primarily to obtain evidence in support of the audit assertion that all
a. Noncapitalizable expenditures for repairs and maintenance have been recorded in the proper period.
b. Expenditures for property and equipment have been recorded in the proper period.
c. Noncapitalizable expenditures for repairs and maintenance have been properly charged to expense.
d. Expenditures for property and equipment have **not** been charged to expense.

N94#74. Which of the following procedures would an accountant **least** likely perform during an engagement to review the financial statements of a nonpublic entity?
a. Observing the safeguards over access to and use of assets and records.
b. Comparing the financial statements with anticipated results in budgets and forecasts.
c. Inquiring of management about actions taken at the board of directors' meetings.
d. Studying the relationships of financial statement elements expected to conform to predictable patterns.

M94#39. An auditor concluded that no excessive costs for idle plant were charged to inventory. This conclusion most likely related to the auditor's objective to obtain evidence about the financial statement assertions regarding inventory, including presentation and disclosure and

a. Valuation and allocation.
b. Completeness.
c. Existence or occurrence.
d. Rights and obligations.

M94#40. Auditors try to identify predictable relationships when using analytical procedures. Relationships involving transactions from which of the following accounts most likely would yield the highest level of evidence?
a. Accounts receivable.
b. Interest expense.
c. Accounts payable.
d. Travel and entertainment expense.

M94#41. An auditor selected items for test counts while observing a client's physical inventory. The auditor then traced the test counts to the client's inventory listing. This procedure most likely obtained evidence concerning management's assertion of
a. Rights and obligations.
b. Completeness.
c. Existence or occurrence.
d. Valuation.

M94#42. In testing plant and equipment balances, an auditor examines new additions listed on an analysis of plant and equipment. This procedure most likely obtains evidence concerning management's assertion of
a. Completeness.
b. Existence or occurrence.
c. Presentation and disclosure.
d. Valuation or allocation.

M94#43. While performing a test of details during an audit, an auditor determined that the sample results supported the conclusion that the recorded account balance was materially misstated. It was, in fact, not materially misstated. This situation illustrates the risk of
a. Assessing control risk too high.
b. Assessing control risk too low.
c. Incorrect rejection.
d. Incorrect acceptance.

M94#47. Which of the following audit procedures is best for identifying unrecorded trade accounts payable?
a. Reviewing cash disbursements recorded subsequent to the balance sheet date to determine whether the related payables apply to the prior period.
b. Investigating payables recorded just prior to and just subsequent to the balance sheet date to determine whether they are supported by receiving reports.
c. Examining unusual relationships between monthly accounts payable balances and recorded cash payments.
d. Reconciling vendors' statements to the file of receiving reports to identify items received just prior to the balance sheet date.

M94#48. In testing for unrecorded retirements of equipment, an auditor most likely would

a. Select items of equipment from the accounting records and then locate them during the plant tour.
b. Compare depreciation journal entries with similar prior-year entries in search of fully depreciated equipment.
c. Inspect items of equipment observed during the plant tour and then trace them to the equipment subsidiary ledger.
d. Scan the general journal for unusual equipment additions and excessive debits to repairs and maintenance expense.

M94#49. An auditor most likely would extend substantive tests of payroll when
a. Payroll is extensively audited by the state government.
b. Payroll expense is substantially higher than in the prior year.
c. Overpayments are discovered in performing tests of details.
d. Employees complain to management about too much overtime.

M94#50. A client has a large and active investment portfolio that is kept in a bank safe deposit box. If the auditor is unable to count the securities at the balance sheet date, the auditor most likely will
a. Request the bank to confirm to the auditor the contents of the safe deposit box at the balance sheet date.
b. Examine supporting evidence for transactions occurring during the year.
c. Count the securities at a subsequent date and confirm with the bank whether securities were added or removed since the balance sheet date.
d. Request the client to have the bank seal the safe deposit box until the auditor can count the securities at a subsequent date.

M94#59. An accountant should perform analytical procedures during an engagement to

	Compile a nonpublic entity's financial statements	Review a nonpublic entity's financial statements
a.	No	No
b.	Yes	Yes
c.	Yes	No
d.	No	Yes

M94#60. Which of the following procedures most likely would **not** be included in a review engagement of a nonpublic entity?
a. Obtaining a management representation letter.
b. Considering whether the financial statements conform with GAAP.
c. Assessing control risk.
d. Inquiring about subsequent events.

N93#26. To determine whether accounts payable are complete, an auditor performs a test to verify that all

merchandise received is recorded. The population of documents for this test consists of all
a. Payment vouchers.
b. Receiving reports.
c. Purchase requisitions.
d. Vendor's invoices.

N93#35. When performing an engagement to review a nonpublic entity's financial statements, an accountant most likely would
a. Confirm a sample of significant accounts receivable balances.
b. Ask about actions taken at board of directors' meetings.
c. Obtain an understanding of internal control.
d. Limit the distribution of the accountant's report.

N93#36. Which of the following statements concerning audit evidence is correct?
a. To be competent, audit evidence should be either persuasive or relevant, but need **not** be both.
b. The measure of the validity of audit evidence lies in the auditor's judgment.
c. The difficulty and expense of obtaining audit evidence concerning an account balance is a valid basis for omitting the test.
d. A client's accounting data can be sufficient audit evidence to support the financial statements.

N93#37. In auditing accounts payable, an auditor's procedures most likely would focus primarily on management's assertion of
a. Existence or occurrence.
b. Presentation and disclosure.
c. Completeness.
d. Valuation or allocation.

N93#40. In which of the following circumstances would the use of the negative form of accounts receivable confirmation most likely be justified?
a. A substantial number of accounts may be in dispute and the accounts receivable balance arises from sales to a few major customers.
b. A substantial number of accounts may be in dispute and the accounts receivable balance arises from sales to many customers with small balances.
c. A small number of accounts may be in dispute and the accounts receivable balance arises from sales to a few major customers.
d. A small number of accounts may be in dispute and the accounts receivable balance arises from sales to many customers with small balances.

N93#44. Which of the following is a documentation requirement that an auditor should follow when auditing in accordance with *Government Auditing Standards?*

a. The auditor should obtain written representations from management acknowledging responsibility for correcting instances of fraud, abuse, and waste.
b. The auditor's working papers should contain sufficient information so that supplementary oral explanations are **not** required.
c. The auditor should document the procedures that assure discovery of all illegal acts and contingent liabilities resulting from noncompliance.
d. The auditor's working papers should contain a caveat that all instances of material errors and fraud may **not** be identified.

M93#26. Which of the following procedures would provide the most reliable audit evidence?
a. Inquiries of the client's internal audit staff held in private.
b. Inspection of prenumbered client purchase orders filed in the vouchers payable department.
c. Analytical procedures performed by the auditor on the entity's trial balance.
d. Inspection of bank statements obtained directly from the client's financial institution.

M93#27. An auditor most likely would review an entity's periodic accounting for the numerical sequence of shipping documents and invoices to support management's financial statement assertion of
a. Existence or occurrence.
b. Rights and obligations.
c. Valuation or allocation.
d. Completeness.

M93#28. When auditing inventories, an auditor would **least** likely verify that
a. The financial statement presentation of inventories is appropriate.
b. Damaged goods and obsolete items have been properly accounted for.
c. All inventory owned by the client is on hand at the time of the count.
d. The client has used proper inventory pricing.

M93#29. In evaluating the adequacy of the allowance for doubtful accounts, an auditor most likely reviews the entity's aging of receivables to support management's financial statement assertion of
a. Existence or occurrence.
b. Valuation or allocation.
c. Completeness.
d. Rights and obligations.

M93#31. In testing long-term investments, an auditor ordinarily would use analytical procedures to ascertain the reasonableness of the
a. Completeness of recorded investment income.
b. Classification between current and noncurrent portfolios.

c. Valuation of marketable equity securities.
d. Existence of unrealized gains or losses in the portfolio.

M93#34. The primary purpose of sending a standard confirmation request to financial institutions with which the client has done business during the year is to
a. Detect kiting activities that may otherwise **not** be discovered.
b. Corroborate information regarding deposit and loan balances.
c. Provide the data necessary to prepare a proof of cash.
d. Request information about contingent liabilities and secured transactions.

M93#35. Which of the following procedures would an auditor most likely perform for year-end accounts receivable confirmations when the auditor did **not** receive replies to second requests?
a. Review the cash receipts journal for the month prior to the year end.
b. Intensify the study of internal control concerning the revenue cycle.
c. Increase the assessed level of detection risk for the existence assertion.
d. Inspect the shipping records documenting the merchandise sold to the debtors.

M93#36. Which of the following is a substantive test that an auditor most likely would perform to verify the existence and valuation of recorded accounts payable?
a. Investigating the open purchase order file to ascertain that prenumbered purchase orders are used and accounted for.
b. Receiving the client's mail, unopened, for a reasonable period of time after the year end to search for unrecorded vendor's invoices.
c. Vouching selected entries in the accounts payable subsidiary ledger to purchase orders and receiving reports.
d. Confirming accounts payable balances with known suppliers who have zero balances.

M93#43. Which of the following most likely would be an advantage in using classical variables sampling rather than probability-proportional-to-size (PPS) sampling?
a. An estimate of the standard deviation of the population's recorded amounts is **not** required.
b. The auditor rarely needs the assistance of a computer program to design an efficient sample.
c. Inclusion of zero and negative balances generally does **not** require special design considerations.
d. Any amount that is individually significant is automatically identified and selected.

N92#26. Which of the following types of audit evidence is the **least** persuasive?
a. Prenumbered purchase order forms.
b. Bank statements obtained from the client.
c. Test counts of inventory performed by the auditor.
d. Correspondence from the client's attorney about litigation.

N92#27. Which of the following combinations of procedures would an auditor most likely perform to obtain evidence about fixed asset additions?
a. Inspecting documents and physically examining assets.
b. Recomputing calculations and obtaining written management representations.
c. Observing operating activities and comparing balances to prior period balances.
d. Confirming ownership and corroborating transactions through inquiries of client personnel.

N92#29. An auditor most likely would analyze inventory turnover rates to obtain evidence concerning management's assertions about
a. Existence or occurrence.
b. Rights and obligations.
c. Presentation and disclosure.
d. Valuation or allocation.

N92#30. Which of the following procedures would an auditor most likely perform to verify management's assertion of completeness?
a. Compare a sample of shipping documents to related sales invoices.
b. Observe the client's distribution of payroll checks.
c. Confirm a sample of recorded receivables by direct communication with the debtors.
d. Review standard bank confirmations for indications of kiting.

N92#31. An auditor's decision either to apply analytical procedures as substantive tests or to perform tests of transactions and account balances usually is determined by the
a. Availability of data aggregated at a high level.
b. Relative effectiveness and efficiency of the tests.
c. Timing of tests performed after the balance sheet date.
d. Auditor's familiarity with industry trends.

N92#38. An auditor may decide to increase the risk of incorrect rejection when
a. Increased reliability from the sample is desired.
b. Many differences (audit value minus recorded value) are expected.
c. Initial sample results do **not** support the planned level of control risk.
d. The cost and effort of selecting additional sample items is low.

N92#43. Which of the following inquiry or analytical procedures ordinarily is performed in an engagement to review a nonpublic entity's financial statements?

a. Analytical procedures designed to test the accounting records by obtaining corroborating evidential matter.
b. Inquiries concerning the entity's procedures for recording and summarizing transactions.
c. Analytical procedures designed to test management's assertions regarding continued existence.
d. Inquiries of the entity's attorney concerning contingent liabilities.

N92#45. Which of the following procedures is **not** usually performed by the accountant during a review engagement of a nonpublic entity?
a. Inquiring about actions taken at meetings of the board of directors that may affect the financial statements.
b. Issuing a report stating that the review was performed in accordance with standards established by the AICPA.
c. Reading the financial statements to consider whether they conform with generally accepted accounting principles.
d. Communicating any material weaknesses discovered during the consideration of internal control.

M92#17. Which of the following audit procedures probably would provide the most reliable evidence concerning the entity's assertion of rights and obligations related to inventories?
a. Trace test counts noted during the entity's physical count to the entity's summarization of quantities.
b. Inspect agreements to determine whether any inventory is pledged as collateral or subject to any liens.
c. Select the last few shipping advices used before the physical count and determine whether the shipments were recorded as sales.
d. Inspect the open purchase order file for significant commitments that should be considered for disclosure.

M92#18. During an audit of an entity's stockholders' equity accounts, the auditor determines whether there are restrictions on retained earnings resulting from loans, agreements, or state law. This audit procedure most likely is intended to verify management's assertion of
a. Existence or occurrence.
b. Completeness.
c. Valuation or allocation.
d. Presentation and disclosure.

M92#19. Which of the following most likely would give the most assurance concerning the valuation assertion of accounts receivable?
a. Tracing amounts in the subsidiary ledger to details on shipping documents.
b. Comparing receivable turnover ratios to industry statistics for reasonableness.
c. Inquiring about receivables pledged under loan agreements.
d. Assessing the allowance for uncollectible accounts for reasonableness.

M92#20. Which of the following tends to be most predictable for purposes of analytical procedures applied as substantive tests?
a. Relationships involving balance sheet accounts.
b. Transactions subject to management discretion.
c. Relationships involving income statement accounts.
d. Data subject to audit testing in the prior year.

M92
Items 26 and 27 are based on the following:

The information below was taken from the bank transfer schedule prepared during the audit of Fox Co.'s financial statements for the year ended December 31, 1991. Assume all checks are dated and issued on December 30, 1991.

Check No.	Bank Accounts		Disbursement Date		Receipt Date	
	From	To	Per Books	Per Bank	Per Books	Per Bank
101	National	Federal	Dec. 30	Jan. 4	Dec. 30	Jan. 3
202	County	State	Jan. 3	Jan. 2	Dec. 30	Dec. 31
303	Federal	American	Dec. 31	Jan. 3	Jan. 2	Jan. 2
404	State	Republic	Jan. 2	Jan. 2	Jan. 2	Dec. 31

26. Which of the following checks might indicate kiting?
a. #101 and #303.
b. #202 and #404.
c. #101 and #404.
d. #202 and #303.

27. Which of the following checks illustrate deposits/transfers in transit at December 31, 1991?
a. #101 and #202.
b. #101 and #303.
c. #202 and #404.
d. #303 and #404.

M92#30. In a probability-proportional-to-size sample with a sampling interval of $5,000, an auditor discovered that a selected account receivable with a recorded amount of $10,000 had an audit amount of $8,000. If this were the only error discovered by the auditor, the projected error of this sample would be
a. $1,000
b. $2,000
c. $4,000
d. $5,000

M92#44. Tracing bills of lading to sales invoices provides evidence that
a. Shipments to customers were recorded as sales.
b. Recorded sales were shipped.
c. Invoiced sales were shipped.
d. Shipments to customers were invoiced.

N91#37. As the acceptable level of detection risk decreases, the assurance directly provided from
a. Substantive tests should increase.
b. Substantive tests should decrease.
c. Tests of controls should increase.
d. Tests of controls should decrease.

N91#42. Which of the following statements concerning analytical procedures is correct?
a. Analytical procedures may be omitted entirely for some financial statement audits.
b. Analytical procedures used in planning the audit should **not** use nonfinancial information.
c. Analytical procedures usually are effective and efficient for tests of controls.
d. Analytical procedures alone may provide the appropriate level of assurance for some assertions.

N91#44. To satisfy the valuation assertion when auditing an investment accounted for by the equity method, an auditor most likely would
a. Inspect the stock certificates evidencing the investment.
b. Examine the audited financial statements of the investee company.
c. Review the broker's advice or canceled check for the investment's acquisition.
d. Obtain market quotations from financial newspapers or periodicals.

N91#49. If the objective of a test of details is to detect overstatements of sales, the auditor should trace transactions from the
a. Cash receipts journal to the sales journal.
b. Sales journal to the cash receipts journal.
c. Source documents to the accounting records.
d. Accounting records to the source documents.

M91#17. Which of the following statements is correct concerning probability proportional to size (PPS) sampling, also known as dollar unit sampling?
a. The sampling distribution should approximate the normal distribution.
b. Overstated units have a lower probability of sample selection than units that are understated.
c. The auditor controls the risk of incorrect acceptance by specifying that risk level for the sampling plan.
d. The sampling interval is calculated by dividing the number of physical units in the population by the sample size.

M91#19. When compiling a nonpublic entity's financial statements, an accountant would be **least** likely to
a. Perform analytical procedures designed to identify relationships that appear to be unusual.
b. Read the compiled financial statements and consider whether they appear to include adequate disclosure.
c. Omit substantially all of the disclosures required by generally accepted accounting principles.
d. Issue a compilation report on one or more, but **not** all, of the basic financial statements.

M91#20. Which of the following procedures would most likely be included in a review engagement of a nonpublic entity?
a. Preparing a bank transfer schedule.
b. Inquiring about related party transactions.
c. Assessing internal control.
d. Performing cutoff tests on sales and purchases transactions.

M91#32. The primary responsibility of a bank acting as registrar of capital stock is to
a. Ascertain that dividends declared do **not** exceed the statutory amount allowable in the state of incorporation.
b. Account for stock certificates by comparing the total shares outstanding to the total in the shareholders subsidiary ledger.
c. Act as an independent third party between the board of directors and outside investors concerning mergers, acquisitions, and the sale of treasury stock.
d. Verify that stock is issued in accordance with the authorization of the board of directors and the articles of incorporation.

M91#59. Performing inquiry and analytical procedures is the primary basis for an accountant to issue a
a. Report on compliance with requirements governing major federal assistance programs in accordance with the Single Audit Act.
b. Review report on prospective financial statements that present an entity's expected financial position, given one or more hypothetical assumptions.
c. Management advisory report prepared at the request of a client's audit committee.
d. Review report on comparative financial statements for a nonpublic entity in its second year of operations.

C. Obtain and Evaluate Lawyers' Letters

R96#12. Which of the following statements extracted from a client's lawyer's letter concerning litigation, claims, and assessments most likely would cause the auditor to request clarification?
   a. "I believe that the possible liability to the company is nominal in amount."
   b. "I believe that the action can be settled for less than the damages claimed."
   c. "I believe that the plaintiff's case against the company is without merit."
   d. "I believe that the company will be able to defend this action successfully."

M95#63. The refusal of a client's attorney to provide information requested in an inquiry letter generally is considered
   a. Grounds for an adverse opinion.
   b. A limitation on the scope of the audit.
   c. Reason to withdraw from the engagement.
   d. Equivalent to a reportable condition.

N94#66. The primary reason an auditor requests letters of inquiry be sent to a client's attorneys is to provide the auditor with
   a. The probable outcome of asserted claims and pending or threatened litigation.
   b. Corroboration of the information furnished by management about litigation, claims, and assessments.
   c. The attorneys' opinions of the client's historical experiences in recent similar litigation.
   d. A description and evaluation of litigation, claims, and assessments that existed at the balance sheet date.

N93#39. The primary source of information to be reported about litigation, claims, and assessments is the
   a. Client's lawyer.
   b. Court records.
   c. Client's management.
   d. Independent auditor.

D. Review Subsequent Events

N95#56. Which of the following procedures would an auditor most likely perform to obtain evidence about the occurrence of subsequent events?
   a. Confirming a sample of material accounts receivable established after year end.
   b. Comparing the financial statements being reported on with those of the prior period.
   c. Investigating personnel changes in the accounting department occurring after year end.
   d. Inquiring as to whether any unusual adjustments were made after year end.

M95#65. Which of the following procedures would an auditor most likely perform in obtaining evidence about subsequent events?
   a. Determine that changes in employee pay rates after year end were properly authorized.
   b. Recompute depreciation charges for plant assets sold after year end.
   c. Inquire about payroll checks that were recorded before year end but cashed after year end.
   d. Investigate changes in long-term debt occurring after year end.

N94#67. An auditor issued an audit report that was dual dated for a subsequent event occurring after the completion of field work but before issuance of the auditor's report. The auditor's responsibility for events occurring subsequent to the completion of field work was
   a. Limited to include only events occurring up to the date of the last subsequent event referenced.
   b. Limited to the specific event referenced.
   c. Extended to subsequent events occurring through the date of issuance of the report.
   d. Extended to include all events occurring since the completion of field work.

M94#53. Zero Corp. suffered a loss that would have a material effect on its financial statements on an uncollectible trade account receivable due to a customer's bankruptcy. This occurred suddenly due to a natural disaster ten days after Zero's balance sheet date, but one month before the issuance of the financial statements and the auditor's report. Under these circumstances,

	The financial statements should be adjusted	The event requires financial statement disclosure, but no adjustment	The auditor's report should be modified for a lack of consistency
a.	Yes	No	No
b.	Yes	No	Yes
c.	No	Yes	Yes
d.	No	Yes	No

M93#45. Which of the following procedures should an auditor generally perform regarding subsequent events?
   a. Compare the latest available interim financial statements with the financial statements being audited.
   b. Send second requests to the client's customers who failed to respond to initial accounts receivable confirmation requests.
   c. Communicate material weaknesses in internal control to the client's audit committee.
   d. Review the cut-off bank statements for several months after the year end.

N92#41. Which of the following procedures would an auditor most likely perform to obtain evidence about the occurrence of subsequent events?
   a. Recomputing a sample of large-dollar transactions occurring after year end for arithmetic accuracy.
   b. Investigating changes in stockholders' equity occurring after year end.

c. Inquiring of the entity's legal counsel concerning litigation, claims, and assessments arising after year end.
d. Confirming bank accounts established after year end.

M92#12. Wilson, CPA, completed the field work of the audit of Abco's December 31, 1991, financial statements on March 6, 1992. A subsequent event requiring adjustment to the 1991 financial statements occurred on April 10, 1992, and came to Wilson's attention on April 24, 1992. If the adjustment is made without disclosure of the event, Wilson's report ordinarily should be dated
a. March 6, 1992.
b. April 10, 1992.
c. April 24, 1992.
d. Using dual dating.

E. Obtain Representations From Management

R97#8. "There have been no communications from regulatory agencies concerning noncompliance with, or deficiencies in, financial reporting practices that could have a material effect on the financial statements." The foregoing passage is most likely from a
a. Report on internal control.
b. Special report.
c. Management representation letter.
d. Letter for underwriters.

N95#57. Which of the following matters would an auditor most likely include in a management representation letter?
a. Communications with the audit committee concerning weaknesses in internal control.
b. The completeness and availability of minutes of stockholders' and directors' meetings.
c. Plans to acquire or merge with other entities in the subsequent year.
d. Management's acknowledgment of its responsibility for the detection of employee fraud.

M95#66. To which of the following matters would materiality limits **not** apply in obtaining written management representations?
a. The availability of minutes of stockholders' and directors' meetings.
b. Losses from purchase commitments at prices in excess of market value.
c. The disclosure of compensating balance arrangements involving related parties.
d. Reductions of obsolete inventory to net realizable value.

M95#67. The date of the management representation letter should coincide with the date of the
a. Balance sheet.
b. Latest interim financial information.
c. Auditor's report.
d. Latest related party transaction.

N94#64. "There are no violations or possible violations of laws or regulations whose effects should be considered for disclosure in the financial statements or as a basis for recording a loss contingency." The foregoing passage most likely is from a(an)
a. Client engagement letter.
b. Report on compliance with laws and regulations.
c. Management representation letter.
d. Attestation report on internal control.

N94#75. Which of the following procedures should an accountant perform during an engagement to review the financial statements of a nonpublic entity?
a. Communicating reportable conditions discovered during the assessment of control risk.
b. Obtaining a client representation letter from members of management.
c. Sending bank confirmation letters to the entity's financial institutions.
d. Examining cash disbursements in the subsequent period for unrecorded liabilities.

M94#54. Which of the following statements ordinarily is included among the written client representations obtained by the auditor?
a. Compensating balances and other arrangements involving restrictions on cash balances have been disclosed.
b. Management acknowledges responsibility for illegal actions committed by employees.
c. Sufficient evidential matter has been made available to permit the issuance of an unqualified opinion.
d. Management acknowledges that there are **no** material weaknesses in the internal control.

M93#32. A purpose of a management representation letter is to reduce
a. Audit risk to an aggregate level of misstatement that could be considered material.
b. An auditor's responsibility to detect material misstatements only to the extent that the letter is relied on.
c. The possibility of a misunderstanding concerning management's responsibility for the financial statements.
d. The scope of an auditor's procedures concerning related party transactions and subsequent events.

N92#34. To which of the following matters would materiality limits **not** apply when obtaining written client representations?
a. Losses from sales commitments.
b. Unasserted claims and assessments.
c. Fraud involving management.
d. Noncompliance with contractual agreements.

M92#35. Which of the following procedures is more likely to be performed in a review engagement of a nonpublic entity than in a compilation engagement?

a. Gaining an understanding of the entity's business transactions.
b. Making a preliminary assessment of control risk.
c. Obtaining a representation letter from the chief executive officer.
d. Assisting the entity in adjusting the accounting records.

F. Identify Reportable Conditions and Other Control Deficiencies

N95#34. A weakness in internal control over recording retirements of equipment may cause an auditor to
a. Inspect certain items of equipment in the plant and trace those items to the accounting records.
b. Review the subsidiary ledger to ascertain whether depreciation was taken on each item of equipment during the year.
c. Trace additions to the "other assets" account to search for equipment that is still on hand but **no** longer being used.
d. Select certain items of equipment from the accounting records and locate them in the plant.

N95#35. An auditor's letter issued on reportable conditions relating to an entity's internal control observed during a financial statement audit should
a. Include a brief description of the tests of controls performed in searching for reportable conditions and material weaknesses.
b. Indicate that the reportable conditions should be disclosed in the annual report to the entity's shareholders.
c. Include a paragraph describing management's assertion concerning the effectiveness of internal control.
d. Indicate that the audit's purpose was to report on the financial statements and **not** to provide assurance on internal control.

N91#43. Which of the following statements is correct concerning reportable conditions noted in an audit?
a. Reportable conditions are material weaknesses in the design or operation of specific internal control components.
b. The auditor is obligated to search for reportable conditions that could adversely affect the entity's ability to record and report financial data.
c. Reportable conditions should be recommunicated each year, even if management has acknowledged its understanding of such deficiencies.
d. The auditor may separately communicate those reportable conditions considered to be material weaknesses.

G. Identify Matters for Communication With Audit Committees

R96#6. In identifying matters for communication with an entity's audit committee, an auditor most likely would ask management whether

a. The turnover in the accounting department was unusually high.
b. It consulted with another CPA firm about accounting matters.
c. There were any subsequent events of which the auditor was unaware.
d. It agreed with the auditor's assessed level of control risk.

N94#84. Which of the following matters is an auditor required to communicate to an entity's audit committee?
a. The basis for assessing control risk below the maximum.
b. The process used by management in formulating sensitive accounting estimates.
c. The auditor's preliminary judgments about materiality levels.
d. The justification for performing substantive procedures at interim dates.

N93#60. An auditor is obligated to communicate a proposed audit adjustment to an entity's audit committee only if the adjustment
a. Has **not** been recorded before the end of the auditor's field work.
b. Has a significant effect on the entity's financial reporting process.
c. Is a recurring matter that was proposed to management the prior year.
d. Results from the correction of a prior period's departure from GAAP.

N92#60. Which of the following matters is an auditor required to communicate to an entity's audit committee?

I. Disagreements with management about matters significant to the entity's financial statements that have been satisfactorily resolved.
II. Initial selection of significant accounting policies in emerging areas that lack authoritative guidance.

a. I only.
b. II only.
c. Both I and II.
d. Neither I nor II.

M92#15. Should an auditor communicate the following matters to an audit committee of a public entity?

	Significant audit adjustments recorded by the entity	Management's consultation with other accountants about significant accounting matters
a.	Yes	Yes
b.	Yes	No
c.	No	Yes
d.	No	No

Selected Questions

III. Review the Engagement

A. Perform Analytical Procedures

R97#9. Analytical procedures performed in the overall review stage of an audit suggest that several accounts have unexpected relationships. The results of these procedures most likely would indicate that
    a. Irregularities exist among the relevant account balances.
    b. Internal control activities are **not** operating effectively.
    c. Additional tests of details are required.
    d. The communication with the audit committee should be revised.

M95#47. Analytical procedures used in the overall review stage of an audit generally include
    a. Gathering evidence concerning account balances that have **not** changed from the prior year.
    b. Retesting control activities that appeared to be ineffective during the assessment of control risk.
    c. Considering unusual or unexpected account balances that were **not** previously identified.
    d. Performing tests of transactions to corroborate management's financial statement assertions.

N93#38. For audits of financial statements made in accordance with generally accepted auditing standards, the use of analytical procedures is required to some extent

	As a substantive test	In the final review stage
a.	Yes	Yes
b.	Yes	No
c.	No	Yes
d.	No	No

M92#34. Which of the following procedures is usually performed by the accountant in a review engagement of a nonpublic entity?
    a. Sending a letter of inquiry to the entity's lawyer.
    b. Comparing the financial statements with statements for comparable prior periods.
    c. Confirming a significant percentage of receivables by direct communication with debtors.
    d. Communicating reportable conditions discovered during the study of internal control.

M91#4. A basic premise underlying the application of analytical procedures is that
    a. The study of financial ratios is an acceptable alternative to the investigation of unusual fluctuations.
    b. Statistical tests of financial information may lead to the discovery of material errors in the financial statements.
    c. Plausible relationships among data may reasonably be expected to exist and continue in the absence of known conditions to the contrary.
    d. These procedures **cannot** replace tests of balances and transactions.

M91#5. Which of the following comparisons would be most useful to an auditor in evaluating the results of an entity's operations?
    a. Prior year accounts payable to current year accounts payable.
    b. Prior year payroll expense to budgeted current year payroll expense.
    c. Current year revenue to budgeted current year revenue.
    d. Current year warranty expense to current year contingent liabilities.

B. Evaluate the Sufficiency and Competence of Audit Evidence and Document Engagement Conclusions

R98#13. Which of the following conditions or events most likely would cause an auditor to have substantial doubt about an entity's ability to continue as a going concern?
    a. Significant related party transactions are pervasive.
    b. Usual trade credit from suppliers is denied.
    c. Arrearages in preferred stock dividends are paid.
    d. Restrictions on the disposal of principal assets are present.

N95#59. Cooper, CPA, believes there is substantial doubt about the ability of Zero Corp. to continue as a going concern for a reasonable period of time. In evaluating Zero's plans for dealing with the adverse effects of future conditions and events, Cooper most likely would consider, as a mitigating factor, Zero's plans to
    a. Discuss with lenders the terms of all debt and loan agreements.
    b. Strengthen internal controls over cash disbursements.
    c. Purchase production facilities currently being leased from a related party.
    d. Postpone expenditures for research and development projects.

N94#71. Which of the following conditions or events most likely would cause an auditor to have substantial doubt about an entity's ability to continue as a going concern?
    a. Cash flows from operating activities are negative.
    b. Research and development projects are postponed.
    c. Significant related party transactions are pervasive.
    d. Stock dividends replace annual cash dividends.

M94#55. Which of the following auditing procedures most likely would assist an auditor in identifying conditions and events that may indicate substantial doubt about an entity's ability to continue as a going concern?
 a. Inspecting title documents to verify whether any assets are pledged as collateral.
 b. Confirming with third parties the details of arrangements to maintain financial support.
 c. Reconciling the cash balance per books with the cut-off bank statement and the bank confirmation.
 d. Comparing the entity's depreciation and asset capitalization policies to other entities in the industry.

M94#62. When an auditor concludes there is substantial doubt about a continuing audit client's ability to continue as a going concern for a reasonable period of time, the auditor's responsibility is to
 a. Issue a qualified or adverse opinion, depending upon materiality, due to the possible effects on the financial statements.
 b. Consider the adequacy of disclosure about the client's possible inability to continue as a going concern.
 c. Report to the client's audit committee that management's accounting estimates may need to be adjusted.
 d. Reissue the prior year's auditor's report and add an explanatory paragraph that specifically refers to "substantial doubt" and "going concern."

M93#53. Davis, CPA, believes there is substantial doubt about the ability of Hill Co. to continue as a going concern for a reasonable period of time. In evaluating Hill's plans for dealing with the adverse effects of future conditions and events, Davis most likely would consider, as a mitigating factor, Hill's plans to
 a. Accelerate research and development projects related to future products.
 b. Accumulate treasury stock at prices favorable to Hill's historic price range.
 c. Purchase equipment and production facilities currently being leased.
 d. Negotiate reductions in required dividends being paid on preferred stock.

N92#49. Green, CPA, concludes that there is substantial doubt about JKL Co.'s ability to continue as a going concern. If JKL's financial statements adequately disclose its financial difficulties, Green's auditor's report should

	Include an explanatory paragraph following the opinion paragraph	Specifically use the words "going concern"	Specifically use the words "substantial doubt"
a.	Yes	Yes	Yes
b.	Yes	Yes	No
c.	Yes	No	Yes
d.	No	Yes	Yes

M91#43. The adverse effects of events causing an auditor to believe there is substantial doubt about an entity's ability to continue as a going concern would most likely be mitigated by evidence relating to the
 a. Ability to expand operations into new product lines in the future.
 b. Feasibility of plans to purchase leased equipment at less than market value.
 c. Marketability of assets that management plans to sell.
 d. Committed arrangements to convert preferred stock to long-term debt.

C. Review the Work Performed

R96#14. Which of the following ratios would an engagement partner most likely calculate when reviewing the balance sheet in the overall review stage of an audit?
 a. Quick assets/current assets.
 b. Accounts receivable/inventory.
 c. Interest payable/interest receivable.
 d. Total debt/total assets.

N95#60. The permanent (continuing) file of an auditor's working papers most likely would include copies of the
 a. Lead schedules.
 b. Attorney's letters.
 c. Bank statements.
 d. Debt agreements.

N94#5. After field work audit procedures are completed, a partner of the CPA firm who has not been involved in the audit performs a second or wrap-up working paper review. This second review usually focuses on
 a. The fair presentation of the financial statements in conformity with GAAP.
 b. Fraud involving the client's management and its employees.
 c. The materiality of the adjusting entries proposed by the audit staff.
 d. The communication of internal control weaknesses to the client's audit committee.

M94#56. Using microcomputers in auditing may affect the methods used to review the work of staff assistants because
 a. The audit field work standards for supervision may differ.
 b. Documenting the supervisory review may require assistance of consulting services personnel.
 c. Supervisory personnel may **not** have an understanding of the capabilities and limitations of microcomputers.
 d. Working paper documentation may **not** contain readily observable details of calculations.

M92#33. An auditor concludes that a substantive auditing procedure considered necessary during the prior period's audit was omitted. Which of the following factors would most likely cause the auditor promptly to apply the omitted procedure?

a. There are **no** alternative procedures available to provide the same evidence as the omitted procedure.
b. The omission of the procedure impairs the auditor's present ability to support the previously expressed opinion.
c. The source documents needed to perform the omitted procedure are still available.
d. The auditor's opinion on the prior period's financial statements was unqualified.

IV. Prepare Communications to Satisfy Engagement Objectives

A. Prepare Reports

R98#14. An auditor concludes that there is substantial doubt about an entity's ability to continue as a going concern for a reasonable period of time. If the entity's financial statements adequately disclose its financial difficulties, the auditor's report is required to include an explanatory paragraph that specifically uses the phrase(s)

	"Reasonable period of time, not to exceed one year"	*"Going concern"*
a.	Yes	Yes
b.	Yes	No
c.	No	Yes
d.	No	No

R98#15. In the first audit of a client, an auditor was not able to gather sufficient evidence about the consistent application of accounting principles between the current and the prior year, as well as the amounts of assets or liabilities at the beginning of the current year. This was due to the client's record retention policies. If the amounts in question could materially affect current operating results, the auditor would
a. Be unable to express an opinion on the current year's results of operations and cash flows.
b. Express a qualified opinion on the financial statements because of a client-imposed scope limitation.
c. Withdraw from the engagement and refuse to be associated with the financial statements.
d. Specifically state that the financial statements are **not** comparable to the prior year due to an uncertainty.

R98#16. What is an auditor's reporting responsibility concerning information accompanying the basic financial statements in an auditor-submitted document?
a. The auditor should report on all the accompanying information included in the document.
b. The auditor should report on the accompanying information only if the auditor participated in its preparation.
c. The auditor should report on the accompanying information only if the auditor did **not** participate in its preparation.
d. The auditor should report on the accompanying information only if it contains obvious material misstatements.

R96#7. During an engagement to review the financial statements of a nonpublic entity, an accountant becomes aware that several leases that should be capitalized are not capitalized. The accountant considers these leases to be material to the financial statements. The accountant decides to modify the standard review report because management will not capitalize the leases. Under these circumstances, the accountant should
a. Issue an adverse opinion because of the departure from GAAP.
b. Express **no** assurance of any kind on the entity's financial statements.
c. Emphasize that the financial statements are for limited use only.
d. Disclose the departure from GAAP in a separate paragraph of the accountant's report.

R96#8. An auditor may express an opinion on an entity's accounts receivable balance even if the auditor has disclaimed an opinion on the financial statements taken as a whole provided the
a. Report on the accounts receivable discloses the reason for the disclaimer of opinion on the financial statements.
b. Distribution of the report on the accounts receivable is restricted to internal use only.
c. Auditor also reports on the current asset portion of the entity's balance sheet.
d. Report on the accounts receivable is presented separately from the disclaimer of opinion on the financial statements.

R96#15. For which of the following events would an auditor issue a report that omits any reference to consistency?
a. A change in the method of accounting for inventories.
b. A change from an accounting principle that is **not** generally accepted to one that is generally accepted.
c. A change in the useful life used to calculate the provision for depreciation expense.
d. Management's lack of reasonable justification for a change in accounting principle.

N95#63. An auditor may **not** issue a qualified opinion when
a. An accounting principle at variance with GAAP is used.
b. The auditor lacks independence with respect to the audited entity.

c. A scope limitation prevents the auditor from completing an important audit procedure.
d. The auditor's report refers to the work of a specialist.

N95#64. An auditor most likely would express an unqualified opinion and would **not** add explanatory language to the report if the auditor
a. Wishes to emphasize that the entity had significant transactions with related parties.
b. Concurs with the entity's change in its method of computing depreciation.
c. Discovers that supplementary information required by FASB has been omitted.
d. Believes that there is a remote likelihood of a material loss resulting from an uncertainty.

N95#65. An auditor would express an unqualified opinion with an explanatory paragraph added to the auditor's report for

	An unjustified accounting change	A material weakness in internal control
a.	Yes	Yes
b.	Yes	No
c.	No	Yes
d.	No	No

N95#66. Under which of the following circumstances would a disclaimer of opinion **not** be appropriate?
a. The auditor is unable to determine the amounts associated with an employee fraud scheme.
b. Management does **not** provide reasonable justification for a change in accounting principles.
c. The client refuses to permit the auditor to confirm certain accounts receivable or apply alternative procedures to verify their balances.
d. The chief executive officer is unwilling to sign the management representation letter.

N95#67. Digit Co. uses the FIFO method of costing for its international subsidiary's inventory and LIFO for its domestic inventory. Under these circumstances, the auditor's report on Digit's financial statements should express an
a. Unqualified opinion.
b. Opinion qualified because of a lack of consistency.
c. Opinion qualified because of a departure from GAAP.
d. Adverse opinion.

N95#68. The fourth standard of reporting requires the auditor's report to contain either an expression of opinion regarding the financial statements taken as a whole or an assertion to the effect that an opinion cannot be expressed. The objective of the fourth standard is to prevent
a. An auditor from expressing different opinions on each of the basic financial statements.
b. Restrictions on the scope of the audit, whether imposed by the client or by the inability to obtain evidence.
c. Misinterpretations regarding the degree of responsibility the auditor is assuming.
d. An auditor from reporting on one basic financial statement and **not** the others.

N95#69. In which of the following circumstances would an auditor **not** express an unqualified opinion?
a. There has been a material change between periods in accounting principles.
b. Quarterly financial data required by the SEC has been omitted.
c. The auditor wishes to emphasize an unusually important subsequent event.
d. The auditor is unable to obtain audited financial statements of a consolidated investee.

N95#70. An explanatory paragraph following the opinion paragraph of an auditor's report describes an uncertainty as follows:

As discussed in Note X to the financial statements, the Company is a defendant in a lawsuit alleging infringement of certain patent rights and claiming damages. Discovery proceedings are in progress. The ultimate outcome of the litigation cannot presently be determined. Accordingly, no provision for any liability that may result upon adjudication has been made in the accompanying financial statements.

What type of opinion should the auditor express under these circumstances?
a. Adverse.
b. Qualified due to a scope limitation.
c. Qualified due to a GAAP violation.
d. Unqualified.

N95#71. Which of the following phrases would an auditor most likely include in the auditor's report when expressing a qualified opinion because of inadequate disclosure?
a. Subject to the departure from generally accepted accounting principles, as described above.
b. With the foregoing explanation of these omitted disclosures.
c. Except for the omission of the information discussed in the preceding paragraph.
d. Does **not** present fairly in all material respects.

N95#72. Kane, CPA, concludes that there is substantial doubt about Lima Co.'s ability to continue as a going concern for a reasonable period of time. If Lima's financial statements adequately disclose its financial difficulties, Kane's auditor's report is required to include an explanatory paragraph that specifically uses the phrase(s)

	"Possible discontinuance of operations"	"Reasonable period of time, **not** to exceed one year"
a.	Yes	Yes
b.	Yes	No
c.	No	Yes
d.	No	No

N95#73. Mead, CPA, had substantial doubt about Tech Co.'s ability to continue as a going concern when reporting on Tech's audited financial statements for the year ended June 30, 1994. That doubt has been removed in 1995. What is Mead's reporting responsibility if Tech is presenting its financial statements for the year ended June 30, 1995, on a comparative basis with those of 1994?
    a. The explanatory paragraph included in the 1994 auditor's report should **not** be repeated.
    b. The explanatory paragraph included in the 1994 auditor's report should be repeated in its entirety.
    c. A different explanatory paragraph describing Mead's reasons for the removal of doubt should be included.
    d. A different explanatory paragraph describing Tech's plans for financial recovery should be included.

N95#74. In the first audit of a new client, an auditor was able to extend auditing procedures to gather sufficient evidence about consistency. Under these circumstances, the auditor should
    a. Not report on the client's income statement.
    b. Not refer to consistency in the auditor's report.
    c. State that the consistency standard does **not** apply.
    d. State that the accounting principles have been applied consistently.

N95#75. When reporting on comparative financial statements, an auditor ordinarily should change the previously issued opinion on the prior-year's financial statements if the
    a. Prior year's financial statements are restated to conform with generally accepted accounting principles.
    b. Auditor is a predecessor auditor who has been requested by a former client to reissue the previously issued report.
    c. Prior year's opinion was unqualified and the opinion on the current year's financial statements is modified due to a lack of consistency.
    d. Prior year's financial statements are restated following a pooling of interests in the current year.

N95#76. Jewel, CPA, audited Infinite Co.'s prior-year financial statements. These statements are presented with those of the current year for comparative purposes without Jewel's auditor's report, which expressed a qualified opinion. In drafting the current year's auditor's report, Crain, CPA, the successor auditor, should

I. Not name Jewel as the predecessor auditor.
II. Indicate the type of report issued by Jewel.
III. Indicate the substantive reasons for Jewel's qualification.

    a. I only.
    b. I and II only.
    c. II and III only.
    d. I, II, and III.

N95#77. The introductory paragraph of an auditor's report contains the following sentences:

We did not audit the financial statements of EZ Inc., a wholly-owned subsidiary, which statements reflect total assets and revenues constituting 27 percent and 29 percent, respectively, of the related consolidated totals. Those statements were audited by other auditors whose report has been furnished to us, and our opinion, insofar as it relates to the amounts included for EZ Inc., is based solely on the report of the other auditors.

These sentences
    a. Indicate a division of responsibility.
    b. Assume responsibility for the other auditor.
    c. Require a departure from an unqualified opinion.
    d. Are an improper form of reporting.

N95#78. March, CPA, is engaged by Monday Corp., a client, to audit the financial statements of Wall Corp., a company that is not March's client. Monday expects to present Wall's audited financial statements with March's auditor's report to 1st Federal Bank to obtain financing in Monday's attempt to purchase Wall. In these circumstances, March's auditor's report would usually be addressed to
    a. Monday Corp., the client that engaged March.
    b. Wall Corp., the entity audited by March.
    c. 1st Federal Bank.
    d. Both Monday Corp. and 1st Federal Bank.

N95#79. Financial statements of a nonpublic entity that have been reviewed by an accountant should be accompanied by a report stating that a review
    a. Provides only limited assurance that the financial statements are fairly presented.
    b. Includes examining, on a test basis, information that is the representation of management.
    c. Consists principally of inquiries of company personnel and analytical procedures applied to financial data.
    d. Does **not** contemplate obtaining corroborating evidential matter or applying certain other procedures ordinarily performed during an audit.

N95#80. Financial statements of a nonpublic entity compiled without audit or review by an accountant should be accompanied by a report stating that
    a. The scope of the accountant's procedures has **not** been restricted in testing the financial information that is the representation of management.
    b. The accountant assessed the accounting principles used and significant estimates made by management.
    c. The accountant does **not** express an opinion or any other form of assurance on the financial statements.
    d. A compilation consists principally of inquiries of entity personnel and analytical procedures applied to financial data.

N95#81. A CPA's report on agreed-upon procedures related to management's assertion about an entity's compliance with specified requirements should contain
a. A statement of limitations on the use of the report.
b. An opinion about whether management's assertion is fairly stated.
c. Negative assurance that control risk has **not** been assessed.
d. An acknowledgement of responsibility for the sufficiency of the procedures.

N95#82. When an accountant examines projected financial statements, the accountant's report should include a separate paragraph that
a. Describes the limitations on the usefulness of the presentation.
b. Provides an explanation of the differences between an examination and an audit.
c. States that the accountant is responsible for events and circumstances up to one year after the report's date.
d. Disclaims an opinion on whether the assumptions provide a reasonable basis for the projection.

N95#88. In auditing a not-for-profit entity that receives governmental financial assistance, the auditor has a responsibility to
a. Issue a separate report that describes the expected benefits and related costs of the auditor's suggested changes to the entity's internal control.
b. Assess whether management has identified laws and regulations that have a direct and material effect on the entity's financial statements.
c. Notify the governmental agency providing the financial assistance that the audit is **not** designed to provide any assurance of detecting errors and fraud.
d. Render an opinion concerning the entity's continued eligibility for the governmental financial assistance.

N95#90. Which of the following statements represents a quality control requirement under government auditing standards?
a. A CPA who conducts government audits is required to undergo an annual external quality control review when an appropriate internal quality control system is **not** in place.
b. A CPA seeking to enter into a contract to perform an audit should provide the CPA's most recent external quality control review report to the party contracting for the audit.
c. An external quality control review of a CPA's practice should include a review of the working papers of each government audit performed since the prior external quality control review.
d. A CPA who conducts government audits may **not** make the CPA's external quality control review report available to the public.

M95#38. Which of the following statements is correct concerning reportable conditions in an audit?
a. An auditor is required to search for reportable conditions during an audit.
b. All reportable conditions are also considered to be material weaknesses.
c. An auditor may communicate reportable conditions during an audit or after the audit's completion.
d. An auditor may report that **no** reportable conditions were noted during an audit.

M95#76. An auditor most likely would be responsible for communicating significant deficiencies in the design of internal control
a. To the Securities and Exchange Commission when the client is a publicly-held entity.
b. To specific legislative and regulatory bodies when reporting under *Government Auditing Standards*.
c. To a court-appointed creditors' committee when the client is operating under Chapter 11 of the Federal Bankruptcy Code.
d. To shareholders with significant influence (more than 20% equity ownership) when the reportable conditions are deemed to be material weaknesses.

M95#77. A principal auditor decides not to refer to the audit of another CPA who audited a subsidiary of the principal auditor's client. After making inquiries about the other CPA's professional reputation and independence, the principal auditor most likely would
a. Add an explanatory paragraph to the auditor's report indicating that the subsidiary's financial statements are **not** material to the consolidated financial statements.
b. Document in the engagement letter that the principal auditor assumes **no** responsibility for the other CPA's work and opinion.
c. Obtain written permission from the other CPA to omit the reference in the principal auditor's report.
d. Contact the other CPA and review the audit programs and working papers pertaining to the subsidiary.

M95#78. Compiled financial statements should be accompanied by an accountant's report stating that
a. A compilation includes assessing the accounting principles used and significant management estimates, as well as evaluating the overall financial statement presentation.
b. The accountant compiled the financial statements in accordance with Statements on Standards for Accounting and Review Services.
c. A compilation is substantially less in scope than an audit in accordance with GAAS, the objective of which is the expression of an opinion.
d. The accountant is **not** aware of any material modifications that should be made to the financial statements to conform with GAAP.

M95#79. Moore, CPA, has been asked to issue a review report on the balance sheet of Dover Co., a nonpublic entity. Moore will not be reporting on Dover's statements of income, retained earnings, and cash flows. Moore may issue the review report provided the
- a. Balance sheet is presented in a prescribed form of an industry trade association.
- b. Scope of the inquiry and analytical procedures has **not** been restricted.
- c. Balance sheet is **not** to be used to obtain credit or distributed to creditors.
- d. Specialized accounting principles and practices of Dover's industry are disclosed.

M95#80. Baker, CPA, was engaged to review the financial statements of Hall Co., a nonpublic entity. During the engagement Baker uncovered a complex scheme involving client illegal acts and fraud that materially affect Hall's financial statements. If Baker believes that modification of the standard review report is **not** adequate to indicate the deficiencies in the financial statements, Baker should
- a. Disclaim an opinion.
- b. Issue an adverse opinion.
- c. Withdraw from the engagement.
- d. Issue a qualified opinion.

M95#81. Each page of a nonpublic entity's financial statements reviewed by an accountant should include the following reference:
- a. See Accompanying Accountant's Footnotes.
- b. Reviewed, **No** Material Modifications Required.
- c. See Accountant's Review Report.
- d. Reviewed, **No** Accountant's Assurance Expressed.

M95#89. In reporting on compliance with laws and regulations during a financial statement audit in accordance with *Government Auditing Standards,* an auditor should include in the auditor's report
- a. A statement of assurance that all controls over fraud and illegal acts were tested.
- b. Material instances of fraud and illegal acts that were discovered.
- c. The materiality criteria used by the auditor in considering whether instances of noncompliance were significant.
- d. An opinion on whether compliance with laws and regulations affected the entity's goals and objectives.

M95#90. Which of the following statements is a standard applicable to financial statement audits in accordance with *Government Auditing Standards*?
- a. An auditor should assess whether the entity has reportable measures of economy and efficiency that are valid and reliable.
- b. An auditor should report on the scope of the auditor's testing of internal controls.
- c. An auditor should briefly describe in the auditor's report the method of statistical sampling used in performing tests of controls and substantive tests.
- d. An auditor should determine the extent to which the entity's programs achieve the desired level of results.

N94#45. Which of the following statements is correct concerning an auditor's required communication of reportable conditions?
- a. A reportable condition previously communicated during the prior year's audit that remains uncorrected causes a scope limitation.
- b. An auditor should perform tests of controls on reportable conditions before communicating them to the client.
- c. An auditor's report on reportable conditions should include a restriction on the distribution of the report.
- d. An auditor should communicate reportable conditions after tests of controls, but before commencing substantive tests.

N94#76. When an independent CPA is associated with the financial statements of a publicly held entity but has **not** audited or reviewed such statements, the appropriate form of report to be issued must include a(an)
- a. Regulation S-X exemption.
- b. Report on pro forma financial statements.
- c. Unaudited association report.
- d. Disclaimer of opinion.

N94#77. Before reissuing the prior year's auditor's report on the financial statements of a former client, the predecessor auditor should obtain a letter of representations from the
- a. Former client's management.
- b. Former client's attorney.
- c. Former client's board of directors.
- d. Successor auditor.

N94#78. An accountant who had begun an audit of the financial statements of a nonpublic entity was asked to change the engagement to a review because of a restriction on the scope of the audit. If there is reasonable justification for the change, the accountant's review report should include reference to the

	Scope limitation that caused the changed engagement	Original engagement that was agreed to
a.	Yes	No
b.	No	Yes
c.	No	No
d.	Yes	Yes

N94#79. Gole, CPA, is engaged to review the 1994 financial statements of North Co., a nonpublic entity. Previously, Gole audited North's 1993 financial statements and expressed an unqualified opinion. Gole decides to include a separate paragraph in the 1994 review report because North plans to present comparative financial

statements for 1994 and 1993. This separate paragraph should indicate that
- a. The 1994 review report is intended solely for the information of management and the board of directors.
- b. The 1993 auditor's report may **no** longer be relied on.
- c. No auditing procedures were performed after the date of the 1993 auditor's report.
- d. There are justifiable reasons for changing the level of service from an audit to a review.

N94#80. Which of the following statements should be included in an accountant's standard report based on the compilation of a nonpublic entity's financial statements?
- a. A compilation consists principally of inquiries of company personnel and analytical procedures applied to financial data.
- b. A compilation is limited to presenting in the form of financial statements information that is the representation of management.
- c. A compilation is **not** designed to detect material modifications that should be made to the financial statements.
- d. A compilation is substantially less in scope than an audit in accordance with generally accepted auditing standards.

N94#81. Miller, CPA, is engaged to compile the financial statements of Web Co., a nonpublic entity, in conformity with the income tax basis of accounting. If Web's financial statements do **not** disclose the basis of accounting used, Miller should
- a. Disclose the basis of accounting in the accountant's compilation report.
- b. Clearly label each page "Distribution Restricted—Material Modifications Required."
- c. Issue a special report describing the effect of the incomplete presentation.
- d. Withdraw from the engagement and provide **no** further services to Web.

N94#82. When an accountant is engaged to compile a nonpublic entity's financial statements that omit substantially all disclosures required by GAAP, the accountant should indicate in the compilation report that the financial statements are
- a. Not designed for those who are uninformed about the omitted disclosures.
- b. Prepared in conformity with a comprehensive basis of accounting other than GAAP.
- c. Not compiled in accordance with Statements on Standards for Accounting and Review Services.
- d. Special-purpose financial statements that are **not** comparable to those of prior periods.

N94#83. An accountant's compilation report on a financial forecast should include a statement that
- a. The forecast should be read only in conjunction with the audited historical financial statements.
- b. The accountant expresses only limited assurance on the forecasted statements and their assumptions.
- c. There will usually be differences between the forecasted and actual results.
- d. The hypothetical assumptions used in the forecast are reasonable in the circumstances.

N94#86. An auditor concludes that there is a material inconsistency in the other information in an annual report to shareholders containing audited financial statements. If the auditor concludes that the financial statements do **not** require revision, but the client refuses to revise or eliminate the material inconsistency, the auditor may
- a. Revise the auditor's report to include a separate explanatory paragraph describing the material inconsistency.
- b. Issue an "except for" qualified opinion after discussing the matter with the client's board of directors.
- c. Consider the matter closed since the other information is **not** in the audited financial statements.
- d. Disclaim an opinion on the financial statements after explaining the material inconsistency in a separate explanatory paragraph.

N94#90. An auditor was engaged to conduct a performance audit of a governmental entity in accordance with *Government Auditing Standards*. These standards do **not** require, as part of this auditor's report
- a. A statement of the audit objectives and a description of the audit scope.
- b. Indications or instances of illegal acts that could result in criminal prosecution discovered during the audit.
- c. The pertinent views of the entity's responsible officials concerning the auditor's findings.
- d. A concurrent opinion on the financial statements taken as a whole.

M94#36. Lake, CPA, is auditing the financial statements of Gill Co. Gill uses the EDP Service Center, Inc. to process its payroll transactions. EDP's financial statements are audited by Cope, CPA, who recently issued a report on EDP's internal control. Lake is considering Cope's report on EDP's internal control in assessing control risk on the Gill engagement. What is Lake's responsibility concerning making reference to Cope as a basis, in part, for Lake's own opinion?
- a. Lake may refer to Cope only if Lake is satisfied as to Cope's professional reputation and independence.
- b. Lake may refer to Cope only if Lake relies on Cope's report in restricting the extent of substantive tests.
- c. Lake may refer to Cope only if Lake's report indicates the division of responsibility.
- d. Lake may **not** refer to Cope under the circumstances above.

M94#61. When an independent CPA assists in preparing the financial statements of a publicly held entity, but has **not** audited or reviewed them, the CPA should issue a disclaimer of opinion. In such situations, the CPA has **no** responsibility to apply any procedures beyond
- a. Documenting that internal control is **not** being relied on.
- b. Reading the financial statements for obvious material misstatements.
- c. Ascertaining whether the financial statements are in conformity with GAAP.
- d. Determining whether management has elected to omit substantially all required disclosures.

M94#63. Investment and property schedules are presented for purposes of additional analysis in an auditor-submitted document. The schedules are not required parts of the basic financial statements, but accompany the basic financial statements. When reporting on such additional information, the measurement of materiality is the
- a. Same as that used in forming an opinion on the basic financial statements taken as a whole.
- b. Lesser of the individual schedule of investments or schedule of property taken by itself.
- c. Greater of the individual schedule of investments or schedule of property taken by itself.
- d. Combined total of both the individual schedules of investments and property taken as a whole.

M94#66. In May 1994, an auditor reissues the auditor's report on the 1992 financial statements at a continuing client's request. The 1992 financial statements are not restated and the auditor does not revise the wording of the report. The auditor should
- a. Dual date the reissued report.
- b. Use the release date of the reissued report.
- c. Use the original report date on the reissued report.
- d. Use the current-period auditor's report date on the reissued report.

M94#69. An auditor includes a separate paragraph in an otherwise unmodified report to emphasize that the entity being reported on had significant transactions with related parties. The inclusion of this separate paragraph
- a. Is considered an "except for" qualification of the opinion.
- b. Violates generally accepted auditing standards if this information is already disclosed in footnotes to the financial statements.
- c. Necessitates a revision of the opinion paragraph to include the phrase "with the foregoing explanation."
- d. Is appropriate and would **not** negate the unqualified opinion.

M94#70. On March 15, 1994, Kent, CPA, issued an unqualified opinion on a client's audited financial statements for the year ended December 31, 1993. On May 4, 1994, Kent's internal inspection program disclosed that engagement personnel failed to observe the client's physical inventory. Omission of this procedure impairs Kent's present ability to support the unqualified opinion. If the stockholders are currently relying on the opinion, Kent should first
- a. Advise management to disclose to the stockholders that Kent's unqualified opinion should **not** be relied on.
- b. Undertake to apply alternative procedures that would provide a satisfactory basis for the unqualified opinion.
- c. Reissue the auditor's report and add an explanatory paragraph describing the departure from generally accepted auditing standards.
- d. Compensate for the omitted procedure by performing tests of controls to reduce audit risk to a sufficiently low level.

M94#71. For an entity that does **not** receive governmental financial assistance, an auditor's standard report on financial statements generally would **not** refer to
- a. Significant estimates made by management.
- b. An assessment of the entity's accounting principles.
- c. Management's responsibility for the financial statements.
- d. The entity's internal control.

M94#72. Due to a scope limitation, an auditor disclaimed an opinion on the financial statements taken as a whole, but the auditor's report included a statement that the current asset portion of the entity's balance sheet was fairly stated. The inclusion of this statement is
- a. Not appropriate because it may tend to overshadow the auditor's disclaimer of opinion.
- b. Not appropriate because the auditor is prohibited from reporting on only one basic financial statement.
- c. Appropriate provided the auditor's scope paragraph adequately describes the scope limitation.
- d. Appropriate provided the statement is in a separate paragraph preceding the disclaimer of opinion paragraph.

M94#73. When there has been a change in accounting principles, but the effect of the change on the comparability of the financial statements is **not** material, the auditor should
- a. Refer to the change in an explanatory paragraph.
- b. Explicitly concur that the change is preferred.
- c. Not refer to consistency in the auditor's report.
- d. Refer to the change in the opinion paragraph.

M94#74. When single-year financial statements are presented, an auditor ordinarily would express an unqualified opinion in an unmodified report if the
- a. Auditor is unable to obtain audited financial statements supporting the entity's investment in a foreign affiliate.
- b. Entity declines to present a statement of cash flows with its balance sheet and related statements of income and retained earnings.

c. Auditor wishes to emphasize an accounting matter affecting the comparability of the financial statements with those of the prior year.
d. Prior year's financial statements were audited by another CPA whose report, which expressed an unqualified opinion, is **not** presented.

M94#75. When financial statements contain a departure from GAAP because, due to unusual circumstances, the statements would otherwise be misleading, the auditor should explain the unusual circumstances in a separate paragraph and express an opinion that is
a. Unqualified.
b. Qualified.
c. Adverse.
d. Qualified or adverse, depending on materiality.

M94#76. Park, CPA, was engaged to audit the financial statements of Tech Co., a new client, for the year ended December 31, 1993. Park obtained sufficient audit evidence for all of Tech's financial statement items except Tech's opening inventory. Due to inadequate financial records, Park could not verify Tech's January 1, 1993, inventory balances. Park's opinion on Tech's 1993 financial statements most likely will be

	Balance sheet	*Income statement*
a.	Disclaimer	Disclaimer
b.	Unqualified	Disclaimer
c.	Disclaimer	Adverse
d.	Unqualified	Adverse

M94#77. Which paragraphs of an auditor's standard report on financial statements should refer to generally accepted auditing standards (GAAS) and generally accepted accounting principles (GAAP) in which paragraphs?

	GAAS	*GAAP*
a.	Opening	Scope
b.	Scope	Scope
c.	Scope	Opinion
d.	Opening	Opinion

M94#79. An accountant may compile a nonpublic entity's financial statements that omit all of the disclosures required by GAAP only if the omission is

I. Clearly indicated in the accountant's report.
II. Not undertaken with the intention of misleading the financial statement users.

a. I only.
b. II only.
c. Both I and II.
d. Either I or II.

M94#80. An accountant's standard report on a review of the financial statements of a nonpublic entity should state that the accountant

a. Does **not** express an opinion or any form of limited assurance on the financial statements.
b. Is **not** aware of any material modifications that should be made to the financial statements for them to conform with GAAP.
c. Obtained reasonable assurance about whether the financial statements are free of material misstatement.
d. Examined evidence, on a test basis, supporting the amounts and disclosures in the financial statements.

M94#82. What is an auditor's responsibility for supplementary information, such as segment information, which is outside the basic financial statements, but required by the FASB?
a. The auditor has **no** responsibility for required supplementary information as long as it is outside the basic financial statements.
b. The auditor's only responsibility for required supplementary information is to determine that such information has **not** been omitted.
c. The auditor should apply certain limited procedures to the required supplementary information, and report deficiencies in, or omissions of, such information.
d. The auditor should apply tests of details of transactions and balances to the required supplementary information, and report any material misstatements in such information.

M94#84. Because of the pervasive effects of laws and regulations on the financial statements of governmental units, an auditor should obtain written management representations acknowledging that management has
a. Identified and disclosed all laws and regulations that have a direct and material effect on its financial statements.
b. Implemented internal control activities designed to detect all illegal acts.
c. Expressed both positive and negative assurance to the auditor that the entity complied with all laws and regulations.
d. Employed internal auditors who can report their findings, opinions, and conclusions objectively without fear of political repercussion.

M94#87. In which of the following circumstances would an auditor be most likely to express an adverse opinion?
a. The chief executive officer refuses the auditor access to minutes of board of directors' meetings.
b. Tests of controls show that the entity's internal control is so poor that it **cannot** be relied upon.
c. The financial statements are **not** in conformity with the FASB Statements regarding the capitalization of leases.
d. Information comes to the auditor's attention that raises substantial doubt about the entity's ability to continue as a going concern.

M94#88. When qualifying an opinion because of an insufficiency of audit evidence, an auditor should refer to the situation in the

	Opening (introductory) paragraph	Scope paragraph
a.	No	No
b.	Yes	No
c.	Yes	Yes
d.	No	Yes

M94#89. When unaudited financial statements of a nonpublic entity are presented in comparative form with audited financial statements in the subsequent year, the unaudited financial statements should be clearly marked to indicate their status and

I. The report on the unaudited financial statements should be reissued.
II. The report on the audited financial statements should include a separate paragraph describing the responsibility assumed for the unaudited financial statements.

a. I only.
b. II only.
c. Both I and II.
d. Either I or II.

M94#90. An auditor expressed a qualified opinion on the prior year's financial statements because of a lack of adequate disclosure. These financial statements are properly restated in the current year and presented in comparative form with the current year's financial statements. The auditor's updated report on the prior year's financial statements should

a. Be accompanied by the auditor's original report on the prior year's financial statements.
b. Continue to express a qualified opinion on the prior year's financial statements.
c. Make **no** reference to the type of opinion expressed on the prior year's financial statements.
d. Express an unqualified opinion on the restated financial statements of the prior year.

N93#45. When auditing an entity's financial statements in accordance with *Government Auditing Standards*, an auditor should prepare a written report on the auditor's

a. Identification of the causes of performance problems and recommendations for actions to improve operations.
b. Understanding of internal control and assessment of control risk.
c. Field work and procedures that substantiated the auditor's specific findings and conclusions.
d. Opinion on the entity's attainment of the goals and objectives specified by applicable laws and regulations.

N93#46. When disclaiming an opinion due to a client-imposed scope limitation, an auditor should indicate in a separate paragraph why the audit did not comply with generally accepted auditing standards. The auditor should also omit the

	Scope paragraph	Opinion paragraph
a.	No	Yes
b.	Yes	Yes
c.	No	No
d.	Yes	No

N93#48. Comparative financial statements include the financial statements of the prior year that were audited by a predecessor auditor whose report is not presented. If the predecessor's report was qualified, the successor should

a. Indicate the substantive reasons for the qualification in the predecessor auditor's opinion.
b. Request the client to reissue the predecessor's report on the prior year's statements.
c. Issue an updated comparative audit report indicating the division of responsibility.
d. Express an opinion only on the current year's statements and make **no** reference to the prior year's statements.

N93#49. An auditor decides to issue a qualified opinion on an entity's financial statements because a major inadequacy in its computerized accounting records prevents the auditor from applying necessary procedures. The opinion paragraph of the auditor's report should state that the qualification pertains to

a. A client-imposed scope limitation.
b. A departure from generally accepted auditing standards.
c. The possible effects on the financial statements.
d. Inadequate disclosure of necessary information.

N93#51. When an auditor qualifies an opinion because of inadequate disclosure, the auditor should describe the nature of the omission in a separate explanatory paragraph and modify the

	Introductory paragraph	Scope paragraph
a.	Yes	Yes
b.	Yes	No
c.	No	Yes
d.	No	No

N93#52. Several sources of GAAP consulted by an auditor are in conflict as to the application of an accounting principle. Which of the following should the auditor consider the most authoritative?

a. FASB Technical Bulletins.
b. AICPA Accounting Interpretations.
c. FASB Statements of Financial Accounting Concepts.
d. AICPA Technical Practice Aids.

N93#53. During an engagement to review the financial statements of a nonpublic entity, an accountant becomes

aware of a material departure from GAAP. If the accountant decides to modify the standard review report because management will **not** revise the financial statements, the accountant should
a. Express negative assurance on the accounting principles that do **not** conform with GAAP.
b. Disclose the departure from GAAP in a separate paragraph of the report.
c. Issue an adverse or an "except for" qualified opinion, depending on materiality.
d. Express positive assurance on the accounting principles that conform with GAAP.

N93#54. Which of the following representations does an accountant make implicitly when issuing the standard report for the compilation of a nonpublic entity's financial statements?
a. The accountant is independent with respect to the entity.
b. The financial statements have **not** been audited.
c. A compilation consists principally of inquiries and analytical procedures.
d. The accountant does **not** express any assurance on the financial statements.

N93#55. An entity changed from the straight-line method to the declining balance method of depreciation for all newly acquired assets. This change has no material effect on the current year's financial statements, but is reasonably certain to have a substantial effect in later years. If the change is disclosed in the notes to the financial statements, the auditor should issue a report with a(an)
a. "Except for" qualified opinion.
b. Explanatory paragraph.
c. Unqualified opinion.
d. Consistency modification.

N93#57. An accountant's standard report on a compilation of a projection should **not** include a
a. Statement that a compilation of a projection is limited in scope.
b. Disclaimer of responsibility to update the report for events occurring after the report's date.
c. Statement that the accountant expresses only limited assurance that the results may be achieved.
d. Separate paragraph that describes the limitations on the presentation's usefulness.

N93#58. In performing a financial statement audit in accordance with *Government Auditing Standards,* an auditor is required to report on the entity's compliance with laws and regulations. This report should
a. State that compliance with laws and regulations is the responsibility of the entity's management.
b. Describe the laws and regulations that the entity must comply with.
c. Provide an opinion on overall compliance with laws and regulations.
d. Indicate that the auditor does **not** possess legal skills and **cannot** make legal judgments.

M93#24. Reporting on internal control under *Government Auditing Standards* differs from reporting under generally accepted auditing standards in that *Government Auditing Standards* requires a
a. Written report describing the entity's internal control activities specifically designed to prevent fraud, abuse, and illegal acts.
b. Written report describing each reportable condition observed including identification of those considered material weaknesses.
c. Statement of negative assurance that the internal control activities **not** tested have an immaterial effect on the entity's financial statements.
d. Statement of positive assurance that internal control activities designed to detect material errors and fraud were tested.

M93#44. An auditor most likely would modify an unqualified opinion if the entity's financial statements include a footnote on related party transactions
a. Disclosing loans to related parties at interest rates significantly below prevailing market rates.
b. Describing an exchange of real estate for similar property in a nonmonetary related party transaction.
c. Stating that a particular related party transaction occurred on terms equivalent to those that would have prevailed in an arm's-length transaction.
d. Presenting the dollar volume of related party transactions and the effects of any change in the method of establishing terms from prior periods.

M93#46. If a publicly held company issues financial statements that purport to present its financial position and results of operations but omits the statement of cash flows, the auditor ordinarily will express a(an)
a. Disclaimer of opinion.
b. Qualified opinion.
c. Review report.
d. Unqualified opinion with a separate explanatory paragraph.

M93#47. In which of the following circumstances would an auditor most likely add an explanatory paragraph to the standard report while **not** affecting the auditor's unqualified opinion?
a. The auditor is asked to report on the balance sheet, but **not** on the other basic financial statements.
b. There is substantial doubt about the entity's ability to continue as a going concern.
c. Management's estimates of the effects of future events are unreasonable.
d. Certain transactions **cannot** be tested because of management's records retention policy.

M93#48. Which of the following best describes the auditor's reporting responsibility concerning information

accompanying the basic financial statements in an auditor-submitted document?
- a. The auditor has **no** reporting responsibility concerning information accompanying the basic financial statements.
- b. The auditor should report on the information accompanying the basic financial statements only if the auditor participated in its preparation.
- c. The auditor should report on the information accompanying the basic financial statements only if the auditor did **not** participate in its preparation.
- d. The auditor should report on all the information included in the document.

M93#49. When an entity changes its method of accounting for income taxes, which has a material effect on comparability, the auditor should refer to the change in an explanatory paragraph added to the auditor's report. This paragraph should identify the nature of the change and
- a. Explain why the change is justified under generally accepted accounting principles.
- b. Describe the cumulative effect of the change on the audited financial statements.
- c. State the auditor's explicit concurrence with or opposition to the change.
- d. Refer to the financial statement note that discusses the change in detail.

M93#50. Green, CPA, was engaged to audit the financial statements of Essex Co. after its fiscal year had ended. The timing of Green's appointment as auditor and the start of field work made confirmation of accounts receivable by direct communication with the debtors ineffective. However, Green applied other procedures and was satisfied as to the reasonableness of the account balances. Green's auditor's report most likely contained a(an)
- a. Unqualified opinion.
- b. Unqualified opinion with an explanatory paragraph.
- c. Qualified opinion due to a scope limitation.
- d. Qualified opinion due to a departure from generally accepted auditing standards.

M93#55. In the auditor's report, the principal auditor decides not to make reference to another CPA who audited a client's subsidiary. The principal auditor could justify this decision if, among other requirements, the principal auditor
- a. Issues an unqualified opinion on the consolidated financial statements.
- b. Learns that the other CPA issued an unqualified opinion on the subsidiary's financial statements.
- c. Is unable to review the audit programs and working papers of the other CPA.
- d. Is satisfied as to the independence and professional reputation of the other CPA.

M93#56. A limitation on the scope of an audit sufficient to preclude an unqualified opinion will usually result when management
- a. Is unable to obtain audited financial statements supporting the entity's investment in a foreign subsidiary.
- b. Refuses to disclose in the notes to the financial statements related party transactions authorized by the Board of Directors.
- c. Does **not** sign an engagement letter specifying the responsibilities of both the entity and the auditor.
- d. Fails to correct a reportable condition communicated to the audit committee after the prior year's audit.

M93#58. In which of the following situations would an auditor ordinarily choose between expressing an "except for" qualified opinion or an adverse opinion?
- a. The auditor did **not** observe the entity's physical inventory and is unable to become satisfied as to its balance by other auditing procedures.
- b. The financial statements fail to disclose information that is required by generally accepted accounting principles.
- c. The auditor is asked to report only on the entity's balance sheet and **not** on the other basic financial statements.
- d. Events disclosed in the financial statements cause the auditor to have substantial doubt about the entity's ability to continue as a going concern.

N92#23. Which of the following representations should **not** be included in a report on internal control related matters noted in an audit?
- a. Reportable conditions related to internal control design exist, but **none** is deemed to be a material weakness.
- b. There are **no** significant deficiencies in the design or operation of internal control.
- c. Corrective follow-up action is recommended due to the relative significance of material weaknesses discovered during the audit.
- d. The auditor's consideration of internal control would **not** necessarily disclose all reportable conditions that exist.

N92#46. Which of the following phrases should be included in the opinion paragraph when an auditor expresses a qualified opinion?

	When read in conjunction with Note X	*With the foregoing explanation*
a.	Yes	No
b.	No	Yes
c.	Yes	Yes
d.	No	No

N92#47. When an auditor expresses an adverse opinion, the opinion paragraph should include

a. The principal effects of the departure from generally accepted accounting principles.
b. A direct reference to a separate paragraph disclosing the basis for the opinion.
c. The substantive reasons for the financial statements being misleading.
d. A description of the uncertainty or scope limitation that prevents an unqualified opinion.

N92#48. Under which of the following circumstances would a disclaimer of opinion **not** be appropriate?
a. The financial statements fail to contain adequate disclosure of related party transactions.
b. The client refuses to permit its attorney to furnish information requested in a letter of audit inquiry.
c. The auditor is engaged after fiscal year-end and is unable to observe physical inventories or apply alternative procedures to verify their balances.
d. The auditor is unable to determine the amounts associated with illegal acts committed by the client's management.

N92#52. Jones Retailing, a nonpublic entity, has asked Winters, CPA, to compile financial statements that omit substantially all disclosures required by generally accepted accounting principles. Winters may compile such financial statements provided the
a. Reason for omitting the disclosures is explained in the engagement letter and acknowledged in the management representation letter.
b. Financial statements are prepared on a comprehensive basis of accounting other than generally accepted accounting principles.
c. Distribution of the financial statements is restricted to internal use only.
d. Omission is **not** undertaken to mislead the users of the financial statements and is properly disclosed in the accountant's report.

M92#1. When engaged to audit a governmental entity in accordance with *Government Auditing Standards,* an auditor prepares a written report on internal control
a. In all audits, regardless of circumstances.
b. Only when the auditor has noted reportable conditions.
c. Only when requested by the governmental entity being audited.
d. Only when requested by the federal government funding agency.

M92#3. When a predecessor auditor reissues the report on the prior period's financial statements at the request of the former client, the predecessor auditor should
a. Indicate in the introductory paragraph of the reissued report that the financial statements of the subsequent period were audited by another CPA.
b. Obtain an updated management representation letter and compare it to that obtained during the prior period audit.
c. Compare the prior period's financial statements that the predecessor reported on with the financial statements to be presented for comparative purposes.
d. Add an explanatory paragraph to the reissued report stating that the predecessor has **not** performed additional auditing procedures concerning the prior period's financial statements.

M92#4. Clark, CPA, compiled and properly reported on the financial statements of Green Co., a nonpublic entity, for the year ended March 31, 1991. These financial statements omitted substantially all disclosures required by generally accepted accounting principles (GAAP). Green asked Clark to compile the statements for the year ended March 31, 1992, and to include all GAAP disclosures for the 1992 statements only, but otherwise present both years' financial statements in comparative form. What is Clark's responsibility concerning the proposed engagement?
a. Clark may **not** report on the comparative financial statements because the 1991 statements are **not** comparable to the 1992 statements that include the GAAP disclosures.
b. Clark may report on the comparative financial statements provided the 1991 statements do **not** contain any obvious material misstatements.
c. Clark may report on the comparative financial statements provided an explanatory paragraph is added to Clark's report on the comparative financial statements.
d. Clark may report on the comparative financial statements provided Clark updates the report on the 1991 statements that do **not** include the GAAP disclosures.

M92#5. Which of the following statements should **not** be included in an accountant's standard report based on the compilation of an entity's financial statements?
a. A statement that the compilation was performed in accordance with standards established by the American Institute of CPAs.
b. A statement that the accountant has **not** audited or reviewed the financial statements.
c. A statement that the accountant does **not** express an opinion but expresses only limited assurance on the financial statements.
d. A statement that a compilation is limited to presenting, in the form of financial statements, information that is the representation of management.

M92#9. An accountant's compilation report on a financial forecast should include a statement that the
a. Compilation does **not** include evaluation of the support of the assumptions underlying the forecast.
b. Hypothetical assumptions used in the forecast are reasonable.

c. Range of assumptions selected is one in which one end of the range is less likely to occur than the other.
d. Prospective statements are limited to presenting, in the form of a forecast, information that is the accountant's representation.

M92#11. An auditor's responsibility to express an opinion on the financial statements is
a. Implicitly represented in the auditor's standard report.
b. Explicitly represented in the opening paragraph of the auditor's standard report.
c. Explicitly represented in the scope paragraph of the auditor's standard report.
d. Explicitly represented in the opinion paragraph of the auditor's standard report.

M92#32. In an audit in accordance with *Government Auditing Standards* an auditor is required to report on the auditor's tests of the entity's compliance with applicable laws and regulations. This requirement is satisfied by designing the audit to provide
a. Positive assurance that the internal control activities tested by the auditor are operating as prescribed.
b. Reasonable assurance of detecting misstatements that are material to the financial statements.
c. Negative assurance that reportable conditions communicated during the audit do **not** prevent the auditor from expressing an opinion.
d. Limited assurance that the internal controls designed by management will prevent or detect errors, fraud, and illegal acts.

M92#51. Which of the following statements concerning an auditor's communication of reportable conditions is correct?
a. The auditor should request a meeting with management one level above the source of the reportable conditions to discuss suggestions for remedial action.
b. Any report issued on reportable conditions should indicate that providing assurance on internal control was **not** the purpose of the audit.
c. Reportable conditions discovered and communicated at an interim date should be reexamined with tests of controls before completing the engagement.
d. Suggestions concerning administration efficiencies and business strategies should **not** be communicated in the same report with reportable conditions.

N91#16. An auditor may reasonably issue an "except for" qualified opinion for a(an)

	Scope limitation	Unjustified accounting change
a.	Yes	No
b.	No	Yes
c.	Yes	Yes
d.	No	No

N91#21. How does an auditor make the following representations when issuing the standard auditor's report on comparative financial statements?

	Examination of evidence on a test basis	Consistent application of accounting principles
a.	Explicitly	Explicitly
b.	Implicitly	Implicitly
c.	Implicitly	Explicitly
d.	Explicitly	Implicitly

N91#22. An auditor was unable to obtain sufficient competent evidential matter concerning certain transactions due to an inadequacy in the entity's accounting records. The auditor would choose between issuing a(an)
a. Qualified opinion and an unqualified opinion with an explanatory paragraph.
b. Unqualified opinion with an explanatory paragraph and an adverse opinion.
c. Adverse opinion and a disclaimer of opinion.
d. Disclaimer of opinion and a qualified opinion.

N91#23. For an entity's financial statements to be presented fairly in conformity with generally accepted accounting principles, the principles selected should
a. Be applied on a basis consistent with those followed in the prior year.
b. Be approved by the Auditing Standards Board or the appropriate industry subcommittee.
c. Reflect transactions in a manner that presents the financial statements within a range of acceptable limits.
d. Match the principles used by most other entities within the entity's particular industry.

N91#26. How does an accountant make the following representations when issuing the standard report for the compilation of a nonpublic entity's financial statements?

	The financial statements have **not** been audited	The accountant has compiled the financial statements
a.	Implicitly	Implicitly
b.	Explicitly	Explicitly
c.	Implicitly	Explicitly
d.	Explicitly	Implicitly

N91#27. The objective of a review of interim financial information of a public entity is to provide the accountant with a basis for
a. Determining whether the prospective financial information is based on reasonable assumptions.

b. Expressing a limited opinion that the financial information is presented in conformity with generally accepted accounting principles.
c. Deciding whether to perform substantive audit procedures prior to the balance sheet date.
d. Reporting whether material modifications should be made for such information to conform with generally accepted accounting principles.

M91#35. A previously communicated reportable condition that has not been corrected ordinarily should be communicated again if
a. The deficiency has a material effect on the auditor's assessment of control risk.
b. The entity accepts that degree of risk because of cost-benefit considerations.
c. The weakness could adversely affect the entity's ability to report financial data.
d. There has been major turnover in upper-level management and the board of directors.

M91#38. Green, CPA, is aware that Green's name is to be included in the interim report of National Company, a publicly-held entity. National's quarterly financial statements are contained in the interim report. Green has not audited or reviewed these interim financial statements. Green should request that

I. Green's name not be included in the communication.
II. The financial statements be marked as unaudited with a notation that **no** opinion is expressed on them.

a. I only.
b. II only.
c. Both I and II.
d. Either I or II.

M91#42. An auditor was unable to obtain audited financial statements or other evidence supporting an entity's investment in a foreign subsidiary. Between which of the following opinions should the entity's auditor choose?
a. Adverse and unqualified with an explanatory paragraph added.
b. Disclaimer and unqualified with an explanatory paragraph added.
c. Qualified and adverse.
d. Qualified and disclaimer.

M91#46. When an auditor qualifies an opinion because of inadequate disclosure, the auditor should describe the nature of the omission in a separate explanatory paragraph and modify the

	Introductory paragraph	*Scope paragraph*	*Opinion paragraph*
a.	Yes	No	No
b.	Yes	Yes	No
c.	No	Yes	Yes
d.	No	No	Yes

B. Prepare Letters and Other Required Communications

R98#17. An auditor may report on condensed financial statements that are derived from complete financial statements if the
a. Condensed financial statements are distributed to stockholders along with the complete financial statements.
b. Auditor describes the additional procedures performed on the condensed financial statements.
c. Auditor indicates whether the information in the condensed financial statements is fairly stated in all material respects in relation to the complete financial statements from which it has been derived.
d. Condensed financial statements are presented in comparative form with the prior year's condensed financial statements.

R96#16. Financial information is presented in a printed form that prescribes the wording of the independent auditor's report. The form is not acceptable to the auditor because the form calls for statements that are inconsistent with the auditor's responsibility. Under these circumstances, the auditor most likely would
a. Withdraw from the engagement.
b. Reword the form or attach a separate report.
c. Express a qualified opinion with an explanation.
d. Limit distribution of the report to the party who designed the form.

N95#83. Field is an employee of Gold Enterprises. Hardy, CPA, is asked to express an opinion on Field's profit participation in Gold's net income. Hardy may accept this engagement only if
a. Hardy also audits Gold's complete financial statements.
b. Gold's financial statements are prepared in conformity with GAAP.
c. Hardy's report is available for distribution to Gold's other employees.
d. Field owns controlling interest in Gold.

N95#84. Which of the following statements is correct about an auditor's required communication with an entity's audit committee?
a. Any matters communicated to the entity's audit committee also are required to be communicated to the entity's management.
b. The auditor is required to inform the entity's audit committee about significant errors discovered by the auditor and subsequently corrected by management.
c. Disagreements with management about the application of accounting principles are required to be communicated in writing to the entity's audit committee.
d. Weaknesses in internal control previously reported to the entity's audit committee are

required to be communicated to the audit committee after each subsequent audit until the weaknesses are corrected.

N95#86. A registration statement filed with the SEC contains the reports of two independent auditors on their audits of financial statements for different periods. The predecessor auditor who audited the prior-period financial statements generally should obtain a letter of representation from the
    a. Successor independent auditor.
    b. Client's audit committee.
    c. Principal underwriter.
    d. Securities and Exchange Commission.

N95#87. An auditor is engaged to report on selected financial data that are included in a client-prepared document containing audited financial statements. Under these circumstances, the report on the selected data should
    a. Be limited to data derived from the audited financial statements.
    b. Be distributed only to senior management and the board of directors.
    c. State that the presentation is a comprehensive basis of accounting other than GAAP.
    d. Indicate that the data are **not** fairly stated in all material respects.

M95#19. An auditor would **least** likely initiate a discussion with a client's audit committee concerning
    a. The methods used to account for significant unusual transactions.
    b. The maximum dollar amount of misstatements that could exist without causing the financial statements to be materially misstated.
    c. Indications of fraud and illegal acts committed by a corporate officer that were discovered by the auditor.
    d. Disagreements with management as to accounting principles that were resolved during the current year's audit.

M95#82. An auditor's report on financial statements prepared on the cash receipts and disbursements basis of accounting should include all of the following **except**
    a. A reference to the note to the financial statements that describes the cash receipts and disbursements basis of accounting.
    b. A statement that the cash receipts and disbursements basis of accounting is **not** a comprehensive basis of accounting.
    c. An opinion as to whether the financial statements are presented fairly in conformity with the cash receipts and disbursements basis of accounting.
    d. A statement that the audit was conducted in accordance with generally accepted auditing standards.

M95#86. Which of the following statements is correct concerning letters for underwriters, commonly referred to as comfort letters?
    a. Letters for underwriters are required by the Securities Act of 1933 for the initial public sale of registered securities.
    b. Letters for underwriters typically give negative assurance on unaudited interim financial information.
    c. Letters for underwriters usually are included in the registration statement accompanying a prospectus.
    d. Letters for underwriters ordinarily update auditors' opinions on the prior year's financial statements.

M95#87. If information accompanying the basic financial statements in an auditor-submitted document has been subjected to auditing procedures, the auditor may include in the auditor's report on the financial statements an opinion that the accompanying information is fairly stated in
    a. Accordance with generally accepted auditing standards.
    b. Conformity with generally accepted accounting principles.
    c. All material respects in relation to the basic financial statements taken as a whole.
    d. Accordance with attestation standards expressing a conclusion about management's assertions.

M95#88. Which of the following statements is correct concerning an auditor's required communication with an entity's audit committee?
    a. This communication is required to occur before the auditor's report on the financial statements is issued.
    b. This communication should include management changes in the application of significant accounting policies.
    c. Any significant matter communicated to the audit committee also should be communicated to management.
    d. Significant audit adjustments proposed by the auditor and recorded by management need **not** be communicated to the audit committee.

N94#87. In the standard report on condensed financial statements that are derived from a public entity's audited financial statements, a CPA should indicate that the
    a. Condensed financial statements are prepared in conformity with another comprehensive basis of accounting.
    b. CPA has audited and expressed an opinion on the complete financial statements.
    c. Condensed financial statements are **not** fairly presented in all material respects.
    d. CPA expresses limited assurance that the financial statements conform with GAAP.

N94#88. Before reporting on the financial statements of a U.S. entity that have been prepared in conformity with another country's accounting principles, an auditor practicing in the U.S. should

a. Understand the accounting principles generally accepted in the other country.
b. Be certified by the appropriate auditing or accountancy board of the other country.
c. Notify management that the auditor is required to disclaim an opinion on the financial statements.
d. Receive a waiver from the auditor's state board of accountancy to perform the engagement.

M94#64. An independent accountant's report is based on a review of interim financial information. If this report is presented in a registration statement, a prospectus should include a statement clarifying that the
a. Accountant's review report is **not** a part of the registration statement within the meaning of the Securities Act of 1933.
b. Accountant assumes **no** responsibility to update the report for events and circumstances occurring after the date of the report.
c. Accountant's review was performed in accordance with standards established by the Securities and Exchange Commission.
d. Accountant obtained corroborating evidence to determine whether material modifications are needed for such information to conform with GAAP.

M94#67. In connection with a proposal to obtain a new client, an accountant in public practice is asked to prepare a written report on the application of accounting principles to a specific transaction. The accountant's report should include a statement that
a. Any difference in the facts, circumstances, or assumptions presented may change the report.
b. The engagement was performed in accordance with Statements on Standards for Consulting Services.
c. The guidance provided is for management use only and may **not** be communicated to the prior or continuing auditors.
d. Nothing came to the accountant's attention that caused the accountant to believe that the accounting principles violated GAAP.

M94#68. An accountant's report on a review of pro forma financial information should include a
a. Statement that the entity's internal control was **not** relied on in the review.
b. Disclaimer of opinion on the financial statements from which the pro forma financial information is derived.
c. Caveat that it is uncertain whether the transaction or event reflected in the pro forma financial information will ever occur.
d. Reference to the financial statements from which the historical financial information is derived.

M94#83. When an auditor reports on financial statements prepared on an entity's income tax basis, the auditor's report should

a. Disclaim an opinion on whether the statements were examined in accordance with generally accepted auditing standards.
b. Not express an opinion on whether the statements are presented in conformity with the comprehensive basis of accounting used.
c. Include an explanation of how the results of operations differ from the cash receipts and disbursements basis of accounting.
d. State that the basis of presentation is a comprehensive basis of accounting other than GAAP.

N93#50. When unaudited financial statements are presented in comparative form with audited financial statements in a document filed with the Securities and Exchange Commission, such statements should be

	Marked as "unaudited"	Withheld until audited	Referred to in the auditor's report
a.	Yes	No	No
b.	Yes	No	Yes
c.	No	Yes	Yes
d.	No	Yes	No

M93#51. Which of the following matters is covered in a typical comfort letter?
a. Negative assurance concerning whether the entity's internal control activities operated as designed during the period being audited.
b. An opinion regarding whether the entity complied with laws and regulations under *Government Auditing Standards* and the Single Audit Act of 1984.
c. Positive assurance concerning whether unaudited condensed financial information complied with generally accepted accounting principles.
d. An opinion as to whether the audited financial statements comply in form with the accounting requirements of the SEC.

M93#57. Delta Life Insurance Co. prepares its financial statements on an accounting basis insurance companies use pursuant to the rules of a state insurance commission. If Wall, CPA, Delta's auditor, discovers that the statements are **not** suitably titled, Wall should
a. Disclose any reservations in an explanatory paragraph and qualify the opinion.
b. Apply to the state insurance commission for an advisory opinion.
c. Issue a special statutory basis report that clearly disclaims any opinion.
d. Explain in the notes to the financial statements the terminology used.

M93#59. Which of the following statements is correct concerning an auditor's required communication with an entity's audit committee?
a. This communication should include disagreements with management about significant audit

adjustments, whether or **not** satisfactorily resolved.
   b. If matters are communicated orally, it is necessary to repeat the communication of recurring matters each year.
   c. If matters are communicated in writing, the report is required to be distributed to both the audit committee and management.
   d. This communication is required to occur before the auditor's report on the financial statements is issued.

N92#50. Blue, CPA, has been asked to render an opinion on the application of accounting principles to a specific transaction by an entity that is audited by another CPA. Blue may accept this engagement, but should
   a. Consult with the continuing CPA to obtain information relevant to the transaction.
   b. Report the engagement's findings to the entity's audit committee, the continuing CPA, and management.
   c. Disclaim any opinion that the hypothetical application of accounting principles conforms with generally accepted accounting principles.
   d. Notify the entity that the report is for the restricted use of management and outside parties who are aware of all relevant facts.

N92#54. An auditor's special report on financial statements prepared in conformity with the cash basis of accounting should include a separate explanatory paragraph before the opinion paragraph that
   a. Justifies the reasons for departing from generally accepted accounting principles.
   b. States whether the financial statements are fairly presented in conformity with another comprehensive basis of accounting.
   c. Refers to the note to the financial statements that describes the basis of accounting.
   d. Explains how the results of operations differ from financial statements prepared in conformity with generally accepted accounting principles.

N92#58. Comfort letters ordinarily are signed by the client's
   a. Independent auditor.
   b. Underwriter of securities.
   c. Audit committee.
   d. Senior management.

M92#8. When an accountant issues to an underwriter a comfort letter containing comments on data that have **not** been audited, the underwriter most likely will receive
   a. Negative assurance on capsule information.
   b. Positive assurance on supplementary disclosures.
   c. A limited opinion on "pro forma" financial statements.
   d. A disclaimer on prospective financial statements.

N91#29. An auditor may report on condensed financial statements that are derived from complete audited financial statements if the
   a. Auditor indicates whether the information in the condensed financial statements is fairly stated in all material respects.
   b. Condensed financial statements are presented in comparative form with the prior year's condensed financial statements.
   c. Auditor describes the additional review procedures performed on the condensed financial statements.
   d. Condensed financial statements are distributed only to management and the board of directors.

M91#49. The financial statements of KCP America, a U.S. entity, are prepared for inclusion in the consolidated financial statements of its non-U.S. parent. These financial statements are prepared in conformity with the accounting principles generally accepted in the parent's country and are for use only in that country. How may KCP America's auditor report on these financial statements?

I. A U.S.-style report (unmodified).
II. A U.S.-style report modified to report on the accounting principles of the parent's country.
III. The report form of the parent's country.

	I	*II*	*III*
a.	Yes	No	No
b.	No	Yes	No
c.	Yes	No	Yes
d.	No	Yes	Yes

M91#54. Comfort letters ordinarily are addressed to
   a. Creditor financial institutions.
   b. The client's audit committee.
   c. The Securities and Exchange Commission.
   d. Underwriters of securities.

C. Other Matters

N95#85. Which of the following events occurring after the issuance of an auditor's report most likely would cause the auditor to make further inquiries about the previously issued financial statements?
   a. An uninsured natural disaster occurs that may affect the entity's ability to continue as a going concern.
   b. A contingency is resolved that had been disclosed in the audited financial statements.
   c. New information is discovered concerning undisclosed lease transactions of the audited period.
   d. A subsidiary is sold that accounts for 25% of the entity's consolidated net income.

M95#85. An auditor is considering whether the omission of a substantive procedure considered necessary at the time of an audit may impair the auditor's present

ability to support the previously expressed opinion. The auditor need **not** apply the omitted procedure if the
a. Financial statements and auditor's report were **not** distributed beyond management and the board of directors.
b. Auditor's previously expressed opinion was qualified because of a departure from GAAP.
c. Results of other procedures that were applied tend to compensate for the procedure omitted.
d. Omission is due to unreasonable delays by client personnel in providing data on a timely basis.

SELECTED MULTIPLE CHOICE ITEMS — UNOFFICIAL ANSWERS

I. Plan, Evaluate, and Accept the Engagement

A. Determine Nature and Scope of Engagement

R98# 1 a
R96# 1 d
N95# 36 c
N95# 61 c
M95# 1 d
M95# 20 b
M95# 21 d
M95# 22 d
N94# 18 b
N94# 19 b
N94# 20 a
N94# 22 d
N94# 23 a
M94# 9 a
M94# 10 a
M94# 11 c
M94# 14 c
M94# 37 a
N93# 2 d
N93# 9 c
N93# 12 d
N93# 56 a
M93# 4 d
N92# 5 c
M92# 60 a
N91# 13 d
N91# 59 a
M91# 51 b

B. Assess Engagement Risk and the CPA Firm's Ability to Perform the Engagement

R98# 2 c
R97# 1 b
N95# 4 b
M95# 5 a
M95# 6 a
M95# 7 b
M95# 23 d
N94# 4 a
N94# 24 c
M94# 3 b
N93# 3 b

N93# 4 b
N92# 3 a

C. Communicate With the Predecessor Accountant/Auditor

R97# 2 d
R96# 9 c
M95# 2 d
M95# 18 d
N94# 3 a
M94# 1 b

D. Decide Whether to Accept or Continue the Client and Engagement

R96# 10 a
N94# 2 c
M94# 2 c

E. Enter Into an Agreement With the Client as to the Terms of the Engagement

M95# 3 d
M94# 12 b

F. Obtain an Understanding of the Client's Operations, Business, and Industry

N94# 6 b
N94# 7 a
M94# 4 d
M94# 46 d
N92# 44 b

G. Perform Analytical Procedures

R97# 3 c
M95# 4 b
M95# 8 c
M94# 5 a

M93# 30 b
N91# 3 b

H. Consider Preliminary Engagement Materiality

R97# 10 c
R97# 11 b
M95# 11 b
N94# 11 b
N93# 6 a
N92# 42 c
M91# 52 c

I. Assess Inherent Risk and Risk of Misstatements

R97# 12 a
R97# 13 b
N95# 17 c
M95# 9 a
M95# 10 c
M95# 12 b
M95# 13 b
M95# 14 c
N94# 8 c
N94# 9 d
N94# 10 b
N94# 12 c
N94# 13 d
M94# 6 a
M94# 7 d
N93# 11 b
N93# 15 a
N92# 4 a
N92# 10 c
N92# 56 c
M92# 57 d
N91# 7 b
N91# 12 a
M91# 26 a

J. Consider Internal Control

R98# 3 b
R98# 4 d
R98# 5 a
R98# 6 d

R98# 7 c
R98# 8 d
R98# 9 c
R98# 10 a
R97# 4 d
R97# 14 c
R96# 2 a
N95# 2 a
N95# 3 b
N95# 5 b
N95# 6 c
N95# 7 c
N95# 8 d
N95# 9 a
N95# 10 c
N95# 11 c
N95# 12 a
N95# 14 b
N95# 15 a
N95# 16 b
N95# 18 b
N95# 19 d
N95# 20 a
N95# 21 d
N95# 22 d
N95# 23 d
N95# 24 c
N95# 25 d
N95# 26 d
N95# 30 d
N95# 32 c
M95# 24 a
M95# 25 c
M95# 27 c
M95# 28 d
M95# 30 c
M95# 33 a
N94# 27 b
N94# 28 b
N94# 30 b
N94# 32 c
N94# 33 a
N94# 34 c
N94# 35 d
N94# 37 c
N94# 38 a
N94# 39 b
N94# 40 d
N94# 41 d
N94# 42 d

A-63

Auditing

N94# 43 b	M93#16 a	**K. Consider Other Planning Matters**	N95# 38 a
N94# 70 a	M93#17 d		M95#16 c
M94#16 b	M93#18 b		M95#69 d
M94#18 d	M93#20 b	R97# 5 b	N94# 57 d
M94#22 a	M93#21 a	R96# 3 d	M94# 8 a
M94#23 c	M93#22 d	N95# 1 d	M94#45 d
M94#25 a	M93#25 d	N95# 53 d	
M94#27 b	M93#41 c	N95# 54 d	
M94#28 a	N92# 12 b	N95# 58 c	**M. Determine and Prepare the Work Program**
M94#29 c	N92# 13 d	M95#59 c	
M94#31 c	N92# 14 d	M95#60 d	
M94#32 c	N92# 16 b	M95#62 a	
M94#33 d	N92# 17 b	M95#68 d	N95# 52 a
M94#34 a	N92# 19 a	N94# 1 d	M95#17 a
M94#35 a	N92# 20 c	N94# 25 b	M95#70 a
M94#44 d	N92# 21 c	N94# 65 d	M95#71 a
N93# 16 b	N92# 22 a	N94# 68 d	N94# 16 d
N93# 18 d	N92# 25 d	N94# 69 c	N94# 17 c
N93# 20 c	N92# 36 b	M94#52 b	N94# 72 c
N93# 21 a	N92# 37 c	M94#57 c	N94# 73 d
N93# 22 a	M92#45 c	M93# 6 d	M94#51 b
N93# 23 c	M92#48 a	N92# 40 d	M94#58 c
N93# 27 c	M92#53 d	N92# 51 b	M93# 2 c
N93# 28 b	M92#54 d	M92#22 a	M93#39 d
N93# 30 c	M92#55 b	N91# 30 a	M93#40 d
N93# 32 d	N91# 32 c	N91# 56 c	N92# 35 a
N93# 33 b	N91# 35 d		M92#24 c
N93# 34 c	N91# 36 b	**L. Identify Financial Statement Assertions and Formulate Audit Objectives**	M92#47 b
M93# 7 c	N91# 55 b		M91#13 a
M93# 8 b	M91#16 c		M91#15 a
M93#14 c	M91#28 c		
M93#15 a	M91#31 b	R97# 6 a	

II. Obtain and Document Information to Form a Basis for Conclusions

A. Perform Planned Procedures Including Planned Applications of Audit Sampling	N95# 43 c	M95#52 d	N94# 74 a
	N95# 44 c	M95#53 c	M94#39 a
	N95# 45 d	M95#54 d	M94#40 b
	N95# 46 b	M95#55 a	M94#41 b
	N95# 47 c	M95#56 d	M94#42 b
R98# 11 c	N95# 48 c	M95#57 c	M94#43 c
R98# 12 a	N95# 49 b	M95#58 c	M94#47 a
R97# 7 b	N95# 50 a	M95#72 b	M94#48 a
R97# 15 a	N95# 51 c	M95#73 a	M94#49 c
R97# 16 a	M95#32 b	M95#74 c	M94#50 d
R97# 17 b	M95#34 b	M95#75 a	M94#59 d
R97# 18 b	M95#35 a	N94# 47 d	M94#60 c
R97# 19 d	M95#37 b	N94# 48 a	N93# 26 b
R96# 4 b	M95#39 c	N94# 49 c	N93# 35 b
R96# 5 c	M95#40 a	N94# 51 a	N93# 36 b
R96# 11 a	M95#41 a	N94# 52 b	N93# 40 d
N95# 27 c	M95#42 c	N94# 53 a	N93# 44 b
N95# 28 a	M95#43 a	N94# 54 c	M93#26 d
N95# 29 d	M95#44 b	N94# 55 b	M93#27 d
N95# 31 a	M95#45 a	N94# 56 b	M93#28 c
N95# 33 a	M95#46 c	N94# 58 b	M93#29 b
N95# 39 c	M95#48 b	N94# 59 d	M93#31 a
N95# 40 b	M95#49 b	N94# 60 c	M93#34 b
N95# 41 b	M95#50 b	N94# 61 d	M93#35 d
N95# 42 b	M95#51 a	N94# 62 d	M93#36 c

Unofficial Answers

M93#43 c	N91# 44 b	N94# 67 b	M92#35 c
N92# 26 a	N91# 49 d	M94#53 d	
N92# 27 a	M91#17 c	M93#45 a	**F. Identify Reportable Conditions and Other Control Deficiencies**
N92# 29 d	M91#19 a	N92# 41 c	
N92# 30 a	M91#20 b	M92#12 a	
N92# 31 b	M91#32 d		
N92# 38 d	M91#59 d		N95# 34 d
N92# 43 b		**E. Obtain Representations From Management**	N95# 35 d
N92# 45 d	**C. Obtain and Evaluate Lawyers' Letters**		N91# 43 d
M92#17 b			
M92#18 d			**G. Identify Matters for Communication With Audit Committees**
M92#19 d	R96# 12 b	R97# 8 c	
M92#20 c	M95#63 b	N95# 57 b	
M92#26 b	N94# 66 b	M95#66 a	
M92#27 b	N93# 39 c	M95#67 c	R96# 6 b
M92#30 b		N94# 64 c	N94# 84 b
M92#44 d	**D. Review Subsequent Events**	N94# 75 b	N93# 60 b
N91# 37 a		M94#54 a	N92# 60 c
N91# 42 d		M93#32 c	M92#15 a
	N95# 56 d	N92# 34 c	
	M95#65 d		

III. Review the Engagement

A. Perform Analytical Procedures	**B. Evaluate the Sufficiency and Competence of Audit Evidence and Document Engagement Conclusions**	N95# 59 d	**C. Review the Work Performed**
		N94# 71 a	
R97# 9 c		M94#55 b	
M95#47 c		M94#62 b	R96# 14 d
N93# 38 c		M93#53 d	N95# 60 d
M92#34 b		N92# 49 a	N94# 5 a
M91# 4 c		M91#43 c	M94#56 d
M91# 5 c			M92#33 b
	R98# 13 b		

IV. Prepare Communications to Satisfy Engagement Objectives

A. Prepare Reports	N95# 78 a	N94# 82 a	M94#89 d
	N95# 79 c	N94# 83 c	M94#90 d
R98# 14 c	N95# 80 c	N94# 86 a	N93# 45 b
R98# 15 a	N95# 81 a	N94# 90 d	N93# 46 d
R98# 16 a	N95# 82 a	M94#36 d	N93# 48 a
R96# 7 d	N95# 88 b	M94#61 b	N93# 49 c
R96# 8 d	N95# 90 b	M94#63 a	N93# 51 d
R96# 15 c	M95#38 c	M94#66 c	N93# 52 a
N95# 63 b	M95#76 b	M94#69 d	N93# 53 b
N95# 64 d	M95#77 d	M94#70 b	N93# 54 a
N95# 65 d	M95#78 b	M94#71 d	N93# 55 c
N95# 66 b	M95#79 b	M94#72 a	N93# 57 c
N95# 67 a	M95#80 c	M94#73 c	N93# 58 a
N95# 68 c	M95#81 c	M94#74 d	M93#24 b
N95# 69 d	M95#89 b	M94#75 a	M93#44 c
N95# 70 d	M95#90 b	M94#76 b	M93#46 b
N95# 71 c	N94# 45 c	M94#77 c	M93#47 b
N95# 72 d	N94# 76 d	M94#79 c	M93#48 d
N95# 73 a	N94# 77 d	M94#80 b	M93#49 d
N95# 74 b	N94# 78 c	M94#82 c	M93#50 a
N95# 75 a	N94# 79 c	M94#84 a	M93#55 d
N95# 76 d	N94# 80 b	M94#87 c	M93#56 a
N95# 77 a	N94# 81 a	M94#88 d	M93#58 b

A-65

Auditing

N92# 23 b	N91# 22 d	N95# 86 a	M93#57 a
N92# 46 d	N91# 23 c	N95# 87 a	M93#59 a
N92# 47 b	N91# 26 b	M95#19 b	N92# 50 a
N92# 48 a	N91# 27 d	M95#82 b	N92# 54 c
N92# 52 d	M91#35 d	M95#86 b	N92# 58 a
M92# 1 a	M91#38 d	M95#87 c	M92# 8 a
M92# 3 c	M91#42 d	M95#88 b	N91# 29 a
M92# 4 a	M91#46 d	N94# 87 b	M91#49 d
M92# 5 c		N94# 88 a	M91#54 d
M92# 9 a	**B. Prepare Letters and Other Required Communications**	M94#64 a	
M92#11 b		M94#67 a	**C. Other Matters**
M92#32 b		M94#68 d	
M92#51 b	R98# 17 c	M94#83 d	N95# 85 c
N91# 16 c	R96# 16 b	N93# 50 a	M95#85 c
N91# 21 d	N95# 83 a	M93#51 d	
	N95# 84 b		

OTHER OBJECTIVE ANSWER FORMATS — SELECTED QUESTIONS

I. Plan, Evaluate, and Accept the Engagement

B. Assess Engagement Risk and the CPA Firm's Ability to Perform the Engagement

M94
Number 3 (Estimated time — — 15 to 25 minutes)

Instructions

Question Number 3 consists of 15 items pertaining to an auditor's risk analysis of an entity. Select the **best** answer for each item. Use a No. 2 pencil to blacken the appropriate ovals on the Objective Answer Sheet to indicate your answers. **Answer all items.** Your grade will be based on the total number of correct answers.

Bond, CPA, is considering audit risk at the financial statement level in planning the audit of Toxic Waste Disposal (TWD) Company's financial statements for the year ended December 31, 1993. TWD is a privately-owned entity that contracts with municipal governments to remove environmental wastes. Audit risk at the financial statement level is influenced by the risk of material misstatements, which may be indicated by a combination of factors related to management, the industry, and the entity.

Required:
Based only on the information below, indicate whether each of the following factors (**Items 106 through 120**) would most likely increase audit risk Ⓘ, decrease audit risk Ⓓ, or have **no** effect on audit risk Ⓝ, and blacken the corresponding oval on the Objective Answer Sheet.

Items to be Answered:

Company Profile

106. This was the first year TWD operated at a profit since 1989 because the municipalities received increased federal and state funding for environmental purposes.

107. TWD's Board of Directors is controlled by Mead, the majority stockholder, who also acts as the chief executive officer.

108. The internal auditor reports to the controller and the controller reports to Mead.

109. The accounting department has experienced a high rate of turnover of key personnel.

110. TWD's bank has a loan officer who meets regularly with TWD's CEO and controller to monitor TWD's financial performance.

111. TWD's employees are paid biweekly.

112. Bond has audited TWD for five years.

Recent developments

113. During 1993, TWD changed its method of preparing its financial statements from the cash basis to generally accepted accounting principles.

114. During 1993, TWD sold one half of its controlling interest in United Equipment Leasing (UEL) Co. TWD retained significant interest in UEL.

115. During 1993, litigation filed against TWD in 1988 alleging that TWD discharged pollutants into state waterways was dropped by the state. Loss contingency disclosures that TWD included in prior years' financial statements are being removed for the 1993 financial statements.

116. During December 1993, TWD signed a contract to lease disposal equipment from an entity owned by Mead's parents. This related party transaction is not disclosed in TWD's notes to its 1993 financial statements.

117. During December 1993, TWD completed a barter transaction with a municipality. TWD removed waste from a municipally-owned site and acquired title to another contaminated site at below market price. TWD intends to service this new site in 1994.

118. During December 1993, TWD increased its casualty insurance coverage on several pieces of sophisticated machinery from historical cost to replacement cost.

119. Inquiries about the substantial increase in revenue TWD recorded in the fourth quarter of 1993 disclosed a new policy. TWD guaranteed to several municipalities that it would refund the federal and state funding paid to TWD if any municipality fails federal or state site clean-up inspection in 1994.

120. An initial public offering of TWD's stock is planned for late 1994.

G. Perform Analytical Procedures

R96
Number 1 (Estimated time —— 15 to 25 minutes)

Question Number 1 consists of 15 items pertaining to analytical procedures. Select the **best** answer for each item. Use a No. 2 pencil to blacken the appropriate ovals on the *Objective Answer Sheet* to indicate your answers. **Answer all items.** Your grade will be based on the total number of correct answers.

Analytical procedures are evaluations of financial information made by a study of plausible relationships among financial and nonfinancial data. Understanding and evaluating such relationships are essential to the audit process.

The following financial statements were prepared by Holiday Manufacturing Co. for the year ended December 31, 1995. Also presented are various financial statement ratios for Holiday as calculated from the prior year's financial statements. Sales represent net credit sales. The total assets and the receivables and inventory balances at December 31, 1995, were the same as at December 31, 1994.

Holiday Manufacturing Co.
Balance Sheet
December 31, 1995

Assets		Liabilities and Capital	
Cash	$ 240,000	Accounts payable	$ 160,000
Receivables	400,000	Notes payable	100,000
Inventory	600,000	Other current liabilities	140,000
Total current assets	$1,240,000	Total current liabilities	$ 400,000
Plant and equipment—net	760,000	Long-term debt	350,000
		Common stock	750,000
		Retained earnings	500,000
Total assets	$2,000,000	Total liabilities and capital	$2,000,000

Holiday Manufacturing Co.
Income Statement
Year Ended December 31, 1995

Sales		$3,000,000
Cost of goods sold		
Material	$800,000	
Labor	700,000	
Overhead	300,000	1,800,000
Gross margin		$1,200,000
Selling expenses	$240,000	
General and administrative expenses	300,000	540,000
Operating income		$ 660,000
Less interest expense		40,000
Income before taxes		$ 620,000
Less federal income taxes		220,000
Net income		$ 400,000

Selected Questions

Required:

a. Items 1 through 9 below represent financial ratios that the auditor calculated during the prior year's audit. For each ratio, calculate the current year's ratio from the financial statements presented above, select the answer from List A, and blacken the corresponding oval on the *Objective Answer Sheet*. Calculations should be rounded, if necessary, to the same number of places as the prior year's ratios. Answers on the list may be selected once, more than once, or not at all.

	Ratio	Holiday Mfg. Co. 12/31/95	Holiday Mfg. Co. 12/31/94	List A Ratio calculations
1.	Current ratio		2.5	Ⓐ 0.6
2.	Quick ratio		1.3	Ⓑ 0.7
3.	Accounts receivable turnover		5.5	Ⓒ 1.0
4.	Inventory turnover		2.5	Ⓓ 1.5
5.	Total asset turnover		1.2	Ⓔ 1.6
6.	Gross margin percentage		35%	Ⓕ 2.0
7.	Net operating margin percentage		25%	Ⓖ 3.0
				Ⓗ 3.1
8.	Times interest earned		10.3	Ⓘ 4.5
9.	Total debt to equity percentage		50%	Ⓙ 5.0
				Ⓚ 7.5
				Ⓛ 10.0
				Ⓜ 15.5
				Ⓝ 16.5
				Ⓞ 13%
				Ⓟ 22%
				Ⓠ 28%
				Ⓡ 33%
				Ⓢ 38%
				Ⓣ 40%
				Ⓤ 60%
				Ⓥ 67%

b. Items 10 through 15 represent an auditor's observed changes in certain financial statement ratios or amounts from the prior year's ratios or amounts. For each observed change, select the most likely explanation or explanations from List B, and blacken the corresponding oval or ovals on the *Objective Answer Sheet*. Select only the number of explanations as indicated. **The observed changes are not related to the calculations in requirement a, above, and are independent of each other.** Answers on the list may be selected once, more than once, or not at all.

R96
Number 1 (cont.)

Auditor's observed changes (**not related to Items 1–9 and independent of each other**).

10. Inventory turnover increased substantially from the prior year. (Select 3 explanations)

11. Accounts receivable turnover decreased substantially from the prior year. (Select 3 explanations)

12. Allowance for doubtful accounts increased from the prior year, but allowance for doubtful accounts as a percentage of accounts receivable decreased from the prior year. (Select 3 explanations)

13. Long-term debt increased from the prior year, but interest expense increased a larger-than-proportionate amount than long-term debt. (Select 1 explanation)

14. Operating income increased from the prior year although the entity was less profitable than in the prior year. (Select 2 explanations)

15. Gross margin percentage was unchanged from the prior year although gross margin increased from the prior year. (Select 1 explanation)

List B
Explanations

Ⓐ Items shipped on consignment during the last month of the year were recorded as sales.

Ⓑ A significant number of credit memos for returned merchandise that were issued during the last month of the year were not recorded.

Ⓒ Year-end purchases of inventory were overstated by incorrectly including items received in the first month of the subsequent year.

Ⓓ Year-end purchases of inventory were understated by incorrectly excluding items received before the year end.

Ⓔ A larger percentage of sales occurred during the last month of the year, as compared to the prior year.

Ⓕ A smaller percentage of sales occurred during the last month of the year, as compared to the prior year.

Ⓖ The same percentage of sales occurred during the last month of the year, as compared to the prior year.

Ⓗ Sales increased at the same percentage as cost of goods sold, as compared to the prior year.

Ⓘ Sales increased at a greater percentage than cost of goods sold increased, as compared to the prior year.

Ⓙ Sales increased at a lower percentage than cost of goods sold increased, as compared to the prior year.

Ⓚ Interest expense decreased, as compared to the prior year.

Ⓛ The effective income tax rate increased, as compared to the prior year.

Ⓜ The effective income tax rate decreased, as compared to the prior year.

Ⓝ Short-term borrowing was refinanced on a long-term basis at the same interest rate.

Ⓞ Short-term borrowing was refinanced on a long-term basis at lower interest rates.

Ⓟ Short-term borrowing was refinanced on a long-term basis at higher interest rates.

J. Consider Internal Control

M95
Number 3 (Estimated time —— 15 to 25 minutes)

Question Number 3 consists of 15 items. Select the **best** answer for each item. Use a No. 2 pencil to blacken the appropriate ovals on the *Objective Answer Sheet* to indicate your answers. **Answer all items.** Your grade will be based on the total number of correct answers.

Field, CPA, is auditing the financial statements of Miller Mailorder, Inc. (MMI) for the year ended January 31, 1995. Field has compiled a list of possible errors and fraud that may result in the misstatement of MMI's financial statements, and a corresponding list of internal control activities that, if properly designed and implemented, could assist MMI in preventing or detecting the errors and fraud.

Required:

For each possible error and fraud numbered **106 through 120,** select one internal control activity from the answer list that, if properly designed and implemented, most likely could assist MMI in preventing or detecting the errors and fraud. Blacken the corresponding oval on the *Objective Answer Sheet*. Each response in the list of internal control activities may be selected once, more than once, or not at all.

Possible Errors and Fraud

106. Invoices for goods sold are posted to incorrect customer accounts.

107. Goods ordered by customers are shipped, but are **not** billed to anyone.

108. Invoices are sent for shipped goods, but are **not** recorded in the sales journal.

109. Invoices are sent for shipped goods and are recorded in the sales journal, but are **not** posted to any customer account.

110. Credit sales are made to individuals with unsatisfactory credit ratings.

111. Goods are removed from inventory for unauthorized orders.

112. Goods shipped to customers do **not** agree with goods ordered by customers.

113. Invoices are sent to allies in a fraudulent scheme and sales are recorded for fictitious transactions.

114. Customers' checks are received for less than the customers' full account balances, but the customers' full account balances are credited.

115. Customers' checks are misappropriated before being forwarded to the cashier for deposit.

116. Customers' checks are credited to incorrect customer accounts.

117. Different customer accounts are each credited for the same cash receipt.

118. Customers' checks are properly credited to customer accounts and are properly deposited, but errors are made in recording receipts in the cash receipts journal.

119. Customers' checks are misappropriated after being forwarded to the cashier for deposit.

120. Invalid transactions granting credit for sales returns are recorded.

Internal Control Activities

A. Shipping clerks compare goods received from the warehouse with the details on the shipping documents.

B. Approved sales orders are required for goods to be released from the warehouse.

C. Monthly statements are mailed to all customers with outstanding balances.

D. Shipping clerks compare goods received from the warehouse with approved sales orders.

E. Customer orders are compared with the inventory master file to determine whether items ordered are in stock.

F. Daily sales summaries are compared with control totals of invoices.

G. Shipping documents are compared with sales invoices when goods are shipped.

H. Sales invoices are compared with the master price file.

I. Customer orders are compared with an approved customer list.

J. Sales orders are prepared for each customer order.

K. Control amounts posted to the accounts receivable ledger are compared with control totals of invoices.

L. Sales invoices are compared with shipping documents and approved customer orders before invoices are mailed.

M. Prenumbered credit memos are used for granting credit for goods returned.

N. Goods returned for credit are approved by the supervisor of the sales department.

O. Remittance advices are separated from the checks in the mailroom and forwarded to the accounting department.

P. Total amounts posted to the accounts receivable ledger from remittance advices are compared with the validated bank deposit slip.

Q. The cashier examines each check for proper endorsement.

R. Validated deposit slips are compared with the cashier's daily cash summaries.

S. An employee, other than the bookkeeper, periodically prepares a bank reconciliation.

T. Sales returns are approved by the same employee who issues receiving reports evidencing actual return of goods.

N93
Number 2 (Estimated time —— 15 to 25 minutes)

Instructions

Question Number 2 consists of 13 items. Select the **best** answer for each item. Use a No. 2 pencil to blacken the appropriate ovals on the Objective Answer Sheet to indicate your answers. **Answer all items.** Your grade will be based on the total number of correct answers.

Required:
The flowchart on the right depicts part of a client's revenue cycle. Some of the flowchart symbols are labeled to indicate control activities and records. For each symbol numbered 61 through 73, select one response from the answer lists below and blacken the corresponding oval on the Objective Answer Sheet. Each response in the lists may be selected once or **not** at all.

Answer Lists

Operations and control activities

A. Enter shipping data
B. Verify agreement of sales order and shipping document
C. Write off accounts receivable
D. To warehouse and shipping department
E. Authorize account receivable write-off
F. Prepare aged trial balance
G. To sales department
H. Release goods for shipment
I. To accounts receivable department
J. Enter price data
K. Determine that customer exists
L. Match customer purchase order with sales order
M. Perform customer credit check
N. Prepare sales journal
O. Prepare sales invoice

Documents, journals, ledgers, and files

P. Shipping document
Q. General ledger master file
R. General journal
S. Master price file
T. Sales journal
U. Sales invoice
V. Cash receipts journal
W. Uncollectible accounts file
X. Shipping file
Y. Aged trial balance
Z. Open order file

Selected Questions

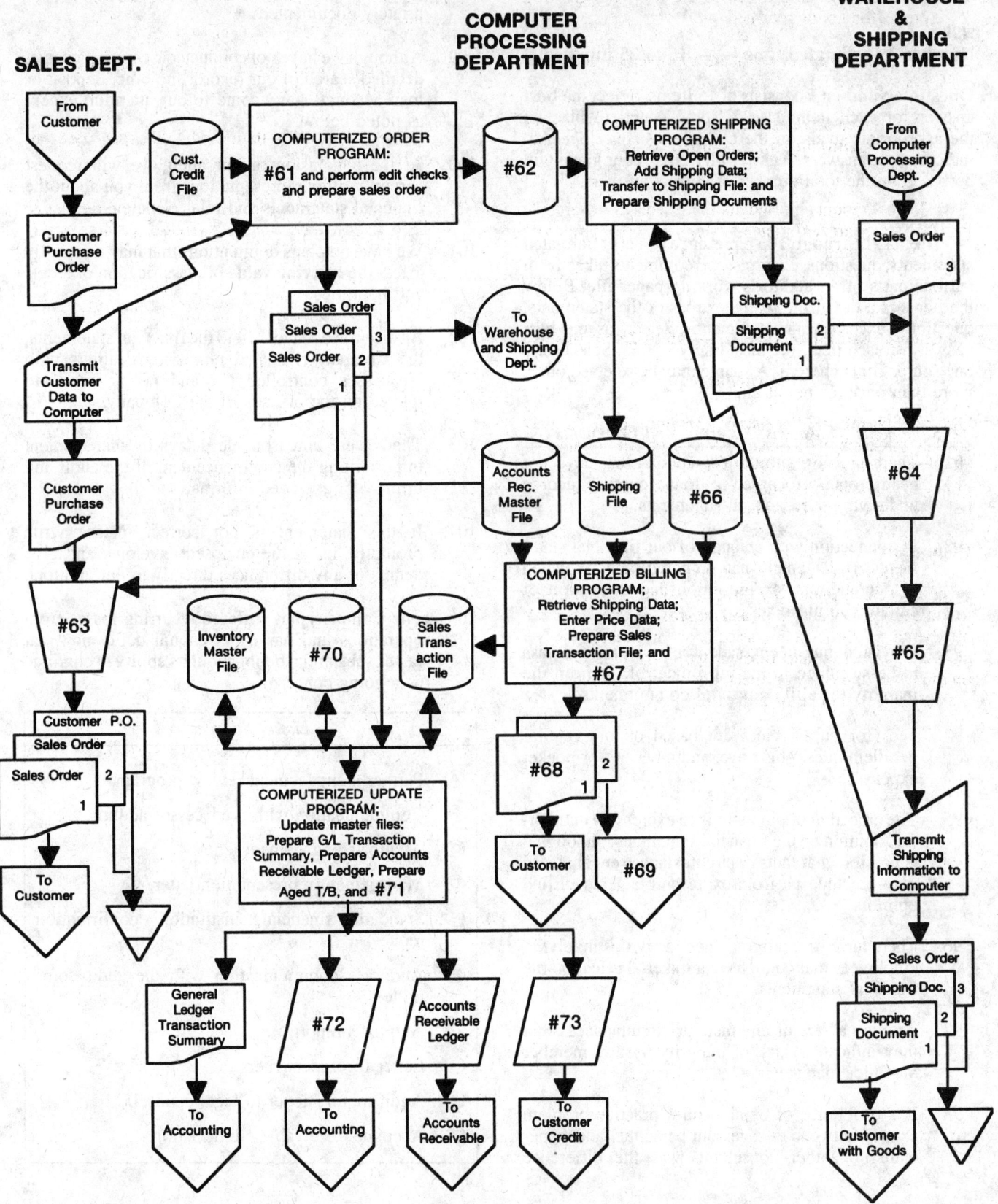

M. Determine and Prepare the Work Program

N95
Number 2 (Estimated time — — 15 to 25 minutes)

Question Number 2 consists of 15 items. Select the **best** answer for each item. Use a No. 2 pencil to blacken the appropriate ovals on the *Objective Answer Sheet* to indicate your answers. **Answer all items**. Your grade will be based on the total number of correct answers.

Required:
Items 91 through 105 represent a series of unrelated statements, questions, excerpts, and comments taken from various parts of an auditor's working paper file. Below the items is a list of the likely sources of the statements, questions, excerpts, and comments. Select, as the best answer for each item, the most likely source. Select only one source for each item. A source may be selected once, more than once, or not at all.

Statements, Questions, Excerpts, and Comments

91. There are no material transactions that have not been properly recorded in the accounting records underlying the financial statements.

92. In connection with an audit of our financial statements, management has prepared, and furnished to our auditors, a description and evaluation of certain contingencies.

93. Provision has been made for any material loss to be sustained in the fulfillment of, or from the inability to fulfill, any sales commitments.

94. Fees for our services are based on our regular per diem rates, plus travel and other out-of-pocket expenses.

95. The objective of our audit is to express an unqualified opinion on the financial statements, although it is possible that facts or circumstances encountered may preclude us from expressing an unqualified opinion.

96. There have been no fraudulent activities involving employees that could have a material effect on the financial statements.

97. Are you aware of any facts or circumstances that may indicate a lack of integrity by any member of senior management?

98. If a difference of opinion on a practice problem existed between engagement personnel and a specialist or other consultant, was the difference resolved in accordance with firm policy and appropriately documented?

99. Although we have not conducted a comprehensive, detailed search of our records, no other deposit or loan accounts have come to our attention except as noted below.

100. At the conclusion of our audit, we will request certain written representations from you about the financial statements and related matters.

101. We have no plans or intentions that may materially affect the carrying value or classification of assets and liabilities.

102. As discussed in Note 14 to the financial statements, the Company has had numerous dealings with businesses controlled by, and people who are related to, the officers of the Company.

103. There were unreasonable delays by management in permitting the commencement of the audit and in providing needed information.

104. If this statement is not correct, please write promptly, using the enclosed envelope, and give details of any differences directly to our auditors.

105. The Company has suffered recurring losses from operations and has a net capital deficiency that raises substantial doubt about its ability to continue as a going concern.

List of Sources

Ⓐ Partner's engagement review program.

Ⓑ Communication with predecessor auditor.

Ⓒ Auditor's engagement letter.

Ⓓ Management representation letter.

Ⓔ Standard financial institution confirmation request.

Ⓕ Auditor's communication with the audit committee.

Ⓖ Auditor's report.

Ⓗ Letter for underwriters.

Ⓘ Audit inquiry letter to legal counsel.

Ⓙ Accounts receivable confirmation.

The next question begins on page A-76.

Auditing

II. Obtain and Document Information to Form a Basis for Conclusions

A. Perform Planned Procedures Including Planned Applications of Audit Sampling

R97
Number 1

Question Number 1 consists of 12 items. Select the **best** answer for each item. Use a No. 2 pencil to blacken the appropriate ovals on the *Objective Answer Sheet* to indicate your answers. **Answer all items.** Your grade will be based on the total number of correct answers.

Required:
  Items 1 through 12 represent possible errors and irregularities that an auditor suspects are present. The accompanying *List of Auditing Procedures* represents procedures that the auditor would consider performing to gather evidence concerning possible errors and irregularities. For each item, select one or two procedures, as indicated, that the auditor most likely would perform to gather evidence in support of that item. The procedures on the list may be selected once, more than once, or not at all.

Possible Errors and Irregularities

1. The auditor suspects that a kiting scheme exists because an accounting department employee who can issue and record checks seems to be leading an unusually luxurious lifestyle. **(Select only 1 procedure)**

2. The auditor suspects that the controller wrote several checks and recorded the cash disbursements just before the year end but did not mail the checks until after the first week of the subsequent year. **(Select only 1 procedure)**

3. The entity borrowed funds from a financial institution. Although the transaction was properly recorded, the auditor suspects that the loan created a lien on the entity's real estate that is not disclosed in its financial statements. **(Select only 1 procedure)**

4. The auditor discovered an unusually large receivable from one of the entity's new customers. The auditor suspects that the receivable may be fictitious because the auditor has never heard of the customer and because the auditor's initial attempt to confirm the receivable has been ignored by the customer. **(Select only 2 procedures)**

5. The auditor suspects that fictitious employees have been placed on the payroll by the entity's payroll supervisor, who has access to payroll records and to the paychecks. **(Select only 1 procedure)**

6. The auditor suspects that selected employees of the entity received unauthorized raises from the entity's payroll supervisor, who has access to payroll records. **(Select only 1 procedure)**

7. The entity's cash receipts of the first few days of the subsequent year were properly deposited in its general operating account after the year end. However, the auditor suspects that the entity recorded the cash receipts in its books during the last week of the year under audit. **(Select only 1 procedure)**

8. The auditor suspects that vouchers were prepared and processed by an accounting department employee for merchandise that was neither ordered nor received by the entity. **(Select only 1 procedure)**

9. The details of invoices for equipment repairs were not clearly identified or explained to the accounting department employees. The auditor suspects that the bookkeeper incorrectly recorded the repairs as fixed assets. **(Select only 1 procedure)**

10. The auditor suspects that a lapping scheme exists because an accounting department employee who has access to cash receipts also maintains the accounts receivable ledger and refuses to take any vacation or sick days. **(Select only 2 procedures)**

11. The auditor suspects that the entity is inappropriately increasing the cash reported on its balance sheet by drawing a check on one account and not recording it as an outstanding check on that account, and simultaneously recording it as a deposit in a second account. **(Select only 1 procedure)**

12. The auditor suspects that the entity's controller has overstated sales and accounts receivable by recording fictitious sales to regular customers in the entity's books. **(Select only 2 procedures)**

List of Auditing Procedures

Ⓐ Compare the details of the cash receipts journal entries with the details of the corresponding daily deposit slips.

Ⓑ Scan the debits to the fixed asset accounts and vouch selected amounts to vendors' invoices and management's authorization.

Ⓒ Perform analytical procedures that compare documented authorized pay rates to the entity's budget and forecast.

Ⓓ Obtain the cutoff bank statement and compare the cleared checks to the year-end bank reconciliation.

Ⓔ Prepare a bank transfer schedule.

Ⓕ Inspect the entity's deeds to its real estate.

Ⓖ Make inquiries of the entity's attorney concerning the details of real estate transactions.

Ⓗ Confirm the terms of borrowing arrangements with the lender.

Ⓘ Examine selected equipment repair orders and supporting documentation to determine the propriety of the charges.

Ⓙ Send requests to confirm the entity's accounts receivable on a surprise basis at an interim date.

Ⓚ Send a second request for confirmation of the receivable to the customer and make inquiries of a reputable credit agency concerning the customer's creditworthiness.

Ⓛ Examine the entity's shipping documents to verify that the merchandise that produced the receivable was actually sent to the customer.

Ⓜ Inspect the entity's correspondence files for indications of customer disputes or for evidence that certain shipments were on consignment.

Ⓝ Perform edit checks of data on the payroll transaction tapes.

Ⓞ Inspect payroll check endorsements for similar handwriting.

Ⓟ Observe payroll check distribution on a surprise basis.

Ⓠ Vouch data in the payroll register to documented authorized pay rates in the human resources department's files.

Ⓡ Reconcile the payroll checking account and determine if there were unusual time lags between the issuance and payment of payroll checks.

Ⓢ Inspect the file of prenumbered vouchers for consecutive numbering and proper approval by an appropriate employee.

Ⓣ Determine that the details of selected prenumbered vouchers match the related vendors' invoices.

Ⓤ Examine the supporting purchase orders and receiving reports for selected paid vouchers.

R97
Number 2

Question Number 2 consists of 2 parts. **Part A.** consists of 10 items and **Part B.** consists of 8 items. Select the **best** answer for each item. Use a No. 2 pencil to blacken the appropriate ovals on the *Objective Answer Sheet* to indicate your answers. **Answer all items.** Your grade will be based on the total number of correct answers.

Required:

A. Items **1 through 10** represent tick marks (symbols) that indicate procedures performed or comments documented in auditing the **Long-term debt** account of American Manufacturers, Inc. Select, from the list of procedures/comments below, the procedure/comment that the auditor most likely performed/documented at each point of the audit where a tick mark was made on the working papers. Select only one procedure/comment for each item. A procedure/comment may be selected once or not at all. Assume that the working papers foot and crossfoot.

American Manufacturers, Inc.
Long-Term Debt
October 31, 1997

Lender	Interest rate	Collateral	Payment terms	Balance 10/31/96	Current year borrowings	Current year reductions	Balance 10/31/97	Interest paid to	Accrued interest payable 10/31/97	Comments
◀ First National Bank	10%	Manufacturing equipment	Interest only on last day of each quarter; principal due in full on 9/30/99.	500,000 ■	200,000 ◆ 3/31/97	(100,000) ✪ 6/30/97	600,000	9/30/97	5,000 ◳	First National confirms that interest payments are current and agrees with account balance.
◀ Second State Bank	9%	First mortgage on production facilities	$10,000 principal plus interest due on the 1st of each month; due in full on 1/1/00.	380,000 ■	0	(110,000) ✚	270,000 ✓★	9/30/97	2,025 ◳	Monthly payment for $12,025 was mailed on 11/3/97; Second State agrees with account balance.
◀ Third Savings & Loan	12%	Second mortgage on production facilities	$5,000 principal plus interest due on the 15th of each month; due in full on 10/15/99.	180,000 ■	0	(60,000)	120,000 ✱★	10/15/97	600	Third Savings & Loan claims 10/15/97 payment wasn't received as of 11/5/97; adjusting entry proposed to increase balance $5,000 and increase accrued interest payable.
◀ A. Clark, majority stockholder	0%	Unsecured	Due in full 10/31/99.	700,000	0	(200,000) 10/28/97	500,000 ✓		0	Borrowed additional $200,000 from Clark on 11/5/97; need to investigate reborrowing just after year end and consider imputed interest on 0% stockholder loan.
				1,760,000	200,000	(470,000)	1,490,000 ●		7,625 ●	

List of procedures/comments—Long-Term Debt

(A) Confirmed, without exception.
(B) Confirmed, with exception.
(C) Traced amount to prior year's working papers.
(D) Traced amount to current year's trial balance and general ledger.
(E) Does not recompute correctly.
(F) Tested reasonableness of calculations.
(G) Agreed to canceled checks and lender's monthly statements.
(H) Agreed to canceled check and board of directors' authorization.
(I) Agreed interest rate, terms, and collateral to note & loan agreement.
(J) Agreed to loan agreement, validated bank deposit ticket, and board of directors' authorization.
(K) Reclassification entry proposed for current portion of long-term debt.

Items to be Answered

1. ◀	2. ■	3. ◆	4. ✪	5. ✚
6. ✓	7. ★	8. ✱	9. ●	10. ◳

Selected Questions

B. Items 11 through 18 represent tick marks (symbols) that indicate procedures performed or comments documented in auditing the Property, plant, and equipment and Accumulated depreciation accounts of American Manufacturers, Inc. During the year under audit, American Manufacturers purchased new computers directly from wholesalers and constructed an addition to one of its buildings. The company's employees also refurbished the fixtures of several older buildings. Select, from the list of procedures/comments below, the procedure/comment that the auditor most likely performed/documented at each point of the audit where a tick mark was made on the working papers. Select only one procedure/comment for each item. A procedure/comment may be selected once or not at all. Assume that the working papers foot and crossfoot.

American Manufacturers, Inc.
Property, Plant, and Equipment and Accumulated Depreciation
October 31, 1997

		Property, Plant, and Equipment					Depreciation		Accumulated Depreciation			
Account	Balance 10/31/96	Additions	Disposals	Other	Balance 10/31/97		Rate	Method	Balance 10/31/96	Provision	Disposal	Balance 10/31/97
Land	650,000 ▲	70,000 ↔	0	0	720,000							
Buildings	3,270,000 ▲	230,000 ✓	0	(30,000) ⊗	3,470,000 ↑		5%	S/L	1,144,500 ▲	168,500 ▲	0	1,313,000 ↑
Equipment	1,750,000 ▲	90,000 ∨	(12,000) ↕	0	1,828,000 ↑		10%	S/L	700,000 ▲	179,500 ⌐	(12,000) ⌐	867,500 ↑
Fixtures	850,000 ▲	200,000 ✓	0	30,000 ⊗	1,080,000 ↑		15%	S/L	510,000 ▲	144,750 ⌐	0	654,750 ↑
	6,520,000	590,000	(12,000)	0	7,098,000				2,354,500	492,750	(12,000)	2,835,250

Items to be Answered

11. ▲
12. ↔
13. ✓
14. ∨
15. ↕
16. ⊗
17. ↑
18. ⌐

List of procedures/comments: Property, Plant and Equipment and Accumulated Depreciation

Ⓐ Does not recompute correctly.
Ⓑ Tested reasonableness of calculation.
Ⓒ Traced amount to current year's trial balance and general ledger.
Ⓓ Reclassification entry for fixtures erroneously recorded as buildings.
Ⓔ Reclassification entry for buildings erroneously recorded as fixtures.
Ⓕ Traced amount to prior year's working papers.
Ⓖ Sold six fully-depreciated computers to employees; no audit procedures necessary.
Ⓗ Confirmed, with exception.
Ⓘ Confirmed, without exception.
Ⓙ Examined supporting vendors' invoices, canceled checks, asset subsidiary ledger and board of directors' minutes of meetings authorizing transactions.
Ⓚ Examined supporting work orders and engineers' reports, canceled checks, asset subsidiary ledger, and board of directors' minutes of meetings authorizing transactions.
Ⓛ Examined supporting deed and purchase contract, canceled checks, asset subsidiary ledger, and board of directors' minutes of meetings authorizing transactions.

N95
Number 3 (Estimated time —— 15 to 25 minutes)

Question Number 3 consists of 15 items. Select the **best** answer for each item. Use a No. 2 pencil to blacken the appropriate ovals on the *Objective Answer Sheet* to indicate your answers. **Answer all items**. Your grade will be based on the total number of correct answers.

Required:
Items 106 through 120 represent a series of unrelated procedures that an accountant may consider performing in separate engagements to review the financial statements of a nonpublic entity (a review) and to compile the financial statements of a nonpublic entity (a compilation). Select, as the best answer for each item, whether the procedure is required ® or not required Ⓝ for both review and compilation engagements. Make two selections for each item.

Procedures

106. The accountant should establish an understanding with the entity regarding the nature and limitations of the services to be performed.

107. The accountant should make inquiries concerning actions taken at the board of directors' meetings.

108. The accountant, as the entity's successor accountant, should communicate with the predecessor accountant to obtain access to the predecessor's working papers.

109. The accountant should obtain a level of knowledge of the accounting principles and practices of the entity's industry.

110. The accountant should obtain an understanding of the entity's internal control.

111. The accountant should perform analytical procedures designed to identify relationships that appear to be unusual.

112. The accountant should make an assessment of control risk.

113. The accountant should send a letter of inquiry to the entity's attorney to corroborate the information furnished by management concerning litigation.

114. The accountant should obtain a management representation letter from the entity.

115. The accountant should study the relationships of the financial statement elements that would be expected to conform to a predictable pattern.

116. The accountant should communicate to the entity's senior management illegal employee acts discovered by the accountant that are clearly inconsequential.

117. The accountant should make inquiries about events subsequent to the date of the financial statements that would have a material effect on the financial statements.

118. The accountant should modify the accountant's report if there is a change in accounting principles that is adequately disclosed.

119. The accountant should submit a hard copy of the financial statements and accountant's report when the financial statements and accountant's report are submitted on a computer disk.

120. The accountant should perform specific procedures to evaluate whether there is substantial doubt about the entity's ability to continue as a going concern.

The next question begins on page A-82.

Auditing

N94
Number 3 (Estimated time — — 15 to 25 minutes)

Instructions

Question Number 3 consists of 6 items. Select the **best** answers for each item. Use a No. 2 pencil to blacken the appropriate ovals on the Objective Answer Sheet to indicate your answers. **Answer all items.** Your grade will be based on the total number of correct answers.

Required:
  Items **99 through 104** represent the items that an auditor ordinarily would find on a client-prepared bank reconciliation. The accompanying **List of Auditing Procedures** represents substantive auditing procedures. For each item, select one or more procedures, as indicated, that the auditor most likely would perform to gather evidence in support of that item. The procedures on the **List** may be selected once, more than once, or not at all.

Assume:

- The client prepared the bank reconciliation on 10/2/94.

- The bank reconciliation is mathematically accurate.

- The auditor received a cutoff bank statement dated 10/7/94 directly from the bank on 10/11/94.

- The 9/30/94 deposit in transit, outstanding checks #1281, #1285, #1289, and #1292, and the correction of the error regarding check #1282 appeared on the cutoff bank statement.

- The auditor assessed control risk concerning the financial statement assertions related to cash at the maximum.

Selected Questions

General Company
Bank Reconciliation
1st National Bank of U.S. Bank Account
September 30, 1994

99. Select 2 Procedures –	Balance per bank			$28,375
100. Select 5 Procedures –	Deposits in transit			
	9/29/94		$4,500	
	9/30/94		1,525	6,025
				34,400
101. Select 5 Procedures –	Outstanding checks			
	# 988	8/31/94	2,200	
	#1281	9/26/94	675	
	#1285	9/27/94	850	
	#1289	9/29/94	2,500	
	#1292	9/30/94	7,225	(13,450)
				20,950
102. Select 1 Procedure –	Customer note collected by bank			(3,000)
103. Select 2 Procedures –	Error: Check #1282, written on 9/26/94 for $270 was erroneously charged by bank as $720; bank was notified on 10/2/94			450
104. Select 1 Procedure –	Balance per books			$18,400

List of Auditing Procedures

A. Trace to cash receipts journal.

B. Trace to cash disbursements journal.

C. Compare to 9/30/94 general ledger.

D. Confirm directly with bank.

E. Inspect bank credit memo.

F. Inspect bank debit memo.

G. Ascertain reason for unusual delay.

H. Inspect supporting documents for reconciling item **not** appearing on cutoff statement.

I. Trace items on the bank reconciliation to cutoff statement.

J. Trace items on the cutoff statement to bank reconciliation.

Auditing

N92
Number 2 (Estimated time —— 15 to 25 minutes)

Instructions:

Question Number 2 consists of 10 items. Select the **best** answer for each item. Use a No. 2 pencil to blacken the appropriate ovals on the Objective Answer Sheet to indicate your answers. **Answer all items.** Your grade will be based on the total number of correct answers.

To support financial statement assertions, an auditor develops specific audit objectives. The auditor then designs substantive tests to satisfy or accomplish each objective.

Required:

Items 61 through 70 represent audit objectives for the investments, accounts receivable, and property and equipment accounts. To the right of each set of audit objectives is a listing of possible audit procedures for that account. For each audit objective, select the audit procedure that would primarily respond to the objective and blacken the corresponding oval on the Objective Answer Sheet. Select only one procedure for each audit objective. A procedure may be selected only once, or not at all.

Example:
The following is an example of the manner in which the answer sheet should be marked.

Item

Audit Objectives for Cash	Audit Procedures for Cash
99. Recorded cash represents cash on hand at the balance sheet date.	C. Count cash on hand.

Answer Sheet

Item	Audit Procedures (select one per item)
99	Ⓐ Ⓑ ● Ⓓ Ⓔ Ⓕ Ⓖ

Items to be Answered:

Audit Objectives for Investments

61. Investments are properly described and classified in the financial statements.

62. Recorded investments represent investments actually owned at the balance sheet date.

63. Investments are properly valued at the lower of cost or market at the balance sheet date.

Audit Procedures for Investments

A. Trace opening balances in the subsidiary ledger to prior year's audit working papers.

B. Determine that employees who are authorized to sell investments do not have access to cash.

C. Examine supporting documents for a sample of investment transactions to verify that prenumbered documents are used.

D. Determine that any impairments in the price of investments have been properly recorded.

E. Verify that transfers from the current to the non-current investment portfolio have been properly recorded.

F. Obtain positive confirmations as of the balance sheet date of investments held by independent custodians.

G. Trace investment transactions to minutes of the Board of Directors meetings to determine that transactions were properly authorized.

Audit Objectives for Accounts Receivable

64. Accounts receivable represent all amounts owed to the entity at the balance sheet date.

65. The entity has legal right to all accounts receivable at the balance sheet date.

66. Accounts receivable are stated at net realizable value.

67. Accounts receivable are properly described and presented in the financial statements.

Audit Procedures for Accounts Receivable

A. Analyze the relationship of accounts receivable and sales and compare it with relationships for preceding periods.

B. Perform sales cut-off tests to obtain assurance that sales transactions and corresponding entries for inventories and cost of goods sold are recorded in the same and proper period.

C. Review the aged trial balance for significant past due accounts.

D. Obtain an understanding of the business purpose of transactions that resulted in accounts receivable balances.

E. Review loan agreements for indications of whether accounts receivable have been factored or pledged.

F. Review the accounts receivable trial balance for amounts due from officers and employees.

G. Analyze unusual relationships between monthly accounts receivable balances and monthly accounts payable balances.

Audit Objectives for Property & Equipment

68. The entity has legal right to property and equipment acquired during the year.

69. Recorded property and equipment represent assets that actually exist at the balance sheet date.

70. Net property and equipment are properly valued at the balance sheet date.

Audit Procedures for Property & Equipment

A. Trace opening balances in the summary schedules to the prior year's audit working papers.

B. Review the provision for depreciation expense and determine that depreciable lives and methods used in the current year are consistent with those used in the prior year.

C. Determine that the responsibility for maintaining the property and equipment records is segregated from the responsibility for custody of property and equipment.

D. Examine deeds and title insurance certificates.

E. Perform cut-off tests to verify that property and equipment additions are recorded in the proper period.

F. Determine that property and equipment is adequately insured.

G. Physically examine all major property and equipment additions.

Auditing

IV. Prepare Communications to Satisfy Engagement Objectives

A. Prepare Reports

R96
Number 2 (Estimated time — — 15 to 25 minutes)

Question Number 2 consists of 17 items pertaining to possible deficiencies in an accountant's report on comparative financial statements. Select the **best** answer for each item. Use a No. 2 pencil to blacken the appropriate ovals on the *Objective Answer Sheet* to indicate your answers. **Answer all items.** Your grade will be based on the total number of correct answers.

Wallace & Wallace, CPAs, audited the financial statements of West Co., a nonpublic entity, for the year ended September 30, 1995, and expressed an unqualified opinion. For the year ended September 30, 1996, West issued comparative financial statements. Wallace & Wallace reviewed West's 1996 financial statements and Gordon, an assistant on the engagement, drafted the accountant's review report below. Martin, the engagement supervisor, decided not to reissue the prior year's auditor's report, but instructed Gordon to include a separate paragraph in the current year's review report describing the responsibility assumed for the prior year's audited financial statements.

Martin reviewed Gordon's draft and indicated in *Martin's Review Notes* that there were many deficiencies in Gordon's draft.

Accountant's Review Report

We have reviewed the accompanying balance sheet of West Company as of September 30, 1996, and the related statements of income and cash flows for the year then ended, in accordance with standards issued by the American Institute of Certified Public Accountants. All information included in these financial statements is the representation of the management of West Company. Our responsibility is to express limited assurance on these financial statements based on our review.

A review consists principally of inquiries of company personnel and analytical procedures applied to financial data. A review also includes assessing the accounting principles used and significant estimates made by management, as well as evaluating the overall financial statement presentation.

Based on our review, we are not aware of any material modifications that should be made to the accompanying financial statements. Accordingly, the accompanying financial statements have been prepared assuming that the company will continue as a going concern. Furthermore, we have no responsibility to update this report for events and circumstances occurring after the date of this report.

The financial statements for the year ended September 30, 1995, were audited by us and we expressed an unqualified opinion on them in our report dated November 7, 1995, but we have not performed any auditing procedures since that date. In our opinion, the financial statements referred to above are presented fairly, in all material respects, for the year then ended in conformity with generally accepted accounting principles.

Wallace & Wallace, CPAs
November 6, 1996

Required:
Items 1 through 17 represent the deficiencies noted by Martin. For each deficiency, indicate whether Martin is correct and Gordon is incorrect **Ⓜ**; Gordon is correct and Martin is incorrect **Ⓖ**; or both Martin and Gordon are incorrect **Ⓑ**. Blacken the corresponding oval on the *Objective Answer Sheet*.

Martin's Review Notes

1. There should be a reference to the prior year's audited financial statements in the first (introductory) paragraph.

2. All of the current year's basic financial statements are **not** properly identified in the first (introductory) paragraph.

3. The standards referred to in the first (introductory) paragraph should **not** be standards issued by the American Institute of Certified Public Accountants, but should be standards for the compilation and review of financial statements.

4. The accountant's responsibility to express limited assurance on the financial statements, mentioned in the first (introductory) paragraph, should be in the second (scope) paragraph.

5. There should be a reference to the prior year's audited financial statements in the second (scope) paragraph.

6. There should be a comparison of the scope of a review to an audit in the second (scope) paragraph.

7. There should be **no** reference to "assessing the accounting principles used," "significant estimates made by management," and "evaluating the overall financial statement presentation" in the second (scope) paragraph.

8. There should be a statement that **no** opinion is expressed on the current year's financial statements in the second (scope) paragraph.

9. There should be a reference to "conformity with generally accepted accounting principles" in the third paragraph.

10. There should be a reference to consistency in the third paragraph.

11. There should be a restriction on the distribution of the accountant's review report in the third paragraph.

12. The reference to "going concern" in the third paragraph should be in the second (scope) paragraph.

13. The accountant's lack of responsibility to update the report in the third paragraph should be in the second (scope) paragraph.

14. There should be **no** mention of the type of opinion expressed on the prior year's audited financial statements in the fourth (separate) paragraph.

15. All of the prior year's basic financial statements are **not** properly identified in the fourth (separate) paragraph.

16. The reference in the fourth (separate) paragraph to the fair presentation of the prior year's audited financial statements in accordance with generally accepted accounting principles should be omitted.

17. The report should be dual dated to indicate the date of the prior year's auditor's report.

M95
Number 2 (Estimated time — — 15 to 25 minutes)

Question Number 2 consists of 15 items pertaining to possible deficiencies in an auditor's report. Select the **best** answer for each item. Use a No. 2 pencil to blacken the appropriate ovals on the *Objective Answer Sheet* to indicate your answers. **Answer all items.** Your grade will be based on the total number of correct answers.

Perry & Price, CPAs, audited the consolidated financial statements of Bond Company for the year ended December 31, 1993, and expressed an adverse opinion because Bond carried its plant and equipment at appraisal values, and provided for depreciation on the basis of such values.

Perry & Price also audited Bond's financial statements for the year ended December 31, 1994. These consolidated financial statements are being presented on a comparative basis with those of the prior year and an unqualified opinion is being expressed.

Smith, the engagement supervisor, instructed Adler, an assistant on the engagement, to draft the auditor's report on May 3, 1995, the date of completion of the field work. In drafting the report below, Adler considered the following:

- Bond recently changed its method of accounting for plant and equipment and restated its 1993 consolidated financial statements to conform with GAAP. Consequently, the CPA firm's present opinion on those statements is different (unqualified) from the opinion expressed on May 12, 1994.

- Larkin & Lake, CPAs, audited the financial statements of BX, Inc., a consolidated subsidiary of Bond, for the year ended December 31, 1994. The subsidiary's financial statements reflected total assets and revenues of 2% and 3%, respectively, of the consolidated totals. Larkin & Lake expressed an unqualified opinion and furnished Perry & Price with a copy of the auditor's report. Perry & Price has decided to assume responsibility for the work of Larkin & Lake insofar as it relates to the expression of an opinion on the consolidated financial statements taken as a whole.

- Bond is a defendant in a lawsuit alleging patent infringement. This is adequately disclosed in the notes to Bond's financial statements, but no provision for liability has been recorded because the ultimate outcome of the litigation cannot presently be determined.

Auditor's Report

We have audited the accompanying consolidated balance sheets of Bond Company and subsidiaries as of December 31, 1994 and 1993, and the related consolidated statements of income, retained earnings, and cash flows for the years then ended. These financial statements are the responsibility of the Company's management. Our responsibility is to express an opinion on these financial statements based on our audits.

We conducted our audits in accordance with generally accepted auditing standards. Those standards require that we plan and perform the audit to obtain reasonable assurance about whether the financial statements are free of material misstatement. An audit includes examining, on a test basis, evidence supporting the amounts and disclosures in the financial statements. An audit also includes assessing the accounting principles used, as well as evaluating the overall financial statement presentation. We believe that our audits provide a reasonable basis for our opinion.

In our previous report, we expressed an opinion that the 1993 financial statements did not fairly present financial position, results of operations, and cash flows in conformity with generally accepted accounting principles because the Company carried its plant and equipment at appraisal values and provided for depreciation on the basis of such values. As described in Note 12, the Company has changed its method of accounting for these items and restated its 1993 financial statements to conform with generally accepted accounting principles. Accordingly, our present opinion on the 1993 financial statements, as presented herein, is different from that expressed in our previous report.

In our opinion, the consolidated financial statements referred to above present fairly, in all material respects, the financial position of Bond Company and subsidiaries as of December 31, 1994 and 1993, and the results of its operations and its cash flows for the years then ended in conformity with generally accepted accounting principles except for the change in accounting principles with which we concur and the uncertainty, which is discussed in the following explanatory paragraph.

The Company is a defendant in a lawsuit alleging infringement of certain patent rights. The Company has filed a counteraction, and preliminary hearings and discovery proceedings are in progress. The ultimate outcome of the litigation cannot presently be determined. Accordingly, no provision for any liability that may result upon adjudication has been made in the accompanying financial statements.

Perry & Price, CPAs
May 3, 1995

Required:

Smith reviewed Adler's draft and indicated in the *Supervisor's Review Notes* below that there were deficiencies in Adler's draft. **Items 91 through 105** represent the deficiencies noted by Smith. For each deficiency, indicate whether Smith is correct © or incorrect ① in the criticism of Adler's draft and blacken the corresponding oval on the *Objective Answer Sheet*.

Supervisor's Review Notes

91. The report is improperly titled.

92. All the basic financial statements are **not** properly identified in the introductory paragraph.

93. There is **no** reference to the American Institute of Certified Public Accountants in the introductory paragraph.

94. Larkin & Lake are **not** identified in the introductory and opinion paragraphs.

95. The subsidiary, BX Inc., is **not** identified and the magnitude of BX's financial statements is **not** disclosed in the introductory paragraph.

96. The report does **not** state in the scope paragraph that generally accepted auditing standards require analytical procedures to be performed in planning an audit.

97. The report does **not** state in the scope paragraph that an audit includes assessing internal control.

98. The report does **not** state in the scope paragraph that an audit includes assessing significant estimates made by management.

99. The date of the previous report (May 12, 1994) is **not** disclosed in the first explanatory paragraph.

100. It is inappropriate to disclose in the first explanatory paragraph the circumstances that caused Perry & Price to express a different opinion on the 1993 financial statements.

101. The concurrence with the accounting change is inappropriate in the opinion paragraph.

102. Reference to the (litigation) uncertainty should **not** be made in the opinion paragraph.

103. Bond's disclosure of the (litigation) uncertainty in the notes to the financial statements is **not** referred to in the second explanatory paragraph.

104. The letter of inquiry to Bond's lawyer concerning litigation, claims, and assessments is **not** referred to in the second explanatory paragraph.

105. The report is **not** dual dated, but it should be because of the change of opinion on the 1993 financial statements.

The next question begins on page A-90.

Auditing

N94
Number 2 (Estimated time —— 15 to 25 minutes)

Instructions

Question Number 2 consists of 8 items. Select the **best** answers for each item. Use a No. 2 pencil to blacken the appropriate ovals on the Objective Answer Sheet to indicate your answers. **Answer all items.** Your grade will be based on the total number of correct answers.

Required:
   Items 91 through 98 present various independent factual situations an auditor might encounter in conducting an audit. List A represents the types of opinions the auditor ordinarily would issue and List B represents the report modifications (if any) that would be necessary. For each situation, select one response from List A and one from List B and blacken the corresponding ovals on the Objective Answer Sheet. Select as the **best** answers for each item, the action the auditor normally would take. The types of opinions in List A and the report modifications in List B may be selected once, more than once, or not at all.

Assume:

- The auditor is independent.

- The auditor previously expressed an unqualified opinion on the prior year's financial statements.

- Only single-year (not comparative) statements are presented for the current year.

- The conditions for an unqualified opinion exist unless contradicted by the facts.

- The conditions stated in the factual situations are material.

- No report modifications are to be made except in response to the factual situation.

Selected Questions

91. An auditor hires an actuary to assist in corroborating a client's complex pension calculations concerning accrued pension liabilities that account for 35% of the client's total liabilities. The actuary's findings are reasonably close to the client's calculations and support the financial statements.

92. A client holds a note receivable consisting of principal and accrued interest payable in 1998. The note's maker recently filed a voluntary bankruptcy petition, but the client failed to reduce the recorded value of the note to its net realizable value, which is approximately 20% of the recorded amount.

93. An auditor is engaged to audit a client's financial statements after the annual physical inventory count. The accounting records are not sufficiently reliable to enable the auditor to become satisfied as to the year-end inventory balances.

94. Big City is required by GASB to present supplementary information outside the basic financial statements concerning the disclosure of pension information. Big City's auditor determines that the supplementary information, which is **not** required to be part of the basic financial statements, is omitted.

95. A client's financial statements do not disclose certain long-term lease obligations. The auditor determines that the omitted disclosures are required by FASB.

96. A principal auditor decides not to take responsibility for the work of another CPA who audited a wholly-owned subsidiary of the principal auditor's client. The total assets and revenues of the subsidiary represent 27% and 28%, respectively, of the related consolidated totals.

97. A client changes its method of accounting for the cost of inventories from FIFO to LIFO. The auditor concurs with the change although it has a material effect on the comparability of the financial statements.

98. Due to losses and adverse key financial ratios, an auditor has substantial doubt about a client's ability to continue as a going concern for a reasonable period of time. The client has adequately disclosed its financial difficulties in a note to its financial statements, which do **not** include any adjustments that might result from the outcome of this uncertainty.

List A	List B
Types of Opinions	**Report Modifications**
A. Either an "except for" qualified opinion or an adverse opinion	H. Describe the circumstances in an explanatory paragraph *without modifying* the three standard paragraphs.
B. Either a disclaimer of opinion or an "except for" qualified opinion	I. Describe the circumstances in an explanatory paragraph and *modify* the *opinion* paragraph.
C. Either an adverse opinion or a disclaimer of opinion	J. Descibe the circumstances in an explanatory paragraph and *modify* the *scope* and *opinion* paragraphs.
D. An "except for" qualified opinion	K. Describe the circumstances in an explanatory paragraph and *modify* the *introductory, scope,* and *opinion* paragraphs.
E. An unqualified opinion	L. Describe the circumstances within the *scope* paragraph without adding an explanatory paragraph.
F. An adverse opinion	M. Describe the circumstances within the *opinion* paragraph without adding an explanatory paragraph.
G. A disclaimer of opinion	N. Describe the circumstances within the *scope* and *opinion* paragraphs without adding an explanatory paragraph.
	O. Describe the circumstances within the *introductory, scope,* and *opinion* paragraphs without adding an explanatory paragraph.
	P. Issue the *standard* auditor's report *without modification.*

M93
Number 2 (Estimated time —— 15 to 25 minutes)

Instructions

Question Number 2 consists of 13 items pertaining to possible deficiencies in an accountant's review report. Select the **best** answer for each item. Use a No. 2 pencil to blacken the appropriate ovals on the Objective Answer Sheet to indicate your answers. **Answer all items**. Your grade will be based on the total number of correct answers.

Jordan & Stone, CPAs, audited the financial statements of Tech Co., a nonpublic entity, for the year ended December 31, 1991, and expressed an unqualified opinion. For the year ended December 31, 1992, Tech issued comparative financial statements. Jordan & Stone reviewed Tech's 1992 financial statements and Kent, an assistant on the engagement, drafted the accountants' review report below. Land, the engagement supervisor, decided not to reissue the prior year's auditors' report, but instructed Kent to include a separate paragraph in the current year's review report describing the responsibility assumed for the prior year's audited financial statements. This is an appropriate reporting procedure.

Land reviewed Kent's draft and indicated in the *Supervisor's Review Notes* below that there were several deficiencies in Kent's draft.

Accountant's Review Report

We have reviewed and audited the accompanying balance sheets of Tech Co. as of December 31, 1992 and 1991, and the related statements of income, retained earnings, and cash flows for the years then ended, in accordance with Statements on Standards for Accounting and Review Services issued by the American Institute of Certified Public Accountants and generally accepted auditing standards. All information included in these financial statements is the representation of the management of Tech Co.

A review consists principally of inquiries of company personnel and analytical procedures applied to financial data. It is substantially less in scope than an audit in accordance with generally accepted auditing standards, the objective of which is the expression of an opinion regarding the financial statements taken as a whole.

Based on our review, we are not aware of any material modifications that should be made to the accompanying financial statements. Because of the inherent limitations of a review engagement, this report is intended for the information of management and should not be used for any other purpose.

The financial statements for the year ended December 31, 1991, were audited by us and our report was dated March 2, 1992. We have no responsibility for updating that report for events and circumstances occurring after that date.

Jordan and Stone, CPAs
March 1, 1993

Required:

Items 61 through 73 represent deficiencies noted by Land. For each deficiency, indicate whether Land is correct © or incorrect ① in the criticism of Kent's draft and blacken the corresponding oval on the Objective Answer Sheet.

Items to be Answered:

Supervisor's Review Notes

61. There should be **no** reference to the prior year's audited financial statements in the first (introductory) paragraph.
62. All the current-year basic financial statements are **not** properly identified in the first (introductory) paragraph.
63. There should be **no** reference to the American Institute of Certified Public Accountants in the first (introductory) paragraph.
64. The accountant's review and audit responsibilities should follow management's responsibilities in the first (introductory) paragraph.
65. There should be **no** comparison of the scope of a review to an audit in the second (scope) paragraph.
66. Negative assurance should be expressed on the current year's reviewed financial statements in the second (scope) paragraph.
67. There should be a statement that **no** opinion is expressed on the current year's financial statements in the second (scope) paragraph.
68. There should be a reference to "conformity with generally accepted accounting principles" in the third paragraph.
69. There should be **no** restriction on the distribution of the accountant's review report in the third paragraph.
70. There should be **no** reference to "material modifications" in the third paragraph.
71. There should be an indication of the type of opinion expressed on the prior year's audited financial statements in the fourth (separate) paragraph.
72. There should be an indication that **no** auditing procedures were performed after the date of the report on the prior year's financial statements in the fourth (separate) paragraph.
73. There should be **no** reference to "updating the prior year's auditor's report for events and circumstances occurring after that date" in the fourth (separate) paragraph.

SELECTED OTHER OBJECTIVE ANSWER FORMATS — UNOFFICIAL ANSWERS

I. Plan, Evaluate, and Accept the Engagement

B. Assess Engagement Risk and the CPA Firm's Ability to Perform the Engagement

M94
Answer 3 (10 points)

ANSWER 3

		Factor's Effect									
Item	Incr	Decr	No Effect	Item	Incr	Decr	No Effect	Item	Incr	Decr	No Effect
106	○	●	○	111	○	○	●	116	●	○	○
107	●	○	○	112	○	●	○	117	●	○	○
108	●	○	○	113	●	○	○	118	○	○	●
109	●	○	○	114	●	○	○	119	●	○	○
110	○	●	○	115	○	●	○	120	●	○	○

G. Perform Analytical Procedures

R96
Answer 1 (10 points)

ANSWER 1

a. Item	Select one
1	H
2	E
3	L
4	G
5	D
6	T
7	N
8	N
9	U

b. Item		Select one, two, or three, as indicated
10	Blacken 3 ovals only	A, B, D
11	Blacken 3 ovals only	A, B, E
12	Blacken 3 ovals only	A, B, E
13	Blacken 1 oval only	P
14	Blacken 2 ovals only	K, P
15	Blacken 1 oval only	H

J. Consider Internal Control

M95
Answer 3 (10 points)

Item	Answer
106	C
107	G
108	F
109	K
110	I
111	B
112	D
113	L
114	O
115	C
116	C
117	N
118	R
119	P
120	N

N93
Answer 2 (10 points)

Item	Select one
61	M
62	Z
63	L
64	B
65	H
66	S
67	O
68	U
69	I
70	Q
71	N
72	T
73	Y

M. Determine and Prepare the Work Program

N95
Answer 2 (10 points)

Item	Select one
91	D
92	I
93	D
94	C
95	C
96	D
97	B
98	A
99	E
100	C
101	D
102	G
103	F
104	J
105	G

Auditing

II. Obtain and Document Information to Form a Basis for Conclusions

A. Perform Planned Procedures Including Planned Applications of Audit Sampling

R97
Answer 1 (10 points)

Select one or two, as indicated

#		Answer
1	Select 1	E
2	Select 1	D
3	Select 1	H
4	Select 2	K, L
5	Select 1	O
6	Select 1	Q
7	Select 1	A
8	Select 1	U
9	Select 1	B
10	Select 2	A, J
11	Select 1	E
12	Select 2	J, L

R97
Answer 2 (10 points)

ANSWER 2

A.			Select one
1	▲		Ⓐ Ⓑ Ⓒ Ⓓ Ⓔ Ⓕ Ⓖ Ⓗ ● Ⓙ Ⓚ
2	■		Ⓐ Ⓑ ● Ⓓ Ⓔ Ⓕ Ⓖ Ⓗ Ⓘ Ⓙ Ⓚ
3	◆		Ⓐ Ⓑ Ⓒ Ⓓ Ⓔ Ⓕ Ⓖ Ⓗ Ⓘ ● Ⓚ
4	✪		Ⓐ Ⓑ Ⓒ Ⓓ Ⓔ Ⓕ Ⓖ ● Ⓘ Ⓙ Ⓚ
5	✚		Ⓐ Ⓑ Ⓒ Ⓓ Ⓔ Ⓕ ● Ⓗ Ⓘ Ⓙ Ⓚ
6	✓		● Ⓑ Ⓒ Ⓓ Ⓔ Ⓕ Ⓖ Ⓗ Ⓘ Ⓙ Ⓚ
7	★		Ⓐ Ⓑ Ⓒ Ⓓ Ⓔ Ⓕ Ⓖ Ⓗ Ⓘ ● Ⓚ
8	✱		Ⓐ ● Ⓒ Ⓓ Ⓔ Ⓕ Ⓖ Ⓗ Ⓘ Ⓙ Ⓚ
9	●		Ⓐ Ⓑ Ⓒ ● Ⓔ Ⓕ Ⓖ Ⓗ Ⓘ Ⓙ Ⓚ
10	◪		Ⓐ Ⓑ Ⓒ Ⓓ Ⓔ ● Ⓖ Ⓗ Ⓘ Ⓙ Ⓚ

B.			Select one
11	▶		Ⓐ Ⓑ Ⓒ Ⓓ Ⓔ ● Ⓖ Ⓗ Ⓘ Ⓙ Ⓚ Ⓛ
12	↕		Ⓐ Ⓑ Ⓒ Ⓓ Ⓔ Ⓕ Ⓖ Ⓗ Ⓘ Ⓙ Ⓚ ●
13	√		Ⓐ Ⓑ Ⓒ Ⓓ Ⓔ Ⓕ Ⓖ Ⓗ Ⓘ Ⓙ ● Ⓛ
14	∠		Ⓐ Ⓑ Ⓒ Ⓓ Ⓔ Ⓕ Ⓖ Ⓗ Ⓘ ● Ⓚ Ⓛ
15	↔		Ⓐ Ⓑ Ⓒ Ⓓ Ⓔ Ⓕ Ⓖ ● Ⓘ Ⓙ Ⓚ Ⓛ
16	⊗		Ⓐ Ⓑ Ⓒ ● Ⓔ Ⓕ Ⓖ Ⓗ Ⓘ Ⓙ Ⓚ Ⓛ
17	→		Ⓐ Ⓑ ● Ⓓ Ⓔ Ⓕ Ⓖ Ⓗ Ⓘ Ⓙ Ⓚ Ⓛ
18	↵		Ⓐ ● Ⓒ Ⓓ Ⓔ Ⓕ Ⓖ Ⓗ Ⓘ Ⓙ Ⓚ Ⓛ

N95
Answer 3 (10 points)

Item	Review		Compilation	
106	●	N	●	N
107	●	N	H	●
108	H	●	H	●
109	●	N	●	N
110	H	●	H	●
111	●	N	●	N
112	H	●	H	●
113	H	●	H	●
114	●	N	●	N
115	●	N	H	●
116	H	●	H	●
117	●	N	●	N
118	H	●	H	●
119	H	●	H	●
120	H	●	H	●

N94
Answer 3 (10 points)

Item		List (Select at least one)
99	Blacken two ovals only	Ⓐ Ⓑ Ⓒ ● Ⓔ Ⓕ Ⓖ Ⓗ ● Ⓙ
100	Blacken five ovals only	● Ⓑ Ⓒ Ⓓ Ⓔ Ⓕ ● ● ● ●
101	Blacken five ovals only	Ⓐ ● Ⓒ Ⓓ Ⓔ Ⓕ ● ● ● ●
102	Blacken one oval only	Ⓐ Ⓑ Ⓒ Ⓓ ● Ⓕ Ⓖ Ⓗ Ⓘ Ⓙ
103	Blacken two ovals only	Ⓐ Ⓑ Ⓒ Ⓓ ● Ⓕ Ⓖ ● Ⓘ Ⓙ
104	Blacken one oval only	Ⓐ Ⓑ ● Ⓓ Ⓔ Ⓕ Ⓖ Ⓗ Ⓘ Ⓙ

N92
Answer 2 (10 points)

Item	Investments (select one)	Item	Accounts Receivable (select one)	Item	Property and Equipment (select one)
61	Ⓐ Ⓑ Ⓒ Ⓓ ● Ⓕ Ⓖ	64	Ⓐ ● Ⓒ Ⓓ Ⓔ Ⓕ Ⓖ	68	Ⓐ Ⓑ Ⓒ ● Ⓔ Ⓕ Ⓖ
62	Ⓐ Ⓑ Ⓒ Ⓓ Ⓔ ● Ⓖ	65	Ⓐ Ⓑ Ⓒ Ⓓ ● Ⓕ Ⓖ	69	Ⓐ Ⓑ Ⓒ Ⓓ Ⓔ Ⓕ ●
63	Ⓐ Ⓑ Ⓒ ● Ⓔ Ⓕ Ⓖ	66	Ⓐ Ⓑ ● Ⓓ Ⓔ Ⓕ Ⓖ	70	Ⓐ ● Ⓒ Ⓓ Ⓔ Ⓕ Ⓖ
		67	Ⓐ Ⓑ Ⓒ Ⓓ Ⓔ ● Ⓖ		

Unofficial Answers

IV. Prepare Communications to Satisfy Engagement Objectives

A. Prepare Reports

R96
Answer 2 (10 points)

Item	Select one				Item	Select one		
1	Ⓜ	●	Ⓑ		10	Ⓜ	●	Ⓑ
2	●	Ⓖ	Ⓑ		11	Ⓜ	●	Ⓑ
3	Ⓜ	Ⓖ	●		12	Ⓜ	Ⓖ	●
4	Ⓜ	Ⓖ	●		13	Ⓜ	Ⓖ	●
5	Ⓜ	●	Ⓑ		14	Ⓜ	●	Ⓑ
6	●	Ⓖ	Ⓑ		15	Ⓜ	●	Ⓑ
7	●	Ⓖ	Ⓑ		16	●	Ⓖ	Ⓑ
8	●	Ⓖ	Ⓑ		17	Ⓜ	●	Ⓑ
9	●	Ⓖ	Ⓑ					

M95
Answer 2 (10 points)

Item	Select one			Item	Select one	
91	●	Ⓓ		99	●	Ⓓ
92	Ⓒ	●		100	Ⓒ	●
93	Ⓒ	●		101	●	Ⓓ
94	Ⓒ	●		102	●	Ⓓ
95	Ⓒ	●		103	●	Ⓓ
96	Ⓒ	●		104	Ⓒ	●
97	Ⓒ	●		105	Ⓒ	●
98	●	Ⓓ				

N94
Answer 2 (10 points)

Item	List A (Select one)	List B (Select one)
91	E	P
92	A	I
93	B	J
94	E	H
95	A	I
96	E	O
97	E	H
98	E	H

M93
Answer 2 (10 points)

Land's criticism is Correct/Incorrect

Item	Correct	Incorrect	Item	Correct	Incorrect
61	●	I	68	●	I
62	C	●	69	●	I
63	C	●	70	C	●
64	C	●	71	●	I
65	C	●	72	●	I
66	C	●	73	●	I
67	●	I			

ESSAYS — SELECTED QUESTIONS

I. Plan, Evaluate and Accept the Engagement

A. Determine Nature and Scope of Engagement

R97
Number 1

On September 3, 1997, Larkin, CPA, was engaged to audit the financial statements of Modern Minerals Co. for the year ended October 31, 1997. Modern purchases precious metals at wholesale prices and resells them to craft clubs at retail. Modern is a new client whose common stock was first offered to the public in 1994. Modern received an unqualified opinion on its financial statements in each of the prior three years but changed auditors after each engagement. In accepting the engagement, Larkin completed all the appropriate client-acceptance procedures. Larkin instructed Johnson, an assistant on the engagement, to draft a planning checklist that would assist Larkin in preparing the audit staff for the field work that is scheduled to begin on October 17, 1997. On October 5, 1997, Johnson prepared the planning checklist below.

Planning checklist for the Modern Minerals (MM) engagement:

I. Understanding the assignment

In planning the audit, have engagement personnel considered:

- MM's accounting policies and procedures?
- Financial statement items likely to require adjustment?
- The nature of the reports expected to be rendered?
- The effects of accounting and auditing pronouncements, particularly new ones?
- The method of sampling likely to be approved by MM?
- The extent of involvement of other independent auditors or internal auditors?

In planning the audit, have engagement personnel discussed:

- The general scope and timing of the audit work with MM's management, board of directors, or audit committee?
- The expected level of detection risk with MM's management, board of directors, or audit committee?

II. Assigning personnel to the engagement

Has a time budget for the engagement been prepared to determine the staffing requirements and to schedule the field work and has it been approved by:

- The engagement partner?
- MM's controller and audit committee?

Has the engagement staffing schedule been approved by the engagement partner?

Have the following factors been considered:

- Engagement size and complexity?
- Personnel available?
- Timing of the work to be performed?
- Continuity and periodic rotation of personnel?
- Opportunities for on-the-job training?

III. Knowledge of the entity's business

Has an overall understanding of MM's operations been obtained by reviewing:

- Minutes of stockholders' and board of directors' meetings?
- Filings with regulatory agencies?
- Recent management letters?
- The Codification of Statements on Auditing Standards?

Have engagement personnel obtained knowledge of MM's organization and operating characteristics?

Have the methods that MM uses to process accounting information been considered?

Have the extent, complexity, and organizational structure of MM's computer activities and their effects on the audit been considered and evaluated?

IV. **Assessing auditability**

Has the adequacy of the accounting records been assessed for proper:

- Descriptions of transactions to permit the appropriate financial statement classification?

- Information about transactions to permit the recording of appropriate monetary amounts?

- Recording of transactions in the appropriate accounting period?

Have the following factors regarding the integrity of management been considered in planning the audit:

- Responses to previous inquiries of local attorneys, bankers, and other business leaders regarding MM's standing in the community?

- MM's credit rating?

Have inquiries of a sample of MM's customers regarding MM's credit-granting policies been made?

V. **Engagement letter**

Have the following items been addressed in the engagement letter:

- Name of the entity and its year end?

- Statements to be audited?

- Scope of services?

- Type of report to be rendered?

- Larkin's responsibilities for detecting fraud?

- Larkin's responsibility for assuring that MM meets its SEC filing deadlines?

- MM's obligations to prepare statements and schedules?

- Requirement that Larkin read all printed material in which the auditor's report appears?

- Larkin's responsibility for the preparation or review of tax returns?

- Provision for MM's acceptance signature and date?

Have the following items been considered for inclusion in the engagement letter:

- Name of MM's personnel to be contacted during the engagement?

- Description of particular audit procedure(s) requested by MM?

- Cooperation with the internal auditors?

- Date when Larkin's detailed audit program will be available for MM's review?

- List of certain services specifically excluded?

- MM's acknowledgment of its responsibility for the financial statements?

- A statement that MM will be informed of any reportable conditions that come to Larkin's attention?

VI. **Assessing risk**

Have inherent risk and control risk been assessed to determine how much detection risk can be accepted?

Has consideration been given to permitting MM's internal auditors to make judgments about the assessment of inherent risk and evaluations of significant accounting estimates?

If control risk is assessed at below the maximum level for some or all financial statement assertions, has that conclusion been documented?

If control risk is assessed at the maximum level for some or all assertions:

- Have specific internal control activities that are likely to prevent or detect material misstatements in those assertions been identified?

- Have tests of controls to evaluate the design and operation of such activities been performed?

- If a further reduction in the assessed level of control risk is desired for some assertions, have additional tests of relevant controls been performed?

- Has the basis for the conclusion that control risk is assessed at the maximum level for some or all assertions been documented?

VII. **Illegal acts**

Have the following matters been considered in assessing the risk that MM has not complied with laws and regulations that have a direct and material effect on the financial statements:

- MM's policy relative to the prevention of illegal acts?
- MM's understanding of the requirements of laws and regulations pertinent to its business?
- Internal control components designed to give MM reasonable assurance that MM complies with those laws and regulations?

VIII. **Analytical procedures**

In planning the audit, have analytical procedures been used that focus on:

- Enhancing an understanding of MM's business and the transactions and events of the year under audit?
- Identifying areas that may represent specific risks relevant to the audit?
- Achieving particular audit objectives?
- Evaluating the overall financial statement presentation?

IX. **Audit strategies and the audit program**

Has the audit program been developed for the engagement and approved by the engagement partner?

Required:

a. Identify the inappropriate comments and misconceptions that exist in Johnson's planning checklist and describe why each is inappropriate or a misconception.

b. Describe the additional considerations and comments that should be addressed in Johnson's planning checklist.

M95
Number 4 (Estimated time — — 25 to 35 minutes)

Hart, CPA, has been approached by Unidyne Co. to accept an attest engagement to examine and report on management's written assertion about the effectiveness of Unidyne's internal control over financial reporting as of June 30, 1995, the end of its fiscal year.

Required:

a. Describe the required conditions that must be met for Hart to accept an attest engagement to examine and report on management's assertion about the effectiveness of Unidyne's internal control.

b. Describe the broad engagement activities that would be involved in Hart's performing an examination of management's assertion about the effectiveness of Unidyne's internal control.

c. Describe the other types of attest services that Hart may provide and those specifically **not** permitted in connection with Unidyne's internal control.

B. **Assess Engagement Risk and the CPA Firm's Ability to Perform the Engagement**

M91
Number 5 (Estimated time — — 15 to 25 minutes)

Green, CPA, is considering audit risk at the financial statement level in planning the audit of National Federal Bank (NFB) Company's financial statements for the year ended December 31, 1990. Audit risk at the financial statement level is influenced by the risk of material misstatements, which may be indicated by a combination of factors related to management, the industry, and the entity. In assessing such factors Green has gathered the following information concerning NFB's environment.

Company profile:

NFB is a federally-insured bank that has been consistently more profitable than the industry average by marketing mortgages on properties in a prosperous rural area, which has experienced considerable growth in recent years. NFB packages its mortgages and sells them to large mortgage investment trusts. Despite recent volatility of interest rates, NFB has been able to continue selling its mortgages as a source of new lendable funds.

NFB's board of directors is controlled by Smith, the majority stockholder, who also acts as the chief executive officer. Management at the bank's branch offices has authority for directing and controlling NFB's operations and is compensated based on branch profitability. The internal auditor reports directly to Harris, a minority shareholder, who also acts as chairman of the board's audit committee.

The accounting department has experienced little turnover in personnel during the five years Green has audited NFB. NFB's formula consistently underestimates the allowance for loan losses, but its controller has always been receptive to Green's suggestions to increase the allowance during each engagement.

Recent developments:

During 1990, NFB opened a branch office in a suburban town thirty miles from its principal place of business. Although this branch is not yet profitable due to competition from several well-established regional banks, management believes that the branch will be profitable by 1992.

Also, during 1990, NFB increased the efficiency of its accounting operations by installing a new, sophisticated computer system.

Required:
Based only on the information above, describe the factors that most likely would have an effect on the risk

of material misstatements. Indicate whether each factor increases or decreases the risk. Use the format illustrated below.

Environmental factor	Effect on risk of material misstatements
Branch management has authority for directing and controlling operations.	Increase

G. Perform Analytical Procedures

N94
Number 4 (Estimated time — — 25 to 35 minutes)

Analytical procedures are an important part of the audit process and consist of evaluations of financial information made by the study of plausible relationships among both financial and nonfinancial data. Analytical procedures are used to assist in planning other auditing procedures, as substantive tests in obtaining evidential matter, and as an overall review of the financial information.

Required:
    a. Describe the objectives and the characteristics of analytical procedures used in planning an audit.

    b. Describe the factors that influence an auditor's decision to select analytical procedures as substantive tests, including the factors that affect their effectiveness and efficiency.

    c. Describe an auditor's objectives in applying analytical procedures in the overall review stage of an audit and which analytical procedures generally would be included in the overall review stage.

I. Assess Inherent Risk and Risk of Misstatements

R98
Number 1

Kent, CPA, is the engagement partner on the financial statement audit of Super Computer Services Co. (SCS) for the year ended April 30, 1998. On May 6, 1998, Smith, the senior auditor assigned to the engagement, had the following conversation with Kent concerning the planning phase of the audit:

Kent: Do you have all the audit programs updated yet for the SCS engagement?

Smith: Mostly. I still have work to do on the fraud risk assessment.

Kent: Why? Our "errors and irregularities" program from last year is still OK. It's passed peer review several times. Besides, we don't have specific duties regarding fraud. If we find it, we'll deal with it then.

Smith: I don't think so. That new CEO, Mint, has almost no salary, mostly bonuses and stock options. Doesn't that concern you?

Kent: No. Mint's employment contract was approved by the Board of Directors just three months ago. It was passed unanimously.

Smith: I guess so, but Mint told those stock analysts that SCS's earnings would increase 30% next year. Can Mint deliver numbers like that?

Kent: Who knows? We're auditing the '98 financial statements, not '99. Mint will probably amend that forecast every month between now and next May.

Smith: Sure, but all this may change our other audit programs.

Kent: No, it won't. The programs are fine as is. If you find fraud in any of your tests, just let me know. Maybe we'll have to extend the tests. Or maybe we'll just report it to the audit committee.

Smith: What would they do? Green is the audit committee's chair, and remember, Green hired Mint. They've been best friends for years. Besides, Mint is calling all the shots now. Brown, the old CEO, is still on the Board, but Brown's never around. Brown's even been skipping the Board meetings. Nobody in management or on the Board would stand up to Mint.

Kent: That's nothing new. Brown was like that years ago. Brown caused frequent disputes with Jones, CPA, the predecessor auditor. Three years ago, Jones told Brown how ineffective the internal audit department was then. Next thing you know, Jones is out and I'm in. Why bother? I'm just as happy that those understaffed internal auditors don't get in our way. Just remember, the bottom line is . . . are the financial statements fairly presented? And they always have been. We don't provide any assurances about fraud. That's management's job.

Smith: But what about the lack of segregation of duties in the cash disbursements department? That clerk could write a check for anything.

Kent: Sure. That's a reportable condition every year and probably will be again this year. But we're talking cost-effectiveness here, not fraud. We just have to do lots of testing on cash disbursements and report it again.

Smith: What about the big layoffs coming up next month? It's more than a rumor. Even the employees know it's going to happen, and they're real uptight about it.

Kent: I know, it's the worst kept secret at SCS, but we don't have to consider that now. Even if it happens, it will only improve next year's financial results. Brown should have let these people go years ago. Let's face it, how else can Mint even come close to the 30% earnings increase next year?

Required:
Begin the answer to each requirement (i.e., A, B, and C) on the top of a new page.

a. Describe the fraud risk factors that are indicated in the dialogue above.

b. Describe Kent's misconceptions regarding the consideration of fraud in the audit of SCS's financial statements that are contained in the dialogue above **and** explain why each is a misconception.

c. Describe an auditor's working paper documentation requirements regarding the assessment of the risk of material misstatement due to fraud.

J. Consider Internal Control

N94
Number 5 (Estimated time —— 25 to 35 minutes)

An auditor's working papers include the narrative description below of the cash receipts and billing portions of the internal control of Rural Building Supplies, Inc. Rural is a single-store retailer that sells a variety of tools, garden supplies, lumber, small appliances, and electrical fixtures to the public, although about half of Rural's sales are to construction contractors on account. Rural employs 12 salaried sales associates, a credit manager, three full-time clerical workers, and several part-time cash register clerks and assistant bookkeepers. The full-time clerical workers perform such tasks as cash receipts, billing, and accounting and are adequately bonded. They are referred to in the narrative as "accounts receivable supervisor," "cashier," and "bookkeeper."

NARRATIVE

Retail customers pay for merchandise by cash or credit card at cash registers when merchandise is purchased. A contractor may purchase merchandise on account if approved by the credit manager based only on the manager's familiarity with the contractor's reputation. After credit is approved, the sales associate files a prenumbered charge form with the accounts receivable (A/R) supervisor to set up the receivable.

The A/R supervisor independently verifies the pricing and other details on the charge form by reference to a management-authorized price list, corrects any errors, prepares the invoice, and supervises a part-time employee who mails the invoice to the contractor. The A/R supervisor electronically posts the details of the invoice in the A/R subsidiary ledger; simultaneously, the transaction's details are transmitted to the bookkeeper. The A/R supervisor also prepares a monthly computer-generated A/R subsidiary ledger without a reconciliation with the A/R control account and a monthly report of overdue accounts.

The cash receipts functions are performed by the cashier who also supervises the cash register clerks. The cashier opens the mail, compares each check with the enclosed remittance advice, stamps each check "for deposit only," and lists checks for deposit. The cashier then gives the remittance advices to the bookkeeper for recording. The cashier deposits the checks daily separate from the daily deposit of cash register receipts. The cashier retains the verified deposit slips to assist in reconciling the monthly bank statements, but forwards to the bookkeeper a copy of the daily cash register summary. The cashier does not have access to the journals or ledgers.

The bookkeeper receives the details of transactions from the A/R supervisor and the cashier for journalizing and posting to the general ledger. After recording the remittance advices received from the cashier, the bookkeeper electronically transmits the remittance information to the A/R supervisor for subsidiary ledger updating. The bookkeeper sends monthly statements to contractors with unpaid balances upon receipt of the monthly report of overdue balances from the A/R supervisor. The bookkeeper authorizes the A/R supervisor to write off accounts as uncollectible when six months have passed since the initial overdue notice was sent. At this time, the credit manager is notified by the bookkeeper not to grant additional credit to that contractor.

Required:
Based only on the information in the narrative, describe the internal control weaknesses in Rural's internal control concerning the cash receipts and billing functions. Organize the weaknesses by employee job function: Credit manager, A/R supervisor, Cashier, and Bookkeeper. Do **not** describe how to correct the weaknesses.

M93
Number 3 (Estimated time —— 15 to 25 minutes)

Butler, CPA, has been engaged to audit the financial statements of Young Computer Outlets, Inc., a new client. Young is a privately-owned chain of retail stores that sells a variety of computer software and video products. Young uses an in-house payroll department at its corporate headquarters to compute payroll data, and to prepare and distribute payroll checks to its 300 salaried employees.

Butler is preparing an internal control questionnaire to assist in obtaining an understanding of Young's internal control and in assessing control risk.

Required:
Prepare a "Payroll" segment of Butler's internal control questionnaire that would assist in obtaining an understanding of Young's internal control and in assessing control risk.

Do **not** prepare questions relating to cash payrolls, EDP applications, payments based on hourly rates, piecework, commissions, employee benefits (pensions, health care, vacations, etc.), or payroll tax accruals other than withholdings.

Use the format in the following example:

Question	Yes	No
Are paychecks prenumbered and accounted for?		

M92
Number 3 (Estimated time — — 15 to 25 minutes)

Harris, CPA, has accepted an engagement to audit the financial statements of Grant Manufacturing Co., a new client. Grant has an adequate control environment and a reasonable segregation of duties. Harris is about to assess control risk for the assertions related to Grant's property and equipment.

Required:
Describe the key internal control structure activities related to Grant's property, equipment, and related transactions (additions, transfers, major maintenance and repairs, retirements, and dispositions) that Harris may consider in assessing control risk.

K. Consider Other Planning Matters

M94
Number 4 (Estimated time — — 25 to 35 minutes)

North, CPA, is planning an audit of the financial statements of General Co. In determining the nature, timing, and extent of the auditing procedures, North is considering General's internal audit function, which is staffed by Tyler.

Required:
a. In what ways may Tyler's work be relevant to North, the independent auditor?

b. What factors should North consider and what inquiries should North make in deciding whether to use Tyler's work?

L. Identify Financial Statement Assertions and Formulate Audit Objectives

N95
Number 5 (Estimated time — — 25 to 35 minutes)

Most of an auditor's work in forming an opinion on financial statements consists of obtaining and evaluating evidential matter concerning the financial statement assertions.

Required:
a. What is the definition of "financial statement assertions?"
Do not list the assertions.

b. What is the relationship between audit objectives and financial statement assertions?

c. What should an auditor consider in developing the audit objectives of a particular engagement?

d. What is the relationship between audit objectives and audit procedures?

e. What are an auditor's primary considerations when selecting particular substantive tests to achieve audit objectives?

M. Determine and Prepare the Work Program

N92
Number 5 (Estimated time — — 15 to 25 minutes)

Cook, CPA, has been engaged to audit the financial statements of General Department Stores, Inc., a continuing audit client, which is a chain of medium-sized retail stores. General's fiscal year will end on June 30, 1993, and General's management has asked Cook to issue the auditor's report by August 1, 1993. Cook will not have sufficient time to perform all of the necessary field work in July 1993, but will have time to perform most of the field work as of an interim date, April 30, 1993.

For the accounts to be tested at the interim date, Cook will also perform substantive tests covering the transactions of the final two months of the year. This will be necessary to extend Cook's conclusions to the balance sheet date.

Required:
a. Describe the factors Cook should consider before applying principal substantive tests to General's balance sheet accounts at April 30, 1993.

b. For accounts tested at April 30, 1993, describe how Cook should design the substantive tests covering the balances as of June 30, 1993, and the transactions of the final two months of the year.

Selected Questions

II. Obtain and Document Information to Form a Basis for Conclusions

A. Perform Planned Procedures Including Planned Applications of Audit Sampling

R97
Number 2

Miller, CPA, is engaged to audit the financial statements of Superior Wholesaling for the year ended December 31, 1996. Miller obtained and documented an understanding of Superior's internal control relating to accounts receivable and assessed control risk relating to accounts receivable at the maximum level. Miller requested and obtained from Superior an aged accounts receivable schedule listing the total amount owed by each customer as of December 31, 1996, and sent positive confirmation requests to a sample of the customers. Subsequently, Miller tested the accuracy of the aged accounts receivable schedule. Miller has asked Adler, the staff assistant assigned to the engagement, to follow up on the eight returned confirmations that appear on the following two pages. Assume that each confirmation is material if the potential misstatement is projected to the population.

Required:

   a. Describe the procedure(s), if any, that Adler should perform to resolve each of the eight confirmations that were returned. Assume that Superior will record any necessary adjusting entries and that Adler will verify that they are appropriate.

   b. Assume that Miller sent second requests for accounts receivable balances initially selected for confirmation for which no responses were received. Describe the alternative substantive procedures that Miller should consider applying to the accounts receivable selected for confirmation for which no responses were received to Miller's second requests. Assume that these accounts receivable in the aggregate, when projected as misstatements to the population, would affect Miller's decision about whether the financial statements are materially misstated.

   c. In addition to performing the confirmation procedures and alternative procedures described in requirements **a.** and **b.** and the procedures described in the first paragraph above, what additional substantive procedures should Miller consider performing to complete the audit of Superior's accounts receivable and related allowances? Assume that all accounts receivable are trade receivables.

Superior Wholesaling, Inc.
123 Commercial Blvd.
Anytown, USA

January 15, 1997

Atom Co.
362 Main Street
Anytown, USA

Confirm #11

Dear *C.L. Adams:*

Our auditor, Miller, CPA, is currently auditing our financial statements. To facilitate this audit, please confirm the balance due us as of December 31, 1996, which is shown on our records as $15,000. Indicate in the space below whether this is in agreement with your records. If there are exceptions, please provide any information that will assist the auditor in reconciling the difference.

Please mail your reply directly to Miller, CPA. A stamped, self-addressed envelope is enclosed for your convenience.

Sincerely,

J. Blake

J. Blake, Controller
Superior Wholesaling, Inc.

To Miller, CPA:
The amount shown above is correct as of December 31, 1996, except as follows:
Yes, we ordered $15,000 worth of merchandise from Superior in November. However, we mailed Superior a check for $15,000 on 12/18/96.
Name *C.L. Adams* Position *Accounting Mgr.* Date *1/22/97*

Note to files: Blake indicates that the check was received and deposited on 12/28/96, but posted to the wrong customer's account.
C. Miller

Superior Wholesaling, Inc.
123 Commercial Blvd.
Anytown, USA

January 15, 1997

Clark Retailing
35 Lincoln Avenue
Jackson, USA

Confirm #34

Dear *J.P. Cummings:*

Our auditor, Miller, CPA, is currently auditing our financial statements. To facilitate this audit, please confirm the balance due us as of December 31, 1996, which is shown on our records as $32,000. Indicate in the space below whether this is in agreement with your records. If there are exceptions, please provide any information that will assist the auditor in reconciling the difference.

Please mail your reply directly to Miller, CPA. A stamped, self-addressed envelope is enclosed for your convenience.

Sincerely,

J. Blake

J. Blake, Controller
Superior Wholesaling, Inc.

To Miller, CPA:
The amount shown above is correct as of December 31, 1996, except as follows:
We received $24,000 of goods on consignment from Superior on 12/10/96, but they're not sold yet!
Name *J. Cummings* Position *President* Date *1/19/97*

Superior Wholesaling, Inc.
123 Commercial Blvd.
Anytown, USA

January 15, 1997

Baker Co.
18 Lakeview Drive
Central City, USA

Confirm #28

Dear *S. Brown:*

Our auditor, Miller, CPA, is currently auditing our financial statements. To facilitate this audit, please confirm the balance due us as of December 31, 1996, which is shown on our records as $25,000. Indicate in the space below whether this is in agreement with your records. If there are exceptions, please provide any information that will assist the auditor in reconciling the difference.

Please mail your reply directly to Miller, CPA. A stamped, self-addressed envelope is enclosed for your convenience.

Sincerely,

J. Blake

J. Blake, Controller
Superior Wholesaling, Inc.

To Miller, CPA:
The amount shown above is correct as of December 31, 1996, except as follows:
Sure we ordered $25,000 of merchandise on Oct. 10, 1996, but Superior was out-of-stock until recently. They back-ordered the goods and we finally received them on Jan. 6, 1997.
Name *S. Brown* Position *A/P Supervisor* Date *Jan. 18, 1997*

Superior Wholesaling, Inc.
123 Commercial Blvd.
Anytown, USA

January 15, 1997

Delta Outlet Stores, Inc.
Sunshine Mall
River City, USA

Confirm #41

Dear *R. Dunn:*

Our auditor, Miller, CPA, is currently auditing our financial statements. To facilitate this audit, please confirm the balance due us as of December 31, 1996, which is shown on our records as $45,000. Indicate in the space below whether this is in agreement with your records. If there are exceptions, please provide any information that will assist the auditor in reconciling the difference.

Please mail your reply directly to Miller, CPA. A stamped, self-addressed envelope is enclosed for your convenience.

Sincerely,

J. Blake

J. Blake, Controller
Superior Wholesaling, Inc.

To Miller, CPA:
The amount shown above is correct as of December 31, 1996, except as follows:
No way! Superior promised these goods in 10 days on Dec. 2nd. When we didn't receive them, I canceled the order on Dec. 12th. General Wholesaling shipped us similar goods overnight!
Name *R. Dunn* Position *General Manager* Date *Jan. 18th*

Selected Questions

Superior Wholesaling, Inc.
123 Commercial Blvd.
Anytown, USA

January 15, 1997

Eagle Distributors
2700 Ocean Shore Blvd.
Ocean City, USA

Confirm #58

Dear T. Engle:

Our auditor, Miller, CPA, is currently auditing our financial statements. To facilitate this audit, please confirm the balance due us as of December 31, 1996, which is shown on our records as $59,000. Indicate in the space below whether this is in agreement with your records. If there are exceptions, please provide any information that will assist the auditor in reconciling the difference.

Please mail your reply directly to Miller, CPA. A stamped, self-addressed envelope is enclosed for your convenience.

Sincerely,

J. Blake

J. Blake, Controller
Superior Wholesaling, Inc.

To Miller, CPA:
    The amount shown above is correct as of December 31, 1996, except as follows:

I use an accounts payable voucher system by individual invoice. I can't verify $59,000, but Superior is one of my regular suppliers. I am sure I probably owe them something.

Name *T. Engle*   Position *Accounting Mgr.*   Date *1-20-97*

Superior Wholesaling, Inc.
123 Commercial Blvd.
Anytown, USA

January 15, 1997

Grove Retailing
3838 Curtis Blvd.
Union Center, USA

Confirm #71

Dear H. Gates:

Our auditor, Miller, CPA, is currently auditing our financial statements. To facilitate this audit, please confirm the balance due us as of December 31, 1996, which is shown on our records as $75,000. Indicate in the space below whether this is in agreement with your records. If there are exceptions, please provide any information that will assist the auditor in reconciling the difference.

Please mail your reply directly to Miller, CPA. A stamped, self-addressed envelope is enclosed for your convenience.

Sincerely,

J. Blake

J. Blake, Controller
Superior Wholesaling, Inc.

To Miller, CPA:
    The amount shown above is correct as of December 31, 1996, except as follows:

Our records show that a check for $75,000 was mailed on 12/27/96.

Name *H. Gates*   Position *Controller*   Date *1/22/97*

Superior Wholesaling, Inc.
123 Commercial Blvd.
Anytown, USA

January 15, 1997

Franklin Co.
17 United Street
Industry City, USA

Confirm #67

Dear S. Brown:

Our auditor, Miller, CPA, is currently auditing our financial statements. To facilitate this audit, please confirm the balance due us as of December 31, 1996, which is shown on our records as $65,000. Indicate in the space below whether this is in agreement with your records. If there are exceptions, please provide any information that will assist the auditor in reconciling the difference.

Please mail your reply directly to Miller, CPA. A stamped, self-addressed envelope is enclosed for your convenience.

Sincerely,

J. Blake

J. Blake, Controller
Superior Wholesaling, Inc.

To Miller, CPA:
    The amount shown above is correct as of December 31, 1996, except as follows:

_____

Name   Position   Date

Note to files: This confirmation was returned by the postal service as "return to sender-no such addressee at this location."

C. Miller

Superior Wholesaling, Inc.
123 Commercial Blvd.
Anytown, USA

January 15, 1997

Hall Enterprises, Inc.
55 Green St.
Grant City, USA

Confirm #86

Dear K. Hines:

Our auditor, Miller, CPA, is currently auditing our financial statements. To facilitate this audit, please confirm the balance due us as of December 31, 1996, which is shown on our records as $80,000. Indicate in the space below whether this is in agreement with your records. If there are exceptions, please provide any information that will assist the auditor in reconciling the difference.

Please mail your reply directly to Miller, CPA. A stamped, self-addressed envelope is enclosed for your convenience.

Sincerely,

J. Blake

J. Blake, Controller
Superior Wholesaling, Inc.

To Miller, CPA:
    The amount shown above is correct as of December 31, 1996, except as follows:

Mailed that check for full amount on 1-3-97; merchandise was only received on 12-23-96.

Name *K. Hines*   Position *Accountant*   Date *1-18-97*

R96
Number 1 (Estimated time — — 25 to 35 minutes)

Cook, CPA, is auditing the financial statements of DollarMart, a local retailer of clothes, appliances, sporting goods, and electronics. During prior years' audits of DollarMart, Cook noticed that management was less concerned about the timely recording of expenses and liabilities than revenues and assets. As a result, very little of DollarMart's internal control resources were expended in assuring an accurate and timely recording of accounts payable. Cook also believes that DollarMart's management may be motivated to delay recording its liabilities at year end, so Cook is approaching the search for unrecorded liabilities with caution.

Required:
   a. What substantive auditing procedures would Cook most likely consider performing in searching for DollarMart's unrecorded liabilities?

   b. How would the nature, timing, and extent of Cook's substantive auditing procedures most likely be affected by DollarMart's deficient control environment?

M94
Number 5 (Estimated time — — 25 to 35 minutes)

King, CPA, is auditing the financial statements of Cycle Co., an entity that has receivables from customers, which have arisen from the sale of goods in the normal course of business. King is aware that the confirmation of accounts receivable is a generally accepted auditing procedure.

Required:
   a. Under what circumstances could King justify omitting the confirmation of Cycle's accounts receivable?

   b. In designing confirmation requests, what factors are likely to affect King's assessment of the reliability of confirmations that King sends?

   c. What alternative procedures would King consider performing when replies to positive confirmation requests are **not** received?

N93
Number 5 (Estimated time — — 15 to 25 minutes)

Mead, CPA, was engaged to audit Jiffy Co.'s financial statements for the year ended August 31, 1993. Mead is applying sampling procedures.

Required:
   Describe each incorrect assumption, statement, and inappropriate application of sampling in Mead's procedures.

During the prior years' audits Mead used classical variables sampling in performing tests of controls on Jiffy's accounts receivable. For the current year Mead decided to use probability-proportional-to-size (PPS) sampling (also known as dollar-unit sampling) in confirming accounts receivable because PPS sampling uses each account in the population as a separate sampling unit. Mead expected to discover many overstatements, but presumed that the PPS sample still would be smaller than the corresponding size for classical variables sampling.

Mead reasoned that the PPS sample would automatically result in a stratified sample because each account would have an equal chance of being selected for confirmation. Additionally, the selection of negative (credit) balances would be facilitated without special considerations.

Mead computed the sample size using the risk of incorrect acceptance, the total recorded book amount of the receivables, and the number of misstated accounts allowed. Mead divided the total recorded book amount of the receivables by the sample size to determine the sampling interval. Mead then calculated the standard deviation of the dollar amounts of the accounts selected for evaluation of the receivables.

Mead's calculated sample size was 60 and the sampling interval was determined to be $10,000. However, only 58 different accounts were selected because two accounts were so large that the sampling interval caused each of them to be selected twice. Mead proceeded to send confirmation requests to 55 of the 58 customers. Three selected accounts each had insignificant recorded balances under $20. Mead ignored these three small accounts and substituted the three largest accounts that had not been selected in the sample. Each of these accounts had balances in excess of $7,000, so Mead sent confirmation requests to those customers.

The confirmation process revealed two differences. One account with an audited amount of $3,000 had been recorded at $4,000. Mead projected this to be a $1,000 misstatement. Another account with an audited amount of $2,000 had been recorded at $1,900. Mead did not count the $100 difference because the purpose of the test was to detect overstatements.

In evaluating the sample results, Mead determined that the accounts receivable balance was not overstated because the projected misstatement was less than the allowance for sampling risk.

M92
Number 4 (Estimated time — — 15 to 25 minutes)

Brown, CPA, is auditing the financial statements of Big Z Wholesaling, Inc., a continuing audit client, for the year ended January 31, 1992. On January 5, 1992, Brown observed the tagging and counting of Big Z's physical inventory and made appropriate test counts. These test counts have been recorded on a computer file. As in prior years, Big Z gave Brown two computer files. One file represents the perpetual inventory (FIFO) records for the year ended January 31, 1992. The other file represents the January 5 physical inventory count.

Assume:

- Brown issued an unqualified opinion on the prior year's financial statements.

- All inventory is purchased for resale and located in a single warehouse.

- Brown has appropriate computerized audit software.

- The perpetual inventory file contains the following information in item number sequence:

  - Beginning balances at February 1, 1991: Item number, item description, total quantity, and prices.

  - For each item purchased during the year: Date received, receiving report number, vendor, item number, item description, quantity, and total dollar amount.

  - For each item sold during the year: Date shipped, invoice number, item number, item description, quantity shipped, and dollar amount of the cost removed from inventory.

  - For each item adjusted for physical inventory count differences: Date, item number, item description, quantity, and dollar amount.

- The physical inventory file contains the following information in item number sequence: Tag number, item number, item description, and count quantity.

Required:
Describe the substantive auditing procedures Brown may consider performing with computerized audit software using Big Z's two computer files and Brown's computer file of test counts. The substantive auditing procedures described may indicate the reports to be printed out for Brown's follow-up by subsequent application of manual procedures. Do **not** describe subsequent manual auditing procedures.

Group the procedures by those using a) the perpetual inventory file and b) the physical inventory and test count files.

N91
Number 4 (Estimated time —— 15 to 25 minutes)

Larkin, CPA, has been engaged to audit the financial statements of Vernon Distributors, Inc., a continuing audit client, for the year ended September 30, 1991. After obtaining an understanding of Vernon's internal control, Larkin assessed control risk at the maximum level for all financial statement assertions concerning investments. Larkin determined that Vernon is unable to exercise significant influence over any investee and none are related parties.

Larkin obtained from Vernon detailed analyses of its investments in domestic securities showing:

- The classification between current and noncurrent portfolios;

- A description of each security, including the interest rate and maturity date of bonds and par value and dividend rate on stocks;

- A notation of the location of each security, either in the Treasurer's safe or held by an independent custodian;

- The number of shares of stock or face amount of bonds held at the beginning and end of the year;

- The beginning and ending balances at cost and at market, and the unamortized premium or discount on bonds;

- Additions to and sales from the portfolios for the year, including date, number of shares, face amount of bonds, cost, proceeds, and realized gain or loss;

- Valuation allowances at the beginning and end of the year and changes therein;

- Accrued investment income for each investment at the beginning and end of the year, and income earned and collected during the year.

Larkin then prepared the following partial audit program of substantive auditing procedures:

1. Foot and crossfoot the analyses.

2. Trace the ending totals to the general ledger and financial statements.

3. Trace the beginning balances to the prior year's working papers.

4. Obtain positive confirmation as of the balance sheet date of the investments held by any independent custodian.

5. Determine that income from investments has been properly recorded as accrued or collected by reference to published sources, by computation, and by tracing to recorded amounts.

6. For investments in nonpublic entities, compare carrying value to information in the most recently available audited financial statements.

7. Determine that all transfers between the current and noncurrent portfolios have been properly authorized and recorded.

8. Determine that any other-than-temporary decline in the price of an investment has been properly recorded.

Required:
a. Identify the primary financial statement assertion relative to investments that would be addressed by

each of the procedures #4 through #8 and describe the primary audit objective of performing that procedure. Use the format illustrated below.

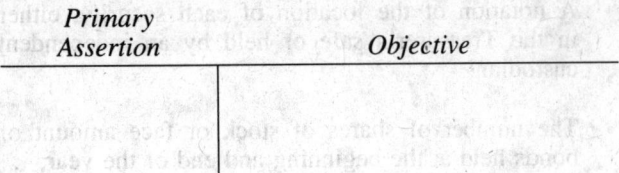

b. Describe three additional substantive auditing procedures Larkin should consider in auditing Vernon's investments.

N91
Number 5 (Estimated time — — 15 to 25 minutes)

Baker, CPA, was engaged to audit Mill Company's financial statements for the year ended September 30, 1991. After obtaining an understanding of Mill's internal control, Baker decided to obtain evidential matter about the effectiveness of both the design and operation of the activities that may support a low assessed level of control risk concerning Mill's shipping and billing functions. During the prior years' audits Baker used nonstatistical sampling, but for the current year Baker used a statistical sample in the tests of controls to eliminate the need for judgment.

Baker wanted to assess control risk at a low level, so a tolerable rate of deviation or acceptable upper precision limit (UPL) of 20% was established. To estimate the population deviation rate and the achieved UPL, Baker decided to apply a discovery sampling technique of attribute sampling that would use a population expected error rate of 3% for the 8,000 shipping documents, and decided to defer consideration of allowable risk of assessing control risk too low (risk of overreliance) until evaluating the sample results. Baker used the tolerable rate, the population size, and the expected population error rate to determine that a sample size of 80 would be sufficient. When it was subsequently determined that the actual population was about 10,000 shipping documents, Baker increased the sample size to 100.

Baker's objective was to ascertain whether Mill's shipments had been properly billed. Baker took a sample of 100 invoices by selecting the first 25 invoices from the first month of each quarter. Baker then compared the invoices to the corresponding prenumbered shipping documents.

When Baker tested the sample, eight errors were discovered. Additionally, one shipment that should have been billed at $10,443 was actually billed at $10,434. Baker considered this $9 to be immaterial and did not count it as an error.

In evaluating the sample results Baker made the initial determination that a reliability level of 95% (risk of assessing control risk too low 5%) was desired and, using the appropriate statistical sampling table, determined that for eight observed deviations from a sample size of 100, the achieved UPL was 14%. Baker then calculated the allowance for sampling risk to be 5%, the difference between the actual sample deviation rate (8%) and the expected error rate (3%). Baker reasoned that the actual sample deviation rate (8%) plus the allowance for sampling risk (5%) was less than the achieved UPL (14%); therefore, the sample supported a low level of control risk.

Required:
Describe each incorrect assumption, statement, and inappropriate application of attribute sampling in Baker's procedures.

M91
Number 3 (Estimated time — — 15 to 25 minutes)

Taylor, CPA, has been engaged to audit the financial statements of Palmer Co., a continuing audit client. Taylor is about to perform substantive audit procedures on Palmer's goodwill (excess of cost over the fair value of net assets purchased) that was acquired in prior years' business combinations. An industry slowdown has occurred recently and purchased operations have not met profit expectations.

During the planning process, Taylor determined that there is a high risk that material misstatements in the assertions related to goodwill could occur. Taylor obtained an understanding of internal control and assessed control risk at the maximum level for the assertions related to goodwill.

Required:
a. Describe the substantive audit procedures Taylor should consider performing in auditing Palmer's goodwill. Do **not** discuss Palmer's internal control.
b. Describe the two significant assertions that Taylor would be most concerned with relative to Palmer's goodwill. Do **not** describe more than two.

C. Obtain and Evaluate Lawyers' Letters

M93
Number 5 (Estimated time — — 15 to 25 minutes)

Cole & Cole, CPAs are auditing the financial statements of Consolidated Industries Co. for the year ended December 31, 1992. On April 2, 1993, an inquiry letter to J.J. Young, Consolidated's outside attorney, was drafted to corroborate the information furnished to Cole by management concerning pending and threatened litigation, claims, and assessments, and unasserted claims and assessments. On May 6, 1993, C.R. Brown, Consolidated's Chief Financial Officer, gave Cole a draft of the inquiry letter below for Cole's review before mailing it to Young.

Required:
Describe the omissions, ambiguities, and inappropriate statements and terminology in Brown's letter below.

Selected Questions

May 6, 1993

J. J. Young, Attorney at Law
123 Main Street
Anytown, USA

Dear J. J. Young:

In connection with an audit of our financial statements at December 31, 1992, and for the year then ended, management of the Company has prepared, and furnished to our auditors, Cole & Cole, CPAs, 456 Broadway, Anytown, USA, a description and evaluation of certain contingencies, including those set forth below involving matters with respect to which you have been engaged and to which you have devoted substantive attention on behalf of the Company in the form of legal consultation or representation. Your response should include matters that existed at December 31, 1992. Because of the confidentiality of all these matters, your response may be limited.

In November 1992, an action was brought against the Company by an outside salesman alleging breach of contract for sales commissions and pleading a second cause of action for an accounting with respect to claims for fees and commissions. The causes of action claim damages of $300,000, but the Company believes it has meritorious defenses to the claims. The possible exposure of the Company to a successful judgment on behalf of the plaintiff is slight.

In July 1988, an action was brought against the Company by Industrial Manufacturing Co. (Industrial) alleging patent infringement and seeking damages of $20,000,000. The action in U.S. District Court resulted in a decision on October 16, 1992, holding that the Company infringed seven Industrial patents and awarded damages of $14,000,000. The Company vigorously denies these allegations and has filed an appeal with the U.S. Court of Appeals for the Federal Circuit. The appeal process is expected to take approximately two years, but there is some chance that Industrial may ultimately prevail.

Please furnish to our auditors such explanation, if any, that you consider necessary to supplement the foregoing information, including an explanation of those matters as to which your views may differ from those stated and an identification of the omission of any pending or threatened litigation, claims, and assessments or a statement that the list of such matters is complete. Your response may be quoted or referred to in the financial statements without further correspondence with you.

You also consulted on various other matters considered pending or threatened litigation. However, you may not comment on these matters because publicizing them may alert potential plaintiffs to the strengths of their cases. In addition, various other matters probable of assertion that have some chance of an unfavorable outcome, as of December 31, 1992, are unasserted claims and assessments.

C. R. Brown
Chief Financial Officer

E. Obtain Representations From Management

N93
Number 4 (Estimated time — — 15 to 25 minutes)

Hart, an assistant accountant with the firm of Better & Best, CPAs, is auditing the financial statements of Tech Consolidated Industries, Inc. The firm's audit program calls for the preparation of a written management representation letter.

Required:

a. 1. In an audit of financial statements, in what circumstances is the auditor required to obtain a management representation letter?
   2. What are the purposes of obtaining the letter?

b. 1. To whom should the representation letter be addressed and as of what date should it be dated?
   2. Who should sign the letter and what would be the effect of their refusal to sign the letter?

c. In what respects may an auditor's other responsibilities be relieved by obtaining a management representation letter?

G. Identify Matters for Communication With Audit Committees

R96
Number 2 (Estimated time — — 25 to 35 minutes)

Smith, CPA, is the supervising partner of the financial statement audit of Digit Sales Co., a publicly-held entity that files reports with the SEC. Hall, the senior auditor assigned to the engagement, had the following conversation with Smith at the end of the field work:

Smith: Don't you think that Digit's board of directors would be surprised with those huge inventory adjustments that we had Digit book last week?

Hall: I guess so, but what about that new assistant controller, Green? What incompetence!

Smith: Well, I suppose Green has a bit to learn about GAAP, but I was really upset when Dodd, the controller, contacted that other CPA firm about the contingent liability I wanted booked.

Hall: Which one was that?

Smith: You know, the employment discrimination suit filed by the union.

Hall: Oh, now I remember. Digit's going to lose that one big time.

Smith: Right! You know it. I know it. The lawyer knows it. Even Dodd knows it. But it wasn't booked until the other CPAs agreed with me.

Hall: Well, the important thing is that they did book it. I was more upset about their two-week delay in having the financial statements completed on time.

Smith: I know it cost us a lot of time, but Dodd was never late on that before. Maybe I should change the dates on next year's engagement letter rather than complain to the board.

Hall: How about that large receivable?

Smith: What a joke! Dodd wouldn't write that overdue account off and Digit doesn't even sell that model anymore. At least Green was on our side.

Hall: They never did collect a penny on that account.

Smith: I heard that the customer finally filed for bankruptcy last month.

Hall: At least Dodd finally booked the write-off after that poorly-timed vacation.

Smith: I suppose so, but I still can't believe that Dodd took two weeks off near the end of our field work.

Hall: Actually, that was great. With Dodd gone, Green booked that inventory adjustment without much of a battle.

Smith: Sure, but we couldn't finish the field work until Dodd signed the rep letter and booked that receivable write-off. The report was late and it caused me grief with our managing partner.

Hall: But that's not fair. It wasn't our fault. The bottom line is they got a clean opinion and this job is history.

Smith: Not really. We haven't communicated with the audit committee yet.

Hall: What do we have to tell them? They got an unqualified opinion . . . and remember, there were only a few reportable conditions. I'm out of here.

Required:
    a. From the discussion above, what specific matters is Smith **required** to communicate to Digit's audit committee? Do **not** include matters that are **not required** to be communicated under GAAS.

    b. What other matters (omitted from the discussion above) is Smith **required** to communicate to Digit's audit committee under GAAS?

III. Review the Engagement

B. Evaluate the Sufficiency and Competence of Audit Evidence and Document Engagement Conclusions

M95
Number 5 (Estimated time —— 25 to 35 minutes)

On November 19, 1994, Wall, CPA, was engaged to audit the financial statements of Trendy Auto Imports, Inc. for the year ended December 31, 1994. Wall is considering Trendy's ability to continue as a going concern.

Required:
    a. Describe Wall's basic responsibility in considering Trendy's ability to continue as a going concern.

    b. Describe the audit procedures Wall most likely would perform to identify conditions and events that may indicate that Trendy has a going concern problem.

    c. Describe the management plans that Wall should consider that could mitigate the adverse effects of Trendy's financial difficulties if Wall identified conditions and events that indicated a potential going concern problem.

Selected Questions

C. Review the Work Performed

M92
Number 5 (Estimated time — — 15 to 25 minutes)

The following Accounts Receivable — Confirmation Statistics working paper (indexed B-3) was prepared by an audit assistant during the calendar year 1991 audit of Lewis County Water Co., Inc., a continuing audit client. The engagement supervisor is reviewing the working papers.

Lewis County Water Co., Inc.
ACCOUNTS RECEIVABLE — CONFIRMATION STATISTICS
12/31/91

Index	B-3

	Accounts		Dollars	
	Number	Percent	Amount	Percent
Confirmation Requests				
Positives	54	2.7%	$ 260,000	13.0%
Negatives	140	7.0%	20,000	10.0%
Total sent	194	9.7%	280,000	23.0%
Accounts selected/client asked us not to confirm	6	0.3%		
Total selected for testing	200	10.0%		
Total accounts receivable at 12/31/91, confirm date	2,000	100.0%	$2,000,000 ✓★	100.0%
RESULTS				
Replies received through 2/25/92				
Positives — no exception	44 C	2.2%	180,000	9.0%
Negatives — did not reply or replied "no exception"	120 C	6.0%	16,000	.8%
Total confirmed without exception	164	8.2%	196,000	9.8%
Differences reported and resolved, no adjustment				
Positives	6 Ø	.3%	30,000	1.5%
Negatives	12	.6%	2,000	.1%
Total	18 ‡	.9%	32,000	1.6%
Differences found to be potential adjustments				
Positives	2 CX	.1%	10,000	.5%
Negatives	8 CX	.4%	2,000	.1%
Total — .6% adjustment, immaterial	10	.5%	12,000	.6%
Accounts selected/client asked us not to confirm	6	.3%		

Tickmark Legend

- ✓ Agreed to accounts receivable subsidiary ledger
- ★ Agreed to general ledger and lead schedule
- Ø Includes one related party transaction
- C Confirmed without exception, W/P B-4
- CX Confirmed with exception, W/P B-5

Overall conclusion — The potential adjustment of $12,000 or .6% is below materiality threshold; therefore, the accounts receivable balance is fairly stated.

Required: Describe the deficiencies in the working paper that the engagement supervisor should discover. Assume that the accounts were selected for confirmation on the basis of a sample that was properly planned and documented on working paper B-2.

Auditing

IV. Prepare Communications to Satisfy Engagement Objectives

A. Prepare Reports

N93
Number 3 (Estimated time — — 15 to 25 minutes)

The auditor's report below was drafted by Miller, a staff accountant of Pell & Pell, CPAs, at the completion of the audit of the consolidated financial statements of Bond Co. for the year ended July 31, 1993. The report was submitted to the engagement partner who reviewed the audit working papers and properly concluded that an unqualified opinion should be issued. In drafting the report, Miller considered the following:

- Bond's consolidated financial statements for the year ended July 31, 1992, are to be presented for comparative purposes. Pell previously audited these statements and appropriately rendered an unmodified report.

- Bond has suffered recurring losses from operations and has adequately disclosed these losses and management's plans concerning the losses in a note to the consolidated financial statements. Although Bond has prepared the financial statements assuming it will continue as a going concern, Miller has substantial doubt about Bond's ability to continue as a going concern.

- Smith & Smith, CPAs, audited the financial statements of BC Services, Inc., a consolidated subsidiary of Bond, for the year ended July 31, 1993. The subsidiary's financial statements reflected total assets and revenues of 15% and 18%, respectively, of the consolidated totals. Smith expressed an unqualified opinion and furnished Miller with a copy of the auditor's report. Smith also granted permission to present the report together with the principal auditor's report. Miller decided not to present Smith's report with that of Pell, but instead to make reference to Smith.

Independent Auditor's Report

We have audited the consolidated balance sheets of Bond Co. and subsidiaries as of July 31, 1993, and 1992, and the related consolidated statements of income and retained earnings for the years then ended. Our responsibility is to express an opinion on these financial statements based on our audits. We did not audit the financial statements of BC Services, Inc., a wholly-owned subsidiary. Those statements were audited by Smith & Smith, CPAs, whose report has been furnished to us, and our opinion, insofar as it relates to the amounts included for BC Services, Inc., is based solely on the report of Smith & Smith.

We conducted our audits in accordance with generally accepted auditing standards. Those standards require that we plan and perform the audit to obtain reasonable assurance about whether the financial statements are free of material misstatement. An audit includes assessing control risk, the accounting principles used, and significant estimates made by management, as well as evaluating the overall financial statement presentation. We believe that our audits provide a reasonable basis for our opinion.

In our opinion, based on our audits and the report of Smith & Smith, CPAs, the consolidated financial statements referred to above present fairly, in all material respects except for the matter discussed below, the financial position of Bond Co. as of July 31, 1993, and 1992, and the results of its operations for the years then ended.

The accompanying consolidated financial statements have been prepared with the disclosure in Note 13 that the company has suffered recurring losses from operations. Management's plans in regard to those matters are also discussed in Note 13. The financial statements do not include any adjustments that might result from the outcome of this uncertainty.

Pell & Pell, CPAs
November 4, 1993

Required:
Identify the deficiencies in the auditor's report as drafted by Miller. Group the deficiencies by paragraph and in the order in which the deficiencies appear. Do **not** redraft the report.

N92
Number 3 (Estimated time — — 15 to 25 minutes)

The auditors' report below was drafted by Moore, a staff accountant of Tyler & Tyler, CPAs, at the completion of the audit of the financial statements of Park Publishing Co., Inc., for the year ended September 30, 1992. The report was submitted to the engagement partner who reviewed the audit working papers and properly concluded that an unqualified opinion should be issued. In drafting the report, Moore considered the following:

- During fiscal year 1992, Park changed its depreciation method. The engagement partner concurred with this change in accounting principle and its justification and Moore included an explanatory paragraph in the auditors' report.

- The 1992 financial statements are affected by an uncertainty concerning a lawsuit, the outcome of which cannot presently be estimated. Moore has included an explanatory paragraph in the auditors' report.

- The financial statements for the year ended September 30, 1991, are to be presented for comparative purposes. Tyler & Tyler previously audited these statements and expressed an unqualified opinion.

Selected Questions

Independent Auditors' Report

To the Board of Directors of Park Publishing Co., Inc.:

We have audited the accompanying balance sheets of Park Publishing Co., Inc. as of September 30, 1992, and 1991, and the related statements of income and cash flows for the years then ended. These financial statements are the responsibility of the company's management.

We conducted our audits in accordance with generally accepted auditing standards. Those standards require that we plan and perform the audit to obtain reasonable assurance about whether the financial statements are fairly presented. An audit includes examining, on a test basis, evidence supporting the amounts and disclosures in the financial statements. An audit also includes assessing significant estimates made by management, as well as evaluating the overall financial statement presentation. We believe that our audits provide a basis for determining whether any material modifications should be made to the accompanying financial statements.

As discussed in Note X to the financial statements, the company changed its method of computing depreciation in fiscal 1992.

In our opinion, except for the accounting change, with which we concur, the financial statements referred to above present fairly, in all material respects, the financial position of Park Publishing Co., Inc. as of September 30, 1992, and the results of its operations and its cash flows for the year then ended in conformity with generally accepted accounting principles.

As discussed in Note Y to the financial statements, the company is a defendant in a lawsuit alleging infringement of certain copyrights. The company has filed a counteraction, and preliminary hearings on both actions are in progress. Accordingly, any provision for liability is subject to adjudication of this matter.

Tyler & Tyler, CPAs
November 5, 1992

Required:
Identify the deficiencies in the auditors' report as drafted by Moore. Group the deficiencies by paragraph and in the order in which the deficiencies appear. Do **not** redraft the report.

M91
Number 2 (Estimated time —— 15 to 25 minutes)

The auditors' report below was drafted by a staff accountant of Baker and Baker, CPAs, at the completion of the audit of the comparative financial statements of Ocean Shore Partnership for the years ended December 31, 1990 and 1989. Ocean Shore prepares its financial statements on the income tax basis of accounting. The report was submitted to the engagement partner who reviewed matters thoroughly and properly concluded that an unqualified opinion should be expressed.

Auditor's Report

We have audited the accompanying statements of assets, liabilities, and capital—income tax basis of Ocean Shore Partnership as of December 31, 1990 and 1989, and the related statements of revenue and expenses—income tax basis and changes in partners' capital accounts—income tax basis for the years then ended.

We conducted our audits in accordance with standards established by the American Institute of Certified Public Accountants. Those standards require that we plan and perform the audit to obtain reasonable assurance about whether the financial statements are free of material misstatement. An audit includes examining, on a test basis, evidence supporting the amounts and disclosures in the financial statements. An audit also includes assessing the accounting principles used as well as evaluating the overall financial statement presentation.

As described in Note A, these financial statements were prepared on the basis of accounting the Partnership uses for income tax purposes. Accordingly, these financial statements are not designed for those who do not have access to the Partnership's tax returns.

In our opinion, the financial statements referred to above present fairly, in all material respects, the assets, liabilities, and capital of Ocean Shore Partnership as of December 31, 1990 and 1989, and its revenue and expenses and changes in partners' capital accounts for the years then ended, in conformity with generally accepted accounting principles applied on a consistent basis.

Baker and Baker, CPAs
April 3, 1991

Required:
Identify the deficiencies contained in the auditors' report as drafted by the staff accountant. Group the deficiencies by paragraph, where applicable. Do **not** redraft the report.

SELECTED ESSAYS — UNOFFICIAL ANSWERS

I. Plan, Evaluate, and Accept the Engagement

A. Determine Nature and Scope of Engagement

R97
Answer 1 (20 points)

a. In section I, Understanding the assignment, Johnson's planning checklist includes a question implying that the method of sampling used by Larkin, the auditor, should be approved by MM, the client. Evaluating the competence of evidential matter is solely a matter of the auditor's professional judgment. Therefore, the choice of statistical or nonstatistical sampling in achieving audit objectives will be controlled by Larkin without MM's approval.

Also, in section I, the checklist implies that Larkin's engagement personnel will discuss the expected level of detection risk with MM's management, board of directors, or audit committee. It is usually inappropriate for an auditor to discuss this with a client, especially with management, because the level of detection risk is a matter of the auditor's professional judgment.

In section II, Assigning personnel to the engagement, the checklist includes a question concerning MM's approval of Larkin's time budget. The time budget may be discussed with the audit committee and the controller, but its approval is solely within the CPA firm and it should not be subject to approval by the client because the CPA firm controls the nature, timing, and extent of the work to be done.

In section III, Knowledge of the entity's business, Johnson has included the Codification of Statements on Auditing Standards (SASs) as a source of understanding MM's operations. Although the SASs are interpretations of the generally accepted auditing standards, they do not provide an auditor with specific knowledge about an entity or a specific industry.

In section IV, Assessing auditability, the inquiries of MM's customers about MM's credit-granting policies are inappropriate. This is not the type of information ordinarily obtained from a client's customers.

In section V, Engagement letter, the reference to Larkin's responsibility for assuring that MM meets its SEC filing deadlines is inappropriate because it is the client's responsibility to meet its SEC filing deadlines.

Also, in section V, Johnson's checklist implies that Larkin's detailed audit program will be made available for MM's review. The auditor's audit program and the corresponding working papers document the work done during the engagement and are not ordinarily shared with the client. The client neither reviews the audit program before nor after the procedures are performed.

In section VI, Assessing risk, Johnson mistakenly allows the internal auditors to make judgments about the assessment of inherent risk and evaluations of significant accounting estimates. These matters are solely within the exercise of the independent auditor's professional judgment and may not be delegated to the internal auditors.

Also, in section VI, the concept of control risk assessed at the maximum level is confused with control risk assessed at **below** the maximum. If control risk is assessed at the maximum level for some or all of the assertions, the auditor need only document that conclusion. If control risk is assessed at **below** the maximum, internal control activities must be identified and tested to evaluate the design and operation of the activities, and the basis for that conclusion must be documented.

Finally, in section VIII, some of Johnson's questions have missed the purpose of analytical procedures in the planning phase of an audit. Achieving particular audit objectives and evaluating the overall financial statement presentation are not the purposes of analytical procedures performed in the planning stage of the audit.

b. In preparing the planning checklist, Johnson has omitted any questions about the need to consider engaging specialists in determining the value of MM's inventory of precious metals. Closely associated with this need is the consideration of whether special expertise may be required by Larkin's staff members who are assigned to the engagement. This consideration also has not been addressed in the checklist.

Johnson has not included any questions regarding the method of audit sampling to be used on the engagement.

Johnson has not prepared any questions addressing the coordination and cooperation of MM's employees who most likely will be assisting Larkin's staff members in data preparation and in obtaining documents and the time required for MM's employees to perform these functions.

Johnson's checklist omitted any reference to reviewing the predecessor auditor's working papers. Johnson also omitted any reference to Larkin's use of the predecessor auditor's responses to Larkin's inquiries.

Johnson should have included questions about the review of the prior year's financial statements and the current year's interim financial statements to assure that Larkin has sufficient knowledge of MM's business.

To obtain an understanding of MM's business, Johnson should have included questions about the engagement personnel's familiarity with economic conditions, government regulations, and specialized accounting practices.

Johnson has omitted any reference to obtaining an understanding of internal control sufficient to plan the audit, including the control environment, risk assessment, control activities, information and communication, such as MM's computer system, and monitoring.

Johnson's section of the checklist that covers engagement letter issues should have addressed the need for determining fees and any arrangements agreed-upon for the frequency of billing.

Although audit risk has been considered in preparing the checklist, materiality has not. Johnson has not prepared questions concerning whether a preliminary judgment about the dollar amount of misstatement that would be material to MM's financial statements has been made.

Johnson has substantially omitted all questions concerning assessing the risk that errors and irregularities/fraud may be present in MM's financial statements. Management characteristics such as unduly aggressive financial reporting and engagement characteristics such as the existence of related party transactions should be addressed. Questions also should be prepared concerning management's predisposition to distort financial statements and change auditors annually, lack of control over computer processing, and indications of constant crisis conditions in operating and accounting areas.

Finally, Johnson has omitted any questions that could assist Larkin in assessing the competence and objectivity of MM's internal auditors. Larkin most likely would be interested in such factors as the professional experience and certification of the internal auditors and their organizational status.

M95
Answer 4 (10 points)

a. Hart may accept the attest engagement to examine and report on management's assertion about the effectiveness of Unidyne's internal control over financial reporting only if Unidyne's management accepts responsibility for its effectiveness. Management then would evaluate its effectiveness using reasonable benchmarks or criteria established by a recognized body such as the AICPA, COSO, or a regulatory agency.

Sufficient evidential matter would have to exist or be developed to support management's evaluation. Finally, management would present its written assertion about the effectiveness of Unidyne's internal control based upon the control criteria.

b. Performing an examination of management's assertion about the effectiveness of Unidyne's internal control initially would involve planning the engagement, which includes developing an overall strategy for the scope and performance of the engagement. Hart then would obtain an understanding of Unidyne's internal control by making inquiries of management and employees, by inspecting documents, and by observing Unidyne's activities and operations.

Next, Hart would test and evaluate the design effectiveness of the internal control structure activities within each component, and then test and evaluate the operating effectiveness of the activities. Hart would perform tests of relevant controls to obtain evidence that supports the report's opinion by focusing on how the activities are applied, the consistency with which they are applied, and by whom they are applied.

Finally, Hart would consider all the evidence obtained, including the results of tests of controls and any control deficiencies identified, in forming an opinion on management's assertion about the effectiveness of Unidyne's internal control.

c. In addition to the proposed engagement to examine and report on management's written assertion about the effectiveness of Unidyne's internal control over financial reporting, Hart may also be engaged to perform agreed-upon procedures relating to management's assertion about the effectiveness of Unidyne's internal control. Hart's report on agreed-upon procedures would be in the form of procedures and findings.

Hart should not accept an engagement to review and report on management's assertion about the effectiveness of Unidyne's internal control or provide negative assurance about whether management's assertion is fairly stated in an agreed-upon procedures engagement.

B. Assess Engagement Risk and the CPA Firm's Ability to Perform the Engagement

M91
Answer 5 (10 points)

The factors most likely to have an effect on the risk of material misstatements and their resulting effect include the following:

Environmental factor	Effect on risk of material misstatements
Government regulation over the banking industry is extensive.	Decrease
NFB operates profitably in a growing prosperous area.	Decrease
Overall demand for the industry's product is high.	Decrease
Interest rates have been volatile recently.	Increase
The availability of funds for additional mortgages is promising.	Decrease
The principal shareholder is also the chief executive officer and controls the board of directors.	Increase

Environmental factor	Effect on risk of material misstatements
Branch management is compensated based on branch profitability.	Increase
The internal auditor reports directly to the chairman of the board's audit committee, a minority shareholder.	Decrease
The accounting department has experienced little turnover in personnel recently.	Decrease
NFB is a continuing audit client.	Decrease
Management fails to establish proper procedures to provide reasonable assurance of reliable accounting estimates.	Increase
Management has been receptive to Green's suggestions relating to accounting adjustments.	Decrease
NFB recently opened a new branch office that is not yet profitable.	Increase
NFB recently installed a new sophisticated computer system.	Increase

G. Perform Analytical Procedures

N94
Answer 4 (10 points)

a. In planning an audit, an auditor should focus on analytical procedures that enhance the auditor's understanding of the client's business and the transactions and events that have occurred since the last audit date, and that identify areas that may represent specific audit risks. The auditor's objective is to identify unusual transactions and events, and amounts, ratios, and trends having financial statement and audit planning ramifications.

Analytical procedures used in planning an audit generally use data aggregated at a high level. They may consist of reviewing changes in account balances from the prior year to the current year using the general ledger or unadjusted working trial balance, and analyzing quarterly financial statements. Sometimes relevant nonfinancial information, such as the number of employees, the square footage of selling space, and the volume of goods produced, is considered as well.

b. In deciding to select analytical procedures as substantive tests, an auditor considers the level of assurance desired for particular audit objectives. For higher levels of assurance, more plausible and predictable relationships are required to develop expectations. For example, relationships in a stable environment and those involving income statement accounts tend to be more predictable than relationships in a dynamic environment and those involving balance sheet accounts.

An auditor also considers the nature of the assertions. Analytical procedures may be effective and efficient when potential misstatements would not be apparent from an examination of detailed evidence. For example, differences from expected relationships may indicate omissions when evidence that individual transactions should have been recorded may not be readily available.

The availability and reliability of data also affect an auditor's decision. If data are not readily available or if the source of the data or the conditions under which it was gathered, such as the reliability of the client's internal control structure, is questionable, an auditor is less likely to perform analytical procedures.

Finally, the precision of an auditor's expectations is considered. As expectations become more precise, the range of expected differences becomes narrower and the likelihood increases that significant differences from expectations are due to misstatements. Expectations developed at detailed levels generally have a greater chance of detecting misstatements than do broad comparisons.

c. The objectives of applying analytical procedures in the overall review stage of an audit are to assist the auditor in assessing the conclusions reached and in evaluating the overall financial statement presentation. The overall review generally would include reading the financial statements and notes. The auditor would consider the adequacy of evidence gathered in response to unusual or unexpected balances previously identified. Furthermore, the auditor would consider unusual or unexpected balances or relationships that were not previously identified.

I. Assess Inherent Risk and Risk of Misstatements

R98
Answer 1 (20 points)

a. There are many fraud risk factors that are indicated in the dialogue. Among the fraud risk factors are the following:

- A significant portion of Mint's compensation is represented by bonuses and stock options. Although this arrangement has been approved by SCS's Board of Directors, this may be a motivation for Mint, the new CEO, to engage in fraudulent financial reporting.

- Mint's statement to the stock analysts that SCS's earnings would increase 30% next year may be both an unduly aggressive and unrealistic forecast. That forecast may tempt Mint to intentionally misstate certain ending balances this year that would increase the profitability of the next year.

- SCS's audit committee may not be sufficiently objective because Green, the chair of the audit committee, hired Mint, the new CEO, and they have been best friends for years.

- One individual, Mint, appears to dominate management without any compensating controls. Mint seems to be making all the important decisions without any apparent input from other members of management or resistance from the Board of Directors.

- There were frequent disputes between Brown, the prior CEO, who like Mint apparently dominated management and the Board of Directors, and Jones, the predecessor auditor. This fact may indicate that an environment exists in which management will be reluctant to make any changes that Kent suggests.

- Management seems to be satisfied with an understaffed and ineffective internal audit department. This situation displays an inappropriate attitude regarding the internal control environment.

- Management has failed to properly monitor and correct a significant deficiency in its internal control—the lack of segregation of duties in cash disbursements. This disregard for the control environment is also a risk factor.

- Information about anticipated future layoffs has spread among the employees. This information may cause an increase in the risk of material misstatement arising from the misappropriation of assets by dissatisfied employees.

b. Kent has many misconceptions regarding the consideration of fraud in the audit of SCS's financial statements that are contained in the dialogue. Among Kent's misconceptions are the following:

- Kent states that an auditor does not have specific duties regarding fraud. In fact, an auditor has a responsibility to specifically assess the risk of material misstatement due to fraud and to consider that assessment in designing the audit procedures to be performed.

- Kent is not concerned about Mint's employment contract. Kent should be concerned about a CEO's contract that is based primarily on bonuses and stock options because such an arrangement may indicate a motivation for management to engage in fraudulent financial reporting.

- Kent does not think that Mint's forecast for 1999 has an effect on the financial statement audit for 1998. However, Kent should consider the possibility that Mint may intentionally misstate the 1998 ending balances to increase the reported profit in 1999.

- Kent believes that the audit programs are fine as is. Actually, Kent should modify the audit programs because of the many risk factors that are present in the SCS audit.

- Kent is not concerned that the internal audit department is ineffective and understaffed. In fact, Kent should be concerned that SCS has permitted this situation to continue because it represents a risk factor relating to misstatements arising from fraudulent financial reporting and/or the misappropriation of assets.

- Kent states that an auditor provides no assurances about fraud because that's management's job. In fact, an auditor has a responsibility to plan and perform an audit to obtain reasonable assurance about whether the financial statements are free of material misstatement, whether caused by error or fraud.

- Kent is not concerned that the prior year's reportable condition has not been corrected. However, Kent should be concerned that the lack of segregation of duties in the cash disbursements department represents a risk factor relating to misstatements arising from the misappropriation of assets.

- Kent does not believe that the rumors about big layoffs in the next month have an effect on audit planning. In planning the audit, Kent should consider this risk factor because it may cause an increase in the risk of material misstatement arising from the misappropriation of assets by dissatisfied employees.

c. In planning a financial statement audit, the auditor should document in the working papers evidence of the performance of the assessment of the risk of material misstatement due to fraud. Where risk factors are identified, the documentation should include those risk factors identified and the auditor's response to those risk factors, individually or in combination. In addition, during the performance of the audit, the auditor may identify fraud risk factors or other conditions that cause the auditor to believe that an additional response is required. The auditor should document such risk factors or other conditions, and any further response that the auditor concludes is appropriate.

J. Consider Internal Control

N94
Answer 5 (10 points)

The internal control weaknesses in Rural's internal control concerning the cash receipts and billing functions include the following:

The credit manager has the ability to approve credit without an external credit check from a rating agency such as Dun & Bradstreet or without reference to established credit limits.

The accounts receivable (A/R) supervisor performs the billing process without any independent manual or computer verification. The A/R supervisor has the ability to alter the details of the charge forms prepared by the sales associates and use the altered details in preparing invoices. Additionally, there is no control to assure that the daily totals of the charge forms equal the daily totals of the invoices.

The A/R supervisor also has the ability to cause accounts to be written off as uncollectible because there is no independent verification of the A/R subsidiary ledger and because there is no reconciliation of the A/R subsidiary ledger with the A/R control account in the general ledger that is maintained by the bookkeeper. The A/R supervisor can simply include collectible accounts in the monthly report of overdue accounts to the bookkeeper. Likewise, accounts can remain on the books long after they are overdue and additional credit can be granted if the A/R supervisor omits them from the monthly notification to the bookkeeper.

The cashier processes receipts from cash and credit sales by performing three incompatible duties: initially receiving cash receipts, depositing cash in bank, and recording the receipts. Although the bookkeeper actually records the cash receipts, the cashier supplies the information (remittance advices), which may be delayed, altered, or incomplete. Without the verified deposit slip or the list of checks, there is no independent verification of the accuracy or completeness of cash receipts. Additionally, the cashier reconciles the monthly bank statements, which is also incompatible with handling cash receipts and depositing cash in bank.

The bookkeeper authorizes the write-off of uncollectible accounts without an investigation into the reasons and details of each overdue account. The established criterion for writing off overdue accounts (six months) is too inflexible and does not provide for the prevention of granting additional credit at an earlier date, such as when an account first becomes overdue. The bookkeeper also can indirectly grant additional credit by not notifying the credit manager when a contractor's account has been written off. Additionally, the bookkeeper has the incompatible duties of authorizing write-offs and recording journal entries.

M93
Answer 3 (10 points)

Young Computer Outlets, Inc.
Payroll
Internal Control Questionnaire

Question	Yes	No
1. Are payroll changes (hires, separations, salary changes, overtime, bonuses, promotions, etc.) properly authorized and approved?		
2. Are discretionary payroll deductions and withholdings authorized in writing by employees?		
3. Are the employees who perform each of the following payroll functions independent of the other five functions?		
• personnel and approval of payroll changes		
• preparation of payroll data		
• approval of payroll		
• signing of paychecks		
• distribution of paychecks		
• reconciliation of payroll account		
4. Are changes in standard data on which payroll is based (hires, separations, salary changes, promotions, deduction and withholding changes, etc.) promptly input to the system to process the payroll?		
5. Is gross pay determined by using authorized salary rates and time and attendance records?		
6. Is there a suitable chart of accounts and/or established guidelines for determining salary account distribution and for recording payroll withholding liabilities?		
7. Are clerical operations in payroll preparation verified?		
8. Is payroll preparation and recording reviewed by supervisors or internal audit personnel?		
9. Are payrolls approved by a responsible official before payroll checks are issued?		
10. Are payrolls disbursed through an imprest account?		
11. Is the payroll bank account reconciled monthly to the general ledger?		
12. Are payroll bank reconciliations properly approved and differences promptly followed up?		
13. Is the custody and follow-up of unclaimed salary checks assigned to a responsible official?		

Question	Yes	No

14. Are differences reported by employees followed up on a timely basis by persons not involved in payroll preparation?

15. Are there procedures (e.g. tickler files) to assure proper and timely payment of withholdings to appropriate bodies and to file required information returns?

16. Are employee compensation records reconciled to control accounts?

17. Is access to personnel and payroll records, checks, forms, signature plates, etc. limited?

M92
Answer 3 (10 points)

The key internal control structure activities related to Grant's property, equipment, and related transactions that Harris may consider in assessing control risk include the following:

- Advance approval in accordance with management's criteria is required for property and equipment transactions.

- Approval authority for transactions above an established dollar value is required at a higher level, such as the board of directors.

- Property and equipment transactions are adequately documented.

- There are written policies covering capitalizing expenditures, classifying leases, and determining estimated useful lives, salvage values, and methods of depreciation and amortization.

- There are written policies covering retirement procedures that include serially numbered retirement work orders, stating reasons for retirement and bearing appropriate approvals.

- There are adequate activities to determine whether property and equipment are received and properly recorded, such as a system that matches purchase orders, receiving reports, and vendors' invoices.

- There are adequate activities to determine whether dispositions of property and equipment are properly accounted for and proceeds, if any, are received in accordance with management's authorization.

- A property and equipment subsidiary ledger is maintained showing additions, retirements, and depreciation, and the ledger is periodically reconciled.

- Property and equipment is physically inspected and reconciled at reasonable intervals with independently maintained property and equipment records.

- An annual budget is prepared and monitored to forecast and control acquisitions and retirements of property and equipment.

- Reporting procedures assure prompt identification and analysis of variances between authorized expenditures and actual costs.

- Property and equipment is protected by adequate safeguards.

- Property and equipment is insured in accordance with management's authorization.

- Documents evidencing title and property rights are periodically compared with the detailed property records.

- The entity employs internal auditors to test whether the internal control activities are operating effectively.

K. Consider Other Planning Matters

M94
Answer 4 (10 points)

a. Tyler's work may be relevant to North in obtaining a sufficient understanding of the design of General's internal control activities, in determining whether they have been placed in operation, and in assessing risk. Since an objective of most internal audit functions is to review, assess, and monitor internal control activities, the procedures performed by Tyler in this area may provide useful information to North.

Tyler's work may also provide direct evidence about material misstatements in assertions about specific account balances or classes of transactions. Therefore, Tyler's work may be relevant to North in planning substantive procedures. Consequently, North may be able to change the nature, timing, or extent of certain procedures.

North may request direct assistance from Tyler. This direct assistance relates to work North specifically requests Tyler to perform to complete some aspect of North's work.

b. If North concludes that Tyler's work is relevant to North's audit of General's financial statements, North should consider whether it would be efficient to consider how Tyler's work might affect the nature, timing, and extent of North's audit procedures. If so, North should assess Tyler's competence and objectivity in light of the intended effect of Tyler's work on North's audit.

North ordinarily should inquire about Tyler's organizational status within General and about Tyler's application of the professional internal auditing standards developed by the Institute of Internal Auditors and the General Accounting Office. North also should ask about

Tyler's internal audit plan, including the nature, timing, and extent of the audit work performed. Additionally, North should inquire about Tyler's access to General's records and whether there are any limitations on the scope of Tyler's activities.

L. Identify Financial Statement Assertions and Formulate Audit Objectives

N95
Answer 5 (10 points)

a. Financial statement assertions are representations by management that are embodied in financial statement components.

b. In obtaining evidential matter in support of financial statement assertions, an auditor develops specific audit objectives in the light of those assertions.

c. In developing the audit objectives of a particular engagement, an auditor should consider the specific circumstances of the entity, including the nature of its economic activity and the accounting practices unique to its industry.

d. There is not necessarily a one-to-one relationship between audit objectives and procedures. Some auditing procedures may relate to more than one objective. On the other hand, a combination of auditing procedures may be needed to achieve a single objective. The procedures adopted should be adequate to achieve the audit objectives.

e. In selecting particular substantive tests to achieve audit objectives, an auditor considers, among other things, the risk of material misstatement in the financial statements, including the assessed levels of control risk, and the expected effectiveness and efficiency of such tests. An auditor's considerations also include the nature and materiality of the items being tested, the kinds and competence of available evidential matter, and the nature of the audit objective to be achieved.

M. Determine and Prepare the Work Program

N92
Answer 5 (10 points)

a. Before applying principal substantive tests to balance sheet accounts at April 30, 1993, the interim date, Cook should assess the difficulty in controlling incremental audit risk. Cook should consider whether

- Cook's experience with the reliability of the accounting records and management's integrity has been good;

- Rapidly changing business conditions or circumstances may predispose General's management to misstate the financial statements in the remaining period;

- The year-end balances of accounts selected for interim testing will be predictable;

- General's procedures for analyzing and adjusting its interim balances and for establishing proper accounting cutoffs will be appropriate;

- General's accounting system will provide sufficient information about year-end balances and transactions in the final two months of the year to permit investigation of unusual transactions, significant fluctuations, and changes in balance compositions that may occur between the interim and balance sheet dates;

- The cost of the substantive tests necessary to cover the final two months of the year and provide the appropriate audit assurance at year end is substantial.

Assessing control risk at below the maximum would not be required to extend the audit conclusions from the interim date to the year end; however, if Cook assesses control risk at the maximum during the final two months, Cook should consider whether the effectiveness of the substantive tests to cover that period will be impaired.

b. Cook should design the substantive tests so that the assurance from those tests and the tests to be applied as of the interim date, and any assurance provided from the assessed level of control risk, achieve the audit objectives at year end. Such tests should include the comparison of year-end information with comparable interim information to identify and investigate unusual amounts. Other analytical procedures and/or substantive tests should be performed to extend Cook's conclusions relative to the assertions tested at the interim date to the balance sheet date.

II. Obtain and Document Information to Form a Basis for Conclusions

A. Perform Planned Procedures Including Planned Applications of Audit Sampling

R97
Answer 2 (20 points)

a. Confirmation #11—Atom. Adler should determine that Superior received and deposited Atom's check on December 28, 1996, by examining supporting documentation, e.g., the entry in the cash receipts journal and either Superior's deposit ticket or its bank statement. Adler should also determine the account to which the check was recorded and why it was not credited to Atom's account.

Confirmation #28—Baker. Adler should examine the terms of the sale and the shipping documents, especially whether the sale/shipment was to be FOB shipping point or FOB destination and the date the goods were shipped to Baker, to verify when the criteria for revenue recognition were met.

Confirmation #34—Clark. Adler should read Superior's correspondence files for evidence concerning the terms of the shipment to Clark to determine whether the criteria for revenue recognition were met.

Confirmation #41—Delta. Adler should investigate whether the merchandise was ever shipped to Delta and, if so, whether the sale was ever consummated, or whether the merchandise was returned, or whether Superior expects it to be returned.

Confirmation #58—Eagle. Adler should send a second request to Eagle providing the individual invoice numbers and amounts or attaching copies of the individual unpaid invoices that Eagle's accounts payable voucher system can verify. In the alternative, Adler should examine shipping documents and subsequent cash receipts.

Confirmation #67—Franklin. Adler should determine Franklin's correct address and send a second request.

Confirmation #71—Grove. Adler should determine when the check was received and where it was recorded by examining Superior's cash receipts records, bank statements, and accounts receivable detail.

Confirmation #86—Hall. No additional procedures are necessary to resolve this confirmation request, although Adler may want to trace the cash receipt to verify that Hall's check was actually received, deposited, and credited to Hall's account in January 1997.

b. When replies to positive confirmation requests have not been received, Miller should apply alternative substantive procedures to the nonresponding accounts receivable. Miller most likely would examine subsequent cash receipts for the accounts that have been paid. This would include matching such receipts with the actual items being paid. In addition, especially for receivables that have not been paid, Miller should inspect shipping documents or other client documentation (e.g., sales invoices, customers' purchase orders, etc.) that may provide evidence for the existence assertion. Miller should also consider reading any correspondence in Superior's files that may indicate disagreements with its customers about the amounts billed or the terms of the sales. In addition, Miller may consider contacting a reputable credit agency to verify the existence of customers who are new to the client or who Miller may be unfamiliar with.

c. The additional substantive procedures that Miller should consider performing to complete the audit of Superior's accounts receivable and related allowances include the following:

- Test the cut-off of sales, cash receipts, and sales returns and allowances.

- Evaluate the reasonableness of all allowances against receivables.

- Perform analytical procedures for accounts receivable, such as sales returns and allowances to sales, bad debt expense to net credit sales, accounts receivable turnover, and days' sales in receivables.

- Determine that Superior's revenue recognition policies are appropriate, including policies for consignment sales.

- Review activity after the balance sheet date for unusual transactions, such as large sales returns.

- Determine whether any accounts receivable are pledged or factored.

- Determine that the presentation and disclosure of accounts receivable and related allowances are in conformity with generally accepted accounting principles.

R96
Answer 1 (9 points)

a. In searching for DollarMart's unrecorded liabilities, Cook most likely would review DollarMart's cash disbursements journal near the conclusion of field work for checks written after year end and examine the supporting documentation, such as receiving reports and vendors' invoices, for selected disbursements to determine that the related accounts payable were properly recorded and to verify the cutoff of DollarMart's receipt of inventory. Alternatively, Cook could review DollarMart's voucher register for selected transactions similarly recorded shortly after year end and examine the supporting detail to identify items that should have been recorded at the balance sheet date, but were not.

Cook most likely would consider examining files of receiving reports and comparing them to recorded accounts payable entries. This would assist Cook in searching for significant merchandise received before year end to verify DollarMart's schedule of merchandise received but not yet billed. Cook may also consider inspecting DollarMart's files of unprocessed vendors' invoices, vendors' statements, and outstanding purchase orders, and comparing them with the receiving records and accounts payable entries for unrecorded liabilities.

Although confirmations are usually not the best source of evidence for unrecorded accounts payable, Cook may consider confirming selected accounts payable with vendors, including regular suppliers showing small or zero balances at year end.

Cook most likely would consider performing analytical procedures such as comparing gross margin, purchases, or certain expense account balances with those of the prior year to identify any large changes that should be investigated because they may represent unrecorded liabilities.

Additionally, Cook may tailor the management representation letter to impress upon DollarMart the need to be concerned about unrecorded accounts payable.

b. Cook most likely would perform more substantive auditing procedures at year end because of DollarMart's deficient control environment. For example, Cook would be more likely to confirm DollarMart's accounts payable. Tests would most likely be performed further into the subsequent year and at a lower dollar value or materiality level than otherwise.

M94
Answer 5 (10 points)

a. Although there is a presumption that King will request the confirmation of Cycle's accounts receivable, King could justify omitting this procedure if Cycle's accounts receivable are immaterial to its financial statements. King could also justify omitting this procedure if the expected response rates to properly designed confirmation requests will be inadequate, or if responses will be unreliable. In these circumstances, King may determine that the use of confirmations would be ineffective.

Additionally, King could justify omitting the confirmation of Cycle's accounts receivable if King's combined assessed level of inherent and control risk is low and the assessed level, in conjunction with the evidence expected to be provided by analytical procedures or other substantive tests of details, is sufficient to reduce audit risk to an acceptably low level for the applicable financial statement assertions.

b. Among the factors likely to affect the reliability of confirmations that King sends is King's decision in choosing the confirmation form. Some positive forms request agreement or disagreement with information stated on the form; other positive forms, known as blank forms, request the respondent to fill in the balance or furnish other information; negative forms request a response only if there is disagreement with the information stated on the request.

King's prior experience with Cycle or similar clients is also likely to affect reliability because King probably would have prior knowledge of the expected confirmation response rates, inaccurate information on prior years' confirmations, and misstatements identified during prior audits.

The nature of the information being confirmed may affect the competence of the evidence obtained as well as the response rate. For example, Cycle's customers' accounting systems may permit confirmation of individual transactions, but not account balances, or vice versa.

Additionally, King's sending of each confirmation request to the proper respondent will likely provide meaningful and competent evidence. Each request should be sent to a person who King believes is knowledgeable about the information to be confirmed.

c. The nature of the alternative procedures King would apply when replies to positive confirmation requests are not received varies according to the account and assertion in question. Possible alternative procedures include examining subsequent cash receipts, and matching such receipts with the actual items being paid. King would also consider inspecting Cycle's shipping documents or invoices, or Cycle's customers' purchase orders on file. Inspecting correspondence between Cycle and its customers could provide additional evidence. King may also establish the existence of Cycle's customers by reference to credit sources such as Dun & Bradstreet.

N93
Answer 5 (10 points)

The incorrect assumptions, statements, and inappropriate applications of sampling are as follows:

1. Classical variables sampling is not designed for tests of controls.

2. PPS sampling uses each dollar in the population, not each account, as a separate sampling unit.

3. PPS sampling is not efficient if many misstatements are expected because the sample size can become larger than the corresponding sample size for classical variables sampling as the expected amount of misstatement increases.

4. Each account does not have an equal chance of being selected; the probability of selection of the accounts is proportional to the accounts' dollar amounts.

5. PPS sampling requires special consideration for negative (credit) balances.

6. Tolerable misstatement was not considered in calculating the sample size.

7. Expected (anticipated) misstatement was not considered in calculating the sample size.

8. The standard deviation of the dollar amounts is not required for PPS sampling.

9. The three selected accounts with insignificant balances should not have been ignored or replaced with other accounts.

10. The account with the $1,000 difference (recorded amount of $4,000 and audited amount of $3,000) was incorrectly projected as a $1,000 misstatement; projected misstatement for this difference was actually $2,500 ($1,000/$4,000 x $10,000 interval).

11. The difference in the understated account (recorded amount of $1,900 and audited amount of $2,000) should not have been omitted from the calculation of projected misstatement.

12. The reasoning (the comparison of projected misstatement with the allowance for sampling risk) concerning the decision that the receivable balance was not overstated was erroneous.

M92
Answer 4 (10 points)

The substantive auditing procedures Brown may consider performing include the following:

Using the perpetual inventory file,

- Recalculate the beginning and ending balances (prices × quantities), foot, and print out a report to be used to reconcile the totals with the general ledger (or agree beginning balance with the prior year's working papers).

- Calculate the quantity balances as of the physical inventory date for comparison to the physical inventory file. (Alternatively, update the physical inventory file for purchases and sales from January 6 to January 31, 1992, for comparison to the perpetual inventory at January 31, 1992.)

- Select and print out a sample of items received and shipped for the periods a) before and after January 5 and 31, 1992, for cut-off testing, b) between January 5 and January 31, 1992, for vouching or analytical procedures, and c) prior to January 5, 1992, for tests of details or analytical procedures.

- Compare quantities sold during the year to quantities on hand at year end. Print out a report of items for which turnover is less than expected. (Alternatively, calculate the number of days' sales in inventory for selected items.)

- Select items noted as possibly unsalable or obsolete during the physical inventory observation and print out information about purchases and sales for further consideration.

- Recalculate the prices used to value the year-end FIFO inventory by matching prices and quantities to the most recent purchases.

- Select a sample of items for comparison to current sales prices.

- Identify and print out unusual transactions. (These are transactions other than purchases or sales for the year, or physical inventory adjustments as of January 5, 1992.)

- Recalculate the ending inventory (or selected items) by taking the beginning balances plus purchases, less sales (quantities and/or amounts), and print out the differences.

- Recalculate the cost of sales for selected items sold during the year.

Using the physical inventory and test count files,

- Account for all inventory tag numbers used and print out a report of missing or duplicate numbers for follow-up.

- Search for tag numbers noted during the physical inventory observation as being voided or not used.

- Compare the physical inventory file to the file of test counts and print out a report of differences for auditor follow-up.

- Combine the quantities for each item appearing on more than one inventory tag number for comparison to the perpetual file.

- Compare the quantities on the file to the calculated quantity balances on the perpetual inventory file as of January 5, 1992. (Alternatively, compare the physical inventory file updated to year end to the perpetual inventory file.)

- Calculate the quantities and dollar amounts of the book-to-physical adjustments for each item and the total adjustment. Print out a report to reconcile the total adjustment to the adjustment recorded in the general ledger before year end.

- Using the calculated book-to-physical adjustments for each item, compare the quantities and dollar amounts of each adjustment to the perpetual inventory file as of January 5, 1992, and print out a report of differences for follow-up.

N91
Answer 4 (10 points)

a.

Primary Assertion	Objective
4. Existence or occurrence	To determine that the custodian holds the securities as identified in the confirmation.
5. Completeness	To determine that all income and related collections from the investments are properly recorded.
6. Valuation or allocation	To determine that the market or other value of the investments is fairly stated.
7. Presentation and disclosure	To determine that the financial statement presentation and disclosure of investments is in conformity with generally accepted accounting principles consistently applied.

Primary Assertion	Objective
8. Valuation or allocation	To determine that the market or other value of the investments is fairly stated and the loss is properly recognized and recorded.

b. Larkin should consider applying the following additional substantive auditing procedures in auditing Vernon's investments:

- Inspect securities on hand in the presence of the custodian.

- Examine supporting evidence (broker's advices, etc.) for transactions between the balance sheet date and the inspection date.

- Obtain confirmation from the issuers or trustees for investments in nonpublic entities.

- Examine contractual terms of debt securities and preferred stock.

- Determine that sales and purchases were properly approved by the Board of Directors or its designee.

- Examine broker's advices in support of transactions or confirm transactions with broker.

- Determine that gains and losses on dispositions have been properly computed.

- Trace payments for purchases to canceled checks, and proceeds from sales to entries in the cash receipts journal.

- Determine that the amortization of premium and discount on bonds has been properly computed.

- Determine that market value for both current and long-term portfolios has been properly computed by tracing quoted market prices to competent published or other sources.

- Compute the unrealized gains and losses on both current and long-term portfolios for marketable equity securities.

- Determine that the unrealized gains and losses on the current portfolio have been properly classified in the income statement, and the unrealized gains and losses on the noncurrent portfolio have been properly classified in the equity section of the balance sheet.

- Ascertain whether any investments are pledged as collateral or encumbered by liens, and, if so, are properly disclosed.

N91
Answer 5 (10 points)

1. Statistical sampling does not eliminate the need for professional judgment.

2. The tolerable rate of deviation or acceptable upper precision limit (UPL) is too high (20%) if Baker plans to assess control risk at a low level (substantial reliance).

3. Discovery sampling is not an appropriate sampling technique in this attribute sampling application.

4. The sampling technique employed is not discovery sampling.

5. The increase in the population size has little or no effect on determining sample size.

6. Baker failed to consider the allowable risk of assessing control risk too low (risk of overreliance) in determining the sample size.

7. The population from which the sample was chosen (invoices) was an incorrect population.

8. The sample selected was not randomly selected.

9. Baker failed to consider the difference of an immaterial amount to be an error.

10. The allowance for sampling risk was incorrectly calculated.

11. Baker's reasoning concerning the decision that the sample supported a low assessed level of control risk was erroneous.

M91
Answer 3 (10 points)

a. Taylor should consider performing the following procedures in the audit of Palmer's goodwill:

- Trace the totals in the account analysis for each significant acquisition to the general ledger;
- Trace the opening balance to the audit working papers for the preceding year;
- Examine supporting documents for evidence of continued ownership of the acquisitions that resulted in excess of costs over fair value of net assets;
- Review the reasonableness and consistency of application of the method of amortization used;
- Determine that the amortization period is reasonable;
- Recompute amortization;
- Determine that the carrying amount does not exceed amounts properly allocable to future periods;
- Assess whether there has been a permanent impairment of value;
- Trace amounts amortized during the period to the related general ledger expense accounts;

- Examine evidence supporting additions and reductions during the year (e.g., contingency payments properly capitalizable, reductions due to recovery of preacquisition taxes, etc.);
- Ascertain whether goodwill and amortization are properly described and classified in the financial statements and disclosed in the notes to the financial statements.

b. The two significant assertions that Taylor would be most concerned with relative to Palmer's goodwill are valuation or allocation, and presentation and disclosure. Taylor would be most concerned with the risk of the loss of recoverability of the goodwill's market value due to not meeting profit expectations, and the risk of inadequate disclosure or presentation in the financial statements.

C. Obtain and Evaluate Lawyers' Letters

M93
Answer 5 (10 points)

The omissions, ambiguities, and inappropriate statements and terminology in Brown's letter are as follows:

1. The action that Consolidated intends to take concerning each suit (for example, to contest the matter vigorously, to seek an out-of-court settlement, or to appeal an adverse decision) is omitted.

2. A description of the progress of each case to date is omitted.

3. An evaluation of the likelihood of an unfavorable outcome of each case is omitted.

4. An estimate, if one can be made, of the amount or range of potential loss of each case is omitted.

5. The various other pending or threatened litigation on which Young was consulted is not identified and included.

6. The unasserted claims and assessments probable of assertion that have a reasonable possibility of an unfavorable outcome are not identified.

7. Consolidated's understanding of Young's responsibility to advise Consolidated concerning the disclosure of unasserted possible claims or assessments is omitted.

8. Materiality (or the limits of materiality) is not addressed.

9. The reference to a limitation on Young's response due to confidentiality is inappropriate.

10. Young is not requested to identify the nature of and reasons for any limited response.

11. Young is not requested to include matters that existed after December 31, 1992, up to the date of Young's response.

12. The date by which Young's response is needed is not indicated.

13. The reference to Young's response possibly being quoted or referred to in the financial statements is inappropriate.

14. Vague terminology such as "slight" and "some chance" is included where "remote" and "possible" are more appropriate.

15. There is no inquiry about any unpaid or unbilled charges, services, or disbursements.

E. Obtain Representations From Management

N93
Answer 4 (10 points)

a. 1. An auditor is required to obtain a written management representation letter as part of every audit performed in accordance with generally accepted auditing standards.

2. The purposes of obtaining a written management representation letter are to:

- Confirm the oral representations given to the auditor.

- Indicate and document the continuing appropriateness of management's representations.

- Reduce the possibility of misunderstanding concerning the matters that are the subject of the representations.

- Complement the other auditing procedures by corroborating the information discovered in performing those procedures.

- Obtain evidence concerning management's future plans and intentions, e.g., when refinancing debt or discontinuing a line of business.

b. 1. The representation letter should be addressed to the auditor and dated as of the date of the auditor's report.

2. The letter should be signed by members of management whom the auditor believes are responsible for and knowledgeable, directly or through others in the organization, about the matters covered by the representation. Their refusal to sign the letter would constitute a limitation on the scope of the audit sufficient to preclude an unqualified opinion and affect the auditor's ability to rely on other management representations.

c. Obtaining a management representation letter does not relieve an auditor of any other responsibility for planning or performing an audit. Accordingly, an auditor should still perform all the usual tests to corroborate representations made by management.

G. Identify Matters for Communication With Audit Committees

R96
Answer 2 (10 points)

a. Smith should inform Digit's audit committee about the inventory adjustments arising from the audit. These adjustments probably have a significant effect on the financial statements and should be included among the required matters to be communicated to the audit committee.

Dodd's consultation with another CPA firm concerning the previously unrecorded contingent liability should also be discussed with the audit committee. Smith should make the audit committee aware of Smith's views about any significant matters that were the subject of that consultation.

Smith should also inform the audit committee of any serious difficulties encountered in dealing with management related to the performance of the audit. Specifically, the two-week delay in completing the financial statements and the unavailability of Dodd, the controller, near the end of the field work should be reported to the audit committee.

Smith's disagreement with Dodd over the write-off of the overdue account receivable, even though satisfactorily resolved, should also be discussed with the audit committee.

Finally, the reportable conditions that Smith became aware of during the audit should be communicated to the audit committee.

b. In order for Digit's audit committee to understand the nature of the assurance that an audit provides, Smith should communicate the level of responsibility assumed under generally accepted auditing standards. The audit committee should understand that an audit is designed to obtain reasonable, rather than absolute, assurance about the financial statements.

Smith should also determine that Digit's audit committee is informed about the initial selection of and changes in significant accounting policies and their application. The audit committee would be interested in the methods Digit uses to account for significant unusual transactions and accounting policies in controversial or emerging areas for which there is no authoritative guidance or consensus.

The audit committee should also be informed about the accounting estimates that are based upon management's judgments, the processes used to formulate particularly sensitive estimates, and the basis for Smith's conclusions regarding the reasonableness of those estimates.

Additionally, Smith should discuss with the audit committee Smith's responsibility for other information in documents containing audited financial statements, such as the "Management's Discussion and Analysis of Financial Condition and Results of Operations" that is presented in the annual report to shareholders. Smith should also discuss any procedures performed and the results.

Smith should also discuss with the audit committee any major issues that were discussed with management in connection with the recurring retention of Smith's CPA firm, including discussions regarding the application of accounting principles and auditing standards.

Finally, Smith should be assured that the audit committee is informed about any irregularities and illegal acts that Smith becomes aware of during the audit unless those matters are clearly inconsequential. However, if senior management is involved in an irregularity or illegal act, Smith should communicate directly with the audit committee.

III. Review the Engagement

B. Evaluate the Sufficiency and Competence of Audit Evidence and Document Engagement Conclusions

M95
Answer 5 (10 points)

a. Wall has a responsibility to evaluate whether there is substantial doubt about Trendy's ability to continue as a going concern for a reasonable period of time, not to exceed one year beyond the date of Trendy's audited financial statements. This evaluation is based on Wall's knowledge of conditions and events that exist at, or have occurred before, the completion of field work.

b. While it is not necessary that Wall design specific audit procedures solely to identify conditions and events that may indicate Trendy's has a going concern problem, Wall most likely would perform analytical procedures to identify ratios and patterns indicative of present and future financial difficulties.

Wall most likely would review any debt and loan agreements to ascertain whether Trendy is complying with their terms. Additionally, if there are any agreements with stockholders or creditors to provide or maintain financial support, confirmation of the details of these arrangements would be appropriate.

Wall's review of subsequent events near the completion of field work also would produce evidence about Trendy's financial difficulties. Wall would especially focus on reading the minutes of directors' meetings, inquiring of Trendy's legal counsel concerning litigation, and reading the latest interim financial statements.

c. Wall should consider any management plans to increase sales, reduce costs, or dispose of assets that could mitigate the adverse effects of Trendy's financial difficulties. The marketability of the assets, any restrictions on their disposal, and the possible operational effects of their disposal should be considered in evaluating whether such plans can be effectively implemented.

If management plans to borrow money or restructure its debt, Wall should consider several factors including the availability of financing, the possibility of restructuring or subordinating debt, the effects of existing borrowing restrictions, and the sufficiency of collateral.

Wall should evaluate any management plans to reduce or delay expenditures such as overhead or administrative expenditures. The postponement of maintenance and R&D, and the leasing of assets ordinarily purchased also may be feasible.

Wall also should consider any plans to increase ownership equity and raise capital. Arrangements to reduce current dividend requirements or accelerate cash distributions from subsidiaries or cash infusions from investors also may be possible.

C. Review the Work Performed

M92
Answer 5 (10 points)

The working paper contains the following deficiencies:

The working paper was not initialed and dated by the audit assistant.

Negative confirmations not returned cannot be considered to be accounts "confirmed without exception."

The two positive confirmations that were sent but were unanswered are not accounted for.

There is no documentation of alternate procedures, possible scope limitation, or other working paper reference for the six accounts selected for confirmation that the client asked the auditor not to confirm.

The dollar amount and percent of the six accounts selected for confirmation that the client asked the auditor not to confirm is omitted from the "Dollars" columns for the "Total selected for testing."

The "Dollars—Percent" for "Confirmation Requests—Negatives" is incorrectly calculated at 10%.

There is no indication of follow-up or cross-referencing of the account confirmed—related party transaction.

The tickmark "‡" is used but is not explained in the tickmark legend.

There is no explanation or proposed disposition of the 10 differences aggregating $12,000.

The overall conclusion reached is not appropriate.

There is no notation that a projection from the sample to the population was made.

There is no reference to second requests.

Cross-referencing is incomplete, such as the 18 "Differences reported and resolved, no adjustment" and "Confirmation Requests" to confirmation control schedule.

IV. Prepare Communications to Satisfy Engagement Objectives

A. Prepare Reports

N93
Answer 3 (10 points)

Deficiencies in Miller's draft are as follows:

Within the opening (introductory) paragraph

- The statement of cash flows is not identified in this paragraph or in the opinion paragraph.

- The financial statements are not stated to be the responsibility of management.

- The magnitude of the portion of the consolidated financial statements audited by the other auditors is not disclosed.

- Smith may not be named in this paragraph or in the opinion paragraph unless Smith's report is presented together with Pell's report.

Within the second (scope) paragraph

- The statement that "an audit includes examining, on a test basis, evidence supporting the amounts and disclosures in the financial statements" is omitted.

- It is inappropriate to state that an audit includes "assessing control risk."

- Reference to the audit of the other auditors as part of the basis for the opinion is omitted.

Within the third (opinion) paragraph

- Use of the phrase "except for the matter discussed below" is inappropriate.

- Reference to "conformity with generally accepted accounting principles" is omitted.

Within the fourth (explanatory) paragraph

- The terms "substantial doubt" and "going concern" are omitted.

N92
Answer 3 (10 points)

Deficiencies in the auditors' report are as follows:

First (introductory) paragraph:

- The statement of retained earnings is not identified.
- The auditors' responsibility to express an opinion is omitted.

Second (scope) paragraph:

- The auditor obtains reasonable assurance about whether the financial statements are "free of material misstatement," not "fairly presented."
- The auditors' assessment of the accounting principles used is omitted.
- An audit provides a "reasonable basis for an opinion," not a "basis for determining whether any material modifications should be made."

Third (first explanatory) paragraph:

- An explanatory paragraph added to the report to describe a change in accounting principle (lack of consistency) should follow the opinion paragraph, not precede it.

Fourth (opinion) paragraph:

- The phrase "except for" should not be used.
- The auditor's concurrence with the change in accounting principles is implicit and should not be mentioned.
- Reference to the prior year's (1991) financial statements is omitted.

Fifth (second explanatory) paragraph:

- The fact that the outcome of the lawsuit cannot presently be estimated is omitted.
- It is inappropriate to state that "provision for any liability is subject to adjudication" because the report is ambiguous as to whether a liability has been recorded.

M91
Answer 2 (10 points)

The auditors' report contains the following deficiencies:

1. "Independent" is omitted from the title of the auditors' report.

Introductory paragraph

2. Management's responsibility for the financial statements is omitted.

3. The auditors' responsibility to express an opinion on the financial statements is omitted.

Scope paragraph

4. "Generally accepted auditing standards" should be referred to, not standards established by the AICPA.

5. Reference to assessing "significant estimates made by management" is omitted.

6. The concluding statement that the auditors "believe that our audits provide a reasonable basis for our opinion" is omitted.

Explanatory paragraph

7. Reference to the income tax basis of accounting as "a comprehensive basis of accounting other than generally accepted accounting principles" is omitted.

8. The statement that the financial statements are "not designed for those who do not have access to the Partnership tax returns" is inappropriate.

Opinion paragraph

9. The income tax basis of accounting "described in Note A" should be referred to, not "generally accepted accounting principles."

10. There should be no reference to consistency unless the accounting principles have not been applied consistently.

SUGGESTED REFERENCES

Auditing

AICPA, *Audit and Accounting Guide, Audit Sampling* (AICPA, 1992).

AICPA, *Audit and Accounting Manual, Non-authoritative Practice Aids* (Commerce Clearing House, 1997).

AICPA, *Audit Risk Alerts—1997/98* (AICPA, 1997).

AICPA, *Auditing Procedure Studies* (AICPA, various dates).

AICPA, *Codification of Statements on Auditing Standards,* nos. 1 to 85 (Commerce Clearing House, 1998).

AICPA, *Codification of Statements on Standards for Accounting and Review Services,* nos. 1 to 7 (Commerce Clearing House, 1998).

AICPA, *Codification of Statements on Standards for Attestation Engagements,* nos. 1 to 7 (Commerce Clearing House, 1998).

AICPA, *Compilation and Review Alerts—1997/98* (AICPA, 1997).

AICPA, *The CPA's Guide to Information Security* (AICPA, 1997).

AICPA, *The CPA's Guide to Web Commerce* (AICPA, 1997).

AICPA, *Practice Alerts—Division for CPA Firms* (AICPA, various dates).

AICPA, *Professional Standards,* vols. 1 & 2 (Commerce Clearing House, 1998).

AICPA, *Top 10 Technologies and Their Impact on CPAs* (AICPA, 1997).

AICPA, *Top 10 Technology Opportunities: Tips and Tools* (AICPA, 1998).

Boynton & Kell, *Modern Auditing,* 6th ed. (Wiley, 1996).

General Accounting Office, *Government Auditing Standards* (U.S. Government Printing Office, 1994).

Guy, Alderman, and Winters, *Auditing,* 4th ed. (Harcourt Brace Jovanovich, 1996).

Guy, Carmichael, and Whittington, *Audit Sampling,* 3d ed. (Wiley, 1994).

Konrath, *Auditing Concepts and Applications,* 3d ed. (West, 1996).

O'Reilly, McDonnell, Winograd, Gerson, and Jaenicke, *Montgomery's Auditing,* 12th ed. (Wiley, 1998).

Pany and Whittington, *Auditing* (Irwin, 1994).

Robertson, *Auditing,* 8th ed. (Irwin, 1996).

Taylor and Glezen, *Auditing: Integrated Concepts and Procedures,* 7th ed. (Wiley, 1997).

Weirich and Reinstein, *Accounting & Auditing Research* (South-Western, 1996).

Whittington and Pany, *Principles of Auditing,* 11th ed. (Irwin, 1995).

Uniform CPA Examination

Accounting & Reporting —

Taxation, Managerial, and Governmental and Not-for-Profit Organizations

**Selected Questions
And Unofficial Answers
Indexed To
Content Specification
Outline**

> **Selected Questions and Unofficial Answers in the Taxation area do not reflect the tax law changes enacted by the TAXPAYER RELIEF ACT OF 1997, the BALANCED BUDGET ACT OF 1997, and the TAXPAYER BROWSING PROTECTION ACT enacted on August 5, 1997.**

TABLE OF CONTENTS

	Pages	
	Multiple Choice Items	Other Objective Answer Formats

Selected Questions‡

I. Federal Taxation — Individuals ..... AR-1 ..... AR-61†

    A. Inclusions in Gross Income ..... AR-1 ..... †
    B. Exclusions and Adjustments to Arrive at Adjusted Gross Income ..... AR-4 ..... †
    C. Deductions From Adjusted Gross Income ..... AR-4 ..... †
    D. Filing Status and Exemptions ..... AR-8 ..... †
    E. Tax Accounting Methods ..... AR-9 ..... †
    F. Tax Computations, Credits, and Penalties ..... AR-9 ..... †
    G. Alternative Minimum Tax ..... AR-10 ..... †
    H. Tax Procedures ..... AR-10 ..... †

II. Federal Taxation — Corporations ..... AR-11 ..... AR-68†

    A. Determination of Taxable Income or Loss ..... AR-11 ..... †
    B. Tax Accounting Methods ..... AR-15 ..... †
    C. S Corporations ..... AR-15 ..... †
    D. Personal Holding Companies ..... AR-16 ..... †
    E. Consolidated Returns ..... AR-16 ..... †
    F. Tax Computations, Credits, and Penalties ..... AR-17 ..... †
    G. Alternative Minimum Tax ..... * ..... †
    H. Other ..... AR-18 ..... †

III. Federal Taxation — Partnerships ..... AR-21 ..... AR-74†

    A. Basis of Partner's Interest and Bases of Assets Contributed to the Partnership ..... AR-21 ..... †
    B. Determination of Partner's Share of Income, Credits, and Deductions ..... AR-22 ..... †
    C. Partnership and Partner Elections ..... AR-23 ..... †
    D. Partner Dealing With Own Partnership ..... AR-23 ..... †
    E. Treatment of Partnership Liabilities ..... AR-23 ..... †
    F. Distribution of Partnership Assets ..... AR-24 ..... †
    G. Termination of Partnership ..... AR-25 ..... †

IV. Federal Taxation — Estates and Trusts, Exempt Organizations, and Preparers' Responsibilities ..... AR-26 ..... AR-75†

    A. Estates and Trusts ..... AR-26 ..... †
    B. Exempt Organizations ..... AR-29 ..... †
    C. Preparers' Responsibilities ..... AR-31 ..... †

---

* No questions were indexed for this area or group.
† Questions in this area are not classified according to group.
‡ The ARE section is an all-objective examination.
Note: All previous Accounting Theory and Accounting Practice Part II questions are designated with the letter (T) and the number (2), respectively, before the exam date and question number.

	Pages	
	Multiple Choice Items	Other Objective Answer Formats

Selected Questions‡

V. Accounting for Governmental and Not-for-Profit Organizations — AR-31 — AR-77†

    A. Governmental Entities — AR-31 — †
    B. Nongovernmental Not-for-Profit Organizations — AR-40 — †

VI. Managerial Accounting — AR-43 — AR-87†

    A. Cost Estimation, Cost Determination, and Cost Drivers — AR-43 — †
    B. Job Costing, Process Costing, and Activity Based Costing — AR-44 — †
    C. Standard Costing and Flexible Budgeting — AR-46 — †
    D. Inventory Planning, Inventory Control, and Just-in-Time Purchasing — AR-48 — †
    E. Budgeting and Responsibility Accounting — AR-49 — †
    F. Variable and Absorption Costing — AR-50 — †
    G. Cost-Volume-Profit Analysis — AR-51 — †
    H. Cost Allocation and Transfer Pricing — AR-53 — †
    I. Joint and By-product Costing — AR-53 — †
    J. Capital Budgeting — AR-53 — †
    K. Special Analyses for Decision Making — AR-55 — †
    L. Product and Service Pricing — AR-56 — †

Selected Multiple Choice Items — Unofficial Answers — AR-57

Other Objective Answer Formats — Selected Questions — AR-61

Selected Other Objective Answer Formats — Unofficial Answers — AR-91

Suggested References — AR-103

Content Specification Outline — CSO-6

Summary of Coverage — May 1996 through May 1998 Uniform CPA Examinations — S-5

> Selected Questions in the Taxation area do not reflect the tax law changes enacted by the TAXPAYER RELIEF ACT OF 1997, the BALANCED BUDGET ACT OF 1997, and the TAXPAYER BROWSING PROTECTION ACT enacted on August 5, 1997.

MULTIPLE CHOICE ITEMS — SELECTED QUESTIONS

I. Federal Taxation — Individuals

A. Inclusions in Gross Income

R98#1. Leker exchanged a van that was used exclusively for business and had an adjusted tax basis of $20,000 for a new van. The new van had a fair market value of $10,000, and Leker also received $3,000 in cash. What was Leker's tax basis in the acquired van?
   a. $20,000
   b. $17,000
   c. $13,000
   d. $ 7,000

R97#1. Klein, a master's degree candidate at Briar University, was awarded a $12,000 scholarship from Briar in 1996. The scholarship was used to pay Klein's 1996 university tuition and fees. Also in 1996, Klein received $5,000 for teaching two courses at a nearby college. What amount is includible in Klein's 1996 gross income?
   a. $0
   b. $ 5,000
   c. $12,000
   d. $17,000

M95#1. Which payment(s) is(are) included in a recipient's gross income?

I. Payment to a graduate assistant for a part-time teaching assignment at a university. Teaching is not a requirement toward obtaining the degree.
II. A grant to a Ph.D. candidate for his participation in a university-sponsored research project for the benefit of the university.

   a. I only.
   b. II only.
   c. Both I and II.
   d. Neither I nor II.

M95
Items 3 and 4 are based on the following:

Conner purchased 300 shares of Zinco stock for $30,000 in 1980. On May 23, 1994, Conner sold all the stock to his daughter Alice for $20,000, its then fair market value. Conner realized no other gain or loss during 1994. On July 26, 1994, Alice sold the 300 shares of Zinco for $25,000.

3. What amount of the loss from the sale of Zinco stock can Conner deduct in 1994?

   a. $0
   b. $ 3,000
   c. $ 5,000
   d. $10,000

4. What was Alice's recognized gain or loss on her sale?
   a. $0
   b. $5,000 long-term gain.
   c. $5,000 short-term loss.
   d. $5,000 long-term loss.

M94#1. In December 1993, Davis purchased a new residence for $200,000. During that same month he sold his former residence for $80,000 and paid the realtor a $5,000 commission. The former residence, his first home, had cost $65,000 in 1990. Davis added a bathroom for $5,000 in 1991. What amount of gain is recognized from the sale of the former residence on Davis' 1993 tax return?
   a. $15,000
   b. $10,000
   c. $ 5,000
   d. $0

M94#3. During 1993 Kay received interest income as follows:

On U.S. Treasury certificates $4,000
On refund of 1991 federal income tax   500

The total amount of interest subject to tax in Kay's 1993 tax return is
   a. $4,500
   b. $4,000
   c. $ 500
   d. $0

M94#5. Rich is a cash basis self-employed air-conditioning repairman with 1993 gross business receipts of $20,000. Rich's cash disbursements were as follows:

Air conditioning parts $2,500
Yellow Pages listing   2,000
Estimated federal income taxes on self-
  employment income   1,000
Business long-distance telephone calls   400
Charitable contributions   200

What amount should Rich report as net self-employment income?

AR-1

a. $15,100
b. $14,900
c. $14,100
d. $13,900

2N93#21. Perle, a dentist, billed Wood $600 for dental services. Wood paid Perle $200 cash and built a bookcase for Perle's office in full settlement of the bill. Wood sells comparable bookcases for $350. What amount should Perle include in taxable income as a result of this transaction?

a. $0
b. $200
c. $550
d. $600

2N93#22. Charles and Marcia are married cash-basis taxpayers. In 1992, they had interest income as follows:

- $500 interest on federal income tax refund.
- $600 interest on state income tax refund.
- $800 interest on federal government obligations.
- $1,000 interest on state government obligations.

What amount of interest income is taxable on Charles and Marcia's 1992 joint income tax return?

a. $ 500
b. $1,100
c. $1,900
d. $2,900

2N93#23. Nare, an accrual-basis taxpayer, owns a building which was rented to Mott under a ten-year lease expiring August 31, 1998. On January 2, 1992, Mott paid $30,000 as consideration for cancelling the lease. On November 1, 1992, Nare leased the building to Pine under a five-year lease. Pine paid Nare $10,000 rent for the two months of November and December, and an additional $5,000 for the last month's rent. What amount of rental income should Nare report in its 1992 income tax return?

a. $10,000
b. $15,000
c. $40,000
d. $45,000

2N93#24. John and Mary were divorced in 1991. The divorce decree provides that John pay alimony of $10,000 per year, to be reduced by 20% on their child's 18th birthday. During 1992, John paid $7,000 directly to Mary and $3,000 to Spring College for Mary's tuition. What amount of these payments should be reported as income in Mary's 1992 income tax return?

a. $ 5,600
b. $ 8,000
c. $ 8,600
d. $10,000

2N93#25. Smith, an individual calendar-year taxpayer, purchased 100 shares of Core Co. common stock for $15,000 on December 15, 1992, and an additional 100 shares for $13,000 on December 30, 1992. On January 3, 1993, Smith sold the shares purchased on December 15, 1992, for $13,000. What amount of loss from the sale of Core's stock is deductible on Smith's 1992 and 1993 income tax returns?

	1992	1993
a.	$0	$0
b.	$0	$2,000
c.	$1,000	$1,000
d.	$2,000	$0

2N93#29. In 1992, Fay sold 100 shares of Gym Co. stock to her son, Martin, for $11,000. Fay had paid $15,000 for the stock in 1989. Subsequently in 1992, Martin sold the stock to an unrelated third party for $16,000. What amount of gain from the sale of the stock to the third party should Martin report on his 1992 income tax return?

a. $0
b. $1,000
c. $4,000
d. $5,000

2N92#13. Unless the Internal Revenue Service consents to a change of method, the accrual method of tax reporting is mandatory for a sole proprietor when there are

	Accounts receivable for services rendered	Year-end merchandise inventories
a.	Yes	Yes
b.	Yes	No
c.	No	No
d.	No	Yes

2N92#15. Lee qualified as head of a household for 1991 tax purposes. Lee's 1991 taxable income was $100,000, exclusive of capital gains and losses. Lee had a net long-term loss of $8,000 in 1991. What amount of this capital loss can Lee offset against 1991 ordinary income?

a. $0
b. $3,000
c. $4,000
d. $8,000

2N92#16. Clark filed Form 1040EZ for the 1991 taxable year. In July 1992, Clark received a state income tax refund of $900, plus interest of $10, for overpayment of 1991 state income tax. What amount of the state tax refund and interest is taxable in Clark's 1992 federal income tax return?

a. $0
b. $ 10
c. $900
d. $910

2N92#19. Feld, the sole stockholder of Maki Corp., paid $50,000 for Maki's stock in 1985. In 1991, Feld contributed a parcel of land to Maki but was not given any additional stock for this contribution. Feld's basis for the land was $10,000, and its fair market value was

$18,000 on the date of the transfer of title. What is Feld's adjusted basis for the Maki stock?
a. $50,000
b. $52,000
c. $60,000
d. $68,000

2M91#22. Cobb, an unmarried individual, had an adjusted gross income of $200,000 in 1990 before any IRA deduction, taxable social security benefits, or passive activity losses. Cobb incurred a loss of $30,000 in 1990 from rental real estate in which he actively participated. What amount of loss attributable to this rental real estate can be used in 1990 as an offset against income from nonpassive sources?
a. $0
b. $12,500
c. $25,000
d. $30,000

2M91#23. In a "like-kind" exchange of an investment asset for a similar asset that will also be held as an investment, no taxable gain or loss will be recognized on the transaction if both assets consist of
a. Convertible debentures.
b. Convertible preferred stock.
c. Partnership interests.
d. Rental real estate located in different states.

2M91#24. Lee, an attorney, uses the cash receipts and disbursements method of reporting. In 1990, a client gave Lee 500 shares of a listed corporation's stock in full satisfaction of a $10,000 legal fee the client owed to Lee. This stock had a fair market value of $8,000 on the date it was given to Lee. The client's basis for this stock was $6,000. Lee sold the stock for cash in January 1991. In Lee's 1990 income tax return, what amount of income should be reported in connection with the receipt of the stock?
a. $10,000
b. $ 8,000
c. $ 6,000
d. $0

2N90#26. Dahl Corp. was organized and commenced operations in 1930. At December 31, 1989, Dahl had accumulated earnings and profits of $9,000 before dividend declaration and distribution. On December 31, 1989, Dahl distributed cash of $9,000 and a vacant parcel of land to Green, Dahl's only stockholder. At the date of distribution, the land had a basis of $5,000 and a fair market value of $40,000. What was Green's taxable dividend income in 1989 from these distributions?
a. $ 9,000
b. $14,000
c. $44,000
d. $49,000

2N90#27. Don Wolf became a general partner in Gata Associates on January 1, 1989 with a 5% interest in Gata's profits, losses, and capital. Gata is a distributor of auto parts. Wolf does not materially participate in the partnership business. For the year ended December 31, 1989, Gata had an operating loss of $100,000. In addition, Gata earned interest of $20,000 on a temporary investment. Gata has kept the principal temporarily invested while awaiting delivery of equipment that is presently on order. The principal will be used to pay for this equipment. Wolf's passive loss for 1989 is
a. $0
b. $4,000
c. $5,000
d. $6,000

2N90#29. Fred Berk bought a plot of land with a cash payment of $40,000 and a purchase money mortgage of $50,000. In addition, Berk paid $200 for a title insurance policy. Berk's basis in this land is
a. $40,000
b. $40,200
c. $90,000
d. $90,200

2N90#30. In 1989, Joan Reed exchanged commercial real estate that she owned for other commercial real estate plus cash of $50,000. The following additional information pertains to this transaction:

Property given up by Reed

Fair market value	$500,000
Adjusted basis	300,000

Property received by Reed

Fair market value	450,000

What amount of gain should be recognized in Reed's 1989 income tax return?
a. $200,000
b. $100,000
c. $ 50,000
d. $0

2M89#42. The following information pertains to the sale of Al Oran's principal residence:

Date of sale	May 1989
Date of purchase	May 1979
Net sales price	$260,000
Adjusted basis	$ 70,000

In June 1989, Oran (age 70) bought a smaller residence for $90,000. Oran elected to avail himself of the exclusion of realized gain available to taxpayers age 55 and over. What amount of gain should Oran recognize in 1989 on the sale of his residence?
a. $45,000
b. $65,000
c. $70,000
d. $90,000

2M89#52. On June 1, 1988, Ben Rork sold 500 shares of Kul Corp. stock. Rork had received this stock on May

AR-3

1, 1988 as a bequest from the estate of his uncle, who died on March 1, 1988. Rork's basis was determined by reference to the stock's fair market value on March 1, 1988. Rork's holding period for this stock was
  a. Short-term.
  b. Long-term.
  c. Short-term if sold at a gain; long-term if sold at a loss.
  d. Long-term if sold at a gain; short-term if sold at a loss.

B. Exclusions and Adjustments to Arrive at Adjusted Gross Income

M95#6. Grey, a calendar year taxpayer, was employed and resided in New York. On February 2, 1994, Grey was permanently transferred to Florida by his employer. Grey worked full-time for the entire year. In 1994, Grey incurred and paid the following unreimbursed expenses in relocating.

Lodging and travel expenses while moving	$1,000
Pre-move househunting costs	1,200
Costs of moving household furnishings and personal effects	1,800

What amount was deductible as moving expense on Grey's 1994 tax return?
  a. $4,000
  b. $2,800
  c. $1,800
  d. $1,000

M94#6. The self-employment tax is
  a. Fully deductible as an itemized deduction.
  b. Fully deductible in determining net income from self-employment.
  c. One-half deductible from gross income in arriving at adjusted gross income.
  d. Not deductible.

2N93#27. Which allowable deduction can be claimed in arriving at an individual's adjusted gross income?
  a. Alimony payment.
  b. Charitable contribution.
  c. Personal casualty loss.
  d. Unreimbursed business expense of an outside salesperson.

2N91
Items 28 through 36* are based on the following:

Hall, a divorced person and custodian of her 12-year-old child, filed her 1990 federal income tax return as head of a household. She submitted the following information to the CPA who prepared her 1990 return:

- The divorce agreement, executed in 1983, provides for Hall to receive $3,000 per month, of which $600 is designated as child support. After the child reaches 18, the monthly payments are to be reduced to $2,400 and are to continue until remarriage or death. However, for the year 1990, Hall received a total of only $5,000 from her former husband. Hall paid an attorney $2,000 in 1990 in a suit to collect the alimony owed.

- In June 1990, Hall's mother gifted her 100 shares of a listed stock. The donor's basis for this stock, which she bought in 1970, was $4,000, and market value on the date of the gift was $3,000. Hall sold this stock in July 1990 for $3,500. The donor paid no gift tax.

- During 1990, Hall spent a total of $1,000 for state lottery tickets. Her lottery winnings in 1990 totaled $200.

- Hall earned a salary of $25,000 in 1990. Hall was not covered by any type of retirement plan, but contributed $2,000 to an IRA in 1990.

- In 1990, Hall sold an antique that she bought in 1980 to display in her home. Hall paid $800 for the antique and sold it for $1,400, using the proceeds to pay a court-ordered judgment.

- Hall paid the following expenses in 1990 pertaining to the home that she owns: realty taxes, $3,400; mortgage interest, $7,000; casualty insurance, $490; assessment by city for construction of a sewer system, $910; interest of $1,000 on a personal, unsecured bank loan, the proceeds of which were used for home improvements. Hall does not rent out any portion of the home.

32. Hall's $2,000 contribution to an IRA should be treated as
  a. An adjustment to income in arriving at adjusted gross income.
  b. A deduction from adjusted gross income subject to the 2% of adjusted gross income floor.
  c. A deduction from adjusted gross income **not** subject to the 2% of adjusted gross income floor.
  d. Nondeductible, with the interest income on the $2,000 to be deferred until withdrawal.

C. Deductions From Adjusted Gross Income

R98#2. Jackson owns two residences. The second residence, which has never been used for rental purposes, is the only residence that is subject to a mortgage. The following expenses were incurred for the second residence in 1997:

Mortgage interest	$5,000
Utilities	1,200
Insurance	6,000

For regular income tax purposes, what is the maximum amount allowable as a deduction for Jackson's second residence in 1997?

---
*The omitted items can be found in other Content Specification Groups.

a. $ 6,200 in determining adjusted gross income.
b. $11,000 in determining adjusted gross income.
c. $ 5,000 as an itemized deduction.
d. $12,200 as an itemized deduction.

R98#3. On December 1, 1997, Krest, a self-employed cash basis taxpayer, borrowed $200,000 to use in her business. The loan was to be repaid on November 30, 1998. Krest paid the entire interest amount of $24,000 on December 1, 1997. What amount of interest was deductible on Krest's 1997 income tax return?
a. $0
b. $ 2,000
c. $22,000
d. $24,000

R97#2. Jimet, an unmarried taxpayer, qualified to itemize 1996 deductions. Jimet's 1996 adjusted gross income was $30,000 and he made a $2,000 cash donation directly to a needy family. In 1996, Jimet also donated stock, valued at $3,000, to his church. Jimet had purchased the stock four months earlier for $1,500. What was the maximum amount of the charitable contribution allowable as an itemized deduction on Jimet's 1996 income tax return?
a. $0
b. $1,500
c. $2,000
d. $5,000

R97#3. In 1996, Wood's residence had an adjusted basis of $150,000 and it was destroyed by a tornado. An appraiser valued the decline in market value at $175,000. Later that same year, Wood received $130,000 from his insurance company for the property loss and did not elect to deduct the casualty loss in an earlier year. Wood's 1996 adjusted gross income was $60,000 and he did not have any casualty gains.
  What total amount can Wood deduct as a 1996 itemized deduction for the casualty loss, after the application of the threshold limitations?
a. $39,000
b. $38,900
c. $19,900
d. $13,900

R97#4. Deet, an unmarried taxpayer, qualified to itemize 1996 deductions. Deet's 1996 adjusted gross income was $40,000 and he made a $1,500 substantiated cash donation directly to a needy family. Deet also donated art, valued at $11,000, to a local art museum. Deet had purchased the art work two years earlier for $2,000. What was the maximum amount of the charitable contribution allowable as an itemized deduction on Deet's 1996 income tax return?
a. $12,500
b. $11,000
c. $ 3,500
d. $ 2,000

M95#7. Moore, a single taxpayer, had $50,000 in adjusted gross income for 1994. During 1994 she contributed $18,000 to her church. She had a $10,000 charitable contribution carryover from her 1993 church contribution. What was the maximum amount of properly substantiated charitable contributions that Moore could claim as an itemized deduction for 1994?
a. $10,000
b. $18,000
c. $25,000
d. $28,000

M95#8. Matthews was a cash basis taxpayer whose records showed the following:

1994 state and local income taxes withheld	$1,500
1994 state estimated income taxes paid December 30, 1994	400
1994 federal income taxes withheld	2,500
1994 state and local income taxes paid April 17, 1995	300

What total amount was Matthews entitled to claim for taxes on her 1994 Schedule A of Form 1040?
a. $4,700
b. $2,200
c. $1,900
d. $1,500

M95#9. Which expense, both incurred and paid in 1994, can be claimed as an itemized deduction subject to the two-percent-of-adjusted-gross-income floor?
a. Employee's unreimbursed business car expense.
b. One-half of the self-employment tax.
c. Employee's unreimbursed moving expense.
d. Self-employed health insurance.

M94#9. Which of the following is **not** a miscellaneous itemized deduction?
a. An individual's tax return preparation fee.
b. Education expense to meet minimum entry level education requirements at an individual's place of employment.
c. An individual's subscription to professional journals.
d. Custodial fees for a brokerage account.

M94#10. The Browns borrowed $20,000, secured by their home, to pay their son's college tuition. At the time of the loan, the fair market value of their home was $400,000, and it was unencumbered by other debt. The interest on the loan qualifies as
a. Deductible personal interest.
b. Deductible qualified residence interest.
c. Nondeductible interest.
d. Investment interest expense.

M94#11. On January 2, 1990, the Philips paid $50,000 cash and obtained a $200,000 mortgage to purchase a home. In 1993 they borrowed $15,000 secured by their home, and used the cash to add a new room to their residence. That same year they took out a $5,000 auto loan.

The following information pertains to interest paid in 1993:

Mortgage interest	$17,000
Interest on room construction loan	1,500
Auto loan interest	500

For 1993, how much interest is deductible, prior to any itemized deduction limitations?
- a. $17,000
- b. $17,500
- c. $18,500
- d. $19,000

M94#13. In 1993, Wells paid the following expenses:

Premiums on an insurance policy against loss of earnings due to sickness or accident	$3,000
Physical therapy after spinal surgery	2,000
Premium on an insurance policy that covers reimbursement for the cost of prescription drugs	500

In 1993, Wells recovered $1,500 of the $2,000 that she paid for physical therapy through insurance reimbursement from a group medical policy paid for by her employer. Disregarding the adjusted gross income percentage threshold, what amount could be claimed on Wells' 1993 income tax return for medical expenses?
- a. $4,000
- b. $3,500
- c. $1,000
- d. $ 500

2N93#30. Which itemized deduction is included in the category of unreimbursed expenses that are deductible only to the extent that the aggregate amount of such expenses exceeds 2% of the taxpayer's adjusted gross income?
- a. Tax return preparation fee.
- b. Medical expense.
- c. Employee moving expense.
- d. Interest expense.

2N93#33. In 1992, Farb, a cash basis individual taxpayer, received an $8,000 invoice for personal property taxes. Believing the amount to be overstated by $5,000, Farb paid the invoiced amount under protest and immediately started legal action to recover the overstatement. In November 1993, the matter was resolved in Farb's favor, and he received a $5,000 refund. Farb itemizes his deductions on his tax returns. Which of the following statements is correct regarding the deductibility of the property taxes?
- a. Farb should deduct $8,000 in his 1992 income tax return and should report the $5,000 refund as income in his 1993 income tax return.
- b. Farb should **not** deduct any amount in his 1992 income tax return and should deduct $3,000 in his 1993 income tax return.
- c. Farb should deduct $3,000 in his 1992 income tax return.
- d. Farb should not deduct any amount in his 1992 income tax return when originally filed, and should file an amended 1992 income tax return in 1993.

2N92
Items 1 through 4 are based on the following:

Alex and Myra Burg, married and filing joint income tax returns, derive their entire income from the operation of their retail candy shop. Their 1991 adjusted gross income was $50,000. The Burgs itemized their deductions on Schedule A for 1991. The following unreimbursed cash expenditures were among those made by the Burgs during 1991:

Repair and maintenance of motorized wheelchair for physically handicapped dependent child	$300
Tuition, meals, and lodging at special school for physically handicapped dependent child in the institution primarily for the availability of medical care, with meals and lodging furnished as necessary incidents to that care	4,000
State income tax	1,200
Self-employment tax	7,650
Four tickets to a theatre party sponsored by a qualified charitable organization; not considered a business expense; similar tickets would cost $25 each at the box office	160
Repair of glass vase accidentally broken in home by dog; vase cost $500 in 1989; fair value $600 before accident and $200 after accident	90
Fee for breaking lease on prior apartment residence located 20 miles from new residence	500
Security deposit placed on apartment at new location	900

1. Without regard to the adjusted gross income percentage threshold, what amount may the Burgs claim in their 1991 return as qualifying medical expenses?
- a. $0
- b. $ 300
- c. $4,000
- d. $4,300

2. What amount should the Burgs deduct for taxes in their itemized deductions on Schedule A for 1991?
   a. $1,200
   b. $3,825
   c. $5,025
   d. $7,650

3. What amount should the Burgs deduct for gifts to charity in their itemized deductions on Schedule A for 1991?
   a. $160
   b. $100
   c. $ 60
   d. $0

4. Without regard to the $100 "floor" and the adjusted gross income percentage threshold, what amount should the Burgs deduct for the casualty loss in their itemized deductions on Schedule A for 1991?
   a. $0
   b. $ 90
   c. $300
   d. $400

2N91
Items 28 through 36* are based on the following:

Hall, a divorced person and custodian of her 12-year-old child, filed her 1990 federal income tax return as head of a household. She submitted the following information to the CPA who prepared her 1990 return:

- The divorce agreement, executed in 1983, provides for Hall to receive $3,000 per month, of which $600 is designated as child support. After the child reaches 18, the monthly payments are to be reduced to $2,400 and are to continue until remarriage or death. However, for the year 1990, Hall received a total of only $5,000 from her former husband. Hall paid an attorney $2,000 in 1990 in a suit to collect the alimony owed.

- In June 1990, Hall's mother gifted her 100 shares of a listed stock. The donor's basis for this stock, which she bought in 1970, was $4,000, and market value on the date of the gift was $3,000. Hall sold this stock in July 1990 for $3,500. The donor paid no gift tax.

- During 1990, Hall spent a total of $1,000 for state lottery tickets. Her lottery winnings in 1990 totaled $200.

- Hall earned a salary of $25,000 in 1990. Hall was not covered by any type of retirement plan, but contributed $2,000 to an IRA in 1990.

- In 1990, Hall sold an antique that she bought in 1980 to display in her home. Hall paid $800 for the antique and sold it for $1,400, using the proceeds to pay a court-ordered judgment.

*The omitted items can be found in other Content Specification Groups.

- Hall paid the following expenses in 1990 pertaining to the home that she owns: realty taxes, $3,400; mortgage interest, $7,000; casualty insurance, $490; assessment by city for construction of a sewer system, $910; interest of $1,000 on a personal, unsecured bank loan, the proceeds of which were used for home improvements. Hall does not rent out any portion of the home.

35. The $910 sewer system assessment imposed by the city in 1990 is
    a. Allowed with the realty taxes as an itemized deduction for taxes.
    b. Allowed as an itemized deduction subject to the 2% of adjusted gross income floor.
    c. Deductible in arriving at adjusted gross income.
    d. Not deductible in 1990.

36. The casualty insurance premium of $490 is
    a. Allowed as an itemized deduction subject to the $100 floor and the 10% of adjusted gross income floor.
    b. Allowed as an itemized deduction subject to the 2% of gross income floor.
    c. Deductible in arriving at adjusted gross income.
    d. Not deductible in 1990.

2M91#26. Dale received $1,000 in 1990 for jury duty. In exchange for regular compensation from her employer during the period of jury service, Dale was required to remit the entire $1,000 to her employer in 1990. In Dale's 1990 income tax return, the $1,000 jury duty fee should be
   a. Claimed in full as an itemized deduction.
   b. Claimed as an itemized deduction to the extent exceeding 2% of adjusted gross income.
   c. Deducted from gross income in arriving at adjusted gross income.
   d. Included in taxable income without a corresponding offset against other income.

2M91#27. For regular tax purposes, with regard to the itemized deduction for qualified residence interest, home equity indebtedness incurred in 1991
   a. Includes acquisition indebtedness secured by a qualified residence.
   b. May exceed the fair market value of the residence.
   c. Must exceed the taxpayer's net equity in the residence.
   d. Is limited to $100,000 on a joint income tax return.

2M91#29. An individual's losses on transactions entered into for personal purposes are deductible only if
   a. The losses qualify as casualty or theft losses.
   b. The losses can be characterized as hobby losses.
   c. The losses do not exceed $3,000 ($6,000 on a joint return).
   d. No part of the transactions was entered into for profit.

2M91#30. Ruth and Mark Cline are married and will file a joint 1991 income tax return. Among their expenditures

AR-7

during 1991 were the following discretionary costs that they incurred for the sole purpose of improving their physical appearance and self-esteem:

Face lift for Ruth, performed by a
  licensed surgeon $5,000
Hair transplant for Mark, performed
  by a licensed surgeon   3,600

Disregarding the adjusted gross income percentage threshold, what total amount of the aforementioned doctors' bills may be claimed by the Clines in their 1991 return as qualifying medical expenses?
    a. $0
    b. $3,600
    c. $5,000
    d. $8,600

2M91#31. During 1990, Scott charged $4,000 on his credit card for his dependent son's medical expenses. Payment to the credit card company had not been made by the time Scott filed his income tax return in 1991. However, in 1990, Scott paid a physician $2,800 for the medical expenses of his wife, who died in 1989. Disregarding the adjusted gross income percentage threshold, what amount could Scott claim in his 1990 income tax return for medical expenses?
    a. $0
    b. $2,800
    c. $4,000
    d. $6,800

2N90#33. Which one of the following expenditures qualifies as a deductible medical expense for tax purposes?
    a. Vitamins for general health **not** prescribed by a physician.
    b. Health club dues.
    c. Transportation to physician's office for required medical care.
    d. Mandatory employment taxes for basic coverage under Medicare A.

2M89
Items 43 through 51* are based on the following selected 1988 information pertaining to Sam and Ann Hoyt, who filed a joint federal income tax return for the calendar year 1988:

        Sam — age 72; normal vision.
        Ann — age 67; legally blind.

        Adjusted gross income — $34,000.

The Hoyts itemized their deductions.

Among the Hoyts' cash receipts during 1988 were the following:

---
*The omitted items can be found in other Content Specification Groups.

$1,000 dividends from taxable domestic corporations on stocks held in Sam's name.
$4,000 net proceeds from sale of 100 shares of listed corporation stock bought in 1980 for $9,000. The Hoyts had **no** other capital gains or losses in the current or prior years.
$6,000 first installment on a $75,000 life insurance policy payable to Ann in annual installments of $6,000 each over a 15-year period, as beneficiary of the policy on her uncle, who died in 1987.

Among the Hoyts' cash expenditures during 1988 were the following:

$2,000 transportation expenses required under the terms of Sam's employment contract were paid by Sam, an outside salesman. No reimbursement was received.
$2,500 repairs in connection with 1988 fire damage to the Hoyt residence. This property has a basis of $50,000. Fair market value was $60,000 before the fire and $55,000 after the fire. Insurance on the property had lapsed in 1987 for nonpayment of premium.
$800 appraisal fee to determine amount of fire loss.
$3,000 real estate tax on residence; $400 state and city sales taxes; $900 state income tax.
$100 contribution to a recognized political party.

48. What amount of fire loss were the Hoyts entitled to deduct as an itemized deduction on their 1988 return?
    a. $5,000
    b. $2,500
    c. $1,600
    d. $1,500

49. What total amount was deductible for taxes on the Hoyts' 1988 return?
    a. $4,300
    b. $3,900
    c. $3,400
    d. $3,000

50. The unreimbursed employee's transportation expenses paid by Sam in 1988 were
    a. Deductible from gross income in arriving at adjusted gross income.
    b. Subject to the 2% of adjusted gross income floor for miscellaneous itemized deductions.
    c. Fully deductible as an itemized deduction.
    d. Not deductible.

51. The appraisal fee to determine the amount of the Hoyts' fire loss was
    a. Deductible from gross income in arriving at adjusted gross income.
    b. Subject to the 2% of adjusted gross income floor for miscellaneous itemized deductions.
    c. Deductible after reducing the amount by $100.
    d. Not deductible.

D. Filing Status and Exemptions

M95#14. In 1994, Smith, a divorced person, provided over one half the support for his widowed mother, Ruth,

and his son, Clay, both of whom are U.S. citizens. During 1994, Ruth did not live with Smith. She received $9,000 in social security benefits. Clay, a full-time graduate student, and his wife lived with Smith. Clay had no income but filed a joint return for 1994, owing an additional $500 in taxes on his wife's income. How many exemptions was Smith entitled to claim on his 1994 tax return?
    a. 4
    b. 3
    c. 2
    d. 1

M94#14. Jim and Kay Ross contributed to the support of their two children, Dale and Kim, and Jim's widowed parent, Grant. For 1993, Dale, a 19-year-old full-time college student, earned $4,500 as a baby-sitter. Kim, a 23-year-old bank teller, earned $12,000. Grant received $5,000 in dividend income and $4,000 in nontaxable social security benefits. Grant, Dale, and Kim are U.S. citizens and were over one-half supported by Jim and Kay. How many exemptions can Jim and Kay claim on their 1993 joint income tax return?
    a. Two
    b. Three
    c. Four
    d. Five

2N92#10. For head of household filing status, which of the following costs are considered in determining whether the taxpayer has contributed more than one-half the cost of maintaining the household?

	Food consumed in the home	Value of services rendered in the home by the taxpayer
a.	Yes	Yes
b.	No	No
c.	Yes	No
d.	No	Yes

2M91#34. A husband and wife can file a joint return even if
    a. The spouses have different tax years, provided that both spouses are alive at the end of the year.
    b. The spouses have different accounting methods.
    c. Either spouse was a nonresident alien at any time during the tax year, provided that at least one spouse makes the proper election.
    d. They were divorced before the end of the tax year.

E. Tax Accounting Methods

M95#15. A cash basis taxpayer should report gross income
    a. Only for the year in which income is actually received in cash.
    b. Only for the year in which income is actually received whether in cash or in property.
    c. For the year in which income is either actually or constructively received in cash only.
    d. For the year in which income is either actually or constructively received, whether in cash or in property.

F. Tax Computations, Credits, and Penalties

R98#4. Krete, an unmarried taxpayer with income exclusively from wages, filed her initial income tax return for the 1997 calendar year. By December 31, 1997, Krete's employer had withheld $16,000 in federal income taxes and Krete had made no estimated tax payments. On April 15, 1998, Krete timely filed an extension request to file her individual tax return and paid $300 of additional taxes. Krete's 1997 income tax liability was $16,500 when she timely filed her return on April 30, 1998, and paid the remaining income tax liability balance. What amount would be subject to the penalty for the underpayment of estimated taxes?
    a. $0
    b. $ 200
    c. $ 500
    d. $16,500

M94#16. The credit for prior year alternative minimum tax liability may be carried
    a. Forward for a maximum of 5 years.
    b. Back to the 3 preceding years or carried forward for a maximum of 5 years.
    c. Back to the 3 preceding years.
    d. Forward indefinitely.

M94#17. Which of the following credits can result in a refund even if the individual had **no** income tax liability?
    a. Credit for prior year minimum tax.
    b. Elderly and permanently and totally disabled credit.
    c. Earned income credit.
    d. Child and dependent care credit.

2N93#37. The alternative minimum tax (AMT) is computed as the
    a. Excess of the regular tax over the tentative AMT.
    b. Excess of the tentative AMT over the regular tax.
    c. The tentative AMT plus the regular tax.
    d. Lesser of the tentative AMT or the regular tax.

2N91#22. Kent qualified for the earned income credit in 1990. This credit could result in a
    a. Refund even if Kent had no tax withheld from wages.
    b. Refund only if Kent had tax withheld from wages.
    c. Carryback or carryforward for any unused portion.
    d. Subtraction from adjusted gross income to arrive at taxable income.

2M91#33. An employee who has had social security tax withheld in an amount greater than the maximum for a particular year may claim
   a. Such excess as either a credit or an itemized deduction, at the election of the employee, if that excess resulted from correct withholding by two or more employers.
   b. Reimbursement of such excess from his employers, if that excess resulted from correct withholding by two or more employers.
   c. The excess as a credit against income tax, if that excess resulted from correct withholding by two or more employers.
   d. The excess as a credit against income tax, if that excess was withheld by one employer.

G. Alternative Minimum Tax

M95#17. In 1994, Don Mills, a single taxpayer, had $70,000 in taxable income before personal exemptions. Mills had no tax preferences. His itemized deductions were as follows:

State and local income taxes	$5,000
Home mortgage interest on loan to acquire residence	6,000
Miscellaneous deductions that exceed 2% of adjusted gross income	2,000

What amount did Mills report as alternative minimum taxable income before the AMT exemption?
   a. $72,000
   b. $75,000
   c. $77,000
   d. $83,000

M95#18. Alternative minimum tax preferences include

	Tax exempt interest from private activity bonds issued during 1994	*Charitable contributions of appreciated capital gain property*
a.	Yes	Yes
b.	Yes	No
c.	No	Yes
d.	No	No

H. Tax Procedures

M95#16. An accuracy-related penalty applies to the portion of tax underpayment attributable to

I. Negligence or a disregard of the tax rules or regulations.
II. Any substantial understatement of income tax.

   a. I only.
   b. II only.
   c. Both I and II.
   d. Neither I nor II.

M94#18. A calendar-year taxpayer files an individual tax return for 1992 on March 20, 1993. The taxpayer neither committed fraud nor omitted amounts in excess of 25% of gross income on the tax return. What is the latest date that the Internal Revenue Service can assess tax and assert a notice of deficiency?
   a. March 20, 1996.
   b. March 20, 1995.
   c. April 15, 1996.
   d. April 15, 1995.

2N92#6. On April 15, 1992, a married couple filed their joint 1991 calendar-year return showing gross income of $120,000. Their return had been prepared by a professional tax preparer who mistakenly omitted $45,000 of income, which the preparer in good faith considered to be nontaxable. No information with regard to this omitted income was disclosed on the return or attached statements. By what date must the Internal Revenue Service assert a notice of deficiency before the statute of limitations expires?
   a. April 15, 1998.
   b. December 31, 1997.
   c. April 15, 1995.
   d. December 31, 1994.

2N90#21. Keen, a calendar-year taxpayer, reported a gross income of $100,000 on his 1989 income tax return. Inadvertently omitted from gross income was a $20,000 commission that should have been included in 1989. Keen filed his 1989 return on March 15, 1990. To collect the tax on the $20,000 omission, the Internal Revenue Service must assert a notice of deficiency **no** later than
   a. March 15, 1993.
   b. April 15, 1993.
   c. March 15, 1996.
   d. April 15, 1996.

2N90#22. If an individual paid income tax in 1989 but did **not** file a 1989 return because his income was insufficient to require the filing of a return, the deadline for filing a refund claim is
   a. Two years from the date the tax was paid.
   b. Two years from the date a return would have been due.
   c. Three years from the date the tax was paid.
   d. Three years from the date a return would have been due.

II. Federal Taxation — Corporations

A. Determination of Taxable Income or Loss

R97#5. How are a C corporation's net capital losses used?
  a. Deducted from the corporation's ordinary income only to the extent of $3,000.
  b. Carried back three years and forward five years.
  c. Deductible in full from the corporation's ordinary income.
  d. Carried forward 15 years.

R96#7. On January 2, 1995, Tek Corp., an accrual-basis calendar-year C corporation, purchased all the assets of a sole proprietorship, including $60,000 in goodwill. Tek's 1995 reported book income before federal income taxes was $400,000. A $1,500 deduction for annual amortization of goodwill was taken based on a 40-year amortization period. What should be the amount of Tek's 1995 taxable income, as reconciled on Tek's Schedule M-1 of Form 1120, U.S. Corporation Income Tax Return?
  a. $389,500
  b. $397,500
  c. $400,000
  d. $401,500

N95#1. In 1994, Starke Corp., an accrual-basis calendar year corporation, reported book income of $380,000. Included in that amount was $50,000 municipal bond interest income, $170,000 for federal income tax expense, and $2,000 interest expense on the debt incurred to carry the municipal bonds. What amount should Starke's taxable income be as reconciled on Starke's Schedule M-1 of Form 1120, U.S. Corporation Income Tax Return?
  a. $330,000
  b. $500,000
  c. $502,000
  d. $550,000

N95#2. Lake Corp., an accrual-basis calendar year corporation, had the following 1994 receipts:

1995 advanced rental payments where the lease ends in 1996	$125,000
Lease cancellation payment from a 5-year lease tenant	50,000

Lake had no restrictions on the use of the advanced rental payments and renders no services. What amount of income should Lake report on its 1994 tax return?
  a. $0
  b. $ 50,000
  c. $125,000
  d. $175,000

N95#4. In 1994, Best Corp., an accrual-basis calendar year C corporation, received $100,000 in dividend income from the common stock that it held in an unrelated domestic corporation. The stock was not debt-financed, and was held for over a year. Best recorded the following information for 1994:

Loss from Best's operations	($ 10,000)
Dividends received	100,000
Taxable income (before dividends-received deduction)	$ 90,000

Best's dividends-received deduction on its 1994 tax return was
  a. $100,000
  b. $ 80,000
  c. $ 70,000
  d. $ 63,000

N95#6. Capital assets include
  a. A corporation's accounts receivable from the sale of its inventory.
  b. Seven-year MACRS property used in a corporation's trade or business.
  c. A manufacturing company's investment in U.S. Treasury bonds.
  d. A corporate real estate developer's unimproved land that is to be subdivided to build homes, which will be sold to customers.

N95#8. In 1994, Cable Corp., a calendar year C corporation, contributed $80,000 to a qualified charitable organization. Cable's 1994 taxable income before the deduction for charitable contributions was $820,000 after a $40,000 dividends-received deduction. Cable also had carryover contributions of $10,000 from the prior year. In 1994, what amount can Cable deduct as charitable contributions?
  a. $90,000
  b. $86,000
  c. $82,000
  d. $80,000

N95#9. If a corporation's charitable contributions exceed the limitation for deductibility in a particular year, the excess
  a. Is **not** deductible in any future or prior year.
  b. May be carried back or forward for one year at the corporation's election.
  c. May be carried forward to a maximum of five succeeding years.
  d. May be carried back to the third preceding year.

N95#10. In 1994, Stewart Corp. properly accrued $5,000 for an income item on the basis of a reasonable estimate. In 1995, after filing its 1994 federal income tax return, Stewart determined that the exact amount was $6,000. Which of the following statements is correct?
  a. No further inclusion of income is required as the difference is less than 25% of the original amount reported and the estimate had been made in good faith.
  b. The $1,000 difference is includible in Stewart's 1995 income tax return.

c. Stewart is required to notify the IRS within 30 days of the determination of the exact amount of the item.
d. Stewart is required to file an amended return to report the additional $1,000 of income.

N94#31. Banks Corp., a calendar year corporation, reimburses employees for properly substantiated qualifying business meal expenses. The employees are present at the meals, which are neither lavish nor extravagant, and the reimbursement is not treated as wages subject to withholdings. For 1994, what percentage of the meal expense may Banks deduct?
  a. 0%
  b. 50%
  c. 80%
  d. 100%

N94#32. For the year ended December 31, 1993, Kelly Corp. had net income per books of $300,000 before the provision for Federal income taxes. Included in the net income were the following items:

Dividend income from an unaffiliated
  domestic taxable corporation (taxable
  income limitation does not apply and there
  is no portfolio indebtedness) $50,000

Bad debt expense (represents the increase in
  the allowance for doubtful accounts)   80,000

Assuming no bad debt was written off, what is Kelly's taxable income for the year ended December 31, 1993?
  a. $250,000
  b. $330,000
  c. $345,000
  d. $380,000

N94#33. For the year ended December 31, 1993, Taylor Corp. had a net operating loss of $200,000. Taxable income for the earlier years of corporate existence, computed without reference to the net operating loss, was as follows:

	Taxable income
1988	$ 5,000
1989	$10,000
1990	$20,000
1991	$30,000
1992	$40,000

If Taylor makes **no** special election to waive the net operating loss carryback, what amount of net operating loss will be available to Taylor for the year ended December 31, 1994?
  a. $200,000
  b. $110,000
  c. $100,000
  d. $ 95,000

N94#34. On January 2, 1991, Bates Corp. purchased and placed into service 7-year MACRS tangible property costing $100,000. On December 31, 1993, Bates sold the property for $102,000, after having taken $47,525 in MACRS depreciation deductions. What amount of the gain should Bates recapture as ordinary income?
  a. $0
  b. $ 2,000
  c. $47,525
  d. $49,525

N94#36. Axis Corp. is an accrual basis calendar year corporation. On December 13, 1993, the Board of Directors declared a two percent of profits bonus to all employees for services rendered during 1993 and notified them in writing. None of the employees own stock in Axis. The amount represents reasonable compensation for services rendered and was paid on March 13, 1994. Axis' bonus expense may
  a. Not be deducted on Axis' 1993 tax return because the per share employee amount **cannot** be determined with reasonable accuracy at the time of the declaration of the bonus.
  b. Be deducted on Axis' 1993 tax return.
  c. Be deducted on Axis' 1994 tax return.
  d. Not be deducted on Axis' tax return because payment is a disguised dividend.

N94#37. Tapper Corp., an accrual basis calendar year corporation, was organized on January 2, 1993. During 1993, revenue was exclusively from sales proceeds and interest income. The following information pertains to Tapper:

Taxable income before charitable
  contributions for the year ended December
  31, 1993 $500,000

Tapper's matching contribution to
  employee-designated qualified universities
  made during 1993   10,000

Board of Directors' authorized contribution
  to a qualified charity (authorized
  December 1, 1993, made February 1,
  1994)   30,000

What is the maximum allowable deduction that Tapper may take as a charitable contribution on its tax return for the year ended December 31, 1993?
  a. $0
  b. $10,000
  c. $30,000
  d. $40,000

N94#38. Which of the following costs are amortizable organizational expenditures?
  a. Professional fees to issue the corporate stock.
  b. Printing costs to issue the corporate stock.
  c. Legal fees for drafting the corporate charter.
  d. Commissions paid by the corporation to an underwriter.

Selected Questions

2M93#41. In 1992, Acorn Inc. had the following items of income and expense:

Sales	$500,000
Cost of sales	250,000
Dividends received	25,000

The dividends were received from a corporation of which Acorn owns 30%. In Acorn's 1992 corporate income tax return, what amount should be reported as income before special deductions?
- a. $525,000
- b. $505,000
- c. $275,000
- d. $250,000

2M93#42. Ace Rentals Inc., an accrual-basis taxpayer, reported rent receivable of $35,000 and $25,000 in its 1992 and 1991 balance sheets, respectively. During 1992, Ace received $50,000 in rent payments and $5,000 in nonrefundable rent deposits. In Ace's 1992 corporate income tax return, what amount should Ace include as rent revenue?
- a. $50,000
- b. $55,000
- c. $60,000
- d. $65,000

2M93#44. Brown Corp., a calendar-year taxpayer, was organized and actively began operations on July 1, 1992, and incurred the following costs:

Legal fees to obtain corporate charter	$40,000
Commission paid to underwriter	25,000
Other stock issue costs	10,000

Brown wishes to amortize its organizational costs over the shortest period allowed for tax purposes. In 1992, what amount should Brown deduct for the amortization of organizational expenses?
- a. $8,000
- b. $7,500
- c. $5,000
- d. $4,000

2M93#47. When a corporation has an unused net capital loss that is carried back or carried forward to another tax year,
- a. It retains its original identity as short-term or long-term.
- b. It is treated as a short-term capital loss whether or not it was short-term when sustained.
- c. It is treated as a long-term capital loss whether or not it was long-term when sustained.
- d. It can be used to offset ordinary income up to the amount of the carryback or carryover.

2M93#48. Soma Corp. had $600,000 in compensation expense for book purposes in 1992. Included in this amount was a $50,000 accrual for 1992 nonshareholder bonuses. Soma paid the actual 1992 bonus of $60,000 on March 1, 1993. In its 1992 tax return, what amount should Soma deduct as compensation expense?
- a. $600,000
- b. $610,000
- c. $550,000
- d. $540,000

2N91#46. In a C corporation's computation of the maximum allowable deduction for contributions, what percentage limitation should be applied to the applicable base amount?
- a. 5%
- b. 10%
- c. 30%
- d. 50%

2N91#47. In the case of a corporation that is **not** a financial institution, which of the following statements is correct with regard to the deduction for bad debts?
- a. Either the reserve method or the direct charge-off method may be used, if the election is made in the corporation's first taxable year.
- b. On approval from the IRS, a corporation may change its method from direct charge-off to reserve.
- c. If the reserve method was consistently used in prior years, the corporation may take a deduction for a reasonable addition to the reserve for bad debts.
- d. A corporation is required to use the direct charge-off method rather than the reserve method.

2N91#49. Would the following expense items be reported on Schedule M-1 of the corporation income tax return showing the reconciliation of income per books with income per return?

	Interest incurred on loan to carry U.S. obligations	Provision for state corporation income tax
a.	Yes	Yes
b.	No	No
c.	Yes	No
d.	No	Yes

2M91#44. The rule limiting the allowability of passive activity losses and credits applies to
- a. Partnerships.
- b. S corporations.
- c. Personal service corporations.
- d. Widely-held C corporations.

2M91#47. The corporate dividends-received deduction
- a. Must exceed the applicable percentage of the recipient shareholder's taxable income.
- b. Is affected by a requirement that the investor corporation must own the investee's stock for a specified minimum holding period.

AR-13

c. Is unaffected by the percentage of the investee's stock owned by the investor corporation.
d. May be claimed by S corporations.

2M91#49. Foreign income taxes paid by a corporation
a. May be claimed either as a deduction or as a credit, at the option of the corporation.
b. May be claimed only as a deduction.
c. May be claimed only as a credit.
d. Do **not** qualify either as a deduction or as a credit.

2M91#51. The minimum total voting power that a parent corporation must have in a subsidiary's stock in order to be eligible for the filing of a consolidated return is
a. 20%
b. 50%
c. 51%
d. 80%

2M91#52. With regard to depreciation computations made under the general MACRS method, the half-year convention provides that
a. One-half of the first year's depreciation is allowed in the year in which the property is placed in service, regardless of when the property is placed in service during the year, and a half-year's depreciation is allowed for the year in which the property is disposed of.
b. The deduction will be based on the number of months the property was in service, so that one-half month's depreciation is allowed for the month in which the property is placed in service and for the month in which it is disposed of.
c. Depreciation will be allowed in the first year of acquisition of the property only if the property is placed in service **no** later than June 30 for calendar-year corporations.
d. Depreciation will be allowed in the last year of the property's economic life only if the property is disposed of after June 30 of the year of disposition for calendar-year corporations.

2M90#35. For the year ended December 31, 1989, Maple Corp.'s book income, before federal income tax, was $100,000. Included in this $100,000 were the following:

Provision for state income tax	$1,000
Interest earned on U.S. Treasury Bonds	6,000
Interest expense on bank loan to purchase U.S. Treasury Bonds	2,000

Maple's taxable income for 1989 was
a. $ 96,000
b. $ 97,000
c. $100,000
d. $101,000

2N89
Items 41 through 45 are based on the following:

Kell Corp.
INCOME STATEMENT
For the Year Ended December 31, 1988

Sales		$900,000
Cost of sales		600,000
Gross margin		300,000
Operating expenses		250,000
Operating income		50,000
Other income:		
Gain on sale of investments	$15,000	
Life insurance policy proceeds	10,000	
Dividends	3,000	28,000
Total		78,000
Other expense:		
Contributions		8,000
Income before income tax		$ 70,000

41. The gain on sale of investments resulted from the sale of stock of an unrelated taxable domestic corporation. This stock had been purchased in 1980. In its 1988 income tax return, Kell should claim a long-term capital gain deduction of
a. $0
b. $ 6,000
c. $ 9,000
d. $12,000

42. This question has not been selected.

43. The dividends were declared and received in 1988 from an unrelated taxable domestic corporation in which Kell owned less than 1% of the investee's stock. Kell had no portfolio indebtedness. In its 1988 income tax return, Kell should claim a dividends-received deduction of
a. $0
b. $ 100
c. $2,100
d. $2,400

44. All of the contributions were to qualified charitable organizations. When Kell computes the maximum allowable deduction for contributions, what percentage of contribution base income should Kell use?
a. 50%
b. 30%
c. 10%
d. 5%

45. Included in Kell's operating expenses were the following life insurance premiums:

AR-14

Term life insurance premiums paid on the life of Kell's controller, with Kell as owner and beneficiary of the policy	$ 2,000
Group-term life insurance premiums paid on employees' lives, with the employees' dependents as owners and beneficiaries of the policies	18,000

In its 1988 income tax return, what amount should Kell deduct for life insurance premiums?
- a. $20,000
- b. $18,000
- c. $ 2,000
- d. $0

B. Tax Accounting Methods

N94#40. Under the uniform capitalization rules applicable to property acquired for resale, which of the following costs should be capitalized with respect to inventory if **no** exceptions are met?

	Marketing costs	Off-site storage costs
a.	Yes	Yes
b.	Yes	No
c.	No	No
d.	No	Yes

C. S Corporations

M95#21. Village Corp., a calendar year corporation, began business in 1990. Village made a valid S Corporation election on December 5, 1993, with the unanimous consent of its shareholders. The eligibility requirements for S status continued to be met throughout 1994. On what date did Village's S status become effective?
- a. January 1, 1993.
- b. January 1, 1994.
- c. December 5, 1993.
- d. December 5, 1994.

M95#22. A shareholder's basis in the stock of an S corporation is increased by the shareholder's pro rata share of income from

	Tax-exempt interest	Taxable interest
a.	No	No
b.	No	Yes
c.	Yes	No
d.	Yes	Yes

N94#41. Zinco Corp. was a calendar year S corporation. Zinco's S status terminated on April 1, 1993, when Case Corp. became a shareholder. During 1993 (365-day calendar year), Zinco had nonseparately computed income of $310,250. If no election was made by Zinco, what amount of the income, if any, was allocated to the S short year for 1993?

- a. $233,750
- b. $155,125
- c. $ 76,500
- d. $0

M94#21. An S Corporation has 30,000 shares of voting common stock and 20,000 shares of non-voting common stock issued and outstanding. The S election can be revoked voluntarily with the consent of the shareholders holding, on the day of the revocation,

	Shares of voting stock	Shares of nonvoting stock
a.	0	20,000
b.	7,500	5,000
c.	10,000	16,000
d.	20,000	0

M94#22. The Haas Corp., a calendar year S corporation, has two equal shareholders. For the year ended December 31, 1993, Haas had taxable income and current earnings and profits of $60,000, which included $50,000 from operations and $10,000 from investment interest income. There were no other transactions that year. Each shareholder's basis in the stock of Haas will increase by
- a. $50,000
- b. $30,000
- c. $25,000
- d. $0

2N93#44. If an S corporation has **no** accumulated earnings and profits, the amount distributed to a shareholder
- a. Must be returned to the S corporation.
- b. Increases the shareholder's basis for the stock.
- c. Decreases the shareholder's basis for the stock.
- d. Has **no** effect on the shareholder's basis for the stock.

2M91#56. Bern Corp., an S corporation, had an ordinary loss of $36,500 for the year ended December 31, 1990. At January 1, 1990, Meyer owned 50% of Bern's stock. Meyer held the stock for 40 days in 1990 before selling the entire 50% interest to an unrelated third party. Meyer's basis for the stock was $10,000. Meyer was a full-time employee of Bern until the stock was sold. Meyer's share of Bern's 1990 loss was
- a. $0
- b. $ 2,000
- c. $10,000
- d. $18,250

2N89#50. With regard to S corporations and their stockholders, the "at risk" rules applicable to losses
- a. Depend on the type of income reported by the S corporation.
- b. Are subject to the elections made by the S corporation's stockholders.
- c. Take into consideration the S corporation's ratio of debt to equity.
- d. Apply at the shareholder level rather than at the corporate level.

D. Personal Holding Companies

M95#23. Edge Corp. met the stock ownership requirements of a personal holding company. What sources of income must Edge consider to determine if the income requirements for a personal holding company have been met?

I. Interest earned on tax-exempt obligations.
II. Dividends received from an unrelated domestic corporation.

a. I only.
b. II only.
c. Both I and II.
d. Neither I nor II.

2M93#52. Acme Corp. has two common stockholders. Acme derives all of its income from investments in stocks and securities, and it regularly distributes 51% of its taxable income as dividends to its stockholders. Acme is a

a. Corporation subject to tax only on income **not** distributed to stockholders.
b. Corporation subject to the accumulated earnings tax.
c. Regulated investment company.
d. Personal holding company.

2M91#54. The following information pertains to Hull, Inc., a personal holding company, for the year ended December 31, 1990:

Undistributed personal holding company income	$100,000
Dividends paid during 1990	20,000
Consent dividends reported in the 1990 individual income tax returns of the holders of Hull's common stock, but **not** paid by Hull to its stockholders	10,000

In computing its 1990 personal holding company tax, what amount should Hull deduct for dividends paid?
a. $0
b. $10,000
c. $20,000
d. $30,000

E. Consolidated Returns

N95#13. Bank Corp. owns 80% of Shore Corp.'s outstanding capital stock. Shore's capital stock consists of 50,000 shares of common stock issued and outstanding. Shore's 1994 net income was $140,000. During 1994, Shore declared and paid dividends of $60,000. In conformity with generally accepted accounting principles, Bank recorded the following entries in 1994:

	Debit	Credit
Investment in Shore Corp. common stock	$112,000	
Equity in earnings of subsidiary		$112,000
Cash	48,000	
Investment in Shore Corp. common stock		48,000

In its 1994 consolidated tax return, Bank should report dividend revenue of
a. $48,000
b. $14,400
c. $ 9,600
d. $0

N94#46. With regard to consolidated tax returns, which of the following statements is correct?
a. Operating losses of one group member may be used to offset operating profits of the other members included in the consolidated return.
b. Only corporations that issue their audited financial statements on a consolidated basis may file consolidated returns.
c. Of all intercompany dividends paid by the subsidiaries to the parent, 70% are excludible from taxable income on the consolidated return.
d. The common parent must directly own 51% or more of the total voting power of all corporations included in the consolidated return.

N94#47. In the filing of a consolidated tax return for a corporation and its wholly owned subsidiaries, intercompany dividends between the parent and subsidiary corporations are
a. Not taxable.
b. Included in taxable income to the extent of 20%.
c. Included in taxable income to the extent of 80%.
d. Fully taxable.

M94#23. Tech Corp. files a consolidated return with its wholly-owned subsidiary, Dow Corp. During 1993, Dow paid a cash dividend of $20,000 to Tech. What amount of this dividend is taxable on the 1993 consolidated return?
a. $20,000
b. $14,000
c. $ 6,000
d. $0

2M93#43. In 1992, Portal Corp. received $100,000 in dividends from Sal Corp., its 80%-owned subsidiary. What net amount of dividend income should Portal include in its 1992 consolidated tax return?
a. $100,000
b. $ 80,000
c. $ 70,000
d. $0

2M93#49. Potter Corp. and Sly Corp. file consolidated tax returns. In January 1991, Potter sold land, with a basis of $60,000 and a fair value of $75,000, to Sly for $100,000. Sly sold the land in December 1992 for $125,000. In its 1992 and 1991 tax returns, what amount of gain should be reported for these transactions in the consolidated return?

	1992	1991
a.	$25,000	$40,000
b.	$50,000	$0
c.	$50,000	$25,000
d.	$65,000	$0

2M91#53. When a consolidated return is filed by an affiliated group of includible corporations connected from inception through the requisite stock ownership with a common parent,
    a. Intercompany dividends are excludible to the extent of 80%.
    b. Operating losses of one member of the group offset operating profits of other members of the group.
    c. The parent's basis in the stock of its subsidiaries is unaffected by the earnings and profits of its subsidiaries.
    d. Each of the subsidiaries is entitled to an accumulated earnings tax credit.

2M90#36. In the consolidated income tax return of a corporation and its wholly-owned subsidiary, what percentage of cash dividends paid by the subsidiary to the parent is tax-free?
    a. 0%
    b. 70%
    c. 80%
    d. 100%

F. Tax Computations, Credits, and Penalties

N95#14. Dart Corp., a calendar year domestic C corporation, is not a personal holding company. For purposes of the accumulated earnings tax, Dart has accumulated taxable income for 1994. Which step(s) can Dart take to eliminate or reduce any 1994 accumulated earnings tax?

I. Demonstrate that the "reasonable needs" of its business require the retention of all or part of the 1994 accumulated taxable income.
II. Pay dividends by March 15, 1995.

    a. I only.
    b. II only.
    c. Both I and II.
    d. Neither I nor II.

N95#15. Eastern Corp., a calendar year corporation, was formed January 3, 1994, and on that date placed five-year property in service. The property was depreciated under the general MACRS system. Eastern did not elect to use the straight-line method. The following information pertains to Eastern:

Eastern's 1994 taxable income	$300,000
Adjustment for the accelerated depreciation taken on 1994 five-year property	1,000
1994 tax-exempt interest from specified private activity bonds issued after August 7, 1986	5,000

What was Eastern's 1994 alternative minimum taxable income before the adjusted current earnings (ACE) adjustment?
    a. $306,000
    b. $305,000
    c. $304,000
    d. $301,000

N95#17. A corporation may reduce its regular income tax by taking a tax credit for
    a. Dividends-received exclusion.
    b. Foreign income taxes.
    c. State income taxes.
    d. Accelerated depreciation.

N95#18. The accumulated earnings tax can be imposed
    a. On both partnerships and corporations.
    b. On companies that make distributions in excess of accumulated earnings.
    c. On personal holding companies.
    d. Regardless of the number of stockholders in a corporation.

N94#48. A corporation's penalty for underpaying federal estimated taxes is
    a. Not deductible.
    b. Fully deductible in the year paid.
    c. Fully deductible if reasonable cause can be established for the underpayment.
    d. Partially deductible.

N94#49. Which of the following credits is a combination of several tax credits to provide uniform rules for the current and carryback-carryover years?
    a. General business credit.
    b. Foreign tax credit.
    c. Minimum tax credit.
    d. Enhanced oil recovery credit.

N94#50. Blink Corp., an accrual basis calendar year corporation, carried back a net operating loss for the tax year ended December 31, 1993. Blink's gross revenues have been under $500,000 since inception. Blink expects to have profits for the tax year ending December 31, 1994. Which method(s) of estimated tax payment can Blink use for its quarterly payments during the 1994 tax year to avoid underpayment of federal estimated taxes?

I. 100% of the preceding tax year method
II. Annualized income method

a. I only.
b. Both I and II.
c. II only.
d. Neither I nor II.

2N93#43. When computing a corporation's income tax expense for estimated income tax purposes, which of the following should be taken into account?

	Corporate tax credits	Alternative minimum tax
a.	No	No
b.	No	Yes
c.	Yes	No
d.	Yes	Yes

2M93#50. Which of the following tax credits **cannot** be claimed by a corporation?
a. Foreign tax credit.
b. Earned income credit.
c. Alternative fuel production credit.
d. General business credit.

2M93#55. Kari Corp., a manufacturing company, was organized on January 2, 1992. Its 1992 federal taxable income was $400,000 and its federal income tax was $100,000. What is the maximum amount of accumulated taxable income that may be subject to the accumulated earnings tax for 1992 if Kari takes only the minimum accumulated earnings credit?
a. $300,000
b. $150,000
c. $ 50,000
d. $0

2M93#57. If a corporation's tentative minimum tax exceeds the regular tax, the excess amount is
a. Carried back to the first preceding taxable year.
b. Carried back to the third preceding taxable year.
c. Payable in addition to the regular tax.
d. Subtracted from the regular tax.

H. Other

R97#6. Elm Corp. is an accrual-basis calendar-year C corporation with 100,000 shares of voting common stock issued and outstanding as of December 28, 1995. On Friday, December 29, 1995, Hall surrendered 2,000 shares of Elm stock to Elm in exchange for $33,000 cash. Hall had no direct or indirect interest in Elm after the stock surrender. Additional information follows:

Hall's adjusted basis in 2,000 shares of Elm
  on December 29, 1995 ($8 per share) $16,000
Elm's accumulated earnings and profits
  at January 1, 1995   25,000
Elm's 1995 net operating loss   (7,000)

What amount of income did Hall recognize from the stock surrender?

a. $33,000 dividend.
b. $25,000 dividend.
c. $18,000 capital gain.
d. $17,000 capital gain.

R97#7. Mintee Corp., an accrual-basis calendar-year C corporation, had no corporate shareholders when it liquidated in 1996. In cancellation of all their Mintee stock, each Mintee shareholder received in 1996, a liquidating distribution of $2,000 cash and land with a tax basis of $5,000 and a fair market value of $10,500. Before the distribution, each shareholder's tax basis in Mintee stock was $6,500. What amount of gain should each Mintee shareholder recognize on the liquidating distribution?
a. $0
b. $ 500
c. $4,000
d. $6,000

R96
Items 8 through 10 are based on the following:

Lind and Post organized Ace Corp., which issued voting common stock with a fair market value of $120,000. They each transferred property in exchange for stock as follows:

	Property	Adjusted basis	Fair market value	Percentage of Ace stock acquired
Lind	Building	$40,000	$82,000	60%
Post	Land	$ 5,000	$48,000	40%

8. The building was subject to a $10,000 mortgage that was assumed by Ace. What amount of gain did Lind recognize on the exchange?
a. $0
b. $10,000
c. $42,000
d. $52,000

9. What was Ace's basis in the building?
a. $30,000
b. $40,000
c. $72,000
d. $82,000

10. What was Lind's basis in Ace stock?
a. $82,000
b. $40,000
c. $30,000
d. $0

N95#19. The following information pertains to Dahl Corp.:

Accumulated earnings and profits
  at January 1, 1994 $120,000
Earnings and profits for the year
  ended December 31, 1994   160,000
Cash distributions to individual
  stockholders during 1994   360,000

What is the total amount of distributions taxable as dividend income to Dahl's stockholders in 1994?
a. $0
b. $160,000
c. $280,000
d. $360,000

N95#20. Ridge Corp., a calendar year C corporation, made a nonliquidating cash distribution to its shareholders of $1,000,000 with respect to its stock. At that time, Ridge's current and accumulated earnings and profits totaled $750,000 and its total paid-in capital for tax purposes was $10,000,000. Ridge had no corporate shareholders. Ridge's cash distribution

I. Was taxable as $750,000 in ordinary income to its shareholders.
II. Reduced its shareholders' adjusted bases in Ridge stock by $250,000.

a. I only.
b. II only.
c. Both I and II.
d. Neither I nor II.

N95#21. Clark and Hunt organized Jet Corp. with authorized voting common stock of $400,000. Clark contributed $60,000 cash. Both Clark and Hunt transferred other property in exchange for Jet stock as follows:

	Other property		
	Adjusted basis	Fair market value	Percentage of Jet stock acquired
Clark	$ 50,000	$100,000	40%
Hunt	120,000	240,000	60%

What was Clark's basis in Jet stock?
a. $0
b. $100,000
c. $110,000
d. $160,000

N95#22. Ace Corp. and Bate Corp. combine in a qualifying reorganization and form Carr Corp., the only surviving corporation. This reorganization is tax-free to the

	Shareholders	Corporation
a.	Yes	Yes
b.	Yes	No
c.	No	Yes
d.	No	No

M95#24. Kent Corp. is a calendar year, accrual basis C corporation. In 1994, Kent made a nonliquidating distribution of property with an adjusted basis of $150,000 and a fair market value of $200,000 to Reed, its sole shareholder. The following information pertains to Kent:

Reed's basis in Kent stock at January 1, 1994	$500,000
Accumulated earnings and profits at January 1, 1994	125,000
Current earnings and profits for 1994	60,000

What was taxable as dividend income to Reed for 1994?
a. $ 60,000
b. $150,000
c. $185,000
d. $200,000

M95#25. Jaxson Corp. has 200,000 shares of voting common stock issued and outstanding. King Corp. has decided to acquire 90 percent of Jaxson's voting common stock solely in exchange for 50 percent of its voting common stock and retain Jaxson as a subsidiary after the transaction. Which of the following statements is true?
a. King must acquire 100 percent of Jaxson stock for the transaction to be a tax-free reorganization.
b. The transaction will qualify as a tax-free reorganization.
c. King must issue at least 60 percent of its voting common stock for the transaction to qualify as a tax-free reorganization.
d. Jaxson must surrender assets for the transaction to qualify as a tax-free reorganization.

N94#51. Tank Corp., which had earnings and profits of $500,000, made a nonliquidating distribution of property to its shareholders in 1993 as a dividend in kind. This property, which had an adjusted basis of $20,000 and a fair market value of $30,000 at the date of distribution, did not constitute assets used in the active conduct of Tank's business. How much gain did Tank recognize on this distribution?
a. $30,000
b. $20,000
c. $10,000
d. $0

N94#52. Adams, Beck, and Carr organized Flexo Corp. with authorized voting common stock of $100,000. Adams received 10% of the capital stock in payment for the organizational services that he rendered for the benefit of the newly formed corporation. Adams did not contribute property to Flexo and was under no obligation to be paid by Beck or Carr. Beck and Carr transferred property in exchange for stock as follows:

	Adjusted basis	Fair market value	Percentage of Flexo stock acquired
Beck	5,000	20,000	20%
Carr	60,000	70,000	70%

What amount of gain did Carr recognize from this transaction?

a. $40,000
b. $15,000
c. $10,000
d. $0

N94#53. In a type B reorganization, as defined by the Internal Revenue Code, the

I. Stock of the target corporation is acquired solely for the voting stock of either the acquiring corporation or its parent.
II. Acquiring corporation must have control of the target corporation immediately after the acquisition.

a. I only.
b. II only.
c. Both I and II.
d. Neither I nor II.

M94#25. On January 1, 1993, Kee Corp., a C corporation, had a $50,000 deficit in earnings and profits. For 1993 Kee had current earnings and profits of $10,000 and made a $30,000 cash distribution to its stockholders. What amount of the distribution is taxable as dividend income to Kee's stockholders?
a. $30,000
b. $20,000
c. $10,000
d. $0

2N93#45. Jones incorporated a sole proprietorship by exchanging all the proprietorship's assets for the stock of Nu Co., a new corporation. To qualify for tax-free incorporation, Jones must be in control of Nu immediately after the exchange. What percentage of Nu's stock must Jones own to qualify as "control" for this purpose?
a. 50.00%
b. 51.00%
c. 66.67%
d. 80.00%

2N93#46. A corporation was completely liquidated and dissolved during 1992. The filing fees, professional fees, and other expenditures incurred in connection with the liquidation and dissolution are
a. Deductible in full by the dissolved corporation.
b. Deductible by the shareholders and **not** by the corporation.
c. Treated as capital losses by the corporation.
d. Not deductible either by the corporation or shareholders.

2M93#53. In 1992, Stone, a cash basis taxpayer, incorporated her CPA practice. No liabilities were transferred. The following assets were transferred to the corporation:

Cash (checking account)	$ 500
Computer equipment	
Adjusted basis	30,000
Fair market value	34,000
Cost	40,000

Immediately after the transfer, Stone owned 100% of the corporation's stock. The corporation's total basis for the transferred assets is
a. $30,000
b. $30,500
c. $34,500
d. $40,500

2N91#48. The costs of organizing a corporation
a. May be deducted in full in the year in which these costs are incurred even if paid in later years.
b. May be deducted only in the year in which these costs are paid.
c. May be amortized over a period of not less than 60 months even if these costs are capitalized on the company's books.
d. Are nondeductible capital expenditures.

2M91#43. Pursuant to a plan of corporate reorganization adopted in July 1990, Gow exchanged 500 shares of Lad Corp. common stock that he had bought in January 1990 at a cost of $5,000 for 100 shares of Rook Corp. common stock having a fair market value of $6,000. Gow's recognized gain on this exchange was
a. $1,000 long-term capital gain.
b. $1,000 short-term capital gain.
c. $1,000 ordinary income.
d. $0.

2M91#45. Nyle Corp. owned 100 shares of Beta Corp. stock that it bought in 1980 for $9 per share. In 1990, when the fair market value of the Beta stock was $20 per share, Nyle distributed this stock to a noncorporate shareholder. Nyle's recognized gain on this distribution was
a. $2,000
b. $1,100
c. $ 900
d. $0

2M90#28. Krol Corp. distributed marketable securities in redemption of its stock in a complete liquidation. On the date of distribution, these securities had a basis of $100,000 and a fair market value of $150,000. What gain does Krol have as a result of the distribution?
a. $0.
b. $50,000 capital gain.
c. $50,000 Section 1231 gain.
d. $50,000 ordinary gain.

2N89#52. How does a noncorporate shareholder treat the gain on a redemption of stock that qualifies as a partial liquidation of the distributing corporation?
a. Entirely as capital gain.
b. Entirely as a dividend.
c. Partly as capital gain and partly as a dividend.
d. As a tax-free transaction.

2N89#53. Rela Associates, a partnership, transferred all of its assets, with a basis of $300,000, subject to liabilities of $50,000, to a newly formed corporation in return for

all of the corporation's stock. Rela then distributed this stock to the partners in liquidation. In connection with this incorporation of the partnership, Rela recognizes
   a. No gain or loss on the transfer of its assets nor on the assumption of Rela's liabilities by the corporation.
   b. Gain on the assumption of Rela's liabilities by the corporation.
   c. Gain or loss on the transfer of its assets to the corporation.
   d. Gain, but **not** loss, on the transfer of its assets to the corporation.

III. Federal Taxation — Partnerships

A. Basis of Partner's Interest and Bases of Assets Contributed to the Partnership

R96
Items 1 and 2 are based on the following:

Jones and Curry formed Major Partnership as equal partners by contributing the assets below:

Asset		Adjusted basis	Fair market value
Jones	Cash	$45,000	$45,000
Curry	Land	30,000	57,000

The land was held by Curry as a capital asset, subject to a $12,000 mortgage, that was assumed by Major.

1. What was Curry's initial basis in the partnership interest?
   a. $45,000
   b. $30,000
   c. $24,000
   d. $18,000

2. What was Jones' initial basis in the partnership interest?
   a. $51,000
   b. $45,000
   c. $39,000
   d. $33,000

M95#26. Dean is a 25 percent partner in Target Partnership. Dean's tax basis in Target on January 1, 1994, was $20,000. At the end of 1994, Dean received a nonliquidating cash distribution of $8,000 from Target. Target's 1994 accounts recorded the following items:

Municipal bond interest income	$12,000
Ordinary income	40,000

What was Dean's tax basis in Target on December 31, 1994?
   a. $15,000
   b. $23,000
   c. $25,000
   d. $30,000

M95#27. Strom acquired a 25 percent interest in Ace Partnership by contributing land having an adjusted basis of $16,000 and a fair market value of $50,000. The land was subject to a $24,000 mortgage, which was assumed by Ace. No other liabilities existed at the time of the contribution. What was Strom's basis in Ace?
   a. $0
   b. $16,000
   c. $26,000
   d. $32,000

M94#26. On January 2, 1993, Black acquired a 50% interest in New Partnership by contributing property with an adjusted basis of $7,000 and a fair market value of $9,000, subject to a mortgage of $3,000. What was Black's basis in New at January 2, 1993?
   a. $3,500
   b. $4,000
   c. $5,500
   d. $7,500

M94#27. Gray is a 50% partner in Fabco Partnership. Gray's tax basis in Fabco on January 1, 1993, was $5,000. Fabco made no distributions to the partners during 1993, and recorded the following:

Ordinary income	$20,000
Tax exempt income	8,000
Portfolio income	4,000

What is Gray's tax basis in Fabco on December 31, 1993?
   a. $21,000
   b. $16,000
   c. $12,000
   d. $10,000

2N93#48. Pert contributed land with a fair market value of $20,000 to a new partnership in exchange for a 50% partnership interest. The land had an adjusted basis to Pert of $12,000 and was subject to a $4,000 mortgage, which the partnership assumed. What is the adjusted basis of Pert's partnership interest?
   a. $10,000
   b. $12,000
   c. $18,000
   d. $20,000

2N93#50. Lee inherited a partnership interest from Dale. The adjusted basis of Dale's partnership interest was $50,000, and its fair market value on the date of Dale's death (the estate valuation date) was $70,000. What was Lee's original basis for the partnership interest?

a. $70,000
b. $50,000
c. $20,000
d. $0

2N91#58. The following information pertains to property contributed by Gray on July 1, 1990, for a 40% interest in the capital and profits of Kag & Gray, a partnership:

As of June 30, 1990	
Adjusted basis	Fair market value
$24,000	$30,000

After Gray's contribution, Kag & Gray's capital totaled $150,000. What amount of gain was reportable in Gray's 1990 return on the contribution of property to the partnership?
a. $0
b. $ 6,000
c. $30,000
d. $36,000

2N91#59. Which of the following should be used in computing the basis of a partner's interest acquired from another partner?

	Cash paid by transferee to transferor	Transferee's share of partnership liabilities
a.	No	Yes
b.	Yes	No
c.	No	No
d.	Yes	Yes

2N91#60. The holding period of a partnership interest acquired in exchange for a contributed capital asset begins on the date
a. The partner is admitted to the partnership.
b. The partner transfers the asset to the partnership.
c. The partner's holding period of the capital asset began.
d. The partner is first credited with the proportionate share of partnership capital.

2M91#58. Eng contributed the following assets to a partnership in exchange for a 50% interest in the partnership's capital and profits:

Cash	$50,000
Equipment:	
Fair market value	35,000
Carrying amount (adjusted basis)	25,000

The basis for Eng's interest in the partnership is
a. $37,500
b. $42,500
c. $75,000
d. $85,000

B. Determination of Partner's Share of Income, Credits, and Deductions

N95#29. Evan, a 25% partner in Vista Partnership, received a $20,000 guaranteed payment in 1994 for deductible services rendered to the partnership. Guaranteed payments were not made to any other partner. Vista's 1994 partnership income consisted of:

Net business income before guaranteed payments	$80,000
Net long-term capital gains	10,000

What amount of income should Evan report from Vista Partnership on her 1994 tax return?
a. $37,500
b. $27,500
c. $22,500
d. $20,000

N94#57. White has a one-third interest in the profits and losses of Rapid Partnership. Rapid's ordinary income for the 1993 calendar year is $30,000, after a $3,000 deduction for a guaranteed payment made to White for services rendered. None of the $30,000 ordinary income was distributed to the partners. What is the total amount that White must include from Rapid as taxable income in his 1993 tax return?
a. $ 3,000
b. $10,000
c. $11,000
d. $13,000

M94#28. On January 2, 1993, Arch and Bean contribute cash equally to form the JK Partnership. Arch and Bean share profits and losses in a ratio of 75% to 25%, respectively. For 1993, the partnership's ordinary income was $40,000. A distribution of $5,000 was made to Arch during 1993. What is Arch's share of taxable income for 1993?
a. $ 5,000
b. $10,000
c. $20,000
d. $30,000

2N93#49. On June 1, 1992, Kelly received a 10% interest in Rock Co., a partnership, for services contributed to the partnership. Rock's net assets at that date had a basis of $70,000 and a fair market value of $100,000. In Kelly's 1992 income tax return, what amount must Kelly include as income from transfer of partnership interest?
a. $ 7,000 ordinary income.
b. $ 7,000 capital gain.
c. $10,000 ordinary income.
d. $10,000 capital gain.

2N93#53. In computing the ordinary income of a partnership, a deduction is allowed for
a. Contributions to recognized charities.
b. The first $100 of dividends received from qualifying domestic corporations.

c. Short-term capital losses.
d. Guaranteed payments to partners.

2N91#55. Which of the following limitations will apply in determining a partner's deduction for that partner's share of partnership losses?

	At-risk	Passive loss
a.	Yes	No
b.	No	Yes
c.	Yes	Yes
d.	No	No

2N91#56. Ola Associates is a limited partnership engaged in real estate development. Hoff, a civil engineer, billed Ola $40,000 in 1990 for consulting services rendered. In full settlement of this invoice, Hoff accepted a $15,000 cash payment plus the following:

	Fair market value	Carrying amount on Ola's books
3% limited partnership interest in Ola	$10,000	N/A
Surveying equipment	7,000	$3,000

What amount should Hoff, a cash-basis taxpayer, report in his 1990 return as income for the services rendered to Ola?
a. $15,000
b. $28,000
c. $32,000
d. $40,000

2M90#24. Dale's distributive share of income from the calendar-year partnership of Dale & Eck was $50,000 in 1989. On December 15, 1989, Dale, who is a cash-basis taxpayer, received a $27,000 distribution of the partnership's 1989 income, with the $23,000 balance paid to Dale in May 1990. In addition, Dale received a $10,000 interest-free loan from the partnership in 1989. This $10,000 is to be offset against Dale's share of 1990 partnership income. What total amount of partnership income is taxable to Dale in 1989?
a. $27,000
b. $37,000
c. $50,000
d. $60,000

C. Partnership and Partner Elections

R96#3. Basic Partnership, a cash-basis calendar year entity, began business on February 1, 1995. Basic incurred and paid the following in 1995:

Filing fees incident to the creation of the partnership	$ 3,600
Accounting fees to prepare the representations in offering materials	12,000

Basic elected to amortize costs. What was the maximum amount that Basic could deduct on the 1995 partnership return?

a. $11,000
b. $ 3,300
c. $ 2,860
d. $ 660

D. Partner Dealing With Own Partnership

M95#29. A guaranteed payment by a partnership to a partner for services rendered, may include an agreement to pay

I. A salary of $5,000 monthly without regard to partnership income.
II. A 25 percent interest in partnership profits.

a. I only.
b. II only.
c. Both I and II.
d. Neither I nor II.

M94#29. Guaranteed payments made by a partnership to partners for services rendered to the partnership, that are deductible business expenses under the Internal Revenue Code, are

I. Deductible expenses on the U.S. Partnership Return of Income, Form 1065, in order to arrive at partnership income (loss).
II. Included on schedules K-1 to be taxed as ordinary income to the partners.

a. I only.
b. II only.
c. Both I and II.
d. Neither I nor II.

2M91#59. Under the Internal Revenue Code sections pertaining to partnerships, guaranteed payments are payments to partners for
a. Payments of principal on secured notes honored at maturity.
b. Timely payments of periodic interest on bona fide loans that are **not** treated as partners' capital.
c. Services or the use of capital without regard to partnership income.
d. Sales of partners' assets to the partnership at guaranteed amounts regardless of market values.

E. Treatment of Partnership Liabilities

R98#5. On January 1, 1997, Kane was a 25% equal partner in Maze General Partnership, which had partnership liabilities of $300,000. On January 2, 1997, a new partner was admitted and Kane's interest was reduced to 20%. On April 1, 1997, Maze repaid a $100,000 general partnership loan. Ignoring any income, loss, or distributions for 1997, what was the *net* effect of the two transactions on Kane's tax basis in Maze partnership interest?

a. Has **no** effect.
b. Decrease of $20,000.
c. Increase of $15,000.
d. Decrease of $75,000.

N95#30. On January 4, 1994, Smith and White contributed $4,000 and $6,000 in cash, respectively, and formed the Macro General Partnership. The partnership agreement allocated profits and losses 40% to Smith and 60% to White. In 1994, Macro purchased property from an unrelated seller for $10,000 cash and a $40,000 mortgage note that was the general liability of the partnership. Macro's liability
a. Increases Smith's partnership basis by $16,000.
b. Increases Smith's partnership basis by $20,000.
c. Increases Smith's partnership basis by $24,000.
d. Has **no** effect on Smith's partnership basis.

2N93#54. When a partner's share of partnership liabilities increases, that partner's basis in the partnership
a. Increases by the partner's share of the increase.
b. Decreases by the partner's share of the increase.
c. Decreases, but **not** to less than zero.
d. Is **not** affected.

2M91#60. Beck and Nilo are equal partners in B&N Associates, a general partnership. B&N borrowed $10,000 from a bank on an unsecured note, thereby increasing each partner's share of partnership liabilities. As a result of this loan, the basis of each partner's interest in B&N was
a. Increased.
b. Decreased.
c. Unaffected.
d. Dependent on each partner's ability to meet the obligation if called upon to do so.

F. Distribution of Partnership Assets

N95#31. Hart's adjusted basis in Best Partnership was $9,000 at the time he received the following nonliquidating distributions of partnership property:

Cash	$ 5,000
Land	
Adjusted basis	7,000
Fair market value	10,000

What was the amount of Hart's basis in the land?
a. $0
b. $ 4,000
c. $ 7,000
d. $10,000

N95#32. Stone's basis in Ace Partnership was $70,000 at the time he received a nonliquidating distribution of partnership capital assets. These capital assets had an adjusted basis of $65,000 to Ace, and a fair market value of $83,000. Ace had no unrealized receivables, appreciated inventory, or properties which had been contributed by its partners. What was Stone's recognized gain or loss on the distribution?

a. $18,000 ordinary income.
b. $13,000 capital gain.
c. $ 5,000 capital loss.
d. $0.

M95#30. Curry's adjusted basis in Vantage Partnership was $5,000 at the time he received a nonliquidating distribution of land. The land had an adjusted basis of $6,000 and a fair market value of $9,000 to Vantage. What was the amount of Curry's basis in the land?
a. $9,000
b. $6,000
c. $5,000
d. $1,000

M94#31. Day's adjusted basis in LMN Partnership interest is $50,000. During the year Day received a nonliquidating distribution of $25,000 cash plus land with an adjusted basis of $15,000 to LMN, and a fair market value of $20,000. How much is Day's basis in the land?
a. $10,000
b. $15,000
c. $20,000
d. $25,000

2N93
Items 55 and 56 are based on the following:

The adjusted basis of Jody's partnership interest was $50,000 immediately before Jody received a current distribution of $20,000 cash and property with an adjusted basis to the partnership of $40,000 and a fair market value of $35,000.

55. What amount of taxable gain must Jody report as a result of this distribution?
a. $0
b. $ 5,000
c. $10,000
d. $20,000

56. What is Jody's basis in the distributed property?
a. $0
b. $30,000
c. $35,000
d. $40,000

2N93#57. The adjusted basis of Vance's partnership interest in Lex Associates was $180,000 immediately before receiving the following distribution in complete liquidation of Lex:

	Basis to Lex	Fair market value
Cash	$100,000	$100,000
Real estate	70,000	96,000

What is Vance's basis in the real estate?
a. $96,000
b. $83,000
c. $80,000
d. $70,000

2N91#54. The basis to a partner of property distributed "in kind" in complete liquidation of the partner's interest is the
   a. Adjusted basis of the partner's interest increased by any cash distributed to the partner in the same transaction.
   b. Adjusted basis of the partner's interest reduced by any cash distributed to the partner in the same transaction.
   c. Adjusted basis of the property to the partnership.
   d. Fair market value of the property.

2M90#26. Hart's adjusted basis of his interest in a partnership was $30,000. He received a nonliquidating distribution of $24,000 cash plus a parcel of land with a fair market value and partnership basis of $9,000. Hart's basis for the land is
   a. $9,000
   b. $6,000
   c. $3,000
   d. $0

G. Termination of Partnership

R97#8. Under which of the following circumstances is a partnership that is **not** an electing large partnership considered terminated for income tax purposes?

I. Fifty-five percent of the total interest in partnership capital and profits is sold within a 12-month period.
II. The partnership's business and financial operations are discontinued.

   a. I only.
   b. II only.
   c. Both I and II.
   d. Neither I nor II.

N95#33. On January 3, 1994, the partners' interests in the capital, profits, and losses of Able Partnership were:

	% of capital, profits and losses
Dean	25%
Poe	30%
Ritt	45%

On February 4, 1994, Poe sold her entire interest to an unrelated party. Dean sold his 25% interest in Able to another unrelated party on December 20, 1994. No other transactions took place in 1994. For tax purposes, which of the following statements is correct with respect to Able?
   a. Able terminated as of February 4, 1994.
   b. Able terminated as of December 20, 1994.
   c. Able terminated as of December 31, 1994.
   d. Able did **not** terminate.

N95#34. Curry's sale of her partnership interest causes a partnership termination. The partnership's business and financial operations are continued by the other members. What is(are) the effect(s) of the termination?

I. There is a deemed distribution of assets to the remaining partners and the purchaser.
II. There is a hypothetical recontribution of assets to a new partnership.

   a. I only.
   b. II only.
   c. Both I and II.
   d. Neither I nor II.

2N93#58. Cobb, Danver, and Evans each owned a one-third interest in the capital and profits of their calendar-year partnership. On September 18, 1991, Cobb and Danver sold their partnership interests to Frank, and immediately withdrew from all participation in the partnership. On March 15, 1992, Cobb and Danver received full payment from Frank for the sale of their partnership interests. For tax purposes, the partnership
   a. Terminated on September 18, 1991.
   b. Terminated on December 31, 1991.
   c. Terminated on March 15, 1992.
   d. Did **not** terminate.

2N93#59. On December 31, 1992, after receipt of his share of partnership income, Clark sold his interest in a limited partnership for $30,000 cash and relief of all liabilities. On that date, the adjusted basis of Clark's partnership interest was $40,000, consisting of his capital account of $15,000 and his share of the partnership liabilities of $25,000. The partnership has no unrealized receivables or substantially appreciated inventory. What is Clark's gain or loss on the sale of his partnership interest?
   a. Ordinary loss of $10,000.
   b. Ordinary gain of $15,000.
   c. Capital loss of $10,000.
   d. Capital gain of $15,000.

2N93#60. On June 30, 1993, Berk retired from his partnership. At that time, his capital account was $50,000 and his share of the partnership's liabilities was $30,000. Berk's retirement payments consisted of being relieved of his share of the partnership liabilities and receipt of cash payments of $5,000 per month for 18 months, commencing July 1, 1993. Assuming Berk makes **no** election with regard to the recognition of gain from the retirement payments, he should report income therefrom of

	1993	1994
a.	$13,333	$26,667
b.	20,000	20,000
c.	40,000	—
d.	—	40,000

2M90#21. Partnership Abel, Benz, Clark & Day is in the real estate and insurance business. Abel owns a 40% interest in the capital and profits of the partnership, while Benz, Clark, and Day each owns a 20% interest. All use a calendar year. At November 1, 1989, the real estate

and insurance business is separated, and two partnerships are formed: Partnership Abel & Benz takes over the real estate business, and Partnership Clark & Day takes over the insurance business. Which one of the following statements is correct for tax purposes?
- a. Partnership Abel & Benz is considered to be a continuation of Partnership Abel, Benz, Clark & Day.
- b. In forming Partnership Clark & Day, partners Clark and Day are subject to a penalty surtax if they contribute their entire distributions from Partnership Abel, Benz, Clark & Day.
- c. Before separating the two businesses into two distinct entities, the partners must obtain approval from the IRS.
- d. Before separating the two businesses into two distinct entities, Partnership Abel, Benz, Clark & Day must file a formal dissolution with the IRS on the prescribed form.

2M90
Items 22 and 23 are based on the following:

The personal service partnership of Allen, Baker & Carr had the following cash basis balance sheet at December 31, 1989:

Assets

	Adjusted basis per books	Market value
Cash	$102,000	$102,000
Unrealized accounts receivable	—	420,000
Totals	$102,000	$522,000

Liability and Capital

Note payable	$ 60,000	$ 60,000
Capital accounts:		
Allen	14,000	154,000
Baker	14,000	154,000
Carr	14,000	154,000
Totals	$102,000	$522,000

Carr, an equal partner, sold his partnership interest to Dole, an outsider, for $154,000 cash on January 1, 1990. In addition, Dole assumed Carr's share of the partnership's liability.

22. What was the total amount realized by Carr on the sale of his partnership interest?
- a. $174,000
- b. $154,000
- c. $140,000
- d. $134,000

23. What amount of ordinary income should Carr report in his 1990 income tax return on the sale of his partnership interest?
- a. $0
- b. $ 20,000
- c. $ 34,000
- d. $140,000

2N89#55. The following information pertains to Carr's admission to the Smith & Jones partnership on July 1, 1988:

Carr's contribution of capital: 800 shares of Ed Corp. stock bought in 1975 for $30,000; fair market value $150,000 on July 1, 1988.

Carr's interest in capital and profits of Smith & Jones: 25%.

Fair market value of net assets of Smith & Jones on July 1, 1988 after Carr's admission: $600,000.

Carr's gain in 1988 on the exchange of the Ed stock for Carr's partnership interest was
- a. $120,000 ordinary income.
- b. $120,000 long-term capital gain.
- c. $120,000 Section 1231 gain.
- d. $0.

IV. Federal Taxation — Estates and Trusts, Exempt Organizations, and Preparers' Responsibilities

A. Estates and Trusts

R98#6. Gem Trust, a simple trust, reported the following items of income and expenses during 1997:

Interest income from corporate bonds	$4,000
Taxable dividend income	2,000
Trustee fees allocable to income	1,500

What is Gem's 1997 distributable net income (DNI)?
- a. $6,000
- b. $4,500
- c. $2,500
- d. $ 500

R97#9. Under the provisions of a decedent's will, the following cash disbursements were made by the estate's executor:

I. A charitable bequest to the American Red Cross.
II. Payment of the decedent's funeral expenses.

What deduction(s) is(are) allowable in determining the decedent's taxable estate?
- a. I only.
- b. II only.
- c. Both I and II.
- d. Neither I nor II.

Selected Questions

N95#36. Steve and Kay Briar, U.S. citizens, were married for the entire 1994 calendar year. In 1994, Steve gave a $30,000 cash gift to his sister. The Briars made no other gifts in 1994. They each signed a timely election to treat the $30,000 gift as made one-half by each spouse. Disregarding the unified credit and estate tax consequences, what amount of the 1994 gift is taxable to the Briars?
    a. $30,000
    b. $20,000
    c. $10,000
    d. $0

M95#31. Lyon, a cash basis taxpayer, died on January 15, 1994. In 1994, the estate executor made the required periodic distribution of $9,000 from estate income to Lyon's sole heir. The following pertains to the estate's income and disbursements in 1994:

1994 Estate Income

$20,000	Taxable interest
10,000	Net long-term capital gains allocable to corpus

1994 Estate Disbursements

$5,000	Administrative expenses attributable to taxable income

For the 1994 calendar year, what was the estate's distributable net income (DNI)?
    a. $15,000
    b. $20,000
    c. $25,000
    d. $30,000

M95#33. A distribution from estate income, that was *currently* required, was made to the estate's sole beneficiary during its calendar year. The maximum amount of the distribution to be included in the beneficiary's gross income is limited to the estate's
    a. Capital gain income.
    b. Ordinary gross income.
    c. Distributable net income.
    d. Net investment income.

N94#56. Bell, a cash basis calendar year taxpayer, died on June 1, 1993. In 1993, prior to her death, Bell incurred $2,000 in medical expenses. The executor of the estate paid the medical expenses, which were a claim against the estate, on July 1, 1993. If the executor files the appropriate waiver, the medical expenses are deductible on
    a. The estate tax return.
    b. Bell's final income tax return.
    c. The estate income tax return.
    d. The executor's income tax return.

N94#58. If the executor of a decedent's estate elects the alternate valuation date and none of the property included in the gross estate has been sold or distributed, the estate assets must be valued as of how many months after the decedent's death?
    a. 12
    b. 9
    c. 6
    d. 3

M94#33. In 1993, Sayers, who is single, gave an outright gift of $50,000 to a friend, Johnson, who needed the money to pay medical expenses. In filing the 1993 gift tax return, Sayers was entitled to a maximum exclusion of
    a. $0
    b. $ 3,000
    c. $10,000
    d. $20,000

2N93#39. What amount of a decedent's taxable estate is effectively tax-free if the maximum unified estate and gift credit is taken?
    a. $0
    b. $ 10,000
    c. $192,800
    d. $600,000

2N93#40. Which of the following is(are) deductible from a decedent's gross estate?

  I. Expenses of administering and settling the estate.
 II. State inheritance or estate tax.

    a. I only.
    b. II only.
    c. Both I and II.
    d. Neither I nor II.

2N91#23. The federal estate tax may be reduced by a credit for state
    a. Death taxes.
    b. Gift taxes on gifts made two years before death.
    c. Income taxes paid in the year of death.
    d. Intangible property taxes.

2N91#25. Which of the following fiduciary entities are required to use the calendar year as their taxable period for income tax purposes?

	Estates	Trusts (except those that are tax-exempt)
a.	Yes	Yes
b.	No	No
c.	Yes	No
d.	No	Yes

2N91#26. During 1990, Blake transferred a corporate bond with a face amount and fair market value of $20,000 to a trust for the benefit of her 16-year-old child. Annual interest on this bond is $2,000, which is to be accumulated in the trust and distributed to the child on reaching the age of 21. The bond is then to be distributed to the donor or her successor-in-interest in liquidation of the trust. Present value of the total interest to be received by the child is $8,710. The amount of the gift that is excludable from taxable gifts is

a. $20,000
b. $10,000
c. $ 8,710
d. $0

2N91#37. Under the unified rate schedule,
a. Lifetime taxable gifts are taxed on a noncumulative basis.
b. Transfers at death are taxed on a noncumulative basis.
c. Lifetime taxable gifts and transfers at death are taxed on a cumulative basis.
d. The gift tax rates are 5% higher than the estate tax rates.

2N91#38. The generation-skipping transfer tax is imposed
a. Instead of the gift tax.
b. Instead of the estate tax.
c. As a separate tax in addition to the gift and estate taxes.
d. On transfers of future interest to beneficiaries who are more than one generation above the donor's generation.

2N91#39. Ordinary and necessary administration expenses paid by the fiduciary of an estate are deductible
a. Only on the fiduciary income tax return (Form 1041) and never on the federal estate tax return (Form 706).
b. Only on the federal estate tax return and never on the fiduciary income tax return.
c. On the fiduciary income tax return only if the estate tax deduction is waived for these expenses.
d. On both the fiduciary income tax return and on the estate tax return by adding a tax computed on the proportionate rates attributable to both returns.

2N91#40. Which of the following requires filing a gift tax return, if the transfer exceeds the available annual gift tax exclusion?
a. Medical expenses paid directly to a physician on behalf of an individual unrelated to the donor.
b. Tuition paid directly to an accredited university on behalf of an individual unrelated to the donor.
c. Payments for college books, supplies, and dormitory fees on behalf of an individual unrelated to the donor.
d. Campaign expenses paid to a political organization.

2M91#35. Fred and Amy Kehl, both U.S. citizens, are married. All of their real and personal property is owned by them as tenants by the entirety or as joint tenants with right of survivorship. The gross estate of the first spouse to die

a. Includes 50% of the value of all property owned by the couple, regardless of which spouse furnished the original consideration.
b. Includes only the property that had been acquired with the funds of the deceased spouse.
c. Is governed by the federal statutory provisions relating to jointly held property, rather than by the decedent's interest in community property vested by state law, if the Kehls reside in a community property state.
d. Includes one-third of the value of all real estate owned by the Kehls, as the dower right in the case of the wife or curtesy right in the case of the husband.

2M91#36. In connection with a "buy-sell" agreement funded by a cross-purchase insurance arrangement, business associate Adam bought a policy on Burr's life to finance the purchase of Burr's interest. Adam, the beneficiary, paid the premiums and retained all incidents of ownership. On the death of Burr, the insurance proceeds will be
a. Includible in Burr's gross estate, if Burr owns 50% or more of the stock of the corporation.
b. Includible in Burr's gross estate only if Burr had purchased a similar policy on Adam's life at the same time and for the same purpose.
c. Includible in Burr's gross estate, if Adam has the right to veto Burr's power to borrow on the policy that Burr owns on Adam's life.
d. Excludible from Burr's gross estate.

2M91#38. The charitable contribution deduction on an estate's fiduciary income tax return is allowable
a. If the decedent died intestate.
b. To the extent of the same adjusted gross income limitation as that on an individual income tax return.
c. Only if the decedent's will specifically provides for the contribution.
d. Subject to the 2% threshold on miscellaneous itemized deductions.

2M91#39. Raff died in 1989 leaving her entire estate to her only child. Raff's will gave full discretion to the estate's executor with regard to distributions of income. For 1990, the estate's distributable net income was $15,000, of which $9,000 was paid to the beneficiary. None of the income was tax exempt. What amount can be claimed on the estate's 1990 fiduciary income tax return for the distributions deduction?
a. $0
b. $ 6,000
c. $ 9,000
d. $15,000

2M91#40. On July 1, 1989, Vega made a transfer by gift in an amount sufficient to require the filing of a gift tax return. Vega was still alive in 1990. If Vega did **not** request an extension of time for filing the 1989 gift tax return, the due date for filing was

a. March 15, 1990.
b. April 15, 1990.
c. June 15, 1990.
d. June 30, 1990.

2N90#35. Jan, an unmarried individual, gave the following outright gifts in 1989:

Donee	Amount	Use by donee
Jones	$15,000	Downpayment on house
Craig	12,000	College tuition
Kande	5,000	Vacation trip

Jan's 1989 exclusions for gift tax purposes should total
   a. $27,000
   b. $25,000
   c. $20,000
   d. $ 9,000

2N90#36. When Jim and Nina became engaged in April 1989, Jim gave Nina a ring that had a fair market value of $50,000. After their wedding in July 1989, Jim gave Nina $75,000 in cash so that Nina could have her own bank account. Both Jim and Nina are U.S. citizens. What was the amount of Jim's 1989 marital deduction?
   a. $0
   b. $ 75,000
   c. $115,000
   d. $125,000

2N90#37. Following are the fair market values of Wald's assets at the date of death:

Personal effects and jewelry	$150,000
Land bought by Wald with Wald's funds five years prior to death and held with Wald's sister as joint tenants with right of survivorship	800,000

The executor of Wald's estate did not elect the alternate valuation date. The amount includible as Wald's gross estate in the federal estate tax return is
   a. $150,000
   b. $550,000
   c. $800,000
   d. $950,000

2N90#39. Income in respect of a cash basis decedent
   a. Covers income earned before the taxpayer's death but **not** collected until after death.
   b. Receives a stepped-up basis in the decedent's estate.
   c. Must be included in the decedent's final income tax return.
   d. Cannot receive capital gain treatment.

2N90#40. Which one of the following is a valid deduction from a decedent's gross estate?
   a. Expenses of administering and settling the estate.
   b. State inheritance tax.
   c. Income tax paid on income earned and received after the decedent's death.
   d. Federal estate tax.

2M89#58. If an individual donor makes a gift of future interest whereby the donee is to receive possession of the gift at some future time, the annual exclusion for gift tax purposes is
   a. $0
   b. $ 3,000
   c. $ 5,000
   d. $10,000

B. Exempt Organizations

R97#10. Maple Avenue Assembly, a tax-exempt religious organization, operates an outreach program for the poor in its community. A candidate for the local city council has endorsed Maple's anti-poverty program. Which of the following activities is(are) consistent with Maple's tax-exempt status?

I. Endorsing the candidate to members.
II. Collecting contributions from members for the candidate.

   a. I only.
   b. II only.
   c. Both I and II.
   d. Neither I nor II.

N95#37. The organizational test to qualify a public service charitable entity as tax exempt requires the articles of organization to

I. Limit the purpose of the entity to the charitable purpose.
II. State that an information return should be filed annually with the Internal Revenue Service.

   a. I only.
   b. II only.
   c. Both I and II.
   d. Neither I nor II.

N95#38. Which of the following activities regularly conducted by a tax exempt organization will result in unrelated business income?

I. Selling articles made by handicapped persons as part of their rehabilitation, when the organization is involved exclusively in their rehabilitation.
II. Operating a grocery store almost fully staffed by emotionally handicapped persons as part of a therapeutic program.

   a. I only.
   b. II only.
   c. Both I and II.
   d. Neither I nor II.

M95#34. The private foundation status of an exempt organization will terminate if it
a. Becomes a public charity.
b. Is a foreign corporation.
c. Does **not** distribute all of its net assets to one or more public charities.
d. Is governed by a charter that limits the organization's exempt purposes.

M95#35. Which of the following exempt organizations must file annual information returns?
a. Churches.
b. Internally supported auxiliaries of churches.
c. Private foundations.
d. Those with gross receipts of less than $5,000 in each taxable year.

N94#59. An organization that operates for the prevention of cruelty to animals will fail to meet the operational test to qualify as an exempt organization if

	The organization engages in insubstantial nonexempt activities	The organization directly participates in any political campaign
a.	Yes	Yes
b.	Yes	No
c.	No	Yes
d.	No	No

N94#60. Which one of the following statements is correct with regard to unrelated business income of an exempt organization?
a. An exempt organization that earns any unrelated business income in excess of $100,000 during a particular year will lose its exempt status for that particular year.
b. An exempt organization is not taxed on unrelated business income of less than $1,000.
c. The tax on unrelated business income can be imposed even if the unrelated business activity is intermittent and is carried on once a year.
d. An unrelated trade or business activity that results in a loss is excluded from the definition of unrelated business.

M94#34. To qualify as an exempt organization other than a church or an employees' qualified pension or profit-sharing trust, the applicant
a. Cannot operate under the "lodge system" under which payments are made to its members for sick benefits.
b. Need **not** be specifically identified as one of the classes on which exemption is conferred by the Internal Revenue Code, provided that the organization's purposes and activities are of a nonprofit nature.
c. Is barred from incorporating and issuing capital stock.
d. Must file a written application with the Internal Revenue Service.

M94#35. Which of the following activities regularly carried out by an exempt organization will **not** result in unrelated business income?
a. The sale of laundry services by an exempt hospital to other hospitals.
b. The sale of heavy duty appliances to senior citizens by an exempt senior citizen's center.
c. Accounting and tax services performed by a local chapter of a labor union for its members.
d. The sale by a trade association of publications used as course materials for the association's seminars which are oriented towards its members.

2N93#47. Which of the following statements is correct regarding the unrelated business income of exempt organizations?
a. If an exempt organization has any unrelated business income, it may result in the loss of the organization's exempt status.
b. Unrelated business income relates to the performance of services, but **not** to the sale of goods.
c. An unrelated business does **not** include any activity where all the work is performed for the organization by unpaid volunteers.
d. Unrelated business income tax will **not** be imposed if profits from the unrelated business are used to support the exempt organization's charitable activities.

2M93#58. If an exempt organization is a corporation, the tax on unrelated business taxable income is
a. Computed at corporate income tax rates.
b. Computed at rates applicable to trusts.
c. Credited against the tax on recognized capital gains.
d. Abated.

2M93#60. During 1992, Help, Inc., an exempt organization, derived income of $15,000 from conducting bingo games. Conducting bingo games is legal in Help's locality and is confined to exempt organizations in Help's state. Which of the following statements is true regarding this income?
a. The entire $15,000 is subject to tax at a lower rate than the corporate income tax rate.
b. The entire $15,000 is exempt from tax on unrelated business income.
c. Only the first $5,000 is exempt from tax on unrelated business income.
d. Since Help has unrelated business income, Help automatically forfeits its exempt status for 1992.

2M90#38. An incorporated exempt organization subject to tax on its 1989 unrelated business income
a. Must make estimated tax payments if its tax can reasonably be expected to be $100 or more.
b. Must comply with the Code provisions regarding installment payments of estimated income tax by corporations.

c. Must pay at least 70% of the tax due as shown on the return when filed, with the balance of tax payable in the following quarter.
d. May defer payment of the tax for up to nine months following the due date of the return.

2M90#40. To qualify as an exempt organization, the applicant
a. May be organized and operated for the primary purpose of carrying on a business for profit, provided that all of the organization's net earnings are turned over to one or more tax exempt organizations.
b. Need **not** be specifically identified as one of the classes upon which exemption is conferred by the Internal Revenue Code, provided that the organization's purposes and activities are of a nonprofit nature.
c. Must **not** be classified as a social club.
d. Must **not** be a private foundation organized and operated exclusively to influence legislation pertaining to protection of the environment.

C. Preparers' Responsibilities

R97#11. Morgan, a sole practitioner CPA, prepares individual and corporate income tax returns. What documentation is Morgan required to retain concerning each return prepared?
a. An unrelated party compliance statement.
b. Taxpayer's name and identification number or a copy of the tax return.
c. Workpapers associated with the preparation of each tax return.
d. A power of attorney.

N94#55. A tax return preparer is subject to a penalty for knowingly or recklessly disclosing corporate tax return information, if the disclosure is made
a. To enable a third party to solicit business from the taxpayer.
b. To enable the tax processor to electronically compute the taxpayer's liability.
c. For peer review.
d. Under an administrative order by a state agency that registers tax return preparers.

M94#19. A tax return preparer may disclose or use tax return information without the taxpayer's consent to
a. Facilitate a supplier's or lender's credit evaluation of the taxpayer.
b. Accommodate the request of a financial institution that needs to determine the amount of taxpayer's debt to it, to be forgiven.
c. Be evaluated by a quality or peer review.
d. Solicit additional nontax business.

M94#20. Which, if any, of the following could result in penalties against an income tax return preparer?

I. Knowing or reckless disclosure or use of tax information obtained in preparing a return.
II. A willful attempt to understate any client's tax liability on a return or claim for refund.

a. Neither I nor II.
b. I only.
c. II only.
d. Both I and II.

V. Accounting for Governmental and Not-for-Profit Organizations

A. Governmental Entities

R97#12. Receipts from a special tax levy to retire and pay interest on general obligation bonds should be recorded in which fund?
a. General.
b. Capital projects.
c. Debt service.
d. Special revenue.

R97#13. South City School District has a separately elected governing body that administers the public school system. The district's budget is subject to the approval of the city council. The district's financial activity should be reported in the City's financial statements by
a. Blending only.
b. Discrete presentation.
c. Inclusion as a footnote only.
d. Either blending or inclusion as a footnote.

R97#14. Marta City's school district is a legally separate entity, but two of its seven board members are also city council members and the district is financially dependent upon the city. The school district should be reported as a
a. Blended unit.
b. Discrete presentation.
c. Note disclosure.
d. Primary government.

R96#4. The measurement focus of governmental-type funds is on the determination of

	Flow of financial resources	Financial position
a.	Yes	No
b.	No	Yes
c.	No	No
d.	Yes	Yes

R96#12. Which of the following journal entries should a city use to record $250,000 for fire department salaries and wages incurred during the month of May?

	Dr.	Cr.
a. Salaries and wages expense	$250,000	
Appropriations		$250,000
b. Salaries and wages expense	$250,000	
Encumbrances		$250,000
c. Encumbrances	$250,000	
Salaries payable		$250,000
d. Expenditures—salaries and wages	$250,000	
Salaries payable		$250,000

N95#62. What is the basic criterion used to determine the reporting entity for a governmental unit?
   a. Special financing arrangement.
   b. Geographic boundaries.
   c. Scope of public services.
   d. Financial accountability.

N95#64. Fish Road property owners in Sea County are responsible for special assessment debt that arose from a storm sewer project. If the property owners default, Sea has no obligation regarding debt service, although it does bill property owners for assessments and uses the monies it collects to pay debt holders. What fund type should Sea use to account for these collection and servicing activities?
   a. Agency.
   b. Debt service.
   c. Expendable trust funds.
   d. Capital projects.

N95#65. The revenues control account of a governmental unit is increased when
   a. The encumbrance account is decreased.
   b. Appropriations are recorded.
   c. Property taxes are recorded.
   d. The budget is recorded.

N95#66. Tuston Township issued the following bonds during the year ended June 30, 1995:

Bonds issued for the garbage collection enterprise fund that will service the debt	$700,000
Revenue bonds to be repaid from admission fees collected by the Township zoo enterprise fund	500,000

What amount of these bonds should be accounted for in Tuston's general long-term debt account group?
   a. $1,200,000
   b. $ 700,000
   c. $ 500,000
   d. $0

N95#67. Frome City signed a 20-year office property lease for its general staff. Frome could terminate the lease at any time after giving one year's notice, but termination is considered a remote possibility. The lease meets the criteria for a capital lease. What is the effect of the lease on the asset amount in Frome's general fixed assets account group and the liability amount in Frome's general long-term debt account group?

	Asset amount	Liability amount
a.	Increase	Increase
b.	Increase	No effect
c.	No effect	Increase
d.	No effect	No effect

N95#71. Which account should Spring Township credit when it issues a purchase order for supplies?
   a. Appropriations control.
   b. Vouchers payable.
   c. Encumbrance control.
   d. Reserve for encumbrances.

N95#72. The estimated revenues control account of a governmental unit is debited when
   a. Actual revenues are recorded.
   b. Actual revenues are collected.
   c. The budget is recorded.
   d. The budget is closed at the end of the year.

M95#51. For governmental fund types, which item is considered the primary measurement focus?
   a. Income determination.
   b. Flows and balances of financial resources.
   c. Capital maintenance.
   d. Cash flows and balances.

M95#52. Governmental financial reporting should provide information to assist users in which situation(s)?

I. Making social and political decisions.
II. Assessing whether current-year citizens received services but shifted part of the payment burden to future-year citizens.

   a. I only.
   b. II only.
   c. Both I and II.
   d. Neither I nor II.

M95#53. In preparing combined financial statements for a governmental entity, interfund receivables and payables should be
   a. Reported as reservations of fund balance.
   b. Reported as additions to or reductions from the unrestricted fund balance.
   c. Reported as amounts due to and due from other funds.
   d. Eliminated.

M95#54. The expenditure element "salaries and wages" is an example of which type of classification?

a. Object.
b. Program.
c. Function.
d. Activity.

M95#55. Cy City's Municipal Solid Waste Landfill Enterprise Fund was established when a new landfill was opened January 3, 1994. The landfill is expected to close December 31, 2015. Cy's 1994 expenses would include a portion of which of the year 2016 expected disbursements?

I. Cost of a final cover to be applied to the landfill.
II. Cost of equipment to be installed to monitor methane gas buildup.

a. I only.
b. II only.
c. Both I and II.
d. Neither I nor II.

N94#1. The governmental fund measurement focus is on the determination of

	Income	Financial position	Flow of financial resources
a.	Yes	Yes	Yes
b.	No	Yes	No
c.	No	Yes	Yes
d.	Yes	No	Yes

N94#3. The orientation of accounting and reporting for all proprietary funds of governmental units is
a. Income determination.
b. Project.
c. Flow of funds.
d. Program.

N94#4. On what accounting basis does GASB recommend that governmental fund budgets be prepared?
a. Cash.
b. Modified cash.
c. Accrual.
d. Modified accrual.

N94#5. If a primary government's general fund has an equity interest in a joint venture, all or a portion of this equity interest should be reported in the
a. General fixed assets account group.
b. Trust fund.
c. Agency fund.
d. Internal service fund.

N94#7. Fixed assets of a governmental unit, other than those accounted for in proprietary funds or trust funds, should be accounted for in the
a. General fund.
b. Capital projects fund.
c. General long-term debt account group.
d. General fixed assets account group.

N94#8. It is inappropriate to record depreciation expense in a(an)
a. Enterprise fund.
b. Internal service fund.
c. Nonexpendable trust fund.
d. Capital projects fund.

N94#9. When a snowplow purchased by a governmental unit is received, it should be recorded in the general fund as a(an)
a. Encumbrance.
b. Expenditure.
c. Fixed Asset.
d. Appropriation.

N94#11. For which of the following funds do operating transfers affect the results of operations?

	Governmental funds	Proprietary funds
a.	No	No
b.	No	Yes
c.	Yes	Yes
d.	Yes	No

N94#12. The debt service fund of a governmental unit is used to account for the accumulation of resources for, and the payment of, principal and interest in connection with a

	Trust fund	Proprietary fund
a.	No	No
b.	No	Yes
c.	Yes	Yes
d.	Yes	No

N94#13. The portion of special assessment debt maturing in 5 years, to be repaid from general resources of the government, should be reported in the
a. General fund.
b. General long-term debt account group.
c. Agency fund.
d. Capital projects fund.

N94#16. During the year, a city's electric utility, which is operated as an enterprise fund, rendered billings for electricity supplied to the general fund. Which of the following accounts should be debited by the general fund?
a. Appropriations.
b. Expenditures.
c. Due to electric utility enterprise fund.
d. Other financing uses-operating transfers out.

N94#17. In which situation(s) should property taxes due to a governmental unit be recorded as deferred revenue?

I. Property taxes receivable are recognized in advance of the year for which they are levied.
II. Property taxes receivable are collected in advance of the year in which they are levied.

a. I only.
b. Both I and II.
c. II only.
d. Neither I nor II.

N94#19. Which of the following transactions is an expenditure of a governmental unit's general fund?
a. Contribution of enterprise fund capital by the general fund.
b. Transfer from the general fund to a capital projects fund.
c. Operating subsidy transfer from the general fund to an enterprise fund.
d. Routine employer contributions from the general fund to a pension trust fund.

N94#20. Operating transfers received by a governmental-type fund should be reported in the Statement of Revenues, Expenditures, and Changes in Fund Balance as a(an)
a. Addition to contributed capital.
b. Addition to retained earnings.
c. Other financing source.
d. Reimbursement.

N94#21. The following transactions were among those reported by Corfe City's electric utility enterprise fund for 1993:

Capital contributed by subdividers	$ 900,000
Cash received from customer households	2,700,000
Proceeds from sale of revenue bonds	4,500,000

In the electric utility enterprise fund's statement of cash flows for the year ended December 31, 1993, what amount should be reported as cash flows from capital and related financing activities?
a. $4,500,000
b. $5,400,000
c. $7,200,000
d. $8,100,000

N94#23. Deferred compensation plans, for other than proprietary fund employees, adopted under IRC Sec. 457 should be reported in a(an)
a. Governmental fund.
b. Agency fund.
c. Trust fund.
d. Account group.

N94#25. Which type of fund can be either nonexpendable or expendable?
a. Trust fund.
b. Special revenue fund.
c. Enterprise fund.
d. Debt service fund.

M94#52. For which of the following governmental entities that use proprietary fund accounting should a statement of cash flows be presented?

	Public benefit corporations	Governmental utilities
a.	No	No
b.	No	Yes
c.	Yes	Yes
d.	Yes	No

M94#57. Taxes collected and held by Franklin County for a separate school district would be accounted for in which fund?
a. Special revenue.
b. Internal service.
c. Trust.
d. Agency.

TN93#51. The encumbrance account of a governmental unit is debited when
a. The budget is recorded.
b. A purchase order is approved.
c. Goods are received.
d. A voucher payable is recorded.

TN93#52. A budgetary fund balance reserved for encumbrances in excess of a balance of encumbrances indicates
a. An excess of vouchers payable over encumbrances.
b. An excess of purchase orders over invoices received.
c. An excess of appropriations over encumbrances.
d. A recording error.

TN93#53. Which of the following accounts of a governmental unit is credited when taxpayers are billed for property taxes?
a. Appropriations.
b. Taxes receivable—current.
c. Estimated revenues.
d. Revenues.

TN93#54. Which of the following funds of a governmental unit uses the modified accrual basis of accounting?
a. Internal service funds.
b. Enterprise funds.
c. Special revenue funds.
d. Nonexpendable trust funds.

2N93#3. For the budgetary year ending December 31, 1993, Maple City's general fund expects the following inflows of resources:

Property taxes, licenses, and fines	$9,000,000
Proceeds of debt issue	5,000,000
Interfund transfers for debt service	1,000,000

In the budgetary entry, what amount should Maple record for estimated revenues?
a. $ 9,000,000
b. $10,000,000
c. $14,000,000
d. $15,000,000

Selected Questions

2N93#4. During its fiscal year ended June 30, 1993, Cliff City issued purchase orders totaling $5,000,000, which were properly charged to encumbrances at that time. Cliff received goods and related invoices at the encumbered amounts totaling $4,500,000 before year end. The remaining goods of $500,000 were not received until after year end. Cliff paid $4,200,000 of the invoices received during the year. What amount of Cliff's encumbrances were outstanding at June 30, 1993?
- a. $0
- b. $300,000
- c. $500,000
- d. $800,000

2N93#5. Elm City issued a purchase order for supplies with an estimated cost of $5,000. When the supplies were received, the accompanying invoice indicated an actual price of $4,950. What amount should Elm debit (credit) to the reserve for encumbrances after the supplies and invoice were received?
- a. ($ 50)
- b. $ 50
- c. $4,950
- d. $5,000

2N93#6. Wood City, which is legally obligated to maintain a debt service fund, issued the following general obligation bonds on July 1, 1992:

Term of bonds	10 years
Face amount	$1,000,000
Issue price	101
Stated interest rate	6%

Interest is payable January 1 and July 1. What amount of bond premium should be amortized in Wood's debt service fund for the year ended December 31, 1992?
- a. $1,000
- b. $ 500
- c. $ 250
- d. $0

2N93#8. Cal City maintains several major fund types. The following were among Cal's cash receipts during 1993:

Unrestricted state grant	$1,000,000
Interest on bank accounts held for employees' pension plan	200,000

What amount of these cash receipts should be accounted for in Cal's general fund?
- a. $1,200,000
- b. $1,000,000
- c. $ 200,000
- d. $0

2N93#9. The following information pertains to Grove City's interfund receivables and payables at December 31, 1992:

Due to special revenue fund from general fund	$10,000
Due to agency fund from special revenue fund	4,000

In Grove's special revenue fund balance sheet at December 31, 1992, how should these interfund amounts be reported?
- a. As an asset of $6,000.
- b. As a liability of $6,000.
- c. As an asset of $4,000 and a liability of $10,000.
- d. As an asset of $10,000 and a liability of $4,000.

2N93#11. Financing for the renovation of Fir City's municipal park, begun and completed during 1992, came from the following sources:

Grant from state government	$400,000
Proceeds from general obligation bond issue	500,000
Transfer from Fir's general fund	100,000

In its 1992 capital projects fund operating statement, Fir should report these amounts as

	Revenues	Other financing sources
a.	$1,000,000	$0
b.	$ 900,000	$ 100,000
c.	$ 400,000	$ 600,000
d.	$0	$1,000,000

2N93#13. Through an internal service fund, New County operates a centralized data processing center to provide services to New's other governmental units. In 1992, this internal service fund billed New's parks and recreation fund $150,000 for data processing services. What account should New's internal service fund credit to record this $150,000 billing to the parks and recreation fund?
- a. Data processing department expenses.
- b. Intergovernmental transfers.
- c. Interfund exchanges.
- d. Operating revenues control.

2N93#14. Arlen City's fiduciary funds contained the following cash balances at December 31, 1992:

Under the Forfeiture Act—cash confiscated from illegal activities; disbursements can be used only for law enforcement activities	$300,000
Sales taxes collected by Arlen to be distributed to other governmental units	500,000

What amount of cash should Arlen report in its expendable trust funds at December 31, 1992?
- a. $0
- b. $300,000
- c. $500,000
- d. $800,000

AR-35

2N93#18. The following information pertains to certain monies held by Blair County at December 31, 1992, that are legally restricted to expenditures for specified purposes:

Proceeds of short-term notes to be used
for advances to expendable trust funds $ 8,000
Proceeds of long-term debt to be used
for a major capital project   90,000

What amount of these restricted monies should Blair account for in special revenue funds?
    a. $0
    b. $ 8,000
    c. $90,000
    d. $98,000

TM93#52. The estimated revenues control account balance of a governmental fund type is eliminated when
    a.   The budget is recorded.
    b.   The budgetary accounts are closed.
    c.   Appropriations are closed.
    d.   Property taxes are recorded.

TM93#53. Encumbrances outstanding at year-end in a state's general fund should be reported as a
    a.   Liability in the general fund.
    b.   Fund balance reserve in the general fund.
    c.   Liability in the general long-term debt account group.
    d.   Fund balance designation in the general fund.

TM93#54. When equipment was purchased with general fund resources, an appropriate entry was made in the general fixed asset account group. Which of the following accounts would have been increased in the general fund?
    a.   Due from general fixed asset account group.
    b.   Expenditures.
    c.   Appropriations.
    d.   No entry should be made in the general fund.

TM93#55. Which of the following funds of a governmental unit recognizes revenues in the accounting period in which they become available and measurable?

	General fund	Enterprise fund
a.	Yes	No
b.	No	Yes
c.	Yes	Yes
d.	No	No

TM93#58. Which of the following statements is correct concerning a governmental entity's combined statement of cash flows?
    a.   Cash flows from capital financing activities are reported separately from cash flows from non-capital financing activities.
    b.   The statement format is the same as that of a business enterprise's statement of cash flows.
    c.   Cash flows from operating activities may **not** be reported using the indirect method.
    d.   The statement format includes columns for the general, governmental, and proprietary fund types.

TM93#59. In a government's comprehensive annual financial report (CAFR), proprietary fund types are included in which of the following combined financial statements?

	Statement of revenues, expenditures, and changes in fund balances	Balance sheet
a.	Yes	Yes
b.	No	No
c.	No	Yes
d.	Yes	No

2M93#28. The town of Hill operates municipal electric and water utilities. In which of the following funds should the operations of the utilities be accounted for?
    a.   Enterprise fund.
    b.   Internal service fund.
    c.   Agency fund.
    d.   Special revenue fund.

2M93#32. Bay Creek's municipal motor pool maintains all city-owned vehicles and charges the various departments for the cost of rendering those services. In which of the following funds should Bay account for the cost of such maintenance?
    a.   General fund.
    b.   Internal service fund.
    c.   Special revenue fund.
    d.   Special assessment fund.

2M93#34. Central County received proceeds from various towns and cities for capital projects financed by Central's long-term debt. A special tax was assessed by each local government, and a portion of the tax was restricted to repay the long-term debt of Central's capital projects. Central should account for the restricted portion of the special tax in which of the following funds?
    a.   Internal service fund.
    b.   Enterprise fund.
    c.   Capital projects fund.
    d.   Debt service fund.

2M93#39. Stone Corp. donated investments to Pine City and stipulated that the income from the investments be used to acquire art for the city's museum. Which of the following funds should be used to account for the investments?
    a.   Endowment fund.
    b.   Special revenue fund.
    c.   Expendable trust fund.
    d.   Nonexpendable trust fund.

TN92#51. Interperiod equity is an objective of financial reporting for governmental entities. According to the

Governmental Accounting Standards Board, is interperiod equity fundamental to public administration and is it a component of accountability?

	Fundamental to public administration	Component of accountability
a.	Yes	No
b.	No	No
c.	No	Yes
d.	Yes	Yes

TN92#52. The appropriations control account of a governmental unit is debited when
- a. Supplies are purchased.
- b. Expenditures are recorded.
- c. The budgetary accounts are closed.
- d. The budget is recorded.

TN92#53. The budgetary fund balance reserved for encumbrances account of a governmental-type fund is increased when
- a. The budget is recorded.
- b. Appropriations are recorded.
- c. Supplies previously ordered are received.
- d. A purchase order is approved.

TN92#55. In what fund type should the proceeds from special assessment bonds issued to finance construction of sidewalks in a new subdivision be reported?
- a. Agency fund.
- b. Special revenue fund.
- c. Enterprise fund.
- d. Capital projects fund.

TM92#57. Under the modified accrual basis of accounting for a governmental unit, revenues that are measurable should be recognized in the accounting period in which they are
- a. Earned.
- b. Available.
- c. Budgeted.
- d. Collected.

TN92#58. River City has a defined contribution pension plan. How should River report the pension plan in its financial statements?
- a. Amortize any transition asset over the estimated number of years of current employees' service.
- b. Disclose in the notes to the financial statements the amount of the pension benefit obligation and the net assets available for benefits.
- c. Identify in the notes to financial statements the types of employees covered and the employer's and employees' obligations to contribute to the fund.
- d. Accrue a liability for benefits earned but **not** paid to fund participants.

2M92#22. Maple City's public employee retirement system (PERS) reported the following account balances at June 30, 1991:

Reserve for employer's contributions	$5,000,000
Actuarial deficiency in reserve for employer's contributions	300,000
Reserve for employees' contributions	9,000,000

Maple's PERS fund balance at June 30, 1991, should be
- a. $ 5,000,000
- b. $ 5,300,000
- c. $14,000,000
- d. $14,300,000

2M92#27. Lake County received the following proceeds that are legally restricted to expenditure for specified purposes:

Levies on affected property owners to install sidewalks	$500,000
Gasoline taxes to finance road repairs	900,000

What amount should be accounted for in Lake's special revenue funds?
- a. $1,400,000
- b. $ 900,000
- c. $ 500,000
- d. $0

2M92#28. On April 1, 1992, Oak County incurred the following expenditures in issuing long-term bonds:

Issue costs	$400,000
Debt insurance	90,000

When Oak establishes the accounting for operating debt service, what amount should be deferred and amortized over the life of the bonds?
- a. $0
- b. $ 90,000
- c. $400,000
- d. $490,000

2M92#29. At December 31, 1991, the following balances were due from the state government to Clare City's various funds:

Capital projects	$300,000
Trust and agency	100,000
Enterprise	80,000

In Clare's December 31, 1991, combined balance sheet for all fund types and account groups, what amount should be classified under governmental funds?
- a. $100,000
- b. $180,000
- c. $300,000
- d. $480,000

2M92#31. Gem City's internal service fund received a residual equity transfer of $50,000 cash from the general fund. This $50,000 transfer should be reported in Gem's internal service fund as a credit to

a. Revenues.
b. Other financing sources.
c. Accounts payable.
d. Contributed capital.

2M92#32. Glen County uses governmental fund accounting and is the administrator of a multiple-jurisdiction deferred compensation plan covering both its own employees and those of other governments participating in the plan. This plan is an eligible deferred compensation plan under the U.S. Internal Revenue Code and Income Tax Regulations. Glen has legal access to the plan's $40,000,000 in assets, comprising $2,000,000 pertaining to Glen and $38,000,000 pertaining to the other participating governments. In Glen's balance sheet, what amount should be reported in an agency fund for plan assets and as a corresponding liability?
a. $0
b. $ 2,000,000
c. $38,000,000
d. $40,000,000

2M92#33. The following are Boa City's fixed assets:

Fixed assets used in proprietary fund activities	$1,000,000
Fixed assets used in governmental-type trust funds	1,800,000
All other fixed assets	9,000,000

What aggregate amount should Boa account for in the general fixed assets account group?
a. $ 9,000,000
b. $10,000,000
c. $10,800,000
d. $11,800,000

2M92#34. The following obligations were among those reported by Fern Village at December 31, 1991:

Vendor financing with a term of 10 months when incurred, in connection with a capital asset acquisition that is not part of a long-term financing plan	$ 150,000
Long-term bonds for financing of capital asset acquisition	3,000,000
Bond anticipation notes due in six months, issued as part of a long-term financing plan for capital purposes	400,000

What aggregate amount should Fern report as general long-term capital debt at December 31, 1991?
a. $3,000,000
b. $3,150,000
c. $3,400,000
d. $3,550,000

2M92#36. Dale City is accumulating financial resources that are legally restricted to payments of general long-term debt principal and interest maturing in future years. At December 31, 1991, $5,000,000 has been accumulated for principal payments and $300,000 has been accumulated for interest payments. These restricted funds should be accounted for in the

	Debt service fund	General fund
a.	$0	$5,300,000
b.	$ 300,000	$5,000,000
c.	$5,000,000	$ 300,000
d.	$5,300,000	$0

TN91#53. Gold County received goods that had been approved for purchase but for which payment had not yet been made. Should the accounts listed below be increased?

	Encumbrances	Expenditures
a.	No	No
b.	No	Yes
c.	Yes	No
d.	Yes	Yes

TN91#56. On June 28, 1991, Silver City's debt service fund received funds for the future repayment of bond principal. As a consequence, the long-term debt account group reported
a. An increase in the amount available in debt service funds and an increase in the fund balance.
b. An increase in the amount available in debt service funds and an increase in the amount to be provided for bonds.
c. An increase in the amount available in debt service funds and a decrease in the amount to be provided for bonds.
d. No changes in any amount until the bond principal is actually paid.

TM91#54. Tott City's serial bonds are serviced through a debt service fund with cash provided by the general fund. In a debt service fund's statements, how are cash receipts and cash payments reported?

	Cash receipts	Cash payments
a.	Revenues	Expenditures
b.	Revenues	Operating transfers
c.	Operating transfers	Expenditures
d.	Operating transfers	Operating transfers

TM91#56. Old equipment, which is recorded in the general fixed asset account group, is sold for less than its carrying amount. The sale reduces the investments in general fixed assets' balance by the
a. Difference between the cost of the equipment and the sales price.
b. Difference between the carrying amount of the equipment and the sales price.
c. Selling price of the equipment.
d. Carrying amount of the equipment.

TN90#52. Which of the following fund types used by a government most likely would have a Fund Balance Reserved for Inventory of Supplies?
a. General.
b. Internal service.
c. Nonexpendable trust.
d. Capital projects.

TN90#53. Should a special revenue fund with a legally adopted budget maintain its accounts on an accrual basis and integrate budgetary accounts into its accounting system?

	Maintain on accrual basis	Integrate budgetary accounts
a.	Yes	Yes
b.	Yes	No
c.	No	Yes
d.	No	No

TN90
Items 54 through 57 are based on the following:

On March 2, 1990, Finch City issued 10-year general obligation bonds at face amount, with interest payable March 1 and September 1. The proceeds were to be used to finance the construction of a civic center over the period April 1, 1990, to March 31, 1991. During the fiscal year ended June 30, 1990, no resources had been provided to the debt service fund for the payment of principal and interest.

54. On June 30, 1990, Finch's debt service fund should include interest payable on the general obligation bonds for
a. 0 months.
b. 3 months.
c. 4 months.
d. 6 months.

55. Proceeds from the general obligation bonds should be recorded in the
a. General fund.
b. Capital projects fund.
c. General long-term debt account group.
d. Debt service fund.

56. The liability for the general obligation bonds should be recorded in the
a. General fund.
b. Capital projects fund.
c. General long-term debt account group.
d. Debt service fund.

57. On June 30, 1990, Finch's combined balance sheet should report the construction in progress for the civic center in the

	Capital projects fund	General fixed assets account group
a.	Yes	Yes
b.	Yes	No
c.	No	No
d.	No	Yes

2N90#42. On December 31, 1989, Elm Village paid a contractor $4,500,000 for the total cost of a new Village Hall built in 1989 on Village-owned land. Financing for the capital project was provided by a $3,000,000 general obligation bond issue sold at face amount on December 31, 1989, with the remaining $1,500,000 transferred from the general fund. What account and amount should be reported in Elm's 1989 financial statements for the general fund?
a. Other financing sources control $4,500,000.
b. Expenditures control $4,500,000.
c. Other financing sources control $3,000,000.
d. Other financing uses control $1,500,000.

2N90#43. During 1989, Spruce City reported the following receipts from self-sustaining activities paid for by users of the services rendered:

Operation of water supply plant $5,000,000
Operation of bus system 900,000

What amount should be accounted for in Spruce's enterprise funds?
a. $0
b. $ 900,000
c. $5,000,000
d. $5,900,000

2N90#46. The following information pertains to Pine City's general fund for 1989:

Appropriations $6,500,000
Expenditures 5,000,000
Other financing sources 1,500,000
Other financing uses 2,000,000
Revenues 8,000,000

After Pine's general fund accounts were closed at the end of 1989, the fund balance increased by
a. $3,000,000
b. $2,500,000
c. $1,500,000
d. $1,000,000

2N90#47. Kew City received a $15,000,000 federal grant to finance the construction of a center for rehabilitation of drug addicts. The proceeds of this grant should be accounted for in the
a. Special revenue funds.
b. General fund.
c. Capital projects funds.
d. Trust funds.

2N90#48. Lisa County issued $5,000,000 of general obligation bonds at 101 to finance a capital project. The

$50,000 premium was to be used for payment of principal and interest. This transaction should be accounted for in the

a. Capital projects funds, debt service funds, and the general long-term debt account group.
b. Capital projects funds and debt service funds only.
c. Debt service funds and the general long-term debt account group only.
d. Debt service funds only.

2N90#49. In 1989, a state government collected income taxes of $8,000,000 for the benefit of one of its cities that imposes an income tax on its residents. The state remitted these collections periodically to the city. The state should account for the $8,000,000 in the

a. General fund.
b. Agency funds.
c. Internal service funds.
d. Special assessment funds.

2N90#51. The following revenues were among those reported by Ariba Township in 1989:

Net rental revenue (after depreciation) from a parking garage owned by Ariba	$ 40,000
Interest earned on investments held for employees' retirement benefits	100,000
Property taxes	6,000,000

What amount of the foregoing revenues should be accounted for in Ariba's governmental-type funds?

a. $6,140,000
b. $6,100,000
c. $6,040,000
d. $6,000,000

2N90#53. The following financial resources were among those received by Seco City during 1989:

For acquisition of major capital facilities	$6,000,000
To create an expendable trust	2,000,000

With respect to the foregoing resources, what amount should be recorded in special revenue funds?

a. $0
b. $2,000,000
c. $6,000,000
d. $8,000,000

2N90#56. At December 31, 1989, Alto Township's committed appropriations that had not been expended in 1989 totaled $10,000. These appropriations do not lapse at year-end. Alto reports on a calendar-year basis. On its December 31, 1989 balance sheet, the $10,000 should be reported as

a. Vouchers payable — prior year.
b. Deferred expenditures.
c. Fund balance reserved for encumbrances.
d. Budgetary fund balance — reserved for encumbrances.

TM90#56. Revenues that are legally restricted to expenditures for specified purposes should be accounted for in special revenue funds, including

a. Accumulation of resources for payment of general long-term debt principal and interest.
b. Pension trust fund revenues.
c. Gasoline taxes to finance road repairs.
d. Proprietary fund revenues.

TM90#57. The basis of accounting for a capital projects fund is the

a. Cash basis.
b. Accrual basis.
c. Modified cash basis.
d. Modified accrual basis.

TN89#57. Customers' security deposits that cannot be spent for normal operating purposes were collected by a governmental unit and accounted for in the enterprise fund. A portion of the amount collected was invested in marketable debt securities and a portion in marketable equity securities. How would each portion be classified in the balance sheet?

	Portion in marketable debt securities	Portion in marketable equity securities
a.	Unrestricted asset	Restricted asset
b.	Unrestricted asset	Unrestricted asset
c.	Restricted asset	Unrestricted asset
d.	Restricted asset	Restricted asset

TM89#52. The encumbrances control account of a governmental unit is increased when

	A voucher payable is recorded	The budgetary accounts are closed
a.	No	No
b.	No	Yes
c.	Yes	Yes
d.	Yes	No

2M89#28. On December 31, 1988, Park Township paid a contractor $4,000,000 for the total cost of a new police building built in 1988. Financing was by means of a $3,000,000 general obligation bond issue sold at face amount on December 31, 1988, with the remaining $1,000,000 transferred from the general fund. What amount should Park record as revenues in the capital projects fund in connection with the bond issue proceeds and the transfer?

a. $0
b. $1,000,000
c. $3,000,000
d. $4,000,000

B. Nongovernmental Not-for-Profit Organizations

R97#15. Child Care Centers, Inc., a not-for-profit organization, receives revenue from various sources during the year to support its day care centers. The following cash amounts were received during 1996.

—$2,000 restricted by the donor to be used for meals for the children.
—$1,500 received for subscriptions to a monthly child care magazine with a fair market value to subscribers of $1,000.
—$10,000 to be used only upon completion of a new playroom that was 75% complete at December 31, 1996.

What amount should Child Care Centers record as contribution revenue in its 1996 Statement of Activities?
- a. $ 2,000
- b. $ 2,500
- c. $10,000
- d. $11,000

R97#16. A not-for-profit organization receives $150 from a donor. The donor receives two tickets to a theater show and an acknowledgment in the theater program. The tickets have a fair market value of $100. What amount is recorded as contribution revenue?
- a. $0
- b. $ 50
- c. $100
- d. $150

R97#17. Which of the following classifications is required for reporting of expenses by all not-for-profit organizations?
- a. Natural classification in the statement of activities or notes to the financial statements.
- b. Functional classification in the statement of activities or notes to the financial statements.
- c. Functional classification in the statement of activities and natural classification in a matrix format in a separate statement.
- d. Functional classification in the statement of activities and natural classification in the notes to the financial statements.

R97#18. The Jackson Foundation, a not-for-profit organization, received contributions in 1996 as follows:

- Unrestricted cash contributions of $500,000.
- Cash contributions of $200,000 to be restricted to acquisition of property.

Jackson's statement of cash flows should include which of the following amounts?

	Operating activities	Investing activities	Financing activities
a.	$700,000	$0	$0
b.	$500,000	$200,000	$0
c.	$500,000	$0	$200,000
d.	$0	$500,000	$200,000

R96#5. In its fiscal year ended June 30, 1995, Barr College, a large private institution, received $100,000 designated by the donor for scholarships for superior students. On July 26, 1995, Barr selected the students and awarded the scholarships. How should the July 26 transaction be reported in Barr's statement of activities for the year ended June 30, 1996?
- a. As both an increase and a decrease of $100,000 in unrestricted net assets.
- b. As a decrease only in unrestricted net assets.
- c. By footnote disclosure only.
- d. Not reported.

R96#6. A storm damaged the roof of a new building owned by K-9 Shelters, a not-for-profit organization. A supporter of K-9, a professional roofer, repaired the roof at no charge. In K-9's statement of activities, the damage and repair of the roof should
- a. Be reported by note disclosure only.
- b. Be reported as an increase in both expenses and contributions.
- c. Be reported as an increase in both net assets and contributions.
- d. Not be reported.

R96#11. In 1995, Gamma, a not-for-profit organization, deposited at a bank $1,000,000 given to it by a donor to purchase endowment securities. The securities were purchased January 2, 1996. At December 31, 1995, the bank recorded $2,000 interest on the deposit. In accordance with the bequest, this $2,000 was used to finance ongoing program expenses in March 1996. At December 31, 1995, what amount of the bank balance should be included as current assets in Gamma's classified balance sheet?
- a. $0
- b. $ 2,000
- c. $1,000,000
- d. $1,002,000

N95#74. A large not-for-profit organization's statement of activities should report the net change for net assets that are

	Unrestricted	Permanently restricted
a.	Yes	Yes
b.	Yes	No
c.	No	No
d.	No	Yes

M95#60. In April 1995, Delta Hospital purchased medicines from Field Pharmaceutical Co. at a cost of $5,000. However, Field notified Delta that the invoice was being canceled and that the medicines were being donated to Delta. Delta should record this donation of medicines as
- a. A memorandum entry only.
- b. A $5,000 credit to nonoperating expenses.
- c. A $5,000 credit to operating expenses.
- d. Other operating revenue of $5,000.

N94#26. Cancer Educators, a not-for-profit organization, incurred costs of $10,000 when it combined program functions with fund raising functions. Which of the following cost allocations might Cancer report in its statement of activities?

	Program services	Fund raising	General services
a.	$0	$0	$10,000
b.	$0	$6,000	$ 4,000
c.	$ 6,000	$4,000	$0
d.	$10,000	$0	$0

N94#28. Which of the following normally would be included in other operating revenues of a hospital?

	Revenues from educational programs	Unrestricted gifts
a.	No	No
b.	No	Yes
c.	Yes	No
d.	Yes	Yes

N94#30. FASB Statement No. 117, *Financial Statements of Not-for-Profit Organizations,* focuses on
  a. Basic information for the organization as a whole.
  b. Standardization of funds nomenclature.
  c. Inherent differences of not-for-profit organizations that impact reporting presentations.
  d. Distinctions between current fund and non-current fund presentations.

M94#60. Valley's community hospital normally includes proceeds from sale of cafeteria meals in
  a. Deductions from dietary service expenses.
  b. Ancillary service revenues.
  c. Patient service revenues.
  d. Other revenues.

TM93#60. When a nonprofit organization combines fund-raising efforts with educational materials or program services, the total combined costs incurred are
  a. Reported as program services expenses.
  b. Allocated between fund-raising and program services expenses using an appropriate allocation basis.
  c. Reported as fund-raising costs.
  d. Reported as management and general expenses.

2M93#21. In 1991, Citizens' Health, a voluntary health and welfare organization, received a bequest of a $200,000 certificate of deposit maturing in 1992. The testator's only stipulations were that this certificate be held until maturity and that the interest revenue be used to finance salaries for a preschool program. Interest revenue for 1992 was $16,000. When the certificate matured and was redeemed, the board of trustees adopted a formal resolution designating $40,000 of the proceeds for the future purchase of equipment for the preschool program. What amount should Citizen report in its 1992 year-end current funds balance sheet as fund balance designated for the preschool program?
  a. $0
  b. $16,000
  c. $40,000
  d. $56,000

2M93#24. The following expenditures were made by Green Services, a society for the protection of the environment:

Printing of the annual report	$12,000
Unsolicited merchandise sent to encourage contributions	25,000
Cost of an audit performed by a CPA firm	3,000

What amount should be classified as fund-raising costs in the society's activity statement?
  a. $37,000
  b. $28,000
  c. $25,000
  d. $0

2M93#27. At the end of the year, Cramer University's unrestricted current funds comprised $15,000,000 of assets and $9,000,000 of liabilities (including deferred revenues of $300,000). What is the fund balance of Cramer's unrestricted current funds?
  a. $ 5,700,000
  b. $ 6,000,000
  c. $ 6,300,000
  d. $15,000,000

2M93#29. In hospital accounting, restricted funds are
  a. **Not** available unless the board of directors remove the restrictions.
  b. Restricted as to use only for board-designated purposes.
  c. **Not** available for current operating use; however, the income generated by the funds is available for current operating use.
  d. Restricted as to use by the donor, grantor, or other source of the resources.

2M93#35. The League, a not-for-profit organization, received the following pledges:

Unrestricted	$200,000
Restricted for capital additions	150,000

All pledges are legally enforceable; however, the League's experience indicates that 10% of all pledges prove to be uncollectible. What amount should the League report as pledges receivable, net of any required allowance account?
  a. $135,000
  b. $180,000
  c. $315,000
  d. $350,000

Selected Questions

TM92#59. Is the recognition of depreciation expense required for public colleges and private not-for-profit colleges?

	Public	Private
a.	No	Yes
b.	No	No
c.	Yes	Yes
d.	Yes	No

VI. Managerial Accounting

A. Cost Estimation, Cost Determination, and Cost Drivers

R97#19. To determine the best cost driver of warranty costs relating to glass breakage during shipments, Wymer Co. used simple linear regression analysis to study the relationship between warranty costs and each of the following variables: type of packaging, quantity shipped, type of carrier, and distance shipped. The analysis yielded the following statistics:

Independent variable	Coefficient of determination	Standard error of regression
Type of packaging	0.60	1,524
Quantity shipped	0.48	1,875
Type of carrier	0.45	2,149
Distance shipped	0.20	4,876

Based on these analyses, the best driver of warranty costs for glass breakage is
 a. Type of packaging.
 b. Quantity shipped.
 c. Type of carrier.
 d. Distance shipped.

R96#13. Multiple regression differs from simple regression in that it
 a. Provides an estimated constant term.
 b. Has more dependent variables.
 c. Allows the computation of the coefficient of determination.
 d. Has more independent variables.

N95#39. Sender, Inc. estimates parcel mailing costs using data shown on the chart below.

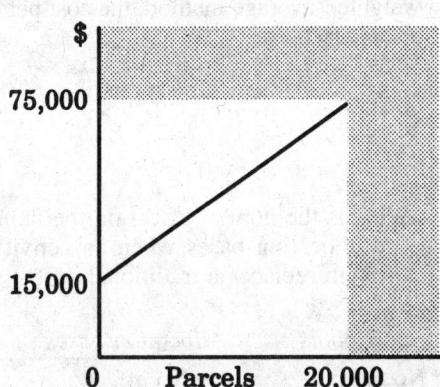

What is Sender's estimated cost for mailing 12,000 parcels?

 a. $36,000
 b. $45,000
 c. $51,000
 d. $60,000

M95#36. Day Mail Order Co. applied the high-low method of cost estimation to customer order data for the first 4 months of 1995. What is the estimated variable order filling cost component per order?

Month	Orders	Cost
January	1,200	$ 3,120
February	1,300	3,185
March	1,800	4,320
April	1,700	3,895
	6,000	$14,520

 a. $2.00
 b. $2.42
 c. $2.48
 d. $2.50

M95#37. A 1995 cash budget is being prepared for the purchase of Toyi, a merchandise item. Budgeted data are:

Cost of goods sold for 1995	$300,000
Accounts payable 1/1/95	20,000
Inventory—1/1/95	30,000
12/31/95	42,000

Purchases will be made in 12 equal monthly amounts and paid for in the following month. What is the 1995 budgeted cash payment for purchases of Toyi?
 a. $295,000
 b. $300,000
 c. $306,000
 d. $312,000

M94#36. Mat Co. estimated its material handling costs at two activity levels as follows:

Kilos handled	Cost
80,000	$160,000
60,000	132,000

What is Mat's estimated cost for handling 75,000 kilos?
 a. $150,000
 b. $153,000
 c. $157,500
 d. $165,000

AR-43

2N92#22. Sago Co. uses regression analysis to develop a model for predicting overhead costs. Two different cost drivers (machine hours and direct materials weight) are under consideration as the independent variable. Relevant data were run on a computer using one of the standard regression programs, with the following results:

	Coefficient
Machine hours	
Y Intercept	2,500
B	5.0
$R^2 = .70$	
Direct materials weight	
Y Intercept	4,600
B	2.6
$R^2 = .50$	

Which regression equation should be used?
  a. Y = 2,500 + 5.0X
  b. Y = 2,500 + 3.5X
  c. Y = 4,600 + 2.6X
  d. Y = 4,600 + 1.3X

B. Job Costing, Process Costing, and Activity Based Costing

R97#20. Mason Company uses a job-order cost system and applies manufacturing overhead to jobs using a predetermined overhead rate based on direct-labor dollars. The rate for the current year is 200 percent of direct-labor dollars. This rate was calculated last December and will be used throughout the current year.

Mason had one job, No. 150, in process on August 1 with raw materials costs of $2,000 and direct-labor costs of $3,000. During August, raw materials and direct labor added to jobs were as follows:

	No. 150	No. 151	No. 152
Raw materials	$ —	$4,000	$1,000
Direct labor	1,500	5,000	2,500

Actual manufacturing overhead for the month of August was $20,000. During the month, Mason completed Job Nos. 150 and 151.

For August, manufacturing overhead was
  a. Overapplied by $4,000.
  b. Underapplied by $7,000.
  c. Underapplied by $2,000.
  d. Underapplied by $1,000.

R97#21. A basic assumption of activity-based costing (ABC) is that
  a. All manufacturing costs vary directly with units of production.
  b. Products or services require the performance of activities, and activities consume resources.
  c. Only costs that respond to unit-level drivers are product costs.
  d. Only variable costs are included in activity-cost pools.

N95#45. Gram Co. develops computer programs to meet customers' special requirements. How should Gram categorize payments to employees who develop these programs?

	Direct costs	Value-adding costs
a.	Yes	Yes
b.	Yes	No
c.	No	No
d.	No	Yes

M95#41. In its April 1995 production, Hern Corp., which does not use a standard cost system, incurred total production costs of $900,000, of which Hern attributed $60,000 to normal spoilage and $30,000 to abnormal spoilage. Hern should account for this spoilage as
  a. Period cost of $90,000.
  b. Inventoriable cost of $90,000.
  c. Period cost of $60,000 and inventoriable cost of $30,000.
  d. Inventoriable cost of $60,000 and period cost of $30,000.

M95#44. In an activity-based costing system, what should be used to assign a department's manufacturing overhead costs to products produced in varying lot sizes?
  a. A single cause and effect relationship.
  b. Multiple cause and effect relationships.
  c. Relative net sales values of the products.
  d. A product's ability to bear cost allocations.

M94#40. The following information pertains to Lap Co.'s Palo Division for the month of April:

	Number of units	Cost of materials
Beginning work-in-process	15,000	$ 5,500
Started in April	40,000	18,000
Units completed	42,500	
Ending work-in-process	12,500	

All materials are added at the beginning of the process. Using the weighted-average method, the cost per equivalent unit for materials is
  a. $0.59
  b. $0.55
  c. $0.45
  d. $0.43

M94#41. What is the normal effect on the numbers of cost pools and allocation bases when an activity-based cost (ABC) system replaces a traditional cost system?

	Cost pools	Allocation bases
a.	No effect	No effect
b.	Increase	No effect
c.	No effect	Increase
d.	Increase	Increase

Selected Questions

M94#42. Under Pick Co.'s job order costing system manufacturing overhead is applied to work in process using a predetermined annual overhead rate. During January 1994, Pick's transactions included the following:

Direct materials issued to production	$90,000
Indirect materials issued to production	8,000
Manufacturing overhead incurred	125,000
Manufacturing overhead applied	113,000
Direct labor costs	107,000

Pick had neither beginning nor ending work-in-process inventory. What was the cost of jobs completed in January 1994?
 a. $302,000
 b. $310,000
 c. $322,000
 d. $330,000

TN93#45. In an activity-based costing system, cost reduction is accomplished by identifying and eliminating

	All cost drivers	Nonvalue-adding activities
a.	No	No
b.	Yes	Yes
c.	No	Yes
d.	Yes	No

TM93#41. In a traditional job order cost system, the issue of indirect materials to a production department increases
 a. Stores control.
 b. Work in process control.
 c. Factory overhead control.
 d. Factory overhead applied.

TN92#45. Nile Co.'s cost allocation and product costing procedures follow activity-based costing principles. Activities have been identified and classified as being either value-adding or nonvalue-adding as to each product. Which of the following activities, used in Nile's production process, is nonvalue-adding?
 a. Design engineering activity.
 b. Heat treatment activity.
 c. Drill press activity.
 d. Raw materials storage activity.

TN92#47. In computing the current period's manufacturing cost per equivalent unit, the FIFO method of process costing considers current period costs
 a. Only.
 b. Plus cost of beginning work-in-process inventory.
 c. Less cost of beginning work-in-process inventory.
 d. Plus cost of ending work-in-process inventory.

2N92#30. Following are Mill Co.'s production costs for October:

Direct materials	$100,000
Direct labor	90,000
Factory overhead	4,000

What amount of costs should be traced to specific products in the production process?
 a. $194,000
 b. $190,000
 c. $100,000
 d. $ 90,000

2N92#33. Cay Co.'s 1991 fixed manufacturing overhead costs totaled $100,000, and variable selling costs totaled $80,000. Under direct costing, how should these costs be classified?

	Period costs	Product costs
a.	$0	$180,000
b.	$ 80,000	$100,000
c.	$100,000	$ 80,000
d.	$180,000	$0

TM92#51. In a process cost system, the application of factory overhead usually would be recorded as an increase in
 a. Finished goods inventory control.
 b. Factory overhead control.
 c. Cost of goods sold.
 d. Work-in-process inventory control.

TM92#55. Book Co. uses the activity-based costing approach for cost allocation and product costing purposes. Printing, cutting, and binding functions make up the manufacturing process. Machinery and equipment are arranged in operating cells that produce a complete product starting with raw materials. Which of the following are characteristic of Book's activity-based costing approach?

 I. Cost drivers are used as a basis for cost allocation.
 II. Costs are accumulated by department or function for purposes of product costing.
 III. Activities that do not add value to the product are identified and reduced to the extent possible.

 a. I only.
 b. I and II.
 c. I and III.
 d. II and III.

2M92#42. Fab Co. manufactures textiles. Among Fab's 1991 manufacturing costs were the following salaries and wages:

Loom operators	$120,000
Factory foremen	45,000
Machine mechanics	30,000

What was the amount of Fab's 1991 direct labor?
 a. $195,000
 b. $165,000
 c. $150,000
 d. $120,000

2M92#44. Birk Co. uses a job order cost system. The following debits (credits) appeared in Birk's work-in-process account for the month of April 1992:

April	Description	Amount
1	Balance	$ 4,000
30	Direct materials	24,000
30	Direct labor	16,000
30	Factory overhead	12,800
30	To finished goods	(48,000)

Birk applies overhead to production at a predetermined rate of 80% of direct labor cost. Job No. 5, the only job still in process on April 30, 1992, has been charged with direct labor of $2,000. What was the amount of direct materials charged to Job No. 5?
- a. $ 3,000
- b. $ 5,200
- c. $ 8,800
- d. $24,000

2M92#45. Yarn Co.'s inventories in process were at the following stages of completion at April 30, 1992:

No. of units	Percent complete
100	90
50	80
200	10

Equivalent units of production amounted to
- a. 150
- b. 180
- c. 330
- d. 350

2M92#48. Hoyt Co. manufactured the following units:

Saleable	5,000
Unsaleable (normal spoilage)	200
Unsaleable (abnormal spoilage)	300

Manufacturing costs totaled $99,000. What amount should Hoyt debit to finished goods?
- a. $90,000
- b. $93,600
- c. $95,400
- d. $99,000

TN91#41. In a job cost system, manufacturing overhead is

	An indirect cost of jobs	A necessary element in production
a.	No	Yes
b.	No	No
c.	Yes	Yes
d.	Yes	No

TN91#43. A direct labor overtime premium should be charged to a specific job when the overtime is caused by the

- a. Increased overall level of activity.
- b. Customer's requirement for early completion of job.
- c. Management's failure to include the job in the production schedule.
- d. Management's requirement that the job be completed before the annual factory vacation closure.

TM91#41. A department adds material at the beginning of a process and identifies defective units when the process is 40% complete. At the beginning of the period, there was no work in process. At the end of the period, the number of work in process units equaled the number of units transferred to finished goods. If all units in ending work in process were $66 \frac{2}{3}\%$ complete, then ending work in process should be allocated
- a. 50% of all normal defective unit costs.
- b. 40% of all normal defective unit costs.
- c. 50% of the material costs and 40% of the conversion costs of all normal defective unit costs.
- d. None of the normal defective unit costs.

TM91#42. A process costing system was used for a department that began operations in January 1991. Approximately the same number of physical units, at the same degree of completion, were in work in process at the end of both January and February. Monthly conversion costs are allocated between ending work in process and units completed. Compared to the FIFO method, would the weighted average method use the same or a greater number of equivalent units to calculate the monthly allocations?

	Equivalent units for weighted average compared to FIFO	
	January	February
a.	Same	Same
b.	Greater number	Greater number
c.	Greater number	Same
d.	Same	Greater number

C. Standard Costing and Flexible Budgeting

N95#47. The standard direct material cost to produce a unit of Lem is 4 meters of material at $2.50 per meter. During May 1995, 4,200 meters of material costing $10,080 were purchased and used to produce 1,000 units of Lem. What was the material price variance for May 1995?
- a. $400 favorable.
- b. $420 favorable.
- c. $ 80 unfavorable.
- d. $480 unfavorable.

M95#42. Companies in what type of industry may use a standard cost system for cost control?

Selected Questions

	Mass production industry	Service industry
a.	Yes	Yes
b.	Yes	No
c.	No	No
d.	No	Yes

M94#37. A flexible budget is appropriate for a

	Marketing budget	Direct material usage budget
a.	No	No
b.	No	Yes
c.	Yes	Yes
d.	Yes	No

TN93#46. When production levels are expected to increase within a relevant range, and a flexible budget is used, what effect would be anticipated with respect to each of the following costs?

	Fixed costs per unit	Variable costs per unit
a.	Decrease	Decrease
b.	No change	No change
c.	No change	Decrease
d.	Decrease	No change

TM93#43. Which of the following standard costing variances would be **least** controllable by a production supervisor?
 a. Overhead volume.
 b. Overhead efficiency.
 c. Labor efficiency.
 d. Material usage.

TM93#46. The basic difference between a master budget and a flexible budget is that a master budget is
 a. Based on one specific level of production and a flexible budget can be prepared for any production level within a relevant range.
 b. Only used before and during the budget period and a flexible budget is only used after the budget period.
 c. Based on a fixed standard, whereas a flexible budget allows management latitude in meeting goals.
 d. For an entire production facility whereas a flexible budget is applicable to single departments only.

2N92#21. Yola Co. manufactures one product with a standard direct labor cost of four hours at $12.00 per hour. During June, 1,000 units were produced using 4,100 hours at $12.20 per hour. The unfavorable direct labor efficiency variance was
 a. $1,220
 b. $1,200
 c. $ 820
 d. $ 400

2N92#24. Carr Co. had an unfavorable materials usage variance of $900. What amounts of this variance should be charged to each department?

	Purchasing	Warehousing	Manufacturing
a.	$0	$0	$900
b.	$0	$900	$0
c.	$300	$300	$300
d.	$900	$0	$0

2N92#25. The following information pertains to Roe Co.'s 1991 manufacturing operations:

Standard direct labor hours per unit	2
Actual direct labor hours	10,500
Number of units produced	5,000
Standard variable overhead per standard direct labor hour	$3
Actual variable overhead	$28,000

Roe's 1991 unfavorable variable overhead efficiency variance was
 a. $0
 b. $1,500
 c. $2,000
 d. $3,500

2N92#31. In connection with a standard cost system being developed by Flint Co., the following information is being considered with regard to standard hours allowed for output of one unit of product:

	Hours
Average historical performance for the past three years	1.85
Production level to satisfy average consumer demand over a seasonal time span	1.60
Engineering estimates based on attainable performance	1.50
Engineering estimates based on ideal performance	1.25

To measure controllable production inefficiencies, what is the best basis for Flint to use in establishing standard hours allowed?
 a. 1.25
 b. 1.50
 c. 1.60
 d. 1.85

2N92#34. Cook Co.'s total costs of operating five sales offices last year were $500,000, of which $70,000 represented fixed costs. Cook has determined that total costs are significantly influenced by the number of sales offices operated. Last year's costs and number of sales offices can be used as the bases for predicting annual costs. What would be the budgeted costs for the coming year if Cook were to operate seven sales offices?
 a. $700,000
 b. $672,000
 c. $614,000
 d. $586,000

TM92#53. When using a flexible budget, a decrease in production levels within a relevant range
  a. Decreases variable cost per unit.
  b. Decreases total costs.
  c. Increases total fixed costs.
  d. Increases variable cost per unit.

2M92#46. The following direct labor information pertains to the manufacture of product Glu:

Time required to make one unit	2 direct labor hours
Number of direct workers	50
Number of productive hours per week, per worker	40
Weekly wages per worker	$500
Workers' benefits treated as direct labor costs	20% of wages

What is the standard direct labor cost per unit of product Glu?
  a. $30
  b. $24
  c. $15
  d. $12

TN91#42. A standard cost system may be used in
  a. Neither process costing nor job order costing.
  b. Process costing but **not** job order costing.
  c. Either job order costing or process costing.
  d. Job order costing but **not** process costing.

TM91#43. During 1990, a department's three-variance overhead standard costing system reported unfavorable spending and volume variances. The activity level selected for allocating overhead to the product was based on 80% of practical capacity. If 100% of practical capacity had been selected instead, how would the reported unfavorable spending and volume variances be affected?

	Spending variance	Volume variance
a.	Increased	Unchanged
b.	Increased	Increased
c.	Unchanged	Increased
d.	Unchanged	Unchanged

D. Inventory Planning, Inventory Control, and Just-in-Time Purchasing

R97#22. In computing the reorder point for an item of inventory, which of the following is used?

  I. Cost.
  II. Usage per day.
  III. Lead time.

  a. I and II.
  b. II and III.
  c. I and III.
  d. I, II, and III.

N95#52. The economic order quantity formula assumes that
  a. Periodic demand for the good is known.
  b. Carrying costs per unit vary with quantity ordered.
  c. Costs of placing an order vary with quantity ordered.
  d. Purchase costs per unit differ due to quantity discounts.

M95#47. Which changes in costs are most conducive to switching from a traditional inventory ordering system to a just-in-time ordering system?

	Cost per purchase order	Inventory unit carrying costs
a.	Increasing	Increasing
b.	Decreasing	Increasing
c.	Decreasing	Decreasing
d.	Increasing	Decreasing

M94#46. As a consequence of finding a more dependable supplier, Dee Co. reduced its safety stock of raw materials by 80%. What is the effect of this safety stock reduction on Dee's economic order quantity?
  a. 80% decrease.
  b. 64% decrease.
  c. 20% increase.
  d. No effect.

M94#50. Bell Co. changed from a traditional manufacturing philosophy to a just-in-time philosophy. What are the expected effects of this change on Bell's inventory turnover and inventory as a percentage of total assets reported on Bell's balance sheet?

	Inventory turnover	Inventory percentage
a.	Decrease	Decrease
b.	Decrease	Increase
c.	Increase	Decrease
d.	Increase	Increase

2N92#26. In Belk Co.'s "just-in-time" production system, costs per set-up were reduced from $28 to $2. In the process of reducing inventory levels, Belk found that there were fixed facility and administrative costs that previously had not been included in the carrying cost calculation. The result was an increase from $8 to $32 per unit per year. What were the effects of these changes on Belk's economic lot size and relevant costs?

	Lot size	Relevant costs
a.	Decrease	Increase
b.	Increase	Decrease
c.	Increase	Increase
d.	Decrease	Decrease

TM91#50. The economic order quantity formula assumes that

a. Purchase costs per unit differ due to quantity discounts.
b. Costs of placing an order vary with quantity ordered.
c. Periodic demand for the good is known.
d. Erratic usage rates are cushioned by safety stocks.

E. Budgeting and Responsibility Accounting

N95#40. Mien Co. is budgeting sales of 53,000 units of product Nous for October 1995. The manufacture of one unit of Nous requires 4 kilos of chemical Loire. During October 1995, Mien plans to reduce the inventory of Loire by 50,000 kilos and increase the finished goods inventory of Nous by 6,000 units. There is no Nous work-in-process inventory. How many kilos of Loire is Mien budgeting to purchase in October 1995?
a. 138,000
b. 162,000
c. 186,000
d. 238,000

M95#45. Select Co. had the following 1994 financial statement relationships:

Asset turnover   5
Profit margin on sales   0.02

What was Select's 1994 percentage return on assets?
a. 0.1%
b. 0.4%
c. 2.5%
d. 10.0%

M95#46. Which measures would be useful in evaluating the performance of a manufacturing system?

I. Throughput time.
II. Total setup time for machines/Total production time.
III. Number of rework units/Total number of units completed.

a. I and II only.
b. II and III only.
c. I and III only.
d. I, II, and III.

M94#43. The following information pertains to Quest Co.'s Gold Division for 1993:

Sales $311,000
Variable cost   250,000
Traceable fixed costs   50,000
Average invested capital   40,000
Imputed interest rate   10%

Quest's return on investment was
a. 10.00%
b. 13.33%
c. 27.50%
d. 30.00%

M94#45. In a quality control program, which of the following is(are) categorized as internal failure costs?

I. Rework.
II. Responding to customer complaints.
III. Statistical quality control procedures.

a. I only.
b. II only.
c. III only.
d. I, II, and III.

TN93#49. Controllable revenue would be included in a performance report for a

	Profit center	Cost center
a.	No	No
b.	No	Yes
c.	Yes	No
d.	Yes	Yes

TM93#49. Nonfinancial performance measures are important to engineering and operations managers in assessing the quality levels of their products. Which of the following indicators can be used to measure product quality?

I. Returns and allowances.
II. Number and types of customer complaints.
III. Production cycle time.

a. I and II only.
b. I and III only.
c. II and III only.
d. I, II, and III.

TN92#48. Residual income of an investment center is the center's
a. Income plus the imputed interest on its invested capital.
b. Income less the imputed interest on its invested capital.
c. Contribution margin plus the imputed interest on its invested capital.
d. Contribution margin less the imputed interest on its invested capital.

2N92#27. Spar Co. calculated the following ratios for one of its profit centers:

Gross margin   30%
Return on sales   25%
Capital turnover   .5 times

What is Spar's return on investment for this profit center?
a. 7.5%
b. 12.5%
c. 15.0%
d. 25.0%

Taxation, Managerial, and Governmental and Not-for-Profit Organizations

2N92#28. Kim Co.'s profit center Zee had 1991 operating income of $200,000 before a $50,000 imputed interest charge for using Kim's assets. Kim's aggregate net income from all of its profit centers was $2,000,000. During 1991, Kim declared and paid dividends of $30,000 and $70,000 on its preferred and common stock, respectively. Zee's 1991 residual income was
    a. $140,000
    b. $143,000
    c. $147,000
    d. $150,000

2N92#35. Lon Co.'s budget committee is preparing its master budget on the basis of the following projections:

Sales	$2,800,000
Decrease in inventories	70,000
Decrease in accounts payable	150,000
Gross margin	40%

What are Lon's estimated cash disbursements for inventories?
    a. $1,040,000
    b. $1,200,000
    c. $1,600,000
    d. $1,760,000

2M92#51. The following is a summarized income statement of Carr Co.'s profit center No. 43 for March 1992:

Contribution margin		$70,000
Period expenses:		
Manager's salary	$20,000	
Facility depreciation	8,000	
Corporate expense allocation	5,000	33,000
Profit center income		$37,000

Which of the following amounts would most likely be subject to the control of the profit center's manager?
    a. $70,000
    b. $50,000
    c. $37,000
    d. $33,000

2M92#52. Following is information relating to Kew Co.'s Vale Division for 1991:

Sales	$500,000
Variable costs	300,000
Traceable fixed costs	50,000
Average invested capital	100,000
Imputed interest rate	6%

Vale's residual income was
    a. $144,000
    b. $150,000
    c. $156,000
    d. $200,000

2M92#53. The following information pertains to Bala Co. for the year ended December 31, 1991:

Sales	$600,000
Net income	100,000
Capital investment	400,000

Which of the following equations should be used to compute Bala's return on investment?
    a. (4/6) × (6/1) = ROI
    b. (6/4) × (1/6) = ROI
    c. (4/6) × (1/6) = ROI
    d. (6/4) × (6/1) = ROI

TN91#50. Which combination of changes in asset turnover and income as a percentage of sales will maximize the return on investment?

	Asset turnover	Income as a percentage of sales
a.	Increase	Decrease
b.	Increase	Increase
c.	Decrease	Increase
d.	Decrease	Decrease

TM91#44. Lanta Restaurant compares monthly operating results with a static budget. When actual sales are less than budget, would Lanta usually report favorable variances on variable food costs and fixed supervisory salaries?

	Variable food costs	Fixed supervisory salaries
a.	Yes	Yes
b.	Yes	No
c.	No	Yes
d.	No	No

TM91#47. Controllable revenues would be included in the performance reports of which of the following types of responsibility centers?

	Cost centers	Investment centers
a.	Yes	No
b.	Yes	Yes
c.	No	No
d.	No	Yes

F. Variable and Absorption Costing

R98#7. In its first year of operations, Magna Manufacturers had the following costs when it produced 100,000 and sold 80,000 units of its only product:

Manufacturing costs—Fixed	$180,000
Variable	160,000
Selling & admin. costs—Fixed	90,000
Variable	40,000

How much lower would Magna's net income be if it used variable costing instead of full absorption costing?

AR-50

a. $36,000
b. $54,000
c. $68,000
d. $94,000

M95#40. Using the variable costing method, which of the following costs are assigned to inventory?

	Variable selling and administrative costs	Variable factory overhead costs
a.	Yes	Yes
b.	Yes	No
c.	No	No
d.	No	Yes

TN93#47. In an income statement prepared as an internal report using the direct (variable) costing method, fixed selling and administrative expenses would
  a. Not be used.
  b. Be treated the same as variable selling and administrative expenses.
  c. Be used in the computation of operating income but **not** in the computation of the contribution margin.
  d. Be used in the computation of the contribution margin.

TM93#45. A manufacturing company prepares income statements using both absorption and variable costing methods. At the end of a period actual sales revenues, total gross profit, and total contribution margin approximated budgeted figures; whereas net income was substantially greater than the budgeted amount. There were no beginning or ending inventories. The most likely explanation of the net income increase is that, compared to budget, actual
  a. Manufacturing fixed costs had increased.
  b. Selling and administrative fixed expenses had decreased.
  c. Sales prices and variable costs had increased proportionately.
  d. Sales prices had declined proportionately less than variable costs.

TM92#52. In calculating the break-even point for a multi-product company, which of the following assumptions are commonly made when variable costing is used?

I. Sales volume equals production volume.
II. Variable costs are constant per unit.
III. A given sales mix is maintained for all volume changes.

  a. I and II.
  b. I and III.
  c. II and III.
  d. I, II, and III.

2M92#49. At the end of Killo Co.'s first year of operations, 1,000 units of inventory remained on hand. Variable and fixed manufacturing costs per unit were $90 and $20, respectively. If Killo uses absorption costing rather than direct (variable) costing, the result would be a higher pretax income of
  a. $0
  b. $20,000
  c. $70,000
  d. $90,000

TN91#45. A single-product company prepares income statements using both absorption and variable costing methods. Manufacturing overhead cost applied per unit produced in 1990 was the same as in 1989. The 1990 variable costing statement reported a profit whereas the 1990 absorption costing statement reported a loss. The difference in reported income could be explained by units produced in 1990 being
  a. Less than units sold in 1990.
  b. Less than the activity level used for allocating overhead to the product.
  c. In excess of the activity level used for allocating overhead to the product.
  d. In excess of units sold in 1990.

G. Cost-Volume-Profit Analysis

R98#8. The following information is taken from Wampler Co.'s 1997 contribution income statement:

Sales	$200,000
Contribution margin	120,000
Fixed costs	90,000
Income taxes	12,000

What was Wampler's margin of safety?
  a. $ 50,000
  b. $150,000
  c. $168,000
  d. $182,000

N95#43. Product Cott has sales of $200,000, a contribution margin of 20%, and a margin of safety of $80,000. What is Cott's fixed cost?
  a. $16,000
  b. $24,000
  c. $80,000
  d. $96,000

N95#44. Break-even analysis assumes that over the relevant range
  a. Unit revenues are nonlinear.
  b. Unit variable costs are unchanged.
  c. Total costs are unchanged.
  d. Total fixed costs are nonlinear.

M95#39. Del Co. has fixed costs of $100,000 and break-even sales of $800,000. What is its projected profit at $1,200,000 sales?
  a. $ 50,000
  b. $150,000
  c. $200,000
  d. $400,000

M94#39. During 1993, Thor Lab supplied hospitals with a comprehensive diagnostic kit for $120. At a volume of 80,000 kits, Thor had fixed costs of $1,000,000 and a profit before income taxes of $200,000. Due to an adverse legal decision, Thor's 1994 liability insurance increased by $1,200,000 over 1993. Assuming the volume and other costs are unchanged, what should the 1994 price be if Thor is to make the same $200,000 profit before income taxes?
a. $120.00
b. $135.00
c. $150.00
d. $240.00

TN92#46. The most likely strategy to reduce the breakeven point would be to
a. Increase both the fixed costs and the contribution margin.
b. Decrease both the fixed costs and the contribution margin.
c. Decrease the fixed costs and increase the contribution margin.
d. Increase the fixed costs and decrease the contribution margin.

2N92#36. The following information pertains to Syl Co.:

Sales	$800,000
Variable costs	160,000
Fixed costs	40,000

What is Syl's breakeven point in sales dollars?
a. $200,000
b. $160,000
c. $ 50,000
d. $ 40,000

TM92#54. On January 1, 1992, Lake Co. increased its direct labor wage rates. All other budgeted costs and revenues were unchanged. How did this increase affect Lake's budgeted break-even point and budgeted margin of safety?

	Budgeted break-even point	Budgeted margin of safety
a.	Increase	Increase
b.	Increase	Decrease
c.	Decrease	Decrease
d.	Decrease	Increase

2M92#50. The following information pertains to Clove Co. for the year ending December 31, 1992:

Budgeted sales	$1,000,000
Breakeven sales	700,000
Budgeted contribution margin	600,000
Cashflow breakeven	200,000

Clove's margin of safety is
a. $300,000
b. $400,000
c. $500,000
d. $800,000

TN91#47. In the budgeted profit/volume chart below, EG represents a two-product company's profit path. EH and HG represent the profit paths of products #1 and #2, respectively.

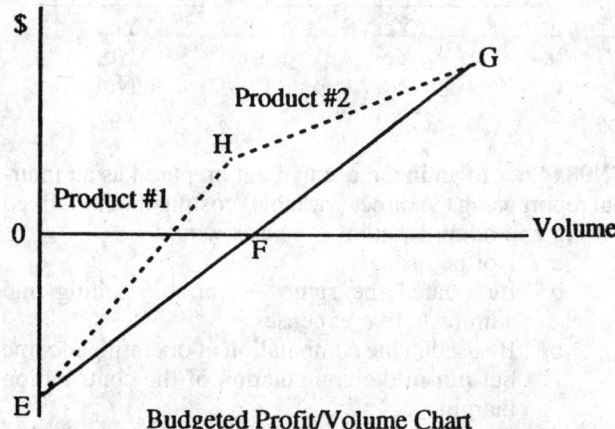

Budgeted Profit/Volume Chart

Sales prices and cost behavior were as budgeted, actual total sales equaled budgeted sales, and there were no inventories. Actual profit was greater than budgeted profit. Which product had actual sales in excess of budget, and what margin does OE divided by OF represent?

	Product with excess sales	OE/OF
a.	#1	Contribution margin
b.	#1	Gross margin
c.	#2	Contribution margin
d.	#2	Gross margin

TM91#49. In the profit-volume chart below, EF and GH represent the profit-volume graphs of a single-product company for 1989 and 1990, respectively.

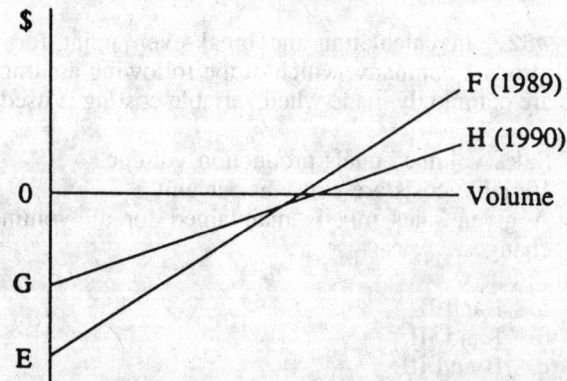

If 1989 and 1990 unit sales prices are identical, how did total fixed costs and unit variable costs of 1990 change compared to 1989?

	1990 total fixed costs	1990 unit variable costs
a.	Decreased	Increased
b.	Decreased	Decreased
c.	Increased	Increased
d.	Increased	Decreased

H. Cost Allocation and Transfer Pricing

M94#44. Brent Co. has intracompany service transfers from Division Core, a cost center, to Division Pro, a profit center. Under stable economic conditions, which of the following transfer prices is likely to be most conducive to evaluating whether both divisions have met their responsibilities?
    a. Actual cost.
    b. Standard variable cost.
    c. Actual cost plus mark-up.
    d. Negotiated price.

I. Joint and By-product Costing

R96#14. A processing department produces joint products Ajac and Bjac, each of which incurs separable production costs after split-off. Information concerning a batch produced at a $60,000 joint cost before split-off follows:

Product	Separable costs	Sales value
Ajac	$ 8,000	$ 80,000
Bjac	22,000	40,000
Total	$30,000	$120,000

What is the joint cost assigned to Ajac if costs are assigned using the relative net realizable value?
    a. $16,000
    b. $40,000
    c. $48,000
    d. $52,000

M95#43. Kode Co. manufactures a major product that gives rise to a by-product called May. May's only separable cost is a $1 selling cost when a unit is sold for $4. Kode accounts for May's sales by deducting the $3 net amount from the cost of goods sold of the major product. There are no inventories. If Kode were to change its method of accounting for May from a by-product to a joint product, what would be the effect on Kode's overall gross margin?
    a. No effect.
    b. Gross margin increases by $1 for each unit of May sold.
    c. Gross margin increases by $3 for each unit of May sold.
    d. Gross margin increases by $4 for each unit of May sold.

TM93#42. For purposes of allocating joint costs to joint products, the sales price at point of sale, reduced by cost to complete after split-off, is assumed to be equal to the
    a. Total costs.
    b. Joint costs.
    c. Sales price less a normal profit margin at point of sale.
    d. Relative sales value at split-off.

2N92#32. Mig Co., which began operations in 1991, produces gasoline and a gasoline by-product. The following information is available pertaining to 1991 sales and production:

Total production costs to split-off point	$120,000
Gasoline sales	270,000
By-product sales	30,000
Gasoline inventory, 12/31/91	15,000
Additional by-product costs:	
Marketing	10,000
Production	15,000

Mig accounts for the by-product at the time of production. What are Mig's 1991 cost of sales for gasoline and the by-product?

	Gasoline	By-product
a.	$105,000	$25,000
b.	$115,000	$0
c.	$108,000	$37,000
d.	$100,000	$0

2M92#47. The following information pertains to a by-product called Moy:

Sales in 1991	5,000 units
Selling price per unit	$6
Selling costs per unit	2
Processing costs	0

Inventory of Moy was recorded at net realizable value when produced in 1990. No units of Moy were produced in 1991. What amount should be recognized as profit on Moy's 1991 sales?
    a. $0
    b. $10,000
    c. $20,000
    d. $30,000

J. Capital Budgeting

R97#23. Oak Company bought a machine which they will depreciate on the straight-line basis over an estimated useful life of seven years. The machine has no salvage value. They expect the machine to generate after-tax net cash inflows from operations of $110,000 in each of the seven years. Oak's minimum rate of return is 12%. Information on present value factors is as follows:

Present value of $1 at 12% at the end of seven periods	.0452
Present value of an ordinary annuity of $1 at 12% for seven periods	4.564

Assuming a positive net present value of $12,000, what was the cost of the machine?
a. $480,000
b. $490,040
c. $502,040
d. $514,040

M95#38. Pole Co. is investing in a machine with a 3-year life. The machine is expected to reduce annual cash operating costs by $30,000 in each of the first 2 years and by $20,000 in year 3. Present values of an annuity of $1 at 14% are:

        Period 1   0.88
               2   1.65
               3   2.32

Using a 14% cost of capital, what is the present value of these future savings?
a. $59,600
b. $60,800
c. $62,900
d. $69,500

M94#38. Para Co. is reviewing the following data relating to an energy saving investment proposal:

Cost	$50,000
Residual value at the end of 5 years	10,000
Present value of an annuity of 1 at 12% for 5 years	3.60
Present value of 1 due in 5 years at 12%	0.57

What would be the annual savings needed to make the investment realize a 12% yield?
a. $ 8,189
b. $11,111
c. $12,306
d. $13,889

TM93#47. A project's net present value, ignoring income tax considerations, is normally affected by the
a. Proceeds from the sale of the asset to be replaced.
b. Carrying amount of the asset to be replaced by the project.
c. Amount of annual depreciation on the asset to be replaced.
d. Amount of annual depreciation on fixed assets used directly on the project.

TN92#49. Which of the following characteristics represent an advantage of the internal rate of return technique over the accounting rate of return technique in evaluating a project?

I. Recognition of the project's salvage value.
II. Emphasis on cash flows.
III. Recognition of the time value of money.

a. I only.
b. I and II.
c. II and III.
d. I, II, and III.

2N92#37. Neu Co. is considering the purchase of an investment that has a positive net present value based on Neu's 12% hurdle rate. The internal rate of return would be
a. 0.
b. 12%.
c. > 12%.
d. < 12%.

2N92#38. Major Corp. is considering the purchase of a new machine for $5,000 that will have an estimated useful life of five years and no salvage value. The machine will increase Major's after-tax cash flow by $2,000 annually for five years. Major uses the straight-line method of depreciation and has an incremental borrowing rate of 10%. The present value factors for 10% are as follows:

Ordinary annuity with five payments	3.79
Annuity due for five payments	4.17

Using the payback method, how many years will it take to pay back Major's initial investment in the machine?
a. 2.50
b. 5.00
c. 7.58
d. 8.34

2N92#39. Lin Co. is buying machinery it expects will increase average annual operating income by $40,000. The initial increase in the required investment is $60,000, and the average increase in required investment is $30,000. To compute the accrual accounting rate of return, what amount should be used as the numerator in the ratio?
a. $20,000
b. $30,000
c. $40,000
d. $60,000

2N92#40. The following information pertains to Krel Co.'s computation of net present value relating to a contemplated project:

Discounted expected cash inflows	$1,000,000
Discounted expected cash outflows	700,000

Net present value is
a. $ 300,000
b. $ 700,000
c. $ 850,000
d. $1,000,000

2M92
Items 57 through 60 are based on the following:

Tam Co. is negotiating for the purchase of equipment that would cost $100,000, with the expectation that

$20,000 per year could be saved in after-tax cash costs if the equipment were acquired. The equipment's estimated useful life is 10 years, with no residual value, and would be depreciated by the straight-line method. Tam's predetermined minimum desired rate of return is 12%. Present value of an annuity of 1 at 12% for 10 periods is 5.65. Present value of 1 due in 10 periods at 12% is .322.

57. Net present value is
   a. $5,760
   b. $6,440
   c. $12,200
   d. $13,000

58. Payback period is
   a. 4.0 years
   b. 4.4 years
   c. 4.5 years
   d. 5.0 years

59. Accrual accounting rate of return based on initial investment is
   a. 30%
   b. 20%
   c. 12%
   d. 10%

60. In estimating the internal rate of return, the factors in the table of present values of an annuity should be taken from the columns closest to
   a. 0.65
   b. 1.30
   c. 5.00
   d. 5.65

TN91#49. How are the following used in the calculation of the internal rate of return of a proposed project? Ignore income tax considerations.

	Residual sales value of project	Depreciation expense
a.	Exclude	Include
b.	Include	Include
c.	Exclude	Exclude
d.	Include	Exclude

TM91#48. The discount rate (hurdle rate of return) must be determined in advance for the
   a. Payback period method.
   b. Time adjusted rate of return method.
   c. Net present value method.
   d. Internal rate of return method.

K. Special Analyses for Decision Making

N95#55. Based on potential sales of 500 units per year, a new product has estimated traceable costs of $990,000. What is the target price to obtain a 15% profit margin on sales?

   a. $2,329
   b. $2,277
   c. $1,980
   d. $1,935

M95#48. Dough Distributors has decided to increase its daily muffin purchases by 100 boxes. A box of muffins costs $2 and sells for $3 through regular stores. Any boxes not sold through regular stores are sold through Dough's thrift store for $1. Dough assigns the following probabilities to selling additional boxes:

Additional sales	Probability
60	.6
100	.4

What is the expected value of Dough's decision to buy 100 additional boxes of muffins?
   a. $28
   b. $40
   c. $52
   d. $68

M95#49. Jago Co. has 2 products that use the same manufacturing facilities and cannot be subcontracted. Each product has sufficient orders to utilize the entire manufacturing capacity. For short-run profit maximization, Jago should manufacture the product with the
   a. Lower total manufacturing costs for the manufacturing capacity.
   b. Lower total variable manufacturing costs for the manufacturing capacity.
   c. Greater gross profit per hour of manufacturing capacity.
   d. Greater contribution margin per hour of manufacturing capacity.

M94#47. Probability (risk) analysis is
   a. Used only for situations involving five or fewer possible outcomes.
   b. Used only for situations in which the summation of probability weights is greater than one.
   c. An extension of sensitivity analysis.
   d. Incompatible with sensitivity analysis.

M94#49. Clay Co. has considerable excess manufacturing capacity. A special job order's cost sheet includes the following applied manufacturing overhead costs:

Fixed costs	$21,000
Variable costs	33,000

The fixed costs include a normal $3,700 allocation for in-house design costs, although no in-house design will be done. Instead the job will require the use of external designers costing $7,750. What is the total amount to be included in the calculation to determine the minimum acceptable price for the job?
   a. $36,700
   b. $40,750
   c. $54,000
   d. $58,050

TM93#50. Using regression analysis, Fairfield Co. graphed the following relationship of its cheapest product line's sales with its customers' income levels:

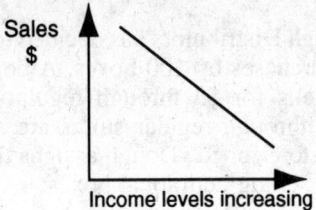

If there is a strong statistical relationship between the sales and customers' income levels, which of the following numbers best represents the correlation coefficient for this relationship?
- a. −9.00
- b. −0.93
- c. +0.93
- d. +9.00

TN92#50. To assist in an investment decision, Gift Co. selected the most likely sales volume from several possible outcomes. Which of the following attributes would that selected sales volume reflect?
- a. The mid-point of the range.
- b. The median.
- c. The greatest probability.
- d. The expected value.

TM92#56. Buff Co. is considering replacing an old machine with a new machine. Which of the following items is economically relevant to Buff's decision? (Ignore income tax considerations.)

	Carrying amount of old machine	Disposal value of new machine
a.	Yes	No
b.	No	Yes
c.	No	No
d.	Yes	Yes

2M92#55. Kane Corp. estimates that it would incur a $100,000 cost to prepare a bid proposal. Kane estimates also that there would be an 80% chance of being awarded the contract if the bid is low enough to result in a net profit of $250,000. What is the expected value of the payoff?
- a. $0
- b. $150,000
- c. $180,000
- d. $220,000

2M92#56. For the year ended December 31, 1991, Abel Co. incurred direct costs of $500,000 based on a particular course of action during the year. If a different course of action had been taken, direct costs would have been $400,000. In addition, Abel's 1991 fixed costs were $90,000. The incremental cost was
- a. $ 10,000
- b. $ 90,000
- c. $100,000
- d. $190,000

L. Product and Service Pricing

M95#50. Cuff Caterers quotes a price of $60 per person for a dinner party. This price includes the 6% sales tax and the 15% service charge. Sales tax is computed on the food plus the service charge. The service charge is computed on the food only. At what amount does Cuff price the food?
- a. $56.40
- b. $51.00
- c. $49.22
- d. $47.40

M94#48. Briar Co. signed a government construction contract providing for a formula price of actual cost plus 10%. In addition, Briar was to receive one-half of any savings resulting from the formula price being less than the target price of $2,200,000. Briar's actual costs incurred were $1,920,000. How much should Briar receive from the contract?
- a. $2,060,000
- b. $2,112,000
- c. $2,156,000
- d. $2,200,000

TN93#50. Vince Inc. has developed and patented a new laser disc reading device that will be marketed internationally. Which of the following factors should Vince consider in pricing the device?

- I. Quality of the new device.
- II. Life of the new device.
- III. Customers' relative preference for quality compared to price.

- a. I and II only.
- b. I and III only.
- c. II and III only.
- d. I, II, and III.

2N92#23. Ral Co.'s target gross margin is 60% of the selling price of a product that costs $5.00 per unit. The product's selling price per unit should be
- a. $17.50
- b. $12.50
- c. $ 8.33
- d. $ 7.50

> Unofficial Answers in the Taxation area do not reflect the tax law changes enacted by the TAXPAYER RELIEF ACT OF 1997, the BALANCED BUDGET ACT OF 1997, and the TAXPAYER BROWSING PROTECTION ACT enacted on August 5, 1997.

SELECTED MULTIPLE CHOICE ITEMS — UNOFFICIAL ANSWERS

I. Federal Taxation — Individuals

A. Inclusions in Gross Income

- R98# 1 b
- R97# 1 b
- M95# 1 c
- M95# 3 a
- M95# 4 a
- M94# 1 d
- M94# 3 a
- M94# 5 a
- 2N93# 21 c
- 2N93# 22 c
- 2N93# 23 d
- 2N93# 24 b
- 2N93# 25 a
- 2N93# 29 b
- 2N92# 13 d
- 2N92# 15 b
- 2N92# 16 b
- 2N92# 19 c
- 2M91#22 a
- 2M91#23 d
- 2M91#24 b
- 2N90# 26 c
- 2N90# 27 c
- 2N90# 29 d
- 2N90# 30 c
- 2M89#42 a
- 2M89#52 b

B. Exclusions and Adjustments to Arrive at Adjusted Gross Income

- M95# 6 b
- M94# 6 c
- 2N93# 27 a
- 2N91# 32 a

C. Deductions From Adjusted Gross Income

- R98# 2 c
- R98# 3 b
- R97# 2 b
- R97# 3 d
- R97# 4 b
- M95# 7 c
- M95# 8 c
- M95# 9 a
- M94# 9 b
- M94#10 b
- M94#11 c
- M94#13 c
- 2N93# 30 a
- 2N93# 33 a
- 2N92# 1 d
- 2N92# 2 a
- 2N92# 3 c
- 2N92# 4 a
- 2N91# 35 d
- 2N91# 36 d
- 2M91#26 c
- 2M91#27 d
- 2M91#29 a
- 2M91#30 a
- 2M91#31 d
- 2N90# 33 c
- 2M89#48 d
- 2M89#49 b
- 2M89#50 b
- 2M89#51 b

D. Filing Status and Exemptions

- M95#14 c
- M94#14 b
- 2N92# 10 c
- 2M91#34 b

E. Tax Accounting Methods

- M95#15 d

F. Tax Computations, Credits, and Penalties

- R98# 4 a
- M94#16 d
- M94#17 c
- 2N93# 37 b
- 2N91# 22 a
- 2M91#33 c

G. Alternative Minimum Tax

- M95#17 c
- M95#18 b

H. Tax Procedures

- M95#16 c
- M94#18 c
- 2N92# 6 a
- 2N90# 21 b
- 2N90# 22 a

II. Federal Taxation — Corporations

A. Determination of Taxable Income or Loss

- R97# 5 b
- R96# 7 b
- N95# 1 c
- N95# 2 d
- N95# 4 d
- N95# 6 c
- N95# 8 b
- N95# 9 c
- N95# 10 b
- N94# 31 b
- N94# 32 c
- N94# 33 b
- N94# 34 c
- N94# 36 b
- N94# 37 d
- N94# 38 c
- 2M93#41 c
- 2M93#42 d
- 2M93#44 d
- 2M93#47 b
- 2M93#48 b
- 2N91# 46 b
- 2N91# 47 d
- 2N91# 49 b
- 2M91#44 c
- 2M91#47 b
- 2M91#49 a
- 2M91#51 d
- 2M91#52 a
- 2M90#35 c
- 2N89# 41 a
- 2N89# 43 c
- 2N89# 44 c
- 2N89# 45 b

B. Tax Accounting Methods

- N94# 40 d

C. S Corporations

- M95#21 b
- M95#22 d
- N94# 41 c
- M94#21 c
- M94#22 b
- 2N93# 44 c

Note: (T)—Questions are from previous Accounting Theory Exams.
(2)—Questions are from previous Accounting Practice Part II Exams.

Taxation, Managerial, and Governmental and Not-for-Profit Organizations

2M91#56 b	2M93#43 d	2N93# 43 d	M95#24 c
2N89# 50 d	2M93#49 d	2M93#50 b	M95#25 b
	2M91#53 b	2M93#55 c	N94# 51 c
D. Personal Holding Companies	2M90#36 d	2M93#57 c	N94# 52 d
			N94# 53 c
	F. Tax Computations, Credits, and Penalties	**H. Other**	M94#25 c
M95#23 b			2N93# 45 d
2M93#52 d		R97# 6 d	2N93# 46 a
2M91#54 d	N95# 14 c	R97# 7 d	2M93#53 b
	N95# 15 a	R96# 8 a	2N91# 48 c
E. Consolidated Returns	N95# 17 b	R96# 9 b	2M91#43 d
	N95# 18 d	R96# 10 c	2M91#45 b
N95# 13 d	N94# 48 a	N95# 19 c	2M90#28 b
N94# 46 a	N94# 49 a	N95# 20 c	2N89# 52 a
N94# 47 a	N94# 50 c	N95# 21 c	2N89# 53 a
M94#23 d		N95# 22 a	

III. Federal Taxation — Partnerships

A. Basis of Partner's Interest and Bases of Assets Contributed to the Partnership	B. Determination of Partner's Share of Income, Credits, and Deductions	D. Partner Dealing With Own Partnership	M95#30 c
			M94#31 b
			2N93# 55 a
		M95#29 a	2N93# 56 b
		M94#29 c	2N93# 57 c
R96# 1 c	N95# 29 a	2M91#59 c	2N91# 54 b
R96# 2 a	N94# 57 d		2M90#26 b
M95#26 c	M94#28 d	**E. Treatment of Partnership Liabilities**	
M95#27 a	2N93# 49 c		**G. Termination of Partnership**
M94#26 c	2N93# 53 d		
M94#27 a	2N91# 55 c		
2N93# 48 a	2N91# 56 c	R98# 5 b	R97# 8 c
2N93# 50 a	2M90#24 c	N95# 30 a	N95# 33 b
2N91# 58 a		2N93# 54 a	N95# 34 c
2N91# 59 d	**C. Partnership and Partner Elections**	2M91#60 a	2N93# 58 a
2N91# 60 c			2N93# 59 d
2M91#58 c		**F. Distribution of Partnership Assets**	2N93# 60 d
	R96# 3 d		2M90#21 a
			2M90#22 a
		N95# 31 b	2M90#23 d
		N95# 32 d	2N89# 55 d

IV. Federal Taxation — Estates and Trusts, Exempt Organizations, and Preparers' Responsibilities

A. Estates and Trusts	2N91# 26 d	2N90# 40 a	M94#35 d
	2N91# 37 c	2M89#58 a	2N93# 47 c
	2N91# 38 c		2M93#58 a
R98# 6 b	2N91# 39 c	**B. Exempt Organizations**	2M93#60 b
R97# 9 c	2N91# 40 c		2M90#38 b
N95# 36 c	2M91#35 a		2M90#40 d
M95#31 a	2M91#36 d		
M95#33 c	2M91#38 c	R97# 10 d	
N94# 56 b	2M91#39 c	N95# 37 a	**C. Preparers' Responsibilities**
N94# 58 c	2M91#40 b	N95# 38 d	
M94#33 c	2N90# 35 b	M95#34 a	
2N93# 39 d	2N90# 36 b	M95#35 c	R97# 11 b
2N93# 40 a	2N90# 37 d	N94# 59 c	N94# 55 a
2N91# 23 a	2N90# 39 a	N94# 60 b	M94# 19 c
2N91# 25 d		M94#34 d	M94# 20 d

Note: (T)—Questions are from previous Accounting Theory Exams.
(2)—Questions are from previous Accounting Practice Part II Exams.

AR-58

Unofficial Answers

V. Accounting for Governmental and Not-for-Profit Organizations

A. Governmental Entities

R97# 12 c
R97# 13 b
R97# 14 b
R96# 4 d
R96# 12 d
N95# 62 d
N95# 64 a
N95# 65 c
N95# 66 d
N95# 67 a
N95# 71 d
N95# 72 c
M95# 51 b
M95# 52 c
M95# 53 c
M95# 54 a
M95# 55 c
N94# 1 c
N94# 3 a
N94# 4 d
N94# 5 a
N94# 7 d
N94# 8 d
N94# 9 b
N94# 11 c
N94# 12 a
N94# 13 b
N94# 16 b
N94# 17 b

N94# 19 d
N94# 20 c
N94# 21 b
N94# 23 b
N94# 25 a
M94# 52 c
M94# 57 d
TN93# 51 b
TN93# 52 d
TN93# 53 d
TN93# 54 c
2N93# 3 a
2N93# 4 c
2N93# 5 d
2N93# 6 d
2N93# 8 b
2N93# 9 d
2N93# 11 c
2N93# 13 d
2N93# 14 b
2N93# 18 a
TM93# 52 b
TM93# 53 b
TM93# 54 b
TM93# 55 a
TM93# 58 a
TM93# 59 c
2M93# 28 a
2M93# 32 b
2M93# 34 d
2M93# 39 d
TN92# 51 d

TN92# 52 c
TN92# 53 d
TN92# 55 d
TM92# 57 b
TN92# 58 c
2M92# 22 d
2M92# 27 b
2M92# 28 a
2M92# 29 c
2M92# 31 d
2M92# 32 d
2M92# 33 a
2M92# 34 c
2M92# 36 d
TN91# 53 b
TN91# 56 c
TM91# 54 c
TM91# 56 d
TN90# 52 a
TN90# 53 c
TN90# 54 a
TN90# 55 b
TN90# 56 c
TN90# 57 d
2N90# 42 d
2N90# 43 d
2N90# 46 b
2N90# 47 c
2N90# 48 a
2N90# 49 b
2N90# 51 d
2N90# 53 a

2N90# 56 c
TM90# 56 c
TM90# 57 d
TN89# 57 d
TM89# 52 a
2M89# 28 a

B. Nongovernmental Not-for-Profit Organizations

R97# 15 b
R97# 16 b
R97# 17 b
R97# 18 c
R96# 5 a
R96# 6 b
R96# 11 b
N95# 74 a
M95# 60 d
N94# 26 c
N94# 28 c
N94# 30 a
M94# 60 d
TM93# 60 b
2M93# 21 c
2M93# 24 c
2M93# 27 b
2M93# 29 d
2M93# 35 c
TM92# 59 a

VI. Managerial Accounting

A. Cost Estimation, Cost Determination, and Cost Drivers

R97# 19 a
R96# 13 d
N95# 39 c
M95# 36 a
M95# 37 c
M94# 36 b
2N92# 22 a

B. Job Costing, Process Costing, and Activity Based Costing

R97# 20 c
R97# 21 b
N95# 45 a

M95# 41 d
M95# 44 b
M94# 40 d
M94# 41 d
M94# 42 b
TN93# 45 c
TM93# 41 c
TN92# 45 d
TN92# 47 a
2N92# 30 b
2N92# 33 d
TM92# 51 d
TM92# 55 c
2M92# 42 d
2M92# 44 b
2M92# 45 a
2M92# 48 b
TN91# 41 c

TN91# 43 b
TM91# 41 a
TM91# 42 d

C. Standard Costing and Flexible Budgeting

N95# 47 b
M95# 42 a
M94# 37 c
TN93# 46 d
TM93# 43 a
TM93# 46 a
2N92# 21 b
2N92# 24 a
2N92# 25 b
2N92# 31 b

2N92# 34 b
TM92# 53 b
2M92# 46 a
TN91# 42 c
TM91# 43 c

D. Inventory Planning, Inventory Control, and Just-in-Time Purchasing

R97# 22 b
N95# 52 a
M95# 47 b
M94# 46 d
M94# 50 c
2N92# 26 d
TM91# 50 c

Note: (T)—Questions are from previous Accounting Theory Exams.
(2)—Questions are from previous Accounting Practice Part II Exams.

Taxation, Managerial, and Governmental and Not-for-Profit Organizations

E. **Budgeting and Responsibility Accounting**

  N95# 40 c
  M95#45 d
  M95#46 d
  M94#43 c
  M94#45 a
  TN93#49 c
  TM93#49 a
  TN92#48 b
  2N92# 27 b
  2N92# 28 d
  2N92# 35 d
  2M92#51 a
  2M92#52 a
  2M92#53 b
  TN91#50 b
  TM91#44 b
  TM91#47 d

F. **Variable and Absorption Costing**

  R98# 7 a

  M95#40 d
  TN93#47 c
  TM93#45 b
  TM92#52 c
  2M92#49 b
  TN91#45 a

G. **Cost-Volume-Profit Analysis**

  R98# 8 a
  N95# 43 b
  N95# 44 b
  M95#39 a
  M94#39 b
  TN92#46 c
  2N92# 36 c
  TM92#54 b
  2M92#50 a
  TN91#47 a
  TM91#49 a

H. **Cost Allocation and Transfer Pricing**

  M94#44 b

I. **Joint and By-product Costing**

  R96# 14 c
  M95#43 b
  TM93#42 d
  2N92# 32 d
  2M92#47 a

J. **Capital Budgeting**

  R97# 23 b
  M95#38 c
  M94#38 c
  TM93#47 a
  TN92#49 c
  2N92# 37 c
  2N92# 38 a
  2N92# 39 c
  2N92# 40 a
  2M92#57 d
  2M92#58 d
  2M92#59 d
  2M92#60 c
  TN91#49 d
  TM91#48 c

K. **Special Analyses for Decision Making**

  N95# 55 a
  M95#48 c
  M95#49 d
  M94#47 c
  M94#49 b
  TM93#50 b
  TN92# 50 c
  TM92#56 b
  2M92#55 c
  2M92#56 c

L. **Product and Service Pricing**

  M95#50 c
  M94#48 c
  TN93# 50 d
  2N92# 23 b

Note: (T)—Questions are from previous Accounting Theory Exams.
  (2)—Questions are from previous Accounting Practice Part II Exams.

Selected Questions in the Taxation area do not reflect the tax law changes enacted by the **TAXPAYER RELIEF ACT OF 1997**, the **BALANCED BUDGET ACT OF 1997**, and the **TAXPAYER BROWSING PROTECTION ACT** enacted on August 5, 1997.

OTHER OBJECTIVE ANSWER FORMATS — SELECTED QUESTIONS

I. Federal Taxation—Individuals

N95
Number 3 (Estimated time — — 25 to 40 minutes)

Question Number 3 consists of 29 items. Select the **best** answer for each item. Use a No. 2 pencil to blacken the appropriate ovals on the *Objective Answer Sheet* to indicate your answers. **Answer all items.** Your grade will be based on the total number of correct answers.

Tom and Joan Moore, both CPAs, filed a joint 1994 federal income tax return showing $70,000 in taxable income. During 1994, Tom's daughter Laura, age 16, resided with Tom's former spouse. Laura had no income of her own and was not Tom's dependent.

Required:

a. For **Items 82 through 91**, determine the amount of income or loss, if any, that should be included on page one of the Moores' 1994 Form 1040. To record your answer, blacken the ovals on the *Objective Answer Sheet*. If zeros precede your numerical answer, blacken the zeros in the ovals preceding your answer. **You cannot receive credit for your answers if you fail to blacken an oval in each column.** You may write the numbers in the boxes provided to facilitate blackening the ovals; however, the numbers written in the boxes will **not** be graded.

82. The Moores had no capital loss carryovers from prior years. During 1994 the Moores had the following stock transactions which resulted in a net capital loss:

	Date acquired	Date sold	Sales price	Cost
Revco	2-1-93	3-17-94	$15,000	$25,000
Abbco	2-18-94	4-1-94	8,000	4,000

83. In 1992, Joan received an acre of land as an inter-vivos gift from her grandfather. At the time of the gift, the land had a fair market value of $50,000. The grandfather's adjusted basis was $60,000. Joan sold the land in 1994 to an unrelated third party for $56,000.

84. The Moores received a $500 security deposit on their rental property in 1994. They are required to return the amount to the tenant.

85. Tom's 1994 wages were $53,000. In addition, Tom's employer provided group-term life insurance on Tom's life in excess of $50,000. The value of such excess coverage was $2,000.

86. During 1994, the Moores received a $2,500 federal tax refund and a $1,250 state tax refund for 1993 overpayments. In 1993, the Moores were not subject to the alternative minimum tax and were not entitled to any credit against income tax. The Moores' 1993 adjusted gross income was $80,000 and itemized deductions were $1,450 in excess of the standard deduction. The state tax deduction for 1993 was $2,000.

87. In 1994, Joan received $1,300 in unemployment compensation benefits. Her employer made a $100 contribution to the unemployment insurance fund on her behalf.

88. The Moores received $8,400 in gross receipts from their rental property during 1994. The expenses for the residential rental property were:

Bank mortgage interest	$1,200
Real estate taxes	700
Insurance	500
MACRS depreciation	3,500

N95
Number 3 (cont.)

89. The Moores received a stock dividend in 1994 from Ace Corp. They had the option to receive either cash or Ace stock with a fair market value of $900 as of the date of distribution. The par value of the stock was $500.

90. This question has not been selected.

91. Tom received $10,000, consisting of $5,000 each of principal and interest, when he redeemed a Series EE savings bond in 1994. The bond was issued in his name in 1987 and the proceeds were used to pay for Laura's college tuition. Tom had not elected to report the yearly increases in the value of the bond.

Required:
    b. For **Item 92**, determine the amount of the adjustment, if any, to arrive at adjusted gross income. To record your answer, blacken the ovals on the *Objective Answer Sheet*. If zeros precede your numerical answer, blacken the zeros in the ovals preceding your answer. **You cannot receive credit for your answers if you fail to blacken an oval in each column.** You may write the numbers in the boxes provided to facilitate blackening the ovals; however, the numbers written in the boxes will **not** be graded.

92. As required by a 1990 divorce agreement, Tom paid an annual amount of $8,000 in alimony and $10,000 in child support during 1994.

Required:
    c. During 1994, the following events took place. For **Items 93 to 104**, select the appropriate tax treatment and blacken the corresponding oval on the *Objective Answer Sheet*. A tax treatment may be selected once, more than once, or not at all.

Event

93. On March 23, 1994, Tom sold 50 shares of Zip stock at a $1,200 loss. He repurchased 50 shares of Zip on April 15, 1994.

94. Payment of a personal property tax based on the value of the Moores' car.

95. Used clothes were donated to church organizations.

96. Premiums were paid covering insurance against Tom's loss of earnings.

97. Tom paid for subscriptions to accounting journals.

98. Interest was paid on a $10,000 home-equity line of credit secured by the Moores' residence. The fair market value of the home exceeded the mortgage by $50,000. Tom used the proceeds to purchase a sailboat.

99. Amounts were paid in excess of insurance reimbursement for prescription drugs.

100. Funeral expenses were paid by the Moores for Joan's brother.

101. Theft loss was incurred on Joan's jewelry in excess of insurance reimbursement. There were no 1994 personal casualty gains.

102. Loss on the sale of the family's sailboat.

103. Interest was paid on the $300,000 acquisition mortgage on the Moores' home. The mortgage is secured by their home.

104. Joan performed free accounting services for the Red Cross. The estimated value of the services was $500.

Tax Treatment
Ⓐ   Not deductible on Form 1040.
Ⓑ   Deductible in full in Schedule A-Itemized Deductions.
Ⓒ   Deductible in Schedule A-Itemized Deductions, subject to a threshold of 7.5% of adjusted gross income.
Ⓓ   Deductible in Schedule A-Itemized Deductions, subject to a limitation of 50% of adjusted gross income.
Ⓔ   Deductible in Schedule A-Itemized Deductions, subject to a $100 floor and a threshold of 10% of adjusted gross income.
Ⓕ   Deductible in Schedule A-Itemized Deductions, subject to a threshold of 2% of adjusted gross income.

Required:

d. For **Items 105 to 110**, indicate if the statement is true Ⓣ or false Ⓕ regarding the Moores' 1994 tax return. Blacken the corresponding oval on the *Objective Answer Sheet*.

105. For 1994, the Moores were subject to the phaseout of half their personal exemptions for regular tax because their adjusted gross income was $75,000.

106. The Moores' unreimbursed medical expenses for AMT had to exceed 10% of adjusted gross income.

107. The Moores' personal exemption amount for regular tax was not permitted for determining 1994 AMT.

108. The Moores paid $1,200 in additional 1994 taxes when they filed their return on Friday, April 14, 1995. Their 1994 federal tax withholdings equalled 100% of 1993 tax liability. Therefore, they were not subject to the underpayment of tax penalty.

109. The Moores, both being under age 50, were subject to an early withdrawal penalty on their IRA withdrawals used for medical expenses.

110. The Moores were allowed an earned income credit against their 1994 tax liability equal to a percentage of their wages.

N94
Number 3 (Estimated time —— 25 to 40 minutes)

Question Number 3 consists of 31 items. Select the **best** answer for each item. Use a No. 2 pencil to blacken the appropriate ovals on the Objective Answer Sheet to indicate your answers. **Answer all items.** Your grade will be based on the total number of correct answers.

Mrs. Vick, a 40-year-old cash basis taxpayer, earned $45,000 as a teacher and $5,000 as a part-time real estate agent in 1993. Mr. Vick, who died on July 1, 1993, had been permanently disabled on his job and collected state disability benefits until his death. For all of 1993 and 1994, the Vick's residence was the principal home of both their 11-year old daughter Joan and Mrs. Vick's unmarried cousin, Fran Phillips, who had no income in either year. During 1993, Joan received $200 a month in survivor social security benefits that began on August 1, 1993, and will continue at least until her 18th birthday. In 1993 and 1994, Mrs. Vick provided over one-half the support for Joan and Fran, both of whom were U.S. citizens. Mrs. Vick did not remarry. Mr. and Mrs. Vick received the following in 1993:

Earned income	$50,000
State disability benefits	1,500
Interest on:	
Refund from amended tax return	50
Savings account and certificates of deposit	350
Municipal bonds	100
Gift	3,000
Pension benefits	900
Jury duty pay	200
Gambling winnings	450
Life insurance proceeds	5,000

Additional information:

- Mrs. Vick received the $3,000 cash gift from her uncle.

- Mrs. Vick received the pension distributions from a qualified pension plan, paid for exclusively by her husband's employer. The $5,000 death benefit exclusion did not apply.

- Mrs. Vick had $100 in gambling losses in 1993.

- Mrs. Vick was the beneficiary of the life insurance policy on her husband's life. She received a lump-sum distribution. The Vicks had paid $500 in premiums.

- Mrs. Vick received Mr. Vick's accrued vacation pay of $500 in 1994.

For items 69 and 70, determine and select from the choices below, **BOTH** the filing status and the number of exemptions for each item. Blacken the corresponding oval on the Objective Answer Sheet.

Filing Status
Ⓢ Single
Ⓜ Married filing joint
Ⓗ Head of household
Ⓠ Qualifying widow with dependent child

Exemptions
①
②
③
④

69. Determine the filing status and the number of exemptions that Mrs. Vick can claim on the 1993 federal income tax return, to get the most favorable tax results.

70. Determine the filing status and the number of exemptions that Mrs. Vick can claim on the 1994 federal income tax return to get the most favorable tax results, if she solely maintains the costs of her home.

For items 71 through 77, determine the amount, if any, that is taxable and should be included in Adjusted Gross Income (AGI) on the 1993 federal income tax return filed by Mrs. Vick. To record your answer, write the number in the boxes on the Objective Answer Sheet **and** blacken the corresponding oval below each box. Write zeros in any blank boxes preceding your numerical answer, and blacken the zero in the oval below the box. **You cannot**

receive credit for your answers if you fail to blacken an oval in each column.

71. State disability benefits
72. Interest income
73. Pension benefits
74. Gift
75. Life insurance proceeds
76. Jury duty pay
77. Gambling winnings

During 1993 the following payments were made or losses were incurred. **For items 78 through 91,** select the appropriate tax treatment and blacken the corresponding oval on the Objective Answer Sheet. A tax treatment may be selected once, more than once, or not at all.

Payments and Losses

78. Premiums on Mr. Vick's personal life insurance policy.

79. Penalty on Mrs. Vick's early withdrawal of funds from a certificate of deposit.

80. Mrs. Vick's substantiated cash donation to the American Red Cross.

81. Payment of estimated state income taxes.

82. Payment of real estate taxes on the Vick home.

83. Loss on the sale of the family car.

84. Cost in excess of the increase in value of residence, for the installation of a stairlift in January 1993, related directly to the medical care of Mr. Vick.

85. The Vick's health insurance premiums for hospitalization coverage.

86. CPA fees to prepare the 1992 tax return.

87. Amortization over the life of the loan of points paid to refinance the mortgage at a lower rate on the Vick home.

88. One-half the self-employment tax paid by Mrs. Vick.

89. Mrs. Vick's $100 in gambling losses.

90. Mrs. Vick's union dues.

91. 1992 federal income tax paid with the Vick's tax return on April 15, 1993.

Tax Treatment

A. Not deductible.

B. Deductible in Schedule A—Itemized Deductions, subject to threshold of 7.5% of adjusted gross income.

C. Deductible in Schedule A—Itemized Deductions, subject to threshold of 2% of adjusted gross income.

D. Deductible on page 1 of Form 1040 to arrive at adjusted gross income.

E. Deductible in full in Schedule A—Itemized Deductions.

F. Deductible in Schedule A—Itemized Deductions, subject to threshold of 50% of adjusted gross income.

Selected Questions

For items 92 through 99, determine whether the statement is true Ⓣ or false Ⓕ regarding the Vicks' 1993 income tax return. Blacken the corresponding oval on the Objective Answer Sheet.

92. The funeral expenses paid by Mr. Vick's estate is a 1993 itemized deduction.

93. Any federal estate tax on the income in respect of decedent, to be distributed to Mrs. Vick, may be taken as a miscellaneous itemized deduction **not** subject to the 2% of adjusted gross income floor.

94. A casualty loss deduction on property used in Mrs. Vick's part-time real estate business is reported as an itemized deduction.

95. The Vicks' income tax liability will be reduced by the credit for the elderly or disabled.

96. The CPA preparer is required to furnish a completed copy of the 1993 income tax return to Mrs. Vick.

97. Since Mr. Vick died during the year, the income limitation for the earned income credit does **not** apply.

98. Mr. Vick's accrued vacation pay, at the time of his death, is to be distributed to Mrs. Vick in 1994. This income should be included in the 1993 Federal income tax return.

99. The Vicks paid alternative minimum tax in 1992. The amount of alternative minimum tax that is attributable to "deferral adjustments and preferences" can be used to offset the alternative minimum tax in the following years.

2M92
Number 4 (Estimated time —— 45 to 55 minutes)

Instructions

Question Number 4 consists of 20 items. Select the **best** answer for each item. Use a No. 2 pencil to blacken the appropriate ovals on the Objective Answer Sheet to indicate your answers. **Answer all items.** Your grade will be based on the total number of correct answers.

Cole, a newly licensed CPA, opened an office in 1991 as a sole practitioner engaged in the practice of public accountancy. Cole reports on the cash basis for income tax purposes. Listed on page AR-79 are Cole's 1991 business and nonbusiness transactions, as well as possible tax treatments.

Required:
For each of Cole's transactions (Items 61 through 80), select the appropriate tax treatment and blacken the corresponding oval on the Objective Answer Sheet. A tax treatment may be selected once, more than once, or not at all.

Example:
The following is an example of the manner in which the answer sheet should be marked.

Item

Transactions	Tax Treatments
99. Dues paid to a local health club.	P. Not deductible.

Answer Sheet

Item	Tax Treatments (select one)
99	Ⓐ Ⓑ Ⓒ Ⓓ Ⓔ Ⓕ Ⓖ Ⓗ Ⓘ Ⓙ Ⓚ Ⓛ Ⓜ Ⓝ Ⓞ ●

Selected Questions

Items to be Answered:

Transactions

61. Fees received for jury duty.
62. Interest income on mortgage loan receivable.
63. Penalty paid to bank on early withdrawal of savings.
64. Writeoffs of uncollectible accounts receivable from accounting practice.
65. Cost of attending review course in preparation for the Uniform CPA Examination.
66. Fee for the biennial permit to practice as a CPA.
67. Costs of attending CPE courses in fulfillment of state board requirements.
68. Contribution to a qualified Keogh retirement plan.
69. Loss sustained from nonbusiness bad debt.
70. Loss sustained on sale of "Small Business Corporation" (Section 1244) stock.
71. Taxes paid on land owned by Cole and rented out as a parking lot.
72. Interest paid on installment purchases of household furniture.
73. Alimony paid to former spouse who reports the alimony as taxable income.
74. Personal medical expenses charged on credit card in December 1991 but not paid until January 1992.
75. Personal casualty loss sustained.
76. State inheritance tax paid on bequest received.
77. Foreign income tax withheld at source on dividend received.
78. Computation of self-employment tax.
79. One-half of self-employment tax paid with 1991 return filed in April 1992.
80. Insurance premiums paid on Cole's life.

Tax Treatments

A. Taxable as interest income in Schedule B — Interest and Dividend Income.
B. Taxable as other income on page 1 of Form 1040.
C. Not taxable.
D. Deductible on page 1 of Form 1040 to arrive at adjusted gross income.
E. Deductible in Schedule A — Itemized Deductions, subject to threshold of 7.5% of adjusted gross income.
F. Deductible in Schedule A — Itemized Deductions, subject to threshold of 10% of adjusted gross income and additional threshold of $100.
G. Deductible in full in Schedule A — Itemized Deductions (cannot be claimed as a credit).
H. Deductible in Schedule B — Interest and Dividend Income.
I. Deductible in Schedule C — Profit or Loss from Business.
J. Deductible in Schedule D — Capital Gains or Losses.
K. Deductible in Schedule E — Supplemental Income and Loss.
L. Deductible in Form 4797 — Sales of Business Property.
M. Claimed in Form 1116 — Foreign Tax Credit, or in Schedule A — Itemized Deductions, at taxpayer's option.
N. Based on gross self-employment income.
O. Based on net earnings from self-employment.
P. Not deductible.

AR-67

II. Federal Taxation—Corporations

R97
Number 1

Question Number 1 consists of 11 items about C Corporations. Select the **best** answer for each item. Use a No. 2 pencil to blacken the appropriate ovals on the *Objective Answer Sheet* to indicate your answers. **Answer all items.** Your grade will be based on the total number of correct answers.

Capital Corp., an accrual-basis calendar-year C corporation, began operations on January 2, 1995. Capital timely filed its 1996 federal income tax return on Monday, March 17, 1997.

Required:
Items 1 through 4 each require **two** responses:

a. For each item below, determine the amount of Capital's 1996 Schedule M-1 adjustment necessary to reconcile book income to taxable income. **The ones, tens, and hundreds** columns **do not appear** on the *Objective Answer Sheet*. To record your answer, blacken the ovals on the *Objective Answer Sheet*. To record a **zero** answer for an item, you must blacken all the **zero ovals** for that particular item. If zeros precede your numerical answer, blacken the zeros in the ovals preceding your answer. **You cannot receive credit for your answers if you fail to blacken an oval in each column.** You may write the numbers in the boxes provided to facilitate blackening the ovals; however, the numbers written in the boxes will **not** be graded.

Example:
The following are examples of the manner in which numeric responses for **Items 1(A) through 4(A)** should be recorded on the *Objective Answer Sheet*.

Answer	$0	$5,000	$18,000	$610,000
Objective Answer Sheet	0 0 0	0 0 5	0 1 8	6 1 0

b. In addition, determine if the Schedule M-1 adjustment necessary to reconcile book income to taxable income increases, decreases, or has no effect on Capital's 1996 taxable income. Blacken the corresponding oval on the *Objective Answer Sheet*. An answer may be selected once, more than once, or not at all.

Selections
(I) Increases Capital's 1996 taxable income.
(D) Decreases Capital's 1996 taxable income.
(N) Has no effect on Capital's 1996 taxable income.

1. At its corporate inception in 1995, Capital incurred and paid $40,000 in organizational costs for legal fees to draft the corporate charter. In 1995, Capital correctly elected, for book purposes, to amortize the organizational expenditures over 40 years and for the minimum required period on its federal income tax return. For 1996 Capital amortized $1,000 of the organizational costs on its books.

2. Capital's 1996 disbursements included $10,000 for reimbursed employees' expenses for business meals and entertainment. The reimbursed expenses met the conditions of deductibility and were properly substantiated under an accountable plan. The reimbursement was not treated as employee compensation.

3. Capital's 1996 disbursements included $15,000 for life insurance premium expense paid for its executives as part of their taxable compensation. Capital is neither the direct nor the indirect beneficiary of the policy, and the amount of the compensation is reasonable.

4. In 1996, Capital increased its allowance for uncollectible accounts by $10,000. No bad debt was written off in 1996.

Sunco Corp., an accrual-basis calendar-year C corporation, timely filed its 1996 federal income tax return on Monday, March 17, 1997.

Required:
 c. For **Items 5 and 6,** determine if the following items are fully taxable, partially taxable, or nontaxable for regular income tax purposes on Sunco's 1996 federal income tax return. Blacken the corresponding oval on the *Objective Answer Sheet*. An answer may be selected once, more than once, or not at all.

	Selections
Ⓕ	Fully taxable for regular income tax purposes on Sunco's 1996 federal income tax return.
Ⓟ	Partially taxable for regular income tax purposes on Sunco's 1996 federal income tax return.
Ⓝ	Nontaxable for regular income tax purposes on Sunco's 1996 federal income tax return.

5. In 1996, Sunco received dividend income from a 35%-owned domestic corporation. The dividends were not from debt-financed portfolio stock, and the taxable income limitation did not apply.

6. In 1996, Sunco received a $2,800 lease cancellation payment from a three-year lease tenant.

Quest Corp., an accrual-basis calendar-year C corporation, timely filed its 1996 federal income tax return on Monday, March 17, 1997.

Required:
 d. For **Items 7 and 8,** determine if the following items are fully deductible, partially deductible, or nondeductible for regular income tax purposes on Quest's 1996 federal income tax return. Blacken the corresponding oval on the *Objective Answer Sheet*. An answer may be selected once, more than once, or not at all.

	Selections
Ⓕ	Fully deductible for regular income tax purposes on Quest's 1996 federal income tax return.
Ⓟ	Partially deductible for regular income tax purposes on Quest's 1996 federal income tax return.
Ⓝ	Nondeductible for regular income tax purposes on Quest's 1996 federal income tax return.

7. Quest's 1996 taxable income before charitable contributions and dividends-received deduction was $200,000. Quest's Board of Directors authorized a $38,000 contribution to a qualified charity on December 1, 1996. The payment was made on February 1, 1997. All charitable contributions were properly substantiated.

8. During 1996 Quest was assessed and paid a $300 uncontested penalty for failure to pay its 1995 federal income taxes on time.

On its 1996 federal income tax return, Gelco Corp., an accrual-basis calendar-year C corporation, reported the same amounts for regular income tax and alternative minimum tax purposes.

Required:
 e. For **Items 9 through 11,** determine if each item, taken separately, contributes to overstating, understating, or correctly stating Gelco's 1996 alternative minimum taxable income (AMTI) prior to the adjusted current earnings adjustment (ACE). Blacken the corresponding oval on the *Objective Answer Sheet*. An answer may be selected once, more than once, or not at all.

	Selections
Ⓞ	Overstating Gelco's 1996 AMTI prior to the ACE.
Ⓤ	Understating Gelco's 1996 AMTI prior to the ACE.
Ⓒ	Correctly stating Gelco's 1996 AMTI prior to the ACE.

9. For regular tax purposes, Gelco deducted the maximum MACRS depreciation on seven-year personal property placed in service on January 1, 1996. Gelco made no Internal Revenue Code Section 179 election to expense the property in 1996.

10. For regular income tax purposes, Gelco depreciated nonresidential real property placed in service on January 1, 1996, under the general MACRS depreciation system for a 39-year depreciable life.

11. Gelco excluded state highway construction general obligation bond interest income earned in 1996 for regular income tax and alternative minimum tax (AMT) purposes.

N95
Number 2 (Estimated time —— 5 to 10 minutes)

Question Number 2 consists of 6 items. Select the best answer for each item. Use a No. 2 pencil to blacken the appropriate ovals on the *Objective Answer Sheet* to indicate your answers. **Answer all items.** Your grade will be based on the total number of correct answers.

Lan Corp., an accrual-basis calendar year repair-service corporation, began business on Monday, January 3, 1994. Lan's valid S corporation election took effect retroactively on January 3, 1994.

Required:

a. For **Items 76 through 79**, determine the amount, if any, using the fact pattern for each item. To record your answer, blacken the ovals on the *Objective Answer Sheet*. If zeros precede your numerical answer, blacken the zeros in the ovals preceding your answer. **You cannot receive credit for your answers if you fail to blacken an oval in each column**. You may write the numbers in the boxes provided to facilitate blackening the ovals; however, the numbers written in the boxes will **not** be graded.

76. Assume the following facts:

Lan's 1994 books recorded the following items:

Gross receipts	$7,260
Interest income on investments	50
Charitable contributions	1,000
Supplies	1,120

What amount of net business income should Lan report on its 1994 Form 1120S, U.S. Income Tax Return for an S Corporation, Schedule K?

77. Assume the following facts:

As of January 3, 1994, Taylor and Barr each owned 100 shares of the 200 issued shares of Lan stock. On January 31, 1994, Taylor and Barr each sold 20 shares to Pike. No election was made to terminate the tax year. Lan had net business income of $14,520 for the year ended December 31, 1994, and made no distributions to its shareholders. Lan's 1994 calendar year had 363 days.

What amount of net business income should have been reported on Pike's 1994 Schedule K-1 from Lan? (1994 is a 363-day tax year.) Round the answer to the nearest hundred.

78. Assume the following facts:

Pike purchased 40 Lan shares on January 31, 1994, for $4,000. Lan made no distributions to shareholders, and Pike's 1994 Schedule K-1 from Lan reported:

Ordinary business loss	($1,000)
Municipal bond interest income	150

What was Pike's basis in his Lan stock at December 31, 1994?

79. Assume the following facts:

On January 3, 1994, Taylor and Barr each owned 100 shares of the 200 issued shares of Lan stock. Taylor's basis in Lan shares on that date was $10,000. Taylor sold all of his Lan shares to Pike on January 31, 1994, and Lan made a valid election to terminate its tax year. Taylor's share of ordinary income from Lan prior to the sale was $2,000. Lan made a cash distribution of $3,000 to Taylor on January 30, 1994.

What was Taylor's basis in Lan shares for determining gain or loss from the sale to Pike?

Required:

b. For **Items 80 and 81**, indicate if the statement is true Ⓣ or false Ⓕ regarding Lan's S corporation status. Blacken the corresponding oval on the *Objective Answer Sheet*.

80. Lan issues shares of both preferred and common stock to shareholders at inception on January 3, 1994. This will **not** affect Lan's S corporation eligibility.

81. Lan, an S corporation since inception, has passive investment income for 3 consecutive years following the year a valid S corporation election takes effect. Lan's S corporation election is terminated as of the first day of the fourth year.

M95
Number 3 (Estimated time — — 25 to 40 minutes)

Question Number 3 consists of 28 items. Select the **best** answer for each item. Use a No. 2 pencil to blacken the appropriate ovals on the *Objective Answer Sheet* to indicate your answers. **Answer all items.** Your grade will be based on the total number of correct answers.

Reliant Corp., an accrual basis calendar-year C corporation, filed its 1994 federal income tax return on March 15, 1995.

Required:

The following **two** responses are required for each of the **Items 85 through 90**.

a. Determine the amount of Reliant's 1994 Schedule M-1 adjustment. To record your answer, blacken the ovals on the *Objective Answer Sheet*. If zeros precede your numerical answer, blacken the zeros in the ovals preceding your answer. **You cannot receive credit for your answers if you fail to blacken an oval in each column.** You may write the numbers in the boxes provided to facilitate blackening the ovals; however, the numbers written in the boxes will **not** be graded.

b. Indicate if the adjustment Ⓘ increases, Ⓓ decreases, or Ⓝ has no effect, on Reliant's 1994 taxable income. Blacken the corresponding oval on the *Objective Answer Sheet*.

85. Reliant's disbursements included reimbursed employees' expenses in 1994 for travel of $100,000, and business meals of $30,000. The reimbursed expenses met the conditions of deductibility and were properly substantiated under an accountable plan. The reimbursement was not treated as employee compensation.

86. Reliant's books expensed $7,000 in 1994 for the term life insurance premiums on the corporate officers. Reliant was the policy owner and beneficiary.

87. Reliant's books indicated an $18,000 state franchise tax expense for 1994. Estimated state tax payments for 1994 were $15,000.

88. Book depreciation on computers for 1994 was $10,000. These computers, which cost $50,000, were placed in service on January 2, 1993. Tax depreciation used MACRS with the half-year convention. No election was made to expense part of the computer cost or to use a straight-line method or the alternative depreciation system.

89. For 1994, Reliant's books showed a $4,000 short-term capital gain distribution from a mutual fund corporation and a $5,000 loss on the sale of Retro stock that was purchased in 1992. The stock was an investment in an unrelated corporation. There were no other 1994 gains or losses and no loss carryovers from prior years.

90. Reliant's 1994 taxable income before the charitable contribution and the dividends received deductions was $500,000. Reliant's books expensed $15,000 in board-of-director authorized charitable contributions that were paid on January 5, 1995. Charitable contributions paid and expensed during 1994 were $35,000. All charitable contributions were properly substantiated. There were no net operating losses or charitable contributions that were carried forward.

Required:

c. For **Items 91 through 95,** indicate if the expenses are Ⓕ fully deductible, Ⓟ partially deductible, or Ⓝ nondeductible for regular tax purposes on Reliant's 1994 federal income tax return. Blacken the corresponding oval on the *Objective Answer Sheet*.

91. Reliant purchased theater tickets for its out of town clients. The performances took place after Reliant's substantial and bona fide business negotiations with its clients.

92. Reliant accrued advertising expenses to promote a new product line. Ten percent of the new product line remained in ending inventory.

93. Reliant incurred interest expense on a loan to purchase municipal bonds.

94. Reliant paid a penalty for the underpayment of 1993 estimated taxes.

95. On December 9, 1994, Reliant's board of directors voted to pay a $500 bonus to each non-stockholder employee for 1994. The bonuses were paid on February 3, 1995.

Required:

d. For **Items 96 through 100,** indicate if the following items are Ⓕ fully taxable, Ⓟ partially taxable, or Ⓝ nontaxable for regular tax purposes on Reliant's 1994 federal income tax return. All transactions occurred during 1994. Blacken the corresponding oval on the *Objective Answer Sheet*.

Items 96 and 97 are based on the following:

Reliant filed an amended federal income tax return for 1992 and received a refund that included both the overpayment of the federal taxes and interest.

96. The portion of Reliant's refund that represented the overpayment of the 1992 federal taxes.

97. The portion of Reliant's refund that is attributable to the interest on the overpayment of federal taxes.

98. Reliant received dividend income from a mutual fund that solely invests in municipal bonds.

99. Reliant, the lessor, benefitted from the capital improvements made to its property by the lessee in 1994. The lease agreement is for one year ending December 31, 1994, and provides for a reduction in rental payments by the lessee in exchange for the improvements.

100. Reliant collected the proceeds on the term life insurance policy on the life of a debtor who was not a shareholder. The policy was assigned to Reliant as collateral security for the debt. The proceeds exceeded the amount of the debt.

Required:

e. For **Items 101 through 105,** indicate if the following Ⓘ increase, Ⓓ decrease, or Ⓝ have no effect on Reliant's 1994 alternative minimum taxable income (AMTI) *prior to* the adjusted current earnings adjustment (ACE). Blacken the corresponding oval on the *Objective Answer Sheet*.

101. Reliant used the 70% dividends-received deduction for regular tax purposes.

102. Reliant received interest from a state's general obligation bonds.

103. Reliant used MACRS depreciation on seven-year personal property placed into service January 3, 1994, for regular tax purposes. No expense or depreciation election was made.

104. Depreciation on nonresidential real property placed into service on January 3, 1994, was under the general MACRS depreciation system for regular tax purposes.

105. Reliant had only cash charitable contributions for 1994.

Required:

f. For **Items 106 through 112,** indicate if the statement is true Ⓣ or false Ⓕ regarding Reliant's compliance with tax procedures, tax credits and the alternative minimum tax. Blacken the corresponding oval on the *Objective Answer Sheet*.

106. Reliant's exemption for alternative minimum tax is reduced by 20% of the excess of the alternative minimum taxable income over $150,000.

107. The statute of limitations on Reliant's fraudulent 1990 federal income tax return expires six years after the filing date of the return.

108. The statute of limitations on Reliant's 1991 federal income tax return, which omitted 30% of gross receipts, expires 2 years after the filing date of the return.

109. The targeted job tax credit may be combined with other business credits to form part of Reliant's general business credit.

110. Reliant incurred qualifying expenditures to remove existing access barriers at the place of employment in 1994. As a small business, Reliant qualifies for the disabled access credit.

111. Reliant's tax preparer, a CPA firm, may use the 1994 corporate tax return information to prepare corporate officers' tax returns without the consent of the corporation.

112. Reliant must file an amended return for 1994 within 1 year of the filing date.

M94
Number 2 (Estimated time — — 25 to 40 minutes)

Number 2 consists of 25 items. Select the **best** answer for each item. Use a No. 2 pencil to blacken the appropriate ovals on the Objective Answer Sheet to indicate your answers. **Answer all items.** Your grade will be based on the total number of correct answers.

Kimberly Corp. is a calendar year accrual basis corporation that commenced operations on January 1, 1990. The following adjusted accounts appear on Kimberly's records for the year ended December 31, 1993. Kimberly is not subject to the uniform capitalization rules.

Revenues and gains

Gross sales	$2,000,000
Dividends:	
20%-owned domestic corporation	10,000
XYZ Corp.	10,000
Interest:	
U.S. treasury bonds	26,000
Municipal bonds	25,000
Insurance proceeds	40,000
Gain on sale:	
Unimproved lot (1)	20,000
XYZ stock (2)	5,000
State franchise tax refund	14,000
Total	2,150,000

Costs and expenses

Cost of goods sold	350,000
Salaries and wages	470,000
Depreciation:	
Real property	50,000
Personal property (3)	100,000
Bad debt (4)	10,000
State franchise tax	25,000
Vacation expense	10,000
Interest expense (5)	16,000
Life insurance premiums	20,000
Federal income taxes	200,000
Entertainment expense	20,000
Other expenses	29,000
Total	1,300,000
Net income	$ 850,000

Additional information:

(1) Gain on the sale of unimproved lot—Purchased in 1991 for use in business for $50,000. Sold in 1993 for $70,000. Kimberly has never had any Sec. 1231 losses.

(2) Gain on sale of XYZ Stock—Purchased in 1991.

(3) Personal Property—The book depreciation is the same as tax depreciation for all the property that was placed in service before January 1, 1993. The book depreciation is straight line over the useful life, which is the same as class life. Company policy is to use half-year convention per books for personal property. Furniture and fixtures costing $56,000 were placed in service on January 1, 1993.

(4) Bad Debt—Represents the increase in the allowance for doubtful accounts based on an aging of accounts receivable. Actual bad debts written off were $7,000.

(5) Interest expense on:

Mortgage loan	$10,000
Loan obtained to purchase municipal bonds	4,000
Line of credit loan	2,000

Required:
For items 61 through 65, determine the amount that should be reported on Kimberly corporation's 1993 Federal income tax return. To record your answer, write the number in the boxes on the Objective Answer Sheet **and** blacken the corresponding oval below each box. Write zeros in any blank boxes preceding your numerical

Selected Questions

answer, and blacken the zero in the oval below the box. **You cannot receive credit for your answer if you fail to blacken the ovals.**

Items to be Answered:

61. What amount of interest income is taxable from the U.S. Treasury bonds?

62. Determine the tax depreciation expense under the Modified Accelerated Cost Recovery System (MACRS), for the furniture and fixtures that were placed in service on January 1, 1993. Assume that no irrevocable depreciation election is made. Round the answer to the nearest thousand. Kimberly did **not** use the alternative depreciation system (ADS) or a straight-line method of depreciation. No election was made to expense part of the cost of the property.

63. Determine the amount of bad debt to be included as an expense item.

64. Determine Kimberly's net long-term capital gain.

65. What amount of interest expense is deductible?

Required:

For items **66 through 70**, select whether the following expenses are Ⓕ fully deductible, Ⓟ partially deductible, or Ⓝ nondeductible, for regular tax purposes, on Kimberly's 1993 Federal income tax return. Blacken the corresponding oval on the Objective Answer Sheet to indicate your answer.

Items to be Answered:

66. Organization expense incurred at corporate inception in 1990 to draft the corporate charter. No deduction was taken for the organization expense in 1990.

67. Life insurance premiums paid by the corporation for its executives as part of their compensation for services rendered. The corporation is neither the direct nor the indirect beneficiary of the policy and the amount of compensation is reasonable.

68. Vacation pay earned by employees which vested under a plan by December 31, 1993, and was paid February 1, 1994.

69. State franchise tax liability that has accrued during the year and was paid on March 15, 1994.

70. Entertainment expense to lease a luxury skybox during football season to entertain clients. A bona fide business discussion precedes each game. The cost of regular seats would have been one half the amount paid.

Required:

For items **71 through 75**, select whether the following revenue items are Ⓕ fully taxable, Ⓟ partially taxable, or Ⓝ nontaxable on Kimberly Corp.'s 1993 Federal income tax return for regular tax purposes. Blacken the corresponding oval on the Objective Answer Sheet to indicate your answer.

Items to be Answered:

71. Dividends from the 20%-owned domestic corporation. The taxable income limitation does not apply. Kimberly does not have the ability to exercise significant influence.

72. Recovery of an account from prior year's bad debts. Kimberly uses an estimate of uncollectibles based on an aging of accounts receivable for book purposes. The account was written off for tax purposes and reduced Kimberly's income tax liability.

73. Refund of state franchise tax overpayment, previously expensed on Kimberly's 1991 federal tax return, thereby reducing federal taxes that year.

74. Interest income from municipal bonds purchased by Kimberly in 1992 on the open market.

75. Proceeds paid to Kimberly by reason of death, under a life insurance policy that Kimberly had purchased on the life of one of its vice-presidents. Kimberly was the beneficiary and used the proceeds to pay the premium charges for the group term insurance policy for its other employees.

Required:

Items **76 through 85** refer to Kimberly's need to determine if it will be subject to the alternative minimum tax. Determine whether the statement is true Ⓣ or false Ⓕ. Blacken the corresponding oval on the Objective Answer Sheet.

Items to be Answered:

76. The method of depreciation for commercial real property to arrive at alternative minimum taxable income before the adjusted current earnings (ACE) adjustment, is the straight-line method.

77. The corporate exemption amount reduces the alternative minimum taxable income.

78. The ACE adjustment can be a positive or negative amount.

79. Depreciation on personal property to arrive at alternative minimum taxable income before the ACE adjustment is straight-line over the MACRS recovery period.

80. The alternative minimum tax is the excess of the tentative minimum tax over the regular tax liability.

81. Municipal bond interest, other than from private activity bonds, is includible income to arrive at alternative minimum taxable income before the ACE adjustment.

82. The maximum corporate exemption amount for minimum tax purposes is $150,000.

83. The 70% dividends received deduction is available to determine ACE.

84. Municipal bond interest is includible income to determine ACE.

85. The method of depreciation for personal property placed in service after 1989 for determining ACE is the sum-of-the-years'-digits method.

III. Federal Taxation—Partnerships

R97
Number 3

Question Number 3 consists of 3 parts. Part **A** consists of 9 items, Part **B** consists of 10 items, and Part **C** consists of 1 item. Select the **best** answer for each item. Use a No. 2 pencil to blacken the appropriate ovals on the *Objective Answer Sheet* to indicate your answers. **Answer all items.** Your grade will be based on the total number of correct answers.

    a. The Internal Revenue Service is auditing Oate's 1996 Form 1040—Individual Income Tax Return. During 1996, Oate, an unmarried custodial parent, had one dependent three-year-old child and worked in a CPA firm. For 1996, Oate, who had adjusted gross income of $40,000, qualified to itemize deductions and was subject to federal income tax liability.

Required:
    For **Items 1 through 9**, select from the following list of tax treatments the appropriate tax treatment and blacken the corresponding oval on the *Objective Answer Sheet*. A tax treatment may be selected once, more than once, or not at all.

Tax Treatments
Ⓐ Not deductible on Form 1040.
Ⓑ Deductible in full on Schedule A—Itemized Deductions.
Ⓒ Deductible in Schedule A—Itemized Deductions subject to a limitation of 50% of adjusted gross income.
Ⓓ Deductible in Schedule A—Itemized Deductions as miscellaneous deduction subject to a threshold of 2% of adjusted gross income.
Ⓔ Deductible in Schedule A—Itemized Deductions as miscellaneous deduction **not** subject to a threshold of 2% of adjusted gross income.
Ⓕ Deductible on Schedule E—Supplemental Income and Loss.
Ⓖ A credit is allowable.

1. In 1996, Oate paid $900 toward continuing education courses and was not reimbursed by her employer.

2. For 1996, Oate had a $30,000 cash charitable contribution carryover from her 1995 cash donation to the American Red Cross. Oate made no additional charitable contributions in 1996.

3. During 1996, Oate had investment interest expense that did not exceed her net investment income.

4. Oate's 1996 lottery ticket losses were $450. She had no gambling winnings.

5. During 1996, Oate paid $2,500 in real property taxes on her vacation home, which she used exclusively for personal use.

6. In 1996, Oate paid a $500 premium for a homeowner's insurance policy on her principal residence.

7. For 1996, Oate paid $1,500 to an unrelated baby-sitter to care for her child while she worked.

8. In 1996, Oate paid $4,000 interest on the $60,000 acquisition mortgage of her principal residence. The mortgage is secured by Oate's home.

9. During 1996, Oate paid $3,600 real property taxes on residential rental property in which she actively participates. There was no personal use of the rental property.

    b. Frank and Dale Cumack are married and filing a joint 1996 income tax return. During 1996, Frank, 65, was retired from government service and Dale, 55, was employed as a university instructor. In 1996, the Cumacks contributed all of the support to Dale's father, Jacques, an unmarried French citizen and French resident who had no gross income.

Required:
    For **Items 10 through 19**, select the correct amount of income, loss, or adjustment to income that should be recognized on page 1 of the Cumacks' 1996 Form 1040—Individual Income Tax Return to arrive at the adjusted gross income for each separate transaction and blacken the corresponding oval on the *Objective Answer Sheet*. A response may be selected once, more than once, or not at all.

Selected Questions

Any information contained in an item is unique to that item and is not to be incorporated in your calculations when answering other items.

Amounts			
Ⓐ	$0	Ⓗ	$ 9,000
Ⓑ	$ 1,000	Ⓘ	$ 10,000
Ⓒ	$ 2,000	Ⓙ	$ 25,000
Ⓓ	$ 2,250	Ⓚ	$ 30,000
Ⓔ	$ 3,000	Ⓛ	$125,000
Ⓕ	$ 4,000	Ⓜ	$150,000
Ⓖ	$ 5,000		

10. During 1996, Dale received a $30,000 cash gift from her aunt.

11. Dale contributed $2,000 to her Individual Retirement Account (IRA) on January 15, 1997. In 1996, she earned $60,000 as a university instructor. During 1996, the Cumacks were not active participants in an employer's qualified pension or annuity plan.

12. In 1996, the Cumacks received a $1,000 federal income tax refund.

13. During 1996, Frank, a 50% partner in Diske General Partnership, received a $4,000 guaranteed payment from Diske for services that he rendered to the partnership that year.

14. In 1996, Frank received $10,000 as beneficiary of his deceased brother's life insurance policy.

15. Dale's employer pays 100% of the cost of all employees' group term life insurance under a qualified plan. Policy cost is $5 per $1,000 of coverage. Dale's group term life insurance coverage equals $450,000.

16. In 1996, Frank won $5,000 at a casino and had $2,000 in gambling losses.

17. During 1996, the Cumacks received $1,000 interest income associated with a refund of their prior years' federal income tax.

18. In 1996, the Cumacks sold their first and only residence for $200,000. They purchased their home in 1985 for $50,000 and have lived there since then. There were no other capital gains, losses, or capital loss carryovers. The Cumacks do not intend to buy another residence and they have properly elected the lifetime exclusion.

19. In 1996, Zeno Corp. declared a stock dividend and Dale received one additional share of Zeno common stock for three shares of Zeno common stock that she held. The stock that Dale received had a fair market value of $9,000. There was no provision to receive cash instead of stock.

c. Frank and Dale Cumack are married and filing a joint 1996 income tax return. During 1996, Frank, 65, was retired from government service and Dale, 55, was employed as a university instructor. In 1996, the Cumacks contributed all of the support to Dale's father, Jacques, an unmarried French citizen and French resident who had no gross income.

Required:
For **Item 20**, determine whether the Cumacks overstated, understated, or correctly determined the number of both personal and dependency exemptions and blacken the corresponding oval on the *Objective Answer Sheet*.

Selections
Ⓞ Overstated the number of both personal and dependency exemptions.
Ⓤ Understated the number of both personal and dependency exemptions.
Ⓒ Correctly determined the number of both personal and dependency exemptions.

20. The Cumacks claimed 3 exemptions on their 1996 joint income tax return.

IV. Federal Taxation—Estates and Trusts, Exempt Organizations, and Preparers' Responsibilities

R98
Number 1

Question Number 1 consists of 2 parts concerning federal estate and gift taxation. Part **A** consists of 5 items and Part **B** consists of 5 items. Select the **best** answer for each item. Use a No. 2 pencil to blacken the appropriate ovals on the *Objective Answer Sheet* to indicate your answers. **Answer all items.** Your grade will be based on the total number of correct answers.

Items 1 through 10 are based on the following fact pattern:

Before his death, Remsen, a U.S. citizen, made cash gifts of $7,000 each to his four sisters. In 1997, Remsen also paid $2,000 in tuition directly to his grandchild's university on the grandchild's behalf. Remsen made no other lifetime transfers. Remsen died on January 9, 1997, and was survived by his wife and only child, both of whom were U.S. citizens. The Remsens did not live in a community property state.

At his death, Remsen owned:
Cash	$650,000
Marketable securities (Fair market value)	900,000
Life insurance policy with Remsen's wife named as the beneficiary (fair market value)	500,000

Under the provisions of Remsen's will, the net cash, after payment of executor's fees and medical and funeral expenses, was bequeathed to Remsen's son. The marketable securities were bequeathed to Remsen's spouse. During 1997, Remsen's estate paid:

Executor's fees to distribute the decedent's property (deducted on the fiduciary tax return)	$15,000
Decedent's funeral expenses	25,000

The estate's executor extended the time to file the estate tax return.

On January 3, 1998, the estate's executor paid the decedent's outstanding $10,000 1997 medical expense and filed the extended estate tax return.

Required:
   a. For **Items 1 through 5**, identify the federal estate tax treatment for each item. Blacken the corresponding oval on the *Objective Answer Sheet*. An answer may be selected once, more than once, or not at all.

Estate Tax Treatments
Ⓕ Fully includible in Remsen's gross estate.
Ⓟ Partially includible in Remsen's gross estate.
Ⓝ Not includible in Remsen's gross estate.

1. What is the estate tax treatment of the $7,000 cash gift to each sister?

2. What is the estate tax treatment of the life insurance proceeds?

3. What is the estate tax treatment of the marketable securities?

4. What is the estate tax treatment of the $2,000 tuition payment?

5. What is the estate tax treatment of the $650,000 cash?

Required:
   b. For **Items 6 through 10**, identify the federal estate tax treatment for each item. Blacken the corresponding oval on the *Objective Answer Sheet*. An answer may be selected once, more than once, or not at all.

Estate Tax Treatments
Ⓖ Deductible from Remsen's gross estate to arrive at Remsen's taxable estate.
Ⓘ Deductible on Remsen's 1997 individual income tax return.
Ⓔ Deductible on either Remsen's estate tax return or Remsen's 1997 individual income tax return.
Ⓝ Not deductible on either Remsen's estate tax return or Remsen's 1997 individual income tax return.

6. What is the estate tax treatment of the executor's fees?

7. What is the estate tax treatment of the cash bequest to Remsen's son?

8. What is the estate tax treatment of the life insurance proceeds paid to Remsen's spouse?

9. What is the estate tax treatment of the funeral expenses?

10. What is the estate tax treatment of the $10,000 1997 medical expense incurred before the decedent's death and paid by the executor on January 3, 1998?

R96
Number 1 (Estimated time — — 5 to 10 minutes)

Question Number 1 consists of 9 items. Select the **best** answer for each item. Use a No. 2 pencil to blacken the appropriate ovals on the *Objective Answer Sheet* to indicate your answers. **Answer all items.** Your grade will be based on the total number of correct answers.

A CPA sole practitioner has tax preparers' responsibilities when preparing tax returns for clients.

Required:
   Items 1 through 9 each represent an independent factual situation in which a CPA sole practitioner has prepared and signed the taxpayer's income tax return. For each item, select from the following list the correct response regarding the tax preparer's responsibilities. Blacken the corresponding oval on the *Objective Answer Sheet*. A response may be selected once, more than once, or not at all.

Answer List
Ⓟ The tax preparer's action constitutes an act of tax preparer misconduct subject to the Internal Revenue Code penalty.
Ⓔ The Internal Revenue Service will examine the facts and circumstances to determine whether the reasonable cause exception applies; the good faith exception applies; or both exceptions apply.
Ⓝ The tax preparer's action does **not** constitute an act of tax preparer misconduct.

Selected Questions

1. The tax preparer disclosed taxpayer income tax return information under an order from a state court, without the taxpayer's consent.

2. The tax preparer relied on the advice of an advisory preparer to calculate the taxpayer's tax liability. The tax preparer believed that the advisory preparer was competent and that the advice was reasonable. Based on the advice, the taxpayer had understated income tax liability.

3. The tax preparer did **not** charge a separate fee for the tax return preparation and paid the taxpayer the refund shown on the tax return less a discount. The tax preparer negotiated the actual refund check for the tax preparer's own account after receiving power of attorney from the taxpayer.

4. The tax preparer relied on information provided by the taxpayer regarding deductible travel expenses. The tax preparer believed that the taxpayer's information was correct but inquired about the existence of the travel expense records. The tax preparer was satisfied by the taxpayer's representations that the taxpayer had adequate records for the deduction. Based on this information, the income tax liability was understated.

5. The taxpayer provided the tax preparer with a detailed check register to compute business expenses. The tax preparer knowingly overstated the expenses on the income tax return.

6. The tax preparer disclosed taxpayer income tax return information during a quality review conducted by CPAs. The tax preparer maintained a record of the review.

7. The tax preparer relied on incorrect instructions on an IRS tax form that were contrary to the regulations. The tax preparer was **not** aware of the regulations nor the IRS announcement pointing out the error. The understatement was immaterial as a result of the isolated error.

8. The tax preparer used income tax return information without the taxpayer's consent to solicit additional business.

9. The tax preparer knowingly deducted the expenses of the taxpayer's personal domestic help as wages paid in the taxpayer's business on the taxpayer's income tax return.

V. Accounting for Governmental and Not-for-Profit Organizations

R98
Number 2

Question Number 2 consists of 3 parts concerning nongovernmental not-for-profit organizations. Part **A** consists of 4 items, Part **B** consists of 7 items, and Part **C** consists of 8 items. Select the **best** answer for each item. Use a No. 2 pencil to blacken the appropriate ovals on the *Objective Answer Sheet* to indicate your answers. **Answer all items.** Your grade will be based on the total number of correct answers.

    a. **Items 1 through 4** are based on the following:

Community Service, Inc. is a nongovernmental not-for-profit voluntary health and welfare calendar-year organization that began operations on January 1, 1996. It performs voluntary services and derives its revenue primarily from voluntary contributions from the general public. Community implies a time restriction on all promises to contribute cash in future periods. However, no such policy exists with respect to gifts of long-lived assets.

    Selected transactions that occurred during Community's 1997 calendar year:

- Unrestricted written promises to
  contribute cash—1996 and 1997
  —1996 promises (collected in 1997) $22,000
  —1997 promises (collected in 1997)   95,000
  —1997 promises (uncollected)   28,000

- Written promises to contribute cash
  restricted to use for community
  college scholarships—1996 and 1997
  —1996 promises (collected and
     expended in 1997)   10,000
  —1997 promises (collected and
     expended in 1997)   20,000
  —1997 promises (uncollected)   12,000

- Written promise to contribute $25,000
  if matching funds are raised for
  the capital campaign during 1997
  —Cash received in 1997 from contri-
     butor as a good faith advance   25,000
  —Matching funds received in 1997   0

- Cash received in 1996 with donor's
  only stipulation that a bus be purchased
  —Expenditure of full amount of
     donation 7/1/97   37,000

Required:
    Items 1 through 4 represent the 1997 amounts that Community reported for selected financial statement elements in its December 31, 1997, statement of financial position and 1997 statement of activities. For each item, indicate whether the amount was overstated, understated, or correctly stated. Select your answer from the list below and blacken the corresponding oval on the *Objective*

Answer Sheet. An answer may be selected once, more than once, or not at all.

List
Ⓞ Overstated.
Ⓤ Understated.
Ⓒ Correctly stated.

1. Community reported $28,000 as contributions receivable.

2. Community reported $37,000 as net assets released from restrictions (satisfaction of use restrictions).

3. Community reported $22,000 as net assets released from restrictions (due to the lapse of time restrictions).

4. Community reported $97,000 as contributions—temporarily restricted.

b. Items 5 through 11 are based on the following:

Community Service, Inc. is a nongovernmental not-for-profit voluntary health and welfare calendar-year organization that began operations on January 1, 1996. It performs voluntary services and derives its revenue primarily from voluntary contributions from the general public. Community implies a time restriction on all promises to contribute cash in future periods. However, no such policy exists with respect to gifts of long-lived assets.

Selected transactions that occurred during Community's 1997 calendar year:

- Debt security endowment received in 1997; income to be used for community services
  —Face value $90,000
  —Fair value at time of receipt 88,000
  —Fair value at 12/31/97 87,000
  —Interest earned in 1997 9,000

- 10 concerned citizens volunteered to serve meals to the homeless (400 hrs. free; fair market value of services $5 per hr.) 2,000

- Short-term investment in equity securities in 1997
  —Cost 10,000
  —Fair value 12/31/97 12,000
  —Dividend income 1,000

- Music festival to raise funds for a local hospital
  —Admission fees 5,000
  —Sales of food and drinks 14,000
  —Expenses 4,000

- Reading materials donated to Community and distributed to the children in 1997
  —Fair market value 8,000

- Federal youth training fee for service grant
  —Cash received during 1997 30,000
  —Instructor salaries paid 26,000

- Other cash operating expenses
  —Business manager salary 60,000
  —General bookkeeper salary 40,000
  —Director of community activities salary 50,000
  —Space rental (75% for community activities, 25% for office activities) 20,000
  —Printing and mailing costs for pledge cards 2,000

- Interest payment on short-term bank loan in 1997 1,000

- Principal payment on short-term bank loan in 1997 20,000

Required:
For **Items 5 through 11**, determine the amounts for the following financial statement elements in the 1997 statement of activities. Select your answer from the following list of amounts and blacken the corresponding oval on the *Objective Answer Sheet.* An amount may be selected once, more than once, or not at all.

Amounts		
Ⓐ $0	Ⓕ $9,000	Ⓚ $87,000
Ⓑ $2,000	Ⓖ $14,000	Ⓛ $88,000
Ⓒ $3,000	Ⓗ $16,000	Ⓜ $90,000
Ⓓ $5,000	Ⓘ $26,000	Ⓝ $94,000
Ⓔ $8,000	Ⓙ $50,000	Ⓞ $99,000

5. Contributions—permanently restricted.

6. Revenues—fees.

7. Investment income—debt securities.

8. Program expenses.

9. General fund-raising expenses (excludes special events).

10. Income on long-term investments—unrestricted.

11. Contributed voluntary services.

c. Items 12 through 19 are based on the fact pattern and financial information found in **both Part A and Part B**.

Selected Questions

Required:

Items **12 through 19** represent Community's transactions reportable in the statement of cash flows. For each of the items listed, select the classification that best describes the item, and blacken the corresponding oval on the *Objective Answer Sheet*. A classification may be selected once, more than once, or not at all.

Classifications
Ⓞ   Cash flows from operating activities.
Ⓘ   Cash flows from investing activities.
Ⓕ   Cash flows from financing activities.

12. Unrestricted 1996 promises collected.
13. Cash received from a contributor as a good faith advance on a promise to contribute matching funds.
14. Purchase of bus.
15. Principal payment on short-term bank loan.
16. Purchase of equity securities.
17. Dividend income earned on equity securities.
18. Interest payment on short-term bank loan.
19. Interest earned on endowment.

R97
Number 2

Question Number 2 consists of 5 items. Select the **best** answer for each item. Use a No. 2 pencil to blacken the appropriate ovals on the *Objective Answer Sheet* to indicate your answers. **Answer all items.** Your grade will be based on the total number of correct answers.

Dease City is a governmental organization that has governmental-type funds and account groups.

Required:

Items **1 through 5** represent transactions by governmental-type funds and account groups based on the following selected information taken from Dease City's 1996 financial records:

General fund

Fund balance at beginning of 1996	$ 700,000
1996 estimated revenues	10,000,000
1996 actual revenues	$10,500,000
1996 appropriations	9,000,000
1996 expenditures	8,200,000
Encumbrances at end of 1996	500,000
Vouchers payable at end of 1996	300,000
1996 operating transfers in	100,000
1996 property tax levy	9,500,000
1996 property taxes estimated to be uncollectible when property tax levy for 1996 recorded	100,000
1996 property taxes delinquent at end of 1996	150,000

Capital projects fund

1996 operating transfers in	100,000
Construction of new library wing started and completed in 1996	
• Proceeds from bonds issued at 100 in 1996	2,000,000
• Expenditures for 1996	2,100,000

For **Items 1 through 5,** determine the amounts based solely on the above information. **The ones, tens, and hundreds** columns **do not appear** on the *Objective Answer Sheet*. To record your answer, blacken the ovals on the *Objective Answer Sheet*. To record a **zero** answer for an item, you must blacken all the **zero ovals** for that particular item. If zeros precede your numerical answer, blacken the zeros in the ovals preceding your answer. **You cannot receive credit for your answers if you fail to blacken an oval in each column.** You may write the numbers in the boxes provided to facilitate blackening the ovals; however, the numbers written in the boxes will **not** be graded.

Example:
The following are examples of the manner in which numeric responses for **Items 1 through 5** should be recorded on the *Objective Answer Sheet*.

Answer	$0	$5,000	$18,000	$610,000
Objective Answer Sheet	0 0 0	0 0 5	0 1 8	6 1 0

AR-79

1. What was the net amount credited to the budgetary fund balance when the budget was approved?

2. What was the amount of property taxes collected on the property tax levy for 1996?

3. What amount for the new library wing was included in the capital projects fund balance at the end of 1996?

4. What amount for the new library wing was charged to the general fixed assets account group at the end of 1996?

5. What amount for the new library wing bonds was included in the general long-term debt account group at the end of 1996?

R96
Number 2 (Estimated time — — 20 to 30 minutes)

Question Number 2 consists of 19 items. Select the **best** answer for each item. Use a No. 2 pencil to blacken the appropriate ovals on the *Objective Answer Sheet* to indicate your answers. **Answer all items.** Your grade will be based on the total number of correct answers.

The following selected information is taken from Shar City's general fund statement of revenues, expenditures, and changes in fund balance for the year ended December 31, 1995:

Revenues	
Property taxes—1995	$ 825,000

Expenditures	
Current services	
Public safety	428,000
Capital outlay (police vehicles)	100,000
Debt service	74,000

Expenditures—1995	$1,349,000
Expenditures—1994	56,000
Expenditures	$1,405,000
Excess of revenues over expenditures	$ 153,000
Other financing uses	(125,000)
Excess of revenues over expenditures and other financing uses	$ 28,000
Decrease in reserve for encumbrances during 1995	15,000
Residual equity transfers out	(190,000)
Decrease in unreserved fund balance during 1995	$(147,000)
Unreserved fund balance January 1, 1995	304,000
Unreserved fund balance December 31, 1995	$ 157,000

The following selected information is taken from Shar's December 31, 1995, general fund balance sheet:

Property taxes receivable— delinquent—1995	$34,000
Less: Allowance for estimated uncollectible taxes–delinquent	20,000
Vouchers payable	$89,000
Fund balance—	
reserved for encumbrances—1995	$ 43,000
reserved for supplies inventory	38,000
unreserved	157,000

Additional Information:

- Debt service was for bonds used to finance a library building and included interest of $22,000.

- $8,000 of 1995 property taxes receivable were written-off; otherwise the allowance for uncollectible taxes balance is unchanged from the initial entry at the time of the original tax levy at the beginning of the year.

- Shar reported supplies inventory of $21,000 at December 31, 1994.

Required:
a. For **Items 1 through 3,** indicate the type of classification used by Shar by blackening the corresponding oval according to the item's classification:
  Ⓐ Character.
  Ⓑ Function.
  Ⓒ Object.

1. Expenditures—current services.
2. Expenditures—capital outlay.
3. Expenditures—health.

b. For **Items 4 through 6,** select the best answer to the question by blackening the corresponding oval.

4. What recording method did Shar use for its general fund supplies inventory?
  A. Consumption.
  B. Purchase.
  C. Perpetual inventory.

5. How should fund equity be reported in Shar's electric utility enterprise fund?
  A. A single amount described as fund balance.
  B. Separately for capital and retained income.
  C. Separately for amount due to general fund and retained income.

6. Shar's electric utility enterprise fund borrowed $1,000,000 subject to Shar's general guarantee. Where should the liability be reported?
  A. The electric utility enterprise fund.
  B. The general long-term debt account group.
  C. Both the electric utility enterprise fund and the general long-term debt account group.

Selected Questions

c. For **Items 7 through 13,** indicate the part of Shar's general fund statement of revenues, expenditures, and changes in fund balance affected by the transaction by blackening the corresponding oval:
- Ⓐ Revenues.
- Ⓑ Expenditures.
- Ⓒ Other financing sources and uses.
- Ⓓ Residual equity transfers.
- Ⓔ Statement of revenues, expenditures, and changes in fund balance is **not** affected.

7. An unrestricted state grant is received.

8. The general fund paid pension fund contributions that were recoverable from an internal service fund.

9. The general fund paid $60,000 for electricity supplied by Shar's electric utility enterprise fund.

10. General fund resources were used to subsidize Shar's swimming pool enterprise fund.

11. $90,000 of general fund resources were loaned to an internal service fund.

12. A motor pool internal service fund was established by a transfer of $80,000 from the general fund. This amount will not be repaid unless the motor pool is disbanded.

13. General fund resources were used to pay amounts due on an operating lease.

d. **Items 14 through 19** require numeric responses. For each item, calculate the numeric amount. To record your answer, blacken the ovals on the *Objective Answer Sheet*. If zeros precede your numerical answer, blacken the zeros in the ovals preceding your answer. **You cannot receive credit for your answers if you fail to blacken an oval in each column.** You may write the numbers in the boxes provided to facilitate blackening the ovals; however, the numbers written in the boxes will **not** be graded.

14. What was the reserved fund balance of the 1994 general fund?

15. What amount was collected from 1995 tax assessments?

16. What amount is Shar's liability to general fund vendors and contractors at December 31, 1995?

17. What amount should be included in the general fixed assets account group for the cost of assets acquired in 1995 through the general fund?

18. What amount arising from 1995 transactions decreased liabilities reported in the general long-term debt account group?

19. What amount of total actual expenditures should Shar report in its 1995 general fund statement of revenues, expenditures, and changes in fund balance–budget and actual?

R96
Number 3 (Estimated time —— 15 to 20 minutes)

Question Number 3 consists of 12 items. Select the **best** answer for each item. Use a No. 2 pencil to blacken the appropriate ovals on the *Objective Answer Sheet* to indicate your answers. **Answer all items.** Your grade will be based on the total number of correct answers.

The following events affected the financial statements of Jey City during 1995:

Budgetary activities:

- Total general fund estimated revenues $8,000,000

- Total general fund budgeted expenditures 7,500,000

- Planned construction of a courthouse improvement expected to cost $1,500,000, and to be financed in the following manner: $250,000 from the general fund, $450,000 from state entitlements, and $800,000 from the proceeds of 20-year, 8% bonds dated and expected to be issued at par on June 30, 1995. Interest on the bonds is payable annually on July 1, together with one-twentieth of the bond principal from general fund revenues of the payment period.

- A budgeted general fund payment of $180,000 to subsidize operations of a solid waste landfill enterprise fund.

Actual results included the following:

- Jey recorded property tax revenues of $5,000,000 and a related allowance for uncollectibles–current of $60,000. On December 31, 1995, the remaining $56,000 balance of the allowance for uncollectibles–current was closed, and an adjusted allowance for uncollectibles–delinquent was recorded equal to the property tax receivables balance of $38,000.

- A police car with an original cost of $25,000 was sold for $7,000.

- Office equipment to be used by the city's fire department was acquired through a capital lease. The lease required 10 equal annual payments of $10,000, beginning with the July 1, 1995, acquisition date. Using a 6% discount rate, the 10 payments had a present value of $78,000 at the acquisition date.

- The courthouse was improved and financed as budgeted except for a $27,000 cost overrun that was paid for by the general fund. Jey plans to transfer cash to the debt service fund during 1996 to service the interest and principal payments called for in the bonds.

Taxation, Managerial, and Governmental and Not-for-Profit Organizations

- Information related to the solid waste landfill at December 31, 1995:

Capacity	1,000,000 cubic yards
Usage prior to 1995	500,000 cubic yards
Usage in 1995	40,000 cubic yards
Estimated total life	20 years
Closure costs incurred to date	$ 300,000
Estimated future costs of closure and postclosure care	1,700,000
Expense for closure and postclosure care recognized prior to 1995	973,000

Jey does not record depreciation for nonproprietary fund-type assets.

Required:

For **Items 1 through 10**, determine the amounts based solely on the above information.

For **Items 1 through 10, the ones, tens, and hundreds** columns **do not appear** on the *Objective Answer Sheet*. To record your answer, blacken the ovals on the *Objective Answer Sheet*. To record a **zero** answer for an item, you must blacken all the **zero ovals** for that particular item. If zeros precede your numerical answer, blacken the zeros in the ovals preceding your answer. **You cannot receive credit for your answers if you fail to blacken an oval in each column.** You may write the numbers in the boxes provided to facilitate blackening the ovals; however, the numbers written in the boxes will **not** be graded.

Example:

The following are examples of the manner in which numeric responses for **Items 1 through 10** should be recorded on the *Objective Answer Sheet*.

Answer	$0	$5,000	$18,000	$610,000	$9,090,000

1. What was the net effect of the budgetary activities on the general fund balance at January 1, 1995?

2. What was the total amount of operating transfers out included in the general fund's budgetary accounts at January 1, 1995?

3. What amount of interest payable related to the 20-year bonds should be reported by the general fund at December 31, 1995?

4. What lease payment amount should be included in 1995 general fund expenditures?

5. What amount was collected from 1995 property taxes in 1995?

6. What was the total amount of the capital project fund's 1995 revenues?

7. What amount should be reported as liabilities in the general long-term debt account group at December 31, 1995?

8. What net increase in assets should be reported in the general fixed assets account group at December 31, 1995?

9. What 1995 closure and postclosure care expenses should be reported in the solid waste landfill enterprise fund?

10. What should be the December 31, 1995, closure and postclosure care liability reported in the solid waste landfill enterprise fund?

For **Items 11 and 12,** indicate, by blackening the corresponding oval on the *Objective Answer Sheet*, the measurement focus of the Jey fund mentioned.

- Ⓐ Subsidy restrictions.
- Ⓑ Bond restrictions.
- Ⓒ Expenditures.
- Ⓓ Financial resources.
- Ⓔ Capital maintenance/intergenerational equity.

11. Capital project fund.

12. Solid waste landfill enterprise fund.

N95

Number 5 (Estimated time — — 15 to 20 minutes)

Question Number 5 consists of 10 items. Select the **best** answer for each item. Use a No. 2 pencil to blacken the appropriate ovals on the *Objective Answer Sheet* to indicate your answers. **Answer all items.** Your grade will be based on the total number of correct answers.

The following information relates to Dane City during its fiscal year ended December 31, 1994:

- On October 31, 1994, to finance the construction of a city hall annex, Dane issued 8% 10-year general obligation bonds at their face value of $600,000. Construction expenditures during the period equaled $364,000.

- Dane reported $109,000 from hotel room taxes, restricted for tourist promotion, in a special revenue fund. The fund paid $81,000 for general promotions and $22,000 for a motor vehicle.

- 1994 general fund revenues of $104,500 were transferred to a debt service fund and used to repay $100,000 of 9% 15-year term bonds, and to pay $4,500 of interest. The bonds were used to acquire a citizens' center.

- At December 31, 1994, as a consequence of past services, city firefighters had accumulated entitlements to compensated absences valued at $86,000. General fund resources available at December 31, 1994, are expected to be used to settle $17,000 of this amount, and $69,000 is expected to be paid out of future general fund resources.

- At December 31, 1994, Dane was responsible for $83,000 of outstanding general fund encumbrances, including the $8,000 for supplies indicated below.

- Dane uses the purchases method to account for supplies. The following information relates to supplies:

Inventory—1/1/94	$ 39,000
12/31/94	42,000
Encumbrances outstanding—	
1/1/94	6,000
12/31/94	8,000
Purchase orders during 1994	190,000
Amounts credited to vouchers payable during 1994	181,000

Required:
For **Items 117 through 126**, determine the amounts based solely on the above information. To record your answer, blacken the ovals on the *Objective Answer Sheet*. If zeros precede your numerical answer, blacken the zeros in the ovals preceding your answer. **You cannot receive credit for your answers if you fail to blacken an oval in each column**. You may write the numbers in the boxes provided to facilitate blackening the ovals; however, the numbers written in the boxes will **not** be graded.

117. What is the amount of 1994 general fund operating transfers out?

118. How much should be reported as 1994 general fund liabilities from entitlements for compensated absences?

119. What is the 1994 reserved amount of the general fund balance?

120. What is the 1994 capital projects fund balance?

121. What is the 1994 fund balance on the special revenue fund for tourist promotion?

122. What is the amount of 1994 debt service fund expenditures?

123. What amount should be included in the general fixed assets account group for the cost of assets acquired in 1994?

124. What amount stemming from 1994 transactions and events decreased the liabilities reported in the general long-term debt account group?

125. Using the purchases method, what is the amount of 1994 supplies expenditures?

126. What was the total amount of 1994 supplies encumbrances?

M95
Number 2 (Estimated time — — 25 to 40 minutes)

Question Number 2 consists of 24 items. Select the **best** answer for each item. Use a No. 2 pencil to blacken the appropriate ovals on the *Objective Answer Sheet* to indicate your answers. **Answer all items.** Your grade will be based on the total number of correct answers.

The following information relates to Bel City, whose first fiscal year ended December 31, 1994. Assume Bel has only the long-term debt specified in the information and only the funds necessitated by the information.

1. General fund:
- The following selected information is taken from Bel's 1994 general fund financial records:

	Budget	Actual
Property taxes	$5,000,000	$4,700,000
Other revenues	1,000,000	1,050,000
Total revenues	$6,000,000	$5,750,000
Total expenditures	$5,600,000	$5,700,000

Property taxes receivable—delinquent		$ 420,000
Less: Allowance for estimated uncollectible taxes—delinquent		50,000
		$ 370,000

AR-83

- There were no amendments to the budget as originally adopted.

- No property taxes receivable have been written off, and the allowance for uncollectibles balance is unchanged from the initial entry at the time of the original tax levy.

- There were no encumbrances outstanding at December 31, 1994.

2. *Capital project fund:*

- Finances for Bel's new civic center were provided by a combination of general fund transfers, a state grant, and an issue of general obligation bonds. Any bond premium on issuance is to be used for the repayment of the bonds at their $1,200,000 par value. At December 31, 1994, the capital project fund for the civic center had the following closing entries:

Revenues	$ 800,000
Other financing sources—bond proceeds	1,230,000
Other financing sources—operating transfers in	500,000
Expenditures	$1,080,000
Other financing uses—operating transfers out	30,000
Unreserved fund balance	1,420,000

- Also, at December 31, 1994, capital project fund entries reflected Bel's intention to honor the $1,300,000 purchase orders and commitments outstanding for the center.

- During 1994, total capital project fund encumbrances exceeded the corresponding expenditures by $42,000. All expenditures were previously encumbered.

- During 1995, the capital project fund received no revenues and no other financing sources. The civic center building was completed in early 1995 and the capital project fund was closed by a transfer of $27,000 to the general fund.

3. *Water utility enterprise fund:*

- Bel issued $4,000,000 revenue bonds at par. These bonds, together with a $700,000 transfer from the general fund, were used to acquire a water utility. Water utility revenues are to be the sole source of funds to retire these bonds beginning in year 1999.

Required:

For **Items 61 through 76,** indicate if the answer to each item is yes Ⓨ or no Ⓝ and blacken the corresponding oval on the *Objective Answer Sheet.*

Items 61 through 68 relate to Bel's general fund.

61. Did recording budgetary accounts at the beginning of 1994 increase the fund balance by $50,000?

62. Should the budgetary accounts for 1994 include an entry for the expected transfer of funds from the general fund to the capital projects fund?

63. Should the $700,000 payment from the general fund, which was used to help to establish the water utility fund, be reported as an "other financing use—operating transfers out"?

64. Did the general fund receive the $30,000 bond premium from the capital projects fund?

65. Should a payment from the general fund for water received for normal civic center operations be reported as an "other financing use—operating transfers out"?

66. Not selected.

67. Would closing budgetary accounts cause the fund balance to increase by $400,000?

68. Would the interaction between budgetary and actual amounts cause the fund balance to decrease by $350,000?

Items 69 through 76 relate to Bel's account groups and funds other than the general fund.

69. In the general fixed assets account group, should a credit amount be recorded for 1994 in "Investment in general fixed assets—capital projects fund"?

70. In the general fixed assets account group, could Bel elect to record depreciation in 1995 on the civic center?

71. In the general fixed assets account group, could Bel elect to record depreciation on water utility equipment?

72. Should the capital project fund be included in Bel's combined statement of revenues, expenditures, and changes in fund balances?

73. Should the water utility enterprise fund be included in Bel's combined balance sheet?

In which fund should Bel report capital and related financing activities in its 1994 statement of cash flows?

74. Debt service fund.

75. Capital project fund.

76. Water utility enterprise fund.

For **Items 77 through 84,** determine the amount. To record your answer, blacken the ovals on the *Objective Answer Sheet.* If zeros precede your numerical answer, blacken the zeros in the ovals preceding your answer.

Selected Questions

You cannot receive credit for your answers if you fail to blacken an oval in each column. You may write the numbers in the boxes provided to facilitate blackening the ovals; however, the numbers written in the boxes will **not** be graded.

Items 77 and 78 relate to Bel's general fund.

77. What was the amount recorded in the opening entry for appropriations?

78. What was the total amount debited to property taxes receivable?

Items 79 through 84 relate to Bel's account groups and funds other than the general fund.

79. In the general long-term debt account group, what amount should be reported for bonds payable at December 31, 1994?

80. In the general fixed assets account group, what amount should be recorded for "Investment in general fixed assets—capital project fund" at December 31, 1994?

81. What was the completed cost of the civic center?

82. How much was the state capital grant for the civic center?

83. In the capital project fund, what was the amount of the total encumbrances recorded during 1994?

84. In the capital project fund, what was the unreserved fund balance reported at December 31, 1994?

AR-85

Taxation, Managerial, and Governmental and Not-for-Profit Organizations

TM92
Number 2 (Estimated time — — 15 to 25 minutes)

Instructions

Question Number 2 consists of 9 items.* Select the **best** answer for each item. Use a No. 2 pencil to blacken the appropriate ovals on the Objective Answer Sheet to indicate your answers. **Answer all items.** Your grade will be based on the total number of correct answers.

Items 66 through 69 are based on the following:

During 1991, Krona City issued bonds for financing the construction of a civic center, and bonds for financing improvements in the environmental controls for its water and sewer enterprise. The latter bonds require a sinking fund for their retirement.

Required:
Financial Statement Items

Items 66 through 69 represent items Krona should report in its 1991 financial statements. For each item, determine whether it would be included in each of the fund types and account groups listed below. On the separate answer sheet, blacken Ⓨ if the item would be included and Ⓝ if the item would not be included.

Krona's Fund Types and Account Groups:

A. General fund
B. Enterprise funds
C. Capital projects funds
D. Debt service funds
E. General fixed assets account group
F. General long-term debt account group

Example:
The following is an example of the manner in which the answer sheet should be marked:

Item

99. Transfer of funds from the general fund to an enterprise fund.

Answer Sheet

Item	General Fund		Enterprise Funds		Capital Projects Funds		Debt Service Funds		General Fixed Assets Account Group		General Long-Term Debt Acct. Group	
	Yes	No	Yes	No	Yes	No	Yes	No	Yes	No	Yes	No
99	●	Ⓝ	●	Ⓝ	Ⓨ	●	Ⓨ	●	Ⓨ	●	Ⓨ	●

Items to be Answered:

66. Bonds payable.
67. Accumulated depreciation.
68. Amounts identified for the repayment of the two bond issues.
69. Reserve for encumbrances.

---

*The omitted items can be found in Content Specification Area IV.

VI. Managerial Accounting

R96
Number 4 (Estimated time — — 5 to 10 minutes)

Question Number 4 consists of 5 items. Select the **best** answer for each item. Use a No. 2 pencil to blacken the appropriate ovals on the *Objective Answer Sheet* to indicate your answers. **Answer all items.** Your grade will be based on the total number of correct answers.

The following information pertains to a product for a 10-week budget period:

- Sales price $11 per unit
  - Materials $3 per unit
  - Manufacturing conversion
    - costs—Fixed $210,000
    - Variable $2 per unit
  - Selling and administrative
    - costs—Fixed $45,000
    - Variable $1 per unit
  - Beginning accounts payable
    - for materials $40,000

- Manufacturing and sales of 70,000 units are expected to occur evenly over the period.
- Materials are paid for in the week following use.
- There are no beginning inventories.

Required:

For **Items 1 through 5,** determine the correct amount using the above information. Any information contained in an item is unique to that item and is **not** to be incorporated in your calculations when answering other items.

For **Items 1 through 5, the ones, tens, and hundreds** columns **do not appear** on the *Objective Answer Sheet.* To record your answer, blacken the ovals on the *Objective Answer Sheet.* To record a **zero** answer for an item, you must blacken all the **zero ovals** for that particular item. If zeros precede your numerical answer, blacken the zeros in the ovals preceding your answer. **You cannot receive credit for your answers if you fail to blacken an oval in each column.** You may write the numbers in the boxes provided to facilitate blackening the ovals; however, the numbers written in the boxes will **not** be graded.

Example:
The following are examples of the manner in which numeric responses for **Items 1 through 5** should be recorded on the *Objective Answer Sheet*.

Answer	$0	$5,000	$18,000	$610,000
Objective Answer Sheet	0 0 0	0 0 5	0 1 8	6 1 0

1. What amount should be budgeted for cash payments to material suppliers during the period?

2. Using variable costing, what is the budgeted income for the period?

3. Using absorption costing, what is the budgeted income for the period?

4. Actual results are as budgeted, except that only 60,000 of the 70,000 units produced were sold. Using absorption costing, what is the difference between the reported income and the budgeted net income?

5. If a special order for 4,000 units would cause the loss of 1,000 regular sales, what minimum amount of revenue must be generated from the special order so that net income is not reduced? (All cost relationships are unchanged.)

TN93
Number 2 (Estimated time — — 15 to 25 minutes)

Question Number 2 consists of 9 items. Select the **best** answer for each item. Use a No. 2 pencil to blacken the appropriate ovals on the Objective Answer Sheet to indicate your answers. **Answer all items.** Your grade will be based on the total number of correct answers.

Items 66 through 69 are based on the following:

A company has two mutually exclusive projects, A and B, which have the same initial investment requirements and lives. Project B has a decrease in estimated net cash inflows each year, and project A has an increase in estimated net cash inflows each year. Project A has a greater total net cash inflow. Diagram I below depicts the net cash inflows of each project by year. Diagram II depicts the net present value (NPV) of each project assuming various discount rates.

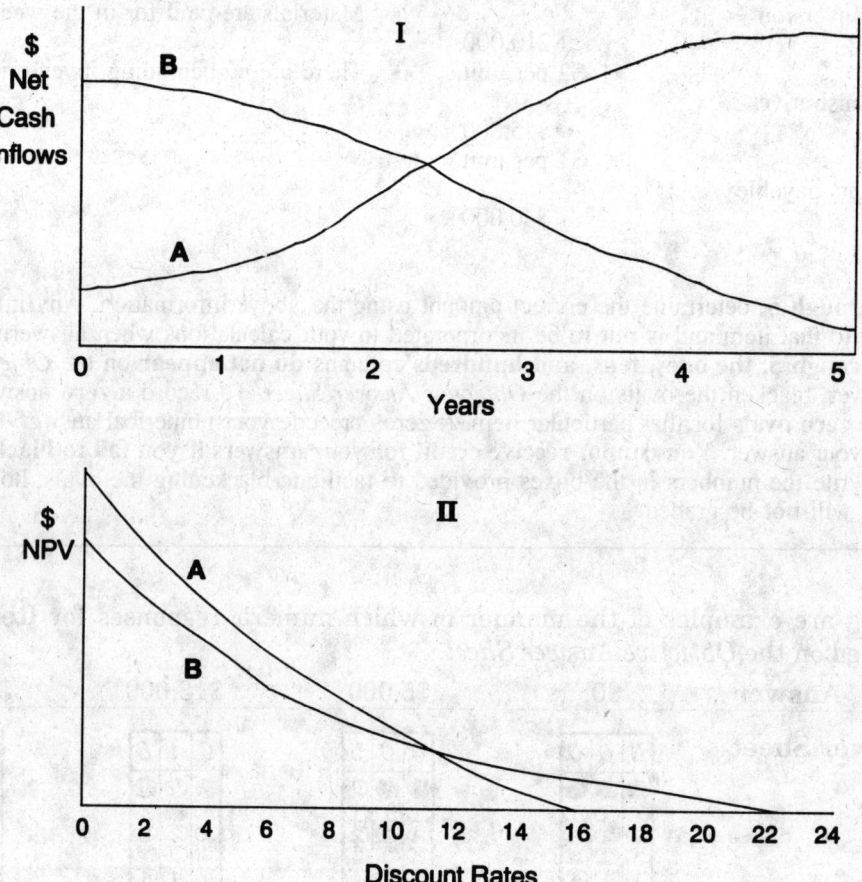

Required:

For **items 66 through 69,** select your answer from the following list and blacken the corresponding oval on the Objective Answer Sheet.

A. Project A
B. Project B
C. Both projects equal

66. Which project would be likely to have the shorter payback period?
67. Which project would have the greater average accounting rate of return?
68. Which project would have the greater internal rate of return?
69. Assume, due to innovation, the projects were to terminate at the end of year 4 with cash flows remaining as projected for the first 4 years and no cash flows in year 5. Which project would have the greater internal rate of return?

Selected Questions

TN92
Number 2 (Estimated time — — 15 to 25 minutes)

Instructions

Question Number 2 consists of 13* items. Select the **best** answer for each item. Use a No. 2 pencil to blacken the appropriate ovals on the Objective Answer Sheet to indicate your answer. **Answer all items.** Your grade will be based on the total number of correct answers.

Items 69 through 73 are based on the following:

The diagram below depicts a manufacturing total cost flexible budget line KI and standard cost line OI. Line OJ is parallel to line KI, and revenues are represented by line OH.

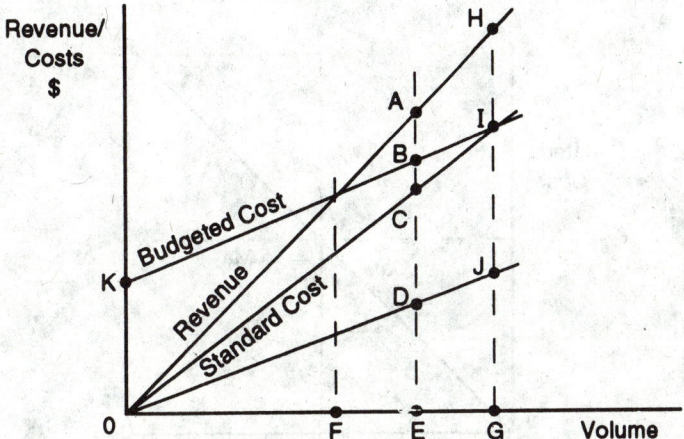

Required:
For Items 69 through 73, identify the line on the graph that represents each item. Indicate your answer by blackening the **two** ovals that define that line.

Example:
The following is an example of the manner in which the answer sheet should be marked.

Item

99. The budgeted revenue at volume OE.

Answer Sheet

Item	Line End Points (select two)
99	● Ⓑ Ⓒ Ⓓ ● Ⓕ Ⓖ Ⓞ

Items to be Answered:

69. The budgeted fixed cost at volume OE.
70. The budgeted variable cost at volume OE.
71. The standard gross profit at volume OE.
72. The budgeted gross profit at volume OE, assuming **no** change between beginning and ending inventories.
73. The normal capacity, assuming standard costs are based on normal capacity.

---

*The items omitted can be found in Financial Accounting and Reporting in Content Specification Area I.

Taxation, Managerial, and Governmental and Not-for-Profit Organizations

TM92
Number 2 (Estimated time — — 15 to 25 minutes)

Instructions

Question Number 2 consists of 9 items.* Select the **best** answer for each item. Use a No. 2 pencil to blacken the appropriate ovals on the Objective Answer Sheet to indicate your answers. **Answer all items.** Your grade will be based on the total number of correct answers.

Items 61 through 65 are based on the following:

Bilco Inc. produces bricks and uses a standard costing system. On the diagram below, the line OP represents Bilco's standard material cost at any output volume expressed in direct material pounds to be used. Bilco had identical outputs in each of the first three months of 1992, with a standard cost of V in each month. Points Ja, Fe, and Ma represent the actual pounds used and actual costs incurred in January, February, and March, respectively.

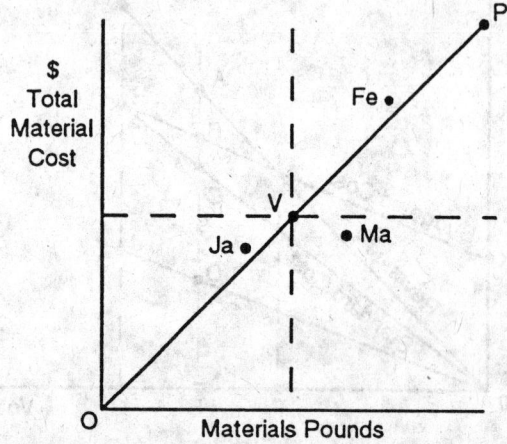

Required:

For Items 61 through 65, determine whether each variance is favorable Ⓕ or unfavorable Ⓤ and blacken the corresponding oval on the answer sheet.

Example:

The following is an example of the manner in which the answer sheet should be marked.

Item

99. January material net variance.

Answer Sheet

Item	Variance
99	● Ⓤ

Items to be Answered:

61. January material price variance.
62. January material usage variance.
63. February material price variance.
64. February material usage variance.
65. March material net variance.

---

*The items omitted can be found in Content Specification Area V.

Unofficial Answers in the Taxation area do not reflect the tax law changes enacted by the TAXPAYER RELIEF ACT OF 1997, the BALANCED BUDGET ACT OF 1997, and the TAXPAYER BROWSING PROTECTION ACT enacted on August 5, 1997.

SELECTED OTHER OBJECTIVE ANSWER FORMATS — UNOFFICIAL ANSWERS

I. Federal Taxation — Individuals

N95
Answer 3 (20 points)

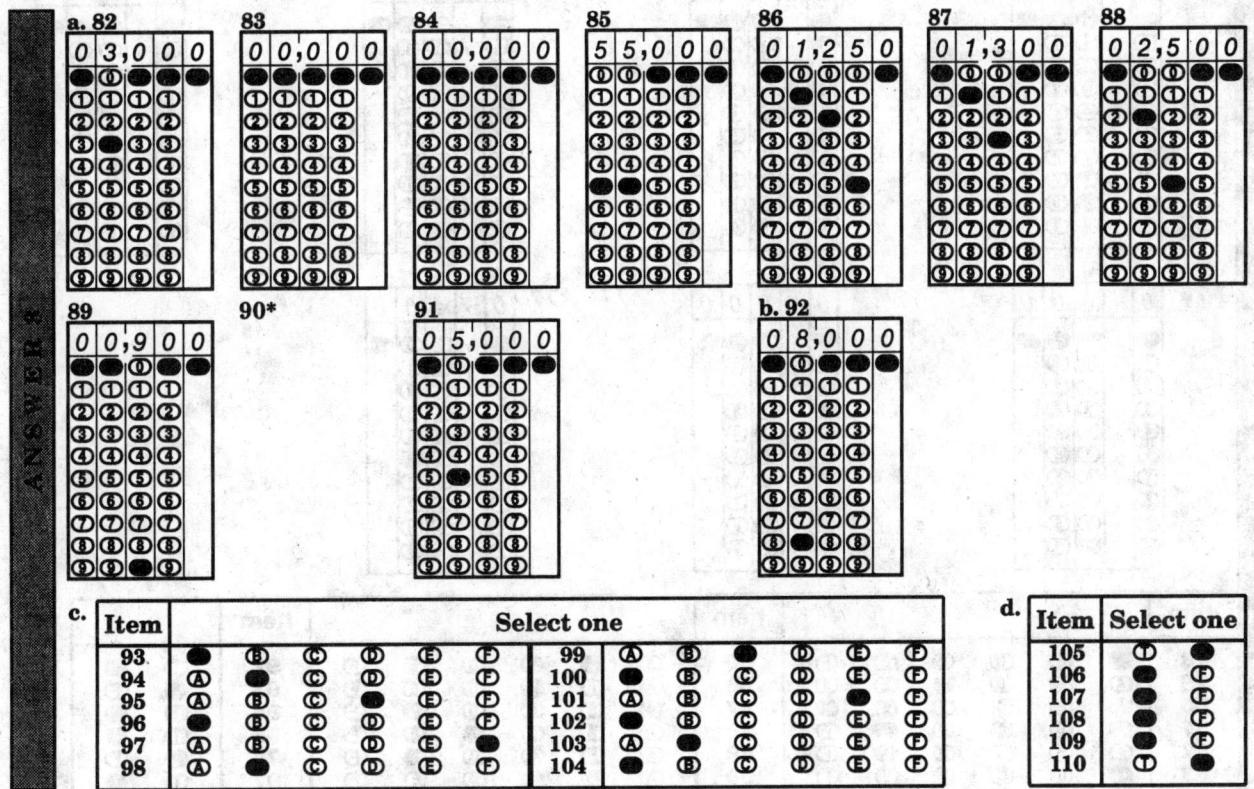

*This question has not been selected.

AR-91

N94
Answer 3 (20 points)

Item
- 69: T, ●, H, Q | 1, 2, 3, ●
- 70: S, ●, H, ● | 1, 2, ●, 4

Zeros have already been preprinted for the ones columns. Write zeros in any blank boxes preceding your numerical answer, and blacken the zero in the oval below the box.

71: 0,000
72: 0,400
73: 0,900
74: 0,000
75: 0,000
76: 0,200
77: 0,450

Item							Item							Item		
78	●	B	C	D	E	F	85	A	●	C	D	E	F	92	D	●
79	A	B	C	●	E	F	86	A	B	●	D	E	F	93	●	F
80	A	B	C	●	E	F	87	A	B	C	●	E	F	94	D	●
81	A	B	C	D	●	F	88	A	B	C	●	E	F	95	D	●
82	A	B	C	D	●	F	89	A	B	C	D	●	F	96	●	F
83	●	B	C	D	E	F	90	●	B	C	D	E	F	97	D	●
84	A	●	C	D	E	F	91	●	B	C	D	E	F	98	D	●
														99	D	●

Unofficial Answers

2M92
Answer 4 (30 points)

	Item	Tax Treatments (select one)	Item	Tax Treatments (select one)
ANSWER 4	61	A ●B C D E F G H I J K L M N O P	71	A B C D E F G H I J ● L M N O P
	62	● B C D E F G H I J K L M N O P	72	A B C D E F G H I J K L M N O ●
	63	A B C ● E F G H I J K L M N O P	73	A B C ● E F G H I J K L M N O P
	64	A B C D E F G H I J K L M N O ●	74	A B C D ● F G H I J K L M N O P
	65	A B C D E F G H I J K L M N O ●	75	A B C D E ● G H I J K L M N O P
	66	A B C D E F G H ● J K L M N O P	76	A B C D E F G H I J K L M N O ●
	67	A B C D E F G H ● J K L M N O P	77	A B C D E F G H I J K L ● N O P
	68	A B C ● E F G H I J K L M N O P	78	A B C D E F G H I J K L M N ● P
	69	A B C D E F G H I ● K L M N O P	79	A B C ● E F G H I J K L M N O P
	70	A B C D E F G H I J K ● M N O P	80	A B C D E F G H I J K L M N O ●

II. Federal Taxation — Corporations

R97
Answer 1 (10 points)

For **Question 1**, you may write the numbers in the boxes provided to facilitate blackening the ovals; however, the numbers written in the boxes will **not** be graded. **Ones, tens, and hundreds columns are not represented in the numeric responses.**

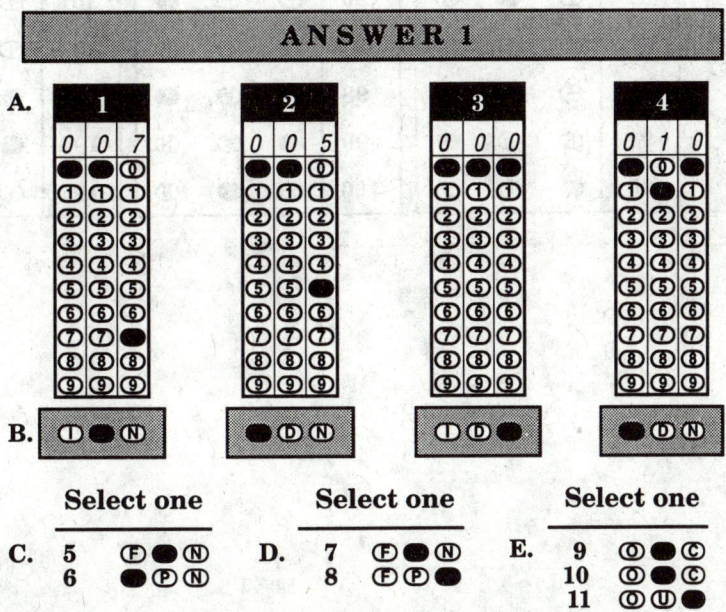

Taxation, Managerial, and Governmental and Not-for-Profit Organizations

N95
Answer 2 (5 points)

M95
Answer 3 (20 points)

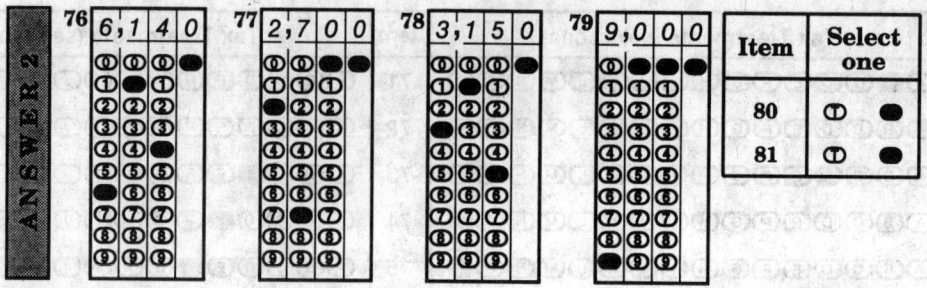

AR-94

M94
Answer 2 (20 points)

Zeros have already been preprinted for the ones, tens, and hundreds columns.

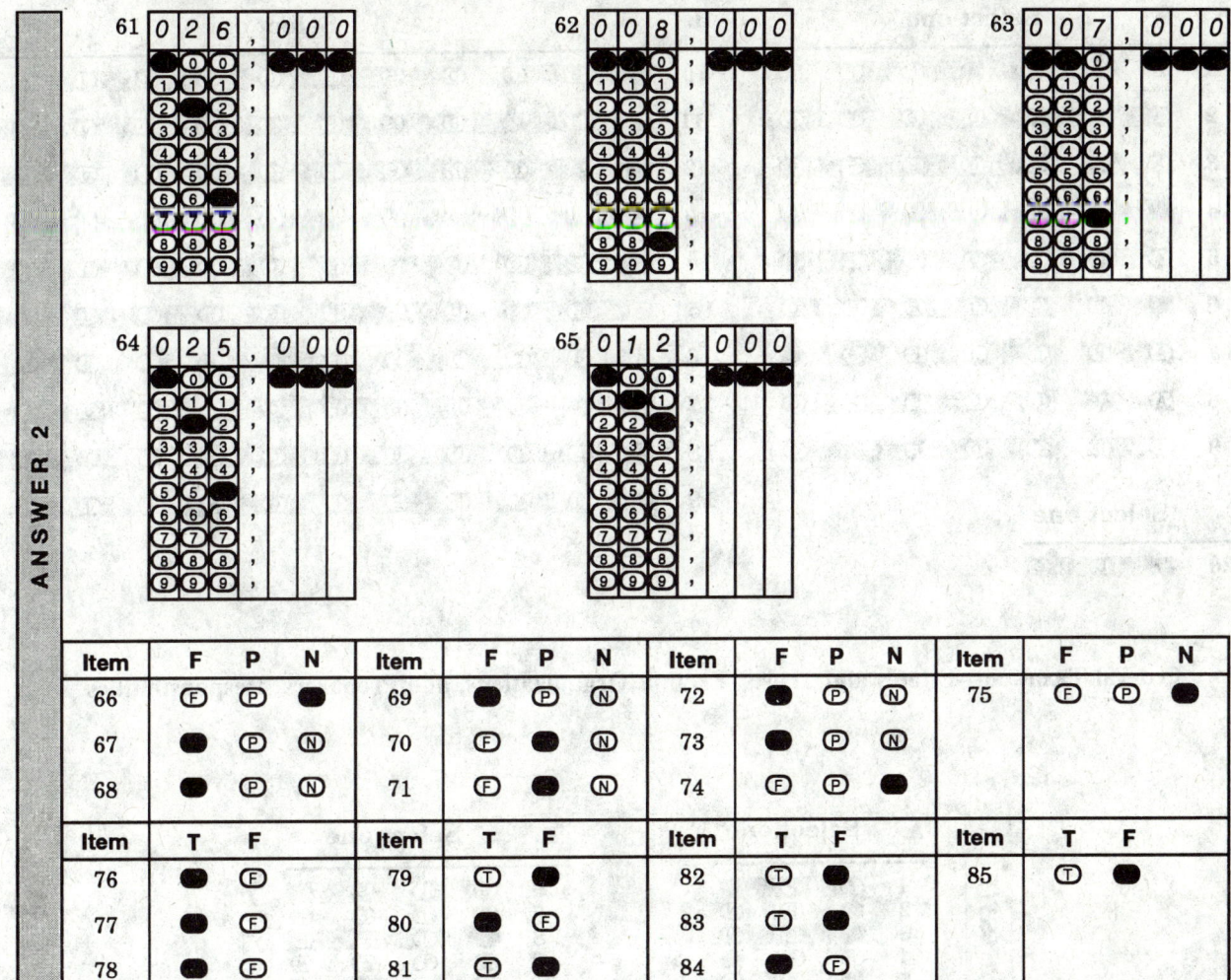

III. Federal Taxation — Partnerships

R97 Answer 3

A. Select one
1. D
2. C
3. B
4. A
5. B
6. A
7. F
8. B
9. F

B. Select one
10. A
11. (none marked clearly)
12. (none marked clearly)
13. F
14. (none marked clearly)
15. C
16. G
17. B
18. I
19. A

C. Select one
20. T

IV. Federal Taxation—Estates and Trusts, Exempt Organizations, and Preparers' Responsibilities

R98 Answer 1

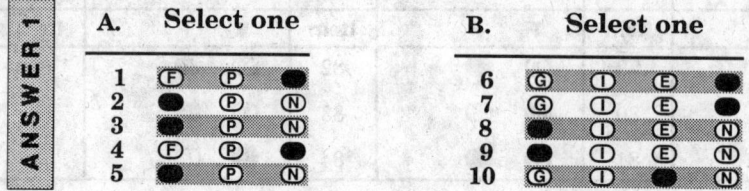

A. Select one
1. N
2. F
3. F
4. N
5. F

B. Select one
6. N
7. N
8. F
9. F
10. E

R96 Answer 1 (5 points)

Item	Select one			Item	Select one			Item	Select one		
1	P	E	●	4	P	E	●	7	P	●	N
2	P	●	N	5	●	E	N	8	●	E	N
3	●	E	N	6	P	E	●	9	●	E	N

Unofficial Answers

V. Accounting for Governmental and Not-for-Profit Organizations

R98 Answer 2

ANSWER 2

A. Select one		B. Select one		C. Select one	
1	O ● C	5	A B C D E F G H I J K ● M N O	12	● I F
2	O ● C	6	A B C ● E F G H I J K L M N O	13	● I F
3	O U ●	7	A B C D ● F G H I J K L M N O	14	O ● F
4	● U C	8	A B C D E F G H I J K L M ●	15	O I ●
		9	A ● C D E F G H I J K L M N O	16	O ● F
		10	● B C D E F G H I J K L M N O	17	● I F
		11	● B C D E F G H I J K L M N O	18	● I F
				19	● I F

R97 Answer 2

For **Question 2**, you may write the numbers in the boxes provided to facilitate blackening the ovals; however, the numbers written in the boxes will **not** be graded. **Ones, tens, and hundreds columns are not represented in the numeric responses.**

ANSWER 2

1	2	3	4
1,000	9,350	0,000	2,100

5
2,000

AR-97

Answer 2 (15 points)

a.
Item	Select one
1	A
2	A
3	B

b.
Item	Select one
4	B
5	B
6	A

c.
Item	Select one
7	A
8	E
9	B
10	C
11	E
12	D
13	B

d.
Item	Amount
14	0,079,000
15	0,811,000
16	0,089,000
17	0,100,000
18	0,052,000
19	1,392,000

Unofficial Answers

R96
Answer 3 (10 points)

For Question 3 you may write the numbers in the boxes provided to facilitate blackening the ovals; however, the numbers written in the boxes will **not** be graded. **Ones, tens, and hundreds columns are not represented in the numeric responses.**

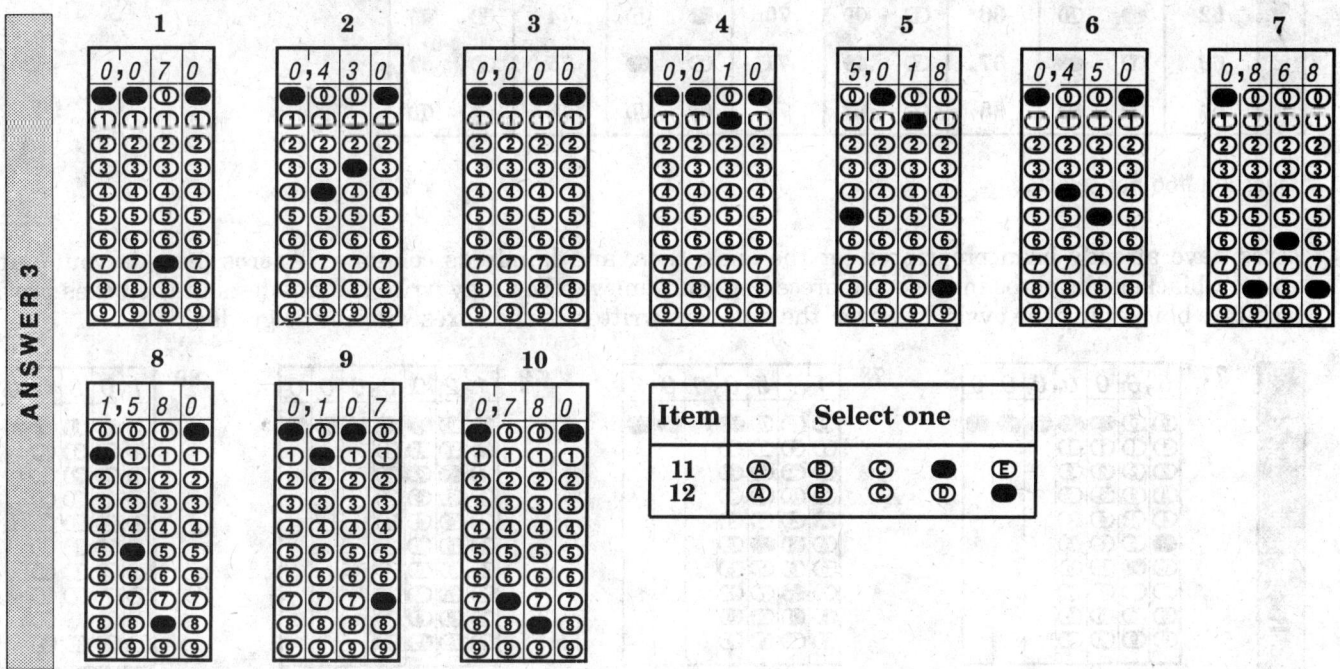

N95
Answer 5 (10 points)

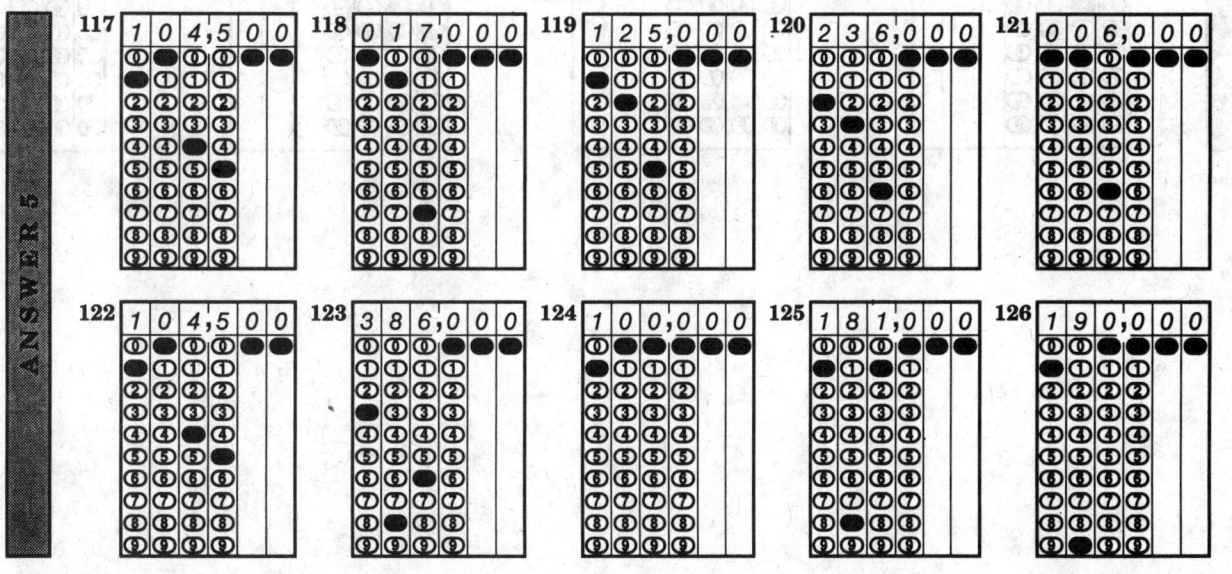

AR-99

M95
Answer 2 (20 points)

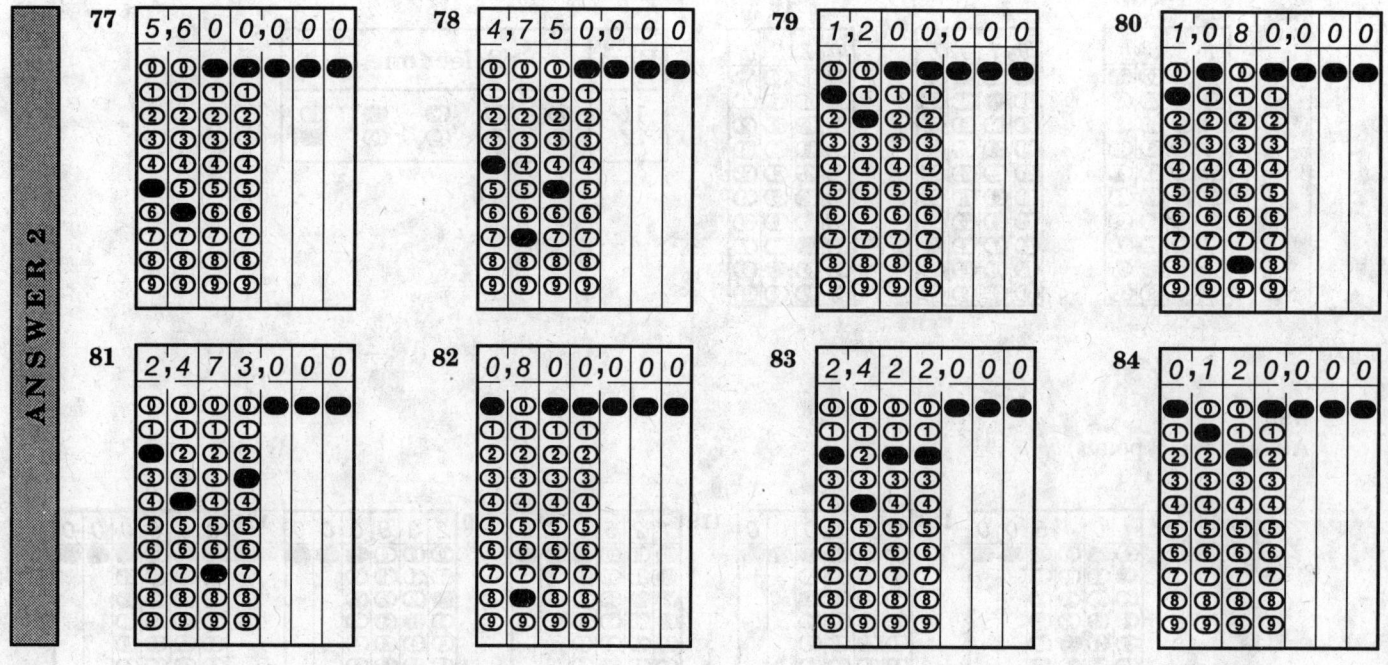

*Question #66 not selected.

Zeros have already been preprinted for the ones, tens, and hundreds columns. If zeros precede your numerical answer, blacken the zeros in the ovals preceding your answer. You may write the numbers in the boxes provided to facilitate blackening the ovals; however, the numbers written in the boxes will **not** be graded.

Unofficial Answers

TM92
Answer 2 (6 points)

Item	General Fund		Enterprise Funds		Capital Projects Funds		Debt Service Funds		General Fixed Assets Account Group		General Long-Term Debt Acct. Group	
	Yes	No	Yes	No	Yes	No	Yes	No	Yes	No	Yes	No
66	Y	●	●	N	Y	●	Y	●	Y	●	●	N
67	Y	●	●	N	Y	●	Y	●	●	N	Y	●
68	Y	●	●	N	Y	●	●	N	Y	●	●	N
69	●	N	Y	●	●	N	Y	●	Y	●	Y	●

VI. Managerial Accounting

R96
Answer 4 (5 points)

For Question 4 you may write the numbers in the boxes provided to facilitate blackening the ovals; however, the numbers written in the boxes will **not** be graded. **Ones, tens, and hundreds columns are not represented in the numeric responses.**

ANSWER 4:

- 128: 2 2 9
- 129: 0 9 5
- 130: 0 9 5
- 131: 0 2 0
- 132: 0 2 9

TN93
Answer 2 (10 points)

Item	Select one		
66	A	●	C
67	●	B	C
68	A	●	C
69	A	●	C

AR-101

TN92
Answer 2 (4 points)

Item	Line End Points (select two)							
69	Ⓐ	●	Ⓒ	●	Ⓔ	Ⓕ	Ⓖ	Ⓤ
70	Ⓐ	Ⓑ	Ⓒ	●	●	Ⓕ	Ⓖ	Ⓤ
71	●	Ⓑ	●	Ⓓ	Ⓔ	Ⓕ	Ⓖ	Ⓤ
72	●	●	Ⓒ	Ⓓ	Ⓔ	Ⓕ	Ⓖ	Ⓤ
73	Ⓐ	Ⓑ	Ⓒ	Ⓓ	Ⓔ	Ⓕ	●	●

TM92
Answer 2 (4 points)

Item	Variance	
61	Ⓕ	●
62	●	Ⓤ
63	Ⓕ	●
64	Ⓕ	●
65	●	Ⓤ

SUGGESTED REFERENCES

Accounting & Reporting—Taxation, Managerial, and Governmental and Not-for-Profit Organizations

Afterman and Jones, *Governmental Accounting and Auditing Disclosure Manual* (Warren, Gorham, and Lamont, 1992).

AICPA, Audit and Accounting Guide, *Audits of Providers of Health Care Services* (AICPA, 1994).

AICPA, Audit and Accounting Guide, *Audits of State and Local Governmental Units* (AICPA, 1994).

AICPA, Industry Audit Guide, *Audits of Colleges and Universities* (AICPA, 1993).

Federal Tax Course 1995 (Commerce Clearing House).

Fischer, Taylor, and Leer, *Advanced Accounting*, 5th ed. (South-Western, 1993).

GASB, *Codification of Governmental Accounting and Financial Reporting Standards* (GASB).

Hammer, Carter, and Usry, *Cost Accounting*, 11th ed. (South-Western, 1994).

Hay and Wilson, *Accounting for Governmental and Nonprofit Entities*, 9th ed. (Irwin, 1992).

Hirsch, *Advanced Management Accounting*, 2nd ed. (South-Western, 1994).

Horngren, Foster, and Datar, *Cost Accounting: A Managerial Emphasis*, 8th ed. (Prentice-Hall, 1994).

Kramer, Pope, Phillips, et al., *Prentice-Hall's Federal Taxation 1997: Corporations, Partnerships, and Trusts* (Prentice-Hall, 1997).

Larsen, *Modern Advanced Accounting*, 6th ed. (McGraw-Hill, 1991).

Maher and Deakin, *Cost Accounting*, 6th ed. (Irwin, 1994).

Morse, Davis, and Hartgraves, *Management Accounting* (Southwestern, 1996).

Pahler and Mori, *Advanced Accounting: Concepts and Practices*, 5th ed. (Dryden, 1994).

Polimeni, Fabozzi, and Adelberg, *Cost Accounting: Concepts and Applications for Managerial Decision Making*, 3d ed. (McGraw-Hill, 1991).

Rayburn, *Cost Accounting: Using a Cost Management Approach*, 5th ed. (Irwin, 1993).

U.S. Master Tax Guide (Commerce Clearing House).

A standard tax service, the Internal Revenue Code, and Income Tax Regulations.

Uniform CPA Examination

Financial Accounting & Reporting

**Selected Questions
And Unofficial Answers
Indexed To
Content Specification
Outline**

TABLE OF CONTENTS

	Pages		
Selected Questions	Multiple Choice Items	Other Objective Answer Formats	Problems/ Essays
I. Concepts and Standards for Financial Statements	FA-1	FA-131	FA-163
A. Financial Accounting Concepts	FA-1	*	FA-163
B. Financial Accounting Standards for Presentation and Disclosure in General Purpose Financial Statements	FA-2	FA-131	FA-163
1. Consolidated and Combined Financial Statements	FA-2	FA-131	FA-163
2. Balance Sheet	FA-10	*	FA-167
3. Statement(s) of Income, Comprehensive Income, and Changes in Equity Accounts	FA-12	FA-134	FA-168
4. Statement of Cash Flows	FA-13	FA-136	FA-172
5. Accounting Policies and Other Notes to Financial Statements	FA-15	*	*
C. Other Presentations of Financial Data	FA-18	*	FA-175
1. Financial Statements Prepared in Conformity With Comprehensive Bases of Accounting Other Than Generally Accepted Accounting Principles	FA-18	*	FA-175
2. Personal Financial Statements	FA-19	*	*
3. Prospective Financial Information	*	*	*
D. Financial Statement Analysis	*	*	*
II. Recognition, Measurement, Valuation, and Presentation of Typical Items in Financial Statements in Conformity With Generally Accepted Accounting Principles	FA-22	FA-140	FA-178
A. Cash, Cash Equivalents, and Marketable Securities	FA-22	*	*
B. Receivables	FA-23	FA-140	FA-178
C. Inventories	FA-28	*	FA-181
D. Property, Plant, and Equipment	FA-32	FA-140	FA-182
E. Investments	FA-36	*	FA-183
F. Intangibles and Other Assets	FA-38	*	FA-183
G. Payables and Accruals	FA-40	*	*
H. Deferred Revenues	FA-43	*	FA-184
I. Notes and Bonds Payable	FA-47	FA-143	FA-184
J. Other Liabilities	FA-52	*	*
K. Equity Accounts	FA-54	*	FA-185
L. Revenue, Cost, and Expense Accounts	FA-64	*	FA-186
III. Recognition, Measurement, Valuation, and Presentation of Specific Types of Transactions and Events in Financial Statements in Conformity With Generally Accepted Accounting Principles	FA-84	FA-144	FA-188
A. Accounting Changes and Corrections of Errors	FA-84	FA-144	FA-188
B. Business Combinations	FA-87	*	FA-188
C. Cash Flow Components—Financing, Investing, and Operating	FA-89	*	*
D. Contingent Liabilities and Commitments	FA-91	FA-147	FA-189
E. Discontinued Operations	FA-94	*	*

* No questions were indexed for this group or topic.
Note: All previous Accounting Theory, Accounting Practice Part I and Accounting Practice Part II questions are designated with the letter (T), and the numbers (1) and (2), respectively, before the exam date and question number.

	Pages		
Selected Questions	Multiple Choice Items	Other Objective Answer Formats	Problems/ Essays
F. Earnings Per Share	FA-96	*	*
G. Employee Benefits	FA-97	FA-149	FA-189
H. Extraordinary Items	FA-102	*	*
I. Financial Instruments	FA-104	*	FA-190
J. Foreign Currency Transactions and Translation	FA-105	*	*
K. Income Taxes	FA-107	FA-150	FA-190
L. Interest Costs	FA-111	*	FA-190
M. Interim Financial Reporting	FA-113	*	*
N. Leases	FA-114	*	FA-191
O. Nonmonetary Transactions	FA-118	*	*
P. Quasi-reorganizations, Reorganizations, and Changes in Entity	FA-120	*	*
Q. Related Parties	FA-121	*	*
R. Research and Development Costs	FA-122	*	FA-192
S. Segment Reporting	FA-123	*	*

Selected Multiple Choice Items — Unofficial Answers   FA-125

Other Objective Answer Formats — Selected Questions   FA-131

Selected Other Objective Answer Formats — Unofficial Answers   FA-151

Problems/Essays — Selected Questions   FA-163

Selected Problems/Essays — Unofficial Answers   FA-193

Suggested References   FA-229

Content Specification Outline   CSO-8

Summary of Coverage — May 1996 through May 1998 Uniform CPA Examinations   S-6

MULTIPLE CHOICE ITEMS — SELECTED QUESTIONS

I. Concepts and Standards for Financial Statements

A. Financial Accounting Concepts

N95#1. According to the FASB conceptual framework, the objectives of financial reporting for business enterprises are based on
    a. Generally accepted accounting principles.
    b. Reporting on management's stewardship.
    c. The need for conservatism.
    d. The needs of the users of the information.

N95#2. According to the FASB conceptual framework, the usefulness of providing information in financial statements is subject to the constraint of
    a. Consistency.
    b. Cost-benefit.
    c. Reliability.
    d. Representational faithfulness.

N95#3. What is the underlying concept governing the generally accepted accounting principles pertaining to recording gain contingencies?
    a. Conservatism.
    b. Relevance.
    c. Consistency.
    d. Reliability.

N95#4. A development stage enterprise should use the same generally accepted accounting principles that apply to established operating enterprises for

	Revenue recognition	Deferral of expenses
a.	Yes	Yes
b.	Yes	No
c.	No	No
d.	No	Yes

N95#5. According to the FASB conceptual framework, which of the following attributes would **not** be used to measure inventory?
    a. Historical cost.
    b. Replacement cost.
    c. Net realizable value.
    d. Present value of future cash flows.

N95#6. Conceptually, interim financial statements can be described as emphasizing
    a. Timeliness over reliability.
    b. Reliability over relevance.
    c. Relevance over comparability.
    d. Comparability over neutrality.

M95#1. According to the FASB conceptual framework, which of the following situations violates the concept of reliability?
    a. Data on segments having the same expected risks and growth rates are reported to analysts estimating future profits.
    b. Financial statements are issued nine months late.
    c. Management reports to stockholders regularly refer to new projects undertaken, but the financial statements never report project results.
    d. Financial statements include property with a carrying amount increased to management's estimate of market value.

M95#2. One of the elements of a financial statement is comprehensive income. Comprehensive income excludes changes in equity resulting from which of the following?
    a. Loss from discontinued operations.
    b. Prior period error correction.
    c. Dividends paid to stockholders.
    d. Unrealized loss on investments in noncurrent marketable equity securities.

N94#1. According to Statements of Financial Accounting Concepts, neutrality is an ingredient of

	Reliability	Relevance
a.	Yes	Yes
b.	Yes	No
c.	No	Yes
d.	No	No

N94#2. In the hierarchy of generally accepted accounting principles, APB Opinions have the same authority as AICPA
    a. Statements of Position.
    b. Industry Audit and Accounting Guides.
    c. Issues Papers.
    d. Accounting Research Bulletins.

N94#3. What is the underlying concept that supports the immediate recognition of a contingent loss?
    a. Substance over form.
    b. Consistency.
    c. Matching.
    d. Conservatism.

M94#1. According to the FASB conceptual framework, the process of reporting an item in the financial statements of an entity is
  a. Allocation.
  b. Matching.
  c. Realization.
  d. Recognition.

M94#2. What are the Statements of Financial Accounting Concepts intended to establish?
  a. Generally accepted accounting principles in financial reporting by business enterprises.
  b. The meaning of "Present fairly in accordance with generally accepted accounting principles."
  c. The objectives and concepts for use in developing standards of financial accounting and reporting.
  d. The hierarchy of sources of generally accepted accounting principles.

M94#4. During a period when an enterprise is under the direction of a particular management, its financial statements will directly provide information about
  a. Both enterprise performance and management performance.
  b. Management performance but **not** directly provide information about enterprise performance.
  c. Enterprise performance but **not** directly provide information about management performance.
  d. Neither enterprise performance nor management performance.

TN92#1. Which of the following accounting pronouncements is the most authoritative?
  a. FASB Statement of Financial Accounting Concepts.
  b. FASB Technical Bulletin.
  c. AICPA Accounting Principles Board Opinion.
  d. AICPA Statement of Position.

TN92#2. According to the FASB conceptual framework, which of the following relates to both relevance and reliability?
  a. Comparability.
  b. Feedback value.
  c. Verifiability.
  d. Timeliness.

TN92#3. According to the FASB conceptual framework, an entity's revenue may result from
  a. A decrease in an asset from primary operations.
  b. An increase in an asset from incidental transactions.
  c. An increase in a liability from incidental transactions.
  d. A decrease in a liability from primary operations.

TM92#1. FASB Interpretations of Statements of Financial Accounting Standards have the same authority as the FASB
  a. Statements of Financial Accounting Concepts.
  b. Emerging Issues Task Force Consensus.
  c. Technical Bulletins.
  d. Statements of Financial Accounting Standards.

TM92#2. According to the FASB conceptual framework, which of the following is an essential characteristic of an asset?
  a. The claims to an asset's benefits are legally enforceable.
  b. An asset is tangible.
  c. An asset is obtained at a cost.
  d. An asset provides future benefits.

TM92#3. According to the FASB conceptual framework, predictive value is an ingredient of

	Reliability	Relevance
a.	Yes	Yes
b.	No	Yes
c.	No	No
d.	Yes	No

TM91#1. Under FASB Statement of Financial Accounting Concepts No. 5, which of the following items would cause earnings to differ from comprehensive income for an enterprise in an industry **not** having specialized accounting principles?
  a. Unrealized loss on investments in noncurrent marketable equity securities.
  b. Unrealized loss on investments in current marketable equity securities.
  c. Loss on exchange of similar assets.
  d. Loss on exchange of dissimilar assets.

B. Financial Accounting Standards for Presentation and Disclosure in General Purpose Financial Statements

1. Consolidated and Combined Financial Statements

N95
Items 49 through 51 are based on the following:

On January 2, 1994, Pare Co. purchased 75% of Kidd Co.'s outstanding common stock. Selected balance sheet data at December 31, 1994, is as follows:

	Pare	Kidd
Total assets	$420,000	$180,000
Liabilities	$120,000	$ 60,000
Common stock	100,000	50,000
Retained earnings	200,000	70,000
	$420,000	$180,000

During 1994, Pare and Kidd paid cash dividends of $25,000 and $5,000, respectively, to their shareholders. There were no other intercompany transactions.

49. In its December 31, 1994, consolidated statement of retained earnings, what amount should Pare report as dividends paid?
   a. $5,000
   b. $25,000
   c. $26,250
   d. $30,000

50. In Pare's December 31, 1994, consolidated balance sheet, what amount should be reported as minority interest in net assets?
   a. $0
   b. $30,000
   c. $45,000
   d. $105,000

51. In its December 31, 1994, consolidated balance sheet, what amount should Pare report as common stock?
   a. $50,000
   b. $100,000
   c. $137,500
   d. $150,000

M95
Items 50 through 52 are based on the following:

Selected information from the separate and consolidated balance sheets and income statements of Pare, Inc. and its subsidiary, Shel Co., as of December 31, 1994, and for the year then ended is as follows:

	Pare	Shel	Consolidated
Balance sheet accounts			
Accounts receivable	$52,000	$38,000	$78,000
Inventory	60,000	50,000	104,000
Income statement accounts			
Revenues	$400,000	$280,000	$616,000
Cost of goods sold	300,000	220,000	462,000
Gross profit	100,000	60,000	154,000

Additional information:
During 1994, Pare sold goods to Shel at the same markup on cost that Pare uses for all sales.

50. What was the amount of intercompany sales from Pare to Shel during 1994?
   a. $6,000
   b. $12,000
   c. $58,000
   d. $64,000

51. At December 31, 1994, what was the amount of Shel's payable to Pare for intercompany sales?
   a. $6,000
   b. $12,000
   c. $58,000
   d. $64,000

52. In Pare's consolidating worksheet, what amount of unrealized intercompany profit was eliminated?
   a. $6,000
   b. $12,000
   c. $58,000
   d. $64,000

N94#56. Sun, Inc. is a wholly-owned subsidiary of Patton, Inc. On June 1, 1993, Patton declared and paid a $1 per share cash dividend to stockholders of record on May 15, 1993. On May 1, 1993, Sun bought 10,000 shares of Patton's common stock for $700,000 on the open market, when the book value per share was $30. What amount of gain should Patton report from this transaction in its consolidated income statement for the year ended December 31, 1993?
   a. $0
   b. $390,000
   c. $400,000
   d. $410,000

M94#7. Consolidated financial statements are typically prepared when one company has a controlling financial interest in another **unless**
   a. The subsidiary is a finance company.
   b. The fiscal year-ends of the two companies are more than three months apart.
   c. Such control is likely to be temporary.
   d. The two companies are in unrelated industries, such as manufacturing and real estate.

M94
Items 55 and 56 are based on the following:

On January 1, 1993, Owen Corp. purchased all of Sharp Corp.'s common stock for $1,200,000. On that date, the fair values of Sharp's assets and liabilities equaled their carrying amounts of $1,320,000 and $320,000, respectively. Owen's policy is to amortize intangibles over 10 years. During 1993, Sharp paid cash dividends of $20,000.

Selected information from the separate balance sheets and income statements of Owen and Sharp as of December 31, 1993, and for the year then ended follows:

	Owen	Sharp
Balance sheet accounts		
Investment in subsidiary	$1,300,000	—
Retained earnings	1,240,000	560,000
Total stockholders' equity	2,620,000	1,120,000
Income statement accounts		
Operating income	420,000	200,000
Equity in earnings of Sharp	120,000	—
Net income	400,000	140,000

55. In Owen's 1993 consolidated income statement, what amount should be reported for amortization of goodwill?

a. $0
b. $12,000
c. $18,000
d. $20,000

56. In Owen's December 31, 1993, consolidated balance sheet, what amount should be reported as total retained earnings?
    a. $1,240,000
    b. $1,360,000
    c. $1,380,000
    d. $1,800,000

TN93#11. Perez, Inc. owns 80% of Senior, Inc. During 1992, Perez sold goods with a 40% gross profit to Senior. Senior sold all of these goods in 1992. For 1992 consolidated financial statements, how should the summation of Perez and Senior income statement items be adjusted?
    a. Sales and cost of goods sold should be reduced by the intercompany sales.
    b. Sales and cost of goods sold should be reduced by 80% of the intercompany sales.
    c. Net income should be reduced by 80% of the gross profit on intercompany sales.
    d. No adjustment is necessary.

TM93#4. Port Inc. owns 100% of Salem Inc. On January 1, 1992, Port sold Salem delivery equipment at a gain. Port had owned the equipment for two years and used a five-year straight-line depreciation rate with no residual value. Salem is using a three-year straight-line depreciation rate with no residual value for the equipment. In the consolidated income statement, Salem's recorded depreciation expense on the equipment for 1992 will be decreased by
    a. 20% of the gain on sale.
    b. 33 1/3% of the gain on sale.
    c. 50% of the gain on sale.
    d. 100% of the gain on sale.

TM93#5. When a parent-subsidiary relationship exists, consolidated financial statements are prepared in recognition of the accounting concept of
    a. Reliability.
    b. Materiality.
    c. Legal entity.
    d. Economic entity.

TM93#6. On September 1, 1990, Phillips, Inc. issued common stock in exchange for 20% of Sago, Inc.'s outstanding common stock. On July 1, 1992, Phillips issued common stock for an additional 75% of Sago's outstanding common stock. Sago continues in existence as Phillips' subsidiary. How much of Sago's 1992 net income should be reported as accruing to Phillips?
    a. 20% of Sago's net income to June 30 and all of Sago's net income from July 1 to December 31.
    b. 20% of Sago's net income to June 30 and 95% of Sago's net income from July 1 to December 31.
    c. 95% of Sago's net income.
    d. All of Sago's net income.

TM93#7. PDX Corp. acquired 100% of the outstanding common stock of Sea Corp. in a purchase transaction. The cost of the acquisition exceeded the fair value of the identifiable assets and assumed liabilities. The general guidelines for assigning amounts to the inventories acquired provide for
    a. Raw materials to be valued at original cost.
    b. Work in process to be valued at the estimated selling prices of finished goods, less both costs to complete and costs of disposal.
    c. Finished goods to be valued at replacement cost.
    d. Finished goods to be valued at estimated selling prices, less both costs of disposal and a reasonable profit allowance.

TM93#8. Combined statements may be used to present the results of operations of

	Companies under common management	Commonly controlled companies
a.	No	Yes
b.	Yes	No
c.	No	No
d.	Yes	Yes

1M93#9. Clark Co. had the following transactions with affiliated parties during 1992:

- Sales of $60,000 to Dean, Inc., with $20,000 gross profit. Dean had $15,000 of this inventory on hand at year end. Clark owns a 15% interest in Dean and does not exert significant influence.

- Purchases of raw materials totaling $240,000 from Kent Corp., a wholly-owned subsidiary. Kent's gross profit on the sale was $48,000. Clark had $60,000 of this inventory remaining on December 31, 1992.

Before eliminating entries, Clark had consolidated current assets of $320,000. What amount should Clark report in its December 31, 1992, consolidated balance sheet for current assets?
    a. $320,000
    b. $317,000
    c. $308,000
    d. $303,000

1M93#14. Wright Corp. has several subsidiaries that are included in its consolidated financial statements. In its December 31, 1992, trial balance, Wright had the following intercompany balances before eliminations:

	Debit	Credit
Current receivable due from Main Co.	$ 32,000	
Noncurrent receivable from Main	114,000	
Cash advance to Corn Corp.	6,000	
Cash advance from King Co.		$ 15,000
Intercompany payable to King		101,000

In its December 31, 1992, consolidated balance sheet, what amount should Wright report as intercompany receivables?
- a. $152,000
- b. $146,000
- c. $ 36,000
- d. $0

2M93#8. Penn Corp. paid $300,000 for the outstanding common stock of Star Co. At that time, Star had the following condensed balance sheet:

	Carrying amounts
Current assets	$ 40,000
Plant and equipment, net	380,000
Liabilities	200,000
Stockholders' equity	220,000

The fair value of the plant and equipment was $60,000 more than its recorded carrying amount. The fair values and carrying amounts were equal for all other assets and liabilities. What amount of goodwill, related to Star's acquisition, should Penn report in its consolidated balance sheet?
- a. $20,000
- b. $40,000
- c. $60,000
- d. $80,000

TN92#31. Penn, Inc., a manufacturing company, owns 75% of the common stock of Sell, Inc., an investment company. Sell owns 60% of the common stock of Vane, Inc., an insurance company. In Penn's consolidated financial statements, should consolidation accounting or equity method accounting be used for Sell and Vane?
- a. Consolidation used for Sell and equity method used for Vane.
- b. Consolidation used for both Sell and Vane.
- c. Equity method used for Sell and consolidation used for Vane.
- d. Equity method used for both Sell and Vane.

TN92#33. On January 1, 1991, Prim, Inc. acquired all the outstanding common shares of Scarp, Inc. for cash equal to the book value of the stock. The carrying amounts of Scarp's assets and liabilities approximated their fair values, except that the carrying amount of its building was more than fair value. In preparing Prim's 1991 consolidated income statement, which of the following adjustments would be made?

- a. Depreciation expense would be decreased and goodwill amortization would be recognized.
- b. Depreciation expense would be increased and goodwill amortization would be recognized.
- c. Depreciation expense would be decreased and **no** goodwill amortization would be recognized.
- d. Depreciation expense would be increased and **no** goodwill amortization would be recognized.

TN92#34. A 70%-owned subsidiary company declares and pays a cash dividend. What effect does the dividend have on the retained earnings and minority interest balances in the parent company's consolidated balance sheet?
- a. No effect on either retained earnings or minority interest.
- b. No effect on retained earnings and a decrease in minority interest.
- c. Decreases in both retained earnings and minority interest.
- d. A decrease in retained earnings and **no** effect on minority interest.

1N92
Items 14 through 18 are based on the following:

Selected information from the separate and consolidated balance sheets and income statements of Pard, Inc. and its subsidiary, Spin Co., as of December 31, 1991, and for the year then ended is as follows:

	Pard	Spin	Consolidated
Balance sheet accounts			
Accounts receivable	$ 26,000	$ 19,000	$ 39,000
Inventory	30,000	25,000	52,000
Investment in Spin	67,000	—	—
Goodwill	—	—	30,000
Minority interest	—	—	10,000
Stockholders' equity	154,000	50,000	154,000
Income statement accounts			
Revenues	$200,000	$140,000	$308,000
Cost of goods sold	150,000	110,000	231,000
Gross profit	50,000	30,000	77,000
Equity in earnings of Spin	11,000	—	—
Amortization of goodwill	—	—	2,000
Net income	36,000	20,000	40,000

Additional information:

- During 1991, Pard sold goods to Spin at the same markup on cost that Pard uses for all sales. At December 31, 1991, Spin had not paid for all of these goods and still held 37.5% of them in inventory.

- Pard acquired its interest in Spin on January 2, 1988. Pard's policy is to amortize goodwill by the straight-line method.

FA-5

Financial Accounting and Reporting

14. What was the amount of intercompany sales from Pard to Spin during 1991?
    a. $ 3,000
    b. $ 6,000
    c. $29,000
    d. $32,000

15. At December 31, 1991, what was the amount of Spin's payable to Pard for intercompany sales?
    a. $ 3,000
    b. $ 6,000
    c. $29,000
    d. $32,000

16. In Pard's consolidated balance sheet, what was the carrying amount of the inventory that Spin purchased from Pard?
    a. $ 3,000
    b. $ 6,000
    c. $ 9,000
    d. $12,000

17. What is the percent of minority interest ownership in Spin?
    a. 10%
    b. 20%
    c. 25%
    d. 45%

18. Over how many years has Pard chosen to amortize goodwill?
    a. 15
    b. 19
    c. 23
    d. 40

2N92#60. The following information pertains to shipments of merchandise from Home Office to Branch during 1991:

Home Office's cost of merchandise	$160,000
Intracompany billing	200,000
Sales by Branch	250,000
Unsold merchandise at Branch on December 31, 1991	20,000

In the combined income statement of Home Office and Branch for the year ended December 31, 1991, what amount of the above transactions should be included in sales?
    a. $250,000
    b. $230,000
    c. $200,000
    d. $180,000

TM92#40. Matt Co. included a foreign subsidiary in its 1991 consolidated financial statements. The subsidiary was acquired in 1985 and was excluded from previous consolidations. The change was caused by the elimination of foreign exchange controls. Including the subsidiary in the 1991 consolidated financial statements results in an accounting change that should be reported

a. By footnote disclosure only.
b. Currently and prospectively.
c. Currently with footnote disclosure of pro forma effects of retroactive application.
d. By restating the financial statements of all prior periods presented.

1M92
Items 6 and 7 are based on the following:

On January 1, 1991, Dallas, Inc. purchased 80% of Style, Inc.'s outstanding common stock for $120,000. On that date, the carrying amounts of Style's assets and liabilities approximated their fair values. During 1991, Style paid $5,000 cash dividends to its stockholders. Summarized balance sheet information for the two companies follows:

	Dallas	Style	
	12/31/91	12/31/91	1/1/91
Investment in Style (equity method)	$132,000		
Other assets	138,000	$115,000	$100,000
	$270,000	$115,000	$100,000
Common stock	$ 50,000	$ 20,000	$ 20,000
Additional paid-in capital	80,250	44,000	44,000
Retained earnings	139,750	51,000	36,000
	$270,000	$115,000	$100,000

6. What amount should Dallas report as earnings from subsidiary, before amortization of goodwill, in its 1991 income statement?
    a. $12,000
    b. $15,000
    c. $16,000
    d. $20,000

7. What amount of total stockholders' equity should be reported in Dallas' December 31, 1991, consolidated balance sheet?
    a. $270,000
    b. $286,000
    c. $362,000
    d. $385,000

1M92
Items 8 and 9 are based on the following:

Scroll, Inc., a wholly owned subsidiary of Pirn, Inc., began operations on January 1, 1991. The following information is from the condensed 1991 income statements of Pirn and Scroll:

Selected Questions

	Pirn	Scroll
Sales to Scroll	$100,000	$ —
Sales to others	400,000	300,000
	500,000	300,000
Cost of goods sold:		
Acquired from Pirn	—	80,000
Acquired from others	350,000	190,000
Gross profit	150,000	30,000
Depreciation	40,000	10,000
Other expenses	60,000	15,000
Income from operations	50,000	5,000
Gain on sale of equipment to Scroll	12,000	—
Income before income taxes	$ 38,000	$ 5,000

Additional information:

- Sales by Pirn to Scroll are made on the same terms as those made to third parties.
- Equipment purchased by Scroll from Pirn for $36,000 on January 1, 1991, is depreciated using the straight-line method over four years.

8. In Pirn's December 31, 1991, consolidating worksheet, how much intercompany profit should be eliminated from Scroll's inventory?
   a. $30,000
   b. $20,000
   c. $10,000
   d. $ 6,000

9. What amount should be reported as depreciation expense in Pirn's 1991 consolidated income statement?
   a. $50,000
   b. $47,000
   c. $44,000
   d. $41,000

1M92#10. Lion, Inc. owns 60% of Gray Corp.'s common stock. On December 31, 1991, Gray owes Lion $400,000 for a cash advance. In preparing the consolidated balance sheet at that date, what amount of the advance should be eliminated?
   a. $400,000
   b. $240,000
   c. $160,000
   d. $0

1M92#11. Parker Corp. owns 80% of Smith, Inc.'s common stock. During 1991, Parker sold Smith $250,000 of inventory on the same terms as sales made to third parties. Smith sold all of the inventory purchased from Parker in 1991. The following information pertains to Smith's and Parker's sales for 1991:

	Parker	Smith
Sales	$1,000,000	$700,000
Cost of sales	400,000	350,000
	$ 600,000	$350,000

What amount should Parker report as cost of sales in its 1991 consolidated income statement?
   a. $750,000
   b. $680,000
   c. $500,000
   d. $430,000

2M92#20. Ahm Corp. owns 90% of Bee Corp.'s common stock and 80% of Cee Corp.'s common stock. The remaining common shares of Bee and Cee are owned by their respective employees. Bee sells exclusively to Cee, Cee buys exclusively from Bee, and Cee sells exclusively to unrelated companies. Selected 1991 information for Bee and Cee follows:

	Bee Corp.	Cee Corp.
Sales	$130,000	$ 91,000
Cost of sales	100,000	65,000
Beginning inventory	None	None
Ending inventory	None	65,000

What amount should be reported as gross profit in Bee and Cee's combined income statement for the year ended December 31, 1991?
   a. $26,000
   b. $41,000
   c. $47,800
   d. $56,000

TN91#8. For which of the following reporting units is the preparation of combined financial statements most appropriate?
   a. A corporation and a majority-owned subsidiary with nonhomogeneous operations.
   b. A corporation and a foreign subsidiary with nonintegrated homogeneous operations.
   c. Several corporations with related operations with some common individual owners.
   d. Several corporations with related operations owned by one individual.

TN91#9. Pride, Inc. owns 80% of Simba, Inc.'s outstanding common stock. Simba, in turn, owns 10% of Pride's outstanding common stock. What percentage of the common stock cash dividends declared by the individual companies should be reported as dividends declared in the consolidated financial statements?

	Dividends declared by Pride	Dividends declared by Simba
a.	90%	0%
b.	90%	20%
c.	100%	0%
d.	100%	20%

1N91#10. Mr. & Mrs. Dart own a majority of the outstanding capital stock of Wall Corp., Black Co., and West, Inc. During 1990, Wall advanced cash to Black and West in the amounts of $50,000 and $80,000, respectively. West advanced $70,000 in cash to Black. At December 31, 1990, none of the advances was repaid. In the combined December 31, 1990, balance sheet of these companies, what amount would be reported as receivables from affiliates?
    a. $200,000
    b. $130,000
    c. $ 60,000
    d. $0

1N91#53. During 1990, Pard Corp. sold goods to its 80%-owned subsidiary, Seed Corp. At December 31, 1990, one-half of these goods were included in Seed's ending inventory. Reported 1990 selling expenses were $1,100,000 and $400,000 for Pard and Seed, respectively. Pard's selling expenses included $50,000 in freight-out costs for goods sold to Seed. What amount of selling expenses should be reported in Pard's 1990 consolidated income statement?
    a. $1,500,000
    b. $1,480,000
    c. $1,475,000
    d. $1,450,000

2N91#10. Beni Corp. purchased 100% of Carr Corp.'s outstanding capital stock for $430,000 cash. Immediately before the purchase, the balance sheets of both corporations reported the following:

	Beni	Carr
Assets	$2,000,000	$750,000
Liabilities	$ 750,000	$400,000
Common stock	1,000,000	310,000
Retained earnings	250,000	40,000
Liabilities and stockholders' equity	$2,000,000	$750,000

At the date of purchase, the fair value of Carr's assets was $50,000 more than the aggregate carrying amounts. In the consolidated balance sheet prepared immediately after the purchase, the consolidated stockholders' equity should amount to
    a. $1,680,000
    b. $1,650,000
    c. $1,600,000
    d. $1,250,000

1M91#7. On January 1, 1990, Poe Corp. sold a machine for $900,000 to Saxe Corp., its wholly-owned subsidiary. Poe paid $1,100,000 for this machine, which had accumulated depreciation of $250,000. Poe estimated a $100,000 salvage value and depreciated the machine on the straight-line method over 20 years, a policy which Saxe continued. In Poe's December 31, 1990, consolidated balance sheet, this machine should be included in cost and accumulated depreciation as

	Cost	Accumulated depreciation
a.	$1,100,000	$300,000
b.	$1,100,000	$290,000
c.	$ 900,000	$ 40,000
d.	$ 850,000	$ 42,500

1M91
Items 13 through 17 are based on the following:

The separate condensed balance sheets and income statements of Purl Corp. and its wholly-owned subsidiary, Scott Corp., are as follows:

BALANCE SHEETS
December 31, 1990

	Purl	Scott
Assets		
Current assets		
Cash	$ 80,000	$ 60,000
Accounts receivable (net)	140,000	25,000
Inventories	90,000	50,000
Total current assets	310,000	135,000
Property, plant, and equipment (net)	625,000	280,000
Investment in Scott (equity method)	390,000	—
Total assets	$1,325,000	$415,000
Liabilities and Stockholders' Equity		
Current liabilities		
Accounts payable	$ 160,000	$ 95,000
Accrued liabilities	110,000	30,000
Total current liabilities	270,000	125,000
Stockholders' equity		
Common stock ($10 par)	300,000	50,000
Additional paid-in capital	—	10,000
Retained earnings	755,000	230,000
Total stockholders' equity	1,055,000	290,000
Total liabilities and stockholders' equity	$1,325,000	$415,000

INCOME STATEMENTS
For the Year Ended December 31, 1990

	Purl	Scott
Sales	$2,000,000	$750,000
Cost of goods sold	1,540,000	500,000
Gross margin	460,000	250,000
Operating expenses	260,000	150,000
Operating income	200,000	100,000
Equity in earnings of Scott	60,000	—
Income before income taxes	260,000	100,000
Provision for income taxes	60,000	30,000
Net income	$ 200,000	$ 70,000

Additional information:

- On January 1, 1990, Purl purchased for $360,000 all of Scott's $10 par, voting common stock. On January 1, 1990, the fair value of Scott's assets and liabilities equaled their carrying amount of $410,000 and $160,000, respectively, except that the fair values of certain items identifiable in Scott's inventory were $10,000 more than their carrying amounts. These items were still on hand at December 31, 1990. Purl's policy is to amortize intangible assets over a 10-year period, unless a definite life is ascertainable.

- During 1990, Purl and Scott paid cash dividends of $100,000 and $30,000, respectively. For tax purposes, Purl receives the 100% exclusion for dividends received from Scott.

- There were no intercompany transactions, except for Purl's receipt of dividends from Scott and Purl's recording of its share of Scott's earnings.

- Both Purl and Scott paid income taxes at the rate of 30%.

In the December 31, 1990, consolidated financial statements of Purl and its subsidiary:

13. Total current assets should be
    a. $455,000
    b. $445,000
    c. $310,000
    d. $135,000

14. Total assets should be
    a. $1,740,000
    b. $1,450,000
    c. $1,350,000
    d. $1,325,000

15. Total retained earnings should be
    a. $985,000
    b. $825,000
    c. $795,000
    d. $755,000

16. Net income should be
    a. $270,000
    b. $200,000
    c. $190,000
    d. $170,000

17. Goodwill amortization expense should be
    a. $20,000
    b. $10,000
    c. $ 6,000
    d. $0

2M91
Items 19 and 20 are based on the following:

Nolan owns 100% of the capital stock of both Twill Corp. and Webb Corp. Twill purchases merchandise inventory from Webb at 140% of Webb's cost. During 1990, merchandise that cost Webb $40,000 was sold to Twill. Twill sold all of this merchandise to unrelated customers for $81,200 during 1990. In preparing combined financial statements for 1990, Nolan's bookkeeper disregarded the common ownership of Twill and Webb.

19. By what amount was unadjusted revenue overstated in the combined income statement for 1990?
    a. $16,000
    b. $40,000
    c. $56,000
    d. $81,200

20. What amount should be eliminated from cost of goods sold in the combined income statement for 1990?
    a. $56,000
    b. $40,000
    c. $24,000
    d. $16,000

TN90#2. Water Co. owns 80% of the outstanding common stock of Fire Co. On December 31, 1989, Fire sold equipment to Water at a price in excess of Fire's carrying amount, but less than its original cost. On a consolidated balance sheet at December 31, 1989, the carrying amount of the equipment should be reported at
   a. Water's original cost.
   b. Fire's original cost.
   c. Water's original cost less Fire's recorded gain.
   d. Water's original cost less 80% of Fire's recorded gain.

TN90#3. Combined statements may be used to present the results of operations of

	Unconsolidated subsidiaries	Companies under common management
a.	Yes	Yes
b.	Yes	No
c.	No	Yes
d.	No	No

1N90#60. Mr. Cord owns four corporations. Combined financial statements are being prepared for these corporations, which have intercompany loans of $200,000 and intercompany profits of $500,000. What amount of these intercompany loans and profits should be included in the combined financial statements?

	Intercompany Loans	Profits
a.	$200,000	$0
b.	$200,000	$500,000
c.	$0	$0
d.	$0	$500,000

1M90#11. At December 31, 1989, Grey, Inc. owned 90% of Winn Corp., a consolidated subsidiary, and 20% of Carr Corp., an investee in which Grey cannot exercise significant influence. On the same date, Grey had receivables of $300,000 from Winn and $200,000 from Carr. In its December 31, 1989, consolidated balance sheet, Grey should report accounts receivable from affiliates of
- a. $500,000
- b. $340,000
- c. $230,000
- d. $200,000

2. Balance Sheet

R98#1. According to the FASB conceptual framework, comprehensive income includes which of the following?

	Loss on discontinued operations	Investments by owners
a.	Yes	Yes
b.	Yes	No
c.	No	Yes
d.	No	No

N95#60. The following data pertain to Cowl, Inc., for the year ended December 31, 1994:

Net sales	$ 600,000
Net income	150,000
Total assets, January 1, 1994	2,000,000
Total assets, December 31, 1994	3,000,000

What was Cowl's rate of return on assets for 1994?
- a. 5%
- b. 6%
- c. 20%
- d. 24%

M95#5. Cali, Inc., had a $4,000,000 note payable due on March 15, 1995. On January 28, 1995, before the issuance of its 1994 financial statements, Cali issued long-term bonds in the amount of $4,500,000. Proceeds from the bonds were used to repay the note when it came due. How should Cali classify the note in its December 31, 1994, financial statements?
- a. As a current liability, with separate disclosure of the note refinancing.
- b. As a current liability, with no separate disclosure required.
- c. As a noncurrent liability, with separate disclosure of the note refinancing.
- d. As a noncurrent liability, with no separate disclosure required.

N94#5. In analyzing a company's financial statements, which financial statement would a potential investor primarily use to assess the company's liquidity and financial flexibility?
- a. Balance sheet.
- b. Income statement.
- c. Statement of retained earnings.
- d. Statement of cash flows.

N94
Items 8 and 9 are based on the following:

The following trial balance of Trey Co. at December 31, 1993, has been adjusted except for income tax expense.

	Dr.	Cr.
Cash	$ 550,000	
Accounts receivable, net	1,650,000	
Prepaid taxes	300,000	
Accounts payable		$ 120,000
Common stock		500,000
Additional paid-in capital		680,000
Retained earnings		630,000
Foreign currency translation adjustment	430,000	
Revenues		3,600,000
Expenses	2,600,000	
	$5,530,000	$5,530,000

Additional information:
- During 1993, estimated tax payments of $300,000 were charged to prepaid taxes. Trey has not yet recorded income tax expense. There were no differences between financial statement and income tax income, and Trey's tax rate is 30%.
- Included in accounts receivable is $500,000 due from a customer. Special terms granted to this customer require payment in equal semi-annual installments of $125,000 every April 1 and October 1.

8. In Trey's December 31, 1993, balance sheet, what amount should be reported as total current assets?
- a. $1,950,000
- b. $2,200,000
- c. $2,250,000
- d. $2,500,000

9. In Trey's December 31, 1993, balance sheet, what amount should be reported as total retained earnings?
   a. $1,029,000
   b. $1,200,000
   c. $1,330,000
   d. $1,630,000

M94#3. Reporting inventory at the lower of cost or market is a departure from the accounting principle of
   a. Historical cost.
   b. Consistency.
   c. Conservatism.
   d. Full disclosure.

M94#11. Brite Corp. had the following liabilities at December 31, 1993:

Accounts payable	$ 55,000
Unsecured notes, 8%, due 7-1-94	400,000
Accrued expenses	35,000
Contingent liability	450,000
Deferred income tax liability	25,000
Senior bonds, 7%, due 3-31-94	1,000,000

The contingent liability is an accrual for possible losses on a $1,000,000 lawsuit filed against Brite. Brite's legal counsel expects the suit to be settled in 1995, and has estimated that Brite will be liable for damages in the range of $450,000 to $750,000.

The deferred income tax liability is not related to an asset for financial reporting and is expected to reverse in 1995.

What amount should Brite report in its December 31, 1993, balance sheet for current liabilities?
   a. $ 515,000
   b. $ 940,000
   c. $1,490,000
   d. $1,515,000

TN93#2. Deecee Co. adjusted its historical cost income statement by applying specific price indexes to its depreciation expense and cost of goods sold. Deecee's adjusted income statement is prepared according to
   a. Fair value accounting.
   b. General purchasing power accounting.
   c. Current cost accounting.
   d. Current cost/general purchasing power accounting.

1N93#1. Mill Co.'s trial balance included the following account balances at December 31, 1992:

Accounts payable	$15,000
Bonds payable, due 1993	25,000
Discount on bonds payable, due 1993	3,000
Dividends payable 1/31/93	8,000
Notes payable, due 1994	20,000

What amount should be included in the current liability section of Mill's December 31, 1992, balance sheet?
   a. $45,000
   b. $51,000
   c. $65,000
   d. $78,000

1M93#1. The following is Gold Corp.'s June 30, 1992, trial balance:

Cash overdraft		$ 10,000
Accounts receivable, net	$ 35,000	
Inventory	58,000	
Prepaid expenses	12,000	
Land held for resale	100,000	
Property, plant, and equipment, net	95,000	
Accounts payable and accrued expenses		32,000
Common stock		25,000
Additional paid-in capital		150,000
Retained earnings		83,000
	$300,000	$300,000

Additional information:

- Checks amounting to $30,000 were written to vendors and recorded on June 29, 1992, resulting in a cash overdraft of $10,000. The checks were mailed on July 9, 1992.

- Land held for resale was sold for cash on July 15, 1992.

- Gold issued its financial statements on July 31, 1992.

In its June 30, 1992, balance sheet, what amount should Gold report as current assets?
   a. $225,000
   b. $205,000
   c. $195,000
   d. $125,000

1N92
Items 1 through 3 are based on the following:

The following trial balance of Mint Corp. at December 31, 1991, has been adjusted except for income tax expense.

TRIAL BALANCE
December 31, 1991

	Dr.	Cr.
Cash	$ 600,000	
Accounts receivable, net	3,500,000	
Cost in excess of billings on long-term contracts	1,600,000	
Billings in excess of costs on long-term contracts		$ 700,000

	Dr.	Cr.
Prepaid taxes	450,000	
Property, plant, and equipment, net	1,480,000	
Note payable—noncurrent		1,620,000
Common stock		750,000
Additional paid-in capital		2,000,000
Retained earnings— unappropriated		900,000
Retained earnings— restricted for note payable		160,000
Earnings from long-term contracts		6,680,000
Costs and expenses	5,180,000	
	$12,810,000	$12,810,000

Other financial data for the year ended December 31, 1991, are:

- Mint uses the percentage-of-completion method to account for long-term construction contracts for financial statement and income tax purposes. All receivables on these contracts are considered to be collectible within 12 months.

- During 1991, estimated tax payments of $450,000 were charged to prepaid taxes. Mint has not recorded income tax expense. There were no temporary or permanent differences, and Mint's tax rate is 30%.

In Mint's December 31, 1991, balance sheet, what amount should be reported as:

1. Total retained earnings?
    a. $1,950,000
    b. $2,110,000
    c. $2,400,000
    d. $2,560,000

2. Total noncurrent liabilities?
    a. $1,620,000
    b. $1,780,000
    c. $2,320,000
    d. $2,480,000

3. Total current assets?
    a. $5,000,000
    b. $5,450,000
    c. $5,700,000
    d. $6,150,000

1N92#6. Rice Co. was incorporated on January 1, 1991, with $500,000 from the issuance of stock and borrowed funds of $75,000. During the first year of operations, net income was $25,000. On December 15, Rice paid a $2,000 cash dividend. No additional activities affected owners' equity in 1991. At December 31, 1991, Rice's liabilities had increased to $94,000. In Rice's December 31, 1991, balance sheet, total assets should be reported at

a. $598,000
b. $600,000
c. $617,000
d. $692,000

TM92#48. On December 31, 1991, Northpark Co. collected a receivable due from a major customer. Which of the following ratios would be increased by this transaction?
a. Inventory turnover ratio.
b. Receivable turnover ratio.
c. Current ratio.
d. Quick ratio.

2M92#18. Zenk Co. wrote off obsolete inventory of $100,000 during 1991. What was the effect of this write-off on Zenk's ratio analysis?
a. Decrease in current ratio but **not** in quick ratio.
b. Decrease in quick ratio but **not** in current ratio.
c. Increase in current ratio but **not** in quick ratio.
d. Increase in quick ratio but **not** in current ratio.

1M91#2. Mirr, Inc. was incorporated on January 1, 1990, with proceeds from the issuance of $750,000 in stock and borrowed funds of $110,000. During the first year of operations, revenues from sales and consulting amounted to $82,000, and operating costs and expenses totaled $64,000. On December 15, Mirr declared a $3,000 cash dividend, payable to stockholders on January 15, 1991. No additional activities affected owners' equity in 1990. Mirr's liabilities increased to $120,000 by December 31, 1990. On Mirr's December 31, 1990, balance sheet, total assets should be reported at
a. $885,000
b. $882,000
c. $878,000
d. $875,000

3. **Statement(s) of Income, Comprehensive Income, and Changes in Equity Accounts**

M94#8. At December 31, 1992 and 1993, Apex Co. had 3,000 shares of $100 par, 5% cumulative preferred stock outstanding. No dividends were in arrears as of December 31, 1991. Apex did not declare a dividend during 1992. During 1993, Apex paid a cash dividend of $10,000 on its preferred stock. Apex should report dividends in arrears in its 1993 financial statements as a(an)
a. Accrued liability of $15,000.
b. Disclosure of $15,000.
c. Accrued liability of $20,000.
d. Disclosure of $20,000.

M94
Items 9 and 10 are based on the following:

Vane Co.'s trial balance of income statement accounts for the year ended December 31, 1993, included the following:

Selected Questions

	Debit	Credit
Sales		$575,000
Cost of sales	$240,000	
Administrative expenses	70,000	
Loss on sale of equipment	10,000	
Sales commissions	50,000	
Interest revenue		25,000
Freight out	15,000	
Loss on early retirement of long-term debt	20,000	
Uncollectible accounts expense	15,000	
Totals	$420,000	$600,000

Other information

Finished goods inventory:

January 1, 1993	$400,000
December 31, 1993	360,000

Vane's income tax rate is 30%. In Vane's 1993 multiple-step income statement,

9. What amount should Vane report as the cost of goods manufactured?
   a. $200,000
   b. $215,000
   c. $280,000
   d. $295,000

10. What amount should Vane report as income after income taxes from continuing operations?
    a. $126,000
    b. $129,500
    c. $140,000
    d. $147,000

1N93#10. Conn Co. reported a retained earnings balance of $400,000 at December 31, 1991. In August 1992, Conn determined that insurance premiums of $60,000 for the three-year period beginning January 1, 1991, had been paid and fully expensed in 1991. Conn has a 30% income tax rate. What amount should Conn report as adjusted beginning retained earnings in its 1992 statement of retained earnings?
   a. $420,000
   b. $428,000
   c. $440,000
   d. $442,000

1M93#5. Pear Co.'s income statement for the year ended December 31, 1992, as prepared by Pear's controller, reported income before taxes of $125,000. The auditor questioned the following amounts that had been included in income before taxes:

Equity in earnings of Cinn Co.	$40,000
Dividends received from Cinn	8,000
Adjustments to profits of prior years for arithmetical errors in depreciation	(35,000)

Pear owns 40% of Cinn's common stock. Pear's December 31, 1992, income statement should report income before taxes of

a. $85,000
b. $117,000
c. $120,000
d. $152,000

1N92#8. Tack, Inc. reported a retained earnings balance of $150,000 at December 31, 1990. In June 1991, Tack discovered that merchandise costing $40,000 had not been included in inventory in its 1990 financial statements. Tack has a 30% tax rate. What amount should Tack report as adjusted beginning retained earnings in its statement of retained earnings at December 31, 1991?
   a. $190,000
   b. $178,000
   c. $150,000
   d. $122,000

1M91#3. In Baer Food Co.'s 1990 single-step income statement, the section titled "Revenues" consisted of the following:

Net sales revenue		$187,000
Results from discontinued operations:		
Loss from operations of segment (net of $1,200 tax effect)	$(2,400)	
Gain on disposal of segment (net of $7,200 tax effect)	14,400	12,000
Interest revenue		10,200
Gain on sale of equipment		4,700
Cumulative change in 1988 and 1989 income due to change in depreciation method (net of $750 tax effect)		1,500
Total revenues		$215,400

In the revenues section of the 1990 income statement, Baer Food should have reported total revenues of
   a. $216,300
   b. $215,400
   c. $203,700
   d. $201,900

4. Statement of Cash Flows

R97#7. During 1995, Beck Co. purchased equipment for cash of $47,000, and sold equipment with a $10,000 carrying value for a gain of $5,000. How should these transactions be reported in Beck's 1995 statement of cash flows?
   a. Cash outflow of $32,000.
   b. Cash outflow of $42,000.
   c. Cash inflow of $5,000 and cash outflow of $47,000.
   d. Cash inflow of $15,000 and cash outflow of $47,000.

N95#47. Mend Co. purchased a three-month U.S. Treasury bill. Mend's policy is to treat as cash equivalents all highly liquid investments with an original maturity of

three months or less when purchased. How should this purchase be reported in Mend's statement of cash flows?
   a. As an outflow from operating activities.
   b. As an outflow from investing activities.
   c. As an outflow from financing activities.
   d. Not reported.

N95#48. Which of the following is **not** disclosed on the statement of cash flows when prepared under the direct method, either on the face of the statement or in a separate schedule?
   a. The major classes of gross cash receipts and gross cash payments.
   b. The amount of income taxes paid.
   c. A reconciliation of net income to net cash flow from operations.
   d. A reconciliation of ending retained earnings to net cash flow from operations.

M95#49. Which of the following information should be disclosed as supplemental information in the statement of cash flows?

	Cash flow per share	Conversion of debt to equity
a.	Yes	Yes
b.	Yes	No
c.	No	Yes
d.	No	No

N94#7. Which of the following should **not** be disclosed in an enterprise's statement of cash flows prepared using the indirect method?
   a. Interest paid, net of amounts capitalized.
   b. Income taxes paid.
   c. Cash flow per share.
   d. Dividends paid on preferred stock.

M94#5. The primary purpose of a statement of cash flows is to provide relevant information about
   a. Differences between net income and associated cash receipts and disbursements.
   b. An enterprise's ability to generate future positive net cash flows.
   c. The cash receipts and cash disbursements of an enterprise during a period.
   d. An enterprise's ability to meet cash operating needs.

TN93#41. In a statement of cash flows, if used equipment is sold at a gain, the amount shown as a cash inflow from investing activities equals the carrying amount of the equipment
   a. Plus the gain.
   b. Plus the gain and less the amount of tax attributable to the gain.
   c. Plus both the gain and the amount of tax attributable to the gain.
   d. With **no** addition or subtraction.

1N93#9. Duke Co. reported cost of goods sold of $270,000 for 1992. Additional information is as follows:

	December 31	January 1
Inventory	$60,000	$45,000
Accounts payable	26,000	39,000

If Duke uses the direct method, what amount should Duke report as cash paid to suppliers in its 1992 statement of cash flows?
   a. $242,000
   b. $268,000
   c. $272,000
   d. $298,000

TM93#32. On September 1, 1992, Canary Co. sold used equipment for a cash amount equaling its carrying amount for both book and tax purposes. On September 15, 1992, Canary replaced the equipment by paying cash and signing a note payable for new equipment. The cash paid for the new equipment exceeded the cash received for the old equipment. How should these equipment transactions be reported in Canary's 1992 statement of cash flows?
   a. Cash outflow equal to the cash paid less the cash received.
   b. Cash outflow equal to the cash paid and note payable less the cash received.
   c. Cash inflow equal to the cash received and a cash outflow equal to the cash paid and note payable.
   d. Cash inflow equal to the cash received and a cash outflow equal to the cash paid.

TM93#33. How should a gain from the sale of used equipment for cash be reported in a statement of cash flows using the indirect method?
   a. In investment activities as a reduction of the cash inflow from the sale.
   b. In investment activities as a cash outflow.
   c. In operating activities as a deduction from income.
   d. In operating activities as an addition to income.

TN92#21. Deed Co. owns 2% of Beck Cosmetic Retailers. A property dividend by Beck consisted of merchandise with a fair value lower than the listed retail price. Deed in turn gave the merchandise to its employees as a holiday bonus. How should Deed report the receipt and distribution of the merchandise in its statement of cash flows?
   a. As both an inflow and outflow for operating activities.
   b. As both an inflow and outflow for investing activities.
   c. As an inflow for investing activities and outflow for operating activities.
   d. As a noncash activity.

TN92#44. A statement of cash flows for a development stage enterprise

a. Is the same as that of an established operating enterprise and, in addition, shows cumulative amounts from the enterprise's inception.
b. Shows only cumulative amounts from the enterprise's inception.
c. Is the same as that of an established operating enterprise, but does **not** show cumulative amounts from the enterprise's inception.
d. Is **not** presented.

1N92

Items 9 through 13 are based on the following:

Flax Corp. uses the direct method to prepare its statement of cash flows. Flax's trial balances at December 31, 1991 and 1990, are as follows:

	December 31	
	1991	1990
Debits:		
Cash	$ 35,000	$ 32,000
Accounts receivable	33,000	30,000
Inventory	31,000	47,000
Property, plant, & equipment	100,000	95,000
Unamortized bond discount	4,500	5,000
Cost of goods sold	250,000	380,000
Selling expenses	141,500	172,000
General and administrative expenses	137,000	151,300
Interest expense	4,300	2,600
Income tax expense	20,400	61,200
	$756,700	$976,100
Credits:		
Allowance for uncollectible accounts	$ 1,300	$ 1,100
Accumulated depreciation	16,500	15,000
Trade accounts payable	25,000	17,500
Income taxes payable	21,000	27,100
Deferred income taxes	5,300	4,600
8% callable bonds payable	45,000	20,000
Common stock	50,000	40,000
Additional paid-in capital	9,100	7,500
Retained earnings	44,700	64,600
Sales	538,800	778,700
	$756,700	$976,100

- Flax purchased $5,000 in equipment during 1991.

- Flax allocated one-third of its depreciation expense to selling expenses and the remainder to general and administrative expenses.

What amounts should Flax report in its statement of cash flows for the year ended December 31, 1991, for the following:

9. Cash collected from customers?

a. $541,800
b. $541,600
c. $536,000
d. $535,800

10. Cash paid for goods to be sold?
a. $258,500
b. $257,500
c. $242,500
d. $226,500

11. Cash paid for interest?
a. $4,800
b. $4,300
c. $3,800
d. $1,700

12. Cash paid for income taxes?
a. $25,800
b. $20,400
c. $19,700
d. $15,000

13. Cash paid for selling expenses?
a. $142,000
b. $141,500
c. $141,000
d. $140,000

TM92#8. Which of the following cash flows per share should be reported in a statement of cash flows?
a. Primary cash flows per share only.
b. Fully diluted cash flows per share only.
c. Both primary and fully diluted cash flows per share.
d. Cash flows per share should **not** be reported.

1M91#8. The following information was taken from the 1990 financial statements of Planet Corp.:

Accounts receivable, January 1, 1990	$ 21,600
Accounts receivable, December 31, 1990	30,400
Sales on account and cash sales	438,000
Uncollectible accounts	1,000

No accounts receivable were written off or recovered during the year.

If the direct method is used in the 1990 statement of cash flows, Planet should report cash collected from customers as
a. $447,800
b. $446,800
c. $429,200
d. $428,200

5. Accounting Policies and Other Notes to Financial Statements

N94#4. A company that wishes to disclose information about the effect of changing prices in accordance with

Statement of Financial Accounting Standards No. 89, *Financial Accounting and Changing Prices*, should report this information in
    a. The body of the financial statements.
    b. The notes to the financial statements.
    c. Supplementary information to the financial statements.
    d. Management's report to shareholders.

N94#59. Which of the following information should be disclosed in the summary of significant accounting policies?
    a. Refinancing of debt subsequent to the balance sheet date.
    b. Guarantees of indebtedness of others.
    c. Criteria for determining which investments are treated as cash equivalents.
    d. Adequacy of pension plan assets relative to vested benefits.

M94#6. What is the purpose of information presented in notes to the financial statements?
    a. To provide disclosures required by generally accepted accounting principles.
    b. To correct improper presentation in the financial statements.
    c. To provide recognition of amounts **not** included in the totals of the financial statements.
    d. To present management's responses to auditor comments.

M94#57. During 1993, Smith Co. filed suit against West, Inc. seeking damages for patent infringement. At December 31, 1993, Smith's legal counsel believed that it was probable that Smith would be successful against West for an estimated amount in the range of $75,000 to $150,000, with all amounts in the range considered equally likely. In March 1994, Smith was awarded $100,000 and received full payment thereof. In its 1993 financial statements, issued in February 1994, how should this award be reported?
    a. As a receivable and revenue of $100,000.
    b. As a receivable and deferred revenue of $100,000.
    c. As a disclosure of a contingent gain of $100,000.
    d. As a disclosure of a contingent gain of an undetermined amount in the range of $75,000 to $150,000.

M94#58. In its financial statements, Hila Co. discloses supplemental information on the effects of changing prices in accordance with Statement of Financial Accounting Standards No. 89, *Financial Reporting and Changing Prices*. Hila computed the increase in current cost of inventory as follows:

Increase in current
   cost (nominal dollars) $15,000
Increase in current
   cost (constant dollars) $12,000

What amount should Hila disclose as the inflation component of the increase in current cost of inventories?

    a. $ 3,000
    b. $12,000
    c. $15,000
    d. $27,000

TN93#19. Which of the following information should be included in Melay, Inc.'s 1992 summary of significant accounting policies?
    a. Property, plant, and equipment is recorded at cost with depreciation computed principally by the straight-line method.
    b. During 1992, the Delay Segment was sold.
    c. Business segment 1992 sales are Alay $1M, Belay $2M, and Celay $3M.
    d. Future common share dividends are expected to approximate 60% of earnings.

1N93#42. On July 1, 1992, South Co. entered into a ten-year operating lease for a warehouse facility. The annual minimum lease payments are $100,000. In addition to the base rent, South pays a monthly allocation of the building's operating expenses, which amounted to $20,000 for the year ended June 30, 1993. In the notes to South's June 30, 1993, financial statements, what amounts of subsequent years' lease payments should be disclosed?
    a. $100,000 per annum for each of the next five years and $500,000 in the aggregate.
    b. $120,000 per annum for each of the next five years and $600,000 in the aggregate.
    c. $100,000 per annum for each of the next five years and $900,000 in the aggregate.
    d. $120,000 per annum for each of the next five years and $1,080,000 in the aggregate.

TM93#31. The summary of significant accounting policies should disclose the
    a. Maturity dates of noncurrent debts.
    b. Terms for convertible debt to be exchanged for common stock.
    c. Concentration of credit risk of all financial instruments by geographical region.
    d. Criteria for determining which investments are treated as cash equivalents.

2M93#11. During 1992, Leader Corp. sued Cape Co. for patent infringement. On December 31, 1992, Leader was awarded a $500,000 favorable judgment in the suit. On that date, Cape offered to settle out of court for $300,000 and not appeal the judgment. In February 1993, after the issuance of its 1992 financial statements, Leader agreed to the out-of-court settlement and received a certified check for $300,000. In its 1992 financial statements, how should Leader have reported these events?
    a. As a gain of $300,000.
    b. As a receivable and deferred credit of $300,000.
    c. As a disclosure in the notes to the financial statements only.
    d. It should **not** be reported in the financial statements.

Selected Questions

TN92#37. Which of the following should be disclosed in a summary of significant accounting policies?

I. Management's intention to maintain or vary the dividend payout ratio.
II. Criteria for determining which investments are treated as cash equivalents.
III. Composition of the sales order backlog by segment.

a. I only.
b. I and III.
c. II only.
d. II and III.

TN92#40. Manhof Co. prepares supplementary reports on income from continuing operations on a current cost basis in accordance with FASB Statement No. 89, *Financial Reporting and Changing Prices*. How should Manhof compute cost of goods sold on a current cost basis?
a. Number of units sold times average current cost of units during the year.
b. Number of units sold times current cost of units at year end.
c. Number of units sold times current cost of units at the beginning of the year.
d. Beginning inventory at current cost plus cost of goods purchased less ending inventory at current cost.

2N92#51. Brad Corp. has unconditional purchase obligations associated with product financing arrangements. These obligations are reported as liabilities on Brad's balance sheet, with the related assets also recognized. In the notes to Brad's financial statements, the aggregate amount of payments for these obligations should be disclosed for each of how many years following the date of the latest balance sheet?
a. 0
b. 1
c. 5
d. 10

TM92
Items 4 and 5 are based on the following:

In a period of rising general price levels, Pollard Corp. discloses income on a current cost basis in accordance with FASB Statement No. 89, *Financial Reporting and Changing Prices*.

4. Compared to historical cost income from continuing operations, which of the following conditions increases Pollard's current cost income from continuing operations?
a. Current cost of equipment is greater than historical cost.
b. Current cost of land is greater than historical cost.
c. Current cost of cost of goods sold is less than historical cost.
d. Ending net monetary assets are less than beginning net monetary assets.

5. Which of the following contributes to Pollard's purchasing power loss on net monetary items?
a. Refundable deposits with suppliers.
b. Equity investment in unconsolidated subsidiaries.
c. Warranty obligations.
d. Wages payable.

TM92#49. Financial reporting by a development stage enterprise differs from financial reporting for an established operating enterprise in regard to footnote disclosures
a. Only.
b. And expense recognition principles only.
c. And revenue recognition principles only.
d. And revenue and expense recognition principles.

2M92#13. The following information pertains to each unit of merchandise purchased for resale by Vend Co.:

March 1, 1991
Purchase price	$ 8
Selling price	$12
Price level index	110

December 31, 1991
Replacement cost	$10
Selling price	$15
Price level index	121

Under current cost accounting, what is the amount of Vend's holding gain on each unit of this merchandise?
a. $0
b. $0.80
c. $1.20
d. $2.00

TM91#32. The summary of significant accounting policies should disclose the
a. Pro forma effect of retroactive application of an accounting change.
b. Basis of profit recognition on long-term construction contracts.
c. Adequacy of pension plan assets in relation to vested benefits.
d. Future minimum lease payments in the aggregate and for each of the five succeeding fiscal years.

1N90#54. Witt Corp. has outstanding at December 31, 1989 two long-term borrowings with annual sinking fund requirements and maturities as follows:

	Sinking fund requirements	Maturities
1989	$1,000,000	$ —
1990	1,500,000	2,000,000
1991	1,500,000	2,000,000
1992	2,000,000	2,500,000
1993	2,000,000	3,000,000
	$8,000,000	$9,500,000

In the notes to its December 31, 1989 balance sheet, how should Witt report the above data?

FA-17

a. No disclosure is required.
b. Only sinking fund payments totaling $8,000,000 for the next five years detailed by year need be disclosed.
c. Only maturities totaling $9,500,000 for the next five years detailed by year need be disclosed.
d. The combined aggregate of $17,500,000 of maturities and sinking fund requirements detailed by year should be disclosed.

TM90#30. Which of the following facts concerning fixed assets should be included in the summary of significant accounting policies?

	Depreciation method	Composition
a.	No	Yes
b.	Yes	Yes
c.	Yes	No
d.	No	No

TM90#35. Grim Corporation operates a plant in a foreign country. It is probable that the plant will be expropriated. However, the foreign government has indicated that Grim will receive a definite amount of compensation for the plant. The amount of compensation is less than the fair market value but exceeds the carrying amount of the plant. The contingency should be reported
a. As a valuation allowance as a part of stockholders' equity.
b. As a fixed asset valuation allowance account.
c. In the notes to the financial statements.
d. In the income statement.

2M90#50. The following assets were among those that appeared on Baird Co.'s books at the end of the year:

Demand bank deposits	$650,000
Net long-term receivables	400,000
Patents and trademarks	150,000

In preparing constant dollar financial statements, how much should Baird classify as monetary assets?
a. $1,200,000
b. $1,050,000
c. $ 800,000
d. $ 650,000

C. Other Presentations of Financial Data

1. Financial Statements Prepared in Conformity With Comprehensive Bases of Accounting Other Than Generally Accepted Accounting Principles

N95#57. Financial statements prepared under which of the following methods include adjustments for both specific price changes and general price-level changes?
a. Historical cost/nominal dollar.
b. Current cost/nominal dollar.
c. Current cost/constant dollar.
d. Historical cost/constant dollar.

N94#58. The following information pertains to Eagle Co.'s 1993 sales:

Cash sales

| Gross | $ 80,000 |
| Returns and allowances | 4,000 |

Credit sales

| Gross | 120,000 |
| Discounts | 6,000 |

On January 1, 1993, customers owed Eagle $40,000. On December 31, 1993, customers owed Eagle $30,000. Eagle uses the direct writeoff method for bad debts. No bad debts were recorded in 1993. Under the cash basis of accounting, what amount of net revenue should Eagle report for 1993?
a. $ 76,000
b. $170,000
c. $190,000
d. $200,000

M94#42. Compared to the accrual basis of accounting, the cash basis of accounting understates income by the net decrease during the accounting period of

	Accounts receivable	Accrued expenses
a.	Yes	Yes
b.	Yes	No
c.	No	No
d.	No	Yes

M94#54. Which of the following accounting bases may be used to prepare financial statements in conformity with a comprehensive basis of accounting other than generally accepted accounting principles?

I. Basis of accounting used by an entity to file its income tax return.
II. Cash receipts and disbursements basis of accounting.

a. I only.
b. II only.
c. Both I and II.
d. Neither I nor II.

TN93#40. Compared to its 1992 cash basis net income, Potoma Co.'s 1992 accrual basis net income increased when it
a. Declared a cash dividend in 1991 that it paid in 1992.
b. Wrote off more accounts receivable balances than it reported as uncollectible accounts expense in 1992.
c. Had lower accrued expenses on December 31, 1992, than on January 1, 1992.
d. Sold used equipment for cash at a gain in 1992.

1N93#43. On April 1, 1993, Ivy began operating a service proprietorship with an initial cash investment of

$1,000. The proprietorship provided $3,200 of services in April and received full payment in May. The proprietorship incurred expenses of $1,500 in April which were paid in June. During May, Ivy drew $500 against her capital account.

What was the proprietorship's income for the two months ended May 31, 1993, under the following methods of accounting?

	Cash-basis	Accrual-basis
a.	$1,200	$1,200
b.	$1,700	$1,700
c.	$2,700	$1,200
d.	$3,200	$1,700

1M93#40. Class Corp. maintains its accounting records on the cash basis but restates its financial statements to the accrual method of accounting. Class had $60,000 in cash-basis pretax income for 1992. The following information pertains to Class's operations for the years ended December 31, 1992 and 1991:

	1992	1991
Accounts receivable	$40,000	$20,000
Accounts payable	15,000	30,000

Under the accrual method, what amount of income before taxes should Class report in its December 31, 1992, income statement?
- a. $25,000
- b. $55,000
- c. $65,000
- d. $95,000

TN92#6. White Co. wants to convert its 1991 financial statements from the accrual basis of accounting to the cash basis. Both supplies inventory and office salaries payable increased between January 1, 1991, and December 31, 1991. To obtain 1991 cash basis net income, how should these increases be added to or deducted from accrual basis net income?

	Supplies inventory	Office salaries payable
a.	Deducted	Deducted
b.	Deducted	Added
c.	Added	Deducted
d.	Added	Added

1N92#41. Reid Partners, Ltd., which began operations on January 1, 1990, has elected to use cash-basis accounting for tax purposes and accrual-basis accounting for its financial statements. Reid reported sales of $175,000 and $80,000 in its tax returns for the years ended December 31, 1991 and 1990, respectively. Reid reported accounts receivable of $30,000 and $50,000 in its balance sheets as of December 31, 1991 and 1990, respectively. What amount should Reid report as sales in its income statement for the year ended December 31, 1991?

- a. $145,000
- b. $155,000
- c. $195,000
- d. $205,000

TM92#6. Before 1991, Droit Co. used the cash basis of accounting. As of December 31, 1991, Droit changed to the accrual basis. Droit cannot determine the beginning balance of supplies inventory. What is the effect of Droit's inability to determine beginning supplies inventory on its 1991 accrual basis net income and December 31, 1991, accrual basis owners' equity?

	1991 net income	12/31/91 owners' equity
a.	No effect	No effect
b.	No effect	Overstated
c.	Overstated	No effect
d.	Overstated	Overstated

1M92#39. Zeta Co. reported sales revenue of $4,600,000 in its income statement for the year ended December 31, 1991. Additional information is as follows:

	12/31/90	12/31/91
Accounts receivable	$1,000,000	$1,300,000
Allowance for uncollectible accounts	(60,000)	(110,000)

Zeta wrote off uncollectible accounts totaling $20,000 during 1991. Under the cash basis of accounting, Zeta would have reported 1991 sales of
- a. $4,900,000
- b. $4,350,000
- c. $4,300,000
- d. $4,280,000

TM90#18. Compared to the accrual basis of accounting, the cash basis of accounting overstates income by the net increase during the accounting period of the

	Accounts receivable	Accrued expenses payable
a.	No	No
b.	No	Yes
c.	Yes	No
d.	Yes	Yes

2. **Personal Financial Statements**

R98#2. Which statements are usually included in a set of personal financial statements?
- a. A statement of net worth and an income statement.
- b. A statement of financial condition and a statement of changes in net worth.
- c. A statement of net worth, an income statement, and a statement of cash flows.
- d. A statement of financial condition, a statement of changes in net worth, and a statement of cash flows.

R98#3. At May 31, 1997, Quay owned a $10,000 whole-life insurance policy with a cash-surrender value of $4,500, net of loans of $2,500. In Quay's May 31, 1997, personal statement of financial condition, what amount should be reported as investment in life insurance?
a. $ 4,500
b. $ 7,000
c. $ 7,500
d. $10,000

N95#54. A business interest that constitutes a large part of an individual's total assets should be presented in a personal statement of financial condition as
a. A separate listing of the individual assets and liabilities at cost.
b. Separate line items of both total assets and total liabilities at cost.
c. A single amount equal to the proprietorship equity.
d. A single amount equal to the estimated current value of the business interest.

N95#55. Quinn is preparing a personal statement of financial condition as of April 30, 1995. Included in Quinn's assets are the following:

- 50% of the voting stock of Ink Corp. A stockholders' agreement restricts the sale of the stock and, under certain circumstances, requires Ink to repurchase the stock. Quinn's tax basis for the stock is $430,000, and at April 30, 1995, the buyout value is $675,000.

- Jewelry with a fair value aggregating $70,000 based on an independent appraisal on April 30, 1995, for insurance purposes. This jewelry was acquired by purchase and gift over a 10-year period and has a total tax basis of $40,000.

What is the total amount at which the Ink stock and jewelry should be reported in Quinn's April 30, 1995, personal statement of financial condition?
a. $470,000
b. $500,000
c. $715,000
d. $745,000

M95#55. Personal financial statements usually consist of
a. A statement of net worth and a statement of changes in net worth.
b. A statement of net worth, an income statement, and a statement of changes in net worth.
c. A statement of financial condition and a statement of changes in net worth.
d. A statement of financial condition, a statement of changes in net worth, and a statement of cash flows.

M94#53. For the purpose of estimating income taxes to be reported in personal financial statements, assets and liabilities measured at their tax bases should be compared to assets and liabilities measured at their

	Assets	Liabilities
a.	Estimated current value	Estimated current amount
b.	Historical cost	Historical cost
c.	Estimated current value	Historical cost
d.	Historical cost	Estimated current amount

TN93#44. Personal financial statements should report assets and liabilities at
a. Estimated current values at the date of the financial statements and, as additional information, at historical cost.
b. Estimated current values at the date of the financial statements.
c. Historical cost and, as additional information, at estimated current values at the date of the financial statements.
d. Historical cost.

TN92#43. Smith owns several works of art. At what amount should these art works be reported in Smith's personal financial statements?
a. Original cost.
b. Insured amount.
c. Smith's estimate.
d. Appraised value.

2N92#57. Clint owns 50% of Vohl Corp.'s common stock. Clint paid $20,000 for this stock in 1986. At December 31, 1991, Clint's 50% stock ownership in Vohl had a fair value of $180,000. Vohl's cumulative net income and cash dividends declared for the five years ended December 31, 1991, were $300,000 and $40,000, respectively. In Clint's personal statement of financial condition at December 31, 1991, what amount should be shown as the investment in Vohl?
a. $ 20,000
b. $150,000
c. $170,000
d. $180,000

2N92#58. Jen has been employed by Komp, Inc. since February 1, 1989. Jen is covered by Komp's Section 401(k) deferred compensation plan. Jen's contributions have been 10% of salaries. Komp has made matching contributions of 5%. Jen's salaries were $21,000 in 1989, $23,000 in 1990, and $26,000 in 1991. Employer contributions vest after an employee completes three years of continuous employment. The balance in Jen's 401(k) account was $11,900 at December 31, 1991, which included earnings of $1,200 on Jen's contributions. What amount should be reported for Jen's vested interest in the 401(k) plan in Jen's December 31, 1991, personal statement of financial condition?

a. $11,900
b. $ 8,200
c. $ 7,000
d. $ 1,200

2N92#59. The following information pertains to an insurance policy that Barton owns on his life:

Face amount	$100,000
Accumulated premiums paid up to December 31, 1991	8,000
Cash value at December 31, 1991	12,000
Policy loan	3,000

In Barton's personal statement of financial condition at December 31, 1991, what amount should be reported for the investment in life insurance?
a. $97,000
b. $12,000
c. $ 9,000
d. $ 8,000

TM92#50. In personal financial statements, how should estimated income taxes on the excess of the estimated current values of assets over their tax bases be reported in the statement of financial condition?
a. As liabilities.
b. As deductions from the related assets.
c. Between liabilities and net worth.
d. In a footnote disclosure only.

2M92#19. Shea, a calendar-year taxpayer, is preparing a personal statement of financial condition as of April 30, 1992. Shea's 1991 income tax liability was paid in full on April 15, 1992. Shea's tax on income earned from January through April 1992 is estimated at $30,000. In addition, $25,000 is estimated for income tax on the differences between the estimated current values of Shea's assets and the current amounts of liabilities and their tax bases at April 30, 1992. No withholdings or payments have been made towards the 1992 income tax liability. In Shea's statement of financial condition at April 30, 1992, what is the total of the amount or amounts that should be reported for income taxes?
a. $0
b. $25,000
c. $30,000
d. $55,000

TM91#40. Personal financial statements should report an investment in life insurance at the
a. Face amount of the policy less the amount of premiums paid.
b. Cash value of the policy less the amount of any loans against it.
c. Cash value of the policy less the amount of premiums paid.
d. Face amount of the policy less the amount of any loans against it.

2M91#9. The following information pertains to marketable equity securities owned by Kent:

	Fair value at December 31,		Cost in
Stock	1990	1989	1988
City Mfg., Inc.	$95,500	$93,000	$89,900
Tri Corp.	3,400	5,600	3,600
Zee, Inc.		10,300	15,000

The Zee stock was sold in January 1990 for $10,200. In Kent's personal statement of financial condition at December 31, 1990, what amount should be reported for marketable equity securities?
a. $93,300
b. $93,500
c. $94,100
d. $98,900

2M91#10. The estimated current values of Lane's personal assets at December 31, 1990, totaled $1,000,000, with tax bases aggregating $600,000. Included in these assets was a vested interest in a deferred profit-sharing plan with a current value of $80,000 and a tax basis of $70,000. The estimated current amounts of Lane's personal liabilities equaled their tax bases at December 31, 1990. Lane's 1990 effective income tax rate was 30%. In Lane's personal statement of financial condition at December 31, 1990, what amount should be provided for estimated income taxes relating to the excess of current values over tax bases?
a. $120,000
b. $117,000
c. $ 3,000
d. $0

1N90#59. Mrs. Taft owns a $150,000 insurance policy on her husband's life. The cash value of the policy is $125,000, and there is a $50,000 loan against the policy. In the Tafts' personal statement of financial condition at December 31, 1989, what amount should be shown as an investment in life insurance?
a. $150,000
b. $125,000
c. $100,000
d. $ 75,000

2M90#59. Dale Hall's holdings at December 31, 1989 included the following:

- 5,000 shares of Arno Corp. common stock purchased in 1984 for $85,000. The market value of the stock was $120,000 at December 31, 1989.
- A life insurance policy with a cash value of $50,000 at December 31, 1989.

In Hall's December 31, 1989 personal statement of financial condition, the above items should be reported at
a. $170,000
b. $135,000
c. $120,000
d. $ 85,000

Financial Accounting and Reporting

II. Recognition, Measurement, Valuation, and Presentation of Typical Items in Financial Statements in Conformity With Generally Accepted Accounting Principles

A. Cash, Cash Equivalents, and Marketable Securities

M95#6. A company has adopted Statement of Financial Accounting Standards No. 115, *Accounting for Certain Investments in Debt and Equity Securities*. It should report the marketable equity securities that it has classified as trading at
  a. Lower of cost or market, with holding gains and losses included in earnings.
  b. Lower of cost or market, with holding gains included in earnings only to the extent of previously recognized holding losses.
  c. Fair value, with holding gains included in earnings only to the extent of previously recognized holding losses.
  d. Fair value, with holding gains and losses included in earnings.

N94#10. Kale Co. has adopted Statement of Financial Accounting Standards No. 115, *Accounting for Certain Investments in Debt and Equity Securities*. Kale purchased bonds at a discount on the open market as an investment and intends to hold these bonds to maturity. Kale should account for these bonds at
  a. Cost.
  b. Amortized cost.
  c. Fair value.
  d. Lower of cost or market.

M94#12. The following information pertains to Grey Co. at December 31, 1993:

Checkbook balance	$12,000
Bank statement balance	16,000
Check drawn on Grey's account, payable to a vendor, dated and recorded 12/31/93 but not mailed until 1/10/94	1,800

On Grey's December 31, 1993, balance sheet, what amount should be reported as cash?
  a. $12,000
  b. $13,800
  c. $14,200
  d. $16,000

M94#13. At December 31, 1993, Kale Co. had the following balances in the accounts it maintains at First State Bank:

Checking account #101	$175,000
Checking account #201	(10,000)
Money market account	25,000
90-day certificate of deposit, due 2-28-94	50,000
180-day certificate of deposit, due 3-15-94	80,000

Kale classifies investments with original maturities of three months or less as cash equivalents. In its December 31, 1993, balance sheet, what amount should Kale report as cash and cash equivalents?
  a. $190,000
  b. $200,000
  c. $240,000
  d. $320,000

1M93#10. Cook Co. had the following balances at December 31, 1992:

Cash in checking account	$350,000
Cash in money-market account	250,000
U.S. Treasury bill, purchased 12/1/92, maturing 2/28/93	800,000
U.S. Treasury bond, purchased 3/1/92, maturing 2/28/93	500,000

Cook's policy is to treat as cash equivalents all highly-liquid investments with a maturity of three months or less when purchased. What amount should Cook report as cash and cash equivalents in its December 31, 1992, balance sheet?
  a. $ 600,000
  b. $1,150,000
  c. $1,400,000
  d. $1,900,000

1N91#9. On March 15, 1990, Ashe Corp. adopted a plan to accumulate $1,000,000 by September 1, 1994. Ashe plans to make four equal annual deposits to a fund that will earn interest at 10% compounded annually. Ashe made the first deposit on September 1, 1990. Future value and future amount factors are as follows:

Future value of 1 at 10% for 4 periods	1.46
Future amount of ordinary annuity of 1 at 10% for 4 periods	4.64
Future amount of annuity in advance of 1 at 10% for 4 periods	5.11

Ashe should make four annual deposits (rounded) of
  a. $250,000
  b. $215,500
  c. $195,700
  d. $146,000

TM91#38. At December 30, 1990, Solomon Co. had a current ratio greater than 1:1 and a quick ratio less than 1:1. On December 31, 1990, all cash was used to reduce accounts payable. How did these cash payments affect the ratios?

	Current ratio	Quick ratio
a.	Decreased	Decreased
b.	Decreased	Increased
c.	Increased	Decreased
d.	Increased	Increased

Selected Questions

1N90#1. In preparing its August 31, 1990 bank reconciliation, Apex Corp. has available the following information:

Balance per bank statement, 8/31/90	$18,050
Deposit in transit, 8/31/90	3,250
Return of customer's check for insufficient funds, 8/31/90	600
Outstanding checks, 8/31/90	2,750
Bank service charges for August	100

At August 31, 1990, Apex's correct cash balance is
- a. $18,550
- b. $17,950
- c. $17,850
- d. $17,550

1M90#1. Poe, Inc. had the following bank reconciliation at March 31, 1990:

Balance per bank statement, 3/31/90	$46,500
Add deposit in transit	10,300
	56,800
Less outstanding checks	12,600
Balance per books, 3/31/90	$44,200

Data per bank for the month of April 1990 follow:

Deposits	$58,400
Disbursements	49,700

All reconciling items at March 31, 1990 cleared the bank in April. Outstanding checks at April 30, 1990 totaled $7,000. There were no deposits in transit at April 30, 1990. What is the cash balance per books at April 30, 1990?
- a. $48,200
- b. $52,900
- c. $55,200
- d. $58,500

B. Receivables

R96#7. When a loan receivable is impaired but foreclosure is **not** probable, which of the following may the creditor use to measure the impairment?

I. The loan's observable market price.
II. The fair value of the collateral if the loan is collateral dependent.

- a. I only.
- b. II only.
- c. Either I or II.
- d. Neither I nor II.

M95#7. Gar Co. factored its receivables without recourse with Ross Bank. Gar received cash as a result of this transaction, which is best described as a
- a. Loan from Ross collateralized by Gar's accounts receivable.
- b. Loan from Ross to be repaid by the proceeds from Gar's accounts receivable.
- c. Sale of Gar's accounts receivable to Ross, with the risk of uncollectible accounts retained by Gar.
- d. Sale of Gar's accounts receivable to Ross, with the risk of uncollectible accounts transferred to Ross.

M95#8. On December 30, 1994, Chang Co. sold a machine to Door Co. in exchange for a noninterest-bearing note requiring ten annual payments of $10,000. Door made the first payment on December 30, 1994. The market interest rate for similar notes at date of issuance was 8%. Information on present value factors is as follows:

Period	Present value of $1 at 8%	Present value of ordinary annuity of $1 at 8%
9	0.50	6.25
10	0.46	6.71

In its December 31, 1994, balance sheet, what amount should Chang report as note receivable?
- a. $45,000
- b. $46,000
- c. $62,500
- d. $67,100

M95#9. At January 1, 1994, Jamin Co. had a credit balance of $260,000 in its allowance for uncollectible accounts. Based on past experience, 2% of Jamin's credit sales have been uncollectible. During 1994, Jamin wrote off $325,000 of uncollectible accounts. Credit sales for 1994 were $9,000,000. In its December 31, 1994, balance sheet, what amount should Jamin report as allowance for uncollectible accounts?
- a. $115,000
- b. $180,000
- c. $245,000
- d. $440,000

N94#11. Mare Co.'s December 31, 1993, balance sheet reported the following current assets:

Cash	$ 70,000
Accounts receivable	120,000
Inventories	60,000
Total	$250,000

An analysis of the accounts disclosed that accounts receivable consisted of the following:

Trade accounts	$ 96,000
Allowance for uncollectible accounts	(2,000)
Selling price of Mare's unsold goods out on consignment, at 130% of cost, **not** included in Mare's ending inventory	26,000
Total	$120,000

FA-23

At December 31, 1993, the total of Mare's current assets is
- a. $224,000
- b. $230,000
- c. $244,000
- d. $270,000

N94#12. When the allowance method of recognizing uncollectible accounts is used, the entry to record the write-off of a specific account
- a. Decreases both accounts receivable and the allowance for uncollectible accounts.
- b. Decreases accounts receivable and increases the allowance for uncollectible accounts.
- c. Increases the allowance for uncollectible accounts and decreases net income.
- d. Decreases both accounts receivable and net income.

M94#15. Delta, Inc. sells to wholesalers on terms of 2/15, net 30. Delta has no cash sales but 50% of Delta's customers take advantage of the discount. Delta uses the gross method of recording sales and trade receivables. An analysis of Delta's trade receivables balances at December 31, 1993, revealed the following:

Age	Amount	Collectible
0 – 15 days	$100,000	100%
16 – 30 days	60,000	95%
31 – 60 days	5,000	90%
Over 60 days	2,500	$500
	$167,500	

In its December 31, 1993, balance sheet, what amount should Delta report for allowance for discounts?
- a. $1,000
- b. $1,620
- c. $1,675
- d. $2,000

M94#16. In its financial statements, Pare, Inc. uses the cost method of accounting for its 15% ownership of Sabe Co. At December 31, 1993, Pare has a receivable from Sabe. How should the receivable be reported in Pare's December 31, 1993, balance sheet?
- a. The total receivable should be reported separately.
- b. The total receivable should be included as part of the investment in Sabe, without separate disclosure.
- c. Eighty-five percent of the receivable should be reported separately, with the balance offset against Sabe's payable to Pare.
- d. The total receivable should be offset against Sabe's payable to Pare, without separate disclosure.

1N93#15. Roth, Inc. received from a customer a one-year, $500,000 note bearing annual interest of 8%. After holding the note for six months, Roth discounted the note at Regional Bank at an effective interest rate of 10%. What amount of cash did Roth receive from the bank?
- a. $540,000
- b. $523,810
- c. $513,000
- d. $495,238

1N93#16. Luge Co., which began operations on January 2, 1992, appropriately uses the installment sales method of accounting. The following information is available for 1992:

Installment accounts receivable,
December 31, 1992 $800,000
Deferred gross profit, December 31,
1992 (before recognition of realized
gross profit for 1992)   560,000
Gross profit on sales   40%

For the year ended December 31, 1992, cash collections and realized gross profit on sales should be

	Cash collections	Realized gross profit
a.	$400,000	$320,000
b.	$400,000	$240,000
c.	$600,000	$320,000
d.	$600,000	$240,000

1N93#17. Frame Co. has an 8% note receivable dated June 30, 1991, in the original amount of $150,000. Payments of $50,000 in principal plus accrued interest are due annually on July 1, 1992, 1993, and 1994. In its June 30, 1993, balance sheet, what amount should Frame report as a current asset for interest on the note receivable?
- a. $0
- b. $ 4,000
- c. $ 8,000
- d. $12,000

1N93#18. On March 31, 1993, Vale Co. had an unadjusted credit balance of $1,000 in its allowance for uncollectible accounts. An analysis of Vale's trade accounts receivable at that date revealed the following:

Age	Amount	Estimated uncollectible
0 – 30 days	$60,000	5%
31 – 60 days	4,000	10%
Over 60 days	2,000	$1,400

What amount should Vale report as allowance for uncollectible accounts in its March 31, 1993, balance sheet?
- a. $4,800
- b. $4,000
- c. $3,800
- d. $3,000

TM93#24. On Merf's April 30, 1993, balance sheet a note receivable was reported as a noncurrent asset and its accrued interest for eight months was reported as a

current asset. Which of the following terms would fit Merf's note receivable?
a. Both principal and interest amounts are payable on August 31, 1993, and August 31, 1994.
b. Principal and interest are due December 31, 1993.
c. Both principal and interest amounts are payable on December 31, 1993, and December 31, 1994.
d. Principal is due August 31, 1994, and interest is due August 31, 1993, and August 31, 1994.

1M93#12. The following information relates to Jay Co.'s accounts receivable for 1992:

Accounts receivable, 1/1/92	$ 650,000
Credit sales for 1992	2,700,000
Sales returns for 1992	75,000
Accounts written off during 1992	40,000
Collections from customers during 1992	2,150,000
Estimated future sales returns at 12/31/92	50,000
Estimated uncollectible accounts at 12/31/92	110,000

What amount should Jay report for accounts receivable, before allowances for sales returns and uncollectible accounts, at December 31, 1992?
a. $1,200,000
b. $1,125,000
c. $1,085,000
d. $ 925,000

1M93#17. The following information pertains to Tara Co.'s accounts receivable at December 31, 1992:

Days outstanding	Amount	Estimated % uncollectible
0 – 60	$120,000	1%
61 – 120	90,000	2%
Over 120	100,000	6%
	$310,000	

During 1992, Tara wrote off $7,000 in receivables and recovered $4,000 that had been written off in prior years. Tara's December 31, 1991, allowance for uncollectible accounts was $22,000. Under the aging method, what amount of allowance for uncollectible accounts should Tara report at December 31, 1992?
a. $ 9,000
b. $10,000
c. $13,000
d. $19,000

TN92#4. After being held for 40 days, a 120-day 12% interest-bearing note receivable was discounted at a bank at 15%. The proceeds received from the bank equal
a. Maturity value less the discount at 12%.
b. Maturity value less the discount at 15%.
c. Face value less the discount at 12%.
d. Face value less the discount at 15%.

TN92#11. When the allowance method of recognizing bad debt expense is used, the allowance would decrease when a(an)
a. Account previously written off is collected.
b. Account previously written off becomes collectible.
c. Specific uncollectible account is written off.
d. Provision for uncollectible accounts is recorded.

TM92#21. On August 15, 1991, Benet Co. sold goods for which it received a note bearing the market rate of interest on that date. The four-month note was dated July 15, 1991. Note principal, together with all interest, is due November 15, 1991. When the note was recorded on August 15, which of the following accounts increased?
a. Unearned discount.
b. Interest receivable.
c. Prepaid interest.
d. Interest revenue.

TM92#41. In its financial statements, Pulham Corp. uses the equity method of accounting for its 30% ownership of Angles Corp. At December 31, 1991, Pulham has a receivable from Angles. How should the receivable be reported in Pulham's 1991 financial statements?
a. None of the receivable should be reported, but the entire receivable should be offset against Angles' payable to Pulham.
b. Seventy percent of the receivable should be separately reported, with the balance offset against 30% of Angles' payable to Pulham.
c. The total receivable should be disclosed separately.
d. The total receivable should be included as part of the investment in Angles, without separate disclosure.

TM92#47. When the allowance method of recognizing uncollectible accounts is used, the entries at the time of collection of a small account previously written off would
a. Increase the allowance for uncollectible accounts.
b. Increase net income.
c. Decrease the allowance for uncollectible accounts.
d. Have **no** effect on the allowance for uncollectible accounts.

1M92#15. On December 31, 1991, Jet Co. received two $10,000 notes receivable from customers in exchange for services rendered. On both notes, interest is calculated on the outstanding principal balance at the annual rate of 3% and payable at maturity. The note from Hart Corp., made under customary trade terms, is due in nine months and the note from Maxx, Inc. is due in five years. The market interest rate for similar notes on December 31, 1991, was 8%. The compound interest factors to convert future values into present values at 8% follow:

Present value of $1 due in nine months: .944
Present value of $1 due in five years: .680

At what amounts should these two notes receivable be reported in Jet's December 31, 1991, balance sheet?

	Hart	Maxx
a.	$ 9,440	$6,800
b.	$ 9,652	$7,820
c.	$10,000	$6,800
d.	$10,000	$7,820

1M92#16. On December 1, 1991, Tigg Mortgage Co. gave Pod Corp. a $200,000, 12% loan. Pod received proceeds of $194,000 after the deduction of a $6,000 nonrefundable loan origination fee. Principal and interest are due in 60 monthly installments of $4,450, beginning January 1, 1992. The repayments yield an effective interest rate of 12% at a present value of $200,000 and 13.4% at a present value of $194,000. What amount of accrued interest receivable should Tigg include in its December 31, 1991, balance sheet?
- a. $4,450
- b. $2,166
- c. $2,000
- d. $0

1M92#21. Dolce Co., which began operations on January 1, 1990, appropriately uses the installment method of accounting to record revenues. The following information is available for the years ended December 31, 1990 and 1991:

	1990	1991
Sales	$1,000,000	$2,000,000
Gross profit realized on sales made in:		
1990	150,000	90,000
1991	—	200,000
Gross profit percentages	30%	40%

What amount of installment accounts receivable should Dolce report in its December 31, 1991, balance sheet?
- a. $1,225,000
- b. $1,300,000
- c. $1,700,000
- d. $1,775,000

TN91#6. For financial statement purposes, the installment method of accounting may be used if the
- a. Collection period extends over more than 12 months.
- b. Installments are due in different years.
- c. Ultimate amount collectible is indeterminate.
- d. Percentage-of-completion method is inappropriate.

1N91#17. On July 1, 1991, Lee Co. sold goods in exchange for a $200,000, 8-month, noninterest-bearing note receivable. At the time of the sale, the note's market rate of interest was 12%. What amount did Lee receive when it discounted the note at 10% on September 1, 1991?
- a. $194,000
- b. $193,800
- c. $190,000
- d. $188,000

TM91#10. Gibbs Co. uses the allowance method for recognizing uncollectible accounts. Ignoring deferred taxes, the entry to record the write-off of a specific uncollectible account
- a. Affects **neither** net income **nor** working capital.
- b. Affects **neither** net income **nor** accounts receivable.
- c. Decreases both net income and accounts receivable.
- d. Decreases both net income and working capital.

2M91#14. Seco Corp. was forced into bankruptcy and is in the process of liquidating assets and paying claims. Unsecured claims will be paid at the rate of forty cents on the dollar. Hale holds a $30,000 noninterest-bearing note receivable from Seco collateralized by an asset with a book value of $35,000 and a liquidation value of $5,000. The amount to be realized by Hale on this note is
- a. $ 5,000
- b. $12,000
- c. $15,000
- d. $17,000

2M91#15. On November 1, 1990, Beni Corp. was awarded a judgment of $1,500,000 in connection with a lawsuit. The decision is being appealed by the defendant, and it is expected that the appeal process will be completed by the end of 1991. Beni's attorney feels that it is highly probable that an award will be upheld on appeal, but that the judgment may be reduced by an estimated 40%. In addition to footnote disclosure, what amount should be reported as a receivable in Beni's balance sheet at December 31, 1990?
- a. $1,500,000
- b. $ 900,000
- c. $ 600,000
- d. $0

1N90#5. On the December 31, 1989 balance sheet of Mann Co., the current receivables consisted of the following:

Trade accounts receivable	$ 93,000
Allowance for uncollectible accounts	(2,000)
Claim against shipper for goods lost in transit (November 1989)	3,000
Selling price of unsold goods sent by Mann on consignment at 130% of cost (**not** included in Mann's ending inventory)	26,000
Security deposit on lease of warehouse used for storing some inventories	30,000
Total	$150,000

At December 31, 1989, the correct total of Mann's current net receivables was

FA-26

a. $94,000
b. $120,000
c. $124,000
d. $150,000

1N90#6. Kemp, Inc. appropriately uses the installment method of accounting to recognize income in its financial statements. Some pertinent data relating to this method of accounting include:

	1987	1988	1989
Installment sales	$300,000	$375,000	$360,000
Cost of installment sales	225,000	285,000	252,000
Gross profit	$75,000	$90,000	$108,000
Rate of gross profit on installment sales	25%	24%	30%
Balance of deferred gross profit at year end:			
1987	$52,500	$15,000	$ –0–
1988		54,000	9,000
1989			72,000
Total	$52,500	$69,000	$81,000

What amount of installment accounts receivable should be presented in Kemp's December 31, 1989 balance sheet?
a. $270,000
b. $277,500
c. $279,000
d. $300,000

1N90#56. On January 3, 1989, Ard Corp. owned a machine that had cost $60,000. The accumulated depreciation was $50,000, estimated salvage value was $5,000, and fair market value was $90,000. On January 4, 1989, this machine was irreparably damaged by Rice Corp. and became worthless. In October 1989, a court awarded damages of $90,000 against Rice in favor of Ard. At December 31, 1989, the final outcome of this case was awaiting appeal and was, therefore, uncertain. However, in the opinion of Ard's attorney, Rice's appeal will be denied. At December 31, 1989, what amount should Ard accrue for this gain contingency?
a. $90,000
b. $80,000
c. $75,000
d. $0

2N90#1. On July 1, 1989, Kay Corp. sold equipment to Mando Co. for $100,000. Kay accepted a 10% note receivable for the entire sales price. This note is payable in two equal installments of $50,000 plus accrued interest on December 31, 1989 and December 31, 1990. On July 1, 1990, Kay discounted the note at a bank at an interest rate of 12%. Kay's proceeds from the discounted note were
a. $48,400
b. $49,350
c. $50,350
d. $51,700

2N90#3. On June 1, 1989, Yola Corp. loaned Dale $500,000 on a 12% note, payable in five annual installments of $100,000 beginning January 2, 1990. In connection with this loan, Dale was required to deposit $5,000 in a noninterest-bearing escrow account. The amount held in escrow is to be returned to Dale after all principal and interest payments have been made. Interest on the note is payable on the first day of each month beginning July 1, 1989. Dale made timely payments through November 1, 1989. On January 2, 1990, Yola received payment of the first principal installment plus all interest due. At December 31, 1989, Yola's interest receivable on the loan to Dale should be
a. $0
b. $5,000
c. $10,000
d. $15,000

2N90#9. Mill Co.'s allowance for uncollectible accounts was $100,000 at the end of 1989 and $90,000 at the end of 1988. For the year ended December 31, 1989, Mill reported bad debt expense of $16,000 in its income statement. What amount did Mill debit to the appropriate account in 1989 to write off actual bad debts?
a. $6,000
b. $10,000
c. $16,000
d. $26,000

1M90#5. Garr Co. received a $60,000, 6-month, 10% interest-bearing note from a customer. After holding the note for two months, Garr was in need of cash and discounted the note at the United Local Bank at 12%. The amount of cash Garr received from the bank was
a. $60,480
b. $60,630
c. $61,740
d. $62,520

1M90#9. The following accounts were abstracted from Roxy Co.'s unadjusted trial balance at December 31, 1989:

	Debit	Credit
Accounts receivable	$1,000,000	
Allowance for uncollectible accounts		8,000
Net credit sales		$3,000,000

Roxy estimates that 3% of the gross accounts receivable will become uncollectible. After adjustment at December 31, 1989, the allowance for uncollectible accounts should have a credit balance of

a. $90,000
b. $82,000
c. $38,000
d. $30,000

1M90#10. On June 1, 1989, Pitt Corp. sold merchandise with a list price of $5,000 to Burr on account. Pitt allowed trade discounts of 30% and 20%. Credit terms were 2/15, n/40 and the sale was made FOB shipping point. Pitt prepaid $200 of delivery costs for Burr as an accommodation. On June 12, 1989, Pitt received from Burr a remittance in full payment amounting to
a. $2,744
b. $2,940
c. $2,944
d. $3,140

1M90#12. Rand, Inc. accepted from a customer a $40,000, 90-day, 12% interest-bearing note dated August 31, 1989. On September 30, 1989, Rand discounted the note at the Apex State Bank at 15%. However, the proceeds were not received until October 1, 1989. In Rand's September 30, 1989 balance sheet, the amount receivable from the bank, based on a 360-day year, includes accrued interest revenue of
a. $170
b. $200
c. $300
d. $400

C. Inventories

R97#1. The original cost of an inventory item is below the net realizable value and above the net realizable value less a normal profit margin. The inventory item's replacement cost is below the net realizable value less a normal profit margin. Under the lower of cost or market method, the inventory item should be valued at
a. Original cost.
b. Replacement cost.
c. Net realizable value.
d. Net realizable value less normal profit margin.

N95#9. A company decided to change its inventory valuation method from FIFO to LIFO in a period of rising prices. What was the result of the change on ending inventory and net income in the year of the change?

	Ending inventory	Net income
a.	Increase	Increase
b.	Increase	Decrease
c.	Decrease	Decrease
d.	Decrease	Increase

M95#11. Walt Co. adopted the dollar-value LIFO inventory method as of January 1, 1994, when its inventory was valued at $500,000. Walt's entire inventory constitutes a single pool. Using a relevant price index of 1.10, Walt determined that its December 31, 1994, inventory was $577,500 at current year cost, and $525,000 at base year cost. What was Walt's dollar-value LIFO inventory at December 31, 1994?
a. $525,000
b. $527,500
c. $552,500
d. $577,500

N94#13. Herc Co.'s inventory at December 31, 1993, was $1,500,000 based on a physical count priced at cost, and before any necessary adjustment for the following:

- Merchandise costing $90,000, shipped FOB shipping point from a vendor on December 30, 1993, was received and recorded on January 5, 1994.

- Goods in the shipping area were excluded from inventory although shipment was not made until January 4, 1994. The goods, billed to the customer FOB shipping point on December 30, 1993, had a cost of $120,000.

What amount should Herc report as inventory in its December 31, 1993, balance sheet?
a. $1,500,000
b. $1,590,000
c. $1,620,000
d. $1,710,000

N94#14. Which of the following statements are correct when a company applying the lower of cost or market method reports its inventory at replacement cost?

I. The original cost is less than replacement cost.
II. The net realizable value is greater than replacement cost.

a. I only.
b. II only.
c. Both I and II.
d. Neither I nor II.

TN93#3. Estimates of price-level changes for specific inventories are required for which of the following inventory methods?
a. Conventional retail.
b. Dollar-value LIFO.
c. Weighted average cost.
d. Average cost retail.

TN93#4. The lower of cost or market rule for inventories may be applied to total inventory, to groups of similar items, or to each item. Which application generally results in the lowest inventory amount?
a. All applications result in the same amount.
b. Total inventory.
c. Groups of similar items.
d. Separately to each item.

TN93#20. In a comparison of 1992 to 1991, Neir Co.'s inventory turnover ratio increased substantially although sales and inventory amounts were essentially unchanged. Which of the following statements explains the increased inventory turnover ratio?

a. Cost of goods sold decreased.
b. Accounts receivable turnover increased.
c. Total asset turnover increased.
d. Gross profit percentage decreased.

1N93#19. Drew Co. uses the average cost inventory method for internal reporting purposes and LIFO for financial statement and income tax reporting. At December 31, 1992, the inventory was $375,000 using average cost and $320,000 using LIFO. The unadjusted credit balance in the LIFO Reserve account on December 31, 1992, was $35,000. What adjusting entry should Drew record to adjust from average cost to LIFO at December 31, 1992?

	Debit	Credit
a. Cost of Goods Sold	$55,000	
Inventory		$55,000
b. Cost of Goods Sold	$55,000	
LIFO Reserve		$55,000
c. Cost of Goods Sold	$20,000	
Inventory		$20,000
d. Cost of Goods Sold	$20,000	
LIFO Reserve		$20,000

1N93#20. Brock Co. adopted the dollar-value LIFO inventory method as of January 1, 1991. A single inventory pool and an internally computed price index are used to compute Brock's LIFO inventory layers. Information about Brock's dollar value inventory follows:

	Inventory		
Date	at base year cost	at current year cost	at dollar value LIFO
1/ 1/91	$40,000	$40,000	$40,000
1991 layer	5,000	14,000	6,000
12/31/91	45,000	54,000	46,000
1992 layer	15,000	26,000	?
12/31/92	$60,000	$80,000	?

What was Brock's dollar value LIFO inventory at December 31, 1992?
a. $80,000
b. $74,000
c. $66,000
d. $60,000

1N93#21. Based on a physical inventory taken on December 31, 1992, Chewy Co. determined its chocolate inventory on a FIFO basis at $26,000 with a replacement cost of $20,000. Chewy estimated that, after further processing costs of $12,000, the chocolate could be sold as finished candy bars for $40,000. Chewy's normal profit margin is 10% of sales. Under the lower of cost or market rule, what amount should Chewy report as chocolate inventory in its December 31, 1992, balance sheet?
a. $28,000
b. $26,000
c. $24,000
d. $20,000

1M93
Items 18 and 19 are based on the following:

During January 1993, Metro Co., which maintains a perpetual inventory system, recorded the following information pertaining to its inventory:

	Units	Unit cost	Total cost	Units on hand
Balance on 1/1/93	1,000	$1	$1,000	1,000
Purchased on 1/7/93	600	3	1,800	1,600
Sold on 1/20/93	900			700
Purchased on 1/25/93	400	5	2,000	1,100

18. Under the moving-average method, what amount should Metro report as inventory at January 31, 1993?
a. $2,640
b. $3,225
c. $3,300
d. $3,900

19. Under the LIFO method, what amount should Metro report as inventory at January 31, 1993?
a. $1,300
b. $2,700
c. $3,900
d. $4,100

1M93#20. The following items were included in Opal Co.'s inventory account at December 31, 1992:

Merchandise out on consignment, at sales price, including 40% markup on selling price	$40,000
Goods purchased, in transit, shipped f.o.b. shipping point	36,000
Goods held on consignment by Opal	27,000

By what amount should Opal's inventory account at December 31, 1992, be reduced?
a. $103,000
b. $ 67,000
c. $ 51,000
d. $ 43,000

1M93#21. Moss Co. has determined its December 31, 1992, inventory on a FIFO basis to be $400,000. Information pertaining to that inventory follows:

Estimated selling price	$408,000
Estimated cost of disposal	20,000
Normal profit margin	60,000
Current replacement cost	360,000

Moss records losses that result from applying the lower of cost or market rule. At December 31, 1992, what should be the net carrying value of Moss' inventory?
a. $400,000
b. $388,000
c. $360,000
d. $328,000

TN92#12. Jel Co., a consignee, paid the freight costs for goods shipped from Dale Co., a consignor. These freight costs are to be deducted from Jel's payment to Dale when the consignment goods are sold. Until Jel sells the goods, the freight costs should be included in Jel's
   a. Cost of goods sold.
   b. Freight-out costs.
   c. Selling expenses.
   d. Accounts receivable.

TN92#14. The original cost of an inventory item is below both replacement cost and net realizable value. The net realizable value less normal profit margin is below the original cost. Under the lower of cost or market method, the inventory item should be valued at
   a. Replacement cost.
   b. Net realizable value.
   c. Net realizable value less normal profit margin.
   d. Original cost.

TN92#15. Jones Wholesalers stocks a changing variety of products. Which inventory costing method will be most likely to give Jones the lowest ending inventory when its product lines are subject to specific price increases?
   a. Specific identification.
   b. Weighted average.
   c. Dollar-value LIFO.
   d. FIFO periodic.

TM92#23. Southgate Co. paid the in-transit insurance premium for consignment goods shipped to Hendon Co., the consignee. In addition, Southgate advanced part of the commissions that will be due when Hendon sells the goods. Should Southgate include the in-transit insurance premium and the advanced commissions in inventory costs?

	Insurance premium	Advanced commissions
a.	Yes	Yes
b.	No	No
c.	Yes	No
d.	No	Yes

TM92#24. During periods of rising prices, when the FIFO inventory method is used, a perpetual inventory system results in an ending inventory cost that is
   a. The same as in a periodic inventory system.
   b. Higher than in a periodic inventory system.
   c. Lower than in a periodic inventory system.
   d. Higher or lower than in a periodic inventory system, depending on whether physical quantities have increased or decreased.

TM92#25. Kahn Co., in applying the lower of cost or market method, reports its inventory at replacement cost. Which of the following statements are correct?

	The original cost is greater than replacement cost	The net realizable value, less a normal profit margin, is greater than replacement cost
a.	Yes	Yes
b.	Yes	No
c.	No	Yes
d.	No	No

1M92#17. Stone Co. had the following consignment transactions during December 1991:

Inventory shipped on consignment to Beta Co.	$18,000
Freight paid by Stone	900
Inventory received on consignment from Alpha Co.	12,000
Freight paid by Alpha	500

No sales of consigned goods were made through December 31, 1991. Stone's December 31, 1991, balance sheet should include consigned inventory at
   a. $12,000
   b. $12,500
   c. $18,000
   d. $18,900

1M92#18. Anders Co. uses the moving-average method to determine the cost of its inventory. During January 1992, Anders recorded the following information pertaining to its inventory:

	Units	Unit cost	Total cost
Balance on 1/1/92	40,000	$5	$200,000
Sold on 1/17/92	35,000		
Purchased on 1/28/92	20,000	8	160,000

What amount of inventory should Anders report in its January 31, 1992, balance sheet?
   a. $200,000
   b. $185,000
   c. $162,500
   d. $150,000

TN91#7. Generally, which inventory costing method approximates most closely the current cost for each of the following?

	Cost of goods sold	Ending inventory
a.	LIFO	FIFO
b.	LIFO	LIFO
c.	FIFO	FIFO
d.	FIFO	LIFO

TN91#27. Thread Co. is selecting its inventory system in preparation for its first year of operations. Thread intends to use either the periodic weighted average method or the perpetual moving average method, and to apply the lower of cost or market rule either to individual items or to the total inventory. Inventory prices are expected to generally increase throughout 1991, although a few individual prices will decrease. What inventory system should Thread select if it wants to maximize the inventory carrying amount at December 31, 1991?

	Inventory method	Cost or market application
a.	Perpetual	Total inventory
b.	Perpetual	Individual item
c.	Periodic	Total inventory
d.	Periodic	Individual item

TN91#28. When the double extension approach to the dollar value LIFO inventory method is used, the inventory layer added in the current year is multiplied by an index number. Which of the following correctly states how components are used in the calculation of this index number?
 a. In the numerator, the average of the ending inventory at base year cost and at current year cost.
 b. In the numerator, the ending inventory at current year cost, and, in the denominator, the ending inventory at base year cost.
 c. In the numerator, the ending inventory at base year cost, and, in the denominator, the ending inventory at current year cost.
 d. In the denominator, the average of the ending inventory at base year cost and at current year cost.

1N91#13. In 1989, Cobb adopted the dollar-value LIFO inventory method. At that time, Cobb's ending inventory had a base-year cost and an end-of-year cost of $300,000. In 1990, the ending inventory had a $400,000 base-year cost and a $440,000 end-of-year cost. What dollar-value LIFO inventory cost would be reported in Cobb's December 31, 1990, balance sheet?
 a. $440,000
 b. $430,000
 c. $410,000
 d. $400,000

2N91#18. Tod Corp. wrote off $100,000 of obsolete inventory at December 31, 1990. The effect of this write-off was to decrease
 a. Both the current and acid-test ratios.
 b. Only the current ratio.
 c. Only the acid-test ratio.
 d. Neither the current nor the acid-test ratios.

TN90#15. How should the following costs affect a retailer's inventory?

	Freight in	Interest on inventory loan
a.	Increase	No effect
b.	Increase	Increase
c.	No effect	Increase
d.	No effect	No effect

TN90#16. The retail inventory method includes which of the following in the calculation of both cost and retail amounts of goods available for sale?
 a. Purchase returns.
 b. Sales returns.
 c. Net markups.
 d. Freight in.

TN90#17. The replacement cost of an inventory item is below the net realizable value and above the net realizable value less the normal profit margin. The original cost of the inventory item is below the net realizable value less the normal profit margin. Under the lower of cost or market method, the inventory item should be valued at
 a. Net realizable value.
 b. Net realizable value less the normal profit margin.
 c. Original cost.
 d. Replacement cost.

1N90#7. The following information applied to Fenn, Inc. for 1989:

Merchandise purchased for resale	$400,000
Freight in	10,000
Freight out	5,000
Purchase returns	2,000

Fenn's 1989 inventoriable cost was
 a. $400,000
 b. $403,000
 c. $408,000
 d. $413,000

1N90#8. Ashe Co. recorded the following data pertaining to raw material X during January 1990:

		Units		
Date	Received	Cost	Issued	On hand
1/1/90 Inventory		$8.00		3,200
1/11/90 Issue			1,600	1,600
1/22/90 Purchase	4,800	$9.60		6,400

The moving-average unit cost of X inventory at January 31, 1990 is
 a. $8.80
 b. $8.96
 c. $9.20
 d. $9.60

1N90#57. During 1989, Rand Co. purchased $960,000 of inventory. The cost of goods sold for 1989 was $900,000, and the ending inventory at December 31, 1989 was $180,000. What was the inventory turnover for 1989?
 a. 6.4
 b. 6.0
 c. 5.3
 d. 5.0

TM90#38. How is the average inventory used in the calculation of each of the following?

	Acid test (quick) ratio	Inventory turnover rate
a.	Numerator	Numerator
b.	Numerator	Denominator
c.	Not used	Denominator
d.	Not used	Numerator

1M90#14. West Retailers purchased merchandise with a list price of $20,000, subject to trade discounts of 20% and 10%, with no cash discounts allowable. West should record the cost of this merchandise as
 a. $14,000
 b. $14,400
 c. $15,600
 d. $20,000

D. Property, Plant, and Equipment

R97#8. During January 1995 Yana Co. incurred landscaping costs of $120,000 to improve leased property. The estimated useful life of the landscaping is fifteen years. The remaining term of the lease is eight years, with an option to renew for an additional four years. However, Yana has not reached a decision with regard to the renewal option. In Yana's December 31, 1995, balance sheet, what should be the net carrying amount of landscaping costs?
 a. $0
 b. $105,000
 c. $110,000
 d. $112,000

M95#12. Theoretically, which of the following costs incurred in connection with a machine purchased for use in a company's manufacturing operations would be capitalized?

	Insurance on machine while in transit	Testing and preparation of machine for use
a.	Yes	Yes
b.	Yes	No
c.	No	Yes
d.	No	No

M94#17. Cole Co. began constructing a building for its own use in January 1993. During 1993, Cole incurred interest of $50,000 on specific construction debt, and $20,000 on other borrowings. Interest computed on the weighted-average amount of accumulated expenditures for the building during 1993 was $40,000. What amount of interest cost should Cole capitalize?
 a. $20,000
 b. $40,000
 c. $50,000
 d. $70,000

M94#18. Turtle Co. purchased equipment on January 2, 1991, for $50,000. The equipment had an estimated five-year service life. Turtle's policy for five-year assets is to use the 200% double-declining depreciation method for the first two years of the asset's life, and then switch to the straight-line depreciation method. In its December 31, 1993, balance sheet, what amount should Turtle report as accumulated depreciation for equipment?
 a. $30,000
 b. $38,000
 c. $39,200
 d. $42,000

1N93#22. Merry Co. purchased a machine costing $125,000 for its manufacturing operations and paid shipping costs of $20,000. Merry spent an additional $10,000 testing and preparing the machine for use. What amount should Merry record as the cost of the machine?
 a. $155,000
 b. $145,000
 c. $135,000
 d. $125,000

1N93#23. Weir Co. uses straight-line depreciation for its property, plant, and equipment, which, stated at cost, consisted of the following:

	12/31/92	12/31/91
Land	$ 25,000	$ 25,000
Buildings	195,000	195,000
Machinery and equipment	695,000	650,000
	915,000	870,000
Less accumulated depreciation	400,000	370,000
	$515,000	$500,000

Weir's depreciation expense for 1992 and 1991 was $55,000 and $50,000, respectively. What amount was debited to accumulated depreciation during 1992 because of property, plant, and equipment retirements?
 a. $40,000
 b. $25,000
 c. $20,000
 d. $10,000

1N93#24. Gei Co. determined that, due to obsolescence, equipment with an original cost of $900,000 and accumulated depreciation at January 1, 1992, of $420,000 had suffered permanent impairment, and as a result should have a carrying value of only $300,000 as of the beginning of the year. In addition, the remaining useful life of the equipment was reduced from 8 years to 3. In its December 31, 1992, balance sheet, what amount should Gei report as accumulated depreciation?
 a. $100,000
 b. $520,000
 c. $600,000
 d. $700,000

TM93#26. A building suffered uninsured fire damage. The damaged portion of the building was refurbished with

higher quality materials. The cost and related accumulated depreciation of the damaged portion are identifiable. To account for these events, the owner should
   a. Reduce accumulated depreciation equal to the cost of refurbishing.
   b. Record a loss in the current period equal to the sum of the cost of refurbishing and the carrying amount of the damaged portion of the building.
   c. Capitalize the cost of refurbishing and record a loss in the current period equal to the carrying amount of the damaged portion of the building.
   d. Capitalize the cost of refurbishing by adding the cost to the carrying amount of the building.

TM93#27. On January 1, 1988, Crater, Inc. purchased equipment having an estimated salvage value equal to 20% of its original cost at the end of a 10-year life. The equipment was sold December 31, 1992, for 50% of its original cost. If the equipment's disposition resulted in a reported loss, which of the following depreciation methods did Crater use?
   a. Double-declining balance.
   b. Sum-of-the-years'-digits.
   c. Straight-line.
   d. Composite.

1M93#22. Star Co. leases a building for its product showroom. The ten-year non-renewable lease will expire on December 31, 1997. In January 1992, Star redecorated its showroom and made leasehold improvements of $48,000. The estimated useful life of the improvements is 8 years. Star uses the straight-line method of amortization. What amount of leasehold improvements, net of amortization, should Star report in its June 30, 1992, balance sheet?
   a. $45,600
   b. $45,000
   c. $44,000
   d. $43,200

1M93#24. On January 2, 1989, Reed Co. purchased a machine for $800,000 and established an annual depreciation charge of $100,000 over an eight-year life. During 1992, after issuing its 1991 financial statements, Reed concluded that: (1) the machine suffered permanent impairment of its operational value, and (2) $200,000 is a reasonable estimate of the amount expected to be recovered through use of the machine for the period January 1, 1992, through December 31, 1996. In Reed's December 31, 1992, balance sheet, the machine should be reported at a carrying amount of
   a. $0
   b. $100,000
   c. $160,000
   d. $400,000

TM92#11. Derby Co. incurred costs to modify its building and to rearrange its production line. As a result, an overall reduction in production costs is expected. However, the modifications did not increase the building's market value, and the rearrangement did not extend the production line's life. Should the building modification costs and the production line rearrangement costs be capitalized?

	Building modification costs	Production line rearrangement costs
a.	Yes	No
b.	Yes	Yes
c.	No	No
d.	No	Yes

TM92#12. Land was purchased to be used as the site for the construction of a plant. A building on the property was sold and removed by the buyer so that construction on the plant could begin. The proceeds from the sale of the building should be
   a. Netted against the costs to clear the land and expensed as incurred.
   b. Netted against the costs to clear the land and amortized over the life of the plant.
   c. Deducted from the cost of the land.
   d. Classified as other income.

TM92#13. Lano Corp.'s forest land was condemned for use as a national park. Compensation for the condemnation exceeded the forest land's carrying amount. Lano purchased similar, but larger, replacement forest land for an amount greater than the condemnation award. As a result of the condemnation and replacement, what is the net effect on the carrying amount of forest land reported in Lano's balance sheet?
   a. The amount is increased by the excess of the replacement forest land's cost over the condemned forest land's carrying amount.
   b. The amount is increased by the excess of the replacement forest land's cost over the condemnation award.
   c. The amount is increased by the excess of the condemnation award over the condemned forest land's carrying amount.
   d. No effect, because the condemned forest land's carrying amount is used as the replacement forest land's carrying amount.

TM92#16. A machine with a 5-year estimated useful life and an estimated 10% salvage value was acquired on January 1, 1988. On December 31, 1991, accumulated depreciation, using the sum-of-the-years' digits method, would be
   a. (Original cost less salvage value) multiplied by $1/15$.
   b. (Original cost less salvage value) multiplied by $14/15$.
   c. Original cost multiplied by $14/15$.
   d. Original cost multiplied by $1/15$.

1M92#22. On December 1, 1991, Boyd Co. purchased a $400,000 tract of land for a factory site. Boyd razed an old building on the property and sold the materials it salvaged from the demolition. Boyd incurred additional costs and realized salvage proceeds during December 1991, as follows:

Demolition of old building	$50,000
Legal fees for purchase contract and recording ownership	10,000
Title guarantee insurance	12,000
Proceeds from sale of salvaged materials	8,000

In its December 31, 1991, balance sheet, Boyd should report a balance in the land account of
- a. $464,000
- b. $460,000
- c. $442,000
- d. $422,000

TN91#33. During January 1990, Vail Co. made long-term improvements to a recently leased building. The lease agreement provides for neither a transfer of title to Vail nor a bargain purchase option. The present value of the minimum lease payments equals 85% of the building's market value, and the lease term equals 70% of the building's economic life. Should assets be recognized for the building and the leasehold improvements?

	Building	Leasehold improvements
a.	Yes	Yes
b.	No	Yes
c.	Yes	No
d.	No	No

1N91#15. On January 1, 1990, Dix Co. replaced its old boiler. The following information was available on that date:

Carrying amount of old boiler	$ 8,000
Fair value of old boiler	2,000
Purchase and installation price of new boiler	100,000

The old boiler was sold for $2,000. What amount should Dix capitalize as the cost of the new boiler?
- a. $ 92,000
- b. $ 94,000
- c. $ 98,000
- d. $100,000

1N91#16. On January 1, 1989, Bay Co. acquired a land lease for a 21-year period with no option to renew. The lease required Bay to construct a building in lieu of rent. The building, completed on January 1, 1990, at a cost of $840,000, will be depreciated using the straight-line method. At the end of the lease, the building's estimated market value will be $420,000. What is the building's carrying amount in Bay's December 31, 1990, balance sheet?
- a. $798,000
- b. $800,000
- c. $819,000
- d. $820,000

1N91#18. On January 1, 1986, Lane, Inc. acquired equipment for $100,000 with an estimated 10-year useful life. Lane estimated a $10,000 salvage value and used the straight-line method of depreciation. During 1990, after its 1989 financial statements had been issued, Lane determined that, due to obsolescence, this equipment's remaining useful life was only four more years and its salvage value would be $4,000. In Lane's December 31, 1990, balance sheet, what was the carrying amount of this asset?
- a. $51,500
- b. $49,000
- c. $41,500
- d. $39,000

1N91#19. A state government condemned Cory Co.'s parcel of real estate. Cory will receive $750,000 for this property, which has a carrying amount of $575,000. Cory incurred the following costs as a result of the condemnation:

Appraisal fees to support a $750,000 value	$2,500
Attorney fees for the closing with the state	3,500
Attorney fees to review contract to acquire replacement property	3,000
Title insurance on replacement property	4,000

What amount of cost should Cory use to determine the gain on the condemnation?
- a. $581,000
- b. $582,000
- c. $584,000
- d. $588,000

1M91#23. On October 1, 1990, Shaw Corp. purchased a machine for $126,000 that was placed in service on November 30, 1990. Shaw incurred additional costs for this machine, as follows:

Shipping	$3,000
Installation	4,000
Testing	5,000

In Shaw's December 31, 1990, balance sheet, the machine's cost should be reported as
- a. $126,000
- b. $129,000
- c. $133,000
- d. $138,000

1M91#24. During 1990, Burr Co. had the following transactions pertaining to its new office building:

Purchase price of land	$ 60,000
Legal fees for contracts to purchase land	2,000
Architects' fees	8,000
Demolition of old building on site	5,000
Sale of scrap from old building	3,000
Construction cost of new building (fully completed)	350,000

In Burr's December 31, 1990, balance sheet, what amounts should be reported as the cost of land and cost of building?

	Land	Building
a.	$60,000	$360,000
b.	$62,000	$360,000
c.	$64,000	$358,000
d.	$65,000	$362,000

1M91#26. In January 1988, Winn Corp. purchased equipment at a cost of $500,000. The equipment had an estimated salvage value of $100,000, an estimated 8-year useful life, and was being depreciated by the straight-line method. Two years later, it became apparent to Winn that this equipment suffered a permanent impairment of value. In January 1990, management determined the carrying amount should be only $175,000, with a 2-year remaining useful life, and the salvage value should be reduced to $25,000. In Winn's December 31, 1990, balance sheet, the equipment should be reported at a carrying amount of
- a. $350,000
- b. $175,000
- c. $150,000
- d. $100,000

1M91#27. On December 31, 1990, a building owned by Carr, Inc. was destroyed by fire. Carr paid $12,000 for removal and clean-up costs. The building had a book value of $250,000 and a fair value of $280,000 on December 31, 1990. What amount should Carr use to determine the gain or loss on this involuntary conversion?
- a. $250,000
- b. $262,000
- c. $280,000
- d. $292,000

TN90#13. A building suffered uninsured water and related damage. The damaged portion of the building was refurbished with upgraded materials. The cost and related accumulated depreciation of the damaged portion are identifiable. To account for these events, the owner should
- a. Capitalize the cost of refurbishing and record a loss in the current period equal to the carrying amount of the damaged portion of the building.
- b. Capitalize the cost of refurbishing by adding the cost to the carrying amount of the building.
- c. Record a loss in the current period equal to the cost of refurbishing and continue to depreciate the original cost of the building.
- d. Record a loss in the current period equal to the sum of the cost of refurbishing and the carrying amount of the damaged portion of the building.

2N90#4. During 1988, Yvo Corp. installed a production assembly line to manufacture furniture. In 1989, Yvo purchased a new machine and rearranged the assembly line to install this machine. The rearrangement did not increase the estimated useful life of the assembly line, but it did result in significantly more efficient production. The following expenditures were incurred in connection with this project:

Machine	$75,000
Labor to install machine	14,000
Parts added in rearranging the assembly line to provide future benefits	40,000
Labor and overhead to rearrange the assembly line	18,000

What amount of the above expenditures should be capitalized in 1989?
- a. $147,000
- b. $107,000
- c. $89,000
- d. $75,000

2N90#5. On July 1, 1986, Rey Corp. purchased computer equipment at a cost of $360,000. This equipment was estimated to have a six-year life with no residual value and was depreciated by the straight-line method. On January 3, 1989, Rey determined that this equipment could no longer process data efficiently, that its value had been permanently impaired, and that $70,000 could be recovered over the remaining useful life of the equipment. What carrying amount should Rey report on its December 31, 1989 balance sheet for this equipment?
- a. $0
- b. $50,000
- c. $70,000
- d. $150,000

2N90#13. Vore Corp. bought equipment on January 2, 1988 for $200,000. This equipment had an estimated useful life of five years and a salvage value of $20,000. Depreciation was computed by the 150% declining balance method. The accumulated depreciation balance at December 31, 1989 should be
- a. $102,000
- b. $98,000
- c. $91,800
- d. $72,000

1M90#15. On December 1, 1989, East Co. purchased a tract of land as a factory site for $300,000. The old building on the property was razed, and salvaged materials resulting from demolition were sold. Additional costs incurred and salvage proceeds realized during December 1989 were as follows:

Cost to raze old building	$25,000
Legal fees for purchase contract and to record ownership	5,000
Title guarantee insurance	6,000
Proceeds from sale of salvaged materials	4,000

In East's December 31, 1989 balance sheet, what amount should be reported as land?
- a. $311,000
- b. $321,000
- c. $332,000
- d. $336,000

1M90#16. On June 18, 1989, Dell Printing Co. incurred the following costs for one of its printing presses:

Purchase of collating and stapling attachment $84,000
Installation of attachment 36,000
Replacement parts for overhaul of press 26,000
Labor and overhead in connection with
  overhaul 14,000

The overhaul resulted in a significant increase in production. Neither the attachment nor the overhaul increased the estimated useful life of the press. What amount of the above costs should be capitalized?
  a. $0
  b. $ 84,000
  c. $120,000
  d. $160,000

1M90#17. On April 1, 1988, Kew Co. purchased new machinery for $300,000. The machinery has an estimated useful life of five years, and depreciation is computed by the sum-of-the-years'-digits method. The accumulated depreciation on this machinery at March 31, 1990 should be
  a. $192,000
  b. $180,000
  c. $120,000
  d. $100,000

1M90#18. On January 2, 1989, Ames Corp. signed an eight-year lease for office space. Ames has the option to renew the lease for an additional four-year period on or before January 2, 1996. During January 1989, Ames incurred the following costs:

- $120,000 for general improvements to the leased premises with an estimated useful life of ten years.
- $50,000 for office furniture and equipment with an estimated useful life of ten years.

At December 31, 1989, Ames' intentions as to exercise of the renewal option are uncertain. A full year's amortization of leasehold improvements is taken for calendar year 1989. In Ames' December 31, 1989 balance sheet, accumulated amortization should be
  a. $10,000
  b. $15,000
  c. $17,000
  d. $21,250

E. Investments

R97#2. On January 2, 1993, Jann Co. purchased a $150,000 whole-life insurance policy on its president. The annual premium is $4,000. The company is both the owner and the beneficiary. Jann charged officers' life insurance expense as follows:

	1993	$ 4,000
	1994	3,600
	1995	3,000
	1996	2,200
	Total	$12,800

In its December 31, 1996, balance sheet, what amount should Jann report as investment in cash surrender value of officers' life insurance?
  a. $0
  b. $ 3,200
  c. $12,800
  d. $16,000

R96#6. When the fair value of an investment in debt securities exceeds its amortized cost, how should each of the following debt securities be reported at the end of the year?

	Debt securities classified as	
	Held-to-maturity	Available-for-sale
a.	Amortized cost	Amortized cost
b.	Amortized cost	Fair value
c.	Fair value	Fair value
d.	Fair value	Amortized cost

N95#27. Grant, Inc. acquired 30% of South Co.'s voting stock for $200,000 on January 2, 1993. Grant's 30% interest in South gave Grant the ability to exercise significant influence over South's operating and financial policies. During 1993, South earned $80,000 and paid dividends of $50,000. South reported earnings of $100,000 for the six months ended June 30, 1994, and $200,000 for the year ended December 31, 1994. On July 1, 1994, Grant sold half of its stock in South for $150,000 cash. South paid dividends of $60,000 on October 1, 1994. In Grant's December 31, 1993, balance sheet, what should be the carrying amount of this investment?
  a. $200,000
  b. $209,000
  c. $224,000
  d. $230,000

N94#16. On January 2, 1993, Well Co. purchased 10% of Rea, Inc.'s outstanding common shares for $400,000. Well is the largest single shareholder in Rea, and Well's officers are a majority on Rea's board of directors. Rea reported net income of $500,000 for 1993, and paid dividends of $150,000. In its December 31, 1993, balance sheet, what amount should Well report as investment in Rea?
  a. $450,000
  b. $435,000
  c. $400,000
  d. $385,000

M94#19. On January 2, 1993, Kean Co. purchased a 30% interest in Pod Co. for $250,000. On this date, Pod's stockholders' equity was $500,000. The carrying amounts of Pod's identifiable net assets approximated their fair values, except for land whose fair value exceeded its carrying amount by $200,000. Pod reported net income of $100,000 for 1993, and paid no dividends. Kean accounts for this investment using the equity method and amortizes goodwill over ten years. In its December 31, 1993, balance sheet, what amount should Kean report as investment in subsidiary?

a. $210,000
b. $220,000
c. $270,000
d. $276,000

TN93#9. Peel Co. received a cash dividend from a common stock investment. Should Peel report an increase in the investment account if it uses the cost method or the equity method of accounting?

	Cost	Equity
a.	No	No
b.	Yes	Yes
c.	Yes	No
d.	No	Yes

1N93#12. On March 4, 1992, Evan Co. purchased 1,000 shares of LVC common stock at $80 per share. On September 26, 1992, Evan received 1,000 stock rights to purchase an additional 1,000 shares at $90 per share. The stock rights had an expiration date of February 1, 1993. On September 30, 1992, LVC's common stock had a market value, ex-rights, of $95 per share and the stock rights had a market value of $5 each. What amount should Evan report on its September 30, 1992, balance sheet for investment in stock rights?
a. $ 4,000
b. $ 5,000
c. $10,000
d. $15,000

1N93#14. Pare, Inc. purchased 10% of Tot Co.'s 100,000 outstanding shares of common stock on January 2, 1992, for $50,000. On December 31, 1992, Pare purchased an additional 20,000 shares of Tot for $150,000. There was no goodwill as a result of either acquisition, and Tot had not issued any additional stock during 1992. Tot reported earnings of $300,000 for 1992. What amount should Pare report in its December 31, 1992, balance sheet as investment in Tot?
a. $170,000
b. $200,000
c. $230,000
d. $290,000

TM93#11. In 1991, Lee Co. acquired, at a premium, Enfield, Inc. 10-year bonds as a long-term investment. At December 31, 1992, Enfield's bonds were quoted at a small discount. Which of the following situations is the most likely cause of the decline in the bonds' market value?
a. Enfield issued a stock dividend.
b. Enfield is expected to call the bonds at a premium, which is less than Lee's carrying amount.
c. Interest rates have declined since Lee purchased the bonds.
d. Interest rates have increased since Lee purchased the bonds.

1M93#16. The following information relates to noncurrent investments that Fall Corp. placed in trust as required by the underwriter of its bonds:

Bond sinking fund balance, 12/31/91	$ 450,000
1992 additional investment	90,000
Dividends on investments	15,000
Interest revenue	30,000
Administration costs	5,000
Carrying amount of bonds payable	1,025,000

What amount should Fall report in its December 31, 1992, balance sheet related to its noncurrent investment for bond sinking fund requirements?
a. $585,000
b. $580,000
c. $575,000
d. $540,000

TN92#30. Pal Corp.'s 1991 dividend income included only part of the dividend received from its Ima Corp. investment. The balance of the dividend reduced Pal's carrying amount for its Ima investment. This reflects that Pal accounts for its Ima investment by the
a. Cost method, and only a portion of Ima's 1991 dividends represent earnings after Pal's acquisition.
b. Cost method, and its carrying amount exceeded the proportionate share of Ima's market value.
c. Equity method, and Ima incurred a loss in 1991.
d. Equity method, and its carrying amount exceeded the proportionate share of Ima's market value.

1M92#12. On July 1, 1991, Cody Co. paid $1,198,000 for 10%, 20-year bonds with a face amount of $1,000,000. Interest is paid on December 31 and June 30. The bonds were purchased to yield 8%. Cody uses the effective interest rate method to recognize interest income from this investment. What should be reported as the carrying amount of the bonds in Cody's December 31, 1991, balance sheet?
a. $1,207,900
b. $1,198,000
c. $1,195,920
d. $1,193,050

TN91#36. An issuer of bonds uses a sinking fund for the retirement of the bonds. Cash was transferred to the sinking fund and subsequently used to purchase investments. The sinking fund

I. Increases by revenue earned on the investments.
II. Is **not** affected by revenue earned on the investments.
III. Decreases when the investments are purchased.

a. I only.
b. I and III.
c. II and III.
d. III only.

TM91#4. An investor purchased a bond classified as a long-term investment between interest dates at a discount. At the purchase date, the carrying amount of the bond is more than the

	Cash paid to seller	Face amount of bond
a.	No	Yes
b.	No	No
c.	Yes	No
d.	Yes	Yes

1M90#4. On January 1, 1988, Purl Corp. purchased as a long-term investment $500,000 face value of Shaw, Inc.'s 8% bonds for $456,200. The bonds were purchased to yield 10% interest. The bonds mature on January 1, 1994 and pay interest annually on January 1. Purl uses the interest method of amortization. What amount (rounded to nearest $100) should Purl report on its December 31, 1989 balance sheet for this long-term investment?
 a. $468,000
 b. $466,200
 c. $461,800
 d. $456,200

F. Intangibles and Other Assets

M95#13. During 1994, Jase Co. incurred research and development costs of $136,000 in its laboratories relating to a patent that was granted on July 1, 1994. Costs of registering the patent equalled $34,000. The patent's legal life is 17 years, and its estimated economic life is 10 years. In its December 31, 1994, balance sheet, what amount should Jase report as patent, net of accumulated amortization?
 a. $ 32,300
 b. $ 33,000
 c. $161,500
 d. $165,000

M95#14. Roro, Inc. paid $7,200 to renew its only insurance policy for three years on March 1, 1995, the effective date of the policy. At March 31, 1995, Roro's unadjusted trial balance showed a balance of $300 for prepaid insurance and $7,200 for insurance expense. What amounts should be reported for prepaid insurance and insurance expense in Roro's financial statements for the three months ended March 31, 1995?

	Prepaid insurance	Insurance expense
a.	$7,000	$300
b.	$7,000	$500
c.	$7,200	$300
d.	$7,300	$200

M94#20. On January 2, 1993, Rafa Co. purchased a franchise with a useful life of ten years for $50,000. An additional franchise fee of 3% of franchise operation revenues must be paid each year to the franchisor. Revenues from franchise operations amounted to $400,000 during 1993. In its December 31, 1993, balance sheet, what amount should Rafa report as an intangible asset-franchise?
 a. $33,000
 b. $43,800
 c. $45,000
 d. $50,000

TN93#10. Which of the following costs of goodwill should be capitalized and amortized?

	Maintaining goodwill	Developing goodwill
a.	Yes	No
b.	No	No
c.	Yes	Yes
d.	No	Yes

1N93#25. On January 2, 1992, Judd Co. bought a trademark from Krug Co. for $500,000. Judd retained an independent consultant, who estimated the trademark's remaining life to be 50 years. Its unamortized cost on Krug's accounting records was $380,000. Judd decided to amortize the trademark over the maximum period allowed. In Judd's December 31, 1992, balance sheet, what amount should be reported as accumulated amortization?
 a. $ 7,600
 b. $ 9,500
 c. $10,000
 d. $12,500

TM93#25. Which of the following statements concerning patents is correct?
 a. Legal costs incurred to successfully defend an internally developed patent should be capitalized and amortized over the patent's remaining economic life.
 b. Legal fees and other direct costs incurred in registering a patent should be capitalized and amortized on a straight-line basis over a five-year period.
 c. Research and development contract services purchased from others and used to develop a patented manufacturing process should be capitalized and amortized over the patent's economic life.
 d. Research and development costs incurred to develop a patented item should be capitalized and amortized on a straight-line basis over 17 years.

1M93#25. On November 30, 1992, Parlor, Inc. purchased for cash at $15 per share all 250,000 shares of the outstanding common stock of Shaw Co. At November 30, 1992, Shaw's balance sheet showed a carrying amount of net assets of $3,000,000. At that date, the fair value of Shaw's property, plant and equipment exceeded its carrying amount by $400,000. In its November 30, 1992, consolidated balance sheet, what amount should Parlor report as goodwill?

a. $750,000
b. $400,000
c. $350,000
d. $0

1M93#27. An analysis of Thrift Corp.'s unadjusted prepaid expense account at December 31, 1992, revealed the following:

- An opening balance of $1,500 for Thrift's comprehensive insurance policy. Thrift had paid an annual premium of $3,000 on July 1, 1991.

- A $3,200 annual insurance premium payment made July 1, 1992.

- A $2,000 advance rental payment for a warehouse Thrift leased for one year beginning January 1, 1993.

In its December 31, 1992, balance sheet, what amount should Thrift report as prepaid expenses?
a. $5,200
b. $3,600
c. $2,000
d. $1,600

TN92#29. Malden, Inc. has two patents that have allegedly been infringed by competitors. After investigation, legal counsel informed Malden that it had a weak case on patent A34 and a strong case in regard to patent B19. Malden incurred additional legal fees to stop infringement on B19. Both patents have a remaining legal life of 8 years. How should Malden account for these legal costs incurred relating to the two patents?
a. Expense costs for A34 and capitalize costs for B19.
b. Expense costs for both A34 and B19.
c. Capitalize costs for both A34 and B19.
d. Capitalize costs for A34 and expense costs for B19.

TM92#14. On December 31, 1990, Bit Co. had capitalized costs for a new computer software product with an economic life of five years. Sales for 1991 were 30 percent of expected total sales of the software. At December 31, 1991, the software had a net realizable value equal to 90 percent of the capitalized cost. What percentage of the original capitalized cost should be reported as the net amount on Bit's December 31, 1991, balance sheet?
a. 70%
b. 72%
c. 80%
d. 90%

1M92#20. Hy Corp. bought Patent A for $40,000 and Patent B for $60,000. Hy also paid acquisition costs of $5,000 for Patent A and $7,000 for Patent B. Both patents were challenged in legal actions. Hy paid $20,000 in legal fees for a successful defense of Patent A and $30,000 in legal fees for an unsuccessful defense of Patent B. What amount should Hy capitalize for patents?

a. $162,000
b. $112,000
c. $65,000
d. $45,000

1M92#23. On November 1, 1991, Key Co. paid $3,600 to renew its insurance policy for three years. At December 31, 1991, Key's unadjusted trial balance showed a balance of $90 for prepaid insurance and $4,410 for insurance expense. What amounts should be reported for prepaid insurance and insurance expense in Key's December 31, 1991, financial statements?

	Prepaid insurance	Insurance expense
a.	$3,300	$1,200
b.	$3,400	$1,200
c.	$3,400	$1,100
d.	$3,490	$1,010

TN91#13. Say Co. purchased Ivy Co. at a cost that resulted in recognition of goodwill having an expected 10-year benefit period. However, Say plans to make additional expenditures to maintain goodwill for a total of 40 years. What costs should be capitalized and over how many years should they be amortized?

	Costs capitalized	Amortization period
a.	Acquisition costs only	10 years
b.	Acquisition costs only	40 years
c.	Acquisition and maintenance costs	10 years
d.	Acquisition and maintenance costs	40 years

1M91#28. On June 30, 1990, Union, Inc. purchased goodwill of $125,000 when it acquired the net assets of Apex Corp. During 1990, Union incurred additional costs of developing goodwill, by training Apex employees ($50,000) and hiring additional Apex employees ($25,000). Before amortization of goodwill, Union's December 31, 1990, balance sheet should report goodwill of
a. $200,000
b. $175,000
c. $150,000
d. $125,000

1M91#29. On July 1, 1990, Roxy Co. obtained fire insurance for a 3-year period at an annual premium of $72,000 payable on July 1 of each year. The first premium payment was made July 1, 1990. On October 1, 1990, Roxy paid $24,000 for real estate taxes to cover the period ending September 30, 1991. This prepayment was made to obtain a discount. In its December 31, 1990, balance sheet, Roxy should report prepaid expenses of
a. $60,000
b. $54,000
c. $48,000
d. $36,000

1M91#30. Under East Co.'s accounting system, all insurance premiums paid are debited to prepaid insurance. For interim financial reports, East makes monthly estimated charges to insurance expense with credits to prepaid insurance. Additional information for the year ended December 31, 1990, is as follows:

Prepaid insurance at December 31, 1989	$105,000
Charges to insurance expense during 1990 (including a year-end adjustment of $17,500)	437,500
Prepaid insurance at December 31, 1990	122,500

What was the total amount of insurance premiums paid by East during 1990?
- a. $332,500
- b. $420,000
- c. $437,500
- d. $455,000

1M90#20. On January 1, 1986, Taft Co. purchased a patent for $714,000. The patent is being amortized over its remaining legal life of 15 years expiring on January 1, 2001. During 1989, Taft determined that the economic benefits of the patent would not last longer than ten years from the date of acquisition. What amount should be reported in the balance sheet for the patent, net of accumulated amortization, at December 31, 1989?
- a. $428,400
- b. $489,600
- c. $504,000
- d. $523,600

2M90#52. Lind Corp. was a development stage enterprise from its inception on October 10, 1987 to December 31, 1988. The following were among Lind's expenditures for this period:

Leasehold improvements, equipment, and furniture	$1,200,000
Research and development	850,000
Laboratory operations	175,000
General and administrative	275,000

The year ended December 31, 1989 was the first year in which Lind was an established operating enterprise. For the period ended December 31, 1988, what total amount of expenditures should Lind have capitalized?
- a. $2,500,000
- b. $2,225,000
- c. $2,050,000
- d. $1,200,000

2M90#58. On June 30, 1989, Finn, Inc. exchanged 2,000 shares of Edlow Corp. $30 par value common stock for a patent owned by Bisk Co. The Edlow stock was acquired in 1987 at a cost of $50,000. At the exchange date, Edlow common stock had a fair value of $40 per share, and the patent had a net carrying amount of $100,000 on Bisk's books. Finn should record the patent at
- a. $ 50,000
- b. $ 60,000
- c. $ 80,000
- d. $100,000

G. Payables and Accruals

M95#15. Ivy Co. operates a retail store. All items are sold subject to a 6% state sales tax, which Ivy collects and records as sales revenue. Ivy files quarterly sales tax returns when due, by the 20th day following the end of the sales quarter. However, in accordance with state requirements, Ivy remits sales tax collected by the 20th day of the month following any month such collections exceed $500. Ivy takes these payments as credits on the quarterly sales tax return. The sales taxes paid by Ivy are charged against sales revenue.

Following is a monthly summary appearing in Ivy's first quarter 1995 sales revenue account:

	Debit	Credit
January	$ —	$10,600
February	600	7,420
March	—	8,480
	$600	$26,500

In its March 31, 1995, balance sheet, what amount should Ivy report as sales taxes payable?
- a. $ 600
- b. $ 900
- c. $1,500
- d. $1,590

N94#19. On July 1, 1993, Ran County issued realty tax assessments for its fiscal year ended June 30, 1994. On September 1, 1993, Day Co. purchased a warehouse in Ran County. The purchase price was reduced by a credit for accrued realty taxes. Day did not record the entire year's real estate tax obligation, but instead records tax expenses at the end of each month by adjusting prepaid real estate taxes or real estate taxes payable, as appropriate. On November 1, 1993, Day paid the first of two equal installments of $12,000 for realty taxes. What amount of this payment should Day record as a debit to real estate taxes payable?
- a. $ 4,000
- b. $ 8,000
- c. $10,000
- d. $12,000

M94#21. Hudson Hotel collects 15% in city sales taxes on room rentals, in addition to a $2 per room, per night, occupancy tax. Sales taxes for each month are due at the end of the following month, and occupancy taxes are due 15 days after the end of each calendar quarter. On January 3, 1994, Hudson paid its November 1993 sales taxes and its fourth quarter 1993 occupancy taxes. Additional information pertaining to Hudson's operations is:

1993	Room rentals	Room nights
October	$100,000	1,100
November	110,000	1,200
December	150,000	1,800

What amounts should Hudson report as sales taxes payable and occupancy taxes payable in its December 31, 1993, balance sheet?

	Sales taxes	Occupancy taxes
a.	$39,000	$6,000
b.	$39,000	$8,200
c.	$54,000	$6,000
d.	$54,000	$8,200

M94#22. Under state law, Acme may pay 3% of eligible gross wages or it may reimburse the state directly for actual unemployment claims. Acme believes that actual unemployment claims will be 2% of eligible gross wages and has chosen to reimburse the state. Eligible gross wages are defined as the first $10,000 of gross wages paid to each employee. Acme had five employees each of whom earned $20,000 during 1993. In its December 31, 1993, balance sheet, what amount should Acme report as accrued liability for unemployment claims?
   a. $1,000
   b. $1,500
   c. $2,000
   d. $3,000

1N93#30. Lyle, Inc. is preparing its financial statements for the year ended December 31, 1992. Accounts payable amounted to $360,000 before any necessary year-end adjustment related to the following:

- At December 31, 1992, Lyle has a $50,000 debit balance in its accounts payable to Ross, a supplier, resulting from a $50,000 advance payment for goods to be manufactured to Lyle's specifications.

- Checks in the amount of $100,000 were written to vendors and recorded on December 29, 1992. The checks were mailed on January 5, 1993.

What amount should Lyle report as accounts payable in its December 31, 1992, balance sheet?
   a. $510,000
   b. $410,000
   c. $310,000
   d. $210,000

1M93#29. On December 1, 1992, Alt Department Store received 505 sweaters on consignment from Todd. Todd's cost for the sweaters was $80 each, and they were priced to sell at $100. Alt's commission on consigned goods is 10%. At December 31, 1992, 5 sweaters remained. In its December 31, 1992, balance sheet, what amount should Alt report as payable for consigned goods?

   a. $49,000
   b. $45,400
   c. $45,000
   d. $40,400

TN92#5. On December 31, 1991, Deal, Inc. failed to accrue the December 1991 sales salaries that were payable on January 6, 1992. What is the effect of the failure to accrue sales salaries on working capital and cash flows from operating activities in Deal's 1991 financial statements?

	Working capital	Cash flows from operating activities
a.	Overstated	No effect
b.	Overstated	Overstated
c.	No effect	Overstated
d.	No effect	No effect

TN92#42. Buc Co. receives deposits from its customers to protect itself against nonpayments for future services. These deposits should be classified by Buc as
   a. A liability.
   b. Revenue.
   c. A deferred credit deducted from accounts receivable.
   d. A contra account.

1N92#5. Able, Inc. had the following amounts of long-term debt outstanding at December 31, 1991:

14$^{1}/_{2}$% term note, due 1992	$ 3,000
11$^{1}/_{8}$% term note, due 1995	107,000
8% note, due in 11 equal annual principal payments, plus interest beginning December 31, 1992	110,000
7% guaranteed debentures, due 1996	100,000
Total	$320,000

Able's annual sinking-fund requirement on the guaranteed debentures is $4,000 per year. What amount should Able report as current maturities of long-term debt in its December 31, 1991, balance sheet?
   a. $ 4,000
   b. $ 7,000
   c. $10,000
   d. $13,000

1N92#21. Rabb Co. records its purchases at gross amounts but wishes to change to recording purchases net of purchase discounts. Discounts available on purchases recorded from October 1, 1991, to September 30, 1992, totaled $2,000. Of this amount, $200 is still available in the accounts payable balance. The balances in Rabb's accounts as of and for the year ended September 30, 1992, before conversion are:

Purchases	$100,000
Purchase discounts taken	800
Accounts payable	30,000

What is Rabb's accounts payable balance as of September 30, 1992, after the conversion?
 a. $29,800
 b. $29,200
 c. $28,800
 d. $28,200

TM92#19. On October 1, 1991, Fleur Retailers signed a 4-month, 16% note payable to finance the purchase of holiday merchandise. At that date, there was no direct method of pricing the merchandise, and the note's market rate of interest was 11%. Fleur recorded the purchase at the note's face amount. All of the merchandise was sold by December 1, 1991. Fleur's 1991 financial statements reported interest payable and interest expense on the note for three months at 16%. All amounts due on the note were paid February 1, 1992.

As a result of Fleur's accounting treatment of the note, interest, and merchandise, which of the following items was reported correctly?

	12/31/91 retained earnings	12/31/91 interest payable
a.	Yes	Yes
b.	No	No
c.	Yes	No
d.	No	Yes

TM92#26. On March 31, 1992, Dallas Co. received an advance payment of 60% of the sales price for special order goods to be manufactured and delivered within five months. At the same time, Dallas subcontracted for production of the special order goods at a price equal to 40% of the main contract price. What liabilities should be reported in Dallas' March 31, 1992, balance sheet?

	Deferred revenues	Payables to subcontractor
a.	None	None
b.	60% of main contract price	40% of main contract price
c.	60% of main contract price	None
d.	None	40% of main contract price

TM91#14. At the end of 1989, Ritzcar Co. failed to accrue sales commissions earned during 1989 but paid in 1990. The error was not repeated in 1990. What was the effect of this error on 1989 ending working capital and on the 1990 ending retained earnings balance?

	1989 ending working capital	1990 ending retained earnings
a.	Overstated	Overstated
b.	No effect	Overstated
c.	No effect	No effect
d.	Overstated	No effect

1M91#34. Kew Co.'s accounts payable balance at December 31, 1990, was $2,200,000 before considering the following data:

- Goods shipped to Kew F.O.B. shipping point on December 22, 1990, were lost in transit. The invoice cost of $40,000 was not recorded by Kew. On January 7, 1991, Kew filed a $40,000 claim against the common carrier.

- On December 27, 1990, a vendor authorized Kew to return, for full credit, goods shipped and billed at $70,000 on December 3, 1990. The returned goods were shipped by Kew on December 28, 1990. A $70,000 credit memo was received and recorded by Kew on January 5, 1991.

- Goods shipped to Kew F.O.B. destination on December 20, 1990, were received on January 6, 1991. The invoice cost was $50,000.

What amount should Kew report as accounts payable in its December 31, 1990, balance sheet?
 a. $2,170,000
 b. $2,180,000
 c. $2,230,000
 d. $2,280,000

1M91#37. Kemp Co. must determine the December 31, 1990, year-end accruals for advertising and rent expenses. A $500 advertising bill was received January 7, 1991, comprising costs of $375 for advertisements in December 1990 issues, and $125 for advertisements in January 1991 issues of the newspaper.

A store lease, effective December 16, 1989, calls for fixed rent of $1,200 per month, payable one month from the effective date and monthly thereafter. In addition, rent equal to 5% of net sales over $300,000 per calendar year is payable on January 31 of the following year. Net sales for 1990 were $550,000.

In its December 31, 1990, balance sheet, Kemp should report accrued liabilities of
 a. $12,875
 b. $13,000
 c. $13,100
 d. $13,475

TN90#22. Which of the following is generally associated with payables classified as accounts payable?

	Periodic payment of interest	Secured by collateral
a.	No	No
b.	No	Yes
c.	Yes	No
d.	Yes	Yes

Selected Questions

1N90#10. Black Corp.'s accounts payable at December 31, 1989, totaled $900,000 before any necessary year-end adjustments relating to the following transactions:

- On December 27, 1989, Black wrote and recorded checks to creditors totaling $400,000 causing an overdraft of $100,000 in Black's bank account at December 31, 1989. The checks were mailed out on January 10, 1990.

- On December 28, 1989, Black purchased and received goods for $153,061, terms 2/10, n/30. Black records purchases and accounts payable at net amounts. The invoice was recorded and paid January 3, 1990.

- Goods shipped F.O.B. destination on December 20, 1989 from a vendor to Black were received January 2, 1990. The invoice cost was $65,000.

At December 31, 1989, what amount should Black report as total accounts payable?
- a. $1,515,000
- b. $1,450,000
- c. $1,153,061
- d. $1,053,061

1N90#12. Bloy Corp.'s payroll for the pay period ended October 31, 1989 is summarized as follows:

Department payroll	Total wages	Federal income tax withheld	Amount of wages subject to payroll taxes	
			F.I.C.A.	Unemployment
Factory	$ 60,000	$ 7,000	$56,000	$18,000
Sales	22,000	3,000	16,000	2,000
Office	18,000	2,000	8,000	—
	$100,000	$12,000	$80,000	$20,000

Assume the following payroll tax rates:

F.I.C.A. for employer and employee	7% each
Unemployment	3%

What amount should Bloy accrue as its share of payroll taxes in its October 31, 1989 balance sheet?
- a. $18,200
- b. $12,600
- c. $11,800
- d. $ 6,200

1M90#22. Rice Co. salaried employees are paid biweekly. Advances made to employees are paid back by payroll deductions. Information relating to salaries follows:

	12/31/88	12/31/89
Employee advances	$24,000	$ 36,000
Accrued salaries payable	40,000	?
Salaries expense during the year		420,000
Salaries paid during the year (gross)		390,000

In Rice's December 31, 1989 balance sheet, accrued salaries payable was
- a. $94,000
- b. $82,000
- c. $70,000
- d. $30,000

1M90#23. At December 31, 1988, a $1,200,000 note payable was included in Cobb Corp.'s liability account balances. The note is dated October 1, 1988, bears interest at 15%, and is payable in three equal annual payments of $400,000. The first interest and principal payment was made on October 1, 1989. In its December 31, 1989 balance sheet, what amount should Cobb report as accrued interest payable for this note?
- a. $135,000
- b. $ 90,000
- c. $ 45,000
- d. $ 30,000

1M90#27. The balance in Kemp Corp.'s accounts payable account at December 31, 1989 was $900,000 before any necessary year-end adjustment relating to the following:

- Goods were in transit to Kemp from a vendor on December 31, 1989. The invoice cost was $50,000. The goods were shipped F.O.B. shipping point on December 29, 1989 and were received on January 4, 1990.
- Goods shipped F.O.B. destination on December 21, 1989 from a vendor to Kemp were received on January 6, 1990. The invoice cost was $25,000.
- On December 27, 1989, Kemp wrote and recorded checks to creditors totaling $40,000 that were mailed on January 10, 1990.

In Kemp's December 31, 1989 balance sheet, the accounts payable should be
- a. $940,000
- b. $950,000
- c. $975,000
- d. $990,000

H. Deferred Revenues

N95#10. Lang Co. uses the installment method of revenue recognition. The following data pertain to Lang's installment sales for the years ended December 31, 1993 and 1994:

	1993	1994
Installment receivables at year-end on 1993 sales	$60,000	$30,000
Installment receivables at year-end on 1994 sales	—	69,000
Installment sales	80,000	90,000
Cost of sales	40,000	60,000

What amount should Lang report as deferred gross profit in its December 31, 1994, balance sheet?
 a. $23,000
 b. $33,000
 c. $38,000
 d. $43,000

N95#11. In a sale-leaseback transaction, a gain resulting from the sale should be deferred at the time of the sale-leaseback and subsequently amortized when

I. The seller-lessee has transferred substantially all the risks of ownership.
II. The seller-lessee retains the right to substantially all of the remaining use of the property.

 a. I only.
 b. II only.
 c. Both I and II.
 d. Neither I nor II.

N94#21. For $50 a month, Rawl Co. visits its customers' premises and performs insect control services. If customers experience problems between regularly scheduled visits, Rawl makes service calls at no additional charge. Instead of paying monthly, customers may pay an annual fee of $540 in advance. For a customer who pays the annual fee in advance, Rawl should recognize the related revenue
 a. When the cash is collected.
 b. At the end of the fiscal year.
 c. At the end of the contract year after all of the services have been performed.
 d. Evenly over the contract year as the services are performed.

M94#23. Since there is no reasonable basis for estimating the degree of collectibility, Astor Co. uses the installment method of revenue recognition for the following sales:

	1993	1992
Sales	$900,000	$600,000
Collections from:		
1992 sales	100,000	200,000
1993 sales	300,000	—
Accounts written off:		
1992 sales	150,000	50,000
1993 sales	50,000	—
Gross profit percentage	40%	30%

What amount should Astor report as deferred gross profit in its December 31, 1993, balance sheet for the 1992 and 1993 sales?
 a. $150,000
 b. $160,000
 c. $225,000
 d. $250,000

1N93#38. Dunne Co. sells equipment service contracts that cover a two-year period. The sales price of each contract is $600. Dunne's past experience is that, of the total dollars spent for repairs on service contracts, 40% is incurred evenly during the first contract year and 60% evenly during the second contract year. Dunne sold 1,000 contracts evenly throughout 1992. In its December 31, 1992, balance sheet, what amount should Dunne report as deferred service contract revenue?
 a. $540,000
 b. $480,000
 c. $360,000
 d. $300,000

1N93#45. On January 2, 1991, Blake Co. sold a used machine to Cooper, Inc. for $900,000, resulting in a gain of $270,000. On that date, Cooper paid $150,000 cash and signed a $750,000 note bearing interest at 10%. The note was payable in three annual installments of $250,000 beginning January 2, 1992. Blake appropriately accounted for the sale under the installment method. Cooper made a timely payment of the first installment on January 2, 1992, of $325,000, which included accrued interest of $75,000. What amount of deferred gross profit should Blake report at December 31, 1992?
 a. $150,000
 b. $172,500
 c. $180,000
 d. $225,000

TM93#40. Delect Co. provides repair services for the AZ195 TV set. Customers prepay the fee on the standard one-year service contract. The 1991 and 1992 contracts were identical, and the number of contracts outstanding was substantially the same at the end of each year. However, Delect's December 31, 1992, deferred revenues' balance on unperformed service contracts was significantly less than the balance at December 31, 1991. Which of the following situations might account for this reduction in the deferred revenue balance?
 a. Most 1992 contracts were signed later in the calendar year than were the 1991 contracts.
 b. Most 1992 contracts were signed earlier in the calendar year than were the 1991 contracts.
 c. The 1992 contract contribution margin was greater than the 1991 contract contribution margin.
 d. The 1992 contribution margin was less than the 1991 contract contribution margin.

1M93#13. Taylor Corp., which began operations in 1992, accounts for revenues using the installment method. Taylor's sales and collections for the year were $60,000 and $35,000, respectively. Uncollectible accounts receivable of $5,000 were written off during 1992. Taylor's gross profit rate is 30%. In its December 31, 1992, balance

sheet, what amount should Taylor report as deferred revenue?
a. $10,500
b. $ 9,000
c. $ 7,500
d. $ 6,000

TN92#7. In June 1992, Northan Retailers sold refundable merchandise coupons. Northan received $10 for each coupon redeemable from July 1 to December 31, 1992, for merchandise with a retail price of $11. At June 30, 1992, how should Northan report these coupon transactions?
a. Unearned revenues at the merchandise's retail price.
b. Unearned revenues at the cash received amount.
c. Revenues at the merchandise's retail price.
d. Revenues at the cash received amount.

1N92#28. Gant Co., which began operations on January 1, 1991, appropriately uses the installment method of accounting. The following information pertains to Gant's operations for the year 1991:

Installment sales	$500,000
Regular sales	300,000
Cost of installment sales	250,000
Cost of regular sales	150,000
General and administrative expenses	50,000
Collections on installment sales	100,000

In its December 31, 1991, balance sheet, what amount should Gant report as deferred gross profit?
a. $250,000
b. $200,000
c. $160,000
d. $ 75,000

1N92#29. Toddler Care Co. offers three payment plans on its 12-month contracts. Information on the three plans and the number of children enrolled in each plan for the September 1, 1991, through August 31, 1992, contract year follows:

Plan	Initial payment per child	Monthly fees per child	Number of children
#1	$500	$ —	15
#2	200	30	12
#3	—	50	9
			36

Toddler received $9,900 of initial payments on September 1, 1991, and $3,240 of monthly fees during the period September 1 through December 31, 1991. In its December 31, 1991, balance sheet, what amount should Toddler report as deferred revenues?
a. $3,300
b. $4,380
c. $6,600
d. $9,900

1N92#30. Regal Department Store sells gift certificates, redeemable for store merchandise, that expire one year after their issuance. Regal has the following information pertaining to its gift certificates sales and redemptions:

Unredeemed at 12/31/90	$ 75,000
1991 sales	250,000
1991 redemptions of prior year sales	25,000
1991 redemptions of current year sales	175,000

Regal's experience indicates that 10% of gift certificates sold will not be redeemed. In its December 31, 1991, balance sheet, what amount should Regal report as unearned revenue?
a. $125,000
b. $112,500
c. $100,000
d. $ 50,000

1N92#35. On June 30, 1992, Lang Co. sold equipment with an estimated useful life of eleven years and immediately leased it back for ten years. The equipment's carrying amount was $450,000; the sales price was $430,000; and the present value of the lease payments, which is equal to the fair value of the equipment, was $465,000. In its June 30, 1992, balance sheet, what amount should Lang report as deferred loss?
a. $35,000
b. $20,000
c. $15,000
d. $0

TM92#32. Rig Co. sold its factory at a gain, and simultaneously leased it back for 10 years. The factory's remaining economic life is 20 years. The lease was reported as an operating lease. At the time of sale, Rig should report the gain as
a. An extraordinary item, net of income tax.
b. An asset valuation allowance.
c. A separate component of stockholders' equity.
d. A deferred credit.

1M92
Items 27 and 28 are based on the following:

Baker Co. is a real estate developer that began operations on January 2, 1990. Baker appropriately uses the installment method of revenue recognition. Baker's sales are made on the basis of a 10% downpayment, with the balance payable over 30 years. Baker's gross profit percentage is 40%. Relevant information for Baker's first two years of operations is as follows:

	1991	1990
Sales	$16,000,000	$14,000,000
Cash collections	2,020,000	1,400,000

27. At December 31, 1990, Baker's deferred gross profit was

a. $ 5,040,000
b. $ 5,600,000
c. $ 8,400,000
d. $12,600,000

28. Baker's realized gross profit for 1991 was
    a. $6,400,000
    b. $2,020,000
    c. $1,212,000
    d. $ 808,000

1M92#31. The following information pertains to a sale and leaseback of equipment by Mega Co. on December 31, 1991:

Sales price	$400,000
Carrying amount	$300,000
Monthly lease payment	$3,250
Present value of lease payments	$36,900
Estimated remaining life	25 years
Lease term	1 year
Implicit rate	12%

What amount of deferred gain on the sale should Mega report at December 31, 1991?
a. $0
b. $ 36,900
c. $ 63,100
d. $100,000

TN91#19. How would the proceeds received from the advance sale of nonrefundable tickets for a theatrical performance be reported in the seller's financial statements before the performance?
a. Revenue for the entire proceeds.
b. Revenue to the extent of related costs expended.
c. Unearned revenue to the extent of related costs expended.
d. Unearned revenue for the entire proceeds.

1N91#27. Each of Potter Pie Co.'s 21 new franchisees contracted to pay an initial franchise fee of $30,000. By December 31, 1991, each franchisee had paid a nonrefundable $10,000 fee and signed a note to pay $10,000 principal plus the market rate of interest on December 31, 1992, and December 31, 1993. Experience indicates that one franchisee will default on the additional payments. Services for the initial fee will be performed in 1992. What amount of net unearned franchise fees would Potter report at December 31, 1991?
a. $400,000
b. $600,000
c. $610,000
d. $630,000

1N91#29. Winn Co. sells subscriptions to a specialized directory that is published semiannually and shipped to subscribers on April 15 and October 15. Subscriptions received after the March 31 and September 30 cutoff dates are held for the next publication. Cash from subscribers is received evenly during the year and is credited to deferred subscription revenue. Data relating to 1990 are as follows:

Deferred subscription revenue, 1/1/90	$ 750,000
Cash receipts from subscribers	3,600,000

In its December 31, 1990, balance sheet, Winn should report deferred subscription revenue of
a. $2,700,000
b. $1,800,000
c. $1,650,000
d. $ 900,000

TM91#15. An automobile dealer sells service contracts. The contracts stipulate that the dealer will perform specific repairs on covered vehicles. The contracts vary in length from 12 to 36 months. Do the following increase when service contracts are sold?

	Deferred revenue	Service revenue
a.	Yes	Yes
b.	No	No
c.	No	Yes
d.	Yes	No

1M91#40. On December 31, 1990, Rice, Inc. authorized Graf to operate as a franchisee for an initial franchise fee of $150,000. Of this amount, $60,000 was received upon signing the agreement and the balance, represented by a note, is due in three annual payments of $30,000 each beginning December 31, 1991. The present value on December 31, 1990, of the three annual payments appropriately discounted is $72,000. According to the agreement, the nonrefundable down payment represents a fair measure of the services already performed by Rice; however, substantial future services are required of Rice. Collectibility of the note is reasonably certain. In Rice's December 31, 1990, balance sheet, unearned franchise fees from Graf's franchise should be reported as
a. $132,000
b. $100,000
c. $ 90,000
d. $ 72,000

1M91#43. Aneen's Video Mart sells 1- and 2-year mail order subscriptions for its video-of-the-month business. Subscriptions are collected in advance and credited to sales. An analysis of the recorded sales activity revealed the following:

	1989	1990
Sales	$420,000	$500,000
Less cancellations	20,000	30,000
Net sales	$400,000	$470,000
Subscriptions expirations:		
1989	$120,000	
1990	155,000	$130,000
1991	125,000	200,000
1992		140,000
	$400,000	$470,000

In Aneen's December 31, 1990, balance sheet, the balance for unearned subscription revenue should be

a. $495,000
b. $470,000
c. $465,000
d. $340,000

1M91#44. On January 1, 1990, Hooks Oil Co. sold equipment with a carrying amount of $100,000, and a remaining useful life of 10 years, to Maco Drilling for $150,000. Hooks immediately leased the equipment back under a 10-year capital lease with a present value of $150,000 and will depreciate the equipment using the straight-line method. Hooks made the first annual lease payment of $24,412 in December 1990. In Hooks' December 31, 1990, balance sheet, the unearned gain on equipment sale should be
a. $50,000
b. $45,000
c. $25,588
d. $0

TN90#23. Jersey, Inc. is a retailer of home appliances and offers a service contract on each appliance sold. Jersey sells appliances on installment contracts, but all service contracts must be paid in full at the time of sale. Collections received for service contracts should be recorded as an increase in a
a. Deferred revenue account.
b. Sales contracts receivable valuation account.
c. Stockholders' valuation account.
d. Service revenue account.

1N90#17. Ryan Co. sells major household appliance service contracts for cash. The service contracts are for a one-year, two-year, or three-year period. Cash receipts from contracts are credited to unearned service contract revenues. This account had a balance of $720,000 at December 31, 1989 before year-end adjustment. Service contract costs are charged as incurred to the service contract expense account, which had a balance of $180,000 at December 31, 1989. Outstanding service contracts at December 31, 1989 expire as follows:

During 1990	—	$150,000
During 1991	—	225,000
During 1992	—	100,000

What amount should be reported as unearned service contract revenues in Ryan's December 31, 1989 balance sheet?
a. $540,000
b. $475,000
c. $295,000
d. $245,000

1N90#34. On January 1, 1988, Rex Co. sold a used machine to Lake, Inc. for $525,000. On this date, the machine had a depreciated cost of $367,500. Lake paid $75,000 cash on January 1, 1988 and signed a $450,000 note bearing interest at 10%. The note was payable in three annual installments of $150,000 beginning January 1, 1989. Rex appropriately accounted for the sale under the installment method. Lake made a timely payment of the first installment on January 1, 1989 of $195,000, which included interest of $45,000 to date of payment. At December 31, 1989, Rex has deferred gross profit of
a. $105,000
b. $ 99,000
c. $ 90,000
d. $ 76,500

TM90#9. A retail store received cash and issued gift certificates that are redeemable in merchandise. The gift certificates lapse one year after they are issued. How would the deferred revenue account be affected by each of the following transactions?

	Redemption of certificates	Lapse of certificates
a.	Decrease	No effect
b.	Decrease	Decrease
c.	No effect	No effect
d.	No effect	Decrease

I. Notes and Bonds Payable

R97#9. The market price of a bond issued at a premium is equal to the present value of its principal amount
a. Only, at the stated interest rate.
b. And the present value of all future interest payments, at the stated interest rate.
c. Only, at the market (effective) interest rate.
d. And the present value of all future interest payments, at the market (effective) interest rate.

N95#59. Barr Co. has total debt of $420,000 and stockholders' equity of $700,000. Barr is seeking capital to fund an expansion. Barr is planning to issue an additional $300,000 in common stock, and is negotiating with a bank to borrow additional funds. The bank is requiring a debt-to-equity ratio of .75. What is the maximum additional amount Barr will be able to borrow?
a. $225,000
b. $330,000
c. $525,000
d. $750,000

M95#19. On July 1, 1994, Eagle Corp. issued 600 of its 10%, $1,000 bonds at 99 plus accrued interest. The bonds are dated April 1, 1994 and mature on April 1, 2004. Interest is payable semiannually on April 1 and October 1. What amount did Eagle receive from the bond issuance?
a. $579,000
b. $594,000
c. $600,000
d. $609,000

M95#20. On January 2, 1994, Nast Co. issued 8% bonds with a face amount of $1,000,000 that mature on January 2, 2000. The bonds were issued to yield 12%, resulting in a discount of $150,000. Nast incorrectly used the straight-line method instead of the effective interest method to amortize the discount. How is the carrying amount of the bonds affected by the error?

	At December 31, 1994	At January 2, 2000
a.	Overstated	Understated
b.	Overstated	No effect
c.	Understated	Overstated
d.	Understated	No effect

N94#22. House Publishers offered a contest in which the winner would receive $1,000,000, payable over 20 years. On December 31, 1993, House announced the winner of the contest and signed a note payable to the winner for $1,000,000, payable in $50,000 installments every January 2. Also on December 31, 1993, House purchased an annuity for $418,250 to provide the $950,000 prize monies remaining after the first $50,000 installment, which was paid on January 2, 1994. In its December 31, 1993, balance sheet, what amount should House report as note payable-contest winner, net of current portion?
  a. $368,250
  b. $418,250
  c. $900,000
  d. $950,000

N94#24. On January 2, 1994, West Co. issued 9% bonds in the amount of $500,000, which mature on January 2, 2004. The bonds were issued for $469,500 to yield 10%. Interest is payable annually on December 31. West uses the interest method of amortizing bond discount. In its June 30, 1994, balance sheet, what amount should West report as bonds payable?
  a. $469,500
  b. $470,475
  c. $471,025
  d. $500,000

M94#29. On January 1, 1994, Oak Co. issued 400 of its 8%, $1,000 bonds at 97 plus accrued interest. The bonds are dated October 1, 1993, and mature on October 1, 2003. Interest is payable semiannually on April 1 and October 1. Accrued interest for the period October 1, 1993, to January 1, 1994, amounted to $8,000. On January 1, 1994, what amount should Oak report as bonds payable, net of discount?
  a. $380,300
  b. $388,000
  c. $388,300
  d. $392,000

M94#30. The discount resulting from the determination of a note payable's present value should be reported on the balance sheet as a(an)
  a. Addition to the face amount of the note.
  b. Deferred charge separate from the note.
  c. Deferred credit separate from the note.
  d. Direct reduction from the face amount of the note.

1N93#27. On December 31, 1992, Roth Co. issued a $10,000 face value note payable to Wake Co. in exchange for services rendered to Roth. The note, made at usual trade terms, is due in nine months and bears interest, payable at maturity, at the annual rate of 3%. The market interest rate is 8%. The compound interest factor of $1 due in nine months at 8% is .944. At what amount should the note payable be reported in Roth's December 31, 1992, balance sheet?
  a. $10,300
  b. $10,000
  c. $ 9,652
  d. $ 9,440

1N93#33. On December 30, 1992, Fort, Inc. issued 1,000 of its 8%, 10-year, $1,000 face value bonds with detachable stock warrants at par. Each bond carried a detachable warrant for one share of Fort's common stock at a specified option price of $25 per share. Immediately after issuance, the market value of the bonds without the warrants was $1,080,000 and the market value of the warrants was $120,000. In its December 31, 1992, balance sheet, what amount should Fort report as bonds payable?
  a. $1,000,000
  b. $ 975,000
  c. $ 900,000
  d. $ 880,000

1N93#34. On January 2, 1992, Gill Co. issued $2,000,000 of 10-year, 8% bonds at par. The bonds, dated January 1, 1992, pay interest semiannually on January 1 and July 1. Bond issue costs were $250,000. What amount of bond issue costs are unamortized at June 30, 1993?
  a. $237,500
  b. $225,000
  c. $220,800
  d. $212,500

1N93#36. Webb Co. has outstanding a 7%, 10-year $100,000 face-value bond. The bond was originally sold to yield 6% annual interest. Webb uses the effective interest rate method to amortize bond premium. On June 30, 1992, the carrying amount of the outstanding bond was $105,000. What amount of unamortized premium on bond should Webb report in its June 30, 1993, balance sheet?
  a. $1,050
  b. $3,950
  c. $4,300
  d. $4,500

1N93#37. On July 1, 1992, after recording interest and amortization, York Co. converted $1,000,000 of its 12% convertible bonds into 50,000 shares of $1 par value common stock. On the conversion date the carrying amount of the bonds was $1,300,000, the market value of the bonds was $1,400,000, and York's common stock was publicly trading at $30 per share. Using the book value method, what amount of additional paid-in capital should York record as a result of the conversion?
  a. $ 950,000
  b. $1,250,000
  c. $1,350,000
  d. $1,500,000

1M93#2. On December 31, 1992, Largo, Inc. had a $750,000 note payable outstanding, due July 31, 1993. Largo borrowed the money to finance construction of a new plant. Largo planned to refinance the note by issuing long-term bonds. Because Largo temporarily had excess cash, it prepaid $250,000 of the note on January 12, 1993. In February 1993, Largo completed a $1,500,000 bond offering. Largo will use the bond offering proceeds to repay the note payable at its maturity and to pay construction costs during 1993. On March 3, 1993, Largo issued its 1992 financial statements. What amount of the note payable should Largo include in the current liabilities section of its December 31, 1992, balance sheet?
 a. $750,000
 b. $500,000
 c. $250,000
 d. $0

1M93#32. On March 1, 1992, Evan Corp. issued $500,000 of 10% nonconvertible bonds at 103, due on February 28, 2002. Each $1,000 bond was issued with 30 detachable stock warrants, each of which entitled the holder to purchase, for $50, one share of Evan's $25 par common stock. On March 1, 1992, the market price of each warrant was $4. By what amount should the bond issue proceeds increase stockholders' equity?
 a. $0
 b. $15,000
 c. $45,000
 d. $60,000

TN92#9. Pie Co. uses the installment sales method to recognize revenue. Customers pay the installment notes in 24 equal monthly amounts, which include 12% interest. What is an installment note's receivable balance six months after the sale?
 a. 75% of the original sales price.
 b. Less than 75% of the original sales price.
 c. The present value of the remaining monthly payments discounted at 12%.
 d. Less than the present value of the remaining monthly payments discounted at 12%.

1N92#22. On August 1, 1991, Vann Corp.'s $500,000, one-year, noninterest-bearing note due July 31, 1992, was discounted at Homestead Bank at 10.8%. Vann uses the straight-line method of amortizing bond discount. What amount should Vann report for notes payable in its December 31, 1991, balance sheet?
 a. $500,000
 b. $477,500
 c. $468,500
 d. $446,000

1N92#36. On April 1, 1992, Hill Corp. issued 200 of its $1,000 face value bonds at 101 plus accrued interest. The bonds were dated November 1, 1991, and bear interest at an annual rate of 9% payable semiannually on November 1 and May 1. What amount did Hill receive from the bond issuance?

 a. $194,500
 b. $200,000
 c. $202,000
 d. $209,500

1N92#37. During 1992, Lake Co. issued 3,000 of its 9%, $1,000 face value bonds at 101 1/2. In connection with the sale of these bonds, Lake paid the following expenses:

Promotion costs	$ 20,000
Engraving and printing	25,000
Underwriters' commissions	200,000

What amount should Lake record as bond issue costs to be amortized over the term of the bonds?
 a. $0
 b. $220,000
 c. $225,000
 d. $245,000

1N92#38. On May 1, 1992, Bolt Corp. issued 11% bonds in the face amount of $1,000,000 that mature on May 1, 2002. The bonds were issued to yield 10%, resulting in bond premium of $62,000. Bolt uses the effective interest method of amortizing bond premium. Interest is payable semiannually on November 1 and May 1. In its October 31, 1992, balance sheet, what amount should Bolt report as unamortized bond premium?
 a. $62,000
 b. $60,100
 c. $58,900
 d. $58,590

1N92#39. Blue Corp.'s December 31, 1991, balance sheet contained the following items in the long-term liabilities section:

9 3/4% registered debentures, callable in 2002, due in 2007	$700,000
9 1/2% collateral trust bonds, convertible into common stock beginning in 2000, due in 2010	600,000
10% subordinated debentures ($30,000 maturing annually beginning in 1997)	300,000

What is the total amount of Blue's term bonds?
 a. $ 600,000
 b. $ 700,000
 c. $1,000,000
 d. $1,300,000

1M92#29. Dixon Co. incurred costs of $3,300 when it issued, on August 31, 1991, 5-year debenture bonds dated April 1, 1991. What amount of bond issue expense should Dixon report in its income statement for the year ended December 31, 1991?
 a. $ 220
 b. $ 240
 c. $ 495
 d. $3,300

1M92#30. The following information pertains to Camp Corp.'s issuance of bonds on July 1, 1991:

Face amount	$800,000
Term	10 years
Stated interest rate	6%
Interest payment dates	Annually on July 1
Yield	9%

	At 6%	At 9%
Present value of 1 for 10 periods	0.558	0.422
Future value of 1 for 10 periods	1.791	2.367
Present value of ordinary annuity of 1 for 10 periods	7.360	6.418

What should be the issue price for each $1,000 bond?
   a. $1,000
   b. $ 864
   c. $ 807
   d. $ 700

TN91#35. The market price of a bond issued at a discount is the present value of its principal amount at the market (effective) rate of interest
   a. Less the present value of all future interest payments at the market (effective) rate of interest.
   b. Less the present value of all future interest payments at the rate of interest stated on the bond.
   c. Plus the present value of all future interest payments at the market (effective) rate of interest.
   d. Plus the present value of all future interest payments at the rate of interest stated on the bond.

TN91#37. Bonds with detachable stock warrants were issued by Flack Co. Immediately after issue the aggregate market value of the bonds and the warrants exceeds the proceeds. Is the portion of the proceeds allocated to the warrants less than their market value, and is that amount recorded as contributed capital?

	Less than warrants' market value	Contributed capital
a.	No	Yes
b.	Yes	No
c.	Yes	Yes
d.	No	No

1N91#28. On October 1, 1990, Brock, Inc. issued 200 of its 10%, $1,000 bonds at 101 plus accrued interest. The bonds are dated July 1, 1990, and mature on July 1, 2000. Interest is payable semiannually on January 1 and July 1. At the time of issuance, Brock received cash of
   a. $207,000
   b. $205,000
   c. $202,000
   d. $197,000

1N91#36. On January 1, 1990, Celt Corp. issued 9% bonds in the face amount of $1,000,000, which mature on January 1, 2000. The bonds were issued for $939,000 to yield 10%, resulting in a bond discount of $61,000. Celt uses the interest method of amortizing bond discount. Interest is payable annually on December 31. At December 31, 1990, Celt's unamortized bond discount should be
   a. $51,000
   b. $51,610
   c. $52,000
   d. $57,100

TM91#5. A 15-year bond was issued in 1980 at a discount. During 1990, a 10-year bond was issued at face amount with the proceeds used to retire the 15-year bond at its face amount. The net effect of the 1990 bond transactions was to increase long-term liabilities by the excess of the 10-year bond's face amount over the 15-year bond's
   a. Face amount.
   b. Carrying amount.
   c. Face amount less the deferred loss on bond retirement.
   d. Carrying amount less the deferred loss on bond retirement.

TM91#6. On March 1, 1990, Clark Co. issued bonds at a discount. Clark incorrectly used the straight-line method instead of the effective interest method to amortize the discount. How were the following amounts, as of December 31, 1990, affected by the error?

	Bond carrying amount	Retained earnings
a.	Overstated	Overstated
b.	Understated	Understated
c.	Overstated	Understated
d.	Understated	Overstated

1M91#35. Ames, Inc. has $500,000 of notes payable due June 15, 1991. Ames signed an agreement on December 1, 1990, to borrow up to $500,000 to refinance the notes payable on a long-term basis with no payments due until 1992. The financing agreement stipulated that borrowings may not exceed 80% of the value of the collateral Ames was providing. At the date of issuance of the December 31, 1990, financial statements, the value of the collateral was $600,000 and is not expected to fall below this amount during 1991. In Ames' December 31, 1990, balance sheet, the obligation for these notes payable should be classified as

	Short-term	Long-term
a.	$500,000	$0
b.	$100,000	$400,000
c.	$ 20,000	$480,000
d.	$0	$500,000

1M91#46. On December 31, 1990, Cobb issued 2,000 of its 10%, $1,000 bonds at 99. The issuance price established a bond discount of $20,000. In connection with the sale of these bonds, Cobb paid the following expenses:

Legal and accounting fees	$45,000
Printing of the prospectus	55,000
Underwriting fees	85,000

FA-50

In Cobb's December 31, 1990, balance sheet, bond issue costs should be reported as
   a. $120,000
   b. $130,000
   c. $160,000
   d. $185,000

1M91#47. Hancock Co.'s December 31, 1990, balance sheet contained the following items in the long-term liabilities section:

Unsecured

9.375% registered bonds ($25,000 maturing annually beginning in 1994)	$275,000
11.5% convertible bonds, callable beginning in 1999, due 2010	125,000

Secured

9.875% guaranty security bonds, due 2010	$250,000
10.0% commodity backed bonds ($50,000 maturing annually beginning in 1995)	200,000

What are the total amounts of serial bonds and debenture bonds?

	Serial bonds	Debenture bonds
a.	$475,000	$400,000
b.	$475,000	$125,000
c.	$450,000	$400,000
d.	$200,000	$650,000

TN90
Items 29 and 30 are based on the following:

On January 2, 1986, Chard Co. issued 10-year convertible bonds at 105. During 1989, these bonds were converted into common stock having an aggregate par value equal to the total face amount of the bonds. At conversion, the market price of Chard's common stock was 50 percent above its par value.

29. On January 2, 1986, cash proceeds from the issuance of the convertible bonds should be reported as
   a. Contributed capital for the entire proceeds.
   b. Contributed capital for the portion of the proceeds attributable to the conversion feature and as a liability for the balance.
   c. A liability for the face amount of the bonds and contributed capital for the premium over the face amount.
   d. A liability for the entire proceeds.

30. Depending on whether the book value method or the market value method was used, Chard would recognize gains or losses on conversion when using the

	Book value method	Market value method
a.	Either gain or loss	Gain
b.	Either gain or loss	Loss
c.	Neither gain **nor** loss	Loss
d.	Neither gain **nor** loss	Gain

TN90#31. Main Co. issued bonds with detachable common stock warrants. Only the warrants had a known market value. The sum of the fair value of the warrants and the face amount of the bonds exceeds the cash proceeds. This excess is reported as
   a. Discount on bonds payable.
   b. Premium on bonds payable.
   c. Common stock subscribed.
   d. Contributed capital in excess of par-stock warrants.

1N90#11. Included in Lee Corp.'s liability account balances at December 31, 1989, were the following:

14% note payable issued October 1, 1989, maturing September 30, 1990	$125,000
16% note payable issued April 1, 1987, payable in six equal annual installments of $50,000 beginning April 1, 1988	200,000

Lee's December 31, 1989 financial statements were issued on March 31, 1990. On January 15, 1990, the entire $200,000 balance of the 16% note was refinanced by issuance of a long-term obligation payable in a lump sum. In addition, on March 10, 1990, Lee consummated a noncancelable agreement with the lender to refinance the 14%, $125,000 note on a long-term basis, on readily determinable terms that have not yet been implemented. Both parties are financially capable of honoring the agreement, and there have been no violations of the agreement's provisions. On the December 31, 1989 balance sheet, the amount of the notes payable that Lee should classify as short-term obligations is
   a. $175,000
   b. $125,000
   c. $ 50,000
   d. $0

1N90#23. On March 1, 1990, Cain Corp. issued at 103 plus accrued interest, two hundred of its 9%, $1,000 bonds. The bonds are dated January 1, 1990 and mature on January 1, 2000. Interest is payable semiannually on January 1 and July 1. Cain paid bond issue costs of $10,000. Cain should realize net cash receipts from the bond issuance of
   a. $216,000
   b. $209,000
   c. $206,000
   d. $199,000

1N90#24. On June 30, 1990, Huff Corp. issued at 99, one thousand of its 8%, $1,000 bonds. The bonds were issued through an underwriter to whom Huff paid bond issue costs of $35,000. On June 30, 1990, Huff should report the bond liability at
   a. $ 955,000
   b. $ 990,000
   c. $1,000,000
   d. $1,025,000

1N90#25. On January 1, 1989, Wolf Corp. issued its 10% bonds in the face amount of $1,000,000, which

mature on January 1, 1999. The bonds were issued for $1,135,000 to yield 8%, resulting in bond premium of $135,000. Wolf uses the interest method of amortizing bond premium. Interest is payable annually on December 31. At December 31, 1989, Wolf's adjusted unamortized bond premium should be
- a. $135,000
- b. $125,800
- c. $121,500
- d. $101,500

1N90#26. On April 1, 1989, Ward Corp. issued $750,000 of 10% nonconvertible bonds at 102 that are due on March 31, 1999. Each $1,000 bond was issued with 40 detachable stock warrants, each of which entitled the bondholder to purchase one share of Ward $10 par common stock for $25. On April 1, 1989, the market value of Ward's common stock was $20 per share, and the market value of each warrant was $4. What amount of the proceeds from the bond issue should Ward record as an increase in stockholders' equity?
- a. $ 15,000
- b. $120,000
- c. $300,000
- d. $750,000

1M90#29. On December 30, 1989, Bart, Inc. purchased a machine from Fell Corp. in exchange for a noninterest bearing note requiring eight payments of $20,000. The first payment was made on December 30, 1989, and the others are due annually on December 30. At date of issuance, the prevailing rate of interest for this type of note was 11%. Present value factors are as follows:

Period	Present value of ordinary annuity of 1 at 11%	Present value of annuity in advance of 1 at 11%
7	4.712	5.231
8	5.146	5.712

On Bart's December 31, 1989 balance sheet, the note payable to Fell was
- a. $ 94,240
- b. $102,920
- c. $104,620
- d. $114,240

1M90#37. During 1989, Eddy Corp. incurred the following costs in connection with the issuance of bonds:

Printing and engraving	$ 30,000
Legal fees	160,000
Fees paid to independent accountants for registration information	20,000
Commissions paid to underwriter	300,000

What amount should be recorded as a deferred charge to be amortized over the term of the bonds?
- a. $510,000
- b. $480,000
- c. $300,000
- d. $210,000

1M90#38. On January 1, 1989, Kay Inc. issued its 10% bonds in the face amount of $400,000, which mature on January 1, 1999. The bonds were issued for $354,000 to yield 12%, resulting in a bond discount of $46,000. Kay uses the interest method of amortizing bond discount. Interest is payable semiannually on July 1 and January 1. At June 30, 1989, Kay's unamortized bond discount would be
- a. $46,000
- b. $44,760
- c. $43,700
- d. $42,000

1M90#40. On January 1, 1984, Fox Corp. issued 1,000 of its 10%, $1,000 bonds for $1,040,000. These bonds were to mature on January 1, 1994 but were callable at 101 any time after December 31, 1987. Interest was payable semiannually on July 1 and January 1. On July 1, 1989, Fox called all of the bonds and retired them. Bond premium was amortized on a straight-line basis. Before income taxes, Fox's gain or loss in 1989 on this early extinguishment of debt was
- a. $30,000 gain.
- b. $12,000 gain.
- c. $10,000 loss.
- d. $ 8,000 gain.

J. Other Liabilities

N95#13. Lime Co.'s payroll for the month ended January 31, 1995, is summarized as follows:

Total wages	$10,000
Federal income tax withheld	1,200

All wages paid were subject to FICA. FICA tax rates were 7% each for employee and employer. Lime remits payroll taxes on the 15th of the following month. In its financial statements for the month ended January 31, 1995, what amounts should Lime report as total payroll tax liability and as payroll tax expense?

	Liability	Expense
a.	$1,200	$1,400
b.	$1,900	$1,400
c.	$1,900	$ 700
d.	$2,600	$ 700

N95#16. On March 1, 1993, Fine Co. borrowed $10,000 and signed a two-year note bearing interest at 12% per annum compounded annually. Interest is payable in full at maturity on February 28, 1995. What amount should Fine report as a liability for accrued interest at December 31, 1994?
- a. $0
- b. $1,000
- c. $1,200
- d. $2,320

M95#21. In December 1994, Mill Co. began including one coupon in each package of candy that it sells and

offering a toy in exchange for 50 cents and five coupons. The toys cost Mill 80 cents each. Eventually 60% of the coupons will be redeemed. During December, Mill sold 110,000 packages of candy and no coupons were redeemed. In its December 31, 1994, balance sheet, what amount should Mill report as estimated liability for coupons?
- a. $ 3,960
- b. $10,560
- c. $19,800
- d. $52,800

N94#25. Black Co. requires advance payments with special orders for machinery constructed to customer specifications. These advances are nonrefundable. Information for 1993 is as follows:

Customer advances — balance 12/31/92	$118,000
Advances received with orders in 1993	184,000
Advances applied to orders shipped in 1993	164,000
Advances applicable to orders cancelled in 1993	50,000

In Black's December 31, 1993, balance sheet, what amount should be reported as a current liability for advances from customer?
- a. $0
- b. $ 88,000
- c. $138,000
- d. $148,000

1N93#32. Kent Co., a division of National Realty, Inc., maintains escrow accounts and pays real estate taxes for National's mortgage customers. Escrow funds are kept in interest-bearing accounts. Interest, less a 10% service fee, is credited to the mortgagee's account and used to reduce future escrow payments. Additional information follows:

Escrow accounts liability, 1/1/92	$ 700,000
Escrow payments received during 1992	1,580,000
Real estate taxes paid during 1992	1,720,000
Interest on escrow funds during 1992	50,000

What amount should Kent report as escrow accounts liability in its December 31, 1992, balance sheet?
- a. $510,000
- b. $515,000
- c. $605,000
- d. $610,000

1N92#24. Case Cereal Co. frequently distributes coupons to promote new products. On October 1, 1991, Case mailed 1,000,000 coupons for $.45 off each box of cereal purchased. Case expects 120,000 of these coupons to be redeemed before the December 31, 1991, expiration date. It takes 30 days from the redemption date for Case to receive the coupons from the retailers. Case reimburses the retailers an additional $.05 for each coupon redeemed. As of December 31, 1991, Case had paid retailers $25,000 related to these coupons and had 50,000 coupons on hand that had not been processed for payment. What amount should Case report as a liability for coupons in its December 31, 1991, balance sheet?
- a. $35,000
- b. $29,000
- c. $25,000
- d. $22,500

1N92#26. Barnel Corp. owns and manages 19 apartment complexes. On signing a lease, each tenant must pay the first and last months' rent and a $500 refundable security deposit. The security deposits are rarely refunded in total, because cleaning costs of $150 per apartment are almost always deducted. About 30% of the time, the tenants are also charged for damages to the apartment, which typically cost $100 to repair. If a one-year lease is signed on a $900 per month apartment, what amount would Barnel report as refundable security deposit?
- a. $1,400
- b. $ 500
- c. $ 350
- d. $ 320

1N92#40. On April 1, 1992, Ash Corp. began offering a new product for sale under a one-year warranty. Of the 5,000 units in inventory at April 1, 1992, 3,000 had been sold by June 30, 1992. Based on its experience with similar products, Ash estimated that the average warranty cost per unit sold would be $8. Actual warranty costs incurred from April 1 through June 30, 1992, were $7,000. At June 30, 1992, what amount should Ash report as estimated warranty liability?
- a. $ 9,000
- b. $16,000
- c. $17,000
- d. $33,000

1N91#26. On the first day of each month, Bell Mortgage Co. receives from Kent Corp. an escrow deposit of $2,500 for real estate taxes. Bell records the $2,500 in an escrow account. Kent's 1990 real estate tax is $28,000, payable in equal installments on the first day of each calendar quarter. On December 31, 1989, the balance in the escrow account was $3,000. On September 30, 1990, what amount should Bell show as an escrow liability to Kent?
- a. $ 1,500
- b. $ 4,500
- c. $ 8,500
- d. $11,500

1M91#39. Fell, Inc. operates a retail grocery store that is required by law to collect refundable deposits of $.05 on soda cans. Information for 1990 follows:

Liability for returnable deposits—12/31/89	$150,000
Cans of soda sold in 1990	10,000,000
Soda cans returned in 1990	11,000,000

On February 1, 1990, Fell subleased space and received a $25,000 deposit to be applied toward rent at the expiration of the lease in 1994. In Fell's December 31, 1990, balance sheet, the current and noncurrent liabilities for deposits were

	Current	Noncurrent
a.	$125,000	$0
b.	$100,000	$ 25,000
c.	$100,000	$0
d.	$ 25,000	$100,000

1N90#14. On January 1, 1989, Glen Co. leased a building to Dix Corp. for a ten-year term at an annual rental of $50,000. At inception of the lease, Glen received $200,000 covering the first two years' rent of $100,000 and a security deposit of $100,000. This deposit will not be returned to Dix upon expiration of the lease but will be applied to payment of rent for the last two years of the lease. What portion of the $200,000 should be shown as a current and long-term liability, respectively, in Glen's December 31, 1989 balance sheet?

	Current liability	Long-term liability
a.	$0	$200,000
b.	$ 50,000	$100,000
c.	$100,000	$100,000
d.	$100,000	$ 50,000

1M90#30. Marr Co. sells its products in reusable containers. The customer is charged a deposit for each container delivered and receives a refund for each container returned within two years after the year of delivery. Marr accounts for the containers not returned within the time limit as being retired by sale at the deposit amount. Information for 1989 is as follows:

Container deposits at December 31, 1988 from deliveries in:

1987	$150,000	
1988	430,000	$580,000

Deposits for containers delivered in 1989   780,000

Deposits for containers returned in 1989 from deliveries in:

1987	$ 90,000	
1988	250,000	
1989	286,000	626,000

In Marr's December 31, 1989 balance sheet, the liability for deposits on returnable containers should be
a. $494,000
b. $584,000
c. $674,000
d. $734,000

K. Equity Accounts

R98#4. Eagle and Falk are partners with capital balances of $45,000 and $25,000, respectively. They agree to admit Robb as a partner. After the assets of the partnership are revalued, Robb will have a 25% interest in capital and profits, for an investment of $30,000. What amount should be recorded as goodwill to the original partners?
a. $0
b. $ 5,000
c. $ 7,500
d. $20,000

R96#1. Selected information from the accounts of Row Co. at December 31, 1995, follows:

Total income since incorporation	$420,000
Total cash dividends paid	130,000
Total value of property dividends distributed	30,000
Excess of proceeds over cost of treasury stock sold, accounted for using the cost method	110,000

In its December 31, 1995, financial statements, what amount should Row report as retained earnings?
a. $260,000
b. $290,000
c. $370,000
d. $400,000

N95#15. The following information pertains to Hall Co.'s defined-benefit pension plan at December 31, 1994:

Unfunded accumulated benefit obligation	$25,000
Unrecognized prior service cost	12,000
Net periodic pension cost	8,000

Hall made no contributions to the pension plan during 1994. In its December 31, 1994, statement of stockholders' equity, what amount should Hall report as excess of additional pension liability over unrecognized prior service cost?
a. $ 5,000
b. $13,000
c. $17,000
d. $25,000

N95#18. Nest Co. issued 100,000 shares of common stock. Of these, 5,000 were held as treasury stock at December 31, 1993. During 1994, transactions involving Nest's common stock were as follows:

May 3 — 1,000 shares of treasury stock were sold.
August 6 — 10,000 shares of previously unissued stock were sold.
November 18 — A 2-for-1 stock split took effect.

Laws in Nest's state of incorporation protect treasury stock from dilution. At December 31, 1994, how many shares of Nest's common stock were issued and outstanding?

	Shares	
	Issued	Outstanding
a.	220,000	212,000
b.	220,000	216,000
c.	222,000	214,000
d.	222,000	218,000

N95#19. Cyan Corp. issued 20,000 shares of $5 par common stock at $10 per share. On December 31, 1993, Cyan's retained earnings were $300,000. In March 1994, Cyan reacquired 5,000 shares of its common stock at $20 per share. In June 1994, Cyan sold 1,000 of these shares to its corporate officers for $25 per share. Cyan uses the cost method to record treasury stock. Net income for the year ended December 31, 1994, was $60,000. At December 31, 1994, what amount should Cyan report as retained earnings?
 a. $360,000
 b. $365,000
 c. $375,000
 d. $380,000

N95#20. Asp Co. was organized on January 2, 1994, with 30,000 authorized shares of $10 par common stock. During 1994 the corporation had the following capital transactions:

January 5 — issued 20,000 shares at $15 per share.
July 14 — purchased 5,000 shares at $17 per share.
December 27 — reissued the 5,000 shares held in treasury at $20 per share.

Asp used the par value method to record the purchase and reissuance of the treasury shares. In its December 31, 1994, balance sheet, what amount should Asp report as additional paid-in capital in excess of par?
 a. $100,000
 b. $125,000
 c. $140,000
 d. $150,000

N95#21. A company issued rights to its existing shareholders without consideration. The rights allowed the recipients to purchase unissued common stock for an amount in excess of par value. When the rights are issued, which of the following accounts will be increased?

	Common stock	Additional paid-in capital
a.	Yes	Yes
b.	Yes	No
c.	No	No
d.	No	Yes

N95#23. During 1994, Young and Zinc maintained average capital balances in their partnership of $160,000 and $100,000, respectively. The partners receive 10% interest on average capital balances, and residual profit or loss is divided equally. Partnership profit before interest was $4,000. By what amount should Zinc's capital account change for the year?

 a. $ 1,000 decrease.
 b. $ 2,000 increase.
 c. $11,000 decrease.
 d. $12,000 increase.

M95
Items 23 and 24 are based on the following:

The following condensed balance sheet is presented for the partnership of Alfa and Beda, who share profits and losses in the ratio of 60:40, respectively:

Cash	$ 45,000
Other assets	625,000
Beda, loan	30,000
	$700,000
Accounts payable	$120,000
Alfa, capital	348,000
Beda, capital	232,000
	$700,000

23. The assets and liabilities are fairly valued on the balance sheet. Alfa and Beda decide to admit Capp as a new partner with a 20% interest. No goodwill or bonus is to be recorded. What amount should Capp contribute in cash or other assets?
 a. $110,000
 b. $116,000
 c. $140,000
 d. $145,000

24. Instead of admitting a new partner, Alfa and Beda decide to liquidate the partnership. If the other assets are sold for $500,000, what amount of the available cash should be distributed to Alfa?
 a. $255,000
 b. $273,000
 c. $327,000
 d. $348,000

N94#28. East Co. issued 1,000 shares of its $5 par common stock to Howe as compensation for 1,000 hours of legal services performed. Howe usually bills $160 per hour for legal services. On the date of issuance, the stock was trading on a public exchange at $140 per share. By what amount should the additional paid-in capital account increase as a result of this transaction?
 a. $135,000
 b. $140,000
 c. $155,000
 d. $160,000

N94#29. During 1992, Brad Co. issued 5,000 shares of $100 par convertible preferred stock for $110 per share. One share of preferred stock can be converted into three shares of Brad's $25 par common stock at the option of the preferred shareholder. On December 31, 1993, when the market value of the common stock was $40 per share, all of the preferred stock was converted. What amount should Brad credit to Common Stock and to Additional

Paid-in Capital—Common Stock as a result of the conversion?

	Common stock	Additional paid-in capital
a.	$375,000	$175,000
b.	$375,000	$225,000
c.	$500,000	$ 50,000
d.	$600,000	$0

N94#30. When a company declares a cash dividend, retained earnings is decreased by the amount of the dividend on the date of
  a. Declaration.
  b. Record.
  c. Payment.
  d. Declaration or record, whichever is earlier.

N94#31. Long Co. had 100,000 shares of common stock issued and outstanding at January 1, 1993. During 1993, Long took the following actions:

March 15 — Declared a 2-for-1 stock split, when the fair value of the stock was $80 per share.
December 15 — Declared a $.50 per share cash dividend.

In Long's statement of stockholders' equity for 1993, what amount should Long report as dividends?
  a. $ 50,000
  b. $100,000
  c. $850,000
  d. $950,000

N94#32. If a corporation sells some of its treasury stock at a price that exceeds its cost, this excess should be
  a. Reported as a gain in the income statement.
  b. Treated as a reduction in the carrying amount of remaining treasury stock.
  c. Credited to additional paid-in capital.
  d. Credited to retained earnings.

N94#35. When Mill retired from the partnership of Mill, Yale, and Lear, the final settlement of Mill's interest exceeded Mill's capital balance. Under the bonus method, the excess
  a. Was recorded as goodwill.
  b. Was recorded as an expense.
  c. Reduced the capital balances of Yale and Lear.
  d. Had **no** effect on the capital balances of Yale and Lear.

M94#31. East Corp., a calendar-year company, had sufficient retained earnings in 1993 as a basis for dividends, but was temporarily short of cash. East declared a dividend of $100,000 on April 1, 1993, and issued promissory notes to its stockholders in lieu of cash. The notes, which were dated April 1, 1993, had a maturity date of March 31, 1994, and a 10% interest rate. How should East account for the scrip dividend and related interest?

  a. Debit retained earnings for $110,000 on April 1, 1993.
  b. Debit retained earnings for $110,000 on March 31, 1994.
  c. Debit retained earnings for $100,000 on April 1, 1993, and debit interest expense for $10,000 on March 31, 1994.
  d. Debit retained earnings for $100,000 on April 1, 1993, and debit interest expense for $7,500 on December 31, 1993.

M94#32. On January 2, 1994, Lake Mining Co.'s board of directors declared a cash dividend of $400,000 to stockholders of record on January 18, 1994, payable on February 10, 1994. The dividend is permissible under law in Lake's state of incorporation. Selected data from Lake's December 31, 1993, balance sheet are as follows:

Accumulated depletion	$100,000
Capital stock	500,000
Additional paid-in capital	150,000
Retained earnings	300,000

The $400,000 dividend includes a liquidating dividend of
  a. $0
  b. $100,000
  c. $150,000
  d. $300,000

M94#35. When property other than cash is invested in a partnership, at what amount should the noncash property be credited to the contributing partner's capital account?
  a. Fair value at the date of contribution.
  b. Contributing partner's original cost.
  c. Assessed valuation for property tax purposes.
  d. Contributing partner's tax basis.

M94#36. Red and White formed a partnership in 1992. The partnership agreement provides for annual salary allowances of $55,000 for Red and $45,000 for White. The partners share profits equally and losses in a 60/40 ratio. The partnership had earnings of $80,000 for 1993 before any allowance to partners. What amount of these earnings should be credited to each partner's capital account?

	Red	White
a.	$40,000	$40,000
b.	$43,000	$37,000
c.	$44,000	$36,000
d.	$45,000	$35,000

M94#37. The following condensed balance sheet is presented for the partnership of Smith and Jones, who share profits and losses in the ratio of 60:40, respectively:

Other assets	$450,000
Smith, loan	20,000
	$470,000
Accounts payable	$120,000
Smith, capital	195,000
Jones, capital	155,000
	$470,000

The partners have decided to liquidate the partnership. If the other assets are sold for $385,000, what amount of the available cash should be distributed to Smith?
 a. $136,000
 b. $156,000
 c. $159,000
 d. $195,000

TN93#15. On November 2, 1992, Finsbury, Inc. issued warrants to its stockholders giving them the right to purchase additional $20 par value common shares at a price of $30. The stockholders exercised all warrants on March 1, 1993. The shares had market prices of $33, $35, and $40 on November 2, 1992, December 31, 1992, and March 1, 1993, respectively. What were the effects of the warrants on Finsbury's additional paid-in capital and net income?

	Additional paid-in capital	Net income
a.	Increased in 1993	No effect
b.	Increased in 1992	No effect
c.	Increased in 1993	Decreased in 1992 and 1993
d.	Increased in 1992	Decreased in 1992 and 1993

TM93#2. A property dividend should be recorded in retained earnings at the property's
 a. Market value at date of declaration.
 b. Market value at date of issuance (payment).
 c. Book value at date of declaration.
 d. Book value at date of issuance (payment).

TM93#9. On April 30, 1993, Algee, Belger, and Ceda formed a partnership by combining their separate business proprietorships. Algee contributed cash of $50,000. Belger contributed property with a $36,000 carrying amount, a $40,000 original cost, and $80,000 fair value. The partnership accepted responsibility for the $35,000 mortgage attached to the property. Ceda contributed equipment with a $30,000 carrying amount, a $75,000 original cost, and $55,000 fair value. The partnership agreement specifies that profits and losses are to be shared equally but is silent regarding capital contributions. Which partner has the largest April 30, 1993, capital account balance?
 a. Algee.
 b. Belger.
 c. Ceda.
 d. All capital account balances are equal.

TM93#10. In 1990, Fogg, Inc. issued $10 par value common stock for $25 per share. No other common stock transactions occurred until March 31, 1992, when Fogg acquired some of the issued shares for $20 per share and retired them. Which of the following statements correctly states an effect of this acquisition and retirement?
 a. 1992 net income is decreased.
 b. 1992 net income is increased.
 c. Additional paid-in capital is decreased.
 d. Retained earnings is increased.

TM93#13. Quoit, Inc. issued preferred stock with detachable common stock warrants. The issue price exceeded the sum of the warrants' fair value and the preferred stocks' par value. The preferred stocks' fair value was not determinable. What amount should be assigned to the warrants outstanding?
 a. Total proceeds.
 b. Excess of proceeds over the par value of the preferred stock.
 c. The proportion of the proceeds that the warrants' fair value bears to the preferred stocks' par value.
 d. The fair value of the warrants.

1M93#6. On April 1, 1993, Hyde Corp., a newly formed company, had the following stock issued and outstanding:

• Common stock, no par, $1 stated value, 20,000 shares originally issued for $30 per share.

• Preferred stock, $10 par value, 6,000 shares originally issued for $50 per share.

Hyde's April 1, 1993, statement of stockholders' equity should report

	Common stock	Preferred stock	Additional paid-in capital
a.	$ 20,000	$ 60,000	$820,000
b.	$ 20,000	$300,000	$580,000
c.	$600,000	$300,000	$0
d.	$600,000	$ 60,000	$240,000

2M93#1. Rudd Corp. had 700,000 shares of common stock authorized and 300,000 shares outstanding at December 31, 1991. The following events occurred during 1992:

January 31	Declared 10% stock dividend
June 30	Purchased 100,000 shares
August 1	Reissued 50,000 shares
November 30	Declared 2-for-1 stock split

At December 31, 1992, how many shares of common stock did Rudd have outstanding?
 a. 560,000
 b. 600,000
 c. 630,000
 d. 660,000

2M93#2. Beck Corp. issued 200,000 shares of common stock when it began operations in 1990 and issued an additional 100,000 shares in 1991. Beck also issued preferred stock convertible to 100,000 shares of common stock. In 1992, Beck purchased 75,000 shares of its common stock and held it in Treasury. At December 31, 1992, how many shares of Beck's common stock were outstanding?
- a. 400,000
- b. 325,000
- c. 300,000
- d. 225,000

2M93#3. The following changes in Vel Corp.'s account balances occurred during 1992:

	Increase
Assets	$89,000
Liabilities	27,000
Capital stock	60,000
Additional paid-in capital	6,000

Except for a $13,000 dividend payment and the year's earnings, there were no changes in retained earnings for 1992. What was Vel's net income for 1992?
- a. $ 4,000
- b. $ 9,000
- c. $13,000
- d. $17,000

2M93#4. At December 31, 1991 and 1992, Carr Corp. had outstanding 4,000 shares of $100 par value 6% cumulative preferred stock and 20,000 shares of $10 par value common stock. At December 31, 1991, dividends in arrears on the preferred stock were $12,000. Cash dividends declared in 1992 totaled $44,000. Of the $44,000, what amounts were payable on each class of stock?

	Preferred stock	Common stock
a.	$44,000	$0
b.	$36,000	$ 8,000
c.	$32,000	$12,000
d.	$24,000	$20,000

2M93#5. At December 31, 1991, Eagle Corp. reported $1,750,000 of appropriated retained earnings for the construction of a new office building, which was completed in 1992 at a total cost of $1,500,000. In 1992, Eagle appropriated $1,200,000 of retained earnings for the construction of a new plant. Also, $2,000,000 of cash was restricted for the retirement of bonds due in 1993. In its 1992 balance sheet, Eagle should report what amount of appropriated retained earnings?
- a. $1,200,000
- b. $1,450,000
- c. $2,950,000
- d. $3,200,000

2M93#13. Roberts and Smith drafted a partnership agreement that lists the following assets contributed at the partnership's formation:

	Contributed by	
	Roberts	Smith
Cash	$20,000	$30,000
Inventory	—	15,000
Building	—	40,000
Furniture & Equipment	15,000	—

The building is subject to a mortgage of $10,000, which the partnership has assumed. The partnership agreement also specifies that profits and losses are to be distributed evenly. What amounts should be recorded as capital for Roberts and Smith at the formation of the partnership?

	Roberts	Smith
a.	$35,000	$85,000
b.	$35,000	$75,000
c.	$55,000	$55,000
d.	$60,000	$60,000

2M93#18. On December 30, 1992, Hale Corp. paid $400,000 cash and issued 80,000 shares of its $1 par value common stock to its unsecured creditors on a pro rata basis pursuant to a reorganization plan under Chapter 11 of the bankruptcy statutes. Hale owed these unsecured creditors a total of $1,200,000. Hale's common stock was trading at $1.25 per share on December 30, 1992. As a result of this transaction, Hale's total stockholder's equity had a net increase of
- a. $1,200,000
- b. $ 800,000
- c. $ 100,000
- d. $ 80,000

2M93#19. Kern and Pate are partners with capital balances of $60,000 and $20,000, respectively. Profits and losses are divided in the ratio of 60:40. Kern and Pate decided to form a new partnership with Grant, who invested land valued at $15,000 for a 20% capital interest in the new partnership. Grant's cost of the land was $12,000. The partnership elected to use the bonus method to record the admission of Grant into the partnership. Grant's capital account should be credited for
- a. $12,000
- b. $15,000
- c. $16,000
- d. $19,000

TN92#18. When collectibility is reasonably assured, the excess of the subscription price over the stated value of the no par common stock subscribed should be recorded as
- a. No par common stock.
- b. Additional paid-in capital when the subscription is recorded.
- c. Additional paid-in capital when the subscription is collected.
- d. Additional paid-in capital when the common stock is issued.

TN92#22. A corporation issuing stock should charge retained earnings for the market value of the shares issued in a(an)

a. Employee stock bonus.
b. Pooling of interests.
c. 10% stock dividend.
d. 2-for-1 stock split.

1N92#7. On September 1, 1992, Hyde Corp., a newly formed company, had the following stock issued and outstanding:

- Common stock, no par, $1 stated value, 5,000 shares originally issued for $15 per share.

- Preferred stock, $10 par value, 1,500 shares originally issued for $25 per share.

Hyde's September 1, 1992, statement of stockholders' equity should report

	Common stock	Preferred stock	Additional paid-in capital
a.	$ 5,000	$15,000	$92,500
b.	$ 5,000	$37,500	$70,000
c.	$75,000	$37,500	$0
d.	$75,000	$15,000	$22,500

2N92#41. On May 18, 1992, Sol Corp.'s board of directors declared a 10% stock dividend. The market price of Sol's 3,000 outstanding shares of $2 par value common stock was $9 per share on that date. The stock dividend was distributed on July 21, 1992, when the stock's market price was $10 per share. What amount should Sol credit to additional paid-in capital for this stock dividend?
a. $2,100
b. $2,400
c. $2,700
d. $3,000

2N92#42. Cross Corp. had outstanding 2,000 shares of 11% preferred stock, $50 par. On August 8, 1992, Cross redeemed and retired 25% of these shares for $22,500. On that date, Cross' additional paid-in capital from preferred stock totaled $30,000. To record this transaction, Cross should debit (credit) its capital accounts as follows:

	Preferred stock	Additional paid-in capital	Retained earnings
a.	$25,000	$7,500	($10,000)
b.	$25,000	—	($ 2,500)
c.	$25,000	($2,500)	—
d.	$22,500	—	—

2N92#43. Boe Corp.'s stockholders' equity at December 31, 1991, was as follows:

6% noncumulative preferred stock,
  $100 par (liquidation value $105
  per share) $100,000
Common stock, $10 par 300,000
Retained earnings 95,000

At December 31, 1991, Boe's book value per common share was
a. $13.17
b. $13.00
c. $12.97
d. $12.80

2N92#44. On July 1, 1992, Cove Corp., a closely-held corporation, issued 6% bonds with a maturity value of $60,000, together with 1,000 shares of its $5 par value common stock, for a combined cash amount of $110,000. The market value of Cove's stock cannot be ascertained. If the bonds were issued separately, they would have sold for $40,000 on an 8% yield to maturity basis. What amount should Cove report for additional paid-in capital on the issuance of the stock?
a. $75,000
b. $65,000
c. $55,000
d. $45,000

2N92#47. In September 1987, Cal Corp. made a dividend distribution of one right for each of its 240,000 shares of outstanding common stock. Each right was exercisable for the purchase of 1/100 of a share of Cal's $50 variable rate preferred stock at an exercise price of $80 per share. On March 20, 1992, none of the rights had been exercised, and Cal redeemed them by paying each stockholder $0.10 per right. As a result of this redemption, Cal's stockholders' equity was reduced by
a. $ 240
b. $ 4,800
c. $24,000
d. $72,000

2N92
Items 48 and 49 are based on the following:

Cor-Eng Partnership was formed on January 2, 1991. Under the partnership agreement, each partner has an equal initial capital balance accounted for under the goodwill method. Partnership net income or loss is allocated 60% to Cor and 40% to Eng. To form the partnership, Cor originally contributed assets costing $30,000 with a fair value of $60,000 on January 2, 1991, while Eng contributed $20,000 in cash. Drawings by the partners during 1991 totaled $3,000 by Cor and $9,000 by Eng. Cor-Eng's 1991 net income was $25,000.

48. Eng's initial capital balance in Cor-Eng is
a. $20,000
b. $25,000
c. $40,000
d. $60,000

49. Cor's share of Cor-Eng's 1991 net income is
a. $15,000
b. $12,500
c. $12,000
d. $ 7,800

2N92#50. On December 31, 1991, Pack Corp.'s board of directors canceled 50,000 shares of $2.50 par value common stock held in treasury at an average cost of $13 per share. Before recording the cancellation of the treasury stock, Pack had the following balances in its stockholder's equity accounts:

Common stock	$540,000
Additional paid-in capital	750,000
Retained earnings	900,000
Treasury stock, at cost	650,000

In its balance sheet at December 31, 1991, Pack should report common stock outstanding of
   a. $0
   b. $250,000
   c. $415,000
   d. $540,000

TM92#35. In the Adel-Brick partnership, Adel and Brick had a capital ratio of 3:1 and a profit and loss ratio of 2:1, respectively. The bonus method was used to record Colter's admittance as a new partner. What ratio would be used to allocate, to Adel and Brick, the excess of Colter's contribution over the amount credited to Colter's capital account?
   a. Adel and Brick's new relative capital ratio.
   b. Adel and Brick's new relative profit and loss ratio.
   c. Adel and Brick's old capital ratio.
   d. Adel and Brick's old profit and loss ratio.

TM92#37. A retained earnings appropriation can be used to
   a. Absorb a fire loss when a company is self-insured.
   b. Provide for a contingent loss that is probable and reasonable.
   c. Smooth periodic income.
   d. Restrict earnings available for dividends.

1M92
Items 2 and 3 are based on the following:

The following format was used by Gee, Inc. for its 1991 statement of owners' equity:

	Common stock, $1 par	Additional paid-in capital	Retained earnings
Balance at 1/1/91	$90,000	$800,000	$175,000
Additions and deductions:			
100% stock dividend			
5% stock dividend			
Balance at 12/31/91			

When both the 100% and the 5% stock dividends were declared, Gee's common stock was selling for more than its $1 par value.

2. How would the 100% stock dividend affect the additional paid-in capital and retained earnings amounts reported in Gee's 1991 statement of owners' equity?

	Additional paid-in capital	Retained earnings
a.	Increase	Increase
b.	Increase	Decrease
c.	No change	Increase
d.	No change	Decrease

3. How would the 5% stock dividend affect the additional paid-in capital and retained earnings amounts reported in Gee's 1991 statement of owners' equity?

	Additional paid-in capital	Retained earnings
a.	Increase	Decrease
b.	Increase	Increase
c.	No change	Decrease
d.	No change	Increase

2M92#1. On March 1, 1992, Rya Corp. issued 1,000 shares of its $20 par value common stock and 2,000 shares of its $20 par value convertible preferred stock for a total of $80,000. At this date, Rya's common stock was selling for $36 per share, and the convertible preferred stock was selling for $27 per share. What amount of the proceeds should be allocated to Rya's convertible preferred stock?
   a. $60,000
   b. $54,000
   c. $48,000
   d. $44,000

2M92#3. Bal Corp. declared a $25,000 cash dividend on May 8, 1991, to stockholders of record on May 23, 1991, payable on June 3, 1991. As a result of this cash dividend, working capital
   a. Was **not** affected.
   b. Decreased on June 3.
   c. Decreased on May 23.
   d. Decreased on May 8.

2M92#5. Ray Corp. declared a 5% stock dividend on its 10,000 issued and outstanding shares of $2 par value common stock, which had a fair value of $5 per share before the stock dividend was declared. This stock dividend was distributed 60 days after the declaration date. By what amount did Ray's current liabilities increase as a result of the stock dividend declaration?
   a. $0
   b. $ 500
   c. $1,000
   d. $2,500

2M92#6. The following information pertains to Meg Corp.:

- Dividends on its 1,000 shares of 6%, $10 par value cumulative preferred stock have not been declared or paid for 3 years.

- Treasury stock that cost $15,000 was reissued for $8,000.

What amount of retained earnings should be appropriated as a result of these items?
- a. $0
- b. $1,800
- c. $7,000
- d. $8,800

2M92#8. On July 1, 1991, Vail Corp. issued rights to stockholders to subscribe to additional shares of its common stock. One right was issued for each share owned. A stockholder could purchase one additional share for 10 rights plus $15 cash. The rights expired on September 30, 1991. On July 1, 1991, the market price of a share with the right attached was $40, while the market price of one right alone was $2. Vail's stockholders' equity on June 30, 1991, comprised the following:

Common stock, $25 par value, 4,000 shares issued and outstanding	$100,000
Additional paid-in capital	60,000
Retained earnings	80,000

By what amount should Vail's retained earnings decrease as a result of issuance of the stock rights on July 1, 1991?
- a. $0
- b. $ 5,000
- c. $ 8,000
- d. $10,000

TN91#15. The Flat and Iron partnership agreement provides for Flat to receive a 20% bonus on profits before the bonus. Remaining profits and losses are divided between Flat and Iron in the ratio of 2 to 3, respectively. Which partner has a greater advantage when the partnership has a profit or when it has a loss?

	Profit	Loss
a.	Flat	Iron
b.	Flat	Flat
c.	Iron	Flat
d.	Iron	Iron

TN91#38. Tem Co. issued rights to its existing stockholders without consideration. A stockholder received a right to buy one share for each 20 shares held. The exercise price was in excess of par value, but less than the current market price. Retained earnings decreases when

	Rights are issued	Rights are exercised
a.	Yes	Yes
b.	Yes	No
c.	No	Yes
d.	No	No

TN91#39. Posy Corp. acquired treasury shares at an amount greater than their par value, but less than their original issue price. Compared to the cost method of accounting for treasury stock, does the par value method report a greater amount for additional paid-in capital and a greater amount for retained earnings?

	Additional paid-in capital	Retained earnings
a.	Yes	Yes
b.	Yes	No
c.	No	No
d.	No	Yes

TN91#40. Grid Corp. acquired some of its own common shares at a price greater than both their par value and original issue price but less than their book value. Grid uses the cost method of accounting for treasury stock. What is the impact of this acquisition on total stockholders' equity and the book value per common share?

	Total stockholders' equity	Book value per share
a.	Increase	Increase
b.	Increase	Decrease
c.	Decrease	Increase
d.	Decrease	Decrease

1N91#37. Clay Corp. had $600,000 convertible 8% bonds outstanding at June 30, 1990. Each $1,000 bond was convertible into 10 shares of Clay's $50 par value common stock. On July 1, 1990, the interest was paid to bondholders, and the bonds were converted into common stock, which had a fair market value of $75 per share. The unamortized premium on these bonds was $12,000 at the date of conversion. Under the book value method, this conversion increased the following elements of the stockholders' equity section by

	Common stock	Additional paid-in capital
a.	$300,000	$312,000
b.	$306,000	$306,000
c.	$450,000	$162,000
d.	$600,000	$ 12,000

2N91#1. Of the 125,000 shares of common stock issued by Vey Corp., 25,000 shares were held as treasury stock at December 31, 1989. During 1990, transactions involving Vey's common stock were as follows:

January 1 through October 31 — 13,000 treasury shares were distributed to officers as part of a stock compensation plan.
November 1 — A 3-for-1 stock split took effect.
December 1 — Vey purchased 5,000 of its own shares to discourage an unfriendly takeover. These shares were not retired.

At December 31, 1990, how many shares of Vey's common stock were issued and outstanding?

	Shares	
	Issued	Outstanding
a.	375,000	334,000
b.	375,000	324,000
c.	334,000	334,000
d.	324,000	324,000

2N91#3. Hoyt Corp.'s current balance sheet reports the following stockholders' equity:

5% cumulative preferred stock, par value $100 per share; 2,500 shares issued and outstanding	$250,000
Common stock, par value $3.50 per share; 100,000 shares issued and outstanding	350,000
Additional paid-in capital in excess of par value of common stock	125,000
Retained earnings	300,000

Dividends in arrears on the preferred stock amount to $25,000. If Hoyt were to be liquidated, the preferred stockholders would receive par value plus a premium of $50,000. The book value per share of common stock is
- a. $7.75
- b. $7.50
- c. $7.25
- d. $7.00

2N91#11. The partnership agreement of Axel, Berg & Cobb provides for the year-end allocation of net income in the following order:

- First, Axel is to receive 10% of net income up to $100,000 and 20% over $100,000.

- Second, Berg and Cobb each are to receive 5% of the remaining income over $150,000.

- The balance of income is to be allocated equally among the three partners.

The partnership's 1990 net income was $250,000 before any allocations to partners. What amount should be allocated to Axel?
- a. $101,000
- b. $103,000
- c. $108,000
- d. $110,000

TM91#17. A company declared a cash dividend on its common stock on December 15, 1990, payable on January 12, 1991. How would this dividend affect stockholders' equity on the following dates?

	December 15, 1990	December 31, 1990	January 12, 1991
a.	Decrease	No effect	Decrease
b.	Decrease	No effect	No effect
c.	No effect	Decrease	No effect
d.	No effect	No effect	Decrease

TM91#18. On incorporation, Dee Inc. issued common stock at a price in excess of its par value. No other stock transactions occurred except treasury stock was acquired for an amount exceeding this issue price. If Dee uses the par value method of accounting for treasury stock appropriate for retired stock, what is the effect of the acquisition on the following?

	Net common stock	Additional paid-in capital	Retained earnings
a.	No effect	Decrease	No effect
b.	Decrease	Decrease	Decrease
c.	Decrease	No effect	Decrease
d.	No effect	Decrease	Decrease

TM91#19. Cricket Corp. issued, without consideration, rights allowing stockholders to subscribe for additional shares at an amount greater than par value but less than both market and book values. When the rights are exercised, how are the following accounts affected?

	Retained earnings	Additional paid-in capital
a.	Decreased	Not affected
b.	Not affected	Not affected
c.	Decreased	Increased
d.	Not affected	Increased

TM91#39. Four individuals who were previously sole proprietors form a partnership. Each partner contributes inventory and equipment for use by the partnership. What basis should the partnership use to record the contributed assets?
- a. Inventory at the lower of FIFO cost or market.
- b. Inventory at the lower of weighted average cost or market.
- c. Equipment at each proprietor's carrying amount.
- d. Equipment at fair value.

1M91
Items 19 and 20 are based on the following:

Pugh Co. reported the following in its statement of stockholders' equity on January 1, 1990:

Common stock, $5 par value, authorized 200,000 shares, issued 100,000 shares	$ 500,000
Additional paid-in capital	1,500,000
Retained earnings	516,000
	2,516,000
Less treasury stock, at cost, 5,000 shares	40,000
Total stockholders' equity	$2,476,000

The following events occurred in 1990:

May 1 — 1,000 shares of treasury stock were sold for $10,000.
July 9 — 10,000 shares of previously unissued common stock were sold for $12 per share.
October 1 — The distribution of a 2-for-1 stock split resulted in the common stock's per share par value being halved.

Pugh accounts for treasury stock under the cost method. Laws in the state of Pugh's incorporation protect shares held in treasury from dilution when stock dividends or stock splits are declared.

19. In Pugh's December 31, 1990, statement of stockholders' equity, the par value of the issued common stock should be
   a. $550,000
   b. $518,000
   c. $291,000
   d. $275,000

20. The number of outstanding common shares at December 31, 1990, should be
   a. 222,000
   b. 220,000
   c. 216,000
   d. 212,000

2M91#2. Dunn and Grey are partners with capital account balances of $60,000 and $90,000, respectively. They agree to admit Zorn as a partner with a one-third interest in capital and profits, for an investment of $100,000, after revaluing the assets of Dunn and Grey. Goodwill to the original partners should be
   a. $0
   b. $33,333
   c. $50,000
   d. $66,667

2M91#3. The partnership agreement of Reid and Simm provides that interest at 10% per year is to be credited to each partner on the basis of weighted-average capital balances. A summary of Simm's capital account for the year ended December 31, 1990, is as follows:

Balance, January 1	$140,000
Additional investment, July 1	40,000
Withdrawal, August 1	(15,000)
Balance, December 31	165,000

What amount of interest should be credited to Simm's capital account for 1990?
   a. $15,250
   b. $15,375
   c. $16,500
   d. $17,250

TN90#32. How would the declaration of a 15% stock dividend by a corporation affect each of the following?

	Retained earnings	Total stockholders' equity
a.	No effect	No effect
b.	No effect	Decrease
c.	Decrease	No effect
d.	Decrease	Decrease

TN90#33. At its date of incorporation, Glean, Inc. issued 100,000 shares of its $10 par common stock at $11 per share. During the current year, Glean acquired 30,000 shares of its common stock at a price of $16 per share and accounted for them by the cost method. Subsequently, these shares were reissued at a price of $12 per share. There have been no other issuances or acquisitions of its own common stock. What effect does the reissuance of the stock have on the following accounts?

	Retained earnings	Additional paid-in capital
a.	Decrease	Decrease
b.	No effect	Decrease
c.	Decrease	No effect
d.	No effect	No effect

TN90#40. Hayes and Jenkins formed a partnership, each contributing assets to the business. Hayes contributed inventory with a current market value in excess of its carrying amount. Jenkins contributed real estate with a carrying amount in excess of its current market value. At what amount should the partnership record each of the following assets?

	Inventory	Real estate
a.	Market value	Market value
b.	Market value	Carrying amount
c.	Carrying amount	Market value
d.	Carrying amount	Carrying amount

TM90#13. The acquisition of treasury stock will cause the number of shares outstanding to decrease if the treasury stock is accounted for by the

	Cost method	Par value method
a.	Yes	No
b.	No	No
c.	Yes	Yes
d.	No	Yes

TM90#14. Pott Co. owned shares in Rose Co. On December 1, 1989, Pott declared and distributed a property dividend of Rose shares when their fair value exceeded the carrying amount. As a consequence of the dividend declaration and distribution, the accounting effects would be

	Property dividends recorded at	Retained earnings
a.	Fair value	Decreased
b.	Fair value	Increased
c.	Cost	Increased
d.	Cost	Decreased

TM90#15. Treasury stock was acquired for cash at a price in excess of its original issue price. The treasury stock was subsequently reissued for cash at a price in excess of its acquisition price. Assuming that the par value method of accounting for treasury stock transactions is used, what is the effect on total stockholders' equity of each of the following events?

	Acquisition of treasury stock	Reissuance of treasury stock
a.	Decrease	No effect
b.	Decrease	Increase
c.	Increase	Decrease
d.	No effect	No effect

TM90#16. Blue Co. issued preferred stock with detachable common stock warrants at a price which exceeded both the par value and the market value of the preferred stock. At the time the warrants are exercised, Blue's total stockholders' equity is increased by the

	Cash received upon exercise of the warrants	Carrying amount of warrants
a.	Yes	No
b.	Yes	Yes
c.	No	No
d.	No	Yes

1M90#42. On June 30, 1989, Hamm Corp. had outstanding $2,000,000 face amount of 8% convertible bonds maturing on June 30, 1994. Interest is payable on June 30 and December 31. Each $1,000 bond is convertible into 40 shares of Hamm's $20 par common stock. After amortization through June 30, 1989, the unamortized balance in the premium on bonds payable account was $50,000. On June 30, 1989, all of the bonds were converted when Hamm's common stock had a market price of $30 per share. Under the book value method, what amount should Hamm credit to additional paid-in capital in recording the conversion?
 a. $350,000
 b. $400,000
 c. $450,000
 d. $800,000

L. Revenue, Cost, and Expense Accounts

R97#10. Ichor Co. reported equipment with an original cost of $379,000 and $344,000, and accumulated depreciation of $153,000 and $128,000, respectively, in its comparative financial statements for the years ended December 31, 1995, and 1994. During 1995, Ichor purchased equipment costing $50,000, and sold equipment with a carrying value of $9,000. What amount should Ichor report as depreciation expense for 1995?
 a. $19,000
 b. $25,000
 c. $31,000
 d. $34,000

R96#2. When the equity method is used to account for investments in common stock, which of the following affect(s) the investor's reported investment income?

	A change in market value of investee's common stock	Cash dividends from investee
a.	Yes	Yes
b.	Yes	No
c.	No	Yes
d.	No	No

R96#5. On December 1, 1995, Money Co. gave Home Co. a $200,000, 11% loan. Money paid proceeds of $194,000 after the deduction of a $6,000 nonrefundable loan origination fee. Principal and interest are due in 60 monthly installments of $4,310, beginning January 1, 1996. The repayments yield an effective interest rate of 11% at a present value of $200,000 and 12.4% at a present value of $194,000. What amount of income from this loan should Money report in its 1995 income statement?
 a. $0
 b. $1,833
 c. $2,005
 d. $7,833

N95
Items 26 and 28 are based on the following:

Grant, Inc. acquired 30% of South Co.'s voting stock for $200,000 on January 2, 1993. Grant's 30% interest in South gave Grant the ability to exercise significant influence over South's operating and financial policies. During 1993, South earned $80,000 and paid dividends of $50,000. South reported earnings of $100,000 for the six months ended June 30, 1994, and $200,000 for the year ended December 31, 1994. On July 1, 1994, Grant sold half of its stock in South for $150,000 cash. South paid dividends of $60,000 on October 1, 1994.

26. Before income taxes, what amount should Grant include in its 1993 income statement as a result of the investment?
 a. $15,000
 b. $24,000
 c. $50,000
 d. $80,000

28. In its 1994 income statement, what amount should Grant report as gain from the sale of half of its investment?
 a. $24,500
 b. $30,500
 c. $35,000
 d. $45,500

N95#29. Glade Co. leases computer equipment to customers under direct-financing leases. The equipment has no residual value at the end of the lease and the leases do not contain bargain purchase options. Glade wishes to earn 8% interest on a five-year lease of equipment with a fair value of $323,400. The present value of an

annuity due of $1 at 8% for five years is 4.312. What is the total amount of interest revenue that Glade will earn over the life of the lease?
- a. $ 51,600
- b. $ 75,000
- c. $129,360
- d. $139,450

N95#30. Rill Co. owns a 20% royalty interest in an oil well. Rill receives royalty payments on January 31 for the oil sold between the previous June 1 and November 30, and on July 31 for oil sold between the previous December 1 and May 31. Production reports show the following oil sales:

June 1, 1993—November 30, 1993	$300,000
December 1, 1993—December 31, 1993	50,000
December 1, 1993—May 31, 1994	400,000
June 1, 1994—November 30, 1994	325,000
December 1, 1994—December 31, 1994	70,000

What amount should Rill report as royalty revenue for 1994?
- a. $140,000
- b. $144,000
- c. $149,000
- d. $159,000

N95#31. It is proper to recognize revenue prior to the sale of merchandise when

I. The revenue will be reported as an installment sale.
II. The revenue will be reported under the cost recovery method.

- a. I only.
- b. II only.
- c. Both I and II.
- d. Neither I nor II.

N95#33. Gray Co. was granted a patent on January 2, 1991, and appropriately capitalized $45,000 of related costs. Gray was amortizing the patent over its estimated useful life of fifteen years. During 1994, Gray paid $15,000 in legal costs in successfully defending an attempted infringement of the patent. After the legal action was completed, Gray sold the patent to the plaintiff for $75,000. Gray's policy is to take no amortization in the year of disposal. In its 1994 income statement, what amount should Gray report as gain from sale of patent?
- a. $15,000
- b. $24,000
- c. $27,000
- d. $39,000

N95#34. When should a lessor recognize in income a nonrefundable lease bonus paid by a lessee on signing an operating lease?
- a. When received.
- b. At the inception of the lease.
- c. At the expiration of the lease.
- d. Over the life of the lease.

N95#35. Upon the death of an officer, Jung Co. received the proceeds of a life insurance policy held by Jung on the officer. The proceeds were not taxable. The policy's cash surrender value had been recorded on Jung's books at the time of payment. What amount of revenue should Jung report in its statements?
- a. Proceeds received.
- b. Proceeds received less cash surrender value.
- c. Proceeds received plus cash surrender value.
- d. None.

M95#10. On July 1, 1994, Casa Development Co. purchased a tract of land for $1,200,000. Casa incurred additional costs of $300,000 during the remainder of 1994 in preparing the land for sale. The tract was subdivided into residential lots as follows:

Lot Class	Number of lots	Sales price per lot
A	100	$24,000
B	100	16,000
C	200	10,000

Using the relative sales value method, what amount of costs should be allocated to the Class A lots?
- a. $300,000
- b. $375,000
- c. $600,000
- d. $720,000

M95#25. Ward, a consultant, keeps her accounting records on a cash basis. During 1994, Ward collected $200,000 in fees from clients. At December 31, 1993, Ward had accounts receivable of $40,000. At December 31, 1994, Ward had accounts receivable of $60,000, and unearned fees of $5,000. On an accrual basis, what was Ward's service revenue for 1994?
- a. $175,000
- b. $180,000
- c. $215,000
- d. $225,000

M95#26. Which of the following is used in calculating the income recognized in the fourth and final year of a contract accounted for by the percentage-of-completion method?

	Actual total costs	Income previously recognized
a.	Yes	Yes
b.	Yes	No
c.	No	Yes
d.	No	No

M95#27. According to the installment method of accounting, gross profit on an installment sale is recognized in income
- a. On the date of sale.
- b. On the date the final cash collection is received.

c. In proportion to the cash collection.
d. After cash collections equal to the cost of sales have been received.

M95#28. Farm Co. leased equipment to Union Co. on July 1, 1994, and properly recorded the sales-type lease at $135,000, the present value of the lease payments discounted at 10%. The first of eight annual lease payments of $20,000 due at the beginning of each year was received and recorded on July 3, 1994. Farm had purchased the equipment for $110,000. What amount of interest revenue from the lease should Farm report in its 1994 income statement?
    a. $0
    b. $5,500
    c. $5,750
    d. $6,750

M95#29. Wood Co. owns 2,000 shares of Arlo, Inc.'s 20,000 shares of $100 par, 6% cumulative, nonparticipating preferred stock and 1,000 shares (2%) of Arlo's common stock. During 1994, Arlo declared and paid dividends of $240,000 on preferred stock. No dividends had been declared or paid during 1993. In addition, Wood received a 5% common stock dividend from Arlo when the quoted market price of Arlo's common stock was $10 per share. What amount should Wood report as dividend income in its 1994 income statement?
    a. $12,000
    b. $12,500
    c. $24,000
    d. $24,500

M95#33. During 1994, Kam Co. began offering its goods to selected retailers on a consignment basis. The following information was derived from Kam's 1994 accounting records:

Beginning inventory	$122,000
Purchases	540,000
Freight in	10,000
Transportation to consignees	5,000
Freight out	35,000
Ending inventory—held by Kam	145,000
—held by consignees	20,000

In its 1994 income statement, what amount should Kam report as cost of goods sold?
    a. $507,000
    b. $512,000
    c. $527,000
    d. $547,000

M95#34. Which of the following should be included in general and administrative expenses?

	Interest	Advertising
a.	Yes	Yes
b.	Yes	No
c.	No	Yes
d.	No	No

M95#35. Which method of recording uncollectible accounts expense is consistent with accrual accounting?

	Allowance	Direct write-off
a.	Yes	Yes
b.	Yes	No
c.	No	Yes
d.	No	No

M95#36. In January 1994, Vorst Co. purchased a mineral mine for $2,640,000 with removable ore estimated at 1,200,000 tons. After it has extracted all the ore, Vorst will be required by law to restore the land to its original condition at an estimated cost of $180,000. Vorst believes it will be able to sell the property afterwards for $300,000. During 1994, Vorst incurred $360,000 of development costs preparing the mine for production and removed and sold 60,000 tons of ore. In its 1994 income statement, what amount should Vorst report as depletion?
    a. $135,000
    b. $144,000
    c. $150,000
    d. $159,000

M95#37. Rye Co. purchased a machine with a four-year estimated useful life and an estimated 10% salvage value for $80,000 on January 1, 1992. In its income statement, what would Rye report as the depreciation expense for 1994 using the double-declining-balance method?
    a. $ 9,000
    b. $10,000
    c. $18,000
    d. $20,000

M95#38. Under a royalty agreement with another company, Wand Co. will pay royalties for the assignment of a patent for three years. The royalties paid should be reported as expense
    a. In the period paid.
    b. In the period incurred.
    c. At the date the royalty agreement began.
    d. At the date the royalty agreement expired.

M95#40. A material loss should be presented separately as a component of income from continuing operations when it is
    a. An extraordinary item.
    b. A cumulative effect type change in accounting principle.
    c. Unusual in nature and infrequent in occurrence.
    d. Not unusual in nature but infrequent in occurrence.

N94#23. House Publishers offered a contest in which the winner would receive $1,000,000, payable over 20 years. On December 31, 1993, House announced the winner of the contest and signed a note payable to the winner for $1,000,000, payable in $50,000 installments every January 2. Also on December 31, 1993, House purchased

an annuity for $418,250 to provide the $950,000 prize monies remaining after the first $50,000 installment, which was paid on January 2, 1994. In its 1993 income statement, what should House report as contest prize expense?
- a. $0
- b. $ 418,250
- c. $ 468,250
- d. $1,000,000

N94#38. Leaf Co. purchased from Oak Co. a $20,000, 8%, 5-year note that required five equal annual year-end payments of $5,009. The note was discounted to yield a 9% rate to Leaf. At the date of purchase, Leaf recorded the note at its present value of $19,485. What should be the total interest revenue earned by Leaf over the life of this note?
- a. $5,045
- b. $5,560
- c. $8,000
- d. $9,000

N94#39. Stock dividends on common stock should be recorded at their fair market value by the investor when the related investment is accounted for under which of the following methods?

	Cost	Equity
a.	Yes	Yes
b.	Yes	No
c.	No	Yes
d.	No	No

N94#40. Wren Corp.'s trademark was licensed to Mont Co. for royalties of 15% of sales of the trademarked items. Royalties are payable semiannually on March 15 for sales in July through December of the prior year, and on September 15 for sales in January through June of the same year. Wren received the following royalties from Mont:

	March 15	September 15
1992	$10,000	$15,000
1993	12,000	17,000

Mont estimated that sales of the trademarked items would total $60,000 for July through December 1993.

In Wren's 1993 income statement, the royalty revenue should be
- a. $26,000
- b. $29,000
- c. $38,000
- d. $41,000

N94#41. As an inducement to enter a lease, Graf Co., a lessor, granted Zep, Inc., a lessee, twelve months of free rent under a five year operating lease. The lease was effective on January 1, 1993, and provides for monthly rental payments to begin January 1, 1994. Zep made the first rental payment on December 30, 1993. In its 1993 income statement, Graf should report rental revenue in an amount equal to
- a. Zero.
- b. Cash received during 1993.
- c. One-fourth of the total cash to be received over the life of the lease.
- d. One-fifth of the total cash to be received over the life of the lease.

N94#43. Bren Co.'s beginning inventory at January 1, 1993, was understated by $26,000, and its ending inventory was overstated by $52,000. As a result, Bren's cost of goods sold for 1993 was
- a. Understated by $26,000.
- b. Overstated by $26,000.
- c. Understated by $78,000.
- d. Overstated by $78,000.

N94#45. Inge Co. determined that the net value of its accounts receivable at December 31, 1993, based on an aging of the receivables, was $325,000. Additional information is as follows:

Allowance for uncollectible accounts—1/1/93	$ 30,000
Uncollectible accounts written off during 1993	18,000
Uncollectible accounts recovered during 1993	2,000
Accounts receivable at 12/31/93	350,000

For 1993, what would be Inge's uncollectible accounts expense?
- a. $ 5,000
- b. $11,000
- c. $15,000
- d. $21,000

N94#46. An increase in the cash surrender value of a life insurance policy owned by a company would be recorded by
- a. Decreasing annual insurance expense.
- b. Increasing investment income.
- c. Recording a memorandum entry only.
- d. Decreasing a deferred charge.

N94#47. Clark Co.'s advertising expense account had a balance of $146,000 at December 31, 1993, before any necessary year-end adjustment relating to the following:

- Included in the $146,000 is the $15,000 cost of printing catalogs for a sales promotional campaign in January 1994.

- Radio advertisements broadcast during December 1993 were billed to Clark on January 2, 1994. Clark paid the $9,000 invoice on January 11, 1994.

What amount should Clark report as advertising expense in its income statement for the year ended December 31, 1993?

a. $122,000
b. $131,000
c. $140,000
d. $155,000

N94#48. Able Co. provides an incentive compensation plan under which its president receives a bonus equal to 10% of the corporation's income before income tax but after deduction of the bonus. If the tax rate is 40% and net income after bonus and income tax was $360,000, what was the amount of the bonus?
a. $36,000
b. $60,000
c. $66,000
d. $90,000

M94#40. The effect of a material transaction that is infrequent in occurrence but **not** unusual in nature should be presented separately as a component of income from continuing operations when the transaction results in a

	Gain	Loss
a.	Yes	Yes
b.	Yes	No
c.	No	No
d.	No	Yes

M94#41. Wren Co. sells equipment on installment contracts. Which of the following statements best justifies Wren's use of the cost recovery method of revenue recognition to account for these installment sales?
a. The sales contract provides that title to the equipment only passes to the purchaser when all payments have been made.
b. No cash payments are due until one year from the date of sale.
c. Sales are subject to a high rate of return.
d. There is **no** reasonable basis for estimating collectibility.

M94#43. Jent Corp. purchased bonds at a discount of $10,000. Subsequently, Jent sold these bonds at a premium of $14,000. During the period that Jent held this investment, amortization of the discount amounted to $2,000. What amount should Jent report as gain on the sale of bonds?
a. $12,000
b. $22,000
c. $24,000
d. $26,000

M94#44. In 1993, Gar Corp. collected $300,000 as beneficiary of a keyman life insurance policy carried on the life of Gar's controller, who had died in 1993. The life insurance proceeds are not subject to income tax. At the date of the controller's death, the policy's cash surrender value was $90,000. What amount should Gar report as revenue in its 1993 income statement?
a. $0
b. $ 90,000
c. $210,000
d. $300,000

M94#45. On January 2, 1993, Lem Corp. bought machinery under a contract that required a down payment of $10,000, plus 24 monthly payments of $5,000 each, for total cash payments of $130,000. The cash equivalent price of the machinery was $110,000. The machinery has an estimated useful life of ten years and estimated salvage value of $5,000. Lem uses straight-line depreciation. In its 1993 income statement, what amount should Lem report as depreciation for this machinery?
a. $10,500
b. $11,000
c. $12,500
d. $13,000

TN93#24. A material loss should be presented separately as a component of income from continuing operations when it is
a. An extraordinary item.
b. A cumulative effect-type change in accounting principle.
c. Infrequent in occurrence and unusual in nature.
d. Infrequent in occurrence but **not** unusual in nature.

TN93#34. In which of the following situations is the units-of-production method of depreciation most appropriate?
a. An asset's service potential declines with use.
b. An asset's service potential declines with the passage of time.
c. An asset is subject to rapid obsolescence.
d. An asset incurs increasing repairs and maintenance with use.

TN93#38. The calculation of the income recognized in the third year of a five-year construction contract accounted for using the percentage-of-completion method includes the ratio of
a. Total costs incurred to date to total estimated costs.
b. Total costs incurred to date to total billings to date.
c. Costs incurred in year 3 to total estimated costs.
d. Costs incurred in year 3 to total billings to date.

TN93#39. Cash collection is a critical event for income recognition in the

	Cost-recovery method	Installment method
a.	No	No
b.	Yes	Yes
c.	No	Yes
d.	Yes	No

1N93
Items 46 and 47 are based on the following:

On January 2, 1992, Emme Co. sold equipment with a carrying amount of $480,000 in exchange for a $600,000 noninterest bearing note due January 2, 1995. There was no established exchange price for the equipment. The prevailing rate of interest for a note of this type at January 2, 1992, was 10%. The present value of 1 at 10% for three periods is 0.75.

46. In Emme's 1992 income statement, what amount should be reported as interest income?
   a. $ 9,000
   b. $45,000
   c. $50,000
   d. $60,000

47. In Emme's 1992 income statement, what amount should be reported as gain (loss) on sale of machinery?
   a. ($ 30,000) loss.
   b. $ 30,000 gain.
   c. $120,000 gain.
   d. $270,000 gain.

1N93#48. Cobb Co. purchased 10,000 shares (2% ownership) of Roe Co. on February 12, 1993. Cobb received a stock dividend of 2,000 shares on March 31, 1993, when the carrying amount per share on Roe's books was $35 and the market value per share was $40. Roe paid a cash dividend of $1.50 per share on September 15, 1993. In Cobb's income statement for the year ended October 31, 1993, what amount should Cobb report as dividend income?
   a. $98,000
   b. $88,000
   c. $18,000
   d. $15,000

1N93#50. Wall Co. leased office premises to Fox, Inc. for a five-year term beginning January 2, 1992. Under the terms of the operating lease, rent for the first year is $8,000 and rent for years 2 through 5 is $12,500 per annum. However, as an inducement to enter the lease, Wall granted Fox the first six months of the lease rent-free. In its December 31, 1992, income statement, what amount should Wall report as rental income?
   a. $12,000
   b. $11,600
   c. $10,800
   d. $ 8,000

1N93#51. On December 30, 1992, Astor Corp. sold merchandise for $75,000 to Day Co. The terms of the sale were net 30, FOB shipping point. The merchandise was shipped on December 31, 1992, and arrived at Day on January 5, 1993. Due to a clerical error, the sale was not recorded until January 1993 and the merchandise, sold at a 25% markup, was included in Astor's inventory at December 31, 1992. As a result, Astor's cost of goods sold for the year ended December 31, 1992, was
   a. Understated by $75,000.
   b. Understated by $60,000.
   c. Understated by $15,000.
   d. Correctly stated.

1N93#52. The following costs were incurred by Griff Co., a manufacturer, during 1992:

Accounting and legal fees	$ 25,000
Freight-in	175,000
Freight-out	160,000
Officers salaries	150,000
Insurance	85,000
Sales representatives salaries	215,000

What amount of these costs should be reported as general and administrative expenses for 1992?
   a. $260,000
   b. $550,000
   c. $635,000
   d. $810,000

1N93#53. In Yew Co.'s 1992 annual report, Yew described its social awareness expenditures during the year as follows:

"The Company contributed $250,000 in cash to youth and educational programs. The Company also gave $140,000 to health and human-service organizations, of which $80,000 was contributed by employees through payroll deductions. In addition, consistent with the Company's commitment to the environment, the Company spent $100,000 to redesign product packaging."

What amount of the above should be included in Yew's income statement as charitable contributions expense?
   a. $310,000
   b. $390,000
   c. $410,000
   d. $490,000

1N93#54. On January 2, 1989, Lava, Inc. purchased a patent for a new consumer product for $90,000. At the time of purchase, the patent was valid for 15 years; however, the patent's useful life was estimated to be only 10 years due to the competitive nature of the product. On December 31, 1992, the product was permanently withdrawn from sale under governmental order because of a potential health hazard in the product. What amount should Lava charge against income during 1992, assuming amortization is recorded at the end of each year?
   a. $ 9,000
   b. $54,000
   c. $63,000
   d. $72,000

1N93#55. On January 2, 1992, Nori Mining Co. (lessee) entered into a 5-year lease for drilling equipment. Nori accounted for the acquisition as a capital lease for $240,000, which includes a $10,000 bargain purchase option. At the end of the lease, Nori expects to exercise the bargain purchase option. Nori estimates that the equipment's fair value will be $20,000 at the end of its 8-year life. Nori regularly uses straight-line depreciation on similar equipment. For the year ended December 31, 1992, what amount should Nori recognize as depreciation expense on the leased asset?

a. $48,000
b. $46,000
c. $30,000
d. $27,500

1N93#59. On June 1, 1993, Oren Co. entered into a five-year nonrenewable lease, commencing on that date, for office space and made the following payments to Cant Properties:

Bonus to obtain lease	$30,000
First month's rent	10,000
Last month's rent	10,000

In its income statement for the year ended June 30, 1993, what amount should Oren report as rent expense?
a. $10,000
b. $10,500
c. $40,000
d. $50,000

TM93#28. Which of the following uses the straight-line depreciation method?

	Group depreciation	Composite depreciation
a.	No	No
b.	Yes	No
c.	Yes	Yes
d.	No	Yes

TM93#35. In 1992, hail damaged several of Toncan Co.'s vans. Hailstorms had frequently inflicted similar damage to Toncan's vans. Over the years, Toncan had saved money by not buying hail insurance and either paying for repairs, or selling damaged vans and then replacing them. In 1992, the damaged vans were sold for less than their carrying amount. How should the hail damage cost be reported in Toncan's 1992 financial statements?
a. The actual 1992 hail damage loss as an extraordinary loss, net of income taxes.
b. The actual 1992 hail damage loss in continuing operations, with **no** separate disclosure.
c. The expected average hail damage loss in continuing operations, with **no** separate disclosure.
d. The expected average hail damage loss in continuing operations, with separate disclosure.

TM93#39. Quo Co. rented a building to Hava Fast Food. Each month Quo receives a fixed rental amount plus a variable rental amount based on Hava's sales for that month. As sales increase so does the variable rental amount, but at a reduced rate. Which of the following curves reflects the monthly rentals under the agreement?

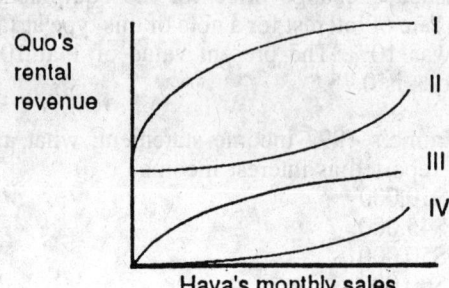

a. I
b. II
c. III
d. IV

1M93#37. Fenn Stores, Inc. had sales of $1,000,000 during December, 1992. Experience has shown that merchandise equalling 7% of sales will be returned within 30 days and an additional 3% will be returned within 90 days. Returned merchandise is readily resalable. In addition, merchandise equalling 15% of sales will be exchanged for merchandise of equal or greater value. What amount should Fenn report for net sales in its income statement for the month of December 1992?
a. $900,000
b. $850,000
c. $780,000
d. $750,000

1M93
Items **38** and **39** are based on the following data pertaining to Pell Co.'s construction jobs, which commenced during 1992:

	Project 1	Project 2
Contract price	$420,000	$300,000
Costs incurred during 1992	240,000	280,000
Estimated costs to complete	120,000	40,000
Billed to customers during 1992	150,000	270,000
Received from customers during 1992	90,000	250,000

38. If Pell used the completed contract method, what amount of gross profit (loss) would Pell report in its 1992 income statement?
a. $(20,000)
b. $ 0
c. $ 340,000
d. $ 420,000

39. If Pell used the percentage-of-completion method, what amount of gross profit (loss) would Pell report in its 1992 income statement?
a. $(20,000)
b. $ 20,000
c. $ 22,500
d. $ 40,000

Selected Questions

1M93#41. Haft Construction Co. has consistently used the percentage-of-completion method. On January 10, 1991, Haft began work on a $3,000,000 construction contract. At the inception date, the estimated cost of construction was $2,250,000. The following data relate to the progress of the contract:

Income recognized at 12/31/91	$ 300,000
Costs incurred 1/10/91 through 12/31/92	1,800,000
Estimated cost to complete at 12/31/92	600,000

In its income statement for the year ended December 31, 1992, what amount of gross profit should Haft report?
    a. $450,000
    b. $300,000
    c. $262,500
    d. $150,000

1M93#42. On January 2, 1992, Yardley Co. sold a plant to Ivory, Inc. for $1,500,000. On that date, the plant's carrying cost was $1,000,000. Ivory gave Yardley $300,000 cash and a $1,200,000 note, payable in 4 annual installments of $300,000 plus 12% interest. Ivory made the first principal and interest payment of $444,000 on December 31, 1992. Yardley uses the installment method of revenue recognition. In its 1992 income statement, what amount of realized gross profit should Yardley report?
    a. $344,000
    b. $200,000
    c. $148,000
    d. $100,000

1M93#43. On July 1, 1992, Denver Corp. purchased 3,000 shares of Eagle Co.'s 10,000 outstanding shares of common stock for $20 per share. On December 15, 1992, Eagle paid $40,000 in dividends to its common stockholders. Eagle's net income for the year ended December 31, 1992, was $120,000, earned evenly throughout the year. In its 1992 income statement, what amount of income from this investment should Denver report?
    a. $36,000
    b. $18,000
    c. $12,000
    d. $ 6,000

1M93#44. In 1990, Super Comics Corp. sold a comic strip to Fantasy, Inc. and will receive royalties of 20% of future revenues associated with the comic strip. At December 31, 1991, Super reported royalties receivable of $75,000 from Fantasy. During 1992, Super received royalty payments of $200,000. Fantasy reported revenues of $1,500,000 in 1992 from the comic strip. In its 1992 income statement, what amount should Super report as royalty revenue?
    a. $125,000
    b. $175,000
    c. $200,000
    d. $300,000

1M93#47. Hall Co.'s allowance for uncollectible accounts had a credit balance of $24,000 at December 31, 1991. During 1992, Hall wrote off uncollectible accounts of $96,000. The aging of accounts receivable indicated that a $100,000 allowance for doubtful accounts was required at December 31, 1992. What amount of uncollectible accounts expense should Hall report for 1992?
    a. $172,000
    b. $120,000
    c. $100,000
    d. $ 96,000

1M93#48. The following information pertains to Deal Corp.'s 1992 cost of goods sold:

Inventory, 12/31/91	$ 90,000
1992 purchases	124,000
1992 write-off of obsolete inventory	34,000
Inventory, 12/31/92	30,000

The inventory written off became obsolete due to an unexpected and unusual technological advance by a competitor. In its 1992 income statement, what amount should Deal report as cost of goods sold?
    a. $218,000
    b. $184,000
    c. $150,000
    d. $124,000

1M93#49. Zach Corp. pays commissions to its sales staff at the rate of 3% of net sales. Sales staff are not paid salaries but are given monthly advances of $15,000. Advances are charged to commission expense, and reconciliations against commissions are prepared quarterly. Net sales for the year ended March 31, 1992, were $15,000,000. The unadjusted balance in the commissions expense account on March 31, 1992, was $400,000. March advances were paid on April 3, 1992. In its income statement for the year ended March 31, 1992, what amount should Zach report as commission expense?
    a. $465,000
    b. $450,000
    c. $415,000
    d. $400,000

1M93#50. On February 12, 1992, VIP Publishing, Inc. purchased the copyright to a book for $15,000 and agreed to pay royalties equal to 10% of book sales, with a guaranteed minimum royalty of $60,000. VIP had book sales of $800,000 in 1992. In its 1992 income statement, what amount should VIP report as royalty expense?
    a. $60,000
    b. $75,000
    c. $80,000
    d. $95,000

1M93#51. Ward Co. estimates its uncollectible accounts expense to be 2% of credit sales. Ward's credit sales for 1992 were $1,000,000. During 1992, Ward wrote off $18,000 of uncollectible accounts. Ward's allowance for uncollectible accounts had a $15,000 balance on January 1, 1992. In its December 31, 1992, income statement,

what amount should Ward report as uncollectible accounts expense?
- a. $23,000
- b. $20,000
- c. $18,000
- d. $17,000

1M93#52. Dana Co.'s officers' compensation expense account had a balance of $224,000 at December 31, 1992, before any appropriate year-end adjustment relating to the following:

- No salary accrual was made for December 30-31, 1992. Salaries for the two-day period totalled $3,500.

- 1992 officers' bonuses of $62,500 were paid on January 31, 1993.

In its 1992 income statement, what amount should Dana report as officers' compensation expense?
- a. $290,000
- b. $286,500
- c. $227,500
- d. $224,000

2M93#7. In May 1989, Caso Co. filed suit against Wayne, Inc. seeking $1,900,000 damages for patent infringement. A court verdict in November 1992 awarded Caso $1,500,000 in damages, but Wayne's appeal is not expected to be decided before 1994. Caso's counsel believes it is probable that Caso will be successful against Wayne for an estimated amount in the range between $800,000 and $1,100,000, with $1,000,000 considered the most likely amount. What amount should Caso record as income from the lawsuit in the year ended December 31, 1992?
- a. $0
- b. $ 800,000
- c. $1,000,000
- d. $1,500,000

TN92#8. A company used the percentage-of-completion method of accounting for a 5-year construction contract. Which of the following items will the company use to calculate the income recognized in the third year?

	Progress billings to date	Income previously recognized
a.	Yes	No
b.	No	Yes
c.	No	No
d.	Yes	Yes

TN92#10. During 1991, Peg Construction Co. recognized substantial gains from:

- An increase in value of a foreign customer's remittance caused by a major foreign currency revaluation.

- A court-ordered increase in a completed long-term construction contract's price due to design changes.

Should these gains be included in continuing operations or reported as an extraordinary item in Peg's 1991 income statement?

	Gain from major currency revaluation	Gain from increase in contract's price
a.	Continuing operations	Continuing operations
b.	Extraordinary item	Continuing operations
c.	Extraordinary item	Extraordinary item
d.	Continuing operations	Extraordinary item

TN92#28. On January 1, 1991, Sip Co. signed a 5-year contract enabling it to use a patented manufacturing process beginning in 1991. A royalty is payable for each product produced, subject to a minimum annual fee. Any royalties in excess of the minimum will be paid annually. On the contract date, Sip prepaid a sum equal to two years' minimum annual fees. In 1991, only minimum fees were incurred. The royalty prepayment should be reported in Sip's December 31, 1991, financial statements as
- a. An expense only.
- b. A current asset and an expense.
- c. A current asset and noncurrent asset.
- d. A noncurrent asset.

1N92#42. Lance Corp.'s statement of cash flows for the year ended September 30, 1992, was prepared using the indirect method and included the following:

Net income	$60,000
Noncash adjustments:	
Depreciation expense	9,000
Increase in accounts receivable	(5,000)
Decrease in inventory	40,000
Decrease in accounts payable	(12,000)
Net cash flows from operating activities	$92,000

Lance reported revenues from customers of $75,000 in its 1992 income statement. What amount of cash did Lance receive from its customers during the year ended September 30, 1992?
- a. $80,000
- b. $70,000
- c. $65,000
- d. $55,000

1N92#43. Several of Fox, Inc.'s customers are having cash flow problems. Information pertaining to these customers for the years ended March 31, 1991 and 1992, follows:

	3/31/91	3/31/92
Sales	$10,000	$15,000
Cost of sales	8,000	9,000
Cash collections		
on 1991 sales	7,000	3,000
on 1992 sales	—	12,000

If the cost recovery method is used, what amount would Fox report as gross profit from sales to these customers for the year ended March 31, 1992?
 a. $ 2,000
 b. $ 3,000
 c. $ 5,000
 d. $15,000

1N92#44. Information pertaining to dividends from Wray Corp.'s common stock investments for the year ended December 31, 1991, follows:

- On September 8, 1991, Wray received a $50,000 cash dividend from Seco, Inc., in which Wray owns a 30% interest. A majority of Wray's directors are also directors of Seco.

- On October 15, 1991, Wray received a $6,000 liquidating dividend from King Co. Wray owns a 5% interest in King Co.

- Wray owns a 2% interest in Bow Corp., which declared a $200,000 cash dividend on November 27, 1991, to stockholders of record on December 15, 1991, payable on January 5, 1992.

What amount should Wray report as dividend income in its income statement for the year ended December 31, 1991?
 a. $60,000
 b. $56,000
 c. $10,000
 d. $ 4,000

1N92#45. Conn Corp. owns an office building and normally charges tenants $30 per square foot per year for office space. Because the occupancy rate is low, Conn agreed to lease 10,000 square feet to Hanson Co. at $12 per square foot for the first year of a three-year operating lease. Rent for remaining years will be at the $30 rate. Hanson moved into the building on January 1, 1992, and paid the first year's rent in advance. What amount of rental revenue should Conn report from Hanson in its income statement for the year ended September 30, 1992?
 a. $ 90,000
 b. $120,000
 c. $180,000
 d. $240,000

1N92#51. In 1986, Chain, Inc. purchased a $1,000,000 life insurance policy on its president, of which Chain is the beneficiary. Information regarding the policy for the year ended December 31, 1991, follows:

Cash surrender value, 1/1/91	$ 87,000
Cash surrender value, 12/31/91	108,000
Annual advance premium paid 1/1/91	40,000

During 1991, dividends of $6,000 were applied to increase the cash surrender value of the policy. What amount should Chain report as life insurance expense for 1991?
 a. $40,000
 b. $25,000
 c. $19,000
 d. $13,000

1N92#55. On January 2, 1991, Cole Co. signed an eight-year noncancelable lease for a new machine, requiring $15,000 annual payments at the beginning of each year. The machine has a useful life of 12 years, with no salvage value. Title passes to Cole at the lease expiration date. Cole uses straight-line depreciation for all of its plant assets. Aggregate lease payments have a present value on January 2, 1991, of $108,000, based on an appropriate rate of interest. For 1991, Cole should record depreciation (amortization) expense for the leased machine at
 a. $0
 b. $ 9,000
 c. $13,500
 d. $15,000

1N92#56. On December 1, 1991, Clark Co. leased office space for five years at a monthly rental of $60,000. On the same date, Clark paid the lessor the following amounts:

First month's rent	$ 60,000
Last month's rent	60,000
Security deposit (refundable at lease expiration)	80,000
Installation of new walls and offices	360,000

What should be Clark's 1991 expense relating to utilization of the office space?
 a. $ 60,000
 b. $ 66,000
 c. $120,000
 d. $140,000

2N92#53. During January 1992, Haze Corp. won a litigation award for $15,000 which was tripled to $45,000 to include punitive damages. The defendant, who is financially stable, has appealed only the $30,000 punitive damages. Haze was awarded $50,000 in an unrelated suit it filed, which is being appealed by the defendant. Counsel is unable to estimate the outcome of these appeals. In its 1992 financial statements, Haze should report what amount of pretax gain?
 a. $15,000
 b. $45,000
 c. $50,000
 d. $95,000

TM92#15. What factor must be present to use the units-of-production (activity) method of depreciation?
 a. Total units to be produced can be estimated.
 b. Production is constant over the life of the asset.
 c. Repair costs increase with use.
 d. Obsolescence is expected.

TM92#17. On January 1, 1991, Brecon Co. installed cabinets to display its merchandise in customers' stores. Brecon expects to use these cabinets for five years. Brecon's 1991 multi-step income statement should include

a. One-fifth of the cabinet costs in cost of goods sold.
b. One-fifth of the cabinet costs in selling, general, and administrative expenses.
c. All of the cabinet costs in cost of goods sold.
d. All of the cabinet costs in selling, general, and administrative expenses.

TM92#18. On October 1, 1991, Fleur Retailers signed a 4-month, 16% note payable to finance the purchase of holiday merchandise. At that date, there was no direct method of pricing the merchandise, and the note's market rate of interest was 11%. Fleur recorded the purchase at the note's face amount. All of the merchandise was sold by December 1, 1991. Fleur's 1991 financial statements reported interest payable and interest expense on the note for three months at 16%. All amounts due on the note were paid February 1, 1992.

Fleur's 1991 cost of goods sold for the holiday merchandise was

a. Overstated by the difference between the note's face amount and the note's October 1, 1991, present value.
b. Overstated by the difference between the note's face amount and the note's October 1, 1991, present value plus 11% interest for two months.
c. Understated by the difference between the note's face amount and the note's October 1, 1991, present value.
d. Understated by the difference between the note's face amount and the note's October 1, 1991, present value plus 16% interest for two months.

TM92#29. The effect of a transaction that is infrequent in occurrence but **not** unusual in nature should be presented separately as a component of income from continuing operations when the transaction results in a

	Loss	Gain
a.	Yes	Yes
b.	No	Yes
c.	No	No
d.	Yes	No

TM92#43. For the last 10 years, Woody Co. has owned cumulative preferred stock issued by Hadley, Inc. During 1991, Hadley declared and paid both the 1991 dividend and the 1990 dividend in arrears. How should Woody report the 1990 dividend in arrears that was received in 1991?

a. As a reduction in cumulative preferred dividends receivable.
b. As a retroactive change of the prior period financial statements.
c. Include, net of income taxes, after 1991 income from continuing operations.
d. Include in 1991 income from continuing operations.

TM92#44. A company uses the completed-contract method to account for a long-term construction contract. Revenue is recognized when recorded progress billings

	Are collected	Exceed recorded costs
a.	Yes	Yes
b.	No	No
c.	Yes	No
d.	No	Yes

TM92#45. Income recognized using the installment method of accounting generally equals cash collected multiplied by the

a. Net operating profit percentage.
b. Net operating profit percentage adjusted for expected uncollectible accounts.
c. Gross profit percentage.
d. Gross profit percentage adjusted for expected uncollectible accounts.

TM92#46. Under a royalty agreement with another enterprise, a company will receive royalties from the assignment of a patent for three years. The royalties received should be reported as revenue

a. At the date of the royalty agreement.
b. In the period earned.
c. In the period received.
d. Evenly over the life of the royalty agreement.

1M92#40. Sage, Inc. bought 40% of Adams Corp.'s outstanding common stock on January 2, 1991, for $400,000. The carrying amount of Adams' net assets at the purchase date totaled $900,000. Fair values and carrying amounts were the same for all items except for plant and inventory, for which fair values exceeded their carrying amounts by $90,000 and $10,000, respectively. The plant has an 18-year life. All inventory was sold during 1991. Goodwill, if any, is to be amortized over 40 years. During 1991, Adams reported net income of $120,000 and paid a $20,000 cash dividend. What amount should Sage report in its income statement from its investment in Adams for the year ended December 31, 1991?

a. $48,000
b. $42,000
c. $36,000
d. $32,000

1M92#41. Ace Co. sold to King Co. a $20,000, 8%, 5-year note that required five equal annual year-end payments. This note was discounted to yield a 9% rate to King. The present value factors of an ordinary annuity of $1 for five periods are as follows:

8%	3.992
9%	3.890

What should be the total interest revenue earned by King on this note?

a. $9,000
b. $8,000
c. $5,560
d. $5,050

1M92#43. Bort Co. purchased 2,000 shares of Crel Co. common stock on March 5, 1991, for $72,000. Bort received a $1,000 cash dividend on the Crel stock on July 15, 1991. Crel declared a 10% stock dividend on December 15, 1991, to stockholders of record as of December 31, 1991. The dividend was distributed on January 15, 1992. The market price of the stock was $38 on December 15, 1991, $40 on December 31, 1991, and $42 on January 15, 1992. What amount should Bort record as dividend revenue for the year ended December 31, 1991?
 a. $1,000
 b. $8,600
 c. $9,000
 d. $9,400

1M92#44. On January 1, 1991, Denver Corp. entered into a 4-year licensing agreement with Akins Co. allowing Akins to use Denver's cartoon characters on all the lunchboxes that Akins manufactures. Akins is required to pay Denver royalties equal to 10% of annual lunchbox sales. Akins guaranteed Denver a $120,000 minimum royalty over the life of the agreement and paid Denver the minimum amount on January 1, 1991. For the year ended December 31, 1991, Akins's lunchbox sales totaled $500,000. What amount of royalty income should Denver report in 1991?
 a. $ 30,000
 b. $ 50,000
 c. $ 80,000
 d. $120,000

1M92#45. On July 1, 1991, one of Rudd Co.'s delivery vans was destroyed in an accident. On that date, the van's carrying value was $2,500. On July 15, 1991, Rudd received and recorded a $700 invoice for a new engine installed in the van in May 1991, and another $500 invoice for various repairs. In August, Rudd received $3,500 under its insurance policy on the van, which it plans to use to replace the van. What amount should Rudd report as gain (loss) on disposal of the van in its 1991 income statement?
 a. $1,000
 b. $ 300
 c. $0
 d. $ (200)

1M92#46. Ocean Corp.'s comprehensive insurance policy allows its assets to be replaced at current value. The policy has a $50,000 deductible clause. One of Ocean's waterfront warehouses was destroyed in a winter storm. Such storms occur approximately every four years. Ocean incurred $20,000 of costs in dismantling the warehouse and plans to replace it. The following data relate to the warehouse:

Current carrying amount	$ 300,000
Replacement cost	1,100,000

What amount of gain should Ocean report as a separate component of income before extraordinary items?
 a. $1,030,000
 b. $ 780,000
 c. $ 730,000
 d. $0

1M92#47. The following balances were reported by Mall Co. at December 31, 1991 and 1990:

	12/31/91	12/31/90
Inventory	$260,000	$290,000
Accounts payable	75,000	50,000

Mall paid suppliers $490,000 during the year ended December 31, 1991. What amount should Mall report for cost of goods sold in 1991?
 a. $545,000
 b. $495,000
 c. $485,000
 d. $435,000

1M92#48. Pak Co.'s professional fees expense account had a balance of $82,000 at December 31, 1991, before considering year-end adjustments relating to the following:

- Consultants were hired for a special project at a total fee not to exceed $65,000. Pak has recorded $55,000 of this fee based on billings for work performed in 1991.

- The attorney's letter requested by the auditors dated January 28, 1992, indicated that legal fees of $6,000 were billed on January 15, 1992, for work performed in November 1991, and unbilled fees for December 1991 were $7,000.

What amount should Pak report for professional fees expense for the year ended December 31, 1991?
 a. $105,000
 b. $ 95,000
 c. $ 88,000
 d. $ 82,000

1M92#49. Hutch, Inc. uses the conventional retail inventory method to account for inventory. The following information relates to 1991 operations:

	Average	
	Cost	Retail
Beginning inventory and purchases	$600,000	$920,000
Net markups		40,000
Net markdowns		60,000
Sales		780,000

What amount should be reported as cost of sales for 1991?
 a. $480,000
 b. $487,500
 c. $520,000
 d. $525,000

1M92#50. South Co. purchased a machine that was installed and placed in service on January 1, 1990, at a cost of $240,000. Salvage value was estimated at $40,000. The machine is being depreciated over 10 years by the double-declining-balance method. For the year ended December 31, 1991, what amount should South report as depreciation expense?
  a. $48,000
  b. $38,400
  c. $32,000
  d. $21,600

1M92#54. Kent Co. incurred the following infrequent losses during 1991:

- A $300,000 loss was incurred on disposal of one of four dissimilar factories.

- A major currency devaluation caused a $120,000 exchange loss on an amount remitted by a foreign customer.

- Inventory valued at $190,000 was made worthless by a competitor's unexpected product innovation.

In its 1991 income statement, what amount should Kent report as losses that are **not** considered extraordinary?
  a. $610,000
  b. $490,000
  c. $420,000
  d. $310,000

TN91#5. During 1990, Tidal Co. began construction on a project scheduled for completion in 1992. At December 31, 1990, an overall loss was anticipated at contract completion. What would be the effect of the project on 1990 operating income under the percentage-of-completion method and the completed-contract method?

	Percentage-of-completion	Completed-contract
a.	No effect	No effect
b.	No effect	Decrease
c.	Decrease	No effect
d.	Decrease	Decrease

TN91#10. An investor uses the cost method to account for an investment in common stock. Dividends received this year exceeded the investor's share of investee's undistributed earnings since the date of investment. The amount of dividend revenue that should be reported in the investor's income statement for this year would be
  a. The portion of the dividends received this year that were in excess of the investor's share of investee's undistributed earnings since the date of investment.
  b. The portion of the dividends received this year that were **not** in excess of the investor's share of investee's undistributed earnings since the date of investment.
  c. The total amount of dividends received this year.
  d. Zero.

TN91#14. When the equity method is used to account for investments in common stock, which of the following affects the investor's reported investment income?

	Goodwill amortization related to purchase	Cash dividends from investee
a.	Yes	Yes
b.	No	Yes
c.	No	No
d.	Yes	No

TN91#20. Dee's inventory and accounts payable balances at December 31, 1990, increased over their December 31, 1989, balances. Should these increases be added to or deducted from cash payments to suppliers to arrive at 1990 cost of goods sold?

	Increase in inventory	Increase in accounts payable
a.	Added to	Deducted from
b.	Added to	Added to
c.	Deducted from	Deducted from
d.	Deducted from	Added to

1N91#31. On January 1, 1990, Dell, Inc. contracted with the city of Little to provide custom built desks for the city schools. The contract made Dell the city's sole supplier and required Dell to supply no less than 4,000 desks and no more than 5,500 desks per year for two years. In turn, Little agreed to pay a fixed price of $110 per desk. During 1990, Dell produced 5,000 desks for Little. At December 31, 1990, 500 of these desks were segregated from the regular inventory and were accepted and awaiting pickup by Little. Little paid Dell $450,000 during 1990. What amount should Dell recognize as contract revenue in 1990?
  a. $450,000
  b. $495,000
  c. $550,000
  d. $605,000

1N91#42. Cap Corp. reported accrued investment interest receivable of $38,000 and $46,500 at January 1 and December 31, 1990, respectively. During 1990, cash collections from the investments included the following:

Capital gains distributions	$145,000
Interest	152,000

What amount should Cap report as interest revenue from investments for 1990?
  a. $160,500
  b. $153,500
  c. $152,000
  d. $143,500

Selected Questions

1N91#44. In 1990, Neil Co. held the following investments in common stock:

- 25,000 shares of B & K, Inc.'s 100,000 outstanding shares. Neil's level of ownership gives it the ability to exercise significant influence over the financial and operating policies of B & K.

- 6,000 shares of Amal Corp.'s 309,000 outstanding shares.

During 1990, Neil received the following distributions from its common stock investments:

November 6 — $30,000 cash dividend from B & K.

November 11 — $1,500 cash dividend from Amal.

December 26 — 3% common stock dividend from Amal. The closing price of this stock on a national exchange was $15 per share.

What amount of dividend revenue should Neil report for 1990?
- a. $ 1,500
- b. $ 4,200
- c. $31,500
- d. $34,200

1N91#54. Loeb Corp. frequently borrows from the bank in order to maintain sufficient operating cash. The following loans were at a 12% interest rate, with interest payable at maturity. Loeb repaid each loan on its scheduled maturity date.

Date of loan	Amount	Maturity date	Term of loan
11/1/89	$ 5,000	10/31/90	1 Year
2/1/90	15,000	7/31/90	6 Months
5/1/90	8,000	1/31/91	9 Months

Loeb records interest expense when the loans are repaid. As a result, interest expense of $1,500 was recorded in 1990. If no correction is made, by what amount would 1990 interest expense be understated?
- a. $540
- b. $620
- c. $640
- d. $720

1N91#57. E & S partnership purchased land for $500,000 on May 1, 1987, paying $100,000 cash and giving a $400,000 note payable to Big State Bank. E & S made three annual payments on the note totaling $179,000, which included interest of $89,000. E & S then defaulted on the note. Title to the land was transferred by E & S to Big State, which cancelled the note, releasing the partnership from further liability. At the time of the default, the fair value of the land approximated the note balance. In E & S's 1990 income statement, the amount of the loss should be

- a. $279,000
- b. $221,000
- c. $190,000
- d. $100,000

1N91#58. On August 1, 1990, Metro, Inc. leased a luxury apartment unit to Klum. The parties signed a 1-year lease beginning September 1, 1990, for a $1,000 monthly rent payable on the first day of the month. At the August 1 signing date, Metro collected $540 as a nonrefundable fee for allowing Klum to sign a 1-year lease (the normal lease term is three years) and $1,000 rent for September. Klum has made timely payments each month, but prepaid January's rent on December 20. In Metro's 1990 income statement, rent revenue should be reported as
- a. $4,000
- b. $4,180
- c. $4,540
- d. $5,180

TM91#8. Drew Co. produces expensive equipment for sale on installment contracts. When there is doubt about eventual collectibility, the income recognition method **least** likely to overstate income is
- a. At the time the equipment is completed.
- b. The installment method.
- c. The cost recovery method.
- d. At the time of delivery.

TM91#9. Bee Co. uses the direct write-off method to account for uncollectible accounts receivable. During an accounting period, Bee's cash collections from customers equal sales adjusted for the addition or deduction of the following amounts:

	Accounts written-off	Increase in accounts receivable balance
a.	Deduction	Deduction
b.	Addition	Deduction
c.	Deduction	Addition
d.	Addition	Addition

TM91#25. A transaction that is unusual, but **not** infrequent, should be reported separately as a(an)
- a. Extraordinary item, net of applicable income taxes.
- b. Extraordinary item, but **not** net of applicable income taxes.
- c. Component of income from continuing operations, net of applicable income taxes.
- d. Component of income from continuing operations, but **not** net of applicable income taxes.

TM91#28. Tay Co. uses the percentage-of-completion method to account for a five-year construction contract. Third year progress billings collected in the fourth year would
- a. Be included in the calculation of third year income.
- b. Be included in the calculation of third year income insofar as they exceeded second year billings collected in the third year.

c. Be included in the calculation of fourth year income.
d. Not be included in the calculation of third, fourth, or fifth year incomes.

1M91#48. Marr Corp. reported rental revenue of $2,210,000 in its cash basis federal income tax return for the year ended November 30, 1990. Additional information is as follows:

Rents receivable — November 30, 1990	$1,060,000
Rents receivable — November 30, 1989	800,000
Uncollectible rents written off during the fiscal year	30,000

Under the accrual basis, Marr should report rental revenue of
a. $1,920,000
b. $1,980,000
c. $2,440,000
d. $2,500,000

1M91#49. Barr Corp. started a long-term construction project in 1990. The following data relate to this project:

Contract price	$4,200,000
Costs incurred in 1990	1,750,000
Estimated costs to complete	1,750,000
Progress billings	900,000
Collections on progress billings	800,000

The project is accounted for by the percentage of completion method of accounting. In Barr's 1990 income statement, what amount of gross profit should be reported for this project?
a. $350,000
b. $150,000
c. $133,333
d. $100,000

1M91#50. The following information pertains to a sale of real estate by Ryan Co. to Sud Co. on December 31, 1989:

Carrying amount		$2,000,000
Sales price:		
Cash	$ 300,000	
Purchase money mortgage	2,700,000	3,000,000

The mortgage is payable in nine annual installments of $300,000 beginning December 31, 1990, plus interest of 10%. The December 31, 1990, installment was paid as scheduled, together with interest of $270,000. Ryan uses the cost recovery method to account for the sale. What amount of income should Ryan recognize in 1990 from the real estate sale and its financing?
a. $570,000
b. $370,000
c. $270,000
d. $0

1M91#52. Huff Co. acquired 30% of the voting common stock of Flax, Inc. on January 1, 1990, for $100,000. Huff has the ability to exercise significant influence over operating and financial policies of Flax. During 1990, Flax earned $40,000 and paid dividends of $25,000. Before income taxes, Huff should include what amount in its 1990 income statement pertaining to this investment?
a. $40,000
b. $25,000
c. $12,000
d. $ 7,500

1M91#53. Tara Co. owns an office building and leases the offices under a variety of rental agreements involving rent paid in advance monthly or annually. Not all tenants make timely payments of their rent. Tara's balance sheets contained the following data:

	1989	1990
Rentals receivable	$ 9,600	$12,400
Unearned rentals	32,000	24,000

During 1990, Tara received $80,000 cash from tenants. What amount of rental revenue should Tara record for 1990?
a. $90,800
b. $85,200
c. $74,800
d. $69,200

1M91#54. At December 31, 1990, Ashe Co. had a $990,000 balance in its advertising expense account before any year-end adjustments relating to the following:

- Radio advertising spots broadcast during December 1990 were billed to Ashe on January 4, 1991. The invoice cost of $50,000 was paid on January 15, 1991.

- Included in the $990,000 is $60,000 for newspaper advertising for a January 1991 sales promotional campaign.

Ashe's advertising expense for the year ended December 31, 1990, should be
a. $ 930,000
b. $ 980,000
c. $1,000,000
d. $1,040,000

1M91#56. Based on 1990 sales of compact discs recorded by an artist under a contract with Bain Co., the artist earned $100,000 after an adjustment of $8,000 for anticipated returns. In addition, Bain paid the artist $75,000 in 1990 as a reasonable estimate of the amount recoverable from future royalties to be earned by the artist. What amount should Bain report in its 1990 income statement for royalty expense?
a. $100,000
b. $108,000
c. $175,000
d. $183,000

1M91#57. On December 1, 1990, Tell Co. leased office space for five years at a monthly rental of $60,000. On the same date, Tell paid the lessor the following amounts:

First month's rent	$ 60,000
Last month's rent	60,000
Security deposit (refundable at lease expiration)	80,000
Installation of new walls and offices	360,000

Tell's 1990 expense relating to utilization of the office space should be
- a. $140,000
- b. $120,000
- c. $ 66,000
- d. $ 60,000

TN90#14. The graph below depicts three depreciation expense patterns over time.

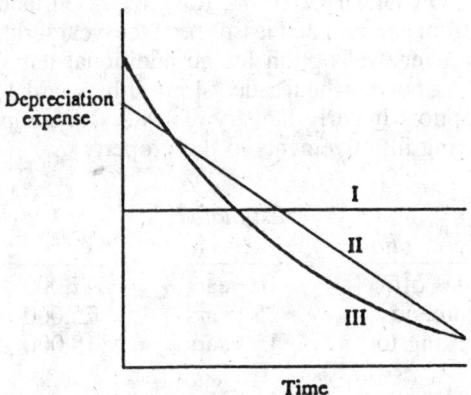

Which depreciation expense pattern corresponds to the sum-of-the-years'-digits method and which corresponds to the double-declining-balance method?

	Sum-of-the-years'-digits	Double-declining-balance
a.	III	II
b.	II	I
c.	I	III
d.	II	III

TN90#19. Under the allowance method of recognizing uncollectible accounts, the entry to write off an uncollectible account
- a. Increases the allowance for uncollectible accounts.
- b. Has **no** effect on the allowance for uncollectible accounts.
- c. Has **no** effect on net income.
- d. Decreases net income.

TN90#37. Gown, Inc. sold a warehouse and used the proceeds to acquire a new warehouse. The excess of the proceeds over the carrying amount of the warehouse sold should be reported as a(an)

- a. Extraordinary gain, net of income taxes.
- b. Part of continuing operations.
- c. Gain from discontinued operations, net of income taxes.
- d. Reduction of the cost of the new warehouse.

1N90#32. In November and December 1989, Dorr Co., a newly organized magazine publisher, received $72,000 for 1,000 three-year subscriptions at $24 per year, starting with the January 1990 issue. Dorr elected to include the entire $72,000 in its 1989 income tax return. What amount should Dorr report in its 1989 income statement for subscriptions revenue?
- a. $0
- b. $ 4,000
- c. $24,000
- d. $72,000

1N90#35. On January 1, 1988, Mill Co. exchanged equipment for a $200,000 noninterest bearing note due on January 1, 1991. The prevailing rate of interest for a note of this type at January 1, 1988 was 10%. The present value of $1 at 10% for three periods is 0.75. What amount of interest revenue should be included in Mill's 1989 income statement?
- a. $0
- b. $15,000
- c. $16,500
- d. $20,000

1N90#36. Day Co. received dividends from its common stock investments during the year ended December 31, 1989 as follows:

- A stock dividend of 400 shares from Parr Corp. on July 25, 1989 when the market price of Parr's shares was $20 per share. Day owns less than 1% of Parr's common stock.

- A cash dividend of $15,000 from Lark Corp. in which Day owns a 25% interest. A majority of Lark's directors are also directors of Day.

What amount of dividend revenue should Day report in its 1989 income statement?
- a. $23,000
- b. $15,000
- c. $ 8,000
- d. $0

1N90#37. On January 1, 1989, Wren Co. leased a building to Brill under an operating lease for ten years at $50,000 per year, payable the first day of each lease year. Wren paid $15,000 to a real estate broker as a finder's fee. The building is depreciated $12,000 per year. For 1989, Wren incurred insurance and property tax expense totaling $9,000. Wren's net rental income for 1989 should be
- a. $27,500
- b. $29,000
- c. $35,000
- d. $36,500

1N90#39. Adam Corp. had the following infrequent transactions during 1989:

- A $190,000 gain on reacquisition and retirement of bonds.

- A $260,000 gain on the disposal of a segment of a business. Adam continues similar operations at another location.

- A $90,000 loss on the abandonment of equipment.

In its 1989 income statement, what amount should Adam report as total infrequent net gains that are **not** considered extraordinary?
    a. $100,000
    b. $170,000
    c. $360,000
    d. $450,000

1N90#40. Brock Corp. reports operating expenses in two categories: (1) selling and (2) general and administrative. The adjusted trial balance at December 31, 1989 included the following expense and loss accounts:

Accounting and legal fees	$120,000
Advertising	150,000
Freight out	80,000
Interest	70,000
Loss on sale of long-term investment	30,000
Officers' salaries	225,000
Rent for office space	220,000
Sales salaries and commissions	140,000

One-half of the rented premises is occupied by the sales department.

Brock's total selling expenses for 1989 are
    a. $480,000
    b. $400,000
    c. $370,000
    d. $360,000

1N90#45. Orr Co. prepared an aging of its accounts receivable at December 31, 1989 and determined that the net realizable value of the receivables was $250,000. Additional information is available as follows:

Allowance for uncollectible accounts at 1/1/89 — credit balance	$28,000
Accounts written off as uncollectible during 1989	23,000
Accounts receivable at 12/31/89	270,000
Uncollectible accounts recovery during 1989	5,000

For the year ended December 31, 1989, Orr's uncollectible accounts expense would be
    a. $23,000
    b. $20,000
    c. $15,000
    d. $10,000

1N90#47. Strand, Inc. incurred the following infrequent losses during 1989:

- A $90,000 write-down of equipment leased to others.

- $50,000 adjustment of accruals on long-term contracts.

- A $75,000 write-off of obsolete inventory.

In its 1989 income statement, what amount should Strand report as total infrequent losses that are **not** considered extraordinary?
    a. $215,000
    b. $165,000
    c. $140,000
    d. $125,000

2N90#2. On January 2, 1988, Ral Co. leased land and building from an unrelated lessor for a ten-year term. The lease has a renewal option for an additional ten years, but Ral has not reached a decision with regard to the renewal option. In early January of 1988, Ral completed the following improvements to the property:

Description	Estimated life	Cost
Sales office	10 years	$47,000
Warehouse	25 years	75,000
Parking lot	15 years	18,000

Amortization of leasehold improvements for 1989 should be
    a. $ 7,000
    b. $ 8,900
    c. $12,200
    d. $14,000

2N90#6. Amar Farms produced 300,000 pounds of cotton during the 1989 season. Amar sells all of its cotton to Brye Co., which has agreed to purchase Amar's entire production at the prevailing market price. Recent legislation assures that the market price will not fall below $.70 per pound during the next two years. Amar's costs of selling and distributing the cotton are immaterial and can be reasonably estimated. Amar reports its inventory at expected exit value. During 1989, Amar sold and delivered to Brye 200,000 pounds at the market price of $.70. Amar sold the remaining 100,000 pounds during 1990 at the market price of $.72. What amount of revenue should Amar recognize in 1989?
    a. $140,000
    b. $144,000
    c. $210,000
    d. $216,000

2N90#8. The following information was derived from the 1989 accounting records of Clem Co.:

Selected Questions

	Clem's central warehouse	Clem's goods held by consignees
Beginning inventory	$110,000	$12,000
Purchases	480,000	60,000
Freight in	10,000	
Transportation to consignees		5,000
Freight out	30,000	8,000
Ending inventory	145,000	20,000

Clem's 1989 cost of sales was
- a. $455,000
- b. $485,000
- c. $507,000
- d. $512,000

2N90#10. The following items were among those that were reported on Lee Co.'s income statement for the year ended December 31, 1989:

Legal and audit fees	$170,000
Rent for office space	240,000
Interest on inventory floorplan	210,000
Loss on abandoned data processing equipment used in operations	35,000

The office space is used equally by Lee's sales and accounting departments. What amount of the above-listed items should be classified as general and administrative expenses in Lee's multiple-step income statement?
- a. $290,000
- b. $325,000
- c. $410,000
- d. $500,000

2N90#12. Zahn Corp.'s comparative balance sheet at December 31, 1989 and 1988 reported accumulated depreciation balances of $800,000 and $600,000, respectively. Property with a cost of $50,000 and a carrying amount of $40,000 was the only property sold in 1989. Depreciation charged to operations in 1989 was
- a. $190,000
- b. $200,000
- c. $210,000
- d. $220,000

2N90#15. Gow Constructors, Inc. has consistently used the percentage-of-completion method of recognizing income. In 1989, Gow started work on an $18,000,000 construction contract that was completed in 1990. The following information was taken from Gow's 1989 accounting records:

Progress billings	$6,600,000
Costs incurred	5,400,000
Collections	4,200,000
Estimated costs to complete	10,800,000

What amount of gross profit should Gow have recognized in 1989 on this contract?
- a. $1,400,000
- b. $1,200,000
- c. $ 900,000
- d. $ 600,000

2N90#20. During 1989, property owned by Arp Co. was acquired by the city in connection with a condemnation proceeding, resulting in a payment of $100,000 to Arp. The property's carrying amount was $70,000. Arp paid $45,000 in 1989 for replacement property. In Arp's income statement for the year ended December 31, 1989, what amount of gain should be reported on this involuntary conversion, disregarding income tax considerations?
- a. $0
- b. $15,000
- c. $25,000
- d. $30,000

TM90#20. A fixed asset with a five-year estimated useful life and no residual value is sold at the end of the second year of its useful life. How would using the sum-of-the-years'-digits method of depreciation instead of the double declining balance method of depreciation affect a gain or loss on the sale of the fixed asset?

	Gain	Loss
a.	Decrease	Decrease
b.	Decrease	Increase
c.	Increase	Decrease
d.	Increase	Increase

TM90#21. Net income is understated if, in the first year, estimated salvage value is excluded from the depreciation computation when using the

	Straight-line method	Production or use method
a.	Yes	No
b.	Yes	Yes
c.	No	No
d.	No	Yes

TM90#34. Advertising costs may be accrued or deferred to provide an appropriate expense in each period for

	Interim financial reporting	Year-end financial reporting
a.	Yes	No
b.	Yes	Yes
c.	No	No
d.	No	Yes

TM90#39. ABC Co. was organized on July 15, 1987, and earned no significant revenues until the first quarter of 1990. During the period 1987–89, ABC acquired plant and equipment, raised capital, obtained financing, trained employees, and developed markets. In its financial statements as of December 31, 1989, ABC should defer all costs incurred during 1987–89,
- a. Net of revenues earned, which are recoverable in future periods.

FA-81

b. Net of revenues earned.
c. Which are recoverable in future periods.
d. Without regard to net revenues earned or recoverability in future periods.

1M90#44. On October 20, 1989, Grimm Co. consigned 40 freezers to Holden Co. for sale at $1,000 each and paid $800 in transportation costs. On December 30, 1989, Holden reported the sale of 10 freezers and remitted $8,500. The remittance was net of the agreed 15% commission. What amount should Grimm recognize as consignment sales revenue for 1989?
a. $ 7,700
b. $ 8,500
c. $ 9,800
d. $10,000

1M90#45. On December 31, 1988, Mill Co. sold construction equipment to Drew, Inc. for $1,800,000. The equipment had a carrying amount of $1,200,000. Drew paid $300,000 cash on December 31, 1988 and signed a $1,500,000 note bearing interest at 10%, payable in five annual installments of $300,000. Mill appropriately accounts for the sale under the installment method. On December 31, 1989, Drew paid $300,000 principal and $150,000 interest. For the year ended December 31, 1989, what total amount of revenue should Mill recognize from the construction equipment sale and financing?
a. $250,000
b. $150,000
c. $120,000
d. $100,000

1M90#46. On July 1, 1989, Pell Co. purchased Green Corp. ten-year, 8% bonds with a face amount of $500,000 for $420,000. The bonds mature on June 30, 1997 and pay interest semiannually on June 30 and December 31. Using the interest method, Pell recorded bond discount amortization of $1,800 for the six months ended December 31, 1989. From this long-term investment, Pell should report 1989 revenue of
a. $16,800
b. $18,200
c. $20,000
d. $21,800

1M90#47. Simpson Co. received dividends from its common stock investments during the year ended December 31, 1989 as follows:

- A cash dividend of $8,000 from Wren Corp., in which Simpson owns a 2% interest.
- A cash dividend of $45,000 from Brill Corp., in which Simpson owns a 30% interest. This investment is appropriately accounted for using the equity method.
- A stock dividend of 500 shares from Paul Corp. was received on December 15, 1989, when the quoted market value of Paul's shares was $10 per share. Simpson owns less than 1% of Paul's common stock.

In Simpson's 1989 income statement, dividend revenue should be

a. $58,000
b. $53,000
c. $13,000
d. $ 8,000

1M90#48. Rapp Co. leased a new machine to Lake Co. on January 1, 1989. The lease expires on January 1, 1994. The annual rental is $90,000. Additionally, on January 1, 1989, Lake paid $50,000 to Rapp as a lease bonus and $25,000 as a security deposit to be refunded upon expiration of the lease. In Rapp's 1989 income statement, the amount of rental revenue should be
a. $140,000
b. $125,000
c. $100,000
d. $ 90,000

1M90#49. The following information was taken from Cody Co.'s accounting records for the year ended December 31, 1989:

Decrease in raw materials inventory	$ 15,000
Increase in finished goods inventory	35,000
Raw materials purchased	430,000
Direct labor payroll	200,000
Factory overhead	300,000
Freight-out	45,000

There was no work-in-process inventory at the beginning or end of the year. Cody's 1989 cost of goods sold is
a. $895,000
b. $910,000
c. $950,000
d. $955,000

1M90#54. For the year ended December 31, 1989, Beal Co. estimated its allowance for uncollectible accounts using the year-end aging of accounts receivable. The following data are available:

Allowance for uncollectible accounts, 1/1/89	$42,000
Provision for uncollectible accounts during 1989 (2% on credit sales of $2,000,000)	40,000
Uncollectible accounts written off, 11/30/89	46,000
Estimated uncollectible accounts per aging, 12/31/89	52,000

After year-end adjustment, the uncollectible accounts expense for 1989 should be
a. $46,000
b. $48,000
c. $52,000
d. $56,000

1M90#56. On January 1, 1989, Park Co. signed a 10-year operating lease for office space at $96,000 per year. The lease included a provision for additional rent of 5% of annual company sales in excess of $500,000. Park's sales for the year ended December 31, 1989 were $600,000. Upon execution of the lease, Park paid $24,000 as a bonus for the lease. Park's rent expense for the year ended December 31, 1989 is

a. $98,400
b. $101,000
c. $103,400
d. $125,000

1M90#57. During 1988, Wall Co. purchased 2,000 shares of Hemp Corp. common stock for $31,500 as a short-term investment. The market value of this investment was $29,500 at December 31, 1988. Wall sold all of the Hemp common stock for $14 per share on December 15, 1989, incurring $1,400 in brokerage commissions and taxes. On the sale, Wall should report a realized loss of

a. $4,900
b. $3,500
c. $2,900
d. $1,500

1M90#58. Witt Co. incurred the following infrequent losses during 1989:

- $175,000 from a major strike by employees.
- $150,000 from an early extinguishment of debt.
- $125,000 from the abandonment of equipment used in the business.

In Witt's 1989 income statement, the total amount of infrequent losses **not** considered extraordinary should be

a. $275,000
b. $300,000
c. $325,000
d. $450,000

2M90#41. During 1988, Mitchell Corp. started a construction job with a total contract price of $600,000. The job was completed on December 15, 1989. Additional data are as follows:

	1988	1989
Actual costs incurred	$225,000	$255,000
Estimated remaining costs	225,000	—
Billed to customer	240,000	360,000
Received from customer	200,000	400,000

Under the completed contract method, what amount should Mitchell recognize as gross profit for 1989?

a. $45,000
b. $72,000
c. $80,000
d. $120,000

2M90#45. Bolte Corp. had the following infrequent gains during 1989:

- $210,000 on reacquisition and retirement of bonds.
- $75,000 on repayment at maturity of a long-term note denominated in a foreign currency.
- $240,000 on sale of a plant facility (Bolte continues similar operations at another location.)

In its 1989 income statement, what amount should Bolte report as total infrequent gains which are **not** considered extraordinary?

a. $450,000
b. $315,000
c. $285,000
d. $240,000

2M90#46. Doren Co.'s officers' compensation expense account had a balance of $490,000 at December 31, 1989 before any appropriate year-end adjustment relating to the following:

- No salary accrual was made for the week of December 25–31, 1989. Officers' salaries for this period totaled $18,000 and were paid on January 5, 1990.
- Bonuses to officers for 1989 were paid on January 31, 1990 in the total amount of $175,000.

The adjusted balance for officers' compensation expense for the year ended December 31, 1989 should be

a. $683,000
b. $665,000
c. $508,000
d. $490,000

2M90#48. Casey Co.'s adjusted trial balance at December 31, 1989 included the following expense accounts:

Advertising	$250,000
Freight-out	75,000
Rent for office space	180,000
Sales salaries and commissions	200,000

One-half of the office space is occupied by the sales department.

What total amount of the expenses listed above should be included in Casey's selling and delivery expenses for 1989?

a. $450,000
b. $525,000
c. $540,000
d. $615,000

2M90#49. On January 1, 1988, Layton Co. acquired the copyright to a book owned by Garner for royalties of 15% of future book sales. Royalties are payable on September 30 for sales in January through June of the same year, and on March 31 for sales in July through December of the preceding year. During 1988 and 1989, Layton remitted royalty checks to Garner as follows:

	March 31	September 30
1988	$ —	$25,000
1989	22,000	40,000

Layton's sales of the Garner book totaled $300,000 for the last half of 1989. In its 1989 income statement, Layton should report royalty expense of

a. $85,000
b. $67,000
c. $62,000
d. $45,000

2M90#55. The following data pertain to Ruhl Corp.'s operations for the year ended December 31, 1989:

Operating income	$800,000
Interest expense	100,000
Income before income tax	700,000
Income tax expense	210,000
Net income	$490,000

The times interest earned ratio is

a. 8.0 to 1
b. 7.0 to 1
c. 5.6 to 1
d. 4.9 to 1

2M90#57. Mill Construction Co. uses the percentage-of-completion method of accounting. During 1989, Mill contracted to build an apartment complex for Drew for $20,000,000. Mill estimated that total costs would amount to $16,000,000 over the period of construction. In connection with this contract, Mill incurred $2,000,000 of construction costs during 1989. Mill billed and collected $3,000,000 from Drew in 1989. What amount should Mill recognize as gross profit for 1989?
a. $250,000
b. $375,000
c. $500,000
d. $600,000

III. Recognition, Measurement, Valuation, and Presentation of Specific Types of Transactions and Events in Financial Statements in Conformity With Generally Accepted Accounting Principles

A. Accounting Changes and Corrections of Errors

R97#4. How should the effect of a change in accounting principle that is inseparable from the effect of a change in accounting estimate be reported?
 a. As a component of income from continuing operations.
 b. By restating the financial statements of all prior periods presented.
 c. As a correction of an error.
 d. By footnote disclosure only.

N95#44. Oak Co. offers a three-year warranty on its products. Oak previously estimated warranty costs to be 2% of sales. Due to a technological advance in production at the beginning of 1994, Oak now believes 1% of sales to be a better estimate of warranty costs. Warranty costs of $80,000 and $96,000 were reported in 1992 and 1993, respectively. Sales for 1994 were $5,000,000. What amount should be disclosed in Oak's 1994 financial statements as warranty expense?
 a. $ 50,000
 b. $ 88,000
 c. $100,000
 d. $138,000

M95
Items **45** and **46** are based on the following:

During 1994, Orca Corp. decided to change from the FIFO method of inventory valuation to the weighted-average method. Inventory balances under each method were as follows:

	FIFO	Weighted-average
January 1, 1994	$71,000	$77,000
December 31, 1994	79,000	83,000

Orca's income tax rate is 30%.

45. In its 1994 financial statements, what amount should Orca report as the cumulative effect of this accounting change?
 a. $2,800
 b. $4,000
 c. $4,200
 d. $6,000

46. Orca should report the cumulative effect of this accounting change as a(an)
 a. Prior period adjustment.
 b. Component of income from continuing operations.
 c. Extraordinary item.
 d. Component of income after extraordinary items.

N94#54. How should the effect of a change in accounting estimate be accounted for?
 a. By restating amounts reported in financial statements of prior periods.
 b. By reporting pro forma amounts for prior periods.
 c. As a prior period adjustment to beginning retained earnings.
 d. In the period of change and future periods if the change affects both.

N94#55. Foy Corp. failed to accrue warranty costs of $50,000 in its December 31, 1992, financial statements. In addition, a change from straight-line to accelerated depreciation made at the beginning of 1993 resulted in a cumulative effect of $30,000 on Foy's retained earnings. Both the $50,000 and the $30,000 are net of related income taxes. What amount should Foy report as prior period adjustments in 1993?

a. $0
b. $30,000
c. $50,000
d. $80,000

TN93#22. The correction of an error in the financial statements of a prior period should be reported, net of applicable income taxes, in the current
a. Retained earnings statement after net income but before dividends.
b. Retained earnings statement as an adjustment of the opening balance.
c. Income statement after income from continuing operations and before extraordinary items.
d. Income statement after income from continuing operations and after extraordinary items.

TN93#23. For 1991, Pac Co. estimated its two-year equipment warranty costs based on $100 per unit sold in 1991. Experience during 1992 indicated that the estimate should have been based on $110 per unit. The effect of this $10 difference from the estimate is reported
a. In 1992 income from continuing operations.
b. As an accounting change, net of tax, below 1992 income from continuing operations.
c. As an accounting change requiring 1991 financial statements to be restated.
d. As a correction of an error requiring 1991 financial statements to be restated.

TN93#26. The cumulative effect of a change in accounting principle should be recorded separately as a component of income after continuing operations, when the change is from the
a. Cash basis of accounting for vacation pay to the accrual basis.
b. Straight-line method of depreciation for previously recorded assets to the double declining balance method.
c. Presentation of statements of individual companies to their inclusion in consolidated statements.
d. Completed-contract method of accounting for long-term construction-type contracts to the percentage-of-completion method.

1N93#4. On January 2, 1992, to better reflect the variable use of its only machine, Holly, Inc. elected to change its method of depreciation from the straight-line method to the units of production method. The original cost of the machine on January 2, 1990, was $50,000, and its estimated life was 10 years. Holly estimates that the machine's total life is 50,000 machine hours.

Machine hours usage was 8,500 during 1991 and 3,500 during 1990.

Holly's income tax rate is 30%. Holly should report the accounting change in its 1992 financial statements as a(an)
a. Cumulative effect of a change in accounting principle of $2,000 in its income statement.
b. Adjustment to beginning retained earnings of $2,000.
c. Cumulative effect of a change in accounting principle of $1,400 in its income statement.
d. Adjustment to beginning retained earnings of $1,400.

1N93#60. On January 2, 1989, Union Co. purchased a machine for $264,000 and depreciated it by the straight-line method using an estimated useful life of eight years with no salvage value. On January 2, 1992, Union determined that the machine had a useful life of six years from the date of acquisition and will have a salvage value of $24,000. An accounting change was made in 1992 to reflect the additional data. The accumulated depreciation for this machine should have a balance at December 31, 1992, of
a. $176,000
b. $160,000
c. $154,000
d. $146,000

TM93#19. During 1992, Krey Co. increased the estimated quantity of copper recoverable from its mine. Krey uses the units of production depletion method. As a result of the change, which of the following should be reported in Krey's 1992 financial statements?

	Cumulative effect of a change in accounting principle	Pro forma effects of retroactive application of new depletion base
a.	Yes	Yes
b.	Yes	No
c.	No	No
d.	No	Yes

TM93#20. On August 31, 1992, Harvey Co. decided to change from the FIFO periodic inventory system to the weighted average periodic inventory system. Harvey is on a calendar year basis. The cumulative effect of the change is determined
a. As of January 1, 1992.
b. As of August 31, 1992.
c. During the eight months ending August 31, 1992, by a weighted average of the purchases.
d. During 1992 by a weighted average of the purchases.

1M93#53. On January 1, 1990, Warren Co. purchased a $600,000 machine, with a five-year useful life and no salvage value. The machine was depreciated by an accelerated method for book and tax purposes. The machine's carrying amount was $240,000 on December 31, 1991. On January 1, 1992, Warren changed retroactively to the straight-line method for financial statement purposes. Warren can justify the change. Warren's income tax rate is 30%. In its 1992 income statement, what amount should Warren report as the cumulative effect of this change?

a. $120,000
b. $ 84,000
c. $ 36,000
d. $0

1N92#60. Milton Co. began operations on January 1, 1989. On January 1, 1991, Milton changed its inventory method from LIFO to FIFO for both financial and income tax reporting. If FIFO had been used in prior years, Milton's inventories would have been higher by $60,000 and $40,000 at December 31, 1991 and 1990, respectively. Milton has a 30% income tax rate. What amount should Milton report as the cumulative effect of this accounting change in its income statement for the year ended December 31, 1991?
    a. $0
    b. $14,000
    c. $28,000
    d. $42,000

2N92#46. On January 2, 1991, Air, Inc. agreed to pay its former president $300,000 under a deferred compensation arrangement. Air should have recorded this expense in 1990 but did not do so. Air's reported income tax expense would have been $70,000 lower in 1990 had it properly accrued this deferred compensation. In its December 31, 1991, financial statements, Air should adjust the beginning balance of its retained earnings by a
    a. $230,000 credit.
    b. $230,000 debit.
    c. $300,000 credit.
    d. $370,000 debit.

2M92#2. While preparing its 1991 financial statements, Dek Corp. discovered computational errors in its 1990 and 1989 depreciation expenses. These errors resulted in overstatement of each year's income by $25,000, net of income taxes. The following amounts were reported in the previously issued financial statements:

	1990	1989
Retained earnings, 1/1	$700,000	$500,000
Net income	150,000	200,000
Retained earnings, 12/31	$850,000	$700,000

Dek's 1991 net income is correctly reported at $180,000. Which of the following amounts should be reported as prior period adjustments and net income in Dek's 1991 and 1990 comparative financial statements?

	Year	Prior period adjustment	Net income
a.	1990	—	$150,000
	1991	($50,000)	180,000
b.	1990	($50,000)	$150,000
	1991	—	180,000
c.	1990	($25,000)	$125,000
	1991	—	180,000
d.	1990	—	$125,000
	1991	—	180,000

TN91#25. In single period statements, which of the following should be reflected as an adjustment to the opening balance of retained earnings?
    a. Effect of a failure to provide for uncollectible accounts in the previous period.
    b. Effect of a decrease in the estimated useful life of depreciable equipment.
    c. Cumulative effect of a change of income recognition from the installment sale method to recognition at point of sale.
    d. Cumulative effect of a change from an accelerated method to straight-line depreciation.

TN91#26. In 1990, Brighton Co. changed from the individual item approach to the aggregate approach in applying the lower of FIFO cost or market to inventories. The cumulative effect of this change should be reported in Brighton's financial statements as a
    a. Prior period adjustment, with separate disclosure.
    b. Component of income from continuing operations, with separate disclosure.
    c. Component of income from continuing operations, without separate disclosure.
    d. Component of income after continuing operations, with separate disclosure.

2N91#2. During 1990, Dale Corp. made the following accounting changes:

Method used in 1989	Method used in 1990	After-tax effect
Sum-of-the-years' digits depreciation	Straight-line depreciation	$30,000
Weighted-average for inventory valuation	First-in, first-out for inventory valuation	98,000

What amount should be classified in 1990 as prior period adjustments?
    a. $0
    b. $ 30,000
    c. $ 98,000
    d. $128,000

TM91#27. When a company changes the expected service life of an asset because additional information has been obtained, which of the following should be reported?

	Pro forma effects of retroactive application	Cumulative effect of a change in accounting principle
a.	Yes	Yes
b.	No	Yes
c.	Yes	No
d.	No	No

TM91#34. Is the cumulative effect of an inventory pricing change on prior years earnings reported separately between extraordinary items and net income for a change from

	LIFO to weighted average?	FIFO to weighted average?
a.	Yes	Yes
b.	Yes	No
c.	No	No
d.	No	Yes

1M91#59. On December 31, 1990, Rapp Co. changed inventory cost methods to FIFO from LIFO for financial statement and income tax purposes. The change will result in a $175,000 increase in the beginning inventory at January 1, 1990. Assuming a 30% income tax rate, the cumulative effect of this accounting change reported in the income statement for the year ended December 31, 1990, is

  a. $175,000
  b. $122,500
  c. $ 52,500
  d. $0

1M91#60. On January 1, 1985, Pell Corp. purchased a machine having an estimated useful life of 10 years and no salvage. The machine was depreciated by the double declining balance method for both financial statement and income tax reporting. On January 1, 1990, Pell changed to the straight-line method for financial statement reporting but not for income tax reporting. Accumulated depreciation at December 31, 1989, was $560,000. If the straight-line method had been used, the accumulated depreciation at December 31, 1989, would have been $420,000. Pell's enacted income tax rate for 1990 and thereafter is 30%. The amount shown in the 1990 income statement for the cumulative effect of changing to the straight-line method should be

  a. $ 98,000 debit.
  b. $ 98,000 credit.
  c. $140,000 credit.
  d. $140,000 debit.

TN90#36. Which of the following should be reported as a prior period adjustment?

	Change in estimated lives of depreciable assets	Change from unaccepted principle to accepted principle
a.	Yes	Yes
b.	No	Yes
c.	Yes	No
d.	No	No

B. Business Combinations

R96#3. Mega, Inc. was organized to consolidate the resources of Lone Co. and Small Co. in a business combination accounted for by the pooling of interests method. Mega issued 31,000 shares of its $10 par voting stock in exchange for all the outstanding capital stock of Lone and Small. The equity accounts of Lone and Small on the date of the exchange were:

	Lone	Small	Total
Common stock, at par	$100,000	$200,000	$300,000
Additional paid-in capital	12,500	17,500	30,000
Retained earnings	60,000	105,000	165,000
	$172,500	$322,500	$495,000

What is the balance in Mega's additional paid-in capital account immediately after the business combination?
  a. $0
  b. $ 20,000
  c. $ 30,000
  d. $195,000

N95#52. In a business combination, how should long-term debt of the acquired company generally be reported under each of the following methods?

	Pooling of interest	Purchase
a.	Fair value	Carrying amount
b.	Fair value	Fair value
c.	Carrying amount	Fair value
d.	Carrying amount	Carrying amount

N95#53. In a business combination accounted for as a purchase, the appraised values of the identifiable assets acquired exceeded the acquisition price. How should the excess appraised value be reported?
  a. As negative goodwill.
  b. As additional paid-in capital.
  c. As a reduction of the values assigned to noncurrent assets and a deferred credit for any unallocated portion.
  d. As positive goodwill.

M95#53. A business combination is accounted for properly as a purchase. Direct costs of combination, other than registration and issuance costs of equity securities, should be
  a. Capitalized as a deferred charge and amortized.
  b. Deducted directly from the retained earnings of the combined corporation.
  c. Deducted in determining the net income of the combined corporation for the period in which the costs were incurred.
  d. Included in the acquisition cost to be allocated to identifiable assets according to their fair values.

M95#54. Poe, Inc. acquired 100% of Shaw Co. in a business combination on September 30, 1994. During 1994, Poe declared quarterly dividends of $25,000 and Shaw declared quarterly dividends of $10,000. Under each of the following methods of accounting for the business combination, what amount should be reported as dividends declared in the December 31, 1994, consolidated statement of retained earnings?

	Purchase	Pooling of interests
a.	$100,000	$130,000
b.	$100,000	$140,000
c.	$130,000	$130,000
d.	$130,000	$140,000

M94#51. Kiwi, Inc.'s planned combination with Mori Co. on January 1, 1994, can be structured either as a purchase or a pooling of interests. In a purchase, Kiwi would acquire Mori's identifiable net assets for more than their book values. These book values approximate fair values. Mori's assets consist of current assets and depreciable noncurrent assets. Ignoring costs required to effect the combination and income tax expense, how would the combined entity's 1994 net income under purchase accounting compare to that under pooling of interests accounting?
   a. Less than pooling.
   b. Equal to pooling.
   c. Greater than pooling.
   d. Not determinable from information given.

M94#52. A business combination occurs in the middle of the year. Results of operations for the year of combination would include the combined results of operations of the separate companies for the entire year if the business combination is a

	Purchase	Pooling of interests
a.	Yes	Yes
b.	Yes	No
c.	No	No
d.	No	Yes

TN93#12. In a business combination accounted for as a pooling
   a. Income is combined only from date of combination, **not** for prior periods presented.
   b. Income is combined for all periods presented.
   c. After the combination, balance sheet amounts are carried at fair market value.
   d. Direct acquisition costs are recorded as part of the cost of the investment.

TN93#13. Which of the following statements is supportive of the pooling of interests method in accounting for a business combination?
   a. Bargaining between the parties is based on current values for assets and liabilities.
   b. Stockholder groups remain intact but combine.
   c. Goodwill is generally a part of any acquisition.
   d. A portion of the total cost is assigned to individual assets acquired on the basis of their fair value.

1M93
Items 7 and 8 are based on the following:

On June 30, 1992, Pane Corp. exchanged 150,000 shares of its $20 par value common stock for all of Sky Corp.'s common stock. At that date, the fair value of Pane's common stock issued was equal to the book value of Sky's net assets. Both corporations continued to operate as separate businesses, maintaining accounting records with years ending December 31. Information from separate company operations follows:

	Pane	Sky
Retained earnings — 12/31/91	$3,200,000	$925,000
Net income — six months ended 6/30/92	800,000	275,000
Dividends paid — 3/25/92	750,000	—

7. If the business combination is accounted for as a pooling of interest, what amount of retained earnings would Pane report in its June 30, 1992, consolidated balance sheet?
   a. $5,200,000
   b. $4,450,000
   c. $3,525,000
   d. $3,250,000

8. If the business combination is accounted for as a purchase, what amount of retained earnings would Pane report in its June 30, 1992, consolidated balance sheet?
   a. $5,200,000
   b. $4,450,000
   c. $3,525,000
   d. $3,250,000

TN92#32. Which of the following conditions would cause a business combination to be accounted for by the purchase method?
   a. The combined corporation intends to dispose of duplicate facilities within one year of the combination.
   b. Cash is to be used to acquire 2% of the outstanding stock of one of the combining companies.
   c. After the combination is consummated, one of the combining companies will be a subsidiary of another combining company.
   d. Before the combination is consummated, one of the combining companies holds 15% of the outstanding stock of another of the combining companies.

TN92#35. On September 30, 1991, Payne, Inc. exchanged some of its shares for all of the common stock of Salem, Inc. in a business combination accounted for as a pooling of interests. Salem continued as a wholly-owned subsidiary of Payne. How should Salem's January 1, 1991, retained earnings and income for January 1 to September 30 be reported in 1991 consolidated statements?

Selected Questions

	1/1/91 Retained earnings	Income for 1/1 to 9/30/91
a.	Added to consolidated retained earnings	Added to consolidated income
b.	Added to consolidated retained earnings	Excluded from consolidated income
c.	Added to consolidated additional paid-in capital	Added to consolidated income
d.	Added to consolidated additional paid-in capital	Excluded from consolidated income

TN91#11. Cedar Co.'s planned combination with Birch Co. on January 1, 1992, can be structured as either a purchase or a pooling of interests. In a purchase, Cedar would acquire Birch's identifiable net assets for less than their book values. These book values approximate fair values. Birch's assets consist of current assets and depreciable noncurrent assets. How would the combined entity's 1992 net income and operating cash flows under purchase accounting compare to those under pooling of interests accounting? Ignore costs required to effect the combination and income tax expense.

	Purchase accounting net income	Purchase accounting operating cash flows
a.	Equal to pooling	Greater than pooling
b.	Equal to pooling	Equal to pooling
c.	Greater than pooling	Greater than pooling
d.	Greater than pooling	Equal to pooling

TN91#12. A business combination is accounted for as a pooling of interests. Costs of furnishing information to stockholders related to effecting the business combination should be
   a. Deducted directly from retained earnings of the combined corporation.
   b. Deducted in determining net income of the combined corporation for the period in which the costs were incurred.
   c. Capitalized but **not** amortized.
   d. Capitalized and subsequently amortized over a period **not** exceeding forty years.

1N91#20. On January 1, 1990, Neal Co. issued 100,000 shares of its $10 par value common stock in exchange for all of Frey, Inc.'s outstanding stock. This business combination was accounted for as a pooling of interests. The fair value of Neal's common stock on December 31, 1989, was $19 per share. The carrying amounts and fair values of Frey's assets and liabilities on December 31, 1989, were as follows:

	Carrying amount	Fair value
Cash	$ 240,000	$ 240,000
Receivables	270,000	270,000
Inventory	435,000	405,000
Property, plant, and equipment	1,305,000	1,440,000
Liabilities	(525,000)	(525,000)
Net assets	$1,725,000	$1,830,000

What is the amount of goodwill resulting from the business combination?
   a. $175,000
   b. $105,000
   c. $ 70,000
   d. $0

2N91#17. Mill Corp. acquired Vore Corp. in a business combination. At the acquisition date, Vore's plant and equipment had a carrying amount of $750,000 and a fair value of $875,000. What amount should the combined entity report for Vore's plant and equipment under each of the following methods at the date of acquisition?

	Pooling of interests	Purchase
a.	$750,000	$875,000
b.	$750,000	$750,000
c.	$875,000	$875,000
d.	$875,000	$750,000

TM90#32. In order to report a business combination as a pooling of interests, the minimum amount of an investee's common stock that must be acquired during the combination period in exchange for the investor's common stock is
   a. 51 percent.
   b. 80 percent.
   c. 90 percent.
   d. 100 percent.

C. Cash Flow Components—Financing, Investing, and Operating

R97#3. In its 1996 income statement, Kilm Co. reported cost of goods sold of $450,000. Changes occurred in several balance sheet accounts as follows:

Inventory	$160,000 decrease
Accounts payable—suppliers	40,000 decrease

What amount should Kilm report as cash paid to suppliers in its 1996 cash flow statement, prepared under the direct method?
   a. $250,000
   b. $330,000
   c. $570,000
   d. $650,000

M95
Items 47 and 48 are based on the following:

In preparing its cash flow statement for the year ended December 31, 1994, Reve Co. collected the following data:

Gain on sale of equipment	$ (6,000)
Proceeds from sale of equipment	10,000
Purchase of A.S., Inc. bonds (par value $200,000)	(180,000)
Amortization of bond discount	2,000
Dividends declared	(45,000)
Dividends paid	(38,000)
Proceeds from sale of treasury stock (carrying amount $65,000)	75,000

In its December 31, 1994, statement of cash flows,

47. What amount should Reve report as net cash used in investing activities?
    a. $170,000
    b. $176,000
    c. $188,000
    d. $194,000

48. What amount should Reve report as net cash provided by financing activities?
    a. $20,000
    b. $27,000
    c. $30,000
    d. $37,000

M94#50. Fara Co. reported bonds payable of $47,000 at December 31, 1992, and $50,000 at December 31, 1993. During 1993, Fara issued $20,000 of bonds payable in exchange for equipment. There was no amortization of bond premium or discount during the year. What amount should Fara report in its 1993 statement of cash flows for redemption of bonds payable?
    a. $ 3,000
    b. $17,000
    c. $20,000
    d. $23,000

1N93#5. Lino Co.'s worksheet for the preparation of its 1992 statement of cash flows included the following:

	December 31	January 1
Accounts receivable	$29,000	$23,000
Allowance for uncollectible accounts	1,000	800
Prepaid rent expense	8,200	12,400
Accounts payable	22,400	19,400

Lino's 1992 net income is $150,000. What amount should Lino include as net cash provided by operating activities in the statement of cash flows?
    a. $151,400
    b. $151,000
    c. $148,600
    d. $145,400

1N93
Items 6 and 7 are based on the following:

Karr, Inc. reported net income of $300,000 for 1992. Changes occurred in several balance sheet accounts as follows:

Equipment	$25,000 increase
Accumulated depreciation	40,000 increase
Note payable	30,000 increase

Additional information:
- During 1992, Karr sold equipment costing $25,000, with accumulated depreciation of $12,000, for a gain of $5,000.
- In December 1992, Karr purchased equipment costing $50,000 with $20,000 cash and a 12% note payable of $30,000.
- Depreciation expense for the year was $52,000.

6. In Karr's 1992 statement of cash flows, net cash provided by operating activities should be
    a. $340,000
    b. $347,000
    c. $352,000
    d. $357,000

7. In Karr's 1992 statement of cash flows, net cash used in investing activities should be
    a. $ 2,000
    b. $12,000
    c. $22,000
    d. $35,000

1N93#8. During 1992, Xan, Inc. had the following activities related to its financial operations:

Payment for the early retirement of long-term bonds payable (carrying amount $370,000)	$375,000
Distribution in 1992 of cash dividend declared in 1991 to preferred shareholders	31,000
Carrying amount of convertible preferred stock in Xan, converted into common shares	60,000
Proceeds from sale of treasury stock (carrying amount at cost, $43,000)	50,000

In Xan's 1992 statement of cash flows, net cash used in financing operations should be
    a. $265,000
    b. $296,000
    c. $356,000
    d. $358,000

TM92#7. In a statement of cash flows, which of the following would increase reported cash flows from operating activities using the direct method? (Ignore income tax considerations.)
    a. Dividends received from investments.
    b. Gain on sale of equipment.
    c. Gain on early retirement of bonds.
    d. Change from straight-line to accelerated depreciation.

TN91#21. Would the following be added back to net income when reporting operating activities' cash flows by the indirect method?

	Excess of treasury stock acquisition cost over sales proceeds (cost method)	Bond discount amortization
a.	Yes	Yes
b.	No	No
c.	No	Yes
d.	Yes	No

TM91#30. In a statement of cash flows, if used equipment is sold at a loss, the amount shown as a cash inflow from investing activities equals the carrying amount of the equipment
   a. Less the loss and plus the amount of tax attributable to the loss.
   b. Less both the loss and the amount of tax attributable to the loss.
   c. Less the loss.
   d. With **no** addition or subtraction.

TM91#31. In a statement of cash flows, which of the following items is reported as a cash outflow from financing activities?

   I. Payments to retire mortgage notes.
   II. Interest payments on mortgage notes.
   III. Dividend payments.
      a. I, II, and III.
      b. II and III.
      c. I only.
      d. I and III.

1M91#4. In 1990, a tornado completely destroyed a building belonging to Holland Corp. The building cost $100,000 and had accumulated depreciation of $48,000 at the time of the loss. Holland received a cash settlement from the insurance company and reported an extraordinary loss of $21,000. In Holland's 1990 cash flow statement, the net change reported in the cash flows from investing activities section should be a
   a. $10,000 increase.
   b. $21,000 decrease.
   c. $31,000 increase.
   d. $52,000 decrease.

1M91#6. Metro, Inc. reported net income of $150,000 for 1990. Changes occurred in several balance sheet accounts during 1990 as follows:

Investment in Videogold, Inc. stock, carried on the equity basis	$5,500 increase
Accumulated depreciation, caused by major repair to projection equipment	2,100 decrease
Premium on bonds payable	1,400 decrease
Deferred income tax liability (long-term)	1,800 increase

In Metro's 1990 cash flow statement, the reported net cash provided by operating activities should be
   a. $150,400
   b. $148,300
   c. $144,900
   d. $142,800

1M91#11. Alp, Inc. had the following activities during 1990:

- Acquired 2,000 shares of stock in Maybel, Inc. for $26,000.

- Sold an investment in Rate Motors for $35,000 when the carrying value was $33,000.

- Acquired a $50,000, 4-year certificate of deposit from a bank. (During the year, interest of $3,750 was paid to Alp.)

- Collected dividends of $1,200 on stock investments.

In Alp's 1990 statement of cash flows, net cash used in investing activities should be
   a. $37,250
   b. $38,050
   c. $39,800
   d. $41,000

2N90#17. Rory Co.'s prepaid insurance was $50,000 at December 31, 1989 and $25,000 at December 31, 1988. Insurance expense was $20,000 for 1989 and $15,000 for 1988. What amount of cash disbursements for insurance would be reported in Rory's 1989 net cash flows from operating activities presented on a direct basis?
   a. $55,000
   b. $45,000
   c. $30,000
   d. $20,000

TM90
Items 27 and 28 are based on the following:

A company acquired a building, paying a portion of the purchase price in cash and issuing a mortgage note payable to the seller for the balance.

27. In a statement of cash flows, what amount is included in investing activities for the above transaction?
   a. Cash payment.
   b. Acquisition price.
   c. Zero.
   d. Mortgage amount.

28. In a statement of cash flows, what amount is included in financing activities for the above transaction?
   a. Cash payment.
   b. Acquisition price.
   c. Zero.
   d. Mortgage amount.

D. Contingent Liabilities and Commitments

N95#17. Eagle Co. has cosigned the mortgage note on the home of its president, guaranteeing the indebtedness in the event that the president should default. Eagle considers the likelihood of default to be remote. How should the guarantee be treated in Eagle's financial statements?
   a. Disclosed only.
   b. Accrued only.
   c. Accrued and disclosed.
   d. Neither accrued nor disclosed.

M95#22. During 1994, Haft Co. became involved in a tax dispute with the IRS. At December 31, 1994, Haft's

tax advisor believed that an unfavorable outcome was probable. A reasonable estimate of additional taxes was $200,000 but could be as much as $300,000. After the 1994 financial statements were issued, Haft received and accepted an IRS settlement offer of $275,000. What amount of accrued liability should Haft have reported in its December 31, 1994 balance sheet?
a. $200,000
b. $250,000
c. $275,000
d. $300,000

N94#26. Management can estimate the amount of loss that will occur if a foreign government expropriates some company assets. If expropriation is reasonably possible, a loss contingency should be
a. Disclosed but **not** accrued as a liability.
b. Disclosed and accrued as a liability.
c. Accrued as a liability but **not** disclosed.
d. Neither accrued as a liability **nor** disclosed.

TN93#21. At December 31, 1992, Date Co. awaits judgment on a lawsuit for a competitor's infringement of Date's patent. Legal counsel believes it is probable that Date will win the suit and indicated the most likely award together with a range of possible awards. How should the lawsuit be reported in Date's 1992 financial statements?
a. In note disclosure only.
b. By accrual for the most likely award.
c. By accrual for the lowest amount of the range of possible awards.
d. Neither in note disclosure **nor** by accrual.

1N93#41. On November 1, 1992, Davis Co. discounted with recourse at 10% a one-year, noninterest bearing, $20,500 note receivable maturing on January 31, 1993. What amount of contingent liability for this note must Davis disclose in its financial statements for the year ended December 31, 1992?
a. $0
b. $20,000
c. $20,333
d. $20,500

TM93#29. In 1991, a contract dispute between Dollis Co. and Brooks Co. was submitted to binding arbitration. In 1991, each party's attorney indicated privately that the probable award in Dollis' favor could be reasonably estimated. In 1992, the arbitrator decided in favor of Dollis. When should Dollis and Brooks recognize their respective gain and loss?

	Dollis' gain	Brooks' loss
a.	1991	1991
b.	1991	1992
c.	1992	1991
d.	1992	1992

1M93#33. On February 5, 1993, an employee filed a $2,000,000 lawsuit against Steel Co. for damages suffered when one of Steel's plants exploded on December 29, 1992. Steel's legal counsel expects the company will lose the lawsuit and estimates the loss to be between $500,000 and $1,000,000. The employee has offered to settle the lawsuit out of court for $900,000, but Steel will not agree to the settlement. In its December 31, 1992, balance sheet, what amount should Steel report as liability from lawsuit?
a. $2,000,000
b. $1,000,000
c. $ 900,000
d. $ 500,000

1M93#34. In 1991, a personal injury lawsuit was brought against Halsey Co. Based on counsel's estimate, Halsey reported a $50,000 liability in its December 31, 1991, balance sheet. In November 1992, Halsey received a favorable judgment, requiring the plaintiff to reimburse Halsey for expenses of $30,000. The plaintiff has appealed the decision, and Halsey's counsel is unable to predict the outcome of the appeal. In its December 31, 1992, balance sheet, Halsey should report what amounts of asset and liability related to these legal actions?

	Asset	Liability
a.	$30,000	$50,000
b.	$30,000	$0
c.	$0	$20,000
d.	$0	$0

2M93#20. On January 1, 1992, Card Corp. signed a three-year, noncancelable purchase contract, which allows Card to purchase up to 500,000 units of a computer part annually from Hart Supply Co. at $.10 per unit and guarantees a minimum annual purchase of 100,000 units. During 1992, the part unexpectedly became obsolete. Card had 250,000 units of this inventory at December 31, 1992, and believes these parts can be sold as scrap for $.02 per unit. What amount of probable loss from the purchase commitment should Card report in its 1992 income statement?
a. $24,000
b. $20,000
c. $16,000
d. $ 8,000

TN92#17. Invern, Inc. has a self-insurance plan. Each year, retained earnings is appropriated for contingencies in an amount equal to insurance premiums saved less recognized losses from lawsuits and other claims. As a result of a 1991 accident, Invern is a defendant in a lawsuit in which it will probably have to pay damages of $190,000. What are the effects of this lawsuit's probable outcome on Invern's 1991 financial statements?
a. An increase in expenses and **no** effect on liabilities.
b. An increase in both expenses and liabilities.
c. No effect on expenses and an increase in liabilities.
d. No effect on either expenses or liabilities.

1N92#31. During 1990, Manfred Corp. guaranteed a supplier's $500,000 loan from a bank. On October 1,

1991, Manfred was notified that the supplier had defaulted on the loan and filed for bankruptcy protection. Counsel believes Manfred will probably have to pay between $250,000 and $450,000 under its guarantee. As a result of the supplier's bankruptcy, Manfred entered into a contract in December 1991 to retool its machines so that Manfred could accept parts from other suppliers. Retooling costs are estimated to be $300,000. What amount should Manfred report as a liability in its December 31, 1991, balance sheet?
- a. $250,000
- b. $450,000
- c. $550,000
- d. $750,000

TM92#27. Snelling Co. did not record an accrual for a contingent loss, but disclosed the nature of the contingency and the range of the possible loss. How likely is the loss?
- a. Remote.
- b. Reasonably possible.
- c. Probable.
- d. Certain.

1M92#35. During 1990, Gum Co. introduced a new product carrying a two-year warranty against defects. The estimated warranty costs related to dollar sales are 2% within 12 months following the sale and 4% in the second 12 months following the sale. Sales and actual warranty expenditures for the years ended December 31, 1990 and 1991, are as follows:

	Sales	Actual warranty expenditures
1990	$150,000	$2,250
1991	250,000	7,500
	$400,000	$9,750

What amount should Gum report as estimated warranty liability in its December 31, 1991, balance sheet?
- a. $ 2,500
- b. $ 4,250
- c. $11,250
- d. $14,250

1M92#36. On January 17, 1991, an explosion occurred at a Sims Co. plant causing extensive property damage to area buildings. Although no claims had yet been asserted against Sims by March 10, 1991, Sims' management and counsel concluded that it is likely that claims will be asserted and that it is reasonably possible Sims will be responsible for damages. Sims' management believed that $1,250,000 would be a reasonable estimate of its liability. Sims' $5,000,000 comprehensive public liability policy has a $250,000 deductible clause. In Sims' December 31, 1990, financial statements, which were issued on March 25, 1991, how should this item be reported?
- a. As an accrued liability of $250,000.
- b. As a footnote disclosure indicating the possible loss of $250,000.
- c. As a footnote disclosure indicating the possible loss of $1,250,000.
- d. No footnote disclosure or accrual is necessary.

1N91#39. East Corp. manufactures stereo systems that carry a two-year warranty against defects. Based on past experience, warranty costs are estimated at 4% of sales for the warranty period. During 1990, stereo system sales totaled $3,000,000, and warranty costs of $67,500 were incurred. In its income statement for the year ended December 31, 1990, East should report warranty expense of
- a. $ 52,500
- b. $ 60,000
- c. $ 67,500
- d. $120,000

TM91#16. A manufacturer of household appliances may incur a loss due to the discovery of a defect in one of its products. The occurrence of the loss is reasonably possible and the resulting costs can be reasonably estimated. This possible loss should be

	Accrued	Disclosed in footnotes
a.	Yes	No
b.	Yes	Yes
c.	No	Yes
d.	No	No

TN90#35. Wyatt Co. has a probable loss that can only be reasonably estimated within a range of outcomes. No single amount within the range is a better estimate than any other amount. The loss accrual should be
- a. Zero.
- b. The maximum of the range.
- c. The mean of the range.
- d. The minimum of the range.

1N90#28. Dunn Trading Stamp Co. records stamp service revenue and provides for the cost of redemptions in the year stamps are sold to licensees. Dunn's past experience indicates that only 80% of the stamps sold to licensees will be redeemed. Dunn's liability for stamp redemptions was $6,000,000 at December 31, 1988. Additional information for 1989 is as follows:

Stamp service revenue from stamps
  sold to licensees $4,000,000
Cost of redemptions (stamps
  sold prior to 1/1/89)   2,750,000

If all the stamps sold in 1989 were presented for redemption in 1990, the redemption cost would be $2,250,000. What amount should Dunn report as a liability for stamp redemptions at December 31, 1989?
- a. $7,250,000
- b. $5,500,000
- c. $5,050,000
- d. $3,250,000

1M90#60. On November 25, 1989, an explosion occurred at a Rex Co. plant causing extensive property damage to area buildings. By March 10, 1990, claims had been asserted against Rex. Rex's management and counsel concluded that it is probable Rex will be responsible for damages, and that $3,500,000 would be a reasonable estimate of its liability. Rex's $10,000,000 comprehensive public liability policy has a $500,000 deductible clause. Rex's December 31, 1989 financial statements, issued on March 25, 1990, should report this item as
   a. A footnote disclosure indicating the probable loss of $3,500,000.
   b. An accrued liability of $3,500,000.
   c. An accrued liability of $500,000.
   d. A footnote disclosure indicating the probable loss of $500,000.

E. Discontinued Operations

N95#40. On April 30, 1994, Deer Corp. approved a plan to dispose of a segment of its business. For the period January 1 through April 30, 1994, the segment had revenues of $500,000 and expenses of $800,000. The assets of the segment were sold on October 15, 1994, at a loss for which no tax benefit is available. In its income statement for the year ended December 31, 1994, how should Deer report the segment's operations from January 1 to April 30, 1994?
   a. $500,000 and $800,000 should be included with revenues and expenses, respectively, as part of continuing operations.
   b. $300,000 should be reported as part of the loss on disposal of a segment.
   c. $300,000 should be reported as an extraordinary loss.
   d. $300,000 should be reported as a loss from operations of a discontinued segment.

M95#44. On October 1, 1994, Host Co. approved a plan to dispose of a segment of its business. Host expected that the sale would occur on April 1, 1995, at an estimated gain of $350,000. The segment had actual and estimated operating losses as follows:

1/1/94 to 9/30/94	$(300,000)
10/1/94 to 12/31/94	(200,000)
1/1/95 to 3/31/95	(400,000)

In its 1994 income statement, what should Host report as a loss on disposal of the segment before income taxes?
   a. $200,000
   b. $250,000
   c. $500,000
   d. $600,000

N94#52. On October 1, 1993, Wand, Inc. committed itself to a formal plan to sell its Kam division's assets. On that date, Wand estimated that the loss from the disposal of assets in February 1994 would be $25,000. Wand also estimated that Kam would incur operating losses of $100,000 for the period of October 1, 1993, through December 31, 1993, and $50,000 for the period January 1, 1994 through February 28, 1994. These estimates were materially correct. Disregarding income taxes, what should Wand report as loss from discontinued operations in its comparative 1993 and 1994 income statements?

	1993	1994
a.	$175,000	$0
b.	$125,000	$ 50,000
c.	$100,000	$ 75,000
d.	$0	$175,000

TN93#18. On November 1, 1992, Smith Co. contracted to dispose of an industry segment on February 28, 1993. Throughout 1992 the segment had operating losses. These losses were expected to continue until the segment's disposition. If a loss is anticipated on final disposition, how much of the operating losses should be included in the loss on disposal reported in Smith's 1992 income statements?

   I. Operating losses for the period January 1 to October 31, 1992.
   II. Operating losses for the period November 1 to December 31, 1992.
   III. Estimated operating losses for the period January 1 to February 28, 1993.

   a. II only.
   b. II and III only.
   c. I and III only.
   d. I and II only.

TM93#3. On December 31, 1992, Brooks Co. decided to end operations and dispose of its assets within three months. At December 31, 1992, the net realizable value of the equipment was below historical cost. What is the appropriate measurement basis for equipment included in Brooks' December 31, 1992, balance sheet?
   a. Historical cost.
   b. Current reproduction cost.
   c. Net realizable value.
   d. Current replacement cost.

TM93#37. A segment of Ace Inc. was discontinued during 1992. Ace's loss on disposal should
   a. Exclude employee relocation costs associated with the decision to dispose.
   b. Exclude operating losses during the phaseout period.
   c. Include additional pension costs associated with the decision to dispose.
   d. Include operating losses of the current period up to the measurement date.

1M93
Items 57 and 58 are based on the following:

On December 31, 1992, the Board of Directors of Maxx Manufacturing, Inc. committed to a plan to discontinue the operations of its Alpha division in 1993. Maxx estimated that Alpha's 1993 operating loss would be

$500,000 and that Alpha's facilities would be sold for $300,000 less than their carrying amounts. Alpha's 1992 operating loss was $1,400,000. Maxx's effective tax rate is 30%.

57. In its 1992 income statement, what amount should Maxx report as loss from discontinued operations?
   a. $ 980,000
   b. $1,330,000
   c. $1,400,000
   d. $1,900,000

58. In its 1992 income statement, what amount should Maxx report as loss on disposal of discontinued operations?
   a. $210,000
   b. $300,000
   c. $560,000
   d. $800,000

1M93#59. Midway Co. had the following transactions during 1992:

- $1,200,000 pretax loss on foreign currency exchange due to a major unexpected devaluation by the foreign government.

- $500,000 pretax loss from discontinued operations of a division.

- $800,000 pretax loss on equipment damaged by a hurricane. This was the first hurricane ever to strike in Midway's area. Midway also received $1,000,000 from its insurance company to replace a building, with a carrying value of $300,000, that had been destroyed by the hurricane.

What amount should Midway report in its 1992 income statement as extraordinary loss before income taxes?
   a. $ 100,000
   b. $1,300,000
   c. $1,800,000
   d. $2,500,000

1M92#57. On December 31, 1990, Greer Co. entered into an agreement to sell its Hart segment's assets. On that date, Greer estimated the gain from the disposition of the assets in 1991 would be $700,000 and Hart's 1991 operating losses would be $200,000. Hart's actual operating losses were $300,000 in both 1990 and 1991, and the actual gain on disposition of Hart's assets in 1991 was $650,000. Disregarding income taxes, what net gain (loss) should be reported for discontinued operations in Greer's comparative 1991 and 1990 income statements?

	1991	1990
a.	$ 50,000	$(300,000)
b.	$ 0	$ 50,000
c.	$ 350,000	$(300,000)
d.	$(150,000)	$ 200,000

1N91#45. Munn Corp.'s income statements for the years ended December 31, 1990 and 1989, included the following, before adjustments:

	1990	1989
Operating income	$ 800,000	$600,000
Gain on sale of division	450,000	—
	1,250,000	600,000
Provision for income taxes	375,000	180,000
Net income	$ 875,000	$420,000

On January 1, 1990, Munn agreed to sell the assets and product line of one of its operating divisions for $1,600,000. The sale was consummated on December 31, 1990, and resulted in a gain on disposition of $450,000. This division's net losses were $320,000 in 1990 and $250,000 in 1989. The income tax rate for both years was 30%. In preparing revised comparative income statements, Munn should report which of the following amounts of gain (loss) from discontinued operations

	1990	1989
a.	$130,000	$0
b.	$130,000	$(250,000)
c.	$ 91,000	$0
d.	$ 91,000	$(175,000)

1N91
Items 50 and 51 are based on the following:

During 1990, Fuqua Steel Co. had the following unusual financial events occur:

- Bonds payable were retired five years before their scheduled maturity, resulting in a $260,000 gain. Fuqua has frequently retired bonds early when interest rates declined significantly.

- A steel forming segment suffered $255,000 in losses due to hurricane damage. This was the fourth similar loss sustained in a 5-year period at that location.

- A segment of Fuqua's operations, steel transportation, was sold at a net loss of $350,000. This was Fuqua's first divestiture of one of its operating segments.

50. Before income taxes, what amount of gain (loss) should be reported separately as a component of income from continuing operations in 1990?
   a. $ 260,000
   b. $ 5,000
   c. $(255,000)
   d. $(350,000)

51. Before income taxes, what amount should be disclosed as the gain (loss) from extraordinary items in 1990?

a. $ 260,000
b. $ 5,000
c. $(90,000)
d. $(350,000)

1N90#49. On May 15, 1989, Munn, Inc. approved a plan to dispose of a segment of its business. It is expected that the sale will occur on February 1, 1990 at a selling price of $500,000. During 1989, disposal costs incurred by Munn totaled $75,000. The segment had actual or estimated operating losses as follows:

1/1/89 to 5/14/89	$130,000
5/15/89 to 12/31/89	50,000
1/1/90 to 1/31/90	15,000

The carrying amount of the segment at the date of sale was expected to be $850,000. Before income taxes, what amount should Munn report as a loss on disposal of the segment in its 1989 income statement?
   a. $490,000
   b. $475,000
   c. $440,000
   d. $425,000

TM90#26. On September 30, 1989, a commitment was made to dispose of a business segment in early 1990. The segment operating loss for the period October 1 to December 31, 1989, should be included in the 1989 income statement as part of
   a. Loss on disposal of the discontinued segment.
   b. Operating loss of the discontinued segment.
   c. Income or loss from continuing operations.
   d. Extraordinary gains or losses.

2M90#47. On April 30, 1989, Carty Corp. approved a plan to dispose of a segment of its business. The estimated disposal loss is $480,000, including severance pay of $55,000 and employee relocation costs of $25,000, both of which are directly associated with the decision to dispose of the segment. Also included is the segment's estimated operating loss of $100,000 for the period from May 1, 1989 to the disposal date. A $120,000 operating loss from January 1, 1989 to April 30, 1989 is **not** included in the estimated disposal loss of $480,000. Before income taxes, what amount should be reported in Carty's income statement for the year ended December 31, 1989 as the loss from discontinued operations?
   a. $600,000
   b. $480,000
   c. $455,000
   d. $425,000

F. Earnings Per Share

R98#5. In computing the weighted-average number of shares outstanding during the year, which of the following midyear events must be treated as if it had occurred at the beginning of the year?
   a. Declaration and distribution of stock dividend.
   b. Purchase of treasury stock.
   c. Sale of additional common stock.
   d. Sale of preferred convertible stock.

N95#45. Ute Co. had the following capital structure during 1993 and 1994:

Preferred stock, $10 par, 4% cumulative, 25,000 shares issued and outstanding	$ 250,000
Common stock, $5 par, 200,000 shares issued and outstanding	1,000,000

Preferred stock is not considered a common stock equivalent. Ute reported net income of $500,000 for the year ended December 31, 1994. Ute paid no preferred dividends during 1993 and paid $16,000 in preferred dividends during 1994. In its December 31, 1994, income statement, what amount should Ute report as earnings per share?
   a. $2.42
   b. $2.45
   c. $2.48
   d. $2.50

M94#49. On December 1, 1993, Clay Co. declared and issued a 6% stock dividend on its 100,000 shares of outstanding common stock. There was no other common stock activity during 1993. What number of shares should Clay use in determining earnings per share for 1993?
   a. 100,000
   b. 100,500
   c. 103,000
   d. 106,000

1M93#60. The following information pertains to Jet Corp.'s outstanding stock for 1992:

Common stock, $5 par value

Shares outstanding, 1/1/92	20,000
2-for-1 stock split, 4/1/92	20,000
Shares issued, 7/1/92	10,000

Preferred stock, $10 par value, 5% cumulative

Shares outstanding, 1/1/92	4,000

What are the number of shares Jet should use to calculate 1992 earnings per share?
   a. 40,000
   b. 45,000
   c. 50,000
   d. 54,000

TN92#23. On January 31, 1992, Pack, Inc. split its common stock 2 for 1, and Young, Inc. issued a 5% stock dividend. Both companies issued their December 31, 1991, financial statements on March 1, 1992. Should Pack's 1991 earnings per share (EPS) take into consideration the stock split, and should Young's 1991 EPS take into consideration the stock dividend?

	Pack's 1991 EPS	Young's 1991 EPS
a.	Yes	No
b.	No	No
c.	Yes	Yes
d.	No	Yes

1M92#59. Timp, Inc. had the following common stock balances and transactions during 1991:

1/1/91	Common stock outstanding	30,000
2/1/91	Issued a 10% common stock dividend	3,000
3/1/91	Issued common stock in a pooling of interests	9,000
7/1/91	Issued common stock for cash	8,000
12/31/91	Common stock outstanding	50,000

What was Timp's 1991 weighted average shares outstanding?
 a. 40,000
 b. 44,250
 c. 44,500
 d. 46,000

TN91#16. Earnings per share data should be reported on the income statement for

	Cumulative effect of a change in accounting principle	Income before extraordinary items
a.	Yes	No
b.	Yes	Yes
c.	No	Yes
d.	No	No

1N90#52. Poe Co. had 300,000 shares of common stock issued and outstanding at December 31, 1988. No common stock was issued during 1989. On January 1, 1989, Poe issued 200,000 shares of nonconvertible preferred stock. During 1989, Poe declared and paid $75,000 cash dividends on the common stock and $60,000 on the preferred stock. Net income for the year ended December 31, 1989 was $330,000. What should be Poe's 1989 earnings per common share?
 a. $1.10
 b. $0.90
 c. $0.85
 d. $0.65

G. Employee Benefits

N95#14. The following information pertains to Hall Co.'s defined-benefit pension plan at December 31, 1994:

Unfunded accumulated benefit obligation	$25,000
Unrecognized prior service cost	12,000
Net periodic pension cost	8,000

Hall made no contributions to the pension plan during 1994. At December 31, 1994, what amount should Hall record as additional pension liability?
 a. $5,000
 b. $13,000
 c. $17,000
 d. $25,000

N95#22. In September 1989, West Corp. made a dividend distribution of one right for each of its 120,000 shares of outstanding common stock. Each right was exercisable for the purchase of $1/100$ of a share of West's $50 variable rate preferred stock at an exercise price of $80 per share. On March 20, 1993, none of the rights had been exercised, and West redeemed them by paying each stockholder $0.10 per right. As a result of this redemption, West's stockholders' equity was reduced by
 a. $120
 b. $2,400
 c. $12,000
 d. $36,000

M95#18. The following information pertains to Kane Co.'s defined benefit pension plan:

Prepaid pension cost, January 1, 1994	$2,000
Service cost	19,000
Interest cost	38,000
Actual return on plan assets	22,000
Amortization of unrecognized prior service cost	52,000
Employer contributions	40,000

The fair value of plan assets exceeds the accumulated benefit obligation. In its December 31, 1994, balance sheet, what amount should Kane report as unfunded accrued pension cost?
 a. $45,000
 b. $49,000
 c. $67,000
 d. $87,000

M95#39. The following information pertains to Gali Co.'s defined benefit pension plan for 1994:

Fair value of plan assets, beginning of year	$350,000
Fair value of plan assets, end of year	525,000
Employer contributions	110,000
Benefits paid	85,000

In computing pension expense, what amount should Gali use as actual return on plan assets?
 a. $65,000
 b. $150,000
 c. $175,000
 d. $260,000

N94#33. On January 2, 1993, Farm Co. granted an employee an option to purchase 1,000 shares of Farm's common stock at $40 per share. The option became exercisable on December 31, 1993, after the employee had completed one year of service, and was exercised on that date. The market prices of Farm's stock were as follows:

    January 2, 1993 $50
    December 31, 1993   65

What amount should Farm recognize as compensation expense for 1993?
- a. $0
- b. $10,000
- c. $15,000
- d. $25,000

N94#34. The following data relates to Nola Co.'s defined benefit pension plan as of December 31, 1993:

Unfunded accumulated benefit obligation	$140,000
Unrecognized prior service cost	45,000
Accrued pension cost	80,000

What amount should Nola report as excess of additional pension liability over unrecognized prior service cost in its statement of stockholders' equity?
- a. $ 15,000
- b. $ 35,000
- c. $ 95,000
- d. $175,000

M94#27. An employer's obligation for postretirement health benefits that are expected to be provided to or for an employee must be fully accrued by the date the
- a. Employee is fully eligible for benefits.
- b. Employee retires.
- c. Benefits are utilized.
- d. Benefits are paid.

M94#28. Payne, Inc. implemented a defined-benefit pension plan for its employees on January 2, 1993. The following data are provided for 1993, as of December 31, 1993:

Accumulated benefit obligation	$103,000
Plan assets at fair value	78,000
Net periodic pension cost	90,000
Employer's contribution	70,000

What amount should Payne record as additional minimum pension liability at December 31, 1993?
- a. $0
- b. $ 5,000
- c. $20,000
- d. $45,000

M94#33. On January 2, 1993, Kine Co. granted Morgan, its president, compensatory stock options to buy 1,000 shares of Kine's $10 par common stock. The options call for a price of $20 per share and are exercisable for 3 years following the grant date. Morgan exercised the options on December 31, 1993. The market price of the stock was $50 on January 2, 1993, and $70 on December 31, 1993. By what net amount should stockholders' equity increase as a result of the grant and exercise of the options?
- a. $20,000
- b. $30,000
- c. $50,000
- d. $70,000

M94#34. On December 31, 1993, Moss Co. issued $1,000,000 of 11% bonds at 109. Each $1,000 bond was issued with 50 detachable stock warrants, each of which entitled the bondholder to purchase one share of $5 par common stock for $25. Immediately after issuance, the market value of each warrant was $4. On December 31, 1993, what amount should Moss record as discount or premium on issuance of bonds?
- a. $ 40,000 premium.
- b. $ 90,000 premium.
- c. $110,000 discount.
- d. $200,000 discount.

TN93#28. If the payment of employees' compensation for future absences is probable, the amount can be reasonably estimated, and the obligation relates to rights that accumulate, the compensation should be
- a. Accrued if attributable to employees' services **not** already rendered.
- b. Accrued if attributable to employees' services already rendered.
- c. Accrued if attributable to employees' services whether already rendered or not.
- d. Recognized when paid.

TN93#29. A company that maintains a defined benefit pension plan for its employees reports an unfunded accrued pension cost. This cost represents the amount that the
- a. Cumulative net pension cost accrued exceeds contributions to the plan.
- b. Cumulative net pension cost accrued exceeds the vested benefit obligation.
- c. Vested benefit obligation exceeds plan assets.
- d. Vested benefit obligation exceeds contributions to the plan.

TN93#30. Visor Co. maintains a defined benefit pension plan for its employees. The service cost component of Visor's net periodic pension cost is measured using the
- a. Unfunded accumulated benefit obligation.
- b. Unfunded vested benefit obligation.
- c. Projected benefit obligation.
- d. Expected return on plan assets.

1N93#26. On January 2, 1992, Loch Co. established a noncontributory defined benefit plan covering all employees and contributed $1,000,000 to the plan. At December 31, 1992, Loch determined that the 1992 service and interest costs on the plan were $620,000. The expected and the actual rate of return on plan assets for 1992 was 10%. There are no other components of Loch's pension expense. What amount should Loch report in its December 31, 1992, balance sheet as prepaid pension cost?

Selected Questions

a. $280,000
b. $380,000
c. $480,000
d. $620,000

1N93#28. Ross Co. pays all salaried employees on a Monday for the five-day workweek ended the previous Friday. The last payroll recorded for the year ended December 31, 1992, was for the week ended December 25, 1992. The payroll for the week ended January 1, 1993, included regular weekly salaries of $80,000 and vacation pay of $25,000 for vacation time earned in 1992 not taken by December 31, 1992. Ross had accrued a liability of $20,000 for vacation pay at December 31, 1991. In its December 31, 1992, balance sheet, what amount should Ross report as accrued salary and vacation pay?
a. $64,000
b. $68,000
c. $69,000
d. $89,000

TM93#14. In a compensatory stock option plan for which the grant, measurement, and exercise date are all different, the stock options outstanding account should be reduced at the
a. Date of grant.
b. Measurement date.
c. Beginning of the service period.
d. Exercise date.

1M93#28. On January 2, 1992, East Corp. adopted a defined benefit pension plan. The plan's service cost of $150,000 was fully funded at the end of 1992. Prior service cost was funded by a contribution of $60,000 in 1992. Amortization of prior service cost was $24,000 for 1992. At December 31, 1992, what amount should East report as prepaid pension cost?
a. $90,000
b. $84,000
c. $60,000
d. $36,000

1M93#30. North Corp. has an employee benefit plan for compensated absences that gives employees 10 paid vacation days and 10 paid sick days. Both vacation and sick days can be carried over indefinitely. Employees can elect to receive payment in lieu of vacation days; however, no payment is given for sick days not taken. At December 31, 1992, North's unadjusted balance of liability for compensated absences was $21,000. North estimated that there were 150 vacation days and 75 sick days available at December 31, 1992. North's employees earn an average of $100 per day. In its December 31, 1992, balance sheet, what amount of liability for compensated absences is North required to report?
a. $36,000
b. $22,500
c. $21,000
d. $15,000

TN92#25. At December 31, 1991, Taos Co. estimates that its employees have earned vacation pay of $100,000. Employees will receive their vacation pay in 1992. Should Taos accrue a liability at December 31, 1991, if the rights to this compensation accumulated over time or if the rights are vested?

	Accumulated	Vested
a.	Yes	No
b.	No	No
c.	Yes	Yes
d.	No	Yes

TN92#26. On July 31, 1991, Tern Co. amended its single employee defined benefit pension plan by granting increased benefits for services provided prior to 1991. This prior service cost will be reflected in the financial statement(s) for
a. Years before 1991 only.
b. Year 1991 only.
c. Year 1991, and years before and following 1991.
d. Year 1991, and following years only.

1N92#25. Nome Co. sponsors a defined benefit plan covering all employees. Benefits are based on years of service and compensation levels at the time of retirement. Nome determined that, as of September 30, 1992, its accumulated benefit obligation was $380,000, and its plan assets had a $290,000 fair value. Nome's September 30, 1992, trial balance showed prepaid pension cost of $20,000. In its September 30, 1992, balance sheet, what amount should Nome report as additional pension liability?
a. $110,000
b. $360,000
c. $380,000
d. $400,000

TM92#20. Interest cost included in the net pension cost recognized by an employer sponsoring a defined benefit pension plan represents the
a. Amortization of the discount on unrecognized prior service costs.
b. Increase in the fair value of plan assets due to the passage of time.
c. Increase in the projected benefit obligation due to the passage of time.
d. Shortage between the expected and actual returns on plan assets.

1M92#25. Webb Co. implemented a defined benefit pension plan for its employees on January 1, 1988. During 1988 and 1989, Webb's contributions fully funded the plan. The following data are provided for 1991 and 1990:

	1991 Estimated	1990 Actual
Projected benefit obligation, December 31	$750,000	$700,000
Accumulated benefit obligation, December 31	520,000	500,000
Plan assets at fair value, December 31	675,000	600,000
Projected benefit obligation in excess of plan assets	75,000	100,000
Pension expense	90,000	75,000
Employer's contribution	?	50,000

What amount should Webb contribute in order to report an accrued pension liability of $15,000 in its December 31, 1991, balance sheet?
    a. $ 50,000
    b. $ 60,000
    c. $ 75,000
    d. $100,000

2M92#14. The following information pertains to Lee Corp.'s defined benefit pension plan for 1991:

Service cost	$160,000
Actual and expected gain on plan assets	35,000
Unexpected loss on plan assets related to a 1991 disposal of a subsidiary	40,000
Amortization of unrecognized prior service cost	5,000
Annual interest on pension obligation	50,000

What amount should Lee report as pension expense in its 1991 income statement?
    a. $250,000
    b. $220,000
    c. $210,000
    d. $180,000

2M92#15. The following information pertains to Rik Co.'s two employees:

Name	Weekly salary	Number of weeks worked in 1991	Vacation rights vest or accumulate
Ryan	$800	52	Yes
Todd	600	52	No

Neither Ryan nor Todd took the usual two-week vacation in 1991. In Rik's December 31, 1991, financial statements, what amount of vacation expense and liability should be reported?
    a. $2,800
    b. $1,600
    c. $1,400
    d. $0

TN91#29. Compensatory stock options were granted to executives on May 1, 1988, with a measurement date of October 31, 1989, for services rendered during 1988, 1989, and 1990. The excess of the market value of the stock over the option price at the measurement date was reasonably estimable at the date of grant. The stock options were exercised on June 30, 1991. Compensation expense should be recognized in which of the following years?

	1988	1990
a.	Yes	No
b.	No	No
c.	Yes	Yes
d.	No	Yes

TN91#31. An employer sponsoring a defined benefit pension plan is subject to the minimum pension liability recognition requirement. An additional liability must be recorded equal to the unfunded
    a. Accumulated benefit obligation plus the previously recognized accrued pension cost.
    b. Accumulated benefit obligation less the previously recognized accrued pension cost.
    c. Projected benefit obligation plus the previously recognized accrued pension cost.
    d. Projected benefit obligation less the previously recognized accrued pension cost.

1N91#23. On June 1, 1988, Ward Corp. established a defined benefit pension plan for its employees. The following information was available at May 31, 1990:

Projected benefit obligation	$14,500,000
Accumulated benefit obligation	12,000,000
Unfunded accrued pension cost	200,000
Plan assets at fair market value	7,000,000
Unrecognized prior service cost	2,550,000

To report the proper pension liability in Ward's May 31, 1990, balance sheet, what is the amount of the adjustment required?
    a. $2,250,000
    b. $4,750,000
    c. $4,800,000
    d. $7,300,000

TM91#37. For a defined benefit pension plan, the discount rate used to calculate the projected benefit obligation is determined by the

	Expected return on plan assets	Actual return on plan assets
a.	Yes	Yes
b.	No	No
c.	Yes	No
d.	No	Yes

1M91#32. Dell Co. adopted a defined benefit pension plan on January 1, 1990. Dell amortizes the prior service cost over 16 years and funds prior service cost by making equal payments to the fund trustee at the end of each of the first ten years. The service (normal) cost is fully funded at the end of each year. The following data are available for 1990:

Service (normal) cost for 1990 $220,000
Prior service cost:
  Amortized 83,400
  Funded 114,400

Dell's prepaid pension cost at December 31, 1990, is
  a. $114,400
  b. $ 83,400
  c. $ 31,000
  d. $0

1M91#36. Pine Corp. is required to contribute, to an employee stock ownership plan (ESOP), 10% of its income after deduction for this contribution but before income tax. Pine's income before charges for the contribution and income tax was $75,000. The income tax rate is 30%. What amount should be accrued as a contribution to the ESOP?
  a. $7,500
  b. $6,818
  c. $5,250
  d. $4,773

2M91#17. The following information pertains to the 1990 activity of Ral Corp.'s defined benefit pension plan:

Service cost	$300,000
Return on plan assets	80,000
Interest cost on pension benefit obligation	164,000
Amortization of actuarial loss	30,000
Amortization of unrecognized net obligation	70,000

Ral's 1990 pension cost was
  a. $316,000
  b. $484,000
  c. $574,000
  d. $644,000

TN90#20. Mercer, Inc. maintains a defined benefit pension plan for its employees. As of December 31, 1989, the market value of the plan assets is less than the accumulated benefit obligation, and less than the projected benefit obligation. The projected benefit obligation exceeds the accumulated benefit obligation. In its balance sheet as of December 31, 1989, Mercer should report a minimum liability in the amount of the
  a. Excess of the projected benefit obligation over the value of the plan assets.
  b. Excess of the accumulated benefit obligation over the value of the plan assets.
  c. Projected benefit obligation.
  d. Accumulated benefit obligation.

TN90#21. Effective January 1, 1989, Flood Co. established a defined benefit pension plan with no retroactive benefits. The first of the required equal annual contributions was paid on December 31, 1989. A 10% discount rate was used to calculate service cost and a 10% rate of return was assumed for plan assets. All information on covered employees for 1989 and 1990 is the same. How should the service cost for 1990 compare with 1989, and should the 1989 balance sheet report an accrued or a prepaid pension cost?

	Service cost for 1990 compared to 1989	Pension cost reported on the 1989 balance sheet
a.	Equal to	Accrued
b.	Equal to	Prepaid
c.	Greater than	Accrued
d.	Greater than	Prepaid

1N90#15. At December 31, 1989, the following information was provided by the Kerr Corp. pension plan administrator:

Fair value of plan assets	$3,450,000
Accumulated benefit obligation	4,300,000
Projected benefit obligation	5,700,000

What is the amount of the pension liability that should be shown on Kerr's December 31, 1989 balance sheet?
  a. $5,700,000
  b. $2,250,000
  c. $1,400,000
  d. $ 850,000

2N90#16. The following information pertains to Seda Co.'s pension plan:

Actuarial estimate of projected benefit obligation at 1/1/89	$72,000
Assumed discount rate	10%
Service costs for 1989	18,000
Pension benefits paid during 1989	15,000

If **no** change in actuarial estimates occurred during 1989, Seda's projected benefit obligation at December 31, 1989 was
  a. $64,200
  b. $75,000
  c. $79,200
  d. $82,200

TM90#37. Barrett Co. maintains a defined benefit pension plan for its employees. At each balance sheet date, Barrett should report a minimum liability at least equal to the
  a. Accumulated benefit obligation.
  b. Projected benefit obligation.
  c. Unfunded accumulated benefit obligation.
  d. Unfunded projected benefit obligation.

2M90#53. Gavin Co. grants all employees two weeks of paid vacation for each full year of employment. Unused vacation time can be accumulated and carried forward to succeeding years and will be paid at the salaries in effect when vacations are taken or when employment is terminated. There was no employee turnover in 1989. Additional information relating to the year ended December 31, 1989 is as follows:

Liability for accumulated vacations
at 12/31/88 $35,000
Pre-1989 accrued vacations taken
from 1/1/89 to 9/30/89 (the authorized
period for vacations) 20,000
Vacations earned for work in 1989
(adjusted to current rates) 30,000

Gavin granted a 10% salary increase to all employees on October 1, 1989, its annual salary increase date. For the year ended December 31, 1989, Gavin should report vacation pay expense of
- a. $45,000
- b. $33,500
- c. $31,500
- d. $30,000

H. Extraordinary Items

R97#5. In September 1996, Koff Co.'s operating plant was destroyed by an earthquake. Earthquakes are rare in the area in which the plant was located. The portion of the resultant loss not covered by insurance was $700,000. Koff's income tax rate for 1996 is 40%. In its 1996 income statement, what amount should Koff report as extraordinary loss?
- a. $0
- b. $280,000
- c. $420,000
- d. $700,000

N95#41. In open market transactions, Gold Corp. simultaneously sold its long-term investment in Iron Corp. bonds and purchased its own outstanding bonds. The broker remitted the net cash from the two transactions. Gold's gain on the purchase of its own bonds exceeded its loss on the sale of the Iron bonds. Gold should report the
- a. Net effect of the two transactions as an extraordinary gain.
- b. Net effect of the two transactions in income before extraordinary items.
- c. Effect of its own bond transaction gain in income before extraordinary items, and report the Iron bond transaction as an extraordinary loss.
- d. Effect of its own bond transaction as an extraordinary gain, and report the Iron bond transaction loss in income before extraordinary items.

N95#42. During 1994 both Raim Co. and Cane Co. suffered losses due to the flooding of the Mississippi River. Raim is located two miles from the river and sustains flood losses every two to three years. Cane, which has been located fifty miles from the river for the past twenty years, has never before had flood losses. How should the flood losses be reported in each company's 1994 income statement?

	Raim	Cane
a.	As a component of income from continuing operations	As an extraordinary item
b.	As a component of income from continuing operations	As a component of income from continuing operations
c.	As an extraordinary item	As a component of income from continuing operations
d.	As an extraordinary item	As an extraordinary item

N94#42. On July 31, 1993, Dome Co. issued $1,000,000 of 10%, 15-year bonds at par and used a portion of the proceeds to call its 600 outstanding 11%, $1,000 face value bonds, due on July 31, 2003, at 102. On that date, unamortized bond premium relating to the 11% bonds was $65,000. In its 1993 income statement, what amount should Dome report as gain or loss, before income taxes, from retirement of bonds?
- a. $ 53,000 gain.
- b. $0.
- c. $(65,000) loss.
- d. $(77,000) loss.

N94#53. A transaction that is unusual in nature and infrequent in occurrence should be reported separately as a component of income
- a. After cumulative effect of accounting changes and before discontinued operations of a segment of a business.
- b. After cumulative effect of accounting changes and after discontinued operations of a segment of a business.
- c. Before cumulative effect of accounting changes and before discontinued operations of a segment of a business.
- d. Before cumulative effect of accounting changes and after discontinued operations of a segment of a business.

M94#48. An extraordinary item should be reported separately on the income statement as a component of income

	Net of income taxes	Before discontinued operations of a segment of a business
a.	Yes	Yes
b.	Yes	No
c.	No	No
d.	No	Yes

TN93#25. On March 1, 1987, Somar Co. issued 20-year bonds at a discount. By September 1, 1992, the bonds were quoted at 106 when Somar exercised its right to retire the bonds at 105. How should Somar report the bond retirement on its 1992 income statement?
- a. A gain in continuing operations.
- b. A loss in continuing operations.
- c. An extraordinary gain.
- d. An extraordinary loss.

1N93
Items 57 and 58 are based on the following:

The following information pertains to the transfer of real estate pursuant to a troubled debt restructuring by Knob Co. to Mene Corp. in full liquidation of Knob's liability to Mene:

Carrying amount of liability liquidated	$150,000
Carrying amount of real estate transferred	100,000
Fair value of real estate transferred	90,000

57. What amount should Knob report as a pretax extraordinary gain (loss) on restructuring of payables?
   a. ($10,000)
   b. $0
   c. $50,000
   d. $60,000

58. What amount should Knob report as ordinary gain (loss) on transfer of real estate?
   a. ($10,000)
   b. $0
   c. $50,000
   d. $60,000

TM93#12. On March 31, 1992, Ashley, Inc.'s bondholders exchanged their convertible bonds for common stock. The carrying amount of these bonds on Ashley's books was less than the market value but greater than the par value of the common stock issued. If Ashley used the book value method of accounting for the conversion, which of the following statements correctly states an effect of this conversion?
   a. Stockholders' equity is increased.
   b. Additional paid-in capital is decreased.
   c. Retained earnings is increased.
   d. An extraordinary loss is recognized.

TM93#18. Weald Co. took advantage of market conditions to refund debt. This was the fifth refunding operation carried out by Weald within the last four years. The excess of the carrying amount of the old debt over the amount paid to extinguish it should be reported as a(an)
   a. Deferred credit to be amortized over life of new debt.
   b. Part of continuing operations.
   c. Extraordinary gain, net of income taxes.
   d. Extraordinary loss, net of income taxes.

1N92#47. On June 30, 1992, King Co. had outstanding 9%, $5,000,000 face value bonds maturing on June 30, 1997. Interest was payable semiannually every June 30 and December 31. On June 30, 1992, after amortization was recorded for the period, the unamortized bond premium and bond issue costs were $30,000 and $50,000, respectively. On that date, King acquired all its outstanding bonds on the open market at 98 and retired them. At June 30, 1992, what amount should King recognize as gain before income taxes on redemption of bonds?
   a. $ 20,000
   b. $ 80,000
   c. $120,000
   d. $180,000

1M92#53. Nu Corp. agreed to give Rand Co. a machine in full settlement of a note payable to Rand. The machine's original cost was $140,000. The note's face amount was $110,000. On the date of the agreement:

- The note's carrying amount was $105,000, and its present value was $96,000.

- The machine's carrying amount was $109,000, and its fair value was $96,000.

What amount of gains (losses) should Nu recognize, and how should these be classified in its income statement?

	Extraordinary	Other
a.	$(4,000)	$ 0
b.	$ 0	$(4,000)
c.	$ 5,000	$(4,000)
d.	$ 9,000	$(13,000)

1M92#55. Ray Finance, Inc. issued a 10-year, $100,000, 9% note on January 1, 1989. The note was issued to yield 10% for proceeds of $93,770. Interest is payable semiannually. The note is callable after two years at a price of $96,000. Due to a decline in the market rate to 8%, Ray retired the note on December 31, 1991. On that date, the carrying amount of the note was $94,582, and the discounted market rate was $105,280. What amount should Ray report as gain (loss) from retirement of the note for the year ended December 31, 1991?
   a. $ 9,280
   b. $ 4,000
   c. $(2,230)
   d. $(1,418)

1M92#58. On December 31, 1991, Wright Corp. placed cash of $875,000 in an irrevocable trust that meets the necessary defeasance requirements. The trust's assets are to be used solely for satisfying obligations on Wright's 6%, $1,100,000, 30-year bond payable. Wright has not been legally released from its obligations under the bond agreement, but any additional liability is considered remote. On December 31, 1991, the bond's carrying amount was $1,050,000, and its present value was $800,000. Disregarding income taxes, what amount of extraordinary gain (loss) should Wright report in its 1991 income statement?
   a. $(75,000)
   b. $175,000
   c. $225,000
   d. $250,000

2M92#9. Wood Corp., a debtor-in-possession under Chapter 11 of the Federal Bankruptcy Code, granted an equity interest to a creditor in full settlement of a $28,000 debt owed to the creditor. At the date of this transaction,

the equity interest had a fair value of $25,000. What amount should Wood recognize as an extraordinary gain on restructuring of debt?
- a. $0
- b. $ 3,000
- c. $25,000
- d. $28,000

TN91#23. In 1990, Teller Co. incurred losses arising from its guilty plea in its first antitrust action, and from a substantial increase in production costs caused when a major supplier's workers went on strike. Which of these losses should be reported as an extraordinary item?

	Antitrust action	Production costs
a.	No	No
b.	No	Yes
c.	Yes	No
d.	Yes	Yes

1N91#24. On September 1, 1991, Hall Corp. redeemed $500,000 of its 12%, 15-year bonds. Related unamortized bond premium and issue costs at that date were $8,000 and $10,000, respectively. What amount should Hall use to determine gain or loss on redemption?
- a. $518,000
- b. $508,000
- c. $502,000
- d. $498,000

1N91#43. During 1990, Colt Co. experienced financial difficulties and is likely to default on a $1,000,000, 15%, 3-year note dated January 1, 1989, payable to Cain National Bank. On December 31, 1990, the bank agreed to settle the note and unpaid 1990 interest of $150,000 for $820,000 cash payable on January 31, 1991. What is the amount of gain, before income taxes, from the debt restructuring?
- a. $0
- b. $150,000
- c. $180,000
- d. $330,000

1N91#52. In 1985, May Corp. acquired land by paying $75,000 down and signing a note with a maturity value of $1,000,000. On the note's due date, December 31, 1990, May owed $40,000 of accrued interest and $1,000,000 principal on the note. May was in financial difficulty and was unable to make any payments. May and the bank agreed to amend the note as follows:

- The $40,000 of interest due on December 31, 1990, was forgiven.

- The principal of the note was reduced from $1,000,000 to $950,000 and the maturity date extended 1 year to December 31, 1991.

- May would be required to make one interest payment totaling $30,000 on December 31, 1991.

As a result of the troubled debt restructuring, May should report a gain, before taxes, in its 1990 income statement of
- a. $40,000
- b. $50,000
- c. $60,000
- d. $90,000

TM91#26. Gains or losses from the early extinguishment of debt, if material, should be
- a. Recognized in income before taxes in the period of extinguishment.
- b. Recognized as an extraordinary item in the period of extinguishment.
- c. Amortized over the life of the new issue.
- d. Amortized over the remaining original life of the extinguished issue.

1N90#27. On June 30, 1989, Town Co. had outstanding 8%, $2,000,000 face amount, 15-year bonds maturing on June 30, 1999. Interest is payable on June 30 and December 31. The unamortized balances in the bond discount and deferred bond issue costs accounts on June 30, 1989 were $70,000 and $20,000, respectively. On June 30, 1989, Town acquired all of these bonds at 94 and retired them. What net carrying amount should be used in computing gain or loss on this early extinguishment of debt?
- a. $1,980,000
- b. $1,930,000
- c. $1,910,000
- d. $1,880,000

1N90#50. On January 1, 1990, Hart, Inc. redeemed its 15-year bonds of $500,000 par value for 102. They were originally issued on January 1, 1978 at 98 with a maturity date of January 1, 1993. The bond issue costs relating to this transaction were $20,000. Hart amortizes discounts, premiums, and bond issue costs using the straight-line method. What amount of extraordinary loss should Hart recognize on the redemption of these bonds?
- a. $16,000
- b. $12,000
- c. $10,000
- d. $0

2N90#11. On its December 31, 1988 balance sheet, Nilo Corp. reported bonds payable of $8,000,000 and related unamortized bond issue costs of $430,000. The bonds had been issued at par. On January 2, 1989, Nilo retired $4,000,000 of the outstanding bonds at par plus a call premium of $100,000. What amount should Nilo report in its 1989 income statement as loss on extinguishment of debt?
- a. $0
- b. $100,000
- c. $215,000
- d. $315,000

I. Financial Instruments

R96#8. Which of the following risks are inherent in an interest rate swap agreement?

I. The risk of exchanging a lower interest rate for a higher interest rate.
II. The risk of nonperformance by the counterparty to the agreement.

 a. I only.
 b. II only.
 c. Both I and II.
 d. Neither I nor II.

R96#9. If it is **not** practicable for an entity to estimate the fair value of a financial instrument, which of the following should be disclosed?

I. Information pertinent to estimating the fair value of the financial instrument.
II. The reasons it is not practicable to estimate fair value.

 a. I only.
 b. II only.
 c. Both I and II.
 d. Neither I nor II.

M95#4. Disclosure of information about significant concentrations of credit risk is required for
 a. All financial instruments.
 b. Financial instruments with off-balance-sheet credit risk only.
 c. Financial instruments with off-balance-sheet market risk only.
 d. Financial instruments with off-balance-sheet risk of accounting loss only.

J. Foreign Currency Transactions and Translation

N95#32. Fogg Co., a U.S. company, contracted to purchase foreign goods. Payment in foreign currency was due one month after the goods were received at Fogg's warehouse. Between the receipt of goods and the time of payment, the exchange rates changed in Fogg's favor. The resulting gain should be included in Fogg's financial statements as a(an)
 a. Component of income from continuing operations.
 b. Extraordinary item.
 c. Deferred credit.
 d. Separate component of stockholders' equity.

M95#31. Park Co.'s wholly-owned subsidiary, Schnell Corp., maintains its accounting records in German marks. Because all of Schnell's branch offices are in Switzerland, its functional currency is the Swiss franc. Remeasurement of Schnell's 1994 financial statements resulted in a $7,600 gain, and translation of its financial statements resulted in an $8,100 gain. What amount should Park report as a foreign exchange gain in its income statement for the year ended December 31, 1994?
 a. $0
 b. $ 7,600
 c. $ 8,100
 d. $15,700

M95#32. On September 22, 1994, Yumi Corp. purchased merchandise from an unaffiliated foreign company for 10,000 units of the foreign company's local currency. On that date, the spot rate was $.55. Yumi paid the bill in full on March 20, 1995, when the spot rate was $.65. The spot rate was $.70 on December 31, 1994. What amount should Yumi report as a foreign currency transaction loss in its income statement for the year ended December 31, 1994?
 a. $0
 b. $ 500
 c. $1,000
 d. $1,500

TN93#35. On October 1, 1992, Mild Co., a U.S. company, purchased machinery from Grund, a German company, with payment due on April 1, 1993. If Mild's 1992 operating income included no foreign exchange transaction gain or loss, then the transaction could have
 a. Resulted in an extraordinary gain.
 b. Been denominated in U.S. dollars.
 c. Caused a foreign currency gain to be reported as a contra account against machinery.
 d. Caused a foreign currency translation gain to be reported as a separate component of stockholders' equity.

TN93#36. When remeasuring foreign currency financial statements into the functional currency, which of the following items would be remeasured using historical exchange rates?
 a. Inventories carried at cost.
 b. Marketable equity securities reported at market values.
 c. Bonds payable.
 d. Accrued liabilities.

1N93#49. Hunt Co. purchased merchandise for £300,000 from a vendor in London on November 30, 1992. Payment in British pounds was due on January 30, 1993. The exchange rates to purchase one pound were as follows:

	November 30, 1992	December 31, 1992
Spot-rate	$1.65	$1.62
30-day rate	1.64	1.59
60-day rate	1.63	1.56

In its December 31, 1992, income statement, what amount should Hunt report as foreign exchange gain?
 a. $12,000
 b. $ 9,000
 c. $ 6,000
 d. $0

TM93#34. On October 1, 1992, Velec Co., a U.S. company, contracted to purchase foreign goods requiring payment in francs one month after their receipt at Velec's factory. Title to the goods passed on December 15, 1992. The goods were still in transit on December 31, 1992.

Exchange rates were one dollar to 22 francs, 20 francs, and 21 francs on October 1, December 15, and December 31, 1992, respectively. Velec should account for the exchange rate fluctuation in 1992 as
    a. A loss included in net income before extraordinary items.
    b. A gain included in net income before extraordinary items.
    c. An extraordinary gain.
    d. An extraordinary loss.

1M93#46. On September 1, 1992, Brady Corp. entered into a foreign exchange contract for speculative purposes by purchasing 50,000 deutsche marks for delivery in 60 days. The rates to exchange $1 for 1 deutsche mark follow:

	9/1/92	9/30/92
Spot rate	.75	.70
30-day forward rate	.73	.72
60-day forward rate	.74	.73

In its September 30, 1992, income statement, what amount should Brady report as foreign exchange loss?
    a. $2,500
    b. $1,500
    c. $1,000
    d. $ 500

TM92#39. A foreign subsidiary's functional currency is its local currency, which has not experienced significant inflation. The weighted average exchange rate for the current year would be the appropriate exchange rate for translating

	Sales to customers	Wages expense
a.	No	No
b.	Yes	Yes
c.	No	Yes
d.	Yes	No

1M92#52. The following information pertains to Flint Co.'s sale of 10,000 foreign currency units under a forward contract dated November 1, 1991, for delivery on January 31, 1992:

	11/1/91	12/31/91
Spot rates	$0.80	$0.83
30-day future rates	0.79	0.82
90-day future rates	0.78	0.81

Flint entered into the forward contract in order to speculate in the foreign currency. In Flint's income statement for the year ended December 31, 1991, what amount of loss should be reported from this forward contract?
    a. $400
    b. $300
    c. $200
    d. $0

TN91#18. Shore Co. records its transactions in U.S. dollars. A sale of goods resulted in a receivable denominated in Japanese yen, and a purchase of goods resulted in a payable denominated in French francs. Shore recorded a foreign exchange gain on collection of the receivable and an exchange loss on settlement of the payable. The exchange rates are expressed as so many units of foreign currency to one dollar. Did the number of foreign currency units exchangeable for a dollar increase or decrease between the contract and settlement dates?

	Yen exchangeable for $1	Francs exchangeable for $1
a.	Increase	Increase
b.	Decrease	Decrease
c.	Decrease	Increase
d.	Increase	Decrease

1N91#46. On September 1, 1990, Cano & Co., a U.S. corporation, sold merchandise to a foreign firm for 250,000 francs. Terms of the sale require payment in francs on February 1, 1991. On September 1, 1990, the spot exchange rate was $.20 per franc. At December 31, 1990, Cano's year end, the spot rate was $.19, but the rate increased to $.22 by February 1, 1991, when payment was received. How much should Cano report as foreign exchange gain or loss in its 1991 income statement?
    a. $0.
    b. $2,500 loss.
    c. $5,000 gain.
    d. $7,500 gain.

1N90#38. On November 15, 1989, Celt, Inc., a U.S. company, ordered merchandise FOB shipping point from an East German company for 200,000 marks. The merchandise was shipped and invoiced to Celt on December 10, 1989. Celt paid the invoice on January 10, 1990. The spot rates for marks on the respective dates are as follows:

November 15, 1989	$.4955
December 10, 1989	.4875
December 31, 1989	.4675
January 10, 1990	.4475

In Celt's December 31, 1989 income statement, the foreign exchange gain is
    a. $9,600
    b. $8,000
    c. $4,000
    d. $1,600

1N90#43. Ball Corp. had the following foreign currency transactions during 1989:

- Merchandise was purchased from a foreign supplier on January 20, 1989 for the U.S. dollar equivalent of $90,000. The invoice was paid on March 20, 1989 at the U.S. dollar equivalent of $96,000.

- On July 1, 1989, Ball borrowed the U.S. dollar equivalent of $500,000 evidenced by a note that was payable in the lender's local currency on July 1, 1991. On December 31, 1989, the U.S. dollar equivalents of the principal amount and accrued interest were $520,000 and $26,000, respectively. Interest on the note is 10% per annum.

In Ball's 1989 income statement, what amount should be included as foreign exchange loss?
   a. $0
   b. $ 6,000
   c. $21,000
   d. $27,000

TM90#22. A balance arising from the translation or remeasurement of a subsidiary's foreign currency financial statements is reported in the consolidated income statement when the subsidiary's functional currency is the

	Foreign currency	U.S. dollar
a.	No	No
b.	No	Yes
c.	Yes	No
d.	Yes	Yes

1M90#52. Fay Corp. had a realized foreign exchange loss of $15,000 for the year ended December 31, 1989 and must also determine whether the following items will require year-end adjustment:

- Fay had an $8,000 loss resulting from the translation of the accounts of its wholly owned foreign subsidiary for the year ended December 31, 1989.
- Fay had an account payable to an unrelated foreign supplier payable in the supplier's local currency. The U.S. dollar equivalent of the payable was $64,000 on the October 31, 1989 invoice date, and it was $60,000 on December 31, 1989. The invoice is payable on January 30, 1990.

In Fay's 1989 consolidated income statement, what amount should be included as foreign exchange loss?
   a. $11,000
   b. $15,000
   c. $19,000
   d. $23,000

2M90#44. Certain balance sheet accounts of a foreign subsidiary of Rowan, Inc., at December 31, 1989, have been translated into U.S. dollars as follows:

	Translated at	
	Current rates	Historical rates
Note receivable, long-term	$240,000	$200,000
Prepaid rent	85,000	80,000
Patent	150,000	170,000
	$475,000	$450,000

The subsidiary's functional currency is the currency of the country in which it is located. What total amount should be included in Rowan's December 31, 1989 consolidated balance sheet for the above accounts?
   a. $450,000
   b. $455,000
   c. $475,000
   d. $495,000

K. Income Taxes

R97#11. Hut Co. has temporary taxable differences that will reverse during the next year and add to taxable income. These differences relate to noncurrent assets. Deferred income taxes based on these temporary differences should be classified in Hut's balance sheet as a
   a. Current asset.
   b. Noncurrent asset.
   c. Current liability.
   d. Noncurrent liability.

N95#36. On its December 31, 1994, balance sheet, Shin Co. had income taxes payable of $13,000 and a current deferred tax asset of $20,000 before determining the need for a valuation account. Shin had reported a current deferred tax asset of $15,000 at December 31, 1993. No estimated tax payments were made during 1994. At December 31, 1994, Shin determined that it was more likely than not that 10% of the deferred tax asset would not be realized. In its 1994 income statement, what amount should Shin report as total income tax expense?
   a. $ 8,000
   b. $ 8,500
   c. $10,000
   d. $13,000

N95
Items 37 and 38 are based on the following:

Zeff Co. prepared the following reconciliation of its pretax financial statement income to taxable income for the year ended December 31, 1994, its first year of operations:

Pretax financial income	$160,000
Nontaxable interest received on municipal securities	(5,000)
Long-term loss accrual in excess of deductible amount	10,000
Depreciation in excess of financial statement amount	(25,000)
Taxable income	$140,000

Zeff's tax rate for 1994 is 40%.

37. In its 1994 income statement, what amount should Zeff report as income tax expense—current portion?
   a. $52,000
   b. $56,000
   c. $62,000
   d. $64,000

38. In its December 31, 1994, balance sheet, what should Zeff report as deferred income tax liability?
   a. $2,000
   b. $4,000
   c. $6,000
   d. $8,000

M95#16. As a result of differences between depreciation for financial reporting purposes and tax purposes, the financial reporting basis of Noor Co.'s sole depreciable asset, acquired in 1994, exceeded its tax basis by $250,000 at December 31, 1994. This difference will reverse in future years. The enacted tax rate is 30% for 1994, and 40% for future years. Noor has no other temporary differences. In its December 31, 1994, balance sheet, how should Noor report the deferred tax effect of this difference?
   a. As an asset of $75,000.
   b. As an asset of $100,000.
   c. As a liability of $75,000.
   d. As a liability of $100,000.

M95#17. At December 31, 1994, Bren Co. had the following deferred income tax items:

- A deferred income tax liability of $15,000 related to a noncurrent asset

- A deferred income tax asset of $3,000 related to a noncurrent liability

- A deferred income tax asset of $8,000 related to a current liability

Which of the following should Bren report in the noncurrent section of its December 31, 1994, balance sheet?
   a. A noncurrent asset of $3,000 and a noncurrent liability of $15,000.
   b. A noncurrent liability of $12,000.
   c. A noncurrent asset of $11,000 and a noncurrent liability of $15,000.
   d. A noncurrent liability of $4,000.

M95#41. For the year ended December 31, 1994, Tyre Co. reported pretax financial statement income of $750,000. Its taxable income was $650,000. The difference is due to accelerated depreciation for income tax purposes. Tyre's effective income tax rate is 30%, and Tyre made estimated tax payments during 1994 of $90,000. What amount should Tyre report as current income tax expense for 1994?
   a. $105,000
   b. $135,000
   c. $195,000
   d. $225,000

M95#42. Quinn Co. reported a net deferred tax asset of $9,000 in its December 31, 1993, balance sheet. For 1994, Quinn reported pretax financial statement income of $300,000. Temporary differences of $100,000 resulted in taxable income of $200,000 for 1994. At December 31, 1994, Quinn had cumulative taxable differences of $70,000. Quinn's effective income tax rate is 30%. In its December 31, 1994, income statement, what should Quinn report as deferred income tax expense?
   a. $12,000
   b. $21,000
   c. $30,000
   d. $60,000

M95#43. Mobe Co. reported the following operating income (loss) for its first three years of operations:

1992	$ 300,000
1993	(700,000)
1994	1,200,000

For each year, there were no deferred income taxes, and Mobe's effective income tax rate was 30%. In its 1993 income tax return, Mobe elected to carry back the maximum amount of loss possible. In its 1994 income statement, what amount should Mobe report as total income tax expense?
   a. $120,000
   b. $150,000
   c. $240,000
   d. $360,000

N94#6. Thorn Co. applies Statement of Financial Accounting Standards No. 109, *Accounting for Income Taxes*. At the end of 1993, the tax effects of temporary differences were as follows:

	Deferred tax assets (liabilities)	Related asset classification
Accelerated tax depreciation	($75,000)	Noncurrent asset
Additional costs in inventory for tax purposes	25,000	Current asset
	($50,000)	

A valuation allowance was not considered necessary. Thorn anticipates that $10,000 of the deferred tax liability will reverse in 1994. In Thorn's December 31, 1993, balance sheet, what amount should Thorn report as noncurrent deferred tax liability?
   a. $40,000
   b. $50,000
   c. $65,000
   d. $75,000

N94
Items 49 and 50 are based on the following:

Kent, Inc.'s reconciliation between financial statement and taxable income for 1993 follows:

Pretax financial income	$150,000	
Permanent difference	(12,000)	
	138,000	
Temporary difference—depreciation	(9,000)	
Taxable income	$129,000	

Additional information:

	At 12/31/92	12/31/93
Cumulative temporary differences (future taxable amounts)	$11,000	$20,000

The enacted tax rate was 34% for 1992, and 40% for 1993 and years thereafter.

49. In its December 31, 1993, balance sheet, what amount should Kent report as deferred income tax liability?
   a. $3,600
   b. $6,800
   c. $7,340
   d. $8,000

50. In its 1993 income statement, what amount should Kent report as current portion of income tax expense?
   a. $51,600
   b. $55,200
   c. $55,860
   d. $60,000

N94#51. In its 1993 income statement, Cere Co. reported income before income taxes of $300,000. Cere estimated that, because of permanent differences, taxable income for 1993 would be $280,000. During 1993 Cere made estimated tax payments of $50,000, which were debited to income tax expense. Cere is subject to a 30% tax rate. What amount should Cere report as income tax expense?
   a. $34,000
   b. $50,000
   c. $84,000
   d. $90,000

M94#24. Because Jab Co. uses different methods to depreciate equipment for financial statement and income tax purposes, Jab has temporary differences that will reverse during the next year and add to taxable income. Deferred income taxes that are based on these temporary differences should be classified in Jab's balance sheet as a
   a. Contra account to current assets.
   b. Contra account to noncurrent assets.
   c. Current liability.
   d. Noncurrent liability.

M94#47. For the year ended December 31, 1993, Grim Co.'s pretax financial statement income was $200,000 and its taxable income was $150,000. The difference is due to the following:

Interest on municipal bonds	$ 70,000
Premium expense on keyman life insurance	(20,000)
Total	$ 50,000

Grim's enacted income tax rate is 30%. In its 1993 income statement, what amount should Grim report as current provision for income tax expense?
   a. $45,000
   b. $51,000
   c. $60,000
   d. $66,000

TN93#32. In its first four years of operations ending December 31, 1992, Alder, Inc.'s depreciation for income tax purposes exceeded its depreciation for financial statement purposes. This temporary difference was expected to reverse in 1993, 1994, and 1995. Alder had no other temporary difference and elected early adoption of FASB 109. Alder's 1992 balance sheet should include
   a. A noncurrent contra asset for the effects of the difference between asset bases for financial statement and income tax purposes.
   b. Both current and noncurrent deferred tax assets.
   c. A current deferred tax liability only.
   d. A noncurrent deferred tax liability only.

1M93#26. West Corp. leased a building and received the $36,000 annual rental payment on June 15, 1992. The beginning of the lease was July 1, 1992. Rental income is taxable when received. West's tax rates are 30% for 1992 and 40% thereafter. West has elected early adoption of FASB Statement No. 109, *Accounting for Income Taxes*. West had no other permanent or temporary differences. West determined that no valuation allowance was needed. What amount of deferred tax asset should West report in its December 31, 1992, balance sheet?
   a. $ 5,400
   b. $ 7,200
   c. $10,800
   d. $14,400

1M93#35. Taft Corp. uses the equity method to account for its 25% investment in Flame, Inc. During 1992, Taft received dividends of $30,000 from Flame and recorded $180,000 as its equity in the earnings of Flame. Additional information follows:

• All the undistributed earnings of Flame will be distributed as dividends in future periods.

• The dividends received from Flame are eligible for the 80% dividends received deduction.

• There are no other temporary differences.

• Enacted income tax rates are 30% for 1992 and thereafter.

Taft elected early application of FASB Statement No. 109, *Accounting for Income Taxes*. In its December 31, 1992, balance sheet, what amount should Taft report for deferred income tax liability?
   a. $ 9,000
   b. $10,800
   c. $45,000
   d. $54,000

1M93#36. Stone Co. began operations in 1992 and reported $225,000 in income before income taxes for the year. Stone's 1992 tax depreciation exceeded its book depreciation by $25,000. Stone also had nondeductible book expenses of $10,000 related to permanent differences. Stone's tax rate for 1992 was 40%, and the enacted rate for years after 1992 is 35%. Stone elected early adoption of FASB Statement No. 109, *Accounting for Income Taxes*. In its December 31, 1992, balance sheet, what amount of deferred income tax liability should Stone report?
   a. $ 8,750
   b. $10,000
   c. $12,250
   d. $14,000

1M93#54. On January 1, 1990, Warren Co. purchased a $600,000 machine, with a five-year useful life and no salvage value. The machine was depreciated by an accelerated method for book and tax purposes. The machine's carrying amount was $240,000 on December 31, 1991. On January 1, 1992, Warren changed retroactively to the straight-line method for financial statement purposes. Warren can justify the change. Warren's income tax rate is 30%. On January 1, 1992, what amount should Warren report as deferred income tax liability as a result of the change?
   a. $120,000
   b. $ 72,000
   c. $ 36,000
   d. $0

1M93#55. Venus Corp.'s worksheet for calculating current and deferred income taxes for 1992 follows:

	1992	1993	1994
Pretax income	$ 1,400		
Temporary differences:			
Depreciation	(800)	(1,200)	$2,000
Warranty costs	400	(100)	(300)
Taxable income	$ 1,000	(1,300)	1,700
Loss carryback		(1,000)	1,000
Loss carryforward			300	(300)
	$ 0	$ 0	$1,400
Enacted rate	30%	30%	25%
Deferred tax liability (asset):			
Current	$ (300)		
Noncurrent			$ 350

Venus elected early adoption of FASB Statement No. 109, *Accounting for Income Taxes*. Venus had no prior deferred tax balances. In its 1992 income statement, what amount should Venus report as current income tax expense?
   a. $420
   b. $350
   c. $300
   d. $0

TN92#41. Rein Inc. reported deferred tax assets and deferred tax liabilities at the end of 1990 and at the end of 1991. According to FASB Statements No. 96 and No. 109, *Accounting for Income Taxes*, for the year ended 1991 Rein should report deferred income tax expense or benefit equal to the
   a. Decrease in the deferred tax assets.
   b. Increase in the deferred tax liabilities.
   c. Amount of the current tax liability plus the sum of the net changes in deferred tax assets and deferred tax liabilities.
   d. Sum of the net changes in deferred tax assets and deferred tax liabilities.

1N92#27. For the year ended December 31, 1991, Mont Co.'s books showed income of $600,000 before provision for income tax expense. To compute taxable income for federal income tax purposes, the following items should be noted:

Income from exempt municipal bonds	$ 60,000
Depreciation deducted for tax purposes in excess of depreciation recorded on the books	120,000
Proceeds received from life insurance on death of officer	100,000
Estimated tax payments	0
Enacted corporate tax rate	30%

Ignoring the alternative minimum tax provisions, what amount should Mont report at December 31, 1991, as its current federal income tax liability?
   a. $ 96,000
   b. $114,000
   c. $150,000
   d. $162,000

1N92#32. Tower Corp. began operations on January 1, 1990. For financial reporting, Tower recognizes revenues from all sales under the accrual method. However, in its income tax returns, Tower reports qualifying sales under the installment method. Tower's gross profit on these installment sales under each method was as follows:

Year	Accrual method	Installment method
1990	$1,600,000	$ 600,000
1991	2,600,000	1,400,000

The income tax rate is 30% for 1990 and future years. There are no other temporary or permanent differences.

In its December 31, 1991, balance sheet, what amount should Tower report as a liability for deferred income taxes?
- a. $840,000
- b. $660,000
- c. $600,000
- d. $360,000

1M92#26. On January 2, 1990, Ross Co. purchased a machine for $70,000. This machine has a 5-year useful life, a residual value of $10,000, and is depreciated using the straight-line method for financial statement purposes. For tax purposes, depreciation expense was $25,000 for 1990 and $20,000 for 1991. Ross elected early application of FASB Statement No. 96, *Accounting for Income Taxes*. Ross' 1991 income, before income taxes and depreciation expense, was $100,000 and its tax rate was 30%. If Ross had made **no** estimated tax payments during 1991, what amount of current income tax liability would Ross report in its December 31, 1991, balance sheet?
- a. $26,400
- b. $25,800
- c. $24,000
- d. $22,500

1N91#25. Dunn Co.'s 1990 income statement reported $90,000 income before provision for income taxes. To compute the provision for federal income taxes, the following 1990 data are provided:

Rent received in advance	$16,000
Income from exempt municipal bonds	20,000
Depreciation deducted for income tax purposes in excess of depreciation reported for financial statement purposes	10,000
Enacted corporate income tax rate	30%

If the alternative minimum tax provisions are ignored, what amount of current federal income tax liability should be reported in Dunn's December 31, 1990, balance sheet?
- a. $18,000
- b. $22,800
- c. $25,800
- d. $28,800

1N90#16. Pine Corp.'s books showed pretax income of $800,000 for the year ended December 31, 1989. In the computation of federal income taxes, the following data were considered:

Gain on an involuntary conversion (Pine has elected to replace the property within the statutory period using total proceeds.)	$350,000
Depreciation deducted for tax purposes in excess of depreciation deducted for book purposes	50,000
Federal estimated tax payments, 1989	70,000
Enacted federal tax rates, 1989	30%

What amount should Pine report as its current federal income tax liability on its December 31, 1989 balance sheet?
- a. $50,000
- b. $65,000
- c. $120,000
- d. $135,000

2N90#7. Ram Corp. prepared the following reconciliation of income per books with income per tax return for the year ended December 31, 1989:

Book income before income taxes	$750,000
Add temporary difference Construction contract revenue which will reverse in 1993	100,000
Deduct temporary difference Depreciation expense which will reverse in equal amounts in each of the next four years	(400,000)
Taxable income	$450,000

Ram's effective income tax rate is 34% for 1989. What amount should Ram report in its 1989 income statement as the current provision for income taxes?
- a. $ 34,000
- b. $153,000
- c. $255,000
- d. $289,000

1M90#26. Graf Corp.'s 1989 income statement showed pretax accounting income of $200,000. To compute the federal income tax liability, the following 1989 data are provided:

Income from exempt municipal bonds	$10,000
Depreciation deducted for tax purposes in excess of depreciation deducted for financial statement purposes	20,000
Estimated federal income tax payments made	40,000
Enacted corporate income tax rate	30%

If the alternate minimum tax provisions are ignored, what amount of current federal income tax liability should be included in Graf's December 31, 1989 balance sheet?
- a. $11,000
- b. $20,000
- c. $39,000
- d. $51,000

L. Interest Costs

R97#6. Troop Co. frequently borrows from the bank to maintain sufficient operating cash. The following loans were at a 12% interest rate, with interest payable at maturity. Troop repaid each loan on its scheduled maturity date.

Date of loan	Amount	Maturity date	Term of loan
11/1/95	$10,000	10/31/96	1 year
2/1/96	30,000	7/31/96	6 months
5/1/96	16,000	1/31/97	9 months

Troop records interest expense when the loans are repaid. Accordingly, interest expense of $3,000 was recorded in 1996. If **no** correction is made, by what amount would 1996 interest expense be understated?
a. $1,080
b. $1,240
c. $1,280
d. $1,440

N94#18. In its 1993 financial statements, Cris Co. reported interest expense of $85,000 in its income statement and cash paid for interest of $68,000 in its cash flow statement. There was no prepaid interest or interest capitalization either at the beginning or end of 1993. Accrued interest at December 31, 1992, was $15,000. What amount should Cris report as accrued interest payable in its December 31, 1993, balance sheet?
a. $ 2,000
b. $15,000
c. $17,000
d. $32,000

M94#46. A bond issued on June 1, 1993, has interest payment dates of April 1 and October 1. Bond interest expense for the year ended December 31, 1993, is for a period of
a. Three months.
b. Four months.
c. Six months.
d. Seven months.

TN93#33. Which of the following is reported as interest expense?
a. Pension cost interest.
b. Postretirement healthcare benefits interest.
c. Imputed interest on non-interest bearing note.
d. Interest incurred to finance construction of machinery for own use.

1N93#29. On January 31, 1992, Beau Corp. issued $300,000 maturity value, 12% bonds for $300,000 cash. The bonds are dated December 31, 1991, and mature on December 31, 2001. Interest will be paid semiannually on June 30 and December 31. What amount of accrued interest payable should Beau report in its September 30, 1992, balance sheet?
a. $27,000
b. $24,000
c. $18,000
d. $ 9,000

1N93#31. On September 1, 1991, Brak Co. borrowed on a $1,350,000 note payable from Federal Bank. The note bears interest at 12% and is payable in three equal annual principal payments of $450,000. On this date, the bank's prime rate was 11%. The first annual payment for interest and principal was made on September 1, 1992. At December 31, 1992, what amount should Brak report as accrued interest payable?
a. $54,000
b. $49,500
c. $36,000
d. $33,000

1N92#23. On November 1, 1991, Mason Corp. issued $800,000 of its 10-year, 8% term bonds dated October 1, 1991. The bonds were sold to yield 10%, with total proceeds of $700,000 plus accrued interest. Interest is paid every April 1 and October 1. What amount should Mason report for interest payable in its December 31, 1991, balance sheet?
a. $17,500
b. $16,000
c. $11,667
d. $10,667

TM91#23. During 1990, Bay Co. constructed machinery for its own use and for sale to customers. Bank loans financed these assets both during construction and after construction was complete. How much of the interest incurred should be reported as interest expense in the 1990 income statement?

	Interest incurred for machinery for own use	Interest incurred for machinery held for sale
a.	All interest incurred	All interest incurred
b.	All interest incurred	Interest incurred after completion
c.	Interest incurred after completion	Interest incurred after completion
d.	Interest incurred after completion	All interest incurred

1M91#33. Mann Corp.'s liability account balances at June 30, 1989, included a 10% note payable in the amount of $3,600,000. The note is dated October 1, 1988, and is payable in three equal annual payments of $1,200,000 plus interest. The first interest and principal payment was made on October 1, 1989. In Mann's June 30, 1990, balance sheet, what amount should be reported as accrued interest payable for this note?
a. $270,000
b. $180,000
c. $ 90,000
d. $ 60,000

1M91#55. On July 1, 1990, Day Co. received $103,288 for $100,000 face amount, 12% bonds, a price that yields 10%. Interest expense for the six months ended December 31, 1990, should be
a. $6,197
b. $6,000
c. $5,164
d. $5,000

1N90#41. On January 1, 1990, Korn Co. sold to Kay Corp. $400,000 of its 10% bonds for $354,118 to yield 12%. Interest is payable semiannually on January 1 and

July 1. What amount should Korn report as interest expense for the six months ended June 30, 1990?
 a. $17,706
 b. $20,000
 c. $21,247
 d. $24,000

TM90#8. A company issued a short-term note payable with a stated 12% rate of interest to a bank. The bank charged a .5% loan origination fee and remitted the balance to the company. The effective interest rate paid by the company in this transaction would be
 a. Equal to 12.5%.
 b. More than 12.5%.
 c. Less than 12.5%.
 d. Independent of 12.5%.

M. Interim Financial Reporting

TN93#31. For interim financial reporting, a company's income tax provision for the second quarter of 1992 should be determined using the
 a. Effective tax rate expected to be applicable for the full year of 1992 as estimated at the end of the first quarter of 1992.
 b. Effective tax rate expected to be applicable for the full year of 1992 as estimated at the end of the second quarter of 1992.
 c. Effective tax rate expected to be applicable for the second quarter of 1992.
 d. Statutory tax rate for 1992.

2M93#17. During the first quarter of 1993, Tech Co. had income before taxes of $200,000, and its effective income tax rate was 15%. Tech's 1992 effective annual income tax rate was 30%, but Tech expects its 1993 effective annual income tax rate to be 25%. In its first quarter interim income statement, what amount of income tax expense should Tech report?
 a. $0
 b. $30,000
 c. $50,000
 d. $60,000

TN92#16. An inventory loss from a market price decline occurred in the first quarter, and the decline was not expected to reverse during the fiscal year. However, in the third quarter the inventory's market price recovery exceeded the market decline that occurred in the first quarter. For interim financial reporting, the dollar amount of net inventory should
 a. Decrease in the first quarter by the amount of the market price decline and increase in the third quarter by the amount of the decrease in the first quarter.
 b. Decrease in the first quarter by the amount of the market price decline and increase in the third quarter by the amount of the market price recovery.
 c. Decrease in the first quarter by the amount of the market price decline and **not** be affected in the third quarter.
 d. Not be affected in either the first quarter or the third quarter.

2N92#52. On March 15, 1992, Krol Co. paid property taxes of $90,000 on its office building for the calendar year 1992. On April 1, 1992, Krol paid $150,000 for unanticipated repairs to its office equipment. The repairs will benefit operations for the remainder of 1992. What is the total amount of these expenses that Krol should include in its quarterly income statement for the three months ended June 30, 1992?
 a. $172,500
 b. $ 97,500
 c. $ 72,500
 d. $ 37,500

2M92#12. On June 30, 1991, Mill Corp. incurred a $100,000 net loss from disposal of a business segment. Also, on June 30, 1991, Mill paid $40,000 for property taxes assessed for the calendar year 1991. What amount of the foregoing items should be included in the determination of Mill's net income or loss for the six-month interim period ended June 30, 1991?
 a. $140,000
 b. $120,000
 c. $ 90,000
 d. $ 70,000

2N91#13. Kell Corp.'s $95,000 net income for the quarter ended September 30, 1990, included the following after-tax items:

- A $60,000 extraordinary gain, realized on April 30, 1990, was allocated equally to the second, third, and fourth quarters of 1990.

- A $16,000 cumulative-effect loss resulting from a change in inventory valuation method was recognized on August 2, 1990.

In addition, Kell paid $48,000 on February 1, 1990, for 1990 calendar-year property taxes. Of this amount, $12,000 was allocated to the third quarter of 1990.

For the quarter ended September 30, 1990, Kell should report net income of
 a. $ 91,000
 b. $103,000
 c. $111,000
 d. $115,000

1N90#55. Farr Corp. had the following transactions during the quarter ended March 31, 1990:

Loss on early extinguishment of debt	$ 70,000
Payment of fire insurance premium for calendar year 1990	100,000

What amount should be included in Farr's income statement for the quarter ended March 31, 1990?

	Extraordinary loss	Insurance expense
a.	$70,000	$100,000
b.	$70,000	$ 25,000
c.	$17,500	$ 25,000
d.	$0	$100,000

2M90#43. An inventory loss from a permanent market decline of $360,000 occurred in May 1989. Cox Co. appropriately recorded this loss in May 1989 after its March 31, 1989 quarterly report was issued. What amount of inventory loss should be reported in Cox's quarterly income statement for the three months ended June 30, 1989?
- a. $0
- b. $ 90,000
- c. $180,000
- d. $360,000

N. Leases

R96#4. On January 2, 1995, Marx Co. as lessee signed a five-year noncancelable equipment lease with annual payments of $200,000 beginning December 31, 1995. Marx treated this transaction as a capital lease. The five lease payments have a present value of $758,000 at January 2, 1995, based on interest of 10%. What amount should Marx report as interest expense for the year ended December 31, 1995?
- a. $0
- b. $48,400
- c. $55,800
- d. $75,800

N95#12. A six-year capital lease entered into on December 31, 1994, specified equal minimum annual lease payments due on December 31 of each year. The first minimum annual lease payment, paid on December 31, 1994, consists of which of the following?

	Interest expense	Lease liability
a.	Yes	Yes
b.	Yes	No
c.	No	Yes
d.	No	No

N94#20. At the inception of a capital lease, the guaranteed residual value should be
- a. Included as part of minimum lease payments at present value.
- b. Included as part of minimum lease payments at future value.
- c. Included as part of minimum lease payments only to the extent that guaranteed residual value is expected to exceed estimated residual value.
- d. Excluded from minimum lease payments.

M94#25. In the long-term liabilities section of its balance sheet at December 31, 1992, Mene Co. reported a capital lease obligation of $75,000, net of current portion of $1,364. Payments of $9,000 were made on both January 2, 1993, and January 2, 1994. Mene's incremental borrowing rate on the date of the lease was 11% and the lessor's implicit rate, which was known to Mene, was 10%. In its December 31, 1993, balance sheet, what amount should Mene report as capital lease obligation, net of current portion?
- a. $66,000
- b. $73,500
- c. $73,636
- d. $74,250

M94#26. One criterion for a capital lease is that the term of the lease must equal a minimum percentage of the leased property's estimated economic life at the inception of the lease. What is this minimum percentage?
- a. 51%
- b. 75%
- c. 80%
- d. 90%

TN93#42. On July 1, 1992, Dewey Co. signed a 20-year building lease that it reported as a capital lease. Dewey paid the monthly lease payments when due. How should Dewey report the effect of the lease payments in the financing activities section of its 1992 statement of cash flows?
- a. An inflow equal to the present value of future lease payments at July 1, 1992, less 1992 principal and interest payments.
- b. An outflow equal to the 1992 principal and interest payments on the lease.
- c. An outflow equal to the 1992 principal payments only.
- d. The lease payments should **not** be reported in the financing activities section.

1N93#35. Oak Co. leased equipment for its entire nine-year useful life, agreeing to pay $50,000 at the start of the lease term on December 31, 1991, and $50,000 annually on each December 31 for the next eight years. The present value on December 31, 1991, of the nine lease payments over the lease term, using the rate implicit in the lease which Oak knows to be 10%, was $316,500. The December 31, 1991, present value of the lease payments using Oak's incremental borrowing rate of 12% was $298,500. Oak made a timely second lease payment. What amount should Oak report as capital lease liability in its December 31, 1992, balance sheet?
- a. $350,000
- b. $243,150
- c. $228,320
- d. $0

1N93#39. Neal Corp. entered into a nine-year capital lease on a warehouse on December 31, 1992. Lease payments of $52,000, which includes real estate taxes of $2,000, are due annually, beginning on December 31, 1993, and every December 31 thereafter. Neal does not know the interest rate implicit in the lease; Neal's incremental borrowing rate is 9%. The rounded present value of an ordinary annuity for nine years at 9% is 5.6. What amount should Neal report as capitalized lease liability at December 31, 1992?

a. $280,000
b. $291,200
c. $450,000
d. $468,000

1N93#44. Howe Co. leased equipment to Kew Corp. on January 2, 1992, for an eight-year period expiring December 31, 1999. Equal payments under the lease are $600,000 and are due on January 2 of each year. The first payment was made on January 2, 1992. The list selling price of the equipment is $3,520,000 and its carrying cost on Howe's books is $2,800,000. The lease is appropriately accounted for as a sales-type lease. The present value of the lease payments at an imputed interest rate of 12% (Howe's incremental borrowing rate) is $3,300,000. What amount of profit on the sale should Howe report for the year ended December 31, 1992?
a. $720,000
b. $500,000
c. $ 90,000
d. $0

TM93#38. On January 1, 1990, JCK Co. signed a contract for an eight-year lease of its equipment with a 10-year life. The present value of the 16 equal semiannual payments in advance equaled 85% of the equipment's fair value. The contract had no provision for JCK, the lessor, to give up legal ownership of the equipment. Should JCK recognize rent or interest revenue in 1992, and should the revenue recognized in 1992 be the same or smaller than the revenue recognized in 1991?

	1992 revenues recognized	1992 amount recognized compared to 1991
a.	Rent	The same
b.	Rent	Smaller
c.	Interest	The same
d.	Interest	Smaller

TN92#27. Lease M does not contain a bargain purchase option, but the lease term is equal to 90% of the estimated economic life of the leased property. Lease P does not transfer ownership of the property to the lessee at the end of the lease term, but the lease term is equal to 75% of the estimated economic life of the leased property. How should the lessee classify these leases?

	Lease M	Lease P
a.	Capital lease	Operating lease
b.	Capital lease	Capital lease
c.	Operating lease	Capital lease
d.	Operating lease	Operating lease

1N92#33. On December 29, 1991, Action Corp. signed a 7-year capital lease for an airplane to transport its sports team around the country. The airplane's fair value was $841,500. Action made the first annual lease payment of $153,000 on December 31, 1991. Action's incremental borrowing rate was 12%, and the interest rate implicit in the lease, which was known by Action, was 9%. The following are the rounded present value factors for an annuity due:

9% for 7 years 5.5
12% for 7 years 5.1

What amount should Action report as capital lease liability in its December 31, 1991, balance sheet?
a. $841,500
b. $780,300
c. $688,500
d. $627,300

1N92#34. On December 30, 1990, Ames Co. leased equipment under a capital lease for 10 years. It contracted to pay $40,000 annual rent on December 31, 1990, and on December 31 of each of the next nine years. The capital lease liability was recorded at $270,000 on December 30, 1990, before the first payment. The equipment's useful life is 12 years, and the interest rate implicit in the lease is 10%. Ames uses the straight-line method to depreciate all equipment. In recording the December 31, 1991, payment, by what amount should Ames reduce the capital lease liability?
a. $27,000
b. $23,000
c. $22,500
d. $17,000

TM92#33. For a capital lease, the amount recorded initially by the lessee as a liability should normally
a. Exceed the total of the minimum lease payments.
b. Exceed the present value of the minimum lease payments at the beginning of the lease.
c. Equal the total of the minimum lease payments.
d. Equal the present value of the minimum lease payments at the beginning of the lease.

TM92#34. On January 1, 1991, Mollat Co. signed a 7-year lease for equipment having a 10-year economic life. The present value of the monthly lease payments equaled 80% of the equipment's fair value. The lease agreement provides for neither a transfer of title to Mollat nor a bargain purchase option. In its 1991 income statement Mollat should report
a. Rent expense equal to the 1991 lease payments.
b. Rent expense equal to the 1991 lease payments less interest expense.
c. Lease amortization equal to one-tenth of the equipment's fair value.
d. Lease amortization equal to one-seventh of 80% of the equipment's fair value.

1M92#34. Robbins, Inc. leased a machine from Ready Leasing Co. The lease qualifies as a capital lease and requires 10 annual payments of $10,000 beginning immediately. The lease specifies an interest rate of 12% and a purchase option of $10,000 at the end of the tenth year, even though the machine's estimated value on that date is $20,000. Robbins' incremental borrowing rate is 14%.

The present value of an annuity due of 1 at:
12% for 10 years is 6.328
14% for 10 years is 5.946

The present value of 1 at:
12% for 10 years is .322
14% for 10 years is .270

What amount should Robbins record as lease liability at the beginning of the lease term?
a. $62,160
b. $64,860
c. $66,500
d. $69,720

TN91#34. Jay's lease payments are made at the end of each period. Jay's liability for a capital lease would be reduced periodically by the
a. Minimum lease payment less the portion of the minimum lease payment allocable to interest.
b. Minimum lease payment plus the amortization of the related asset.
c. Minimum lease payment less the amortization of the related asset.
d. Minimum lease payment.

1N91#14. On July 1, 1990, Glen Corp. leased a new machine from Ryan Corp. The lease contains the following information:

Lease term	10 years
Useful life of the machine	12 years
Present value of the minimum lease payments	$120,000
Fair value of the machine	200,000
Executory costs	3,000

No bargain purchase option is provided, and the machine reverts to Ryan when the lease expires. What amount should Glen record as a capitalized leased asset at inception of the lease?
a. $0
b. $120,000
c. $123,000
d. $200,000

1N91#33. On December 31, 1990, Day Co. leased a new machine from Parr with the following pertinent information:

Lease term	6 years
Annual rental payable at beginning of each year	$50,000
Useful life of machine	8 years
Day's incremental borrowing rate	15%
Implicit interest rate in lease (known by Day)	12%
Present value of an annuity of 1 in advance for 6 periods at	
12%	4.61
15%	4.35

The lease is not renewable, and the machine reverts to Parr at the termination of the lease. The cost of the machine on Parr's accounting records is $375,500. At the beginning of the lease term, Day should record a lease liability of
a. $375,500
b. $230,500
c. $217,500
d. $0

1N91#34. On December 31, 1989, Adam Co. leased a machine under a capital lease for a period of ten years, contracting to pay $50,000 on signing the lease and $50,000 annually on December 31 of the next nine years. The present value at December 31, 1989, of the ten lease payments over the lease term discounted at 10% was $338,000. At December 31, 1990, Adam's total capital lease liability is
a. $303,980
b. $266,800
c. $259,200
d. $243,000

1M91#25. On January 1, 1988, Nobb Corp. signed a 12-year lease for warehouse space. Nobb has an option to renew the lease for an additional 8-year period on or before January 1, 1992. During January 1990, Nobb made substantial improvements to the warehouse. The cost of these improvements was $540,000, with an estimated useful life of 15 years. At December 31, 1990, Nobb intended to exercise the renewal option. Nobb has taken a full year's amortization on this leasehold. In Nobb's December 31, 1990, balance sheet, the carrying amount of this leasehold improvement should be
a. $486,000
b. $504,000
c. $510,000
d. $513,000

1M91#42. On January 1, 1990, Babson, Inc. leased two automobiles for executive use. The lease requires Babson to make five annual payments of $13,000 beginning January 1, 1990. At the end of the lease term, December 31, 1994, Babson guarantees the residual value of the automobiles will total $10,000. The lease qualifies as a capital lease. The interest rate implicit in the lease is 9%. Present value factors for the 9% rate implicit in the lease are as follows:

For an annuity due with 5 payments	4.240
For an ordinary annuity with 5 payments	3.890
Present value of $1 for 5 periods	0.650

Babson's recorded capital lease liability immediately after the first required payment should be
a. $48,620
b. $44,070
c. $35,620
d. $31,070

1M91#45. On January 1, 1990, Blaugh Co. signed a long-term lease for an office building. The terms of the lease required Blaugh to pay $10,000 annually, beginning

December 30, 1990, and continuing each year for 30 years. The lease qualifies as a capital lease. On January 1, 1990, the present value of the lease payments is $112,500 at the 8% interest rate implicit in the lease. In Blaugh's December 31, 1990, balance sheet, the capital lease liability should be
- a. $102,500
- b. $111,500
- c. $112,500
- d. $290,000

TN90#26. In a lease that is recorded as a sales-type lease by the lessor, interest revenue
- a. Should be recognized in full as revenue at the lease's inception.
- b. Should be recognized over the period of the lease using the straight-line method.
- c. Should be recognized over the period of the lease using the effective interest method.
- d. Does **not** arise.

1N90#21. On December 31, 1989, Neal, Inc. leased machinery with a fair value of $105,000 from Frey Rentals Co. The agreement is a six-year noncancelable lease requiring annual payments of $20,000 beginning December 31, 1989. The lease is appropriately accounted for by Neal as a capital lease. Neal's incremental borrowing rate is 11%. Neal knows the interest rate implicit in the lease payments is 10%.

- The present value of an annuity due of 1 for 6 years at 10% is 4.7908.

- The present value of an annuity due of 1 for 6 years at 11% is 4.6959.

In its December 31, 1989 balance sheet, Neal should report a lease liability of
- a. $75,816
- b. $85,000
- c. $93,918
- d. $95,816

1N90#22. On December 31, 1988, Roe Co. leased a machine from Colt for a five-year period. Equal annual payments under the lease are $105,000 (including $5,000 annual executory costs) and are due on December 31 of each year. The first payment was made on December 31, 1988, and the second payment was made on December 31, 1989. The five lease payments are discounted at 10% over the lease term. The present value of minimum lease payments at the inception of the lease and before the first annual payment was $417,000. The lease is appropriately accounted for as a capital lease by Roe. In its December 31, 1989 balance sheet, Roe should report a lease liability of
- a. $317,000
- b. $315,000
- c. $285,300
- d. $248,700

1N90#33. Winn Co. manufactures equipment that is sold or leased. On December 31, 1989, Winn leased equipment to Bart for a five-year period ending December 31, 1994, at which date ownership of the leased asset will be transferred to Bart. Equal payments under the lease are $22,000 (including $2,000 executory costs) and are due on December 31 of each year. The first payment was made on December 31, 1989. Collectibility of the remaining lease payments is reasonably assured, and Winn has no material cost uncertainties. The normal sales price of the equipment is $77,000, and cost is $60,000. For the year ended December 31, 1989, what amount of income should Winn realize from the lease transaction?
- a. $17,000
- b. $22,000
- c. $23,000
- d. $33,000

1N90#46. Kew Apparel, Inc. leases and operates a retail store. The following information relates to the lease for the year ended December 31, 1989:

- The store lease, an operating lease, calls for a base monthly rent of $1,500 on the first day of each month.

- Additional rent is computed at 6% of net sales over $300,000 up to $600,000 and 5% of net sales over $600,000, per calendar year.

- Net sales for 1989 were $900,000.

- Kew paid executory costs to the lessor for property taxes of $12,000 and insurance of $5,000.

For 1989, Kew's expenses relating to the store lease are
- a. $71,000
- b. $68,000
- c. $54,000
- d. $35,000

TM90#11. A lessee had a ten-year capital lease requiring equal annual payments. The reduction of the lease liability in year 2 should equal
- a. The current liability shown for the lease at the end of year 1.
- b. The current liability shown for the lease at the end of year 2.
- c. The reduction of the lease obligation in year 1.
- d. One-tenth of the original lease liability.

TM90#24. A twenty-year property lease, classified as an operating lease, provides for a 10% increase in annual payments every five years. In the sixth year compared to the fifth year, the lease will cause the following expenses to increase

	Rent	Interest
a.	No	Yes
b.	Yes	No
c.	Yes	Yes
d.	No	No

1M90#33. On December 31, 1988, Ball Co. leased a machine from Cook for a ten-year period expiring December 30, 1998. Annual payments of $100,000 are due on December 31. The first payment was made on December 31, 1988, and the second payment was made on December 31, 1989. The present value at the inception of the lease for the ten lease payments discounted at 10% was $676,000. The lease is appropriately accounted for as a capital lease by Ball. In its December 31, 1989 balance sheet, Ball should report a lease liability of
- a. $643,600
- b. $608,400
- c. $533,600
- d. $518,400

1M90#35. On January 1, 1989, Day Corp. entered into a 10-year lease agreement with Ward, Inc. for industrial equipment. Annual lease payments of $10,000 are payable at the end of each year. Day knows that the lessor expects a 10% return on the lease. Day has a 12% incremental borrowing rate. The equipment is expected to have an estimated useful life of 10 years. In addition, a third party has guaranteed to pay Ward a residual value of $5,000 at the end of the lease.

The present value of an ordinary annuity of $1 at

12% for 10 years is 5.6502
10% for 10 years is 6.1446

The present value of $1 at

12% for 10 years is .3220
10% for 10 years is .3855

In Day's October 31, 1989 balance sheet, the principal amount of the lease obligation was
- a. $63,374
- b. $61,446
- c. $58,112
- d. $56,502

1M90
Items 50 and 51 are based on the following:

On January 2, 1989, Dix Machine Shops, Inc. signed a ten-year noncancellable lease for a heavy duty drill press. The lease stipulated annual payments of $30,000 starting at the end of the first year, with title passing to Dix at the expiration of the lease. Dix treated this transaction as a capital lease. The drill press has an estimated useful life of 15 years, with no salvage value. Dix uses straight-line depreciation for all of its fixed assets. Aggregate lease payments were determined to have a present value of $180,000, based on implicit interest of 10%.

50. In its 1989 income statement, what amount of interest expense should Dix report from this lease transaction?
- a. $0
- b. $12,000
- c. $15,000
- d. $18,000

51. In its 1989 income statement, what amount of depreciation expense should Dix report from this lease transaction?
- a. $30,000
- b. $20,000
- c. $18,000
- d. $12,000

O. Nonmonetary Transactions

M95#30. Slate Co. and Talse Co. exchanged similar plots of land with fair values in excess of carrying amounts. In addition, Slate received cash from Talse to compensate for the difference in land values. As a result of the exchange, Slate should recognize
- a. A gain equal to the difference between the fair value and the carrying amount of the land given up.
- b. A gain in an amount determined by the ratio of cash received to total consideration.
- c. A loss in an amount determined by the ratio of cash received to total consideration.
- d. Neither a gain nor a loss.

TN93#37. Bensol Co. and Sable Co. exchanged similar trucks with fair values in excess of carrying amounts. In addition, Bensol paid Sable to compensate for the difference in truck values. As a consequence of the exchange, Sable recognizes
- a. A gain equal to the difference between the fair value and carrying amount of the truck given up.
- b. A gain determined by the proportion of cash received to the total consideration.
- c. A loss determined by the proportion of cash received to the total consideration.
- d. Neither a gain **nor** a loss.

TM93#16. In an exchange of similar assets, Transit Co. received equipment with a fair value equal to the carrying amount of equipment given up. Transit also contributed cash. As a result of the exchange, Transit recognized
- a. A loss equal to the cash given up.
- b. A loss determined by the proportion of cash paid to the total transaction value.
- c. A gain determined by the proportion of cash paid to the total transaction value.
- d. Neither gain **nor** loss.

1M93#45. On June 27, 1992, Brite Co. distributed to its common stockholders 100,000 outstanding common shares of its investment in Quik, Inc., an unrelated party. The carrying amount on Brite's books of Quik's $1 par common stock was $2 per share. Immediately after the distribution, the market price of Quik's stock was $2.50 per share. In its income statement for the year ended June 30, 1992, what amount should Brite report as gain before income taxes on disposal of the stock?
- a. $250,000
- b. $200,000
- c. $ 50,000
- d. $0

Selected Questions

2M93#9. During 1992, Beam Co. paid $1,000 cash and traded inventory, which had a carrying amount of $20,000 and a fair value of $21,000, for other inventory in the same line of business with a fair value of $22,000. What amount of gain (loss) should Beam record related to the inventory exchange?
a. $2,000
b. $1,000
c. $0
d. ($1,000)

2M93#10. Amble, Inc. exchanged a truck with a carrying amount of $12,000 and a fair value of $20,000 for a truck and $5,000 cash. The fair value of the truck received was $15,000. At what amount should Amble record the truck received in the exchange?
a. $ 7,000
b. $ 9,000
c. $12,000
d. $15,000

TN92#20. Deed Co. owns 2% of Beck Cosmetic Retailers. A property dividend by Beck consisted of merchandise with a fair value lower than the listed retail price. Deed in turn gave the merchandise to its employees as a holiday bonus. How should Deed report the receipt and distribution of the merchandise in its income statement?
a. At fair value for both dividend revenue and employee compensation expense.
b. At listed retail price for both dividend revenue and employee compensation expense.
c. At fair value for dividend revenue and listed retail price for employee compensation expense.
d. By disclosure only.

TN92#24. Vik Auto and King Clothier exchanged goods, held for resale, with equal fair values. Each will use the other's goods to promote their own products. The retail price of the car that Vik gave up is less than the retail price of the clothes received. What profit should Vik recognize for the nonmonetary exchange?
a. A profit is **not** recognized.
b. A profit equal to the difference between the retail prices of the clothes received and the car.
c. A profit equal to the difference between the retail price and the cost of the car.
d. A profit equal to the difference between the fair value and the cost of the car.

1N92#20. On July 1, 1991, Balt Co. exchanged a truck for 25 shares of Ace Corp.'s common stock. On that date, the truck's carrying amount was $2,500, and its fair value was $3,000. Also, the book value of Ace's stock was $60 per share. On December 31, 1991, Ace had 250 shares of common stock outstanding and its book value per share was $50. What amount should Balt report in its December 31, 1991, balance sheet as investment in Ace?
a. $3,000
b. $2,500
c. $1,500
d. $1,250

1N92#46. Dahl Co. traded a delivery van and $5,000 cash for a newer van owned by West Corp. The following information relates to the values of the vans on the exchange date:

	Carrying value	Fair value
Old van	$30,000	$45,000
New van	40,000	50,000

Dahl's income tax rate is 30%. What amounts should Dahl report as gain on exchange of the vans?
a. $15,000
b. $ 1,000
c. $ 700
d. $0

2N92#45. Mio Corp. was the sole stockholder of Plasti Corp. On September 30, 1991, Mio declared a property dividend of Plasti's 2,000 outstanding shares of $1 par value common stock, distributable to Mio's stockholders. On that date, the book value of Plasti's stock was $1.50 per share. Immediately after the distribution, the market value of Plasti's stock was $4.50 per share. What amount should Mio report in its 1991 financial statements as gain on disposal of the Plasti stock?
a. $1,000
b. $2,000
c. $3,000
d. $6,000

TM92#36. Instead of the usual cash dividend, Evie Corp. declared and distributed a property dividend from its overstocked merchandise. The excess of the merchandise's carrying amount over its market value should be
a. Ignored.
b. Reported as a separately disclosed reduction of retained earnings.
c. Reported as an extraordinary loss, net of income taxes.
d. Reported as a reduction in income before extraordinary items.

1M92#19. On December 31, 1991, Vey Co. traded equipment with an original cost of $100,000 and accumulated depreciation of $40,000 for similar productive equipment with a fair value of $60,000. In addition, Vey received $30,000 cash in connection with this exchange. What should be Vey's carrying amount for the equipment received at December 31, 1991?
a. $30,000
b. $40,000
c. $60,000
d. $80,000

2M92#11. Yola Co. and Zaro Co. are fuel oil distributors. To facilitate the delivery of oil to their customers, Yola and Zaro exchanged ownership of 1,200 barrels of oil without physically moving the oil. Yola paid Zaro $30,000 to compensate for a difference in the grade of oil. On the date of the exchange, cost and market values of the oil were as follows:

	Yola Co.	Zaro Co.
Cost	$100,000	$126,000
Market values	120,000	150,000

In Zaro's income statement, what amount of gain should be reported from the exchange of the oil?
- a. $0
- b. $ 4,800
- c. $24,000
- d. $30,000

2N91#9. Pine City owned a vacant plot of land zoned for industrial use. Pine gave this land to Medi Corp. solely as an incentive for Medi to build a factory on the site. The land had a fair value of $300,000 at the date of the gift. This nonmonetary transaction should be reported by Medi as
- a. Extraordinary income.
- b. Additional paid-in capital.
- c. A credit to retained earnings.
- d. A memorandum entry.

TM91#35. May Co. and Sty Co. exchanged nonmonetary assets. The exchange did not culminate an earning process for either May or Sty. May paid cash to Sty in connection with the exchange. To the extent that the amount of cash exceeds a proportionate share of the carrying amount of the asset surrendered, a realized gain on the exchange should be recognized by

	May	Sty
a.	Yes	Yes
b.	Yes	No
c.	No	Yes
d.	No	No

TN90#12. Solen Co. and Nolse Co. exchanged similar trucks with fair values in excess of carrying amounts. In addition, Solen paid Nolse to compensate for the difference in truck values. As a consequence of the exchange, Solen recognizes
- a. A gain equal to the difference between the fair value and carrying amount of the truck given up.
- b. A gain determined by the proportion of cash paid to the total consideration.
- c. A loss determined by the proportion of cash paid to the total consideration.
- d. Neither a gain **nor** a loss.

2N90#18. Slad Co. exchanged similar productive assets with Gil Co. and, in addition, paid Gil cash of $100,000. The following information pertains to this exchange:

Assets	Carrying amounts	Fair values
Relinquished by Gil	$75,000	$140,000
Relinquished by Slad	40,000	40,000

On Slad's books, the assets acquired should be recorded at what amount?

- a. $ 75,000
- b. $100,000
- c. $140,000
- d. $175,000

TM90#31. Scott Co. exchanged similar nonmonetary assets with Dale Co. No cash was exchanged. The carrying amount of the asset surrendered by Scott exceeded both the fair value of the asset received and Dale's carrying amount of that asset. Scott should recognize the difference between the carrying amount of the asset it surrendered and
- a. The fair value of the asset it received as a loss.
- b. The fair value of the asset it received as a gain.
- c. Dale's carrying amount of the asset it received as a loss.
- d. Dale's carrying amount of the asset it received as a gain.

P. Quasi-reorganizations, Reorganizations, and Changes in Entity

N95#25. The stockholders' equity section of Brown Co.'s December 31, 1994, balance sheet consisted of the following:

Common stock, $30 par, 10,000 shares authorized and outstanding	$ 300,000
Additional paid-in capital	150,000
Retained earnings (deficit)	(210,000)

On January 2, 1995, Brown put into effect a stockholder-approved quasi-reorganization by reducing the par value of the stock to $5 and eliminating the deficit against additional paid-in capital. Immediately after the quasi-reorganization, what amount should Brown report as additional paid-in capital?
- a. $(60,000)
- b. $150,000
- c. $190,000
- d. $400,000

N94#37. The primary purpose of a quasi-reorganization is to give a corporation the opportunity to
- a. Obtain relief from its creditors.
- b. Revalue understated assets to their fair values.
- c. Eliminate a deficit in retained earnings.
- d. Distribute the stock of a newly-created subsidiary to its stockholders in exchange for part of their stock in the corporation.

M94#39. Which of the following statements is correct regarding accounting changes that result in financial statements that are, in effect, the statements of a different reporting entity?
- a. Cumulative-effect adjustments should be reported as separate items on the financial statements pertaining to the year of change.
- b. No restatements or adjustments are required if the changes involve consolidated methods of accounting for subsidiaries.

c. No restatements or adjustments are required if the changes involve the cost or equity methods of accounting for investments.
d. The financial statements of all prior periods presented should be restated.

2M93#6. The condensed balance sheet of Adams & Gray, a partnership, at December 31, 1992, follows:

Current assets	$250,000
Equipment (net)	30,000
Total assets	$280,000
Liabilities	$ 20,000
Adams, capital	160,000
Gray, capital	100,000
Total liabilities and capital	$280,000

On December 31, 1992, the fair values of the assets and liabilities were appraised at $240,000 and $20,000, respectively, by an independent appraiser. On January 2, 1993, the partnership was incorporated and 1,000 shares of $5 par value common stock were issued. Immediately after the incorporation, what amount should the new corporation report as additional paid-in capital?
a. $275,000
b. $260,000
c. $215,000
d. $0

TN92#19. When a company goes through a quasi-reorganization, its balance sheet carrying amounts are stated at:
a. Original cost.
b. Original book value.
c. Replacement value.
d. Fair value.

2N91#8. Jay & Kay partnership's balance sheet at December 31, 1990, reported the following:

Total assets	$100,000
Total liabilities	20,000
Jay, capital	40,000
Kay, capital	40,000

On January 2, 1991, Jay and Kay dissolved their partnership and transferred all assets and liabilities to a newly formed corporation. At the date of incorporation, the fair value of the net assets was $12,000 more than the carrying amount on the partnership's books, of which $7,000 was assigned to tangible assets and $5,000 was assigned to goodwill. Jay and Kay were each issued 5,000 shares of the corporation's $1 par value common stock. Immediately following incorporation, additional paid-in capital in excess of par should be credited for

a. $68,000
b. $70,000
c. $77,000
d. $82,000

Q. Related Parties

R98#6. Lemu Co. and Young Co. are under the common management of Ego Co. Ego can significantly influence the operating results of both Lemu and Young. While Lemu had no transactions with Ego during the year, Young sold merchandise to Ego under the same terms given to unrelated parties. In the notes to their respective financial statements, should Lemu and Young disclose their relationship with Ego?

	Lemu	Young
a.	Yes	Yes
b.	Yes	No
c.	No	Yes
d.	No	No

R96#10. Which of the following related party transactions by a company should be disclosed in the notes to the financial statements?

I. Payment of per diem expenses to members of the board of directors.
II. Consulting fees paid to a marketing research firm, one of whose partners is also a director of the company.

a. I only.
b. II only.
c. Both I and II.
d. Neither I nor II.

N95#7. For which type of material related-party transactions does Statement of Financial Accounting Standard No. 57, *Related Party Disclosures,* require disclosure?
a. Only those not reported in the body of the financial statements.
b. Only those that receive accounting recognition.
c. Those that contain possible illegal acts.
d. All those other than compensation arrangements, expense allowances, and other similar items in the ordinary course of business.

1N90#53. Dean Co. acquired 100% of Morey Corp. prior to 1989. During 1989, the individual companies included in their financial statements the following:

	Dean	Morey
Officers' salaries	$ 75,000	$ 50,000
Officers' expenses	20,000	10,000
Loans to officers	125,000	50,000
Intercompany sales	150,000	—

What amount should be reported as related party disclosures in the notes to Dean's 1989 consolidated financial statements?

a. $150,000
b. $155,000
c. $175,000
d. $330,000

R. Research and Development Costs

N94#44. During 1993, Orr Co. incurred the following costs:

Research and development services performed by Key Corp. for Orr	$150,000
Design, construction, and testing of preproduction prototypes and models	200,000
Testing in search for new products or process alternatives	175,000

In its 1993 income statement, what should Orr report as research and development expense?
a. $150,000
b. $200,000
c. $350,000
d. $525,000

1N93#56. Brill Co. made the following expenditures during 1992:

Costs to develop computer software for internal use in Brill's general management information system	$100,000
Costs of market research activities	75,000

What amount of these expenditures should Brill report in its 1992 income statement as research and development expenses?
a. $175,000
b. $100,000
c. $ 75,000
d. $0

1M93#23. During 1992, Lyle Co. incurred $400,000 of research and development costs in its laboratory to develop a product for which a patent was granted on July 1, 1992. Legal fees and other costs associated with the patent totaled $82,000. The estimated economic life of the patent is 10 years. What amount should Lyle capitalize for the patent on July 1, 1992?
a. $0
b. $ 82,000
c. $400,000
d. $482,000

1N92#53. Heller Co. incurred the following costs in 1991:

Research and development services performed by Kay Corp. for Heller	$150,000
Testing for evaluation of new products	125,000
Laboratory research aimed at discovery of new knowledge	185,000

What amount should Heller report as research and development costs in its income statement for the year ended December 31, 1991?

a. $125,000
b. $150,000
c. $335,000
d. $460,000

TM92#31. Which of the following costs is included in research and development expense?
a. Ongoing efforts to improve existing products.
b. Troubleshooting in connection with breakdowns during commercial production.
c. Periodic design changes to existing products.
d. Design, construction, and testing of preproduction prototypes and models.

1M92#51. West, Inc. made the following expenditures relating to Product Y:

- Legal costs to file a patent on Product Y — $10,000. Production of the finished product would not have been undertaken without the patent.

- Special equipment to be used solely for development of Product Y — $60,000. The equipment has no other use and has an estimated useful life of four years.

- Labor and material costs incurred in producing a prototype model — $200,000.

- Cost of testing the prototype — $80,000.

What is the total amount of costs that will be expensed when incurred?
a. $280,000
b. $295,000
c. $340,000
d. $350,000

TN91#32. On January 1, 1990, Jambon purchased equipment for use in developing a new product. Jambon uses the straight-line depreciation method. The equipment could provide benefits over a 10-year period. However, the new product development is expected to take five years, and the equipment can be used only for this project. Jambon's 1990 expense equals
a. The total cost of the equipment.
b. One-fifth of the cost of the equipment.
c. One-tenth of the cost of the equipment.
d. Zero.

1N91#47. In 1990, Ball Labs incurred the following costs:

Direct costs of doing contract research and development work for the government to be reimbursed by governmental unit	$ 400,000

Research and development costs not included above were:

Depreciation	$300,000
Salaries	700,000
Indirect costs appropriately allocated	200,000
Materials	180,000

What was Ball's total research and development expense in 1990?
- a. $1,080,000
- b. $1,380,000
- c. $1,580,000
- d. $1,780,000

1M91
Items 21 and 22 are based on the following:

During 1990, Pitt Corp. incurred costs to develop and produce a routine, low-risk computer software product, as follows:

Completion of detail program design	$13,000
Costs incurred for coding and testing to establish technological feasibility	10,000
Other coding costs after establishment of technological feasibility	24,000
Other testing costs after establishment of technological feasibility	20,000
Costs of producing product masters for training materials	15,000
Duplication of computer software and training materials from product masters (1,000 units)	25,000
Packaging product (500 units)	9,000

21. In Pitt's December 31, 1990, balance sheet, what amount should be reported in inventory?
- a. $25,000
- b. $34,000
- c. $40,000
- d. $49,000

22. In Pitt's December 31, 1990, balance sheet, what amount should be capitalized as software cost, subject to amortization?
- a. $54,000
- b. $57,000
- c. $59,000
- d. $69,000

1N90#42. Cody Corp. incurred the following costs during 1989:

Design of tools, jigs, molds, and dies involving new technology	$125,000
Modification of the formulation of a process	160,000
Trouble-shooting in connection with breakdowns during commercial production	100,000
Adaptation of an existing capability to a particular customer's need as part of a continuing commercial activity	110,000

In its 1989 income statement, Cody should report research and development expense of
- a. $125,000
- b. $160,000
- c. $235,000
- d. $285,000

1M90#53. During 1989, Vest Co. incurred the following costs:

Testing in search for process alternatives	$280,000
Routine design of tools, jigs, molds, and dies	250,000
Modification of the formulation of a process	410,000
Research and development services performed by Acme Corp. for Vest	325,000

In Vest's 1989 income statement, research and development expense should be
- a. $ 410,000
- b. $ 735,000
- c. $1,015,000
- d. $1,265,000

S. Segment Reporting

N95#8. Terra Co.'s total revenues from its three business segments were as follows:

Segment	Sales to unaffiliated customers	Intersegment sales	Total revenues
Lion	$ 70,000	$30,000	$100,000
Monk	22,000	4,000	26,000
Nevi	8,000	16,000	24,000
Combined	$100,000	$50,000	$150,000
Elimination	—	(50,000)	(50,000)
Consolidated	$100,000	$ —	$100,000

Which business segment(s) is(are) deemed to be reportable segments?
- a. None.
- b. Lion only.
- c. Lion and Monk only.
- d. Lion, Monk, and Nevi.

M95#56. Disclosure is required by publicly-held companies if 10% or more of total revenues are derived from

	Sales to a single customer	Export sales
a.	Yes	Yes
b.	Yes	No
c.	No	Yes
d.	No	No

TN92#36. Cott Co.'s four business segments have revenues and identifiable assets expressed as percentages of Cott's total revenues and total assets as follows:

	Revenues	Assets
Ebon	64%	66%
Fair	14%	18%
Gel	14%	4%
Hak	8%	12%
	100%	100%

Which of these business segments are deemed to be reportable segments?
- a. Ebon only.
- b. Ebon and Fair only.
- c. Ebon, Fair, and Gel only.
- d. Ebon, Fair, Gel, and Hak.

SELECTED MULTIPLE CHOICE ITEMS — UNOFFICIAL ANSWERS

I. Concepts and Standards for Financial Statements

A. Financial Accounting Concepts

N95# 1 d
N95# 2 b
N95# 3 a
N95# 4 a
N95# 5 d
N95# 6 a
M95# 1 d
M95# 2 c
N94# 1 b
N94# 2 d
N94# 3 d
M94# 1 d
M94# 2 c
M94# 4 c
TN92# 1 c
TN92# 2 a
TN92# 3 d
TM92# 1 d
TM92# 2 d
TM92# 3 b
TM91# 1 a

B. Financial Accounting Standards for Presentation and Disclosure in General Purpose Financial Statements

1. Consolidated and Combined Financial Statements

N95# 49 b
N95# 50 b
N95# 51 b
M95#50 d
M95#51 b
M95#52 a
N94# 56 a
M94# 7 c
M94#55 d
M94#56 a

TN93# 11 a
TM93# 4 b
TM93# 5 d
TM93# 6 b
TM93# 7 d
TM93# 8 d
1M93# 9 c
1M93#14 d
2M93# 8 a
TN92#31 b
TN92#33 a
TN92#34 b
1N92# 14 d
1N92# 15 b
1N92# 16 c
1N92# 17 b
1N92# 18 b
2N92# 60 a
TM92#40 d
1M92# 6 c
1M92# 7 a
1M92# 8 d
1M92# 9 b
1M92#10 a
1M92#11 c
2M92#20 b
TN91# 8 d
TN91# 9 a
1N91# 10 d
1N91# 53 d
2N91# 10 d
1M91# 7 a
1M91#13 a
1M91#14 b
1M91#15 d
1M91#16 b
1M91#17 b
2M91#19 c
2M91#20 a
TN90# 2 c
TN90# 3 a
1N90# 60 c
1M90#11 d

2. Balance Sheet

R98# 1 b

N95# 60 b
M95# 5 c
N94# 5 a
N94# 8 a
N94# 9 c
M94# 3 a
M94#11 c
TN93# 2 c
1N93# 1 a
1M93# 1 a
1N92# 1 b
1N92# 2 a
1N92# 3 c
1N92# 6 c
TM92#48 b
2M92#18 a
1M91# 2 a

3. Statement(s) of Income, Comprehensive Income, and Changes in Equity Accounts

M94# 8 d
M94# 9 a
M94#10 c
1N93# 10 b
1M93# 5 d
1N92# 8 b
1M91# 3 d

4. Statement of Cash Flows

R97# 7 d
N95# 47 d
N95# 48 d
M95#49 c
N94# 7 c
M94# 5 c
TN93#41 a
1N93# 9 d
TM93#32 d
TM93#33 c
TN92# 21 d

TN92#44 a
1N92# 9 d
1N92# 10 d
1N92# 11 c
1N92# 12 a
1N92# 13 c
TM92# 8 d
1M91# 8 c

5. Accounting Policies and Other Notes to Financial Statements

N94# 4 c
N94# 59 c
M94# 6 a
M94#57 d
M94#58 a
TN93#19 a
1N93# 42 c
TM93#31 d
2M93#11 c
TN92#37 c
TN92#40 a
2N92# 51 c
TM92# 4 c
TM92# 5 a
TM92#49 a
2M92#13 d
TM91#32 b
1N90# 54 d
TM90#30 c
TM90#35 c
2M90#50 b

C. Other Presentations of Financial Data

1. Financial Statements Prepared in Conformity With Comprehensive Bases of Accounting Other Than Generally Accepted Accounting Principles

N95# 57 c

Note: (T)—Questions are from previous Accounting Theory Exams.
(1)—Questions are from previous Accounting Practice Part I Exams.
(2)—Questions are from previous Accounting Practice Part II Exams.

Financial Accounting and Reporting

N94# 58 d	TM92# 6 c	N95# 54 d	2N92# 59 c
M94#42 d	1M92#39 d	N95# 55 d	TM92#50 c
M94#54 c	TM90#18 b	M95#55 c	2M92#19 d
TN93#40 c	**2. Personal Financial Statements**	M94#53 a	TM91#40 b
1N93# 43 d		TN93#44 b	2M91# 9 d
1M93#40 d		TN92#43 d	2M91#10 a
TN92# 6 b	R98# 2 b	2N92# 57 d	1N90# 59 d
1N92# 41 b	R98# 3 a	2N92# 58 b	2M90#59 a

II. Recognition, Measurement, Valuation, and Presentation of Typical Items in Financial Statements in Conformity With Generally Accepted Accounting Principles

A. Cash, Cash Equivalents, and Marketable Securities

- M95# 6 d
- N94# 10 b
- M94#12 b
- M94#13 c
- 1M93#10 c
- 1N91# 9 c
- TM91#38 c
- 1N90# 1 a
- 1M90# 1 a

B. Receivables

- R96# 7 c
- M95# 7 d
- M95# 8 c
- M95# 9 a
- N94# 11 c
- N94# 12 a
- M94#15 a
- M94#16 a
- 1N93# 15 c
- 1N93# 16 d
- 1N93# 17 c
- 1N93# 18 a
- TM93#24 d
- 1M93#12 c
- 1M93#17 a
- TN92# 4 b
- TN92# 11 c
- TM92#21 b
- TM92#41 c
- TM92#47 a
- 1M92#15 d
- 1M92#16 c
- 1M92#21 c
- TN91# 6 c
- 1N91# 17 c
- TM91#10 a

2M91#14 c
2M91#15 d
1N90# 5 a
1N90# 6 b
1N90# 56 d
2N90# 1 d
2N90# 3 c
2N90# 9 a
1M90# 5 a
1M90# 9 d
1M90#10 c
1M90#12 a

C. Inventories

- R97# 1 d
- N95# 9 c
- M95#11 b
- N94# 13 d
- N94# 14 b
- TN93# 3 b
- TN93# 4 d
- TN93#20 d
- 1N93# 19 d
- 1N93# 20 c
- 1N93# 21 c
- 1M93#18 b
- 1M93#19 b
- 1M93#20 d
- 1M93#21 c
- TN92#12 d
- TN92#14 d
- TN92#15 c
- TM92#23 c
- TM92#24 a
- TM92#25 b
- 1M92#17 d
- 1M92#18 b
- TN91# 7 a
- TN91#27 a
- TN91#28 b
- 1N91# 13 c
- 2N91# 18 b

TN90# 15 a
TN90# 16 a
TN90# 17 c
1N90# 7 c
1N90# 8 c
1N90# 57 b
TM90#38 c
1M90#14 b

D. Property, Plant, and Equipment

- R97# 8 b
- M95#12 a
- M94#17 b
- M94#18 b
- 1N93# 22 a
- 1N93# 23 b
- 1N93# 24 d
- TM93#26 c
- TM93#27 c
- 1M93#22 c
- 1M93#24 c
- TM92#11 b
- TM92#12 c
- TM92#13 a
- TM92#16 b
- 1M92#22 a
- TN91#33 b
- 1N91# 15 d
- 1N91# 16 a
- 1N91# 18 b
- 1N91# 19 a
- 1M91#23 d
- 1M91#24 c
- 1M91#26 d
- 1M91#27 b
- TN90# 13 a
- 2N90# 4 a
- 2N90# 5 b
- 2N90# 13 a
- 1M90#15 c
- 1M90#16 d

1M90#17 b
1M90#18 b

E. Investments

- R97# 2 b
- R96# 6 b
- N95# 27 b
- N94# 16 b
- M94#19 d
- TN93# 9 a
- 1N93# 12 a
- 1N93# 14 c
- TM93#11 d
- 1M93#16 b
- TN92#30 a
- 1M92#12 c
- TN91#36 a
- TM91# 4 b
- 1M90# 4 a

F. Intangibles and Other Assets

- M95#13 a
- M95#14 b
- M94#20 c
- TN93# 10 b
- 1N93# 25 d
- TM93#25 a
- 1M93#25 c
- 1M93#27 b
- TN92#29 a
- TM92#14 a
- 1M92#20 c
- 1M92#23 c
- TN91# 13 a
- 1M91#28 d
- 1M91#29 b
- 1M91#30 d
- 1M90#20 b
- 2M90#52 d
- 2M90#58 c

Note: (T)—Questions are from previous Accounting Theory Exams.
(1)—Questions are from previous Accounting Practice Part I Exams.
(2)—Questions are from previous Accounting Practice Part II Exams.

Unofficial Answers

G. Payables and Accruals

- M95# 15 b
- N94# 19 b
- M94# 21 b
- M94# 22 a
- 1N93# 30 a
- 1M93# 29 c
- TN92# 5 a
- TN92# 42 a
- 1N92# 5 d
- 1N92# 21 a
- TM92# 19 d
- TM92# 26 c
- TM91# 14 d
- 1M91# 34 a
- 1M91# 37 d
- TN90# 22 a
- 1N90# 10 b
- 1N90# 12 d
- 1M90# 22 c
- 1M90# 23 d
- 1M90# 27 d

H. Deferred Revenues

- N95# 10 c
- N95# 11 b
- N94# 21 d
- M94# 23 d
- 1N93# 38 b
- 1N93# 45 a
- TM93# 40 b
- 1M93# 13 d
- TN92# 7 b
- 1N92# 28 b
- 1N92# 29 c
- 1N92# 30 d
- 1N92# 35 b
- TM92# 32 d
- 1M92# 27 a
- 1M92# 28 d
- 1M92# 31 a
- TN91# 19 d
- 1N91# 27 c
- 1N91# 29 a
- TM91# 15 d
- 1M91# 40 d
- 1M91# 43 c
- 1M91# 44 b
- TN90# 23 a
- 1N90# 17 b
- 1N90# 34 c
- TM90# 9 b

I. Notes and Bonds Payable

- R97# 9 d
- N95# 59 b
- M95# 19 d
- M95# 20 b
- N94# 22 b
- N94# 24 b
- M94# 29 b
- M94# 30 d
- 1N93# 27 b
- 1N93# 33 c
- 1N93# 34 d
- 1N93# 36 c
- 1N93# 37 b
- 1M93# 2 c
- 1M93# 32 d
- TN92# 9 c
- 1N92# 22 c
- 1N92# 36 c
- 1N92# 37 d
- 1N92# 38 b
- 1N92# 39 d
- 1M92# 29 b
- 1M92# 30 c
- TN91# 35 c
- TN91# 37 c
- 1N91# 28 a
- 1N91# 36 d
- TM91# 5 b
- TM91# 6 c
- 1M91# 35 c
- 1M91# 46 d
- 1M91# 47 a
- TN90# 29 d
- TN90# 30 c
- TN90# 31 a
- 1N90# 11 d
- 1N90# 23 d
- 1N90# 24 b
- 1N90# 25 b
- 1N90# 26 b
- 1M90# 29 a
- 1M90# 37 a
- 1M90# 38 b
- 1M90# 40 d

J. Other Liabilities

- N95# 13 d
- N95# 16 d
- M95# 21 a
- N94# 25 b
- 1N93# 32 c
- 1N92# 24 a
- 1N92# 26 b
- 1N92# 40 c
- 1N91# 26 b
- 1M91# 39 b
- 1N90# 14 b
- 1M90# 30 c

K. Equity Accounts

- R98# 4 d
- R96# 1 a
- N95# 15 a
- N95# 18 a
- N95# 19 a
- N95# 20 b
- N95# 21 c
- N95# 23 a
- M95# 23 d
- M95# 24 b
- N94# 28 a
- N94# 29 a
- N94# 30 a
- N94# 31 b
- N94# 32 c
- N94# 35 c
- M94# 31 c
- M94# 32 b
- M94# 35 a
- M94# 36 b
- M94# 37 a
- TN93# 15 a
- TM93# 2 a
- TM93# 9 c
- TM93# 10 c
- TM93# 13 d
- 1M93# 6 a
- 2M93# 1 a
- 2M93# 2 d
- 2M93# 3 b
- 2M93# 4 b
- 2M93# 5 a
- 2M93# 13 b
- 2M93# 18 b
- 2M93# 19 d
- TN92# 18 b
- TN92# 22 c
- 1N92# 7 a
- 2N92# 41 a
- 2N92# 42 c
- 2N92# 43 b
- 2N92# 44 b
- 2N92# 47 c
- 2N92# 48 d
- 2N92# 49 a
- 2N92# 50 c
- TM92# 35 d
- TM92# 37 d
- 1M92# 2 d
- 1M92# 3 a
- 2M92# 1 c
- 2M92# 3 d
- 2M92# 5 a
- 2M92# 6 a
- 2M92# 8 a
- TN91# 15 b
- TN91# 38 d
- TN91# 39 c
- TN91# 40 c
- 1N91# 37 a
- 2N91# 1 a
- 2N91# 3 d
- 2N91# 11 c
- TM91# 17 b
- TM91# 18 b
- TM91# 19 d
- TM91# 39 d
- 1M91# 19 a
- 1M91# 20 d
- 2M91# 2 c
- 2M91# 3 b
- TN90# 32 c
- TN90# 33 c
- TN90# 40 a
- TM90# 13 c
- TM90# 14 a
- TM90# 15 b
- TM90# 16 a
- 1M90# 42 c

L. Revenue, Cost, and Expense Accounts

- R97# 10 c
- R96# 2 d
- R96# 5 c
- N95# 26 b
- N95# 28 b
- N95# 29 a
- N95# 30 c
- N95# 31 d
- N95# 33 b
- N95# 34 d
- N95# 35 b
- M95# 10 c
- M95# 25 c
- M95# 26 a
- M95# 27 c
- M95# 28 c
- M95# 29 c
- M95# 33 b
- M95# 34 d
- M95# 35 b
- M95# 36 b
- M95# 37 b
- M95# 38 b
- M95# 40 d
- N94# 23 c
- N94# 38 b
- N94# 39 d
- N94# 40 a
- N94# 41 d
- N94# 43 c
- N94# 45 b

Note: (T)—Questions are from previous Accounting Theory Exams.
(1)—Questions are from previous Accounting Practice Part I Exams.
(2)—Questions are from previous Accounting Practice Part II Exams.

Financial Accounting and Reporting

N94# 46 a	1M93#48 c	1M92#50 b	1N90# 47 a
N94# 47 c	1M93#49 b	1M92#54 a	2N90# 2 d
N94# 48 b	1M93#50 c	TN91# 5 d	2N90# 6 c
M94#40 a	1M93#51 b	TN91#10 b	2N90# 8 d
M94#41 d	1M93#52 a	TN91#14 d	2N90#10 a
M94#43 b	2M93# 7 a	TN91#20 d	2N90#12 c
M94#44 c	TN92# 8 b	1N91#31 c	2N90#15 d
M94#45 a	TN92#10 a	1N91#42 a	2N90#20 d
TN93#24 d	TN92#28 b	1N91#44 a	TM90#20 b
TN93#34 a	1N92#42 b	1N91#54 a	TM90#21 b
TN93#38 a	1N92#43 c	1N91#57 c	TM90#34 b
TN93#39 b	1N92#44 d	1N91#58 b	TM90#39 c
1N93#46 b	1N92#45 c	TM91# 8 c	1M90#44 d
1N93#47 a	1N92#51 c	TM91# 9 a	1M90#45 a
1N93#48 c	1N92#55 b	TM91#25 d	1M90#46 d
1N93#50 c	1N92#56 b	TM91#28 c	1M90#47 d
1N93#51 b	2N92#53 a	1M91#48 c	1M90#48 c
1N93#52 a	TM92#15 a	1M91#49 c	1M90#49 b
1N93#53 a	TM92#17 b	1M91#50 c	1M90#54 d
1N93#54 c	TM92#18 c	1M91#52 c	1M90#56 c
1N93#55 d	TM92#29 a	1M91#53 a	1M90#57 a
1N93#59 b	TM92#43 d	1M91#54 b	1M90#58 b
TM93#28 c	TM92#44 b	1M91#56 a	2M90#41 d
TM93#35 b	TM92#45 c	1M91#57 c	2M90#45 b
TM93#39 a	TM92#46 b	TN90#14 d	2M90#46 a
1M93#37 a	1M92#40 b	TN90#19 c	2M90#48 c
1M93#38 a	1M92#41 c	TN90#37 b	2M90#49 a
1M93#39 b	1M92#43 a	1N90#32 a	2M90#55 a
1M93#41 d	1M92#44 b	1N90#35 c	2M90#57 c
1M93#42 b	1M92#45 b	1N90#36 d	
1M93#43 b	1M92#46 c	1N90#37 a	
1M93#44 d	1M92#47 a	1N90#39 b	
1M93#47 a	1M92#48 b	1N90#40 a	
	1M92#49 d	1N90#45 d	

III. Recognition, Measurement, Valuation, and Presentation of Specific Types of Transactions and Events in Financial Statements in Conformity With Generally Accepted Accounting Principles

A. Accounting Changes and Corrections of Errors

	2M92# 2 c	TN93#12 b	M94#50 b
	TN91#25 a	TN93#13 b	1N93# 5 a
	TN91#26 d	1M93# 7 b	1N93# 6 b
	2N91# 2 a	1M93# 8 d	1N93# 7 a
R97# 4 a	TM91#27 d	TN92#32 d	1N93# 8 c
N95#44 a	TM91#34 d	TN92#35 a	TM92# 7 a
M95#45 c	1M91#59 c	TN91#11 d	TN91#21 c
M95#46 d	1M91#60 b	TN91#12 b	TM91#30 c
N94#54 d	TN90#36 b	1N91#20 d	TM91#31 d
N94#55 c		2N91#17 a	1M91# 4 c
TN93#22 b	**B. Business Combinations**	TM90#32 c	1M91# 6 c
TN93#23 a			1M91#11 d
TN93#26 b		**C. Cash Flow Components—Financing, Investing, and Operating**	2N90#17 b
1N93# 4 c	R96# 3 b		TM90#27 a
1N93#60 d	N95#52 c		TM90#28 c
TM93#19 c	N95#53 c		
TM93#20 a	M95#53 d	R97# 3 b	**D. Contingent Liabilities and Commitments**
1M93#53 b	M95#54 a	M95#47 a	
1N92#60 a	M94#51 a	M95#48 d	
2N92#46 b	M94#52 d		N95#17 a

Note: (T)—Questions are from previous Accounting Theory Exams.
(1)—Questions are from previous Accounting Practice Part I Exams.
(2)—Questions are from previous Accounting Practice Part II Exams.

Unofficial Answers

M95#22 a	M94#28 b	**I. Financial Instruments**	1M90#26 a
N94# 26 a	M94#33 a		
TN93#21 a	M94#34 c	R96# 8 c	**L. Interest Costs**
1N93#41 d	TN93#28 b	R96# 9 c	
TM93#29 c	TN93#29 a	M95# 4 a	R97# 6 a
1M93#33 d	TN93#30 c		N94# 18 d
1M93#34 d	1N93# 26 c	**J. Foreign Currency**	M94#46 d
2M93#20 c	1N93# 28 d	**Transactions and**	TN93#33 c
TN92#17 b	TM93#14 d	**Translation**	1N93# 29 d
1N92# 31 a	1M93#28 d		1N93# 31 c
TM92#27 b	1M93#30 d	N95# 32 a	1N92# 23 b
1M92#35 d	TN92#25 c	M95#31 b	TM91#23 d
1M92#36 b	TN92#26 b	M95#32 d	1M91#33 b
1N91# 39 d	1N92# 25 a	TN93#35 b	1M91#55 c
TM91#16 c	TM92#20 c	TN93#36 a	1N90# 41 c
TN90#35 d	1M92#25 c	1N93# 49 b	TM90# 8 b
1N90# 28 c	2M92#14 d	TM93#34 b	
1M90#60 c	2M92#15 b	1M93#46 c	**M. Interim Financial**
	TN91#29 c	TM92#39 b	**Reporting**
E. Discontinued	TN91#31 b	1M92#52 a	
Operations	1N91# 23 c	TN91#18 b	TN93#31 b
	TM91#37 b	1N91# 46 d	2M93#17 c
N95# 40 d	1M91#32 c	1N90# 38 c	TN92#16 a
M95#44 b	1M91#36 b	1N90# 43 d	2N92# 52 c
N94# 52 a	2M91#17 b	TM90#22 b	2M92#12 b
TN93#18 b	TN90#20 b	1M90#52 a	2N91# 13 a
TM93# 3 c	TN90#21 d	2M90#44 c	1N90# 55 b
TM93#37 c	1N90# 15 d		2M90#43 d
1M93#57 a	2N90# 16 d	**K. Income Taxes**	
1M93#58 c	TM90#37 c		**N. Leases**
1M93#59 a	2M90#53 c	R97# 11 d	
1M92#57 c		N95# 36 c	R96# 4 d
1N91# 45 d	**H. Extraordinary Items**	N95# 37 b	N95# 12 c
1N91# 50 c		N95# 38 c	N94# 20 a
1N91# 51 a	R97# 5 c	M95#16 d	M94#25 b
1N90# 49 a	N95# 41 d	M95#17 b	M94#26 b
TM90#26 a	N95# 42 a	M95#41 c	TN93#42 c
2M90#47 a	N94# 42 a	M95#42 c	1N93# 35 b
	N94# 53 d	M95#43 c	1N93# 39 a
F. Earnings Per Share	M94#48 b	N94# 6 d	1N93# 44 b
	TN93#25 d	N94# 49 d	TM93#38 d
R98# 5 a	1N93# 57 d	N94# 50 a	TN92#27 b
N95# 45 b	1N93# 58 a	N94# 51 c	1N92# 33 c
M94#49 d	TM93#12 a	M94#24 d	1N92# 34 d
1M93#60 b	TM93#18 c	M94#47 a	TM92#33 d
TN92#23 c	1N92# 47 b	TN93#32 d	TM92#34 a
1M92#59 d	1M92#53 d	1M93#26 b	1M92#34 c
TN91#16 b	1M92#55 d	1M93#35 a	TN91#34 a
1N90# 52 b	1M92#58 b	1M93#36 a	1N91# 14 b
	2M92# 9 b	1M93#54 c	1N91# 33 b
G. Employee Benefits	TN91#23 c	1M93#55 c	1N91# 34 b
	1N91# 24 d	TN92#41 d	1M91#25 b
N95# 14 c	1N91# 43 d	1N92# 27 a	1M91#42 a
N95# 22 c	1N91# 52 c	1N92# 32 b	1M91#45 b
M95#18 a	TM91#26 b	1M92#26 c	TN90#26 c
M95#39 b	1N90# 27 c	1N91# 25 b	1N90# 21 a
N94# 33 b	1N90# 50 a	1N90# 16 a	1N90# 22 d
N94# 34 a	2N90# 11 d	2N90# 7 b	1N90# 33 a
M94#27 a			

Note: (T)—Questions are from previous Accounting Theory Exams.
     (1)—Questions are from previous Accounting Practice Part I Exams.
     (2)—Questions are from previous Accounting Practice Part II Exams.

Financial Accounting and Reporting

1N90# 46 b	TN92#24 d	N94# 37 c	1N92# 53 d
TM90#11 a	1N92# 20 a	M94#39 d	TM92#31 d
TM90#24 d	1N92# 46 d	2M93# 6 c	1M92#51 c
1M90#33 c	2N92# 45 d	TN92#19 d	TN91#32 a
1M90#35 b	TM92#36 d	2N91# 8 d	1N91# 47 b
1M90#50 d	1M92#19 b		1M91#21 b
1M90#51 d	2M92#11 b	**Q. Related Parties**	1M91#22 c
	2N91# 9 b		1N90# 42 d
O. Nonmonetary Transactions	TM91#35 c	R98# 6 a	1M90#53 c
	TN90#12 d	R96# 10 b	
	2N90# 18 c	N95# 7 d	
M95#30 b	TM90#31 a	1N90# 53 c	**S. Segment Reporting**
TN93# 37 b			
TM93#16 a	**P. Quasi-reorganizations, Reorganizations, and Changes in Entity**	**R. Research and Development Costs**	N95# 8 d
1M93#45 c			M95#56 a
2M93# 9 c			TN92#36 d
2M93#10 b		N94# 44 d	
TN92#20 a	N95# 25 c	1N93# 56 d	
		1M93#23 b	

Note: (T)—Questions are from previous Accounting Theory Exams.
(1)—Questions are from previous Accounting Practice Part I Exams.
(2)—Questions are from previous Accounting Practice Part II Exams.

OTHER OBJECTIVE ANSWER FORMATS — SELECTED QUESTIONS

I. Concepts and Standards for Financial Statements

B. Financial Accounting Standards for Presentation and Disclosure in General Purpose Financial Statements

   1. Consolidated and Combined Financial Statements

R96
Number 2(b) (Estimated time —— 15 to 25 minutes)

Question Number 2 consists of 2 parts. Part **a*** consists of 5 items and part **b** consists of 10 items. Select the **best** answer for each item. Use a No. 2 pencil to blacken the appropriate ovals on the *Objective Answer Sheet* to indicate your answers. **Answer all items.** Your grade will be based on the total number of correct answers.

Required:
   b. On January 2, 1995, Purl Co. purchased 90% of Strand Co.'s outstanding common stock at a purchase price that was in excess of Strand's stockholders' equity. On that date, the fair values of Strand's assets and liabilities equaled their carrying amounts. Purl has accounted for the acquisition as a purchase. Transactions during 1995 were as follows:

- On February 15, 1995, Strand sold equipment to Purl at a price higher than the equipment's carrying amount. The equipment had a remaining life of three years and was depreciated using the straight-line method by both companies.

- During 1995, Purl sold merchandise to Strand under the same terms it offered to third parties. At December 31, 1995, one-third of this merchandise remained in Strand's inventory.

- On November 15, 1995, both Purl and Strand paid cash dividends to their respective stockholders.

- On December 31, 1995, Purl recorded its equity in Strand's earnings.

Required:
   Items 6 through 15 relate to accounts that may or may not be included in Purl and Strand's consolidated financial statements. The list on the right refers to the possible ways those accounts may be reported in Purl's consolidated financial statements for the year ended December 31, 1995. For each item, blacken one corresponding oval on the *Objective Answer Sheet*. An answer may be selected once, more than once, or not at all.

		Responses to be Selected
6. Cash.	Ⓐ	Sum of the amounts on Purl and Strand's separate unconsolidated financial statements.
7. Equipment.		
8. Investment in subsidiary.		
9. Minority interest.	Ⓑ	Less than the sum of the amounts on Purl and Strand's separate unconsolidated financial statements, but not the same as the amount on either separate unconsolidated financial statement.
10. Common stock.		
11. Beginning retained earnings.		
12. Dividends paid.	Ⓒ	Same as the amount for Purl only.
13. Cost of goods sold.		
14. Interest expense.	Ⓓ	Same as the amount for Strand only.
15. Depreciation expense.		
	Ⓔ	Eliminated entirely in consolidation.
	Ⓕ	Shown in the consolidated financial statements but not in the separate unconsolidated financial statements.

*Part a can be found in another Content Specification Group.

2N93
Number 5 (Estimated time —— 45 to 55 minutes)

Question Number 5 consists of 16 items. Select the **best** answer for each item. Use a No. 2 pencil to blacken the appropriate ovals on the Objective Answer Sheet to indicate your answers. **Answer all items.** Your grade will be based on the total number of correct answers.

Presented below are selected amounts from the separate unconsolidated financial statements of Poe Corp. and its 90%-owned subsidiary, Shaw Co., at December 31, 1992. Additional information follows:

	Poe	Shaw
Selected income statement amounts		
Sales	$710,000	$530,000
Cost of goods sold	490,000	370,000
Gain on sale of equipment	—	21,000
Earnings from investment in subsidiary	61,000	—
Interest expense	—	16,000
Depreciation	25,000	20,000
Selected balance sheet amounts		
Cash	$ 50,000	$ 15,000
Inventories	229,000	150,000
Equipment	440,000	360,000
Accumulated depreciation	(200,000)	(120,000)
Investment in Shaw	189,000	—
Investment in bonds	100,000	—
Discount on bonds	(9,000)	—
Bonds payable	—	(200,000)
Common stock	(100,000)	(10,000)
Additional paid-in capital	(250,000)	(40,000)
Retained earnings	(402,000)	(140,000)
Selected statement of retained earnings amounts		
Beginning balance, December 31, 1991	$272,000	$100,000
Net income	210,000	70,000
Dividends paid	80,000	30,000

Additional information:

- On January 2, 1992, Poe, Inc. purchased 90% of Shaw Co.'s 100,000 outstanding common stock for cash of $155,000. On that date, Shaw's stockholders' equity equalled $150,000 and the fair values of Shaw's assets and liabilities equalled their carrying amounts. Poe has accounted for the acquisition as a purchase. Poe's policy is to amortize intangibles over 10 years.

- On September 4, 1992, Shaw paid cash dividends of $30,000.

- On December 31, 1992, Poe recorded its equity in Shaw's earnings.

Required:
   a. **Items 76 through 78.** Items 76 through 78 below represent transactions between Poe and Shaw during 1992. Determine the dollar amount effect of the consolidating adjustment on 1992 consolidated income before considering minority interest. Ignore income tax considerations. To record your answer, write the number in the boxes on the Objective Answer Sheet and blacken the corresponding oval below each box. These items cannot be graded if you fail to blacken the ovals.

Selected Questions

Items to be Answered:

76. On January 3, 1992, Shaw sold equipment with an original cost of $30,000 and a carrying value of $15,000 to Poe for $36,000. The equipment had a remaining life of three years and was depreciated using the straight-line method by both companies.
77. During 1992, Shaw sold merchandise to Poe for $60,000, which included a profit of $20,000. At December 31, 1992, half of this merchandise remained in Poe's inventory.
78. On December 31, 1992, Poe paid $91,000 to purchase 50% of the outstanding bonds issued by Shaw. The bonds mature on December 31, 1998, and were originally issued at par. The bonds pay interest annually on December 31 of each year, and the interest was paid to the prior investor immediately before Poe's purchase of the bonds.

b. Item 79. Determine the amount recorded by Poe as amortization of goodwill for 1992. To record your answer, write the number in the boxes on the Objective Answer Sheet and blacken the corresponding oval beneath each box. These items cannot be graded if you fail to blacken the ovals.

c. Items 80 through 91. Items 80 through 91 below refer to accounts that may or may not be included in Poe and Shaw's consolidated financial statements. The list on the right refers to the various possibilities of those amounts to be reported in Poe's consolidated financial statements for the year ended December 31, 1992. Consider all transactions stated in items 76 through 79 in determining your answer. Ignore income tax considerations. For each item, blacken the corresponding oval on the Objective Answer Sheet.

Items to be Answered:

80. Cash
81. Equipment
82. Investment in subsidiary
83. Bonds payable
84. Minority interest
85. Common stock
86. Beginning retained earnings
87. Dividends paid
88. Gain on retirement of bonds
89. Cost of goods sold
90. Interest expense
91. Depreciation expense

Responses to be Selected:

A. Sum of amounts on Poe and Shaw's separate unconsolidated financial statements.
B. Less than the sum of amounts on Poe and Shaw's separate unconsolidated financial statements but not the same as the amount on either.
C. Same as amount for Poe only.
D. Same as amount for Shaw only.
E. Eliminated entirely in consolidation.
F. Shown in consolidated financial statements but not in separate unconsolidated financial statements.
G. Neither in consolidated nor in separate unconsolidated financial statements.

3. **Statement(s) of Income, Comprehensive Income, and Changes in Equity Accounts**

M95
Number 2 (Estimated time — — 15 to 25 minutes)

Question Number 2 consists of 10 items. Select the **best** answer for each item. Use a No. 2 pencil to blacken the appropriate ovals on the *Objective Answer Sheet* to indicate your answers. **Answer all items.** Your grade will be based on the total number of correct answers.

Min Co. is a publicly-held company whose shares are traded in the over-the-counter market. The stockholders' equity accounts at December 31, 1993, had the following balances:

Preferred stock, $100 par value, 6% cumulative; 5,000 shares authorized; 2,000 issued and outstanding	$ 200,000
Common stock, $1 par value, 150,000 shares authorized; 100,000 issued and outstanding	100,000
Additional paid-in capital	800,000
Retained earnings	1,586,000
Total stockholders' equity	$2,686,000

Transactions during 1994 and other information relating to the stockholders' equity accounts were as follows:

- February 1, 1994—Issued 13,000 shares of common stock to Ram Co. in exchange for land. On the date issued, the stock had a market price of $11 per share. The land had a carrying value on Ram's books of $135,000, and an assessed value for property taxes of $90,000.

- March 1, 1994—Purchased 5,000 shares of its own common stock to be held as treasury stock for $14 per share. Min uses the cost method to account for treasury stock. Transactions in treasury stock are legal in Min's state of incorporation.

- May 10, 1994—Declared a property dividend of marketable securities held by Min to common shareholders. The securities had a carrying value of $600,000; fair value on relevant dates were:

Date of declaration (May 10, 1994)	$720,000
Date of record (May 25, 1994)	758,000
Date of distribution (June 1, 1994)	736,000

- October 1, 1994—Reissued 2,000 shares of treasury stock for $16 per share.

- November 4, 1994—Declared a cash dividend of $1.50 per share to all common shareholders of record November 15, 1994. The dividend was paid on November 25, 1994.

- December 20, 1994—Declared the required annual cash dividend on preferred stock for 1994. The dividend was paid on January 5, 1995.

- January 16, 1995—Before closing the accounting records for 1994, Min became aware that no amortization had been recorded for 1993 for a patent purchased on July 1, 1993. The patent was properly capitalized at $320,000 and had an estimated useful life of eight years when purchased. Min's income tax rate is 30%. The appropriate correcting entry was recorded on the same day.

- Adjusted net income for 1994 was $838,000.

Required:
Items **61 through 68** represent amounts to be reported in Min's financial statements. Items **69 and 70** represent other financial information. For all items, calculate the amounts requested. To record your answer, blacken the ovals on the *Objective Answer Sheet*. If zeros precede your numerical answer, blacken the zeros in the ovals preceding your answer. **You cannot receive credit for your answers if you fail to blacken an oval in each column.** You may write the numbers in the boxes provided to facilitate blackening the ovals; however, the numbers written in the boxes will **not** be graded.

Items 61 through 64 represent amounts to be reported on Min's 1994 statement of retained earnings.

61. Prior period adjustment.

62. Preferred dividends.

63. Common dividends — cash.

64. Common dividends — property.

Items 65 through 68 represent amounts to be reported on Min's statement of stockholders' equity at December 31, 1994.

65. Number of common shares issued at December 31, 1994.

66. Amount of common stock issued.

67. Additional paid-in capital, including treasury stock transactions.

68. Treasury stock.

Items 69 and 70 represent other financial information for 1993 and 1994.

69. Book value per share at December 31, 1993, before prior period adjustment.

70. Numerator used in calculation of 1994 earnings per share for the year.

M95
Number 3 (Estimated time — — 15 to 25 minutes)

Question Number 3 consists of 6 items. Select the **best** answer for each item. Use a No. 2 pencil to blacken the appropriate ovals on the *Objective Answer Sheet* to indicate your answers. **Answer all items.** Your grade will be based on the total number of correct answers.

Hake Co. is in the process of preparing its financial statements for the year ended December 31, 1994.

Required:

Items 71 through 76 represent various transactions that occurred during 1994. The following **two** responses are required for each item:

- Compute the amount of gain, loss, or adjustment to be reported in Hake's 1994 financial statements. Disregard income taxes. To record your answer, blacken the ovals on the *Objective Answer Sheet*. If zeros precede your numerical answer, blacken the zeros in the ovals preceding your answer. **You cannot receive credit for your answers if you fail to blacken an oval in each column.** You may write the numbers in the boxes provided to facilitate blackening the ovals; however, the numbers written in the boxes will **not** be graded.

- Select from the list below the financial statement category in which the gain, loss, or adjustment should be presented, and blacken the corresponding oval on the *Objective Answer Sheet*. A category may be used once, more than once, or not at all.

Financial Statement Categories

- A. Income from continuing operations.
- B. Extraordinary item.
- C. Cumulative effect of change in accounting principle.
- D. Prior period adjustment to beginning retained earnings.
- E. Separate component of stockholders' equity.

71. On June 30, 1994, after paying the semi-annual interest due and recording amortization of bond discount, Hake redeemed its 15-year, 8% $1,000,000 par bonds at 102. The bonds, which had a carrying amount of $940,000 on January 1, 1994, had originally been issued to yield 10%. Hake uses the effective interest method of amortization, and had paid interest and recorded amortization on June 30. Compute the amount of gain or loss on redemption of the bonds and select the proper financial statement category.

72. As of January 1, 1994, Hake decided to change the method of computing depreciation on its sole piece of equipment from the sum-of-the-years'-digits method to the straight-line method. The equipment, acquired in January 1991 for $520,000, had an estimated life of five years and a salvage value of $20,000. Compute the amount of the accounting change and select the proper financial statement category.

73. In October 1994, Hake paid $375,000 to a former employee to settle a lawsuit out of court. The lawsuit had been filed in 1993, and at December 31, 1993, Hake had recorded a liability from lawsuit based on legal counsel's estimate that the loss from the lawsuit would be between $250,000 and $750,000. Compute the amount of gain or loss from settlement of the lawsuit and select the proper financial statement category.

74. In November 1994, Hake purchased two marketable equity securities, I and II, which it bought and held principally to sell in the near term, and in fact sold on February 28, 1995. Hake has adopted Statement of Financial Accounting Standards No. 115, *Accounting for Certain Investments in Debt and Equity Securities*. Relevant data is as follows:

	Cost	Fair Value 12/31/94	Fair Value 2/28/95
I	$125,000	$145,000	$155,000
II	235,000	205,000	230,000

Compute the amount of holding gain or loss at December 31, 1994, and select the proper financial statement category.

75. During 1994, Hake received $1,000,000 from its insurance company to cover losses suffered during a hurricane. This was the first hurricane ever to strike in Hake's area. The hurricane destroyed a warehouse with a carrying amount of $470,000, containing equipment with a carrying amount of $250,000 and inventory with a carrying amount of $535,000 and a fair value of $600,000. Compute the amount of gain or loss from the hurricane and select the proper financial statement category.

76. At December 31, 1994, Hake prepared the following worksheet summarizing the translation of its wholly-owned foreign subsidiary's financial statements into dollars. Hake had purchased the foreign subsidiary for $324,000 on January 2, 1994. On that date, the carrying amounts of the subsidiary's assets and liabilities equalled their fair values.

	Foreign currency amounts	Applicable exchange rates	Dollars
Net assets at January 2, 1994 (date of purchase)	720,000	$.45	$324,000
Net income, 1994	250,000	.42	105,000
Net assets at December 31, 1994	970,000		$429,000
Net assets at December 31, 1994	970,000	.40	$388,000

Compute the amount of the foreign currency translation adjustment and select the proper financial statement category.

4. Statement of Cash Flows

N94
Number 3 (Estimated time — — 15 to 25 minutes)

The following condensed trial balance of Probe Co., a publicly-held company, has been adjusted except for income tax expense.

Probe Co.
CONDENSED TRIAL BALANCE

	12/31/93 Balances Dr. (Cr.)	12/31/92 Balances Dr. (Cr.)	Net change Dr. (Cr.)
Cash	$ 473,000	$ 817,000	$(344,000)
Accounts receivable, net	670,000	610,000	60,000
Property, plant, and equipment	1,070,000	995,000	75,000
Accumulated depreciation	(345,000)	(280,000)	(65,000)
Dividends payable	(25,000)	(10,000)	(15,000)
Income taxes payable	35,000	(150,000)	185,000
Deferred income tax liability	(42,000)	(42,000)	—
Bonds payable	(500,000)	(1,000,000)	500,000
Unamortized premium on bonds	(71,000)	(150,000)	79,000
Common stock	(350,000)	(150,000)	(200,000)
Additional paid-in capital	(430,000)	(375,000)	(55,000)
Retained earnings	(185,000)	(265,000)	80,000
Sales	(2,420,000)		
Cost of sales	1,863,000		
Selling and administrative expenses	220,000		
Interest income	(14,000)		
Interest expense	46,000		
Depreciation	88,000		
Loss on sale of equipment	7,000		
Gain on extinguishment of bonds	(90,000)		
	$ 0	$ 0	$300,000

Additional information:

- During 1993 equipment with an original cost of $50,000 was sold for cash, and equipment costing $125,000 was purchased.

- On January 1, 1993, bonds with a par value of $500,000 and related premium of $75,000 were redeemed. The $1,000 face value, 10% par bonds had been issued on January 1, 1984, to yield 8%. Interest is payable annually every December 31 through 2003.

- Probe's tax payments during 1993 were debited to Income Taxes Payable. Probe elected early adoption of Statement of Financial Accounting Standards No. 109, *Accounting for Income Taxes,* for the year ended December 31, 1992, and recorded a deferred income tax liability of $42,000 based on temporary differences of $120,000 and an enacted tax rate of 35%. Probe's 1993 financial statement income before income taxes was greater than its 1993 taxable income, due entirely to temporary differences, by $60,000. Probe's cumulative net taxable temporary differences at December 31, 1993, were $180,000. Probe's enacted tax rate for the current and future years is 30%.

- 60,000 shares of common stock, $2.50 par, were outstanding on December 31, 1992. Probe issued an additional 80,000 shares on April 1, 1993.

- There were no changes to retained earnings other than dividends declared.

Selected Questions

Question Number 3 consists of 6 items. Select the **best** answer for each item. Use a No. 2 pencil to blacken the appropriate ovals on the Objective Answer Sheet to indicate your answers. **Answer all items.** Your grade will be based on the total number of correct answers.

Required:

For each transaction in **items 75 through 80,** the following **two** responses are required:

- Determine the amount to be reported in Probe's 1993 statement of cash flows prepared using the indirect method. To record your answer, write the number in the boxes on the Objective Answer Sheet **and** blacken the corresponding oval below each box. Write zeros in any blank boxes preceding your numerical answer, and blacken the zero in the oval below the box. **You cannot receive credit for your answers if you fail to blacken an oval in each column.**

- Select from the list below where the specific item should be separately reported on the statement of cash flows prepared using the indirect method and blacken the corresponding oval on the Objective Answer Sheet.

O. Operating.
I. Investing.
F. Financing.
S. Supplementary information.
N. Not reported on Probe's statement of cash flows.

75. Cash paid for income taxes.
76. Cash paid for interest.
77. Redemption of bonds payable.
78. Issuance of common stock.
79. Cash dividends paid.
80. Proceeds from sale of equipment.

1M92
Number 4 (Estimated time — — 45 to 55 minutes)

Number 4 consists of two unrelated parts.*

Instructions — Number 4(a)

Question Number 4(a) consists of 5 items. Use a No. 2 pencil to indicate your answers on the Objective Answer Sheet. These items require numerical answers and selection of the proper cash flow category. For the numerical answers, you are to both write your numerical answer in the boxes and blacken the corresponding oval below each box. **These items cannot be graded if you fail to blacken the ovals.** Write zeros in any blank boxes preceding your numerical answer. If there is a discrepancy between the amount written in the boxes and the amount indicated by the blackened ovals, the amount indicated by the blackened ovals will prevail. **Answer all items.** Your grade will be based on the total number of correct answers.

Following are selected balance sheet accounts of Zach Corp. at December 31, 1991 and 1990, and the increases or decreases in each account from 1990 to 1991. Also presented is selected income statement information for the year ended December 31, 1991, and additional information.

Selected balance sheet accounts	1991	1990	Increase (Decrease)
Assets:			
Accounts receivable	$ 34,000	$ 24,000	$10,000
Property, plant, and equipment	277,000	247,000	30,000
Accumulated depreciation	(178,000)	(167,000)	(11,000)
Liabilities and stockholders' equity:			
Bonds payable	49,000	46,000	3,000
Dividends payable	8,000	5,000	3,000
Common stock, $1 par	22,000	19,000	3,000
Additional paid-in capital	9,000	3,000	6,000
Retained earnings	104,000	91,000	13,000

Selected income statement information for the year ended December 31, 1991

Sales revenue	$155,000
Depreciation	33,000
Gain on sale of equipment	13,000
Net income	28,000

---

*The omitted item can be found in another Content Specification Group.

Selected Questions

Additional information

- Accounts receivable relate to sales of merchandise.

- During 1991, equipment costing $40,000 was sold for cash.

- During 1991, $20,000 of bonds payable were issued in exchange for property, plant, and equipment. There was no amortization of bond discount or premium.

Required:

Items 61 through 65 represent activities that will be reported in Zach's statement of cash flows for the year ended December 31, 1991. The following two responses are required for each item:

- Determine the amount that should be reported in Zach's 1991 statement of cash flows. To record your answer, write the number in the boxes on the Objective Answer Sheet and blacken the corresponding oval below each box. These items cannot be graded if you fail to blacken the ovals.

- Using the list below, determine the category in which the amount should be reported in the statement of cash flows and blacken the corresponding oval on the Objective Answer Sheet.

    O. Operating activity
    I. Investing activity
    F. Financing activity

Example:
The following is an example of the manner in which the Objective Answer Sheet should be marked. **Zeros have already been marked on the Objective Answer Sheet for the ones, tens, and hundreds columns.**

Item

99. Proceeds from sale of common stock.

Answer Sheet

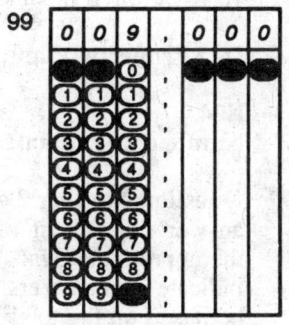
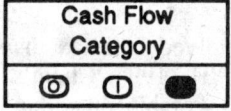

Items to be Answered:

61. Cash collections from customers (direct method).
62. Payments for purchase of property, plant, and equipment.
63. Proceeds from sale of equipment.
64. Cash dividends paid.
65. Redemption of bonds payable.

Financial Accounting and Reporting

II. Recognition, Measurement, Valuation, and Presentation of Typical Items in Financial Statements in Conformity With Generally Accepted Accounting Principles

B. Receivables

R96
Number 1 (Estimated time — — 15 to 25 minutes)

Question Number 1 consists of 10 items to be reported on Chem Co.'s 1995 financial statements. Use a No. 2 pencil to blacken the appropriate ovals on the *Objective Answer Sheet* to indicate your answers. **Answer all items.** Your grade will be based on the total number of correct answers.

Items 1 through 10 are based on the following:

- Accounts receivable at December 31, 1994, were $100,000 before allowance for uncollectible accounts of $10,000. Sales to customers on account (excluding credit card sales) during 1995 were $1,810,000, and collections from customers, excluding recoveries, totaled $1,795,000. During 1995, accounts receivable of $45,000 were written off and $17,000 were recovered. An aging of the accounts receivable at December 31, 1995, indicated that $15,000 may be uncollectible.

- Chem accepts credit cards for payments of sales, and deposits the credit card slips in the bank, which credits Chem's account with the amount of the sale less a 4% commission. For 1995 credit card sales, Chem received proceeds of $600,000, net of commission.

- During 1995, Chem was involved in a tax dispute with the IRS. At December 31, 1995, Chem's tax advisor believed that an unfavorable outcome was probable. A reasonable estimate of additional tax payments was between $45,000 and $95,000, but $60,000 was the best estimate in that range.

- One of Chem's product lines carries a two-year warranty against defects. Based on past experience, warranty costs are estimated at 4% of sales. During 1995, sales of this product totaled $500,000 and warranty costs of $6,000 were incurred and paid.

- On July 1, 1995, Chem issued an 8%, $1,000,000 bond at a discount of $160,000 to yield 10%. The bond is due on June 30, 2010, and pays interest annually on June 30. Chem applies the effective interest method on an annual basis to amortize the discount.

- Chem's 1995 income before income taxes was $300,000. Due to temporary differences, its taxable income was $260,000. During 1995, Chem made estimated tax payments of $45,000. Chem reported deferred tax liabilities of $15,000 and $3,000 at December 31, 1995, and 1994, respectively. Chem is subject to a 30% tax rate.

Required:
For Items 1 through 10, determine the amount to be reported in Chem's 1995 financial statements. To record your answer, blacken the ovals on the *Objective Answer Sheet*. If zeros precede your numerical answer, blacken the zeros in the ovals preceding your answer. **You cannot receive credit for your answers if you fail to blacken an oval in each column.** You may write the numbers in the boxes provided to facilitate blackening the ovals; however, the numbers written in the boxes will **not** be graded.

1. Accounts receivable (excluding credit card sales).
2. Allowance for uncollectible accounts.
3. Uncollectible accounts expense.
4. Credit card commission expense.
5. Estimated liability for tax assessment.
6. Estimated liability for warranty.
7. Bond interest payable.
8. Bond interest expense.
9. Federal income taxes currently payable.
10. Deferred income tax expense.

D. Property, Plant, and Equipment

N94
Number 2 (Estimated time — — 15 to 25 minutes)

Question Number 2 consists of 14 items. Select the **best** answer for each item. Use a No. 2 pencil to blacken the appropriate ovals on the Objective Answer Sheet to indicate your answers. **Answer all items.** Your grade will be based on the total number of correct answers.

Items 61 through 66 represent expenditures for goods held for resale and equipment.

Required:
For items 61 through 66, determine for each item whether the expenditure should be capitalized Ⓒ or expensed as a period cost Ⓔ and blacken the corresponding oval on the Objective Answer Sheet.

61. Freight charges paid for goods held for resale.
62. In-transit insurance on goods held for resale purchased F.O.B. shipping point.
63. Interest on note payable for goods held for resale.
64. Installation of equipment.
65. Testing of newly-purchased equipment.
66. Cost of current year service contract on equipment.

Selected Questions

Items 67 through 70 are based on the following 1993 transactions:

- Link Co. purchased an office building and the land on which it is located by paying $800,000 cash and assuming an existing mortgage of $200,000. The property is assessed at $960,000 for realty tax purposes, of which 60% is allocated to the building.

- Link leased construction equipment under a 7-year capital lease requiring annual year-end payments of $100,000. Link's incremental borrowing rate is 9%, while the lessor's implicit rate, which is not known to Link, is 8%. Present value factors for an ordinary annuity for seven periods are 5.21 at 8% and 5.03 at 9%. Fair value of the equipment is $515,000.

- Link paid $50,000 and gave a plot of undeveloped land with a carrying amount of $320,000 and a fair value of $450,000 to Club Co. in exchange for a plot of undeveloped land with a fair value of $500,000. The land was carried on Club's books at $350,000.

Required:
For items 67 through 70, calculate the amount to be recorded for each item. To record your answer, write the number in the boxes on the Objective Answer Sheet **and** blacken the corresponding oval below each box. Write zeros in any blank boxes preceding your numerical answer, and blacken the zero in the oval below the box. **You cannot receive credit for your answers if you fail to blacken an oval in each column.**

67. Building.
68. Leased equipment.
69. Land received from Club on Link's books.
70. Land received from Link on Club's books.

Items 71 through 74 are based on the following information:

On January 2, 1992, Half, Inc. purchased a manufacturing machine for $864,000. The machine has an 8-year estimated life and a $144,000 estimated salvage value. Half expects to manufacture 1,800,000 units over the life of the machine. During 1993, Half manufactured 300,000 units.

Required:
Items 71 through 74 represent various depreciation methods. For each item, calculate depreciation expense for 1993 (the second year of ownership) for the machine described above under the method listed. To record your answer, write the number in the boxes on the Objective Answer Sheet **and** blacken the corresponding oval below each box. Write zeros in any blank boxes preceding your numerical answer, and blacken the zero in the oval below the box. **You cannot receive credit for your answers if you fail to blacken an oval in each column.**

71. Straight-line.
72. Double-declining balance.
73. Sum-of-the-years'-digits.
74. Units of production.

1N92
Number 4 (Estimated time — — 45 to 55 minutes)

Number 4 consists of two unrelated parts.*

Instructions — Number 4(a)

Question Number 4(a) consists of 8 items. Select the **best** answer for each item. Use a No. 2 pencil to blacken the appropriate ovals on the Objective Answer Sheet to indicate your answers. **Answer all items**. Your grade will be based on the total number of correct answers.

During 1992, Sloan, Inc. began a project to construct new corporate headquarters. Sloan purchased land with an existing building for $750,000. The land was valued at $700,000 and the building at $50,000. Sloan planned to demolish the building and construct a new office building on the site. Items 61 through 68 represent various expenditures by Sloan for this project.

Required:
   For each expenditure in Items 61 through 68, select from the list below the appropriate accounting treatment and blacken the corresponding oval on the Objective Answer Sheet.

   L. Classify as land and do not depreciate.
   B. Classify as building and depreciate.
   E. Expense.

Example:
The following is an example of the manner in which the answer sheet should be marked.

Item

99. Architect's fees of $100,000.

Answer Sheet

Item	Land	Building	Expense
99	Ⓛ	●	Ⓔ

Items to be Answered:

61. Purchase of land for $700,000.
62. Interest of $147,000 on construction financing incurred after completion of construction.
63. Interest of $186,000 on construction financing paid during construction.
64. Purchase of building for $50,000.
65. $18,500 payment of delinquent real estate taxes assumed by Sloan on purchase.
66. $12,000 liability insurance premium during the construction period.
67. $65,000 cost of razing existing building.
68. Moving costs of $136,000.

*The omitted item can be found in another Content Specification Group.

Selected Questions

I. Notes and Bonds Payable

N95
Number 3 (Estimated time — — 15 to 25 minutes)

Question Number 3 consists of 13 items.* Select the **best** answer for each item. Use a No. 2 pencil to blacken the appropriate ovals on the *Objective Answer Sheet* to indicate your answers. **Answer all items.** Your grade will be based on the total number of correct answers.

Items 71 through 77 are based on the following:

On January 2, 1994, North Co. issued bonds payable with a face value of $480,000 at a discount. The bonds are due in 10 years and interest is payable semiannually every June 30 and December 31. On June 30, 1994, and on December 31, 1994, North made the semiannual interest payments due, and recorded interest expense and amortization of bond discount.

Required:

Items 71 through 77, contained in the partially-completed amortization table below, represent information needed to complete the table. For each item, select from the following lists the correct numerical response and blacken the corresponding oval on the *Objective Answer Sheet*. A response may be selected once, more than once, or not at all.

Rates	
Ⓐ	3.0%
Ⓑ	4.5%
Ⓒ	5.0%
Ⓓ	6.0%
Ⓔ	9.0%
Ⓕ	10.0%

Amounts			
Ⓖ	$ 3,420	Ⓟ	$ 21,600
Ⓗ	$ 3,600	Ⓠ	$116,400
Ⓘ	$ 3,780	Ⓡ	$120,000
Ⓙ	$ 3,960	Ⓢ	$123,600
Ⓚ	$ 14,400	Ⓣ	$360,000
Ⓛ	$ 17,820	Ⓤ	$363,600
Ⓜ	$ 18,000	Ⓥ	$367,200
Ⓝ	$ 18,180	Ⓦ	$467,400
Ⓞ	$ 18,360	Ⓧ	$480,000

	Cash	Interest expense	Amortization	Discount	Carrying amount
1/2/94					(73)
6/30/94	(72)	18,000	3,600	(71)	363,600
12/31/94	$14,400	(76)	(77)		

Annual Interest Rates: Stated **(74)**
                        Effective **(75)**

---

*The omitted items can be found in another Content Specification Group.

FA-143

Financial Accounting and Reporting

TN93
Number 2 (Estimated time —— 15 to 25 minutes)

Question Number 2 consists of 5 items. Select the **best** answer for each item. Use a No. 2 pencil to blacken the appropriate ovals on the Objective Answer Sheet to indicate your answers. **Answer all items.** Your grade will be based on the total number of correct answers.

Items 61 through 65 are based on the following:

Hamnoff, Inc.'s $50 par value common stock has always traded above par. During 1992, Hamnoff had several transactions that affected the following balance sheet accounts:

      I. Bond discount
     II. Bond premium
    III. Bonds payable
    IV. Common stock
     V. Additional paid-in capital
    VI. Retained earnings

Required:
    For **items 61 through 65,** determine whether the transaction increased (I), decreased (D), or had no effect (N) on each of the balances in the above accounts, and blacken the corresponding oval on the Objective Answer Sheet.

61. Hamnoff issued bonds payable with a nominal rate of interest that was less than the market rate of interest.
62. Hamnoff issued convertible bonds, which are common stock equivalents, for an amount in excess of the bonds' face amount.
63. Hamnoff issued common stock when the convertible bonds described in item 62 were submitted for conversion. Each $1,000 bond was converted into 20 common shares. The book value method was used for the early conversion.
64. Hamnoff issued bonds, with detachable stock warrants, for an amount equal to the face amount of the bonds. The stock warrants have a determinable value.
65. Hamnoff declared and issued a 2% stock dividend.

III. Recognition, Measurement, Valuation, and Presentation of Specific Types of Transactions and Events in Financial Statements in Conformity With Generally Accepted Accounting Principles

A. Accounting Changes and Corrections of Errors

R97
Number 2

Question Number 2 consists of 4 items. Select the **best** answer for each item. Use a No. 2 pencil to blacken the appropriate ovals on the *Objective Answer Sheet* to indicate your answers. **Answer all items.** Your grade will be based on the total number of correct answers.

    On January 2, 1996, Falk Co. hired a new controller. During the year, the controller, working closely with Falk's president and outside accountants, made changes in existing accounting policies, instituted new accounting policies, and corrected several errors dating from prior to 1996.
    Falk's financial statements for the year ended December 31, 1996, will not be presented in comparative form with its 1995 financial statements.

Required:
    Items 1 through 4 represent Falk's transactions.
    List A represents possible classifications of these transactions as a change in accounting principle, a change in accounting estimate, correction of an error in previously presented financial statements, or neither an accounting change nor an error correction.
    List B represents the general accounting treatment required for these transactions. These treatments are:

- Cumulative effect approach—Include the cumulative effect of the adjustment resulting from the accounting change or error correction in the 1996 financial statements.

Selected Questions

- Retroactive restatement approach—Adjust 1996 beginning retained earnings if the error or change affects a period prior to 1996.

- Prospective approach—Report 1996 and future financial statements on the new basis, but do not adjust beginning retained earnings or include the cumulative effect of the change in the 1996 income statements.

List A (Select one)	List B (Select one)
Type of change	General accounting treatment
Ⓐ Change in accounting principle.	Ⓧ Cumulative effect approach.
Ⓑ Change in accounting estimate.	Ⓨ Retroactive restatement approach.
Ⓒ Correction of an error in previously presented financial statements.	Ⓩ Prospective approach.
Ⓓ Neither an accounting change nor an error correction.	

For **Items 1 and 2**, select a classification for each transaction from List A **and** the general accounting treatment required to report the change from List B, and blacken the corresponding ovals on the *Objective Answer Sheet*.

1. Falk manufactures customized equipment to customer specifications on a contract basis. Falk changed its method of accounting for these long-term contracts from the completed-contract method to the percentage-of-completion method because Falk is now able to make reasonable estimates of future construction costs.

2. Based on improved collection procedures, Falk changed the percentage of credit sales used to determine the allowance for uncollectible accounts from 2% to 1%.

For **Items 3 and 4**, in addition to selecting a classification for each transaction from List A **and** the general accounting treatment required to report the change from List B, a third response is required. For these items, determine the amount, if any, of the cumulative change or prior period adjustment, ignoring income tax effects, and record the amount by blackening the corresponding ovals on the *Objective Answer Sheet*. To record a **zero** answer for an item, you must blacken all the **zero** ovals for that particular item. If zeros precede your numerical answer, blacken the zeros in the ovals preceding your answer. **You cannot receive credit for your answers if you fail to blacken an oval in each column.** You may write the numbers in the boxes provided to facilitate blackening the ovals; however, the numbers written in the boxes will **not** be graded.

3. Effective January 1, 1996, Falk changed from average cost to FIFO to account for its inventory. Cost of goods sold under each method was as follows:

Year	Average cost	FIFO
Years prior to 1995	$71,000	$77,000
1995	79,000	82,000

4. In January 1995, Falk purchased a machine with a five-year life and no salvage value for $40,000. The machine was depreciated using the straight-line method. On December 30, 1996, Falk discovered that depreciation on the machine had been calculated using a 25% rate.

R96
Number 2(a) (Estimated time — — 15 to 25 minutes)

Question Number 2 consists of 2 parts. Part **a** consists of 5 items and part **b*** consists of 10 items. Select the **best** answer for each item. Use a No. 2 pencil to blacken the appropriate ovals on the *Objective Answer Sheet* to indicate your answers. **Answer all items.** Your grade will be based on the total number of correct answers.

Required:
    a. **Items 1 through 5** relate to accounting for business combinations. For each item, determine whether the statement is consistent with:

*Part b can be found in another Content Specification Group.

	List
Ⓐ	Purchase accounting.
Ⓑ	Pooling of interests.
Ⓒ	Either.
Ⓓ	Neither.

Blacken the corresponding oval on the *Objective Answer Sheet*. An answer may be selected once, more than once, or not at all.

1. When the investment cost is lower than the carrying amounts of the target company's net assets, the target

company's assets will be valued on the books of the combined firm at less than their carrying amounts.

2. A combination is finalized within nine months after the combination plan was initiated.

3. Results of operations for the year of combination include the combined results of the separate companies for the entire year.

4. Costs of furnishing information to stockholders related to effecting the business combination are deducted directly from the combined corporation's retained earnings.

5. When the investment cost is higher than the fair value of the target company's net assets, goodwill may appear in the consolidated financial statements.

M94
Number 2 (Estimated time — — 15 to 25 minutes)

Question 2 consists of 10 items. Select the **best** answer for each item. Use a No. 2 pencil to blacken the appropriate ovals on the Objective Answer Sheet to indicate your answers. **Answer all items.** Your grade will be based on the total number of correct answers.

On January 2, 1993, Quo, Inc. hired Reed to be its controller. During the year, Reed, working closely with Quo's president and outside accountants, made changes in accounting policies, corrected several errors dating from 1992 and before, and instituted new accounting policies.

Quo's 1993 financial statements will be presented in comparative form with its 1992 financial statements.

Required:
Items **61 through 70** represent Quo's transactions. List A represents possible classifications of these transactions as: a change in accounting principle, a change in accounting estimate, a correction of an error in previously presented financial statements, or neither an accounting change nor an accounting error.
List B represents the general accounting treatment required for these transactions. These treatments are:

- Cumulative effect approach—Include the cumulative effect of the adjustment resulting from the accounting change or error correction in the 1993 financial statements, and do **not** restate the 1992 financial statements.
- Retroactive restatement approach—Restate the 1992 financial statements and adjust 1992 beginning retained earnings if the error or change affects a period prior to 1992.
- Prospective approach—Report 1993 and future financial statements on the new basis, but do **not** restate 1992 financial statements.

For each item, select one from List A and one from List B and blacken the corresponding ovals on the Objective Answer Sheet.

List A (Select one)	List B (Select one)
A. Change in accounting principle.	X. Cumulative effect approach.
B. Change in accounting estimate.	Y. Retroactive restatement approach.
C. Correction of an error in previously presented financial statements.	Z. Prospective approach.
D. Neither an accounting change nor an accounting error.	

Items to be answered:

61. Quo manufactures heavy equipment to customer specifications on a contract basis. On the basis that it is preferable, accounting for these long-term contracts was switched from the completed-contract method to the percentage-of-completion method.

62. As a result of a production breakthrough, Quo determined that manufacturing equipment previously depreciated over 15 years should be depreciated over 20 years.

63. The equipment that Quo manufactures is sold with a five-year warranty. Because of a production breakthrough, Quo reduced its computation of warranty costs from 3% of sales to 1% of sales.

64. Quo changed from LIFO to FIFO to account for its finished goods inventory.

65. Quo changed from FIFO to average cost to account for its raw materials and work in process inventories.

66. Quo sells extended service contracts on its products. Because related services are performed over several years, in 1993 Quo changed from the cash method to the accrual method of recognizing income from these service contracts.

67. During 1993, Quo determined that an insurance premium paid and entirely expensed in 1992 was for the period January 1, 1992, through January 1, 1994.

68. Quo changed its method of depreciating office equipment from an accelerated method to the straight-line method to more closely reflect costs in later years.

69. Quo instituted a pension plan for all employees in 1993 and adopted Statement of Financial Accounting Standards No. 87, *Employers' Accounting for Pensions*. Quo had not previously had a pension plan.

70. During 1993, Quo increased its investment in Worth, Inc. from a 10% interest, purchased in 1992, to 30%, and acquired a seat on Worth's board of directors. As a result of its increased investment, Quo changed its method of accounting for investment in subsidiary from the cost method to the equity method.

D. Contingent Liabilities and Commitments

N95
Number 3 (Estimated time — — 15 to 25 minutes)

Items 78 through 83 are based on the following:

Town, Inc. is preparing its financial statements for the year ended December 31, 1994.

Required:
Items **78 through 83** represent various commitments and contingencies of Town at December 31, 1994, and events subsequent to December 31, 1994, but prior to the issuance of the 1994 financial statements. For each item, select from the following list the reporting requirement and blacken the corresponding oval on the *Objective Answer Sheet*. A reporting requirement may be selected once, more than once, or not at all.

Reporting Requirement
(D) Disclosure only.
(A) Accrual only.
(B) Both accrual and disclosure.
(N) Neither accrual nor disclosure.

78. On December 1, 1994, Town was awarded damages of $75,000 in a patent infringement suit it brought against a competitor. The defendant did not appeal the verdict, and payment was received in January 1995.

79. A former employee of Town has brought a wrongful-dismissal suit against Town. Town's lawyers believe the suit to be without merit.

80. At December 31, 1994, Town had outstanding purchase orders in the ordinary course of business for purchase of a raw material to be used in its manufacturing process. The market price is currently higher than the purchase price and is not anticipated to change within the next year.

81. A government contract completed during 1994 is subject to renegotiation. Although Town estimates that it is reasonably possible that a refund of approximately $200,000–$300,000 may be required by the government, it does not wish to publicize this possibility.

82. Town has been notified by a governmental agency that it will be held responsible for the cleanup of toxic materials at a site where Town formerly conducted operations. Town estimates that it is probable that its share of remedial action will be approximately $500,000.

83. On January 5, 1995, Town redeemed its outstanding bonds and issued new bonds with a lower rate of interest. The reacquisition price was in excess of the carrying amount of the bonds.

M94
Number 3 (Estimated time — — 15 to 25 minutes)

Question 3 consists of 12 items. Select the **best** answer for each item. Use a No. 2 pencil to blacken the appropriate ovals on the Objective Answer Sheet to indicate your answers. **Answer all items**. Your grade will be based on the total number of correct answers.

Edge Co., a toy manufacturer, is in the process of preparing its financial statements for the year ended December 31, 1993. Edge expects to issue its 1993 financial statements on March 1, 1994.

Required:
Items **71 through 82** represent various information that has not been reflected in the financial statements. For each item, the following two responses are required:

a. Determine if an adjustment is required and select the appropriate amount, if any, from the list below.

b. Determine (Yes/No) if additional disclosure is **required**, either on the face of the financial statements or in the notes to the financial statements.

Blacken the corresponding ovals on the Objective Answer Sheet.

Adjustment amounts

A. No adjustment is required
B. $100,000
C. $150,000
D. $250,000
E. $400,000
F. $500,000

Items to be answered:

71. Edge owns a small warehouse located on the banks of a river in which it stores inventory worth approximately $500,000. Edge is not insured against flood losses. The river last overflowed its banks twenty years ago.

72. During 1993, Edge began offering certain health care benefits to its eligible retired employees. Edge's actuaries have determined that the discounted expected cost of these benefits for current employees is $150,000.

73. Edge offers an unconditional warranty on its toys. Based on past experience, Edge estimates its warranty expense to be 1% of sales. Sales during 1993 were $10,000,000.

74. On October 30, 1993, a safety hazard related to one of Edge's toy products was discovered. It is considered probable that Edge will be liable for an amount in the range of $100,000 to $500,000.

75. On November 22, 1993, Edge initiated a lawsuit seeking $250,000 in damages from patent infringement.

76. On December 17, 1993, a former employee filed a lawsuit seeking $100,000 for unlawful dismissal. Edge's attorneys believe the suit is without merit. No court date has been set.

77. On December 15, 1993, Edge guaranteed a bank loan of $100,000 for its president's personal use.

78. On December 31, 1993, Edge's board of directors voted to discontinue the operations of its computer games division and sell all the assets of the division. The division was sold on February 15, 1994. On December 31, 1993, Edge estimated that losses from operations, net of tax, for the period January 1, 1994, through February 15, 1994, would be $400,000 and that the gain from the sale of the division's assets, net of tax, would be $250,000. These estimates were materially correct.

79. On January 5, 1994, a warehouse containing a substantial portion of Edge's inventory was destroyed by fire. Edge expects to recover the entire loss, except for a $250,000 deductible, from insurance.

80. On January 24, 1994, inventory purchased FOB shipping point from a foreign country was detained at that country's border because of political unrest. The shipment is valued at $150,000. Edge's attorneys have stated that it is probable that Edge will be able to obtain the shipment.

81. On January 30, 1994, Edge issued $10,000,000 bonds at a premium of $500,000.

82. On February 4, 1994, the IRS assessed Edge an additional $400,000 for the 1992 tax year. Edge's tax attorneys and tax accountants have stated that it is likely that the IRS will agree to a $100,000 settlement.

Selected Questions

G. Employee Benefits

1M93
Number 4 (Estimated time —— 40 to 50 minutes)

Number 4 consists of two unrelated parts.*

Instructions — Number 4(a)

Question Number 4(a) consists of 10 items. Select the **best** answer for each item. Use a No. 2 pencil to blacken the appropriate ovals on the Objective Answer Sheet to indicate your answers. **Answer all items.** Your grade will be based on the total number of correct answers.

The following information pertains to Sparta Co.'s defined benefit pension plan.

Discount rate	8%
Expected rate of return	10%
Average service life	12 years

At January 1, 1992:

Projected benefit obligation	$600,000
Fair value of pension plan assets	720,000
Unrecognized prior service cost	240,000
Unamortized prior pension gain	96,000

At December 31, 1992:

Projected benefit obligation	910,000
Fair value of pension plan assets	825,000

Service cost for 1992 was $90,000. There were no contributions made or benefits paid during the year. Sparta's unfunded accrued pension liability was $8,000 at January 1, 1992. Sparta uses the straight-line method of amortization over the maximum period permitted.

Required:
1. **For items 61 through 65,** calculate the amounts to be recognized as components of Sparta's unfunded accrued pension liability at December 31, 1992. To record your entry, write the number in the boxes on the Objective Answer Sheet and blacken the corresponding oval below each box. These items cannot be graded if you fail to blacken the ovals.

Amounts to be Calculated:

61. Interest cost.
62. Expected return on plan assets.
63. Actual return on plan assets.
64. Amortization of prior service costs.
65. Minimum amortization of unrecognized pension gain.

2. **For items 66 through 70,** determine whether the component increases Ⓘ or decreases Ⓓ Sparta's unfunded accrued pension liability and blacken the corresponding oval on the Objective Answer Sheet.

Items to be Answered:

66. Service cost.
67. Deferral of gain on pension plan assets.
68. Actual return on plan assets.
69. Amortization of prior service costs.
70. Amortization of unrecognized pension gain.

---

*The omitted item can be found in another Content Specification Group.

K. Income Taxes

R97 Number 1

Question Number 1 consists of 2 parts. Each part consists of 4 items. Select the **best** answer for each item. Use a No. 2 pencil to blacken the appropriate ovals on the *Objective Answer Sheet* to indicate your answers. **Answer all items.** Your grade will be based on the total number of correct answers.

Required:

a. Items 1 through 4 describe circumstances resulting in differences between financial statement income and taxable income. For each numbered item, determine whether the difference is:

List
Ⓐ A temporary difference resulting in a deferred tax asset.
Ⓑ A temporary difference resulting in a deferred tax liability.
Ⓒ A permanent difference.

Blacken the corresponding oval on the *Objective Answer Sheet*. An answer may be selected once, more than once, or not at all.

1. For plant assets, the depreciation expense deducted for tax purposes is in excess of the depreciation expense used for financial reporting purposes.

2. A landlord collects some rents in advance. Rents received are taxable in the period in which they are received.

3. Interest is received on an investment in tax-exempt municipal obligations.

4. Costs of guarantees and warranties are estimated and accrued for financial reporting purposes.

b. The following partially completed worksheet contains Lane Co.'s reconciliation between financial statement income and taxable income for the three years ended April 30, 1997, and additional information.

Lane Co.
INCOME TAX WORKSHEET
For the Three Years Ended April 30, 1997

	April 30, 1995	April 30, 1996	April 30, 1997
Pretax financial income	$900,000	$1,000,000	$1,200,000
Permanent differences	100,000	100,000	100,000
Temporary differences	200,000	100,000	150,000
Taxable income	$600,000	$800,000	$950,000
Cumulative temporary differences (future taxable amounts)	$200,000	$ (6)	$450,000
Tax rate	20%	25%	30%
Deferred tax liability	$40,000	$75,000	$ (8)
Deferred tax expense	$ —	$ (7)	$ —
Current tax expense	$ (5)	$ —	$ —

The tax rate changes were enacted at the beginning of each tax year and were not known to Lane at the end of the prior year.

Required:

Items 5 through 8 represent amounts omitted from the worksheet. For each item, determine the amount omitted from the worksheet. Select the amount from the following list and blacken the corresponding oval on the *Objective Answer Sheet*. An answer may be used once, more than once, or not at all.

5. Current tax expense for the year ended April 30, 1995.

6. Cumulative temporary differences at April 30, 1996.

7. Deferred tax expense for the year ended April 30, 1996.

8. Deferred tax liability at April 30, 1997.

Amount			
Ⓐ	$25,000	Ⓗ	$135,000
Ⓑ	$35,000	Ⓘ	$140,000
Ⓒ	$45,000	Ⓙ	$160,000
Ⓓ	$75,000	Ⓚ	$180,000
Ⓔ	$100,000	Ⓛ	$200,000
Ⓕ	$112,500	Ⓜ	$300,000
Ⓖ	$120,000	Ⓝ	$400,000

SELECTED OTHER OBJECTIVE ANSWER FORMATS — UNOFFICIAL ANSWERS

I. Concepts and Standards for Financial Statements

B. Financial Accounting Standards for Presentation and Disclosure in General Purpose Financial Statements

    1. Consolidated and Combined Financial Statements

R96
Answer 2(b)

b. Item	Select one
6	● Ⓐ... A selected
7	B selected
8	E selected
9	F selected
10	C selected
11	C selected
12	C selected
13	B selected
14	A selected
15	B selected

FA-151

2N93
Answer 5 (10 points)

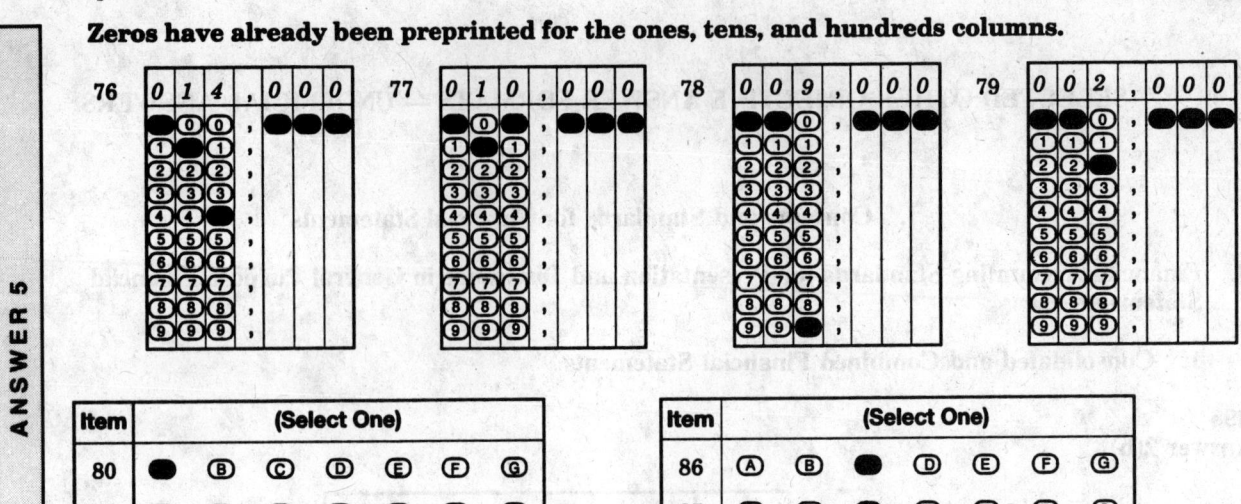

3. Statement(s) of Income, Comprehensive Income, and Changes in Equity Accounts

M95
Answer 2 (10 points)

Zeros have already been preprinted for the ones, tens, and hundreds columns. If zeros precede your numerical answer, blacken the zeros in the ovals preceding your answer. You may write the numbers in the boxes provided to facilitate blackening the ovals; however, the numbers written in the boxes will **not** be graded.

#	Answer
61	014,000
62	012,000
63	165,000
64	720,000
65	113,000
66	113,000
67	934,000
68	042,000
69	24.86
70	826,000

M95
Answer 3 (10 points)

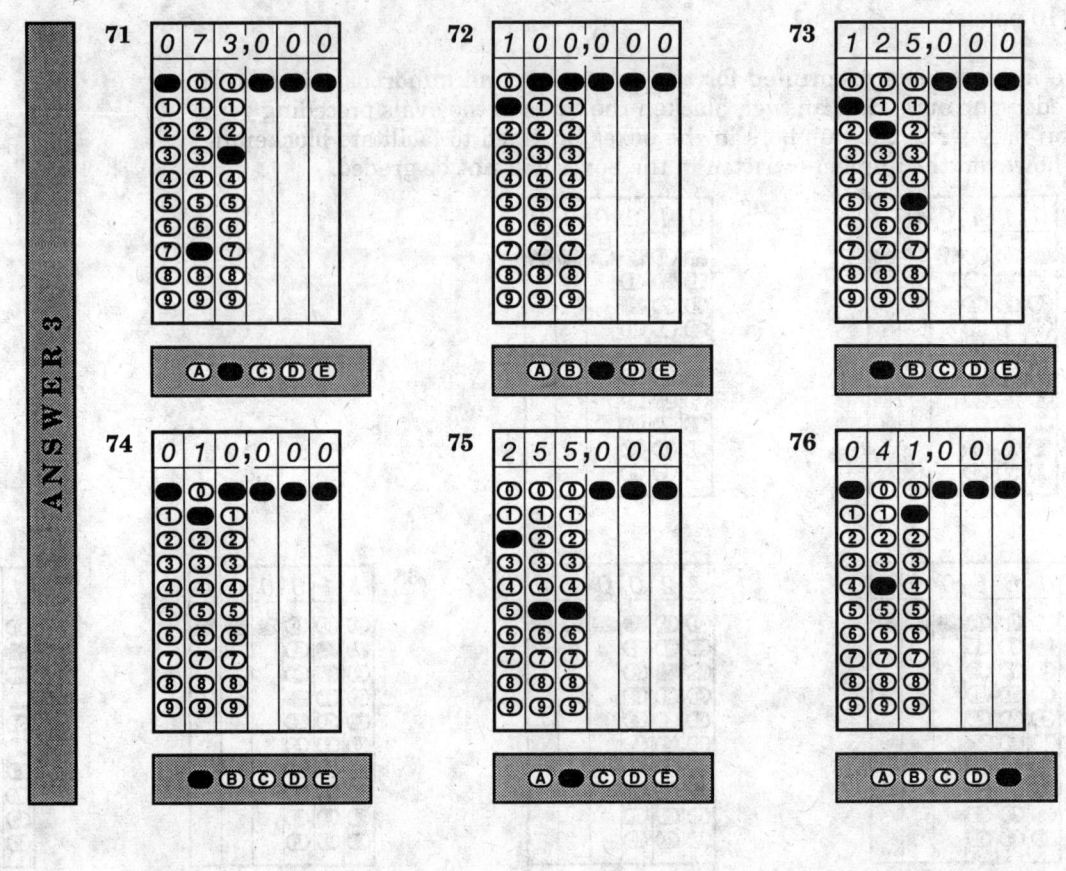

Unofficial Answers

4. **Statement of Cash Flows**

N94
Answer 3 (10 points)

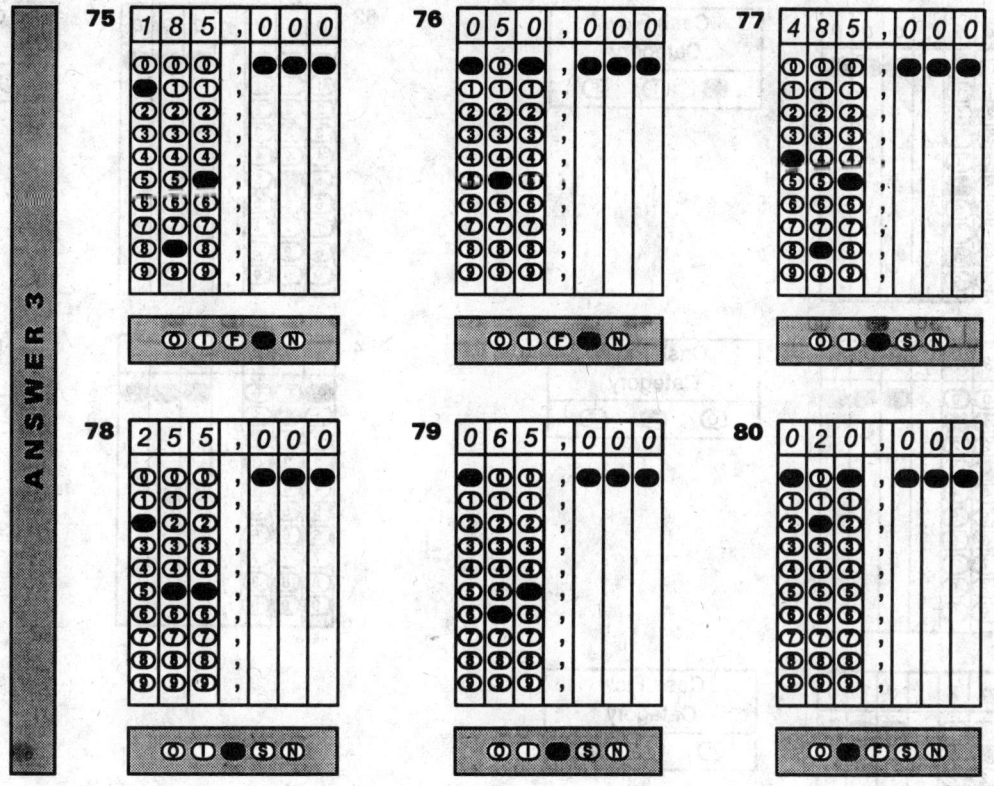

1M92
Answer 4(a) (5 points)

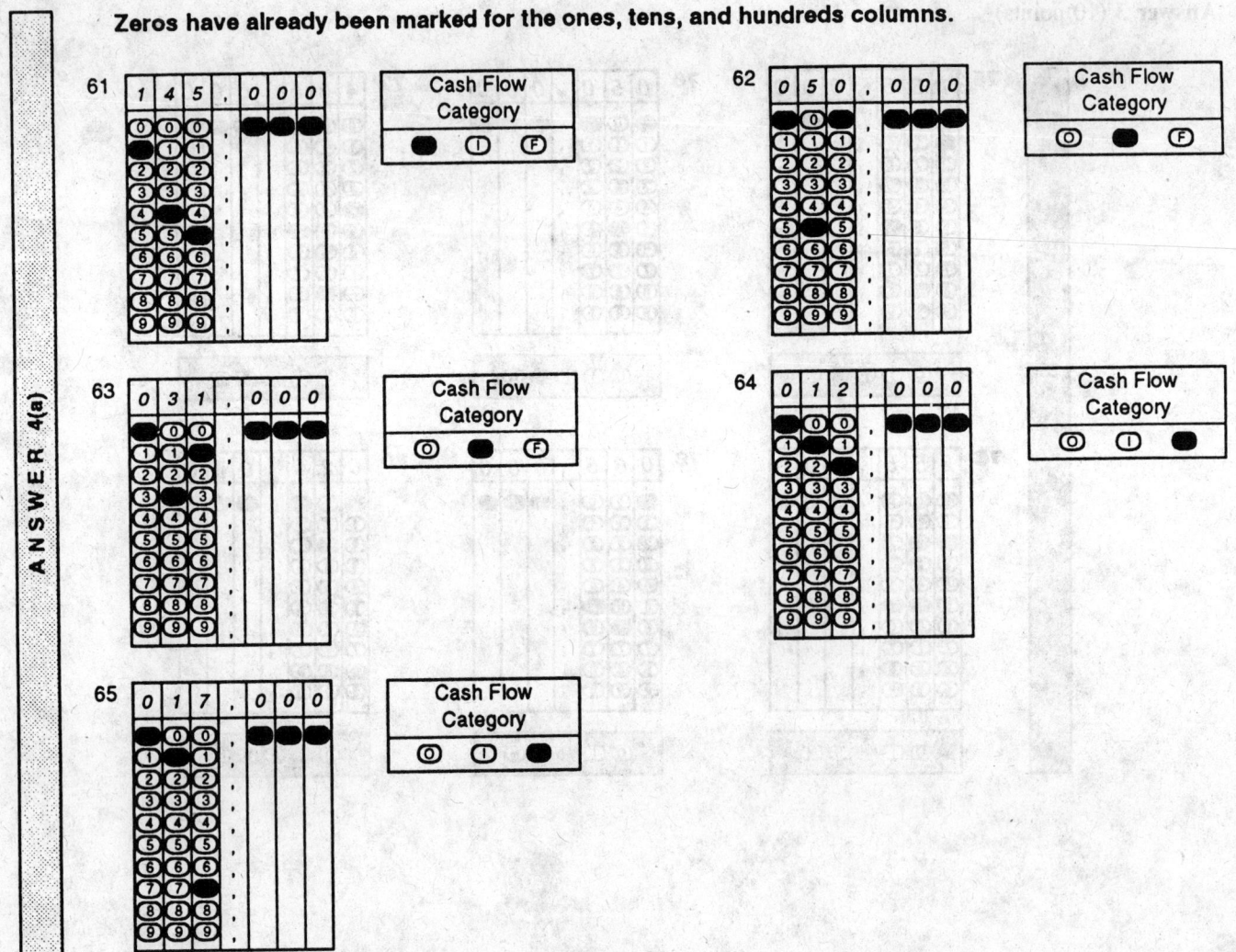

Unofficial Answers

II. Recognition, Measurement, Valuation, and Presentation of Typical Items in Financial Statements in Conformity With Generally Accepted Accounting Principles

B. Receivables

R96
Answer 1 (10 points)

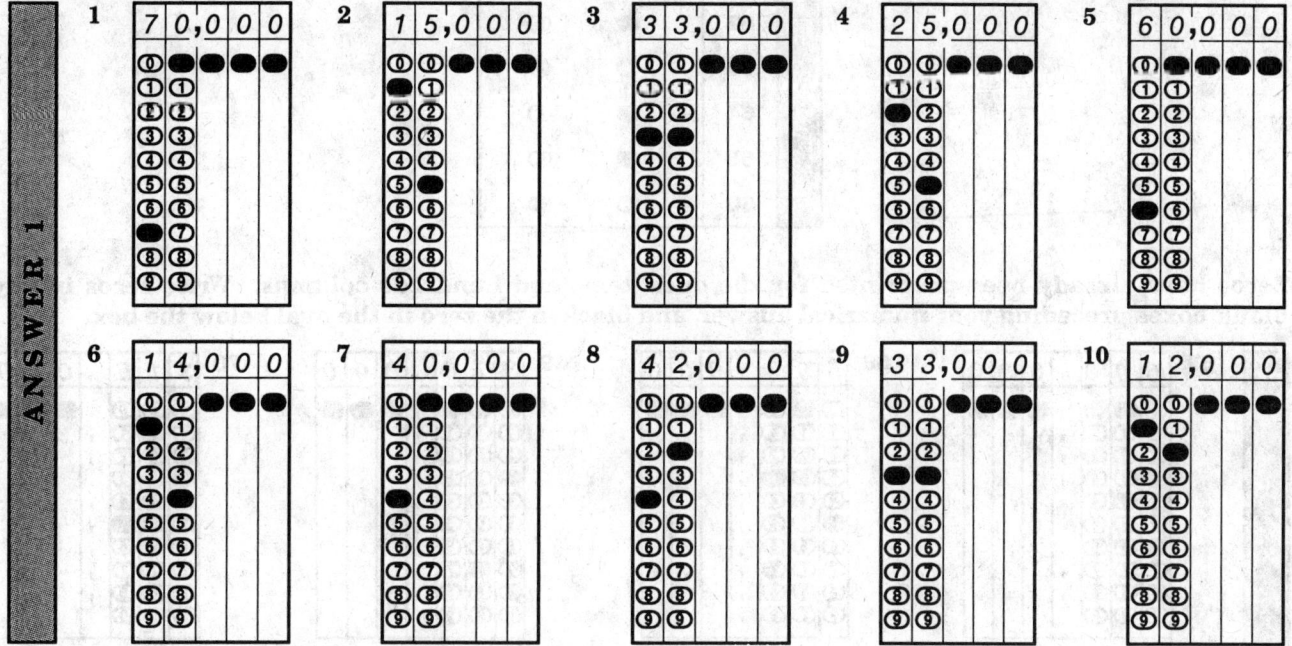

FA-157

D. Property, Plant, and Equipment

N94
Answer 2 (10 points)

Item		
61	●	(E)
62	●	(E)
63	(C)	●
64	●	(E)
65	●	(E)
66	(C)	●

Zeros have already been preprinted for the ones, tens, and hundreds columns. Write zeros in any blank boxes preceding your numerical answer, and blacken the zero in the oval below the box.

67. 600,000
68. 503,000
69. 370,000
70. 315,000
71. 090,000
72. 162,000
73. 140,000
74. 120,000

1N92
Answer 4(a) (5 points)

Item	Land	Building	Expense
61	●	(B)	(E)
62	(L)	(B)	●
63	(L)	●	(E)
64	●	(B)	(E)

Item	Land	Building	Expense
65	●	(B)	(E)
66	(L)	●	(E)
67	●	(B)	(E)
68	(L)	(B)	●

Unofficial Answers

I. Notes and Bonds Payable

N95
Answer 3

Item	Rate	Amount
71	(A) (B) (C) (D) (E) (F)	(G)(H)(I)(J)(K)(L)(M)(N)(O)(P)●(R)(S)(T)(U)(V)(W)(X)
72	(A) (B) (C) (D) (E) (F)	(G)(H)(I)(J)(K)●(M)(N)(O)(P)(Q)(R)(S)(T)(U)(V)(W)(X)
73	(A) (B) (C) (D) (E) (F)	(G)(H)(I)(J)(K)(L)(M)(N)(O)(P)(Q)(R)(S)●(U)(V)(W)(X)
74	(A) (B) (C) ● (E) (F)	(G)(H)(I)(J)(K)(L)(M)(N)(O)(P)(Q)(R)(S)(T)(U)(V)(W)(X)
75	(A) (B) (C) (D) (E) ●	(G)(H)(I)(J)(K)(L)(M)(N)(O)(P)(Q)(R)(S)(T)(U)(V)(W)(X)
76	(A) (B) (C) (D) (E) (F)	(G)(H)(I)(J)(K)(L)(M)●(O)(P)(Q)(R)(S)(T)(U)(V)(W)(X)
77	(A) (B) (C) (D) (E) (F)	(G)(H)●(J)(K)(L)(M)(N)(O)(P)(Q)(R)(S)(T)(U)(V)(W)(X)

TN93
Answer 2 (10 points)

Item	I Incr	I Decr	I No Eff	II Incr	II Decr	II No Eff	III Incr	III Decr	III No Eff	IV Incr	IV Decr	IV No Eff	V Incr	V Decr	V No Eff	VI Incr	VI Decr	VI No Eff
61	●	(D)	(N)	(I)	(D)	●	(I)	(D)	●	(I)	●	(N)	(I)	(D)	●	(I)	(D)	●
62	(I)	(D)	●	●	(D)	(N)	(I)	(D)	●	(I)	(D)	●	(I)	●	(N)	(I)	(D)	●
63	(I)	●	(N)	(I)	●	(N)	(I)	●	(N)	(I)	(D)	●	●	(D)	(N)	(I)	(D)	●
64	●	(D)	(N)	(I)	(D)	●	(I)	●	(N)	(I)	(D)	●	●	(D)	(N)	(I)	(D)	●
65	(I)	(D)	●	(I)	(D)	●	(I)	(D)	●	●	(D)	(N)	(I)	(D)	●	(I)	●	(N)

III. Recognition, Measurement, Valuation, and Presentation of Specific Types of Transactions and Events in Financial Statements in Conformity With Generally Accepted Accounting Principles

A. Accounting Changes and Corrections of Errors

R97
Answer 2

	Select one	Select one		Select one	Select one		Select one	Select one
1	●(B)(C)(D)	(X)●(Z)	3	●(B)(C)(D)	●(Y)(Z)	4	(A)(B)●(D)	(X)●(Z)
2	(A)●(C)(D)	(X)(Y)●						

Item 3: 9,000
Item 4: 2,000

FA-159

R96
Answer 2(b)

ANSWER 2

a. Item	Select one			
1	●	Ⓑ	Ⓒ	Ⓓ
2	Ⓐ	Ⓑ	●	Ⓓ
3	Ⓐ	●	Ⓒ	Ⓓ
4	Ⓐ	Ⓑ	Ⓒ	●
5	●	Ⓑ	Ⓒ	Ⓓ

M94
Answer 2 (10 points)

ANSWER 2

Item	List A (Select one)				List B (Select one)		
61	●	Ⓑ	Ⓒ	Ⓓ	Ⓧ	●	Ⓩ
62	Ⓐ	●	Ⓒ	Ⓓ	Ⓧ	Ⓨ	●
63	Ⓐ	●	Ⓒ	Ⓓ	Ⓧ	Ⓨ	●
64	●	Ⓑ	Ⓒ	Ⓓ	Ⓧ	●	Ⓩ
65	●	Ⓑ	Ⓒ	Ⓓ	●	Ⓨ	Ⓩ
66	Ⓐ	Ⓑ	●	Ⓓ	Ⓧ	●	Ⓩ
67	Ⓐ	Ⓑ	●	Ⓓ	Ⓧ	●	Ⓩ
68	●	Ⓑ	Ⓒ	Ⓓ	●	Ⓨ	Ⓩ
69	Ⓐ	Ⓑ	Ⓒ	●	Ⓧ	Ⓨ	●
70	Ⓐ	Ⓑ	Ⓒ	●	Ⓧ	●	Ⓩ

D. Contingent Liabilities and Commitments

N95
Answer 3

ANSWER 3

Item	Select one			
78	Ⓓ	Ⓐ	●	Ⓝ
79	Ⓓ	Ⓐ	Ⓑ	●
80	Ⓓ	Ⓐ	Ⓑ	●
81	●	Ⓐ	Ⓑ	Ⓝ
82	Ⓓ	Ⓐ	●	Ⓝ
83	●	Ⓐ	Ⓑ	Ⓝ

M94
Answer 3 (10 points)

Item	List A (Select one)	Select One
71	A	Y
72	C	Y
73	B	Y
74	B	Y
75	A	Y
76	A	Y
77	A	Y
78	C	Y
79	A	Y
80	A	Y
81	A	Y
82	B	Y

Financial Accounting and Reporting

G. Employee Benefits

1M93
Answer 4(a) (5 points)

ANSWER 4(a)

Zeros have already been preprinted for the ones, tens, and hundreds columns.

61. 048,000
62. 072,000
63. 105,000
64. 020,000
65. 002,000

66. I ● / D (D)
67. I ● / D (D)
68. I (I) / D ●
69. I ● / D (D)
70. I (I) / D ●

K. Income Taxes

R97
Answer 1 (5 points)

ANSWER 1

A. Select one
1. (A) ● (C)
2. ● (B) (C)
3. (A) (B) ●
4. ● (B) (C)

B. Select one
5. (A) (B) (C) (D) (E) (F) ● (H) (I) (J) (K) (L) (M) (N)
6. (A) (B) (C) (D) (E) (F) (G) (H) (I) (J) (K) (L) ● (N)
7. (A) ● (C) (D) (E) (F) (G) (H) (I) (J) (K) (L) (M) (N)
8. (A) (B) (C) (D) (E) (F) (G) ● (I) (J) (K) (L) (M) (N)

PROBLEMS/ESSAYS — SELECTED QUESTIONS

I. Concepts and Standards for Financial Statements

A. Financial Accounting Concepts

TN93
Number 5 (Estimated time — — 15 to 25 minutes)

Mono Tech Co. began operations in 1989 and confined its activities to one project. It purchased equipment to be used exclusively for research and development on the project, and other equipment that is to be used initially for research and development and subsequently for production. In 1990, Mono constructed and paid for a pilot plant that was used until December 1991 to determine the best manufacturing process for the project's product. In December 1991, Mono obtained a patent and received cash from the sale of the pilot plant. In 1992, a factory was constructed and commercial manufacture of the product began.

Required:
    a. 1. According to the FASB conceptual framework, what are the three essential characteristics of an asset?
    2. How do Mono's project expenditures through 1991 meet the FASB conceptual framework's three essential characteristics of an asset? Do **not** discuss why the expenditures may **not** meet the characteristics of an asset.
    3. Why is it difficult to justify the classification of research and development expenditures as assets?

    b. How should Mono report:

    1. The effects of equipment expenditures in its income statements and balance sheets from 1989 through 1992?
    2. Pilot plant construction costs and sale proceeds in its 1990 and 1991 statements of cash flows using the direct method?

B. Financial Accounting Standards for Presentation and Disclosure in General Purpose Financial Statements

    1. **Consolidated and Combined Financial Statements**

TM92
Number 4 (Estimated time — — 15 to 25 minutes)

On September 1, 1991, Plains Corp. acquired all of Sox Corp.'s outstanding stock for cash. The fair value of Sox's net assets was less than the purchase price but greater than the net carrying amount. During November 1991, Plains sold goods to Sox at a price that included its normal markup. At December 31, 1991, 20% of these goods remained in Sox's inventory. The separate legal entities were maintained and Sox uses push-down accounting for its separate financial statements.

Required:
    Ignore income tax considerations when answering all questions.

    a. 1. Specify three reasons for preparing consolidated financial statements that present operating results, cash flows, and financial position as if a parent company and its subsidiaries were a single entity.
    2. What changes in Plains' September 1, 1991, consolidated balance sheet will result from this acquisition?
    3. In preparing Plains' December 31, 1991, consolidated financial statements, what adjustments or eliminations are required as a consequence of the intercompany sales?

    b. In preparing separate financial statements immediately after acquisition (September 1, 1991), what is the effect of the purchase on the balance sheet of:
    1. Plains?
    2. Sox (which uses push-down accounting)?

1N91
Number 5 (Estimated time — — 40 to 50 minutes)

Pine Corp. issued 200,000 shares of its $10 par common stock on March 31, 1990, to acquire all of the outstanding $25 par value common stock of Strand, Inc. The business combination meets all conditions for a pooling of interests. On March 31, 1990, the market price of Pine's common stock was $35 a share. Both corporations continued to operate as separate businesses, maintaining separate accounting records with years ending December 31.

On March 31, 1990, immediately before the combination, the stockholders' equities were

	Pine	Strand
Common stock	$ 5,500,000	$2,500,000
Additional paid-in capital	4,200,000	470,000
Retained earnings	7,360,000	2,430,000
	$17,060,000	$5,400,000

Additional information

- During March 1990, Pine paid $720,000 for expenditures relating to the business combination with Strand.

- Pine accounts for its investment in Strand using the equity method.

- On March 31, 1990, the fair values of Strand's assets and liabilities equaled their book values, except for its long-term investment in marketable equity securities, for which the aggregate market value exceeded aggregate cost by $600,000.

- On March 10, 1990, Strand paid a cash dividend totaling $250,000 on its common stock.

- On November 15, 1990, Pine paid a cash dividend totaling $1,500,000 on its common stock.

- During August 1990, Pine sold merchandise to Strand at a profit of $800,000. At December 31, 1990, one-fourth of this merchandise remained in Strand's inventory.

- For the period April 1 through December 31, 1990, Strand paid Pine management fees totaling $150,000.

- Strand's 1990 net income was $1,450,000. Pine's 1990 income was $2,240,000, before considering equity in Strand's net income.

- The balances in retained earnings at December 31, 1989, were $6,820,000 and $2,290,000 for Pine and Strand, respectively.

Required:

a. Prepare Pine Corp.'s journal entries to record the business combination with Strand, Inc. and the expenditures relating to the business combination.

b. Prepare a schedule to compute the investment in Strand, Inc., at equity, at December 31, 1990.

c. Prepare a formal consolidated statement of changes in retained earnings of Pine Corp. and its subsidiary Strand, Inc. for the year ended December 31, 1990.

1M90
Number 4 (Estimated time — — 45 to 55 minutes)

Cain Corp. acquired all of the outstanding $10 par value voting common stock of Frey, Inc. on January 1, 1989 in exchange for 25,000 shares of its $10 par value voting common stock. On December 31, 1988, Cain's common stock had a closing market price of $30 per share on a national stock exchange. The acquisition was appropriately accounted for as a purchase. Both companies continued to operate as separate business entities maintaining separate accounting records with years ending December 31.

On December 31, 1989, the companies had condensed financial statements as follows:

	Cain Corp. Dr. (Cr.)	Frey, Inc. Dr. (Cr.)
Income Statement		
Net sales	$(3,800,000)	$(1,500,000)
Dividends from Frey	(40,000)	
Gain on sale of warehouse	(30,000)	
Cost of goods sold	2,360,000	870,000
Operating expenses (including depreciation)	1,100,000	440,000
Net income	$ (410,000)	$ (190,000)
Retained Earnings Statement		
Balance, 1/1/89	$ (440,000)	$ (156,000)
Net income	(410,000)	(190,000)
Dividends paid		40,000
Balance, 12/31/89	$ (850,000)	$ (306,000)
Balance Sheet		
Assets:		
Cash	$ 570,000	$ 150,000
Accounts receivable (net)	860,000	350,000
Inventories	1,060,000	410,000
Land, plant, and equipment	1,320,000	680,000
Accumulated depreciation	(370,000)	(210,000)
Investment in Frey (at cost)	750,000	
Total Assets	$ 4,190,000	$ 1,380,000
Liabilities & Stockholders' Equity:		
Accounts payable & accrued expenses	$(1,340,000)	$ (594,000)
Common stock ($10 par)	(1,700,000)	(400,000)
Additional paid-in capital	(300,000)	(80,000)
Retained earnings	(850,000)	(306,000)
Total Liabilities & Stockholders' Equity	$(4,190,000)	$(1,380,000)

Selected Questions

Additional information follows:

- There were no changes in the common stock and additional paid-in capital accounts during 1989 except the one necessitated by Cain's acquisition of Frey.

- At the acquisition date, the fair value of Frey's machinery exceeded its book value by $54,000. The excess cost will be amortized over the estimated average remaining life of six years. The fair values of all of Frey's other assets and liabilities were equal to their book values. Any goodwill resulting from the acquisition will be amortized over a 20-year period.

- On July 1, 1989, Cain sold a warehouse facility to Frey for $129,000 cash. At the date of sale, Cain's book values were $33,000 for the land and $66,000 for the undepreciated cost of the building. Based on a real estate appraisal, Frey allocated $43,000 of the purchase price to land and $86,000 to building. Frey is depreciating the building over its estimated five-year remaining useful life by the straight-line method with no salvage value.

- During 1989, Cain purchased merchandise from Frey at an aggregate invoice price of $180,000, which included a 100% markup on Frey's cost. At December 31, 1989, Cain owed Frey $86,000 on these purchases, and $36,000 of this merchandise remained in Cain's inventory.

Required: Complete the tear-out worksheet that would be used to prepare a consolidated income statement and a consolidated retained earnings statement for the year ended December 31, 1989, and a consolidated balance sheet as of December 31, 1989. Formal consolidated statements and adjusting entries are **not** required. Ignore income tax considerations. Supporting computations should be in good form. Include the completed tear-out worksheet in the proper sequence and include it with the other answer sheets.

1M90
Number 4 (Tear-out Worksheet)

Cain Corp. and Subsidiary
CONSOLIDATING STATEMENT WORKSHEET
December 31, 1989

Income Statement	Cain Corp. Dr. (Cr.)	Frey, Inc. Dr. (Cr.)	Adjustments & Eliminations Dr.	Adjustments & Eliminations Cr.	Adjusted Balance
Net sales	(3,800,000)	(1,500,000)			
Dividends from Frey	(40,000)				
Gain on sale of warehouse	(30,000)				
Cost of goods sold	2,360,000	870,000			
Operating expenses (including depreciation)	1,100,000	440,000			
Net income	(410,000)	(190,000)			
Retained Earnings Statement					
Balance, 1/1/89	(440,000)	(156,000)			
Net income	(410,000)	(190,000)			
Dividends paid		40,000			
Balance, 12/31/89	(850,000)	(306,000)			
Balance Sheet					
Assets:					
Cash	570,000	150,000			
Accounts receivable (net)	860,000	350,000			
Inventories	1,060,000	410,000			
Land, plant, and equipment	1,320,000	680,000			
Accumulated depreciation	(370,000)	(210,000)			
Investment in Frey (at cost)	750,000				
Total Assets	4,190,000	1,380,000			
Liabilities & Stockholders' Equity:					
Accounts payable & accrued expenses	(1,340,000)	(594,000)			
Common stock ($10 par)	(1,700,000)	(400,000)			
Additional paid-in capital	(300,000)	(80,000)			
Retained earnings	(850,000)	(306,000)			
Total Liabilities & Stockholders' Equity	(4,190,000)	(1,380,000)			

2. Balance Sheet

R98
Number 1

The following information relates to the obligations of Villa Watch Co. as of December 31, 1997:

- Accounts payable for goods and services purchased on open account amounted to $35,000 at December 31, 1997.

- On December 15, 1997, Villa declared a cash dividend of $.05 per common share, payable on January 12, 1998, to shareholders of record as of December 31, 1997. Villa had 1,000,000 shares of common stock issued and outstanding throughout 1997.

- On December 30, 1997, Villa entered into a six-year capital lease on a warehouse and made the first annual lease payment of $100,000. Villa's incremental borrowing rate was 12%, and the interest rate implicit in the lease, which was known to Villa, was 10%. The rounded present value factors for an annuity due for six years are 4.6 at 12% and 4.8 at 10%.

- On July 1, 1997, Villa issued $500,000, 8% bonds for $440,000 to yield 10%. The bonds mature on June 30, 2003, and pay interest annually every June 30. At December 31, 1997, the bonds were trading on the open market at 86 to yield 12%. Villa uses the effective interest method.

- Villa's 1997 pretax financial income was $850,000 and its taxable income was $600,000. The difference is due to $100,000 of permanent differences and $150,000 of temporary differences related to noncurrent assets. At December 31, 1997, Villa had cumulative taxable differences of $300,000 related to noncurrent assets. Villa's effective tax rate is 30%. Villa made no estimated tax payments during the year.

- Contingency information:
  — Villa has been named a liable party for toxic waste cleanup on its land, and must pay an as-yet undetermined amount for environmental remediation activities.
  — An adjoining landowner, Clear Toothpaste Co., sold its property because of possible toxic contamination of the water supply and resulting potential adverse public reaction toward its product. Clear sued Villa for damages. There is a reasonable possibility that Clear will prevail and be awarded between $250,000 and $600,000.
  — As a result of comprehensive risk assessment, Villa has discontinued rockslide insurance for its warehouse, which is located at the base of a mountain. The warehouse has never sustained rockslide damage, and the probability of sustaining future damage is only slight.

Required:
Begin the answer to each requirement (i.e., A, B, and C) on the top of a new page.

a. Prepare the liabilities section of Villa's December 31, 1997, balance sheet.

b. Discuss the information Villa is required to disclose, either in the body of the financial statements or the notes thereto, related to bonds payable and capital leases included in the liabilities presented above.

c. Explain how Villa should account for each contingency in its 1997 financial statements. Discuss the theoretical justification for each accounting treatment.

1M91
Number 4 (Estimated time —— 45 to 55 minutes)

Kern, Inc. had the following long-term receivable account balances at December 31, 1989:

Note receivable from the sale of an
  idle building $750,000
Note receivable from an officer   200,000

Transactions during 1990 and other information relating to Kern's long-term receivables follow:

- The $750,000 note receivable is dated May 1, 1989, bears interest at 9%, and represents the balance of the consideration Kern received from the sale of its idle building to Able Co. Principal payments of $250,000 plus interest are due annually beginning May 1, 1990. Able made its first principal and interest payment on May 1, 1990. Collection of the remaining note installments is reasonably assured.

- The $200,000 note receivable is dated December 31, 1987, bears interest at 8%, and is due on December 31, 1992. The note is due from Frank Black, president of Kern, Inc., and is collateralized by 5,000 shares of Kern's common stock. Interest is payable annually on December 31, and all interest payments were made through December 31, 1990. The quoted market price of Kern's common stock was $45 per share on December 31, 1990.

- On April 1, 1990, Kern sold a patent to Frey Corp. in exchange for a $100,000 noninterest bearing note due on April 1, 1992. There was no established exchange price for the patent, and the note had no ready market. The prevailing interest rate for this type of note was 10% at April 1, 1990. The present value of $1 for two periods at 10% is 0.826. The patent had a carrying amount of $40,000 at January 1, 1990, and the amortization for the year ended December 31, 1990, would have been $8,000. Kern is reasonably assured of collecting the note receivable from Frey.

- On July 1, 1990, Kern sold a parcel of land to Barr Co. for $400,000 under an installment sale contract.

Barr made a $120,000 cash down payment on July 1, 1990, and signed a four-year 10% note for the $280,000 balance. The equal annual payments of principal and interest on the note will be $88,332, payable on July 1 of each year from 1991 through 1994. The fair value of the land at the date of sale was $400,000. The cost of the land to Kern was $300,000. Collection of the remaining note installments is reasonably assured.

Required:

Prepare the following and show supporting computations:

a. Long-term receivables section of Kern's December 31, 1990, balance sheet.

b. Schedule showing current portion of long-term receivables and accrued interest receivable to be reported in Kern's December 31, 1990, balance sheet.

c. Schedule showing interest revenue from long-term receivables and gains recognized on sale of assets to be reported in Kern's 1990 income statement.

3. Statement(s) of Income, Comprehensive Income, and Changes in Equity Accounts

R96
Number 2 (Estimated time —— 30 to 40 minutes)

The following pro forma statement of income and changes in equity accounts was prepared by the newly-hired staff accountant of Topaz, Inc., a nonpublic company, for the year ended December 31, 1995.

Topaz, Inc.
STATEMENT OF INCOME AND CHANGES IN RETAINED EARNINGS
December 31, 1995

Revenues and gains:
Gross sales
Purchase discounts
Recovery of accounts receivable written off in prior years
Interest revenue
Gain on early extinguishment of debt
    Total revenues and gains

Expenses and losses:
Cost of goods sold
Sales returns and allowances
Selling expenses
General and administrative expenses
Cash dividends declared
    Total expenses and losses
Income before discontinued operations and extraordinary item

Discontinued operations:
Loss on disposal of discontinued styles, net of tax effect

Extraordinary item:
Correction of errors in prior years' statements, net of tax effect
Retained earnings at beginning of year
Income taxes
Net income
Retained earnings at end of year

Additional information:
- Topaz uses the allowance method to account for uncollectible accounts.
- The loss on disposal of discontinued styles resulted from the sale of outdated styles within a product line.
- Topaz had no temporary tax differences at the beginning or the end of the year.

Required:
Identify the weaknesses in classification and presentation in the above Statement of Income and Changes in Retained Earnings. Explain the proper classification and presentation. **Do not prepare a corrected statement.**

The next question begins on page FA-170.

N94
Number 4 (Estimated time —— 30 to 40 minutes)

The following condensed trial balance of Probe Co., a publicly-held company, has been adjusted except for income tax expense.

Probe Co.
CONDENSED TRIAL BALANCE

	12/31/93 Balances Dr. (Cr.)	12/31/92 Balances Dr. (Cr.)	Net change Dr. (Cr.)
Cash	$ 473,000	$ 817,000	$(344,000)
Accounts receivable, net	670,000	610,000	60,000
Property, plant, and equipment	1,070,000	995,000	75,000
Accumulated depreciation	(345,000)	(280,000)	(65,000)
Dividends payable	(25,000)	(10,000)	(15,000)
Income taxes payable	35,000	(150,000)	185,000
Deferred income tax liability	(42,000)	(42,000)	—
Bonds payable	(500,000)	(1,000,000)	500,000
Unamortized premium on bonds	(71,000)	(150,000)	79,000
Common stock	(350,000)	(150,000)	(200,000)
Additional paid-in capital	(430,000)	(375,000)	(55,000)
Retained earnings	(185,000)	(265,000)	80,000
Sales	(2,420,000)		
Cost of sales	1,863,000		
Selling and administrative expenses	220,000		
Interest income	(14,000)		
Interest expense	46,000		
Depreciation	88,000		
Loss on sale of equipment	7,000		
Gain on extinguishment of bonds	(90,000)		
	$ 0	$ 0	$300,000

Additional information:

- During 1993 equipment with an original cost of $50,000 was sold for cash, and equipment costing $125,000 was purchased.

- On January 1, 1993, bonds with a par value of $500,000 and related premium of $75,000 were redeemed. The $1,000 face value, 10% par bonds had been issued on January 1, 1984, to yield 8%. Interest is payable annually every December 31 through 2003.

- Probe's tax payments during 1993 were debited to Income Taxes Payable. Probe elected early adoption of Statement of Financial Accounting Standards No. 109, *Accounting for Income Taxes,* for the year ended December 31, 1992, and recorded a deferred income tax liability of $42,000 based on temporary differences of $120,000 and an enacted tax rate of 35%. Probe's 1993 financial statement income before income taxes was greater than its 1993 taxable income, due entirely to temporary differences, by $60,000. Probe's cumulative net taxable temporary differences at December 31, 1993, were $180,000. Probe's enacted tax rate for the current and future years is 30%.

- 60,000 shares of common stock, $2.50 par, were outstanding on December 31, 1992. Probe issued an additional 80,000 shares on April 1, 1993.

- There were no changes to retained earnings other than dividends declared.

Required:

Prepare Probe Co.'s multiple-step income statement for the year ended December 31, 1993, with earnings per share information and supporting computations for current and deferred income tax expense.

1N92
Number 5 (Estimated time — — 40 to 50 minutes)

The following condensed trial balance of Powell Corp., a publicly-owned company, has been adjusted except for income tax expense:

Powell Corp.
CONDENSED TRIAL BALANCE
June 30, 1992

	Debit	Credit
Total assets	$25,080,000	
Total liabilities		$ 9,900,000
5% cumulative preferred stock		2,000,000
Common stock		10,000,000
Retained earnings		2,900,000
Machine sales		750,000
Service revenues		250,000
Interest revenue		10,000
Gain on sale of factory		250,000
Cost of sales—machines	425,000	
Cost of services	100,000	
Administrative expenses	300,000	
Research and development expenses	110,000	
Interest expense	5,000	
Loss from asset disposal	40,000	
	$26,060,000	$26,060,000

Other information and financial data for the year ended June 30, 1992, follows:

- The weighted average number of common shares outstanding during 1992 was 200,000. The potential dilution from the exercise of stock options held by Powell's officers and directors was not material.

- There were no dividends-in-arrears on Powell's preferred stock at July 1, 1991. On May 1, 1992, Powell's directors declared a 5% preferred stock dividend to be paid in August 1992.

- During 1992, one of Powell's foreign factories was expropriated by the foreign government, and Powell received a $900,000 payment from the foreign government in settlement. The carrying value of the plant was $650,000. Powell has never disposed of a factory.

- Administrative expenses includes a $5,000 premium payment for a $1,000,000 life insurance policy on Powell's president, of which the corporation is the beneficiary.

- Powell depreciates its assets using the straight-line method for financial reporting purposes and an accelerated method for tax purposes. The differences between book and tax depreciation are as follows:

June 30	Financial statements over (under) tax depreciation
1992	$(15,000)
1993	10,000
1994	5,000

There were no other temporary differences.

- Powell's enacted tax rate for the current and future years is 30%. Powell elected early application of FASB Statement No. 109, *Accounting for Income Taxes*.**

Required:

a. Using the single-step format, prepare Powell's income statement for the year ended June 30, 1992.

b. Prepare a schedule reconciling Powell's financial statement net income to taxable income for the year ended June 30, 1992.

**Revised to reflect application of accounting pronouncements effective subsequent to examination date.

Financial Accounting and Reporting

4. **Statement of Cash Flows**

1M93
Number 5 (Estimated time — — 45 to 55 minutes)

The following is Omega Corp.'s comparative balance sheet accounts worksheet at December 31, 1992, and 1991, with a column showing the increase (decrease) from 1991 to 1992.

Comparative balance sheet worksheet	1992	1991	Increase (Decrease)
Cash	$ 800,000	$ 700,000	$100,000
Accounts receivable	1,128,000	1,168,000	(40,000)
Inventories	1,850,000	1,715,000	135,000
Property, plant, and equipment	3,307,000	2,967,000	340,000
Accumulated depreciation	(1,165,000)	(1,040,000)	(125,000)
Investment in Belle Co.	305,000	275,000	30,000
Loan receivable	270,000	—	270,000
Total assets	$6,495,000	$5,785,000	$710,000
Accounts payable	$1,015,000	$ 955,000	$ 60,000
Income taxes payable	30,000	50,000	(20,000)
Dividends payable	80,000	90,000	(10,000)
Capital lease obligation	400,000	—	$ 400,000
Capital stock, common, $1 par	500,000	500,000	—
Additional paid-in capital	1,500,000	1,500,000	—
Retained earnings	2,970,000	2,690,000	280,000
Total liabilities and stockholders' equity	$6,495,000	$5,785,000	$710,000

Additional information:

- On December 31, 1991, Omega acquired 25% of Belle Co.'s common stock for $275,000. On that date, the carrying value of Belle's assets and liabilities, which approximated their fair values, was $1,100,000. Belle reported income of $120,000 for the year ended December 31, 1992. No dividend was paid on Belle's common stock during the year.
- During 1992, Omega loaned $300,000 to Chase Co., an unrelated company. Chase made the first semi-annual principal repayment of $30,000, plus interest at 10%, on October 1, 1992.
- On January 2, 1992, Omega sold equipment costing $60,000, with a carrying amount of $35,000, for $40,000 cash.
- On December 31, 1992, Omega entered into a capital lease for an office building. The present value of the annual rental payments is $400,000, which equals the fair value of the building. Omega made the first rental payment of $60,000 when due on January 2, 1993.
- Net income for 1992 was $360,000.
- Omega declared and paid cash dividends for 1992 and 1991 as follows:

	1992	1991
Declared	December 15, 1992	December 15, 1991
Paid	February 28, 1993	February 28, 1992
Amount	$80,000	$90,000

Required:

Prepare a statement of cash flows for Omega, Inc. for the year ended December 31, 1992, using the indirect method. Supplemental schedules and disclosures are **not** required. A worksheet is **not** required.

1N90
Number 5 (Estimated time — — 40 to 50 minutes)

Presented below are the condensed statements of financial position of Linden Consulting Associates as of December 31, 1989 and 1988, and the condensed statement of income for the year ended December 31, 1989.

Linden Consulting Associates
CONDENSED STATEMENTS OF FINANCIAL POSITION
December 31, 1989 and 1988

	1989	1988	Net change increase (decrease)
Assets			
Cash	$ 652,000	$ 280,000	$372,000
Accounts receivable, net	446,000	368,000	78,000
Investment in Zach, Inc., at equity	550,000	466,000	84,000
Property and equipment	1,270,000	1,100,000	170,000
Accumulated depreciation	(190,000)	(130,000)	(60,000)
Excess of cost over book value of investment in Zach, Inc. (net)	152,000	156,000	(4,000)
Total assets	$2,880,000	$2,240,000	$640,000
Liabilities and Partners' Equity			
Accounts payable and accrued expenses	$ 320,000	$ 270,000	$ 50,000
Mortgage payable	250,000	270,000	(20,000)
Partners' equity	2,310,000	1,700,000	610,000
Total liabilities and partners' equity	$2,880,000	$2,240,000	$640,000

Linden Consulting Associates
CONDENSED STATEMENT OF INCOME
For the Year Ended December 31, 1989

Fee revenue	$2,664,000
Operating expenses	1,940,000
Operating income	724,000
Equity in earnings of Zach, Inc. (net of $4,000 amortization of excess of cost over book value)	176,000
Net income	$ 900,000

1N90
Number 5 (cont.)

Additional information:

- On December 31, 1988, partners' capital and profit sharing percentages were as follows:

	Capital	Profit sharing %
Garr	$1,020,000	60%
Pat	680,000	40%
	$1,700,000	

- On January 1, 1989, Garr and Pat admitted Scott to the partnership for a cash payment of $340,000 to Linden Consulting Associates as the agreed amount of Scott's beginning capital account. In addition, Scott paid a $50,000 cash bonus directly to Garr and Pat. This amount was divided $30,000 to Garr and $20,000 to Pat. The new profit sharing arrangement is as follows:

Garr	50%
Pat	30%
Scott	20%

- On October 1, 1989, Linden purchased and paid for an office computer costing $170,000, including $15,000 for sales tax, delivery, and installation. There were no dispositions of property and equipment during 1989.

- Throughout 1989, Linden owned 25% of Zach, Inc.'s common stock. As a result of this ownership interest, Linden can exercise significant influence over Zach's operating and financial policies. During 1989, Zach paid dividends totaling $384,000 and reported net income of $720,000. Linden's 1989 amortization of excess of cost over book value in Zach was $4,000.

- Partners' drawings for 1989 were as follows:

Garr	$280,000
Pat	200,000
Scott	150,000
	$630,000

Required:

a. Using the direct method, prepare Linden's statement of cash flows for the year ended December 31, 1989.

b. Prepare a reconciliation of net income to net cash provided by operating activities.

c. Prepare an analysis of changes in partners' capital accounts for the year ended December 31, 1989.

C. Other Presentations of Financial Data

1. Financial Statements Prepared in Conformity With Comprehensive Bases of Accounting Other Than Generally Accepted Accounting Principles

N95
Number 4 (Estimated time —— 30 to 40 minutes)

The following information pertains to Baron Flowers, a calendar-year sole proprietorship, which maintained its books on the cash basis during the year.

Baron Flowers
TRIAL BALANCE
December 31, 1994

	Dr.	Cr.
Cash	$ 25,600	
Accounts receivable, 12/31/93	16,200	
Inventory, 12/31/93	62,000	
Furniture & fixtures	118,200	
Land improvements	45,000	
Accumulated depreciation, 12/31/93		$ 32,400
Accounts payable, 12/31/93		17,000
Baron, Drawings		
Baron, Capital, 12/31/93		124,600
Sales		653,000
Purchases	305,100	
Salaries	174,000	
Payroll taxes	12,400	
Insurance	8,700	
Rent	34,200	
Utilities	12,600	
Living expenses	13,000	
	$827,000	$827,000

Baron has developed plans to expand into the wholesale flower market and is in the process of negotiating a bank loan to finance the expansion. The bank is requesting 1994 financial statements prepared on the accrual basis of accounting from Baron. During the course of a review engagement, Muir, Baron's accountant, obtained the following additional information.

1. Amounts due from customers totaled $32,000 at December 31, 1994.

2. An analysis of the above receivables revealed that an allowance for uncollectible accounts of $3,800 should be provided.

3. Unpaid invoices for flower purchases totaled $30,500 and $17,000, at December 31, 1994, and December 31, 1993, respectively.

4. The inventory totaled $72,800 based on a physical count of the goods at December 31, 1994. The inventory was priced at cost, which approximates market value.

5. On May 1, 1994, Baron paid $8,700 to renew its comprehensive insurance coverage for one year. The premium on the previous policy, which expired on April 30, 1994, was $7,800.

6. On January 2, 1994, Baron entered into a twenty-five-year operating lease for the vacant lot adjacent to Baron's retail store for use as a parking lot. As agreed in the lease, Baron paved and fenced in the lot at a cost of $45,000. The improvements were completed on April 1, 1994, and have an estimated useful life of fifteen years. No provision for depreciation or amortization has been recorded. Depreciation on furniture and fixtures was $12,000 for 1994.

N95
Number 4 (cont.)

7. Accrued expenses at December 31, 1993 and 1994, were as follows:

	1993	1994
Utilities	$ 900	$1,500
Payroll taxes	1,100	1,600
	$2,000	$3,100

8. Baron is being sued for $400,000. The coverage under the comprehensive insurance policy is limited to $250,000. Baron's attorney believes that an unfavorable outcome is probable and that a reasonable estimate of the settlement is $300,000.

9. The salaries account includes $4,000 per month paid to the proprietor. Baron also receives $250 per week for living expenses.

Required:

  a. Using the worksheet on page 27 of your *Essay Ruled Paper,* prepare the adjustments necessary to convert the trial balance of Baron Flowers to the accrual basis of accounting for the year ended December 31, 1994. Formal journal entries are not required to support your adjustments. However, use the numbers given with the additional information to cross-reference the postings in the adjustment columns on the worksheet.

  b. Write a brief memo to Baron explaining why the bank would require financial statements prepared on the accrual basis instead of the cash basis.

FA-176

Selected Questions

N95
Number 4 (Tear-out Worksheet)

Baron Flowers
WORKSHEET TO CONVERT TRIAL BALANCE TO ACCRUAL BASIS
December 31, 1994

Account title	Cash basis Dr.	Cash basis Cr.	Adjustments Dr.	Adjustments Cr.	Accrual Basis* Dr.*	Accrual Basis* Cr.*
Cash	25,600					
Accounts receivable	16,200					
Inventory	62,000					
Furniture & fixtures	118,200					
Land improvements	45,000					
Accumulated depreciation & amortization		32,400				
Accounts payable		17,000				
Baron, Drawings						
Baron, Capital		124,600				
Sales		653,000				
Purchases	305,100					
Salaries	174,000					
Payroll taxes	12,400					
Insurance	8,700					
Rent	34,200					
Utilities	12,600					
Living expenses	13,000					
	827,000	827,000				

*Completion of these columns is not required.

II. Recognition, Measurement, Valuation and Presentation of Typical Items in Financial Statements in Conformity With Generally Accepted Accounting Principles

B. Receivables

TN93
Number 3 (Estimated time —— 15 to 25 minutes)

Gregor Wholesalers Co. sells industrial equipment for a standard three-year note receivable. Revenue is recognized at time of sale. Each note is secured by a lien on the equipment and has a face amount equal to the equipment's list price. Each note's stated interest rate is below the customer's market rate at date of sale. All notes are to be collected in three equal annual installments beginning one year after sale. Some of the notes are subsequently discounted at a bank with recourse, some are subsequently discounted without recourse, and some are retained by Gregor. At year end, Gregor evaluates all outstanding notes receivable and provides for estimated losses arising from defaults.

Required:

a. What is the appropriate valuation basis for Gregor's notes receivable at the date it sells equipment?

b. How should Gregor account for the discounting, without recourse, of a February 1, 1992, note receivable discounted on May 1, 1992? Why is it appropriate to account for it in this way?

c. At December 31, 1992, how should Gregor measure and account for the impact of estimated losses resulting from notes receivable that it
   1. Retained and did **not** discount?
   2. Discounted at a bank with recourse?

Selected Questions

1M92
Number 4 (Estimated time —— 45 to 55 minutes)

Number 4 consists of two unrelated parts.*

Number 4(b)

Sigma Co. began operations on January 1, 1990. On December 31, 1990, Sigma provided for uncollectible accounts based on 1% of annual credit sales. On January 1, 1991, Sigma changed its method of determining its allowance for uncollectible accounts by applying certain percentages to the accounts receivable aging as follows:

Days past invoice date	Percent deemed to be uncollectible
0 – 30	1
31 – 90	5
91 – 180	20
Over 180	80

In addition, Sigma wrote off all accounts receivable that were over one year old. The following additional information relates to the years ended December 31, 1991, and 1990:

	1991	1990
Credit sales	$3,000,000	$2,800,000
Collections	2,915,000	2,400,000
Accounts written off	27,000	None
Recovery of accounts previously written off	7,000	None

Days past invoice date at 12/31		
0 – 30	300,000	250,000
31 – 90	80,000	90,000
91 – 180	60,000	45,000
Over 180	25,000	15,000

Required:
    a. Prepare a schedule showing the calculation of the allowance for uncollectible accounts at December 31, 1991.

    b. Prepare a schedule showing the computation of the provision for uncollectible accounts for the year ended December 31, 1991.

---

*The omitted item can be found in another Content Specification Group.

TN91
Number 2 (Estimated time — — 15 to 25 minutes)

On September 30, 1989, Industrial Machinery Co. sold a machine and accepted the customer's noninterest-bearing note. Industrial normally makes sales on a cash basis. Since the machine was unique, its sales price was not determinable using Industrial's normal pricing practices.

After receiving the first of two equal annual installments on September 30, 1990, Industrial immediately discounted the note with recourse. On October 9, 1991, Industrial received notice that the note was dishonored, and it paid all amounts due. At all times prior to default, the note was reasonably expected to be paid in full.

Required:

    a. 1. How should Industrial determine the sales price of the machine?

        2. How should Industrial report the effects of the noninterest-bearing note on its income statement for the year ended December 31, 1989? Why is this accounting presentation appropriate?

    b. What are the effects of the discounting of the note receivable with recourse on Industrial's income statement for the year ended December 31, 1990, and its balance sheet at December 31, 1990?

    c. How should Industrial account for the effects of the note being dishonored?

TM90
Number 2 (Estimated time — — 15 to 25 minutes)

Magrath Company has an operating cycle of less than one year and provides credit terms for all of its customers. On April 1, 1989, the company factored, without recourse, some of its accounts receivable.

On July 1, 1989, Magrath sold special order merchandise and received a noninterest-bearing note due June 30, 1991. The market rate of interest for this note is determinable.

Magrath uses the allowance method to account for uncollectible accounts. During 1989, some accounts were written off as uncollectible and other accounts previously written off as uncollectible were collected.

Required:

    a. How should Magrath account for and report the accounts receivable factored on April 1, 1989? Why is this accounting treatment appropriate?

    b. How should Magrath report the effects of the noninterest-bearing note on its income statement for the year ended December 31, 1989, and its December 31, 1989 balance sheet?

    c. How should Magrath account for the collection of the accounts previously written off as uncollectible?

    d. What are the two basic approaches to estimating uncollectible accounts under the allowance method? What is the rationale for each approach?

Selected Questions

C. Inventories

M94
Number 4 (Estimated time — — 30 to 40 minutes)

York Co. sells one product, which it purchases from various suppliers. York's trial balance at December 31, 1993, included the following accounts:

Sales (33,000 units @ $16)	$528,000
Sales discounts	7,500
Purchases	368,900
Purchase discounts	18,000
Freight-in	5,000
Freight-out	11,000

York Co.'s inventory purchases during 1993 were as follows:

	Units	Cost per unit	Total cost
Beginning inventory, January 1	8,000	$8.20	$ 65,600
Purchases, quarter ended March 31	12,000	8.25	99,000
Purchases, quarter ended June 30	15,000	7.90	118,500
Purchases, quarter ended September 30	13,000	7.50	97,500
Purchases, quarter ended December 31	7,000	7.70	53,900
	55,000		$434,500

Additional information:

York's accounting policy is to report inventory in its financial statements at the lower of cost or market, applied to total inventory. Cost is determined under the last-in, first-out (LIFO) method.

York has determined that, at December 31, 1993, the replacement cost of its inventory was $8 per unit and the net realizable value was $8.80 per unit. York's normal profit margin is $1.05 per unit.

Required:
   a. Prepare York's schedule of cost of goods sold, with a supporting schedule of ending inventory. York uses the direct method of reporting losses from market decline of inventory.

   b. Explain the rule of lower of cost or market and its application in this situation.

TM93
Number 3 (Estimated time — — 15 to 25 minutes)

Blaedon Co. makes ongoing design refinements to lawnmowers that are produced for it by contractors. Blaedon stores the lawnmowers in its own warehouse and sells them at list price, directly to retailers. Blaedon uses the FIFO inventory method. Approximately two-thirds of new lawnmower sales involve trade-ins. For each used lawnmower traded in and returned to Blaedon, retailers receive a $40 allowance regardless of whether the trade-in was associated with a sale of a 1992 or 1993 model. Blaedon's net realizable value on a used lawnmower averages $25.

At December 31, 1992, Blaedon's inventory of new lawnmowers includes both 1992 and 1993 models. When the 1993 model was introduced in September 1992, the list price of the remaining 1992 model lawnmowers was reduced below cost. Blaedon is experiencing rising costs.

Required:
    a. At December 31, 1992, how should Blaedon determine the carrying amounts assigned to its lawnmower inventory of
        1. 1993 models?
        2. 1992 models?

    b. Considering only the 1993 model lawnmower, explain the impact of the FIFO cost flow assumptions on Blaedon's 1992
        1. Income statement amounts.
        2. Balance sheet amounts.

TM91
Number 3 (Estimated time — — 15 to 25 minutes)

Happlia Co. imports expensive household appliances. Each model has many variations and each unit has an identification number. Happlia pays all costs for getting the goods from the port to its central warehouse in Des Moines. After repackaging, the goods are consigned to retailers. A retailer makes a sale, simultaneously buys the appliance from Happlia, and pays the balance due within one week.

To alleviate the overstocking of refrigerators at a Minneapolis retailer, some were reshipped to a Kansas City retailer where they were still held in inventory at December 31, 1990. Happlia paid the costs of this reshipment.

Happlia uses the specific identification inventory costing method.

Required:
    a. In regard to the specific identification inventory costing method
        1. Describe its key elements.
        2. Discuss why it is appropriate for Happlia to use this method.

    b. 1. What general criteria should Happlia use to determine inventory carrying amounts at December 31, 1990? Ignore lower of cost or market considerations.
        2. Give four examples of costs included in these inventory carrying amounts.

    c. What costs should be reported in Happlia's 1990 income statement? Ignore lower of cost or market considerations.

TM90
Number 4 (Estimated time — — 15 to 25 minutes)

Huddell Company, which is both a wholesaler and retailer, purchases merchandise from various suppliers FOB destination, and incurs substantial warehousing costs.

The dollar value LIFO method is used for the wholesale inventories.

Huddell determines the estimated cost of its retail ending inventories using the conventional retail inventory method, which approximates lower of average cost or market.

Required:
    a. When should the purchases from various suppliers generally be included in Huddell's inventory? Why?

    b. How should Huddell account for the warehousing costs? Why?

    c. 1. What are the advantages of using the dollar value LIFO method as opposed to the traditional LIFO method?
        2. How does the application of the dollar value LIFO method differ from the application of the traditional LIFO method?

    d. 1. In the calculation of the cost to retail percentage used to determine the estimated cost of its ending retail inventories, how should Huddell use
        • Net markups?
        • Net markdowns?
        2. Why does Huddell's retail inventory method approximate lower of average cost or market?

D. Property, Plant, and Equipment

TN92
Number 5 (Estimated time — — 15 to 25 minutes)

Winter Sports Co. rents winter sports equipment to the public. Snowmobiles are depreciated by the double declining balance method. Before the season began, the estimated lives of several snowmobiles were extended because engines were replaced. Winter was given thirty days to pay for the engines. Winter gave the old engines to a local mechanic who agreed to provide repairs and maintenance service in the next year equal to the fair value of the engines. Rental skis, poles, and boots are capitalized and depreciated according to the inventory (appraisal) method.

Required:
    a. How would Winter account for the purchase of the new engines and the transfer of the old engines to the local mechanic if the old engines' costs are
        1. Known?
        2. Unknown?

    b. 1. What are two assumptions underlying use of an accelerated depreciation method?
        2. How should Winter calculate the snowmobiles' depreciation?

    c. How should Winter calculate and report the costs of the skis, poles, and boots in its balance sheets and income statements?

TN91
Number 3 (Estimated time — — 15 to 25 minutes)

Portland Co. uses the straight-line depreciation method for depreciable assets. All assets are depreciated individually except manufacturing machinery, which is depreciated by the composite method.

During the year, Portland exchanged a delivery truck with Maine Co. for a larger delivery truck. It paid cash equal to 10% of the larger truck's value.

Required:
    a. What factors should have influenced Portland's selection of the straight-line depreciation method?

    b. How should Portland account for and report the truck exchange transaction?

    c. 1. What benefits should Portland derive from using the composite method rather than the individual basis for manufacturing machinery?
        2. How should Portland have calculated the manufacturing machinery's annual depreciation expense in its first year of operation?

E. Investments

M95
Number 4 (Estimated time — — 30 to 40 minutes)

On January 2, 1994, Bing Co. purchased 39,000 shares of Latt Co.'s 200,000 shares of outstanding common stock for $585,000. On that date, the carrying amount of the acquired shares on Latt's books was $405,000. Bing attributed the excess of cost over carrying amount to goodwill. Bing's policy is to amortize intangibles over ten years.

During 1994, Bing's president gained a seat on Latt's board of directors. Latt reported earnings of $400,000 for the year ended December 31, 1994, and declared and paid dividends of $100,000 during 1994. On December 31, 1994, Latt's common stock was trading over-the-counter at $15 per share.

Required:
    a. What criteria should Bing consider in determining whether to account for its investment in Latt under the equity method? Is the equity method consistent with accrual accounting? Explain.

    b. Assuming Bing accounts for the investment using the equity method, prepare a schedule of the amounts related to this investment to be reported on Bing's income statement for the year ended 1994 and the amount in the investment in Latt account in the balance sheet at December 31, 1994. Show all computations. **Disregard income taxes.**

TN90
Number 2 (Estimated time — — 15 to 25 minutes)

Since Grumer Co.'s inception, Monroe Co. has owned 18% of Grumer's outstanding common stock. Monroe provides three key management personnel to Grumer and purchased 25% of Grumer's output during 1989. Grumer is profitable. On January 2, 1990, Monroe purchased additional common stock to finance Grumer's expansion, thereby becoming a 30% owner. Grumer's common stock does not have a quoted market price. The stock has always been issued at its book value, which is assumed to approximate its fair value.

Required:
    a. In general, distinguish between investor income reporting under the cost method and under the equity method. Which method is more consistent with accrual accounting? Why?

    b. Prior to January 2, 1990, what specific factors should Monroe have considered in determining the appropriate method of accounting for its investment in Grumer?

    c. For purposes of your answer to **c** only, assume Monroe used the cost method in accounting for its investment in Grumer prior to January 2, 1990. Describe the book adjustments required on January 2, 1990, when Monroe became owner of 30% of the outstanding common stock of Grumer.

F. Intangibles and Other Assets

N95
Number 5 (Estimated time — — 30 to 40 minutes)

During 1994, Broca Co. had the following transactions:

- On January 2, Broca purchased the net assets of Amp Co. for $360,000. The fair value of Amp's identifiable net assets was $172,000. Broca believes that, due to the popularity of Amp's consumer products, the life of the resulting goodwill is unlimited.

- On February 1, Broca purchased a franchise to operate a ferry service from the state government for $60,000 and an annual fee of 1% of ferry revenues. The franchise expires after five years. Ferry revenues were $20,000 during 1994. Broca projects future revenues of $40,000 in 1995, and $60,000 per annum for the three years thereafter.

- On April 5, Broca was granted a patent that had been applied for by Amp. During 1994, Broca incurred legal costs of $51,000 to register the patent and an additional $85,000 to successfully prosecute a patent infringement suit against a competitor. Broca estimates the patent's economic life to be ten years.

Broca's accounting policy is to amortize all intangibles on the straight-line basis over the maximum period permitted by generally accepted accounting principles, taking a full year's amortization in the year of acquisition.

Required:
    a. 1. Describe the characteristics of intangible assets. Discuss the accounting for the purchase or internal development of intangible assets with an indeterminable life, such as goodwill.
    2. Over what period should intangible assets be amortized? How should this period be determined? Discuss the justification for amortization of intangible assets with indeterminable lives.
    3. Describe the financial statement disclosure requirements relating to Broca's intangible assets and expenses. Do not write the related footnotes.

    b. Prepare a schedule showing the intangibles section of Broca's balance sheet at December 31, 1994, and a schedule showing the related expenses that would appear on Broca's 1994 income statement. Show supporting computations.

H. Deferred Revenues

1N93
Number 5 (Estimated time — — 40 to 50 minutes)

London, Inc. began operation of its construction division on October 1, 1991, and entered into contracts for two separate projects. The Beta project contract price was $600,000 and provided for penalties of $10,000 per week for late completion. Although during 1992 the Beta project had been on schedule for timely completion, it was completed four weeks late in August 1993. The Gamma project's original contract price was $800,000. Change orders during 1993 added $40,000 to the original contract price.

The following data pertains to the separate long-term construction projects in progress:

	Beta	Gamma
As of September 30, 1992:		
Costs incurred to date	$360,000	$410,000
Estimated costs to complete	40,000	410,000
Billings	315,000	440,000
Cash collections	275,000	365,000
As of September 30, 1993:		
Costs incurred to date	450,000	720,000
Estimated costs to complete	—	180,000
Billings	560,000	710,000
Cash collections	560,000	625,000

Additional information:

- London accounts for its long-term construction contracts using the percentage-of-completion method for financial reporting purposes and the completed-contract method for income tax purposes.

- London elected early application of FASB 109, *Accounting for Income Taxes*, for the year ended September 30, 1992. Enacted rates are 25% for 1992 and 30% for future years.

- London's income before income taxes from all divisions, before considering revenues from long-term construction projects, was $300,000 for the year ended September 30, 1992. There were no other temporary or permanent differences.

Required:
    a. Prepare a schedule showing London's gross profit (loss) recognized for the years ended September 30, 1992, and 1993, under the percentage-of-completion method.

    b. Prepare a schedule showing London's balances in the following accounts at September 30, 1992, under the percentage-of-completion method:

- Accounts receivable
- Costs and estimated earnings in excess of billings
- Billings in excess of costs and estimated earnings

    c. Prepare a schedule reconciling London's financial statement income and taxable income for the year ended September 30, 1992, and showing all components of taxes payable and current and deferred income tax expense for the year then ended. Do not consider estimated tax requirements.

I. Notes and Bonds Payable

TN92
Number 3 (Estimated time — — 15 to 25 minutes)

On June 30, 1988, Corval Co. issued 15-year 12% bonds at a premium (effective yield 10%). On November 30, 1991, Corval transferred both cash and property to the bondholders to extinguish the entire debt. The fair value of the transferred property equaled its carrying amount. The fair value of the cash and property transferred exceeded the bonds' carrying amount. [Ignore income taxes.]

Required:
    a. Explain the purpose of the effective interest method and the effect of applying the method in 1988 on Corval's bond premium.

    b. What would have been the effect on 1988 interest expense, net income, and the carrying amount of the bonds if Corval had incorrectly adopted the straight-line interest method instead of the effective interest method?

c. How should Corval calculate and report the effects of the November 30, 1991, transaction in its 1991 income statement? Why is this presentation appropriate?

d. How should Corval report the effects of the November 30, 1991, transaction in its statement of cash flows using the indirect method?

TM92
Number 3 (Estimated time — — 15 to 25 minutes)

Columbine Co.'s 10-year convertible bonds, issued and dated October 1, 1989, were common stock equivalents. Each $1,000 bond is convertible, at the holder's option, into 20 shares of Columbine's $25 par value common stock. The bonds were issued at a premium when the common stock traded at $45 per share. After payment of interest on October 1, 1991, 30% of the bonds were tendered for conversion when the common stock was trading at $57 per share. Columbine used the book value method to account for the conversion.

Required:
a. 1. How would the issue price of Columbine's convertible bonds be determined?
   2. How should Columbine account for the issuance of the convertible bonds? Give the rationale for this accounting practice.
   3. How should Columbine account for the conversion of the bonds into common stock?

b. 1. How should Columbine determine whether to include the convertible bonds, which are common stock equivalents, in computing 1989 primary earnings per share?
   2. How does the inclusion of convertible bonds affect the computation of 1989 primary earnings per share?

TM90
Number 3 (Estimated time — — 15 to 25 minutes)

On January 2, 1987, Drew Company issued 9% term bonds dated January 2, 1987, at an effective annual interest rate (yield) of 10%. Drew uses the effective interest method of amortization. On July 1, 1989, the bonds were extinguished early when Drew acquired them in the open market for a price greater than their face amount.

On September 1, 1989, Drew issued for cash 7% nonconvertible bonds dated September 1, 1989, with detachable stock purchase warrants. Immediately after issuance, both the bonds and the warrants had separately determined market values.

Required:
a. 1. Were the 9% term bonds issued at face amount, at a discount, or at a premium? Why?
   2. Would the amount of interest expense for the 9% term bonds using the effective interest method of amortization be higher in the first or second year of the life of the bond issue? Why?

b. 1. How should gain or loss on early extinguishment of debt be determined? Does the early extinguishment of the 9% term bonds result in a gain or loss? Why?
   2. How should Drew report the early extinguishment of the 9% term bonds on the 1989 income statement?

c. How should Drew account for the issuance of the 7% nonconvertible bonds with detachable stock purchase warrants?

K. Equity Accounts

R97
Number 2

Field Co.'s stockholders' equity account balances at December 31, 1995, were as follows:

Common stock	$ 800,000
Additional paid-in capital	1,600,000
Retained earnings	1,845,000

The following 1996 transactions and other information relate to the stockholders' equity accounts:

- Field had 400,000 authorized shares of $5 par common stock, of which 160,000 shares were issued and outstanding.

- On March 5, 1996, Field acquired 5,000 shares of its common stock for $10 per share to hold as treasury stock. The shares were originally issued at $15 per share. Field uses the cost method to account for treasury stock. Treasury stock is permitted in Field's state of incorporation.

- On July 15, 1996, Field declared and distributed a property dividend of inventory. The inventory had a $75,000 carrying value and a $60,000 fair market value.

- On January 2, 1994, Field granted stock options to employees to purchase 20,000 shares of Field's common stock at $18 per share, which was the market price on that date. The options may be exercised within a three-year period beginning January 2, 1996. The measurement date is the same as the grant date. On October 1, 1996, employees exercised all 20,000 options when the market value of the stock was $25 per share. Field issued new shares to settle the transaction.

- Field's net income for 1996 was $240,000.

- Field intends to issue new stock options to key employees in 1997. Field's management is aware that Statement of Financial Accounting Standards No. 123,

Accounting for Stock-Based Compensation, which was issued in 1995, discusses both the "intrinsic value" method and the "fair value" method of accounting for stock options. Field's management is unsure of the difference between the two methods.

Required:

a. Prepare the stockholders' equity section of Field's December 31, 1996, balance sheet. Support all computations.

b. In a brief memo to Field's management, explain how compensation cost is measured under both the "fair value" method and the "intrinsic value" method of accounting for stock options, and when the measured cost is recognized.

1N93
Number 4 (Estimated time — — 45 to 55 minutes)

Trask Corp., a public company whose shares are traded in the over-the-counter market, had the following stockholders' equity account balances at December 31, 1991:

Common stock	$ 7,875,000
Additional paid-in capital	15,750,000
Retained earnings	16,445,000
Treasury common stock	750,000

Transactions during 1992, and other information relating to the stockholders' equity accounts, were as follows:

- Trask had 4,000,000 authorized shares of $5 par value common stock; 1,575,000 shares were issued, of which 75,000 were held in treasury.

- On January 21, 1992, Trask issued 50,000 shares of $100 par value, 6% cumulative preferred stock in exchange for all of Rover Co.'s assets and liabilities. On that date, the net carrying amount of Rover's assets and liabilities was $5,000,000. The carrying amounts of Rover's assets and liabilities equalled their fair values. On January 22, 1992, Rover distributed the Trask shares to its stockholders in complete liquidation and dissolution of Rover. Trask had 150,000 authorized shares of preferred stock.

- On February 17, 1992, Trask formally retired 25,000 of its 75,000 treasury common stock shares. The shares were originally issued at $15 per share and had been acquired on September 25, 1991, for $10 per share. Trask uses the cost method to account for treasury stock.

- Trask owned 15,000 shares of Harbor, Inc. common stock purchased in 1989 for $600,000. The Harbor stock was included in Trask's short-term marketable securities portfolio. On March 5, 1992, Trask declared a property dividend of one share of Harbor common stock for every 100 shares of Trask common stock held by a stockholder of record on April 16, 1992. The market price of Harbor stock on March 5, 1992, was $60 per share. The property dividend was distributed on April 29, 1992.

- On January 2, 1990, Trask granted stock options to employees to purchase 200,000 shares of the company's common stock at $12 per share, which was also the market price on that date. The options are exercisable within a three-year period beginning January 2, 1992. The measurement date is the same as the grant date. On June 1, 1992, employees exercised 150,000 options when the market value of the stock was $25 per share. Trask issued new shares to settle the transaction.

- On October 27, 1992, Trask declared a 2-for-1 stock split on its common stock and reduced the per share par value accordingly. Trask stockholders of record on August 2, 1992, received one additional share of Trask common stock for each share of Trask common stock held. The laws in Trask's state of incorporation protect treasury stock from dilution.

- On December 12, 1992, Trask declared the yearly cash dividend on preferred stock, payable on January 11, 1993, to stockholders of record on December 31, 1992.

- On January 16, 1993, before the accounting records were closed for 1992, Trask became aware that depreciation expense was understated by $350,000 for the year ended December 31, 1991. The after-tax effect on 1991 net income was $245,000. The appropriate correcting entry was recorded on the same day.

- Net income for 1992 was $2,400,000.

Required:

a. Prepare Trask's statement of retained earnings for the year ended December 31, 1992. Assume that Trask prepares only single-period financial statements for 1992.

b. Prepare the stockholders' equity section of Trask's balance sheet at December 31, 1992.

c. Compute the book value per share of common stock at December 31, 1992.

Show all supporting calculations in good form.

L. Revenue, Cost, and Expense Accounts

N94
Number 5 (Estimated time — — 30 to 40 minutes)

Wyatt, CPA, is meeting with Brown, the controller of Emco, a wholesaler, to discuss the accounting issues regarding two unrelated items:*

---

*The omitted item can be found in another Content Specification Group.

- Emco is considering offering its customers the right to return its products for a full refund within one year of purchase. Emco expects its sales to increase as a result, but is unable to estimate the amount of future returns.

Brown has asked Wyatt to write a brief memo to Brown that Brown can use to explain these issues to Emco's president.

Required:
Write a brief advisory memo from Wyatt to Brown to:

a. Explain the general principle of revenue recognition, the method of revenue recognition when right to return exists, and the impact of offering a right to return on Emco's ability to recognize revenue, if any.

TM93
Number 4 (Estimated time — — 15 to 25 minutes)

On July 1, 1991, Bow Construction Co. commenced operations and began constructing a building for Crecy under a fixed price contract. Anticipated completion date was June 15, 1993. Bow projects a large profit because it purchased most of the contract materials at exceptionally low prices in August 1991.

At the end of each month, Crecy is billed for completed work, for which it pays within 30 days. On December 31, 1992, all costs incurred exceed billings on the contract.

For the Crecy contract, Bow uses the percentage-of-completion (cost-to-cost) method for financial statement purposes. For income tax purposes, Bow qualifies for and uses the completed-contract method. Bow has no other contracts and no other differences between financial statement and income tax reporting.

Required:
a. How should Bow determine that the percentage-of-completion method is appropriate for the Crecy contract?

b. How should Bow calculate its 1992 income to be recognized on the Crecy contract? Explain any special treatment of unused material costs and why it is required.

c. Ignoring income tax effects, specify how the accounts related to the Crecy contract should be reported on Bow's December 31, 1992, balance sheet.

d. Assuming Bow has elected early adoption of FASB Statement No. 109, *Accounting for Income Taxes,* what are the income tax effects of the Crecy contract on Bow's 1992 balance sheet and income statement?

TM93
Number 5 (Estimated time — — 15 to 25 minutes)

At December 31, 1992, Niki Co. reviewed the following situations to consider their impact on its 1992 financial statements:

- In December 1992, Niki became aware of a safety hazard related to one of its products. Estimates of the probable costs resulting from the hazard include highest, most likely, and lowest amounts.

- During 1992, Niki received a note for goods sold to a customer. The note was sold to a bank with recourse. The customer filed for bankruptcy in December 1992, before the note's 1993 due date.

- In 1988, Niki moved and assigned the remaining 10 years of its old lease to Pro Co., an unrelated third party. Pro agreed to make all payments due on the assigned lease, but Niki has prime responsibility for the lease to the lessor. At December 31, 1992, it is reasonably possible that Pro will be unable to make all payments due on the assigned lease.

- On November 30, 1992, Niki received goods with a cost denominated in pounds. During December 1992, the dollar's value declined relative to the pound. Niki believes that the original exchange rate will be restored by the time payment is due in 1993.

Required:
For each of the following occurrences, state how Niki should report the impact, if any, on its 1992 financial statements, and explain why the reporting is appropriate.

a. The safety hazard.

b. The customer's filing for bankruptcy.

c. Pro's reasonably possible inability to make all payments due on the assigned lease.

d. Changes in the exchange rate of the dollar and the pound.

TN90
Number 3 (Estimated time — — 15 to 25 minutes)

At December 31, 1989, Roko Co. has two fixed price construction contracts in progress. Both contracts have monthly billings supported by certified surveys of work completed. The contracts are:

- The Ski Park contract, begun in 1988, is 80% complete, is progressing according to bid estimates, and is expected to be profitable.

The Nassu Village contract, a project to construct 100 condominium units, was begun in 1989. Thirty-five units have been completed. Work on the remaining units is delayed by conflicting recommendations on how to overcome unexpected subsoil problems. While the total cost of the project is uncertain, a loss is not anticipated.

Required:
a. Identify the alternatives available to account for long-term construction contracts, and specify the criteria used to determine which method is applicable to a given contract.

b. Identify the appropriate accounting method for each of Roko's two contracts, and describe each contract's effect on net income for 1989.

c. Indicate how the accounts related to the Ski Park contract should be reported on the balance sheet at December 31, 1989.

III. Recognition, Measurement, Valuation, and Presentation of Specific Types of Transactions and Events in Financial Statements in Conformity With Generally Accepted Accounting Principles

A. Accounting Changes and Corrections of Errors

TN92
Number 4 (Estimated time — — 15 to 25 minutes)

On January 1, 1991, Windsor Corp. made the following changes in its accounting policies:

- Changed from the LIFO inventory method to the FIFO inventory method.

- Adopted the straight-line depreciation method for all future machinery acquisitions, but continued to use sum-of-the-years' digits depreciation method for all machinery purchased before 1991.

- Changed from the cash to the accrual basis of accounting for accumulated vacation pay.

Windsor prepares two-year comparative financial statements.

Required:
a. What type of accounting change is the change from the LIFO to the FIFO inventory costing method? How should Windsor report this change in its 1991 comparative financial statements?

b. What type of accounting change is Windsor's change from the sum-of-the-years' digits to the straight-line depreciation method for all machinery purchased after 1990? How should Windsor report this change?

c. What type of change occurs when recognition of vacation pay expense is changed from the cash basis to the accrual basis? How should Windsor report this change?

TM90
Number 5 (Estimated time — — 15 to 25 minutes)

Boulder Company appropriately changed its depreciation method for its production machinery from the double-declining balance method to the production method effective January 1, 1989.

In addition, effective January 1, 1989, Boulder appropriately changed the salvage values used in computing depreciation for its office equipment.

On December 31, 1989, Boulder appropriately changed the specific subsidiaries constituting the group of companies for which consolidated financial statements are presented.

Required:
a. Identify any accounting changes in the three situations described above. For each accounting change identified, indicate whether Boulder should show:

- The cumulative effect of a change in accounting principle in net income of the period of change.

- Pro forma effects of retroactive application for all prior periods presented currently.

- Restatement of the financial statements of all prior periods presented currently.

b. 1. Why are accounting principles, once adopted, normally continued?
    2. What is the rationale for disclosure of a change from one generally accepted accounting principle to another generally accepted accounting principle?

B. Business Combinations

TM91
Number 2 (Estimated time — — 15 to 25 minutes)

Pap Co. and Sib Co. plan to combine on December 31, 1990, with Sib becoming Pap's subsidiary. Pap's $1 par value common stock will be exchanged, on a 3 for 1 basis, for the majority of Sib's outstanding $1 par value common stock. Johnson continues to hold a minority interest in Sib. There is neither treasury stock nor intercompany holdings. Both companies use the same accounting methods and practices, and have net assets with fair values in excess of carrying amounts. Ignore any expense connected with the combination.

Required:
a. What is the conceptual rationale used to account for a business combination as a pooling of interests? Do **not** discuss accounting entries or specific criteria required for applying pooling-of-interests accounting.

b. What percentage of Sib's outstanding common stock must be exchanged at December 31, 1990, so that pooling-of-interests accounting is used for the combination?

c. If pooling-of-interests accounting is used, how should the December 31, 1990, consolidated balance sheet report:
   1. Assets and liabilities?
   2. Investors' interests?

D. Contingent Liabilities and Commitments

TN91
Number 4 (Estimated time — — 15 to 25 minutes)

Supey Chemical Co. encountered the following two situations in 1990:

- Supey must pay an indeterminate amount for toxic waste cleanup on its land. An adjoining land owner, Gap Toothpaste, sold its property because of possible toxic contamination by Supey of the water supply and resulting potential adverse public reaction towards its product. Gap sued Supey for damages. There is a reasonable possibility that Gap will prevail in the suit.

- At December 31, 1990, Supey had a noncancellable purchase contract for 10,000 pounds of Chemical XZ, for delivery in June 1991. Supey does not hedge its contracts. Supey uses this chemical to make Product 2-Y. In December 1990, the U.S. Food and Drug Administration banned the sale of Product 2-Y in concentrated form. Supey will be allowed to sell Product 2-Y in a diluted form; however, it will take at least five years to use the 10,000 pounds of Chemical XZ. Supey believes the sales price of the diluted product will not be sufficient to recover the contract price of Chemical XZ.

Required:

a. 1. In its 1990 financial statements, how should Supey report the toxic waste cleanup? Why is this reporting appropriate?

2. In its 1990 financial statements, how should Supey report Gap's claim against it? Why is this reporting appropriate?

b. In its 1990 financial statements, how should Supey report the effects of the contract to purchase Chemical XZ? Why is this reporting appropriate?

G. Employee Benefits

R96
Number 1 (Estimated time — — 30 to 40 minutes)

Deck Co. has just hired a new president, Palmer, and is reviewing its employee benefit plans with the new employee. For current employees, Deck offers a compensation plan for future vacations. Deck also provides postemployment benefits to former or inactive employees.

On the date of Palmer's hire, Palmer entered into a deferred compensation contract with Deck. Palmer is expected to retire in ten years. The contract calls for a payment of $150,000 upon termination of employment following a minimum three-year service period. The contract also provides that interest of 10%, compounded annually, be credited on the amount due each year after the third year.

Required:

a. Give an example of postemployment benefits. State the conditions under which Deck is required to accrue liabilities for compensated absences and postemployment benefits. State Deck's disclosure requirements if these conditions, in full or in part, are not met.

b. Describe the general accrual period for amounts to be paid under a deferred compensation contract. State the theoretical rationale for requiring accrual of these liabilities and related expenses.

c. Prepare a schedule of the expense and accrued liability related to Palmer's deferred compensation agreement to be reported in Deck's financial statements for the first four years of the contract.

N94
Number 5 (Estimated time — — 30 to 40 minutes)

Wyatt, CPA, is meeting with Brown, the controller of Emco, a wholesaler, to discuss the accounting issues regarding two unrelated items:*

- Brown is aware that Statement of Financial Accounting Standards (FAS) No. 106, *Employers' Accounting for Postretirement Benefits Other Than Pensions,* is effective for years beginning after December 15, 1992. Brown is uncertain about the benefits and beneficiaries covered by this Statement. Brown believes that, regardless of FAS 106, no estimate of postretirement obligation can be reasonable because it would be based on too many assumptions. For this reason, Brown wishes to continue to account for the postretirement benefits that Emco pays to its retirees on the pay-as-you-go (cash) basis.

Brown has asked Wyatt to write a brief memo to Brown that Brown can use to explain these issues to Emco's president.

Required:
Write a brief advisory memo from Wyatt to Brown to:

b. State the principal benefit covered by FAS 106 and give an example of other benefits covered by FAS 106. Explain the reasoning given in FAS 106 for requiring accruals based on estimates. Indicate the primary recipients of postretirement benefits other than pensions.

TM92
Number 5 (Estimated time — — 15 to 25 minutes)

At December 31, 1991, as a result of its single employer defined benefit pension plan, Bighorn Co. had an unrecognized net loss and an unfunded accrued pension cost. Bighorn's pension plan and its actuarial

---
*The omitted item can be found in another Content Specification Group.

assumptions have not changed since it began operations in 1987. Bighorn has made annual contributions to the plan.

Required:

a. Identify the components of net pension cost that should be recognized in Bighorn's 1991 financial statements.

b. What circumstances caused Bighorn's
1. Unrecognized net loss?
2. Unfunded accrued pension cost?

c. How should Bighorn compute its minimum pension liability and any additional pension liability?

I. Financial Instruments

R97
Number 1

Coyn, CPA, has been approached by Howe, the chief financial officer of Chatham Co. Howe is aware that the Financial Accounting Standards Board is engaged in an ongoing project to improve disclosure of information about financial instruments and has recently issued three related Statements of Financial Accounting Standards (SFAS): SFAS No. 105, *Disclosure of Information about Financial Instruments with Off-Balance-Sheet Risk and Financial Instruments with Concentrations of Credit Risk*; SFAS No. 107, *Disclosures about Fair Value of Financial Instruments*; and SFAS No. 119, *Disclosure about Derivative Financial Instruments and Fair Value of Financial Instruments*. In accordance with these pronouncements, Howe has prepared the following footnote for Chatham's financial statements:

Note 12: Financial Instruments
The Company is party to **financial instruments** with **off-balance-sheet risk of accounting loss** in the normal course of business. The Company uses various financial instruments with off-balance-sheet **market risk,** including **derivative financial instruments,** to manage its interest rate and foreign currency exchange rate risks. Other financial instruments that potentially subject the Company to **concentrations of credit risk** consist principally of trade receivables.

Howe will be meeting with Chatham's board of directors to review the financial statements, and has asked Coyn to prepare a handout for the board explaining the terms used in the footnote.

Required:
Prepare the requested handout. Include the following:

a. What is a *financial instrument*? Define and give an example of *derivative financial instruments*.

b. Define *off-balance-sheet risk of accounting loss* and give an example of a financial instrument having off-balance-sheet risk of accounting loss.

c. Define both *market risk* and *credit risk*. What is meant by the term *concentration of credit risk*?

d. Define *fair value*. Discuss the methods Chatham's management might use to estimate the fair values of its various financial instruments.

K. Income Taxes

and

L. Interest Costs

M94
Number 5 (Estimated time — — 30 to 40 minutes)

Chris Green, CPA, is auditing Rayne Co.'s 1993 financial statements. The controller, Dunn, has provided Green with the following information:

• At December 31, 1992, Rayne had a note payable to Federal Bank with a balance of $90,000. The annual principal payment of $10,000, plus 8% interest on the unpaid balance, was paid when due on March 31, 1993.

• On January 2, 1993, Rayne leased two automobiles for executive use under a capital lease. Five annual lease payments of $15,000 are due beginning January 3, 1993. Rayne's incremental borrowing rate on the date of the lease was 11% and the lessor's implicit rate, which was known by Rayne, was 10%. The lease was properly recorded at $62,500, before the first payment was made.

• On July 1, 1993, Rayne received proceeds of $538,000 from a $500,000 bond issuance. The bonds mature in 15 years and interest of 11% is payable semiannually on June 30 and December 31. The bonds were issued at a price to yield investors 10%. Rayne uses the effective interest method to amortize bond premium.

• For the year ended December 31, 1993, Rayne has adopted Statement of Financial Accounting Standards No. 109, *Accounting for Income Taxes*. Dunn has prepared a schedule of all differences between financial statement and income tax return income. Dunn believes that as a result of pending legislation, the enacted tax rate at December 31, 1993, will be increased for 1994. Dunn is uncertain which differences to include and which rates to apply in computing deferred taxes under FASB 109. Dunn has requested an overview of FAS 109 from Green.

Required:
a. Prepare a schedule of interest expense for the year ended December 31, 1993.

b. Prepare a brief memo to Dunn from Green:
- identifying the objectives of accounting for income taxes,
- defining temporary differences,
- explaining how to measure deferred tax assets and liabilities, and
- explaining how to measure deferred income tax expense or benefit.

N. Leases

M95
Number 5 (Estimated time — — 30 to 40 minutes)

On January 2, 1994, Cody, Inc. sold equipment to Griff Co. for cash of $864,000 and immediately leased it back under a capital lease for 9 years. The carrying amount of the equipment was $540,000, and its estimated remaining economic life is 10 years. Annual year-end payments of $153,000, which include executory costs of $3,000, are based on an implicit interest rate of 10%, which is known to Cody. Cody's incremental borrowing rate is 13%. Cody uses the straight-line method of depreciation. The rounded present value factors of an ordinary annuity for 9 years are 5.76 at 10% and 5.2 at 13%.

Required:
a. What is the theoretical basis for requiring lessees to capitalize certain long-term leases? **Do not discuss the specific criteria for classifying a lease as a capital lease.**

b. Prepare the journal entries that Cody must make to record the sale and the leaseback on January 2, 1994.

c. Prepare the journal entries, including any adjusting entries, that Cody must make at December 31, 1994.

TN93
Number 4 (Estimated time — — 15 to 25 minutes)

On December 31, 1991, Jen, Inc. sold a building for its fair value and leased it back. The building was sold for more than its carrying amount and a gain was recorded. Lease payments are due at the end of each month. Jen accounted for the transaction as a capital lease. The lease's interest rate was equal to Jen's incremental borrowing rate.

Required:
a. How should Jen account for the sale portion of the sale-leaseback transaction at December 31, 1991? Why is this an appropriate method of accounting for this portion of the contract?

b. How should Jen report the leaseback portion of the sale-leaseback transaction on its December 31, 1992, balance sheet? How are these reported amounts determined?

1M93
Number 4 (Estimated time — — 40 to 50 minutes)

Number 4 consists of two unrelated parts.*

Number 4(b)

On January 2, 1992, Elsee Co. leased equipment from Grant, Inc. Lease payments are $100,000, payable annually every December 31 for twenty years. Title to the equipment passes to Elsee at the end of the lease term. The lease is noncancelable.

Additional facts:

- The equipment has a $750,000 carrying amount on Grant's books. Its estimated economic life was 25 years on January 2, 1992.

- The rate implicit in the lease, which is known to Elsee, is 10%. Elsee's incremental borrowing rate is 12%.

- Elsee uses the straight-line method of depreciation.

The rounded present value factors of an ordinary annuity for 20 years are as follows:

12%	7.5
10%	8.5

Required:
Prepare the necessary journal entries, without explanations, to be recorded by Elsee for:
1. entering into the lease on January 2, 1992.
2. making the lease payment on December 31, 1992.
3. expenses related to the lease for the year ended December 31, 1992.

Show supporting calculations for all entries.

TM91
Number 4 (Estimated time — — 15 to 25 minutes)

On December 31, 1989, Port Co. sold six-month old equipment at fair value and leased it back. There was a loss on the sale. Port pays all insurance, maintenance, and taxes on the equipment. The lease provides for eight equal annual payments, beginning December 31, 1990, with a present value equal to 85% of the equipment's fair value and sales price. The lease's term is equal to 80% of the equipment's useful life. There is no provision for Port to reacquire ownership of the equipment at the end of the lease term.

Required:
a. 1. Why is it important to compare an equipment's fair value to its lease payments' present value and its useful life to the lease term?

---
*The omitted item can be found in another Content Specification Group.

2. Evaluate Port's leaseback of the equipment in terms of each of the four criteria for determination of a capital lease.

b. How should Port account for the sale portion of the sale-leaseback transaction at December 31, 1989?

c. How should Port report the leaseback portion of the sale-leaseback transaction on its December 31, 1990, balance sheet?

R. **Research and Development Costs**

TN90
Number 4 (Estimated time —— 15 to 25 minutes)

Clonal, Inc., a biotechnology company, developed and patented a diagnostic product called Trouver. Clonal purchased some research equipment to be used exclusively for Trouver and other research equipment to be used on Trouver and subsequent research projects. Clonal defeated a legal challenge to its Trouver patent, and began production and marketing operations for the product.

Corporate headquarters' costs were allocated to Clonal's research division as a percentage of the division's salaries.

Required:
a. How should the equipment purchased for Trouver be reported in Clonal's income statements and balance sheets?

b. 1. Describe the matching principle.
2. Describe the accounting treatment of research and development costs and consider whether this is consistent with the matching principle. What is the justification for the accounting treatment of research and development costs?

c. How should corporate headquarters' costs allocated to the research division be classified in Clonal's income statement? Why?

d. How should the legal expenses incurred in defending Trouver's patent be reported in Clonal's statement of cash flows (direct method)?

SELECTED PROBLEMS/ESSAYS — UNOFFICIAL ANSWERS

I. Concepts and Standards for Financial Statements

A. Financial Accounting Concepts

TN93
Answer 5 (10 points)

a. 1. According to the FASB conceptual framework, the three essential characteristics of an asset are:

- It embodies a probable future benefit that involves a capacity to contribute to future net cash inflows.

- A particular entity can obtain the benefit and control others' access to it.

- The transaction or other event giving rise to the entity's right to or control of the benefit has already occurred.

2. Mono's project expenditures through 1991 meet the FASB conceptual framework's three essential characteristics of an asset as follows:

- Since Mono intends to produce the product, it presumably anticipates future net cash inflows.

- Mono has obtained a patent that will enable it to control the benefits arising from the product.

- The control is a consequence of past events.

3. It is difficult to justify the classification of research and development expenditures as assets because at the time expenditures are made the future benefits are uncertain, and difficult to measure.

b. 1. Expenditures for equipment to be used exclusively for research and development should be reported as research and development expense in the period incurred. Expenditures for equipment to be used both for research and development and for production should be capitalized and reported as fixed assets, less accumulated depreciation, on Mono's balance sheets from 1989 through 1992. An appropriate depreciation method should be used, with depreciation from 1989 through 1991 reported as research and development expense. Depreciation for 1992 should be added to cost of inventory, via factory overhead, and expensed as cost of goods sold.

2. Cash payments for the pilot plant construction should be reported as cash outflows from operating activities on Mono's 1990 statement of cash flows. Cash received from the sale of the pilot plant should be reported as a cash inflow from operating activities on Mono's 1991 statement of cash flows.

B. Financial Accounting Standards for Presentation and Disclosure in General Purpose Financial Statements

1. Consolidated and Combined Financial Statements

TM92
Answer 4 (10 points)

a. 1. Consolidated operating results, cash flows, and financial position are prepared, as if a parent company and its subsidiaries are a single entity, to provide information that:

- Reflects the operating results, financial status, and central management ties that bind the companies into a single economic and financial unit.
- Is representationally faithful and fair, without the biases caused by exclusions or netting of data.
- Is comparable with information about other economic entities regardless of the companies' legal framework.
- Is relevant and complete for investors and other parties basing decisions on the data.

2. Plains' September 1, 1991, consolidated balance sheet is changed by including all of Sox's identifiable assets and liabilities at their fair values, and cash is decreased by the purchase price. The excess of purchase price over the fair value of the net assets acquired is reported as goodwill.

3. The effect of the intercompany sales is eliminated from Plains' December 31, 1991, consolidated financial statements by:

- Reducing sales by the amount of the intercompany sales.
- Reducing ending inventory by the markup on goods sold by Plains and still held by Sox.
- Reducing cost of goods sold for the difference between the amounts of the two previous adjustments.

b. 1. The effects on Plains' September 1, 1991, balance sheet are the establishment of an investment in Sox and a decrease in cash equal to the purchase price.

2. Using push-down accounting, all of Sox's assets and liabilities, including goodwill, are restated to reflect their fair values on September 1, 1991. The retained earnings balance is eliminated. Additional paid-in capital is adjusted for the difference arising from the restatement of the asset and liability balances and the elimination of retained earnings.

1N91
Answer 5 (10 points)

a.

Pine Corp.
JOURNAL ENTRIES
March 31, 1990

Account	Dr.	Cr.
Investment in Strand, Inc.	5,400,000 [1]	
Common stock		2,000,000
Additional paid-in capital		970,000 [2]
Retained earnings of subsidiary		2,430,000
To record issuance of 200,000 shares of common stock for all the outstanding common stock of Strand, Inc., in a business combination accounted for by the pooling-of-interests method		
Expenses of business combination	720,000	
Cash		720,000
To record payment of the expenses relating to the business combination with Strand, Inc.		

Explanations of Amounts

[1] Investment in Strand, Inc.
    Carrying amount of Strand's stockholders' equity, March 31, 1990

Capital stock	$2,500,000
Additional paid-in capital	470,000
Retained earnings	2,430,000
Total	$5,400,000

[2] Additional paid-in capital
    Strand, Inc. additional paid-in capital, March 31, 1990 $ 470,000

Par value of Strand, Inc. common stock acquired	$2,500,000	
Par value of Pine Corp. common stock issued (200,000 shares × $10)	2,000,000	
Excess added to additional paid-in capital		500,000
Total		$ 970,000

b.

Pine Corp.
INVESTMENT IN STRAND, INC. — AT EQUITY
December 31, 1990

Balance at date of acquisition, 3/31/90		$5,400,000
Net income of Strand, Inc. for period 4/1 through 12/31/90	$1,060,000 [3]	
Less: Elimination of intercompany profit in Strand's inventory	200,000	860,000
Balance, 12/31/90		$6,260,000

FA-194

Explanation of Amounts

[3] Net income of Strand, Inc.
for period 4/1 through 12/31/90

Retained earnings, 12/31/89		$2,290,000
Net income for 1990	$1,450,000	
Less: Dividend paid, 3/10/90	(250,000)	
Net increase in 1990 retained earnings		1,200,000
Retained earnings, 12/31/90		3,490,000
Retained earnings, 3/31/90		(2,430,000)
Net income for period 4/1 through 12/31/90		$1,060,000

c.
Pine Corp. and Subsidiary
CONSOLIDATED STATEMENT OF CHANGES IN RETAINED EARNINGS
For the Year Ended December 31, 1990

Balance, December 31, 1989:

As originally reported		$ 6,820,000
Adjustment for pooling of interests with Strand, Inc.		2,290,000
As restated		9,110,000
Net income		3,490,000 [4]
		12,600,000
Dividends paid:		
By Strand, Inc., before combination		(250,000)
By Pine Corp., after combination		(1,500,000)
		(1,750,000)
Balance, December 31, 1990		$10,850,000

Explanation of Amounts

[4] Consolidated net income for 1990

Pine Corp.'s income before considering equity in Strand's net income	$2,240,000
Strand, Inc.'s separate net income	1,450,000
	3,690,000
Elimination of intercompany profit in Strand's inventory (¹/₄ × $800,000)	(200,000)
Consolidated net income for 1990	$3,490,000

1M90
Answer 4 (10 points)

Cain Corp. and Subsidiary
CONSOLIDATING STATEMENT WORKSHEET
December 31, 1989

Income Statement	Cain Corp. Dr. (Cr.)	Frey, Inc. Dr. (Cr.)	Adjustments & Eliminations Dr.		Adjustments & Eliminations Cr.		Adjusted Balance
Net sales	(3,800,000)	(1,500,000)	[6]	180,000			(5,120,000)
Dividends from Frey	(40,000)		[3]	40,000			
Gain on sale of warehouse	(30,000)		[4]	30,000			
Cost of goods sold	2,360,000	870,000			[6]	162,000	3,068,000
Operating expenses (including depreciation)	1,100,000	440,000	[2]	12,000	[5]	2,000	1,550,000
Net income	(410,000)	(190,000)	[a]	262,000	[a]	164,000	(502,000)
Retained Earnings Statement							
Balance, 1/1/89	(440,000)	(156,000)	[1]	156,000			(440,000)
Net income	(410,000)	(190,000)	[a]	262,000	[a]	164,000	(502,000)
Dividends paid		40,000			[3]	40,000	
Balance, 12/31/89	(850,000)	(306,000)	[b]	418,000	[b]	204,000	(942,000)
Balance Sheet							
Assets:							
Cash	570,000	150,000					720,000
Accounts receivable (net)	860,000	350,000			[7]	86,000	1,124,000
Inventories	1,060,000	410,000			[6]	18,000	1,452,000
Land, plant, and equipment	1,320,000	680,000	[1]	54,000	[4]	30,000	2,024,000
Accumulated depreciation	(370,000)	(210,000)	[5]	2,000	[2]	9,000	(587,000)
Investment in Frey (at cost)	750,000				[1]	750,000	
Goodwill			[1]	60,000	[2]	3,000	57,000
Total Assets	4,190,000	1,380,000					4,790,000
Liabilities & Stockholders' Equity:							
Accounts payable & accrued expenses	(1,340,000)	(594,000)	[7]	86,000			(1,848,000)
Common stock ($10 par)	(1,700,000)	(400,000)	[1]	400,000			(1,700,000)
Additional paid-in capital	(300,000)	(80,000)	[1]	80,000			(300,000)
Retained earnings	(850,000)	(306,000)	[b]	418,000	[b]	204,000	(942,000)
Total Liabilities & Stockholders' Equity	(4,190,000)	(1,380,000)		1,100,000		1,100,000	(4,790,000)

Explanations of Adjustments & Eliminations

[1] To eliminate the reciprocal elements in investment, goodwill, equity, and property accounts. Cain's investment is carried at cost at December 31, 1989.

[2] To record amortization of the fair value in excess of book value of Frey's machinery at date of acquisition ($54,000 ÷ 6) and amortization of goodwill ($60,000 ÷ 20) for the year ended December 31, 1989

[3] To eliminate Cain's dividend revenue from Frey.

[4] To eliminate intercompany profit on the sale of the warehouse by Cain to Frey.

[5] To eliminate the excess depreciation on the warehouse building sold by Cain to Frey [$1/2 \times \$4,000$ ($86,000 - \$66,000 \times 1/5$)].

[6] To eliminate intercompany sales from Cain to Frey and the intercompany profit in Cain's ending inventory as follows:

	Total	On hand
Sales	$180,000	$36,000
Gross profit	90,000	18,000

[7] To eliminate Cain's intercompany balance to Frey for the merchandise it purchased.

2. Balance Sheet

R98
Answer 1 (20 points)

a.
Villa Co.
BALANCE SHEET—LIABILITIES SECTION
December 31, 1997

Accounts payable	$ 35,000	
Accrued interest payable	20,000	[2]
Income taxes payable	180,000	[3]
Dividends payable	50,000	
Current portion, long-term debt	62,000	[1]
Total current liabilities	347,000	
Capital lease payable, less		
$62,000 current portion	318,000	[1]
Bonds payable	442,000	[2]
Deferred tax liability	90,000	[3]
Total liabilities	$1,197,000	

[1] $100,000 × 4.8 = $480,000
$480,000 − $100,000 = $380,000
$380,000 × 10% = $38,000
$100,000 − $38,000 = $62,000
$380,000 − $62,000 = $318,000

[2] 500K × 8% × ½ = 20K
440K × 10% × ½ = 22K
440K + (22K − 20K) = 442,000

[3] 600K × 30% = 180K
300K × 30% = 90K

b. Villa should disclose the following information about the capital leases, either in the body of the financial statements or in the notes thereto:

- The gross amount of assets recorded under the capital leases, presented by major classes. This information may be combined with owned assets.

- Future minimum lease payments as of the balance sheet date, in the aggregate and for each of the five succeeding years.

- A general description of the leasing arrangement, including the existence and terms of renewal, escalation clauses, and restrictions imposed by the lease agreements.

Villa should disclose the following information about the bonds payable, either in the body of the financial statements or in the notes thereto:

- The face amount.

- The nature and terms of the bonds and a discussion of their credit and market risk, cash requirements, and related accounting policies.

- The fair value of the bonds and the method used to estimate their fair value. The price at which the bonds are trading is the most reasonable estimate of their fair value at December 31, 1997.

c. Villa should account for each contingency in a slightly different way because the likelihood of Villa's incurring a loss differs in each situation.

For the toxic waste cleanup, a loss has been incurred. In the notes to its financial statements, Villa should disclose the nature of the loss on cleanup and indicate that an estimate of the loss, or range of the loss, cannot be made. No accrual should be made because the loss cannot be reasonably estimated and accrual of an uncertain amount would impair the integrity of the financial statements.

With regard to Clear's claim it is only reasonably possible, and not probable, that Villa will have to pay. Accordingly, Villa should not accrue the loss. Villa should disclose the existence and nature of Clear's claim in the notes to its financial statements. Disclosure should include an estimate of the potential range of loss.

Regarding the lack of rockslide insurance, no asset has been impaired and no liability has been incurred. Accordingly, Villa should not accrue a loss. Since the likelihood of a rockslide is remote, disclosure of the uninsured risk, while permitted, is not required.

1M91
Answer 4 (10 points)

a.

Kern, Inc.
**LONG-TERM RECEIVABLES SECTION
OF BALANCE SHEET**
December 31, 1990

9% note receivable from sale of idle building, due in annual installments of $250,000 to May 1, 1992, less current installment	$250,000	[1]*
8% note receivable from officer, due December 31, 1992, collateralized by 5,000 shares of Kern, Inc., common stock with a fair value of $225,000	200,000	
Noninterest-bearing note from sale of patent, net of 10% imputed interest, due April 1, 1992	88,795	[2]
Installment contract receivable, due in annual installments of $88,332 to July 1, 1994, less current installment	219,668	[3]
Total long-term receivables	$758,463	

b.

Kern, Inc.
SELECTED BALANCE SHEET ACCOUNTS
December 31, 1990

Current portion of long-term receivables:

Note receivable from sale of idle building	$250,000	[1]
Installment contract receivable	60,332	[3]
Total	$310,332	

Accrued interest receivable:

Note receivable from sale of idle building	$30,000	[4]
Installment contract receivable	14,000	[5]
Total	$44,000	

*Numbers in brackets are keyed to explanations of amounts.

Unofficial Answers

c.
Kern, Inc.
INTEREST REVENUE FROM LONG-TERM RECEIVABLES
AND GAINS RECOGNIZED ON SALE OF ASSETS
For the year ended December 31, 1990

Interest revenue:

Note receivable from sale of idle building	$52,500	[6]
Note receivable from sale of patent	6,195	[2]
Note receivable from officer	16,000	[7]
Installment contract receivable from sale of land	14,000	[5]
Total interest revenue	$88,695	

Gains recognized on sale of assets:

Patent	$ 44,600	[8]
Land	100,000	[9]
Total gains recognized	$144,600	

Explanation of Amounts:

[1] Long-term portion of 9% note receivable at 12/31/90

Face amount, 5/1/89	$750,000
Less installment received 5/1/90	250,000
Balance, 12/31/90	500,000
Less installment due 5/1/91	250,000
Long-term portion, 12/31/90	$250,000

[2] Noninterest-bearing note, net of imputed interest at 12/31/90

Face amount, 4/1/90	$100,000
Less imputed interest [$100,000 − $82,600 ($100,000 × 0.826)]	17,400
Balance, 4/1/90	82,600
Add interest earned to 12/31/90 [$82,600 × 10% × 9/12]	6,195
Balance, 12/31/90	$ 88,795

1M91
Answer 4 (cont.)

[3] Long-term portion of installment contract receivable at 12/31/90
    Contract selling price, 7/1/90 $400,000
    Less cash down payment   120,000
    Balance, 12/31/90   280,000
    Less installment due 7/1/91 [$88,332 − $28,000 ($280,000 × 10%)]   60,332
    Long-term portion, 12/31/90 $219,668

[4] Accrued interest — note receivable, sale of idle building at 12/31/90
    Interest accrued from 5/1 to 12/31/90 [$500,000 × 9% × 8/12] $ 30,000

[5] Accrued interest — installment contract at 12/31/90
    Interest accrued from 7/1 to 12/31/90 [$280,000 × 10% × 1/2] $ 14,000

[6] Interest revenue — note receivable, sale of idle building, for 1990
    Interest earned from 1/1 to 5/1/90 [$750,000 × 9% × 4/12] $ 22,500
    Interest earned from 5/1 to 12/31/90 [$500,000 × 9% × 8/12]   30,000
    Interest revenue $ 52,500

[7] Interest revenue — note receivable, officer, for 1990
    Interest earned 1/1 to 12/31/90 [$200,000 × 8%] $ 16,000

[8] Gain recognized on sale of patent
    Stated selling price $100,000
    Less imputed interest   17,400 [2]
    Actual selling price   82,600
    Less cost of patent (net)
        Carrying value 1/1/90 $40,000
        Less amortization 1/1 to 4/1/90 [$8,000 × 1/4]   2,000   38,000
    Gain recognized $ 44,600

[9] Gain recognized on sale of land
    Selling price $400,000
    Less cost   300,000
    Gain recognized $100,000

3. Statement(s) of Income, Comprehensive Income, and Changes in Equity Accounts

R96
Answer 2 (10 points)

There are a number of weaknesses noted in the Statement of Income and Changes in Retained Earnings.

The first weakness noted is the heading. An income statement reports the results of an entity's earning activities for an accounting period. Accordingly, the statement should be titled "For the Year Ended December 31, 1995."

The Revenues and gains section improperly includes several items. "Purchase discounts" should reduce the cost of purchases or cost of goods sold. It is not theoretically sound to consider as revenue savings on purchases. Also, under the allowance method of accounting for uncollectible accounts, recovery of accounts receivable written off in previous years should be credited to the allowance for uncollectible accounts.

The Expenses and losses section also contains errors. Sales returns and allowances should be offset against or deducted from gross sales. Cash dividends are not an expense, but should be shown as a reduction of retained earnings.

Discounted operations includes a loss that does not meet the criteria for discontinued operations. The loss on disposal of discontinued styles should be classified as ordinary and usual and be reported in the Expenses and losses section of the income statement. An ordinary loss should not be shown net of tax effect.

Income before extraordinary item should be shown before the extraordinary item. The caption for the extraordinary item is properly positioned on the income statement, but contains two errors. First, early extinguishment of debt, incorrectly reported under "Revenues and gains," is always reported as an extraordinary item, net of tax effect.

Second, the error discovered from the previous year is not an extraordinary item, but should be treated as a prior period adjustment. Accordingly, the retained earnings balance at the beginning of the year should be adjusted by the amount of the error correction, net of tax effect, and the income statement should include a subtotal titled "Retained earnings at beginning of year as restated." Cash dividends declared should be deducted from this subtotal.

Income taxes and net income should be shown elsewhere on the Statement. Income taxes should be deducted in arriving at income before extraordinary item, either included as the last item in the expenses section or shown as a separate line item before income before extraordinary item. Net income should be reported immediately before beginning retained earnings.

N94
Answer 4 (10 points)

Probe Co.
INCOME STATEMENT
For the Year Ended December 31, 1993

Sales			$2,420,000
Cost of sales			1,863,000
Gross profit			557,000
Selling and administrative expenses	$220,000		
Depreciation	88,000		308,000
Operating income			249,000
Other income (expenses):			
Interest income		14,000	
Interest expense		(46,000)	
Loss on sale of equipment		(7,000)	(39,000)
Income before income tax and extraordinary item			210,000
Income tax:			
Current		45,000 [1]	
Deferred		12,000 [2]	57,000
Income before extraordinary item			153,000
Extraordinary item:			
Gain on extinguishment of debt, net of income taxes of $27,000			63,000
Net income			$ 216,000
Earnings per share			
Earnings before extraordinary item			$1.275 [3]
Extraordinary item			.525 Optional
Net income			$1.800

[1] Current income tax expense:

Income before income tax and extraordinary item	$210,000
Differences between financial statement and taxable income	(60,000)
Income subject to tax	150,000
Income tax rate	x 30%
Income tax excluding extraordinary item	$ 45,000

[2] Deferred income tax expense:

Cumulative temporary differences—12/31/93	$180,000
Income tax rate	x 30%
Deferred tax liability—12/31/93	54,000
Deferred tax liability—12/31/92	42,000
Deferred tax expense for 1993	$ 12,000

[3] Earnings per share:
    Weighted average number of shares outstanding for 1993:

January thru March	60,000 x 3	180,000
April thru December	140,000 x 9	1,260,000
Total		1,440,000
		÷ 12
		120,000
Income before extraordinary item		153,000
Earnings per share	(153,000 ÷ 120,000)	1.275

1N92
Answer 5 (10 points)

a.

Powell Corp.
INCOME STATEMENT
For the Year Ended June 30, 1992

Revenues:		
Machine sales	$750,000	
Service revenues	250,000	
Interest revenue	10,000	
Total revenues		$1,010,000
Expenses:		
Cost of sales—machines	425,000	
Cost of services	100,000	
Administrative expenses	300,000	
Research and development expenses	110,000	
Interest expense	5,000	
Loss from asset disposal	40,000	
Current income tax expense	6,000	
Deferred income tax expense	4,500	
Total expenses and losses		990,500
Income before extraordinary gain		19,500
Extraordinary gain, net of income taxes of $75,000		175,000
Net income		$ 194,500
Earnings (loss) per share:		
Income before extraordinary gain		($0.40)
Net income		$0.47

b.

Net income	$194,500
Add:	
Taxes on extraordinary gain	75,000
Provision for income taxes	10,500
Financial statement income before income taxes	280,000
Permanent difference — officer's life insurance	5,000
Temporary difference — excess of tax over financial statement depreciation	(15,000)
Taxable income	$270,000

4. Statement of Cash Flows

1M93
Answer 5 (10 points)

Omega Corp.
STATEMENT OF CASH FLOWS
For the year ended December 31, 1992

Cash flows from operating activities:			
Net Income			$360,000
Adjustments to reconcile net income to net cash provided by operating activities:			
Depreciation	$150,000	[1]	
Gain on sale of equipment	(5,000)	[2]	
Undistributed earnings of Belle Co.	(30,000)	[3]	
Changes in assets and liabilities:			
Decrease in accounts receivable	40,000		
Increase in inventories	(135,000)		
Increase in accounts payable	60,000		
Decrease in income taxes payable	(20,000)		
			60,000
Net cash provided by operating activities			420,000
Cash flows from investing activities:			
Proceeds from sale of equipment	40,000		
Loan to Chase Co.	(300,000)		
Principal payment of loan receivable	30,000		
Net cash used in investing activities			(230,000)
Cash flows from financing activities:			
Dividends paid	(90,000)		
Net cash used in financing activities			(90,000)
Net increase in cash			100,000
Cash at beginning of year			700,000
Cash at end of year			$800,000

Unofficial Answers

Explanation of Amounts:

[1] Depreciation
    Net increase in accumulated depreciation
      for the year ended December 31, 1992 $125,000
    Accumulated depreciation on equipment sold:
      Cost $60,000
      Carrying value   35,000   25,000
    Depreciation for 1992 $150,000

[2] Gain on sale of equipment
    Proceeds $ 40,000
    Carrying value   35,000
      Gain $ 5,000

[3] Undistributed earnings of Belle Co.
    Belle's net income for 1992 $120,000
    Omega's ownership   25%
      Undistributed earnings of Belle Co. $ 30,000

1N90
Answer 5 (10 points)

a.

Linden Consulting Associates
STATEMENT OF CASH FLOWS
For the Year Ended December 31, 1989
Increase (Decrease) in Cash

Cash flows from operating activities:		
Cash received from customers	$ 2,586,000 [1]	
Cash paid to suppliers and employees	(1,830,000) [2]	
Dividends received from affiliate	96,000	
Net cash provided by operating activities		$ 852,000
Cash flows from investing activities:		
Purchased property and equipment		(170,000)
Cash flows from financing activities:		
Principal payment of mortgage payable	(20,000)	
Proceeds for admission of new partner	340,000	
Drawings against partners' capital accounts	(630,000)	
Net cash used in financing activities		(310,000)
Net increase in cash		372,000
Cash at beginning of year		280,000
Cash at end of year		$ 652,000

Explanation of amounts:

[1]	Fee revenue		$2,664,000
	Less ending accounts receivable balance		(446,000)
	Add beginning accounts receivable balance		368,000
			$2,586,000
[2]	Operating expenses		$1,940,000
	Less: Depreciation	$ 60,000	
	Ending accounts payable balance	320,000	(380,000)
	Add beginning accounts payable balance		270,000
			$1,830,000

Unofficial Answers

b.

Reconciliation of net income to net cash provided by operating activities:

Net income		$900,000
Adjustments to reconcile net income to net cash provided by operating activities:		
Depreciation and amortization	$ 64,000	
Undistributed earnings of affiliate	(84,000) [1]	
Change in assets and liabilities:		
Increase in accounts receivable	(78,000)	
Increase in accounts payable and accrued expenses	50,000	
Total adjustments		(48,000)
Net cash provided by operating activities		$852,000

[1] Linden's share of Zach, Inc.'s:

Reported net income for 1989 (25% × $720,000)	$180,000
Cash dividends paid for 1989 (25% of $384,000)	96,000
Undistributed earnings for 1989	$ 84,000

c.

Linden Consulting Associates
ANALYSIS OF CHANGES IN PARTNERS' CAPITAL ACCOUNTS
For the Year Ended December 31, 1989

	Total	Garr	Pat	Scott
Balance, December 31, 1988	$1,700,000	$1,020,000	$680,000	$ —
Capital investment	340,000	—	—	340,000
Allocation of net income	900,000	450,000	270,000	180,000
Balance before drawings	2,940,000	1,470,000	950,000	520,000
Drawings	630,000	280,000	200,000	150,000
Balance, December 31, 1989	$2,310,000	$1,190,000	$750,000	$370,000

C. Other Presentations of Financial Data

1. Financial Statements Prepared in Conformity With Comprehensive Bases of Accounting Other Than Generally Accepted Accounting Principles

N95
Answer 4 (10 points)

a.

Baron Flowers
WORKSHEET TO CONVERT TRIAL BALANCE TO ACCRUAL BASIS
December 31, 1994

Account title	Cash basis Dr.	Cash basis Cr.	Adjustments Dr.		Adjustments Cr.		Accrual Basis* Dr.*	Accrual Basis* Cr.*
Cash	25,600						25,600	
Accounts receivable	16,200		[1]	15,800			32,000	
Inventory	62,000		[4]	10,800			72,800	
Furniture & fixtures	118,200						118,200	
Land improvements	45,000						45,000	
Accumulated depreciation & amortization		32,400			[6]	14,250		46,650
Accounts payable		17,000			[3]	13,500		30,500
Baron, Drawings			[9]	61,000			61,000	
Baron, Capital		124,600	[7]	2,000	[5]	2,600		125,200
Allowance for uncollectible accounts					[2]	3,800		3,800
Prepaid insurance			[5]	2,900			2,900	
Accrued expenses					[7]	3,100		3,100
Estimated liability from lawsuit					[8]	50,000		50,000
Sales		653,000			[1]	15,800		668,800
Purchases	305,100		[3]	13,500			318,600	
Salaries	174,000				[9]	48,000	126,000	
Payroll taxes	12,400		[7]	500			12,900	
Insurance	8,700				[5]	300	8,400	
Rent	34,200						34,200	
Utilities	12,600		[7]	600			13,200	
Living expenses	13,000				[9]	13,000		
Income summary—inventory			[4]	62,000	[4]	72,800		10,800
Uncollectible accounts			[2]	3,800			3,800	
Depreciation & amortization			[6]	14,250			14,250	
Estimated loss from lawsuit			[8]	50,000			50,000	
	827,000	827,000		237,150		237,150	938,850	938,850

*Completion of these columns was not required.

Explanations of Adjustments

[1] To convert 1994 sales to accrual basis.

Accounts receivable balances:	
December 31, 1994	$32,000
December 31, 1993	16,200
Increase in sales	$15,800

[2] To record provision for uncollectible accounts.

[3] To convert 1994 purchases to accrual basis.

Accounts payable balances:	
December 31, 1994	$30,500
December 31, 1993	17,000
Increase in purchases	$13,500

[4] To record increase in inventory from 12/31/93 to 12/31/94.

Inventory balances:	
December 31, 1994	$72,800
December 31, 1993	62,000
Increase in inventory	$10,800

[5] To adjust prepaid insurance.

Prepaid balances:	
December 31, 1994 ($8,700 x $4/12$)	$2,900
December 31, 1993 ($7,800 x $4/12$)	2,600
Decrease in insurance expense	$ 300

[6] To record 1994 depreciation and amortization expense.

Cost of leasehold improvement	$45,000
Estimated life	15 years
Amortization ($45,000 x $1/15$ x $9/12$)	2,250
Depreciation expense on fixtures and equipment	12,000
	$14,250

[7] To convert expenses to accrual basis.

	Balances		
	December 31, 1994	1993	Increase in expenses
Utilities	$1,500	$ 900	$ 600
Payroll taxes	1,600	1,100	500
	$3,100	$2,000	$1,100

[8] To record lawsuit liability at 12/31/94.

Attorney's estimate of probable loss	$300,000
Amount covered by insurance	250,000
Baron's estimated liability	$ 50,000

[9] To record Baron's drawings for 1994.

Salary ($4,000 x 12)	$48,000
Living expenses	13,000
	$61,000

b.

To: Baron Flowers

From: Muir

Re: Accrual basis financial statements

You have asked me to explain why the bank would require financial statements prepared on the accrual basis instead of the cash basis. The bank is concerned about your ability to repay the loan. To assess that ability, it wants information about your earnings for the period, total assets, and all claims on those assets. This information about your enterprise's performance and financial position is provided more completely by accrual basis financial statements than by cash-basis financial statements.

Under the cash basis, revenues are recognized when received and expenses when paid. Earnings can be manipulated by the timing of cash receipts and disbursements. Accrual basis accounting, while grounded in cash flows, reports transactions and other events with cash consequences at the time the transactions and events occur. Revenues and expenses are reported in the accounting period benefited and reflect receivables and payables, not just what the enterprise was able to collect or chose to pay.

II. Recognition, Measurement, Valuation, and Presentation of Typical Items in Financial Statements in Conformity With Generally Accepted Accounting Principles

B. Receivables

TN93
Answer 3 (10 points)

a. The appropriate valuation basis of a note receivable at the date of sale is its discounted present value of the future amounts receivable for principal and interest using the customer's market rate of interest, if known or determinable, at the date of the equipment's sale.

b. Gregor should increase the carrying amount of the note receivable by the effective interest revenue earned for the period February 1 to May 1, 1992. Gregor should account for the discounting of the note receivable without recourse by increasing cash for the proceeds received, eliminating the carrying amount of the note receivable, and recognizing a loss(gain) for the resulting difference.

This reporting is appropriate since the note's carrying amount is correctly recorded at the date it was discounted and the discounting of a note receivable without recourse is equivalent to a sale of that note. Thus the difference between the cash received and the carrying amount of the note at the date it is discounted is reported as a loss(gain).

c. 1. For notes receivable not discounted, Gregor should recognize an uncollectible notes expense. The expense equals the adjustment required to bring the balance of the allowance for uncollectible notes receivable equal to the estimated uncollectible amounts less the fair values of recoverable equipment.

2. For notes receivable discounted with recourse, Gregor should recognize an uncollectible notes expense. The expense equals the estimated amounts payable for customers' defaults less the fair values of recoverable equipment.

1M92
Answer 4(b) (5 points)

a.

Sigma Co.
**SCHEDULE OF CALCULATION OF
ALLOWANCE FOR UNCOLLECTIBLE ACCOUNTS**
December 31, 1991

0 to 30 days	$300,000 × 1%	$ 3,000
31 to 90 days	80,000 × 5%	4,000
91 to 180 days	60,000 × 20%	12,000
Over 180 days	25,000 × 80%	20,000
Accounts receivable	$465,000	
Allowance for uncollectible accounts		$39,000

b. Computation of 1991 provision:

Balance December 31, 1990	$28,000
Writeoffs during 1991	(27,000)
Recoveries during 1991	7,000
Balance before 1991 provision	8,000
Required allowance at December 31, 1991	39,000
1991 provision	$31,000

Unofficial Answers

TN91
Answer 2 (10 points)

a. 1. It was not possible to determine the machine's fair value directly, so the sales price of the machine is reported at the note's September 30, 1989, fair value. The note's September 30, 1989, fair value equals the present value at that date of the two installments discounted at the buyer's September 30, 1989, market rate of interest from their due dates of September 30, 1990, and September 30, 1991.

2. Industrial reports 1989 interest revenue determined by multiplying the note's carrying amount at September 30, 1989, times the buyer's market rate of interest at the date of issue, times three-twelfths. Industrial should recognize that there is an interest factor implicit in the note, and this interest is earned with the passage of time. Therefore, interest revenue for 1989 should include three months' revenue. The rate used should be the market rate established by the original present value, and this is applied to the carrying amount of the note.

b. To report the discounting of the note receivable with recourse, Industrial should decrease notes receivable by the carrying amount of the discounted note, increase cash by the amount received, and report the difference as a loss or gain as part of income from continuing operations. The contingent liability with respect to a possible customer default should be disclosed in notes to the financial statements.

c. Industrial should decrease cash, and increase its notes (accounts) receivable past due for all payments caused by the note's dishonor. The note (account) receivable should be written down to its estimated recoverable amount (or an allowance for uncollectibles established), and a loss on uncollectible notes should be recorded for the difference.

TM90
Answer 2 (10 points)

a. To account for the accounts receivable factored on April 1, 1989, Magrath should decrease accounts receivable by the amount of accounts receivable factored, increase cash by the amount received from the factor, and record a loss equal to the difference. The loss should be reported in the income statement. Factoring of accounts receivable on a without recourse basis is equivalent to a sale.

b. The carrying amount of the note at July 1, 1989 is the maturity amount discounted for two years at the market interest rate. For the noninterest-bearing note receivable, the interest revenue for 1989 should be determined by multiplying the carrying amount of the note at July 1, 1989 times the market rate of interest at the date of the note times one-half.

The noninterest-bearing note receivable should be reported in the December 31, 1989 balance sheet, as a noncurrent asset at its face amount less the unamortized discount.

c. Magrath should account for the collection of the accounts previously written off as uncollectible as follows:

- Increase both accounts receivable and the allowance for uncollectible accounts.
- Increase cash and decrease accounts receivable.

d. One approach estimates uncollectible accounts based on credit sales. This approach focuses on income determination by attempting to match uncollectible accounts expense with the revenues generated.

The other allowance approach estimates uncollectible accounts based on the balance in or aging of receivables. The approach focuses on asset valuation by attempting to report receivables at realizable value.

C. Inventories

M94
Answer 4 (10 points)

a.

York Co.
Schedule of Cost of Goods Sold
For the Year Ended December 31, 1993

Beginning inventory	$ 65,600
Add: Purchases	368,900
Less: Purchase discounts	(18,000)
Add: Freight-in	5,000
Goods available for sale	421,500
Less: Ending inventory	(176,000) [1]
Cost of Goods Sold	$245,500

York Co.
Supporting Schedule of Ending Inventory
December 31, 1993

Inventory at cost (LIFO):

	Units	Cost per unit	Total cost
Beginning inventory, January 1	8,000	$8.20	$ 65,600
Purchases, quarter ended March 31	12,000	8.25	99,000
Purchases, quarter ended June 30	2,000	7.90	15,800
	22,000		$180,400

Inventory at market:
22,000 units @ $8 = $176,000 [1]

b. Inventory should be valued at the lower of cost or market. Market means current replacement cost, except that:

(1) Market should not exceed the net realizable value; and
(2) Market should not be less than net realizable value reduced by an allowance for an approximately normal profit margin.

In this situation, because replacement cost ($8 per unit) is less than net realizable value, but greater than net realizable value reduced by a normal profit margin, replacement cost is used as market. Because inventory valued at market ($176,000) is lower than inventory valued at cost ($180,400), inventory should be reported in the financial statements at market.

TM93
Answer 3 (10 points)

a. 1. For its 1993 models, Blaedon should include in inventory carrying amounts all necessary and reasonable costs. These costs may include design costs, purchase price from contractors, freight-in, and warehousing costs.

2. Blaedon's 1992 model inventory should be assigned a carrying amount equal to its net realizable value, which is its current list price reduced by both its disposition costs and two-thirds of the difference between the $40 allowance given and the carrying amount assigned to trade-ins. The trade-ins' carrying amount should equal the $25 average net realizable value less the profit margin, if any, assigned.

b. 1. Using FIFO, Blaedon would assign the earliest lawnmower costs to cost of goods sold. With rising costs, this would result in matching old, relatively low inventory costs against current revenues. Net income would be higher than that reported using certain other inventory methods.

2. Blaedon would assign the latest costs to ending inventory. Normally, the carrying amount of Blaedon's FIFO ending inventory would approximate replacement cost at December 31, 1992. Retained earnings would be higher than that reported using certain other inventory methods.

TM91
Answer 3 (10 points)

a. 1. The specific identification method requires each unit to be clearly distinguished from similar units either by description, identification number, location, or other characteristic. Costs are accumulated for specific units and expensed as the units are sold. Thus, the specific identification method results in recognized cost flows being identical to actual physical flows. Ideally, each unit is relatively expensive and the number of such units relatively few so that recording of costs is not burdensome. Under the specific identification method, if similar items have different costs, cost of goods sold is influenced by the specific units sold.

2. It is appropriate for Happlia to use the specific identification method because each appliance is expensive, and easily identified by number and description. The specific identification method is feasible because Happlia already maintains records of its units held by individual retailers. Management's ability to manipulate cost of goods sold is minimized because once the inventory is in retailer's hands Happlia's management cannot influence the units selected for sales.

b. 1. Happlia should include in inventory carrying amounts all necessary and reasonable costs to get an appliance into a useful condition and place for sale. Common (or joint) costs should be allocated to individual units. Such costs exclude the excess costs incurred in transporting refrigerators to Minneapolis and their reshipment to Kansas City. These units' costs should only include normal freight costs from Des Moines to Kansas City. In addition, costs incurred to provide time utility to the goods, i.e., ensuring that they are available when required, will also be included in inventory carrying amounts.

2. Examples of inventoriable costs include the unit invoice price, plus an allocated proportion of the port handling fees, import duties, freight costs to Des Moines and to retailers, insurance costs, repackaging, and warehousing costs.

c. The 1990 income statement should report in cost of goods sold all inventory costs related to units sold in 1990, regardless of when cash is received from retailers. Excess freight costs incurred for shipping the refrigerators from Minneapolis to Kansas City should be included in determining operating income.

TM90
Answer 4 (10 points)

a. Purchases from various suppliers generally should be included in Huddell's inventory when Huddell receives the goods. Title to goods purchased FOB destination is assumed to pass when the goods are received.

b. Huddell should account for the warehousing costs as additional cost of inventory. All necessary and reasonable costs of readying goods for sale should be included in inventory.

c. 1. The advantages of using the dollar value LIFO method are to reduce the cost of accounting for inventory and to minimize the probability of reporting the liquidation of LIFO inventory layers.

2. The application of dollar value LIFO is based on dollars of inventory, an inventory cost index for each year, and broad inventory pools. The inventory layers are identified with the inventory cost index for the year in which the layer was added. In contrast, traditional LIFO is applied to individual units at their cost.

d. 1. Huddell's net markups should be included only in the retail amounts (denominator) to determine the cost to retail percentage.

Huddell's net markdowns should be ignored in the calculation of the cost to retail percentage.

2. By not deducting net markdowns from the retail amounts to determine the cost to retail percentage, Huddell produces a lower cost to retail percentage than would result if net markdowns were deducted. Applying this lower percentage to ending inventory at retail, the inventory is reported at an amount below cost. This amount is intended to approximate lower of average cost or market.

D. Property, Plant, and Equipment

TN92
Answer 5 (10 points)

a. 1. When the old engines' costs are known, the snowmobiles account is decreased by the old engines' costs, and accumulated depreciation is decreased by the accumulated depreciation on the old engines. A current asset would be recorded for the fair value of the future repair and maintenance services. The net difference between the old engines' carrying amounts and their fair values is recorded as an operating gain or loss. To record the new engines' acquisition, both the snowmobiles account and accounts payable are increased by the new engines' costs.

2. If the old engines' costs are unknown then either the snowmobiles account would be increased or accumulated depreciation would be decreased by the difference between the new engines' costs and the old engines' fair values.

b. 1. Assumptions underlying use of an accelerated depreciation method include:

- An asset is more productive in the earlier years of its estimated useful life. Therefore, greater depreciation charges in the earlier years would be matched against the greater revenues generated in the earlier years.

- Repair and maintenance costs are often higher in later periods and an accelerated depreciation method results in a more nearly annual constant total cost over the years of use.

- An asset may become obsolete before the end of its originally estimated useful life. The risk associated with estimated long-term cash flow is greater than the risk associated with near-term cash flows. Accelerated depreciation recognizes this condition.

2. Winter should calculate snowmobile depreciation by applying twice the straight-line rate to their carrying amounts.

c. Under the inventory (appraisal) method, Winter calculates the ending undepreciated cost on the skis, poles, and boots by multiplying the physical quantities of these items on hand by an appraised amount. This ending undepreciated cost is classified as a noncurrent asset. Depreciation included in continuing operations equals the sum of the beginning balance and purchases for the year less the ending undepreciated cost.

TN91
Answer 3 (10 points)

a. Portland should have selected the straight-line depreciation method when approximately the same amount of an asset's service potential is used up each period. If the reasons for the decline in service potential are unclear, then the selection of the straight-line method could be influenced by the ease of recordkeeping, its use for similar assets, and its use by others in the industry.

b. Portland should record depreciation expense to the date of the exchange. If the original truck's carrying amount is greater than its fair value, a loss results. The truck's capitalized cost and accumulated depreciation are eliminated, and the loss on trade-in is reported as part of income from continuing operations. The newly acquired truck is recorded at fair value. If the original truck's carrying amount is less than its fair value at trade-in, then there is an unrecognized gain. The newly acquired truck is recorded at fair value less the unrecognized gain. Cash is decreased by the amount paid.

c. 1. By associating depreciation with a group of machines instead of each individual machine, Portland's bookkeeping process is greatly simplified. Also, since actual machine lives vary from the average depreciable life, unrecognized net losses on early dispositions are expected to be offset by continuing depreciation on machines usable beyond the average depreciable life. Periodic income does not fluctuate as a result of recognizing gains and losses on manufacturing machine dispositions.

2. Portland should divide the depreciable cost (capitalized cost less residual value) of each machine by its estimated life to obtain its annual depreciation. The sum of the individual annual depreciation amounts should then be divided by the sum of the individual capitalized costs to obtain the annual composite depreciation rate.

E. Investments

M95
Answer 4 (10 points)

a. Bing should consider whether it has the ability to exercise significant influence over operating and financial policies of the investee enterprise. That ability is presumed to exist for investments of 20 percent or more and presumed not to exist for investments of less than 20 percent. Both presumptions may be overcome by predominant evidence to the contrary, such as board of directors or policy making participation, material intercompany transactions, interchange of managerial personnel, or technological dependency.

The equity method is consistent with accrual accounting, because the investor recognizes its share of the earnings and losses of the investee in the periods in which they are reflected in the accounts of the investee.

b.

Income statement:

Equity in earnings of Latt	
(400,000 x 19.5% (39,000 ÷ 200,000))	$ 78,000
Amortization of goodwill	
(180,000(585,000 − 405,000) ÷ 10)	(18,000)
	$ 60,000

Balance sheet:

Investment in Latt	
(585,000 + 78,000 − 18,000 − 19,500	
(100,000 x 19.5%))	$625,500

TN90
Answer 2 (10 points)

a. Under the cost method, the investor recognizes dividends as income when received. Under the equity method, an investor recognizes as income its share of an investee's earnings or losses in the periods in which they are reported by the investee. The amount recognized as income is adjusted for any change in the difference between investment cost and underlying equity in net assets at the investment date. The equity method is more consistent with accrual accounting than is the cost method, because the equity method recognizes income when earned rather than when dividends are received.

b. Monroe should have assessed whether it could have exerted significant influence over Grumer's operating and financial policies. Monroe did not own 20% or more of Grumer's voting stock (which would have given the refutable presumption that it could exercise significant influence); however, the ability to exercise significant influence may be indicated by other factors such as Monroe's provision of three key management personnel and purchase of 25% of Grumer's output.

c. On becoming a 30% owner of Grumer, Monroe should use the equity method to account for its investment. As of January 2, 1990, Monroe's investment and retained earnings accounts must be adjusted retroactively to show balances as if the equity method had been used from the initial purchase date. Both accounts should be increased by 18% of Grumer's undistributed income since formation. [In this case, no adjustment to the undistributed income is necessary since the stock was issued at its book value which was assumed to approximate its fair value.]

F. Intangibles and Other Assets

N95
Answer 5 (10 points)

a. 1. The main characteristics of intangible assets are their lack of physical substance, the difficulty of estimating their value, and the high degree of uncertainty regarding their future life. Accounting for intangible assets depends on whether they have been purchased or developed internally.

Intangible assets purchased from others should be recorded at cost. The costs of developing intangible assets with indeterminable lives, such as goodwill, are ordinarily not distinguishable from the current costs of operations and thus are not assignable to specific assets but are expensed immediately.

2. Intangible assets should be amortized over their estimated useful life. Estimated useful life should be determined by consideration of such factors as legal life; provisions for renewal or extensions of contracts; the effects of obsolescence, demand, and competition; and other economic factors.

An apparently unlimited useful life may in fact be indefinite. The justification for amortizing the cost of goodwill or other intangible assets with an indeterminate life over time is that the value almost inevitably becomes zero at some future date. Since the date at which the value becomes zero is indeterminable, the useful life has been set arbitrarily at a period not to exceed forty years.

3. The financial statements should disclose the method and period of amortization of all intangible assets.

b.

Broca Co.
INTANGIBLES SECTION OF BALANCE SHEET
December 31, 1994

Goodwill, net of accumulated amortization of $4,700	$183,300	[1]
Franchise, net of accumulated amortization of $12,000	48,000	[2]
Patent, net of accumulated amortization of $13,600	122,400	[3]

[1]	Cash paid	$360,000
	Value of net assets	(172,000)
	Goodwill	188,000
	Amortization over 40 years	(4,700)
	Balance	$183,300

[2]	Franchise	$60,000
	Amortization over 5 years	(12,000)
	Balance	$48,000

[3]	Legal costs (51,000 + 85,000)	$136,000
	Amortization over 10 years	(13,600)
	Balance	$122,400

EXPENSES RESULTING FROM INTANGIBLES
For the Year Ended December 31, 1994

Amortization:	
Goodwill	$ 4,700
Franchise	12,000
Patent	13,600
	$30,300
Franchise fee	200
	$30,500

Unofficial Answers

H. Deferred Revenues

1N93
Answer 5 (10 points)

a.

London, Inc.
SCHEDULE OF GROSS PROFIT (LOSS)

	Beta	Gamma
For the Year Ended September 30, 1992:		
Estimated gross profit (loss):		
Contract price	$600,000	$800,000
Less total costs	400,000	820,000
Estimated gross profit (loss)	$200,000	$(20,000)
Percent complete:		
Costs incurred to date	$360,000	$410,000
Total costs	400,000	820,000
Percent complete	90%	50%
Gross profit (loss) recognized	$180,000	$(20,000)
For the Year Ended September 30, 1993:		
Estimated gross profit (loss):		
Contract price	$560,000	$840,000
Less total costs	450,000	900,000
Estimated gross profit (loss)	$110,000	$(60,000)
Percent complete:		
Costs incurred to date	$450,000	$720,000
Total costs	450,000	900,000
Percent complete	100%	80%
Gross profit (loss)	110,000	(60,000)
Less gross profit (loss) recognized in prior year	180,000	(20,000)
Gross profit (loss) recognized	$(70,000)	$(40,000)

1N93
Answer 5 (cont.)

b.

London Inc.
SCHEDULE OF SELECTED BALANCE SHEET ACCOUNTS
September 30, 1992

Accounts receivable		$115,000
Costs and estimated earnings in excess of billings:		
Construction in progress	$540,000	
Less: Billings	315,000	
Costs and estimated earnings in excess of billings		225,000
Billings in excess of costs and estimated earnings		50,000

c.

London, Inc.
SCHEDULE OF INCOME TAXES PAYABLE AND INCOME TAX EXPENSE
September 30, 1992

Financial statement income:		
From other divisions		$300,000
From Beta project		180,000
From Gamma project		(20,000)
Total financial statement income		$460,000
Less temporary differences:		
Beta project income		(180,000)
Gamma project loss		20,000
Total taxable income		$300,000
Taxes payable ($300,000 x 25%)		$ 75,000
Deferred tax liability ($160,000 x 30%)		48,000
Tax expense:		
Current	$75,000	
Deferred	48,000	123,000

I. Notes and Bonds Payable

TN92
Answer 3 (10 points)

a. The purpose of the effective interest method is to provide periodic interest expense based on a constant rate over the life of the bonds. The impact of applying the effective interest method on Corval's bond premium is to decrease the premium by a lesser amount in 1988 compared to using the straight-line method of amortization.

b. Under the straight-line interest method, the premium is amortized at a constant periodic amount, and in 1988 the premium amortization would have been greater than amortization under the effective interest method. Consequently, for 1988, interest expense would have been understated, net income would have been overstated, and the carrying amount of the bonds would have been understated.

c. The November 30, 1991, transaction is reported as an extraordinary loss after income from continuing operations. This loss equals the excess of the fair value of the cash and property transferred over the bonds' carrying amount on November 30, 1991. This presentation is appropriate because this is an early extinguishment of debt.

d. The gross amount of the extraordinary loss is added to net income under cash flows from operating activities. The cash payment is reported as a cash outflow from financing activities.

Corval should disclose details of the noncash elements of the transaction either on the same page as the statement of cash flows or in the notes to the financial statements.

TM92
Answer 3 (10 points)

a. 1. The bond issue price would be determined by the expected future cash flows of principal and interest, discounted at the market rate of interest, plus the value of the conversion option at the date of issuance.

2. Columbine should account for the issuance of the convertible bonds by increasing cash for the issue price, increasing bonds payable by the face amount, and increasing premium on bonds payable for the balance. The convertible debt is accounted for solely as debt. The conversion option is not recognized primarily because it is inseparable from the debt, and secondarily because of the practical difficulty of assigning it a value.

3. Columbine should account for the conversion of the bonds into common stock by decreasing both bonds payable and unamortized bond premium by 30%, increasing common stock by $25 for each share issued, and increasing additional paid-in capital by the difference between the three previous amounts.

b. 1. If the bonds are dilutive, they are included in computing Columbine's 1989 primary earnings per share.

2. Both earnings and number of shares are affected by including the convertible bonds in computing primary earnings per share. Interest expense on convertible bonds, net of income taxes, is added to net income. The number of shares outstanding is increased by the number of shares potentially issuable on conversion (number of bonds times 20), multiplied by the proportion of the year that the bonds were outstanding (one-quarter).

TM90
Answer 3 (10 points)

a. 1. The 9% bonds were issued at a discount (less than face amount). Although the bonds provide for payment of interest of 9% of face amount, this rate was less than the prevailing or market rate for bonds of similar quality at the time the bonds were issued. Thus, the issue price of the bonds, which is the present value of the principal and interest payments discounted at 10%, is less than the face amount.

2. The amount of interest expense would be higher in the second year of the life of the bond issue than in the first year of the life of the bond issue. According to the effective interest method of amortization, the 10% effective interest rate is applied to the bond carrying amount. In a discount situation, the bond carrying amount increases each year, and this results in a greater interest expense in each successive year.

b. 1. Gain or loss on early extinguishment of debt should be determined by comparing the carrying amount of the bonds at the date of extinguishment with the acquisition price. If the carrying amount exceeds the acquisition price, a gain results. If the carrying amount is less than the acquisition price, a loss results.

In this case, a loss results. The term bonds were issued at a discount. Therefore, the carrying amount of the bonds at the date of extinguishment must be less than the face amount, which is less than the acquisition price.

2. Drew should report the loss from early extinguishment of debt in its 1989 income statement as an extraordinary item, net of income taxes.

c. The proceeds from the issuance of the 7% nonconvertible bonds with detachable stock purchase warrants should be recorded as an increase in cash. These proceeds should be allocated between the bonds and the warrants on the basis of their relative market values. The portion of the proceeds allocable to the bonds should be accounted for as long-term debt, while the portion allocable to the warrants should be accounted for as paid-in capital.

K. Equity Accounts

R97
Answer 2 (10 points)

a.

Field Co.
STOCKHOLDERS' EQUITY SECTION OF BALANCE SHEET
December 31, 1996

Common stock, $5 par value, 400,000 shares authorized, 180,000 shares issued, 175,000 shares outstanding		$ 900,000 [1]
Additional paid-in capital		1,860,000 [2]
Retained earnings:		
Beginning balance	$1,845,000	
Add: Net income	240,000	
Less: Property dividend distributed	(60,000)	2,025,000
		4,785,000
Less common stock in treasury, 5,000 shares at cost		(50,000)
Total stockholders' equity		$4,735,000

[1] Shares issued: 160,000 + 20,000 = 180,000 × $5 = $900,000
[2] Additional paid-in capital: 1,600,000 + (20,000 × ($18 − 5)) = 1,600,000 + 260,000

b. To: Management, Field Co.
Re: Accounting for Stock-Based Compensation

As you are aware, Statement of Financial Accounting Standards No. 123 discusses both the "intrinsic value" method and the "fair value" method of accounting for stock options. The purpose of this memo is to inform you of the difference between the two methods and of when the company should record compensation cost associated with 1997 stock option issuances.

Under the "fair value" method of accounting for stock options, compensation cost is measured at the grant date based on the value of the award. This value is computed using an option-pricing model. Under the "intrinsic value" method, compensation cost is the excess, if any, of the quoted market price of the stock at the grant date (or other measurement date) over the amount an employee must pay to acquire the stock.

Under both methods, compensation cost, if any, is recognized over the service period, which is usually the vesting period.

Answer 4 (10 points)

a.

Trask Corp.
STATEMENT OF RETAINED EARNINGS
For the Year Ended December 31, 1992

Balance, December 31, 1991		
As originally reported		$16,445,000
Less prior period adjustment from error understating depreciation	$350,000	
Less income tax effect	105,000	245,000
As restated		16,200,000
Net income		2,400,000
		18,600,000
Deduct dividends		
Cash dividend on preferred stock	300,000 [1]	
Dividend in kind on common stock	900,000 [2]	1,200,000
Balance, December 31, 1992		$17,400,000

b.

Trask Corp.
STOCKHOLDERS' EQUITY SECTION OF BALANCE SHEET
December 31, 1992

Preferred stock, $100 par value, 6% cumulative; 150,000 shares authorized; 50,000 shares issued and outstanding	$ 5,000,000
Common stock, $2.50 par value; 4,000,000 shares authorized; 3,400,000 shares issued	8,500,000 [3]
Additional paid-in capital	16,675,000 [4]
Retained earnings	17,400,000
	47,575,000
Less common stock in treasury, 100,000 shares at cost	500,000
Total stockholders' equity	$47,075,000

c.

Trask Corp.
COMPUTATION OF BOOK VALUE PER SHARE OF COMMON STOCK
December 31, 1992

Total stockholders' equity	$47,075,000
Deduct allocation to preferred stock	5,000,000
Allocation to common stock	$42,075,000
Divided by number of common shares outstanding [3,400,000−100,000]	÷3,300,000
Book value per share of common stock	$12.75

FA-221

1N93
Answer 4 (cont.)

Explanation of Amounts

[1]   Preferred stock dividend
      Par value of outstanding preferred shares $ 5,000,000
      Multiplied by dividend rate   x .06
      Dividends paid on preferred stock $ 300,000

[2]   Dividend in kind on common stock
      Fair market value of Harbor stock distributed [15,000 shares @ $60] $ 900,000

[3]   Number of common shares issued and outstanding
      Number of common shares issued, 12/31/91   1,575,000
      Less: common shares retired   (25,000)
      Number of common shares issued, 6/1/92   150,000
             1,700,000

      Two-for-one stock split, 10/27/92   x 2
      Number of common shares issued after stock split   3,400,000
      Less: common shares held in treasury   100,000
      Total number of common shares outstanding   3,300,000

      Amount of common shares issued
      Amount of common shares issued, 12/31/91 $ 7,875,000
      Less: common shares retired at par value   (125,000)
      Number of common shares issued, 6/1/92   750,000
      Total amount of common shares issued $ 8,500,000

[4]   Amount of additional paid-in capital
      Amount at 12/31/91 (1,575,000 @ $10) $15,750,000
      Less: treasury stock retired [25,000 shares @ $5 ($10 cost − $5 par value)]   (125,000)
      Amount received upon issuance of common shares, 6/1/92 (150,000 shares @ $7)   1,050,000
      Total amount of additional paid-in capital $16,675,000

L. Revenue, Cost, and Expense Accounts

N94
Answer 5a* (10 points)

To: Brown

From: Wyatt

As we discussed, here is a brief overview of revenue recognition and Statement of Financial Accounting Standards No. 106.

a. Revenue recognition.

The revenue recognition principle provides that revenue is recognized when it is realized or realizable and it is earned. Accordingly, revenues from the sale of products ordinarily are recognized at the time of sale. Revenue from sales transactions in which the buyer has a right to return the product are recognized at time of sale only if specified conditions are met. If all these conditions are not met, revenue recognition is postponed; if they are met, sales revenue and cost of sales should be reported in the income statement, reduced to reflect estimated returns.

One of the specified conditions is that the amount of future returns can be reasonably estimated. Since Emco cannot reasonably estimate future returns, Emco should defer recognition of sales revenue and cost of sales until the return privilege has substantially expired or it can reasonably estimate returns, whichever occurs first.

TM93
Answer 4 (10 points)

a. Bow must have a system that is capable of meeting both of the following conditions for the Crecy contract:

---

*The omitted item can be found in another Content Specification Group.

- Reasonable estimates of profitability at completion.
- Reliable measures of progress toward completion.

b. At December 31, 1992, Bow should calculate the percentage of completion by comparing the costs incurred to date, less costs of unused materials, to the estimated total cost to complete Crecy. Income to date equals the percentage-of-completion multiplied by the estimated total profit to be earned on the contract. The 1992 income equals the income to be recognized to December 31, 1992, less the income reported under the contract in 1991.

When contract materials are purchased but not used, costs of the unused materials are excluded from income recognition calculations. Otherwise, the early period income reported may be overstated compared with the income earning efforts of that period.

c. Bow should report a current asset for the Crecy account receivable, and another for the excess of costs incurred plus total profit recognized over contract billings.

d. Assuming Bow has elected early adoption of FASB Statement No. 109, *Accounting for Income Taxes*, Bow should report a current deferred tax liability equal to its total net income reported in 1991 and 1992 multiplied by its enacted 1993 average tax rate. A deferred income tax expense should be recognized for the increase during 1992 in the deferred tax liability balance.

TM93
Answer 5 (10 points)

a. For the safety hazard, Niki should accrue for a loss and a liability equal to the most likely cost. The most likely loss is the best estimate of the expected loss. Accrual of a loss is appropriate because the loss is both probable and can be reasonably estimated. In addition, Niki should separately disclose in the notes to the 1992 financial statements the nature of the hazard and the range of possible loss.

b. Niki should accrue for a loss and a liability for the note sold to a bank. The accrual should equal the amount due on the note plus related costs and less any expected settlement from the bankruptcy. Accrual is appropriate because it is probable that a loss has occurred, as evidenced by the bankruptcy filing, even though this note is not yet due.

c. Niki should disclose the possible loss on the assigned lease in notes to the 1992 financial statements. Disclosures should include details of the assigned lease and the amounts due, estimates of any revenues that might be earned on the property, and any amounts recoverable from Pro. Although disclosure is appropriate for the financial statements not to be misleading, accrual of a loss is inappropriate because the loss is only reasonably possible.

d. Niki should report a foreign exchange loss on its 1992 income statement, and an increase in the account payable to reflect the exchange rate at December 31, 1992. Reporting a foreign exchange loss is appropriate because, consistent with accrual accounting, the exchange rate on December 31, 1992, should be used to value the contract. Niki's beliefs as to future exchange movements are excluded from the financial statements.

TN90
Answer 3 (10 points)

a. The two alternative accounting methods to account for long-term construction contracts are the percentage-of-completion method and the completed-contract method. The percentage-of-completion method must be used if both of the following conditions are met at the statement date:

- Reasonable estimates of profitability at completion.
- Reliable measures of progress toward completion.

If one or both of these conditions are not met at the statement date, the completed-contract method must be used.

b. The Ski Park contract must be accounted for by the percentage-of-completion method. Eighty percent of the estimated total income on the contract should be recognized as of December 31, 1989. Therefore, the 1989 income to be recognized will equal 80% of the estimated total income less the income reported under the contract in 1988.

The Nassu Village contract must be accounted for by the completed-contract method. Therefore no income or loss is recognized in 1989 under this contract.

c. The receivable on the Ski Park contract should be reported as a current asset. If costs plus gross profit to date exceed billings, the difference should be reported as a current asset. If billings exceed cost plus gross profit to date, the difference should be reported as a current liability.

III. Recognition, Measurement, Valuation, and Presentation of Specific Types of Transactions and Events in Financial Statements in Conformity With Generally Accepted Accounting Principles

A. Accounting Changes and Corrections of Errors

TN92
Answer 4 (10 points)

a. A change from the LIFO inventory method to the FIFO inventory method is a change in accounting principle. Windsor should restate the 1990 financial statements, including adjustment for the effect on January 1, 1990, retained earnings, as if the FIFO method had been adopted at the beginning of 1990. The nature and justification for the change in inventory method should be disclosed in the notes to the 1991 financial statements. The effects of the change on income statement components should be disclosed for all periods presented.

b. Windsor's change from sum-of-the-years' digits depreciation method for all future machinery acquisitions is a change in accounting principle. The nature and justification for the change in depreciation methods should be disclosed in the notes to the 1991 comparative financial statements. The 1990 financial statements are unaffected by the change, but the effects of the change on 1991 income components should be disclosed.

c. A change from the cash basis of vacation pay expense recognition to the accrual basis is a change from an accounting principle that is not generally accepted to one that is generally accepted. Such a change is considered an error correction. Windsor should restate the 1990 financial statement, including adjustment for the effect on January 1, 1990, retained earnings, to correct prior errors. Windsor should disclose the nature and details of the corrections in notes to the 1991 financial statements.

TM90
Answer 5 (10 points)

a. Boulder's change in depreciation method is a change in accounting principle. This change in accounting principle should show the cumulative effect of a change in accounting principle in net income of the period of change, and the pro forma effects of retroactive application for all prior periods presented currently. Financial statements of prior periods should not be restated.

Boulder's change in salvage values is a change in accounting estimate. Boulder would not report a cumulative effect, nor pro forma effects, nor would prior period financial statements be restated.

Boulder's change in the specific subsidiaries constituting the group of companies for which consolidated financial statements are presented is a change in reporting entity. Neither the cumulative effect nor the pro forma effects of the change should be reported. However, financial statements of prior periods presented currently should be restated.

b. 1. Consistent use of accounting principles from one accounting period to another enhances the comparability of accounting information across accounting periods, and thus increases the usefulness of financial statements.

2. If a change in accounting principle occurs, the nature and effect of a change in accounting principle should be disclosed to avoid misleading financial statement users. Disclosure is required because there is a presumption that an accounting principle once adopted should not be changed in accounting for events and transactions of a similar type.

B. Business Combinations

TM91
Answer 2 (10 points)

a. A business combination accounted for as a pooling-of-interests is a continuation of ownership interests of previously separate companies. Each stockholder group retains risk and benefit elements from its former investments to which are added risks and benefits obtained through mutual exchanges with the other group or groups. Total resources of the pooled entity remain intact.

b. At least 90% of Sib's outstanding common stock must be exchanged on December 31, 1990, for the combination to be treated as a pooling-of-interests.

c. 1. The December 31, 1990, consolidated balance sheet reports assets and liabilities at the sum of Pap's and Sib's carrying amounts before the combination.

2. Johnson's proportional ownership in Sib is reported as a minority interest regardless of the type of combination accounting. In pooling-of-interests accounting, to report the controlling stockholders' equity, the balance of Sib's stockholders' equity is added to Pap's stockholders' equity before the combination, with components as follows:

- Common stock equals the par value of Pap's common stock outstanding after the combination.

- Additional paid-in capital equals the sum of the two companies' additional paid-in capital before the combination less:

    – Johnson's proportional interest in Sib's additional paid-in capital, and

    – Excess of the par value of new Pap stock issued over par value of Sib stock exchanged.

If a negative amount arises from this calculation it is deducted from combined retained earnings.

- Retained earnings equals the sum of the separate retained earnings before the combination less

Unofficial Answers

- Johnson's proportional interest in Sib's retained earnings, and

- Any deduction, as noted above, required for the issue of Pap's common stock.

D. Contingent Liabilities and Commitments

TN91
Answer 4 (10 points)

a. 1 Notes to Supey's 1990 financial statements should disclose the nature of the loss on cleanup and indicate that an estimate of the loss, or range of the loss, cannot be made. No accrual should be made because the loss cannot be reasonably estimated and accrual of an uncertain amount would impair the integrity of the financial statements.

2. Supey should disclose the nature of Gap's claim in the notes to the 1990 financial statements. Disclosure should include an estimate of the potential loss. Supey should not accrue the loss because it is only reasonably possible that it will have to pay for Gap's losses.

b. An estimated loss on the purchase commitment, equal to the unrecoverable amount of the contract price, should be reported as part of 1990 income from continuing operations and as a current liability at December 31, 1990. The net loss on the purchase commitment should be measured and recognized in the period in which it occurs. Since Supey did not hedge this contract, reporting this loss recognizes the commitment's impact on future cash flows.

G. Employee Benefits

R96
Answer 1 (10 points)

a. An example of postemployment benefits offered by employers is continuation of health care benefits. Deck is required to accrue liabilities for compensated absences and postemployment benefits if all of the following conditions are met:

- the obligation is attributable to employees' services already rendered,

- the employees' rights accumulate or vest,

- payment is probable, and

- the amount of the benefits can be reasonably estimated.

If an obligation cannot be accrued solely because the amount cannot be reasonably estimated, the financial statements should disclose that fact.

b. Estimated amounts to be paid under a deferred compensation contract should be accrued over the period of an employee's active employment from the time the contract is signed to the employee's full eligibility date. The theoretical rationale for accrual of these obligations to be paid in the future is that accrual matches the cost of the benefits to the period in which services are rendered, and results in recognition of a measurable liability.

c.
Deck Co.
Schedule of Deferred Compensation Amounts
For the Years 1995 through 1998

For the year ended	Accrued liability	Deferred compensation expense
12/31/95	$ 50,000	$50,000 [a]
12/31/96	$100,000	$50,000
12/31/97	$150,000	$50,000
12/31/98	$165,000	$15,000 [b]

[a] $150,000 ÷ 3 (straight-line method)
[b] $150,000 × 10%

N94
Answer 5b* (10 points)

To: Brown

From: Wyatt

As we discussed, here is a brief overview of revenue recognition and Statement of Financial Accounting Standards No. 106.

b. Statement of Financial Accounting Standards No. 106, *Employers' Accounting for Postretirement Benefits Other Than Pensions.*

The primary recipients of postretirement benefits other than pensions are retired employees, their beneficiaries, and covered dependents. The principle benefit covered by FAS 106 is postretirement health care benefits. Examples of other benefits include tuition assistance, legal services, life insurance benefits, day care, and housing subsidies.

The reasoning given in FAS 106 is that accrual of the obligation based on best estimates is superior to implying, by a failure to accrue, that no obligation exists prior to the payment of benefits.

TM92
Answer 5 (10 points)

a. The components of Bighorn's 1991 net pension cost calculation are:

---

*The omitted item can be found in another Content Specification Group.

- Service cost.
- Interest cost.
- Actual return on plan assets.
- Gain or loss consisting of:
  - The difference between the actual and expected return on plan assets.
  - Any amortization of the unrecognized gain or loss from previous periods.

b. 1. Bighorn's unrecognized net loss results from differences between actuarial assumptions and experiences for both its projected benefit obligation and returns on plan assets.

2. Bighorn's unfunded accrued pension cost occurs because cumulative net pension expense exceeds cash contributed to the pension fund.

c. Bighorn's minimum pension liability equals the excess of the accumulated benefit obligation over the fair value of plan assets. Bighorn's additional pension liability would equal any excess of this minimum pension liability over the unfunded accrued pension cost.

I. Financial Instruments

R97
Answer 1 (10 points)

a. A financial instrument is cash, evidence of an ownership interest in an entity, or a contractual right to receive or deliver cash or another financial instrument. A derivative financial instrument is a product whose value is derived, at least in part, from the value and characteristics of one or more underlying assets. Examples of derivative financial instruments include: futures; forward, swap, or options contracts; interest-rate caps; and fixed-rate loan commitments.

b. Off-balance-sheet risk of accounting loss is the risk of accounting loss from a financial instrument that exceeds the amount recognized for the financial instrument in the balance sheet. An example of a financial instrument having off-balance-sheet risk of accounting loss would be a noncancelable operating lease with future minimum lease commitments. Other examples include standby loan commitments written, letters of credit, options, interest rate caps and swaps, repurchase agreements, purchase commitments, futures contracts, and obligations arising from financial instruments sold short.

c. Market risk is the possibility that future changes in market prices may make a financial instrument less valuable or more burdensome. Credit risk is the possibility that a loss may occur from the failure of the other party to perform according to the terms of a contract. Concentrations of credit risk exist when receivables have common characteristics that may affect their collection. One common characteristic might be that the receivables are due from companies in the same industry or in the same region of the country.

d. The fair value of a financial instrument is the amount at which the instrument could be exchanged in a current transaction between willing parties, other than in a forced or liquidation sale. Quoted market price, if available, is the best evidence of the fair value of a financial instrument. If quoted prices are not available, Chatham's management's best estimate of fair value might be based on valuation techniques or on the quoted market price of a financial instrument with similar characteristics.

K. Income Taxes

and

L. Interest Costs

M94
Answer 5 (10 points)

a.

Rayne Co.
SCHEDULE OF INTEREST EXPENSE
For the Year Ended December 31, 1993

Note payable	$ 6,600	[1]
Capital lease obligation	4,750	[2]
Bonds payable	26,900	[3]
Total interest expense	$38,250	

[1] 1,800 (90,000 x 8% x $^3/_{12}$) + 4,800 (80,000 x 8% x $^9/_{12}$)
[2] 10% x 47,500 (62,500 – 15,000)
[3] 538,000 x 10% x $^1/_2$

b. To: Dunn
From: Green
Re: Accounting for income taxes

Below is a brief overview of accounting for income taxes in accordance with FAS 109.

The objectives of accounting for income taxes are to recognize (a) the amount of taxes payable or refundable for the current year, and (b) deferred tax liabilities and assets for the estimated future tax consequences of temporary differences and carryforwards. Temporary differences are differences between the tax basis of assets or liabilities and their reported amounts in the financial statements that will result in taxable or deductible amounts in future years.

Deferred tax assets and liabilities are measured based on the provisions of enacted tax law; the effects of future changes in the tax laws or rates are not anticipated. The measurement of deferred tax assets is reduced, if necessary, by a valuation allowance to reflect the net asset

N. Leases

M95
Answer 5 (10 points)

a. The theoretical basis for capitalizing certain long-term leases is that the economic effect or substance of such leases on the lessee is that of an installment purchase. Such a lease transfers substantially all the risks and benefits incident to the ownership of property to the lessee, and obligates the lessee in a manner similar to that created when funds are borrowed.

b.

Cash	864,000	
Deferred gain		324,000
Equipment		540,000
Leased equipment	864,000	
Capital lease obligation		864,000

c.

Interest expense	86,400 [1]	
Capital lease obligation	63,600	
Executory costs	3,000	
Cash		153,000
Depreciation	96,000 [2]	
Accumulated depreciation		96,000
Deferred gain	36,000 [3]	
Depreciation		36,000

[1] 864,000 x 10% implicit interest rate
[2] 864,000 ÷ 9 year lease period
[3] 324,000 ÷ 9 year lease period

TN93
Answer 4 (10 points)

a. Jen should account for the sale portion of the sale-leaseback transaction by increasing cash for the sale price, decreasing property, plant, and equipment for the building's carrying amount, and recording a deferred gain for the excess of the sale price over the building's carrying amount.

This accounting is appropriate because Jen still retains substantial ownership rights and obligations pertaining to the building. Since no earning process occurred, this sale-leaseback is not in substance a sale but a financing transaction. Therefore the gain should be deferred.

b. The leased building is included on Jen's December 31, 1992, balance sheet as leased property at its discounted present value on December 31, 1991, less accumulated depreciation, and less unamortized deferred gain on the sale. Its discounted present value at December 31, 1991, represents the future lease payments, discounted at Jen's interest rate.

The lease obligation on Jen's December 31, 1992, balance sheet equals the building's December 31, 1991, present value less principal repaid in 1992. An amount equal to the principal to be repaid in 1993 should be reported as a current liability. The balance of the obligation should be reported as a noncurrent liability.

1M93
Answer 4(b) (5 points)

	Debits	Credits
1. January 2, 1992— to record lease:		
Equipment	850,000	
Capital lease liability		850,000
2. December 31, 1992— to record payment:		
Capital lease liability	100,000	
Cash		100,000
3. December 31, 1992— to record depreciation:		
Depreciation expense	34,000	
Accumulated depreciation		34,000
Interest expense	85,000	
Capital lease liability		85,000

TM91
Answer 4 (10 points)

a. 1. Comparisons of an equipment's fair value to its lease payments' present value, and of its useful life to the lease term, are used to determine whether the lease is equivalent to an installment sale, and therefore is a capital lease.

2. A lease is categorized as a capital lease, if, at the date of the lease agreement, it meets any one of four criteria. As the lease has no provision for Port to reacquire ownership of the equipment, it fails the two criteria of transfer of ownership at the end of the lease and a bargain purchase option. Port's lease payments, with a present value equaling 85% of the equipment's fair value, fail the criterion for a present value equaling or exceeding 90% of the equipment's fair value. However, the lease would be classified as a capital lease, because its term of 80% of the equipment's estimated useful life exceeds the criterion of being at least 75% of the equipment's estimated useful life.

b. Port should account for the sale portion of the sale-leaseback transaction at December 31, 1989, by increasing cash for the sale price, decreasing equipment by the carrying amount, and recognizing a loss for the excess of the equipment's carrying amount over its sale price.

c. On the December 31, 1990, balance sheet, the equipment should be included as a fixed asset, at the lease payments' present value at December 31, 1989, less 1990 amortization.

On the December 31, 1990, balance sheet, the lease obligation will equal the lease payments' present value at December 31, 1989, less principal repaid December 31, 1990. This amount will be reported in current liabilities for the principal to be repaid in 1991, and the balance in noncurrent liabilities.

R. Research and Development Costs

TN90
Answer 4 (10 points)

a. The costs of research equipment used exclusively for Trouver would be reported as research and development expenses in the period incurred.

The costs of research equipment used on both Trouver and future research projects would be capitalized and shown as equipment (less accumulated depreciation) on the balance sheet. An appropriate method of depreciation should be used. Depreciation on capitalized research equipment should be reported as a research and development expense.

b. 1. Matching refers to the process of expense recognition by associating costs with revenues on a cause and effect basis.

2. Research and development costs are usually expensed in the period incurred and may not be matched with revenues. This accounting treatment is justified by the high degree of uncertainty regarding the amount and timing of future benefits. A direct relationship between research and development costs and future revenues generally cannot be demonstrated.

c. Corporate headquarters' costs allocated to research and development would be classified as general and administrative expenses in the period incurred, because they are not clearly related to research and development activities.

d. On Clonal's statement of cash flows, the legal expenses incurred in defending the patent should be reported under investing activities in the period paid.

SUGGESTED REFERENCES

Financial Accounting & Reporting

AICPA, *Guide for Prospective Financial Information* (AICPA, 1993).

AICPA, *Personal Financial Statements Guide* (AICPA, 1991).

AICPA, *Professional Standards* (AICPA, 1997).

AICPA, *Technical Practice Aids* (AICPA, 1993).

Beams, *Advanced Accounting*, 5th ed. (Prentice-Hall, 1993).

Chasteen, Flaherty, O'Connor, *Intermediate Accounting*, 6th ed. (Random House, 1998).

FASB, *Current Text, Accounting Standards* (FASB).

FASB, *Original Pronouncements, Accounting Standards* (FASB).

Fischer, Taylor, Leer, *Advanced Accounting*, 6th ed. (South-Western, 1995).

Kieso & Weygandt, *Intermediate Accounting*, 9th ed. (Wiley, 1997).

Larson, *Modern Advanced Accounting*, 7th ed. (McGraw-Hill, 1997).

Nikolai & Bazley, *Intermediate Accounting*, 7th ed. (South Western, 1997).

Pahler, Mori, *Advanced Accounting: Concepts and Practice*, 6th ed. (Harcourt Brace Jovanovich, 1997).

Williams, Stanga, Holder, *Intermediate Accounting*, 5th ed. (Harcourt Brace Jovanovich, 1997).

CONTENT SPECIFICATION OUTLINES

Content Specification Outlines

The original content specification outlines were adopted by the Board of Examiners in 1981, effective for the November 1983 examination. In 1984 the Board of Examiners modified the original content specification outlines in order to incorporate the information obtained from an AICPA 1983 practice analysis study.

In March 1987, the Board of Examiners issued an Exposure Draft titled *Proposed Changes in the Uniform CPA Examination.* The recommendations in the Exposure Draft were based on the 1983 practice analysis and three years of study of the Examination's content, structure, and format. In July 1989, the Board of Examiners approved restructuring the Uniform CPA Examination into four new sections. In 1991, the Board of Examiners received the results of a second practice analysis.

In early 1997, the Board of Examiners issued *Invitation to Comment—Updating the Uniform CPA Examination Content Specifications* to assess the content specification outlines (CSOs) and to revise the CSOs to include topics such as information technology. Based on the recommendations of the Examination Content Oversight Task Force, the Board of Examiners made minor adjustments to the CSOs, which encompassed new professional pronouncements and further integration of information technology.

These content specification outlines, effective for the May 1998 Uniform CPA Examination, are based on the results of the two practice analysis studies and the comments received from the *Invitation to Comment*.

Meaning and Use of Content Specification Outlines

The content specification outlines are for technical accounting, auditing, and business law knowledge and skills. The content specification outlines list the areas, groups, and topics to be tested in the following manner:

    I. Area
    A. Group
    1. Topic

The outlines are used to:

1. Ensure consistent coverage of subject matter from one examination to the next.
2. Provide guidance to those who are responsible for preparing the Examination to ensure a balanced examination.
3. Assist candidates in preparing for the Examination by indicating subjects that may be covered by the Examination.
4. Alert accounting educators about the subject matter considered necessary to prepare for the Examination.

The approximate weight given to each area is indicated by the percentage listed. The Examination will sample from the groups and topics listed within each area to meet the approximate percentage allocation. Generally, the group title should be sufficient to indicate the subject matter to be covered. However, in certain instances, topics have been explicitly listed to clarify or limit the subject matter covered within a group.

No weight allocation is given for groups or topics. For example, if there are several groups within an area or several topics within a group, no inference should be drawn about the relative importance or weight to be given to these groups or topics on an examination.

Clear-cut distinctions about subject matter do not always exist. Thus, there may be overlapping subjects in the four sections of the Examination. For example, Auditing questions often require a knowledge of accounting and business law as well as auditing procedures. Also, questions in the Financial Accounting & Reporting section may require the integration of accounting and business law knowledge.

The content specification outlines are considered to be complete with respect to the subjects covered in the Examination, including recent professional developments as they affect these subjects. Candidates should answer examination questions, developed from these outlines, in terms of the most recent developments, pronouncements, and standards in the accounting profession. When new subject matter is identified, the outlines will be amended to include it, which will be communicated to the profession.

Content Specification Outlines

Effective Date of Pronouncements

Candidates are responsible for knowing accounting and auditing pronouncements, including pronouncements in the governmental and not-for-profit organizations areas, six months after a pronouncement's *effective* date, unless early application is permitted. When early application is permitted, candidates are responsible for knowing the new pronouncement six months after the *issuance* date. In this case, candidates are responsible for knowing both the old and new pronouncements until the old pronouncement is superseded.

For the Federal Taxation area, candidates are responsible for knowing the Internal Revenue Code and federal tax regulations in effect six months before the examination date.

For the Business Law & Professional Responsibilities section, candidates are responsible for knowing federal laws six months after their *effective* date and uniform acts one year after their adoption by a simple majority of the jurisdictions.

Writing Skills Content

Answers to selected essay responses from the LPR, AUDIT, and FARE sections are used to assess candidates' writing skills. Five percent of the total points available on each of these sections will be allocated to writing skills. Effective writing skills include the following six characteristics: (1) coherent organization, (2) conciseness, (3) clarity, (4) use of standard English, (5) responsiveness to the requirements of the question, and (6) appropriateness for the reader. The current edition of *Information for Uniform CPA Examination Candidates* includes a discussion on the assessment of writing skills.

Business Law & Professional Responsibilities

The Business Law & Professional Responsibilities section tests candidates' knowledge of a CPA's professional responsibilities and of the legal implications of business transactions, particularly as they relate to accounting and auditing. Content covered in this section includes a CPA's professional responsibilities, business organizations, contracts, debtor-creditor relationships, government regulation of business, the Uniform Commercial Code, and property. Candidates will be required to

- Recognize relevant legal issues
- Recognize the legal implications of certain business situations
- Apply the underlying principles of law to accounting and auditing situations

This section deals with federal and widely adopted uniform laws. If there is no federal or uniform law on a topic, the questions are intended to test knowledge of the law of the majority of jurisdictions. Professional ethics questions are based on the AICPA *Code of Professional Conduct* because it is national in its application, whereas codes of other organizations and jurisdictions may be limited in their application.

In preparing for this section, candidates should study publications such as:

- AICPA *Code of Professional Conduct*
- AICPA Statements on Auditing Standards dealing explicitly with proficiency, independence, and due care
- AICPA Statements on Standards for Consulting Services
- AICPA Statements on Responsibilities in Personal Financial Planning Practice
- Books covering business law, auditing, and accounting

Business Law & Professional Responsibilities Content Specification Outline

I. Professional and Legal Responsibilities (15%)

    A. Code of Professional Conduct
    B. Proficiency, Independence, and Due Care
    C. Responsibilities in Other Professional Services
    D. Disciplinary Systems Imposed by the Profession and State Regulatory Bodies
    E. Common Law Liability to Clients and Third Parties
    F. Federal Statutory Liability
    G. Privileged Communications and Confidentiality
    H. Responsibilities of CPAs in Business and Industry, and in the Public Sector

Content Specification Outlines

II. Business Organizations (20%)

   A. Agency
      1. Formation and Termination
      2. Duties of Agents and Principals
      3. Liabilities and Authority of Agents and Principals
   B. Partnership, Joint Ventures, and Other Unincorporated Associations
      1. Formation, Operation, and Termination
      2. Liabilities and Authority of Partners and Owners
   C. Corporations
      1. Formation and Operation
      2. Stockholders, Directors, and Officers
      3. Financial Structure, Capital, and Distributions
      4. Reorganization and Dissolution
   D. Estates and Trusts
      1. Formation, Operation, and Termination
      2. Allocation Between Principal and Income
      3. Fiduciary Responsibilities
      4. Distributions

III. Contracts (10%)

   A. Formation
   B. Performance
   C. Third Party Assignments
   D. Discharge, Breach, and Remedies

IV. Debtor-Creditor Relationships (10%)

   A. Rights, Duties, and Liabilities of Debtors and Creditors
   B. Rights, Duties, and Liabilities of Guarantors
   C. Bankruptcy

V. Government Regulation of Business (15%)

   A. Federal Securities Acts
   B. Employment Regulation
   C. Environmental Regulation

VI. Uniform Commercial Code (20%)

   A. Negotiable Instruments
   B. Sales
   C. Secured Transactions
   D. Documents of Title

VII. Property (10%)

   A. Real Property Including Insurance
   B. Personal Property Including Bailments and Computer Technology Rights

Auditing

The Auditing section covers knowledge of generally accepted auditing standards and procedures and the skills needed to apply them in auditing and other attestation engagements. This section tests the knowledge and skills, as appropriate, in the context of the four broad engagement tasks that follow.

In preparing for this section, candidates should study publications such as:

- AICPA Statements on Auditing Standards
- AICPA Statements on Standards for Accounting and Review Services

- AICPA Statements on Quality Control Standards
- AICPA Statements on Standards for Attestation Engagements
- U.S. General Accounting Office Government Auditing Standards
- AICPA Audit and Accounting Guides:
  — Audit Sampling
  — Consideration of Internal Control in a Financial Statement Audit
- Textbooks and articles on auditing and other assurance services
- AICPA Auditing Procedure Studies
- AICPA Top 10 Technologies and Their Impact on CPAs
- AICPA Top 10 Technology Opportunities: Tips and Tools
- The CPA's Guide to Web Commerce
- The CPA's Guide to Information Security
- AICPA Risk Alerts
- SECPS Practice Alerts
- Single Audit Act, as amended
- Information on auditing and other assurance services on the AICPA Website

Auditing Content Specification Outline

I. Plan the Engagement, Evaluate the Prospective Client and Engagement, Decide Whether to Accept or Continue the Client and the Engagement, and Enter Into an Agreement With the Client (40%)

    A. Determine Nature and Scope of Engagement
       1. Generally Accepted Auditing Standards
       2. Standards for Accounting and Review Services
       3. Standards for Attestation Engagements
       4. Compliance Auditing Applicable to Governmental Entities and Other Recipients of Governmental Financial Assistance
       5. Other Assurance Services
       6. Appropriateness of Engagement to Meet Client's Needs
    B. Assess Engagement Risk and the CPA Firm's Ability to Perform the Engagement
       1. Engagement Responsibilities
       2. Staffing and Supervision Requirements
       3. Quality Control Considerations
       4. Management Integrity
       5. Researching Information Sources for Planning and Performing the Engagement
    C. Communicate With the Predecessor Accountant/Auditor
    D. Decide Whether to Accept or Continue the Client and Engagement
    E. Enter Into an Agreement With the Client as to the Terms of the Engagement
    F. Obtain an Understanding of the Client's Operations, Business, and Industry
    G. Perform Analytical Procedures
    H. Determine Preliminary Engagement Materiality
    I. Assess Inherent Risk and Risk of Misstatements
       1. Errors
       2. Fraud
       3. Illegal Acts by Clients
    J. Consider Internal Control
       1. Obtain and Document an Understanding of Internal Control—Automated and Manual
       2. Assess Control Risk
       3. Consider Limitations of Internal Control
       4. Consider the Effects of Information Technology on Internal Control
       5. Consider the Effects of Service Organizations on Internal Control
    K. Consider Other Planning Matters
       1. Using the Work of Other Independent Auditors
       2. Using the Work of a Specialist
       3. Internal Audit Function
       4. Related Parties and Related Party Transactions
       5. Electronic Evidence

L. Identify Financial Statement Assertions and Formulate Audit Objectives
   1. Accounting Estimates
   2. Routine Financial Statement Balances, Classes of Transactions, and Disclosures
   3. Unusual Financial Statement Balances, Classes of Transactions, and Disclosures
M. Determine and Prepare the Work Program Defining the Nature, Timing, and Extent of the Auditor's Procedures

II. Obtain and Document Information to Form a Basis for Conclusions (35%)

   A. Perform Planned Procedures Including Planned Applications of Audit Sampling
      1. Tests of Controls
      2. Analytical Procedures
      3. Confirmation of Balances and/or Transactions With Third Parties
      4. Physical Examination of Inventories and Other Assets
      5. Other Tests of Details
      6. Computer Assisted Audit Techniques
      7. Substantive Tests Prior to the Balance Sheet Date
      8. Tests of Unusual Year-end Transactions
   B. Evaluate Contingencies
   C. Obtain and Evaluate Lawyers' Letters
   D. Review Subsequent Events
   E. Obtain Representations From Management
   F. Identify Reportable Conditions and Other Control Deficiencies
   G. Identify Matters for Communication With Audit Committees

III. Review the Engagement to Provide Reasonable Assurance that Objectives are Achieved and Evaluate Information Obtained to Reach and to Document Engagement Conclusions (5%)

   A. Perform Analytical Procedures
   B. Evaluate the Sufficiency and Competence of Audit Evidence and Document Engagement Conclusions
      1. Consider Substantial Doubt About an Entity's Ability to Continue as a Going Concern
      2. Evaluate Whether Financial Statements are Free of Material Misstatements
      3. Consider Other Information in Documents Containing Audited Financial Statements
   C. Review the Work Performed to Provide Reasonable Assurance That Objectives Are Achieved

IV. Prepare Communications to Satisfy Engagement Objectives (20%)

   A. Prepare Reports
      1. Reports on Audited Financial Statements
      2. Reports on Reviewed and Compiled Financial Statements
      3. Reports Required by Government Auditing Standards
      4. Reports on Compliance With Laws and Regulations
      5. Reports on Internal Control
      6. Reports on Prospective Financial Information
      7. Reports on Agreed-Upon Procedures
      8. Reports on Other Attestation Engagements
      9. Reports on the Processing of Transactions by Service Organizations
      10. Reports on Supplementary Financial Information
      11. Other Special Reports
      12. Reissuance of Reports
   B. Prepare Letters and Other Required Communications
      1. Errors and Fraud
      2. Illegal Acts
      3. Special Reports
      4. Communication With Audit Committees
      5. Other Reporting Considerations Covered by Statements on Auditing Standards and Statements on Standards for Attestation Engagements
   C. Other Matters
      1. Subsequent Discovery of Facts Existing at the Date of the Auditor's Report
      2. Consideration of Omitted Procedures After the Report Date

Content Specification Outlines

Accounting & Reporting—Taxation, Managerial, and Governmental and Not-for-Profit Organizations

The Accounting & Reporting—Taxation, Managerial, and Governmental and Not-for-Profit Organizations section tests candidates' knowledge of principles and procedures for federal taxation, managerial accounting, and accounting for governmental and not-for-profit organizations, and the skills needed to apply them in a public accounting engagement.

In preparing for this section, candidates should study publications such as:

Federal Taxation:
- Internal Revenue Code and Income Tax Regulations
- Internal Revenue Service Circular 230
- AICPA Statements on Responsibilities in Tax Practice
- Income tax textbooks

Governmental and Not-for-Profit Organizations:
- Governmental Accounting Standards Board (GASB) Statements, Interpretations, and Technical Bulletins
- Financial Accounting Standards Board (FASB) Statements of Financial Accounting Standards and Interpretations, Accounting Principles Board Opinions, AICPA Accounting Research Bulletins, and FASB Technical Bulletins
- FASB Statement of Financial Accounting Concepts No. 4, "Objectives of Financial Reporting by Nonbusiness Organizations," and FASB Statement of Financial Concepts No. 6, "Elements of Financial Statements"
- AICPA Statement on Auditing Standards No. 69, "The Meaning of *Present Fairly in Conformity with Generally Accepted Accounting Principles* in the Independent Auditor's Report"
- AICPA Audit and Accounting Guides and Statements of Position relating to governmental and not-for-profit organizations
- Governmental and not-for-profit accounting textbooks and other accounting textbooks containing pertinent chapters

Managerial Accounting:
- Managerial accounting textbooks and other accounting textbooks containing pertinent chapters
- Accounting periodicals

Federal Taxation

This portion covers knowledge applicable to federal taxation and its application in practice. Candidates will

- Analyze information and identify data relevant for tax purposes
- Identify issues, elections, and alternative tax treatments
- Perform required calculations
- Formulate conclusions

Federal Taxation Content Specification Outline

I. Federal Taxation—Individuals (20%)

    A. Inclusions in Gross Income
    B. Exclusions and Adjustments to Arrive at Adjusted Gross Income
    C. Deductions From Adjusted Gross Income
    D. Filing Status and Exemptions
    E. Tax Accounting Methods
    F. Tax Computations, Credits, and Penalties
    G. Alternative Minimum Tax
    H. Tax Procedures

II. Federal Taxation—Corporations (20%)

    A. Determination of Taxable Income or Loss
    B. Tax Accounting Methods
    C. S Corporations
    D. Personal Holding Companies
    E. Consolidated Returns
    F. Tax Computations, Credits, and Penalties
    G. Alternative Minimum Tax

H. Other
   1. Distributions
   2. Incorporation, Reorganization, Liquidation, and Dissolution
   3. Tax Procedures

III. Federal Taxation—Partnerships (10%)

   A. Basis of Partner's Interest and Bases of Assets Contributed to the Partnership
   B. Determination of Partner's Share of Income, Credits, and Deductions
   C. Partnership and Partner Elections
   D. Partner Dealing With Own Partnership
   E. Treatment of Partnership Liabilities
   F. Distribution of Partnership Assets
   G. Termination of Partnership

IV. Federal Taxation—Estates and Trusts, Exempt Organizations, and Preparers' Responsibilities (10%)

   A. Estates and Trusts
      1. Income Taxation
      2. Determination of Beneficiary's Share of Taxable Income
      3. Estate and Gift Taxation
   B. Exempt Organizations
      1. Types of Organizations
      2. Requirements for Exemption
      3. Unrelated Business Income Tax
   C. Preparers' Responsibilities

Governmental and Not-for-Profit Organizations

This portion covers knowledge applicable to accounting for governmental and not-for-profit organizations and its application in practice. Candidates will

- Analyze and identify information relevant to governmental and not-for-profit accounting and reporting
- Identify alternative accounting and reporting policies and select those appropriate in specific situations
- Distinguish the relative weight of authority of differing sources of generally accepted accounting principles
- Perform procedures, formulate conclusions, and present results

Governmental and Not-for-Profit Organizations Content Specification Outline

V. Accounting for Governmental and Not-for-Profit Organizations (30%)

   A. Governmental Entities
      1. Measurement Focus and Basis of Accounting
      2. Objectives of Financial Reporting
      3. Uses of Fund Accounting
      4. Budgetary Process
      5. Financial Reporting Entity
      6. Elements of Financial Statements
      7. Conceptual Reporting Issues
      8. Accounting and Reporting for State and Local Governments
         a. Governmental-type Funds and Account Groups
         b. Proprietary-type Funds
         c. Fiduciary-type Funds
      9. Accounting and Financial Reporting for Governmental Not-for-Profit Organizations (Including Hospitals, Colleges and Universities, Voluntary Health and Welfare Organizations and Other Governmental Not-for-Profit Organizations)
   B. Nongovernmental Not-for-Profit Organizations
      1. Objectives of Financial Reporting
      2. Elements of Financial Statements

Content Specification Outlines

    3. Formats of Financial Statements
    4. Accounting and Financial Reporting for Nongovernmental Not-for-Profit Organizations
        a. Revenues and Contributions
        b. Restrictions on Resources
        c. Expenses, Including Depreciation

Managerial Accounting

This portion covers knowledge applicable to managerial accounting and its application in accounting practice. Candidates will

- Analyze and interpret information as a basis for decision making
- Determine product and service costs
- Prepare and interpret information for planning and control

Managerial Accounting Content Specification Outline

VI. Managerial Accounting (10%)

    A. Cost Estimation, Cost Determination, and Cost Drivers
    B. Job Costing, Process Costing, and Activity Based Costing
    C. Standard Costing and Flexible Budgeting
    D. Inventory Planning, Inventory Control, and Just-in-Time Purchasing
    E. Budgeting and Responsibility Accounting
    F. Variable and Absorption Costing
    G. Cost-Volume-Profit Analysis
    H. Cost Allocation and Transfer Pricing
    I. Joint and By-Product Costing
    J. Capital Budgeting
    K. Special Analyses for Decision Making
    L. Product and Service Pricing

Financial Accounting & Reporting

The Financial Accounting & Reporting section tests candidates' knowledge of generally accepted accounting principles for business enterprises and the skills needed to apply them in a public accounting engagement. Content covered in this section includes financial accounting concepts and standards as well as their application in a public accounting engagement. Candidates will

- Obtain and document entity information for use in financial statement presentations
- Evaluate, analyze, and process entity information for reporting in financial statements
- Communicate entity information and conclusions
- Analyze information and identify data relevant to financial accounting and reporting
- Identify financial accounting and reporting methods and select those that are suitable
- Perform calculations and formulate conclusions
- Present results in writing in a financial statement format or other appropriate format

In preparing for this section, candidates should study publications such as:

- Financial Accounting Standards Board (FASB) Statements of Financial Accounting Standards and Interpretations, Accounting Principles Board Opinions, and AICPA Accounting Research Bulletins
- FASB Technical Bulletins
- AICPA Statement on Auditing Standards No. 69, "The Meaning of *Present Fairly in Conformity with Generally Accepted Accounting Principles* in the Independent Auditor's Report," and Statement on Auditing Standards No. 62, "Special Reports"
- AICPA Personal Financial Statements Guide
- FASB Statements of Financial Accounting Concepts
- AICPA Statements of Position
- Books and articles on accounting

Financial Accounting & Reporting Content Specification Outline

I. Concepts and Standards for Financial Statements (20%)

   A. Financial Accounting Concepts
   B. Financial Accounting Standards for Presentation and Disclosures in General Purpose Financial Statements
      1. Consolidated and Combined Financial Statements
      2. Balance Sheet
      3. Statement(s) of Income, Comprehensive Income and Changes in Equity Accounts
      4. Statement of Cash Flows
      5. Accounting Policies and Other Notes to Financial Statements
   C. Other Presentations of Financial Data
      1. Financial Statements Prepared in Conformity With Comprehensive Bases of Accounting Other Than Generally Accepted Accounting Principles
      2. Personal Financial Statements
      3. Prospective Financial Information
   D. Financial Statement Analysis

II. Recognition, Measurement, Valuation, and Presentation of Typical Items in Financial Statements in Conformity With Generally Accepted Accounting Principles (40%)

   A. Cash, Cash Equivalents, and Marketable Securities
   B. Receivables
   C. Inventories
   D. Property, Plant, and Equipment
   E. Investments
   F. Intangible and Other Assets
   G. Payables and Accruals
   H. Deferred Revenues
   I. Notes and Bonds Payable
   J. Other Liabilities
   K. Equity Accounts
   L. Revenue, Cost, and Expense Accounts

III. Recognition, Measurement, Valuation, and Presentation of Specific Types of Transactions and Events in Financial Statements in Conformity With Generally Accepted Accounting Principles (40%)

   A. Accounting Changes and Corrections of Errors
   B. Business Combinations
   C. Cash Flow Components—Financing, Investing, and Operating
   D. Contingent Liabilities and Commitments
   E. Discontinued Operations
   F. Earnings Per Share
   G. Employee Benefits
   H. Extraordinary Items
   I. Financial Instruments
   J. Foreign Currency Transactions and Translation
   K. Income Taxes
   L. Interest Costs
   M. Interim Financial Reporting
   N. Leases
   O. Nonmonetary Transactions
   P. Quasi-reorganizations, Reorganizations, and Changes in Entity
   Q. Related Parties
   R. Research and Development Costs
   S. Segment Reporting

SUMMARY OF COVERAGE
MAY 1996 THROUGH MAY 1998
UNIFORM CPA EXAMINATIONS

Summary of Coverage—May 1996 through May 1998 Uniform CPA Examinations

The following summary of coverage provides an analysis of the Content Specification Outline coverage for the May 1996 through May 1998 Uniform CPA Examinations. This summary is intended only as a study aid and should not be used to predict the content of future Examinations.

How to interpret this chart

The percentages in bold indicate the percentage points allocated to each type of question on these Examinations. For example, on the May 1998 Business Law & Professional Responsibilities section (LPR), 60 percent of the examination points were allocated to multiple-choice questions, 20 percent of the points were allocated to other objective answer format (OOAF), and 20 percent of the points were allocated to the essays.

We have also provided the actual number of multiple-choice questions asked for each part and area of the content specification outlines, e.g., for the May 1998 Examination, under the Professional and Legal Responsibilities part of LPR, there were 10 multiple-choice questions asked; of those 10, 2 dealt with the Code of Professional Conduct area. In addition, we have indicated the percentage of OOAF and essay questions asked for each part of each section. For example, 5 percent of the OOAFs and none of the essays tested the Professional and Legal Responsibilities area of LPR for the May 1998 Examination.

Business Law & Professional Responsibilities	Multiple-Choice						OOAFs						Essays					
	M98 (60%)	N97 (60%)	M97 (60%)	N96 (60%)	M96 (60%)		M98	N97	M97	N96	M96		M98	N97	M97	N96	M96	
I. Professional and Legal Responsibilities	10	5	15	5	15		**20%**	**20%**	**20%**	**20%**	**20%**		**20%**	**20%**	**20%**	**20%**	**20%**	
A. Code of Professional Conduct	2	1	3	0	2		5%	0%	0%	0%	0%		0%	10%	0%	10%	0%	
B. Proficiency, Independence, and Due Care	2	1	3	0	2													
C. Responsibilities in Other Professional Services	2	1	2	0	2													
D. Disciplinary Systems Imposed by the Profession and State Regulatory Bodies	1	1	1	0	1													
E. Common Law Liability to Clients and Third Parties	0	1	3	0	3													
F. Federal Statutory Liability	2	0	3	3	4													
G. Privileged Communications and Confidentiality	1	0	0	2	1													
H. Responsibilities of CPAs in Business and Industry, and in the Public Sector	0	0	0	0	0													
II. Business Organizations	15	10	20	10	10		**0%**	**10%**	**0%**	**10%**	**10%**		**5%**	**0%**	**0%**	**0%**	**0%**	
A. Agency	5	5	5	0	5			5%		5%								
B. Partnership, Joint Ventures, and Other Unincorporated Associations	5	0	5	5	0						5%							
C. Corporations	5	0	5	5	0						5%							
D. Estates and Trusts	0	5	5	0	5					5%								
III. Contracts	0	10	0	0	10		**10%**	**0%**	**0%**	**0%**	**0%**		**0%**	**10%**	**10%**	**10%**	**0%**	
A. Formation	0	3	0	0	2													
B. Performance	0	2	0	0	3													
C. Third Party Assignments	0	3	0	0	2													

Summary of Coverage

Business Law & Professional Responsibilities	Multiple-Choice						OOAFs						Essays					
	M98	N97	M97	N96	M96		M98	N97	M97	N96	M96		M98	N97	M97	N96	M96
D. Discharge, Breach, and Remedies	0	2	0	0	3		0%	0%		0%	0%		0%	0%	0%	0%	0%
IV. Debtor-Creditor Relationships	10	10	0	10	0			0%	10%		0%						10%
A. Rights, Duties, and Liabilities of Debtors and Creditors	3	2	0	2	0				5%								
B. Rights, Duties, and Liabilities of Guarantors	3	2	0	2	0						5%						
C. Bankruptcy	4	6	0	6	0				5%								10%
V. Government Regulation of Business	15	5	15	15	10		0%	0%	0%	0%	5%		0%	10%	0%	0%	0%
A. Federal Securities Acts	5	0	5	7	7					5%				10%			
B. Employment Regulation	5	3	5	5	0						5%						
C. Environmental Regulation	5	2	5	3	3					5%							
VI. Uniform Commercial Code	5	15	10	10	10		5%	5%	10%	10%	0%		10%	0%	0%	0%	10%
A. Negotiable Instruments	4	0	7	2	4			5%		5%							
B. Sales	0	5	0	5	0				5%								10%
C. Secured Transactions	0	7	0	1	4				5%	5%							
D. Documents of Title	1	3	3	2	2												
VII. Property	5	5	0	10	5		0%	5%	0%	0%	5%		5%	0%	10%	0%	0%
A. Real Property Including Insurance	2	4	0	7	2			5%			5%				10%		
B. Personal Property Including Bailments and Computer Technology Rights	3	1	0	3	3												

S-2

Summary of Coverage

Auditing	Multiple-Choice					OOAFs				Essays			
	M98 (50%)	N97 (50%)	M97 (50%)	N96 (50%)	M96 (50%)	M98 30%	N97 30%	M97 30%	N96 30%	M96 30%	M98 20%	N97 20%	M97 20%	N96 20%	M96 20%
I. Plan the Engagement, Evaluate the Prospective Client and Engagement, Decide Whether to Accept or Continue the Client and the Engagement, and Enter into an Agreement with the Client	15	23	30	30	21	10%	5%	20%	20%	15%	20%	20%	0%	0%	11%
A. Determine Nature and Scope of Engagement	3	3	3	3	4							1%			
B. Assess Engagement Risk and the CPA Firm's Ability to Perform the Engagement	2	1	4	2	4				10%			1%			
C. Communicate with the Predecessor Accountant/Auditor	0	0	1	1	1		2%					1%			
D. Decide Whether to Accept or Continue the Client and Engagement	1	0	1	2	1							5%			
E. Enter into an Agreement with the Client as to the Terms of the Engagement	1	0	1	1	0		2%					5%			
F. Obtain an Understanding of the Client's Operations, Business, and Industry	0	0	1	0	0				5%			1%			
G. Perform Analytical Procedures	1	2	2	2	0					5%		1%			
H. Consider Preliminary Engagement Materiality	1	1	2	2	1							1%			
I. Assess Inherent Risk and Risk of Misstatements	0	3	1	3	0			10%				1%			
J. Consider Internal Control	0	8	8	8	7			10%	5%			2%			11%
K. Consider Other Planning Matters	3	1	3	3	2							1%			
L. Identify Financial Statement Assertions and Formulate Audit Objectives	1	3	2	2	0					5%					
M. Determine and Prepare the Work Program Defining the Nature, Timing, and Extent of the Auditor's Procedures	2	1	1	1	0		1%			5%		1%			
II. Obtain and Document Information to Form a Basis for Conclusions	38	37	23	23	32	10%	10%	0%	0%	5%	0%	0%	20%	20%	9%
A. Perform Planned Procedures Including Planned Applications of Audit Sampling	29	32	15	17	23		5%						20%	10%	9%
B. Evaluate Contingencies	1	0	2	1	2		2%								
C. Obtain and Evaluate Lawyers' Letters	1	0	1	1	1										
D. Review Subsequent Events	2	2	2	2	2										
E. Obtain Representations from Management	2	1	1	0	1		2%								
F. Identify Reportable Conditions and Other Control Deficiencies	2	2	1	1	2									10%	
G. Identify Matters for Communication with Audit Committees	1	0	1	1	1		1%								

S-3

Summary of Coverage

Auditing	Multiple-Choice				OOAFs				Essays			
	M98	N97	M97	N96	M96	M98	N97	M97	N96	M96	M98	N97	M97	N96	M96
III. Review the Engagement to Provide Reasonable Assurance That Objectives Are Achieved and Evaluate Information Obtained to Reach and to Document Engagement Conclusions	7	0	7	7	7	0%	5%	0%	0%	0%	0%	0%	0%	0%	0%
A. Perform Analytical Procedures	2	0	3	3	2										
B. Evaluate the Sufficiency and Competence of Audit Evidence and Document Engagement Conclusions	4	0	2	2	4										
C. Review the Work Performed to Provide Reasonable Assurance that Objectives Are Achieved	1	0	2	2	1										
IV. Prepare Communications to Satisfy Engagement Objectives	15	15	15	15	15	10%	10%	10%	10%	10%	0%	0%	0%	0%	0%
A. Prepare Reports	14	12	10	13	12		3%	5%	10%	10%					
B. Prepare Letters and Other Required Communications	1	1	4	1	3		7%	5%							
C. Other Matters	0	2	1	1	0										

S-4

Summary of Coverage

Accounting & Reporting—Taxation, Managerial, and Governmental and Not-for-Profit Organizations	Multiple-Choice					OOAFs				Essays
	M98	N97	M97	N96	M96	M98	N97	M97	N96	M96
	75 (60%)	75 (60%)	75 (60%)	75 (60%)	75 (60%)	40%	40%	40%	40%	40%
I. Federal Taxation—Individuals	25	7	25	0	25	0%	15%	0%	20%	0%
A. Inclusions in Gross Income	10	1	9	0	9					
B. Exclusions and Adjustments to Arrive at Adjusted Gross Income	3	0	2	0	2					
C. Deductions from Adjusted Gross Income	7	2	6	0	6					
D. Filing Status and Exemptions	0	1	0	0	0					
E. Tax Accounting Methods	1	1	0	0	0					
F. Tax Computations, Credits, and Penalties	3	2	3	0	3					
G. Alternative Minimum Tax	1	0	3	0	3					
H. Tax Procedures	0	0	2	0	2					
II. Federal Taxation—Corporations	0	25	0	25	7	20%	0%	20%	0%	15%
A. Determination of Taxable Income or Loss	0	10	0	8	1			5%		
B. Tax Accounting Methods	0	1	0	1	0					
C. S Corporations	0	4	0	3	2			10%		
D. Personal Holding Companies	0	0	0	0	0					
E. Consolidated Returns	0	2	0	1	0					
F. Tax Computations, Credits, and Penalties	0	2	0	3	0					
G. Alternative Minimum Tax	0	0	0	2	0			5%		
H. Other	0	6	0	7	4					
III. Federal Taxation—Partnerships	12	0	12	12	12	0%	10%	0%	0%	0%
A. Basis of Partner's Interest and Bases of Assets Contributed to the Partnership	3	0	3	3	3					
B. Determination of Partner's Share of Income, Credits, and Deductions	3	0	3	2	3					
C. Partnership and Partner Elections	1	0	0	1	1					
D. Partner Dealing with Own Partnership	1	0	1	0	1					
E. Treatment of Partnership Liabilities	1	0	1	2	0					
F. Distribution of Partnership Assets	3	0	3	2	3					
G. Termination of Partnership	0	0	1	2	1					
IV. Federal Taxation—Estates and Trusts, Exempt Organizations, and Preparers' Responsibilities	7	12	7	7	0	5%	0%	5%	5%	10%
A. Estates and Trusts	5	6	3	5	0			5%		
B. Exempt Organizations	1	3	0	1	0					

S-5

Summary of Coverage

Accounting & Reporting—Taxation, Managerial, and Governmental and Not-for-Profit Organizations	Multiple-Choice						OOAFs					Essays
	M98	N97	N97	M97	N96	M96	M98	N97	M97	N96	M96	
C. Preparers' Responsibilities	1	3	4	1	0				5%			
V. Accounting for Governmental and Not-for-Profit Organizations	19	19	19	25	19	15%	15%	15%	10%	15%		
A. Governmental Entities	19	10	10	15	13							
B. Nongovernmental Not-for-Profit Organizations	0	9	9	10	6							
VI. Managerial Accounting	12	12	12	6	12	0%	0%	0%	5%	0%		
A. Cost Estimation, Cost Determination, and Cost Drivers	1	1	2	1	1							
B. Job Costing, Process Costing, and Activity Based Costing	2	2	2	0	1							
C. Standard Costing and Flexible Budgeting	0	0	0	0	1							
D. Inventory Planning, Inventory Control, and Just-in-Time Purchasing	1	1	1	1	1							
E. Budgeting and Responsibility Accounting	2	2	2	0	1							
F. Variable and Absorption Costing	1	1	1	0	1							
G. Cost-Volume-Profit Analysis	1	1	1	0	1							
H. Cost Allocation and Transfer Pricing	1	1	1	1	1							
I. Joint and By-Product Costing	0	0	0	1	1							
J. Capital Budgeting	1	1	1	1	1							
K. Special Analyses for Decision Making	1	1	1	0	1							
L. Product and Service Pricing	1	1	0	1	1							

S-6

Summary of Coverage

Financial Accounting & Reporting	Multiple-Choice					OOAFs					Essays				
	M98	N97	M97	N96	M96	M98	N97	M97	N96	M96	M98	N97	M97	N96	M96
	60 (60%)	60 (60%)	60 (60%)	60 (60%)	60 (60%)	20%	20%	20%	20%	20%	20%	20%	20%	20%	20%
I. Concepts and Standards for Financial Statements	11	14	0	4	7	2%	1%	5%	5%	10%	7%	5%	15%	11%	3%
A. Financial Accounting Concepts	0	0	0	2	0	2%	1%					2%	5%		3%
B. Financial Accounting Standards for Presentation and Disclosure in General Purpose Financial Statements	8	12	0	1	6			5%	5%	10%	7%	3%	10%	11%	
C. Other Presentations of Financial Data	3	2	0	1	1										
D. Financial Statement Analysis	0	0	0	0	0										
II. Recognition, Measurement, Valuation, and Presentation of Typical Items in Financial Statements in Conformity with Generally Accepted Accounting Principles	19	24	28	22	30	18%	0%	0%	10%	10%	4%	12%	5%	6%	0%
A. Cash, Cash Equivalents, and Marketable Securities	2	0	3	3	2							7%			
B. Receivables	2	1	2	1	0				10%	10%					
C. Inventories	2	2	2	0	3				10%					4%	
D. Property, Plant, and Equipment	0	3	3	0	2	5%									
E. Investments	1	0	2	2	2							2%			
F. Intangibles and Other Assets	1	1	1	2	1										
G. Payables and Accruals	2	2	2	1	2										
H. Deferred Revenues	0	1	1	1	1	4%									
I. Notes and Bonds Payable	0	3	2	2	1						4%				
J. Other Liabilities	0	1	2	0	1										
K. Equity Accounts	3	2	3	4	4							3%	3%	2%	
L. Revenue, Cost, and Expense Accounts	6	8	5	6	11	9%									
III. Recognition, Measurement, Valuation, and Presentation of Typical Items in Financial Statements in Conformity with Generally Accepted Accounting Principles	30	22	32	34	23	0%	19%	15%	5%	0%	9%	3%	0%	3%	17%
A. Accounting Changes and Corrections of Errors	2	0	2	0	0		4%								
B. Business Combinations	2	1	3	0	2				5%					1%	6%
C. Cash Flow Components—Financing, Investing, and Operating	2	3	0	2	2			5%							
D. Contingent Liabilities and Commitments	0	1	2	2	0						4%				
E. Discontinued Operations	2	2	2	2	0										
F. Earnings Per Share	2	0	2	1	1		2%								
G. Employee Benefits	3	1	4	6	2			5%				3%			9%

Summary of Coverage

Financial Accounting & Reporting	Multiple-Choice							OOAFs				Essays			
	M98	N97	M97	N96	M96			M98	N97	M97	N96	M98	N97	N96	M96
H. Extraordinary Items	2	3	3	2	2									2%	
I. Financial Instruments	1	1	0	3	2							2%			
J. Foreign Currency Transactions and Translation	1	1	2	1	1										
K. Income Taxes	2	2	0	4	2					5%					2%
L. Interest Costs	2	0	2	2	1										
M. Interim Financial Reporting	2	0	2	1	2				3%						
N. Leases	0	0	2	2	1				10%			3%			
O. Nonmonetary Transactions	1	2	2	2	2										
P. Quasi-reorganizations, Reorganizations, and Changes in Entity	1	1	0	1	0										
Q. Related Parties	2	2	2	1	2										
R. Research and Development Costs	2	2	1	1	1										
S. Segment Reporting	1	0	1	1	0										

S-8